SERIES

(ex•ploring)

1. To investigate in a systematic way: examine. 2. To search
into or range over for the purpose of discovery.

(ex•ploring)

SERIES

1. To investigate in a systematic way: examine. 2. To search into or range over for the purpose of discovery.

Microsoft®

Office 2007

PLUS EDITION

Robert T. Grauer

Michelle Hulett | Cynthia Krebs | Maurie Wigman Lockley

Keith Mulbery | Judy Scheeren

PEARSON

Prentice Hall

**Upper Saddle River
New Jersey 07458**

Library of Congress Cataloging-in-Publication Data
Grauer, Robert T., 1945-
  Exploring Microsoft Office 2007 plus edition / Robert T. Grauer, Michelle Hulett, Cynthia Krebs.
     p. cm.
  ISBN-13: 978-0-13-239381-2
  ISBN-10: 0-13-239381-6
  1. Microsoft Office. 2. Business—Computer programs. I. Hulett, Michelle J. II. Krebs, Cynthia. III. Title.
  HF5548.4.M525G696 2008
  005.5--dc22

                                                                              2007026049

Vice President and Publisher: Natalie E. Anderson
Associate VP/ Executive Acquisitions Editor, Print: Stephanie Wall
Executive Acquisitions Editor, Media: Richard Keaveny
Sr. Acquisitions Editor: Melissa Sabella
Product Development Manager: Eileen Bien Calabro
Sr. Editorial Project Manager/Development: Eileen Clark
Editorial Project Manager/Assistant Editor: Jenelle J. Woodrup
Market Development Editor: Claire Hunter
Editorial Assistant: Rebecca Knauer
Executive Producer: Lisa Strite
Content Development Manager: Cathi Profitko
Project Manager, Media: Ashley Lulling
Director of Marketing: Margaret Waples
Sr. Marketing Manager: Scott Davidson
Sr. Sales Associate: Rebecca Scott
Sr. Managing Editor: Cynthia Zonneveld
Associate Managing Editor: Camille Trentacoste
Senior Operations Specialist: Nick Sklitsis
Production Media Project Manager: Lorena E. Cerisano
Design Director: Maria Lange
Art Director/Interior and Cover Design: Blair Brown
Cover Illustration/Photo: Courtesy of Getty Images/Laurent Hamels
Composition: GGS Book Services
Project Management: GGS Book Services
Project Manager: Kevin Bradley
Production Editors: Blair Woodcock and Andrea Shearer
Cover Printer: Phoenix Color
Printer/Binder: Banta/Menasha

10 9 8 7 6 5 4 3 2 1
ISBN-13: 978-0-13-239381-2
ISBN-10:   0-13-239381-6

Dedications

To Marion—my wife, my lover, and my best friend.

Robert Grauer

I would like to dedicate this book to the memory of my grandmother,
Effie Burrell Marcum. Her love, encouragement, and belief in my abilities got me to this
point and help me endure every day. And also to John. 143

Michelle Hulett

I dedicate this book to those I love in thanks for the joy and support they give me:
My wonderful children: Marshall, Jaron, Jenalee, and Michelle who make it all
worthwhile, and Bradley Behle—my newest son and a welcome addition to our family.

My granddaughter, Ava—her baby cuddles make life a pleasure.
My parents, Neal and Zola Mulhern, who continually do all they can to make life easier.
And to those who have gone before: my father, Reed J. Olsen, and my
Grandparents Waddoups. I would like to dedicate this book to my siblings: my sister,
Vicki O. Ridgway; and my brothers Randy J. and Michael R. Olsen.
Thank you for always being there for me.

Cynthia Krebs

I would like to express appreciation for my family's patience and support as I have
worked on this project. Elizabeth, Aaron, and James were extraordinarily understanding
and cooperative about letting me work. I need to acknowledge Dan Bullard for his
continuing source of motivation and inspiration. Most of all, I need to thank my best friend
and husband, Jim, for always believing in me.

Maurie Wigman Lockley

I would like to dedicate this book to my family and close friends who provided a
strong community of emotional support and patience as I completed my doctorate program
and worked on this edition of the Exploring series.

Keith Mulbery

Thanks for my husband, Bill, for all the support and energy that has helped
me to put ideas on paper. His encouragement made it all possible.

Thanks also to my parents who believe in learning at any age.
And, a special thanks to the following people for their contributions: Frank Lucente, colleague,
friend, and mentor for sharing his tips and unique teaching style; and the students at Westmoreland County
Community College who make it all worthwhile.

Judy Scheeren

About the Authors

Dr. Robert T. Grauer

Dr. Robert T. Grauer is an Associate Professor in the Department of Computer Information Systems at the University of Miami, where he has been honored with the Outstanding Teacher Award in the School of Business. He is the vision behind the Exploring Series, which is about to sell its 3 millionth copy.

Dr. Grauer has written more than 50 books on programming and information systems. His work has been translated into three foreign languages and is used in all aspects of higher education at both national and international levels.

Dr. Grauer also has been a consultant to several major corporations including IBM and American Express. He received his Ph.D. in operations research in 1972 from the Polytechnic Institute of Brooklyn.

Michelle Hulett

Michelle Hulett received a B.S. degree in CIS from the University of Arkansas and a M.B.A. from Missouri State University. She has worked for various organizations as a programmer, network administrator, computer literacy coordinator, and educator. She currently teaches computer literacy and Web design classes at Missouri State University.

When not teaching or writing, she enjoys flower gardening, traveling (Alaska and Hawaii are favorites), hiking, canoeing, and camping with her husband, John, and dog, Dakota.

Cynthia Krebs

Cynthia Krebs is a professor in the Digital Media Department at Utah Valley State College, where she has taught since 1988. In addition to teaching classes in basic computer proficiency using Microsoft Office, she teaches classes in business presentations, business graphics, and an introduction to multimedia. She has received the Teacher-of-the-Year Award in the School of Business twice during her tenure at UVSC.

She has written chapters for many texts, co-authored a text on advanced word processing, and has presented locally and nationally. A graduate of Utah State University, Cynthia lives in Springville, Utah.

She has four children and one granddaughter. When she isn't teaching or writing, she enjoys spending time with her children and spoiling her granddaughter.

Maurie Wigman Lockley

Maurie Wigman Lockley teaches desktop applications and management information systems classes at the University of North Carolina Greensboro. She has been an instructor there since 1990.

She lives in a tiny piedmont North Carolina town with her husband, daughter, and two preschool-aged grandsons. She spends her free time playing with the boys, reading, camping, playing computer games, and singing. She serves on several not-for-profit boards and is active at her church.

Dr. Keith Mulbery

Dr. Keith Mulbery is an Associate Professor in the Information Systems and Technology Department at Utah Valley State College, where he teaches computer applications, programming, and MIS classes. He has written more than 15 software textbooks and business communication test banks. In January 2001, he received the Utah Valley State College Board of Trustees Award of Excellence for authoring *MOUS Essentials Word 2000*. In addition to his series editor and authoring experience, he also served as a developmental editor on two word processing textbooks.

He received his B.S. and M.Ed. (majoring in Business Education) from Southwestern Oklahoma State University and earned his Ph.D. in Education with an emphasis in Business Information Systems at Utah State University in 2006. His dissertation topic was computer-assisted instruction using TAIT to supplement traditional instruction in basic computer proficiency courses.

Judith Scheeren

Judith Scheeren is a professor of computer technology at Westmoreland County Community College in Youngwood, Pennsylvania where she received the Outstanding Teacher award. She holds an M.S.I.S. She holds an M.S. from the University of Pittsburgh and an advanced certificate in online teaching and learning from the University of California at Hayward. She has several years of experience in the computer industry with Fortune 500 companies. She has developed and written training materials for custom applications in both the public and private sectors. She also has written books on desktop publishing.

Contributing Authors

Linda Ericksen, Office Fundamentals Chapter

Linda Ericksen is Associate Professor of Software Engineering at the University of Advancing Technology in Tempe, Arizona. She is the author of over 20 college-level computer text books on topics ranging from the Internet through many software applications, writing for major publishers such as Que, Addison-Wesley, and Course Technology. She was also the author of her own popular series for Prentice Hall, the Quick Simple Series, which featured Microsoft Office 2000.

Lynn Hogan, Windows XP Chapter

Lynn Hogan has taught computer literacy and microcomputer applications classes at Calhoun Community College for 25 years. For the past 18 years, she has served as chair of the Department of Computer Information Systems. She received Calhoun's outstanding instructor award in 2006, and currently teaches computer literacy for senior adults and web design courses. Having developed the first online computer course at Calhoun, she continues to work with the distance education program. She received an M.B.A. from the University of North Alabama and a Ph.D. from the University of Alabama.

She resides in Alabama with her husband and two daughters. Much of her free time is spent traveling to cutting horse shows and dressage shows, watching her daughters compete. In addition to working with horses, she enjoys cooking, reading, and family travel.

A Special Thank You to Maryann Barber

After being a key part of the Exploring series for 15 years, Maryann Barber has retired from authoring. Prentice Hall and Bob Grauer would like to thank her for all of her tremendous work through the years that helped make the series the success it is today. While she will be greatly missed, her contributions will be felt for many editions to come.

Brief Contents

Contents

Microsoft Office Word 2007

Microsoft Office Excel 2007

CHAPTER ONE | Introduction to Excel: What Can I Do with a Spreadsheet? 311

CHAPTER TWO | Formulas and Functions: Math Basics for Spreadsheet Use 379

Microsoft Office Access 2007

CHAPTER TWO | Relational Databases and Multi-Table Queries: Designing Databases and Using Related Data

807

CHAPTER THREE | Customize, Analyze, and Summarize Query Data: Creating and Using Queries to Make Decisions

879

CHAPTER FOUR | Create, Edit, and Perform Calculations in Reports: Creating Professional and Useful Reports 931

CHAPTER FIVE | PivotTables and PivotCharts: Data Mining 995

CHAPTER SIX | Data Protection: Integrity, Validation, and Reliability 1059

Microsoft Office PowerPoint 2007

CHAPTER ONE | Introduction to PowerPoint: Presentations Made Easy 1123

CHAPTER TWO | Presentation Development: Planning and Preparing a Presentation 1197

Windows XP 2007

CHAPTER ONE | Getting Started with Windows XP 1259

Acknowledgments

The success of the Exploring series is attributed to contributions from numerous individuals. First and foremost, our heartfelt appreciation to Melissa Sabella, senior acquisitions editor, for providing new leadership and direction to capitalize on the strength and tradition of the Exploring series while implementing innovative ideas into the Exploring Office 2007 edition. Scott Davidson, senior marketing manager, was an invaluable addition to the team who believes in the mission of this series passionately and did an amazing job communicating its message.

During the first few months of the project, Eileen Clark, senior editorial project manager, kept the team focused on the vision, pedagogy, and voice that has been the driving force behind the success of the Exploring series. Claire Hunter, market development editor, facilitated communication between the editorial team and the reviewers to ensure that this edition meet the changing needs of computer professors and students at the collegiate level. Keith Mulbery gave up many nights and weekends (including Thanksgiving) to jump in and help out with anything that was asked of him, including assisting with topical organization, reviewing and revising content, capturing screenshots, and ensuring chapter manuscripts adhered to series guidelines.

Jenelle Woodrup, editorial project manager/assistant editor, masterfully managed the flow of manuscript files among the authors, editorial team, and production to ensure timely publication of series. Laura Town, developmental editor, provided an objective perspective in reviewing the content and organization of selected chapters. Eileen Calabro, product development manager, facilitated communication among the editorial team, authors, and production during a transitional stage. The team at GGS worked through software delays, style changes and anything else we threw at them to bring the whole thing together. Art director Blair Brown's conversations with students and professors across the country yielded a design that addressed the realities of today's students with function and style.

A special thanks to the following for the use of their work in the PowerPoint section of the text: Cameron Martin, Ph.D., Assistant to the President, Utah Valley State College, for the use of the Institutional Policies and Procedures Approval Process flowchart; Nick Finner, Paralegal Studies, Utah Valley State College, for the use of his research relating to the elderly population residing in the prisons of Utah; Ryan Phillips, Xeric Landscape and Design (XericUtah.com), for sharing Xeric's concepts for creating beautiful, drought-tolerant landscapes and for the photographs illustrating these concepts; Jo Porter, Photographer, Mapleton, Utah, for allowing the use of her beautiful engagement and wedding photographs; and David and Ali Valeti for the photographs of their baby and their family.

The following organizations and individuals generously provided data and structure from their organizational databases: Replacements, Ltd., Shweta Ponnappa, JC Raulston Arboretum at North Carolina State University, and Valerie Tyson. We deeply appreciate the ability to give students a feel for "real" data.

The new members of the Exploring author team would like to especially thank Bob Grauer for his vision in developing Exploring and his leadership in creating this highly successful series.

Maryann Barber would like to thank Bob Grauer for a wonderful collaboration and providing the opportunities through which so much of her life has changed.

The Exploring team would like to especially thank the following instructors who drew on their experience in the classroom and their software expertise to give us daily advice on how to improve this book. Their impact can be seen on every page:

Barbara Stover, Marion Technical College

Bob McCloud, Sacred Heart University

Cassie Georgetti, Florida Technical College

Dana Johnson, North Dakota State University

Jackie Lamoureux, Central New Mexico Community College

Jim Pepe, Bentley College

Judy Brown, The University of Memphis

Lancie Anthony Affonso, College of Charleston

Mimi Duncan, University of Missouri – St. Louis

Minnie Proctor, Indian River Community College

Richard Albright, Goldey-Beacom College

We also want to acknowledge all the reviewers of the Exploring 2007 series. Their valuable comments and constructive criticism greatly improved this edition:

Aaron Schorr
Fashion Institute of Technology

Alicia Stonesifer
La Salle University

Allen Alexander, Delaware
Tech & Community College

Amy Williams, Abraham
Baldwin Agriculture College

Annie Brown
Hawaii Community College

Barbara Cierny
Harper College

Barbara Hearn
Community College of Philadelphia

Barbara Meguro
University of Hawaii at Hilo

Bette Pitts
South Plains College

Beverly Fite
Amarillo College

Bill Wagner
Villanova

Brandi N. Guidry
University of Louisiana at Lafayette

Brian Powell
West Virginia University – Morgantown
Campus

Carl Farrell
Hawaii Pacific University

Carl Penzuil
Ithaca College

Carole Bagley;
University of St. Thomas

Catherine Hain
Central New Mexico CC

Charles Edwards
University of Texas of the Permian Basin

Christine L. Moore
College of Charleston

David Barnes
Penn State Altoona

David Childress;
Ashland Community College

David Law, Alfred
State College

Dennis Chalupa
Houston Baptist

Diane Stark
Phoenix College

Dianna Patterson
Texarkana College

Dianne Ross
University of Louisiana at Lafayette

Dr. Behrooz Saghafi
Chicago State University

Dr. Gladys Swindler
Fort Hays State University

Dr. Joe Teng
Barry University

Dr. Karen Nantz
Eastern Illinois University.

Duane D. Lintner
Amarillo College

Elizabeth Edmiston
North Carolina Central University

Erhan Uskup
Houston Community College

Fred Hills, McClellan
Community College

Gary R. Armstrong
Shippensburg University of Pennsylvania

Glenna Vanderhoof
Missouri State

Gregg Asher
Minnesota State University, Mankato

Hong K. Sung
University of Central Oklahoma

Hyekyung Clark
Central New Mexico CC

J Patrick Fenton
West Valley College

Jana Carver
Amarillo College

Jane Cheng
Bloomfield College

Janos T. Fustos
Metropolitan State College of Denver

Jeffrey A Hassett
University of Utah

Jennifer Pickle
Amarillo College

Jerry Kolata
New England Institute of Technology

Jesse Day
South Plains College

John Arehart
Longwood University

John Lee Reardon
University of Hawaii, Manoa

Joshua Mindel
San Francisco State University

Karen Wisniewski
County College of Morris

Karl Smart
Central Michigan University

Kathryn L. Hatch
University of Arizona

Krista Terry
Radford University

Laura McManamon
University of Dayton

Laura Reid
University of Western Ontario

Linda Johnsonius
Murray State University

Lori Kelley
Madison Area Technical College

Lucy Parker,
California State University, Northridge

Lynda Henrie
LDS Business College

Malia Young
Utah State University

Margie Martyn
Baldwin Wallace

Marianne Trudgeon
Fanshawe College

Marilyn Hibbert
Salt Lake Community College

Marjean Lake
LDS Business College

Mark Olaveson
Brigham Young University

Nancy Sardone
Seton Hall University

Patricia Joseph
Slippery Rock University.

Patrick Hogan
Cape Fear Community College

Paula F. Bell
Lock Haven University of Pennsylvania

Paulette Comet
Community College of Baltimore County,
Catonsville

Pratap Kotala
North Dakota State University

Richard Blamer
John Carroll University

Richard Herschel
St. Joseph's University

Richard Hewer
Ferris State University

Robert Gordon
Hofstra University

Robert Marmelstein
East Stroudsburg University

Robert Stumbur
Northern Alberta Institute of Technology

Roberta I. Hollen
University of Central Oklahoma

Roland Moreira
South Plains College

Ron Murch
University of Calgary

Rory J. de Simone
University of Florida

Ruth Neal
Navarro College

Sandra M. Brown
Finger Lakes Community College

Sharon Mulroney
Mount Royal College

Stephen E. Lunce
Midwestern State University

Steve Schwarz
Raritan Valley Community College

Steven Choy
University of Calgary

Susan Byrne
St. Clair College

Thomas Setaro
Brookdale Community College

Todd McLeod
Fresno City College

Vickie Pickett
Midland College

Vipul Gupta
St Joseph's University

Vivek Shah
Texas State University - San Marcos

Wei-Lun Chuang
Utah State University

William Dorin
Indiana University Northwest

Finally, we wish to acknowledge reviewers of previous editions of the Exploring series—we wouldn't have made it to the 7th edition without you:

Alan Moltz
Naugatuck Valley Technical Community
College

Alok Charturvedi
Purdue University

Antonio Vargas
El Paso Community College

Barbara Sherman
Buffalo State College

Bill Daley
University of Oregon

Bill Morse
DeVry Institute of Technology

Bonnie Homan
San Francisco State University

Carl M. Briggs
Indiana University School of Business

Carlotta Eaton
Radford University

Carolyn DiLeo
Westchester Community College

Cody Copeland
Johnson County Community College

Connie Wells
Georgia State University

Daniela Marghitu
Auburn University

David B. Meinert
Southwest Missouri State University

David Douglas
University of Arkansas

David Langley
University of Oregon

David Rinehard
Lansing Community College

David Weiner
University of San Francisco

Dean Combellick
Scottsdale Community College

Delores Pusins
Hillsborough Community College

Don Belle
Central Piedmont Community College

Douglas Cross
Clackamas Community College

Ernie Ivey
Polk Community College

Gale E. Rand
College Misericordia

Helen Stoloff
Hudson Valley Community College

Herach Safarian
College of the Canyons

Jack Zeller
Kirkwood Community College

James Franck
College of St. Scholastica

James Gips
Boston College

Jane King
Everett Community College

Janis Cox
Tri-County Technical College

Jerry Chin
Southwest Missouri State University

Jill Chapnick
Florida International University

Jim Pruitt
Central Washington University

John Lesson
University of Central Florida

John Shepherd
Duquesne University

Judith M. Fitspatrick
Gulf Coast Community College

Judith Rice
Santa Fe Community College

Judy Dolan
Palomar College

Karen Tracey
Central Connecticut State University

Kevin Pauli
University of Nebraska

Kim Montney
Kellogg Community College

Kimberly Chambers
Scottsdale Community College

Larry S. Corman
Fort Lewis College

Lynn Band
Middlesex Community College

Margaret Thomas
Ohio University

Marguerite Nedreberg
Youngstown State University

Marilyn Salas
Scottsdale Community College

Martin Crossland
Southwest Missouri State University

Mary McKenry Percival
University of Miami

Michael Hassett
Fort Hayes State University

Michael Stewardson
San Jacinto College – North

Midge Gerber
Southwestern Oklahoma State University

Mike Hearn
Community College of Philadelphia

Mike Kelly
Community College of Rhode Island

Mike Thomas
Indiana University School of Business

Paul E. Daurelle
Western Piedmont Community College

Ranette Halverson
Midwestern State University

Raymond Frost
Central Connecticut State University

Robert Spear, Prince
George's Community College

Rose M. Laird
Northern Virginia Community College

Sally Visci
Lorain County Community College

Shawna DePlonty
Sault College of Applied Arts and Technology

Stuart P. Brian
Holy Family College

Susan Fry
Boise State Universtiy

Suzanne Tomlinson
Iowa State University

Vernon Griffin
Austin Community College

Wallace John Whistance-Smith
Ryerson Polytechnic University

Walter Johnson
Community College of Philadelphia

Wanda D. Heller
Seminole Community College

We very much appreciate the following individuals for painstakingly checking every step and every explanation for technical accuracy, while dealing with an entirely new software application:

Barbara Waxer
Bill Daley
Beverly Fite
Dawn Wood
Denise Askew
Elizabeth Lockley

James Reidel
Janet Pickard
Janice Snyder
Jeremy Harris
John Griffin
Joyce Neilsen

LeeAnn Bates
Mara Zebest
Mary E. Pascarella
Michael Meyers
Sue McCrory

The Exploring Series

Exploring has been Prentice Hall's most successful Office Application series of the past 15 years. For Office 2007 Exploring has undergone the most extensive changes in its history, so that it can truly move today's student "beyond the point and click."

The goal of Exploring has always been to teach more than just the steps to accomplish a task – the series provides the theoretical foundation necessary for a student to understand when and why to apply a skill. This way, students achieve a broader understanding of Office.

Today's students are changing and Exploring has evolved with them. Prentice Hall traveled to college campuses across the country and spoke directly to students to determine how they study and prepare for class. We also spoke with hundreds of professors about the best ways to administer materials to such a diverse body of students.

Here is what we learned

Students go to college now with a different set of skills than they did 5 years ago. The new edition of Exploring moves students beyond the basics of the software at a faster pace, without sacrificing coverage of the fundamental skills that everybody needs to know. This ensures that students will be engaged from Chapter 1 to the end of the book.

Students have diverse career goals. With this in mind, we broadened the examples in the text (and the accompanying Instructor Resources) to include the health sciences, hospitality, urban planning, business and more. Exploring will be relevant to every student in the course.

Students read, prepare and study differently than they used to. Rather than reading a book cover to cover students want to easily identify what they need to know, and then learn it efficiently. We have added key features that will bring students into the content and make the text easy to use such as objective mapping, pull quotes, and key terms in the margins.

Moving students beyond the point and click

All of these additions mean students will be more engaged, achieve a higher level of understanding, and successfully complete this course. In addition to the experience and expertise of the series creator and author Robert T. Grauer we have assembled a tremendously talented team of supporting authors to assist with this critical revision. Each of them is equally dedicated to the Exploring mission of **moving students beyond the point and click.**

Key Features of the Office 2007 revision include

- **New** **Office Fundamentals Chapter** efficiently covers skills common among all applications like save, print, and bold to avoid repetition in each Office application's first chapter, along with coverage of problem solving skills to prepare students to apply what they learn in any situation.

- **New** **Moving Beyond the Basics** introduces advanced skills earlier because students are learning basic skills faster.

- **White Pages/Yellow Pages clearly** distinguish the theory (white pages) from the skills covered in the Hands-On exercises (yellow pages) so students always know what they are supposed to be doing.

- **New** **Objective Mapping** enables students to skip the skills and concepts they know, and quickly find those they don't, by scanning the chapter opener page for the page numbers of the material they need.

- **New** **Pull Quotes** entice students into the theory by highlighting the most interesting points.

- **New** **Conceptual Animations** connect the theory with the skills, by illustrating tough to understand concepts with interactive multimedia.

- **New** **More End of Chapter Exercises** offer instructors more options for assessment. Each chapter has approximately 12–15 exercises ranging from Multiple Choice questions to open-ended projects.

- **New** **More Levels of End of Chapter Exercises,** including new Mid-Level Exercises tell students what to do, but not how to do it, and Capstone Exercises cover all of the skills within each chapter.

- **New** **Mini Cases with Rubrics** are open ended exercises that guide both instructors and students to a solution with a specific rubric for each mini case.

Instructor and Student Resources

Instructor Chapter Reference Cards

A four page color card for every chapter that includes a:

- *Concept Summary* that outlines the KEY objectives to cover in class with tips on where students get stuck as well as how to get them un-stuck. It helps bridge the gap between the instructor and student when discussing more difficult topics.

- *Case Study Lecture Demonstration Document* which provides instructors with a lecture sample based on the chapter opening case that will guide students to critically use the skills covered in the chapter, with examples of other ways the skills can be applied.

The Enhanced Instructor's Resource Center on CD-ROM includes:

- **Additional Capstone Production Tests** allow instructors to assess all the skills in a chapter with a single project.

- **Mini Case Rubrics** in Microsoft® Word format enable instructors to customize the assignment for their class.

- **PowerPoint® Presentations** for each chapter with notes included for online student.

- **Lesson Plans** that provide a detailed blueprint for an instructor to achieve chapter learning objectives and outcomes.

- **Student Data Files**

- **Annotated Solution Files**

- **Complete Test Bank**

- **Test Gen Software with QuizMaster**

TestGen is a test generator program that lets you view and easily edit testbank questions, transfer them to tests, and print in a variety of formats suitable to your teaching situation. The program also offers many options for organizing and displaying testbanks and tests. A random number test generator enables you to create multiple versions of an exam.

QuizMaster, also included in this package, allows students to take tests created with TestGen on a local area network. The QuizMaster Utility built into TestGen lets instructors view student records and print a variety of reports. Building tests is easy with Test-Gen, and exams can be easily uploaded into WebCT, BlackBoard, and CourseCompass.

Prentice Hall's Companion Web Site

www.prenhall.com/exploring offers expanded IT resources and downloadable supplements. This site also includes an online study guide for student self-study.

Online Course Cartridges

Flexible, robust and customizable content is available for all major online course platforms that include everything instructors need in one place.

www.prenhall.com/webct
www.prenhall.com/blackboard
www.coursecompass.com

myitlab for Microsoft Office 2007, is a solution designed by professors that allows you to easily deliver Office courses with defensible assessment and outcomes-based training.

The new *Exploring Office 2007* System will seamlessly integrate online assessment and training with the new myitlab for Microsoft Office 2007!

Integrated Assessment and Training

To fully integrate the new myitlab into the *Exploring Office 2007* System we built myitlab assessment and training directly from the *Exploring* instructional content. No longer is the technology just mapped to your textbook.

This 1:1 content relationship between the *Exploring* text and myitlab means that your online assessment and training will work with your textbook to move your students beyond the point and click.

Advanced Reporting

With myitlab you will get advanced reporting capabilities including a detailed student click stream. This ability to see exactly what actions your students took on a test, click-by-click, provides you with true defensible grading.

In addition, myitlab for Office 2007 will feature. . .

Project-based assessment: Test students on Exploring projects, or break down assignments into individual Office application skills.

Outcomes-based training: Students train on what they don't know without having to relearn skills they already know.

Optimal performance and uptime: Provided by world-class hosting environment.

Dedicated student and instructor support: Professional tech support is available by phone and email when you need it.

No installation required! myitlab runs entirely from the Web.

And much more!

www.prenhall.com/myitlab

Office Fundamentals Chapter

efficiently covers skills common among all applications like save, print, and bold to avoid repetition in each 1st application chapter.

chapter 1 | Office Fundamentals

Using Word, Excel, Access, and PowerPoint

bjectives

After you read this chapter you will be able to:

1. Identify common interface components (**page 4**).
2. Use Office 2007 Help (**page 10**).
3. Open a file (**page 18**).
4. Save a file (**page 21**).
5. Print a document (**page 24**).
6. Select text to edit (**page 31**).
7. Insert text and change to the Overtype mode (**page 32**).
8. Move and copy text (**page 34**).
9. Find, replace, and go to text (**page 36**).
10. Use the Undo and Redo commands (**page 39**).
11. Use language tools (**page 39**).
12. Apply font attributes (**page 43**).
13. Copy formats with the Format Painter (**page 47**).

Hands-On Exercises

Exercises	Skills Covered
1. IDENTIFYING PROGRAM INTERFACE COMPONENTS AND USING HELP (page 12)	• Use PowerPoint's Office Button, Get Help in a Dialog Box, and Use the Zoom Slider • Use Excel's Ribbon, Get Help from an Enhanced ScreenTip, and Use the Zoom Dialog Box • Search Help in Access • Use Word's Status Bar • Search Help and Print a Help Topic
2. PERFORMING UNIVERSAL TASKS (page 28) **Open:** chap1_ho2_sample.docx **Save as:** chap1_ho2_solution.docx	• Open a File and Save it with a Different Name • Use Print Preview and Select Options • Print a Document
3. PERFORMING BASIC TASKS (page 48) **Open:** chap1_ho3_internet.docx **Save as:** chap_ho3_internet_solution.docx	• Cut, Copy, Paste, and Undo • Find and Replace Text • Check Spelling • Choose Synonyms and Use Thesaurus • Use the Research Tool • Apply Font Attributes • Use Format Painter

Microsoft Office 2007 Software Office Fundamentals   1

Customize, Analyze, and Summarize Query Data

Creating and Using Queries to Make Decisions

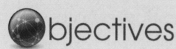bjectives

After you read this chapter you will be able to:

1. Understand the order of precedence (**page 679**).
2. Create a calculated field in a query (**page 679**).
3. Create expressions with the Expression Builder (**page 679**).
4. Create and edit Access functions (**page 690**).
5. Perform date arithmetic (**page 694**).
6. Create and work with data aggregates (**page 704**).

Hands-On Exercises

Exercises	Skills Covered
1. CALCULATED QUERY FIELDS (PAGE 683) **Open:** chap3_ho1-3_realestate.accdb **Save:** chap3_ho1-3_realestate_solution.accdb **Back up as:** chap3_ho1_realestate_solution.accdb	• Copy a Database and Start the Query • Select the Fields, Save, and Open the Query • Create a Calculated Field and Run the Query • Verify the Calculated Results • Recover from a Common Error
2. EXPRESSION BUILDER, FUNCTIONS, AND DATE ARITHMETIC (page 695) **Open:** chap3_ho1-3_realestate.accdb (from Exercise 1) **Save:** chap3_ho1-3_realestate_solution.accdb (additional modifications) **Back up as:** chap3_ho2_realestate_solution.accdb	• Create a Select Query • Use the Expression Builder • Create Calculations Using Input Stored in a Different Query or Table • Edit Expressions Using the Expression Builder • Use Functions • Work with Date Arithmetic
3. DATA AGGREGATES (page 707) **Open:** chap3_ho1-3_realestate.accdb (from Exercise 2) **Save:** chap3_ho1-3_realestate_solution.accdb (additional modifications)	• Add a Total Row • Create a Totals Query Based on a Select Query • Add Fields to the Design Grid • Add Grouping Options and Specify Summary Statistics

Access 2007 | 677

Objective Mapping

allows students to skip the skills and concepts they know and quickly find those they don't by scanning the chapter opening page for the page numbers of the material they need.

Case Study

begins each chapter to provide an effective overview of what students can accomplish by completing the chapter.

CASE STUDY

West Transylvania College Athletic Department

The athletic department of West Transylvania College has reached a fork in the road. A significant alumni contingent insists that the college upgrade its athletic program from NCAA Division II to Division I. This process will involve adding sports, funding athletic scholarships, expanding staff, and coordinating a variety of fundraising activities.

Tom Hunt, the athletic director, wants to determine if the funding support is available both inside and outside the college to accomplish this goal. You are helping Tom prepare the five-year projected budget based on current budget figures. The plan is to increase revenues at a rate of 10% per year for five years while handling an estimated 8% increase in expenses over the same five-year period. Tom feels that a 10% increase in revenue versus an 8% increase in expenses should make the upgrade viable. Tom wants to examine how increased alumni giving, increases in college fees, and grant monies will increase the revenue flow. The Transylvania College's Athletic Committee and its Alumni Association Board of Directors want Tom to present an analysis of funding and expenses to determine if the move to NCAA Division I is feasible. As Tom's student assistant this year, it is your responsibility to help him with special projects. Tom prepared the basic projected budget spreadsheet and has asked you to finish it for him.

Case Study

Your Assignment

- Read the chapter carefully and pay close attention to mathematical operations, formulas, and functions.
- Open *chap2_case_athletics*, which contains the partially completed, projected budget spreadsheet.
- Study the structure of the worksheet to determine what type of formulas you need to complete the financial calculations. Identify how you would perform calculations if you were using a calculator and make a list of formulas using regular language to determine if the financial goals will be met. As you read the chapter, identify formulas and functions that will help you complete the financial analysis. You will insert formulas in the revenue and expenditures sections for column C. Use appropriate cell references in formulas. Do not enter constant values within a formula; instead enter the 10% and 8% increases in an input area. Use appropriate functions for column totals in both the revenue and expenditures sections. Insert formulas for the Net Operating Margin and Net Margin rows. Copy the formulas.
- Review the spreadsheet and identify weaknesses in the formatting. Use your knowledge of good formatting design to improve the appearance of the spreadsheet so that it will be attractive to the Athletic Committee and the alumni board. You will format cells as currency with 0 decimals and widen columns as needed. Merge and center the title and use an attractive fill color. Emphasize the totals and margin rows with borders. Enter your name and current date. Create a custom footer that includes a page number and your instructor's name. Print the worksheet as displayed and again with cell formulas displayed. Save the workbook as **chap2_case_athletics_solution**.

Key Terms

are called out in the margins of the chapter so students can more effectively study definitions.

Pull Quotes

entice students into the theory by highlighting the most interesting points.

Tables

A *table* is a series of rows and columns that organize data.

A *cell* is the intersection of a row and column in a table.

> The table feature is one of the most powerful in Word and is the basis for an almost limitless variety of documents. It is very easy to create once you understand how a table works.

A *table* is a series of rows and columns that organize data effectively. The rows and columns in a table intersect to form *cells*. The table feature is one of the most powerful in Word and is an easy way to organize a series of data in a columnar list format such as employee names, inventory lists, and e-mail addresses. The Vacation Planner in Figure 3.1, for example, is actually a 4x9 table (4 columns and 9 rows). The completed table looks impressive, but it is very easy to create once you understand how a table works. In addition to the organizational benefits, tables make an excellent alignment tool. For example, you can create tables to organize data such as employee lists with phone numbers and e-mail addresses. The Exploring series uses tables to provide descriptions for various software commands. Although you can align text with tabs, you have more format control when you create a table. (See the Practice Exercises at the end of the chapter for other examples.)

Vacation Planner			
Item	Number of Days	Amount per Day (est)	Total Amount
Airline Ticket			449.00
Amusement Park Tickets	4	50.00	200.00
Hotel	5	120.00	600.00
Meals	6	50.00	300.00
Rental Car	5	30.00	150.00
Souvenirs	5	20.00	100.00
TOTAL EXPECTED EXPENSES			$1799.00

Figure 3.1 The Vacation Planner

In this section, you insert a table in a document. After inserting the table, you can insert or delete columns and rows if you need to change the structure. Furthermore, you learn how to merge and split cells within the table. Finally, you change the row height and column width to accommodate data in the table.

Inserting a Table

You can create a table from the Insert tab. Click Table in the Tables group on the Insert tab to see a gallery of cells from which you select the number of columns and rows you require in the table, or you can choose the Insert Table command below the gallery to display the Insert Table dialog box and enter the table composition you prefer. When you select the table dimension from the gallery or from the Insert Table dialog box, Word creates a table structure with the number of columns and rows you specify. After you define a table, you can enter text, numbers, or graphics in individual cells. Text

Keyword for search

Collections to be searched

Type of clips to be included in results

CIS 101 Review Session
Test #2

Monday
7pm
Glass 102

Search results

Link to Microsoft Clip Organizer

Link to more clips online

Figure 3.18 The Clip Art Task Pane

You can access the Microsoft Clip Organizer (to view the various collections) by clicking Organize clips at the bottom of the Clip Art task pane. You also can access the Clip Organizer when you are not using Word; click the Start button on the taskbar, click All Programs, Micros[...] Clip Organizer. Once in the Organi[...] ous collections, reorganize the exi[...] add new clips (with their associate[...] the bottom of the task pane in Figu[...] and tips for finding more relevant c[...]

Insert a Picture

In addition to the collection of clip[...] you also can insert your own pictur[...] ital camera attached to your compu[...] Word. After you save the picture to[...] on the Insert tab to locate and inser[...] opens so that you can navigate to t[...] insert the picture, there are many c[...] mands are discussed in the next sec[...]

Formatting a Grap[...]

When you ins[...]
fined size. For[...]
very large and[...]
resized. Most t[...]
within the d[...]

(Remember that graphical elements should enhance a document, not overpower it.)

Step 2
Move and Resize the Clip Art Object

Refer to Figure 3.24 as you complete Step 2.

a. Click once on the clip art object to select it. Click **Text Wrapping** in the Arrange group on the Picture Tools Format tab to display the text wrapping options, and then select **Square**, as shown in Figure 3.24.

   You must change the layout in order to move and size the object.

b. Click **Position** in the Arrange group, and then click **More Layout Options.** Click the **Picture Position tab** in the Advanced Layout dialog box, if necessary, then click **Alignment** in the *Horizontal* section. Click the **Alignment drop-down arrow** and select **Right.** Deselect the **Allow overlap check box** in the *Options* section. Click **OK.**

c. Click **Crop** in the Size group, then hold your mouse over the sizing handles and notice how the pointer changes to angular shapes. Click the **bottom center handle** and drag it up. Drag the side handles inward to remove excess space surrounding the graphical object.

d. Click the Shape **Height box** in the Size group and type **2.77.**

   Notice the width is changed automatically to retain the proportion.

e. Save the document.

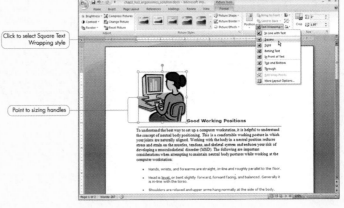

Click to select Square Text Wrapping style

Point to sizing handles

Figure 3.24 Formatting Clip Art

Step 3
Create a WordArt Object

Refer to Figure 3.25 as you complete Step 3.

a. Press **Ctrl+End** to move to the end of the document. Click the **Insert tab**, and then click **WordArt** in the Text group to display the WordArt gallery.

b. Click **WordArt Style 28** on the bottom row of the gallery.

   The Edit WordArt Text dialog box displays, as shown in Figure 3.25.

Summary

1. **Create a presentation using a template.** Using a template saves you a great deal of time and enables you to create a more professional presentation. Templates incorporate a theme, a layout, and content that can be modified. You can use templates that are installed when Microsoft Office is installed, or you can download templates from Microsoft Office Online. Microsoft is constantly adding templates to the online site for your use.

2. **Modify a template.** In addition to changing the content of a template, you can modify the structure and design. The structure is modified by changing the layout of a slide. To change the layout, drag placeholders to new locations or resize placeholders. You can even add placeholders so that elements such as logos can be included.

3. **Create a presentation in Outline view.** When you use a storyboard to determine your content, you create a basic outline. Then you can enter your presentation in Outline view, which enables you to concentrate on the content of the presentation. Using Outline view keeps you from getting buried in design issues at the cost of your content. It also saves you time because you can enter the information without having to move from placeholder to placeholder.

4. **Modify an outline structure.** Because the Outline view gives you a global view of the presentation, it helps you see the underlying structure of the presentation. You are able to see where content needs to be strengthened, or where the flow of information needs to be revised. If you find a slide with content that would be presented better in another location in the slide show, you can use the Collapse and Expand features to easily move it. By collapsing the slide content, you can drag it to a new location and then expand it. To move individual bullet points, cut and paste the bullet point or drag-and-drop it.

5. **Print an outline.** When you present, using the outline version of your slide show as a reference is a boon. No matter how well you know your information, it is easy to forget to present some information when facing an audience. While you would print speaker's notes if you have many details, you can print the outline as a quick reference. The outline can be printed in either the collapsed or the expanded form, giving you far fewer pages to shuffle in front of an audience than printing speaker's notes would.

6. **Import an outline.** You do not need to re-enter information from an outline created in Microsoft Word or another word processor. You can use the Open feature to import any outline that has been saved in a format that PowerPoint can read. In addition to a Word outline, you can use the common generic formats Rich Text Format and Plain Text Format.

7. **Add existing content to a presentation.** After you spend time creating the slides in a slide show, you may find that slides in the slide show would be appropriate in another show at a later date. Any slide you create can be reused in another presentation, thereby saving you considerable time and effort. You simply open the Reuse Slides pane, locate the slide show with the slide you need, and then click on the thumbnail of the slide to insert a copy of it in the new slide show.

8. **Examine slide show design principles.** With a basic understanding of slide show design principles you can create presentations that reflect your personality in a professional way. The goal of applying these principles is to create a slide show that focuses the audience on the message of the slide without being distracted by clutter or unreadable text.

9. **Apply and modify a design theme.** PowerPoint provides you with themes to help you create a clean, professional look for your presentation. Once a theme is applied you can modify the theme by changing the color scheme, the font scheme, the effects scheme, or the background style.

10. **Insert a header or footer.** Identifying information can be included in a header or footer. You may, for example, wish to include the group to whom you are presenting, or the location of the presentation, or a copyright notation for original work. You can apply footers to slides, handouts, and Notes pages. Headers may be applied to handouts and Notes pages.

Summary

links directly back to the objectives so students can more effectively study and locate the concepts that they need to focus on.

More End-of-Chapter Exercises with New Levels of Assessment

offer instructors more options for assessment. Each chapter has approximately 12-15 projects per chapter ranging from multiple choice to open-ended projects.

Practice Exercises

reinforce skills learned in the chapter with specific directions on what to do and how to do it.

New Mid-Level Exercises

assess the skills learned in the chapter by directing the students on what to do but not how to do it.

New Capstone Exercises

cover all of the skills with in each chapter without telling students how to perform the skills.

Mini Cases with Rubrics

are open ended exercises that guide both instructors and students to a solution with a specific rubric for each Mini Case.

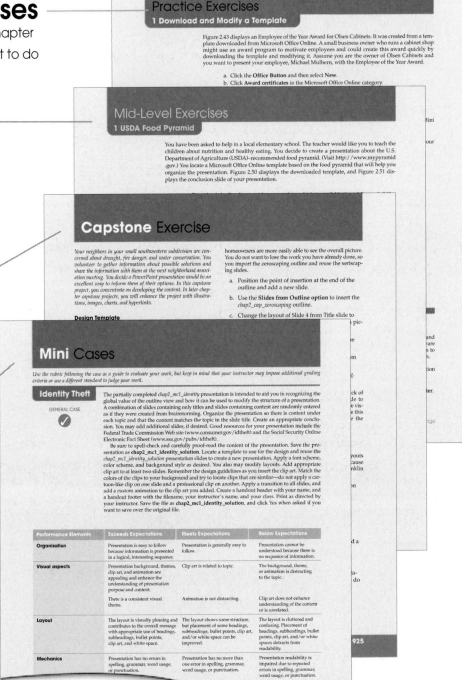

Using Word, Excel, Access, and PowerPoint

bjectives

After you read this chapter, you will be able to:

1. Identify common interface components (page 4).
2. Use Office 2007 Help (page 10).
3. Open a file (page 18).
4. Save a file (page 21).
5. Print a document (page 24).
6. Select text to edit (page 31).
7. Insert text and change to the Overtype mode (page 32).
8. Move and copy text (page 34).
9. Find, replace, and go to text (page 36).
10. Use the Undo and Redo commands (page 39).
11. Use language tools (page 39).
12. Apply font attributes (page 43).
13. Copy formats with the Format Painter (page 47).

Hands-On Exercises

Exercises	Skills Covered
1. IDENTIFYING PROGRAM INTERFACE COMPONENTS AND USING HELP (page 12)	• Use PowerPoint's Office Button, Get Help in a Dialog Box, and Use the Zoom Slider • Use Excel's Ribbon, Get Help from an Enhanced ScreenTip, and Use the Zoom Dialog Box • Search Help in Access • Use Word's Status Bar • Search Help and Print a Help Topic
2. PERFORMING UNIVERSAL TASKS (page 28) Open: chap1_ho2_sample.docx Save as: chap1_ho2_solution.docx	• Open a File and Save It with a Different Name • Use Print Preview and Select Options • Print a Document
3. PERFORMING BASIC TASKS (page 48) Open: chap1_ho3_internet_docx Save as: chap_ho3_internet_solution.docx	• Cut, Copy, Paste, and Undo • Find and Replace Text • Check Spelling • Choose Synonyms and Use Thesaurus • Use the Research Tool • Apply Font Attributes • Use Format Painter

CASE STUDY

Color Theory Design

Natalie Trevino's first job after finishing her interior design degree is with Color Theory Design of San Diego. Her new supervisor has asked her to review a letter written to an important client and to make any changes or corrections she thinks will improve it. Even though Natalie has used word processing software in the past, she is unfamiliar with Microsoft Office 2007. She needs to get up to speed with Word 2007 so that she can open the letter, edit the content, format the appearance, re-save the file, and print the client letter. Natalie wants to successfully complete this important first task, plus she wants to become familiar with all of Office 2007 because she realizes that her new employer, CTD, makes extensive use of all the Office products.

Case Study

In addition, Natalie needs to improve the appearance of an Excel workbook by applying font attributes, correcting spelling errors, changing the zoom magnification, and printing the worksheet. Finally, Natalie needs to modify a short PowerPoint presentation that features supplemental design information for CTD's important client.

Your Assignment

- Read the chapter and open the existing client letter, *chap1_case_design*.
- Edit the letter by inserting and overtyping text and moving existing text to improve the letter's readability.
- Find and replace text that you want to update.
- Check the spelling and improve the vocabulary by using the thesaurus.
- Modify the letter's appearance by applying font attributes.
- Save the file as **chap1_case_design_solution**, print preview, and print a copy of the letter.
- Open the *chap1_case_bid* workbook in Excel, apply bold and blue font color to the column headings, spell-check the worksheet, change the zoom to 125%, print preview, and print the workbook. Save the workbook as **chap1_case_bid_solution**.
- Open the *chap1_case_design* presentation in PowerPoint, spell-check the presentation, format text, and save it as **chap1_case_design_solution**.

Microsoft Office 2007 Software

(Which software application should you choose? You have to start with an analysis of the output required.)

Microsoft Office 2007 is composed of several software applications, of which the primary components are Word, Excel, PowerPoint, and Access. These programs are powerful tools that can be used to increase productivity in creating, editing, saving, and printing files. Each program is a specialized and sophisticated program, so it is necessary to use the correct one to successfully complete a task, much like using the correct tool in the physical world. For example, you use a hammer, not a screwdriver, to pound a nail into the wall. Using the correct tool gets the job done correctly and efficiently the first time; using the wrong tool may require redoing the task, thus wasting time. Likewise, you should use the most appropriate software application to create and work with computer data.

Choosing the appropriate application to use in a situation seems easy to the beginner. If you need to create a letter, you type the letter in Word. However, as situations increase in complexity, so does the need to think through using each application. For example, you can create an address book of names and addresses in Word to create form letters; you can create an address list in Excel and then use spreadsheet commands to manipulate the data; further, you can store addresses in an Access database table and then use database capabilities to manipulate the data. Which software application should you choose? You have to start with an analysis of the output required. If you only want a form letter as the final product, then you might use Word; however, if you want to spot customer trends with the data and provide detailed reports, you would use Access. Table 1.1 describes the main characteristics of the four primary programs in Microsoft Office 2007 to help you decide which program to use for particular tasks.

Table 1.1 Office Products

Office 2007 Product	Application Characteristics
Word 2007	***Word processing software*** is used with text to create, edit, and format documents such as letters, memos, reports, brochures, resumes, and flyers.
Excel 2007	***Spreadsheet software*** is used to store quantitative data and to perform accurate and rapid calculations with results ranging from simple budgets to financial analyses and statistical analyses.
PowerPoint 2007	***Presentation graphics software*** is used to create slide shows for presentation by a speaker, to be published as part of a Web site, or to run as a stand-alone application on a computer kiosk.
Access 2007	***Relational database software*** is used to store data and convert it into information. Database software is used primarily for decision-making by businesses that compile data from multiple records stored in tables to produce informative reports.

Word processing software is used primarily with text to create, edit, and format documents.

Spreadsheet software is used primarily with numbers to create worksheets.

Presentation graphics software is used primarily to create electronic slide shows.

Relational database software is used to store data and convert it into information.

In this section, you explore the common interface among the programs. You learn the names of the interface elements. In addition, you learn how to use Help to get assistance in using the software.

Identifying Common Interface Components

A *user interface* is the meeting point between computer software and the person using it.

A *user interface* is the meeting point between computer software and the person using it and provides the means for a person to communicate with a software program. Word, Excel, PowerPoint, and Access share the overall Microsoft Office 2007 interface. This interface is made up of three main sections of the screen display shown in Figure 1.1.

Office Button, Quick Access Toolbar, and title bar

Ribbon

Status bar

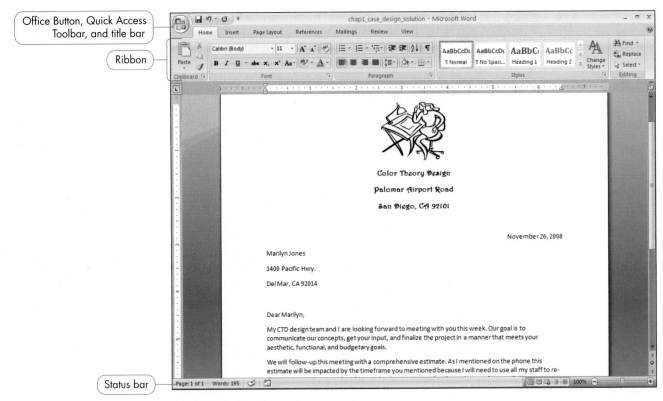

Figure 1.1   Office 2007 Interface

Use the Office Button and Quick Access Toolbar

The first section of the Office 2007 interface contains three distinct items: the Microsoft Office Button (referred to as Office Button in the Exploring series), Quick Access Toolbar, and the title bar. These three items are located at the top of the interface for quick access and reference. The following paragraphs explain each item.

The *Office Button* is an icon that, when clicked, displays the *Office menu*, a list of commands that you can perform on the entire file or for the specific Office program. For example, when you want to perform a task that involves the entire document, such as saving, printing, or sharing a file with others, you use the commands on the Office menu. You also use the Office menu commands to work with the entire program, such as customizing program settings or exiting from the program. Some commands on the Office menu perform a default action when you click them, such as Save—the file open in the active window is saved. However, other commands open a submenu when you point to or click the command. Figure 1.2 displays the Office menu in Access 2007.

Click the *Office Button* to display the Office menu.

The *Office menu* contains commands that work with an entire file or with the program.

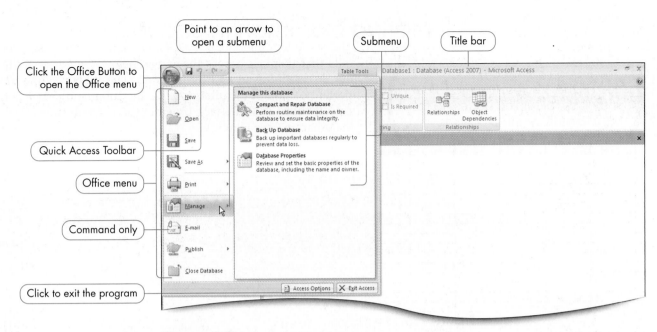

Figure 1.2 Access Office Menu

TIP Displaying the Office Menu from the Keyboard

If you prefer to use a keyboard shortcut to display the Office menu instead of clicking the Office Button, press Alt+F.

The **Quick Access Toolbar** contains buttons for frequently used commands.

The second item at the top of the window is the **Quick Access Toolbar**, which contains buttons for frequently used commands, such as saving a file or undoing an action. This toolbar keeps buttons for common tasks on the screen at all times, enabling you to be more productive in using these frequently used commands.

TIP Customizing the Quick Access Toolbar

As you become more familiar with Microsoft Office 2007, you might find that you need quick access to additional commands, such as Print Preview or Spelling & Grammar. You can easily customize the Quick Access Toolbar by clicking the Customize Quick Access Toolbar drop-down arrow on the right end of the toolbar and adding command buttons from the list that displays. You also can customize the toolbar by changing where it displays. If you want it closer to the document window, you can move the toolbar below the Ribbon.

A **title bar** displays the program name and file name at the top of a window.

The third item at the top of the screen is the **title bar**, which displays the name of the open program and the file name at the top of a window. For example, in Figure 1.1, *chap1_case_design_solution* is the name of a document, and *Microsoft Word* is the name of the program. In Figure 1.2, *Database1* is the name of the file, and *Microsoft Access* is the name of the program.

The **Ribbon** is a large strip of visual commands that enables you to perform tasks.

(The Ribbon is the command center of the Microsoft Office 2007 interface, providing access to the functionality of the programs.)

Familiarize Yourself with the Ribbon

The second section of the Office 2007 interface is the **Ribbon**, a large strip of visual commands that displays across the screen below the Office Button, Quick Access Toolbar, and the title bar. The Ribbon is the most important section of the interface: It is the command center of the Microsoft Office 2007 interface, providing access to the functionality of the programs (see Figure 1.3).

Figure 1.3 The Ribbon

The Ribbon has three main components: tabs, groups, and commands. The following list describes each component.

Tabs, which look like folder tabs, divide the Ribbon into task-oriented categories.

- **Tabs**, which look like folder tabs, divide the Ribbon into task-oriented sections. For example, the Ribbon in Word contains these tabs: Home, Insert, Page Layout, Reference, Mailings, Review, and View. When you click the Home tab, you see a set of core commands for that program. When you click the Insert tab, you see a set of commands that enable you to insert objects, such as tables, clip art, headers, page numbers, etc.

Groups organize similar commands together within each tab.

- **Groups** organize related commands together on each tab. For example, the Home tab in Word contains these groups: Clipboard, Font, Paragraph, Styles, and Editing. These groups help organize related commands together so that you can find them easily. For example, the Font group contains font-related commands, such as Font, Font Size, Bold, Italic, Underline, Highlighter, and Font Color.

A **command** is a visual icon in each group that you click to perform a task.

- **Commands** are specific tasks performed. Commands appear as visual icons or buttons within the groups on the Ribbon. The icons are designed to provide a visual clue of the purpose of the command. For example, the Bold command looks like a bolded B in the Font group on the Home tab. You simply click the desired command to perform the respective task.

The Ribbon has the same basic design—tabs, groups, and commands—across all Microsoft Office 2007 applications. When you first start using an Office 2007 application, you use the Home tab most often. The groups of commands on the Home tab are designed to get you started using the software. For example, the Home tab contains commands to help you create, edit, and format a document in Word, a worksheet in Excel, and a presentation in PowerPoint. In Access, the Home tab contains groups of commands to insert, delete, and edit records in a database table. While three of the four applications contain an Insert tab, the specific groups and commands differ by application. Regardless of the application, however, the Insert tab contains commands to *insert something*, whether it is a page number in Word, a column chart in Excel, or a shape in PowerPoint. One of the best ways to develop an understanding of the Ribbon is to study its structure in each application. As you explore each program, you will notice the similarities in how commands are grouped on tabs, and you will notice the differences specific to each application.

The Ribbon provides an extensive sets of commands that you use when creating and editing documents, worksheets, slides, tables, or other items. Figure 1.4 points out other important components of the Ribbon.

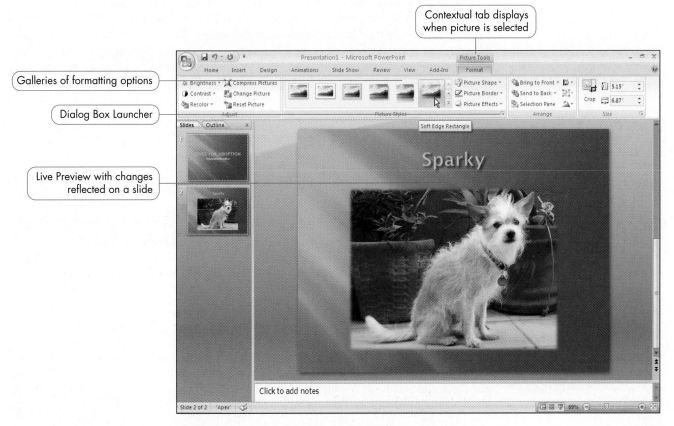

Figure 1.4 PowerPoint with Ribbon

A **dialog box** is a window that provides options related to a group of commands.

A **Dialog Box Launcher** is a small icon that, when clicked, opens a related dialog box.

A **gallery** is a set of options that appears as thumbnail graphics.

Live Preview provides a preview of the results for gallery options.

Figure 1.4 shows examples of four other components of the Ribbon. These components include a Dialog Box Launcher, a gallery, Live Preview, and a contextual tab. The following list describes each component:

- A **Dialog Box Launcher** is a small icon located on the right side of some group names that you click to open a related **dialog box**, which is a window that provides options related to a group of commands.

- A **gallery** is a set of options that appear as thumbnail graphics that visually represent the option results. For example, if you create a chart in Excel, a gallery of chart formatting options provides numerous choices for formatting the chart.

- **Live Preview** works with the galleries, providing a preview of the results of formatting in the document. As you move your mouse pointer over the gallery thumbnails, you see how each formatting option affects the selected item in your document, worksheet, or presentation. This feature increases productivity because you see the results immediately. If you do not like the results, keep moving the mouse pointer over other gallery options until you find a result you like.

A ***contextual tab*** is a tab that provides specialized commands that display only when the object they affect is selected.

• A *contextual tab* provides specialized commands that display only when the object they affect is selected. For example, if you insert a picture on a slide, PowerPoint displays a contextual tab on the Ribbon with commands specifically related to the selected image. When you click outside the picture to deselect it, the contextual tab disappears.

TIP   Using Keyboard Shortcuts

Many people who have used previous Office products like to use the keyboard to initiate commands. Microsoft Office 2007 makes it possible for you to continue to use keyboard shortcuts for commands on the Ribbon. Simply press Alt on the keyboard to display the Ribbon and Quick Access Toolbar with shortcuts called Key Tips. A *Key Tip* is the letter or number that displays over each feature on the Ribbon or Quick Access Toolbar and is the keyboard equivalent that you press. Notice the Key Tips that display in Figure 1.5 as a result of pressing Alt on the keyboard. Other keyboard shortcuts, such as Ctrl+C to copy text, remain the same from previous versions of Microsoft Office.

A ***Key Tip*** is the letter or number that displays over each feature on the Ribbon and Quick Access Toolbar and is the keyboard equivalent that you press.

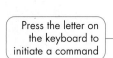

Press the letter on the keyboard to initiate a command

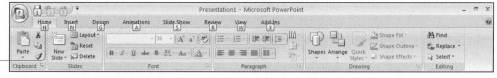

Figure 1.5   Key Tips Displayed for Ribbon and Quick Access Toolbar

---

Use the Status Bar

The ***status bar*** displays below the document and provides information about the open file and buttons for quick access.

The third major section of the Office 2007 user interface is the status bar. The *status bar* displays at the bottom of the program window and contains information about the open file and tools for quick access. The status bar contains details for the file in the specific application. For example, the Word status bar shows the current page, total number of pages, total words in the document, and proofreading status. The PowerPoint status bar shows the slide number, total slides in the presentation, and the applied theme. The Excel status bar provides general instructions and displays the average, count, and sum of values for selected cells. In each program, the status bar also includes View commands from the View tab for quick access. You can use the View commands to change the way the document, worksheet, or presentation displays onscreen. Table 1.2 describes the main characteristics of each Word 2007 view.

Table 1.2 Word Document Views

View Option	Characteristics
Print Layout	Displays the document as it will appear when printed.
Full Screen Reading	Displays the document on the entire screen to make reading long documents easier. To remove Full Screen Reading, press the Esc key on the keyboard.
Web Page	Displays the document as it would look as a Web page.
Outline	Displays the document as an outline.
Draft	Displays the document for quick editing without additional elements such as headers or footers.

The ***Zoom slider*** enables you to increase or decrease the magnification of the file onscreen.

The ***Zoom slider***, located on the right edge of the status bar, enables you to drag the slide control to change the magnification of the current document, worksheet, or presentation. You can change the display to zoom in on the file to get a close up view, or you can zoom out to get an overview of the file. To use the Zoom slider, click and drag the slider control to the right to increase the zoom or to the left to decrease the zoom. If you want to set a specific zoom, such as 78%, you can type the precise value in the Zoom dialog box when you click Zoom on the View tab. Figure 1.6 shows the Zoom dialog box and the elements on Word's status bar. The Zoom dialog box in Excel and PowerPoint looks similar to the Word Zoom dialog box, but it contains fewer options in the other programs.

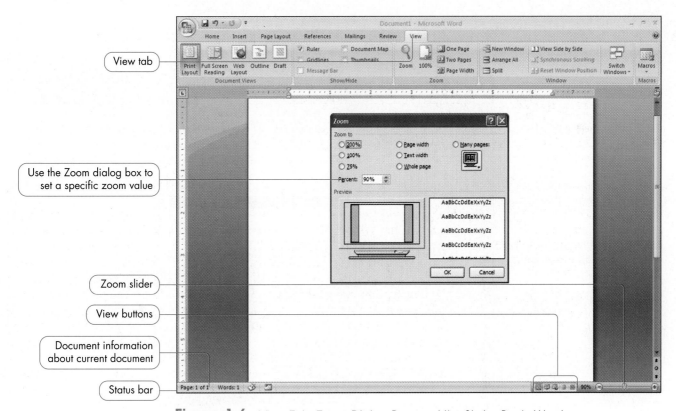

Figure 1.6 View Tab, Zoom Dialog Box, and the Status Bar in Word

Using Office 2007 Help

Help is always available when you use any Office 2007 program.

Have you ever started a project such as assembling an entertainment center and had to abandon it because you had no way to get help when you got stuck? Microsoft Office includes features that keep this type of scenario from happening when you use Word, Excel, Access, or PowerPoint. In fact, several methods are available to locate help when you need assistance performing tasks. Help is always available when you use any Office 2007 program. Help files reside on your computer when you install Microsoft Office, and Microsoft provides additional help files on its Web site. If you link to Microsoft Office Online, you not only have access to help files for all applications, you also have access to up-to-date products, files, and graphics to help you complete projects.

Use Office 2007 Help

To access Help, press F1 on the keyboard or click the Help button on the right edge of the Ribbon shown in Figure 1.7. If you know the topic you want help with, such as printing, you can type the key term in the Search box to display help files on that topic. Help also displays general topics in the lower part of the Help window that are links to further information. To display a table of contents for the Help files, click the Show Table of Contents button, and after locating the desired help topic, you can print the information for future reference by clicking the Print button. Figure 1.7 shows these elements in Excel Help.

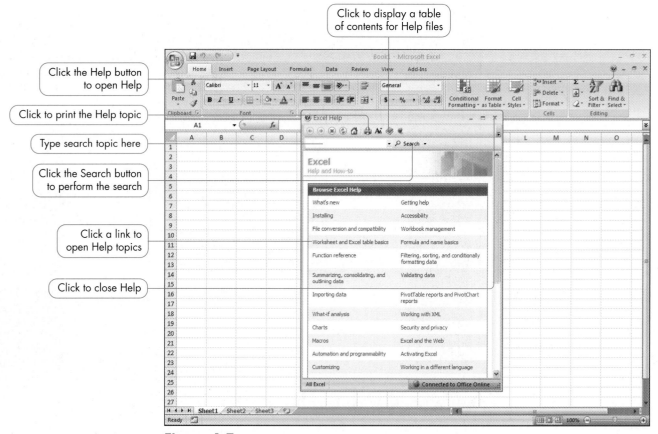

Figure 1.7   Excel Help

Use Enhanced ScreenTips

An **Enhanced ScreenTip**
displays the name and brief
description of a command
when you rest the pointer on a
command.

Another method for getting help is to use the Office 2007 Enhanced ScreenTips. An *Enhanced ScreenTip* displays when you rest the mouse pointer on a command. Notice in Figure 1.8 that the Enhanced ScreenTip provides the command name, a brief description of the command, and a link for additional help. To get help on the specific command, keep the pointer resting on the command and press F1 if the Enhanced ScreenTip displays a Help icon. The advantage of this method is that you do not have to find the correct information yourself because the Enhanced ScreenTip help is context sensitive.

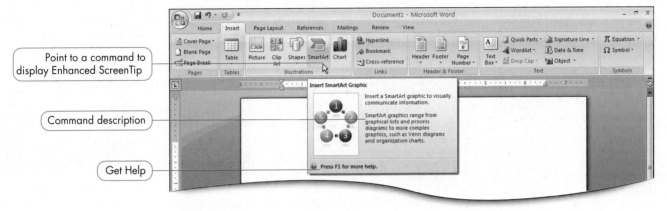

Figure 1.8 Enhanced ScreenTip

Get Help with Dialog Boxes

As you work within a dialog box, you might need help with some of the numerous options contained in that dialog box, but you do not want to close the dialog box to get assistance. For example, if you open the Insert Picture dialog box and want help with inserting files, click the Help button located on the title bar of the dialog box to display specific help for the dialog box. Figure 1.9 shows the Insert Picture dialog box with Help displayed.

Figure 1.9 Help with Dialog Boxes

Hands-On Exercises

1 | Identifying Program Interface Components and Using Help

Skills covered: 1. Use PowerPoint's Office Button, Get Help in a Dialog Box, and Use the Zoom Slider **2.** Use Excel's Ribbon, Get Help from an Enhanced ScreenTip, and Use the Zoom Dialog Box **3.** Search Help in Access **4.** Use Word's Status Bar **5.** Search Help and Print a Help Topic

---

Step 1
Use PowerPoint's Office Button, Get Help in a Dialog Box, and Use the Zoom Slider

Refer to Figure 1.10 as you complete Step 1.

a. Click **Start** to display the Start menu. Click (or point to) **All Programs**, click **Microsoft Office**, then click **Microsoft Office PowerPoint 2007** to start the program.

b. Point to and rest the mouse on the Office Button, and then do the same to the Quick Access Toolbar.

As you rest the mouse pointer on each object, you see an Enhanced ScreenTip for that object.

TROUBLESHOOTING: If you do not see the Enhanced ScreenTip, keep the mouse pointer on the object a little longer.

c. Click the **Office Button** and slowly move your mouse down the list of menu options, pointing to the arrow after any command name that has one.

The Office menu displays, and as you move the mouse down the list, submenus display for menu options that have an arrow.

d. Select **New**.

The New Presentation dialog box displays. Depending on how Microsoft Office 2007 was installed, your screen may vary. If Microsoft Office 2007 was fully installed, you should see a thumbnail to create a Blank Presentation, and you may see additional thumbnails in the *Recently Used Templates* section of the dialog box.

e. Click the **Help button** on the title bar of the New Presentation dialog box.

PowerPoint Help displays the topic *Create a new file from a template*.

f. Click **Close** on the Help Window and click the **Cancel** button in the New Presentation dialog box.

g. Click and drag the **Zoom slider** to the right to increase the magnification. Then click and drag the **Zoom slider** back to the center point for a 100% zoom.

h. To exit PowerPoint, click the **Office Button** to display the Office menu, and then click the **Exit PowerPoint button**.

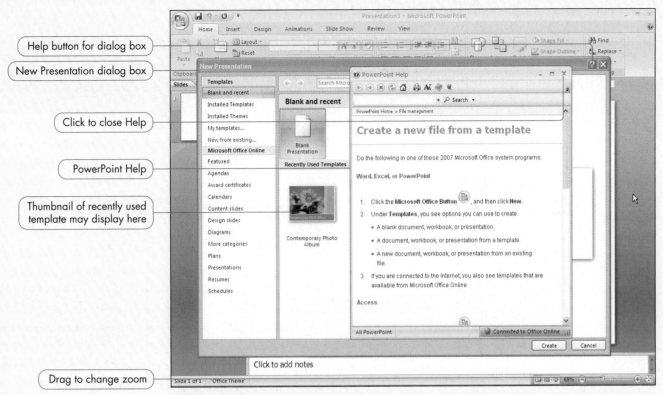

Help button for dialog box

New Presentation dialog box

Click to close Help

PowerPoint Help

Thumbnail of recently used
template may display here

Drag to change zoom

Figure 1.10 PowerPoint Help for New Presentations Dialog Box

Step 2
**Use Excel's Ribbon,
Get Help from an
Enhanced ScreenTip,
and Use the Zoom
Dialog Box**

Refer to Figure 1.11 as you complete Step 2.

a. Click **Start** to display the Start menu. Click (or point to) **All Programs**, click **Microsoft Office**, then click **Microsoft Office Excel 2007** to open the program.

b. Click the **Insert tab** on the Ribbon.

The Insert tab contains groups of commands for inserting objects, such as tables, illustrations, charts, links, and text.

c. Rest the mouse on **Hyperlink** in the Links group on the Insert tab.

The Enhanced ScreenTip for Hyperlinks displays. Notice the Enhanced ScreenTip contains a Help icon.

d. Press **F1** on the keyboard.

Excel Help displays the *Create or remove a hyperlink* Help topic.

TROUBLESHOOTING: If you are not connected to the Internet, you might not see the context-sensitive help.

e. Click the **Close button** on the Help window.

f. Click the **View tab** on the Ribbon and click **Zoom** in the Zoom group.

The Zoom dialog box appears so that you can change the zoom percentage.

g. Click the **200%** option and click **OK**.

The worksheet is now magnified to 200% of its regular size.

h. Click **Zoom** in the Zoom group on the View tab, click the **100%** option, and click **OK**.

The worksheet is now restored to 100%.

i. To exit Excel, click the **Office Button** to display the Office menu, and then click the **Exit Excel button**.

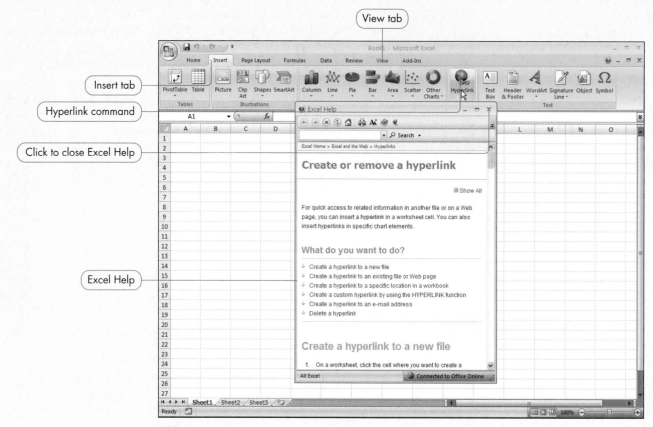

Figure 1.11 Excel Ribbon with Help

Step 3
Search Help in Access

Refer to Figure 1.12 as you complete Step 3.

a. Click **Start** to display the Start menu. Click (or point to) **All Programs**, click **Microsoft Office**, then click **Microsoft Office Access 2007** to start the program.

Access opens and displays the Getting Started with Microsoft Access screen.

TROUBLESHOOTING: If you are not familiar with Access, just use the opening screen that displays and continue with the exercise.

b. Press **F1** on the keyboard.

Access Help displays.

c. Type **table** in the Search box in the Access Help window.

d. Click the **Search** button.

Access displays help topics.

e. Click the topic **Create tables in a database**.

The help topic displays.

f. Click the **Close** button on the Access Help window.

Access Help closes.

g. To exit Access, click the **Office Button** to display the Office menu, and then click the **Exit Access button**.

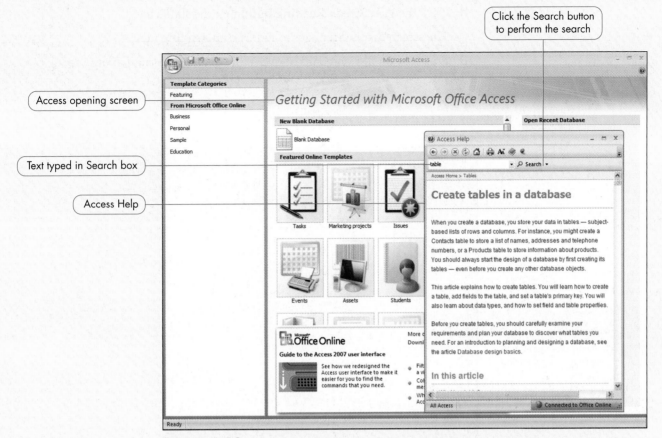

Access opening screen

Text typed in Search box

Access Help

Click the Search button to perform the search

Figure 1.12 Access Help

Step 4
Use Word's Status Bar

Refer to Figure 1.13 as you complete Step 4.

a. Click **Start** to display the Start menu. Click (or point to) **All Programs**, click **Microsoft Office**, then click **Microsoft Office Word 2007** to start the program.

Word opens with a blank document ready for you to start typing.

b. Type your first name.

Your first name displays in the document window.

c. Point your mouse to the **Zoom slider** on the status bar.

d. Click and drag the **Zoom slider** to the right to increase the magnification.

The document with your first name increases in size onscreen.

e. Click and drag the slider control to the left to decrease the magnification.

The document with your first name decreases in size.

f. Click and drag the **Zoom slider** back to the center.

The document returns to 100% magnification.

g. Slowly point the mouse to the buttons on the status bar.

A ScreenTip displays the names of the buttons.

h. Click the **Full Screen Reading button** on the status bar.

The screen display changes to Full Screen Reading view.

i. Press **Esc** on the keyboard to return the display to Print Layout view.

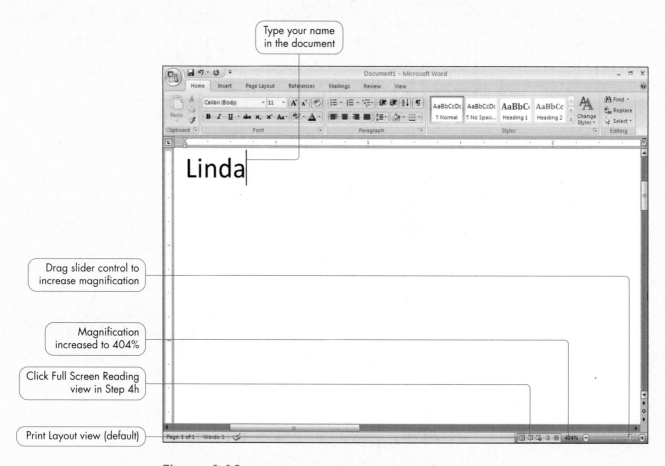

Type your name in the document

Drag slider control to increase magnification

Magnification increased to 404%

Click Full Screen Reading view in Step 4h

Print Layout view (default)

Figure 1.13 The Word Status Bar

Step 5

Search Help and Print a Help Topic

Refer to Figure 1.14 as you complete Step 5.

a. With Word open on the screen, press **F1** on the keyboard.

Word Help displays.

b. Type **zoom** in the Search box in the Word Help window.

c. Click the **Search** button.

Word Help displays related topics.

d. Click the topic **Zoom in or out of a document**.

The help topic displays.

TROUBLESHOOTING: If you do not have a printer that is ready to print, skip Step 5e and continue with the exercise.

e. Turn on the attached. printer, be sure it has paper, and then click the Word Help **Print** button.

The Help topic prints on the attached printer.

f. Click the **Show Table of Contents** button on the Word Help toolbar.

The Table of Contents pane displays on the left side of the Word Help dialog box so that you can click popular Help topics, such as *What's new*. You can click a closed book icon to see specific topics to click for additional information, and you can click an open book icon to close the main Help topic.

g. Click the **Close** button on Word Help.

Word Help closes.

h. To exit Word, click the **Office Button** to display the Office menu, and then click the **Exit Word button**.

A warning appears stating that you have not saved changes to your document.

i. Click **No** in the Word warning box.

You exit Word without saving the document.

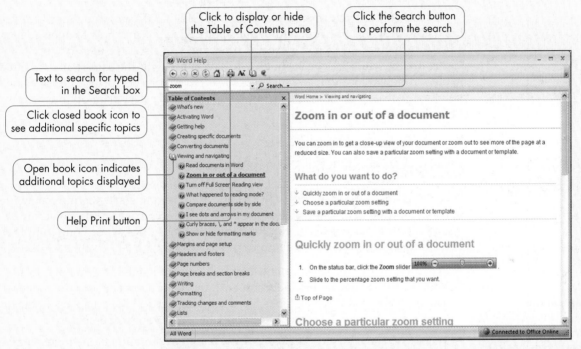

Figure 1.14 Word Help

Universal Tasks

Today, storing large amounts of information on a computer is taken for granted, but in reality, computers would not have become very important if you could not save and re-use the files you create.

One of the most useful and important aspects of using computers is the ability to save and re-use information. For example, you can store letters, reports, budgets, presentations, and databases as files to reopen and use at some time in the future. Today, storing large amounts of information on a computer is taken for granted, but in reality, computers would not have become very important if you could not save and re-use the files you create.

Three fundamental tasks are so important for productivity that they are considered universal to most every computer program, including Office 2007:

- opening files that have been saved
- saving files you create
- printing files

In this section, you open a file within an Office 2007 program. Specifically, you learn how to open a file from within the Open dialog box and how to open a file from a list of recently used files in a specific program. You also save files to keep them for future use. Specifically, you learn how to save a file with the same name, a different name, a different location, or a different file type. Finally, you print a file. Specifically, you learn how to preview a file before printing it and select print options within the Print dialog box.

Opening a File

When you start any program in Office 2007, you need to start creating a new file or open an existing one. You use the Open command to retrieve a file saved on a storage device and place it in the random access memory (RAM) of your computer so you can work on it. For example:

The ***insertion point*** is the blinking vertical line in the document, cell, slide show, or database table designating the current location where text you type displays.

- When you start Word 2007, a new blank document named Document1 opens. You can either start typing in Document1, or you can open an existing document. The ***insertion point***, which looks like a blinking vertical line, displays in the document designating the current location where text you type displays.

- When you start PowerPoint 2007, a new blank presentation named Presentation1 opens. You can either start creating a new slide for the blank presentation, or you can open an existing presentation.

- When you start Excel 2007, a new blank workbook named Book1 opens. You can either start inputting labels and values into Book1, or you can open an existing workbook.

- When you start Access 2007—unlike Word, PowerPoint, and Excel—a new blank database is not created automatically for you. In order to get started using Access, you must create and name a database first or open an existing database.

Open a File Using the Open Dialog Box

Opening a file in any of the Office 2007 applications is an easy process: Use the Open command from the Office menu and specify the file to open. However, locating the file to open can be difficult at times because you might not know where the file you want to use is located. You can open files stored on your computer or on a remote computer that you have access to. Further, files are saved in folders, and you might need to look for files located within folders or subfolders. The Open dialog box, shown in Figure 1.15, contains many features designed for file management; however, two features are designed specifically to help you locate files.

- **Look in**—provides a hierarchical view of the structure of folders and subfolders on your computer or on any computer network you are attached to. Move up or down in the structure to find a specific location or folder and then click the desired location to select it. The file list in the center of the dialog box displays the subfolders and files saved in the location you select. Table 1.3 lists and describes the toolbar buttons.
- **My Places bar**—provides a list of shortcut links to specific folders on your computer and locations on a computer network that you are attached to. Click a link to select it, and the file list changes to display subfolders and files in that location.

Table 1.3 Toolbar Buttons

Buttons	Characteristics
Previous Folder	Returns to the previous folder you viewed.
Up One Level	Moves up one level in the folder structure from the current folder.
Delete	Deletes the selected file or selected folder.
Create New Folder	Creates a new folder within the current folder.
Views	Changes the way the list of folders and files displays in the File list.

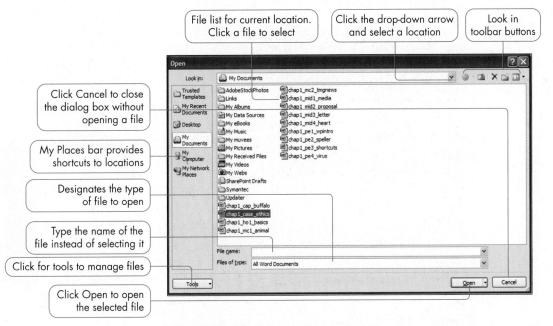

Figure 1.15 Open Dialog Box in Word

After you locate and select the file, click the Open button in the dialog box to display the file on the screen. However, if, for example, you work as part of a workgroup that shares files with each other, you might find the need to open files in a more specialized way. Microsoft Office programs provide several options for opening files when you click the drop-down arrow on the Open button. For example, if you want to keep the original file intact, you might open the file as a copy of the original. Table 1.4 describes the Open options.

Table 1.4 Open Options

Open Options	Characteristics
Open	Opens the selected file with the ability to read and write (edit).
Open Read-Only	Opens the selected file with the ability to read the contents but prevents you from changing or editing it.
Open as Copy	Opens the selected file as a copy of the original so that if you edit the file, the original remains unchanged.
Open in Browser	Opens the selected file in a Web browser.
Open with Transform	Opens a file and provides the ability to transform it into another type of document, such as an HTML document.
Open and Repair	Opens the selected file and attempts to repair any damage. If you have difficulty opening a file, try to open it by selecting Open and Repair.

Open Files Using the Recent Documents List

Office 2007 provides a quick method for accessing files you used recently. The Recent Documents list displays when the Office menu opens and provides a list of links to the last few files you used. The list changes as you work in the application to reflect only the most recent files. Figure 1.16 shows the Office menu with the Recent Documents list.

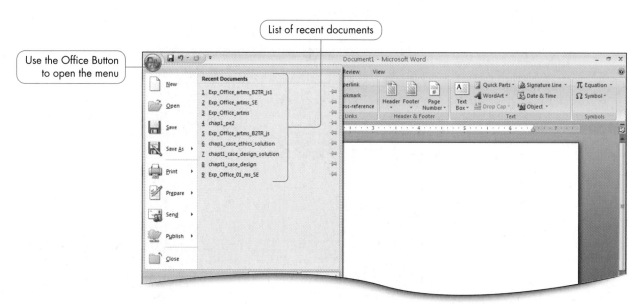

Figure 1.16 The Recent Documents List

TIP Keeping Files on the Recent Documents List

As you use the Office application and open several files, the list of Recent Documents changes; however, you can designate files to keep displayed on the Recent Documents list at all times. Notice the icon of the pushpin that displays immediately following each file name on the Recent Documents list. Just as you use pushpins to post an important notice in the real world, you use pushpins here to designate important files that you want easy access to. To pin a specific file to the Recent Documents list, click the icon of a gray pushpin. The shape of the pin changes as if pushed in, and the color of the pin changes to green designating that the file is pinned permanently on the list. However, if later you decide to remove the file from the list, you can unpin it by simply clicking the green pushpin, changing the icon back to gray, and the file will disappear from the list over time. Notice the Recent Documents list with both gray and green pushpins in Figure 1.17.

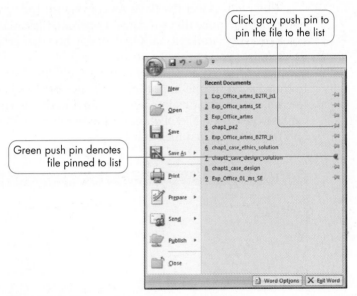

Figure 1.17 The Recent Documents List

Saving a File

As you work with any Office 2007 application and create files, you will need to save them for future use. While you are working on a file, it is stored in the temporary memory or RAM of your computer. When you save a file, the contents of the file stored in RAM are saved to the hard drive of your computer or to a storage device such as a flash drive. As you create, edit, and format a complex file such as a report, slide show, or budget, you should consider saving several versions of it as you work. For example, you might number versions or use the date in the file name to designate each version. Using this method enables you to revert to a previous version of the document if necessary. To save a file you create in Word, PowerPoint, or Excel, click the Office Button to display the Office menu. Office provides two commands that work similarly: Save and Save As. Table 1.5 describes the characteristics of these two commands.

> As you create, edit, and format a complex file such as a report, slide show, or budget, you should consider saving several versions of it as you work.

Table 1.5 Save Options

Command	Characteristics
Save	Saves the open document: • If this is the first time the document is being saved, Office 2007 opens the Save As dialog box so that you can name the file. • If this document was saved previously, the document is automatically saved using the original file name.
Save As	Opens the Save As dialog box: • If this is the first time the document is being saved, use the Save As dialog box to name the file. • If this document was saved previously, use this option to save the file with a new name, in a new location, or as a new file type preserving the original file with its original name.

When you select the Save As command, the Save As dialog box appears (see Figure 1.18). Notice that saving and opening files are related, that the Save As dialog box looks very similar to the Open dialog box that you saw in Figure 1.15. The dialog box requires you to specify the drive or folder in which to store the file, the name of the file, and the type of file you wish the file to be saved as. Additionally, because finding saved files is important, you should always group related files together in folders, so that you or someone else can find them in a location that makes sense. You can use the Create New Folder button in the dialog box to create and name a folder, and then save related files to it.

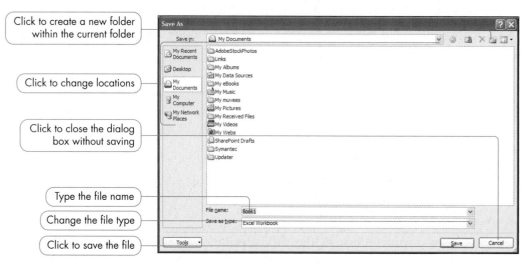

Figure 1.18 Save As Dialog Box in Excel

All subsequent executions of the Save command save the file under the assigned name, replacing the previously saved version with the new version. Pressing Ctrl+S is another way to activate the Save command. If you want to change the name of the file, use the Save As command. Word, PowerPoint, and Excel use the same basic process for saving files, which include the following options:

• naming and saving a previously unsaved file

• saving an updated file with the same name and replacing the original file with the updated one

• saving an updated file with a different name or in a different location to keep the original intact

• saving the file in a different file format

TIP Saving from the Office Menu

You should select the Save As command on the Office menu rather than pointing to the arrow that follows the command. When you point to the arrow, menu options display for saving the file in an alternative format. Always check the Save as type box in the dialog box to be sure that the correct file type is specified.

Office 2007 saves files in a different format from previous versions of the software. Office now makes use of XML formats for files created in Word, PowerPoint, and Excel. For example, in previous versions of Word, all documents were saved with the three-letter extension .doc. Now Word saves default documents with the four-letter extension .docx. The new XML format makes use of file compression to save storage space for the user. The files are compressed automatically when saved and uncompressed when opened. Another important feature is that the XML format makes using the files you create in Office 2007 easier to open in other software. This increased portability of files is a major benefit in any workplace that might have numerous applications to deal with. The new file format also differentiates between files that contain *macros*, which are small programs that automate tasks in a file, and those that do not. This specification of files that contain macros enables a virus checker to rigorously check for damaging programs hidden in files. A *virus checker* is software that scans files for a hidden program that can damage your computer. Table 1.6 lists the file formats with the four-letter extension for Word, PowerPoint, and Excel, and a five-letter extension for Access.

A *macro* is a small program that automates tasks in a file.

A *virus checker* is software that scans files for a hidden program that can damage your computer.

A *template* is a file that contains formatting and design elements.

Table 1.6 Word, PowerPoint, Excel, and Access File Extensions

File Format	Characteristics
Word	.docx—default document format .docm—a document that contains macros .dotx—a template without macros (a **template** is a file that contains formatting and design elements) .dotm—a template with macros
PowerPoint	.pptx—default presentation format .pptm—a presentation that contains macros .potx—a template .potm—a template with macros .ppam—an add-in that contains macros .ppsx—a slide show .ppsm—a slide show with macros .sldx—a slide saved independently of a presentation .sldm—a slide saved independently of a presentation that contains a macro .thmx—a theme used to format a slide
Excel	.xlsx—default workbook .xlsm—a workbook with macros .xltx—a template .xltm—a template with a macro .xlsb—non-XML binary workbook—for previous versions of the software .xlam—an add-in that contains macros
Access	.accdb—default database

Access 2007 saves data differently from Word, PowerPoint, and Excel. When you start Access, which is a relational database, you must create a database and define at least one table for your data. Then as you work, your data is stored automatically. This powerful software enables multiple users access to up-to-date data. The concepts of saving, opening, and printing remain the same, but the process of how data is saved is unique to this powerful environment.

TIP   Changing the Display of the My Places Bar

Sometimes finding saved files can be a time-consuming chore. To help you quickly locate files, Office 2007 provides options for changing the display of the My Places bar. In Word, PowerPoint, Excel, and Access, you can create shortcuts to folders where you store commonly used files and add them to the My Places bar. From the Open or Save As dialog box, select the location in the Look in list you want to add to the bar. With the desired location selected, point to an empty space below the existing shortcuts on the My Places bar. Right-click the mouse to display a *shortcut menu*, which displays when you right-click the mouse on an object and provides a list of commands pertaining to the object you clicked. From the shortcut menu, choose Add (folder name)—the folder name is the name of the location you selected in the Look in box. The new shortcut is added to the bottom of the My Places bar. Notice the shortcut menu in Figure 1.19, which also provides options to change the order of added shortcuts or remove an unwanted shortcut. However, you can only remove the shortcuts that you add to the bar; the default shortcuts cannot be removed.

A ***shortcut menu*** displays when you right-click the mouse on an object and provides a list of commands pertaining to the object you clicked.

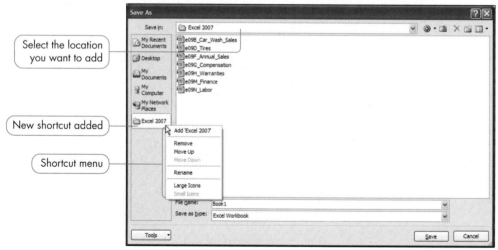

Select the location you want to add

New shortcut added

Shortcut menu

Figure 1.19   Save As Dialog Box with New Shortcut Added to My Places Bar

Printing a Document

As you work with Office 2007 applications, you will need to print hard copies of documents, such as letters to mail, presentation notes to distribute to accompany a slide show, budget spreadsheets to distribute at a staff meeting, or database summary reports to submit. Office provides flexibility so that you can preview the document before you send it to the printer; you also can select from numerous print options, such as changing the number of copies printed; or you can simply and quickly print the current document on the default printer.

Preview Before You Print

It is highly recommended that you preview your document before you print because Print Preview displays all the document elements, such as graphics and formatting, as they will appear when printed on paper. Previewing the document first enables you to make any changes that you need to make without wasting paper. Previewing documents uses the same method in all Office 2007 applications, that is, point to the arrow next to the Print command on the Office menu and select Print Preview to display the current document, worksheet, presentation, or database table in the Print Preview window. Figure 1.20 shows the Print Preview window in Word 2007.

> It is highly recommended that you preview your document before you print because Print Preview displays all the document elements, such as graphics and formatting, as they will appear when printed on paper.

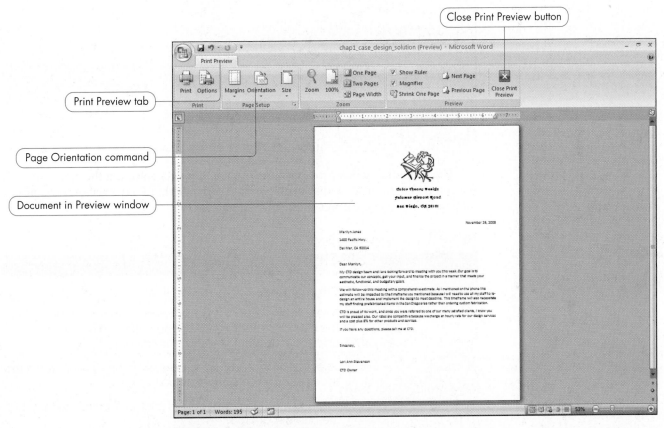

Figure 1.20 Print Preview Window

As you preview the document, you can get a closer look at the results by changing the zoom. Notice that the mouse pointer displays in the Preview window as a magnifying glass with a plus sign, so that you can simply click in the document to increase the zoom. Once clicked, the plus sign changes to a minus sign, enabling you to click in the document again to decrease the zoom. You also can use the Zoom group on the Print Preview tab or the Zoom slider on the status bar to change the view of the document.

Other options on the Print Preview tab change depending on the application that you are using. For example, you might want to change the orientation to switch from portrait to landscape. Refer to Figure 1.20. ***Portrait orientation*** is longer than it is wide, like the portrait of a person; whereas, ***landscape orientation*** is wider than it is long, resembling a landscape scene. You also can change the size of the paper or other options from the Print Preview tab.

Portrait orientation is longer than it is wide—like the portrait of a person.

Landscape orientation is wider than it is long, resembling a landscape scene.

If you need to edit the document before printing, close the Print Preview window and return to the document. However, if you are satisfied with the document and want to print, click Print in the Print group on the Print Preview tab. The Print dialog box displays. Figure 1.21 shows Word's Print dialog box.

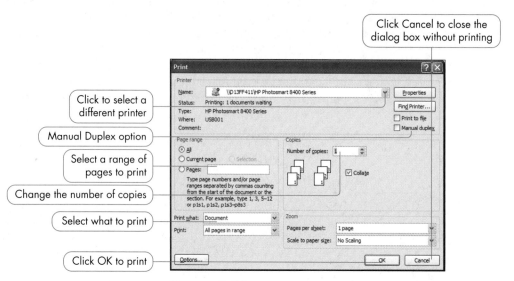

Figure 1.21 Print Dialog Box

The Print dialog box provides numerous options for selecting the correct printer, selecting what to print, and selecting how to print. Table 1.7 describes several important and often-used features of the Print dialog box.

Table 1.7 Print Dialog Box

Print Option	Characteristics
All	Select to print all the pages in the file.
Current page/slide	Select to print only the page or slide with the insertion point. This is a handy feature when you notice an error in a file, and you only want to reprint the corrected page.
Pages	Select to print only specific pages in a document. You must specify page numbers in the text box.
Number of Copies	Change the number of copies printed from the default 1 to the number desired.
Collate	Click if you are printing multiple copies of a multi-page file, and you want to print an entire first copy before printing an entire second copy, and so forth.
Print what	Select from options on what to print, varying with each application.
Selection	Select to print only selected text or objects in an Excel worksheet.
Active sheet(s)	Select to print only the active worksheet(s) in Excel.
Entire workbook	Select to print all worksheets in the Excel workbook.

As you work with other Office 2007 applications, you will notice that the main print options remain unchanged; however, the details vary based on the specific task of the application. For example, the *Print what* option in PowerPoint includes options such as printing the slide, printing handouts, printing notes, or printing an outline of the presentation.

A **duplex printer** prints on both sides of the page.

A **manual duplex** operation allows you to print on both sides of the paper by printing first on one side and then on the other.

TIP   Printing on Both Sides of the Paper

Duplex printers print on both sides of the page. However, if you do not have a duplex printer, you can still print on two sides of the paper by performing a **manual duplex** operation, which prints on both sides of the paper by printing first on one side, and then on the other. To perform a manual duplex print job in Word 2007, select the Manual duplex option in the Print dialog box. Refer to Figure 1.21. With this option selected, Word prints all pages that display on one side of the paper first, then prompts you to turn the pages over and place them back in the printer tray. The print job continues by printing all the pages that appear on the other side of the paper.

Print Without Previewing the File

If you want to print a file without previewing the results, select Print from the Office menu, and the Print dialog box displays. You can still make changes in the Print dialog box, or just immediately send the print job to the printer. However, if you just want to print quickly, Office 2007 provides a quick print option that enables you to send the current file to the default printer without opening the Print dialog box. This is a handy feature to use if you have only one printer attached and you want to print the current file without changing any print options. You have two ways to quick print:

- Select Quick Print from the Office menu.
- Customize the Quick Access toolbar to add the Print icon. Click the icon to print the current file without opening the Print dialog box.

Hands-On Exercises

2 | Performing Universal Tasks

Skills covered: 1. Open a File and Save It with a Different Name **2.** Use Print Preview and Select Options **3.** Print a Document

---

Step 1
Open a File and Save It with a Different Name

Refer to Figure 1.22 as you complete Step 1.

a. Start Word, click the **Office Button** to display the Office menu, and then select **Open**.

The Open dialog box displays.

b. If necessary, click the **Look in drop-down arrow** to locate the files for this text-book to find *chap1_ho2_sample*.

TROUBLESHOOTING: If you have trouble finding the files that accompany this text, you may want to ask your instructor where they are located.

c. Select the file and click **Open**.

The document displays on the screen.

d. Click the **Office Button**, and then select **Save As** on the Office menu.

The Save As dialog box displays.

e. In the *File name* box, type **chap1_ho2_solution**.

f. Check the location listed in the **Save in** box. If you need to change locations to save your files, use the **Save in drop-down arrow** to select the correct location.

g. Make sure that the *Save as type* option is Word Document.

TROUBLESHOOTING: Be sure that you click the **Save As** command rather than pointing to the arrow after the command, and be sure that Word Document is specified in the Save as type box.

h. Click the **Save button** in the dialog box to save the file under the new name.

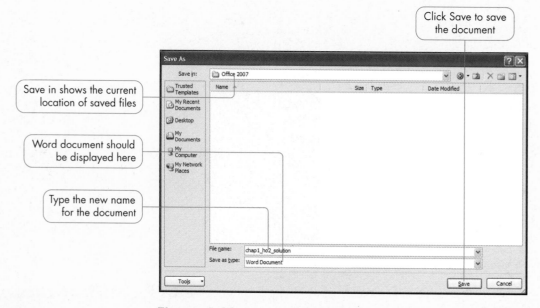

Figure 1.22 Save As Dialog Box

Step 2
Use Print Preview and Select Options

Refer to Figure 1.23 as you complete Step 2.

a. With the document displayed on the screen, click the **Office Button** and point to the arrow following **Print** on the Office menu.

The Print submenu displays.

b. Select **Print Preview**.

The document displays in the Print Preview window.

c. Point the magnifying glass mouse pointer in the document and click the mouse once.

TROUBLESHOOTING: If you do not see the magnifying glass pointer, point the mouse in the document and keep it still for a moment.

The document magnification increases.

d. Point the magnifying glass mouse pointer in the document and click the mouse again.

The document magnification decreases.

e. Click **Orientation** in the Page Setup group on the Print Preview tab.

The orientation options display.

f. Click **Landscape**.

The document orientation changes to landscape.

g. Click **Orientation** a second time, and then choose **Portrait**.

The document returns to portrait orientation.

h. Click the **Close Print Preview** button on the Print Preview tab.

i. The Print Preview window closes.

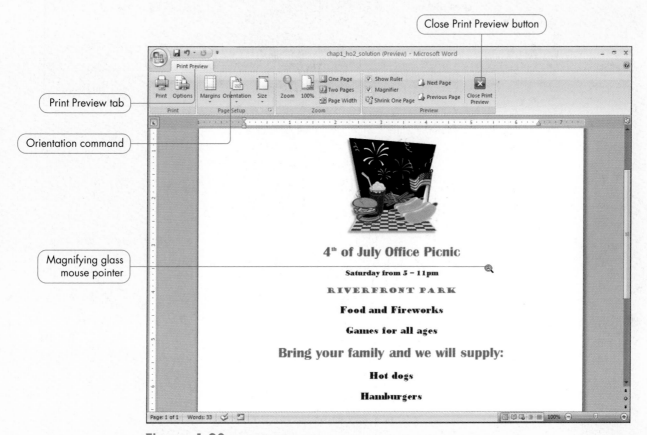

Figure 1.23 Print Preview

Refer to Figure 1.24 as you complete Step 3.

a. Click the **Office Button**, and then point to the arrow next to **Print** on the Office menu.

The print options display.

b. Select **Print**.

The Print dialog box displays.

TROUBLESHOOTING: Be sure that your printer is turned on and has paper loaded.

c. If necessary, select the correct printer in the **Name box** by clicking the drop-down arrow and selecting from the resulting list.

d. Click **OK**.

The Word document prints on the selected printer.

e. To exit Word, click the **Office Button**, and then click the **Exit Word button**.

f. If prompted to save the file, choose **No**.

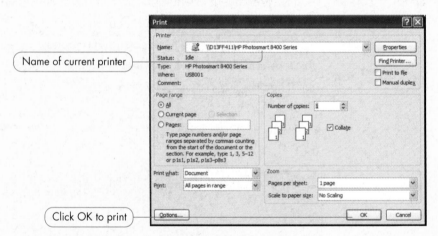

Figure 1.24 The Print Dialog Box

Basic Tasks

Many of the operations you perform in one Office program are the same or similar in all Office applications. These tasks are referred to as basic tasks and include such operations as inserting and typing over, copying and moving items, finding and replacing text, undoing and redoing commands, checking spelling and grammar, using the thesaurus, and using formatting tools. Once you learn the underlying concepts of these operations, you can apply them in different applications.

Most basic tasks in Word fall into two categories:

- editing a document
- formatting a document

Most successful writers use many word processing features to revise and edit documents, and most would agree that the revision process takes more time than the initial writing process. Errors such as spelling and grammar need to be eliminated to produce error-free writing. However, to turn a rough draft into a finished document, such as a report for a class or for a business, requires writers to revise and edit several times by adding text, removing text, replacing text, and moving text around to make the meaning clearer. Writers also improve their writing using tools to conduct research to make the information accurate and to find the most appropriate word using the thesaurus. Modern word processing applications such as Word 2007 provide these tools and more to aid the writer.

> Most successful writers use many word processing features to revise and edit documents, and most would agree that the revision process takes more time than the initial writing process.

The second category of basic tasks is formatting text in a document. Formatting text includes changing the type, the size, and appearance of text. You might want to apply formatting to simply improve the look of a document, or you might want to emphasize particular aspects of your message. Remember that a poorly formatted document or workbook probably will not be read. So whether you are creating your résumé or the income statement for a corporation's annual report, how the output looks is important. Office 2007 provides many tools for formatting documents, but in this section, you will start by learning to apply font attributes and copy those to other locations in the document.

In this section, you learn to perform basic tasks in Office 2007, using Word 2007 as the model. As you progress in learning other Office programs such as PowerPoint, Excel, and Access, you will apply the same principles in other applications.

Selecting Text to Edit

Most editing processes involve identifying the text that the writer wants to work with. For example, to specify which text to edit, you must select it. The most common method used to select text is to use the mouse. Point to one end of the text you want to select (either the beginning or end) and click-and-drag over the text. The selected text displays highlighted with a light blue background so that it stands out from other text and is ready for you to work with. The *Mini toolbar* displays when you select text in Word, Excel, and PowerPoint. It displays above the selected text as semitransparent and remains semitransparent until you point to it. Often-used commands from the Clipboard, Font, and Paragraph groups on the Home tab are repeated on the Mini toolbar for quick access. Figure 1.25 shows selected text with the Mini toolbar fully displayed in the document.

The *Mini toolbar* displays above the selected text as semitransparent and repeats often-used commands.

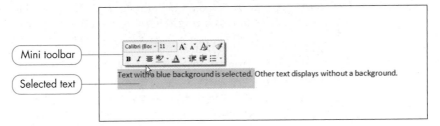

Figure 1.25 Selected Text

Sometimes you want to select only one word or character, and trying to drag over it to select it can be frustrating. Table 1.8 describes other methods used to select text.

Table 1.8 Easy Text Selection in Word

Outcome Desired	Method
Select a word	Double-click the word.
One line of text	Point the mouse to the left of the line, and when the mouse pointer changes to a right-pointing arrow, click the mouse.
A sentence	Hold down Ctrl and click in the sentence to select.
A paragraph	Triple-click the mouse in the paragraph.
One character to the left of the insertion point	Hold down Shift and press the left arrow key.
One character to the right of the insertion point	Hold down Shift and press the right arrow key.

TIP Selecting Large Amounts of Text

As you edit documents, you might need to select a large portion of a document. However, as you click-and-drag over the text, you might have trouble stopping the selection at the desired location because the document scrolls by too quickly. This is actually a handy feature in Word 2007 that scrolls through the document when you drag the mouse pointer at the edge of the document window.

To select a large portion of a document, click the insertion point at the beginning of the desired selection. Then move the display to the end of the selection using the scroll bar at the right edge of the window. Scrolling leaves the insertion point where you placed it. When you reach the end of the text you want to select, hold down Shift and click the mouse. The entire body of text is selected.

Inserting Text and Changing to the Overtype Mode

Insert is adding text in a document.

As you create and edit documents using Word, you will need to *insert* text, which is adding text in a document. To insert or add text, point and click the mouse in the location where the text should display. With the insertion point in the location to insert the text, simply start typing. Any existing text moves to the right, making room for the new inserted text. At times, you might need to add a large amount of text in a document, and you might want to replace or type over existing text instead of inserting text. This task can be accomplished two ways:

- Select the text to replace and start typing. The new text replaces the selected text.

Overtype mode replaces the existing text with text you type character by character.

- Switch to **Overtype mode**, which replaces the existing text with text you type character by character. To change to Overtype mode, select the Word Options button on the Office menu. Select the option Use Overtype Mode in the Editing Options section of the Advanced tab. Later, if you want to return to Insert mode, repeat these steps to deselect the overtype mode option. Figure 1.26 shows the Word Options dialog box.

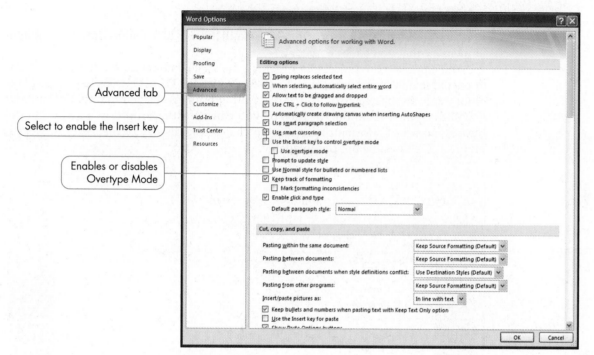

Figure 1.26 The Word Options Dialog Box

TIP Using the Insert Key on the Keyboard

If you find that you need to switch between Insert and Overtype mode often, you can enable Insert on the keyboard by clicking the Word Options button on the Office menu. Select the option Use the Insert Key to Control Overtype Mode in the Editing Options section on the Advanced tab. Refer to Figure 1.26. You can now use Insert on the keyboard to switch between the two modes, and this option stays in effect until you go back to the Word Options dialog box and deselect it.

Moving and Copying Text

As you revise a document, you might find that you need to move text from one location to another to improve the readability of the content. To move text, you must cut the selected text from its original location and then place it in the new location by pasting it there. To duplicate text, you must copy the selected text in its original location and then paste the duplicate in the desired location. To decide whether you should use the Cut or Copy command in the Clipboard group on the Home tab to perform the task, you must notice the difference in the results of each command:

- **Cut** removes the selected original text or object from its current location.
- **Copy** makes a duplicate copy of the text or object, leaving the original text or object intact.

Keep in mind while you work, that by default, Office 2007 retains only the last item in memory that you cut or copied.

You complete the process by invoking the Paste command. **Paste** places the cut or copied text or object in the new location. Notice the Paste Options button displays along with the pasted text. You can simply ignore the Paste Options button, and it will disappear from the display, or you can click the drop-down arrow on the button and select a formatting option to change the display of the text you pasted. Figure 1.27 shows the options available.

Cut removes the original text or object from its current location.

Copy makes a duplicate copy of the text or object, leaving the original intact.

Paste places the cut or copied text or object in the new location.

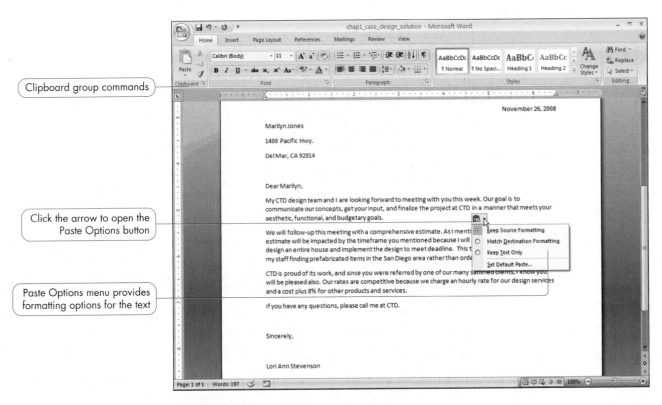

Figure 1.27 Text Pasted in the Document

TIP Moving and Copying Using Shortcuts

You can use alternative methods instead of using the commands located on the Home tab to cut, copy, and paste text. Office 2007 provides the following shortcuts:

- After selecting text, point back to the selected text and right-click the mouse. The shortcut menu displays, allowing you to choose Cut or Copy. Move the insertion point to the desired location, right-click the mouse again, and choose Paste from the shortcut menu.

- After selecting text, use the keyboard shortcut combinations Ctrl+C to copy or Ctrl+X to cut text. Move the insertion point to the new location and press Ctrl+V to paste. These keyboard shortcuts work in most Windows applications, so they can be very useful.

- After selecting text, you can move it a short distance in the document by dragging to the new location. Point to the selected text, hold down the left mouse button, and then drag to the desired location. While you are dragging the mouse, the pointer changes to a left-pointing arrow with a box attached to it. Release the mouse button when you have placed the insertion point in the desired location, and the text displays in the new location.

Use the Office Clipboard

The **Clipboard** is a memory location that holds up to 24 items for you to paste into the current document, another file, or another application.

Office 2007 provides an option that enables you to cut or copy multiple items to the *Clipboard*, which is a memory location that holds up to 24 items for you to paste into the current file, another file, or another application. The Clipboard stays active only while you are using one of the Office 2007 applications. When you exit from all Office 2007 applications, all items on the Clipboard are deleted. To accumulate items on the Clipboard, you must first display it by clicking the Dialog Box Launcher in the Clipboard group on the Home tab. When the Clipboard pane is open on the screen, its memory location is active, and the Clipboard accumulates all items you cut or copy up to the maximum 24. To paste an item from the Clipboard, point to it, click the resulting drop-down arrow, and choose Paste. To change how the Clipboard functions, use the Options button shown in Figure 1.28. One of the most important options allows the Clipboard to accumulate items even when it is not open on the screen. To activate the Clipboard so that it works in the background, click the Options button in the Clipboard, and then select Collect without Showing Office Clipboard.

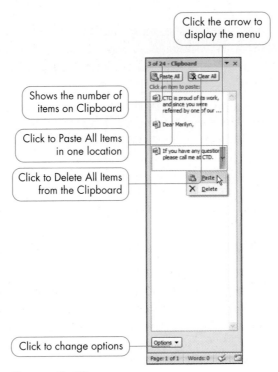

Figure 1.28 Clipboard

Finding, Replacing, and Going to Text

You can waste a great deal of time slowly scrolling through a document trying to locate text or other items. Office 2007 provides features that speed up editing by automatically finding text and objects in a document, thus making you more productive. Office 2007 provides the following three related operations that all use the Find and Replace dialog box:

- The *Find* command enables you to locate a word or group of words in a document quickly.

- The *Replace* command not only finds text quickly, it replaces a word or group of words with other text.

- The *Go To* command moves the insertion point to a specific location in the document.

Find Text

To locate text in an Office file, choose the Find command in the Editing group on the Home tab and type the text you want to locate in the resulting dialog box, as shown in Figure 1.29. After you type the text to locate, you can find the next instance after the insertion point and work through the file until you find the instance of the text you were looking for. Alternatively, you can find all instances of the text in the file at one time. If you decide to find every instance at once, the Office application temporarily highlights each one, and the text stays highlighted until you perform another operation in the file.

Find locates a word or group of words in a document.

Replace not only finds text, it replaces a word or group of words with other text.

Go To moves the insertion point to a specific location in the document.

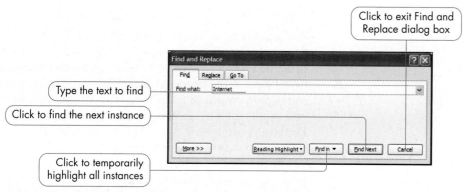

Click to exit Find and Replace dialog box

Type the text to find

Click to find the next instance

Click to temporarily highlight all instances

Figure 1.29 Find Tab of the Find and Replace Dialog Box

TIP Finding and Highlighting Text in Word

Sometimes, temporarily highlighting all instances of text is not sufficient to help you edit the text you find. If you want Word to find all instances of specific text in a document and keep the highlighting from disappearing until you want it to, you can use the Reading Highlight option in the Find dialog box. One nice feature of this option is that even though the text remains highlighted on the screen, the document prints normally without highlighting. Figure 1.30 shows the Find and Replace dialog box with the Reading Highlight options that you use to highlight or remove the highlight from a document.

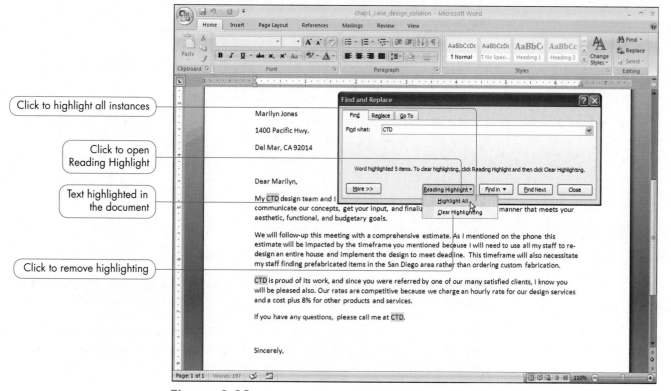

Click to highlight all instances

Click to open Reading Highlight

Text highlighted in the document

Click to remove highlighting

Figure 1.30 Find and Replace Dialog Box with Highlighting Options

Replace Text

While revising a file, you might realize that you have used an incorrect term and need to replace it throughout the entire file. Alternatively, you might realize that you could be more productive by re-using a letter or report that you polished and saved if you replace the previous client's or corporation's name with a new one. While you could perform these tasks manually, it would not be worth the time involved, and you might miss an instance of the old text, which could prove embarrassing. The Replace command in the Editing group on the Home tab can quickly and easily replace the old text with the new text throughout an entire file.

In the Find and Replace dialog box, first type the text to find, using the same process you used with the Find command. Second, type the text to replace the existing text with. Third, specify how you want Word to perform the operation. You can either replace each instance of the text individually, which can be time-consuming but allows you to decide whether to replace each instance one at a time, or you can replace every instance of the text in the document all at once. Word (but not the other Office applications) also provides options in the dialog box that help you replace only the correct text in the document. Click the More button to display these options. The most important one is the Find whole words only option. This option forces the application to find only complete words, not text that is part of other words. For instance, if you are searching for the word *off* to replace with other text, you would not want Word to replace the *off* in *office* with other text. Figure 1.31 shows these options along with the options for replacing text.

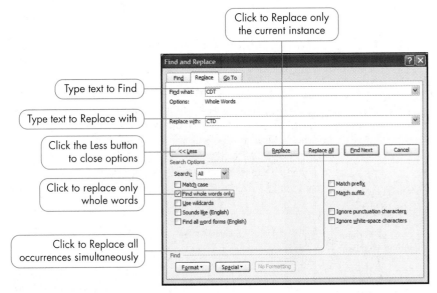

Figure 1.31 Find and Replace Dialog Box

Go Directly to a Location in a File

If you are editing a long document and want to move within it quickly, you can use the Go To command by clicking the down arrow on the Find command in the Editing group on the Home tab rather than slowly scrolling through an entire document or workbook. For example, if you want to move the insertion point to page 40 in a 200-page document, choose the Go To command and type 40 in the *Enter page number* text box. Notice the list of objects you can choose from in the Go to what section of the dialog box in Figure 1.32.

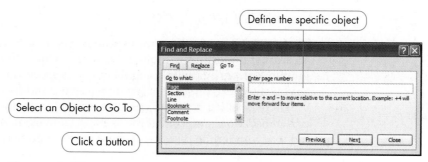

Figure 1.32 Go To Tab of the Find and Replace Dialog Box

Using the Undo and Redo Commands

The **Undo** command cancels your last one or more operations.

The **Redo** command reinstates or reverses an action performed by the Undo command.

As you create and edit files, you may perform an operation by mistake or simply change your mind about an edit you make. Office applications provide the **Undo** command, which can cancel your previous operation or even your last few operations. After using Undo to reverse an action or operation, you might decide that you want to use the **Redo** command to reinstate or reverse the action taken by the Undo command.

To undo the last action you performed, click Undo on the Quick Access Toolbar. For example, if you deleted text by mistake, immediately click Undo to restore it. If, however, you deleted some text and then performed several other operations, you can find the correct action to undo, with the understanding that all actions after that one will also be undone. To review a list of the last few actions you performed, click the Undo drop-down arrow and select the desired one from the list—Undo highlights all actions in the list down to that item and will undo all of the highlighted actions. Figure 1.33 shows a list of recent actions in PowerPoint. To reinstate or reverse an action as a result of using the Undo command, click Redo on the Quick Access Toolbar.

The **Repeat** command repeats only the last action you performed.

The **Repeat** command provides limited use because it repeats only the last action you performed. To repeat the last action, click Repeat on the Quick Access Toolbar. If the Office application is able to repeat your last action, the results will display in the document. Note that the Repeat command is replaced with the Redo command after you use the Undo command. For example, Figure 1.33 shows the Redo command after the Undo command has been used, and Figure 1.34 shows the Repeat command when Undo has not been used.

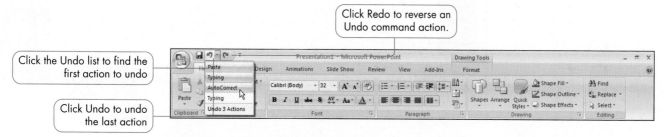

Figure 1.33 Undo and Redo Buttons

Using Language Tools

Documents, spreadsheets, and presentations represent the author, so remember that errors in writing can keep people from getting a desired job, or once on the job, can keep them from getting a desired promotion. To avoid holding yourself back, you should polish your final documents before submitting them electronically or as a hard copy. Office 2007 provides built-in proofing tools to help you fix spelling and grammar errors and help you locate the correct word or information.

Check Spelling and Grammar Automatically

By default, Office applications check spelling as you type and flag potential spelling errors by underlining them with a red wavy line. Word also flags potential grammar errors by underlining them with a green wavy line. You can fix these errors as you enter text, or you can ignore the errors and fix them all at once.

To fix spelling errors as you type, simply move the insertion point to a red wavy underlined word and correct the spelling yourself. If you spell the word correctly, the red wavy underline disappears. However, if you need help figuring out the correct spelling for the flagged word, then point to the error and right-click the mouse. The shortcut menu displays with possible corrections for the error. If you find the correction on the shortcut menu, click it to replace the word in the document. To fix grammar errors, follow the same process, but when the shortcut menu displays, you can choose to view more information to see rules that apply to the potential error. Notice the errors flagged in Figure 1.34. Note that the Mini toolbar also displays automatically.

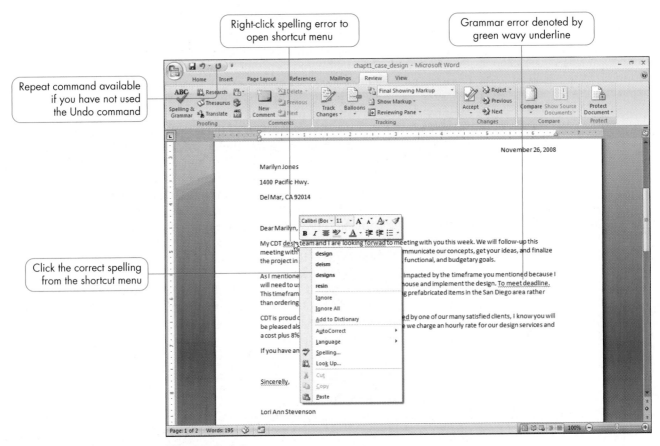

Figure 1.34 Automatic Spell and Grammar Check

Check Spelling and Grammar at Once

Some people prefer to wait until they complete typing the entire document and then check spelling and grammar at once. To check for errors, click Spelling & Grammar in Word (Spelling in Excel or PowerPoint) in the Proofing group on the Review tab. As the checking proceeds through the file and detects any spelling or grammar errors, it displays the Spelling dialog box if you are using Excel or PowerPoint, or the Spelling and Grammar dialog box in Word. You can either correct or ignore the changes that the Spelling checker proposes to your document. For example, Figure 1.35 shows the Spelling and Grammar dialog box with a misspelled word in the top section and Word's suggestions in the bottom section. Select the correction from the list and change the current instance, or you can change all instances of the error throughout the document. However, sometimes the flagged word might be a specialized term or a person's name, so if the flagged word is not a spelling error, you can ignore it once in the current document or throughout the entire document; further, you could add the word to the spell-check list so that it never flags that spelling again.

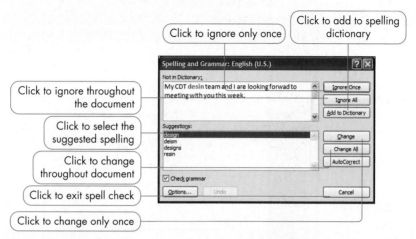

Figure 1.35 Spelling and Grammar Dialog Box

TIP Proofreading Your Document

The spelling and grammar checks available in Word provide great help improving your documents. However, you should not forget that you still have to proofread your document to ensure that the writing is clear, appropriate for the intended audience, and makes sense.

Use the Thesaurus

As you edit a document, spreadsheet, or presentation, you might want to improve your writing by finding a better or different word for a particular situation. For example, say you are stuck and cannot think of a better word for *big*, and you would like to find an alternative word that means the same. Word, Excel, and PowerPoint provide a built-in thesaurus, which is an electronic version of a book of synonyms. Synonyms are different words with the same or similar meaning, and antonyms are words with the opposite meaning.

The easiest method for accessing the Thesaurus is to point to the word in the file that you want to find an alternative for and right-click the mouse. When the shortcut menu displays, point to Synonyms, and the program displays a list of alternatives. Notice the shortcut menu and list of synonyms in Figure 1.36. To select one of the alternative words on the list, click it, and the word you select replaces the original word. If you do not see an alternative on the list that you want to use and you want to investigate further, click Thesaurus on the shortcut menu to open the full Thesaurus.

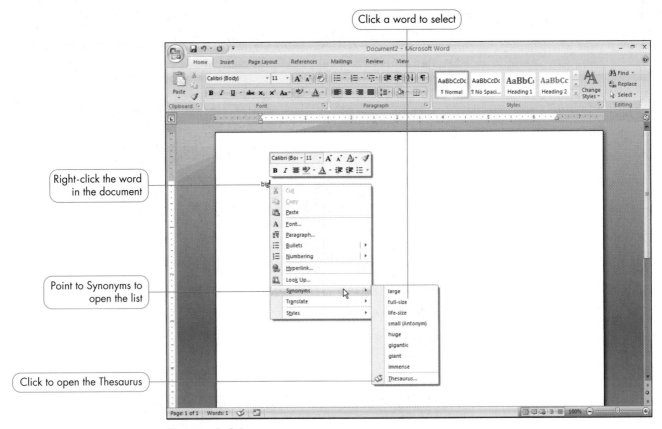

Figure 1.36 Shortcut Menu with Synonyms

An alternative method for opening the full Thesaurus is to place the insertion point in the word you want to look up, and then click the Thesaurus command in the Proofing group on the Review tab. The Thesaurus opens with alternatives for the selected word. You can use one of the words presented in the pane, or you can look up additional words. If you do not find the word you want, use the Search option to find more alternatives. Figure 1.37 shows the Thesaurus.

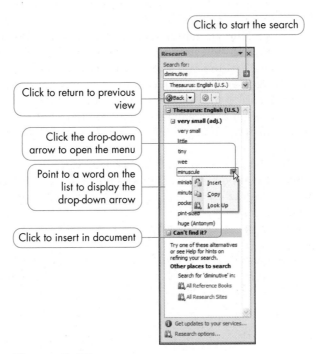

Figure 1.37 The Thesaurus

Conduct Research

As you work in Word, Excel, or PowerPoint, you might need to find the definition of a word or look up an item in the encyclopedia to include accurate information. Office 2007 provides quick access to research tools. To access research tools, click the Research button in the Proofing group on the Review tab. Notice in Figure 1.38 that you can specify what you want to research and specify where to Search. Using this feature, you can choose from reference books, research sites, and business and financial sites.

Figure 1.38 Research Task Pane

TIP Avoiding Plagiarism

If you use the research feature in Office to find information in an encyclopedia or in other locations to help you create your document, then you need to credit the source of that information. Avoid the problem of plagiarism, which is borrowing other people's words or ideas, by citing all sources that you use. You might want to check with your instructor for the exact format for citing sources.

Applying Font Attributes

Taking the time to format text helps the reader find important information in the document by making it stand out and helps the reader understand the message by emphasizing key items.

After you have edited a document, you might want to improve its visual appeal by formatting the text. *Formatting text* changes an individual letter, a word, or a body of selected text. Taking the time to format text helps the reader find important information in the document by making it stand out and helps the reader understand the message by emphasizing key items. You can format the text in the document by changing the following font attributes:

Formatting text changes an individual letter, a word, or a body of selected text.

- font face or size

- font attributes such as bold, underline, or italic

- font color

The Font group on the Home tab—available in Word, Excel, PowerPoint, and Access—provides many formatting options, and Office provides two methods for applying these font attributes:

- Choose the font attributes first, and then type the text. The text displays in the document with the formatting.

- Type the text, select the text to format, and choose the font attributes. The selected text displays with the formatting.

You can apply more than one attribute to text, so you can select one or more attributes either all at once or at any time. Also, it is easy to see which attributes you have applied to text in the document. Select the formatted text and look at the commands in the Font group on the Home tab. The commands in effect display with a gold background. See Figure 1.39. To remove an effect from text, select it and click the command. The gold background disappears for attributes that are no longer in effect.

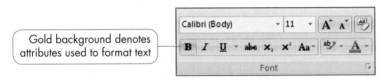

Gold background denotes attributes used to format text

Figure 1.39 Font Group of the Home tab

Change the Font

A *font* is a named set of characters with the same design.

Remember that more is not always better when applied to fonts, so limit the number of font changes in your document.

A *font* is a named set of characters with the same design, and Office 2007 provides many built-in fonts for you to choose from. Remember that more is not always better when applied to fonts, so limit the number of font changes in your document. Additionally, the choice of a font should depend on the intent of the document and should never overpower the message. For example, using a fancy or highly stylized font that may be difficult to read for a client letter might seem odd to the person receiving it and overpower the intended message.

One powerful feature of Office 2007 that can help you decide how a font will look in your document is Live Preview. First, select the existing text, and then click the drop-down arrow on the Font list in the Font group on the Home tab. As you point to a font name in the list, Live Preview changes the selected text in the document to that font. Figure 1.40 shows the selected text displaying in a different font as a result of Live Preview.

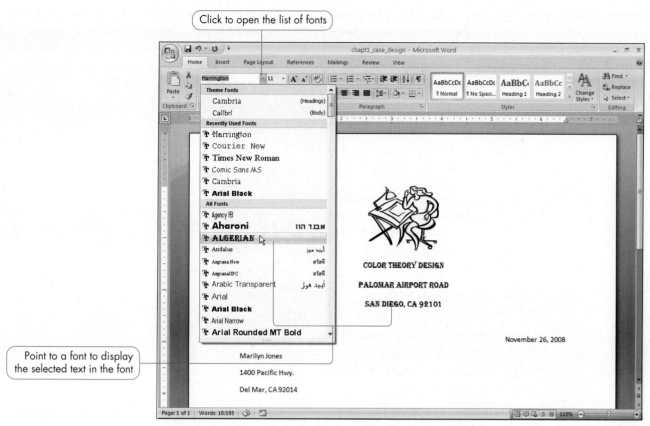

Figure 1.40 Font List

Change the Font Size, Color, and Attributes

Besides changing the font, you also can change the size, color, and other attributes of text in a document. Because these formatting operations are used so frequently, Office places many of these commands in several places for easy access:

- in the Font group on the Home tab
- on the Mini toolbar
- in the Font dialog box

Table 1.9 describes the commands that display in the Font group of the Home tab and in the Font dialog box.

Table 1.9 Font Commands

Command	Description	Example
Font	Enables you to designate the font.	Arial **Comic Sans MS**
Font Size	Enables you to designate an exact font size.	Size 8 Size 18
Grow Font	Each time you click the command, the selected text increases one size.	A **A**
Shrink Font	Each time you click the command, the selected text decreases one size.	B **B**
Clear Formatting	Removes all formatting from the selected text.	*Formatted* Cleared
Bold	Makes the text darker than the surrounding text.	**Bold**
Italic	Places the selected text in italic, that is, slants the letters to the right.	*Italic*
Underline	Places a line under the text. Click the drop-down arrow to change the underline style.	Underline
Strikethrough	Draws a line through the middle of the text.	~~Strikethrough~~
Subscript	Places selected text below the baseline.	Sub$_{script}$
Superscript	Places selected text above the line of letters.	Super^{script}
Change Case	Changes the case of the selected text. Click the drop-down arrow to select the desired case.	lowercase UPPERCASE
Text Highlight Color	Makes selected text look like it was highlighted with a marker pen. Click the drop-down arrow to change color and other options.	Highlighted
Font Color	Changes the color of selected text. Click the drop-down arrow to change colors.	Font Color

If you have several formatting changes to make, click the Dialog Box Launcher in the Font group on the Home tab to display the Font dialog box. The Font dialog box is handy because all the formatting features display in one location, and it provides additional options such as changing the underline color. Figure 1.41 shows the Font dialog box in Word.

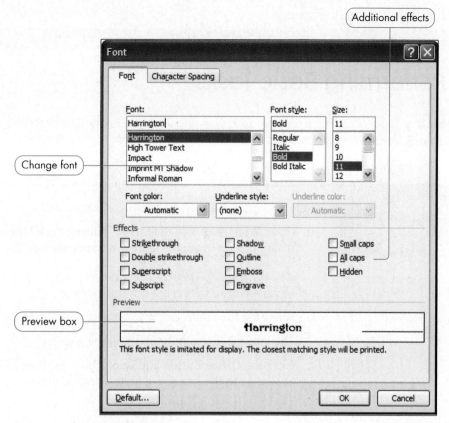

Figure 1.41 Font Dialog Box

Copying Formats with the Format Painter

After formatting text in one part of a document, you might want to apply that same formatting to other text in a different location in the document. You could try to remember all the formatting options you selected, but that process would be time-consuming and could produce inconsistent results. Office 2007 provides a shortcut method called the *Format Painter*, which copies the formatting of text from one location to another.

Select the formatted text you want to copy and click the Format Painter in the Clipboard group on the Home tab to copy the format. Single-click the command to turn it on to copy formatting to one location—the option turns off automatically after one copy—or double-click the command to turn it on for unlimited format copying—you must press Esc on the keyboard to turn it off.

The ***Format Painter*** copies the formatting of text from one location to another.

Hands-On Exercises

3 | Performing Basic Tasks

Skills covered: 1. Cut, Copy, Paste, and Undo **2.** Find and Replace Text **3.** Check Spelling **4.** Choose Synonyms and Use Thesaurus **5.** Use the Research Tool **6.** Apply Font Attributes **7.** Use Format Painter

---

Step 1 Cut, Copy, Paste, and Undo	Refer to Figure 1.42 as you complete Steps 1 and 2. **a.** Open Word and click the **Office Button**, click **Open**, and then using the Open dialog box features, navigate to your classroom file location. **TROUBLESHOOTING:** If you have trouble finding the file, remember to use the Look in feature to find the correct location. **b.** Select the file *chap1_ho3_internet* and click the **Open** button. The Word document displays on the screen. **c.** Click the **Office Button** and select **Save As**. If necessary, use the **Look in** feature to change to the location where you save files. The Save As dialog box displays. **d.** Type the new file name, **chap1_ho3_internet_solution**, be sure that *Word Document* displays in the *Save as type* box, and click **Save**. The file is saved with the new name. **e.** Click to place the insertion point at the beginning of the second sentence in the first paragraph. Type **These developments brought together**, and then press **Spacebar**. The text moves to the right, making room for the new inserted text. **f.** Press and hold down **Ctrl** as you click this sentence below the heading The World Wide Web: *The Netscape browser led in user share until Microsoft Internet Explorer took the lead in 1999.* **g.** Click **Cut** in the Clipboard group on the Home tab. The text disappears from the document. **h.** Move the insertion point to the end of the last paragraph and click **Paste** in the Clipboard group on the Home tab. The text displays in the new location. **i.** Reselect the sentence you just moved and click **Copy** in the Clipboard group on the Home tab. **j.** Move the insertion point to the end of the first paragraph beginning *The idea* and click the right mouse button. The shortcut menu displays. **k.** Select **Paste** from the shortcut menu. The text remains in the original position and is copied to the second location. **l.** Click **Undo** on the Quick Access Toolbar to undo the last paste.

Refer to Figure 1.42 to complete Step 2.

a. Press **Ctrl + Home** to move the insertion point to the beginning of the document. Click **Replace** in the Editing group on the Home tab.

The Find and Replace dialog box displays.

b. Type **Internet** in the *Find what* box and type **World Wide Web** in the *Replace with* box.

c. Click the **Replace All** button. Click **OK** to close the information box that informs you that Word has made seven replacements. Click **Close** to close the Find and Replace dialog box.

All instances of Internet have been replaced with World Wide Web in the document.

d. Click **Undo** on the Quick Access Toolbar.

All instances of *World Wide Web* have changed back to *Internet* in the document.

e. Click **Replace** in the Editing group on the Home tab.

The Find and Replace dialog box displays with the text you typed still in the boxes.

f. Click the **Find Next** button.

The first instance of the text *Internet* is highlighted.

g. Click the **Replace** button.

The first instance of Internet is replaced with World Wide Web, and the next instance of Internet is highlighted.

h. Click the **Find Next** button.

The highlight moves to the next instance of Internet without changing the previous one.

i. Click the **Close** button to close the Find and Replace dialog box.

The Find and Replace dialog box closes.

The World Wide Web

By Linda Ericksen

The idea of a complex computer network that would allow communicatin among users of various computers developed over time. These developments brought together the network of networks known as the Internet, which included both technological developments and the merging together of existing network infrastructure and telecommunication systems. This network provides users with email, chat, file transfer, Web pages and other files.

History of Internet

In 1957, the Soviet Union lanched the first satellite, Sputnik I, triggering President Dwight Eisenhower to create the ARPA agency to regain the technological lead in the arms race. Practical implementations of a large computer network began during the late 1960's and 1970's. By the 1980's, technologies we now recognise as the basis of the modern Internet began to spread over the globe.

In 1990, ARPANET was replaced by NSFNET which connected universities in North America, and later research facilities in Europe were added. Use of the Internet exploded after 1990, causing the US Government to transfer management to independent orginizations.

The World Wide Web

The World Wide Web was developed in the 1980's in Europe and then rapidly spread around the world. The World Wide Web is a set of linked documents on computers connected by the Internet. These documents make use of hyperliks to link documents together. To use hyperlinks, browser software was developed.

Browsers

The first widely used web browser was Mosaic, and the programming team went on to develop the first commercial web browser called Netscape Navigator. The Netscape browser led in user share until Microsoft Internet Explorer took the lead in 1999.

Figure 1.42 Edited Document (Shown in Full Screen Reading View)

Refer to Figure 1.43 as you complete Steps 3–5.

a. Right-click the first word in the document that displays with the red wavy underline: *communicatin*.

> **TROUBLESHOOTING:** If the first word highlighted is the author's last name, ignore it for now. The name is spelled correctly, but if it is not listed in the spell check, then Word flags it.

The shortcut menu displays with correct alternatives.

b. Click **communication** to replace the misspelled word in the document.

The incorrect spelling is replaced, and the red wavy underline disappears.

c. Click the **Review tab**, and then click **Spelling & Grammar** in the Proofing group.

The Spelling and Grammar dialog box opens with the first detected error displayed.

d. Move through the document selecting the correct word from the suggestions provided and choosing to **Change** the errors.

e. Click **OK** to close the Spelling and Grammar checker when the process is complete.

a. Place the insertion point in the word **complex** in the first sentence and right-click the mouse.

The shortcut menu displays.

b. Point to **Synonyms** on the shortcut menu.

The list of alternative words displays.

c. Click the alternative word **multifaceted**.

The new word replaces the word *complex* in the document.

d. Click in the word you just replaced, *multifaceted*, and click the **Thesaurus** button on the Review tab.

The Thesaurus displays with alternatives for **multifaceted**.

e. Scroll down the list and point to the word *comprehensive*.

A box displays around the word with a drop-down arrow on the right.

f. Click the drop-down arrow to display the menu and click **Insert**.

The word *comprehensive* replaces the word in the document.

Refer to Figure 1.43 to complete Step 5.

a. Place the insertion point in the Search for text box and type **browser**.

b. Click the drop-down arrow on the **Reference** list, which currently displays the Thesaurus.

The list of reference sites displays.

c. Click **Encarta Encyclopedia: English (North American)** option.

A definition of the browser displays in the results box.

d. Click the **Close** button on the Research title bar.

The Research pane closes.

The World Wide Web

By Linda Ericksen

The idea of a comprehensive computer network that would allow communication among users of various computers developed over time. These developments brought together the network of networks known as the Internet, which included both technological developments and the merging together of existing network infrastructure and telecommunication systems. This network provides users with email, chat, file transfer, Web pages and other files.

History of Internet

In 1957, the Soviet Union launched the first satellite, Sputnik I, triggering President Dwight Eisenhower to create the ARPA agency to regain the technological lead in the arms race. Practical implementations of a large computer network began during the late 1960's and 1970's. By the 1980's, technologies we now recognize as the basis of the modern Internet began to spread over the globe.

In 1990, ARPANET was replaced by NSFNET which connected universities in North America, and later research facilities in Europe

were added. Use of the Internet exploded after 1990, causing the US Government to transfer management to independent organizations.

The World Wide Web

The World Wide Web was developed in the 1980's in Europe and then rapidly spread around the world. The World Wide Web is a set of linked documents on computers connected by the Internet. These documents make use of hyperlinks to link documents together. To use hyperlinks, browser software was developed.

Browsers

The first widely used web browser was Mosaic, and the programming team went on to develop the first commercial web browser called Netscape Navigator. The Netscape browser led in user share until Microsoft Internet Explorer took the lead in 1999.

Figure 1.43 Language Tools Improved the Document

Step 6
Apply Font Attributes

Refer to Figure 1.44 as you complete Steps 6 and 7.

a. Select the title of the document.

The Mini toolbar displays.

b. Click **Bold** on the Mini toolbar, and then click outside the title.

TROUBLESHOOTING: If the Mini toolbar, is hard to read, remember to point to it to make it display fully.

The text changes to boldface.

c. Select the title again and click the drop-down arrow on the **Font** command in the Font group on the Home tab.

The list of fonts displays.

d. Point to font names on the list.

Live Preview changes the font of the selected sentence to display the fonts you point to.

e. Scroll down, and then select the **Lucinda Bright** font by clicking on the name.

The title changes to the new font.

f. With the title still selected, click the drop-down arrow on the **Font Size** command and select **16**.

The title changes to font size 16.

g. Select the byline that contains the author's name and click the **Underline** command, the **Italic** command, and the **Shrink Font** command once. All are located in the Font group on the Home tab.

The author's byline displays underlined, in italic, and one font size smaller.

h. Select the first heading *History of Internet* and click the **Font Color** down arrow command in the Font group on the Home tab. When the colors display, under Standard Colors, choose **Purple**, and then click outside the selected text.

The heading displays in purple.

i. Select the heading you just formatted as purple text and click **Bold**.

Refer to Figure 1.44 to complete Step 7.

a. Click the **Format Painter** command in the Clipboard group on the Home tab.

The pointer changes to a small paintbrush.

b. Select the second unformatted heading and repeat the process to format the third unformatted heading.

The Format Painter formats that heading as purple and bold and automatically turns off.

c. Press **Ctrl** while you click the last sentence in the document and click the **Dialog Box Launcher** in the Font group.

d. Select **Bold** in the Font style box and **Double strikethrough** in the *Effects* section of the dialog box, then click **OK**.

e. Click outside the selected sentence to remove the selection and view the effects, and then click back in the formatted text.

The sentence displays bold with two lines through the text. The Bold command in the Font group on the Home tab displays with a gold background.

f. Select the same sentence again, click **Bold** in the Font group on the Home tab, and then click outside the sentence.

The Bold format has been removed from the text.

g. Click **Save** on the Quick Access Toolbar.

The document is saved under the same name.

h. To exit Word, click the **Office Button**, and then click the **Exit Word** button.

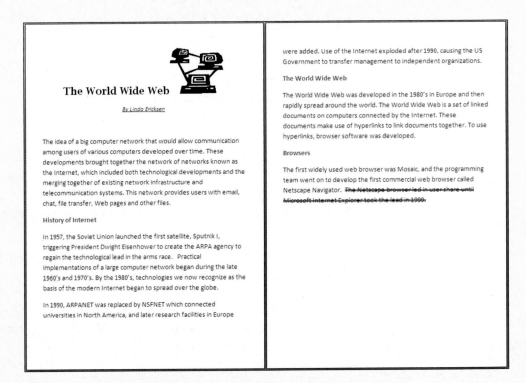

Figure 1.44 Formatted Document

Summary

1. **Identify common interface components.** You learned to identify and use the common elements of the Office 2007 interface and apply them in Word, PowerPoint, Excel, and Access. The top of the application window contains the Office Button that, when clicked, displays the Office menu. The Quick Access Toolbar provides commonly used commands, such as Save and Undo. The primary command center is the Ribbon, which contains tabs to organize major tasks. Each tab contains groups of related commands. The bottom of the window contains a status bar that gives general information, view options, and the Zoom slider.

2. **Use Office 2007 Help.** When you need help to continue working with Office 2007, you can use the Help feature from your computer or get help at Microsoft Office Online. You can position the mouse pointer on a command to see an Enhanced ScreenTip. You can click some Enhanced ScreenTips to display help. You can get context-sensitive help by clicking Help within dialog boxes.

3. **Open a file.** To retrieve a file you have previously saved, you use the Open command. When you open a file, it is copied into RAM so that you can view and work on it.

4. **Save a file.** As you create and edit documents, you should save your work for future use. Use the Save or Save As command to save a file for the first time, giving it a name and location. To continue saving changes to the same file name, use Save. To assign a new name, location, or file type, use Save As.

5. **Print a document.** Producing a perfect hard copy of the document is an important task, and you can make it easier by previewing, selecting options, and printing. You can select the printer, how many copies to print, and the pages you want to print. In addition, each program has specific print options.

6. **Select text to edit.** In order to edit text, you have to identify the body of text you want to work with by selecting it first. You can select text by using the mouse.

7. **Insert text and change to the Overtype mode.** To edit text in the document, you need to be able to insert text and to replace text by typing over it. The Insert mode inserts text without deleting existing text. The Overtype mode types over existing text as you type.

8. **Move and copy text.** You can move text from one location to another to achieve a better flow in a document, worksheet, or presentation. You can use the Copy command to duplicate data in one location and use the Paste command to place the duplicate in another location.

9. **Find, replace, and go to text.** Another editing feature that can save you time is to find text by searching for it or going directly to a specific element in the document. You can also replace text that needs updating.

10. **Use the Undo and redo Commands.** If you make a mistake and want to undo it, you can easily remedy it by using the Undo feature. Likewise, to save time, you can repeat the last action with the Redo command.

11. **Use language tools.** Office 2007 provides tools to help you create and edit error-free documents. You can use the spelling check and grammar check, the built-in thesaurus, and even conduct research all from your Word document. You can check spelling and conduct research in Excel and PowerPoint as well.

12. **Apply font attributes.** Applying font formats can help make the message clearer. For example, you can select a different font to achieve a different look. In addition, you can adjust the font size and change the font color of text. Other font attributes include bold, underline, and italic.

13. **Copy formats with the Format Painter.** You might want to copy the format of text to another location or to several locations in the document. You can easily accomplish that with the Format Painter.

Key Terms

Multiple Choice

1. Software that is used primarily with text to create, edit, and format documents is known as:

   (a) Electronic spreadsheet software

   (b) Word processing software

   (c) Presentation graphics software

   (d) Relational database software

2. Which Office feature displays when you rest the mouse pointer on a command?

   (a) The Ribbon

   (b) The status bar

   (c) An Enhanced ScreenTip

   (d) A dialog box

3. What is the name of the blinking vertical line in a document that designates the current location in the document?

   (a) A command

   (b) Overtype mode

   (c) Insert mode

   (d) Insertion point

4. If you wanted to locate every instance of text in a document and have it temporarily highlighted, which command would you use?

   (a) Find

   (b) Replace

   (c) Go To

   (d) Spell Check

5. The meeting point between computer software and the person using it is known as:

   (a) A file

   (b) Software

   (c) A template

   (d) An interface

6. Which of the following is true about the Office Ribbon?

   (a) The Ribbon displays at the bottom of the screen.

   (b) The Ribbon is only available in the Word 2007 application.

   (c) The Ribbon is the main component of the Office 2007 interface.

   (d) The Ribbon cannot be used for selecting commands.

7. Which element of the Ribbon looks like folder tabs and provides commands that are task oriented?

   (a) Groups

   (b) Tabs

   (c) Status bar

   (d) Galleries

8. Which Office 2007 element provides commands that work with an entire document or file and displays by default in the title bar?

   (a) Galleries

   (b) Ribbon

   (c) Office Button

   (d) Groups

9. If you needed the entire screen to read a document, which document view would you use?

   (a) Outline view

   (b) Draft view

   (c) Print Layout

   (d) Full Screen Reading

10. The default four-letter extension for Word documents that do not contain macros is:

    (a) .docx

    (b) .pptx

    (c) .xlsx

    (d) .dotm

11. Before you can cut or copy text, you must first do which one of the following?

    (a) Preview the document.

    (b) Save the document.

    (c) Select the text.

    (d) Undo the previous command.

12. What is the name of the memory location that holds up to twenty-four items for you to paste into the current document, another document, or another application?

    (a) My Places bar

    (b) My Documents

    (c) Ribbon

    (d) Clipboard

Multiple Choice Continued...

13. Word flags misspelled words by marking them with which one of the following?

(a) A green wavy underline

(b) Boldfacing them

(c) A red wavy underline

(d) A double-underline in black

14. Which of the following displays when you select text in a document?

(a) The Mini toolbar

(b) The Quick Access Toolbar

(c) A shortcut menu

(d) The Ribbon

15. Formatting text allows you to change which of the following text attributes?

(a) The font

(b) The font size

(c) The font type

(d) All of the above

Practice Exercises

1 Using Help and Print Preview in Access 2007

a. Open Access. Click the **Office Button**, and then select **Open**. Use the Look in feature to find the *chap1_pe1* database, and then click **Open**.

b. At the right side of the Ribbon, click the **Help** button. In the Help window, type **table** in the **Type words to search for** box. Click the **Search** button.

c. Click the topic *Create tables in a database*. Browse the content of the Help window, and then click the **Close** button in the Help window.

d. Double-click the **Courses table** in the left pane. The table opens in Datasheet view.

e. Click the **Office Button**, point to the arrow after the **Print** command, and select **Print Preview** to open the Print Preview window with the Courses table displayed.

f. Point the mouse pointer on the table and click to magnify the display. Compare your screen to Figure 1.45.

g. Click the **Close Print Preview** button on the Print Preview tab.

h. Click the **Office Button**, and then click the **Exit Access button**.

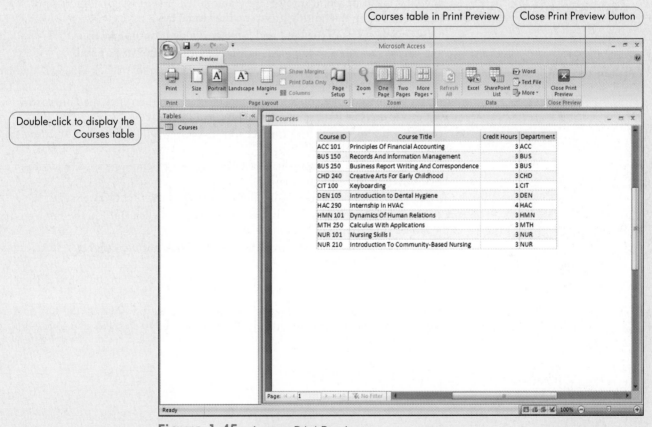

Figure 1.45 Access Print Preview

...continued on Next Page

As part of your Introduction to Computers course, you have prepared an oral report on phishing. You want to provide class members with a handout that summarizes the main points of your report. This handout is in the rough stages, so you need to edit it, and you also realize that you can format some of the text to emphasize the main points.

a. Start Word. Click the **Office Button**, and then select **Open**. Use the *Look in* feature to find the *chap1_pe2* document, and then click **Open**.

b. Click the **Office Button**, and then select **Save As**. In the *File name* box, type the document name, **chap1_pe2_solution**, be sure that Word document displays in the *Save as type* box, and use the *Look in* option to move to the location where you save your class files. Click **Save**.

c. In the document, click after the word Name and type **your name**.

d. Select your name, and then click **Bold** and **Italic** on the Mini toolbar—remember to point to the Mini toolbar to make it display fully. Your name displays in bold and italic.

e. Move the insertion point immediately before the title of the document and click the **Replace** button in the Editing group on the Home tab.

f. In the *Find what* box of the Find and Replace dialog box, type **internet**.

g. In the *Replace with* box of the Find and Replace dialog box, type **email**.

h. Click the **Replace All** button to have Word replace the text. Click **OK**, and then click **Close** to close the dialog boxes.

i. To format the title of the document, first select it, and then click the **Font arrow** in the Font group on the Home tab to display the available fonts.

j. Scroll down and choose the **Impact** font if you have it; otherwise, use one that is available.

k. Place the insertion point in the word *Phishng*. Right-click the word, and then click **Phishing** from the shortcut menu.

l. To emphasize important text in the list, double-click the first **NOT** to select it.

m. Click the **Font Color** arrow and select Red, and then click **Bold** in the Font group on the Home tab to apply bold to the text.

n. With the first instance of NOT selected, double-click **Format Painter** in the Clipboard group on the Home tab.

o. Double-click the second and then the third instance of **NOT** in the list, and then press **Esc** on the keyboard to turn off the Format Painter.

p. Compare your document to Figure 1.46. Save by clicking **Save** on the Quick Access Toolbar. Close the document and exit Word or proceed to the next step to preview and print the document.

...continued on Next Page

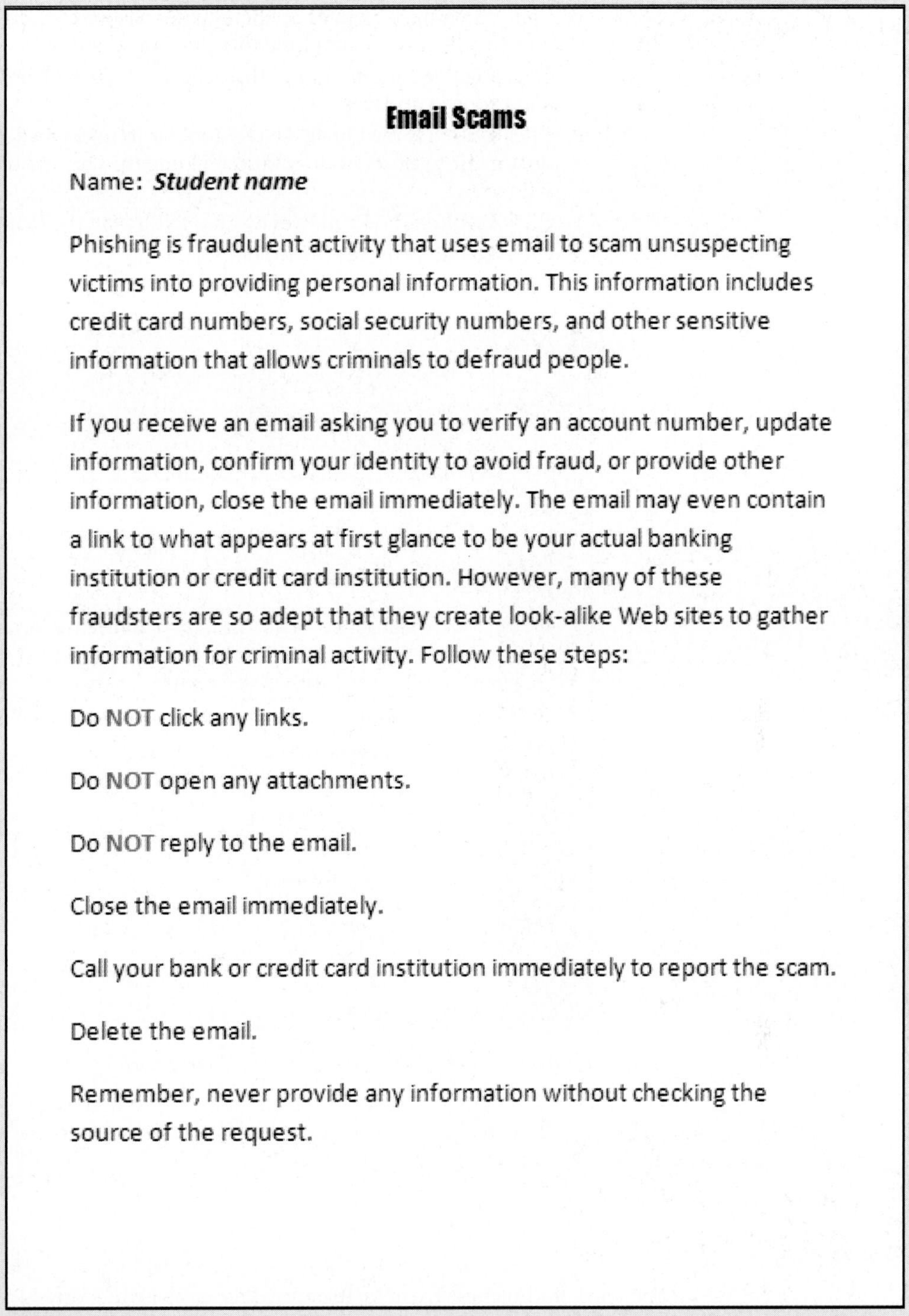

Email Scams

Name: *Student name*

Phishing is fraudulent activity that uses email to scam unsuspecting victims into providing personal information. This information includes credit card numbers, social security numbers, and other sensitive information that allows criminals to defraud people.

If you receive an email asking you to verify an account number, update information, confirm your identity to avoid fraud, or provide other information, close the email immediately. The email may even contain a link to what appears at first glance to be your actual banking institution or credit card institution. However, many of these fraudsters are so adept that they create look-alike Web sites to gather information for criminal activity. Follow these steps:

Do NOT click any links.

Do NOT open any attachments.

Do NOT reply to the email.

Close the email immediately.

Call your bank or credit card institution immediately to report the scam.

Delete the email.

Remember, never provide any information without checking the source of the request.

Figure 1.46 Phishing Document

3 Previewing and Printing a Document

You created a handout to accompany your oral presentation in the previous exercise. Now you want to print it out so that you can distribute it.

a. If necessary, open the *chap1_pe2_solution* document that you saved in the previous exercise.
b. Click the **Office Button**, point to the arrow after the Print command, and select **Print Preview** to open the Print Preview window with the document displayed.

...continued on Next Page

c. Point the mouse pointer in the document and click to magnify the display. Click the mouse pointer a second time to reduce the display.

d. To change the orientation of the document, click **Orientation** in the Page Setup group and choose **Landscape**.

e. Click **Undo** on the Quick Access Toolbar to undo the last command, which returns the document to portrait orientation. Compare your results to the zoomed document in Figure 1.47.

f. Click **Print** on the Print Preview tab to display the Print dialog box.

g. Click **OK** to print the document.

h. Close the document without saving it.

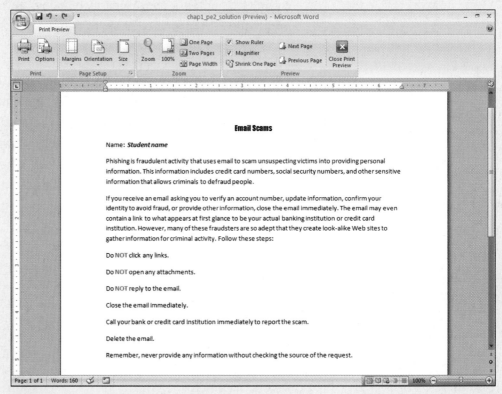

Figure 1.47   Document in Print Preview Window

4 Editing a Promotion Flyer

You work for Business Express, formerly known as Print Express, a regional company specializing in business centers that design and produce documents for local businesses and individuals. Business Express has just undergone a major transition along with a name change. Your job is to edit and refine an existing flyer to inform customers of the new changes. Proceed as follows:

a. Open Word. Click the **Office Button**, and then select **Open**. Use the *Look in* feature to find the *chap1_pe4* document.

b. Click the **Office Button** again and select **Save As**. Type the document name, **chap1_pe4_solution**, be sure that Word document displays in the *Save as type* box, and use the *Look in* option to move to the location where you save your class files.

c. Place the insertion point at the beginning of the document, and then click **Spelling & Grammar** in the Proofing group on the Review tab to open the Spelling and Grammar dialog box.

d. Click the **Change** button three times to correct the spelling errors. Click **OK** to close the completion box.

...continued on Next Page

e. Place the insertion point at the end of the first sentence of the document—just before the period. To insert the following text, press **Spacebar** and type **that offers complete business solutions**.

f. Place the insertion point in *good* in the first sentence of the third paragraph and right-click the mouse.

g. Point to **Synonyms**, and then click **first-rate** to replace the word in the document.

h. Place the insertion point in *bigger* in the last sentence of the third paragraph and click **Thesaurus** in the Proofing group on the Review tab. Point to **superior** and click the drop-down arrow that displays. Click **Insert** from the menu to replace the word in the document, and then click the **Close** button on the Thesaurus.

i. Select the last full paragraph of the document and click **Cut** in the Clipboard group on the Home tab to remove the paragraph from the document.

j. Place the insertion point at the beginning of the new last paragraph and click **Paste** in the Clipboard group on the Home tab to display the text.

k. Click **Undo** on the Quick Access Toolbar twice to undo the paste operation and to undo the cut operation—placing the text back in its original location.

l. Place the insertion point after the colon at the bottom of the document and type **your name**.

m. Compare your results to Figure 1.48, and then save and close the document.

Figure 1.48 Business Flyer

Mid-Level Exercises

1 Updating a Training Document

Your position as trainer for a large building supply company involves training all new employees. It is your job to familiarize new employees with the services provided by Castle Home Building Supply. You distribute a list at the training session and you realize that it needs updating before the next session, so you decide to edit and format it.

a. Start Word. Open the *chap1_mid1* file and save it as **chap1_mid1_solution**.
b. Change the title font to Arial Rounded MT Bold size 16 and change the font color to dark brown.
c. Make the subtitle Arial Unicode MS and italic.
d. Cut the item *Help with permits* and make it the second item on the list.
e. In the first list item, insert **and** after the word *fair*.
f. Change the word *help* in the last list item to **Assistance**.
g. Select the list of items excluding the heading, Services Provided.
h. Bold the list and change the font size to 16.
i. Save the document and compare it to Figure 1.49.

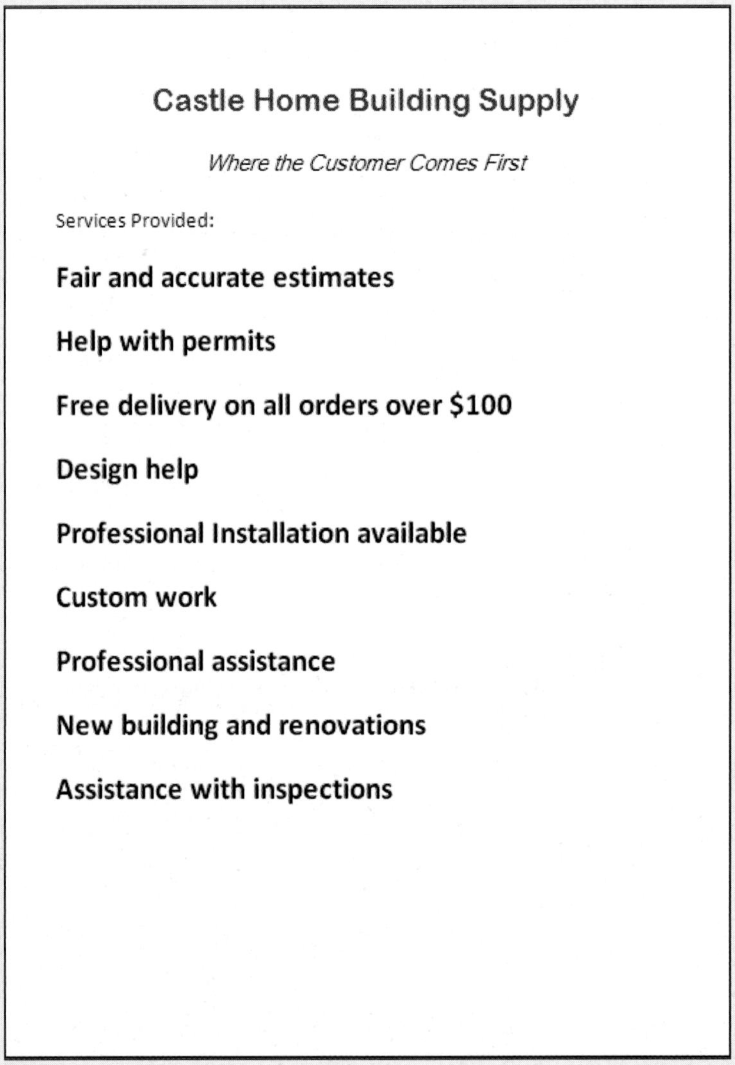

Castle Home Building Supply

Where the Customer Comes First

Services Provided:

Fair and accurate estimates

Help with permits

Free delivery on all orders over $100

Design help

Professional Installation available

Custom work

Professional assistance

New building and renovations

Assistance with inspections

Figure 1.49 Training Document

...continued on Next Page

2 Formatting a Menu

The owner of the Bayside Restaurant wants your help formatting his menu so that it is more pleasing to customers; follow the steps below:

a. Open the *chap1_mid2* document and save it as **chap1_mid2_solution**.

b. Format the menu title as Broadway size 16.

c. Format the three headings: Appetizers, Soups and Salads, and Lunch or Dinner Anytime! as Bodoni MT Black, size 12, and change the font color to Dark Red. Remember to format the first one and use the Format Painter for the second two headings.

d. Format all the dish names, such as Nachos, using the Outline Font Effects.

e. Bold all the prices in the document.

f. Preview the document, compare to Figure 1.50, and then print it.

g. Save and close the document.

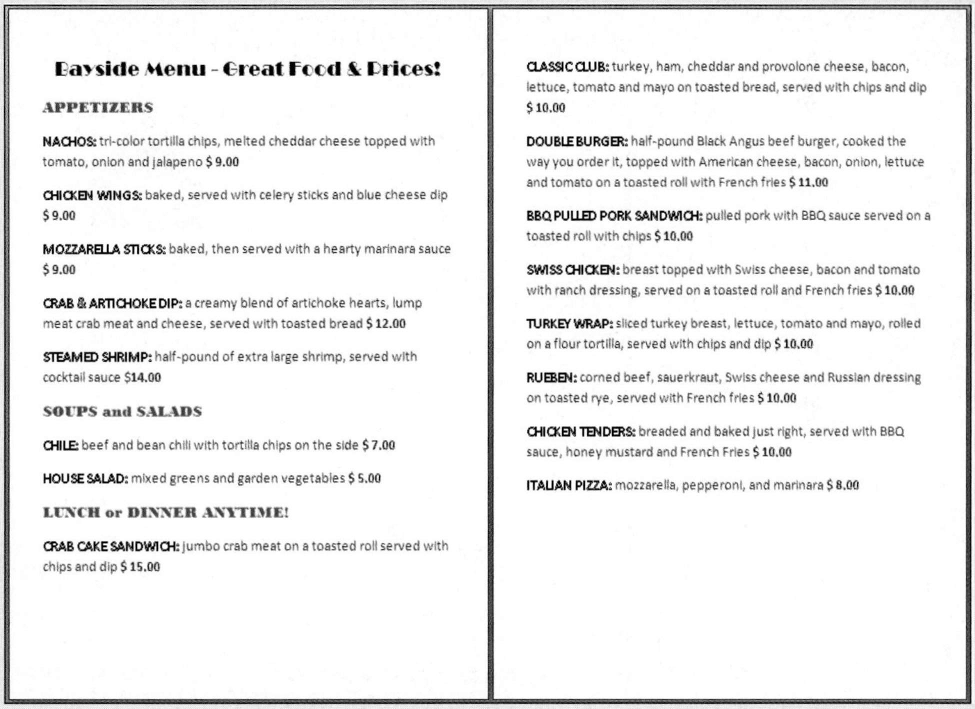

Bayside Menu - Great Food & Prices!

APPETIZERS

NACHOS: tri-color tortilla chips, melted cheddar cheese topped with tomato, onion and jalapeno **$ 9.00**

CHICKEN WINGS: baked, served with celery sticks and blue cheese dip **$ 9.00**

MOZZARELLA STICKS: baked, then served with a hearty marinara sauce **$ 9.00**

CRAB & ARTICHOKE DIP: a creamy blend of artichoke hearts, lump meat crab meat and cheese, served with toasted bread **$ 12.00**

STEAMED SHRIMP: half-pound of extra large shrimp, served with cocktail sauce **$14.00**

SOUPS and SALADS

CHILE: beef and bean chili with tortilla chips on the side **$ 7.00**

HOUSE SALAD: mixed greens and garden vegetables **$ 5.00**

LUNCH or DINNER ANYTIME!

CRAB CAKE SANDWICH: jumbo crab meat on a toasted roll served with chips and dip **$ 15.00**

CLASSIC CLUB: turkey, ham, cheddar and provolone cheese, bacon, lettuce, tomato and mayo on toasted bread, served with chips and dip **$ 10.00**

DOUBLE BURGER: half-pound Black Angus beef burger, cooked the way you order it, topped with American cheese, bacon, onion, lettuce and tomato on a toasted roll with French fries **$ 11.00**

BBQ PULLED PORK SANDWICH: pulled pork with BBQ sauce served on a toasted roll with chips **$ 10.00**

SWISS CHICKEN: breast topped with Swiss cheese, bacon and tomato with ranch dressing, served on a toasted roll and French fries **$ 10.00**

TURKEY WRAP: sliced turkey breast, lettuce, tomato and mayo, rolled on a flour tortilla, served with chips and dip **$ 10.00**

RUEBEN: corned beef, sauerkraut, Swiss cheese and Russian dressing on toasted rye, served with French fries **$ 10.00**

CHICKEN TENDERS: breaded and baked just right, served with BBQ sauce, honey mustard and French Fries **$ 10.00**

ITALIAN PIZZA: mozzarella, pepperoni, and marinara **$ 8.00**

Figure 1.50 The Formatted Menu

...continued on Next Page

3 Enhance the Insurance Letter

Your job duties at Health First Insurance, Inc., involve maintaining the correspondence. You need to update the welcome letter you send to clients to reflect the company's new name, new address, and other important elements, and then address it to a new client. Proceed as follows.

a. Open the *chap1_mid3* document and save it as **chap1_mid3_solution**.

b. Run the Spelling check to eliminate the errors.

c. Use Replace to change **University Insurance, Inc**. to **Health First Insurance, Inc**. throughout the letter.

d. Change the Address from **123 Main St**. to **1717 N. Zapata Way**.

e. Change the inside address that now has **Client name, Client Address, Client City, State and Zip Code** to **your name and complete address**. Also change the salutation to your name.

f. Move the first paragraph so that it becomes the last paragraph in the body of the letter.

g. Preview the letter to be sure that it fits on one page, compare it with Figure 1.51, and then print it.

h. Save and close the document.

Figure 1.51 The Updated Letter

Capstone Exercise

In this project, you work with a business plan for Far East Trading Company that will be submitted to funding sources in order to secure loans. The document requires editing to polish the final product and formatting to enhance readability and emphasize important information.

Editing the Document

This document is ready for editing, so proceed as follows:

a. Open the *chap1_cap* document. Save the document as **chap1_cap_solution**.

b. Run the Spelling and Grammar check to eliminate all spelling and grammar errors in the document.

c. Use the Thesaurus to find a synonym for the word **unique** in the second paragraph of the document.

d. Use the Go To command to move to page 3 and change the $175,000 to $250,000.

e. Move the entire second section of the document (notice the numbers preceding it) now located at the end of the document to its correct location after the first section.

f. Insert the street **1879 Columbia Ave.** before Portland in the first paragraph.

g. Copy the inserted street address to section 2.3 and place it in front of Portland there also.

h. Replace the initials **FET** with **FETC** for every instance in the document.

i. Type over 1998 in the third paragraph so that it says 2008.

Formatting the Document

Next, you will apply formatting techniques to the document. These format options will further increase the readability and attractiveness of your document.

a. Select the two-line title and change the font to Engravers MT, size 14, and change the color to Dark Red.

b. Select the first heading in the document: 1.0 Executive Summary, then change the font to Gautami, bold, and change the color to Dark Blue.

c. Use the Format Painter to make all the main numbered headings the same formatting, that is 2.0, 3.0, 4.0, and 5.0.

d. The first three numbered sections have subsections such as 1.1, 1.2. Select the heading 1.1 and format it for bold, italic, and change the color to a lighter blue—Aqua, Accents, Darker 25%.

e. Use the Format Painter to make all the numbered subsections the same formatting.

Printing the Document

To finish the job, you need to print the business plan.

a. Preview the document to check your results.

b. Print the document.

c. Save your changes and close the document.

Mini Cases

Use the rubric following the case as a guide to evaluate our work, but keep in mind that your instructor may impose additional grading criteria or use a different standard to judge your work.

A Thank-You Letter

GENERAL CASE

As the new volunteer coordinator for Special Olympics in your area, you need to send out information for prospective volunteers, and the letter you were given needs editing and formatting. Open the *chap1_mc1* document and make necessary changes to improve the appearance. You should use Replace to change the text (insert your state name), use the current date and your name and address information, format to make the letter more appealing, and eliminate all errors. Your finished document should be saved as **chap1_mc1_solution**.

Performance Elements	Exceeds Expectations	Meets Expectations	Below Expectations
Corrected all errors	Document contains no errors.	Document contains minimal errors.	Document contains several errors.
Use of character formatting features such as font, font size, font color, or other attributes	Used character formatting options throughout entire document.	Used character formatting options in most sections of document.	Used character formatting options on a small portion of document.
Inserted text where instructed	The letter is complete with all required information inserted.	The letter is mostly complete.	Letter is incomplete.

The Information Request Letter

RESEARCH CASE

Search the Internet for opportunities to teach abroad or for internships available in your major. Have fun finding a dream opportunity. Use the address information you find on the Web site that interests you, and compose a letter asking for additional information. For example, you might want to teach English in China, so search for that information. Your finished document should be saved as **chap1_mc2_solution**.

Performance Elements	Exceeds Expectations	Meets Expectations	Below Expectations
Use of character formatting	Three or more character formats applied to text.	One or two character formats applied to text.	Does not apply character formats to text.
Language tools	No spelling or grammar errors.	One spelling or grammar error.	More than one spelling or grammar error.
Presentation	Information is easy to read and understand.	Information is somewhat unclear.	Letter is unclear.

Movie Memorabilia

Use the following rubrics to guide your evaluation of your work, but keep in mind that your instructor may impose additional grading criteria.

Open the *chap1_mc3* document that can be found in the Exploring folder. The advertising document is over-formatted, and it contains several errors and problems. For example, the text has been formatted in many fonts that are difficult to read. The light color of the text also has made the document difficult to read. You should improve the formatting so that it is consistent, helps the audience read the document, and is pleasing to look at. Your finished document should be saved as **chap1_mc3_solution**.

Performance Elements	Exceeds Expectations	Meets Expectations	Below Expectations
Type of font chosen to format document	Number and style of fonts appropriate for short document.	Number or style of fonts appropriate for short document.	Overused number of fonts or chose inappropriate font.
Color of font chosen to format document	Appropriate font colors for document.	Most font colors appropriate.	Overuse of font colors.
Overall document appeal	Document looks appealing.	Document mostly looks appealing.	Did not improve document much.

Microsoft Word

What Will Word Processing Do for Me?

bjectives

After you read this chapter, you will be able to:

1. Understand Word basics **(page 72)**.
2. Use AutoText **(page 76)**.
3. View a document **(page 78)**.
4. Use the Mini toolbar **(page 80)**.
5. Set margins and specify page orientation **(page 87)**.
6. Insert page breaks **(page 88)**.
7. Add page numbers **(page 90)**.
8. Insert headers and footers **(page 91)**.
9. Create sections **(page 92)**.
10. Insert a cover page **(page 93)**.
11. Use Find and Replace commands **(page 94)**.
12. Check spelling and grammar **(page 103)**.
13. Use save and backup options **(page 104)**.
14. Select printing options **(page 107)**.
15. Customize Word **(page 108)**.

Hands-On Exercises

Exercises	Skills Covered
1. **INTRODUCTION TO MICROSOFT WORD (page 81)** **Open:** chap1_ho1_credit.docx **Save as:** chap1_ho1_credit_solution.docx	• Open and Save a Word Document • Modify the Document • Insert AutoText • Create an AutoText Entry • Change Document Views and Zoom
2. **DOCUMENT ORGANIZATION (page 96)** **Open:** chap1_ho1_credit_solution.docx (from Exercise 1) **Save as:** chap1_ho2_credit_solution.docx (additional modifications)	• Set Page Margins and Orientation • Insert a Page Break • Add a Cover Page and Insert a Document Header • Insert a Section Break • Insert a Page Number in the Footer • Use Find, Replace, and Go To
3. **THE FINAL TOUCHES (page 110)** **Open:** chap1_ho2_credit_solution.docx (from Exercise 2) **Save as:** chap1_ho3_credit_solution.docx (additional modifications), chap1_ho3_credit2_solution.docx, and chap1_ho3_credit_solution.doc	• Perform a Spelling and Grammar Check • Run the Document Inspector and a Compatibility Check • Save in a Compatible Format • Change Word Options • Use Print Preview Features

CASE STUDY

A Question of Ethics

You would never walk into a music store, put a CD under your arm, and walk out without paying for it. What if, however, you could download the same CD from the Web for free? Are you hurting anyone? Or what if you gave a clerk a $5 bill, but received change for a $50? Would you return the extra money? Would you speak up if it was the person ahead of you in line who received change for the $50, when you clearly saw that he or she gave the clerk $5? Ethical conflicts occur all the time and result when one person or group benefits at the expense of another.

Case Study

Your Philosophy 101 instructor assigned a class project whereby students are divided into teams to consider questions of ethics and society. Each team is to submit a single document that represents the collective efforts of all the team members. The completed project is to include a brief discussion of ethical principles followed by five examples of ethical conflicts. Every member of the team will receive the same grade, regardless of his or her level of participation; indeed, this might be an ethical dilemma, in and of itself.

Your Assignment

- Read the chapter, paying special attention to sections that describe how to format a document using page breaks, headers and footers, and page numbers.
- Open the *chap1_case_ethics* document, which contains the results of your team's collaboration, but which requires further formatting before you submit it to your professor.
- Create a cover page for the document. Include the name of the report, the team members, and your course name.
- View the document in draft view and remove any unnecessary page breaks.
- Set the margins on your document to a width and height that allows for binding the document.
- Set page numbers for each page of the document except the cover page. The page numbers should display in the center of the footer. Page numbering should begin on the page that follows the cover page.
- Perform a spelling and grammar check on the document, but proofread it also.
- Save your work in a document named **chap1_case_ethics_solution.docx**.
- Run a compatibility check, and then save it also in Word 97–2003 format, as **chap1_case_ethics_solution.doc**, in case your professor, who does not have Office 2007, requests a digital copy.

Introduction to Word Processing

Word processing software is probably the most commonly used type of software. You can create letters, reports, research papers, newsletters, brochures, and other documents with Word. You can even create and send e-mail, produce Web pages, and update blogs with Word.

Word processing software is probably the most commonly used type of software. People around the world—students, office assistants, managers, and professionals in all areas—use word processing programs such as Microsoft Word for a variety of tasks. You can create letters, reports, research papers, newsletters, brochures, and other documents with Word. You can even create and send e-mail, produce Web pages, and update blogs with Word. Figure 1.1 shows examples of documents created in Word.

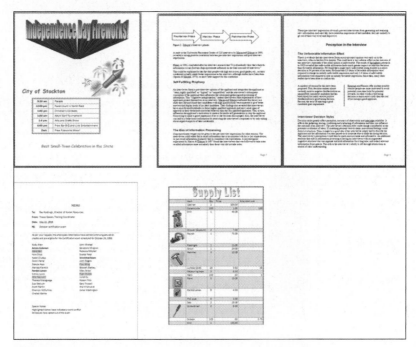

Figure 1.1 The Versatility of Microsoft Word 2007

Microsoft Word provides a multitude of features that enable you to enhance documents with only a few clicks of the mouse. You can change colors, add interesting styles of text, insert graphics, use a table to present data, track changes made to a document, view comments made about document content, combine several documents into one, and quickly create reference pages such as a table of contents, an index, or a bibliography.

This chapter provides a broad-based introduction to word processing in general and Microsoft Word in particular. All word processors adhere to certain basic concepts that must be understood to use the program effectively.

In this section, you learn about the Word interface, word-wrap, and toggles. You learn how to use the AutoText feature to insert text automatically in your document, and then you change document views and learn to use the new Mini toolbar.

Understanding Word Basics

The Exploring series authors used Microsoft Word to write this book. You will use Word to complete the exercises in this chapter. When you start Word, your screen might be different. You will not see the same document shown in Figure 1.2, nor is it likely that you will customize Word in exactly the same way. You should, however, be able to recognize the basic elements that are found in the Microsoft Word window and that are emphasized in Figure 1.2.

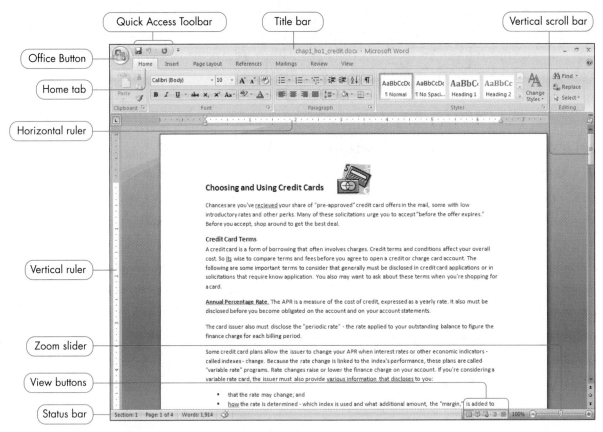

Figure 1.2 The Microsoft Word Window

Figure 1.2 displays two open windows—an application window for Microsoft Word and a document window for the specific document on which you are working. However, only one title bar appears at the top of the application window, and it reflects the application (Microsoft Word) as well as the document name (chap1_ho1_credit.docx). If you want to close the document but not the Word program, click the Office Button and select Close. To close both the document and the application, click Close in the upper-right corner.

The Quick Access Toolbar appears on the left side of the title bar. This toolbar contains commands that are used very frequently, such as Save, Undo, and Repeat. Vertical and horizontal scroll bars appear at the right and bottom of a document window. You use them to view portions of a document that do not display on the screen. Each Microsoft Office application includes the Ribbon, which contains tabs that organize commands into task-oriented groups. The active tab is highlighted, and the commands on that tab display immediately below the title bar. The tab can change according to the current task, or you can display a different tab by clicking the tab name. The tabs in Word are displayed in the Reference on the next two pages.

The status bar at the bottom of the document window displays information about the document such as the section and page where the insertion point is currently positioned, the total number of pages in the document, and the total number of words in the document. At the right side of the status bar, you find command buttons that enable you to quickly change the view and zoom level of the document.

Word Tabs | Reference

Tab and Group	Description

Home
    Clipboard
    Font
    Paragraph
    Styles
    Editing
	The basic Word tab. Contains basic editing functions such as cut and paste along with most formatting actions. Some groups contain Dialog Box Launchers that offer more commands and increase functionality.

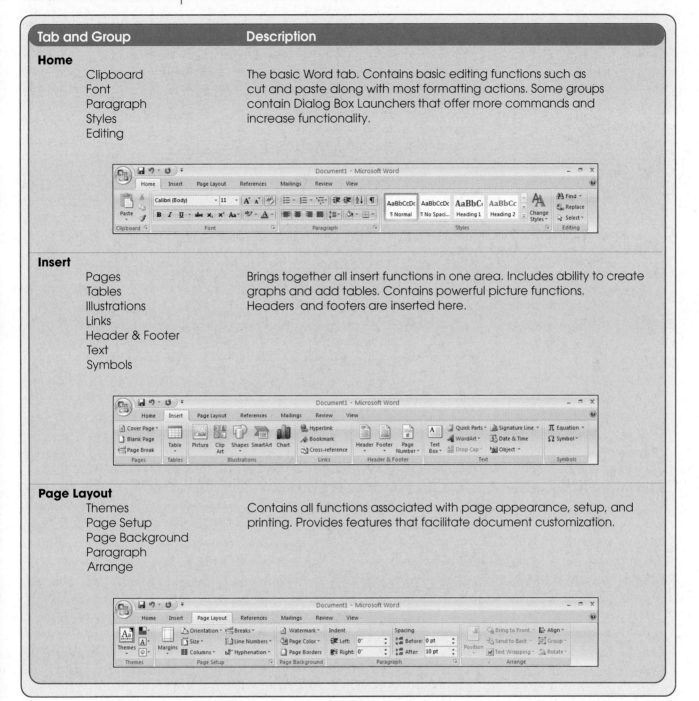

Insert
    Pages
    Tables
    Illustrations
    Links
    Header & Footer
    Text
    Symbols
	Brings together all insert functions in one area. Includes ability to create graphs and add tables. Contains powerful picture functions. Headers and footers are inserted here.

Page Layout
    Themes
    Page Setup
    Page Background
    Paragraph
    Arrange
	Contains all functions associated with page appearance, setup, and printing. Provides features that facilitate document customization.

Tab and Group	Description
References	
Table of Contents	Provides functions for automating references in a document. Includes
Footnotes	assistance using popular writing styles.
Citations &	
Bibliography	
Captions	
Index	
Table of Authorities	

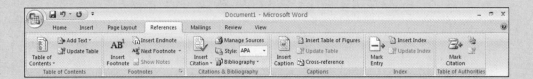

Mailings	
Create	Contains commands used in the process of combining data from
Start Mail Merge	multiple sources and providing useful information.
Write & Insert Fields	
Preview Results	
Finish	

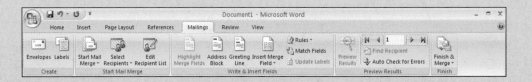

Review	
Proofing	Contains all reviewing tools in Word, including spelling and grammatical
Comments	check, the management of comments, sharing, and protection.
Tracking	
Changes	
Compare	
Protect	

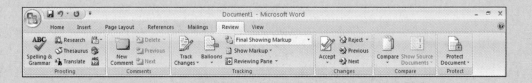

View	
Document Views	Contains basic and advanced view settings. Some of these options also
Show/Hide	appear below the horizontal and vertical scroll bars.
Zoom	
Window	
Macros	

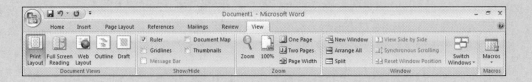

Learn About Word Wrap

A word processor is a software tool that enables you to document your thoughts or other information. Whether you are new to using a word processor or have been using one for a period of time, you will notice that certain functions seem to happen automatically. As you type, you probably don't think about how much text can fit on one line or where the sentences must roll from one line to the other. Fortunately, the word processor takes care of that for you. This function is called *word wrap* and enables you to type continually without pressing Enter at the end of a line within a paragraph. The only time you press Enter is at the end of a paragraph or when you want the insertion point to move to the next line.

Word wrap moves words to the next line if they do not fit on the current line.

Word wrap is closely associated with another concept, that of hard and soft returns. A *hard return* is created by the user when he or she presses the Enter key at the end of a line or paragraph; a *soft return* is created by the word processor as it wraps text from one line to the next. The locations of the soft returns change automatically as a document is edited (e.g., as text is inserted or deleted, or as margins or fonts are changed). The locations of hard returns can be changed only by the user, who must intentionally insert or delete each hard return.

A *hard return* is created when you press Enter to move the insertion point to a new line.

A *soft return* is created by the word processor as it wraps text to a new line.

The paragraphs at the top of Figure 1.3 show two hard returns, one at the end of each paragraph. It also includes four soft returns in the first paragraph (one at the end of every line except the last) and three soft returns in the second paragraph. Now suppose the margins in the document are made smaller (that is, the line is made longer), as shown in the bottom paragraphs of Figure 1.3. The number of soft returns drops to three and two (in the first and second paragraphs, respectively) as more text fits on a line and fewer lines are needed. The revised document still contains the two original hard returns, one at the end of each paragraph.

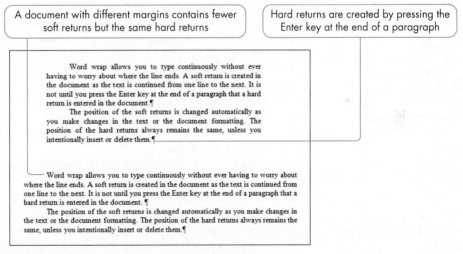

Figure 1.3 Document with Hard and Soft Returns

Use Keyboard Shortcuts to Scroll

The horizontal and vertical scrollbars frequently are used to move around in a document. However, clicking the scroll arrows does not move the insertion point; it merely lets you see different parts of the document in the document window and leaves the insertion point where it was last positioned. You can use the mouse or the keyboard to move the insertion point in a document. Table 1.1 shows useful keyboard shortcuts for moving around in a document and relocating the insertion point.

Table 1.1 Keyboard Scrolling Methods

Key	Moves the Insertion Point …	Key	Moves the Insertion Point …
Left arrow	one character to the left	Ctrl + Home	to the beginning of the document
Right arrow	one character to the right	Ctrl + End	to the end of the document
Up arrow	up one line	Ctrl + Left arrow	one word to the left
Down arrow	down one line	Ctrl + Right arrow	one word to the right
Home	to the beginning of the line	Ctrl + Up arrow	up one paragraph
End	to the end of the line	Ctrl + Down arrow	down one paragraph
PgUp	up one window or page	Ctrl + Pgup	to the top of the previous page
PgDn	down one window or page	Ctrl + PgDn	to the top of the next page

Discover Toggle Switches

Suppose you sat down at the keyboard and typed an entire sentence without pressing Shift; the sentence would be in all lowercase letters. Then you pressed the Caps Lock key and retyped the sentence, again without pressing the Shift key. This time, the sentence would be in all uppercase letters. Each time you pressed the Caps Lock key, the text you type would switch from lowercase to uppercase and vice versa.

The **toggle switch** is a device that causes the computer to alternate between two states.

The point of this exercise is to introduce the concept of a **toggle switch**, a device that causes the computer to alternate between two states. Caps Lock is an example of a toggle switch. Each time you press it, newly typed text will change from uppercase to lowercase and back again. In the Office Fundamentals chapter, you read about other toggle switches. Some toggle switches are physical keys you press, such as the Insert key (which toggles to Overtype). And some toggle switches are software features such as the Bold, Italic, and Underline commands (which can be clicked to turn on and off).

The **Show/Hide feature** reveals where formatting marks such as spaces, tabs, and returns are used in the document.

Another toggle switch that enables you to reveal formatting applied to a document is the **Show/Hide feature**. Click Show/Hide ¶ in the Paragraph group on the Home tab to reveal where formatting marks such as spaces, tabs, and hard returns are used in the document.

The Backspace and Delete keys delete one character immediately to the left or right of the insertion point, respectively. The choice between them depends on when you need to erase a character(s). The Backspace key is easier if you want to delete a character (or characters) immediately after typing. The Delete key is preferable during subsequent editing.

You can delete several characters at one time by selecting (clicking and dragging the mouse over) the characters to be deleted, then pressing the Delete key. You can delete and replace text in one operation by selecting the text to be replaced and then typing the new text in its place. You can also select a block of text by clicking to place the insertion point in front of the first character, holding down Shift and then clicking to the right of the last character. Double-click a word to select it, and triple-click to select a paragraph. These forms of selecting text enable you to quickly format or delete text.

Using AutoText

The **AutoText** feature substitutes a predefined item for specific text but only when the user initiates it.

You learned about the AutoCorrect feature in the Office Fundamentals chapter. The *AutoText* feature is similar in concept to AutoCorrect in that both substitute a predefined item for a specific character string or group of characters. The difference is that the substitution occurs automatically with the AutoCorrect entry, whereas you have to take deliberate action for the AutoText substitution to take place. AutoText entries can also include significantly more text, formatting, and even clip art.

Microsoft Word includes a host of predefined AutoText entries such as days of the week and months of the year. For example, if you start typing today's date, you see a ScreenTip that displays the entire date, as shown in Figure 1.4. Press Enter while the ScreenTip is visible to insert the date automatically.

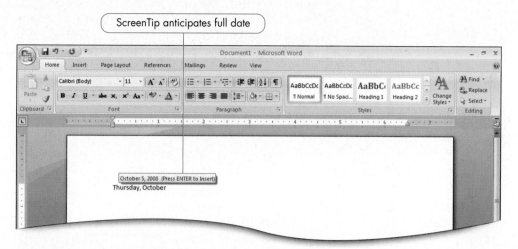

Figure 1.4 Insert AutoText

As with the AutoCorrect feature, you can define additional entries of your own. (However, you may not be able to do this in a computer lab environment.) This is advisable if you use the same piece of text frequently, such as a disclaimer, a return address, a company logo, or a cover page. You first select the text, click Quick Parts in the Text group on the Insert tab, and select Save Selection to Quick Part Gallery. In the Create New Building Block dialog box, make sure the Gallery option displays Quick Parts, and click OK. After you add entries to the Quick Parts gallery, they are included in the **Building Blocks** library, which contains document components you use frequently, such as those mentioned above. After you add the text to the Quick Parts gallery, you can type a portion of the entry, then press F3 to insert the remainder into your document. Figure 1.5 demonstrates the creation of the AutoText entry.

Building Blocks are document components used frequently, such as disclaimers, company addresses, or a cover page.

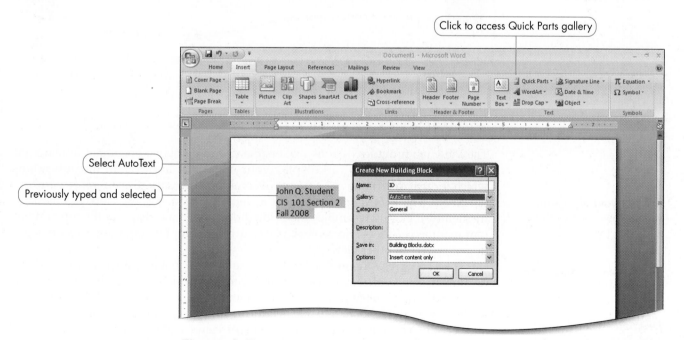

Figure 1.5 Adding an AutoText Building Block

TIP Insert the Date and Time

Some documents include the date and time they were created. A time and date stamp can help determine the most recent edition of a document, which is important if the document is updated frequently. To create a time and date stamp, display the Insert tab, click Insert Date and Time in the Text group to display the Date and Time dialog box, then choose a format. Click the *Update automatically* check box to update the date automatically if you want your document to reflect the date on which it is opened, or clear the box to retain the date on which the date was inserted (see Figure 1.6).

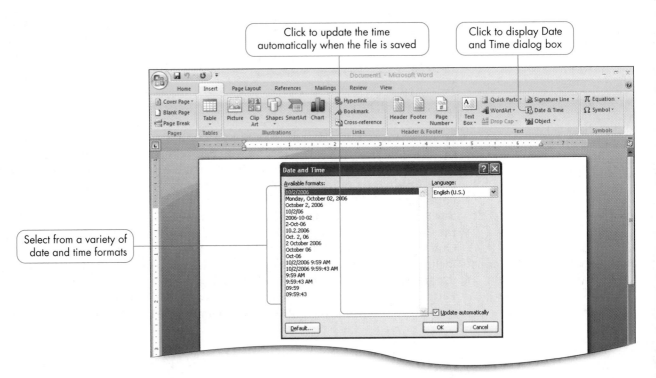

Click to update the time automatically when the file is saved

Click to display Date and Time dialog box

Select from a variety of date and time formats

Figure 1.6 The Date and Time Dialog Box

Viewing a Document

The View tab provides options that enable you to display a document in many different ways. Each view can display your document at different magnifications, which in turn determine the amount of scrolling necessary to see remote parts of a document. The *Print Layout view* is the default view and is the view you use most frequently. It closely resembles the printed document and displays the top and bottom margins, headers and footers, page numbers, graphics, and other features that do not appear in other views.

The *Full Screen Reading view* hides the Ribbon, making it easier to read your document. The *Draft view* creates a simple area in which to work; it removes white space and certain elements from the document, such as headers, footers, and graphics, but leaves the Ribbon. It displays information about some elements, such as page and section breaks, not easily noticed in other views. Because view options are used frequently, buttons for each also are located on the status bar, as shown in Figure 1.2.

The Zoom command displays the document on the screen at different magnifications—for example, 75%, 100%, or 200%. But this command does not affect

Print Layout view is the default view and closely resembles the printed document.

Full Screen Reading view eliminates tabs and makes it easier to read your document.

Draft view shows a simplified work area, removing white space and other elements from view.

the size of the text on the printed page. It is helpful to be able to zoom in to view details or to zoom out and see the effects of your work on a full page. When you click Zoom in the Zoom group on the View tab, a dialog box displays with several zoom options (see Figure 1.7).

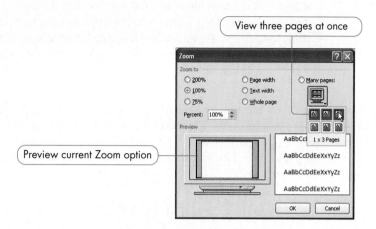

Figure 1.7   The Zoom Dialog Box

Word automatically will determine the magnification if you select one of the Zoom options—Page Width, Text Width, Whole Page, or Many Pages (Whole Page and Many Pages are available only in the Print Layout view). Figure 1.8, for example, displays a four-page document in Print Layout view. The 28% magnification is determined automatically after you specify the number of pages. If you use a wide screen, the magnification size might differ slightly.

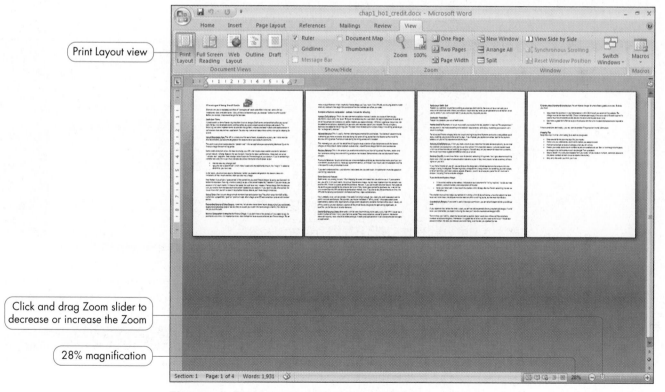

Figure 1.8   View Four Pages of Document

The **Outline view** displays a structural view of the document that can be collapsed or expanded.

The **Web Layout view** is used when creating a Web page.

The View tab also provides access to two additional views—the Outline view and the Web Layout view. The **Outline view** does not display a conventional outline, but rather a structural view of a document that can be collapsed or expanded as necessary. The **Web Layout view** is used when you are creating a Web page.

Using the Mini Toolbar

The **Mini toolbar** contains frequently used formatting commands and displays when you select text.

Several formatting commands, such as Bold, Center, and Italic, are used frequently, and although they can be found on the Home tab, you can also apply them using the Mini toolbar. The **Mini toolbar** contains frequently used formatting commands and displays when you select text or right-click selected text. The Mini toolbar displays faintly at first, then darkens as you move the mouse pointer closer to it, as seen in Figure 1.9. If you move the mouse pointer away from it, it becomes fainter; if you do not want to use the Mini toolbar and prefer it disappear from view, press Esc when it displays. The Mini toolbar reduces the distance your mouse pointer has to travel around the screen and enables you to quickly and easily apply the most frequently used commands.

The Mini toolbar darkens as the mouse pointer moves closer

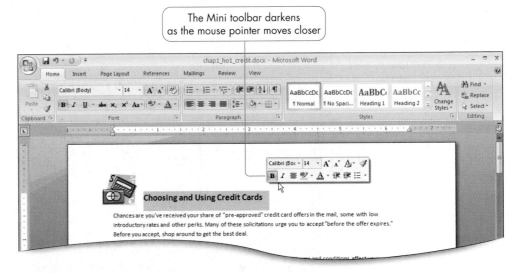

Figure 1.9 The Mini Toolbar

Hands-On Exercises

1 | Introduction to Microsoft Word

Skills covered: 1. Open and Save a Word Document **2.** Modify the Document **3.** Insert AutoText **4.** Create an AutoText Entry **5.** Change Document Views and Zoom

---

Step 1
Open and Save a Word Document

Refer to Figure 1.10 as you complete Step 1.

a. Click **Start** to display the Start menu. Click (or point to) **All Programs**, click **Microsoft Office**, and then click **Microsoft Office Word 2007** to start the program.

b. Click the **Office Button** and select **Open**. Navigate to the Exploring Word folder and open the *chap1_ho1_credit* document.

You should see the document containing the title *Choosing and Using Credit Cards*.

c. Click the **Office Button** and select **Save As.**

The Save As dialog box displays so that you can save the document in a different location, with a different name, or as a different file type. The **Exploring Word folder** is the active folder, as shown in Figure 1.10.

TIP Use Save and Save As

You should practice saving your files often. If you open a document and you do not want to change its name, the easiest way to save it is to click Save on the Quick Access Toolbar. You can also click the Office Button and select Save, but many users press the Ctrl+S keyboard command to save quickly and often. The first time you save a document, use the Save As command from the Microsoft Office menu. The command displays the Save As dialog box that enables you to assign a descriptive file name (*job cover letter*, for example) and indicate where the file will be saved. Subsequent saves will be to the same location and will update the file with new changes.

d. Click the **Save in drop-down arrow**. Click the appropriate drive, such as (C:), where you want to store your completed files.

e. In the **File name** box, click once to position the insertion point at the end of the word *credit*. Type **_solution** to rename the document as *chap1_ho1_credit_solution*.

f. Click **Save** or press **Enter**. The title bar changes to reflect the new document name, *chap1_ho1_credit_solution.docx*.

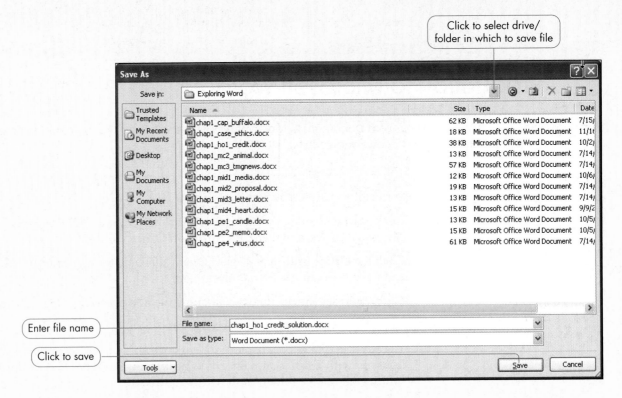

Click to select drive/
folder in which to save file

Enter file name

Click to save

Figure 1.10 Save As Dialog Box

<hr>

Step 2
Modify the Document

Refer to Figure 1.11 as you complete Step 2.

a. Use the vertical scroll bar to move down to the bottom of the third page in the document. Select the text ****Insert Text Here**** and press **Delete**.

You will add the heading and introduction to this paragraph in the next step.

b. Click **Bold** in the Font group on the Home tab to toggle the format on, if necessary, and then type **Unauthorized Charges**.

c. Click **Bold** in the Font group again to toggle the format off. Press **Spacebar** once to insert a space after the period typed in the step above. Then type **If your card is used without your permission, you can be held responsible for up to $50 per card**.

d. Press **Enter** after you complete the sentence. Select the *$50* that you just typed, and then click **Bold** on the Mini toolbar.

You completed the sentence using toggle switches, and you used the Mini toolbar to apply formatting.

e. Click **Show/Hide ¶** in the Paragraph group on the Home tab, if necessary, to display formatting marks in the document.

Notice the formatting marks display to indicate where each space, tab, and soft and hard return occurs.

f. Select the hard return character that follows the sentence typed above, as shown in Figure 1.11. Press **Delete** to delete the unnecessary hard return.

You also can place the insertion point on either side of the formatting mark and press Delete or Backspace to remove it, depending on the location of the insertion point.

g. Click **Save** on the Quick Access Toolbar.

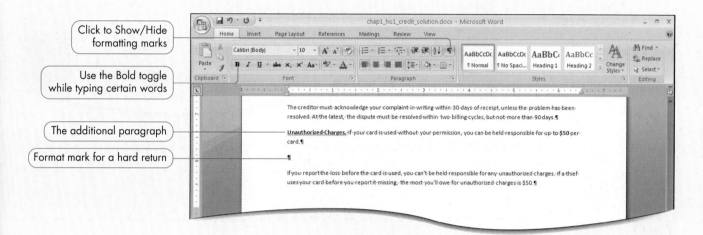

Figure 1.11 The Modified Document

Step 3
Insert AutoText

Refer to Figure 1.12 as you complete Step 3.

a. Press **Ctrl+End** to move to the end of the document and press **Enter** two times.

b. Type the first few letters of the current day of the week, such as **Tues** for *Tuesday*.

Notice that after you type the first few letters, a ScreenTip displays the full name.

c. Press **Enter** to accept the AutoText, and then type a comma.

Now a ScreenTip displays with the complete date—day or week, month, day, and year, as shown in Figure 1.12.

TROUBLESHOOTING: If the complete date does not display, press **Spacebar**, then type the first few letters of the current month, such as **Oct** for October. Press **Enter** to accept the AutoText after a ScreenTip displays with the full name of the month. Then continue until a ScreenTip displays with the complete date—month, day, and year, then press **Enter** to accept and insert the date.

d. Press **Enter** to accept the date. Press **Enter** one more time to insert a hard return.

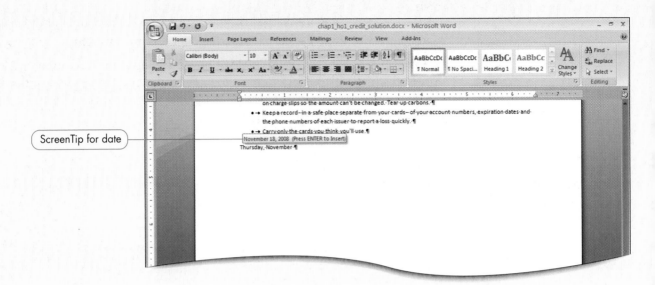

ScreenTip for date

Figure 1.12 Use AutoText to Insert the Date

Step 4
Create an AutoText Entry

Refer to Figure 1.13 as you complete Step 4.

a. Type your name on the line you just added, and then select it.

b. Click the **Insert tab** and click **Quick Parts** in the Text group. Select **Save Selection to Quick Part Gallery**.

The Create New Building Block dialog box displays.

c. In the **Name box**, type your initials.

The text in this box is what you begin to type, then press F3 to insert the actual building block content.

d. Click the **Gallery drop-down arrow**. Select **AutoText**, as shown in Figure 1.13. Click **OK.**

This procedure adds an AutoText entry to the Normal template. If you are in a lab environment, you might not have permission to add this item or save the changes to the Normal template.

e. Select your name in the document, but do not select the hard return mark, and then press **Delete** to remove it. Click **Quick Parts**, and then select **Building Blocks Organizer**.

The Building Blocks Organizer dialog box opens so that you can manage building blocks.

f. Click the **Gallery** heading at the top of the Building Blocks Organizer dialog box to sort the entries.

The AutoText entries display first. You should be able to see your new entry near the top of the list.

g. Select your entry in the Name column. Click **Insert** at the bottom of the dialog box.

Your name displays at the bottom of the page.

h. Click **Undo** in the Quick Access Toolbar to remove your name. Type the first two letters of your initials, and then press **F3**.

Your name, as saved in the Building Block, displays. You now have experience inserting a Building Block using two different methods.

i. Click **Save** on the Quick Access Toolbar.

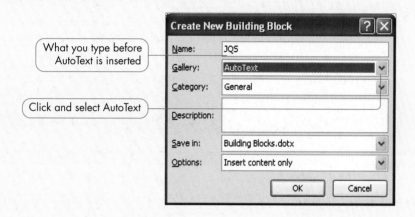

Figure 1.13 The Create New Building Block Dialog Box

<table>
<tr><td>**Step 5**</td><td></td></tr>
<tr><td>Change Document Views and Zoom</td><td></td></tr>
</table>

Step 5
Change Document Views and Zoom

Refer to Figure 1.14 as you complete Step 5.

a. Press **Ctrl+Home** to move the insertion point to the beginning of the document. Click the **View tab** and click **Full Screen Reading** in the Document Views group.

The document looks different, pages one and two display, the Ribbon is removed, and only a few buttons display (see Figure 1.14).

TROUBLESHOOTING: If you do not see two pages, click **View Options** in the upper-right corner and select **Show Two Pages**.

b. Hover your mouse pointer over the arrow in the lower-right corner of the screen, and then click the arrow to scroll to the next set of pages. Click the arrow one more time to view the last pages.

Once you reach the end of the document, the navigation arrow moves to the lower-left side of the screen.

c. Click the left-pointing arrow twice to display the first two pages again.

TIP Return to Print Layout View

Press **Esc** to return to Print Layout view and close the Full Screen Reading view.

d. Click **Close** in the upper-right corner of the screen to return to the default view.

e. Click **Zoom** in the Zoom group on the View tab. Click the icon below **Many pages** and roll your mouse to select 1 × 3 Pages. Click **OK** to change the view and display three pages on the top of the screen and one page at the bottom.

Notice the Zoom slider in the lower-right corner of the window displays 39%. If you use a wide-screen monitor, the size might differ slightly.

f. Save the *chap1_ho1_credit_solution* document and keep it onscreen if you plan to continue with the next exercise. Close the file and exit Word if you do not want to continue with the next exercise at this time.

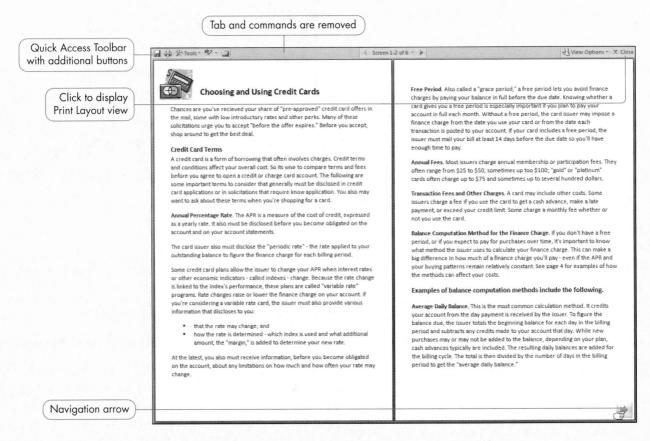

Figure 1.14 Full Screen Reading View

Document Formatting

Throughout your college and professional career, you will create a variety of documents. As you compose and edit large documents, you want to set them up so they have title pages, display a certain way when printed, or include page numbers at the top or bottom of a page. All of these options are available using features in Microsoft Word.

In this section, you make formatting changes to a Word document, such as changing the document margins and orientation. You insert page breaks, page numbers, headers and footers, sections, and cover pages. You also learn how to use the Find and Replace commands.

Setting Margins and Specifying Page Orientation

When you create a document, you consider the content you will insert, but you also should consider how you want the document to look when you print or display it. Many of the settings needed for this purpose are found on the Page Layout tab. The first setting most people change is *margins*. Margins determine the amount of white space from the text to the edges of the page. You should adjust margins to improve the appearance and readability of your document.

Margins are the amount of white space around the top, bottom, left, and right edges of the page.

The default margins, indicated in Figure 1.15, are 1″ on the top, bottom, left, and right of the page. You can select different margin settings from the gallery that displays when you click Margins in the Page Setup group on the Page Layout tab, or you can select the Custom Margins option to enter specific settings.

> When you create a document, you consider the content you will insert, but you should also consider how you want the document to look when you print or display it... to have title pages, or include page numbers at the top or bottom of a page. All of these options are available using features in Microsoft Word.

When you create a short business letter, you want to increase the margins to a larger size, such as 1.5″ on all sides, so the letter contents are balanced on the printed page. When you print a long document, you might want to reduce the margins to a small amount, such as 0.3″ or 0.5″, in order to reduce the amount of paper used. If you print a formal or research paper, you want to use a 1.5″ left margin and a 1″ right margin to allow extra room for binding. The margins you choose will apply to the whole document regardless of the position of the insertion point. You can establish different margin settings for different parts of a document by creating sections. Sections are discussed later in this chapter.

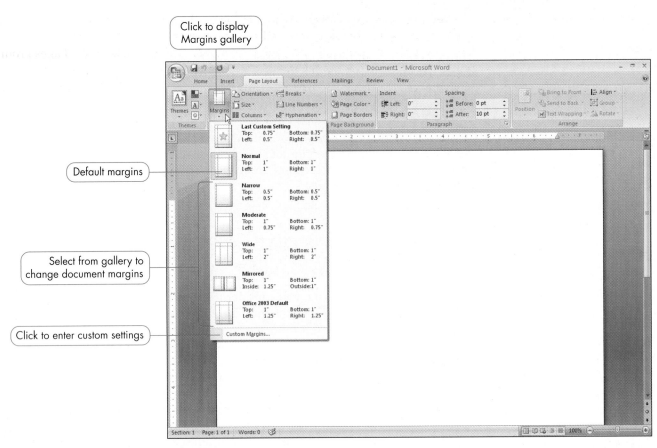

Figure 1.15 Setting Margins

Another setting to consider for a document is orientation. The Page Layout tab contains the Orientation command with two settings—portrait and landscape. *Portrait orientation,* the default setting, positions text parallel with the short side of the page so that the printed page is taller than it is wide. *Landscape orientation* flips the page 90 degrees so that text displays parallel with the longer side of the page, so that the printed page is wider than it is tall. The type of document you create and the manner in which you wish to display the information will dictate which type of orientation you use. Most documents, such as letters and research papers, use portrait orientation, but a brochure, large graphic, chart, or table might display better on a page with landscape orientation.

Portrait orientation positions text parallel with the short side of the page.

Landscape orientation positions text parallel with the long side of the page.

If you need to print a document on special paper, such as legal size (8½" × 14") or on an envelope, you should select the paper size before you create the document text. The Size command in the Page Setup group on the Page Layout tab contains several different document sizes from which you can choose. If you have special paper requirements, you can select More Paper Sizes to enter your own custom size. If you do not select the special size before you print, you will waste paper and find yourself with a very strange looking printout.

Inserting Page Breaks

When you type more text than can fit on a page, Word continues the text on another page using soft and hard page breaks. The *soft page break* is a hidden marker that automatically continues text on the top of a new page when text no longer fits on the current page. These breaks adjust automatically when you add and delete text. For the most part, you rely on soft page breaks to prepare multiple-page documents. However, at times you need to start a new page before Word inserts a soft page break.

A **soft page break** is inserted when text fills an entire page, then continues on the next page.

You can insert a **hard page break**, a hidden marker, to force text to begin on a new page. A hard page break is inserted into a document using the Breaks command in the Page Setup group on the Page Layout tab, or Page Break in the Pages group on the Insert tab. To view the page break markers in Print Layout view, you must click Show/Hide ¶ on the Home tab, to toggle on the formatting marks, as seen in Figure 1.16. You can view the page break markers without the Show/Hide toggled on when you switch to Draft view (see Figure 1.17).

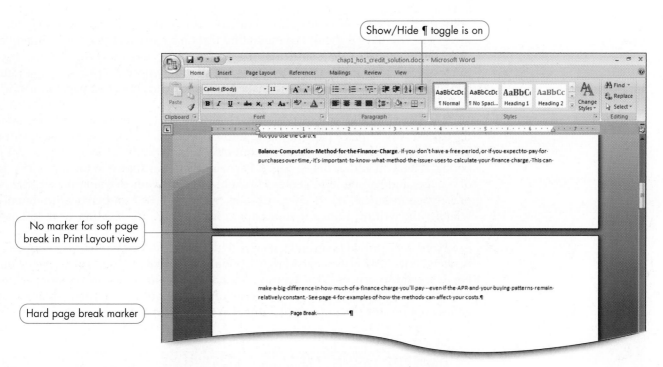

Figure 1.16 View Page Breaks in Print Layout View

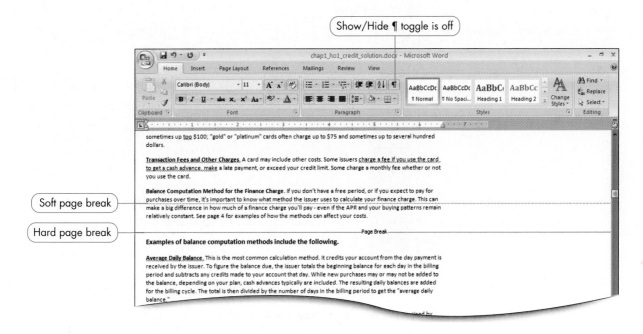

Figure 1.17 View Page Breaks in Draft View

Adding Page Numbers

Page numbers are essential in long documents. They serve as a convenient reference point for the writer and reader. If you do not include page numbers in a long document, you will have difficulty trying to find text on a particular page or trying to tell someone where to locate a particular passage in the document. Have you ever tried to reassemble a long document that was out of order and did not have page numbers? It can be very frustrating and makes a good case for inserting page numbers in your documents.

The Page Number command in the Header & Footer group on the Insert tab is the easiest way to place page numbers into a document. When you use this feature, Word not only inserts page numbers but also automatically adjusts the page numbering when you add or delete pages. Page numbers can appear at the top or bottom of a page, and can be left-, center-, or right-aligned. Your decision on whether to place page numbers in a header or footer might be based on personal preference, whether the writing guide for your paper dictates a specific location, or if you have other information to include in a header or footer also.

Word 2007 provides several galleries with options for formatting page numbers. New to Office 2007 is the Page Margin option, which enables you to put a page number on the side of a page. This feature adds a nice element of style to a multipage document that will be distributed as a flyer or annual report. Figure 1.18 displays a few gallery options for placing a page number at the bottom of a page.

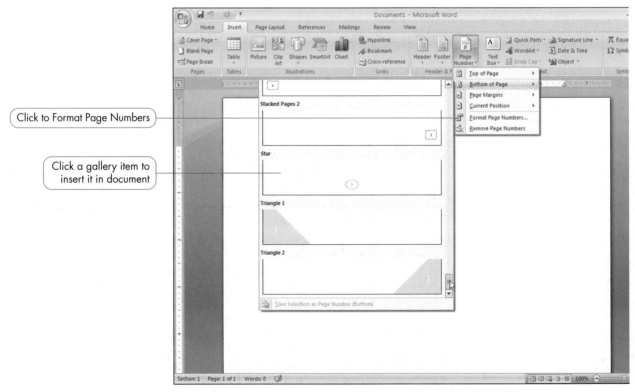

Figure 1.18 Insert Page Numbers at Bottom of Page

Word enables you to customize the number format for page numbers to use Roman rather than Arabic numerals, which often are used for preliminary or preface pages at the beginning of a book. You also can adjust the page numbering so that it starts numbering at a page other than the first. This is useful when you have a report with a cover page; you typically do not consider the cover as page one but instead begin numbering with the page that follows it. You use the Format Page Numbers command to display the Page Number Format dialog box (see Figure 1.19) where you can make these changes. If you are not satisfied with the page numbering in a document, use the Remove Page Numbers command to remove them.

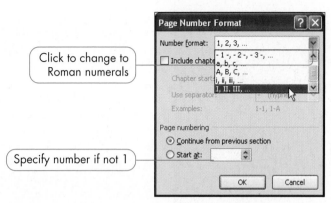

Figure 1.19 Page Number Format Dialog Box

Inserting Headers and Footers

A **header** is information printed at the top of document pages.

A **footer** is information printed at the bottom of document pages.

Headers and footers give a professional appearance to a document. A **header** consists of one or more lines that are printed at the top of a page. A **footer** is printed at the bottom of the page. A document may contain headers but not footers, footers but not headers, both headers and footers, or neither. Footers often contain the page number and a date the document was created. Headers might contain the name of an organization, author, or title of the document. Take a moment to notice the type of information you see in the headers/footers of the books or magazines you are reading.

Headers and footers are added from the Insert tab. You can create a simple header or footer by clicking Insert Page Number, depending on whether the page number is at the top or bottom of a page. Headers and footers are formatted like any other paragraph and can be center, left or right aligned. You can format headers and footers in any typeface or point size and can include special codes to automatically insert the page number, date, and time a document is printed.

The advantage of using a header or footer (over typing the text yourself at the top or bottom of every page) is that you type the text only once, after which it appears automatically according to your specifications. In addition, the placement of the headers and footers is adjusted for changes in page breaks caused by the insertion or deletion of text in the body of the document.

Headers and footers can change continually throughout a document. Once you insert one, the Header & Footer Tools tab displays and contains many options (see Figure 1.20). For instance, you can specify a different header or footer for the first page; this is advisable when you have a cover page and do not want the header (or footer) to display on that page. You also can have different headers and footers for odd and even pages. This feature is useful when you plan to print a document that will be bound as a book. Notice the different information this book prints on the footer of odd versus even pages, and how the page numbers display in the corners of each page. If you want to change the header (or footer) midway through a document, you need to insert a section break at the point where the new header (or footer) is to begin. These breaks are discussed in the next section.

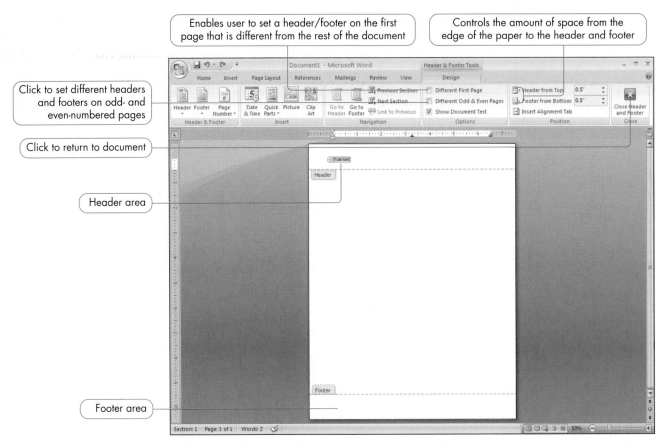

Enables user to set a header/footer on the first page that is different from the rest of the document

Controls the amount of space from the edge of the paper to the header and footer

Click to set different headers and footers on odd- and even-numbered pages

Click to return to document

Header area

Footer area

Figure 1.20 Header and Footer Tools Commands

Creating Sections

Formatting in Word occurs on three levels: character, paragraph, and section. Formatting at the section level controls headers and footers, page numbering, page size and orientation, margins, and columns. All of the documents in the text so far have consisted of a single section, and thus any section formatting applied to the entire document. You can, however, divide a document into sections and format each section independently.

You determine where one section ends and another begins by clicking Breaks in the Page Setup group on the Page Layout tab. A *section break* is a marker that divides a document into sections. It enables you to decide how the section will be formatted on the printed page; that is, you can specify that the new section continues on the same page, that it begins on a new page, or that it begins on the next odd or even page even if a blank page has to be inserted. Formatting at the section level gives you the ability to create more sophisticated documents. You can use section formatting to do the following:

A *section break* is a marker that divides a document into sections, thereby allowing different formatting in each section.

- Change the margins within a multipage letter, where the first page (the letterhead) requires a larger top margin than the other pages in the letter.

- Change the orientation from portrait to landscape to accommodate a wide table at the end of the document.

- Change the page numbering to use Roman numerals at the beginning of the document for a table of contents and Arabic numerals thereafter.

- Change the number of columns in a newsletter, which may contain a single column at the top of a page for the masthead, then two or three columns in the body of the newsletter.

Word stores the formatting characteristics of each section in the section break at the end of a section. Thus, deleting a section break also deletes the section formatting, causing the text above the break to assume the formatting characteristics of the next section.

Figure 1.21 displays a multipage view of a six-page document. The document has been divided into two sections, and the insertion point is currently on the last page of the document, which is also the first page of the second section. Note the corresponding indications on the status bar and the position of the headers and footers throughout the document.

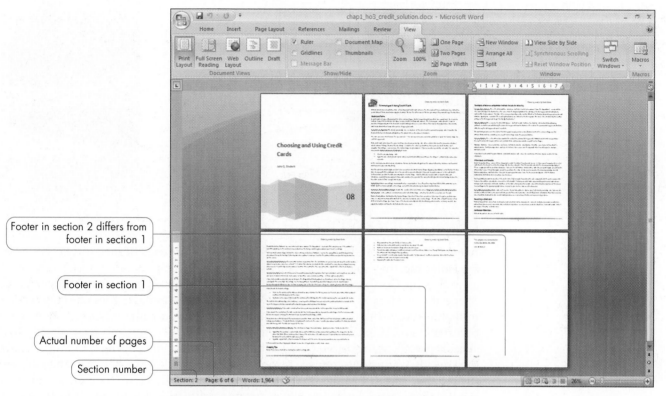

Figure 1.21 A Document with Two Sections

Inserting a Cover Page

You can use commands such as page break and keystrokes such as Ctrl+Enter, mentioned in previous sections, to create a cover page for a document. But Word 2007 offers a feature to quickly insert a preformatted cover page in your document. The Cover Page feature in the Pages group of the Insert tab includes a gallery with several designs, as seen in Figure 1.22. Each design includes building block fields, such as Document Title, Company Name, Date, and Author, which you can personalize. Additionally, the title pages already are formatted with the different first page option in the header and footer, so you don't have to change that setting after you insert the page. After you personalize and make any additional modifications of your choice, your document will include an attractive cover page.

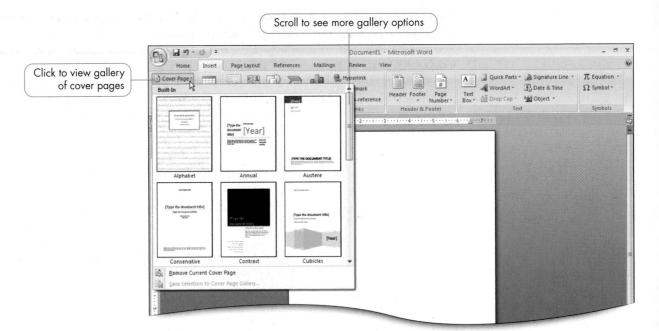

Figure 1.22 Insert a Cover Page

Using Find and Replace Commands

Even though Find and Replace have individual commands in the Editing group, on the Home tab, they share a common dialog box with different tabs for each command as well as the Go To command. The Find command locates one or more occurrences of specific text (e.g., a word or phrase). The Replace command goes one step further in that it locates the text, and then enables you to optionally replace (one or more occurrences of) that text with different text. The Go To command goes directly to a specific place (e.g., a specific page) in the document. If you use the find function and then decide you want to replace text, you can simply click the Replace tab to initiate the process. These functions are very helpful when working in a long document; you can use them to quickly locate text or jump to a different location in the document.

The search in both the Find and Replace commands is case sensitive or case insensitive. A **case-sensitive search**, where the Match Case option is selected, matches not only the text but also the use of upper- and lowercase letters. Thus, *There* is different from *there*, and a search on one will not identify the other. A **case-insensitive search**, where Match Case is *not* selected, is just the opposite and finds both *There* and *there*. A search also may specify whole words only to identify *there*, but not *therefore* or *thereby*. And finally, the search and replacement text also can specify different numbers of characters; for example, you could replace *flower* with *daisy*.

The Replace command implements either **selective replacement**, which lets you examine each occurrence of the character string in context and decide whether to replace it, or **automatic replacement**, where the substitution is made automatically. Selective replacement is implemented by clicking the Find Next command, then clicking (or not clicking) Replace to make the substitution. Automatic replacement (through the entire document) is implemented by clicking Replace All. This feature can save you a great deal of time if you need to make a replacement throughout a document, but it also can produce unintended consequences. For example, if you substitute the word *text* for *book*, the word *textbook* would become *texttext*, which is not what you had in mind.

The Find and Replace commands can include formatting and/or special characters. This command is helpful in situations where you need to make changes to the way text is formatted, but not necessarily to the text itself. You can, for example, change all italicized text to boldface, as shown in Figure 1.23, or you can change five consecutive spaces to a tab character, which makes it easier to align text. You also can

A **case-sensitive search** matches not only the text but also the use of upper- and lowercase letters.

A **case-insensitive search** finds a word regardless of any capitalization used.

Selective replacement lets you decide whether to replace text.

Automatic replacement makes a substitution automatically.

use special characters in the character string, such as the "any character" (consisting of ^?). For example, to find all four-letter words that begin with "f" and end with "l" (such as *fall*, *fill*, or *fail*), search for f^?^?l. (The question mark stands for any character, just like a wildcard in a card game.) You also can search for all forms of a word; for example, if you specify *am*, it will also find *is* and *are*. You can even search for a word based on how it sounds. When searching for *Marion*, for example, check the Sounds like check box, and the search will find both *Marion* and *Marian*.

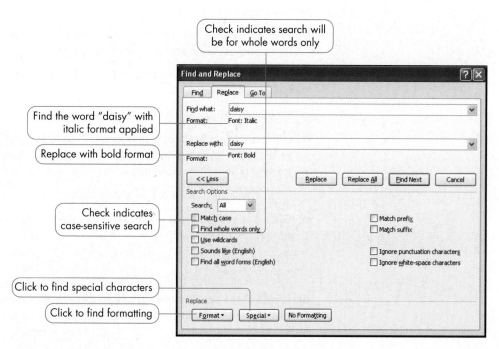

Figure 1.23 The Find and Replace Dialog Box

Hands-On Exercises

2 | Document Organization

Skills covered: 1. Set Page Margins and Orientation **2.** Insert a Page Break **3.** Add a Cover Page and Insert a Document Header **4.** Insert a Section Break **5.** Insert a Page Number in the Footer **6.** Use Find, Replace, and Go To

Step 1 Set Page Margins and Orientation	Refer to Figure 1.24 as you complete Step 1. **a.** Open the *chap1_ho1_credit_solution* document if you closed it after the last hands-on exercise and save it as **chap1_ho2_credit_solution**. **b.** Click the **Page Layout tab** and click **Margins** in the Page Setup group. Click **Custom Margins**. The Page Setup dialog box displays. **c.** Click the **Margins tab**, if necessary. Type **.75** in the Top margin box. Press **Tab** to move the insertion point to the Bottom margin box. Type **.75** and press **Tab** to move to the Left margin box. 0.75″ is the equivalent of ¾ of one inch. **d.** Click the **Left margin down arrow** to reduce the left margin to **0.5″**, and then repeat the procedure to set the right margin to **0.5″**. The top and bottom margins are now set at 0.75″ and the left and right margins are set at 0.5″ (see Figure 1.24). **e.** Check that these settings apply to the **Whole document**, located in the lower portion of the dialog box. Click **OK**. You can see the change in layout as a result of changing the margins. More text displays on the first three pages, and there is only one line of text remaining on the fourth page. **f.** Click **Orientation** in the Page Setup group on the Page Layout tab, and then select **Landscape**. The pages now display in landscape orientation. Whereas the document looks fine, we will return to portrait orientation to prepare for the remaining exercises. **g.** Click **Undo** on the Quick Access Toolbar. Save the document.

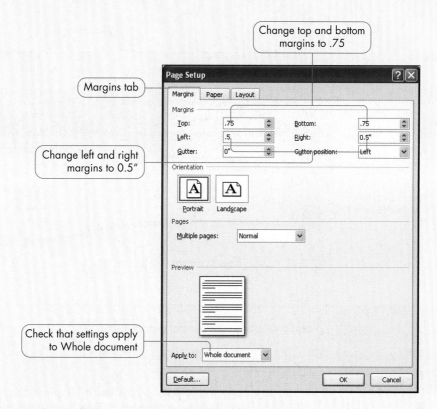

Change top and bottom
margins to .75

Margins tab

Change left and right
margins to 0.5"

Check that settings apply
to Whole document

Figure 1.24 Change the Margins

Step 2
Insert a Page Break

Refer to Figure 1.25 as you complete Step 2.

a. Click the **Zoom slider** and increase the zoom to **100%**.

b. Place the insertion point on the left side of the heading *Examples of balance computation methods include the following* on the bottom of the first page.

c. Press **Ctrl+Enter** to insert a page break.

The heading and paragraph that follows move to the top of the second page. It leaves a gap of space at the bottom of the first page, but you will make other adjustments to compensate for that.

d. Place the insertion point on the left side of the paragraph heading *Prompt Credit for Payment* on the bottom of the second page. Press **Enter** one time.

The hard returns force the paragraph to relocate to the top of the next page.

e. Click the **Zoom slider** and decrease the zoom to **50%**, and then display pages one and two. If necessary, click **Show/Hide ¶** in the Paragraph group on the Home tab to view formatting marks.

Notice the marks that indicate the Page Break and hard return at the bottom of the first and second pages, as seen in Figure 1.25.

f. Save the document.

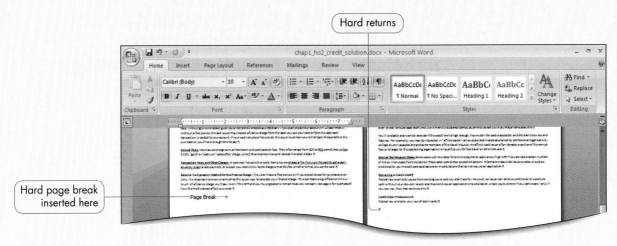

Figure 1.25 Insert a Hard Page Break

Step 3
Add a Cover Page and Insert a Document Header

Refer to Figure 1.26 as you complete Step 3.

a. Click the **Insert tab**, click **Cover Page** in the Pages group, and then click **Cubicles** from the gallery.

You now have a title page that already displays the report title, and the rest of the document begins at the top of page two. The insertion point does not have to be at the beginning of a document to insert a cover page.

TROUBLESHOOTING: If the document title does not display automatically, click the Title field and replace the text *Type the document title* with **Choosing and Using Credit Cards**.

b. Right-click the Subtitle field and click **Cut**. Right-click the company name field at the top of the page, and then click **Cut**. Click the Year field and type the current year. If necessary, click the Author Name field and type your name.

Due to the preset format of the title page, the date 2008 will change to 08 automatically.

c. Click the **Zoom slider** and increase the zoom to **100%**. Click **Header** on the Insert tab and click **Edit Header** at the bottom of the gallery list.

The Design tab displays and the header area of the page is bordered by a blue line.

d. Look at the status bar on the bottom of the page to determine the page where the insertion point is located. If necessary, place your insertion point in the header of page two. Confirm that the **Different First Page** option is selected in the Design tab's Options group.

The cover page you created does not require a heading, and this setting prevents the heading from displaying on that page.

e. Press **Tab** two times to move the insertion point to the right side of the footer. Click **Quick Parts** in the Insert group and point to **Document Property**. Click **Title** at the end of the submenu.

The title of the document, *Choosing and Using Credit Cards*, displays in the header, as seen in Figure 1.26.

f. Scroll down and notice the header on the remaining pages. Click **Close Header and Footer**.

g. Save the document.

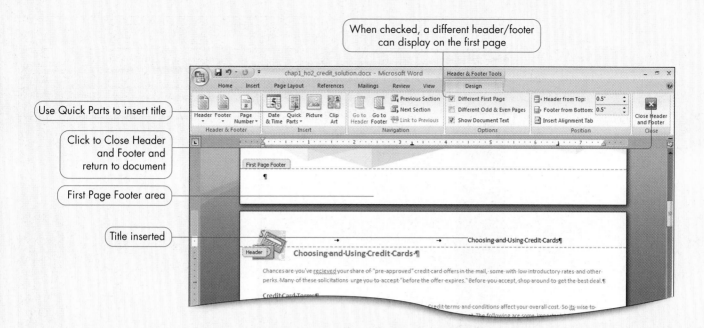

When checked, a different header/footer can display on the first page

Use Quick Parts to insert title

Click to Close Header and Footer and return to document

First Page Footer area

Title inserted

Figure 1.26 Create a Header

Refer to Figure 1.27 as you complete Step 4.

a. Press **Ctrl+End** to move to the end of the document, then place the insertion point on the left side of the date. Click the **Page Layout tab,** click **Breaks** in the Page Setup group, and then click **Next Page** under Section Breaks.

By inserting this section break, you are now free to make modifications to the last page without changing the previous pages.

b. Double-click in the header or footer area of the last page to display the Design tab. Click in the header of the last page, and then click **Link to Previous** in the Navigation group to deselect it.

Even though you insert a section break, the header and footer of this page take on the same formatting as the first section. When you remove that link, you can set up an independent header and/or footer.

c. In the header of the last page, type **This project was completed on**, as shown in Figure 1.27.

d. Click **Go To Footer** in the Navigation group. Click **Link to Previous** to toggle it off. In the Position group, click the **Footer from Bottom** up arrow until **.8"** displays.

This footer is now independent from all other document footers, and the page number at the bottom will print in a different location on the page.

e. Click **Close Header and Footer**. Save the document.

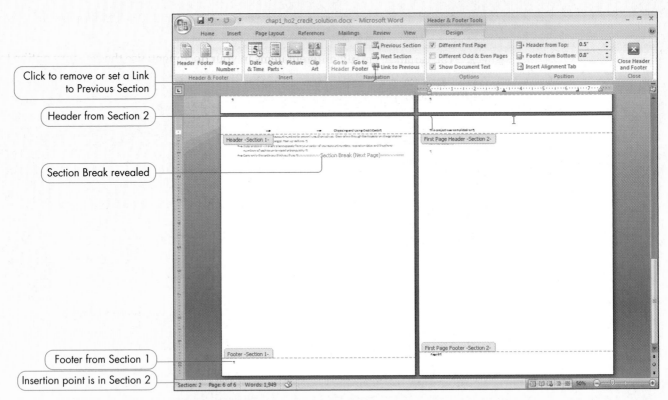

Click to remove or set a Link to Previous Section

Header from Section 2

Section Break revealed

Footer from Section 1

Insertion point is in Section 2

Figure 1.27 Header in Section 2

Step 5

Insert a Page Number in the Footer

Refer to Figure 1.28 as you complete Step 5.

a. Place your insertion point anywhere on the second page. Click the **Insert tab**, if necessary. Click **Page Number** in the Header & Footer group, and then point to **Bottom of Page**. Scroll down to the bottom of the gallery and click **Thick Line**.

A dark line and the page number display on the bottom of each page except the first and last because you changed the Different First Page and Link to Previous options.

TROUBLESHOOTING: If your insertion point was on the first page, the footer will display on that page only. Click Undo on the Quick Access Toolbar, place your insertion point on page two, and repeat the step above to add the footer to the remaining pages.

b. Click **Page Number** in the Header & Footer group of the Design tab and click **Format Page Numbers**.

The Page Number Format dialog box displays.

c. Click **Start at**, then click the down arrow until **0** displays.

If you begin page numbering with zero, the second page, which is the first page of content, displays as page 1.

d. Scroll to the bottom of page 6. Place the insertion point on the left side of the footer area, type **Page**, and then press **Spacebar** one time.

e. Click **Quick Parts** in the Insert group and select **Field**. Click the **Categories drop-down arrow** and select **Numbering**.

You can insert many different items in your document; use the category option to minimize the number of fields to browse through to find the one you want.

f. Select **Page** in the **Field names** list and select the first option displayed in the Format list, as seen in Figure 1.28. Click **OK**.

The end result for this operation will be similar to one that you can reach using the Page Number feature; however, this exercise demonstrates the field feature that allows you to use more customization in headers and footers by combining the field with text of your choice.

g. Click **Close Header and Footer**.

h. Save the document.

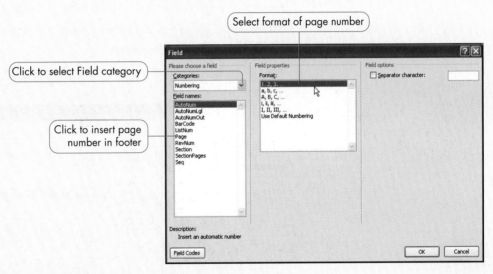

Figure 1.28 Insert a Field in a Footer

Refer to Figure 1.29 as you complete Step 6.

Step 6
Use Find, Replace, and Go To

a. Press **Ctrl+Home** to move to the beginning of the document. Click the **Home tab** and click **Find** in the Editing group.

b. Type **APR** in the *Find what* text box, and then click **Find Next**.

The first occurrence of the text appears on the second page.

c. Click the **Replace tab** in the Find and Replace dialog box. Type **annual percentage rate** in the *Replace with* box. Click **Replace All**.

A dialog box displays, indicating seven replacements were made.

d. Click **OK** to remove the dialog box. In the Find what text box, type **$50**. Click **More**, if necessary, then click **Format** and click **Font**. In the Font dialog box, click **Bold** in the *Font style* list, and then click **OK**.

e. In the *Replace with* text box, type **$50**. Click **Format** and click **Font**. In the Font dialog box, click **Regular** in the *Font style* list, and then click **OK**. Compare your window to Figure 1.29.

TROUBLESHOOTING: If you applied the Bold format to the text in the *Replace with* box instead of the *Find what* box, click **No Formatting** on the bottom of the window, then start again. Be sure the insertion point is in the desired box before you click **Format**.

f. Click **Find Next**.

The bolded occurrence of $50 displays near the bottom of the fourth page.

g. Click **Replace** to remove the formatting from the text, and then click **OK** in the dialog box that informs you Word has finished searching the document.

h. Click the **Go To tab**.

The Go To tab of the Find and Replace dialog box displays, and the insertion point is in the *Enter page number* box.

i. Type **1** in the *Enter page number* box, then click **Go To**.

The top of page 1 displays on your screen, and the Find and Replace dialog box is still onscreen.

j. Click **Section** in the **Go to what** box, type **2** in the *Enter section number* box, and then click **Go To**.

The top of page 6 displays, which is the beginning of the section you added in Step 4.

k. Click **Close**. Save the document.

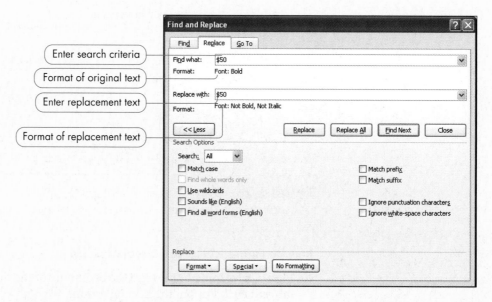

Figure 1.29 Find and Replace Text

The Final Touches

You can create a document that is, for the most part, free of typographical and grammatical errors. Word provides many features that assist in correcting a variety of grammatical mistakes.

As you work on a document, you should save changes frequently. Word even has an option to create backup copies of your work periodically in case of a system failure. When you believe that your document is complete, you should take one last look and run a few diagnostics to check for mistakes in spelling and grammar. If you are sending the document to another person, you also should use the tools that locate compatibility issues your document has with older versions of Word. If you print your document, be sure to use features that avoid wasting paper.

In this section, you check for spelling and grammatical errors. You also revisit the important process of saving files as well as backup options, the Compatibility Checker, and the Document Inspector. You learn different print options, and you learn about the many customization options available in Word 2007.

Checking Spelling and Grammar

You can create a document that is, for the most part, free of typographical and grammatical errors. However, you should always proofread a document at the conclusion of your edits because it is possible the automated spelling and grammar checker did not find every error. Word provides many features that assist in correcting a variety of grammatical mistakes. In the Office Fundamentals chapter, you learned how to use the Spelling and Grammar and the Thesaurus features to assist in writing and proofing. In the following paragraphs, you will learn about other features that help you create error-free documents.

Perform a Spelling and Grammar Check

The **Spelling and Grammar** feature looks for mistakes in spelling, punctuation, writing style, and word usage.

The **Spelling and Grammar** feature attempts to catch mistakes in spelling, punctuation, writing style, and word usage by comparing strings of text within a document to a series of predefined rules. When located, you can accept the suggested correction and make the replacement automatically, or more often, edit the selected text and make your own changes.

You also can ask the grammar check to explain the rule it is attempting to enforce. Unlike the spell check, the grammar check is subjective, and what seems appropriate to you may be objectionable to someone else. Indeed, the grammar check is quite flexible, and can be set to check for different writing styles; that is, you can implement one set of rules to check a business letter and a different set of rules for casual writing. Many times, however, you will find that the English language is just too complex for the grammar check to detect every error, although it will find many. Depending on your reliance on the grammar check, you can set the option for it to run all the time by marking the selection in the Word Options, Proofing category.

TIP Custom Dictionaries

If you work in a field that uses technical terminology, such as nursing or aviation, you need to include those terms with the existing dictionary in the Spelling and Grammar feature. To use the custom dictionary, click the Office Button, click Word Options, click Proofing, click Custom Dictionary, and then navigate to the location where the dictionary is stored.

Check Contextual Spelling

In addition to spelling and grammar checking, Word 2007 has added a contextual spelling feature that attempts to locate a word that is spelled correctly, but used incorrectly. For example, many people confuse the usage of words such as *their* and *there*, *two* and *too*, and *which* and *witch*. The visual indication that a contextual spelling error occurs is a blue wavy line under the word, as shown in Figure 1.30. By default, this feature is not turned on; to invoke the command, click the Office Button, select Word Options at the bottom, select the Proofing category, then click to select the Use contextual spelling check box.

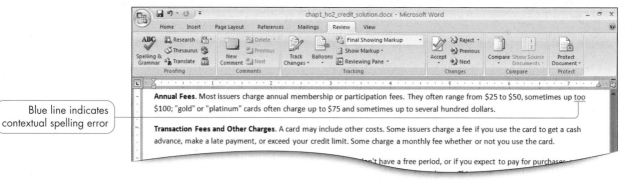

Blue line indicates contextual spelling error

Figure 1.30 Check Contextual Spelling

Using Save and Backup Options

It is not a question of *if* it will happen but *when*. Files are lost, systems crash, and viruses infect a system. That said, we cannot overemphasize the importance of saving your work frequently. Additionally, you should use available resources to provide a backup copy (or two) of your most important documents and back up your files at every opportunity. For example, the Exploring series authors back up all of their manuscript files in case one system crashes. Graduate students periodically back up their lengthy theses and dissertations so that they do not have to recreate these research documents from scratch if one system fails.

Save a Document in Compatible Format

After reading the Office Fundamentals chapter, you know the Save and Save As commands are used to copy your documents to disk and should be used frequently in order to avoid loss of work and data. Because some people may use a different version of Microsoft Word, you should know how to save a document in a format that they can use. People cannot open a Word 2007 document in earlier versions of Word unless they update their earlier version with the Compatibility Pack that contains a converter. If you are not sure if they have installed the Compatibility Pack, it is best to save the document in an older format, such as Word 97–2003.

To save a document so that someone with a different version of Office can open it, click the Office Button and point to the arrow on the right side of the Save As command. The option to save in Word 97–2003 format appears (see Figure 1.31), and after

you click it, you can use the Save As dialog box normally. The saved file will have the .doc extension instead of the Word 2007 extension, .docx. Another way to save in the older format is to double-click Save As, then select the Word 97–2003 format from the *Save as type* list in the Save As dialog box.

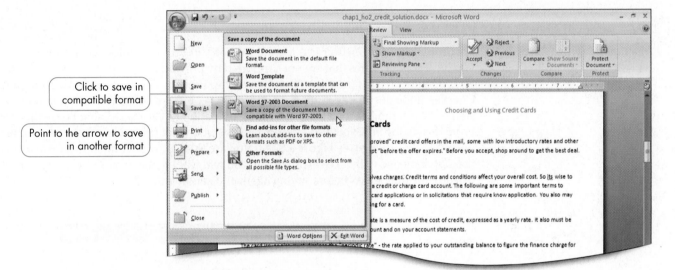

Figure 1.31 Save a File in Compatible Format

If you open a Word document created in an earlier version, such as Word 2003, the title bar will include *(Compatibility Mode)* at the top. You can still work with the document and even save it back in the same format for a Word 97–2003 user. However, some newer features of Word 2007, such as SmartArt and other graphic enhancement options used in the Cover Page and custom headers and footers, are not viewable or available for use in compatibility mode. To remove the file from compatibility mode, click the Office Button and select Convert. It will convert the file and remove the *(Compatibility Mode)* designator, but the .doc extension still displays. The next time you click Save, the extension will change to .docx, indicating that it is converted into a Word 2007 file, and then you can use all of the application features.

Understand Backup Options

Microsoft Word offers several different backup options, the most important of which is to save AutoRecover information periodically. If Microsoft Word crashes, the program will be able to recover a previous version of your document when you restart Word. The only work you will lose is anything you did between the time of the last AutoRecover operation and the time of the crash. The default *Save AutoRecover information every 10 minutes* ensures that you will never lose more than 10 minutes of work.

You also can set Word to create a backup copy in conjunction with every Save. You set these valuable backup and AutoRecover options from the Save and Advanced categories of the Word Options menu. Assume, for example, that you have created the simple document *The fox jumped over the fence* and saved it under the name *Fox*. Assume further that you edit the document to read *The quick brown fox jumped over the fence* and that you saved it a second time. The second Save command changes the name of the original document from *Fox* to *Backup of Fox*, then saves the current contents of memory as *Fox*. In other words, the disk now contains two versions of the document: the current version *Fox* and the most recent previous version *Backup of Fox*.

The cycle goes on indefinitely, with *Fox* always containing the current version and *Backup of Fox* the most recent previous version. So, if you revise and save the document a third time, *Fox* will contain the latest revision while *Backup of Fox* would contain the previous version alluding to the quick brown fox. The original (first) version of the document disappears entirely because only two versions are kept.

The contents of *Fox* and *Backup of Fox* are different, but the existence of the latter enables you to retrieve the previous version if you inadvertently edit beyond repair or accidentally erase the current *Fox* version. Should this situation occur, you can always retrieve its predecessor and at least salvage your work prior to the last save operation. But remember, this process only takes place if you enable the Always create backup copy option in the Advanced category of the Word Options dialog box.

Run the Compatibility Checker

The **Compatibility Checker** looks for features that are not supported by previous versions of Word.

The **Compatibility Checker** is a feature in Word 2007 that enables you to determine if you have used features that are not supported by previous versions. After you complete your document, click the Office Button, point to Prepare, and then select Compatibility Checker. If the document contains anything that could not be opened in a different version of Word, the Microsoft Office Word Compatibility Checker dialog box will list it. From this dialog box, you also can indicate that you want to always check compatibility when saving this file (see Figure 1.32). If you are saving the document in a format to be used by someone with an earlier version, you will want to make corrections to the items listed in the dialog box before saving again and sending the file.

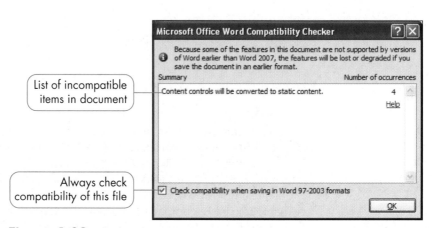

Figure 1.32 The Compatibility Checker

Run the Document Inspector

The **Document Inspector** checks for and removes different kinds of hidden and personal information from a document.

Before you send or give a document to another person, you should run the **Document Inspector** to reveal any hidden or personal data in the file. For privacy or security reasons, you might want to remove certain items contained in the document such as author name, comments made by one or more persons who have access to the document, or document server locations. Some inspectors are specific to individual Office applications, such as Excel and PowerPoint. Word provides inspectors that you can invoke to reveal different types of information, including:

- Comments, Revisions, Versions, and Annotations
- Document Properties and Personal Information
- Custom XML Data
- Headers, Footers, and Watermarks
- Hidden Text

The inspectors also can locate information in documents created in older versions of Word. Because some information that the Document Inspector might remove cannot be recovered with the Undo command, you should save a copy of your original document, using a different name, just before you run any of the inspectors. After you save the copy, click the Office Button, point to Prepare, and then select the Inspect Document option to run the inspector (see Figure 1.33). When it is complete, it will list the results and enable you to choose whether to remove the information from the document. If you forget to save a backup copy of the document, you can use the Save As command to save a copy of the document with a new name after you run the inspector.

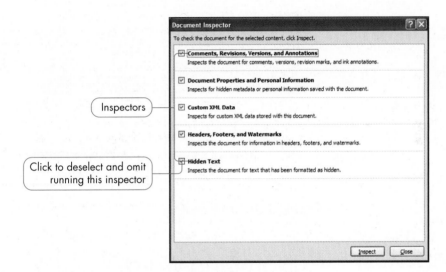

Figure 1.33 The Document Inspector

Selecting Printing Options

People often print an entire document when they want to view only a few pages. All computer users should be mindful of the environment, and limiting printer use is a perfect place to start. Millions of sheets of paper have been wasted because someone did not take a moment to preview his or her work and then had to reprint due to a very minor error that is easily noticed in a preview window.

Click the Office Button and click the Print arrow to see three settings to consider when you are ready to print your work: Print, Quick Print, and Print Preview. You should select the Print Preview option first to see a preview of what the document will look like when you print it. In the Print Preview window, you have several settings that enable you to magnify the page onscreen, display multiple pages, and even make changes to the page layout so you can view the results immediately. If you are satisfied with the document, you can launch the Print dialog box from that window.

The Quick Print option sends a document straight to the printer without prompting you for changes to the printer configuration. If you have only one printer and rarely change printer options, this is an efficient tool.

The final print option is Print, which always displays the Print dialog box and contains many useful options. For example, you can print only the page that contains the insertion point (Current page) or a specific range of pages, such as pages 3–10 (Pages). Furthermore, you can print more than one copy of the document (Number of copies), print miniature copies of pages on a single sheet of paper (Pages per sheet), or adjust the document text size to fit on a particular type of paper (Scale to paper size). If you do not have a duplex printer, you can select the option to print only even numbered pages, flip the paper over and put it back in the printer, then select the option to print only odd pages, as seen in Figure 1.34. This method is used frequently by some of the Exploring authors because they do not own duplex printers and also because they want to conserve paper!

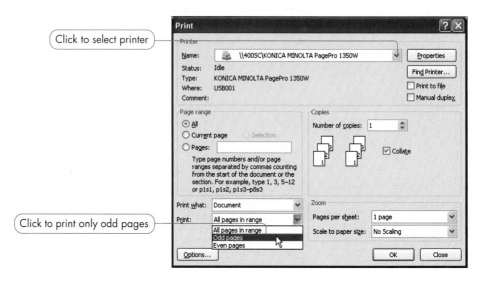

Figure 1.34 Print Options

Customizing Word

As installed, Word is set up to be useful immediately. However, you might find options that you would prefer to customize, add, or remove from the document window. For example, you can add commands to the Quick Access Toolbar (QAT) that do not currently display on any tabs. Or you can add commands that you use so frequently you prefer to access them from the always-visible QAT.

You can customize Word in many ways. To begin the process, or just to view the options available for customization, click the Office Button, then select Word Options. Table 1.2 describes the main categories that you can customize and some of the features in each category. You should take some time to glance through each category as you continue to read this chapter. Keep in mind that if you are working in a school lab, you might not have permission to change options on a permanent basis.

Table 1.2 Word Options

Menu Category	Description	Sample of Options to Change
Popular	Change the most popular options in Word.	Show Mini toolbar; show Enhanced ScreenTips; change color scheme; change user name and initials.
Display	Change how documents are displayed on the screen and in print.	Show white space between pages in Print Layout view; always show formatting marks such as spaces on the screen; print document properties.
Proofing	Modify how Word corrects and formats your text.	Ignore words in uppercase (do not flag as incorrect); use Spellchecker; use contextual spelling (checks for words that sound alike but are spelled differently such as two, too, and to); mark grammatical errors.
Save	Customize how documents are saved.	Default locations and format to save files; AutoRecover file location; Web server location.
Advanced	Specify editing options; cut, copy, and paste options; show document content options; display options; print options; and save options.	Allow text to be dragged and dropped; enable click and type; default paragraph style; show paste option buttons; show smart tags; number of recent documents to show in file menu; print pages in reverse order; always create backup copy; embed smart tags; update automatic links at open; compatibility options.
Customize	Customize the Quick Access Toolbar and other keyboard shortcuts.	Add or remove buttons from the QAT; determine location of QAT; customize keyboard shortcuts.
Add-Ins	View the add-ins previously installed, customize settings for add-ins, and install more add-ins.	View settings for active and inactive application add-ins; manage smart tags, templates, and disabled items.
Trust Center	View online documentation about security and privacy and change settings to protect documents from possible infections.	Enable and disable macros; change ActiveX settings; set privacy options; select trusted publishers and locations.
Resources	Provide links to Microsoft sites where you can find online resources and keep your Office application updated.	Download updates for Office; diagnose and repair problems with Office; contact Microsoft; activate your license for Office; register for free online services; view product specifications.

As you can see, you are able to customize dozens of settings in Word. Table 1.2 mentions only a small sample of them; fortunately, most users do not need to change any settings at all.

3 | The Final Touches

Skills covered: 1. Perform a Spelling and Grammar Check **2.** Run the Document Inspector and a Compatibility Check **3.** Save in a Compatible Format **4.** Change Word Options **5.** Use Print Preview Features

---

Step 1
Perform a Spelling and Grammar Check

Refer to Figure 1.35 as you complete Step 1.

a. Open the *chap1_ho2_credit_solution* document if you closed it after the last hands-on exercise and save it as **chap1_ho3_credit_solution**.

b. Press **Ctrl+Home** to move to the beginning of the document. Click the **Review tab** and click **Spelling & Grammar** in the Proofing group.

The Spelling and Grammar dialog box displays with the first error indicated in red text (see Figure 1.35).

c. Click **Change All** to replace all misspellings of the word *recieved* with the correct *received*, then view the next error.

d. Click **Change** to replace *its* with the correct usage, *it's*.

e. Click **Ignore Once** to keep the heading *Annual Percentage Rate*.

Remember that not all grammar usage flagged may be incorrect. Use your best judgment for those occasions.

f. Remove the check from the **Check grammar** option.

Most of the headings in the document will be flagged for incorrect grammar, so this will let you bypass all of them and check the spelling only.

g. Click **Change** to replace the contextual spelling error *too* with *to* near the bottom of the first page. Click **Change** to replace the incorrect spelling of *Errors* on the third page. Click **OK** in the box that informs you the spelling and grammar check is complete.

h. Save the document.

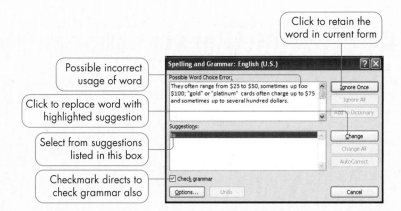

Figure 1.35 Check Spelling and Grammar

Refer to Figure 1.36 as you complete Step 2.

a. Click the **Office Button**, select **Prepare**, and then select **Run Compatibility Checker**.

A list of any non-compatible items in the document will display in the Microsoft Office Word Compatibility Checker dialog box.

b. Click **OK** after you view the incompatible listings.

c. Click the **Office Button** and select **Save As**. Save the document as **chap1_ho3_credit2_solution**.

Before you run the Document Inspector you save the document with a different name in order to have a backup.

d. Click the **Office Button**, point to **Prepare**, and then select **Inspect Document**.

TROUBLESHOOTING: An informational window might display with instructions to save the document before you run the Document Inspector. You should save the document first because the Document Inspector might make changes that you cannot undo.

e. Click to select any inspector check box that is not already checked. Click **Inspect**.

The Document Inspector results are shown, and Remove All buttons are displayed to remove the items found in each category.

f. Click **Close**; do not remove any items at this time.

g. Save the document as **chap1_ho3_credit_solution**. Click **OK** to overwrite the existing file with the same name.

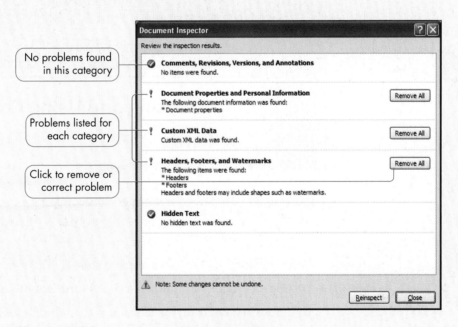

Figure 1.36 Document Inspector Results

Refer to Figure 1.37 as you complete Step 3.

a. Click the **Office Button**, click the **Save As** arrow, and select **Word 97–2003 Format**.

b. Confirm the *Save as type* box displays **Word 97–2003 document (*.doc)**, then click **Save**.

The Compatibility Checker dialog box displays to confirm the compatibility issues you have seen already.

c. Click **Continue** to accept the alteration.

The title bar displays *(Compatibility Mode)* following the file name. If you set the option to display file extensions on your computer, the document extension .doc displays in the title bar instead of .docx, as shown in Figure 1.37.

d. Click the **Office Button** and select **Convert**.

The Compatibility Mode designation is removed from the title bar. If a dialog box displays stating the document will be converted to the newest file format, click OK. You can check the option that prevents the dialog box from displaying each time this situation occurs.

e. Click **Save** on the Quick Access Toolbar. Click **Save** in the Save As dialog box and click **OK** if the authorization to overwrite the current file displays.

The document extension has been restored to .docx.

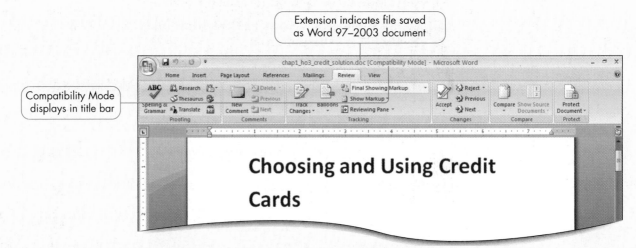

Figure 1.37 File Saved in Word 97–2003 Format

Refer to Figure 1.38 as you complete Step 4.

a. Click the **Office Button**, then click **Word Options** at the bottom of the menu.

b. Click **Customize** on the left side of the Word Options dialog box.

Look at other Word Options also, to view the many different features you can modify.

c. Select **Print Preview** from the *Choose commands from* list and click **Add** in the middle of the dialog box.

Print Preview displays in the Customize Quick Access Toolbar list.

d. Click the *Choose Commands from* drop-down arrow and click **All Commands**. Scroll down the list and click **Inspect Document** from the *Choose commands from* list and click **Add**.

e. Select **Print Preview** from the Customize Quick Access Toolbar list and click **Remove**.

Print Preview no longer displays in the list of icons for the Quick Access Toolbar, as seen in Figure 1.38.

f. Click **OK** at the bottom of the dialog box to return to the document.

The Quick Access Toolbar includes a new icon—the Document Inspector.

TROUBLESHOOTING: If you work in a lab environment, you might not have permission to modify the Word application. Accept any error messages you might see when saving the Word options and proceed to the next step.

g. Click the **Office Button**, click **Word Options** at the bottom of the menu, then click **Customize** on the left side of the Word Options dialog box. Select **Inspect Document** from the Customize Quick Access Toolbar list and click **Remove**. Click **OK** to close the Word Options dialog box.

The Quick Access Toolbar returns to the default setting.

h. Save the document.

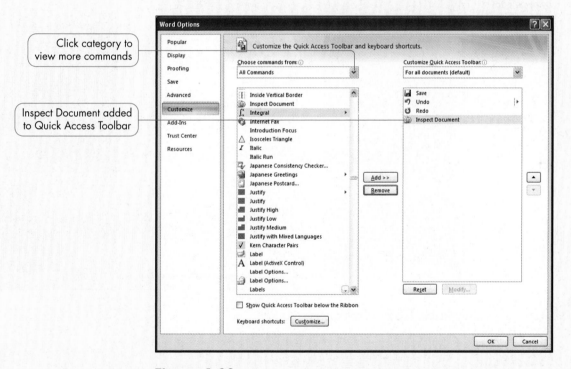

Click category to view more commands

Inspect Document added to Quick Access Toolbar

Figure 1.38 Customize the Quick Access Toolbar

Step 5
Use Print Preview Features

Refer to Figure 1.39 as you complete Step 5.

a. Click **Ctrl+Home**, if necessary, to move to the beginning of the document. Click the **Office Button**, click the **Print** arrow, and then select **Print Preview**.

The Print Preview dialog box displays the first page (see Figure 1.39).

b. Click **Two Pages** in the Zoom group to view the first two pages in this document. Click the check box next to **Magnifier** in the Preview group to remove the check mark.

This step removes the magnifying glass displayed on the mouse pointer and displays the insertion point. When you remove the magnifier, you can edit the file in the Print Preview window.

c. Place the insertion point on the left side of your name and type **Presented by:**. Click anywhere on the second page to move the insertion point out of the field.

d. Click **Margins** and select the **Narrow** setting.

Margins in section one of the document change to .5″ on each side.

e. Click **Next Page** to view each page in the document. Click **Close Print Preview** to return to the document.

f. Save the document and exit Word.

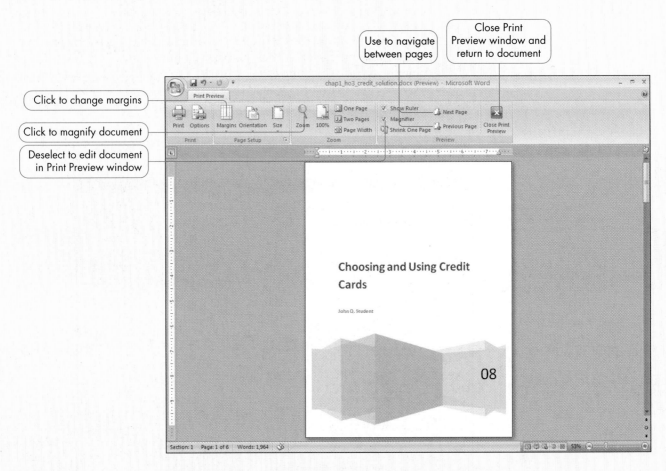

Figure 1.39 Print Preview Options

Summary

1. **Understand Word basics.** A word processing window is made up of several components including the title bar, Quick Access Toolbar, status bar, and the document area. Several tabs contain the commands that you use while working in Word, and the tabs might change according to the current task. As you type in a document, the word wrap feature automatically positions text for you using soft returns; however, you can insert a hard return to force text to the next line. Toggle switches such as the Caps Lock key or Bold feature are often used to alternate between two states while you work. The Show/Hide ¶ feature toggles on to reveal formatting marks in a document. The AutoText feature enables you to quickly insert predefined text or graphics.

2. **Use AutoText.** The AutoText feature substitutes a predefined item for specific text when the user initiates the replacement. Predefined and frequently used items, such as a logo, company name, author name, or return address, are stored as building blocks. You can type a portion of the building block entry, then press F3 to insert the remainder into your document.

3. **View a document.** The View tab provides options that enable you to display a document in many different ways. Views include Print Layout, Full Screen Reading, Web Layout, Outline, and Draft. To quickly change the view, click a button on the status bar in the lower-right corner of the window. You can use the Zoom slider to very quickly change magnification by sliding to a different percentage such as 75%. The Zoom dialog box includes options to change to whole page or multipage view.

4. **Use the Mini toolbar.** The Mini toolbar contains frequently used formatting commands such as Bold, Italic, Underline, Center, and Font Size. It displays faintly when you select text or right-click selected text, but it darkens as you move the mouse pointer closer to it. If you move the mouse pointer away from the Mini toolbar, it becomes fainter; if you do not want to use the Mini toolbar and prefer it disappears from view, press Esc when it displays.

5. **Set margins and specify page orientation.** When you create a document, you should consider how it will look when you print or display it. Margins determine the amount of white space from the text to the edge of the page. Pages can be set to display in portrait or landscape orientation. In portrait orientation, the text runs parallel to the shorter side of the paper. In landscape orientation, the text runs parallel to the longer side of the paper.

6. **Insert page breaks.** Soft page breaks occur when text no longer fits on the current page and automatically wraps to the top of a new page. The break is signified by a hidden marker that you can view using the Show/Hide ¶ feature. Hard page breaks can be used to force text onto a new page. A hard page break is inserted into a document using the Breaks command in the Page Setup group on the Page Layout tab, or Page Break in the Pages group on the Insert tab, but more easily through the Ctrl+Enter keyboard shortcut.

7. **Add page numbers.** Page numbers serve as a convenient reference point and assist in reading through a document. They can appear in the side margins or at the top or bottom of a page and can be left, center, or right aligned. The easiest way to place page numbers into a document is to click Page Number in the Header & Footer group on the Insert tab. When you use this feature, Word not only inserts page numbers but also adjusts automatically the page numbering when you add or delete pages.

8. **Insert headers and footers.** Headers and footers give a professional appearance to a document and are the best location to store page numbers. A header consists of one or more lines that are printed at the top of a page. A footer is printed at the bottom of a page. Footers often contain the page number and the date the document was created. Headers might contain the name of an organization, author, or title of the document. Headers and footers are added from the Insert tab. A simple header or footer also is created automatically by the Insert Page Number command.

9. **Create sections.** A section break is a marker that divides a document into sections, thereby allowing different formatting in each section. You determine where one section ends and another begins by using Breaks in the Page Setup group on the Page Layout tab. By using section breaks, you can change the margins within a multipage letter, where the first page (the letterhead) requires a larger top margin than the other pages in the letter. You also can change the page numbering within a document or even change the number of columns in a newsletter, which may contain a single column at the top of a page for the masthead, then two or three columns in the body of the newsletter.

...continued on Next Page

10. **Insert a cover page.** Word 2007 offers a feature to quickly insert a preformatted cover page in your document. The Cover Page feature includes a gallery with several designs, and each includes building block fields, such as Document Title, Company Name, Date, and Author, which you can personalize.

11. **Use Find and Replace commands.** Find and Replace commands include settings that enable you to look for or replace specific formatting on text. They also include options to conduct a case-sensitive or case-insensitive search. You can also use automatic replacement or selective replacement where you determine on an individual basis whether to replace the text or format. You can search for formatting and special characters. The Go To command moves the insertion point to a designated location in the document. You can go to a page, a section, or specify the number of pages to move forward or backward.

12. **Check spelling and grammar.** The grammar check feature looks for mistakes in punctuation, writing style, and word usage. If it finds an error, it will underline it with a green wavy line. You also can ask the grammar check to explain the rule it is attempting to enforce. When a possible error is found, you can accept the suggested correction, or determine if it is appropriate. The contextual spelling feature attempts to locate a word that is spelled correctly but used incorrectly. For example, it looks for the correct usage of the words *there* and *their*. A contextual spelling error is underlined with a blue wavy line.

13. **Use save and backup options.** To prevent loss of data you should save and back up your work frequently. You also should be familiar with commands that enable you to save your documents in a format compatible with older versions of Microsoft Word. You can use the convert command to alter those files into Word 2007 format, which is more efficient. Several backup options can be set, including an AutoRecover setting you can customize. This feature is useful for recovering a document when the program crashes. You can also require Word to create a backup copy in conjunction with every save operation. Word 2007 includes a compatibility checker to look for features that are not supported by previous versions of Word, and it also offers a Document Inspector that checks for and removes different kinds of hidden or personal information from a document.

14. **Select printing options.** You have three options to consider when you are ready to print your work: Print, Quick Print, and Print Preview. In the Print Preview window, you have several settings that enable you to magnify the page onscreen, display multiple pages, and even make changes to the page layout so you can view the results immediately. The Quick Print option sends a document straight to the printer without prompting you for changes to the printer configuration. The Print dialog box contains many useful options including print only the current page, a specific range of pages, or a specific number of copies.

15. **Customize Word.** After installation, Word is useful immediately. However, many options can be customized. The Word Options dialog box contains nine categories of options you can change including Personalize, Proofing, and Add-Ins. You can add to or remove commands from the Quick Access Toolbar using the Customize section of the Word Options dialog box.

Key Terms

Multiple Choice

1. When entering text within a document, you normally press Enter at the end of every:
   - (a) Line
   - (b) Sentence
   - (c) Paragraph
   - (d) Page

2. How do you display the Print dialog box?
   - (a) Click the Print button on the Quick Access Toolbar.
   - (b) Click the Office Button, and then click the Print command.
   - (c) Click the Print Preview command.
   - (d) Click the Home tab.

3. Which view removes all tabs from the screen?
   - (a) Full Screen Reading
   - (b) Print Layout
   - (c) Draft
   - (d) Print Preview

4. You want to add bold and italic to a phrase that is used several times in a document. What is the easiest way to make this update?
   - (a) Use the Go To feature and specify the exact page for each occurrence.
   - (b) Use the Find feature, then use overtype mode to replace the text.
   - (c) Use the Find and Replace feature and specify the format for the replacement.
   - (d) No way exists to automatically complete this update.

5. You are the only person in your office to upgrade to Word 2007. Before you share documents with co-workers you should
   - (a) Print out a backup copy.
   - (b) Run the Compatibility Checker.
   - (c) Burn all documents to CD.
   - (d) Have no concerns that they can open your documents.

6. A document has been entered into Word using the default margins. What can you say about the number of hard and soft returns if the margins are increased by 0.5" on each side?
   - (a) The number of hard returns is the same, but the number and/or position of the soft returns increases.
   - (b) The number of hard returns is the same, but the number and/or position of the soft returns decreases.
   - (c) The number and position of both hard and soft returns is unchanged.
   - (d) The number and position of both hard and soft returns decreases.

7. Which of the following is detected by the contextual spell checker?
   - (a) Duplicate words
   - (b) Irregular capitalization
   - (c) Use of the word *hear* when you should use *here*
   - (d) Improper use of commas

8. Which option on the Page Layout tab allows you to specify that you are printing on an envelope?
   - (a) Orientation
   - (b) Margins
   - (c) Breaks
   - (d) Size

9. You need to insert a large table into a report, but it is too wide to fit on a standard page. Which of the following is the best option to use in this case?
   - (a) Put the table in a separate document and don't worry about page numbering.
   - (b) Insert section breaks and change the format of the page containing the table to landscape orientation.
   - (c) Change the whole document to use landscape orientation.
   - (d) Change margins to 0" on the right and left.

10. What feature adds organization to your documents?
    - (a) Print Preview
    - (b) Orientation
    - (c) Page Numbers
    - (d) Find and Replace

11. What might cause you to be unsuccessful in finding a specific block of text in your document?

(a) You are performing a case-sensitive search.

(b) You have specified formatting that is not used on the text.

(c) You are not using wildcard characters even though you are uncertain of the proper spelling of your target.

(d) All of the above.

12. Which action below is the result of using the AutoText feature?

(a) When you click the Print button on the Quick Access Toolbar, the document prints.

(b) When you select text, the Mini toolbar displays.

(c) When you press Ctrl+F, the Find dialog box displays.

(d) You start typing the date, a ScreenTip displays the date on the screen, and you press Enter to insert it.

13. If you cannot determine why a block of text starts at the top of the next page, which toggle switch should you invoke to view the formatting marks in use?

(a) Word wrap

(b) Show/Hide

(c) Bold font

(d) Caps Lock

14. If you use the margins feature frequently, what action should you take to make it more accessible?

(a) Use the Customization category of Word Options and add Margins to the Quick Access Toolbar.

(b) Use the Customization category of Word Options and add Margins to the Status bar.

(c) Use the Personalization category of Word Options and add Margins to the Quick Access Toolbar.

(d) No way exists to make it more accessible.

15. You are on page 4 of a five-page document. Which of the following is not a way to move the insertion point to the top of the first page?

(a) Press Ctrl+Home.

(b) Press Ctrl+G, type 1 in the Enter page number box, and click Go To.

(c) Press PageUp on the keyboard one time.

(d) Press Ctrl+F, click the Go To tab, type 1 in the Enter page number box, and click Go To.

16. What visual clue tells you a document is not in Word 2007 format?

(a) The status bar includes the text (Compatibility Mode).

(b) The file extension is .docx.

(c) The title bar is a different color.

(d) The title bar includes (Compatibility Mode) after the file name.

Practice Exercises

1 Impress a Potential Customer

Chapter 1 introduced you to many of the basic features and abilities of a word processor. In the following steps, you use those tools to make modifications and enhancements to a letter that will be sent to a potential customer. It is important to write in a professional manner, even if the letter is casual. In this case, you use Find and Replace to change a misspelled word. You also insert the date and a page number and observe the AutoCorrect feature as you misspell text while typing.

a. Start Word, if necessary, and open the *chap1_pe1_candle* document. Save the file as **chap1_pe1_candle_solution**.

b. Click **Replace** in the Editing group on the Home tab, and then type **cents** in the *Find what* box and type **Scents** in the *Replace with* box. Click **More**, if necessary, to display additional search options. **Click Find whole words only**, and then click **No Formatting**, if necessary, to remove format settings from the previous Find and Replace operation.

c. Click **Find Next** and click **Replace** when the word is found. Click **OK** to close the dialog box that indicates Word has finished searching the document.

The first sentence of the first paragraph contains the first occurrence of the word. You must select *Find whole words only* to prevent replacing the occurrences of *Scents* that are spelled correctly.

d. Move the insertion point to the left of the phrase that starts with *Take a look*. Press **Insert** to change into Insert mode, if necessary, and type the sentence **We offer teh above scented candles in four sizes, just right for any room.** As you enter the word *the*, type **teh** instead and watch as the spelling is automatically corrected.

e. Click the **Insert tab** and click **Page Number** in the Header and Footer group. Point to **Bottom of Page** and select **Plain Number 2** from the gallery.

f. Press **Ctrl + Home** to move the insertion point to the top of the page. Type the current month, then press **Enter** when the ScreenTip displays the full date.

TROUBLESHOOTING: If you begin to type the date and the ScreenTip does not display, continue to manually type the current date.

g. Click the **View tab** and select **Full Screen Reading** in the Document Views group. Compare your document to Figure 1.40. Click **Close** to return to Print Layout view.

h. Click **Ctrl+S** to save the document. Click the **Office Button** and select **Close**.

...continued on Next Page

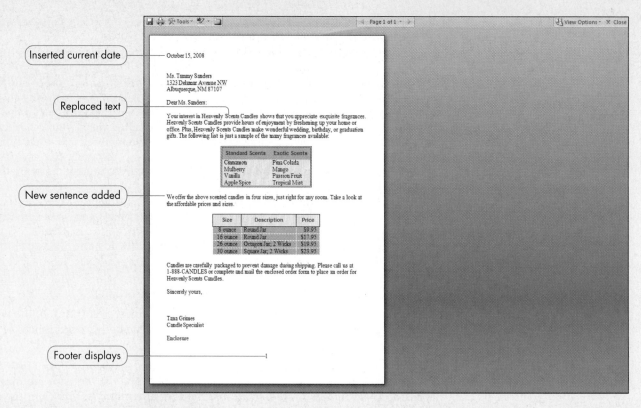

Figure 1.40 Updated Word Processing Document

2 Use Spelling and Grammar Check on a Memo

Mr. McGary, the Human Resources director of a medium-sized company, sends several memos each week to the employees in his company. It is important to communicate effectively with the employees, so he relies heavily on Word to locate errors in spelling, contextual spelling, and grammar as denoted by the wavy red, blue, and green lines, respectively. Even though Word contains these features, some mistakes may go unnoticed by the program. Mr. McGary, as well as anyone who uses a word processor, should always proofread documents carefully in addition to running the electronic spelling and grammar checkers. Your assignment is to correct the document so that it is error free and Mr. McGary can convey his message to employees without the distraction of poor spelling and grammar.

a. Open the *chap1_pe2_memo* document and save it as **chap1_pe2_memo_solution**.

b. Click the **Office Button** and click **Word Options** to display the Word Options dialog box. Click **Proofing** and click **Use contextual spelling**, if necessary, to enable that feature. Click **OK**.

c. Press **Ctrl+Home** to move to the beginning of the document. Click the **Review tab** and click **Spelling & Grammar** to check the document and correct errors. The first error displays in Figure 1.41. Use the following table to validate your corrections.

Error	Correction
Employeees	Employees
As you probably no	As you probably know
seminars are held inn the Cowboy Hat Hotel	seminars are held in the Cowboy Hat Hotel
managers have been instructed too allow employees in their department too attend	managers have been instructed to allow employees in their department to attend
MEntoring	Mentoring
attend..	attend.

...continued on Next Page

d. Right-click the words *These seminars* in the last sentence of the first paragraph. Click **These seminars** to remove the extra space between the words.

e. Click to the right of the letter b in the word *Subrdinate* in the first seminar listed in the table. Type **o** to correct the misspelling of subordinate.

f. Click the **Insert tab** and click **Footer** in the Header and Footer group. Click **Edit Footer** and type **Updated by**, then press **Spacebar** one time. Type your initials, then press **F3** to insert the AutoText entry that contains your name. Click **Close Header and Footer**.

g. Save the document.

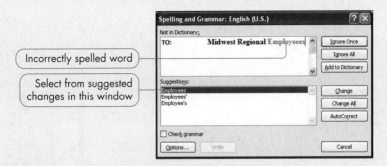

Figure 1.41 The Spell Check Process

3 Keyboard Shortcuts

Keyboard shortcuts are especially useful if you are a good typist because your hands can remain on the keyboard, as opposed to continually moving to and from the mouse. We never set out to memorize the shortcuts; we just learn them along the way as we continue to use Microsoft Office. It is much easier than you think, and the same shortcuts apply to multiple applications, such as Microsoft Excel, PowerPoint, and Access.

a. Open the *chap1_pe3_shortcuts* document. Click the **Office Button** and select **Convert**. Save the document as **chap1_pe3_shortcuts_solution**, paying special attention that it is saved in Word format (*.docx).

b. Click the **Page Layout tab**, click **Margins** in the Page Setup group, and click **Normal**. Click **Orientation**, and then click **Portrait**.

c. Click the **Home tab** and click **Show/Hide ¶** in the Paragraph group, if necessary, to display formatting marks.

   It will be helpful to see the formatting marks when you edit the document in the following steps.

d. Move the insertion point to the left side of the hard return mark at the end of the line containing Ctrl+B. Press **Ctrl+B**, then type the word **Bold**.

e. Move the insertion point to the left side of the hard return mark at the end of the line containing Ctrl+I. Press **Ctrl+I**, then type the word **Italic**.

f. Scroll to the bottom of the first page and place the insertion point on the left side of the title *Other Ctrl Keyboard Shortcuts*. Press **Ctrl+Enter** to insert a hard page break and keep the paragraph together on one page.

g. Click the **Insert tab**, click **Page Number** in the Header & Footer group, point to **Bottom of Page**, and select **Brackets 1** from the gallery.

h. Click **Header** in the Header & Footer group and select **Edit Header**. Click **Different First Page** in the Options group of the Design tab to insert a check mark. Place the insertion point in the header area of the second page and type **Keyboard Shortcuts**.

   Because you selected the *Different First Page* option, the header does not display on the first page as it is not needed there. However, the footer on the first page has been removed, so you will have to reinsert it.

...continued on Next Page

i. Move the insertion point to the first page footer. With the Design tab selected, click **Page Number** in the Header & Footer group, point to **Bottom of Page**, then select **Brackets 1** from the gallery. Click **Close Header and Footer**.

j. Click the **Zoom button** in the status bar, click **Many pages**, then drag to select **1 x 2 pages**. Click **OK** to close the Zoom dialog box. Click **Show/Hide ¶** in the Paragraph group on the Home tab to toggle off the formatting marks. Compare your document to Figure 1.42.

k. Save the document.

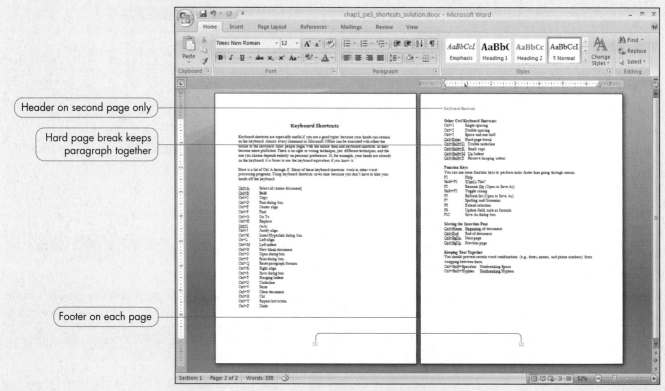

Figure 1.42 Keyboard Shortcut Document

4 Protecting Your System

The document you use in this exercise discusses computer viruses and backup procedures. It is not a question of *if* it will happen, but *when*—hard drives die, removable disks are lost, or viruses may infect a system. You can prepare for the inevitable by creating an adequate backup before the problem occurs. The advice in this document is very important; you should take it very seriously, and then protect yourself and your data.

a. Open the *chap1_pe4_virus* document and save it as **chap1_pe4_virus_solution**.

b. Click **Ctrl+H** to display the Find and Replace dialog box. In the *Find what* box, type **virus**. In the *Replace with* box, type **virus**. Click **More**, if necessary, then click the **Match case** check box.

c. Confirm that the *Replace with* text is selected or that the insertion point is in that box. Click **Format** at the bottom of the window and select **Font**. Click **Bold Italic** under the *Font Style* section, then click **OK**. Click **Replace All**, then click **OK** to confirm 17 replacements in the document. Click **Close** to remove the Find and Replace dialog box.

d. Scroll to the bottom of the first page and place the insertion point on the left side of the title *The Essence of Backup*. Press **Ctrl+Enter** to insert a hard page break.

This step creates a more appropriate break and keeps the heading and content together on one page.

...continued on Next Page

e. Press **Ctrl+End** to move to the end of the document. Type your name, press **Enter**, type the name of your class, then use the mouse to select it. Click **Quick Parts** in the Text group on the **Insert tab**, then click **Save Selection to Quick Part Gallery**.

The Create New Building Block dialog box displays, and you will add your name as an AutoText entry.

f. Replace your name in the *Name* box with the word **me**. Change the *Gallery* option to **AutoText**, and then click **OK**.

Even though you replaced your name in the dialog box, the text that is highlighted in the document will be used when you invoke the AutoText feature.

g. Delete your name at the end of the document. Click **Page Number** in the Header & Footer group on the **Insert tab**, click Bottom of Page, and then click **Circle** from the gallery.

h. The insertion point is on the left margin of the footer. Type **Created by: me** and press **F3**.

When you click F3, the AutoText entry should replace the text *me* with your name and your class displays on the line below.

i. Click **Close Header and Footer**.

j. Click **Zoom** in the status bar, click **Many pages**, then drag to select **1 × 2 pages**. Click **OK** to close the Zoom dialog box. Click **Show/Hide ¶** in the Paragraph group on the Home tab to toggle off the formatting marks, if necessary. Compare your document to Figure 1.43.

k. Save the document. Click the **Office Button**, click **Prepare**, and then click **Run Compatibility Checker**.

The results indicate that some text box positioning will change if opened in an older version of Word. It was good to check this before you save the document in Word 97–2003 format.

l. Click **OK** to close the Compatibility Checker window. Click the **Office Button**, click the **Save As arrow**, and select **Word 97–2003 Format**. Confirm the *Save as type* box displays Word 97–2003 document (*.doc), then click **Save**. Click **Continue** when the Compatibility Checker box shows the information you viewed previously.

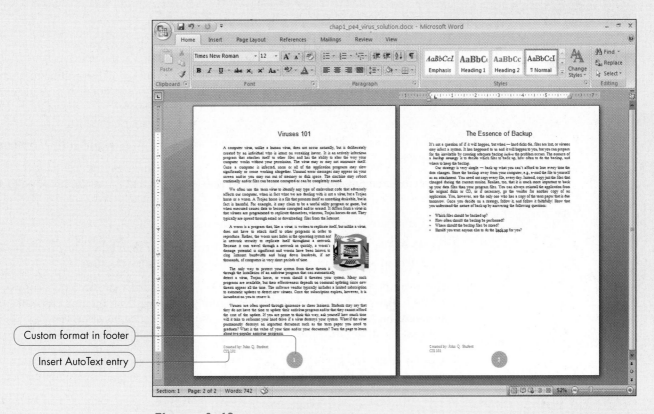

Figure 1.43 Protecting Your System

Mid-Level Exercises

1 Media-Blitz

Media-Blitz is a locally owned store that specializes in both new and used copies of popular music and movies. Its proximity to a local college campus provides a steady flow of customers during the school year. To increase sales during the typically slow summer season, it is offering discounts to students who have already enrolled in classes for the upcoming semester. You are working for the store this summer, and your assistance is needed to put the finishing touches on a flyer it wants to distribute in the area.

a. Open the *chap1_mid1_media* document and save it as **chap1_mid1_media_solution**.

b. Insert hard returns to create a list of discounts using the information below the first paragraph. Use the Mini toolbar to apply Bold and Center formatting to this group of items.

c. Perform a spelling and grammar check on the document to correct errors.

d. Create an AutoText entry for the name and address of the business. Name the entry Blitz. This entry will be useful in other documents you create for the business. Test the entry to make sure it works properly.

e. The school recently changed its name to Greene County Community College. Make appropriate changes in the flyer so each use of the name is updated and bolded.

f. Change to Full Screen Reading view, then change back to Print Layout view.

g. Display the document in the Print Preview window. Change orientation to Landscape.

h. Save and close the document.

2 Training Proposal

All About Training is an established computer training company that actively markets its services to the community. You have the opportunity to preview a document it will be sending to prospective clients and you notice several modifications that would add a professional appearance to the document. Use your skills to make the changes listed in the steps below.

a. Open the *chap1_mid2_proposal* document and save it as **chap1_mid2_proposal_ solution**.

b. Insert a section break at the beginning of the document that forces the proposal to start on the second page.

c. Set 1" margins on all sides of the whole document.

d. At the end of the last page, insert several hard returns, then type a line that says **Last Updated on:** and insert the current date using the AutoText feature.

e. Create a title page, without using the Cover Page feature, that contains a copy of the text *All About Training*. Use a 36 pt bold font and center it on the line. Type **Training Proposal** on the second line; use a 26 pt bold font, and center it on the line. Set 1.5" margins on all sides for this page.

f. Display page numbers on the side margin. The title page should not display a page number, so page numbering should begin on the second page. (Hint: you must change a setting in the Header and Footer Design tab.)

...continued on Next Page

g. Replace each instance of the company name to display in bold, italic, and red font color. Allow the replacement only when it appears in a paragraph, not in the banner that appears at the top of the document.

h. Perform a spelling and grammar check on the document.

i. Save the document in both Word 2007 and Word 97–2003 formats so it will be available for prospective clients regardless of the version of Word they use. Close all documents.

3 Fundraiser

The organizer of a craft fair has contacted your school to request permission to conduct a fundraiser. Your work in the office of College Relations includes returning the responses from administrators on matters such as this. The response letter has been drafted, and you will complete the letter by adding the recipient's name and address; then you create an envelope in which to mail it.

a. Open a blank document and type your name on a blank line. Use your name to create a Building Block AutoText entry.

b. Open the *chap1_mid3_letter* document and save it as **chap1_mid3_letter_solution**.

c. Move the insertion point to the bottom of the letter and replace the text *Your Name Here* with your name using the AutoText entry you created in the first step.

d. Insert a Next Page Section Break at the end of the letter and apply landscape orientation to the second page.

e. Confirm that the headers and footers in the second section are not linked to the first section. Then use the AutoText entry to insert your name in the header.

f. Use copy and paste to insert the recipient's name and address from the letter in the second section. Center the address so it resembles an envelope.

g. Save and close the document.

4 Heart Disease Prevention

Millions of people suffer from heart disease and other cardiac-related illnesses. Of those people, several million will suffer a heart attack each year. Your mother volunteers for the American Heart Association and has brought you a document that explains what causes a heart attack, the signs of an attack, and what you can do to reduce your risk of having one. The information in the document is very valuable, but she needs you to put the finishing touches on this document before she circulates it in the community.

a. Open the *chap1_mid4_heart* document and save it as **chap1_mid4_heart_solution**.

b. Convert the solution file so it does not open in Compatibility Mode.

c. Create a cover page for the report. Use **Tiles** in the cover page gallery. Add text where necessary to display the report title and subtitle (use *What You Should Know* as the subtitle), and your name as author. Delete any unused fields on the cover page.

d. Change the document margins to .75" on all sides.

e. Create a section break between the cover page and the first page of the report. Set appropriate options to prevent a footer from displaying on the cover page. A page number should display at the bottom of the remaining pages, and you should display the number one on the first page of the report that follows the cover page.

...continued on Next Page

f. Create a header that displays the report title. It should not display on the cover or first page of the report (the page that follows the cover page). Confirm that the headers and footers in the second section are not linked to the first section.

g. Toggle the Show/Hide ¶ feature on, then select Draft view. Remove any page breaks that cause the report data to display on separate pages. Do not remove the page break that immediately follows the cover page. View the document in Print Layout view and insert page breaks where necessary to prevent a paragraph or list from breaking across pages.

h. You are investing a lot of time in this project, so confirm that Word is performing back-ups every 5 minutes using the Word Options.

i. Save and close the document.

Capstone Exercise

After a hard week of work, you decide to enjoy the great outdoors by taking a canoe trip with your friends. Your friend researched the Buffalo National River and e-mailed you a document that describes the activities and preparations needed before visiting the area. You want to send the information to others who will accompany you on the trip, but the document needs some formatting modifications.

Spelling and Grammar

The first thing you notice about the report is the number of spelling and grammatical errors detected by Word. You will fix those as well as correct all references to the river that omit its status as a National River.

a. Open the *chap1_cap_buffalo* document, found in the Exploring Word folder. Save the document as **chap1_cap_buffalo_solution**.

b. Display the document in Full Screen Reading view. Use the navigation tool to view each page. Return to Print Layout view.

c. Display the Word Options dialog box and engage the Contextual Spelling feature if it is not already in use.

d. Run the spell checker and correct grammar and contextual spelling errors also.

e. Replace all occurrences of *Buffalo River* with **Buffalo National River**. When you make the replacements, add a bold font.

Revise Page Layout

When you zoom out to view multiple pages of the document, you notice that several lines and paragraphs break at odd places. Use formatting tools and page layout options to improve the readability of this file. Take special consideration of the picture on the last page; it seems to be too wide to display on a standard page.

a. Change the Zoom to 50% and determine where the content makes awkward breaks. Click Show/Hide ¶, if necessary, to display formatting marks that will assist you in determining which format options are in use.

b. Remove any unnecessary hard returns that interfere with word wrapping in the first paragraph.

c. Adjust margins to use the Normal setting (1″ on each side). Insert hard page breaks where necessary to keep paragraphs together.

d. Create a footer that displays page numbers. Select the **Annual** format for the page numbers.

e. Insert a Next Page Section break before the picture of the river. Change the orientation of the last page so the whole picture displays on the page.

Save in Multiple Formats

After improving the readability of the document, you remember that it has not yet been saved. Saving work is very important, and you will save it immediately. Since you will be sharing the document with friends, you also decide to save it in a format compatible with older versions.

a. Save the document again as **chap1_cap_buffalo2_solution**, then run the Compatibility Checker and Document Inspector, but do not take any suggested actions at this time.

b. Save the document in Word 97–2003 format.

c. Use the Print Preview feature to view the document before printing. Do not print unless instructed to by your teacher.

Mini Cases

Use the rubric following the case as a guide to evaluate your work, but keep in mind that your instructor may impose additional grading criteria or use a different standard to judge your work.

Letter of Appreciation

GENERAL CASE

Have you taken time to think about the people who have helped you get to where you are? For some, parents have provided encouragement and financial assistance so their children can enjoy the privileges of a higher education. Many other students receive the moral support of family but are financing their education personally. Regardless of how your education is funded, there are people who deserve your appreciation. Take this opportunity to write a letter that you can send to those people. In the letter you can give an update on your classes, tell them about your future plans, and don't forget to express your appreciation for their support. Create an attractive document using skills learned in this chapter, then save your letter as **chap1_mc1_appreciate_solution**.

Performance Elements	Exceeds Expectations	Meets Expectations	Below Expectations
Completeness	Document contains all required elements.	Document contains most required elements.	Document contains elements not specified in instructions.
Page setup	Modified or added at least three Page Layout elements.	Modified or added at least two Page Layout elements.	Did not modify or add any Page Layout elements.
Accuracy	No errors in spelling, grammar, or punctuation were found.	Fewer than two errors in spelling, grammar, or punctuation were found.	More than two errors in spelling, grammar, or punctuation were found.

Animal Concerns

RESEARCH CASE

As the population of family pets continues to grow, it is imperative that we learn how to be responsible pet owners. Very few people take the time to perform thorough research on the fundamental care of and responsibility for animal populations. Open the *chap1_mc2_animal* document and proceed to search the Internet for information that will contribute to this report on animal care and concerns. Compare information from at least three sources. Give consideration to information that is copyrighted and do not reprint it. Any information used should be cited in the document. As you enter the information and sources into the document, you will be reminded of concepts learned in Chapter 1 such as word wrap and soft returns. Use your knowledge of other formatting techniques, such as hard returns, page numbers, and margin settings, to create an attractive document. Create a cover page for the document, perform a spell check, and view the print preview before submitting this assignment to your instructor. Create headers and/or footers to improve readability. Name your completed document **chap1_mc2_animal_solution**.

Performance Elements	Exceeds Expectations	Meets Expectations	Below Expectations
Research	All sections were completed with comprehensive information and citations.	All sections were updated but with minimal information and no citations.	Sections were not updated, no citations were given.
Page setup	Modified or added at least three Page Layout elements.	Modified or added at least two Page Layout elements.	Did not modify or add any Page Layout elements.
Accuracy	No errors in spelling, grammar, or punctuation were found.	Fewer than two errors in spelling, grammar, or punctuation were found.	More than two errors in spelling, grammar, or punctuation were found.

TMG Newsletter

DISASTER RECOVERY

The *chap1_mc3_tmgnews* document was started by an office assistant, but she quickly gave up on it after she moved paragraphs around until it became unreadable. The document contains significant errors, which cause the newsletter to display in a very disjointed way. Use your knowledge of Page Layout options and other Word features to revise this newsletter in time for the monthly mailing. Save your work as **chap1_mc3_tmgnews_solution**.

Performance Elements	Exceeds Expectations	Meets Expectations	Below Expectations
Page setup	Modified Page Layout options in such a way that newsletter displays on one page.	Few Page Layout modifications applied; newsletter displays on more than one page.	No Page Layout modifications applied; newsletter displays on more than one page.
Accuracy	No errors in spelling, grammar, or punctuation were found.	Fewer than two errors in spelling, grammar, or punctuation were found.	More than two errors in spelling, grammar, or punctuation were found.

Gaining Proficiency

Editing and Formatting

Objectives

After you read this chapter, you will be able to:

1. Apply font attributes through the Font dialog box **(page 133)**.

2. Highlight text **(page 136)**.

3. Control word wrapping with nonbreaking hyphens and nonbreaking spaces **(page 137)**.

4. Copy formats with the Format Painter **(page 139)**.

5. Set off paragraphs with tabs, borders, lists, and columns **(page 143)**.

6. Apply paragraph formats **(page 148)**.

7. Create and modify styles **(page 159)**.

8. Create a table of contents **(page 171)**.

9. Create an index **(page 171)**.

Hands-On Exercises

Exercises	Skills Covered
1. CHARACTER FORMATTING (page 140) **Open:** chap2_ho1_description.docx **Save as:** chap2_ho1_description_solution.docx	• Change Text Appearance • Insert Nonbreaking Spaces and Nonbreaking Hyphens • Highlight Text and Use Format Painter
2. PARAGRAPH FORMATTING (page 152) **Open:** chap2_ho1_description_solution.docx (from Exercise 1) **Save as:** chap2_ho2_description_solution.docx (additional modifications)	• Set Tabs in a Footer • Select Text to Format • Specify Line Spacing, Justification, and Pagination • Indent Text • Apply Borders and Shading • Change Column Structure • Insert a Section Break and Create Columns
3. STYLES (page 164) **Open:** chap2_ho3_gd.docx **Save as:** chap2_ho3_gd_solution.docx	• Apply Style Properties • Modify the Body Text Style • Modify the Heading 3 Style • Select the Outline View • Create a Paragraph Style • Create a Character Style • View the Completed Document
4. REFERENCE PAGES (page 173) **Open:** chap2_ho3_gd_solution.docx (from Exercise 3) **Save as:** chap2_ho4_gd_solution.docx (additional modifications)	• Apply a Style • Insert a Table of Contents • Define an Index Entry • Create the Index • Complete the Index • View the Completed Document

CASE STUDY

Treyserv-Pitkin Enterprises

Treyserv, a consumer products manufacturing company, has recently acquired a competitor, paving the way for a larger, stronger company poised to meet the demands of the market. Each year Treyserv generates a corporate annual report and distributes it to all employees and stockholders. You are the executive assistant to the president of Treyserv and your responsibilities include preparing and distributing the corporate annual report. This year the report emphasizes the importance of acquiring Pitkin Industries to form Treyserv-Pitkin Enterprises.

As with most mergers or acquisitions, the newly created Treyserv-Pitkin organization will enable management to make significant changes to establish a more strategic and profitable company. **Case Study** Management will focus on reorganizing both companies to eliminate duplication of efforts and reduce expenses; it will reduce long-term debt when possible and combine research and development activities. The annual report always provides a synopsis of recent changes to upper management, and this year it will introduce a new Chair and Chief Executive Officer, Mr. Dewey A. Larson. The company also hired Ms. Amanda Wray as chief financial officer; both positions are very high profile and contribute to the stockholders' impression of the company's continued success. Information about these newly appointed executives and other financial data have been gathered, but the report needs to be formatted attractively before it can be distributed to employees and stockholders.

Your Assignment

- Read the chapter, paying special attention to sections that describe how to apply styles, create a table of contents, and create an index.
- Open the document, *chap2_case_treyserv,* which contains the unformatted report that was provided to you by the president of the company.
- Add format features such as borders and shading, line spacing, justification, paragraph indention, and bullet and number lists to enhance the appearance of information in the report.
- Use tabs or columns, when appropriate, to align information in the report.
- Use predefined styles, such as Heading 1 and Heading 2, to format paragraph headings throughout the document.
- Apply paragraph formats such as widow/orphan control to prevent text from wrapping awkwardly when it spans from one page to the next.
- Add a table of contents and page numbering to assist readers in locating information.
- Save your work in a document named **chap2_case_treyserv_solution**.

Text Formatting

> The ultimate success of any document depends greatly on its appearance. Typeface should reinforce the message without calling attention to itself and should be consistent with the information you want to convey.

The arrangement and appearance of printed matter is called *typography*. You also may define it as the process of selecting typefaces, type styles, and type sizes. The importance of these decisions is obvious, for the ultimate success of any document depends greatly on its appearance. Typeface should reinforce the message without calling attention to itself and should be consistent with the information you want to convey. For example, a paper prepared for a professional purpose, such as a résumé, should use a standard typeface and abstain from using one that looks funny or cute. Additionally, you want to minimize the variety of typefaces in a document to maintain a professional look.

A *typeface* or *font* is a complete set of characters—upper- and lowercase letters, numbers, punctuation marks, and special symbols. A definitive characteristic of any typeface is the presence or absence of thin lines that end the main strokes of each letter. A *serif typeface* contains a thin line or extension at the top and bottom of the primary strokes on characters. A *sans serif typeface* (sans from the French for without) does not contain the thin lines on characters. Times New Roman is an example of a serif typeface. Arial is a sans serif typeface.

Serifs help the eye to connect one letter with the next and generally are used with large amounts of text. This book, for example, is set in a serif typeface. A sans serif typeface is more effective with smaller amounts of text such as titles, headlines, corporate logos, and Web pages.

A second characteristic of a typeface is whether it is monospaced or proportional. A *monospaced* typeface (such as Courier New) uses the same amount of horizontal space for every character regardless of its width. A *proportional* typeface (such as Times New Roman or Arial) allocates space according to the width of the character. For example, the lowercase *m* is wider than the lowercase *i*. Monospaced fonts are used in tables and financial projections where text must be precisely lined up, one character underneath the other. Proportional typefaces create a more professional appearance and are appropriate for most documents, such as research papers, status reports, and letters. You can set any typeface in different *type styles* such as regular, **bold**, *italic*, or ***bold italic***.

In this section, you apply font attributes through the Font dialog box, change casing, and highlight text so that it stands out. You also control word wrapping by inserting nonbreaking hyphens and nonbreaking spaces between words. Finally, you copy formats using the Format Painter.

Typography is the appearance of printed matter.

A **typeface** or **font** is a complete set of characters.

A **serif typeface** contains a thin line at the top and bottom of characters.

A **sans serif typeface** does not contain thin lines on characters.

A **monospaced typeface** uses the same amount of horizontal space for every character.

A **proportional typeface** allocates horizontal space to the character.

Type style is the characteristic applied to a font, such as bold.

Applying Font Attributes Through the Font Dialog Box

In the Office Fundamentals chapter, you learned how to use the Font group on the Home tab to apply font attributes. The Font group contains commands to change the font, font size, and font color; and apply bold, italic, and underline. In addition to applying commands from the Font group, you can display the Font dialog box to give you complete control over the typeface, size, and style of the text in a document. Making selections in the Font dialog box before entering text sets the format of the text as you type. You also can change the font of existing text by selecting the text and then applying the desired attributes from the Font dialog box, as shown in Figure 2.1.

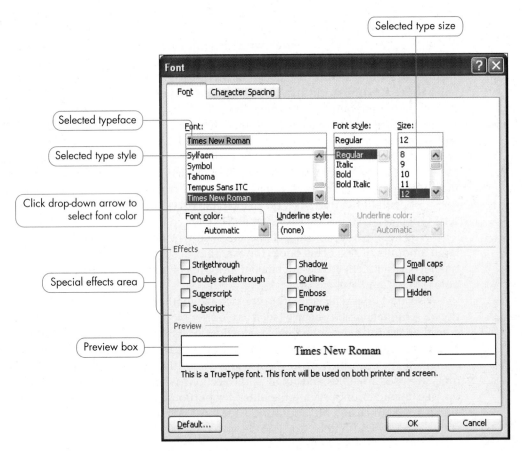

Figure 2.1 Font Dialog Box

Change Text Case (Capitalization)

Use ***Change Case*** to change capitalization of text.

To quickly change the capitalization of text in a document use ***Change Case*** in the Font group on the Home tab. When you click Change Case, the following list of options display:

- **Sentence case.** (capitalizes only the first word of the sentence or phrase)
- **lowercase** (changes the text to lowercase)
- **UPPERCASE** (changes the text to all capital letters)
- **Capitalize Each Word** (capitalizes the first letter of each word; effective for formatting titles, but remember to lowercase first letters of short prepositions, such as *of*)
- **tOGGLE cASE** (changes lowercase to uppercase and uppercase to lowercase)

This feature is useful when generating a list and you want to use the same case formatting for each item. If you do not select text first, the casing format will take effect on the text where the insertion point is located. You can toggle among upper-case, lowercase, and sentence case formats by pressing Shift+F3.

Select Font Options

In addition to changing the font, font style, and size, you can apply other font attributes to text. Although the Font group on the Home tab contains special effects commands such as strikethrough, subscript, and superscript, the *Effects* section in the Font tab in the Font dialog box contains a comprehensive set of options for applying color and special effects, such as SMALL CAPS, superscripts, or subscripts. Table 2.1 lists and defines more of these special effects. You also can change the underline options and indicate if spaces are to be underlined or just words. You can even change the color of the text and underline.

Table 2.1 Font Effects

Effect	Description	Example
Strikethrough	Displays a horizontal line through the middle of the text	~~strikethrough~~
Superscript	Displays text in a smaller size and raised above the baseline	Super^{script}
Subscript	Displays text in a smaller size and lowered below the baseline	Sub$_{script}$
Shadow	Displays text with a 3D shadow effect	Shadow
Emboss	Displays text as if it has been raised from the page	Emboss
Engrave	Displays text as if it has been pressed down into the page	Engrave
Small caps	Displays letters as uppercase but smaller than regular-sized uppercase letters	SMALL CAPS

TIP Hidden Text

Hidden text is document text that does not appear on screen, unless you click Show/Hide ¶ in the Paragraph group on the Home tab. You can use this special effect format to hide confidential information before printing documents for other people. For example, an employer can hide employees' Social Security numbers before printing a company roster.

Set Character Spacing

Hidden text does not appear onscreen.

Character spacing refers to the amount of horizontal space between characters. Although most character spacing is acceptable, some character combinations appear too far apart or too close together in large-sized text when printed. If so, you might want to adjust for this spacing discrepancy. The Character Spacing tab in the Font dialog box contains options in which you manually control the spacing between characters. The Character Spacing tab shown in Figure 2.2 displays four options for adjusting character spacing: Scale, Spacing, Position, and Kerning.

Character spacing is the horizontal space between characters.

Scale increases or decreases the text horizontally as a percentage of its size; it does not change the vertical height of text. You may use the scale feature on justified text, which does not produce the best-looking results—adjust the scale by a low percentage (90%–95%) to improve text flow without a noticeable difference to the reader.

Scale increases or decreases text as a percentage of its size.

You may select the *Expanded* option to stretch a word or sentence so it fills more space; for example, use it on a title you want to span across the top of a page. The *Condensed* option is useful to squeeze text closer together, such as when you want to prevent one word from wrapping to another line.

Position raises or lowers text from the baseline without creating superscript or subscript size. Use this feature when you want text to stand out from other text on the same line; or use it to create a fun title by raising and/or lowering every few letters. *Kerning* automatically adjusts spacing between characters to achieve a more evenly spaced appearance. Kerning primarily allows letters to fit closer together, especially when a capital letter can use space unoccupied by a lowercase letter beside it. For example, you can kern the letters *Va* so the top of the *V* extends into the empty space above the *a* instead of leaving an awkward gap between them.

Position raises or lowers text from the baseline.

Kerning allows more even spacing between characters.

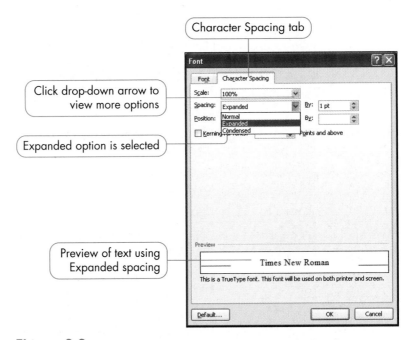

Figure 2.2 Character Spacing Tab in the Font Dialog Box

Highlighting Text

Use the **Highlighter** to mark text that you want to locate easily.

People often use a highlighting marker to highlight important parts of textbooks, magazine articles, and other documents. In Word, you use the *Highlighter* to mark text that you want to stand out or locate easily. Highlighted text draws the reader's attention to important information within the documents you create, as illustrated in Figure 2.3. The Text Highlight Color command is located in the Font group on the Home tab and also on the Mini toolbar. You can click Text Highlight Color before or after selecting text. When you click Text Highlight Color before selecting text, the mouse pointer resembles a pen that you can click and drag across text to highlight it. The feature stays on so you can highlight additional text. When you finish highlighting text, press Esc to turn it off. If you select text first, click Text Highlight Color to apply the color. To remove highlights, select the highlighted text, click the Text Highlight Color arrow, and choose No Color.

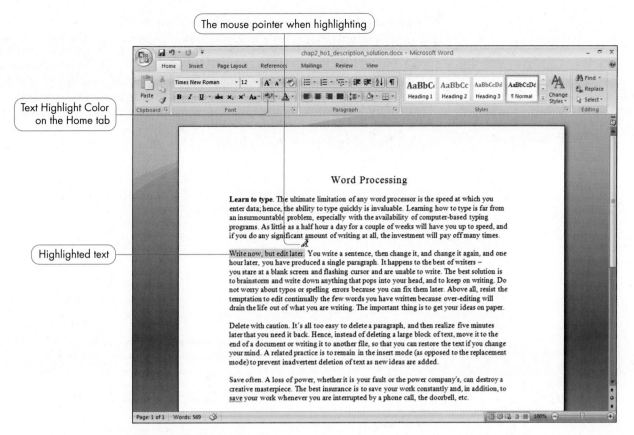

The mouse pointer when highlighting

Text Highlight Color on the Home tab

Highlighted text

Figure 2.3 The Highlight Tool

If you use a color printer, you see the highlight colors on your printout. If you use a monochrome printer, the highlight appears in shades of gray. Be sure that you can easily read the text with the gray highlight. If not, select a lighter highlight color, and print your document again. You can create a unique highlighting effect by choosing a dark highlight color, such as Dark Blue, and applying a light font color, such as White.

TIP Impose a Time Limit

Word 2007 is supposed to save time and make you more productive. It will do exactly that, provided you use Word for its primary purpose—writing and editing. It is all too easy, however, to lose sight of that objective and spend too much time formatting the document. Concentrate on the content of your document rather than its appearance and remember that the success of a document ultimately depends on its content. Impose a limit on the amount of time you will spend on formatting.

Controlling Word Wrapping with Nonbreaking Hyphens and Nonbreaking Spaces

In Word, text wraps to the next line when the current line of text is full. Most of the time, the way words wrap is acceptable. Occasionally, however, text may wrap in an undesirable location. To improve the readability of text, you need to proofread word-wrapping locations and insert special characters. Two general areas of concern are hyphenated words and spacing within proper nouns.

Insert Nonbreaking Hyphens

If a hyphenated word falls at the end of a line, the first word and the hyphen may appear on the first line, and the second word may wrap to the next line. However, certain hyphenated text, such as phone numbers, should stay together to improve the readability of the text. To keep hyphenated words together, replace the regular hyphen with a nonbreaking hyphen. A *nonbreaking hyphen* keeps text on both sides of the hyphen together, thus preventing the hyphenated word from becoming separated at the hyphen, as shown in Figure 2.4. To insert a nonbreaking hyphen, press Ctrl+Shift+Hyphen. When you click Show/Hide ¶ in the Paragraph group on the Home tab to display formatting symbols, a regular hyphen looks like a hyphen, and a nonbreaking hyphen appears as a wider hyphen. However, the nonbreaking hyphen looks like a regular hyphen when printed.

A *nonbreaking hyphen* prevents a word from becoming separated at the hyphen.

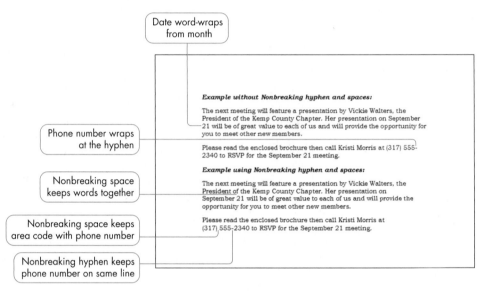

Figure 2.4 Nonbreaking Hyphens and Spaces

Insert Nonbreaking Spaces

Because text will wrap to the next line if a word does not fit at the end of the current line, occasionally word-wrapping between certain types of words is undesirable; that is, some words should be kept together for improved readability. For example, the date *March 31* should stay together instead of word-wrapping after March. Other items that should stay together include names, such as *Ms. Stevenson*, and page references, such as *page 15*. To prevent words from separating due to the word-wrap feature, you can insert a *nonbreaking space*—a special character that keeps two or more words together. To insert a nonbreaking space, press Ctrl+Shift+Spacebar between the two words that you want to keep together. If a space already exists, the result of pressing the Spacebar, you should delete it before you insert the nonbreaking space.

A *nonbreaking space* keeps two or more words together on a line.

Copying Formats with the Format Painter

Use the **Format Painter** to copy existing text formats to other text.

You should format similar headings and text within a document with the same formatting. However, it is time-consuming to select every heading individually and apply the desired format (such as bold, underline, and font color). You can use the *Format Painter* to copy existing text formats to other text to ensure consistency. Using the Format Painter helps you improve your efficiency because you spend less time copying multiple formats rather than applying individual formats to each heading or block of text one at a time. When you single-click Format Painter in the Clipboard group on the Home tab, you can copy the formats only one time, then Word turns off Format Painter. When you double-click Format Painter, it stays activated so you can format an unlimited amount of text. To turn off Format Painter, click Format Painter once or press Esc.

(You can use Format Painter to . . . ensure consistency . . . and improve your efficiency by spending less time copying multiple formats rather than applying individual formats to each heading or block of text one at a time.)

Display Nonprinting Formatting Marks

As you type text, Word inserts nonprinting marks or symbols. While these symbols do not display on printouts, they do affect the appearance. For example, Word inserts a "code" every time you press Spacebar, Tab, and Enter. The paragraph mark ¶ at the end of a paragraph does more than just indicate the presence of a hard return. It also stores all of the formatting in effect for the paragraph. To preserve the formatting when you move or copy a paragraph, you must include the paragraph mark in the selected text. Click Show/Hide ¶ in the Paragraph group on the Home tab to display the paragraph mark and make sure it has been selected. Table 2.2 lists several common formatting marks. Both the hyphen and nonbreaking hyphen look like a regular hyphen when printed.

Table 2.2 Nonprinting Symbols

Symbol	Description	Create by
•	Regular space	Pressing Spacebar
°	Nonbreaking space	Pressing Ctrl+Shift+Spacebar
-	Regular hyphen	Pressing Hyphen
—	Nonbreaking hyphen	Pressing Ctrl+Shift+Hyphen
→	Tab	Pressing Tab
¶	End of paragraph	Pressing Enter
. . .	Hidden text	Selecting Hidden check box in Font dialog box
↵	Line break	Pressing Shift+Enter

Hands-On Exercises

1 | Character Formatting

Skills covered: 1. Change Text Appearance **2.** Insert Nonbreaking Spaces and Nonbreaking Hyphens
3. Highlight Text and Use Format Painter

<table>
<tr>
<td>

Step 1
Change Text
Appearance

</td>
<td>

Refer to Figure 2.5 as you complete Step 1.

a. Start Word. Open the *chap2_ho1_description* document in the **Exploring Word folder** and save it as **chap2_ho1_description_solution**.

You must select the text for which you want to adjust the character spacing.

b. Select the heading *Word Processing*, then click the **Font Dialog Box Launcher** in the Font group on the Home tab.

The Font dialog box displays with the Font tab options.

c. Click the **Character spacing tab** and click the **Spacing drop-down arrow**. Select **Expanded** and notice how the text changes in the preview box. Click **OK**.

Word expands the spacing between letters in the heading *Word Processing*, as shown in Figure 2.5.

d. Save the document.

</td>
</tr>
</table>

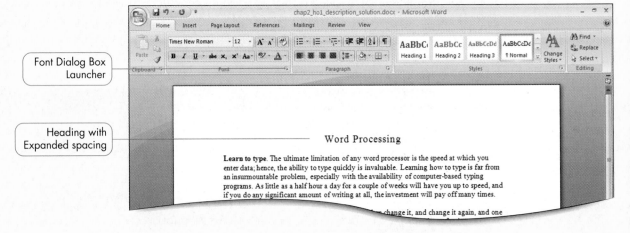

Font Dialog Box Launcher

Heading with Expanded spacing

Figure 2.5 Text Formatting

<table>
<tr>
<td>

Step 2
Insert Nonbreaking
Spaces and
Nonbreaking Hyphens

</td>
<td>

Refer to Figure 2.6 as you complete Step 2.

a. Place the insertion point between the words *you stare* in the third sentence of the second paragraph.

Before inserting a nonbreaking space, you must position the insertion point between the two words you want to keep together.

b. Delete the existing space, and then press **Ctrl+Shift+Spacebar** to insert a nonbreaking space.

The nonbreaking space keeps the words *you stare* together, preventing word wrapping between the two words.

</td>
</tr>
</table>

c. Select the hyphen between the text *five-minute* in the third sentence of the sixth paragraph. Delete the hyphen, and then press **Ctrl+Shift+Hyphen** to insert a nonbreaking hyphen, as shown in Figure 2.6.

> **TROUBLESHOOTING:** If text continues word-wrapping between two words after you insert a nonbreaking space or nonbreaking hyphen, click Show/Hide ¶ in the Paragraph group on the Home tab to display symbols and then identify and delete regular spaces or hyphens that still exist between words.

d. Save the document.

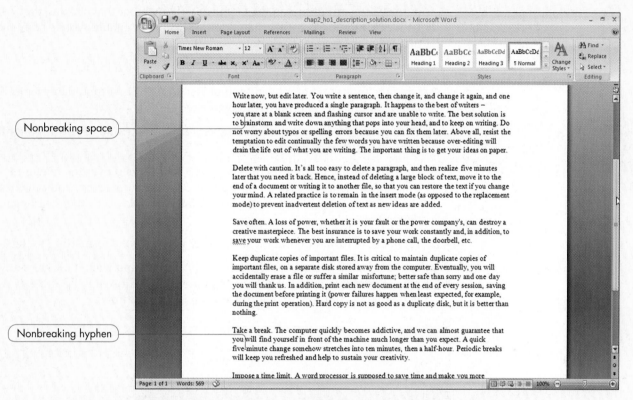

Figure 2.6 Nonbreaking Characters

TIP Another Way to Insert Nonbreaking Spaces and Hyphens

An alternative to using keyboard shortcuts to insert nonbreaking spaces and hyphens is to use the Symbols gallery on the Insert tab. Click **More Symbols** to display the Symbol dialog box, click the Special Characters tab, select the Nonbreaking Hyphen or the Nonbreaking Space character option, and click **Insert** to insert a nonbreaking hyphen or a nonbreaking space, respectively. Close the Symbol dialog box after inserting the nonbreaking hyphen or nonbreaking space.

Refer to Figure 2.7 as you complete Step 3.

a. Select the text *Learn to type.* in the first paragraph.

b. Click **Text Highlight Color** in the Font group on the Home tab.

Word highlighted the selected text in the default highlight color, yellow.

TROUBLESHOOTING: If Word applies a different color to the selected text, that means another highlight color was selected after starting Word. If this happens, select the text again, click the Text Highlight Color arrow, and select Yellow.

c. Click anywhere within the sentence *Learn to type.* Double-click **Format Painter** in the Clipboard group on the Home tab. (Remember that clicking the Format Painter button once, rather than double-clicking it, enables you to copy the format only one time.)

The mouse pointer changes to a paintbrush, as shown in Figure 2.7.

d. Drag the mouse pointer over the first sentence in the second paragraph, *Write now, but edit later.*, and release the mouse.

The formatting from the original sentence (bold font and yellow highlight) is applied to this sentence as well.

e. Drag the mouse pointer (in the shape of a paintbrush) over the remaining titles (the first sentence in each paragraph) to copy the formatting. You can click the scroll down arrow on the vertical scroll bar to display the other headings in the document.

f. Press **Esc** to turn off Format Painter after you copy the formatting to the last tip.

g. Save the *chap2_ho1_description_solution* document and keep it onscreen if you plan to continue with the next hands-on exercise. Close the file and exit Word if you will not continue with the next exercise at this time.

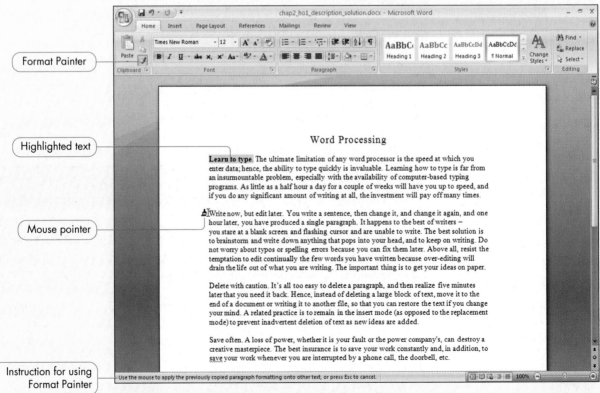

Figure 2.7 The Format Painter

Paragraph Formats

A change in typography is only one way to alter the appearance of a document. You also can change the alignment, indentation, tab stops, or line spacing for any paragraph(s) within the document. You can control the pagination and prevent the occurrence of awkward page breaks by specifying that an entire paragraph must appear on the same page, or that a one-line paragraph (e.g., a heading) should appear on the same page as the next paragraph. You can include borders or shading for added emphasis around selected paragraphs.

Word implements all of these paragraph formats for all selected paragraphs. If no paragraphs are selected, Word applies the formats to the current paragraph (the paragraph containing the insertion point), regardless of the position of the insertion point within the paragraph when you apply the paragraph formats.

> Word implements all of these paragraph formats for all selected paragraphs. If no paragraphs are selected, Word applies the feature to the current paragraph.

In this section, you set tabs, apply borders, create lists, and format text into columns to help offset text for better readability. You also change text alignment, indent paragraphs, set line and paragraph spacing, and control pagination breaks.

Setting Off Paragraphs with Tabs, Borders, Lists, and Columns

Many people agree that their eyes tire and minds wander when they read page after page of plain black text on white paper. To break up long blocks of text or draw attention to an area of a page, you can format text with tabs, borders, lists, or columns. These formatting features enable you to modify positioning, frame a section, itemize for easy reading, order steps in a sequence, or create pillars of text for visual appeal and easy reading. For example, look through the pages of this book and notice the use of bulleted lists, tables for reference points, and borders around TIP boxes to draw your attention and enhance the pages.

Set Tabs

Tabs are markers for aligning text in a document.

Tabs are markers that specify the position for aligning text and add organization to a document. They often are used to create columns of text within a document. When you start a new document, the default tab stops are set every one-half inch across the page and are left aligned. Every time you press Tab, the insertion point moves over ½". You typically press Tab to indent the first line of paragraphs in double-spaced reports or the first line of paragraphs in a modified block style letter.

You access the Tabs feature by first clicking the Paragraph Dialog Box Launcher in the Paragraph group on the Home tab, then click the Tabs button. The Tabs dialog box displays so that you can set left, center, right, decimal, and bar tabs.

A *left tab* marks the position to align text on the left.

- A *left tab* sets the start position on the left so as you type, text moves to the right of the tab setting.

A *center tab* marks where text centers as you type.

- A *center tab* sets the middle point of the text you type; whatever you type will be centered on that tab setting.

A *right tab* marks the position to align text on the right.

- A *right tab* sets the start position on the right so as you type, text moves to the left of that tab setting and aligns on the right.

A *decimal tab* marks where numbers align on a decimal point as you type.

- A *decimal tab* aligns numbers on a decimal point. Regardless of how long the number, each number lines up with the decimal in the same position.

A *bar tab* marks the location of a vertical line between columns.

- A *bar tab* does not position text or decimals, but inserts a vertical bar at the tab setting. This bar is useful as a separator for text printed on the same line.

Instead of setting tabs in the Tabs dialog box, you can set tabs on the ruler. First, click the Tabs button to the left of the ruler (refer to Figure 2.8) until you see the tab alignment you want. Then click on the ruler in the location where you want to set the type of tab you selected. To delete a tab, click the tab marker on the ruler, then drag it down and off the ruler.

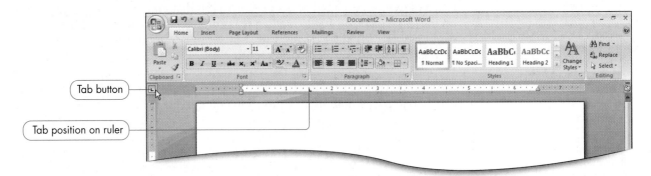

Figure 2.8 Tab Button and Ruler

TIP Deleting Default Tabs

When you set a tab on the ruler, Word deletes all of the default tab settings to the *left* of the tab you set. If you need to delete a single tab setting, click the tab marker on the ruler and drag it down. When you release the mouse, you delete the tab setting.

A *leader character* is dots or hyphens that connect two items.

In the Tabs dialog box, you also can specify a *leader character*, typically dots or hyphens, to draw the reader's eye across the page. For example, in a table of contents you can easily read a topic and the associated page where it is found when tab leaders connect the two, as shown in Figure 2.9. Notice also in Figure 2.9 that the default tab settings have been cleared, and a right tab is set at 5".

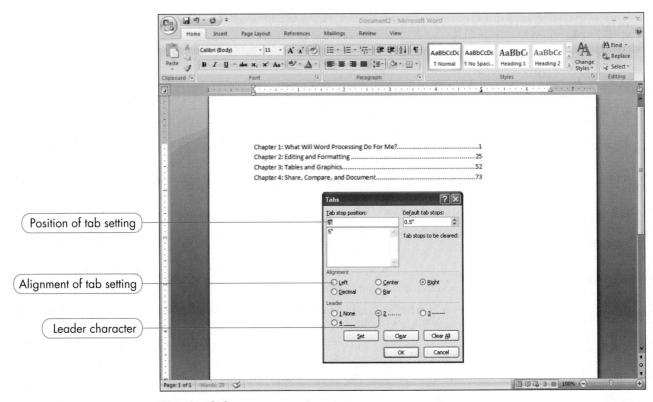

Figure 2.9 The Tabs Dialog Box

Apply Borders and Shading

You can draw attention to a document or an area of a document by using the Borders and Shading command. A **border** is a line that surrounds a paragraph, a page, a table, or an image, similar to how a picture frame surrounds a photograph or piece of art. **Shading** is a background color that appears behind text in a paragraph, a page, or a table. You can apply specific borders, such as top, bottom, or outside, from the Border command in the Paragraph group on the Home tab. To allow more customization of borders, open the Borders and Shading dialog box when you click the Borders arrow in the Paragraph group on the Home tab, as shown in Figure 2.10. Borders or shading is applied to selected text within a paragraph, to the entire paragraph if no text is selected, to the entire page if the Page Border tab is selected, and also can be used on tables and images. You can create boxed and/or shaded text as well as place horizontal or vertical lines around different quantities of text. A good example of this practice is used in the *Exploring* series: The TIP boxes are surrounded by a border with dark shading and a white font color for the headings to attract your attention.

You can choose from several different line styles in any color, but remember you must use a color printer to display the line colors on the printed page. Colored lines appear in gray on a monochrome printer. You can place a uniform border around a paragraph (choose Box), or you can choose a shadow effect with thicker lines at the right and bottom. You also can apply lines to selected sides of a paragraph(s) by selecting a line style, then clicking the desired sides as appropriate.

The horizontal line button at the bottom of the Borders and Shading dialog box provides access to a variety of attractive horizontal line designs.

> (Use page borders on . . . fliers, newsletters, and invitations, but not on formal documents such as research papers and professional reports.)

The Page Border tab enables you to place a decorative border around one or more selected pages. As with a paragraph border, you can place the border around the entire page, or you can select one or more sides. The page border also provides an additional option to use preselected clip art instead of ordinary lines. Note that it is appropriate to use page borders on documents such as fliers, newsletters, and invitations, but not on formal documents such as research papers and professional reports.

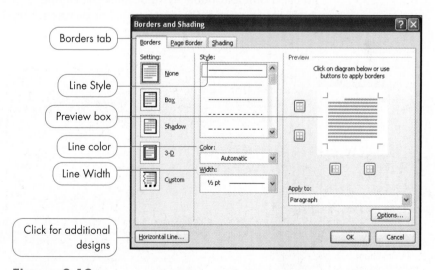

Figure 2.10 Apply a Border Around Text, Paragraphs, or Pages

Shading is applied independently of the border and is accessed from the Borders and Shading dialog box or from Shading in the Paragraph group on the Home tab. Clear (no shading) is the default. Solid (100%) shading creates a solid box where the text is turned white so you can read it. Shading of 10% or 20% generally is most effective to add emphasis to the selected paragraph (see Figure 2.11). The Borders and Shading command is implemented on the paragraph level and affects the entire paragraph unless text has been selected within the paragraph.

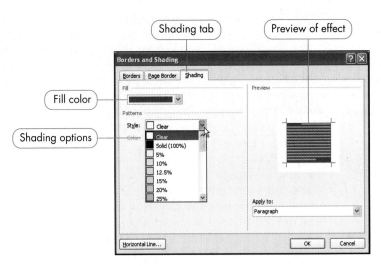

Shading tab

Preview of effect

Fill color

Shading options

Figure 2.11 Apply Shading to Text or a Paragraph

Create Bulleted and Numbered Lists

A **bulleted list** itemizes and separates paragraph text to increase readability.

A **numbered list** sequences and prioritizes items.

A **multilevel list** extends a numbered list to several levels.

A list helps you organize information by highlighting important topics. A **bulleted list** itemizes and separates paragraphs to increase readability. A **numbered list** sequences and prioritizes the items and is automatically updated to accommodate additions or deletions. A **multilevel list** extends a numbered list to several levels, and it too is updated automatically when topics are added or deleted. You create each of these lists from the Paragraph group on the Home tab.

To apply bullet formatting to a list, click the Bullets arrow and choose one of several predefined symbols in the Bullet library (see Figure 2.12). Position your mouse over one of the bullet styles in the Bullet Library and a preview of that bullet style will display in your document. To use that style, simply click the bullet. If you want to use a different bullet symbol, click the Define New Bullet option below the Bullet Library to choose a different symbol or picture for the bullet.

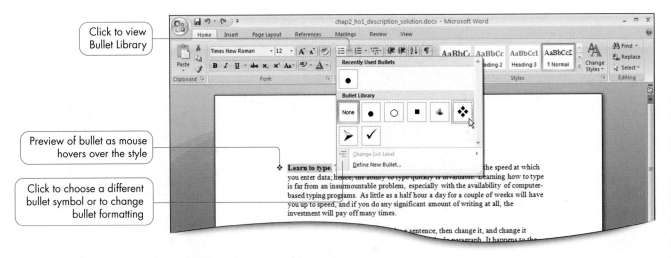

Click to view Bullet Library

Preview of bullet as mouse hovers over the style

Click to choose a different bullet symbol or to change bullet formatting

Figure 2.12 Bulleted List Options

Click the Numbering arrow in the Paragraph group to apply Arabic or Roman numerals, or upper- or lowercase letters, for a numbered list. When you position the mouse pointer over a style in the Numbering Library, you see a preview of that numbering style in your document. As with a bulleted list, you can define a new style by selecting the Define New Number Format option below the Numbering Library. Note, too, the options to restart or continue numbering found by selecting the Set Numbering Value option. These become important if a list appears in multiple places within a document. In other words, each occurrence of a list can start numbering anew, or it can continue from where the previous list left off.

The Mulitlevel List command enables you to create an outline to organize your thoughts in a hierarchical structure. As with the other types of lists, you can choose one of several default styles, and/or modify a style through the Define New Multilevel List option below the My Lists gallery. You also can specify whether each outline within a document is to restart its numbering, or whether it is to continue numbering from the previous outline.

Format Text into Columns

Columns format a section of a document into side-by-side vertical blocks.

Columns format a section of a document into side-by-side vertical blocks in which the text flows down the first column and then continues at the top of the next column. The length of a line of columnar text is shorter, enabling people to read through each article faster. To format text into columns, click the Page Layout tab and click Columns in the Page Setup group. From the Columns gallery, you can specify the number of columns or select More Columns to display the Columns dialog box. The Columns dialog box provides options for setting the number of columns and spacing between columns. Microsoft Word calculates the width of each column according to the left and right document margins on the page and the specified (default) space between columns.

The dialog box in Figure 2.13 implements a design of three equal columns. The 2" width of each column is computed based on current 1" left and right document margins and the ¼" spacing between columns. The width of each column is determined by subtracting the sum of the margins and the space between the columns (a total of 2½" in this example) from the page width of 8½". The result of the subtraction is 6", which is divided by 3 columns, resulting in a column width of 2".

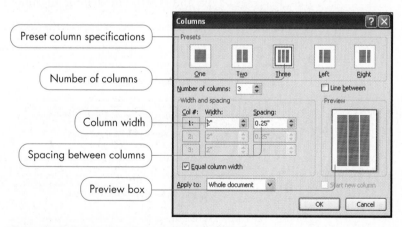

Figure 2.13 The Columns Dialog Box

One subtlety associated with column formatting is the use of sections, which control elements such as the orientation of a page (landscape or portrait), margins, page numbers, and the number of columns. All of the documents you have worked with so far have consisted of a single section, so section formatting was not an issue. It becomes important only when you want to vary an element that is formatted at the section level. You could, for example, use section formatting to create a document that has one column on its title page and two columns on the remaining pages. Creating this type of formatting requires you to divide the document into two sections by inserting a section break. You then format each section independently and specify the number of columns in each section. Table 2.3 guides you in formatting text into columns.

Table 2.3 Formatting with Columns

If your document contains . . .	And you want to apply column formatting to . . .	Do this:
only one section	the entire document	apply column formatting from anywhere within the document
two or more sections	only one section	position the insertion point in that section, and apply column formatting
one or more sections	only part of the document within a section	select the text you want to format, and then apply column formatting

Applying Paragraph Formats

The Paragraph group on the Home tab contains commands to set and control several format options for a paragraph. The options include alignment, indentation, line spacing, and pagination. These features also are found in the Paragraph dialog box. All of these formatting features are implemented at the paragraph level and affect all selected paragraphs. If no paragraphs are selected, Word applies the formatting to the current paragraph—the paragraph containing the insertion point.

Change Text Alignment

Horizontal alignment refers to the placement of text between the left and right margins.

Horizontal alignment refers to the placement of text between the left and right margins. Text is aligned in four different ways as shown in Figure 2.14. Alignment options are justified (flush left/flush right), left aligned (flush left with a ragged right margin), right aligned (flush right with a ragged left margin), or centered within the margins (ragged left and right). The default alignment is left.

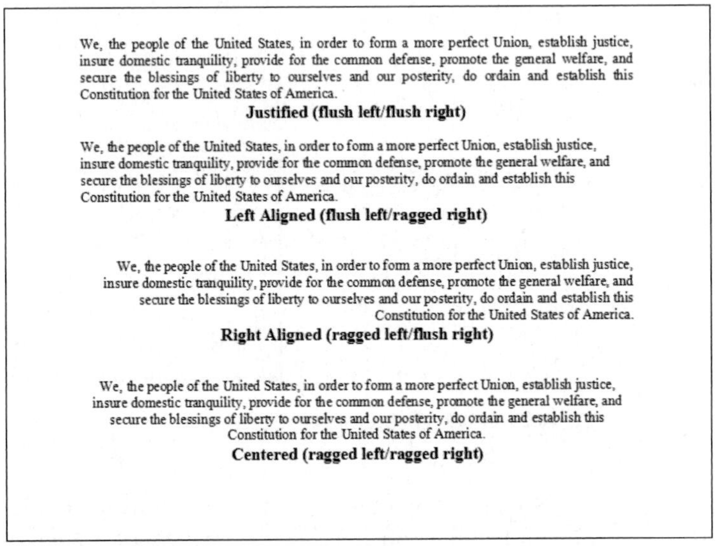

We, the people of the United States, in order to form a more perfect Union, establish justice, insure domestic tranquility, provide for the common defense, promote the general welfare, and secure the blessings of liberty to ourselves and our posterity, do ordain and establish this Constitution for the United States of America.
Justified (flush left/flush right)

We, the people of the United States, in order to form a more perfect Union, establish justice, insure domestic tranquility, provide for the common defense, promote the general welfare, and secure the blessings of liberty to ourselves and our posterity, do ordain and establish this Constitution for the United States of America.
Left Aligned (flush left/ragged right)

We, the people of the United States, in order to form a more perfect Union, establish justice, insure domestic tranquility, provide for the common defense, promote the general welfare, and secure the blessings of liberty to ourselves and our posterity, do ordain and establish this Constitution for the United States of America.
Right Aligned (ragged left/flush right)

We, the people of the United States, in order to form a more perfect Union, establish justice, insure domestic tranquility, provide for the common defense, promote the general welfare, and secure the blessings of liberty to ourselves and our posterity, do ordain and establish this Constitution for the United States of America.
Centered (ragged left/ragged right)

Figure 2.14 Horizontal Alignment

Left-aligned text is perhaps the easiest to read. The first letters of each line align with each other, helping the eye to find the beginning of each line. The lines themselves are of irregular length. Uniform spacing exists between words, and the ragged margin on the right adds white space to the text, giving it a lighter and more informal look.

Justified text, sometimes called fully justified, produces lines of equal length, with the spacing between words adjusted to align at the margins. Look closely and you will see many books, magazines, and newspapers fully justify text to add formality and "neatness" to the text. Some find this style more difficult to read because of the uneven (sometimes excessive) word spacing and/or the greater number of hyphenated words needed to justify the lines. But it also can enable you to pack more information onto a page when space is constrained.

Text that is centered or right aligned is usually restricted to limited amounts of text where the effect is more important than the ease of reading. Centered text, for example, appears frequently on wedding invitations, poems, or formal announcements. In research papers, first-level titles often are centered as well. Right-aligned text is used with figure captions and short headlines.

The Paragraph group on the Home tab contains the four alignment options: Align Left, Center, Align Right, and Justify. To apply the alignment, select text, then click the alignment option on the Home tab. You can also set alignment from the Paragraph dialog box; the Indents and Spacing tab contains an Alignment drop-down box in the General section.

TIP Alignment Keyboard Shortcuts

You can quickly apply alignment by using keyboard shortcuts. After you select the text, click Ctrl+L to align left, click Ctrl+E to align center, click Ctrl+R to align right, or click Ctrl+J to justify.

Indent Paragraphs

You can indent individual paragraphs so they appear to have different margins from the rest of a document. Indentation is established at the paragraph level; thus it is possible to apply different indentation properties to different paragraphs. You can indent one paragraph from the left margin only, another from the right margin only, and a third from both the left and right margins. For example, the fifth edition of the *Publication Manual of the American Psychological Association* specifies that quotations consisting of 40 or more words should be contained in a separate paragraph that is indented ½" from the left margin. Additionally, you can indent the first line of any paragraph differently from the rest of the paragraph. And finally, a paragraph may have no indentation at all, so that it aligns on the left and right margins.

Three settings determine the indentation of a paragraph: the left indent, the right indent, and a special indent, if any (see Figure 2.15). The left and right indents are set to 0 by default, as is the special indent, and produce a paragraph with no indentation at all. Positive values for the left and right indents offset the paragraph from both margins.

A *first line indent* marks the location to indent only the first line in a paragraph.

A *hanging indent* marks how far to indent each line of a paragraph except the first.

The two types of special indentation are first line and hanging. The *first line indent* affects only the first line in the paragraph, and you apply it by pressing the Tab key at the beginning of the paragraph or by setting a specific measurement in the Paragraph dialog box. Remaining lines in the paragraph align at the left margin. A *hanging indent* aligns the first line of a paragraph at the left margin and indents the remaining lines. Hanging indents often are used with bulleted or numbered lists and to format citations on a bibliography page.

Set Line and Paragraph Spacing

Line spacing is the space between the lines in a paragraph.

Line spacing determines the space between the lines in a paragraph and between paragraphs. Word provides complete flexibility and enables you to select any multiple of line spacing (single, double, line and a half, and so on). You also can specify line spacing in terms of points (1" vertical contains 72 points). Click the Line spacing command in the Paragraph group on the Home tab to establish line spacing for the current paragraph. You can also set line spacing in the *Spacing* section on the Indents and Spacing tab in the Paragraph dialog box.

Paragraph spacing is the amount of space before or after a paragraph.

Paragraph spacing is the amount of space before or after a paragraph, as indicated by the paragraph mark when you press Enter between paragraphs. Unlike line spacing that controls *all* spacing within and between paragraphs, paragraph spacing controls only the spacing between paragraphs.

Sometimes you need to single-space text within a paragraph but want to have a blank line between paragraphs. Instead of pressing Enter twice between paragraphs, you can set the paragraph spacing to control the amount of space before or after the paragraph. You can set paragraph spacing in the *Spacing* section on the Indents and Spacing tab in the Paragraph dialog box. Setting a 12-point *After* spacing creates the appearance of a double-space after the paragraph even though the user presses Enter only once between paragraphs.

The Paragraph dialog box is illustrated in Figure 2.15. The Indents and Spacing tab specifies a hanging indent, 1.5 line spacing, and justified alignment. The Preview area within the Paragraph dialog box enables you to see how the paragraph will appear within the document.

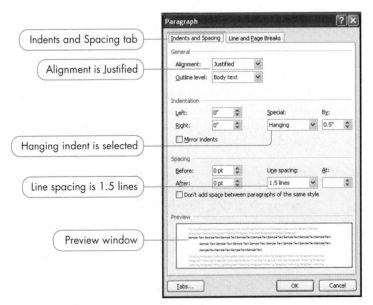

Figure 2.15 Indents and Spacing

Control Widows and Orphans

A **widow** is the last line of a paragraph appearing by itself at the top of a page.

An **orphan** is the first line of a paragraph appearing by itself at the bottom of a page.

Some lines become isolated from the remainder of a paragraph and seem out of place at the beginning or end of a multipage document. A *widow* refers to the last line of a paragraph appearing by itself at the top of a page. An *orphan* is the first line of a paragraph appearing by itself at the bottom of a page. You can prevent these from occurring by clicking the *Widow/Orphan control* check box in the *Pagination* section of the Line and Page Breaks tab of the Paragraph dialog box.

To prevent a page break from occurring within a paragraph and ensure that the entire paragraph appears on the same page use the *Keep lines together* option in the *Pagination* section of the Line and Page Breaks tab of the Paragraph dialog box. The paragraph is moved to the top of the next page if it does not fit on the bottom of the current page. Use the *Keep with next* option in the *Pagination* section to prevent a soft page break between the two paragraphs. This option is typically used to keep a heading (a one-line paragraph) with its associated text in the next paragraph. The check boxes in Figure 2.16 enable you to prevent the occurrence of awkward soft page breaks that detract from the appearance of a document.

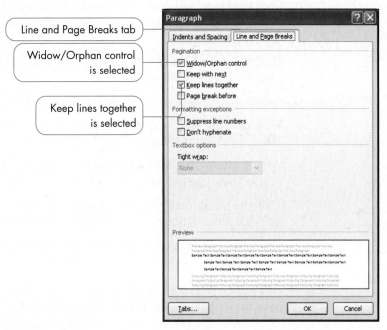

Figure 2.16 Line and Page Breaks

> ### TIP · The Section Versus the Paragraph
>
> Line spacing, alignment, tabs, and indents are implemented at the paragraph level. Change any of these parameters anywhere within the current (or selected) paragraph(s) and you change *only* those paragraph(s). Margins, page numbering, orientation, and columns are implemented at the section level. Change these parameters anywhere within a section and you change the characteristics of every page within that section.

Hands-On Exercises

2 | Paragraph Formatting

Skills covered: 1. Set Tabs in a Footer **2.** Select Text to Format **3.** Specify Line Spacing, Justification, and Pagination **4.** Indent Text **5.** Apply Borders and Shading **6.** Change Column Structure **7.** Insert a Section Break and Create Columns

---

Step 1
Set Tabs in a Footer

Refer to Figure 2.17 as you complete Step 1.

a. Open the *chap2_ho1_description_solution* document if you closed it after the last hands-on exercise and save it as **chap2_ho2_description_solution**.

b. Click the **Insert tab**, and then click **Footer** in the Header & Footer group. Click **Edit Footer** and notice the document text is dimmed except for the footer area.

c. Click the **Home tab**, and then click the **Paragraph Dialog Box Launcher** to display the Paragraph dialog box. Click **Tabs** in the lower-left corner to display the Tabs dialog box.

This footer contains no tab settings. You will add a 3" center tab that will be used for a page number.

d. Type **3** in the *Tab stop position* box. Click **Center**, and then click **OK**.

e. Click near the bottom of your page to display the footer area, if necessary. Press **Tab** one time, type **Page**, and press **Spacebar** one time.

You reposition the insertion point to the middle of the footer area using the tab you set and type the text you want to precede the page number.

f. Click the **Design tab** and click **Quick Parts** in the Insert group, then click **Field** to open the Field dialog box. Click **Page** in the *Field Names* box, then click **OK**.

The actual page number displays in the footer, as shown in Figure 2.17, and will automatically paginate for any additional pages added to your document.

TROUBLESHOOTING: If the page number is not horizontally centered at the 3" position, double-check the tab settings on the ruler. If tab settings appear to the left of the 3" tab setting, drag the tab markers off the ruler to delete them.

g. Click **Close Header and Footer** in the Close group of the Header and Footer Tools tab.

h. Save the document.

Quick Parts command

Center tab set for footer

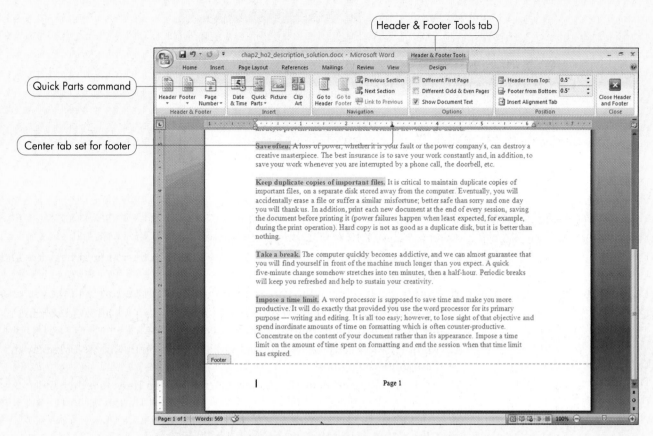

Figure 2.17 Insert Tab in Footer

Step 2
Select Text to Format

Refer to Figure 2.18 as you complete Step 2.

a. Position your insertion point at the end of the title, *Word Processing*, then press **Ctrl+Enter**.

You inserted a manual page break between the title and the list of tips.

b. Click **Zoom** in the status bar to display the Zoom dialog box. Click **Many pages** and drag to select the first two icons that represent two pages, as shown in Figure 2.18. Click **OK**.

You can see the entire document as you select text to format.

c. Select the entire second page.

d. Save the document.

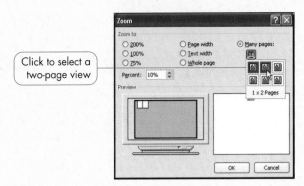

Click to select a two-page view

Figure 2.18 Zoom Dialog Box

Step 3

Specify Line Spacing, Justification, and Pagination

Refer to Figure 2.19 as you complete Step 3.

a. Select page 2, if necessary, and then click **Justify** in the Paragraph group on the Home tab.

b. Click **Line Spacing** in the Paragraph group on the Home tab, and then select **1.5**.

These settings align the text on the right and left margins and add spacing before and after lines of text, making it easier to read.

c. Right-click the selected text and select **Paragraph** on the menu to display the Paragraph dialog box.

d. Click the **Line and Page Breaks tab**. Click the **Keep lines together check box** in the *Pagination* section, if necessary. Click the **Widow/Orphan control check box** in the *Pagination* section, if necessary.

e. Click **OK** to accept the settings and close the dialog box.

These settings prevent paragraphs from being split at a page break.

f. Click anywhere in the document to deselect the text and see the effects of the formatting changes that were just specified.

Three paragraphs now display on a third page, and none are split at the page break, as shown in Figure 2.19.

g. Save the document.

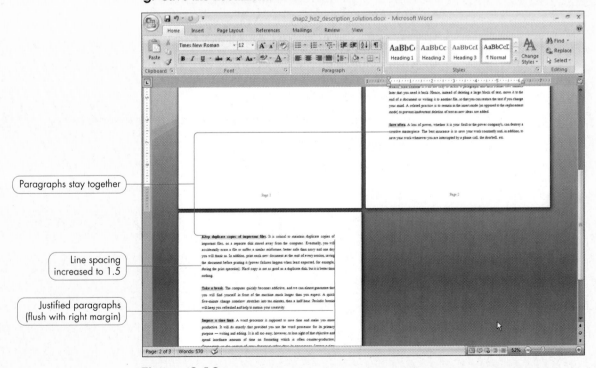

Paragraphs stay together

Line spacing increased to 1.5

Justified paragraphs (flush with right margin)

Figure 2.19 Result of Changing Line Spacing, Alignment, and Pagination

Refer to Figure 2.20 as you complete Step 4.

a. Click the **Zoom slider** in the status bar and select **100%**. Select the second paragraph, as shown in Figure 2.20.

> The second paragraph will not be indented yet.

b. Right-click the selected text and select **Paragraph** from the shortcut menu.

c. If necessary, click the **Indents and Spacing tab** in the Paragraph dialog box.

d. Click the **Left spin box** up arrow to display 0.5" in the *Indentation* section. Set the **Right indention** to 0.5" also. Click **OK**.

> Your document should match Figure 2.20.

e. Save the document.

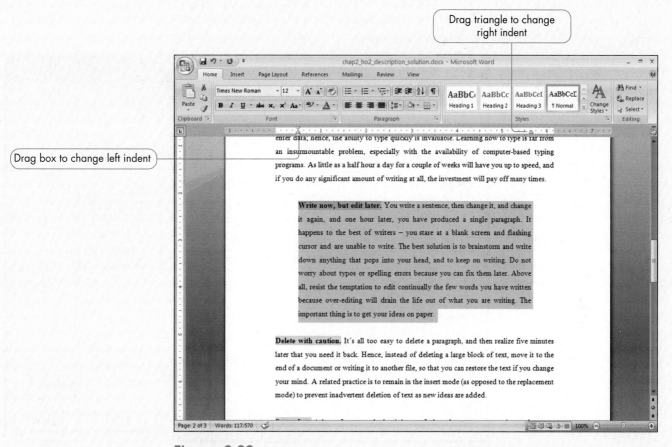

Figure 2.20 Indent

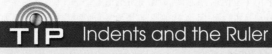 **Indents and the Ruler**

You can use the ruler to change the special, left, and/or right indents. Select the paragraph (or paragraphs) in which you want to change indents, and then drag the appropriate indent markers to the new location(s) on the ruler. If you get a hanging indent when you wanted to change the left indent, it means you dragged the bottom triangle instead of the box. Click Undo on the Quick Access Toolbar and try again. You can always use the Paragraph dialog box rather than the ruler if you continue to have difficulty.

Refer to Figure 2.21 as you complete Step 5.

a. Click the **Home tab**, click the **Borders arrow**, and then click **Borders and Shading** to display the Borders and Shading dialog box shown in Figure 2.21.

b. Click the **Borders tab**, if necessary, then click the double line style in the *Style* list. Click **¾ pt** in the *Width* list, then click **Box** in the *Setting* section.

A preview of these settings will display on the right side of the window in the Preview area.

c. Click the **Shading tab**, then click the **Fill drop-down arrow** and select **Dark Blue, Text 2, Lighter 80%** from the palette. It is located in the fourth column from the left and in the second row from the top. Click **OK** to accept the settings for both Borders and Shading.

The paragraph is surrounded by a ¾ point double-line border, and a light blue shading appears behind the text.

d. Click outside the paragraph to deselect it and view your formatting changes.

e. Save the document.

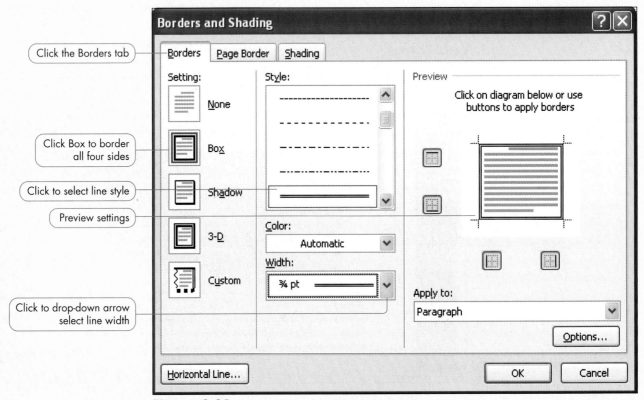

Figure 2.21 Borders and Shading Dialog Box

Refer to Figure 2.22 as you complete Step 6.

a. Click the **Page Layout tab** and click **Margins** in the Page Setup group. Click **Custom Margins** and select the **Margins tab** if necessary.

b. Click the spin arrows to set **1"** left and right margins. Click **OK**.

The document is now formatted by 1" left, right, top, and bottom margins.

c. Click the **Zoom button** in the status bar, select **Page width,** and then click **OK**. Press **PgUp** or **PgDn** on the keyboard to scroll until the second page comes into view.

d. Click anywhere in the paragraph, *Write now, but edit later*. Right-click and select **Paragraph**, click the **Indents and Spacing tab** if necessary, then change left and right to **0"** in the *Indentation* section. Click **OK**.

These settings prepare your document for the changes you make in the next steps.

e. Click the **Page Layout tab** and click **Columns** in the Page Setup group. Click **More Columns** to display the Columns dialog box.

Because you will change several settings related to columns, you clicked the More Columns option instead of clicking the gallery option to create three columns.

f. Click **Three** in the *Presets* section of the dialog box. The default spacing between columns is 0.5", which leads to a column width of 1.83". Change the spacing to **.25"** in the **Spacing** list, which automatically changes the column width to 2".

g. Click the **Line between column check box**, as shown in Figure 2.22. Click **OK**.

The document is now formatted in three columns with 0.25" space between columns. Vertical lines appear between columns.

h. Save the document.

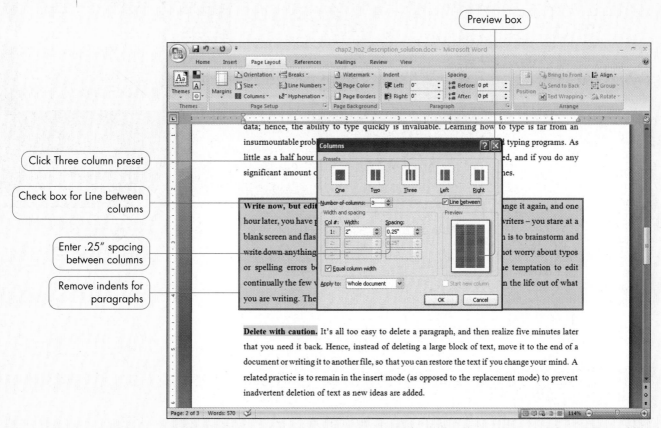

Figure 2.22 Change Column Structure

Refer to Figure 2.23 as you complete Step 7.

a. Click **Zoom** on the status bar to display the Zoom dialog box. Click **Many Pages**, drag to select **1x3** pages, and then click **OK**.

The document displays the column formatting.

b. Place the insertion point immediately to the left of the first paragraph on the second page. Click the **Page Layout tab** and click **Breaks** to display the list shown in Figure 2.23. Click **Continuous** under *Section Breaks*.

c. Click anywhere on the title page, above the section break you just inserted. Click **Columns**, then click **One** to display the content in one column.

The formatting for the first section of the document (the title page) should change to one column; the title of the document is centered across the entire page.

d. Save and close the *chap2_ho2_description_solution* document. Exit Word if you will not continue with the next exercise at this time.

Click to display Breaks options

Continuous Section Break

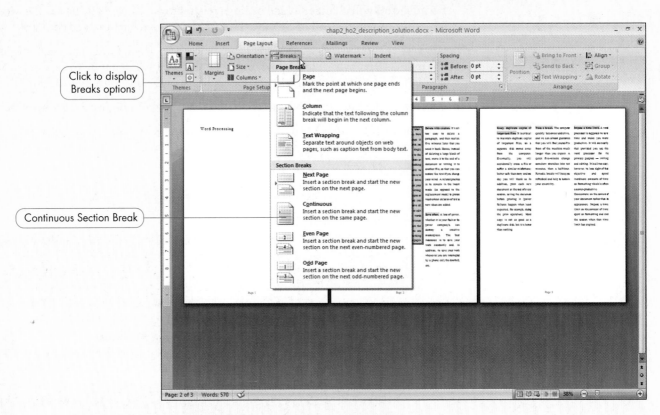

Figure 2.23 Insert a Section Break

Styles and Document References

As you complete reports, assignments, and projects for other classes or in your job, you probably apply the same text, paragraph, table, and list formatting for similar documents. Instead of formatting each document individually, you can create your own custom style to save time in setting particular formats for titles, headings, and paragraphs. Styles and other features in Word then can be used to automatically generate reference pages such as a table of contents and indexes.

In this section, you create and modify styles. You also display a document in the Outline view. Finally, you learn how to use the AutoFormat feature.

Creating and Modifying Styles

> One way to achieve uniformity throughout a document is to store the formatting information as a style. Change the style and you automatically change all text defined by that style.

One characteristic of a professional document is the uniform formatting that is applied to similar elements throughout the document. Different elements have different formatting. For headings you can use one font, color, style, and size, and then use a completely different format design on text below those headings. The headings may be left aligned, while the text is fully justified. You can format lists and footnotes in entirely different styles.

One way to achieve uniformity throughout the document is to use the Format Painter to copy the formatting from one occurrence of each element to the next, but this step is tedious and inefficient. And if you were to change your mind after copying the formatting throughout a document, you would have to repeat the entire process all over again. A much easier way to achieve uniformity is to store all the formatting information together, which is what we refer to as a *style*. Styles automate the formatting process and provide a consistent appearance to a document. It is possible to store any type of character or paragraph formatting within a style, and once a style is defined, you can apply it to any element within a document to produce identical formatting. Change the style and you automatically change all text defined by that style.

A *style* is a set of formatting options you apply to characters or paragraphs.

Styles are created on the character or paragraph level. A *character style* stores character formatting (font, size, and style) and affects only the selected text. A *paragraph style* stores paragraph formatting such as alignment, line spacing, indents, tabs, text flow, and borders and shading, as well as the font, size, and style of the text in the paragraph. A paragraph style affects the current paragraph or, if selected, multiple paragraphs. You create and apply styles from the Styles group on the Home tab, as shown in Figure 2.24.

A *character style* stores character formatting and affects only selected text.

A *paragraph style* stores paragraph formatting of text.

The Normal template contains more than 100 styles. Unless you specify a style, Word uses the Normal style. The Normal style contains these settings: 12-point Calibri, English (U.S.) language, single line spacing, left horizontal alignment, and Widow/Orphan control. You can create your own styles to use in a document, modify or delete an existing style, and even add your new style to the Normal template for use in other documents.

The document in Figure 2.25 is a report about the Great Depression. Each paragraph begins with a one-line heading, followed by the supporting text. The task pane in the figure displays all of the styles used in the document. The Normal style contains the default paragraph settings (left aligned, single spacing, and a default font) and is assigned automatically to every paragraph unless a different style is specified. The Clear Formatting style removes all formatting from selected text. It is the Heading 3 and Body Text styles, however, that are of interest to us, as these styles have been applied throughout the document to the associated elements.

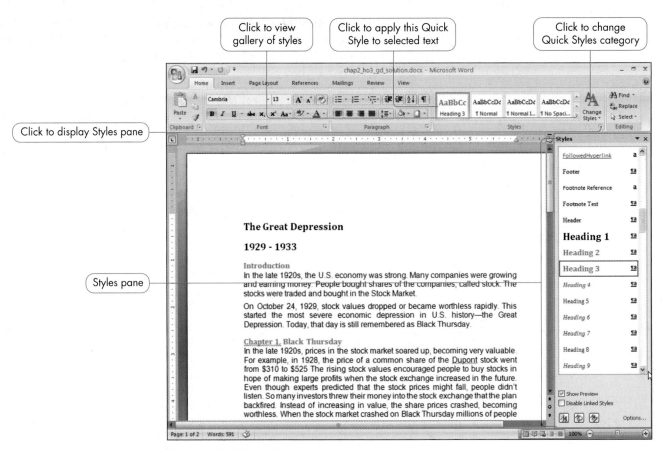

Click to view gallery of styles

Click to apply this Quick Style to selected text

Click to change Quick Styles category

Click to display Styles pane

Styles pane

Figure 2.24 The Styles Group

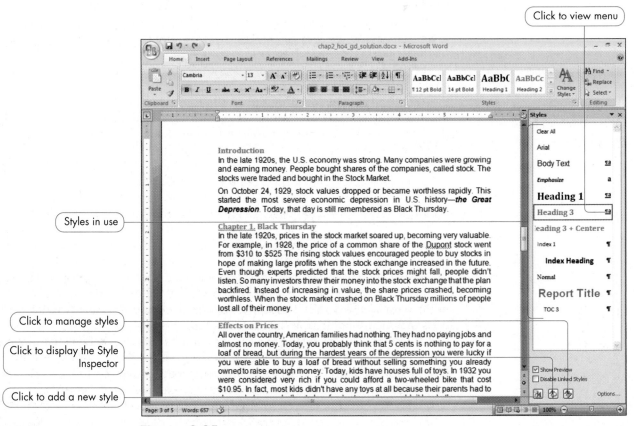

Click to view menu

Styles in use

Click to manage styles

Click to display the Style Inspector

Click to add a new style

Figure 2.25 Styles Task Pane

You can change the specifications of a style by clicking the down arrow for the particular style, then selecting Modify. The specifications for the Heading 3 style are shown in Figure 2.26. The current settings within the Heading 3 style call for 13-point Cambria bold type using a custom color. There is a 12-point space before the text, and the heading appears on the same page as the next paragraph. The preview frame in the dialog box shows how paragraphs formatted in this style display. Click the Format button in the Modify Style dialog box to select and open other dialog boxes where you modify settings that are used in the style. And as indicated earlier, any changes to the style are reflected automatically in any text or element defined by that style.

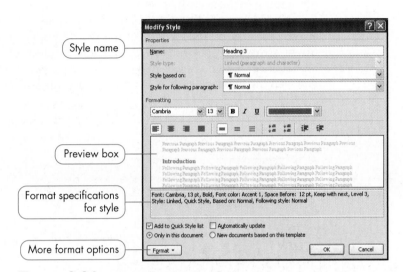

Figure 2.26 Modify a Style

TIP Styles and Paragraphs

A paragraph style affects the entire paragraph; that is, you cannot apply a paragraph style to only part of a paragraph. To apply a style to an existing paragraph, place the insertion point anywhere within the paragraph, click the Styles Dialog Box Launcher on the Home tab to display the Styles pane, then click the name of the style you want to use. The Styles pane can display in several locations. Initially, it might display as a floating window, but you can drag the title bar to move it. Drag to the far left or right side, and it will dock on that side of the window.

Use the Styles Pane Options

When you display the Styles pane in your document, it might contain only the styles used in the document, as in Figure 2.25, or it might list every style in the Word document template. If the Styles pane only displays styles used in the document, you are unable to view or apply other styles. You can change the styles that display in the Styles pane by using the Styles Gallery Options dialog box, which displays when you click *Options* in the lower-right corner of the Styles pane. In the *Select styles to show* box, you select from several options including Recommended, In use, In current document, and All styles. Select *In use* to view only styles used in this document; select *All styles* to view all styles created for the document template as well as any custom styles you create. Other options are available in this dialog box, including how to sort the styles when displayed and whether to show Paragraph or Font or both types of styles. To view the style names with their styles applied, click the *Show Preview* check box near the bottom of the Styles pane.

Reveal Formatting

To display complete format properties for selected text in the document, use the Reveal Formatting task pane as shown in Figure 2.27. The properties are displayed by Font, Paragraph, and Section, enabling you to click the plus or minus sign next to each item to view or hide the underlying details. The properties in each area are links to the associated dialog boxes. Click Alignment or Justification, for example, within the Paragraph area to open the Paragraph dialog box, where you can change the indicated property. This panel is often helpful for troubleshooting a format problem in a document. To view this pane, click the Styles Dialog Box Launcher on the Home tab, click Style Inspector at the bottom of the Styles pane, then click Reveal Formatting in the Style Inspector pane. If you use this feature often, you can add it to the Quick Access Toolbar. To add it, click the Office Button, then click Word Options; select *Customize* on the left side of the Word Options dialog box, then click the drop-down arrow for *Choose commands from* and select *All Commands*. Scroll down the alphabetical list and select *Reveal Formatting*, then click the Add button displayed between the two large lists. Click OK to save the addition.

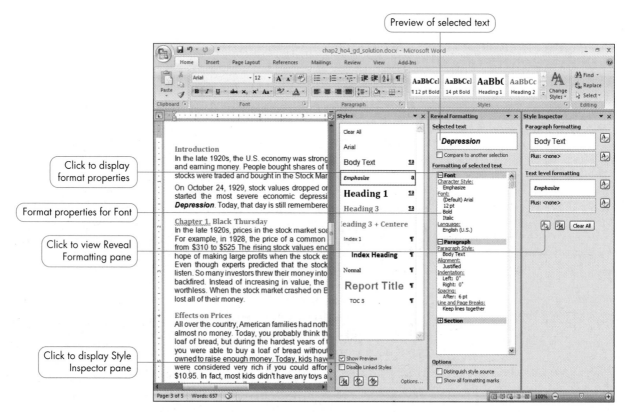

Figure 2.27 Reveal Formatting

Use the Outline View

Outline view is a structural view that displays varying amounts of detail.

One additional advantage of styles is that they enable you to view a document in the Outline view. The **Outline view** does not display a conventional outline, but rather a structural view of a document that can be collapsed or expanded as necessary. Consider, for example, Figure 2.28, which displays the Outline view of a report about the Great Depression. The heading for each tip is formatted according to the Heading 3 style. The text of each tip is formatted according to the Body Text style.

The advantage of Outline view is that you can collapse or expand portions of a document to provide varying amounts of detail. We have, for example, collapsed almost the entire document in Figure 2.28, displaying the headings while suppressing the body text. We also expanded the text for two sections (*Introduction* and *The New Deal*) for purposes of illustration.

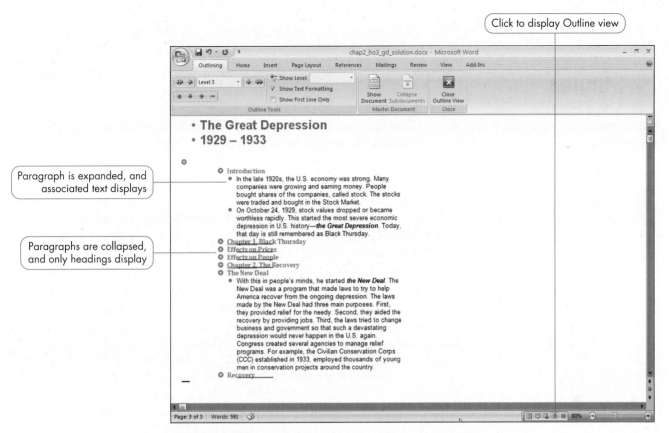

Click to display Outline view

Paragraph is expanded, and associated text displays

Paragraphs are collapsed, and only headings display

Figure 2.28 The Outline View

Now assume that you want to move one paragraph from its present position to a different position in the document. Without the Outline view, the text might stretch over several pages, making it difficult to see the text of both areas at the same time. Using the Outline view, however, you can collapse what you do not need to see, then simply click and drag headings to rearrange the text within the document. The Outline view is very useful with long documents, but it requires the use of styles throughout the document.

> ### TIP   The Outline Versus the Outline View
>
> A conventional outline is created as a multilevel list using the Multilevel List command in the Paragraph group on the Home tab. Text for the outline is entered in the Print Layout view, *not* the Outline view. The latter provides a condensed view of a document that is used in conjunction with styles.

Use the AutoFormat Feature

Styles are extremely powerful. They enable you to impose uniform formatting within a document, and they let you take advantage of the Outline view. What if, however, you have an existing or lengthy document that does not contain any styles (other than the default Normal style, which is applied to every paragraph)? Do you have to manually go through every paragraph in order to apply the appropriate style? Fortunately, the answer is no, because the AutoFormat feature provides a quick solution. The *AutoFormat* feature analyzes a document and formats it for you; it evaluates an entire document and determines how each paragraph is used, then it applies an appropriate style to each paragraph. To use the AutoFormat feature, you must add it to the Quick Access Toolbar using the same procedure explained previously in the Reveal Formatting section.

The *AutoFormat* feature analyzes a document and formats it for you.

Styles and Document References | **Word 2007**   163

Hands-On Exercises

3 | Styles

Skills covered: 1. Apply Style Properties **2.** Modify the Body Text Style **3.** Modify the Heading 3 Style **4.** Select the Outline View **5.** Create a Paragraph Style **6.** Create a Character Style **7.** View the Completed Document

---

Step 1
Apply Style Properties

Refer to Figure 2.29 as you complete Step 1.

a. Open the document *chap2_ho3_gd* in the **Exploring Word folder** and save it as **chap2_ho3_gd_solution**.

b. Press **Ctrl+Home** to move to the beginning of the document.

Notice the headings have been formatted with 14-point and 12-point bold font.

c. Select the first two lines, *The Great Depression* and *1929–1933*, then click **Heading 1** from the Quick Style gallery in the Styles group on the Home tab.

d. Click anywhere in the first paragraph heading, *Introduction*. Click the **Styles Dialog Box Launcher** on the Home tab. Double-click the title bar of the task pane to dock it, if necessary, so it does not float on the screen. Click the down arrow that displays when you hover over the *12 pt Bold* style listed in the Styles pane, then click **Select all 7 instances**.

All paragraph headings in this document are selected, as shown in Figure 2.29.

e. Click the **More button** on the right side of the **Quick Style** gallery to display more styles, then click the **Heading 3** style.

When you hover your mouse over the different styles in the gallery, the Live Preview feature displays the style on your selected text but will not apply it until you click on the style.

f. Save the document.

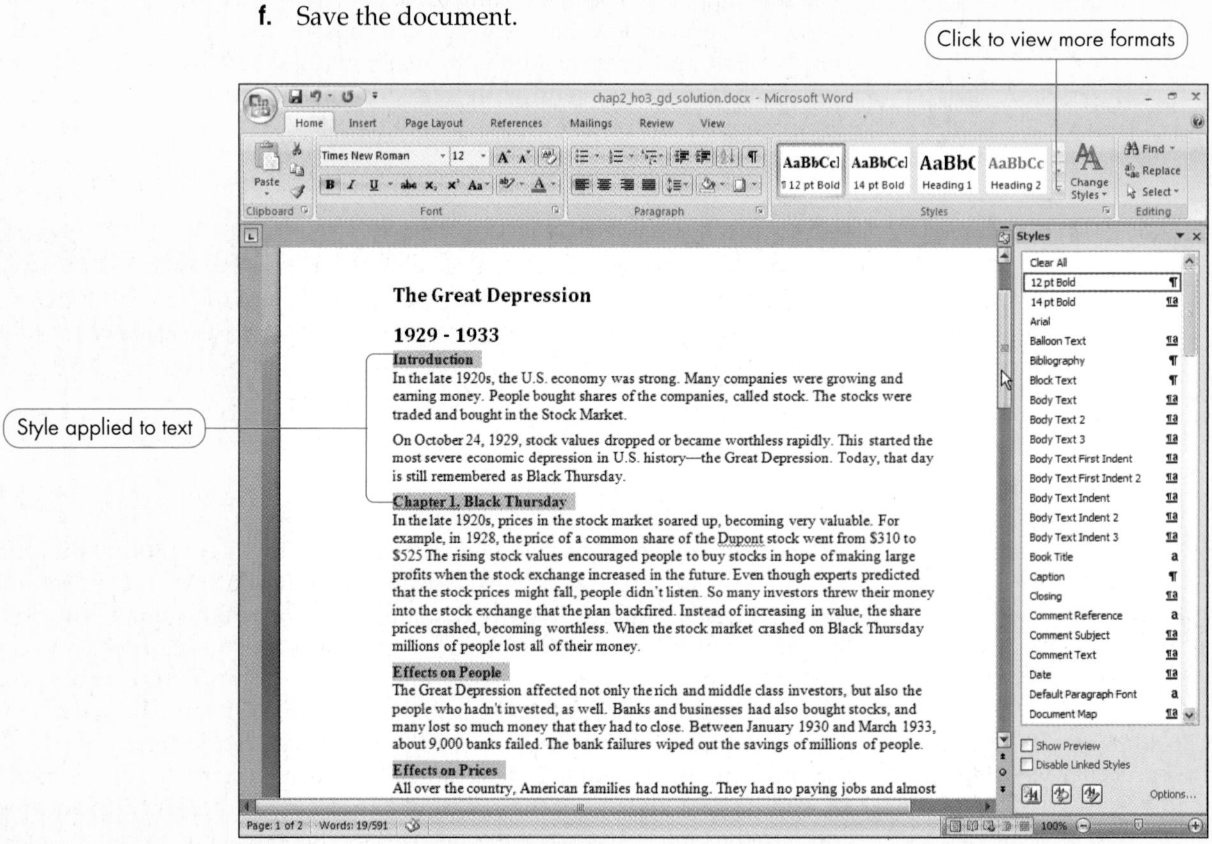

Click to view more formats

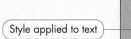
Style applied to text

Figure 2.29 View Style Properties

Refer to Figure 2.30 as you complete Step 2.

a. Press **Ctrl+Home** to move to the beginning of the document. Place the insertion point in the first paragraph, then notice the Body Text style is selected in the Styles pane. Click the down arrow next to the style and click **Modify** to display the Modify Style dialog box.

> **TROUBLESHOOTING:** If you click the style name instead of the down arrow, you will apply the style to the selected text instead of modifying it. Click Undo on the Quick Access Toolbar to cancel the command. Click the down arrow next to the style name to display the associated menu and click the Modify command to display the Modify Style dialog box.

b. Change the font to **Arial**. Click **Justify** to change the alignment of every paragraph in the document formatted with the *Body Text* style.

c. Click **Format** in the lower-left corner of the window, as shown in Figure 2.30, then click **Paragraph** to display the Paragraph dialog box. If necessary, click the **Line and Page Breaks tab**.

The box for Widow/Orphan control is checked by default. This option ensures that any paragraph defined by the Body Text style will not be split, leaving a single line of text at the bottom or top of a page.

d. Click the **Keep lines together check box** in the *Pagination* section.

This option is a more stringent requirement and ensures that the entire paragraph is not split.

e. Click **OK** to close the Paragraph dialog box. Click **OK** to close the Modify Style dialog box.

All of the multiline paragraphs in the document change automatically to reflect the new definition of the Body Text style, which includes full justification, a new font, and ensuring that a paragraph is not split across pages.

f. Save the document.

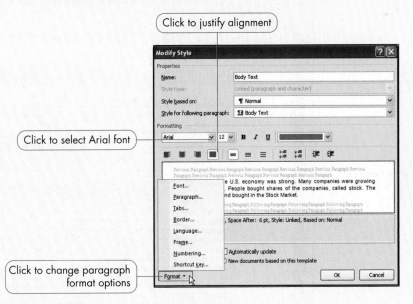

Figure 2.30 Modify the Body Text Style

Refer to Figure 2.31 as you complete Step 3.

a. Place the insertion point in one of the headings that has been formatted with the *Heading 3* style. Scroll, if necessary, to view *Heading 3* in the Styles pane. Hover your mouse over Heading 3, click the down arrow, then click **Modify** to display the Modify Style dialog box.

b. Click the **Font Color drop-down arrow** to display the palette in Figure 2.31. Click **Blue, Accent 1**, the blue color swatch on the first row, to change the color of all of the headings in the document.

You see a preview of the effect as you hover the mouse over the color, but the change will not take effect until you click *OK* to accept the settings and close the dialog box.

c. Click **Format** at the bottom of the dialog box, then click **Paragraph** to display the Paragraph dialog box. Click the **Indents and Spacing tab**, then change the **Spacing After** to **0**. Click **OK** to accept the settings and close the Paragraph dialog box.

You modified the style by changing the spacing after the heading to 0, which forces the paragraph text to display closer to the heading.

d. Click **OK** to close the Modify Style dialog box.

The formatting in your document has changed to reflect the changes in the Heading 3 style.

e. Save the document.

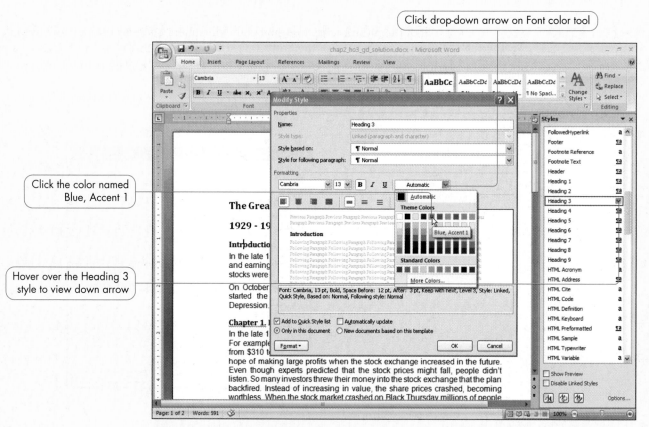

Figure 2.31 Modify the Heading 3 Style

TIP Space Before and After

Within single-spaced text, it is common practice to press the Enter key twice at the end of a paragraph (once to end the paragraph and a second time to insert a blank line before the next paragraph). The same effect is achieved by setting the spacing before or after the paragraph using the Spacing Before or After list boxes in the Paragraph dialog box. The latter technique gives you greater flexibility in that you can specify any amount of spacing (e.g., 6 pt) to leave only half a line before or after a paragraph. It also enables you to change the spacing between paragraphs more easily because the spacing information is stored within the paragraph style.

Step 4
Select the Outline View

Refer to Figure 2.32 as you complete Step 4.

a. Close the Styles pane. Click the **View tab**, then click **Outline** to display the document in Outline view.

b. Place the insertion point to the left of the first paragraph heading, *Introduction*, and select the rest of the document. Click the **Outlining tab**, if necessary, then click **Collapse** in the Outline Tools group.

The entire document collapses so that only the headings display.

c. Click in the heading titled *The New Deal*, as shown in Figure 2.32. Click **Expand** in the Outline Tools group to see the subordinate items under this heading.

d. Select the paragraph heading *Effects on Prices*, then click **Move Up** on the Outline Tools group.

You moved the paragraph above the paragraph that precedes it in the outline. Note that you also can drag and drop a selected paragraph.

e. Save the document.

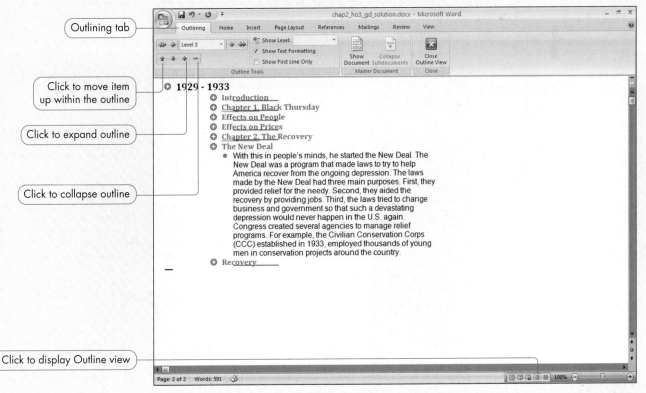

Figure 2.32 The Outline View

Refer to Figure 2.33 as you complete Step 5.

a. Click Close Outline View to change to return to Print Layout view. Click the **Home tab**, if necessary, and then click the **Styles Dialog Box Launcher** to open the Styles pane.

b. Press **Ctrl+Home** to move the insertion point to the beginning of the document, then place the insertion point to the right of *1933* and press **Ctrl+Enter**.

Inserting a page break creates space where you can add a title page.

c. Press **Ctrl+Home** to move the insertion point to the beginning of the new page, then select both lines on the title page. Scroll up if necessary and click **Clear All** in the Styles pane. Click the **Font arrow** on the Home tab and select **Arial**, then click the **Font Size arrow**, select **24** and click **Bold** and **Center** in the Paragraph group on the Home tab. Click the **Font Color arrow** and select **Blue, Accent 1** on the color palette (the blue color swatch on the first row) to change the color of the text to blue.

The Styles task pane displays the specifications for the text you just entered. You have created a new style, but the style is not yet named.

d. Point to the description for the title on the Styles pane (you may only be able to see the first or last few format effects such as Bold, Accent 1), hover your mouse over the description to view the down arrow, click the down arrow, as shown in Figure 2.33, and then select **Modify Style** to display the Modify Style dialog box.

e. Click in the **Name text box** in the Properties area and type **Report Title** as the name of the new style. Click **OK**.

f. Save the document.

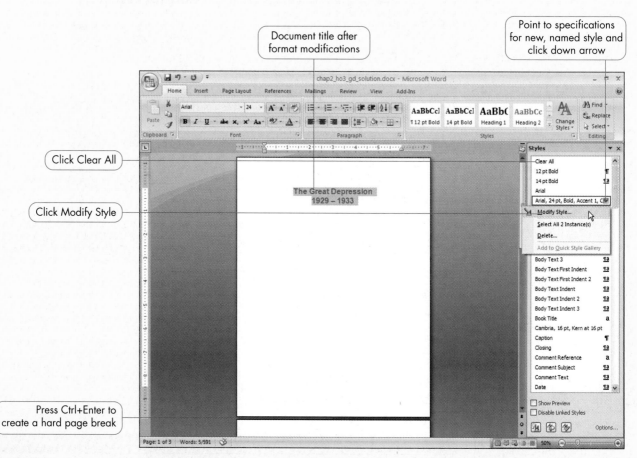

Figure 2.33 Create a Paragraph Style

Refer to Figure 2.34 as you complete Step 6.

a. Select the words *the Great Depression* (that appear within the second paragraph of the Introduction). Click **Bold** and **Italic** in the Font group on the Home tab.

b. Click **New Style** on the bottom of the Styles pane, and then type **Emphasize** as the name of the style.

c. Click the **Style type drop-down arrow** and select **Character** (see Figure 2.34). Click **OK**.

The style named Emphasize is listed in the Style pane and can be used throughout your document.

d. Select the words *the New Deal* in the first sentence of the *New Deal* section. Click **More** in the Quick Style gallery on the Home tab and apply the newly created *Emphasize* character style to the selected text. Close the Styles task pane.

e. Save the document.

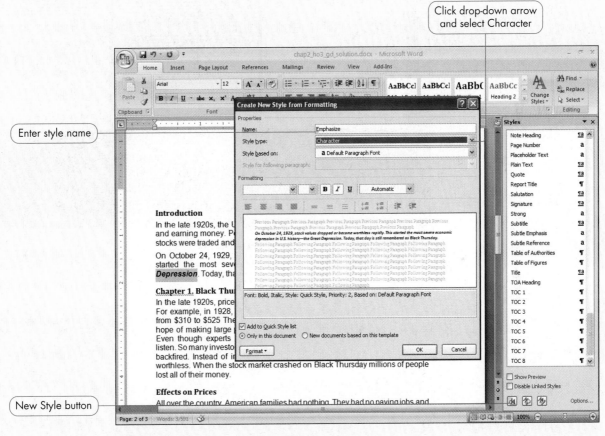

Figure 2.34 Create a Character Style

Refer to Figure 2.35 as you complete Step 7.

a. Click **Zoom** on the status bar, click **Many Pages**, then click and drag to select 1 x 3 pages. Click **OK**.

You should see a multipage display similar to Figure 2.35. The text on the individual pages is too small to read, but you can see the page breaks and overall document flow. According to the specifications in the Body Text style, the paragraphs should all be justified and each should fit completely on one page without spilling over to the next page.

b. Click to the left of the title on the first page and press **Enter** three times to position the title further down the page.

c. Save the *chap2_ho3_gd_solution* document and keep it onscreen if you plan to continue with the next hands-on exercise. Close the file and exit Word if you will not continue with the next exercise at this time.

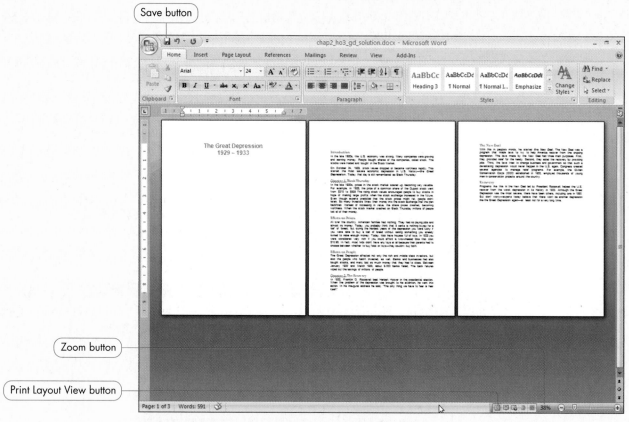

Figure 2.35 The Completed Document

Table of Contents and Indexes

Well-prepared long documents include special features to help readers locate information easily. You can use Word to help you create these supplemental document components with minimal effort.

Well-prepared long documents include special features to help readers locate information easily. For example, people often refer to the table of contents or the index in a long document—such as a book, reference manual, or company policy—to locate particular topics within that document. You can use Word to help you create these supplemental document components with minimal effort.

In this section, you generate a table of contents at the beginning of a document. You then learn how to designate text to include in an index and then generate the index at the end of a document.

Creating a Table of Contents

A *table of contents* lists headings and the page numbers where they appear in a document.

A *table of contents* lists headings in the order they appear in a document and the page numbers where the entries begin. Word can create the table of contents automatically, if you apply a style to each heading in the document. You can use built-in styles, Heading 1 through Heading 9, or identify your own custom styles to use when generating the table of contents. Word also will update the table to accommodate the addition or deletion of headings and/or changes in page numbers brought about through changes in the document.

The table of contents is located on the References tab. You can select from several predefined formats such as Classic and Formal, as well as determine how many levels to display in the table; the latter correspond to the heading styles used within the document. You can determine whether or not to right-align the page numbers; and you also can choose to include a leader character to draw the reader's eyes across the page from a heading to a page number.

Creating an Index

An *index* is a listing of topics and the page numbers where the topic is discussed.

An index puts the finishing touch on a long document. The *index* provides an alphabetical listing of topics covered in a document, along with the page numbers where the topic is discussed. Typically, the index appears at the end of a book or document. Word will create an index automatically, provided that the entries for the index have been previously marked. This result, in turn, requires you to go through a document, select the terms to be included in the index, and mark them accordingly. It is not as tedious as it sounds. You can, for example, select a single occurrence of an entry and tell Word to mark all occurrences of that entry for the index. You also can create cross-references, such as "see also Internet."

After you specify the entries, create the index by choosing the Insert Index command on the References tab. You can choose a variety of styles for the index, just as you can for the table of contents. Word arranges the index entries in alphabetical order and enters the appropriate page references. You also can create additional index entries and/or move text within a document, then update the index with the click of a mouse.

Table of Contents and Index Styles | Reference

Table of Contents

Fancy Format

INDEX

B

Bank failures, 3
Black Thursday, 2, *See Stock Market*

C

Civilian Conservation Corps, 3

D

Dupont, 2

H

Hoover, 3

N

New Deal, 3

R

Roosevelt, 3

S

Stock Market, 2

Bulleted Format

Table of Contents

Formal Format

INDEX

B

Bank failures, 3
Black Thursday, 2, *See Stock Market*

C

Civilian Conservation Corps, 3

D

Dupont, 2

H

Hoover, 3

N

New Deal, 3

R

Roosevelt, 3

S

Stock Market, 2

Classic Format

Table of Contents

Modern Format

INDEX

B

Bank failures, 3
Black Thursday, 2, *See Stock Market*

C

Civilian Conservation Corps, 3

D

Dupont, 2

H

Hoover, 3

N

New Deal, 3

R

Roosevelt, 3

S

Stock Market, 2

Fancy Format

Table of Contents

Simple Format

INDEX

B

Bank failures · 3
Black Thursday · 2, *See Stock Market*

C

Civilian Conservation Corps · 3

D

Dupont · 2

H

Hoover · 3

N

New Deal · 3

R

Roosevelt · 3

S

Stock Market · 2

Modern Format

Hands-On Exercises

4 | Reference Pages

Skills covered: 1. Apply a Style **2.** Insert a Table of Contents **3.** Define an Index Entry **4.** Create the Index **5.** Complete the Index **6.** View the Completed Document

---

Step 1
Apply a Style

Refer to Figure 2.36 as you complete Step 1.

a. Open the *chap2_ho3_gd_solution* document if you closed it after the last hands-on exercise and save it as **chap2_ho4_gd_solution**.

b. Click **Zoom** in the status bar, click **Page Width**, then click **OK**. Scroll to the top of the second page.

c. Click to the left of the *Introduction* title. Type **Table of Contents**, and then press **Enter** two times. Press **Ctrl+Enter** to insert a page break.

The table of contents displays on a page between the title page and the body of the document using the Heading 3 style you modified in the previous exercise.

d. Click anywhere in the *Table of Contents* heading.

TROUBLESHOOTING: If the Heading 3 style does not display, click Heading 3 from the Quick Style gallery on the Home tab.

e. Click **Center** in the Paragraph group on the Home tab and compare your document to Figure 2.36.

f. Save the document.

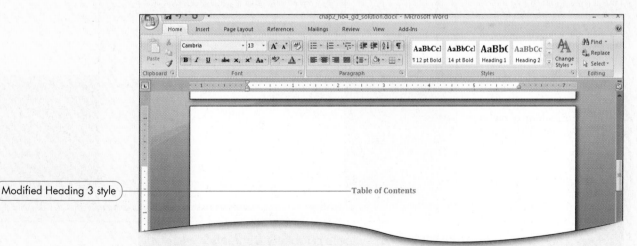

Figure 2.36 Apply a Style to a Heading

Refer to Figure 2.37 as you complete Step 2.

a. Place the insertion point immediately under the *Table of Contents* title, then click **Zoom** on the status bar. Click **Many Pages**, then click and drag to select 1 x 4 pages. Click **OK**.

The display changes to show all four pages in the document.

b. Click the **References tab**, and then click **Table of Contents** in the Table of Contents group. Select **Insert Table of Contents**.

The Table of Contents dialog box displays (see Figure 2.37).

c. If necessary, click the **Show page numbers check box** and the **Right align page numbers check box**.

d. Click the **Formats drop-down arrow** in the *General* section and select **Distinctive**. Click the **Tab leader drop-down arrow** in the *Print Preview* section and choose a **dot leader**. Click **OK**.

Word takes a moment to create the table of contents, and then displays it in the location of your insertion point.

e. Save the document.

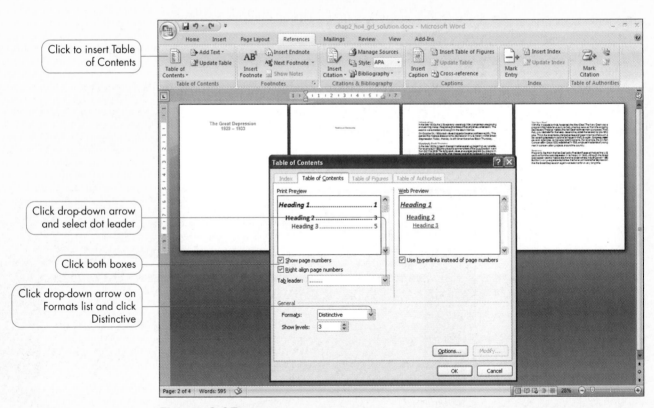

Figure 2.37 Create a Table of Contents

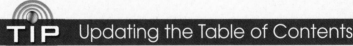

TIP Updating the Table of Contents

You can use a shortcut menu to update the table of contents. Point to any entry in the table of contents, then press the right mouse button to display the menu. Click **Update Field**, click **Update Entire Table**, and then click **OK**. The table of contents is adjusted automatically to reflect page number changes as well as the addition or deletion of any text defined by a style.

Refer to Figure 2.38 as you complete Step 3.

a. Press **Ctrl+Home** to move to the beginning of the document. Drag the Zoom Slider on the task bar to 100%. Click the **Home tab**, then click **Find** in the Editing group. Type **Black Thursday** in the *Find what* box, and then click **Find Next** two times.

You click Find Next two times because the first occurrence of *Black Thursday* is in the table of contents, but that is not the occurrence you want to mark for the index.

b. Click **Cancel** to close the Find and Replace dialog box. Click **Show/Hide ¶** in the Paragraph group on the Home tab so you can see the nonprinting characters in the document.

The index entries that were created by the authors appear in curly brackets and begin with the letters XE.

c. Check that the text *Black Thursday* is selected within the document, then press **Alt+Shift+X** to display the Mark Index Entry dialog box, as shown in Figure 2.38.

TROUBLESHOOTING: If you forget the shortcut, click Mark Entry on the References tab.

d. Click **Mark** to create the index entry.

After you create the index entry, you see the field code, {XE "Black Thursday"}, to indicate that the index entry is created. The Mark Index Entry dialog box stays open so that you can create additional entries by selecting additional text.

e. Click the **Cross-reference check box** in the *Options* section. Type **Stock Market** in the Cross-reference text box, then click **Mark**.

f. Click in the document, scroll down to the next paragraph, select the text *Dupont*, then click in the Mark Index Entry dialog box and notice Main entry automatically changes to Dupont. Click **Mark** to create the index entry, then close the Mark Index Entry dialog box.

g. Save the document.

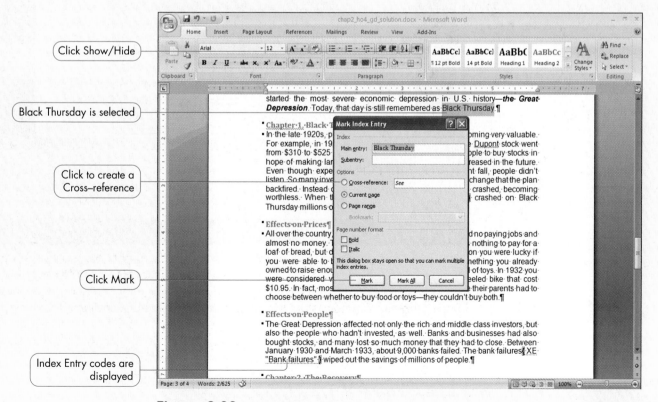

Figure 2.38 Create an Index Entry

Refer to Figure 2.39 as you complete Step 4.

a. Press **Ctrl+End** to move to the end of the document, then press **Enter** to begin a new line.

This spot is where you will insert the index.

b. Click the **References tab**, and then click **Insert Index** in the Index group.

The Index dialog box displays, as shown in Figure 2.39.

c. Click the **Formats drop-down arrow** and select **Classic**. If necessary, click the **Columns spin box arrows** until **2** displays. Click **OK** to create the index.

TROUBLESHOOTING: Click Undo on the Quick Access Toolbar if you are not satisfied with the appearance of the index or if it does not display at the end of the document, then repeat the process.

d. Save the document.

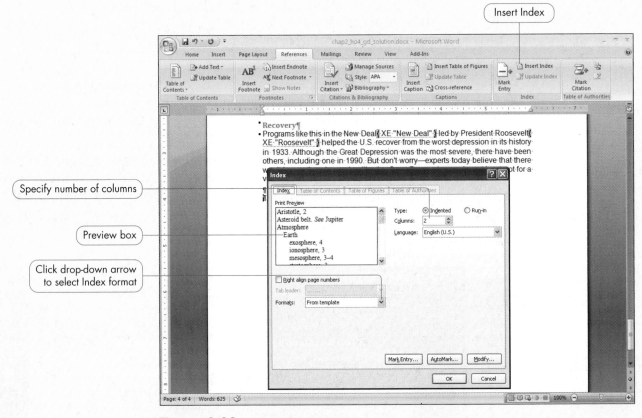

Figure 2.39 Create the Index

TIP   AutoMark Index Entries

The AutoMark command will, as the name implies, automatically mark all occurrences of all entries for inclusion in an index. To use the feature, you have to create a separate document that lists the terms you want to reference, then you execute the AutoMark command from the Index dialog box. The advantage is that it is fast. The disadvantage is that every occurrence of an entry is marked in the index so that a commonly used term may have too many page references. You can, however, delete superfluous entries by manually deleting the field codes. Click **Show/Hide ¶** in the Paragraph group of the Home tab if you do not see the entries in the document.

Refer to Figure 2.40 as you complete Step 5.

a. At the beginning of the index click to position the insertion point on the left of the letter "B".

b. Click the **Page Layout tab**, then click **Breaks** and select **Next Page**.

The index moves to the top of a new page.

c. Click the **Insert tab**, click **Page Number** in the Header & Footer group, and then select **Format Page Numbers** to display the Page Number Format dialog box. Click **Continue from previous section**, if necessary, then click **OK**.

d. Click **Header** in the Header & Footer group, and then click **Edit Header** to display the Design tab as shown in Figure 2.40. Click **Link to Previous**.

When you toggle the Link to Previous indicator off, you create a new header for this section that is independent of and different from the header in the previous section. Notice other Header and Footer options that display in the tab.

e. Type **INDEX** in the header. Select *INDEX* then on the Mini toolbar click **Center**. Click **Close Header and Footer** in the Close group to return to the document. Click **Show/Hide ¶** in the Paragraph group on the Home tab to turn off display of field codes.

f. Save the document.

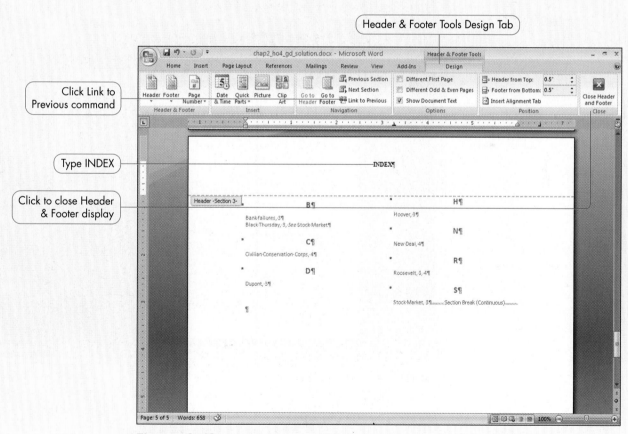

Figure 2.40 Complete the Index

TIP Check the Index Entries

Every entry in the index should begin with an uppercase letter. If this is not the case, it is because the origin entry within the body of the document was marked improperly. Click **Show/Hide ¶** in the Paragraph group on the Home tab to display the indexed entries within the document, which appear within brackets; e.g., {XE "Practice Files"}. Change each entry to begin with an uppercase letter as necessary.

Step 6
View the Completed Document

Refer to Figure 2.41 as you complete Step 6.

a. Click **Zoom** on the status bar. Click **Many pages** and drag to display 2 x 3. Click **OK**.

The completed document is shown in Figure 2.41. The index appears by itself on the last page of the document.

b. Save and close the *chap2_ho4_gd_solution* document.

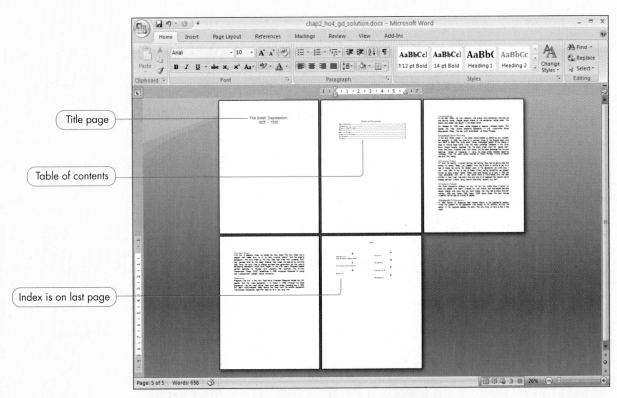

Figure 2.41 The Completed Document

Summary

1. **Apply font attributes through the Font dialog box.** Formatting occurs at the character, paragraph, or section level. The Font dialog box allows you to change spacing of the characters and also provides special formatting options for text that only appears on the screen. Through this dialog box, you can change the font and character spacing attributes including font, font size, font color, underline color, and effects. Use the character spacing options to control horizontal spacing between letters. You also can adjust the scale, position, and kerning of characters.

2. **Highlight text.** The Text Highlight Color command provides the ability to color text on screen so it stands out or resembles highlighting marks you often make in books. The Text Highlight Color command is located on the Home tab and also on the Mini toolbar that appears when you select text.

3. **Control word-wrapping with nonbreaking hyphens and nonbreaking spaces.** Occasionally, text wraps in an undesirable location in your document, or you just want to keep words together for better readability. To keep hyphenated words together on one line, use a nonbreaking hyphen to replace the regular hyphen. You insert a nonbreaking hyphen by pressing Ctrl+Shift+Hyphen in place of a hypen. You also can keep words together on one line by inserting a nonbreaking space instead of using the spacebar. To insert a nonbreaking space, click Ctrl+Shift+Spacebar.

4. **Copy formats with the Format Painter.** Use the Format Painter to copy existing format features to other text for consistency in appearance. The Format Painter uses fewer clicks than formatting from scratch. You can use it one time by single-clicking Format Painter in the Clipboard group on the Home tab, then selecting the text to format. If you double-click Format Painter, it toggles on and you can select many items to format the text. To toggle off the Format Painter, press Esc or click Format Painter again.

5. **Set off paragraphs with tabs, borders, lists, and columns.** You can change the appearance and add interest to documents by using paragraph formatting options. Tabs allow you to set markers in the document to use for aligning text. Borders and shading are set at the character or paragraph level and enable you to use boxes and/or shading to highlight an area of your document. A bulleted or numbered list helps to organize information by emphasizing and/or ordering important topics. Columns add interest to a document by formatting text into side-by-side vertical blocks of text and are implemented at the section level.

6. **Apply paragraph formats.** You can use additional formatting options in the Paragraph dialog box. Paragraph alignment refers to the placement of text between the left and right margins; text can be aligned left, right, centered between, or justified, which allows it to touch both margins. Another option that incorporates the distance from margins is indention. You can specify indention from the left margin, right margin, or both, or use special indents such as hanging or first-line. Line spacing determines the space between lines in a document and can be customized as single, double, or 1.5, for example. You also can specify an amount of space to insert before or after a paragraph, which is more efficient than pressing Enter. Widow/Orphan control prevents a single line from displaying at the top or bottom of a page, separate from the rest of a paragraph.

7. **Create and modify styles.** A style is a set of formatting instructions that has been saved under a distinct name. Styles are created at the character or paragraph level and provide a consistent appearance to similar elements throughout a document. You can modify any existing style to change the formatting of all text defined by that style. You can even create a new style for use in the current or any other document. Styles provide the foundation to use other tools such as outlines and the table of contents. The Outline view displays a condensed view of a document based on styles within the document. Text may be collapsed or expanded as necessary to facilitate moving text within long documents. The Outline view does not display a conventional outline, which is created in Print Layout view using the Multilevel List command on the Home tab.

8. **Create a table of contents.** A table of contents lists headings in the order they appear in a document with their respective page numbers. Word can create it automatically, provided the built-in heading styles were applied previously to the items for inclusion.

9. **Create an index.** Word also will create an index automatically, provided that the entries for the index have been marked previously. This result, in turn, requires you to go through a document, select the appropriate text, and mark the entries accordingly.

Key Terms

Multiple Choice

1. Which of the following can be stored within a paragraph style?
   (a) Tabs and indents
   (b) Line spacing and alignment
   (c) Shading and borders
   (d) All of the above

2. What is the easiest way to change the alignment of five paragraphs scattered throughout a document, each of which is formatted with the same style?
   (a) Select the paragraphs individually, then click the appropriate alignment button.
   (b) Select the paragraphs at the same time, then click the appropriate alignment button on the Home tab.
   (c) Change the format of the existing style, which changes the paragraphs.
   (d) Retype the paragraphs according to the new specifications.

3. Which feature analyzes a document and formats it for you?
   (a) Character styles
   (b) AutoFormat
   (c) Multilevel list
   (d) Table of contents

4. Which of the following is used to create a conventional outline?
   (a) A Numbered list
   (b) The Outline view
   (c) A table of contents
   (d) An index

5. A(n) _____ occurs when the first line of a paragraph is isolated at the bottom of a page and the rest of the paragraph continues on the next page.
   (a) widow
   (b) section break
   (c) footer
   (d) orphan

6. What is the keyboard shortcut to mark an index entry?
   (a) Index entries cannot be marked manually.
   (b) Press Ctrl+Enter
   (c) Ctrl+I
   (d) Alt+Shift+X

7. Which of the following is true regarding the formatting within a document?
   (a) Line spacing and alignment are implemented at the section level.
   (b) Margins, headers, and footers are implemented at the paragraph level.
   (c) Nonbreaking hyphens are implemented at the paragraph level.
   (d) Columns are implemented at the section level.

8. Which tab contains the Table of Contents and Index features?
   (a) Home
   (b) Insert
   (c) View
   (d) References

9. After you create and insert a table of contents into a document,
   (a) any subsequent page changes arising from the insertion or deletion of text to existing paragraphs must be entered manually.
   (b) any additions to the entries in the table arising due to the insertion of new paragraphs defined by a heading style must be entered manually.
   (c) an index can not be added to the document.
   (d) you can right-click, then select Update Field to update the table of contents.

10. Which of the following is a false statement about the Outline view?
    (a) It can be collapsed to display only headings.
    (b) It can be expanded to show the entire document.
    (c) It requires the application of styles.
    (d) It is used to create a conventional outline.

11. What is the best way to create a conventional outline in a Word document?
    (a) Use the Outline view.
    (b) Use the Mulitlevel List command in the Paragraph group in Print Layout view.
    (c) Use the Outlining toolbar.
    (d) All of the above are equally acceptable.

12. Which of the following is not a predefined Word style that is available in every document?

    (a) Normal

    (b) Heading 1

    (c) Body Text

    (d) Special 1

13. What happens if you modify the Body Text style in a Word document?

    (a) Only the paragraph where the insertion point is located is changed.

    (b) All paragraphs in the document will be changed.

    (c) Only those paragraphs formatted with the Body Text style will be changed.

    (d) It is not possible to change a Word default style such as Body Text.

14. Which of the following are not set at the paragraph level?

    (a) Alignment

    (b) Tabs and indents

    (c) Line spacing

    (d) Columns

15. Which of the following is a true statement regarding indents?

    (a) Indents are measured from the edge of the page.

    (b) The left, right, and first line indents must be set to the same value.

    (c) The insertion point can be anywhere in the paragraph when indents are set.

    (d) Indents must be set within the Paragraph dialog box.

16. The default tab stops are set to:

    (a) Left indents every ½".

    (b) Left indents every ¼".

    (c) Right indents every ½".

    (d) Right indents every ¼".

17. The spacing in an existing multipage document is changed from single spacing to double spacing throughout the document. What can you say about the number of hard and soft page breaks before and after the formatting change?

    (a) The number of soft page breaks is the same, but the number and/or position of the hard page breaks is different.

    (b) The number of hard page breaks is the same, but the number and/or position of the soft page breaks is different.

    (c) The number and position of both hard and soft page breaks is the same.

    (d) The number and position of both hard and soft page breaks is different.

18. Which of the following is not a valid use of the Format Painter?

    (a) View formatting codes assigned to a paragraph.

    (b) Copy the font style of a paragraph heading to other paragraph headings.

    (c) Restore character style to a paragraph (whose style was deleted accidentally) using the style from a properly formatted paragraph.

    (d) Copy the format of a paragraph that includes a hanging indent to a paragraph formatted in the Normal style.

19. If you want to be sure the phone number 555-1234 does not word-wrap what should you do?

    (a) Use a nonbreaking hyphen in place of the hyphen.

    (b) Use expanded spacing on the whole number.

    (c) Use a nonbreaking space in place of the hyphen.

    (d) Press Ctrl+Enter before you type the phone number.

Practice Exercises

1 The Purchase of a PC

You can purchase a PC from any number of vendors, each of which offers multiple models and typically enables you to upgrade individual components. You want to remember a few important tips as you shop for your next system. We have provided a few of those tips for you, but the document is difficult to read in its current state. Follow instructions to change the formatting of this document and improve readability. Refer to Figure 2.42 as you complete this exercise.

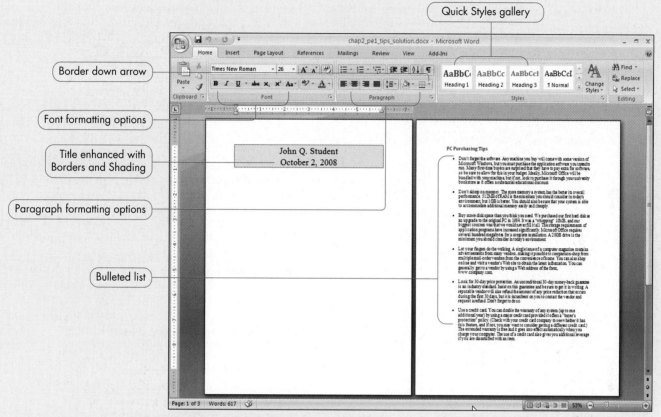

Figure 2.42 PC Purchasing Tips

a. Open the *chap2_pe1_tips* document in the Exploring Word folder and save the document as **chap2_pe1_tips_solution**.

b. Press **Ctrl+Home** to go to the beginning of the document, and then press **Ctrl+Enter** to insert a page break. Press **Ctrl+Home** to move to the beginning of the document and type your name. Press **Enter**, then type today's date. This is your title page.

c. Click the **Home tab**, select your name and date, and then click the **Borders arrow** in the Paragraph group on the Home tab. Select **Borders and Shading** to open the dialog box.

d. In the Borders tab, select **Box** in the *Setting* section. Click the **Color drop-down arrow** and select **Accent 4**, which is purple. Click the **Width drop-down arrow** and select 2¼.

e. Click the **Shading tab**. Click the **Fill drop-down arrow**, then select **Purple, Accent 4** (a shade of purple). Click **OK** to close the Borders and Shading dialog box.

f. Select your name again, if necessary, click the **Font size arrow** in the Font group on the Home tab, and select **26**. Click **Center** in the Paragraph group on the Home tab. Click the **Styles Dialog Box Launcher** to display the Styles Pane, then scroll to find the format applied to your name. Move your mouse over the style, then click the down arrow and select **Modify** to display the Modify Style dialog box. Type **PCTitle** in the Name box, then click **OK**.

g. Select the date, then click **PCTitle** in the Styles pane to apply the style to the second line of your title page. Close the Styles pane.

...continued on Next Page

h. The second page of the document contains various tips that we provide, but it is up to you to complete the formatting. Select the title *PC Purchasing Tips* at the top of this page. Click **Heading 1** in the Quick Styles gallery on the Home tab to format this title.

i. To create a bulleted list for the tips on this page, select all remaining text that has not been formatted, then click the **Bullets arrow** in the Paragraph group on the Home tab. Select a round black circle from the bullet Style gallery.

j. The bullets help differentiate each point, but they are still spaced pretty close together. To make the document easier to read, click the **Paragraph Dialog Box Launcher**, and then click the **After spin box up arrow** until **12 pt** displays. Click the **Don't add space between paragraphs of the same style** check box.

k. One paragraph splits between two pages. To eliminate that split, click the **Line and Page Breaks tab** in the Paragraph dialog box, and then click the **Keep lines together check box**. Click **OK**.

l. Compare your document to Figure 2.42. Save and close the document.

2 Creating a List of Job Descriptions

You work for a major book publisher, and your supervisor asked you to prepare a document that lists key personnel and their job descriptions. This information sheet will be sent to each author on the Microsoft Office 2007 team, so they will know who is responsible for different aspects of the publication process. Refer to Figure 2.43 as you complete this exercise.

Office 2007 Series

Publisher Contact	Job Description
Rachel Starkey	**Executive Editor**: Coordinate all books in the Office 2007 series. Contact potential authors and issue contracts to final authors. Work with all publishing personnel. Determine budgets, sales forecasts, etc.
Marilyn Kay	**Developmental Editor**: Work with author to organize topics for a final TOC. Review incoming chapters and provide suggestions for organization, content, and structure. Ensure that author correctly formats the manuscript according to series specifications.
Scott Umpir	**Project Manager**: Coordinate the publishing process with the authors, developmental editors, technical editors, copy editors, and production team members.
Brittany Shaymonu	**Technical Editor**: Review first-draft of manuscript to ensure technical accuracy of the step-by-step lessons. Make notes of any missing or extra steps. Point out inconsistencies with menu names, options, etc., including capitalization. Make other notes from a student's perspective.
Darleen Terry	**Copy Editor**: Proofread manuscript and correct errors in spelling, grammar, punctuation, wording, etc. Use the tracking feature in Word to make the online edits.

Figure 2.43 Publisher Job Descriptions

a. Click the **Office Button**, click **New**, and then double-click **Blank document** to open a new document. Save as **chap2_pe2_personnel_solution**.

b. Click the **Page Layout tab**, click **Margins** in the Page Setup group, and then click **Custom Margins** to display the Page Setup dialog box. Click the **Top margin spin box up arrow** until **2** displays, and then click **OK**.

...continued on Next Page

c. Type the title shown in Figure 2.43. Press **Enter** three times to triple-space after the title. Select the title, and then on the Mini Toolbar click **Center**, click the **Font arrow** and select **Arial,** click the **Font Size arrow** and select **16**, and click **Bold**.

d. Click the **Font Dialog Box Launcher** on the Home tab and select the **Character Spacing tab**. Click the **Spacing drop-down arrow** and select **Expanded**. Click **OK**. Click on one of the blank lines below the title to deselect it.

e. Click the **View tab** and click the **Ruler check box**, if necessary. The ruler should display at the top of your page.

f. Click on the **2"** mark on the ruler to insert a Left tab. The Left tab mark displays on the ruler.

g. Click the **Home tab**. Click the **Paragraph Dialog Box Launcher**. Click the **Special drop-down arrow** in the *Indention* section and select **Hanging**. Click in the **After text box** in the Spacing section and type **12**. Click **OK**.

h. Type the column heading **Publisher Contact**. Press **Tab** and type the column heading **Job Description**. Press **Enter** to begin on the next line. Select the column headings and on the Mini toolbar, click **Bold**. Finish typing the rest of the columnar text, as shown in Figure 2.43; notice the 12-point After paragraph spacing creates the equivalent of one blank line between rows.

i. Select the first job description, *Executive Editor*, and click **Underline** in the Font group on the Home tab. Double-click **Format Painter** in the Clipboard group on the Home tab, then select the remaining job descriptions to apply the Underline format to each job. After you format the last job description, press **Esc** to turn off the Format Painter.

j. Select the name of each person and apply bold formatting. Save and close the *chap2_pe2_personnel_solution* document.

3 Creating and Updating a Table of Contents and an Index

You have received an ISO 9000 document that lists standards for quality management and assurance and is used by international manufacturing and service organizations. You need to distribute the standards to your employees. It is a multipage document that does not contain a table of contents or index for easy reference. You decide to add each before making copies. After creating the table of contents, you decide only two levels of headings are necessary, so you update it to reflect your changes. After adding the index, you decide to make it more detailed, so you edit and update it as well. Refer to Figure 2.44 as you complete this exercise.

a. Open the *chap2_pe3_iso* document and save it as **chap2_pe3_iso_solution**.

b. Place the insertion point at the end of *ISO 9000* at the top of the first page and press **Ctrl+Enter** to create a hard page break. The page break creates a page for the table of contents.

c. Click the **References tab**, click **Table of Contents** in the Table of Contents group, and then select **Contents Table** from the gallery. Select **Update Entire Table** if the Update Table of Contents dialog box appears.

d. Click to place the insertion point on the left of the heading *I. Introduction* and press **Ctrl+Enter** to create a hard page break.

e. Click one time anywhere in the table of contents to select it, click **Table of Contents** on the References tab, and then click **Insert Table of Contents Field**. Click the **Show Levels spin box down arrow** until **2** displays. Click **OK**, and then click **OK** again at the prompt asking to replace the selected table of contents.

f. Before you insert the index, you must mark several words as entries. Locate, then select the word *quality* in the *Quality Policy* paragraph, and then press **Alt+Shift+X** to display the Mark Index Entry dialog box. Click **Mark** to create the index entry.

g. Locate and select the following words, and then click **Mark** for each one, just as you did in the previous step:

authority	In heading *Responsibility and authority*
procedures	In heading *Quality System Procedures*
supplier	First sentence under heading *Quality System Procedures*
testing	In heading *Inspection and Testing*

...continued on Next Page

h. Press **Ctrl+End** to go to the end of the document. Press **Ctrl+Enter** to insert a new page where you will display the index. Click **Insert Index** from the Index group on the References tab, and then click **OK** to create the Index.

i. You decide your index is incomplete and should include more words. Locate and select the words below. Remember to press **Alt+Shift+X** to display the Mark Index Entry dialog box and click **Mark** to create the index entry.

data control   In heading *Document and Data Control*

training   In heading *Training*

records   In heading *Control of Quality Records*

j. Close the Mark Index Entry dialog box. Position the insertion point anywhere in the index and click **Update index** in the Index group on the References tab. Your additional entries will display in the updated index.

k. Select all entries, then click **Change Case** in the Font group on the Home tab. Select **lowercase** to change the case of all entries.

l. Position the insertion point left of the section break that precedes the first index entry heading and press **Enter** two times. Move the insertion point up to the first empty line and type **INDEX**, and then select it and click **Heading 1** in the Quick Styles gallery on the Home tab.

m. Save the document and compare your results to Figure 2.44.

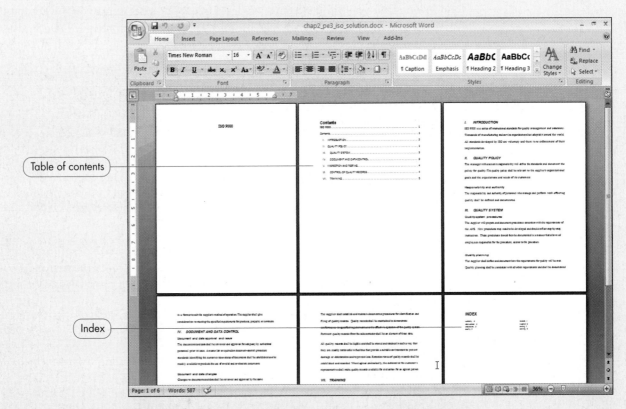

Figure 2.44 Report Including Table of Contents and Index

4 Editing a Memo to the HR Director

Tracey Spears is the training coordinator for a local company, and her responsibilities include tracking employees' continuing education efforts. The company urges employees to pursue educational opportunities that add experience and knowledge to their positions, including taking any certification exams that enhance their credentials. The human resources director has asked Ms. Spears to provide him with a list of employees who have met minimum qualifications to take an upcoming certification exam. In its present state, the memo prints on two pages; you will

...continued on Next Page

format the memo using columns in order to save paper and display the entire list on one page. Refer to Figure 2.45 as you complete this exercise.

a. Open the *chap2_pe4_training* document and save it as **chap2_pe4_training_solution**.

b. Select the word *MEMO*, click **Heading 1** in the Quick Styles gallery on the Home tab, and then click **Center** in the Paragraph group on the Home tab.

c. Several employees have a work conflict and will be unable to sit for the certification exam in October. To specify the people who fall into that category scroll over *Alana Bell* to select her name, and then on the Mini toolbar click **Text Highlight Color** or click **Text Highlight Color** in the Font group on the Home tab. Repeat this process for *Amy Kay Lynn*, *Piau Shing*, and *Ryan Stubbs*.

d. Employees can opt out of the exam for personal reasons, and we need to specify those as well. Hold down **Ctrl** and select the following employees: *Simon Anderson*, *Randall Larsen*, and *Winnifred Roark*. Click the **Font Dialog Box Launcher**, and then click the **Strikethrough check box** in the *Effects* section on the Font tab; click **OK** to return to the memo.

e. Now you list the employees in two columns so you can print the memo on one sheet of paper instead of two. Drag your mouse over the list of employees to select all names. Click the **Page Layout tab**, click **Columns**, and then select **Two**. The names now display in two columns, and the entire memo fits on one page, as shown in Figure 2.45.

f. Save your work and close the document.

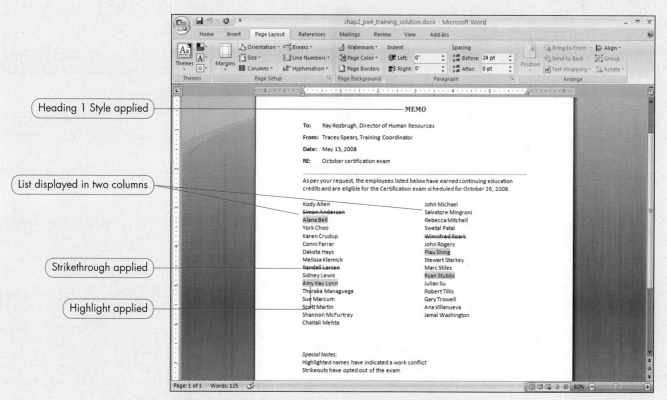

Figure 2.45 The Formatted Memo

You created a status report to inform committee members about an upcoming conference of which you are in charge. You want it to look attractive and professional, and you decide to create and apply your own styles rather than use those already available in Word. You create a paragraph style named Side Heading to format the headings, and then you create a character style named Session to format the names of the conference sessions and apply these formats to document text. You then copy these two styles to the Normal template. Eventually, you delete these two styles from the Normal template. Refer to Figure 2.46 as you complete this exercise.

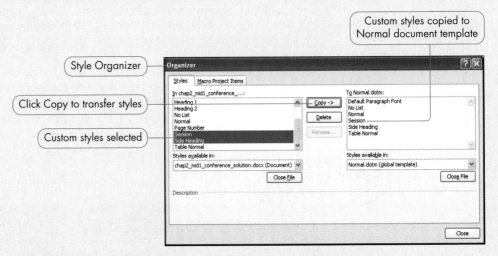

Figure 2.46 Transfer Custom Styles to the Global Template

a. Open the *chap2_mid1_conference* document and save it as **chap2_mid1_conference_solution**.

b. Create a new paragraph style named **Side Heading** using the following properties: Style based on is Normal, Style for following paragraph is Normal. Font properties are Arial, 14-pt, Bold, Red, Accent 2, Darker 50% font color.

c. Set the following paragraph formats: 12-point Before paragraph spacing, 6-point After paragraph spacing.

d. Apply the Side Heading style to the three headings *The Committee, Training Sessions,* and *Training Goal*.

e. Create a new character style named **Session** using the following specifications: Bold and Red, Accent 2, Darker 50% font color.

f. In the bulleted list, apply the Session style to the following: *Word, Web Page Development, Multimedia,* and *Presentations Graphics*.

g. Open the **Manage Styles** dialog box, then click **Import/Export**. In the Organizer dialog box, copy the **Side Heading** and **Session** styles from the **chap2_mid1_conference_solution.docx** list to the **Normal.dotm** list, as shown in Figure 2.46. Close the Organizer dialog box.

h. Save and close *chap2_mid1_conference_solution*.

i. Open a new document. Display the Styles pane, if necessary, then verify that the Session and Side Heading styles are listed. This step proves that you copied the two styles to the Normal template so that they are available for all new documents.

j. Open the **Manage Styles** dialog box, then click the **Import/Export button**. In the Organizer dialog box, delete the two styles from the **In Normal.dotm** list. Click **Yes to All** when prompted. Close the Organizer dialog box.

k. Close the blank document without saving it.

...continued on Next Page

2 Tips for Healthy Living

As a student in the Physician Assistant program at a local university you create a document containing tips for healthier living. The facts have been typed into a Word 2007 document but are thus far unformatted. You will modify it to incorporate styles and add readability as you follow the steps below. Refer to Figure 2.47 as you complete this exercise.

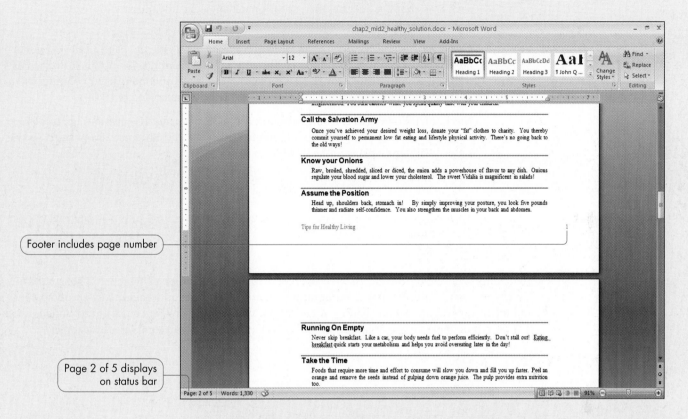

Footer includes page number

Page 2 of 5 displays on status bar

a. Open the *chap2_mid2_healthy* document and save it as **chap2_mid2_healthy_solution**.

b. Apply the **Heading 1** and **Body Text** styles throughout the document. The Format Painter is a useful tool to copy formats.

c. Change the specifications for the *Body Text* and *Heading 1* styles so that your document matches the document in Figure 2.47. The Heading 1 style is 12-point Arial bold with a blue top border. The Body Text style is 10-point Times New Roman, justified, ¼" left indent, and 12-point spacing After.

d. Create a title page for the document consisting of the title, *Tips for Healthy Living*, and an additional line of text that indicates the document was prepared by you. Format the title page content using a custom style named after yourself. The custom style should contain 28-point Times New Roman font that is bold, centered, and colored in Dark Blue, Text 2 (a blue color).

e. Create a footer for the document consisting of the title, **Tips for Healthy Living**, and a page number. (You can see the footer in Figure 2.47.) The footer should not appear on the title page; that is, page 1 is actually the second page of the document. Look closely at the status bar in Figure 2.47 and you will see that you are on page 1, but that this is the second page of a five-page document.

f. Click Outline View, collapse the text, and view the headings only.

g. Save and close the document.

...continued on Next Page

3 Enhance the Healthy Living Document

Your modifications to the Healthy Living document in the last exercise set it up nicely for the next step in creating a comprehensive document that includes a table of contents and index.

a. Open the *chap2_mid2_healthy_solution* document you created in the last exercise and save it as **chap2_mid3_healthy_solution**. Change the document view to Print Layout so the whole document displays.

b. Create a page specifically for the table of contents, then give the page a title and generate a table of contents using the Healthy Living tip headings. Do not include the custom styles you created for the Title page in the table of contents. You should use a dashed leader to connect the headings to the page numbers in the table.

c. Mark the following text for inclusion in the index: *diet, exercise, metabolism, vegetables, fat*. At the end of your document, create the index and take necessary steps so the index heading displays in the table of contents.

d. Save and close the document.

4 Editing a Welcome Letter

You composed a letter to welcome new members to an organization of which you are president. Now, you need to apply various paragraph formatting, such as alignment, paragraph spacing, and a paragraph border and shading. In addition, you want to create a customized bulleted list that describes plans for the organization. Refer to Figure 2.48 as you complete this exercise.

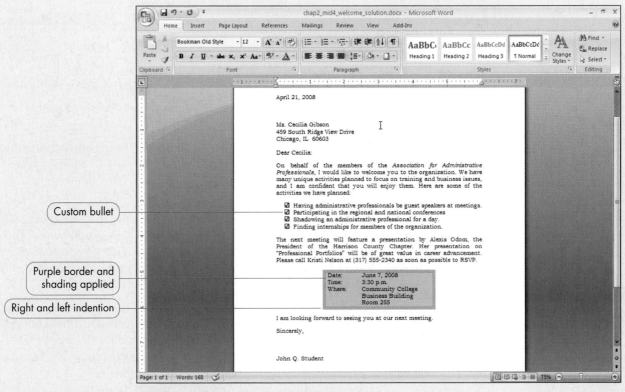

Figure 2.48 Formatted Welcome Letter

...continued on Next Page

a. Open the *chap2_mid4_welcome* document and save it as **chap2_mid4_welcome_solution**. Change Ken's name to your name in the signature block.

b. Apply Justified alignment to the entire document. Delete the asterisk (*) and create a customized bulleted list, selecting a picture bullet of your choice. Type the following items in the bulleted list:

Having administrative professionals be guest speakers at meetings.
Participating in the regional and national conferences.
Shadowing an administrative professional for a day.
Finding internships for members of the organization.

c. Select text from the salutation, *Dear Cecilia*, through the last paragraph that ends with *next meeting*. Set 12-point spacing After paragraph.

d. Select the italicized lines of text and remove the italics. For these lines of text, set 1.5" left and right indents and 0.0-point spacing After paragraph. Apply a triple-line border, Purple, Accent 4 border color, ¾ pt border width, and Purple, Accent 4, Lighter 60% shading color.

e. Click on the line containing the text *Room 255* and set 12-point spacing After paragraph.

f. Select the entire document, and then change the Font to 12-point Bookman Old Style.

g. If needed, delete an extra tab formatting mark to the left of *Community College* to prevent it from word-wrapping. Compare your work to Figure 2.48.

h. Save and close the document.

Capstone Exercise

In this project, you work with a document prepared for managers involved in the hiring process. This report analyzes the validity of the interview process and suggests that selection doesn't depend only on quality information, but on the quality of the interpretation of information. The document requires formatting to enhance readability and important information; you will use skills from this chapter to format multiple levels of headings and figures. To make it easy for readers to locate topics in your document, create and use various supplemental document components such as a table of contents and index.

Adding Style

This document is ready for enhancements, and the styles feature is a good tool that allows you to add them quickly and easily.

a. Open the file *chap2_cap_interview* document and save it as **chap2_cap_interview_solution**.

b. Create a **Title_Page_1** with these formats: 22-point size, Shadow font effect, character spacing expanded by 1 point, horizontally centered, and no Widow/Orphan control. Apply this style to the first line of the title on the title page.

c. Create a paragraph style named **Title_Page_2** based on the first style you created, with these additional formats: 20-point size, custom color 66, 4, 66. Apply this style to the subtitle on the title page.

d. Replace the * at the bottom of the first page with your name. Apply the Heading 3 style to your name and the line that precedes it.

e. Apply the Body Text style to all regular paragraphs.

f. Apply the Heading 2 style to the side headings and the Heading 1 style to the main headings throughout the document.

Formatting the Paragraphs

Next, you will apply paragraph formatting to the document. These format options will further increase the readability and attractiveness of your document.

a. Select the second paragraph in the *Introduction* section and apply these formats: 0.7" left and right indent, 6-point spacing after the paragraph, boxed 1½-point border with a custom color (31, 73, 125 RGB), and custom shading color (210, 218, 229 RGB).

b. Select the second and third paragraphs in *The Unfavorable Information Effect* section and create a two-column format with a line between the columns.

c. Use Keep Lines Together controls to prevent paragraphs from being separated across pages.

d. Insert nonbreaking spaces and nonbreaking hyphens where appropriate.

e. Apply the arrow bulleted-list format for the five-item list in the *Introduction*.

f. Apply the (1) numbered-list format for the three phases in the *Pre-Interview Impressions* section.

Inserting References

To put the finishing touches on your document, you will add a table of contents and index. These additions enable the reader to quickly locate topics in your document and add a level of professionalism to your work.

a. Create a table of contents based on the styles you applied to paragraph headings; do not include the style you used for the title page.

b. Mark these words as index entries: behavior, favorable, impression, interview, interviewer, perceptions, personal interview, reference, unqualified. Add an index to the end of the document. Use the Classic index format.

c. A page number should display in the footer of the document. Use the **Accent Bar 4** format, but prevent it from displaying on the title page and start numbering on the page that contains the table of contents.

d. Save your changes and close the document.

Mini Cases

Use the rubric following the case as a guide to evaluate your work, but keep in mind that your instructor may impose additional grading criteria or use a different standard to judge your work.

A Fundraising Letter

GENERAL CASE

Each year, you update a letter to several community partners soliciting support for an auction. The auction raises funds for your organization, and your letter should impress your supporters by using several formatting styles and options that give it a very professional look. Open the *chap2_mc1_auction* document and make necessary changes to improve the appearance. Consider the use of columns for auction items, bullets to draw attention to the list of forms, and page borders—and that is just for starters! Your finished document should be saved as **chap2_mc1_auction_solution**.

Performance Elements	Exceeds Expectations	Meets Expectations	Below Expectations
Enhanced document using the following paragraph formatting features: columns, bullets/numbering, borders/shading	Document contains at least three of the paragraph formatting features.	Document contains at least two of the paragraph formatting features.	Document contains one or none of the paragraph formatting features.
Use of character formatting features such as Font, Font Size, Font color, or other attributes from Font dialog box	Used character formatting options throughout entire document.	Used character formatting options in most sections of document.	Used character formatting options on a small portion of document.
Overall appearance of document	Used formatting tools to create a very attractive document that is easy to read.	Some formatting has been applied, but more updates are required for an attractive and readable document.	Minimal formatting has been applied, resulting in a plain and somewhat unattractive document.

The Invitation

RESEARCH CASE

Search the Internet for an upcoming local event at your school or in your community and produce the perfect invitation. You can invite people to a charity ball, a fun run, or to a fraternity party. Your laser printer and abundance of fancy fonts enable you to do anything a professional printer can do. Your finished document should be saved as **chap2_mc2_invitation_solution**.

Performance Elements	Exceeds Expectations	Meets Expectations	Below Expectations
Use of character formatting	Three or more character formats applied to text.	One or two character formats applied to text.	Does not apply character formats to text.
Use of styles	Created custom paragraph or character style.	Used at least two predefined styles.	Used one or no predefined style.
Use of paragraph formatting	Two or more paragraph format options used.	Used one paragraph format option.	Does not use paragraph format options.
Presentation	Invitation is formatted attractively; information is easy to read and understand.	Special formatting has been applied, but information is somewhat cluttered.	Invitation lists basic information with no special formatting for attractiveness.

Open the *chap2_mc3_wintips* document. The document is formatted, but it contains several errors and problems. For example, the paragraph titles are not all formatted with the same style, so they do not all display in the table of contents. You will notice most of the problems easily and you must fix them before the document can be useful. Your finished document should be saved as **chap2_mc3_wintips_solution**.

Performance Elements	Exceeds Expectations	Meets Expectations	Below Expectations
Paragraph and text formatting	Standardized style used on all paragraph text and headings.	Standardized style used on either text or headings, but not both.	Did not standardize styles on text or headings.
Table of contents	All appropriate paragraph titles are listed in the TOC.	Most paragraph titles are listed; no inappropriate titles are listed.	Some paragraph titles are not listed, and TOC contains some inappropriate titles.
Updated footer	Made all necessary updates to footer.	Made some updates to footer.	Did not update footer.

Enhancing a Document

Tables and Graphics

 bjectives

After you read this chapter, you will be able to:

1. Insert a table **(page 197)**.

2. Format a table **(page 205)**.

3. Sort and apply formulas to table data **(page 207)**.

4. Convert text to a table **(page 210)**.

5. Insert clip art and images into a document **(page 219)**.

6. Format a graphic element **(page 220)**.

7. Insert WordArt into a document **(page 225)**.

8. Insert symbols into a document **(page 226)**.

Hands-On Exercises

Exercises	Skills Covered
1. INSERT A TABLE (page 201) **Open:** Blank document **Save as:** chap3_ho1_vacation_solution.docx	• Create a Table • Insert Rows and Columns • Change Row Height and Column Width • Merge Cells to Create Header Row
2. ADVANCED TABLE FEATURES (page 212) **Open:** chap3_ho1_vacation_solution.docx (from Exercise 1) **Save as:** chap3_ho2_vacation_solution.docx (additional modifications) **Open:** chap3_ho2_expenses.docx (Step 7) **Save as:** chap3_ho2_expenses_solution.docx	• Apply a Table Style • Add Table Borders and Shading • Enter Formulas to Calculate Totals • Add a Row and Enter a Formula • Sort Data in a Table • Align Table and Data • Convert Text to a Table
3. CLIP ART, WORDART, AND SYMBOLS (page 227) **Open:** chap3_ho3_ergonomics.docx **Save as:** chap3_ho3_ergonomics_solution.docx	• Insert a Clip Art Object • Move and Resize the Clip Art Object • Create a WordArt Object • Modify the WordArt Object • Insert a Symbol

CASE STUDY

The Ozarks Science and Engineering Fair

Each spring Luanne Norgren is responsible for coordinating the Science and Engineering Fair at Southwest State University. The premier science event for the Ozarks region, it attracts middle school and high school students from 28 counties. You have been hired to serve as the assistant coordinator for the event and are responsible for communications with school administrators and faculty. You prepared an informational letter that will be sent to each school explaining the event registration procedures and project criteria. At your suggestion, Luanne

Case Study

agreed to let you develop a one-page flyer that can be mailed independently or with the informational letter. The flyer will be an attractive source of information that will encourage participation by faculty and students at the schools.

The event takes place April 4–6, 2008, on the university campus. The students who participate will be entered into either the Junior or Senior division, depending on their grade (7–9 in Junior, 10–12 in Senior). In both divisions students can enter a science project in any of the following categories: Biochemistry, Botany, Chemistry, Computer Science, Earth and Space Sciences, Engineering, Environmental Sciences, Physics, or Zoology.

Your Assignment

- Read the chapter, paying special attention to sections that describe how to insert and format tables and graphics.
- As assistant coordinator in charge of communications, you develop a flyer in Word that can be used as a quick source of information about the event. The flyer must include the date, divisions, and categories listed above, and contact information.
- You consider the use of a table, primarily as a placeholder for other information that you will add. Merge and split cells as necessary to create the effect you want to portray using the flyer. Use table styles to enhance color and readability of data in the table. Use borders and shading where appropriate or to supplement any table style you use.
- Insert clip art or other science-oriented graphics to add emphasis and excitement to the flyer. Use graphic formatting tools as needed to enhance colors, change styles, and compress the graphics.
- Use WordArt to create an exciting heading and in any other place it can be used to enhance the flyer.
- Add a "For more information" section to the flyer and list your contact information, Phone: (555) 111-2222 and e-mail: yourname@swsu.edu.
- Save the document as **chap3_case_science_solution**.

Tables

A **table** is a series of columns and rows that organize data.

A **cell** is the intersection of a column and row in a table.

A *table* is a series of columns and rows that organize data effectively. The columns and rows in a table intersect to form *cells*. The table feature is one of the most powerful in Word and is an easy way to organize a series of data in a columnar list format such as employee names, inventory lists, and e-mail addresses. The Vacation Planner in Figure 3.1, for example, is actually a 4x9 table (4 columns and 9 rows). The completed table looks impressive, but it is very easy to create once you understand how a table works. In addition to the organizational benefits, tables make an excellent alignment tool. For example, you can create tables to organize data such as employee lists with phone numbers and e-mail addresses. The Exploring series uses tables to provide descriptions for various software commands. Although you can align text with tabs, you have more format control when you create a table. (See the Practice Exercises at the end of the chapter for other examples.)

> The table feature is one of the most powerful in Word and is the basis for an almost limitless variety of documents. It is very easy to create once you understand how a table works.

Vacation Planner			
Item	Number of Days	Amount per Day (est)	Total Amount
Airline Ticket			449.00
Amusement Park Tickets	4	50.00	200.00
Hotel	5	120.00	600.00
Meals	6	50.00	300.00
Rental Car	5	30.00	150.00
Souvenirs	5	20.00	100.00
TOTAL EXPECTED EXPENSES			$1799.00

In this section, you insert a table in a document. After inserting the table, you can insert or delete columns and rows if you need to change the structure. Furthermore, you learn how to merge and split cells within the table. Finally, you change the row height and column width to accommodate data in the table.

Inserting a Table

You can create a table from the Insert tab. Click Table in the Tables group on the Insert tab to see a gallery of cells from which you select the number of columns and rows you require in the table, or you can choose the Insert Table command below the gallery to display the Insert Table dialog box and enter the table composition you prefer. When you select the table dimension from the gallery or from the Insert Table dialog box, Word creates a table structure with the number of columns and rows you specify. After you define a table, you can enter text, numbers, or graphics in individual cells. Text wraps as it is entered within a cell so that you can add or delete text without affecting the entries in other cells.

You format the contents of an individual cell the same way you format an ordinary paragraph; that is, you change the font, apply boldface or italic, change the text alignment, or apply any other formatting command. You can select multiple cells and apply the formatting to all selected cells at once, or you can format a cell independently of every other cell.

After you insert a table in your document, use commands in the Table Tools Design and Layout tabs to modify and enhance it. Place the insertion point anywhere in the table, then click either the Design or Layout tab to view the commands. In either tab, just point to a command and a ScreenTip describes its function.

TIP Tabs and Tables

The Tab key functions differently in a table than in a regular document. Press Tab to move to the next cell in the current row or to the first cell in the next row if you are at the end of a row. Press Tab when you are in the last cell of a table to add a new blank row to the bottom of the table. Press Shift+Tab to move to the previous cell in the current row (or to the last cell in the previous row). You must press Ctrl+Tab to insert a regular tab character within a cell.

Insert and Delete Rows and Columns

You can change the structure of a table after it has been created. If you need more rows or columns to accommodate additional data in your table, it is easy to add or insert them using the Rows & Columns group on the Table Tools Layout tab. The Insert and Delete commands enable you to add new or delete existing rows or columns. When you add a column, you can specify if you want to insert it to the right or left of the current column. Likewise, you can specify where to place a new row— either above or below the currently selected row—based on where you need to add the new row.

You can delete complete rows and columns using the commands mentioned above, or you can delete only the data in those rows and columns using the Delete key on your keyboard. Keep in mind that when you insert or delete complete rows or columns those that remain will adjust positioning. For example, if you delete the third row of a 5x5 table, the data in the fourth and fifth rows move up and become the third and fourth rows. If you delete only the data in the third row, the cells would be blank and the fourth and fifth rows would not change at all.

Merge and Split Cells

You can use the Merge Cells command in the Merge group on the Table Tools Layout tab to join individual cells together (merge) to form a larger cell, as was done in the first and last rows of Figure 3.1. People often merge cells to enter a main title at the top of a table. Conversely, you can use the Split Cells command in the Merge group to split a single cell into multiple cells if you find you require more cells to hold data.

Change Row Height and Column Width

Row height is the vertical space from the top to the bottom of a row.

Column width is the horizontal space or length of a column.

When you create a table, Word builds evenly spaced columns. Frequently you need to change the row height or column width to fit your data. **Row height** is the vertical distance from the top to the bottom of a row. **Column width** is the horizontal space or width of a column. You might increase the column width to display a wide string of text, such as first and last name, to prevent it from wrapping in the cell. You might increase row height to better fit a header that has been enlarged for emphasis.

The table command is easy to master, and as you might have guessed, you will benefit from reviewing the available commands listed in the Design and Layout tabs as shown in the reference pages. You will use many of these commands as you create a table in the hands-on exercises.

Table Tools Layout Ribbon | Reference

Group	Commands	Enables You to
Table	Select ▾ View Gridlines Properties *Table*	• Select particular parts of a table (entire table, column, row, or cell). • Show or hide the gridlines around the table. • Display the Table Properties dialog box to format the table.
Rows & Columns	Delete ▾ · Insert Above · Insert Below · Insert Left · Insert Right *Rows & Columns*	• Delete cells, columns, rows, or the entire table. • Insert rows and columns. • Display the Insert Cells dialog box.
Merge	Merge Cells Split Cells Split Table *Merge*	• Merge (join) selected cells together. • Split cells into additional cells. • Split the table into two tables.
Cell Size	0.22" 6.15" AutoFit ▾ *Cell Size*	• Adjust the row height and column width. • Adjust the column width automatically based on the data in the column. • Display the Table Properties dialog box.
Alignment	Text Direction · Cell Margins *Alignment*	• Specify the combined horizontal and vertical alignment of text within a cell. • Change the text direction. • Set margins within a cell.
Data	Sort · Repeat Heading Rows · Convert to Text · Formula *Data*	• Sort data within a table. • Repeat heading rows when tables span multiple pages. • Convert tabulated text to table format. • Insert a formula in a table.

Hands-On Exercises

1 | Insert a Table

Skills covered: 1. Create a Table **2.** Insert Rows and Columns **3.** Change Row Height and Column Width **4.** Merge Cells to Create Header Row

---

Step 1
Create a Table

Refer to Figure 3.2 as you complete Step 1.

a. Start Word and press **Enter** two times in the blank document, then click the **Insert tab**.

The Insert tab contains the Table command.

b. Click **Table** in the Tables group, and then drag your mouse over the cells until you select 3 columns and 7 rows; you will see the table size, 3x7, displayed above the cells, as shown in Figure 3.2. Click the lower-right cell (where the 3rd column and the 7th row intersect) to insert the table into your document.

Word creates an empty table that contains three columns and seven rows. The default columns have identical widths, and the table spans from the left to the right margin.

c. Practice selecting various elements from the table, something that you will have to do in subsequent steps:

- To select a single cell, click inside the left grid line (the pointer changes to a black slanted arrow when you are in the proper position).
- To select a row, click outside the table to the left of the first cell in that row.
- To select a column, click just above the top of the column (the pointer changes to a small black downward pointing arrow).
- To select adjacent cells, drag the mouse over the cells.
- To select the entire table, drag the mouse over the table or click the table selection box that appears at the upper-left corner of the table.

d. Save the document as **chap3_ho1_vacation_solution**.

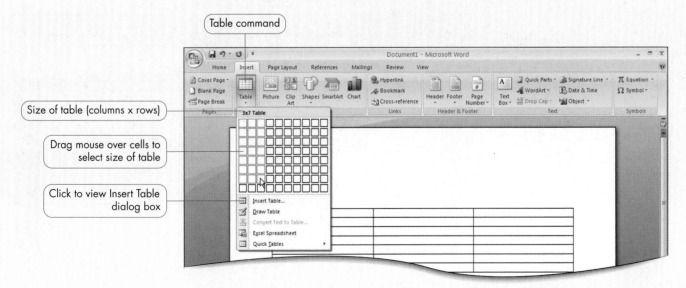

Refer to Figure 3.3 as you complete Step 2.

a. Click in the first cell of the first row and type **Vacation Planner**.

b. Click the first cell in the second row and type **Item**. Press **Tab** (or **right arrow**) to move to the next cell. Type **Number of Days**. Press **Tab** to move to the next cell, and then type **Amount per Day (est)**.

Notice you do not have enough columns to add the last heading, *Total Amount*.

c. Click anywhere in the last column of your table, then click the **Layout tab**. Click **Insert Right** in the Rows & Columns group to add a new column to your table. Click in the second row of the new column and type **Total Amount**.

You added a new column on the right side of the table. Notice that the column widths decrease to make room for the new column you just added.

TROUBLESHOOTING: If the column you insert is not in the correct location within the table, click Undo on the Quick Access Toolbar, confirm your insertion point is in the last column, and then click the appropriate Insert command.

d. Select the text *Vacation Planner* in the first row. On the Mini toolbar, click the **Font Size arrow** and click **18**, click **Bold,** and click **Center** to center the heading within the cell.

The table title stands out with the larger font size, bold, and center horizontal alignment.

e. Click outside and left of the second row to select the entire row. On the Mini toolbar, click the **Font Size arrow** and select **16,** and then click **Bold** and **Center**.

f. Enter the remaining data, as shown in Figure 3.3. When you get to the last row and find the table is too small to hold all the data, place the insertion point in the last cell (in the Total Amount column) and press **Tab** to add a row to the end of your table. Then enter the last item and amounts.

g. Save the document.

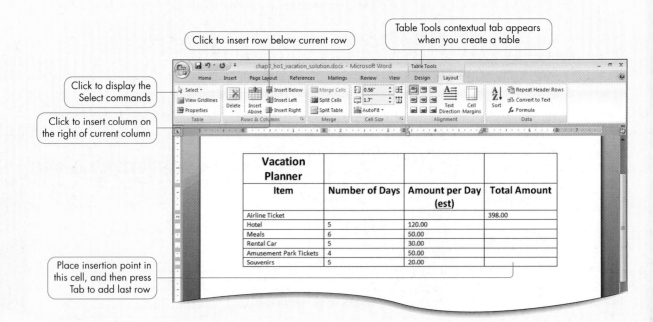

Step 3
Change Row Height and Column Width

Refer to Figure 3.4 as you complete Step 3.

a. Hold your mouse over the second column of data until the small black arrow appears, then hold down your mouse and drag to the right to select the last three columns of the table.

b. Click the **Layout tab**, then type **1.2** in the **Width** box in the Cell Size group, as shown in Figure 3.4.

You changed the width of the last three columns so that they are each 1.2" wide. They are now narrower, and the headings wrap even more in the cells.

c. Place the insertion point anywhere in the cell containing the text *Airline Ticket*, then click **Select** in the Table group on the Layout tab. Click **Select Row**, then hold down **Shift** and press the **down arrow** on your keyboard five times to select the remaining rows in the table. Click the **Height spin arrow** in the Cell Size group on the Layout tab to display 0.3".

You changed the height of some of the rows in the table to 0.3" tall.

d. Save the document.

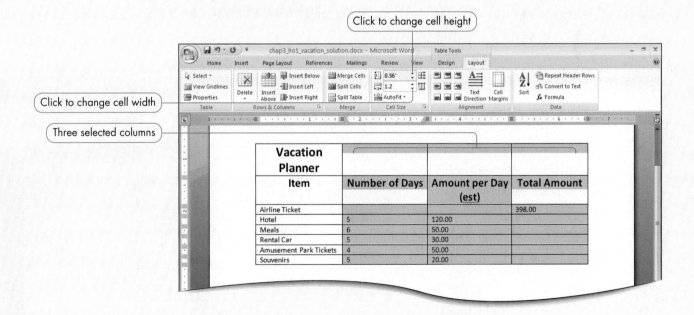

TIP Adjusting Column Width and Row Height

If you are not certain of the exact measurements needed for row height or column width, you can use the mouse to increase or decrease the size. Position the mouse pointer on the gridline that separates the rows (or columns) until the pointer changes to a two-headed arrow. The two-headed arrow indicates you can adjust the height (or width) by clicking and dragging the gridline up or down (right or left) to resize the cell.

Step 4
Merge Cells to Create Header Row

Refer to Figure 3.5 as you complete Step 4.

a. Click outside the table to the left of the first cell in the first row to select the entire first row.

b. Click **Merge Cells** in the Merge group on the Layout tab, as shown in Figure 3.5.

You merged or joined the selected cells. The first row now contains a single cell.

c. Place the insertion point anywhere in the first row, click **Select** in the Table group on the Layout tab, then choose **Select Row**. Click the **Home tab**, click the **Font Size arrow**, and select **24**. Click **Center** in the Paragraph group.

d. Click the **Layout tab**, then click the **Height spin arrow** in the Cell Size group to display **0.5"**.

After increasing the size of the cell contents, you increased the height of the cell so the text is easier to read.

e. Save the *chap3_ho1_vacation_solution* document and keep it onscreen if you plan to continue to the next hands-on exercise. Close the file and exit Word if you do not want to continue with the next exercise at this time.

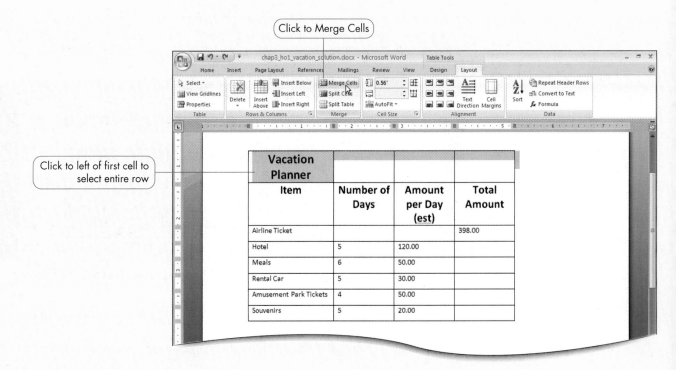

Advanced Table Features

After you create a basic table, you will want to enhance the appearance to create interest for the reader and improve readability. Microsoft Word 2007 provides many predefined styles, which contain borders, shading, font sizes, and other attributes that enhance a table.

You now have a good understanding of the table features and realize there are many uses for them in your Word documents. After you create the basic table, you want to enhance the appearance to create interest for the reader and improve readability. Microsoft Word 2007 includes many tools to assist with these efforts, and you will use several of them to complete the Vacation Planner table.

In this section, you learn how to format a table. Specifically, you apply borders and shading to table cells, apply table styles to the entire table, and select table alignment and position. In addition, you sort data within a table and insert formulas to perform calculations. Finally, you convert text to a table format.

Formatting a Table

You can use basic formatting options to enhance the appearance of your table. The Borders and Shading commands, for example, offer a wide variety of choices for formatting the table structure. *Shading* affects the background color within a cell or group of cells. Table shading is similar to the Highlight feature that places a color behind text. You often apply shading to the header row of a table to make it stand out from the data. *Border* refers to the line style around each cell in the table. The default is a single line, but you can choose from many styles to outline a table such as a double, triple, or a wavy line. You can even choose invisible borders if you want only data to display in your document without the outline of a table. Borders and Shading commands are located on the Design tab so you do not have to return to the Home tab to use them.

Shading affects the background color within a cell.

Border refers to the line style around each cell.

Apply Table Styles

When you do not have time to apply custom borders and shading, you will find the Table Styles feature very helpful. Microsoft Word 2007 provides many predefined *table styles* that contain borders, shading, font sizes, and other attributes that enhance readability of a table. The custom styles are available in the Table Styles group on the Design tab. To use a predefined table style, click anywhere in your table, and then click a style from the Table Styles gallery. A few styles from the gallery display, but you can select from many others by clicking the down arrow on the right side of the gallery, as shown in Figure 3.6. The Live preview of a style displays on your table when you hover your mouse over it in the gallery. To apply a style, click it one time.

A **table style** contains borders, shading, and other attributes to enhance a table.

You can modify a predefined style if you wish to make changes to features such as color or alignment. You also can create your own table style and save it for use in the current document or add it to a document template for use in other Word documents. Click More in the Table Styles group to access the Modify Table Style and New Table Style commands.

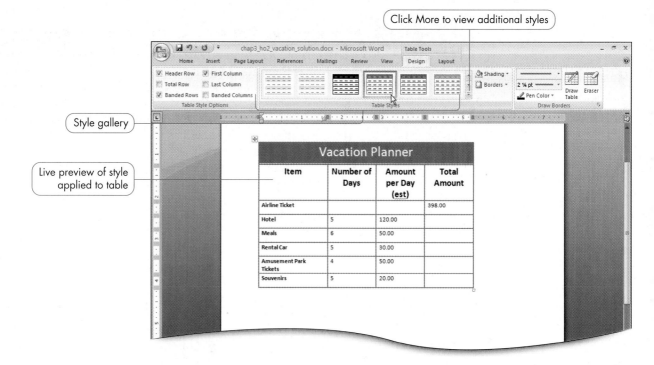

Click More to view additional styles

Style gallery

Live preview of style applied to table

Select the Table Position and Alignment

Table alignment is the position of a table between the left and right margins.

When you insert a table, Word aligns it at the left margin by default. However, you can click Properties in the Table group on the Layout tab to change the *table alignment*, the position of a table between the left and right document margins. For example, you might want to center the table between the margins or align it at the right margin.

You also can change alignment of the data in a table separately from the table itself using the Properties dialog box. The Layout tab includes the Alignment group that contains many options to quickly format table data.

Table data can be formatted to align in many different horizontal and vertical combinations. We often apply horizontal settings, such as center, to our data, but using vertical settings also increases readability. For example, when you want your data to be centered both horizontally and vertically within a cell so it is easy to read and does not appear to be elevated on the top or too close to the bottom, click Align Center in the Alignment group to apply that setting.

Text direction refers to the degree of rotation in which text displays.

The default *text direction* places text in an upright position. However, you can rotate text so it displays sideways. To change text direction, click Text Direction in the Alignment group on the Layout tab. Each time you click Text Direction, the text rotates. This is a useful tool for aligning text that is in the header row of a narrow column.

Cell margins are the amount of space between data and the cell border in a table.

The *Cell margins* command in the Alignment group on the Layout tab enables you to adjust the amount of white space inside a cell as well as spacing between cells. Use this setting to improve readability of cell contents by adjusting white space around your data or between cells if they contain large amounts of text or data. If you increase cell margins, it prevents data from looking squeezed together.

Sorting and Applying Formulas to Table Data

Because tables provide an easy way to arrange numbers within a document, it is important to know how to use table calculations. This feature gives a Word document the power of a simple spreadsheet. Additional organization of table data is possible by the use of *sorting*, or rearranging data based on a certain criteria. Figure 3.7 displays the vacation expenses you created previously, but this table illustrates two additional capabilities of the table feature—sorting and calculating.

Sorting is the process of rearranging data.

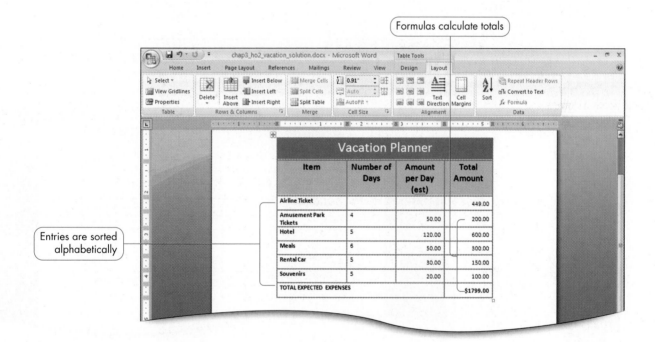

Calculate Using Table Formulas

In this table, the entries in the Total Amount column consist of formulas that were entered into the table to perform a calculation. The entries are similar to those in a spreadsheet. Thus, the rows in the table are numbered from one to nine while the columns are labeled from A to D. The row and column labels do not appear in the table, but are used in the formulas.

You know that the intersection of a row and column forms a cell. Word uses the column letter and row number of that intersection to identify the cell and to give it an address. Cell D5, for example, contains the entry to compute the total hotel expense by multiplying the number of days (in cell B5) by the amount charged per day (in cell C5). In similar fashion, the entry in cell D6 computes the total expense for meals by multiplying the values in cells B6 and C6, respectively. The formula is not entered (typed) into the cell explicitly, but is created using the Formula command in the Data group on the Layout tab.

Figure 3.8 is a slight variation of Figure 3.7 in which the field codes have been toggled on to display the formulas, as opposed to the calculated values. The cells are shaded to emphasize that these cells contain formulas (fields), as opposed to numerical values. The field codes are toggled on and off by selecting the formula and pressing Shift+F9 or by right-clicking the entry and selecting the Toggle Field Codes command.

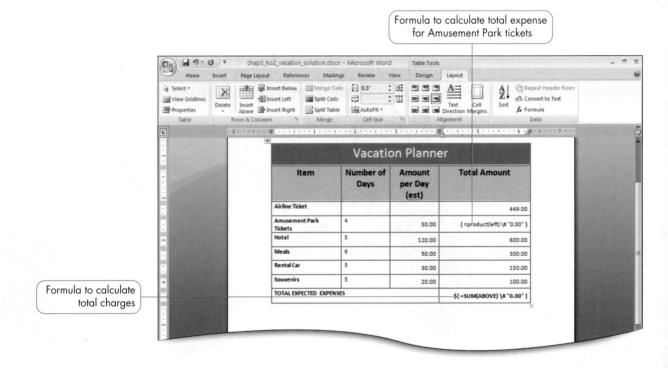

Formula to calculate total expense for Amusement Park tickets

Formula to calculate total charges

The formula in cell D9 has a different syntax and sums the value of all cells directly above it. You do not need to know the syntax because Word provides a dialog box that supplies the entry for you, but once you use it to create the formula, you will find it easy to understand. It is better to use the Formula command to calculate totals than to type a number because if you add data to the table, you can use formula tools to recalculate for you.

Sort Data in a Table

At times, you might need to sort data in a table to enhance order or understand the data. For example, when a list of employees is reviewed, a manager would prefer to view the names in alphabetical order by last name or department. You can sort data according to the entries in a specific column or row of the table. Sort orders include *ascending order*, which arranges text in alphabetical or sequential order starting with the lowest letter or number and continuing to the highest (A–Z or 0–9). Or you can sort in *descending order*, where data is arranged from highest to lowest (Z–A or 9–0).

Ascending order arranges data from lowest to highest.

Descending order arranges data from highest to lowest.

You can sort the rows in a table to display data in different sequences as shown in Figure 3.9, where the vacation items are sorted from lowest to highest expense. You also could sort the data in descending (high to low) sequence according to the Total Amount. In descending order, the hotel (largest expense) displays at the top of the list, and the souvenirs (smallest expense) appear last. The second row of the table contains the field names for each column and is not included in the sort. The next six rows contain the sorted data, while the last row displays the total for all expenses and is not included in the sort.

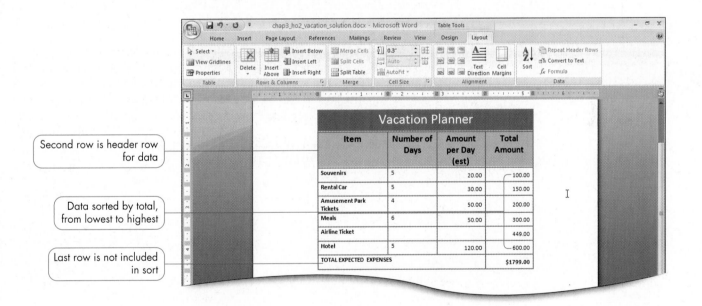

Sorting is accomplished according to the select-then-do methodology that is used for many operations in Microsoft Word. You select the rows that are to be sorted, rows three through nine in this example, and then you click Sort in the Data group on the Layout tab. The Sort dialog box displays, as shown in Figure 3.10, which enables you to select the direction and sort criteria.

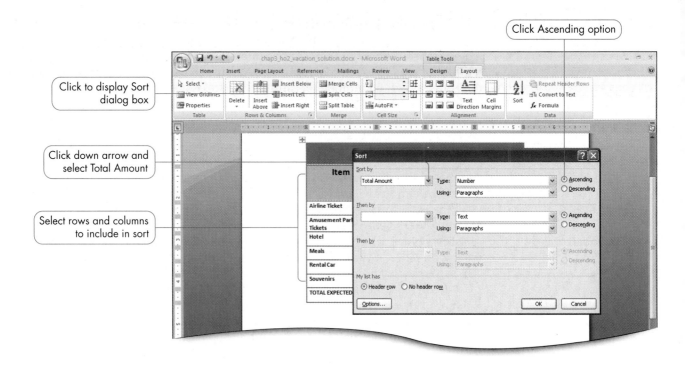

Click Ascending option

Click to display Sort dialog box

Click down arrow and select Total Amount

Select rows and columns to include in sort

Converting Text to a Table

The tables feature is outstanding. But what if you are given a lengthy list of items—for example, two items per line separated by a tab that should have been formatted as a table? The Table command on the Insert tab includes the Convert Text to Table command, and it can aid you in this transformation. After you select the text and choose this command, the Convert Text to Table dialog box displays and offers several options to assist in a quick conversion of text into a table. The command also works in reverse; you can convert a table to text. You will perform a table conversion in the next set of hands-on exercises.

Table Tools Design Ribbon | Reference

Group	Commands	Enables you to
Table Style Options	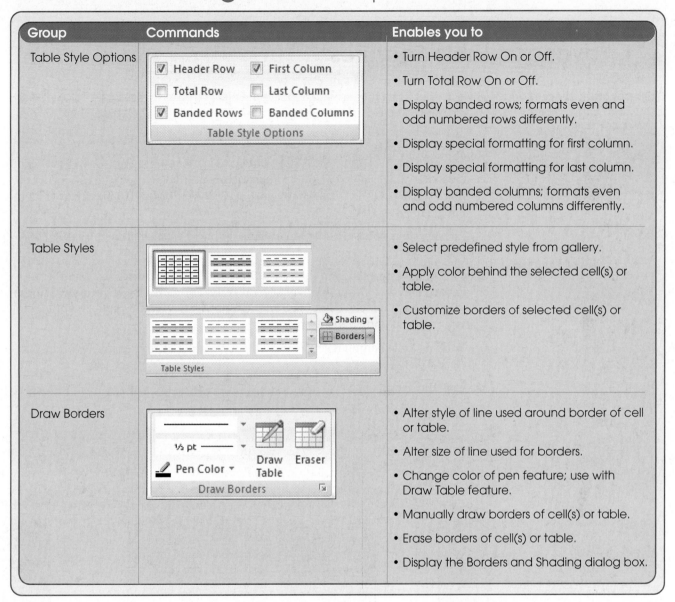	• Turn Header Row On or Off. • Turn Total Row On or Off. • Display banded rows; formats even and odd numbered rows differently. • Display special formatting for first column. • Display special formatting for last column. • Display banded columns; formats even and odd numbered columns differently.
Table Styles		• Select predefined style from gallery. • Apply color behind the selected cell(s) or table. • Customize borders of selected cell(s) or table.
Draw Borders		• Alter style of line used around border of cell or table. • Alter size of line used for borders. • Change color of pen feature; use with Draw Table feature. • Manually draw borders of cell(s) or table. • Erase borders of cell(s) or table. • Display the Borders and Shading dialog box.

Hands-On Exercises

2 | Advanced Table Features

Skills covered: 1. Apply a Table Style **2.** Add Table Borders and Shading **3.** Enter Formulas to Calculate Totals **4.** Add a Row and Enter a Formula **5.** Sort Data in a Table **6.** Align Table and Data **7.** Convert Text to a Table

---

Step 1
Apply a Table Style

Refer to Figure 3.11 as you complete Step 1.

a. Open the *chap3_ho1_vacation_solution* document if you closed it at the end of the first exercise and save it as **chap3_ho2_vacation_solution**. Then click anywhere in the table.

> The insertion point must be somewhere within the table before the Table Tools tabs display.

b. Click the **Design tab**, and then click **More** on the right side of the Table Styles gallery. Hover your mouse over several styles and notice how the table changes to preview that style. Click once on the **Light List – Accent 1** style to apply it to your table, as shown in Figure 3.11.

> Previous cell shading is replaced by the formatting attributes for the **Light List – Accent 1** style.

c. Save the document.

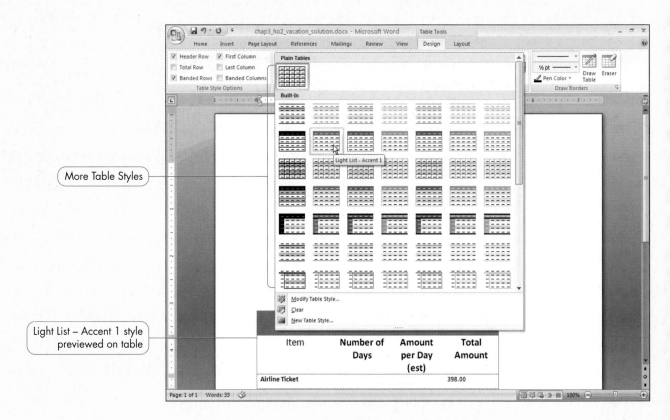

More Table Styles

Light List – Accent 1 style previewed on table

Refer to Figure 3.12 as you complete Step 2.

a. Click anywhere in the Vacation Planner table. Click the **Borders arrow** in the Table Styles group and select **Borders and Shading**.

b. Click **All** in the *Setting* section on the left side of the Borders tab. Then click the **Width drop-down arrow** and select 2¼ pt. Click **OK** to close the Borders and Shading box.

Your table has a darker blue border surrounding each cell.

c. Drag your mouse across the cells in the second row of the table to select them, then click **Shading** in the Table Styles group. Click the swatch in the fourth row of the first column named **White, Background 1, Darker 25%**, as shown in Figure 3.12.

The table now displays a large, blue title row, a gray colored header row, and blue borders around the remaining data.

d. Save the document.

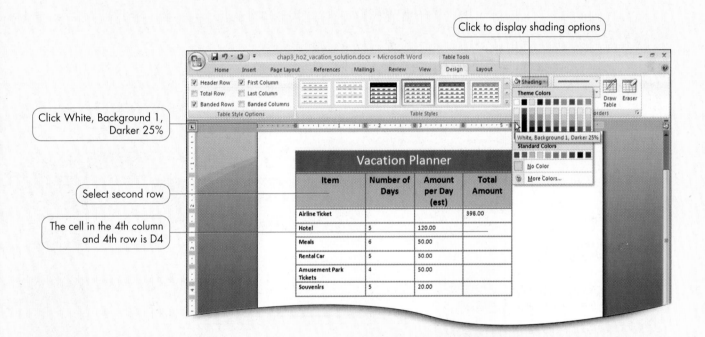

Refer to Figure 3.13 as you complete Step 3.

a. Click in **cell D4**, the cell in the fourth column and fourth row. Click the **Layout tab** and click **Formula** in the Data group to display the formula box.

b. Click and drag to select the =SUM(ABOVE) function, which is entered by default. Type **=b4*c4**, as shown in Figure 3.13, to replace the existing formula and compute the total hotel expense. Click the **Number format drop-down arrow** and select **0.00**, and then click **OK**.

The formula is not case sensitive; you can type formula references in lowercase or capital letters. The total is computed by multiplying the number of days (in cell B4) by the amount per day (in cell C4). The result, 600, displays in a number format with two decimal places because these numbers represent a monetary value in dollars and cents.

c. Click in **cell D5**, directly below the cell you edited in the last step, then click **Formula**. In the Formula box, click and drag to select SUM(ABOVE) but do not select the equal sign, then press **Delete** to remove the formula. Click the **Paste function drop-down arrow**, and then scroll and select **PRODUCT**. Type **left** between the parentheses where the insertion point is blinking in the Formula box. Click the **Number format drop-down arrow**, select **0.00**, and then click **OK**.

This formula performs the same function as the one you used in Step B, but it references cells to the left of the current cell instead of using actual cell addresses.

d. Calculate the total expenses for cells D6, D7, and D8 using either formula used in the previous steps.

e. Save the document.

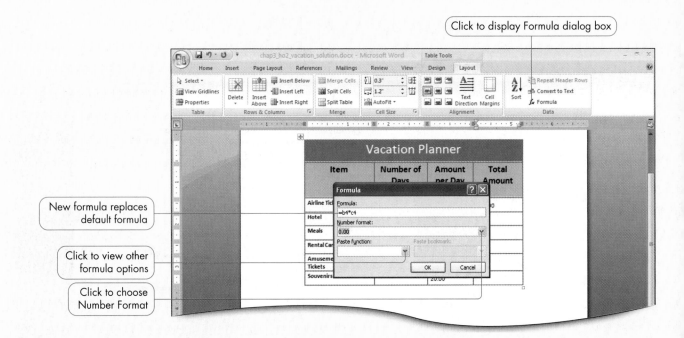

Click to display Formula dialog box

New formula replaces default formula

Click to view other formula options

Click to choose Number Format

Refer to Figure 3.14 as you complete Step 4.

a. Click the last cell in the table and press **Tab** to add another row to the table. Drag your mouse across all four cells in this row to select them, and then click **Merge Cells** in the Merge group on the Layout tab. Type the words **TOTAL EXPECTED EXPENSES** in the newly merged cell.

b. Click **Split Cells** in the Merge group to display the Split Cells dialog box. If necessary, click the **Number of columns spin box** to display **2**, then click **OK**.

The last row displays two cells of equal size. You will display the total vacation expense amount in the last cell, but you need to resize it to the same size as cells in the last column so the numbers will align correctly.

c. Hold your mouse over the border between the cells in the last row until a two-headed arrow displays. Then click and drag to the right until the border aligns with the border of the last column in the rows above, as shown in Figure 3.14.

d. Click in the last cell of the table, click **Formula**, click the **Number format drop-down arrow**, select **0.00**, and then click **OK** to accept the default formula, =SUM(ABOVE).

You should see 1748.00 (the sum of the cells in the last column) displayed in the selected cell.

e. Click the number, 1748.00, one time so that it is shaded in grey, then press **Shift+F9** to display the code {=SUM(ABOVE)\#"0.00"}. Press **Shift+F9** a second time to display the actual value.

f. Click in **cell D3** (the cell containing the airfare). Replace 398.00 with **449.00** and press **Tab** to move out of the cell.

The total expenses are not yet updated in cell D9.

g. Right-click on the number that displays in **cell D9** to display a shortcut menu, then select **Update Field**.

Cell D9 displays 1799.00, the updated total for all expenses.

h. Save the document.

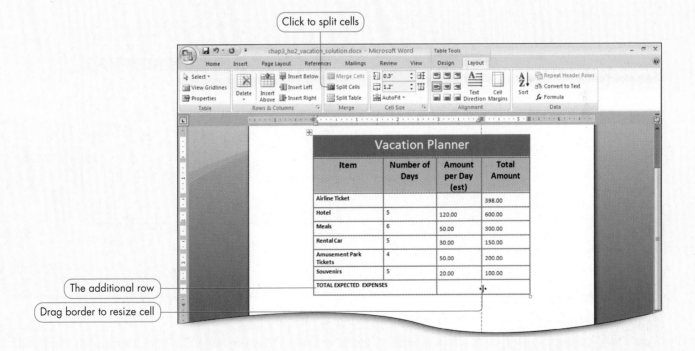

Step 5
Sort Data in a Table

Refer to Figure 3.15 as you complete Step 5.

a. Click and drag to select rows two through eight in the table. Click **Sort** in the Data group on the Layout tab.

b. Click **Header row** in the *My list has* section of the dialog box.

c. If necessary, click the **Sort by drop-down arrow** and select **Item** (the column heading for the first column). The Ascending option is selected by default, as shown in Figure 3.15. Click **OK**.

The entries in the table are rearranged alphabetically according to the entry in the Item column. The Total row remains at the bottom of the table since it was not included in the sort.

TROUBLESHOOTING: If you do not first click Header row, the headings for each column will not display in the Sort by drop-down list; instead, you will see the Column numbers listed. You can sort by Column number (1, 2, 3, or 4), but it is important to click the Header row option before you leave this dialog box so the header row is not included in the sort.

d. Select rows four through six, which have lost formatting along the left and right borders. Click the **Design tab**, click the **Borders arrow** in the Table Styles group, and then select **All Borders**.

The dark blue borders fill the left and right borders of the selected cells, matching the remainder of the table.

e. Save the document.

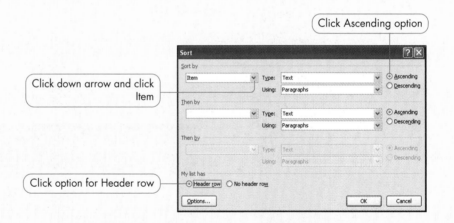

Step 6
Align Table and Data

Refer to Figure 3.16 as you complete Step 6.

a. Click the table selector to select the entire table. Click the **Layout tab**, then click **Properties** in the Table group.

b. Click the **Table tab**, if necessary, and then click **Center** in the *Alignment* section, as shown in Figure 3.16. Click **OK**.

Your table is now centered between the left and right margins.

c. Click anywhere to deselect the whole table, then drag your mouse to select the last two columns of rows three through eight. Select entries listed under Amount Per Day (est) and Total Amount, but do not select data in the header row. Click **Align Center Right** from the Alignment group. Select the last cell in the table and click **Align Center Right** to align it with other data.

Because these columns contain numerical data, you right align them to give the effect of decimal alignment. However, the numbers are not decimal aligned, so if you display an additional digit in a value, it will result in misaligned numbers.

d. Click in the last cell and insert a dollar sign ($) in front of the amount of expected expenses.

e. Save and close the *chap3_ho2_vacation_solution* document.

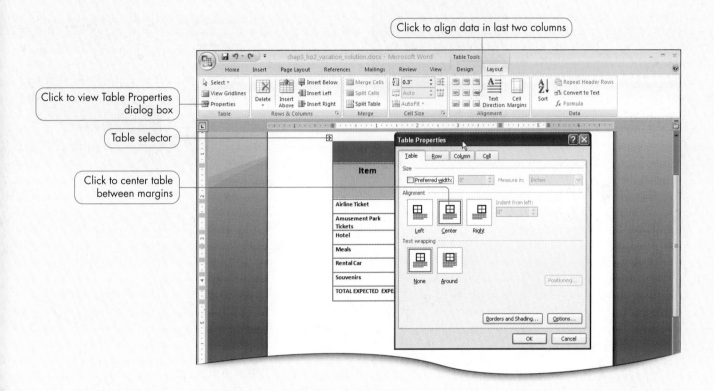

Step 7
Convert Text to a Table

Refer to Figure 3.17 as you complete Step 7.

a. Open the *chap3_ho2_expenses* document and save it as **chap3_ho2_expenses_solution**.

b. Press **Ctrl+A** to select all text in this document and then click the **Insert tab**.

c. Click **Table**, and then select **Convert Text to Table**. View the options in the Convert Text to Table dialog box, as shown in Figure 3.17, but do not make any changes at this time. Click **OK**.

The list of items display in a table that can now be sorted and formatted.

d. Save and close the *chap3_ho2_expenses_solution* document.

Click to change number of columns in table

Click to view Convert Text to Table option

Graphic Tools

One of the most exciting features of Word is its graphic capabilities. You can use clip art, images, drawings, and scanned photographs to visually enhance brochures, newsletters, announcements, and reports. **Clip art** is a graphical image, illustration, drawing, or sketch. In addition to inserting clip art in a document, you can insert photographs from a digital camera or scanner, graphically shaped text, and special boxes to hold text. After inserting a graphical image or text, you can adjust size, choose placement, and perform other graphical format options.

> One of the most exciting features of Word is its graphic capabilities. You can use clip art, images, drawings, and scanned photographs to visually enhance brochures, newsletters, announcements, and reports.

In this section, you insert clip art and an image in a document. Then you format the image by changing the height and width, applying a text-wrapping style, applying a quick style, and adjusting graphic properties. Finally, you insert WordArt and symbols in a document.

Inserting Clip Art and Images into a Document

Clip art and other graphical images or objects may be stored locally, purchased on a CD at a computer supply store, or downloaded from the Internet for inclusion into a document. Whether you use Microsoft's online clip gallery or purchase clip art, you should read the license agreements to know how you may legally use the images.

A **copyright** provides legal protection to a written or artistic work, giving the author exclusive rights to its use and reproduction, except as governed under the fair use exclusion. Anything on the Internet should be considered copyrighted unless the document specifically says it is in the public domain. The Fair Use doctrine allows you to use a portion of the work for educational, nonprofit purposes, or for the purpose of critical review or commentary. All such material should be cited through an appropriate footnote or endnote. Using clip art for a purpose not allowed by the license agreement is illegal.

Manage Clips with the Microsoft Clip Organizer

The Clip Art command displays a task pane through which you can search, select, and insert clip art, photographs, sounds, and movies (collectively called clips). The clips can come from a variety of sources. They may be installed locally in the My Collections folder, they may have been installed in conjunction with Microsoft Office in the Office Collections folder, and/or they may have been downloaded from the Web and stored in the Web Collections folder. You can insert a specific clip into a document if you know its location. You also can search for a clip that will enhance the document on which you are working.

The **Microsoft Clip Organizer** brings order out of potential chaos by cataloging the clips, photos, sounds, and movies that are available to you. You enter a keyword that describes the clip you are looking for, specify the collections that are to be searched, and indicate the type of clip(s) you are looking for. The results are returned in the task pane, as shown in Figure 3.18, which displays the clips that are described by the keyword *computer*. You can restrict the search to selected collections but request that all media types be displayed. If you also specify to search for items stored locally, the search is faster than one that searches online as well. When you see a clip that you want to use, click the clip to insert it into your document. For more options, point to the clip, click the down arrow that appears, and then select from the menu.

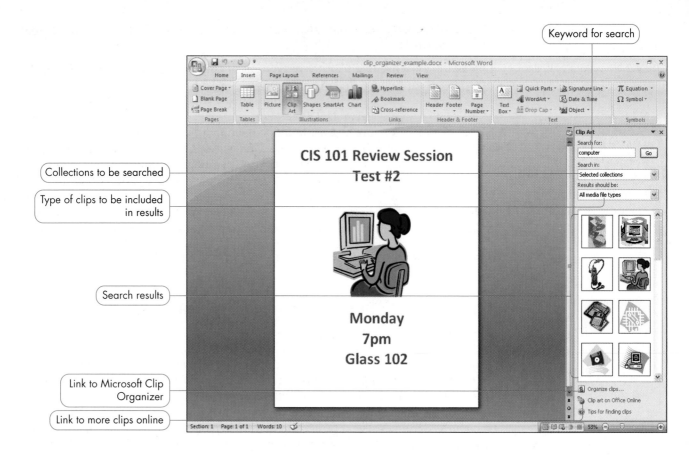

You can access the Microsoft Clip Organizer (to view the various collections) by clicking Organize clips at the bottom of the Clip Art task pane. You also can access the Clip Organizer when you are not using Word; click the Start button on the taskbar, click All Programs, Microsoft Office, Microsoft Office Tools, and Microsoft Clip Organizer. Once in the Organizer, you can search through the clips in the various collections, reorganize the existing collections, add new collections, and even add new clips (with their associated keywords) to the collections. The other links at the bottom of the task pane in Figure 3.18 provide access to additional clip art online and tips for finding more relevant clips.

Insert a Picture

In addition to the collection of clip art and pictures that you can access from Word, you also can insert your own pictures into a document. If you have a scanner or digital camera attached to your computer, you can scan or download a picture for use in Word. After you save the picture to your disk, click Picture in the Illustrations group on the Insert tab to locate and insert it in the document. The Insert Picture dialog box opens so that you can navigate to the location where the picture is saved. After you insert the picture, there are many commands you can use to format it. Those commands are discussed in the next section.

Formatting a Graphic Element

Remember that graphical elements should enhance a document, not overpower it.

When you insert an image in a document, it comes in a predefined size. For example, the clip art image in Figure 3.18 was very large and took up much space on the page before it was resized. Most times, you need to adjust an image's size so it fits within the document and does not greatly increase the document file size. Remember that graphical elements should enhance a document, not overpower it.

Adjust the Height and Width of a Graphic

Sizing handles are the small circles and squares that appear around a selected object and enable you to adjust the height and width of an object.

Word provides different tools you can use to adjust the height or width of an image, depending on how exact you want the measurements. The Picture Tools Format tab contains Height and Width commands that enable you to specify exact measurements. You can use *sizing handles*, the small circles and squares that appear around a selected object, to size an object by clicking and dragging any one of the handles. When you use the circular sizing handles in the corner of a graphic to adjust the height (or width), Word also adjusts the width (or height) simultaneously. If needed, hold down Shift while dragging the corner sizing handle to maintain the correct proportion of the image. If you use square sizing handles on the right, left, top, or bottom, you adjust that measurement without regard to any other sides.

Adjust Text Wrapping

Text wrapping style refers to the way text wraps around an image.

When you first insert an image, Word treats it as a character in the line of text, which leaves a lot of empty space on the left or right side of the image. You may want it to align differently, perhaps allowing text to display very tightly around the object or even behind the text. *Text wrapping style* refers to the way text wraps around an image. Table 3.1 describes the different wrapping options.

Table 3.1 Text Wrapping Styles

Text Wrapping Style	Description
Square	Allows text to wrap around the graphic frame that surrounds the image.
Tight	Allows text to wrap tightly around the outer edges of the image itself instead of the frame.
Through	Select this option to wrap text around the perimeter and inside any open portions of the object.
Top and Bottom	Text wraps to the top and bottom of the image frame, but no text appears on the sides.
Behind Text	Allows the image to display behind the text in such a way that the image appears to float directly behind the text and does not move if text is inserted or deleted.
In Front of Text	Allows the image to display on top of the text in such a way that the image appears to float directly on top of the text and does not move if text is inserted or deleted.
In Line with Text	Graphic displays on the line where inserted so that as you add or delete text, causing the line of text to move, the image moves with it.

Apply Picture Quick Styles

The **Picture Styles** gallery contains preformatted options that can be applied to a graphical object.

Word 2007 introduces the **Picture Styles** gallery that contains many preformatted picture formats. The gallery of styles you can apply to a picture or clip art is extensive, and you also can modify the style after you apply it. The quick styles provide a valuable resource if you want to improve the appearance of a graphic but are not familiar with graphic design and format tools. For example, after you insert a graphic, with one click you can choose a style from the Quick Styles gallery that adds a border and displays a reflection of the picture. You might want to select a style that changes the shape of your graphic to an octagon, or select a style that applies a 3-D effect to the image. To apply a quick style, select the graphical object, then choose a quick style from the Picture Styles group on the Picture Tools Format tab. Other style formatting options, such as Soft Edges or 3-D Rotation, are listed in Picture Effects on the Picture Styles group, as shown in Figure 3.19.

Adjust Graphic Properties

Crop or Cropping is the process of trimming the edges of an image or other graphical object.

Scale or scaling is the adjustment of height or width by a percentage of the image's original size.

Contrast is the difference between light and dark areas of an image.

Brightness is the ratio between lightness and darkness of an image.

After you insert a graphic or an image, you might find that you need to edit it before using a picture style. One of the most common changes includes *crop or cropping*, which is the process of trimming edges or other portions of an image or other graphical object that you do not wish to display. Cropping enables you to call attention to a specific area of a graphical element while omitting any unnecessary detail. When you add images to enhance a document, you may find clip art that has more objects than you desire or you may find an image that has damaged edges that you do not wish to appear in your document. You can solve the problems with these graphics by cropping. The cropping tool is located in the Size group on the Format tab.

Instead of cropping unused portions of a graphic, you may need to enlarge or reduce its size to fit in the desired area. The easiest method for sizing is selecting the image and dragging the selection handles. For more exact measurements, however, you could adjust the *scale or scaling*, which adjusts the height or width of an image by a percentage of its original size. The scale adjustment is located in the Size dialog box, which you display by clicking the Size Dialog Box Launcher on the Format tab.

Other common adjustments to a graphical object include contrast and/or brightness. Adjusting the *contrast* increases or decreases the difference in dark and light areas of the image. Adjusting the *brightness* lightens or darkens the overall image.

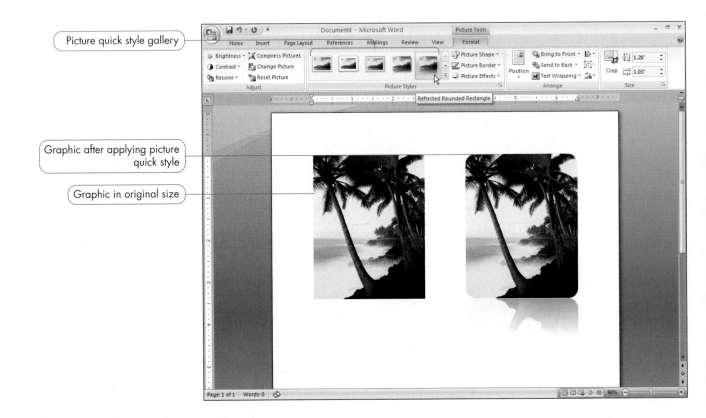

Picture quick style gallery

Graphic after applying picture quick style

Graphic in original size

These adjustments often are made on a picture taken with a digital camera in poor lighting or if a clip art image is too bright or dull to match other objects in your document. Adjusting contrast or brightness can improve the visibility of subjects in a picture. You may want to increase contrast for a dramatic effect or lower contrast to soften an image. The Brightness and Contrast adjustments are in the Picture Tools group on the Format tab.

Even though graphical objects add a great deal of visual enhancement to a document, they also can increase the file size of the document. If you add several graphics to a document, you should view the file size before you copy or save it to a portable storage device, and then confirm the device has enough empty space to hold the large file. Additional consideration should be given to files you send as e-mail attachments. Many people have space limitations in their mailboxes, and a document that contains several graphics can fill their space or take a long time to download. To decrease the size a graphic occupies, you can use the *Compress* feature, which reduces the size of an object. When you select a graphical object, you can click the Compress Pictures command on the Picture Tools group in the Format tab. The Compression Settings dialog box displays, and you can select from options that allow you to reduce the size of the graphical elements, thus reducing the size of the file when you save.

The Picture Tools tab offers many additional graphic editing features, which are described on the following reference page.

Compress reduces the file size of an object.

Graphic Editing Features | Reference

Feature	Button	Description
Height		Height of an object in inches.
Width		Width of an object in inches.
Crop		Remove unwanted portions of the object from top, bottom, left, or right to adjust size.
Align		Adjust edges of object to line up on right or left margin or center between margins.
Group		Process of selecting multiple objects so you can move and format them together.
Rotate		Ability to change the position of an object by rotating it around its own center.
Text Wrapping		Refers to the way text wraps around an object.
Position		Specify location on page where object will reside.
Border		The outline surrounding an object; it can be formatted using color, shapes, or width, or can be set as invisible.
Shadow Effects		Ability to add a shadow to an object.
Compress		Reduce the file size of an object.
Brightness		Increase or decrease brightness of an object.
Contrast		Increase or decrease difference between black and white colors of an object.
Recolor		Change object to give it an effect such as washed-out or grayscale.

Inserting WordArt into a Document

Microsoft WordArt creates decorative text for a document.

Microsoft WordArt is a Microsoft Office application that creates decorative text that can be used to add interest to a document. You can use WordArt in addition to clip art, or in place of clip art if the right image is not available. You can rotate text in any direction, add three-dimensional effects, display the text vertically, slant it, arch it, or even print it upside down.

WordArt is intuitively easy to use. In essence, you choose a style from the gallery (see Figure 3.20). Then you enter the specific text in the Edit WordArt Text dialog box, after which the results display (see Figure 3.21). The WordArt object can be moved and sized, just like any object. A WordArt Tools tab provides many formatting features that enable you to change alignment, add special effects, and change styles quickly. It is fun and easy, and you can create some truly unique documents.

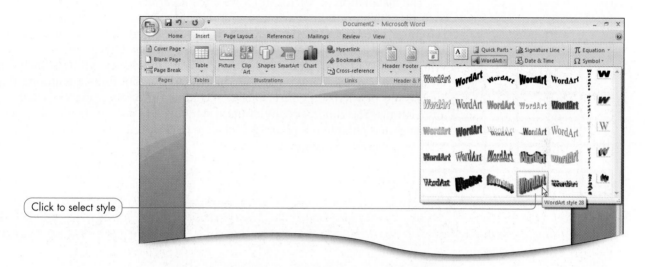

Click to select style

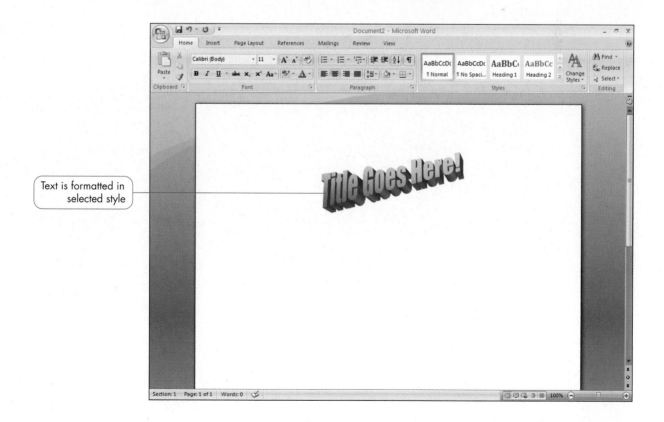

Text is formatted in selected style

Inserting Symbols into a Document

The Symbol command enables you to enter typographic symbols and/or foreign language characters into a document in place of ordinary typing—for example, ® rather than (R), © rather than (c), ½ and ¼, rather than ½ and ¼, or é rather than e (as used in the word résumé). These special characters give a document a very professional look.

You may have already discovered that some of this formatting can be done automatically through the AutoCorrect feature that is built in to Word. If, for example, you type the letter "c" enclosed in parentheses, it will automatically be converted to the copyright symbol. You can use the Symbol command to insert other symbols, such as accented letters like the é in résumé or those in a foreign language (e.g., ¿Cómo está usted?).

The installation of Microsoft Office adds a variety of fonts onto your computer, each of which contains various symbols that can be inserted into a document. Selecting "normal text," however, as was done in Figure 3.22, provides access to the accented characters as well as other common symbols. Other fonts—especially the Wingdings, Webdings, and Symbol fonts—contain special symbols, including the Windows logo. The Wingdings, Webdings, and Symbol fonts are among the best-kept secrets in Microsoft Office. Each font contains a variety of symbols that are actually pictures. You can insert any of these symbols into a document as text, select the character and enlarge the point size, change the color, then copy the modified character to create a truly original document.

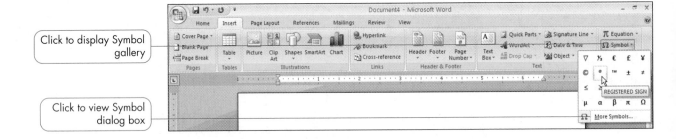

Hands-On Exercises

3 | Clip Art, WordArt, and Symbols

Skills covered: 1. Insert a Clip Art Object **2.** Move and Resize the Clip Art Object **3.** Create a WordArt Object
4. Modify the WordArt Object **5.** Insert a Symbol

<table>
<tr>
<td>

Step 1

Insert a Clip Art Object

</td>
<td>

Refer to Figure 3.23 as you complete Step 1.

a. Open the *chap3_ho3_ergonomics* document and save it as **chap3_ho3_ergonomics_ solution**.

b. Click to move the insertion point to the beginning of the document, if necessary. Click the **Insert tab** and click **Clip Art** in the Illustrations group.

The Clip Art task pane opens, as shown in Figure 3.23.

c. Type **computer** in the **Search for box** to search for any clip art image that is indexed with this keyword. Click the **Search in drop-down arrow** and click **Office Collections**, then click to deselect My Collections and Web Collections, if necessary. Click **Go**.

The images display in the task pane.

d. Point to the first image to display a down arrow, and then click the arrow to display a menu.

e. Click **Insert** to insert the image into the document. Do not be concerned about its size or position at this time. Close the task pane.

f. Save the document.

</td>
</tr>
</table>

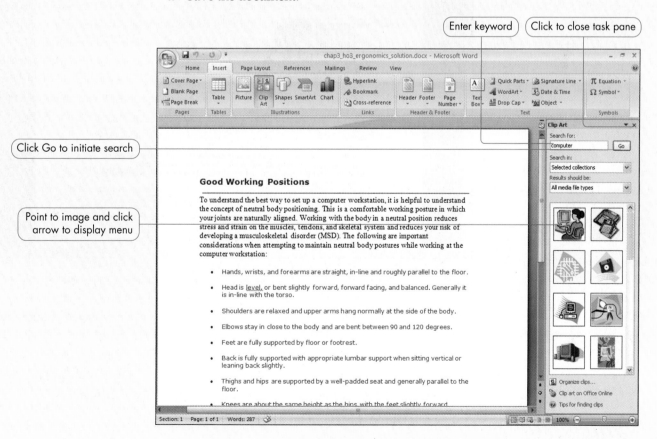

Enter keyword

Click to close task pane

Click Go to initiate search

Point to image and click arrow to display menu

Step 2
Move and Resize the Clip Art Object

Refer to Figure 3.24 as you complete Step 2.

a. Click once on the clip art object to select it. Click **Text Wrapping** in the Arrange group on the Picture Tools Format tab to display the text wrapping options, and then select **Square**, as shown in Figure 3.24.

You must change the layout in order to move and size the object.

b. Click **Position** in the Arrange group, and then click **More Layout Options.** Click the **Picture Position tab** in the Advanced Layout dialog box, if necessary, then click **Alignment** in the *Horizontal* section. Click the **Alignment drop-down arrow** and select **Right**. Deselect the **Allow overlap check box** in the *Options* section. Click **OK**.

c. Click **Crop** in the Size group, then hold your mouse over the sizing handles and notice how the pointer changes to angular shapes. Click the **bottom center handle** and drag it up. Drag the side handles inward to remove excess space surrounding the graphical object.

d. Click the Shape **Height box** in the Size group and type **2.77**.

Notice the width is changed automatically to retain the proportion.

e. Save the document.

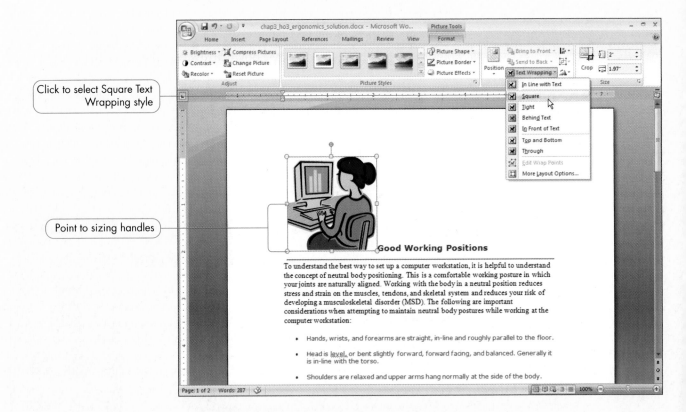

Click to select Square Text Wrapping style

Point to sizing handles

Step 3
Create a WordArt Object

Refer to Figure 3.25 as you complete Step 3.

a. Press **Ctrl+End** to move to the end of the document. Click the **Insert tab**, and then click **WordArt** in the Text group to display the WordArt gallery.

b. Click **WordArt Style 28** on the bottom row of the gallery.

The Edit WordArt Text dialog box displays, as shown in Figure 3.25.

c. Type **WWW.OSHA.GOV**, and then click OK.

The WordArt object appears in your document in the style you selected.

TROUBLESHOOTING: If the WordArt object displays on another page, you can correct it in the next steps.

d. Point to the WordArt object and right-click to display a shortcut menu. Select **Format WordArt** to display the Format WordArt dialog box.

e. Click the **Layout tab** and click **Square** in the *Wrapping style* section. Click **OK**.

It is important to select this wrapping option to facilitate placing the WordArt at the bottom of the first page.

f. Save the document.

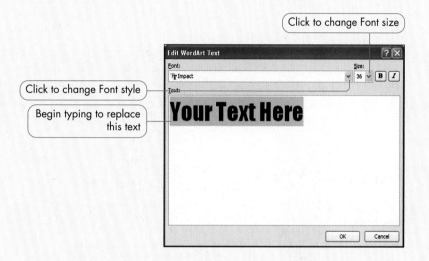

 TIP   Display the Format Tab Quickly

To save time and mouse clicks, you can double-click a WordArt object to quickly display the WordArt Tools Format tab.

Step 4
Modify the WordArt Object

Refer to Figure 3.26 as you complete Step 4.

a. Click and drag the WordArt object to move it to the bottom-right corner of the document, below the text.

The Format WordArt dialog box is not yet visible.

b. Point to the WordArt object, right-click to display a menu, and then click **Format WordArt** to display the Format WordArt dialog box.

Remember that many of the options in this dialog box also are displayed in the WordArt Tools Format tab.

c. Click the **Colors and Lines tab** and click the **Color drop-down arrow** in the *Fill* section to display the color palette. Click **Orange, Accent 6, Lighter 40%**, which is in the last column. Click **OK**.

This action enables you to customize the colors used in the WordArt graphic. In this case, you minimize much of the bright orange tint in the WordArt.

d. Click **3-D Effects** on the Format tab, then click **3-D Effects** to display the 3-D Effects gallery, as shown in Figure 3.26. Click **3-D Style 1** from the Parallel group.

> **TROUBLESHOOTING:** If your monitor uses a high resolution, or if you have a wide monitor, the 3-D Effects gallery might display immediately after you click 3-D Effects the first time. In that case, you will not click 3-D Effects twice, as instructed in Step D.

e. Save the document.

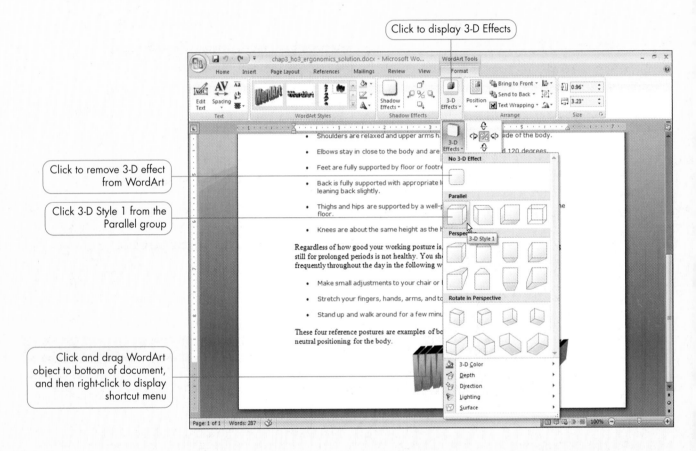

Refer to Figure 3.27 as you complete Step 5.

Step 5
Insert a Symbol

a. Select the word *degrees* that displays at the end of the fourth bullet item in the document. Press **Backspace** to remove the word and the space that follows 120.

b. Click the **Insert tab**, click **Symbol** in the Symbols group, and click **More Symbols** to display the Symbol dialog box. Click the **Font** drop-down box, and then select **Verdana** as shown in Figure 3.27. If necessary, click the *Subset* drop-down box and select **Basic Latin**.

c. Click the **Degree symbol** (the last character in the seventh line), click **Insert**, and close the Symbol dialog box.

d. Save the *chap3_ho3_ergonomics_solution* document and close Word if you do not want to continue with the end-of-chapter exercise at this time.

Click down arrow and click Verdana

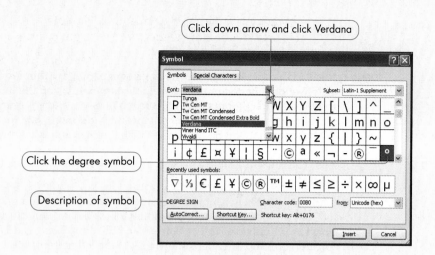

Click the degree symbol

Description of symbol

Summary

1. **Insert a table.** Tables represent a very powerful capability within Word and are used to organize a variety of data in documents. The Table command is on the Insert tab, and tables are made up of rows and columns; the intersection of a row and column is called a cell. You can insert additional rows and columns if you need to add more data to a table, or you can delete a row or column if you no longer need data in the respective row or column. Individual cells can be merged to create a larger cell. Conversely, you can split a single cell into multiple cells. The rows in a table can be different heights and/or each column can be a different width.

2. **Format a table.** Each cell in a table is formatted independently and may contain text, numbers, and/or graphics. To enhance readability of table data, you can apply a predefined style, which Word provides, or use Borders and Shading tools to add color and enhance it. Furthermore, you can align table data—at the left margin, at the right margin, or centered between the margins. You also can change the text direction within a cell.

3. **Sort and apply formulas to table data.** You can sort the rows in a table to display the data in ascending or descending sequence, according to the values in one or more columns in the table. Sorting is accomplished by selecting the rows within the table that are to be sorted, then executing the Sort command in on the Layout tab. Calculations can be performed within a table using the Formula command in that same tab.

4. **Convert text to a table.** If you have a list of tabulated items that would be easier to manipulate in a table, you can use the Convert Text to Table command. The command also works in reverse, enabling you to remove data from a table and format it as tabulated text.

5. **Insert clip art and images into a document.** You often add graphics to enhance a document. When you click the Clip Art command, Office displays a task pane where you enter a keyword to describe the clip you are looking for. The search is made possible by the Microsoft Clip Organizer, which organizes the media files available to you into collections, then enables you to limit the search to specific media types and/or specific collections. Resources (such as clip art or photographs) can be downloaded from the Web for inclusion in a Word document. Although clip art is often acceptable for educational or nonprofit use, it may not be permitted in some advertising situations. You should always assume a graphic is copyrighted unless noted otherwise.

6. **Format a graphic element.** After you insert the clip art object, you can use a variety of tools to refine the object to fit in your document, such as changing height and width, cropping, rotating, or aligning.

7. **Insert WordArt into a document.** Microsoft WordArt is an application within Microsoft Office that creates decorative text that can be used to add interest to a document. WordArt can be used in addition to clip art or in place of clip art if the right image is not available. You can rotate text in any direction, add three-dimensional effects, display the text vertically down the page, or print it upside down.

8. **Insert symbols into a document.** The Insert Symbol command provides access to special characters, making it easy to place typographic characters into a document. The symbols can be taken from any font and can be displayed in any point size.

Key Terms

Multiple Choice

1. You have created a table containing numerical values and have entered the SUM(ABOVE) function at the bottom of a column. You then delete one of the rows included in the sum. Which of the following is true?

   (a) The row cannot be deleted because it contains a cell that is included in the sum function.

   (b) The sum is updated automatically.

   (c) The sum cannot be updated.

   (d) The sum will be updated provided you right-click the cell and click the Update Field command.

2. Which process below is the best option to change the size of a selected object so that the height and width change in proportion to one another?

   (a) Enter the Height and allow Word to establish the Width.

   (b) Click and drag the sizing handle on the top border, then click and drag the sizing handle on the left side.

   (c) Click and drag the sizing handle on the bottom border, then click and drag the sizing handle on the right side.

   (d) Click only the sizing handle in the middle of the left side.

3. How do you search for clip art using the Clip Organizer?

   (a) By entering a keyword that describes the image you want.

   (b) By selecting the photo album option.

   (c) By clicking the Clip Organizer command on the Insert tab.

   (d) There is no such thing as a Clip Organizer.

4. What guideline should you remember when inserting graphics into a document?

   (a) It is distasteful to insert more than two graphics into a document.

   (b) It is not necessary to consider copyright notices if the document is for personal use.

   (c) WordArt should always be center aligned on a page.

   (d) Graphic elements should enhance a document, not overpower it.

5. Which of the following commands in the Picture Tools Format tab would you use to remove portions of a graphic that you do not wish to see in your document?

   (a) Height

   (b) Position

   (c) Crop

   (d) Reset Picture

6. Which of the following is not an example of how to use the Symbols feature in a document?

   (a) You can type (c) to insert the copyright symbol.

   (b) You can insert WordArt from the Symbol dialog box.

   (c) You can insert the Windows logo from the Symbol dialog box.

   (d) You can insert special characters from the Symbol dialog box.

7. Which of the following is true regarding objects and their associated tabs?

   (a) Clicking a WordArt object displays the WordArt Tools tab.

   (b) Right-clicking on a Picture displays the Picture Tools tab.

   (c) You can only display a tab by clicking the tab across the top of the screen.

   (d) Neither (a) nor (b).

8. Which wrap style allows text to wrap around the graphic frame that surrounds the image?

   (a) Top and Bottom

   (b) Tight

   (c) Behind Text

   (d) Square

9. What provides legal protection to the author for a written or artistic work?

   (a) Copyright

   (b) Public domain

   (c) Fair use

   (d) Footnote

10. Microsoft WordArt cannot be used to:

    (a) Arch text, or print it upside down

    (b) Rotate text, or add three-dimensional effects

    (c) Display text vertically down a page

    (d) Insert a copyright symbol

11. What happens when you press Tab from within the last cell of a table?

    (a) A Tab character is inserted just as it would be for ordinary text.

    (b) Word inserts a new row below the current row.

    (c) Word inserts a new column to the right of the current column.

    (d) The insertion point appears in the paragraph below the table.

12. What happens when you type more than one line of text into a cell?

    (a) The cell gets wider to accommodate the extra text.

    (b) The row gets taller as word wrapping occurs to display the additional text.

    (c) The other lines are hidden by default.

    (d) A new column is inserted automatically.

13. Assume you created a table with the names of the months in the first column. Each row lists data for that particular month. The insertion point is in the first cell on the third row—this row lists goals for April. You realize that you left out the goals for March. What should you do?

    (a) Display the Insert tab and click the Table command.

    (b) Display the Table Tools Design tab and click the Insert Cell command.

    (c) Display the Table Tools Layout tab and click the Insert Left command.

    (d) Display the Table Tools Layout tab and click the Insert Above command.

14. You have a list of people who were sent an invitation to a wedding. You are responsible for monitoring their responses to the invitation, whether they will attend or not, and to determine the grand total of those attending. Using skills learned in this chapter, what would be a good way to track this information?

    (a) Use pen and paper to mark through names of those who decline the invitation and put stars by those who accept.

    (b) Convert the list of names to a table; add columns that allow you to mark their response, including the number who will attend, and use a formula to add up the numbers when all responses are received.

    (c) Insert wedding clip art in the document so you will know the purpose of the document.

    (d) Insert a two-column table beside the names and mark the responses as declined or attending.

15. If cell A1 contains the value 2 and A2 contains the value 4, what value will be displayed if cell A3 contains the formula =PRODUCT(ABOVE)?

    (a) 8

    (b) 2

    (c) 6

    (d) This is not a valid formula.

16. What option would you use if you were given a lengthy list of items that are separated by tabs and that would be easier to format in a table?

    (a) Insert Table

    (b) Convert Table to Text

    (c) Convert Text to Table

    (d) Insert Text Box

17. Which option should you use to add color to improve the attractiveness and readability of a table?

    (a) Text wrapping

    (b) Sort

    (c) Add column to right

    (d) Borders and shading

Practice Exercises

1 The Library Station

While working as a volunteer at the local library, you are asked to create a flyer to advertise the upcoming annual book sale, as shown in Figure 3.28. You are required to use a combination of tables, clip art, WordArt, and symbols to create an informative and attractive flyer. If you are unable to find the exact same graphics, find something as similar as possible; you need not match our flyer exactly.

a. Open a new document and save it as **chap3_pe1_flyer_solution**.

b. Click the **Page Layout tab** and click **Margins** in the Page Setup group. Click **Normal**, if necessary, to set all four margins to 1″.

c. Click the **Insert tab** and click **Table** in the Tables group to insert a table. Click only one cell to insert a **1x1** table.

d. Click the **Home tab**, and then click the **Font Dialog Box Launcher**. Select **Comic Sans MS** in the **Font list**, select **Bold** in the **Font style list**, and select **36** in the **Size list**. Click the **Font color drop-down arrow** and select **Red, Accent 2, Darker 25%** (a shade of red). Click **OK** to close the Font dialog box.

e. Type **Annual Book Sale** in the table. Click **Center** in the Paragraph group to center the text within the table cell.

f. Click the **Design tab**, click the **Borders arrow**, and click **Borders and Shading**. Select **None** in the *Setting* section to remove all current borders around the table. Click the **Color drop-down arrow** and select **Red, Accent 2, Darker 50%** (at the bottom of the red column). Then click the **Width drop-down arrow** and select **3 pt**.

g. Click once on the top of the diagram in the *Preview* section to insert a top border, and then click once on the bottom of the diagram to insert a bottom border. If necessary, click the **Apply to drop-down arrow**, select **Table**, and click **OK**.

h. Click below the table to move the insertion point. Click the **Home tab**, and then click the **Font Size arrow** and select **28**. Type the date of the sale, **March 1**, and click **Align Right** in the Paragraph group to move the date to the right side of the flyer.

i. Press **Enter** two times to move the insertion point down the page, click the **Insert tab**, and click **WordArt** in the Text group. Click **WordArt style 28** on the bottom row. In the Edit WordArt Text dialog box, type **The Library Station** and click **OK**.

j. The WordArt object needs to be resized and relocated to have a bigger impact on our flyer. Click **Position** in the Arrange group of the Format tab and click **Position in Middle Center with Tight Text Wrapping**.

k. Click the **Height box** and type **2** to increase the height of the object. Click the **Width box** and type **6** to elongate the object. Click the uppermost handle on the top of the object and notice the insertion point changes to a curved arrow. Click this handle and hold down while rotating the object to the left so that it appears similar to Figure 3.28.

l. Click anywhere to deselect the WordArt object. Click the **Insert** tab, and then click **Clip Art**. When the Clip Art task pane displays, type **book** in the **Search for** box, click the **Search in drop-down arrow**, and click **Office Collections**. Deselect My Collections and Web Collections, if necessary, and click **Go**. Click one time on the first object to insert it in your document, then close the Clip Art task pane.

m. Click the clip art object to display the Format tab, if necessary. Click **Text Wrapping** in the Arrange group, and then select **Square**. Now you can move the object anywhere in your document. Move it to the left side above the WordArt object, as it appears in Figure 3.28.

n. Double-click anywhere in the bottom of your document to reposition the insertion point. Click the **Insert tab**, and then click **Table**. Drag your mouse over the cells until **2x3 Table** displays (a 2 column, 3 row table), and click to insert it in the document.

o. Click the table selector in the upper-left corner to select the whole table and click the **Layout** tab. Click **Properties** in the Table group to display the Table Properties dialog box. Click the **Table tab**, and then click the **Preferred width check box**. Type **8** in the **Preferred width box** and click **OK**.

p. Drag your mouse across the two cells in the first row to select it, then right-click and select **Merge Cells**. Type **Hourly Drawings for FREE Books!** in the first row.

q. Click the **Design tab**, and then click **More** in the **Table Styles** group. Scroll to view the **B2 Dark List Accent 2** style. Click once to apply the style to your table.

...continued on Next Page

r. Right-click the table, click **Table Properties**, click **Center** alignment, and click **OK**.

s. Select the two empty cells in the first (left) column of the table, right-click, and click **Merge Cells**. In this column enter the phrase **Discounts of 50% or More**. Select the two empty cells in the right column of the table, right-click, and select **Merge Cells**. In this column, type the phrase **Only at our North Glenstone Location**.

t. Click anywhere in the table, if necessary, and click the **Layout tab**. Click **Cell Margins**, click the **Allow spacing between cells check box**, then type **.1** as the spacing amount. Click **OK** and notice the improvement.

u. Select only the text in the table, but do not click the table selector; on the Mini toolbar, click **Center**.

v. Make minor adjustments to each element as necessary so your flyer looks attractive and spacing is retained. Save and close the document.

Figure 3.28 The Book Sale Flyer

2 Lost Pet

In an unfortunate mishap, your 3-year-old dog escaped from your fenced yard and is now missing. After calling local shelters and pet stores, you decide to create a flyer to post around the neighborhood and shops so that people will know whom to contact if they see her. Figure 3.29 displays a flyer that is intended to give information about your dog, Dakota, and also provide a tag with contact information that someone can pull from the flyer and take with him or her. The tag displays your name and phone number. Use a table as the basis of this document; you can use the picture of our pet or any other picture you like.

a. Open a new document and save it as **chap3_pe2_lostpet_solution**.

b. Click the **Insert tab** and click **Table** in the Tables group. Drag to select cells to create a table with 10 columns and 4 rows (**10x4 Table**), then click on the last cell to insert the table.

c. Click left of the first cell in the first row to select the entire row. Right-click the selected row and select **Merge Cells** to merge all the cells in the first row. Repeat the step to merge the cells in rows 2, and then the cells in row 3.

d. Click in the first row and enter the text **Lost Pet**. Select the text, and then on the Mini toolbar click the **Font size arrow** and select **26**. The row height will increase automatically to accommodate the larger text. On the Mini toolbar, click **Center** to center the text in the cell.

e. Select the cell in the second row. Click the **Design tab** and click **Shading** in the Table Styles group. Click **Black, Text 1** (the black swatch in the first row), which will place a black background in the cell.

...continued on Next Page

f. Click **Insert tab** and click **Picture** in the Illustrations group. Locate pictures of your pet or pets; we have provided a picture of Dakota, dakota.jpg, in the Exploring Word folder. When you locate the file, double-click to insert the picture. The row height will expand automatically to accommodate the picture. Click once to select the picture, if necessary, and then press **Ctrl+E** to center the picture.

g. Click in the third row and enter text to describe your pet or pets. Feel free to duplicate the information we have provided in Figure 3.29. Select the text, then on the Mini toolbar, click the **Font size arrow**, and select **14**, and click **Center**.

h. Type your name and phone number in the first cell of the fourth row. Display the **Layout tab**, and then click **Text Direction** one time to rotate the text (see Figure 3.29). Click **Align Top Center** to align the text vertically on the top of the cell. Right-click the cell and click **Copy**. Select the empty cells on that row, right-click, and click **Paste Cells** to populate the remaining cells with the owner information.

i. Select the entire row, right-click, and select **Borders and Shading**. Click the **Borders** tab, if necessary, and click a dashed line in the **Style list**. Click **OK**.

j. Click the **Height** box in the Cell Size group and increase the size to at least **1.5"**. The contact information now displays correctly.

k. Click **Zoom** in the task bar, click **Whole page**, and click **OK**.

l. Save and close the document.

3 The Study Schedule

Your midterm grades reveal the need to set up a solid study schedule. The best way to plan your study time is to create a daily schedule, mark the times you are in class or at work, then find the needed study time. Your work in this chapter provided information you can use to create a document that lists days and times and allows you to establish your new study schedule. You can even add colorful borders and shading, as well as graphics, to create a document you can proudly display.

a. Open a new blank document and save it as **chap3_pe3_schedule_solution**.

b. Click the **Page Layout tab**. Click **Margins** in the Page Setup group, and then click **Custom Margins** to display the Page Layout dialog box. Type **.75** in the **Top** and **Bottom** boxes, then type **.5** in the **Left** and **Right** boxes. Click **Landscape** in the *Orientation* section and click **OK**.

...continued on Next Page

c. Click the **Insert tab** and click **Table**. Click **Insert Table** to display the Insert Table dialog box. Type **8** in the **Number of columns** box and type **12** in the **Number of rows** box. Click **OK**.

d. Click left of the first cell in the first row to select the entire first row, then **right-click** and select **Merge Cells**. Click in the merged cell, then type **Weekly Class and Study Schedule**. Select the text you typed. On the Mini toolbar, click the **Font arrow** and select **Arial**, click the **Font size arrow** and select **24**, and click **Bold** and **Center**.

e. Click left of the first cell in the last row to select the entire row, then right-click and select **Merge Cells**. Click in the merged cell, type **Notes:**, then press **Enter** five times. The height of the cell increases to accommodate the blank lines.

f. Select the text you typed. On the Mini toolbar, click the **Font arrow** and select **Arial**, click the **Font size arrow** and select **12**, and click **Bold**.

g. Click the second cell in the second row. Type **Monday**. Press **Tab** (or right arrow key) to move to the next cell. Type **Tuesday**. Continue until the days of the week have been entered. Select the entire row. On the Mini toolbar, click the **Font arrow** and select **Arial**, click the **Font size arrow** and select **10**, and then click **Bold** and **Center**.

h. Click the first cell in the third row. Type **8:00 a.m.** Press the **down arrow key** to move to the first cell in the fourth row. Type **9:00 a.m.** Continue to enter the hourly periods up to **4:00 p.m.**

i. Select the cells containing the hours of the day, and then right-click and select **Table Properties**. Click the **Row tab**, then click the **Specify height check box**. Click the spin button until the height is **0.5"**. Click the **Row height is drop-down arrow** and select **Exactly**.

j. Click the **Cell tab** in the Table Properties dialog box and click **Center** in the *Vertical alignment* section. Click **OK** to accept the settings and close the dialog box.

k. Select the first row, containing the title of your table. Click the **Design tab** and click **Shading**. Click **Orange, Accent 6**, the orange color at the end of the first row.

l. Click and drag to select the first four cells under Sunday, then right-click and select **Merge Cells**. Type **Reserved for services** in the new large cell. Select this text, then click the **Layout tab**. Click **Text Direction** one time to rotate the text, and then click **Align Center** to display the text, as shown in Figure 3.30.

m. Click anywhere in the cell in the last row of the table. Click the **Insert tab** and click **Clip Art** to display the task pane. Type **books** in the **Search for** box, and then click **Go** or press **Enter**. Click the first clip art object to insert it in your table.

n. Click the newly inserted clip art to display the Format tab, if necessary, and click **Text Wrapping** and select **Square**. Click the sizing handle on the upper-right corner, hold down **Shift**, and drag the sizing handle to reduce the size of the object and maintain proportions. Move the object to the lower-right corner of the last row and close the Clip Art task pane.

o. Save and close the document.

...continued on Next Page

You work as a bank consultant for a software firm and must bill for services each month. Traditionally, you type the amount of your invoice in the document, but after a discussion with a coworker you discover how to use table formulas and begin to use them to calculate your total fees on the invoice. In this exercise, you develop a professional-looking invoice and use formulas to calculate totals within the table.

a. Open a blank document and save it as **chap3_pe4_invoice_solution**.

b. Click the **Page Layout tab**, click **Margins**, and click **Office 2003 Default**, which sets 1.25″ left and right margins. Click the **Insert tab** and click **Table**. Drag to select eight rows and two columns (**2x8 Table**).

c. Click left of the first cell in the first row to select the entire first row, right-click, and select **Merge Cells**. Click in the merged cell, and then type **Invoice**. Select the text you typed, click the **Home tab**, and click **Heading 1** from the Styles gallery. Click **Center** in the Paragraph group to complete the first row of the table.

d. Select the second and third cells in the first column, and then click the **Layout tab**. Click **Merge Cells**, click the **Height box** in the Cell Size group, and type **1** to increase the size of the cell. In this cell, enter the following text:

TO:

Jack Hendrix Technologies
4999 Garland Street
Fayetteville, AR 72703

e. Select the second and third cells in the right column and click **Merge Cells**. They inherit the size from the cell on their left. Click **Align Top Right** in the Alignment group and type the following text in the cell:

FROM:
John Q. Student
9444 Elton Lane
Tulsa, OK 74129

f. Select the last five cells in the first column, then click the **Width box** in the Cell Size group and type **5**. The cells on the right might extend beyond the borders of the page, but you will fix that next. Select the five cells in the second column, then click the **Width box** and type **1.15**. Now the cells should align with the cells in the first two rows.

g. Type the following text in the third through sixth cells of the two columns, as shown in Figure 3.31:

Description	Amount
Consulting Fee for June	$5640.00
Travel Expenses	500.00
Supplies	200.00

h. In the first column of the last row, type **TOTAL**. Click in the second column in the last row and click **Formula** on the Layout tab. Click **OK** to accept the formula, =SUM(ABOVE), which is correct for our calculation. The total is $6340.00.

i. Your invoice is correct, but formatting changes are needed to give it a more professional appearance. Select the third row, which contains the Description and Amount titles, and hold down **Ctrl**, and select the last row of the table. Click the **Design tab**

...continued on Next Page

and click **Shading**. Click **White, Background 1, Darker 15%** from the first column. Do not deselect the rows.

j. While the rows are selected, click the **Home tab** and click **Heading 3** from the Styles gallery. You may need to click the **More button** in the Styles group, select **Apply Styles** from the gallery, type **Heading 3** in the Apply Styles dialog box, and click **Apply**. Click anywhere to deselect the rows and view the format changes.

k. Select the last four cells in the second column, click the **Layout tab**, and click **Align Center Right** on the tab. The result gives the effect of decimal alignment. However, the numbers are not decimal aligned, so if you display an additional decimal place, it will result in misaligned numbers.

l. Select the fourth, fifth, and sixth rows, which contain the items you bill for, then click **Sort** in the Data group. Click **OK**. Deselect the rows to view the newly sorted list.

m. You determine the travel expenses were incorrect; change the amount to **550.00**. Right-click the cell that contains the formula and select **Update Field** to recalculate the total. The new total $6390.00 displays.

n. Save and close the document.

Invoice		
TO: Jack Hendrix Technologies 4999 Garland Street Fayetteville, AR 72703		FROM: John Q. Student 9444 Elton Lane Tulsa, OK 74129
Description		**Amount**
Consulting Fee for June		$5640.00
Supplies		200.00
Travel Expenses		550.00
TOTAL		$6390.00

Microsoft Word 2007 includes a Résumé template, but you can achieve an equally good result through the tables feature. In this exercise you create a resume for yourself using the tools learned in this chapter. Follow the instructions below to create a résumé similar to the document in Figure 3.32. Remember that a resume often serves as the first impression between you and a potential employer, so you must include all the information expected by an employer and display it in a manner that is easy to read and follow.

a. Open a new blank document and save it as **chap3_mid1_resume_solution**. Set margins at 1" on the top and bottom, and 1.25" on the left and right. Insert a 2-column, 10-row table into your document. Additional rows can be added as needed. Conversely, rows can be deleted at a later time if they are not needed.

b. Merge the two cells in the first row. Type your name in the cell, and then center it. Change the font to Times New Roman, 24 pt, and bold, as shown in Figure 3.32.

c. Enter your addresses in the second row. Type your campus address, telephone number, and e-mail address in the cell on the left and your permanent address and telephone number in the cell on the right. Format the text in Times New Roman, 12 pt. Left align the text in the cell on the left and right align the text in the cell on the right.

d. Enter the categories in the left cell of each row, being sure to include the following categories: **Objective**, **Professional Accomplishments**, **Education**, **Honors**, and **References**. Format the text in Times New Roman, 12 pt, boldface and right align the text in these cells. (Not all of these categories are visible in Figure 3.32.)

e. Enter the associated information in the right cell of each row. Be sure to include all information that would interest a prospective employer. Format the text in Times New Roman, 12 pt. Left align the text in these cells, using boldface and italics where appropriate.

f. Select rows three through ten in the first column, then change the width of the cells to 1.5". Select the same rows in the second column and increase the width of the cells until they align with the first two rows.

g. Select the entire table and remove the borders surrounding the individual cells. (Figure 3.32 displays gridlines, which—unlike borders—do not appear in the printed document.) For the first row only, set a bottom line border.

h. Save and close the document.

...continued on Next Page

You work as an intern for the Human Resources department of a company that offers home health consulting services. Your manager mentions the need for a new employment application form and asks you to create an application form similar to the document in Figure 3.33. Use the skills you recently acquired about the tables feature in Word to follow our design and create the application form. Remember that the Tables and Borders toolbar can be used in place of the Table menu to execute various commands during the exercise. Proceed as follows:

a. Open a blank document and save it as **chap3_mid2_application_solution**.

b. Create a 9 × 3 (nine rows and three columns) table to match our design. Select the entire table after it is created initially. Change the before paragraph spacing to 6 pt. The result will drop the text in each cell half a line from the top border of the cell, and also determine the spacing between paragraphs within a cell.

c. Merge the cells in the first row to create the title for the application. Enter the text for the first line, press **Shift+Enter** to create a line break instead of a paragraph break (to minimize the spacing between lines), then enter the text on the second line. Center the text. Select the first cell, and then shade the cell with the color **Black, Text 1** to create white letters on a dark background. Increase the font size of the title to 22 pt.

d. Enter the text in the next several cells, as shown in Figure 3.33. Select cells individually and adjust the width to create the offsetting form fields.

e. Move down in the table until you can select the cell for the highest degree attained. Enter the indicated text, click and drag to select all four degrees, and create a custom bulleted list using the check box character in the Wingdings font.

f. Merge the cells in row 7, then enter the text that asks the applicant to describe the skills that qualify him or her for the position. Merge the cells in row 8 (these cells are not visible in Figure 3.33) to create a single cell for employment references.

g. Reduce the zoom setting to view the entire document. Change the row heights as necessary so that the completed application fills the entire page.

h. Complete the finished application as though you were applying for a job. Replace the check box next to the highest degree earned (remove the bullet) with the letter X.

i. Save and close the document.

...continued on Next Page

You are the marketing manager for a private pilot flight school. Periodically, you perform a review of marketing tools used in the company, then make a list of items that must be changed. In your last review, you noticed the company letterhead is quite dated and should be changed. Since the change is being made, all company stationery will be replaced with the new logo. Figure 3.34 displays an envelope and matching letterhead designed by an intern. Replicate that design as closely as possible, creating both the letterhead and matching envelope.

a. Begin with the stationery. Open a blank document and save it as **chap3_mid3_ stationery_solution**.

b. Click the **Narrow** margin setting, which sets 1/2" margins all around. Enter the company name, address, telephone, and e-mail information at the top of the page. Use a larger font and distinguishing color for your name, then center all of the text at the top of the page.

c. After you type your information, convert the text into a table. Split the table into three columns so you can add a logo to each side of your information.

d. Use the Clip Organizer to locate the clip art image shown in Figure 3.34. (If you cannot find the same clip art image, use one with the same theme.) Use that image as a logo by inserting it in the first column of the table. Click the Square text wrap style. Change the image height to **1"**. Crop the image to decrease width to approximately **1.1"**. Select the clip art, click Copy, then Paste the image in the third column of the table on the right side of the page.

e. Center align the information in each cell both horizontally and vertically. Use the Borders command to add a 3-pt wide horizontal line below the text that contains your address information. Do not extend the border below the clip art images.

f. Insert a new page section break at the beginning of the document. (The result creates a new page as well as a new section. The latter enables you to change the page orientation within a document.)

g. Click on the newly inserted page and select landscape orientation. Change the **Size** to **Envelope #10** (the standard business envelope).

h. Copy the clip art and address information from the letterhead to the envelope. Make adjustments as necessary to align your address beside the logo.

i. Save and close the document.

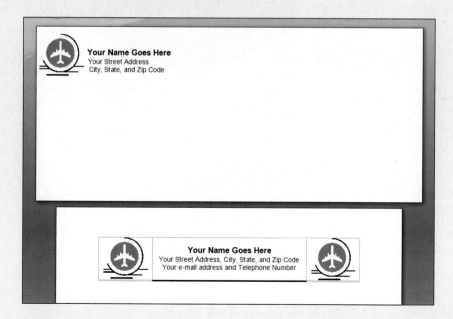

...continued on Next Page

You work as an intern for the mayor's office in City Hall. The office sponsors a yearly fireworks display near the local airport and posts informational flyers in local businesses prior to the event. The community relations director has asked for your help to create the flyers they will distribute because of your experience using Microsoft Word 2007. You are responsible for creating an exciting and attractive flyer for this year's event using the guidelines below.

a. Open a new blank document and save it as **chap3_mid4_fireworks_solution**.

b. Set the following margins: 0.6" top, 0.3" bottom, 0.5" left, and 0.5" right. If a warning appears mentioning that the margins are outside the boundary, choose the option to fix the problem.

c. Create a WordArt object with these settings: Click WordArt style 11 in the WordArt gallery. Type **Independence Day Fireworks!** in the WordArt box. Add the **3-D Style 11** effect. Change the Shape Fill, located in the WordArt Styles group of the Format tab, to use the **Linear Down** gradient color scheme. Change the height to **1.5"** and the width to **7"**, then Format the object to use **Square Text Wrapping**, and center it horizontally on the page.

d. Use the Clip Art task pane and search for **fireworks** in the Web Collections. Find and insert the image, as shown in Figure 3.35. Adjust the height to **3"**, then crop the image to trim white space from the top and bottom of the picture. Adjust the brightness to **+20%**. Apply square text wrapping, and then move the object to the right side of the flyer, as shown in Figure 3.35.

e. Place the insertion point on the left side of the document and type **City of Stockton** on the left side of the Clip art object. Format the text in Comic Sans MS, 26-pt size, and change the font color to red.

f. Insert a table to list the events shown in Figure 3.35. Align text on the left and right as displayed. In addition to increasing Cell Margins, insert an extra column to create the gap between columns. Apply a Dark Red Double-line outside border, then left-align the table.

g. Below the table insert the text **Best Small-Town Celebration in the State**, as shown in Figure 3.35. Format the text using Comic Sans MS 18-pt, change the font color to red, and center the text on the page.

h. Save and close the document.

Capstone Exercise

You are the executive assistant to a general contractor, and your duties include listing the materials that will be used on a home remodeling project. Due to the large number of people who work on the project, from plumbers to electricians to carpenters, it is necessary to keep detailed records of the materials and supplies to use during the remodel. After the first job, you decide to provide the crew with a table of materials that includes pictures. This also might be helpful for any crewmember who does not speak English.

Create the Table

Fortunately, a list of materials has been provided, which will eliminate the need for you to type a list of supplies. However, the preexisting list is weak. You decide to modify the document to increase organization and clarity by putting the list in table format, creating a header row and labels, and also adding visual enhancements with WordArt.

a. Open the *chap3_cap_construction* document and save it as **chap3_cap_construction_solution**. You wisely decide to convert this list to a three-column table so you can organize the list of materials and add more data.

b. Insert two rows at the top to use for a heading and item descriptions.
   - Create a title row on the table by merging cells in the first row.
   - Use WordArt to create a title using the phrase **Supply List**.
   - Use the second row as a header for the columns.
   - Enter an appropriate label for each column.

Format the Table

Your table is functional now, but it would look even better with additional improvements. Enhance the table of materials by aligning the data in columns, sorting the data, and using formulas to calculate costs. Since the table spans more than one page, you also should change the table properties so that the header row repeats on every page.

a. Use the Table Properties dialog box to indicate the first row should repeat as a header row at the top of each page if your table spans more than one page.

b. Align the prices of each item in the third column. The prices should appear to align on the decimal point.

c. Center the data in the second column, which displays the quantity of each item you will use in the project.

d. Sort the data in ascending order by Item.

e. Use the Split cell option to add a column to calculate the total cost of materials.

f. Use a formula to calculate the total cost of any item that has a quantity of 10 or more.

Add Visual Enhancements

Your table is very factual, but to assist members of the crew who need more visual information, you will enhance the table with pictures. Insert pictures from the Clip Organizer and then use formatting tools, when appropriate, to modify the graphics so they will fit into the table cells.

a. Insert a column to the left of the first column.

b. Insert a picture of each item in the first column.
   - Use symbols, clip art, or pictures to visually describe the following materials in your table: Drill, Faucet, Hammer, Paint, Paintbrushes, Screwdriver, Toilet, and Towel holder.
   - You might not be able to locate a graphic for each item, but you should be able to find at least five to use in the table.
   - Crop or resize the graphics as necessary so they do not exceed 2" in height or width.
   - All graphics should align in the center of the cell.

TROUBLESHOOTING: If your Clip Organizer query does not return any results, click Clip art on Office Online. The Online organizer will display in a new Internet Explorer window, but you can return to Word and continue your clip art search. Your search should now return more results.

c. Apply the **Light Grid Accent 1** style to the table. Add a double-line outside border to the table, then center it horizontally on the page. If necessary, click Table Properties and verify that the setting for the first row will repeat as a header row on the top of each page.

d. Save and close the document.

Mini Cases

Use the rubric following the case as a guide to evaluate your work, but keep in mind that your instructor may impose additional grading criteria or use a different standard to judge your work.

Holiday Greetings

GENERAL CASE

After learning how to use the creative tools in Microsoft Word 2007, you decide to create your own holiday greeting card. Your greeting card should include a picture of a family (feel free to use your own or one from the Clip Organizer) and decorative text. Use several editing features on the graphics so the greeting card reflects your personality or sentiment during the holidays. Due to printing constraints for special paper used for cards, design only the cover of your Greeting card. Save the document as **chap3_mc1_greeting_solution**.

Performance Elements	Exceeds Expectations	Meets Expectations	Below Expectations
Use of tables and table formatting	Inserted table; applied two or more table format options.	Inserted table; applied one table format option.	Inserted table; did not apply additional formatting.
Use of graphics	Inserted at least two graphical objects and used at least three formatting options.	Inserted at least one graphical object and applied formatting.	Inserted zero or one graphical object.
Presentation	Greeting card is formatted attractively; information is easy to read and understand.	Special formatting has been applied, but information is somewhat cluttered.	Greeting card lists basic information with no special formatting for attractiveness.

Travel World

RESEARCH CASE

You have been hired at *Let's Go!* Travel Agency and asked to create a flyer to distribute on campus. Search the Internet to find a company that offers cruises to Alaska and sails through the Inside Passage. Then create a flyer that provides information about one of the cruises through the Alaska Inside Passage. You should include your name and e-mail address as the travel agent. Use a combination of clip art, photographs, and/or WordArt to make the flyer as attractive as possible. Use a table to list the Ports of Call in Alaska. Save your work as **chap3_mc2_alaska_solution**.

Performance Elements	Exceeds Expectations	Meets Expectations	Below Expectations
Use of tables and table formatting	Inserted table; applied three or more table formats.	Inserted table; applied one or two table format options.	Inserted table; did not apply additional formatting.
Use of graphics	Inserted at least two graphical objects and applied formatting to objects.	Inserted at least two graphical objects and resized them.	Inserted zero or one graphical object.
Use of research	Two or more pieces of information are included in flyer, reflecting adequate research was performed.	Includes one piece of information reflecting research of topic.	Does not include data that indicate research was performed.
Presentation	Flyer is formatted attractively; information is easy to read and understand.	Special formatting has been applied, but information is somewhat cluttered.	Flyer lists basic information with no special formatting for attractiveness.

Payroll Report

You are assigned the job of proofreading a payroll report before it goes to the department head who issues checks. After looking at the data you find several errors that must be corrected before the report can be submitted. Open the *chap3_mc3_payroll_report* document and correct the errors. Remember to use the keyboard shortcut that reveals formulas in a table. Make further adjustments that enhance your ability to view the information easily and to make the report look more professional. Save your work as **chap3_mc3_payroll_solution**.

Performance Elements	Exceeds Expectations	Meets Expectations	Below Expectations
Use of table formulas	Table formulas applied correctly to all entries.	Table formulas applied correctly to two entries.	Table formulas applied incorrectly to at least one item.
Use of other table formatting options	Used at least three table format options.	Used two table format options.	Does not use table format options.
Presentation	Report is formatted attractively; information is easy to read and understand.	Some report formatting corrections have been applied, but information is somewhat cluttered.	Report contains errors in formatting and presentation is poor.

Share, Compare, and Document

Workgroups, Collaboration, and References

Objectives

After you read this chapter, you will be able to:

1. Insert comments in a document **(page 251)**.
2. Track changes in a document **(page 254)**.
3. View documents side by side **(page 263)**.
4. Compare and combine documents **(page 264)**.
5. Create master documents and subdocuments **(page 265)**.
6. Use navigation tools **(page 267)**.
7. Acknowledge a source **(page 277)**.
8. Create a bibliography **(page 279)**.
9. Select the writing style **(page 280)**.
10. Create and modify footnotes and endnotes **(page 281)**.
11. Add figure references **(page 287)**.
12. Insert a table of figures **(page 288)**.
13. Add legal references **(page 289)**.
14. Create cross-references **(page 289)**.
15. Modify document properties **(page 290)**.

Hands-On Exercises

Exercises	Skills Covered
1. DOCUMENT COLLABORATION (page 258) **Open:** chap4_ho1_proposal.docx **Save as:** chap4_ho1_proposal_solution.docx	• Set User Name and Customize the Track Changes Options • Track Document Changes • View, Add, and Delete Comments • Accept and Reject Changes
2. DOCUMENT COMPARISON, MERGERS, AND NAVIGATION (page 270) **Open:** chap4_ho1_proposal_solution.docx (from Exercise 1) chap4_ho2_proposal2.docx Overview.docx, Ideology.docx, Time Frame.docx, Budget.docx, and Conclusion.docx **Save as:** chap4_ho2_compare_solution.docx and chap4_ho2_combine_solution.docx **Open:** chap4_ho1_proposal_solution.docx (from Exercise 1) **Open:** chap4_ho2_master.docx chap4_ho2_background.docx **Save as:** chap4_ho2_map_solution **Save as:** chap4_ho2_master_solution.docx,	• Compare and Combine Documents • View Documents Side by Side • Create Master Documents and Subdocuments • Modify Master Documents and Subdocuments • Use Document Map and Create Bookmarks
3. REFERENCE RESOURCES (page 283) **Open:** chap4_ho3_plagiarism.docx and chap4_ho3_plmasterlist.xml **Save as:** chap4_ho3_plagiarism_solution.docx	• Create and Search for a Source • Select a Writing Style and Insert a Bibliography • Create and Modify Footnotes • Convert Footnotes to Endnotes and Modify Endnotes
4. ADDITIONAL REFERENCE RESOURCES (page 292) **Open:** chap4_ho4_tables.docx **Save as:** chap4_ho4_tables_solution.docx	• Add Captions and Create a Table of Figures • Create a Table of Authorities • Create a Cross-Reference • Modify Document Properties

CASE STUDY

Compiling an Employee Handbook

After years of planning and saving, Alex Caselman has recently started his own company. He will be hiring 20 employees initially and anticipates hiring 40 more by the end of the first fiscal year. He understands the importance of establishing goals and procedures that the employees can use to guide their efforts, so he has been working with the Small Business Development Center in his community to create these documents. The SBDC suggested Alex partner with a local business college and recruit students to assist him in writing a Staff Handbook for his employees. There are many laws which must be considered for employee hiring and management, and Alex wants to be sure his company stays in compliance with all regulations.

Case Study

The two students who have volunteered to help Alex, Tanner and Elexis, have spent a number of hours researching employee handbooks and the laws that regulate hiring and employee leave in their state. They decide to assign a section to each person; after each section is written and reviewed, they will combine them. Knowing they would be viewing and editing all pages for each section, each person tracked the changes in their respective documents so the person in charge of combining them can easily view the modifications. Their work has been hard and they have only completed the first five sections of the handbook, but so far everyone is pleased with their progress.

Your Assignment

- Read the chapter, paying special attention to sections that describe how to use the Track Changes and Master Document features in Word.
- Open the *chap4_case_handbook* document, which contains the opening section of the employee handbook, and save the file as **chap4_case_handbook_ solution**. This will become the master document for the handbook.
- Insert the following files, in this order, as subdocuments into the master document: *chap4_case_eligibility, chap4_case_employment, chap4_case_leave, chap4_case_ conduct*.
- Display the document in Print Layout view, then turn on track changes. Accept all changes to the eligibility, employment, and leave sections of the document. Reject changes to the conduct section of the document.
- Renumber the conduct section so that all paragraph numbers begin with 5 instead of 7.
- Save and close the *chap4_case_handbook_solution* document.

Workgroups and Collaboration

This chapter introduces several features that go beyond the needs of the typical student and extend to capabilities that you will appreciate in the workplace, especially as you work with others on a collaborative project. This chapter opens with a discussion of workgroup editing, where suggested revisions from one or more individuals can be stored electronically within a document. This feature enables the original author to review each suggestion individually before it is incorporated into the final version of the document, and further, enables multiple people to work on the same document in collaboration with one another.

In this section, you insert comments to provide feedback or to pose questions to the document author. Then you track editing changes you make so that others can see your suggested edits.

Inserting Comments in a Document

In today's organizational environment, teams of people with diverse backgrounds, skills, and knowledge prepare documentation. Team members work together while planning, developing, writing, and editing important documents. If you have not participated in a team project yet, most likely you will. When you work with a team, you can use collaboration tools in Word such as the Comment feature. A *comment* is a note or annotation to ask a question or provide a suggestion to another person about the content of a document.

> In today's organizational environment, teams of people with diverse backgrounds, skills, and knowledge prepare documentation. When you work with a team, you can use collaboration tools in Word such as the Comment feature.

A ***comment*** is a note or annotation about the content of a document.

Before you use the comment and other collaboration features, you should click the Office Button, click Word Options, and then view the Personalize section and confirm that your name is displayed as the user. Word uses this information to indicate the name of the person who uses collaboration tools, such as comments. If you are in a lab environment, you might not have permission to modify settings or change the User name; however, you should be able to change these settings on a home computer.

Add a Comment

Add comments to a document to remind yourself (or a reviewer) of action that needs to be taken. Click in the document where you want the comment to appear, display the Review tab, and click New Comment in the Comments group to open the markup balloon (see Figure 4.1), and enter the text of the comment and click outside the comment area. ***Markup balloons*** are colored circles that contain comments, insertions, and deletions in the margin with a line drawn to where the insertion point was in the document prior to inserting the comment or editing the document. After you complete the comment, the word containing the insertion point is highlighted in the color assigned to the reviewer. If you do not select anything prior to clicking New Comment, Word selects the word or object to the left of the insertion point for the comment reference.

Markup balloons are colored circles that contain comments and display in the margins.

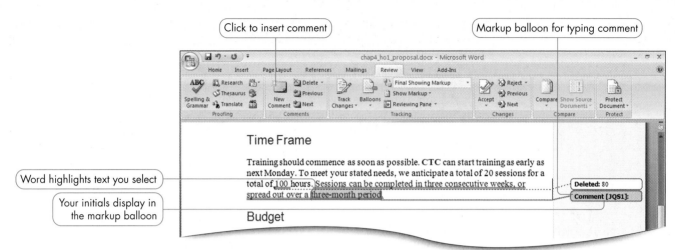

Figure 4.1 Insert a Comment

TIP   Record Voice Comments

You can record voice comments if your computer contains a sound card and a microphone. The Insert Voice command is not found in a tab; therefore, you must add it to the Quick Access Toolbar using the Customize section of the Word Options command. To create the sound comment, position the insertion point where you want to insert the sound comment, click Insert Voice on the Quick Access Toolbar, click the Record button in the Sound Object dialog box, record your voice, and then click the Stop button. Click the Rewind button to rewind the sound clip and click the Play button to hear your recording. People can listen to the voice comment by double-clicking the sound icon within the document.

View, Modify, and Delete Comments

The **Reviewing Pane** displays comments and changes made to a document.

Comments appear in markup balloons in Print Layout, Web Layout, and Full Screen Reading views. In Draft view, comments appear as tags embedded in the document; when you hover the mouse over the tag, it displays the comment. In any view, you can display the **Reviewing Pane**, a pane that displays all comments and editorial changes made to the main document. To display or hide the Reviewing Pane, click Reviewing Pane on the Review tab. You can display the pane vertically on the left side of the document window, as shown in Figure 4.2, or horizontally at the bottom. The Reviewing Pane is useful when the comments are too long to display completely in a markup balloon.

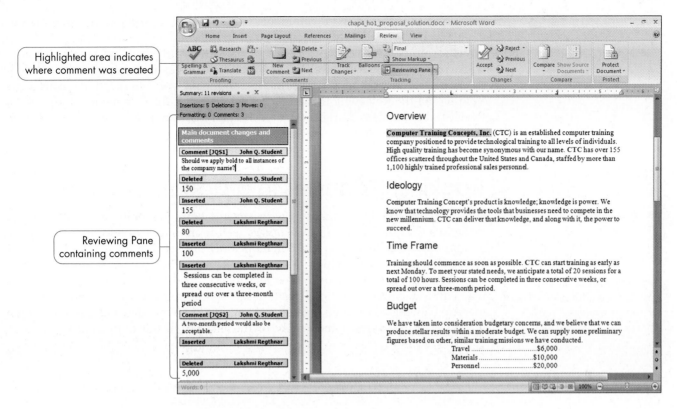

Highlighted area indicates where comment was created

Reviewing Pane containing comments

Figure 4.2 The Reviewing Pane

Show Markup enables you to view document revisions by reviewer.

If you do not see comments initially, click Show Markup on the Review tab and confirm that Comment is toggled on. The *Show Markup* feature enables you to view document revisions by reviewers. It also enables you to choose which type of revisions you want to view, such as Comments, Ink annotations (made on a tablet PC), insertions and deletions, or formatting changes. Each can be toggled on or off and you can view one or all at the same time. Show Markup also color codes each revision or comment with a different color for each reviewer. If you want to view changes by a particular reviewer, you simply toggle off all others in the Show Markup reviewers list, as shown in Figure 4.3.

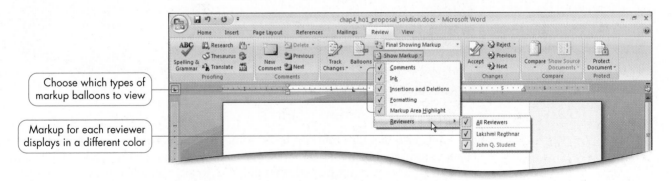

Choose which types of markup balloons to view

Markup for each reviewer displays in a different color

Figure 4.3 Show Markup Features

You can modify comments easily. When you click inside a markup balloon, the insertion point will relocate and you can use word processing formatting features, such as bold, italic, underline, and color, in the comment. If a document contains many comments, or the document is lengthy, you can click Previous and Next in the Comments group of the Review tab to navigate from comment to comment. This is a quick way to move between comments without scrolling through the entire document and it also places the insertion point in the comment automatically. You also can edit comments from the Reviewing Pane. After you edit a comment, click anywhere outside of the balloon or Reviewing Pane to save the changes.

After reading, acting on, or printing comments, you can delete the comments from within the Reviewing Pane by clicking Delete in the Comments group on the Review tab. You also can right-click a comment markup balloon and choose Delete Comment from the shortcut menu.

Tracking Changes in a Document

Use **Track Changes** to insert revision marks and markup balloons for additions, deletions, and formatting changes.

Revision Marks indicate where text is added, deleted, or formatted while the Track Changes feature is active.

Whether you work individually or with a group, you can monitor any revisions you make to a document. The **Track Changes** feature monitors all additions, deletions, and formatting changes you make in a document. When Track Changes is active, it applies **Revision Marks**, which are onscreen elements that indicate locations where a person added, deleted, or formatted text. Word uses colors for different reviewers who edit a document. You can position the mouse pointer over revision marks or markup balloons to see who made the change and on what date and time, as shown in Figure 4.4. The vertical line may be on the left or right side of the screen.

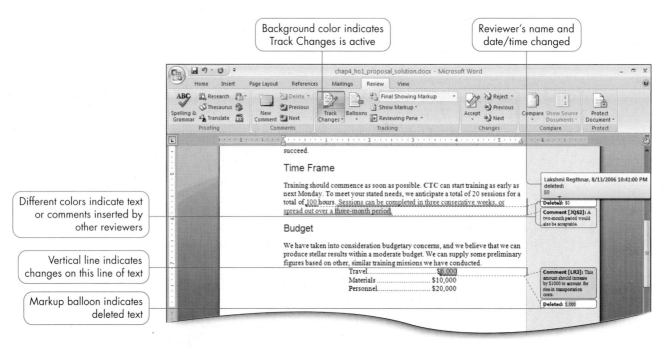

Figure 4.4 An Example of Track Changes

Word also includes markup tools, some of which enable you to accept or reject changes indicated by revision marks. The Changes group on the Review tab includes Accept, to accept a suggested change, and Reject, which removes a suggested change. When you accept or reject a change, the revision marks and markup balloon disappear.

The Track Changes feature is useful in situations where a document must be reviewed by several people, each of whom can offer suggestions or changes, and then returned to one person who must finalize the document. The last person can view all suggestions at the same time, and then accept or reject the suggested changes with the click of a mouse. If the process takes place using paper copies of a document, it is difficult to visualize all the suggested changes at one time, and then the last person must manually change the original document. While writing the Exploring series, the authors, editors, and reviewers each inserted comments and tracked changes to the manuscript for each chapter. Each person's comments or changes displayed in different colored balloons, and because all edits were performed in one document, the last person could accept and reject changes before sending it to the next step of the publishing process.

Select Markup Views

Original Showing Markup view shows a line through deleted text and puts inserted text in a markup balloon.

Final Showing Markup view shows inserted text in the body and puts deleted text in a markup balloon.

The suggested revisions from the various reviewers display in one of two ways, as the Original Showing Markup or as the Final Showing Markup. The *Original Showing Markup* view shows the deleted text within the body of the document (with a line through the deleted text) and displays the inserted text in a balloon to the right of the actual document, as shown in Figure 4.5. The *Final Showing Markup* view is the opposite; that is, it displays the inserted text in the body of the document and shows the deleted text in a balloon. The difference is subtle and depends on personal preference with respect to displaying the insertions and deletions in a document. (All revisions fall into one of these two categories: insertions or deletions. Even if you substitute one word for another, you are deleting the original word and then inserting its replacement.) Both views display revision marks on the edge of any line that has been changed. Comments are optional and enclosed in balloons in the side margin of a document.

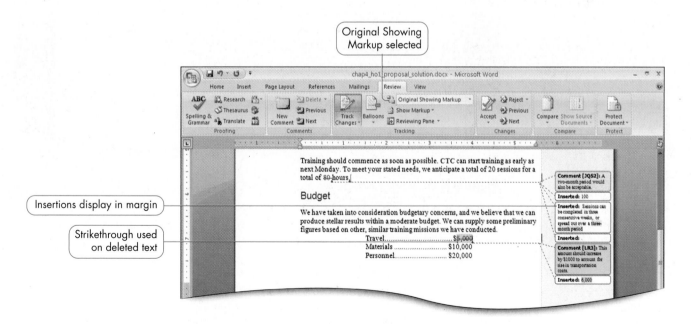

Figure 4.5   Original Showing Markup View

When you click the Display for Review arrow in the Review tab, two additional view options are listed—Final and Original. Final shows how the document looks if you accept and incorporate all tracked changes. Original shows the document prior to using the Track Changes feature.

The review process is straightforward. The initial document is sent for review to one or more individuals, who record their changes by executing the Track Changes command on the Review tab to start (or stop) the recording process. The author of the original document receives the altered document and then uses Accept and Reject in the Changes group on the Review tab to review the document and implement the suggested changes.

Customize Track Changes Options

Although the feature seems to have many options for viewing and displaying changes, you can further customize the Track Changes feature. The following reference page describes the sections and settings you can change in the Track Changes dialog box.

The beginning of this chapter mentioned that you should check the Word Options, making changes if necessary, so your name is associated with any tracked changes you make in the document. You also can access those settings from the Review tab when you click the Track Changes arrow and click Change User Name, as shown in Figure 4.6. This step takes you to the Popular category of the Word Options dialog box, where you have the opportunity to enter your name and initials in the Personalize your copy of Microsoft Office section.

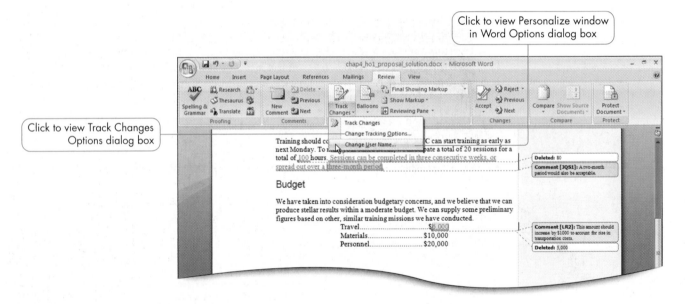

Figure 4.6 Track Changes Customization Options

Track Changes Options Dialog Box | Reference

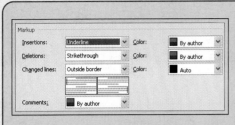

Markup

Specify format property (color, bold, italic, underline, strikethrough) used for insertions and deletions.

Specify location (left border, right border, outside border, none) of marks that indicate a change has been made to text on a line.

Specify color to use for comments, insertions, deletions, and changed lines. Select a standard color for each or assign color by author/reviewer.

Moves

Specify format property (double strikethrough, double underline) used on text that is moved within the document.

Specify color to use for text that is moved within the document.

Select a standard color for each or assign color by author/reviewer.

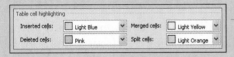

Table cell highlighting

Specify highlight color used to indicate a change in the layout of a table (insert cells, delete cells, merge or split cells).

Select a standard color for each type of modification or assign color by author/reviewer.

Formatting

Turn on Track formatting. Tracks any change made to the format of text or an object.

Specify format property (color, bold, italic, underline, strikethrough) used to indicate a format change.

Specify color of balloon used to indicate a format change.

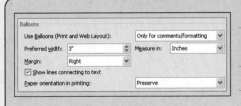

Balloons

Specify when to use balloons in Print and Web Layout views (always, never, only for comments/formatting).

Specify width of balloon.

Specify width measurement (inches or percentage of page width).

Specify in which margin (right or left) to display balloons.

Specify if lines will connect balloons to text.

Hands-On Exercises

1 | Document Collaboration

Skills covered: 1. Set User Name and Customize the Track Changes Options **2.** Track Document Changes **3.** View, Add, and Delete Comments **4.** Accept and Reject Changes

Step 1 **Set User Name and Customize the Track Changes Options**	Refer to Figure 4.7 as you complete Step 1. **a.** Start Word. Open the *chap4_ho1_proposal* document and save it as **chap4_ho1_proposal_solution**. **b.** Click the **Review tab** and click the upper portion of **Track Changes** in the Tracking group. The command should display with an orange background color indicating the feature is turned on. When you click the upper portion of Track Changes, you toggle the feature on or off. When you click the lower portion of Track Changes, a menu of options displays, which you use in the next step. **c.** Click the **Track Changes down arrow**, and then select **Change User Name**. In the *Personalize your copy of Microsoft Office* section, type your name in the **User name** box and type your initials in the **Initials** box, if necessary. Click **OK** to close the Word Options dialog box. You want to be sure your name and initials are correct before you add any comments or initiate any changes in the document. After you update the User information, your initials display with any comments or changes you make. **d.** Click the **Track Changes** arrow and click **Change Tracking Options**. In the *Markup* section, click the **Insertions drop-down arrow**, and then click **Double underline**. In the *Formatting* section, click the **Track formatting check box**. **e.** In the *Balloons* section, click the **Use Balloons (Print and Web Layout) drop-down arrow** and select **Always**, if necessary. Click the **Preferred width spin arrow** until **1.8″** displays. Click the **Margin drop-down arrow** and select **Left**, as shown in Figure 4.7. Click **OK** to close the Track Changes Options dialog box. Your revisions to the Track Changes options enable you to quickly view any additions to the document because they will be identified in balloons and insertions will display with a double underline. Additionally, you altered the location of all comment and editing balloons to display on the left side of your document instead of on the right, which is the default. You also decreased the width of the markup balloons so they will take up less space in the margins. **f.** Save the document.

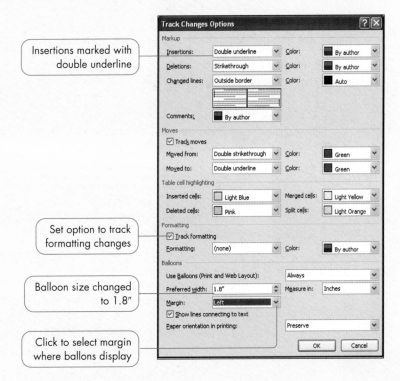

Insertions marked with double underline

Set option to track formatting changes

Balloon size changed to 1.8"

Click to select margin where ballons display

Figure 4.7 Track Changes Options Dialog Box

Refer to Figure 4.8 as you complete Step 2.

a. Click the **Display for Review arrow** in the Tracking group and select **Final Showing Markup**, if necessary. Scroll down to view the bottom of the first page.

One comment and two previous changes display in balloons. Because of the changes you made in Steps 1a and 1b, any future changes you make in the document also display in balloons in the margin of the document.

b. Scroll to the top of the page, select the number 150 in the first paragraph, and replace it with **155**.

TROUBLESHOOTING: If a balloon does not display, indicating the number 150 was deleted, make sure the Track Changes is on. When on, Track Changes is highlighted in an orange color. If necessary, click Track Changes again to turn it on, then repeat Step 2b.

c. Select *Computer Training Concepts, Inc.* in the first sentence of the first paragraph and apply **Bold** from the Mini toolbar.

The changed line appears on the right side of the line you formatted, a markup balloon indicates the formatting change, and the text you inserted in Step 2b is colored with a double underline, as shown in Figure 4.8.

d. Click the **Display for Review arrow** in the Tracking group and select **Final**.

The formatting change indicators do not display, and the text in the first sentence displays in bold.

e. Save the document.

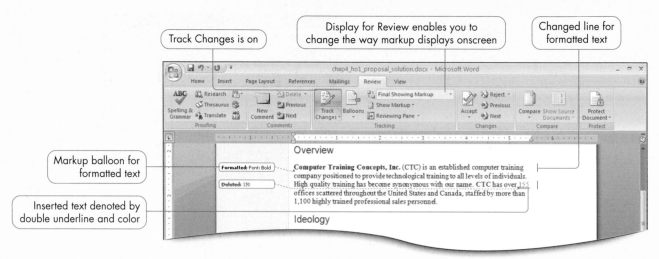

Figure 4.8 View Changes in a Document

Refer to Figure 4.9 as you complete Step 3.

a. Click the **Display for Review arrow** in the Tracking group and select **Final Showing Markup**.

b. Select *three-month period* at the end of the *Time Frame* paragraph. Click **New Comment** in the Comments group, and then type **A four-month period would also be acceptable.**

If you do not select anything prior to clicking New Comment, Word selects the word or object to the left of the insertion point for the comment reference.

c. Select *Computer Training Concepts, Inc.* in the first sentence of the first paragraph. Click **New Comment**, and then type **Should we apply bold to all instances of the company name?** in the markup balloon.

d. Click inside the first markup balloon you created. Edit the comment by replacing *four-month* with **two-month**. Click outside of the balloon to deselect it.

e. Position the mouse pointer over the comment balloon in the Budget paragraph.

When you position the mouse pointer over a markup balloon, Word displays a ScreenTip that tells you who created the comment and when.

f. Click the comment by Lakshmi Regthnar one time to select it, and then click **Delete** in the Comments group of the Review tab (see Figure 4.9).

You removed the selected comment and the markup balloon. If you click the arrow on the right side of Delete, you can select from several options, including Delete all Comments in Document.

g. Save the document.

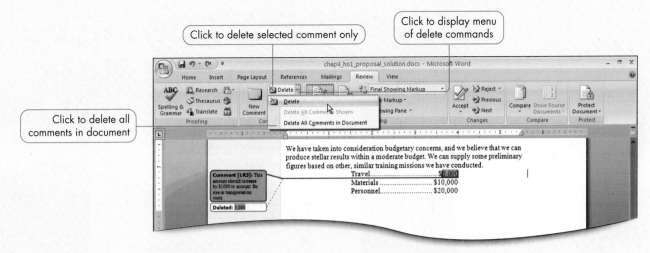

Figure 4.9 Deleting Comments

Step 4
Accept and Reject Changes

Refer to Figure 4.10 as you complete Step 4.

a. Press **Ctrl+Home** to place the insertion point at the beginning of the document.

b. Click **Next** in the Changes group to highlight the first change, and then position the mouse pointer over the tracked change.

When you position the mouse pointer on the revision mark, a ScreenTip appears that tells you who made the change and the date and time the change was made.

TROUBLESHOOTING: If you click Next in the Comments group instead of Next in the Changes group, click Previous in the Comments group, and then click Next in the Changes group.

c. Click **Accept** in the Changes group.

The formatting change is accepted. When the suggested change is accepted, the markup balloons and other Track Changes markups disappear. Additionally, the markup balloon for the next change or comment is highlighted. As with other commands, you can click the upper portion of the Accept command to accept this change only or you can click the lower portion of the command to view a menu of options for accepting changes.

d. Click **Next** in the Changes group to pass the comment and view the next markup balloon. Click **Accept** two times to accept the change to 155 offices.

e. Click **Reject** two times to retain the session time frame of *80 hours*.

f. Click the **Accept arrow** and click **Accept All Changes in Document**. Click the **Display for Review** arrow and select **Final**.

Figure 4.10 shows the first page after accepting and rejecting changes.

g. Save and close *chap4_ho1_proposal_solution*. Exit Word if you will not continue with the next exercise at this time.

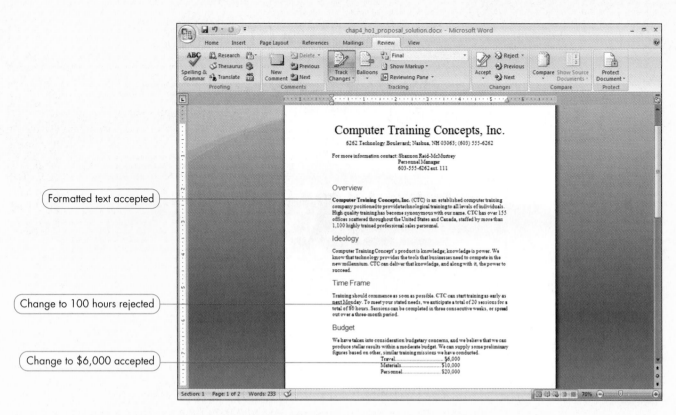

Formatted text accepted

Change to 100 hours rejected

Change to $6,000 accepted

Figure 4.10 The Revised Document

Multiple Documents

(Features in Word enable you to work with multiple documents simultaneously—you can view multiple documents at one time, as well as combine them into one.)

The collaboration features in Word facilitate an easy exchange of ideas and revisions to a document. But some users do not use the collaboration features, which causes the process of combining information into one document to be less efficient. Fortunately, other features in Word enable you to work with multiple documents simultaneously—you can view multiple documents at one time, as well as combine them into one.

In this section, you display multiple documents side by side as well as compare and combine documents into a new file. You create a document that contains subdocuments and then use tools to navigate within lengthy documents. Finally, you create an electronic marker for a location in a document and use the Go To feature.

Viewing Documents Side by Side

View Side by Side enables you to display two documents on the same screen.

The ***View Side by Side*** feature enables you to display two documents on the same screen. This is a useful tool when you want to compare an original to a revised document or when you want to cut or copy a portion from one document to another. To view two documents side by side, you must open both documents. The View Side by Side command is grayed out if only one document is open. When the documents are open, click View Side by Side in the Window group on the View tab, and the Word window will split to display each document, as shown in Figure 4.11. If you have more than two documents open, the Compare Side by Side dialog box displays and you select which document you want to display beside the active document.

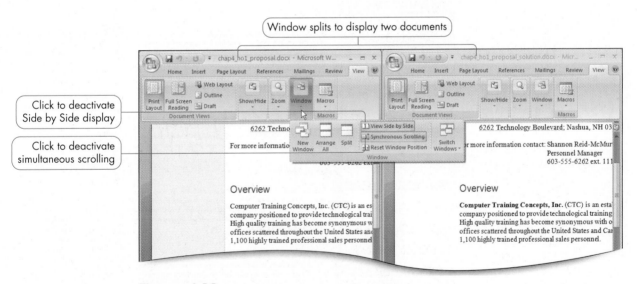

Figure 4.11 View Documents Side by Side

Synchronous scrolling enables you to simultaneously scroll through documents in Side by Side view.

When the documents display side by side, synchronous scrolling is active by default. ***Synchronous scrolling*** enables you to scroll through both documents at the same time. If you want to scroll through each document independently, click Synchronous Scrolling on the View tab to toggle it off. If you are viewing two versions of the same document, synchronous scrolling enables you to view both documents using only one scroll bar. If you scroll through each document asynchronously, you must use the respective scroll bars to navigate through each document.

While in Side by Side view, you can resize and reposition the two document windows. If you want to reset them to the original side-by-side viewing size, click Reset Window Position on the View tab. To close Side by Side view, click View Side by Side to toggle it off. The document that contains the insertion point when you close Side by Side view will display as the active document.

Comparing and Combining Documents

Ideally, when you have a document to submit to others for feedback, you want everyone to use the Track Changes feature in Word. However, sometimes it is necessary to have several people editing their own copy of the document simultaneously before they return it to you. When this occurs, you have several similar documents but with individual changes. Instead of compiling results from printed copies or viewing each one in Side by Side view to determine the differences, you can use a Compare feature. *Compare* automatically evaluates the contents of two or more documents and displays markup balloons that show the differences between the documents. You can display the differences in the original document, the revised document, or in a new document. You also can display query on the screen with the new document, as shown in Figure 4.12. The Compare command is in the Compare group of the Review tab.

The ***Compare*** feature evaluates the contents of two or more documents and displays markup balloons showing the differences.

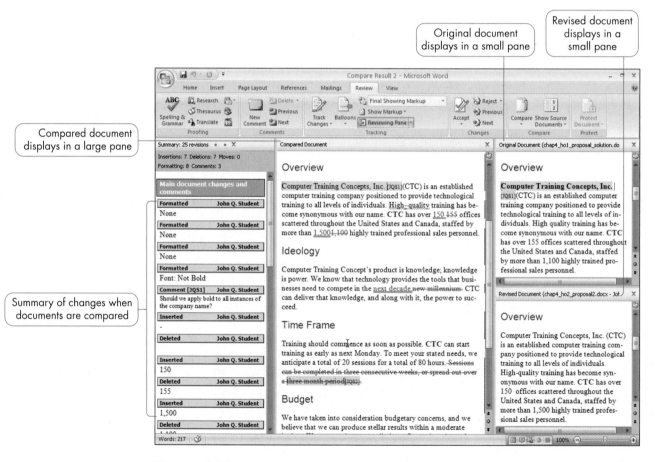

Figure 4.12 Results of Comparing Two Documents

The ***Combine*** feature incorporates all changes from multiple documents into a new document.

If you want to go a step further than just viewing the differences, you can use the *Combine* feature to integrate all changes from multiple documents into one document. To use the Combine feature, click the Compare arrow in the Review tab and select Combine. The Combine Documents dialog box opens displaying a variety of options you can invoke, as shown in Figure 4.13. The option you are most likely to change is in the Show Changes section, where you determine where the Combined documents will display—in the original document, the revised document, or in a new document. If you want to be certain not to modify the original documents, you should combine the changes into a new document.

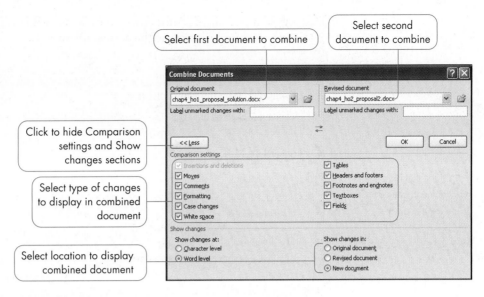

Select first document to combine

Select second document to combine

Click to hide Comparison settings and Show changes sections

Select type of changes to display in combined document

Select location to display combined document

Figure 4.13 The Combine Documents Dialog Box

Creating Master Documents and Subdocuments

Working with long documents can be cumbersome. You may notice your computer slows down when you are working in a lengthy document. Scrolling, finding and replacing, editing, and formatting typically take longer. To improve this situation, you can create a *master document*, a document that acts like a binder for managing smaller documents. A smaller document that is a part of a master document is called a *subdocument*. The advantage of the master document is that you can work with several smaller documents, as opposed to a single large document. Thus, you edit the subdocuments individually and more efficiently than if they were all part of the same document. You can create a master document to hold the chapters of a book, where each chapter is stored as a subdocument. You also can use a master document to hold multiple documents created by others, such as a group project, where each member of the group is responsible for a section of the document.

The Outlining tab contains the Collapse and Expand Subdocuments buttons, as well as other tools associated with master documents. Figure 4.14 displays a master document with five subdocuments. The subdocuments are collapsed in Figure 4.14 and expanded in Figure 4.15. The collapsed structure enables you to see at a glance the subdocuments that comprise the master document. You can insert additional subdocuments or remove existing subdocuments from the master document. Deleting a subdocument from within a master document does not delete the actual subdocument file.

A ***master document*** is a document that acts like a binder for managing smaller documents.

A ***subdocument*** is a smaller document that is a part of a master document.

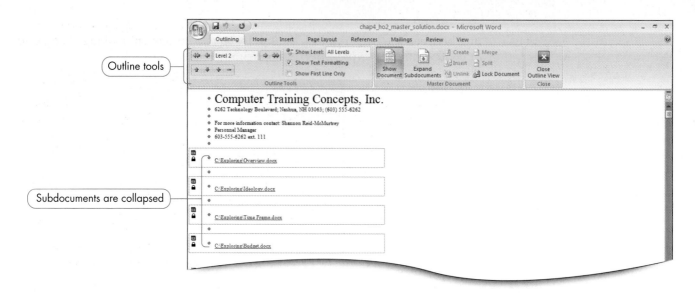

Figure 4.14 Master Document Showing Collapsed Subdocuments

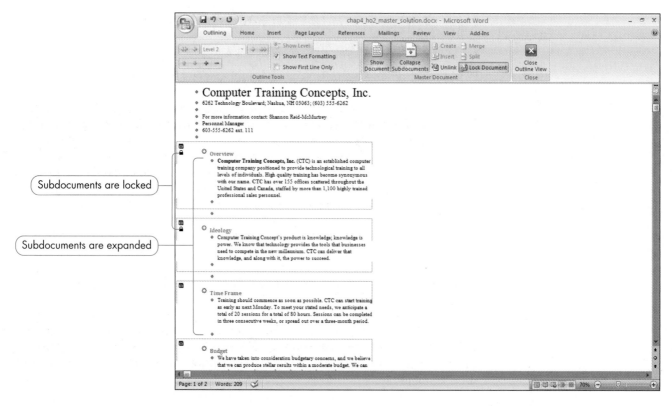

Figure 4.15 Master Document Showing Expanded Subdocuments

The expanded structure enables you to view and/or edit the contents of the sub-documents. Look carefully, however, at the subdocuments in Figure 4.15. A padlock appears to the left of the first line in the first and second subdocuments, whereas it is absent from the third and fourth subdocuments. These subdocuments are locked and unlocked, respectively. (All subdocuments are locked when collapsed, as in Figure 4.14.)

You can make changes to the master document at any time. However, you can make changes to the subdocuments only when the subdocument is unlocked. Note, too, that you can make changes to a subdocument in one of two ways, either when the subdocument is expanded (and unlocked) within a master document, as in Figure 4.15, or by opening the subdocument as an independent document within

Microsoft Word. Both techniques work equally well, and you will find yourself alternating between the two. You lock the subdocuments to prevent making changes to their content but also to prevent the subdocument from being deleted from the master document.

Regardless of how you edit the subdocuments, the attraction of a master document is the ability to work with multiple subdocuments simultaneously. The subdocuments are created independently of one another, with each subdocument stored in its own file. Then, when all of the subdocuments are finished, the master document is created, and the subdocuments are inserted into the master document, from where they are easily accessed. Inserting page numbers into the master document, for example, causes the numbers to run consecutively from one subdocument to the next. You also can create a table of contents or index for the master document that will reflect the entries in all of the subdocuments. And finally, you can print all of the subdocuments from within the master document with a single command.

Alternatively, you can reverse the process by starting with an empty master document and using it as the basis to create the subdocuments. This process is ideal for organizing a group project in school or at work, the chapters in a book, or the sections in a report. Start with a new document, and then enter the topics assigned to each group member. Format each topic in a heading style within the master document, and then use the Create Subdocument command to create subdocuments based on those headings. Saving the master document will automatically save each subdocument in its own file. This is the approach that you will follow in the next hands-on exercise.

TIP Printing a Master Document

If you click Print when a master document is displayed and the subdocuments are collapsed, the message *Do you want to open the subdocuments before continuing with this command?* appears. Click Yes to open the subdocuments so that they will print as one long document. Click No to print the master document that lists the subdocument filenames as they display onscreen.

Using Navigation Tools

Without a reference source, such as a table of contents, it can be difficult to locate information in a long document. Even scrolling through a long document can be inefficient if you are uncertain of the exact location that you want to view. Fortunately, Word provides navigation tools that assist the author and reader in locating content quickly and easily.

Display a Document Map and Thumbnails

The ***Document Map*** is a pane that lists the structure of headings in your document.

You can use the Find and Go To features in Word to move through a document. Another helpful navigation feature is the ***Document Map***, a pane that lists the structure of headings in your document. The headings in a document are displayed in the left pane, and the text of the document is visible in the right pane. You can click a heading in the Document Map to move the insertion point to that heading in the document. When working in long documents, the Document Map provides a way to navigate quickly to a particular topic, as shown in Figure 4.16.

Figure 4.16 The Document Map

To display the Document Map pane, click Document Map in the Show/Hide group on the View tab. If you want to display the Document Map for a master document, be sure the master document is expanded to display the text of the subdocuments. This feature is a toggle; to close the Document Map, remove the check mark from the Document Map check box. The Document Map can be used on any document that uses the styles feature to format headings. The best way to format headings is to apply the built-in Title or Heading styles from the Styles group on the Home tab.

Thumbnails are small pictures of each page in your document that display in a separate window pane.

In lieu of the Document Map, you can display **Thumbnails**—small pictures of each page in your document that display in a pane on the left side of the screen. As with the Document Map, you can click a thumbnail to move the insertion point to the top of that page. This is another method of navigating quickly through a document.

Even though you cannot read the text on a thumbnail, you can see the layout of a page well enough to determine if that is a location you want to display. And if you display markup, the revision marks and comments also display in the thumbnails, as shown in Figure 4.17. The Thumbnails view is a toggle; click the Thumbnails check box on the Show/Hide group of the View tab to display the pane, and remove the check to turn it off.

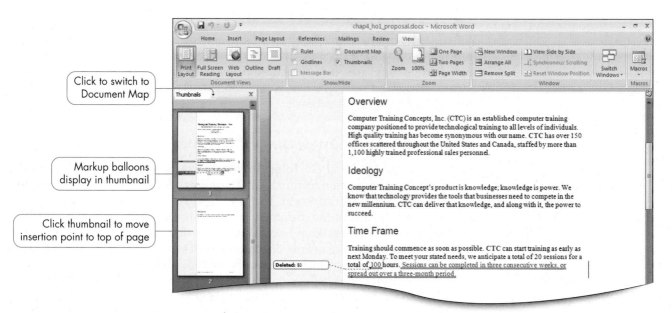

Figure 4.17 Show Markup Features

Insert Bookmarks

The ***bookmark*** feature is an electronic marker for a specific location in a document

When you read a book you use a bookmark to help you return to that location quickly. Word provides the ***bookmark*** feature as an electronic marker for a specific location in a document, enabling the user to go to that location quickly. Bookmarks are helpful to mark a location where you are working. You can scroll to other parts of a document and then quickly go back to the bookmarked location. The Bookmark command is in the Links group on the Insert tab. After you click the command, the Bookmark dialog box displays, and you can designate the name of the bookmark, as shown in Figure 4.18. Bookmarks are inserted at the location of the insertion point. Bookmark names cannot contain spaces or hyphens; however, they may contain the underscore character to improve readability.

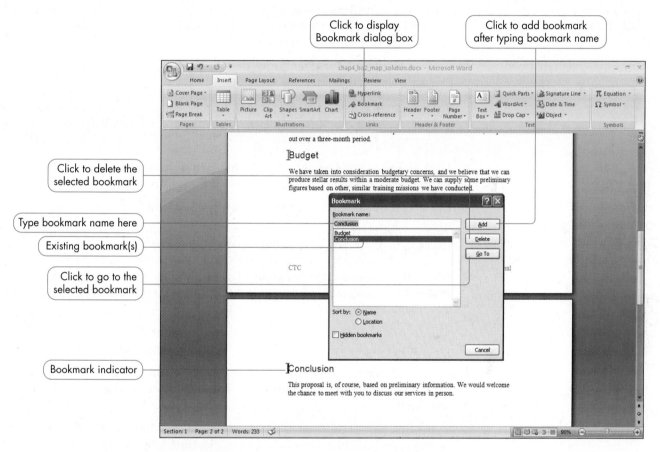

Figure 4.18 Bookmark a Location in the Document

After you insert a bookmark, you can click Bookmark on the Insert tab to see a list of bookmarks in the current document. Click a bookmark in the Bookmark name list, and then click Go To to move the insertion point to that bookmarked location. You can also press Ctrl+G to open the Go To tab of the Find and Replace dialog box. When you click Bookmark in the *Go to what* section, a drop-down list of bookmarks is available to choose from.

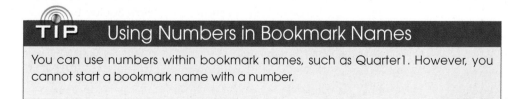

TIP Using Numbers in Bookmark Names

You can use numbers within bookmark names, such as Quarter1. However, you cannot start a bookmark name with a number.

Hands-On Exercises

2 | Document Comparison, Mergers, and Navigation

Skills covered: 1. Compare and Combine Documents **2.** View Documents Side by Side **3.** Create Master Documents and Subdocuments **4.** Modify Master Documents and Subdocuments **5.** Use Document Map and Create Bookmarks

---

Step 1
Compare and Combine Documents

Refer to Figure 4.19 as you complete Step 1.

a. Click the **Office Button**, select **New**, and double-click **Blank document**. Click the **Review tab**. Click **Compare**, and then click **Compare** to display the Compare Documents dialog box.

b. Click the **Original document drop-down arrow** and select the *chap4_ho1_proposal_solution* document.

> **TROUBLESHOOTING:** If the chap4_ho1_proposal_solution document does not display in the drop-down list, click the Browse for Original button to locate the document.

c. Click **Browse for Revised** beside the **Revised document** text box, and then browse to locate and open the *chap4_ho2_proposal2* document.

d. Click **New document** under *Show changes in*, if necessary.

> **TROUBLESHOOTING:** If the Comparison settings and Show changes sections do not display, click More to display them.

e. Click **OK**, and then click **Yes** in the Microsoft Office Word dialog box that explains how the tracked changes in each document will be accepted before the document displays.

The document opens in a new window and contains markup balloons to indicate each difference in the two documents. The Reviewing Pane might also display.

f. Save the document as **chap4_ho2_compare_solution**. If the Reviewing Pane displays, click **Reviewing Pane** in the Tracking group on the Review tab to remove it.

In the first part of this exercise, you compared two documents. In the next series of steps, you combine the documents. Take time to notice how Word tracks the differences in compared versus combined documents.

g. In the Compare group, click **Compare**, and then click **Combine** to display the Combine Documents dialog box.

h. Click the **Original document drop-down arrow** and select the *chap4_ho1_proposal_solution* document. Click **Browse for Revised** and browse to locate the *chap4_ho2_proposal2* document.

i. Click **New document** under *Show changes in*, if necessary. Click **OK**, and then click **Continue with Merge**.

> **TROUBLESHOOTING:** If the two documents you just merged display in small windows on the screen, click **Show Source Documents** in the Compare group on the Review tab, and then click **Hide Source Documents** to close them.

The document opens in a new window and contains markup balloons to indicate each difference in the two documents, as shown in Figure 4.19. Depending on your Track Changes settings, the balloons might display on either the left or right side of your document.

j. Save the document as **chap4_ho2_combine_solution**.

k. Leave both documents open for Step 2. If the two documents you just merged display in small windows on the screen, click **Show Source Documents** in the Compare group on the Review tab, and then click **Hide Source Documents** to close them.

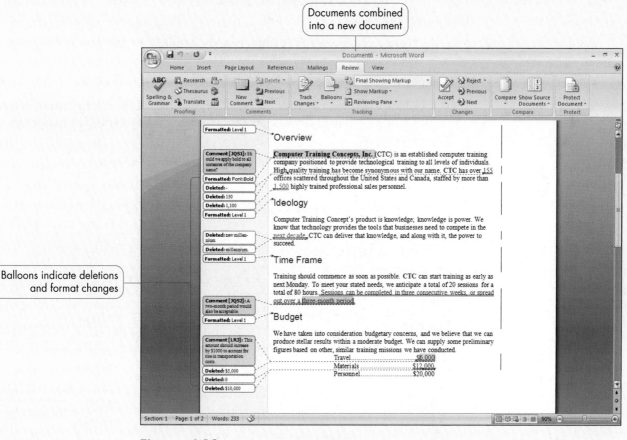

Figure 4.19 Combining Documents

Refer to Figure 4.20 as you complete Step 2.

a. If *chap4_ho2_combine_solution* is not the active document, click the **View tab**, click **Switch Windows**, and then click *chap4_ho2_combine_solution* from the list. Click **View Side by Side** in the Window group.

Two windows display containing the files you created using the compare and combine features. Notice in the Window group on the View tab that Synchronous Scrolling is highlighted in an orange color to indicate the setting is on. As you scroll in one document, the other will scroll also.

TROUBLESHOOTING: If your view of one or both of the documents is insufficient, you can use the mouse to resize the window. Click and drag the border of the window until you reach an acceptable size to view the document information.

b. Scroll down to view the Time Frame paragraph and compare the differences.

In the *chap4_ho2_compare_solution* document, the last sentence in this section is deleted and displays in a markup balloon. In the *chap4_ho2_combine_solution* document, the last sentence displays in the paragraph.

c. Click **Synchronous Scrolling** on the View tab, as shown in Figure 4.20, to turn the toggle off. Scroll down in the *chap4_ho2_combine_solution* document until the Conclusion paragraph displays.

Since the Synchronous Scrolling toggle is off, the *chap4_ho2_compare_solution* document does not scroll, and the Time Frame paragraph remains in view.

d. Scroll to the top of the page. Click the **Review tab**, click the **Tracking arrow**, click the **Display for Review arrow**, and then click **Final**. Do this for both documents.

Notice the bold formatting is only applied to the company name in the *chap4_ho2_combine_solution* document.

e. Close *chap4_ho2_compare_solution* without saving.

f. In the *chap4_ho2_combine_solution* document, click the **Accept arrow** in the Changes group of the Review tab, and then click **Accept All Changes in Document**.

g. Save and close the *chap4_ho2_combine_solution* document.

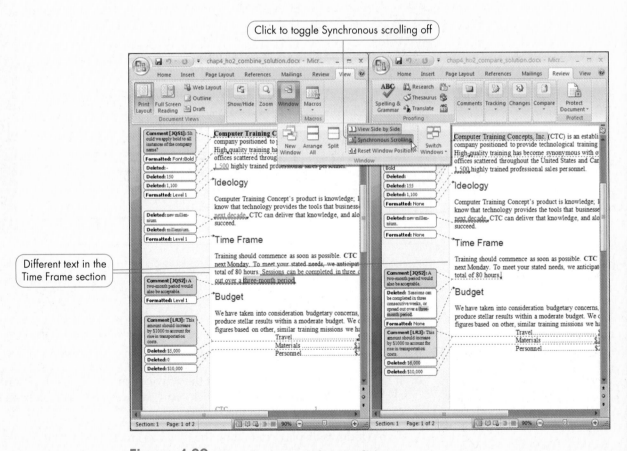

Figure 4.20 View Documents Side by Side

Refer to Figure 4.21 as you complete Step 3.

a. Open the *chap4_ho2_master* document and save it as **chap4_ho2_master_solution**.

b. Press **Ctrl+End** to move to the end of the document. Type the following headings for the subdocuments: **Overview**, **Ideology**, **Time Frame**, **Budget**, and **Conclusion**.

c. Select the topics you just typed, and then click **Heading 2** from the Quick Styles gallery on the Home tab. Click the **Outline** button on the status bar.

The Outlining tab displays and the document text displays in Outline view. Be sure all five headings are still selected before you perform the next step.

d. Click **Show Document** in the Master Document group to display more master document commands. Click **Create**.

Individual subdocuments are created for the selected headings. A box surrounds each subdocument, and you see a subdocument icon in the top-left corner of each subdocument box, as shown in Figure 4.21. You also will see section breaks and other formatting marks if your Show/Hide ¶ feature is turned on.

e. Click **Collapse Subdocuments** in the Master Document group to collapse the subdocuments in the document and display the name and path where each subdocument is saved. Click **OK** if prompted to save changes to the master document.

f. Click **Expand Subdocuments** in the Master Document group to reopen and display the subdocuments.

g. Save the document.

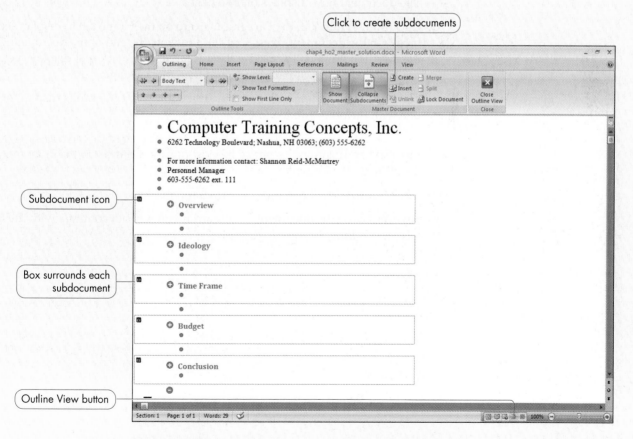

Figure 4.21   View Subdocuments in a Master Document

Refer to Figure 4.22 as you complete Step 4.

a. Press **Ctrl+End** to move to the end of the master document.

b. Click **Insert** in the Master Document group to display the Insert Subdocument dialog box. If necessary, click the **Look in drop-down arrow** to change to the **Exploring Word folder** and select *chap4_ho2_background*. Then click **Open** to insert this document into the master document. If prompted to rename the style in the subdocument, click **Yes**.

The Background Information and Financial Statement paragraphs display as a subdocument at the bottom of the page.

c. Click within the third subdocument, Time Frame, which will eventually summarize the amount of time the company requires for training.

d. Click **Lock Document** in the Master Document group of the Outlining tab. Press the letter **a** on the keyboard.

The padlock icon displays below the subdocument icon and the Lock Document command is highlighted in an orange color to indicate the toggle is on. Attempts to type or edit text are not successful because the document is locked.

e. Click **Lock Document** a second time to unlock the document. Click below the Time Frame heading and type the text, as shown in Figure 4.22. Then click **Save** to save changes to the Master document.

TROUBLESHOOTING: Be sure the subdocument is unlocked so the changes you make will be reflected in the subdocument file as well.

f. Click **Close Outline View** to return to Print Layout view.

The document now displays on two pages.

g. Click **Show/Hide ¶** in the Paragraph group on the Home tab to display section breaks in the document. Press **Ctrl+End** to view the end of the document. Place the insertion point on the *Section Break (Continuous)* mark that displays below the *Financial Statement* paragraph, and then press **Delete**.

The *Background Information* and *Financial Statement* paragraphs display on page one with the other subdocument headings.

TROUBLESHOOTING: If the last two paragraphs still display on page two, position the insertion point on the left of the last paragraph mark in the document and press **Delete** to remove the empty second page.

h. Click **Show/Hide ¶** to toggle off paragraph marks.

i. Save and close the document. Exit Word if you will not continue with the next step at this time.

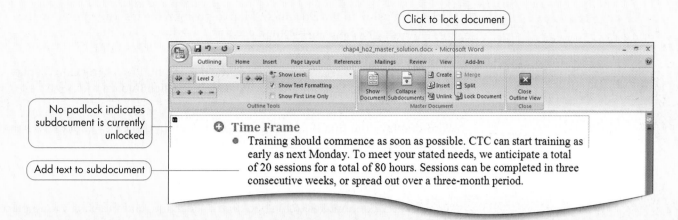

Figure 4.22 Modify a Subdocument

Refer to Figure 4.23 as you complete Step 5.

a. Open the *chap4_ho1_proposal_solution* document you completed in Step 1 and save it as **chap4_ho2_map_solution**. Click the **View tab** and click **Thumbnails** in the Show/Hide group to display the Thumbnails pane on the left side of the screen.

The Thumbnails appear as a separate pane on the left side of your screen. An orange border appears around the thumbnail of the currently viewed page.

b. Click the thumbnail for the second page.

Word positions the insertion point at the beginning of the second page.

c. Click **Thumbnails** to hide the thumbnails pane. Click **Document Map**.

The Document Map contains a list of text formatted with built-in heading styles. Like Thumbnails, it is a toggle. Clicking it again hides the Document Map pane.

d. Click **Overview** in the Document Map. Click **Computer Training Concepts, Inc.** in the Document Map.

Because of your actions, Word moves the insertion point to the left side of the *Overview* heading near the top of the first page, and then moves it to the left of *Computer Training Concepts*. Because *Overview* and other headings are formatted with the Heading 2 style, they display in the Document Map.

e. Click **Budget** in the Document Map.

You moved the insertion point and now you will insert a bookmark in this location.

f. Click the **Insert tab** and click **Bookmark** in the Links group. Type **Budget** in the Bookmark name text box, then click **Add**.

Word inserts a bookmark with the name you entered. A large, gray-colored I-beam indicates the location of the bookmark.

TROUBLESHOOTING: If you do not see the bookmark indicator, you can change a setting that enables it. Click the Office Button, then click Word Options. Click Advanced, and then scroll down and click the *Show bookmarks* check box in the Show document content section. Click OK to save the settings and return to the document.

g. Click **Conclusion** in the Document Map to position the insertion point on the top of the second page next to the *Conclusion* heading. Click **Bookmark**, type **Conclusion** in the Bookmark name text box, and then click **Add**.

h. Press **Ctrl+Home** to return to the top of the document. Press **Ctrl+G** to display the *Go To* tab of the Find and Replace dialog box. Click **Bookmark** in the *Go to what* list.

Word displays the first bookmark name, Budget, in the Enter bookmark name text box, as shown in Figure 4.23. If you click the *Enter bookmark name* drop-down arrow, the Conclusion bookmark also will display in the list.

i. Click **Go To**.

The insertion point moves to the bookmark's location, and the Find and Replace dialog box remains onscreen in case you want to go to another bookmark.

j. Click **Close** to remove the Find and Replace dialog box. Click **Close** in the upper-right corner of the Document Map pane.

k. Save and close the file. Exit Word if you will not continue with the next exercise at this time.

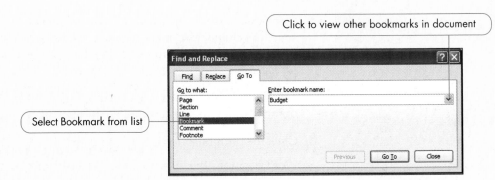

Figure 4.23 Go to a Bookmark

Reference Resources

Well-prepared documents often include notes that provide supplemental information or citations for sources quoted in the document. Some documents also contain other valuable supplemental components, such as a list of figures or legal references. Word 2007 includes many features that can help you create these supplemental references, as well as many others described in the following paragraphs.

In this section, you use Word to create citations used for reference pages, create a bibliography page that displays works cited in the document, and select from a list of writing styles that are commonly used to dictate the format of reference pages. You also create and modify footnote and endnote citations, which display at the bottom or end of the document.

Acknowledging a Source

Failure to acknowledge the source of information you use in a document is a form of plagiarism. Word includes a robust feature for tracking sources and producing the supplemental resources to display them.

Plagiarism is the act of using and documenting the ideas or writings of another as one's own.

It is common practice to use a variety of sources to supplement your own thoughts when writing a paper, report, legal brief, or many other types of document. Failure to acknowledge the source of information you use in a document is a form of plagiarism. *Webster's New Collegiate Dictionary* defines **plagiarism** as the act of using and documenting the ideas or writings of another as one's own. Plagiarism has serious moral and ethical implications and is taken very seriously in the academic community, and is often classified as academic dishonesty. It is also a violation of U.S. Copyright law, so it should be avoided in any professional and personal setting also.

To assist in your efforts to avoid plagiarism, which is frequently a thoughtless oversight rather than a malicious act, Word includes a robust feature for tracking sources and producing the supplemental resources to display them.

Create a Source

A **citation** is a note recognizing a source of information or a quoted passage.

Word provides the citation feature to track, compile, and display your research sources for inclusion in several types of supplemental references. To use this feature you use the Insert Citation command in the Citations & Bibliography group on the References tab to add data about each source, as shown in Figure 4.24. A **citation** is a note recognizing the source of information or a quoted passage. The Create Source dialog box includes fields to catalog information, such as author, date, publication name, page number, or Web site address, from the following types of sources:

- Book
- Book Section
- Journal Article
- Article in a Periodical
- Conference Proceedings
- Report
- Web Site
- Document from Web Site
- Electronic Source
- Art
- Sound Recording
- Performance
- Film
- Interview
- Patent
- Case
- Miscellaneous

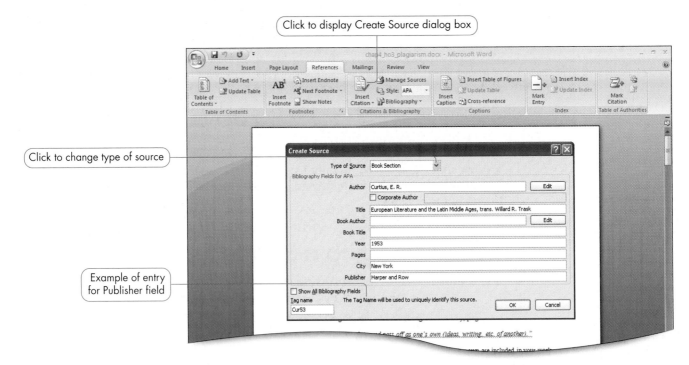

Figure 4.24 Add a Source Citation

After you create the citation sources, you can insert them into a document using the Insert Citation command. When you click the command, a list of your sources displays; click a source from the list, and the proper citation format is inserted in your document.

Share and Search for a Source

The ***Master List*** is a database of all citation sources created in Word.

The ***Current List*** includes all citation sources you use in the current document.

After you add sources, they are saved in a Master List. The ***Master List*** is a database of all citation sources created in Word on a particular computer. The source also is stored in the ***Current List***, which contains all sources you use in the current document. Sources saved in the Master List can be used in any Word document. This feature is very helpful to those who use the same sources on multiple occasions. Master Lists are stored in XML format, so you can share the Master List file with coworkers or other authors, eliminating the need to retype the information and to ensure accuracy. The Master List file is stored in \Application Data\Microsoft\Bibliography, which is a subfolder of the user account folder stored under C:\Documents and Settings. For example, a path to the Master File might be C:\Documents and Settings\John Q. Student\Application Data\Microsoft\Bibliography\Sources.xml.

The Source Manager dialog box (see Figure 4.25) displays the Master List you created, and you also can browse to find others. If you do not have access to a Master List on a local or network drive, you can e-mail the Master List file. After you open the Master List, you can copy sources to your Current List. You also can use the Research and Reference Pane to search external libraries for Master Lists of sources. If a library or host service makes its sources available in a format compatible with Office 2007, you can import its files, open the Master File, and insert a citation, avoiding the need to fill out a new Source form in Word.

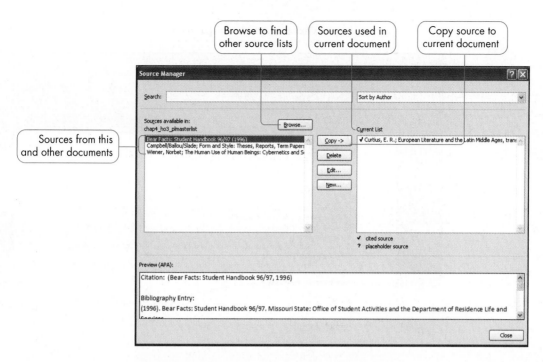

Browse to find other source lists

Sources used in current document

Copy source to current document

Sources from this and other documents

Figure 4.25 Source Manager Dialog Box

Creating a Bibliography

A **bibliography** is a list of works cited or consulted by an author in a document.

A **bibliography** is a list of works cited or consulted by an author and should be included with the document when published. Some reference manuals use the terms Works Cited or References instead of Bibliography. A bibliography is just one form of reference that gives credit to the sources you consulted or quoted in the preparation of your paper. The addition of a bibliography to your completed work demonstrates respect for the material consulted and proves that you are not plagiarizing. It also gives the reader an opportunity to validate your references for accuracy.

Word includes a bibliography feature that makes the addition of this reference page very easy. After you add the sources using the Insert Citation feature, you click Bibliography in the Citations & Bibliography group of the References tab, and then click Insert Bibliography. Any sources used in the current document will display in the appropriate format as a Bibliography, as shown in Figure 4.26.

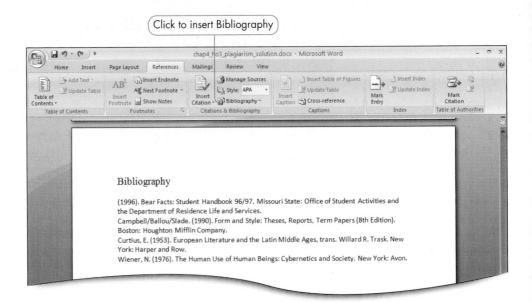

Figure 4.26 Bibliography

Selecting the Writing Style

When research papers are prepared the author often must conform to a particular writing style. The writing style, also called an editorial style, consists of rules and guidelines set forth by a publisher of a research journal to ensure consistency in presentation of research documents. Some of the presentation consistencies that a style enforces are use of punctuation and abbreviations, format of headings and tables, presentation of statistics, and citation of references. The style guidelines differ depending on the discipline the research topic comes from. For example, the APA style originates with the American Psychological Association, but many other disciplines use this style as well. Another common style is MLA, which is sanctioned by the Modern Language Association. The topic of your paper and the audience you write to will determine which style you should use while writing.

Word 2007 incorporates several writing style guidelines, which makes it easier for you to generate supplemental references in the required format. The Style list in the Citations & Bibliography group on the References tab includes the most commonly used international styles, as shown in Figure 4.27. When you select the style before creating the bibliography, the citations that appear in the bibliography will be formatted exactly as required by that style.

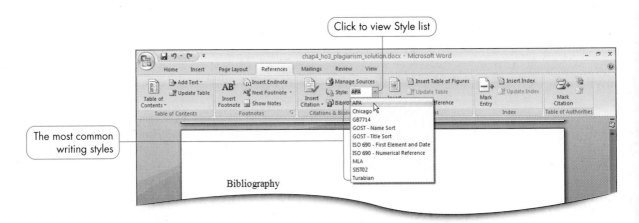

Figure 4.27 Style Options

Creating and Modifying Footnotes and Endnotes

A ***footnote*** is a citation that appears at the bottom of a page.

An ***endnote*** is a citation that appears at the end of a document.

A *footnote* is a citation that appears at the bottom of a page, and an *endnote* is a citation that appears at the end of a document. You use footnotes or endnotes to credit the sources you quote or cite in your document. You also can use footnotes or endnotes to provide supplemental information about a topic that is too distracting to include in the body of the document. Footnotes, endnotes, and bibliographies often contain the same information. Your use of one of the three options is determined by the style of paper (MLA for example) or by the person who oversees your research. When you use a bibliography, the information about a source is displayed only one time at the end of the paper, and the exact location in the document that uses information from the source may not be obvious. When you use a footnote, the information about a source displays on the specific page where a quote or information appears. When you use endnotes, the information about a source displays only at the end of the document; however, the number that identifies the endnote displays on each page, and you can use several references to the same source throughout the document.

The References tab includes the Insert Footnote and Insert Endnote commands. If you click the Footnotes Dialog Box Launcher, the Footnote and Endnote dialog box opens, and you can modify the location of the notes and the format of the numbers. By default, Word sequentially numbers footnotes with Arabic numerals (1, 2, and 3), as shown in Figure 4.28. Endnotes are numbered with lowercase Roman numerals (i, ii, and iii) based on the location of the note within the document. If you add or delete notes, Word renumbers the remaining notes automatically.

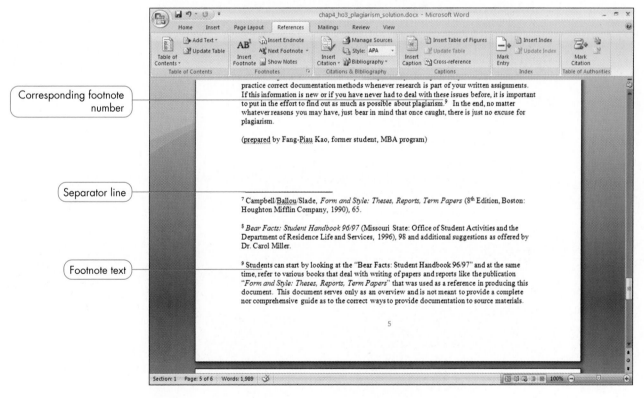

Figure 4.28 Document Containing Footnotes

You can easily make modifications to footnotes and endnotes. In Print Layout view, scroll to the bottom of the page (or for endnotes, to the end of the document or section), click inside the note, and then edit it. In Draft view, double-click the footnote or endnote reference mark to see the Footnotes or Endnotes pane, then edit the note.

TIP   Relocating a Footnote or Endnote

If you created a note in the wrong location, select the note reference mark, cut it from its current location, and then paste it in the correct location within the document text. You also can use the drag-and-drop method to move a selected note reference mark to a different location.

Hands-On Exercises

3 | Reference Resources

Skills covered: 1. Create and Search for a Source **2.** Select a Writing Style and Insert a Bibliography **3.** Create and Modify Footnotes **4.** Convert Footnotes to Endnotes and Modify Endnotes

---

<table>
<tr>
<td>

Step 1

Create and Search for a Source

</td>
<td>

Refer to Figure 4.29 as you complete Step 1.

a. Open the *chap4_ho3_plagiarism* document and save it as **chap4_ho3_ plagiarism_ solution**.

b. Click the **References tab**, click **Manage Sources** in the Citations & Bibliography group, and then click **New** in the middle of the dialog box.

Because you want to create a citation source without inserting it into the document, you use the Source Manager instead of Create Citation. After you click New in the Source Manager, the Create Source dialog box displays.

c. Click the **Type of Source drop-down arrow** and select **Book Section**. Type the source information in the Bibliography fields, as shown in Figure 4.29, and then click **OK** to add the source to your document and return to the Source Manager dialog box.

d. Click **Browse** in the Source Manager dialog box to display the Open Source List dialog box. Click the **Look in drop-down arrow** and navigate to the Exploring Word folder. Select *chap4_ho3_plmasterlist*, and then click **OK**.

You return to the Source Manager dialog box, and three sources display in the *Sources available in* box.

e. Click the first source entry, if necessary, to select it. Then press and hold **Shift** and select the last entry. Click **Copy** to insert the sources into the current document.

The three sources you copied and the one source you created display in the Current List box.

f. Click **Close** to return to the document. Save the document.

</td>
</tr>
</table>

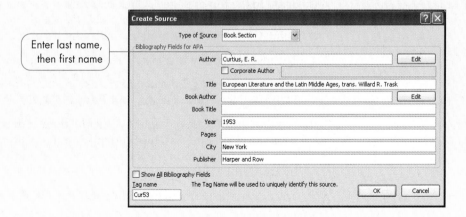

Figure 4.29 Add a New Source

Refer to Figure 4.30 as you complete Step 2.

a. Click the **Style arrow** in the Citations and Bibliography group and select **MLA**.

b. Press **Ctrl+End** to position the insertion point at the end of the document, press **Ctrl+Enter** to add a blank page, type **Bibliography** at the top of the new page, and then press **Enter** two times.

c. Click **Bibliography**, and then click **Insert Bibliography**.

The sources cited in the document display in the MLA format for bibliographies, as shown in Figure 4.30.

d. Click the **Style arrow** again and select **APA**.

The format of the bibliography changes to reflect the standards of the APA style.

e. Save the document.

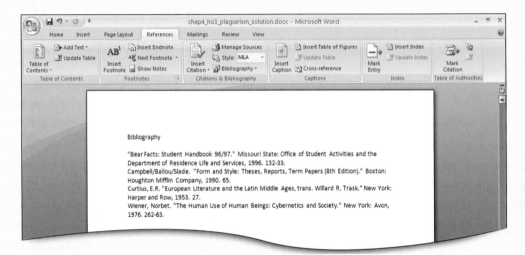

Figure 4.30 Bibliography in MLA Style

Refer to Figure 4.31 as you complete Step 3.

a. Scroll to the top of page 3. Click one time at the end of the paragraph that begins with *Ernst Robert Curtius's term "the Latin Middle Ages"* to move the insertion point. Click **Insert Footnote** in the Footnotes group on the References tab.

The insertion point displays at the bottom of the page, below the horizontal line.

b. Type **E. R. Curtius,** *European Literature and the Latin Middle Ages,* **trans. Willard R. Trask (New York: Harper and Row, 1953), 27.**

c. Scroll to the bottom of page 5. Click one time at the end of the seventh footnote, a reference to *Bear Facts,* the Student Handbook. Remove the period that follows the page number and type the following: **and additional suggestions as offered by Dr. Carol Miller.**

You edited the footnote by adding text to it, as shown in Figure 4.31.

d. Save the document.

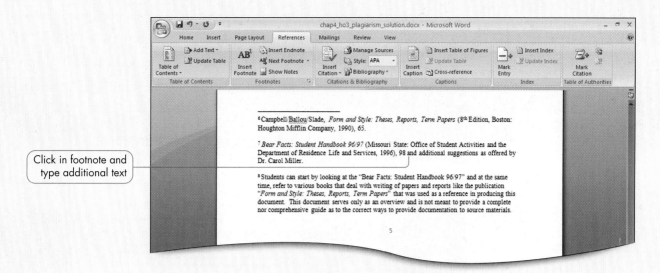

Click in footnote and type additional text

Figure 4.31 Modify a Footnote

Step 4
Convert Footnotes to Endnotes and Modify Endnotes

Refer to Figure 4.32 as you complete Step 4.

a. Click the **Footnotes Dialog Box Launcher**. Click **Convert**, click **Convert all footnotes to endnotes**, and then click **OK**. Click **Close** to close the Footnote and Endnote dialog box.

All footnotes relocate to the last page, below the Bibliography, and the number format is changed to Roman numerals.

b. Scroll to the bottom of page 3. Move the insertion point to the end of the first example paragraph, which ends with *subject to law*. Click **Insert Endnote** and type **Norbet Wiener,** *The Human Use of Human Beings: Cybernetics and Society* **(New York: Avon, 1976), 262–63.**

The endnote displays at the end of the document and the endnote numbers adjust for the addition, as shown in Figure 4.32.

c. Save and close the document. Exit Word if you will not continue with the next exercise at this time.

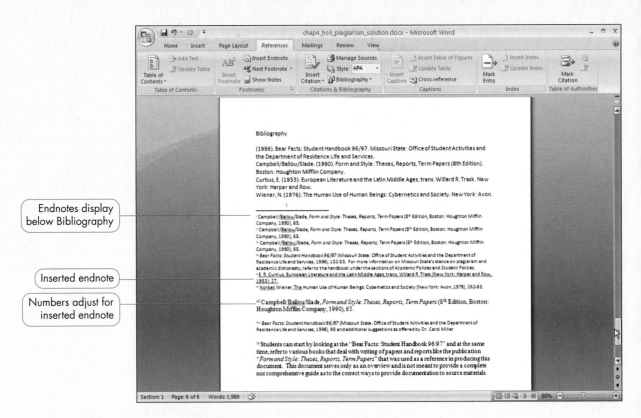

Endnotes display below Bibliography

Inserted endnote

Numbers adjust for inserted endnote

Figure 4.32 Modify an Endnote

Additional Reference Resources

The previous section mentioned several types of reference features that should be used when a document refers to outside information or sources. Some reference features are used less frequently, yet are valuable for creating professional quality documents. These supplements include a list of captions used on figures, a list of figures presented in a document, references to other locations in a document, and a list of legal sources referenced. You also can attach information that refers to the contents and origin of a document.

> Some reference features are used less frequently, yet are valuable for creating professional quality documents. You also can attach information that refers to the contents and origin of a document.

In this section, you add descriptions to visual elements and create a list of the visuals used in a document. You create a cross-reference, or note that refers the reader to another location in the document, and you create a list of references from a legal document. Finally, you modify the properties associated with a document.

Adding Figure References

Documents and books often contain several images, charts, or tables. For example, this textbook contains several screenshots in each project. To help readers refer to the correct image or table, you can insert a caption. A *caption* is a descriptive title for an image, a figure, or a table. To add a caption, click Insert Caption in the Captions group on the References tab. By default, Word assigns a number to the equation, figure, or table at the beginning of the caption. When you click Insert Caption, the Caption dialog box appears, as shown in Figure 4.33, and you can edit the default caption by adding descriptive text.

A *caption* is a descriptive title for an equation, a figure, or a table.

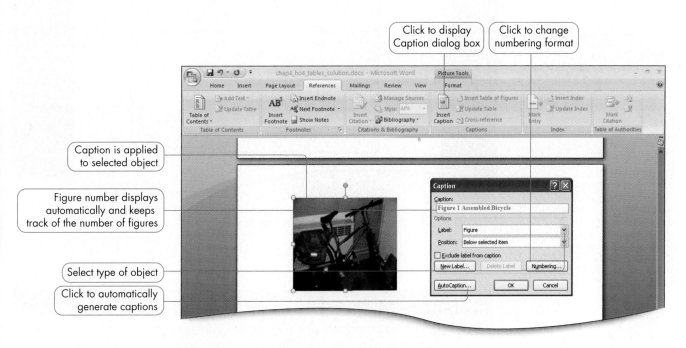

Figure 4.33 Insert Caption Dialog Box

To automatically generate captions, click AutoCaption in the Caption dialog box. In the *Add caption when inserting* list, in the AutoCaption dialog box, click the check box next to the element type for which you want to create AutoCaptions. Specify the default caption text in the *Use label* text box, and specify the location of the caption by clicking the Position drop-down arrow. If your document will contain several captions, this feature helps you to ensure each caption is named and numbered sequentially.

Inserting a Table of Figures

A ***table of figures*** is a list of the captions in a document.

If your document includes pictures, charts and graphs, slides, or other illustrations along with a caption, you can include a ***table of figures***, or list of the captions, as a reference. To build a table of figures, Word searches a document for captions, sorts the captions by number, and displays the table of figures in the document. A table of figures is placed after the table of contents for a document. The Insert Table of Figures command is in the Captions group on the References tab. The Table of Figures dialog box, shown in Figure 4.34, enables you to select page number, format, and caption label options.

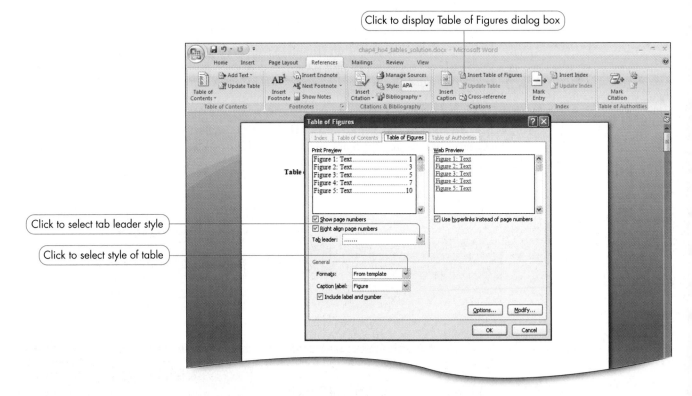

Figure 4.34 The Table of Figures Dialog Box

(((TIP   Update a Table of Figures

If the figures or figure captions in a document change or are removed, you should update the table of figures. To update the table, right-click on any table entry to select the entire table and display a menu. Click Update Field, and then choose between the options Update Page Numbers only or Update entire table. If significant changes have been made, you should update the entire table.

Adding Legal References

A *table of authorities* is used in legal documents to reference cases, rules, treaties, and other documents referred to in a legal brief. You typically compile the table of authorities on a separate page at the beginning of a legal document, as shown in Figure 4.35. Word's table of authorities feature enables you to track, compile, and display citations, or references to specific legal cases and other legal documents, to be included in the table of authorities. Before you generate the table of authorities, you must indicate which citations you want to include using the Mark Citation command in the Table of Authorities group on the References tab. To mark citations, select text and then click Mark Citation. After you mark the citations, click Insert Table of Authorities in the Table of Authorities group on the References tab to generate the table at the location of your insertion point.

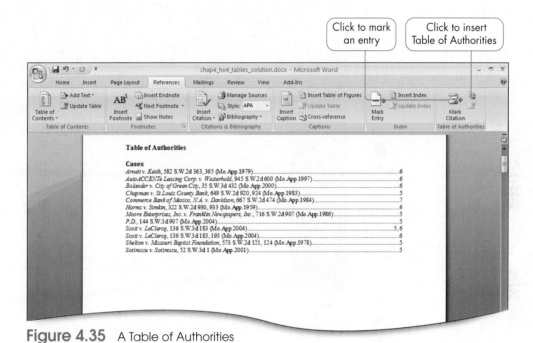

Figure 4.35 A Table of Authorities

To modify a table of authorities entry, you must display the table of authorities fields by clicking Show/Hide ¶ in the Paragraph group on the Home tab. Locate the entry that you wish to modify and edit the text inside the quotation marks. Do not change the entry in the finished table of authorities or the next time you update the table of authorities, your changes will be lost.

To delete a table of authorities entry, select the entire entry field, including the braces {}, and press Delete. After you modify or delete a marked entry, click Update Table in the Table of Authorities group on the References tab to display the changes in the table.

Creating Cross-References

A *cross-reference* is a note that refers the reader to another location for more information about a topic. You can create cross-references to headings, bookmarks, footnotes, endnotes, captions, and tables. A typical cross-reference looks like this: *See page 4 for more information about local recreation facilities.* For files you make available via e-mail or on an intranet, you can create an electronic cross-reference. However, if you are distributing printed copies of your document, you need printed references so the readers can find the location themselves.

To create a cross-reference, position the insertion point in the location where the reference occurs. Display the References tab and click Cross-reference in the Captions group. When the Cross-reference dialog box displays, as shown in Figure 4.36, you choose the type of reference (such as Heading, Bookmark, Figure, or Footnote), and then the reference element to display (such as page number or paragraph text). You can specify whether it displays as a hyperlink in the document, causing a ScreenTip to appear when the mouse pointer is over the cross-reference.

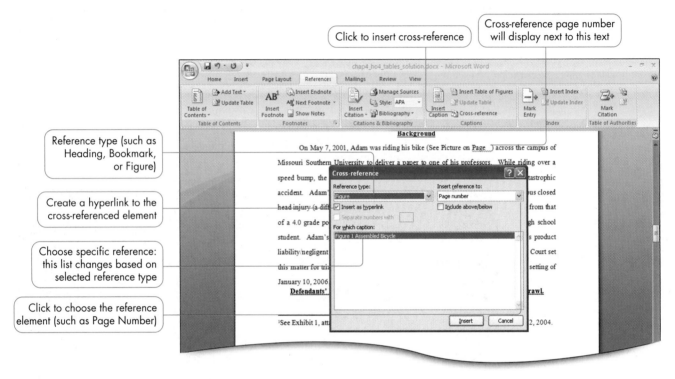

Figure 4.36 Insert a Cross-Reference

Modifying Document Properties

The **_Document Information panel_** allows you to enter descriptive information about a document.

Sometimes, you want to record information about a document but do not want to include the information directly in the document window. For example, you might want to record some notes to yourself about a document, such as the document's author, purpose, or intended audience. To help maintain documents, you can use the **_Document Information panel_** to store descriptive information about a document, such as a title, subject, author, keywords, and comments. When you create a document summary and save the document, Word saves the document summary with the document. You can update the document summary at any time by opening the Document Information panel for the respective document. To display the Document Information panel, as shown in Figure 4.37, click the Office Button, point to Prepare, and then select Properties.

> Sometimes, you want to record information about a document but do not want to include the information directly in the document window . . . you can use the **_Document Information panel_** to store descriptive information about a document, such as a title, subject, author, keywords, and comments.

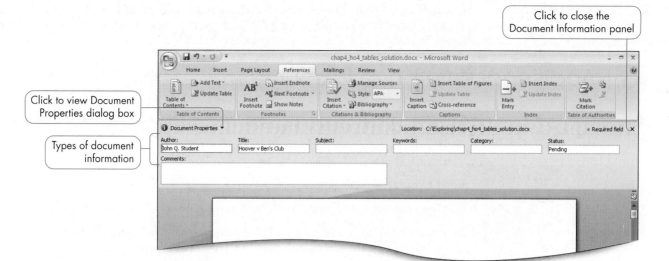

Figure 4.37   Document Information Panel

TIP   Search for a Document Using Document Properties

After you insert information into the Document Information panel, you can use it as search criteria when using the Windows search tool. The information entered as document title, comments, author, or any other field will be searched in the same manner as text that displays in the document.

Customize Document Properties

In addition to creating, modifying, and viewing a document summary, you might want to customize the document properties in the Document Information panel. When you click the arrow next to Document Properties and then click Advanced Properties, the Properties dialog box displays. The Custom tab of the Properties dialog box enables you to add other properties and assign values to those properties. For example, you might want to add the *Date completed* property and specify an exact date for reference. This date would reflect the completion date, not the date the file was last saved—in case someone opens a file and saves it without making changes. You also might create a field to track company information such as warehouse location or product numbers.

You can create and modify document summaries directly from the Open dialog box, through Windows Explorer, or in other file management windows. You do not have to create the document summary when the document is open within Microsoft Word.

Print Document Properties

You can print document properties to have hard copies to store in a filing cabinet for easy reference. To do this, display the Print dialog box, click the Print what drop-down arrow, choose Document properties, and click OK.

Hands-On Exercises

4 | Additional Reference Resources

Skills covered: 1. Add Captions and Create a Table of Figures **2.** Create a Table of Authorities **3.** Create a Cross-Reference **4.** Modify Document Properties

---

Step 1
Add Captions and Create a Table of Figures

Refer to Figure 4.38 as you complete Step 1.

a. Open the *chap4_ho4_tables* document and save it as **chap4_ho4_ tables_solution**.

b. Press **Ctrl+End** to view the end of the document. Click once on the picture to select it. Click the **References tab** and click **Insert Caption** in the Captions group.

The Caption dialog box displays, and the insertion point is positioned at the end of the caption text that displays automatically.

c. Press **Spacebar** to insert a space and then type **Assembled Bicycle** after the existing text in the Caption box, as shown in Figure 4.38. Click **OK**.

The caption *Figure 1 Assembled Bicycle* displays below the picture in a text box.

d. Press **Ctrl+Home** to view page 1. Press **Ctrl+Enter** to insert a page, move your insertion point to the top of the new page, and then type **Table of Figures**. Press **Enter** two times.

e. Click **Insert Table of Figures** in the Captions group to display the Table of Figures dialog box. Click **OK**.

The table displays, showing only one entry at this time.

f. Save the document.

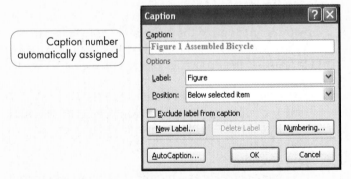

Caption number automatically assigned

Figure 4.38 Add a Caption to a Picture

Refer to Figure 4.39 as you complete Step 2.

a. Go to page 4 in the document. Locate the *Shelton v. Missouri Baptist Foundation* case and select the case information from *Shelton* up to and including the date *(1978)*. Click **Mark Citation** in the Table of Authorities group on the References tab. Click **Mark All**, as shown in Figure 4.39, and then click **Close**.

b. Search through the remainder of the document and mark all case references. Click the **Home tab**, and then click **Show/Hide ¶** to turn off display of formatting marks.

c. Press **Ctrl+Home** to position the insertion point at the beginning of the document, press **Ctrl+Enter** to add a blank page, type **Table of Authorities** at the top of the new page, and then press **Enter** one time. Click the **References tab**, and then click **Insert Table of Authorities** in the Table of Authorities group. Click **OK**.

The Table of Authorities, which lists information about the cases mentioned in the brief, is shown in Figure 4.35.

d. Save the document.

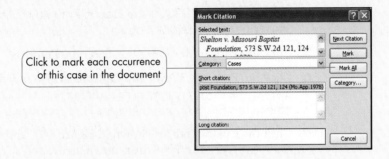

Figure 4.39 Mark Citation Dialog Box

Refer to Figure 4.40 as you complete Step 3.

a. Scroll to page 3 and place the insertion point on the right side of the word *bike* in the first sentence of the *Background* section.

b. Press **Spacebar** and type **(See picture on page**. Click the **References tab**, if necessary, and click **Cross-Reference** in the Captions group. Click the **Reference Type arrow** and click **Figure**, click **Figure 1** in the **For which caption** list, click the **Insert reference to arrow** and select **Page Number**, as shown in Figure 4.40, and then click **Insert**.

The cross-reference displays 8, the page where the picture displays.

c. Click **Close** to close the Cross-reference dialog box. Type **)** to end the cross-reference.

Hold your mouse over the cross-reference page number and view the ScreenTip that instructs you to press **Ctrl** while you click on the number *8* to move the insertion point to the location of the picture.

d. Save the document.

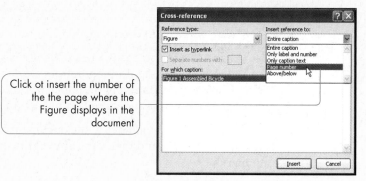

Click ot insert the number of the the page where the Figure displays in the document

Figure 4.40 Insert Cross-Reference

Step 4
Modify Document Properties

Refer to Figure 4.41 as you complete Step 4.

a. Click the **Office Button**, select **Prepare**, and then select **Properties**.

The Document Information panel displays above your document.

TROUBLESHOOTING: If the Document Information panel disappears, repeat Step a. above to display it again.

b. Click one time in the *Status* box and type **Pending**.

c. Click the **Property Views and Options arrow** and click **Advanced Properties** to display the Document Properties dialog box. Click the Summary tab, click one time in the *Title* box, and then type **Hoover v Ben's Club**.

d. Click the **Custom tab,** as shown in Figure 4.41, and select **Date completed** in the *Name list*. Click the **Type drop-down arrow** and select **Date**. Type today's date in the *Value box* using MM/DD/YY format, and then click **Add**. Click **OK** to close the dialog box.

e. Save and close the document.

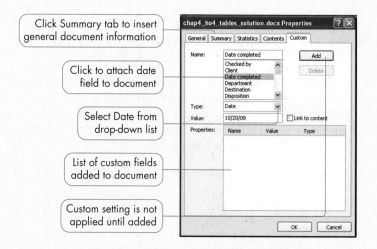

Click Summary tab to insert general document information

Click to attach date field to document

Select Date from drop-down list

List of custom fields added to document

Custom setting is not applied until added

Figure 4.41 Change Document Properties

Summary

1. **Insert comments in a document.** When you work as part of a team you can use the Comment feature to collaborate. Comments enable you to ask a question or provide a suggestion to another person in a document, without modifying the content of the document. Comments are inserted using colored Markup balloons, and a different color is assigned to each reviewer. Comments appear in the Print Layout, Web Layout, and Full Screen Reading views. You can display comments in the margins of a document or in a reading pane.

2. **Track changes in a document.** This feature monitors all additions, deletions, and formatting changes you make to a document. When active, the Track Changes feature applies revision marks to indicate where a change occurs. When you move your mouse over a revision mark, it will display the name of the person who made the change as well as the date and time of change. You can use markup tools to accept or reject changes that have been tracked. These tools are especially helpful when several people make changes to the same document. If comments and tracked changes do not display initially, you can turn on the Show Markup feature to view them. You also can view the document as a final copy if all tracked changes are accepted or as the original before any changes were made and tracked. You can modify the Track Changes options to change settings such as fonts, colors, location, and size of markup balloons.

3. **View documents side by side.** This feature enables you to view two documents on the same screen. It is useful when you want to compare the contents of two documents or if you want to cut or copy and paste text from one document to another. To view two documents side by side, they must both be open in Word. While you display the two documents, you can use synchronous scrolling to move through both using only one scroll bar.

4. **Compare and combine documents.** When you have several copies of the same document submitted from different people, you can use the compare and combine features. The compare feature evaluates the contents of two or more documents and displays markup balloons that show the differences between the documents. You can determine if the differences display in the original document, a revised document, or a new document. The combine feature goes a step further and integrates all changes from multiple documents into one.

5. **Create master documents and subdocuments.** Working with long documents can be cumbersome, and a document that is very long can even slow down your computer. As an alternative to creating long documents, you can create a master document that acts like a binder for managing smaller documents. The smaller document is called a subdocument and can be edited individually at any time. It can be modified when displayed as part of the master document if it is not locked for editing. The Outlining tab contains the Collapse and Expand buttons, as well as other tools used to work on master documents. The great benefit of master and subdocuments is the ability to work with multiple subdocuments simultaneously. For example, you can create page numbers in a master document, and it will cause the numbers to run consecutively from one subdocument to the next.

6. **Use navigation tools.** When you use the Document Map feature, the headings in a document are displayed in a pane on the left, and the text of the document is visible on the right. You can click a heading in the Document Map to move the insertion point to that heading in the document. The feature is only available when headings are formatted using the styles feature. You also can use Thumbnails to navigate quickly through a document. Thumbnails are small pictures of each page that display on the left in a pane when the feature is toggled on. When you click a thumbnail, the insertion point moves to the top of that page. The bookmark feature is an electronic marker for a specific location in a document. You can designate a bookmark in a particular location in a document, then use the Go To feature to return to that bookmark.

7. **Acknowledge a source.** It is common practice to use a variety of sources to supplement your own thoughts when authoring a paper, report, legal brief, or many other types of document. Failure to acknowledge the source of information you use in a document is a form of plagiarism. Word provides the citation feature to track, compile, and display your research sources for inclusion in several types of supplemental references. After you add sources, they are saved in a Master List, a database of all citation sources created in Word on a particular computer. The source also is stored in the Current List, which contains all sources you use in the current document. These lists are stored in XML format and can be used in any Word document.

...continued on Next Page

8. **Create a bibliography.** A bibliography is a list of works cited or consulted by an author and should be included with the document when published. The addition of a bibliography to your completed work demonstrates respect for the material consulted and proves that you are not plagiarizing. It also gives the reader an opportunity to validate your references for accuracy. Any sources added with the citation feature and used in the current document will display in the appropriate format as a bibliography.

9. **Select the writing style.** When research papers are prepared, the author often must conform to a particular writing style. The writing style, also called an editorial style, consists of rules and guidelines set forth by a publisher to ensure consistency in presentation of research documents. The Style list in the Citations & Bibliography group of the References tab includes the most commonly used international styles. When you select the style before creating the bibliography, the citations that appear in the bibliography will be formatted exactly as required by that style.

10. **Create and modify footnotes and endnotes.** A footnote is a citation that appears at the bottom of a page and an endnote is a citation that appears at the end of a document. You use footnotes or endnotes to credit the sources you quote or cite in your document. If you click the Footnotes Dialog Box Launcher, the Footnotes and Endnotes dialog box opens, and you can modify the location of the notes and the format of the numbers.

11. **Add figure references.** Documents and books often contain several images, charts, or tables. To help readers refer to the correct image or table, you can insert a caption that is a descriptive title. To add a caption, click Insert Caption in the Captions group of the References tab. To automatically generate captions, click AutoCaption in the Caption dialog box.

12. **Insert a table of figures.** If your document includes pictures, charts and graphs, slides, or other illustrations along with a caption, you can include a table of figures, or list of the captions, as a reference. To build a table of figures, Word searches a document for captions, sorts the captions by number, and displays the table of figures in the document. A table of figures is commonly placed after the table of contents for a document.

13. **Add legal references.** A table of authorities is used in legal documents to reference cases, rules, treaties, and other documents referred to in a legal brief. Word's Table of Authorities feature enables you to track, compile, and display citations, or references to specific legal cases and other legal documents, to be included in the table of authorities. Before you generate the table of authorities, you must indicate which citations you want to include using the Mark Citation command. To modify a table of authorities entry, locate the entry that you wish to modify and edit the text inside the quotation marks. To delete a table of authorities entry, select the entire entry field, including the braces {}, and then press Delete. If you do not wish to use the existing categories of citations in your table of authorities, you can add or change the categories.

14. **Create cross-references.** A cross-reference is a note that refers the reader to another location for more information about a topic. You can create cross-references to headings, bookmarks, footnotes, endnotes, captions, and tables.

15. **Modify document properties.** You can create a document summary that provides descriptive information about a document, such as a title, subject, author, keywords, and comments. When you create a document summary, Word saves the document summary with the saved document. You can update the document summary at any time by opening the Document Information panel for the respective document. The Custom tab of the Document Properties dialog box enables you to add other properties and assign values to those properties. You also can print document properties from the Print dialog box.

Key Terms

Multiple Choice

1. Which of the following statements about Comments is false?

   (a) Comment balloons appear on the right side in Print Layout view by default.

   (b) A ScreenTip showing the reviewer's name and date/time of comment creation appears when the mouse pointer is over a markup balloon.

   (c) You cannot print comments with the rest of the document.

   (d) You can use the Show Markup feature on the Review tab to filter markup balloons so only comments display on the page.

2. Which dialog box gives you the ability to enter the name of the person using the computer so that person's name appears in ScreenTips for tracked changes and markup balloons?

   (a) View

   (b) File Properties

   (c) Paragraph

   (d) Word Options (located in Office menu)

3. What option enables you to see the document appearance if you accept all tracked changes?

   (a) Final Showing Markup

   (b) Final

   (c) Original Showing Markup

   (d) Original

4. Which of the document elements listed below can you find using the Go To command?

   (a) Bookmark

   (b) Hyperlink

   (c) Table of Contents

   (d) Cross-reference notation

5. Which procedure is a method used to view and edit footnote text?

   (a) By positioning the mouse pointer over the footnote reference mark and clicking inside the ScreenTip that appears

   (b) Through the Footnote and Endnote dialog box

   (c) By double-clicking the footnote reference mark and typing from within the Footnotes pane in Print Layout view

   (d) By clicking Citation on the References tab

6. When you use the styles feature to format headings, you can use this feature to view an outline of your document and click on a heading in the outline to relocate the insertion point in your document.

   (a) Bookmarks

   (b) Document Map

   (c) Thumbnails

   (d) Navigation

7. What navigation tool do you use to display images of document pages that you can click to move the insertion point to the top of a particular page?

   (a) Task pane

   (b) Document Map

   (c) Thumbnails

   (d) Zoom

8. Which option is not true about plagiarism?

   (a) It is the act of using another person's work and claiming it as your own.

   (b) It is an illegal violation of U.S. Copyright law.

   (c) It only applies to written works; ideas, spoken words, or graphics are not included.

   (d) It has serious moral and ethical implications and is taken very seriously in academic communities.

9. What document item directs a reader to another location in a document by mentioning its location?

   (a) Cross-reference

   (b) Bookmark

   (c) Endnote

   (d) Thumbnail

10. A table of figures is generated from what type of entries?

    (a) Bullets

    (b) Bookmarks

    (c) Comments

    (d) Captions

11. What does a table of authorities display?

    (a) A list of pictures, tables, and figures in a document

    (b) A list of cases, rules, treaties, and other documents cited in a legal document

    (c) A list of key words and phrases in the document

    (d) A sequential list of section headings and their page numbers

Multiple Choice Continued...

12. What comprises a master document?

    (a) Subdocuments

    (b) Bibliographies

    (c) Completed document

    (d) Legal citations

13. Which feature enables you to attach information to a document such as author name, subject, title, keywords, and comments?

    (a) Track changes

    (b) Bibliography

    (c) Master document

    (d) Document Information panel

14. Select the sequence of events you undertake to include a bibliography in your document.

    (a) Insert a citation, select writing style, insert bibliography.

    (b) Type citations into document, insert bibliography, select writing style.

    (c) Select writing style, mark legal references, insert bibliography.

    (d) Select writing style, insert bibliography, insert citations.

15. Which feature enables you to display the differences in two documents in a separate document?

    (a) Side by side view

    (b) Compare documents

    (c) Combo documents

    (d) Subdocuments

Practice Exercises

1 Review a Document

Periodically, it is helpful to step back and review the basics. In this case, you have the opportunity to read and work in a document that describes the reviewing features in Word. These features are extremely helpful when working on a group project, and you should take time to evaluate and practice using the feature.

a. Open the *chap4_pe1_review* and *chap4_pe1_review2* document. Click the **View tab** and click **View Side by Side**. After you view the differences in the two documents, click **Window** on the View tab for the *chap4_pe1_review2* document and click **View Side by Side** to close the Side by Side view and display only one file.

b. Click the **Review tab**, click **Compare**, and then click **Combine**. Click **Browse for Original**, navigate to the *chap4_pe1_review* document, and then click **Open**. Click **Browse for Revised**, navigate to the *chap4_pe1_review2* document, and then click **Open**. Click **OK**, and then click **Continue with Merge**.

c. Save the new document as **chap4_pe1_review_solution**.

d. Click **Show Source Documents** in the Compare group on the Review tab, and then click **Hide Source Documents**, if necessary. Click **Reviewing Pane** in the Tracking group to hide the reviewing pane that displays on the left side of the screen, if necessary.

e. Click the **Track Changes arrow** and click **Change Tracking Options**. Take a moment to review the variety of options you can set in this dialog box. In the *Formatting* section, click the **Formatting drop-down arrow** and select **Double underline**, if necessary. Click the **Color drop-down arrow** in the *Formatting* section and select **Violet**. In the *Balloons* section, click the **Margin drop-down arrow** and select **Right**, if necessary. In the Balloons section, click the **Preferred width spin arrow** until **1.8** displays, if necessary. Click **OK** to close the dialog box.

f. Click **Show Markup** in the Tracking group, and then click **Reviewers** to display the names of the reviewers, each of whom is displayed in a different color. Click **All Reviewers** to remove the check mark. Click **Show Markup**, click **Reviewers**, and then click **John Doe**. Only revisions by John Doe display, as shown in Figure 4.42. Click **Show Markup**, click **Reviewers**, and then click **All Reviewers** to display all markup balloons again. Note that reviewer colors may be different on your screen.

g. Click the **Display for Review down arrow** on the Review tab and select **Original Showing Markup**. Click the **Display for Review down arrow** again and select **Final Showing Markup**.

h. Press **Ctrl+Home** to move the insertion point to the beginning of the document, if necessary. Click **Next** in the Changes group to move to the first revision. Click **Accept** in the Changes group to accept this change. Click the **Accept arrow** and select **Accept and Move to Next**.

i. Click to place the insertion point after the letter *A* at the beginning of the second sentence. Press **Spacebar** to insert a space between *A* and *line*. Click the **Accept arrow** and select **Accept All Changes in Document**.

j. Press **Ctrl+End** to move to the end of the document. Click **New Comment** and type **Review completed by** *your name* **on** *current date*. Substitute your name and the current date in the sentence, where appropriate.

k. Save and close the document. Close the *chap4_pe1_review* and *chap4_pe1_review2* documents without saving.

...continued on Next Page

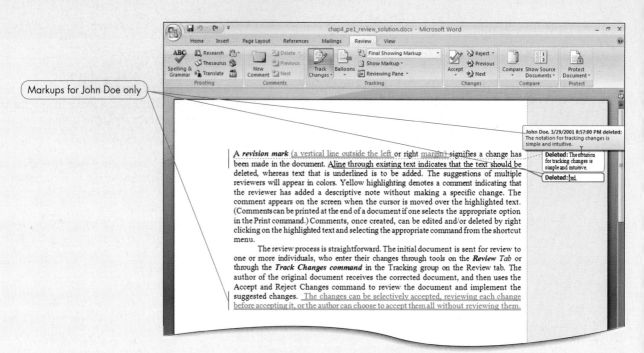

Markups for John Doe only

Figure 4.42 Review a Document

2 Create a Master Document

You volunteer in a middle school library and have the opportunity to observe the computer skill level of many students. You decide to create a document that contains tips for using Windows XP for the students to use as a reference. You found three sources of information and want to combine them into one document. Fortunately, you are familiar with the Master and Subdocument features in Word, so you can easily combine the documents into one.

a. Create a new document. Click the **Outline button** on the status bar. The Outlining tab should display automatically. Save the document as **chap4_pe2_tips_solution**.

b. Type the title of the document, **Tips for Windows XP**, and then apply **24-point Arial** and **Center** it using the Mini toolbar. Click to move the insertion point to the right side of the heading and press **Enter** two times.

c. Click the **Outline button** in the status bar, and then click **Show Document** in the Master Document group on the Outlining tab to display other features. Click **Insert**, and then open the file *chap4_pe2_tips1*. Insert two additional documents, *chap4_pe2_tips2* and *chap4_pe2_tips3*, that are stored in the same folder. When you get a Microsoft Office Word dialog box that asks if you want to rename the style in the subdocument, click **Yes to All**.

d. Click **Close Outline View**, and then click the **View tab**. Click **Document Map** in the Show/Hide group to display the Document Map pane; click **Select Multiple Files** from the list in the pane, as shown in Figure 4.43.

e. After the *Select Multiple Files* heading and paragraph display, click the **Insert tab**, and then in the Links group, click **Bookmark**. Type **multiple** in the Bookmark name box, and then click **Add**.

f. Click the **Switch Navigation Window** arrow in the Document Map pane and click **Thumbnails**. Click the **page 6 thumbnail** and view the *Customize Windows Explorer* paragraph at the top of the page. Click **Bookmark**, type **customize** in the Bookmark name box, and then click **Add**.

g. Click **Close** in the Thumbnails pane. Press **Ctrl+G**, select **Bookmark** in the *Go to what* list, and then select **multiple**, if necessary, in the **Enter bookmark name** list. Click **Go To** and view the *Select Multiple Files* paragraph. Click **Close** to remove the Find and Replace dialog box.

h. Save and close the document.

...continued on Next Page

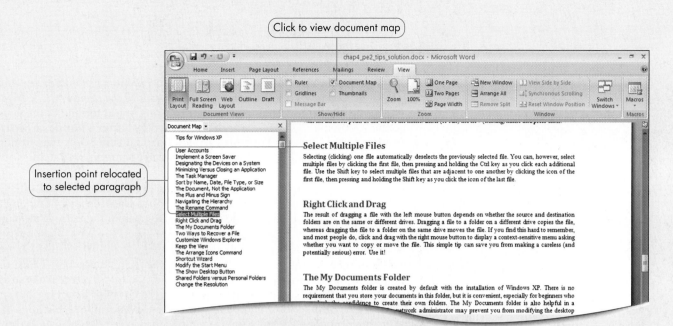

Click to view document map

Insertion point relocated to selected paragraph

Figure 4.43 Use the Document Map

3 Planting Tulips

You are a member of the Izzard County Horticulture Society and have been asked to assist in the development of information packets about a variety of flowers and plants. You are responsible for developing an informational report about tulips that will be distributed at the fall meeting. After viewing sources of information on the Internet, in books, and in journals, you have created a short paper that includes information and pictures. In the following steps, you create additional resources to accompany your report, such as a table of figures and a bibliography.

a. Open the *chap4_pe3_tulip* document and save it as **chap4_pe3_tulip_solution**.

b. Press **Ctrl+End** to view the sources at the bottom of the document. Click the **References tab**, click **Manage Sources**, and then click **New**. Click the **Type of Source drop-down arrow** and click **Article in a Periodical**. In the Author box, type **Lauren Bonar Swezey**. In the Title box, type **A Westerner's Guide to Tulips**. In the Year box, type **1999**. In the Month box, type **October**. Click **OK** to close the dialog box.

c. Select the first Web site listed in the Sources list and press **Ctrl+C** to copy it to the Clipboard. Click **Insert Citation**, and then click **Add New Source**. Click the **Type of Source drop-down arrow** and click **Web site**. Click once in the URL box to move the insertion point, and then press **Ctrl+V** to paste the Web site address. Type **http://americanmeadows.com** in the Name of Web Site box, as shown in Figure 4.44. Click **OK**. Repeat this procedure for the remaining Web site sources in the list.

d. Scroll up to view the page that contains pictures of different varieties of tulips. Click one time on the first image. Click **Insert Caption** in the Captions group on the References tab. The caption number is already entered; press **Spacebar** one time, and then type **Angelique** to add more detail to the caption information. Click **OK** to close the Caption dialog box. Add the following tulip classifications to the captions for the remaining images on the first row: **Beauty of Apeldoorn**, **Black Parrot**. Add the following classifications to the captions for the images on the second row: **Candela**, **Plaisir**. Remember to insert a space between the caption number and tulip classification.

e. Scroll down to the top of the page 4. Click one time on the *Planting Guide at a Glance* graphic. Click **Insert Caption**. Press **Spacebar** one time in the Caption box, which already displays *Figure 6*, and type **Planting Depth Guide**, and then click **OK**. Scroll down to the bottom of the page. Click one time on the cross-section graphic of a bulb. Click **Insert Caption**. Press **Spacebar** one time in the Caption box, which already displays *Figure 7*, type **Dissecting a Bulb**, and then click **OK**.

...continued on Next Page

f. Scroll up to page 3. Click one time to place the insertion point at the end of the third paragraph in the *Planting* section, which ends with *made by the planter*. Click **Insert Endnote** and notice the insertion point blinking on a blank line at the end of the document. Type the following: **Swezey, Lauren Bonar, A Westerner's Guide to Tulips (Sunset, October 1999)**. Click the **Footnotes Dialog Box Launcher**, click the **Number format drop-down arrow**, click **1, 2, 3** to change the format of marks used in the document to denote endnotes, and then click **Apply**.

g. Scroll to the third page and find the sentence *See the depth chart in Figure 6*, which displays in the third paragraph in the *Planting* section. Click to place the insertion point at the end of the sentence, and then add the following text before the period: **on page**. Be sure to include a space before and after the text you type. Now you insert a cross-reference to complete the sentence.

h. Click **Cross-reference** in the Captions group on the References tab. Click the **Reference type drop-down arrow** and click **Figure**. Click the **Insert reference to drop-down arrow** and click **Page Number**. Click **Figure 6** in the **For which caption** list, and then click **Insert**. The number four completes the sentence, informing the reader that the graphic is found on page 4. Click **Close** to remove the Cross-reference dialog box.

i. Place the insertion point at the end of the table of contents. Press **Ctrl+Enter** to insert a page. Type **Table of Figures.** Click at the end of the heading, and then press **Enter** two times. Click **Insert Table of Figures**, and then click **OK**. Select the Table of Figures heading, and then click **Heading 3** from the Styles Quick gallery in the Home tab.

j. Place the insertion point at the end of the last paragraph in the report, *Forcing Tulips*. Press **Ctrl+Enter** to insert a page. Type **Bibliography** and press **Enter** two times. Click the **References tab**. In the Citations & Bibliography group, click the **Style arrow** and click **APA**, if necessary. Click **Bibliography**, and then click **Insert Bibliography**. Select the bibliography heading, and then click **Heading 3** from the Styles Quick gallery in the Home tab.

k. Select the list of sources that were in the document before you inserted the bibliography and press **Delete** to remove them from the document.

l. Scroll to the second page that contains the table of contents. Click one time anywhere in the table of contents and press **F9**. Click **Update Entire Table**, and then click **OK**.

m. Save and close the document.

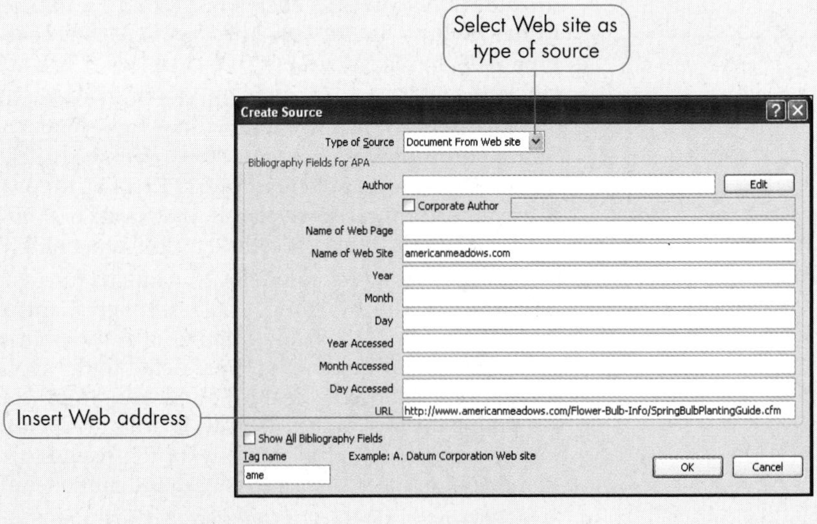

Select Web site as type of source

Insert Web address

Create Source

Figure 4.44 Insert Citation from Web Site

...continued on Next Page

You work as a clerk in a law firm and are responsible for preparing documentation used in all phases of the judicial process. A senior partner in the firm asks you to complete a document by inserting a table of authorities based on the cases cited in the document. You will mark the references to other cases in the document, then prepare a table of authorities based on those cases.

a. Open *chap4_pe4_legal* and save it as **chap4_pe4_legal_solution**.

b. Press **Ctrl+Home** to move the insertion point to the beginning of the document. Display the **Page Layout tab**, click **Breaks** in the Page Setup group, and then click the **Next Page section break**.

c. Press **Ctrl+End** to move the insertion point to the end of the document. Display the **Insert tab**, click **Page Number** in the Header & Footer group, and click **Format Page Numbers**. In the Page Number Format dialog box, click the **Start at** option button to display the number **1.** Click **OK** to close the dialog box.

d. Double-click the footer area on the second page. Click **Link to Previous** in the Navigation group of the Design tab to toggle the setting off. Click **Page Number** in the Header and Footer group, point to **Bottom of Page**, and then select **Plain Number 2** from the gallery. Click **Close Header and Footer**.

e. Press **Ctrl+Home** to move the insertion point to the beginning of the document. Type the title **TABLE OF AUTHORITIES** at the top of the page. Press **Enter** twice, and then click **Align Text Left** in the Paragraph group on the Home tab. Select the *Table of Authorities* title, and then click **Center** and **Underline** on the Home tab.

f. Select the citation *Utah Code Ann.' 33-8-34 (1994)* in the *Statutes Involved* section on the second page. Click the **References tab** and click **Mark Citation** in the Table of Authorities group. Click **Mark All**, and then click **Close**. Click the **Home tab** and click **Show/Hide ¶** on the Paragraph group to turn off the display of formatting marks.

g. Scroll to the top of the document and position the insertion point on the second line following the *Table of Authorities* heading. Click **Insert Table of Authorities** in the Table of Authorities group on the References tab. In the Table of Authorities dialog box, click **Cases** in the Category list, and then click **OK** to display the table in your document, as shown in Figure 4.45.

h. Select the heading **Cases** and the five citations, click the **Home tab**, click **Line spacing** in the Paragraph group, and select **2.0** to double-space the entries in the table.

i. Click the **Office Button** and select **Prepare**. Click **Properties** to display the Document Information Panel above the document. Click one time in the **Author** box, delete the current name if necessary, and type your name. Click once in the Title box and type **Motion for Appeal**. Click once in the Comment box and type **Utah District Court**.

j. Save and close the document.

...continued on Next Page

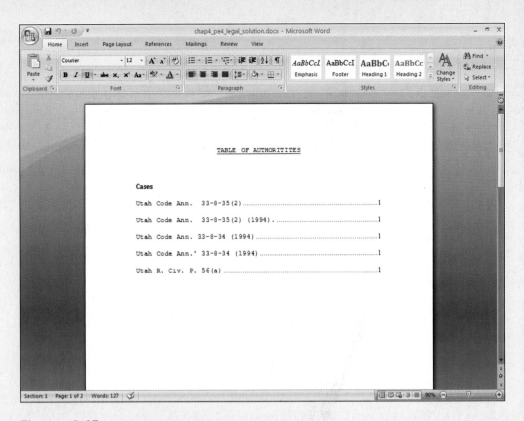

Figure 4.45 Table of Authorities

You work as a volunteer at the local humane society. The board of directors asked you to coordinate a fund-raising effort in which animal recipe books will be sold. You have been receiving recipes from several supporters via e-mail and decide to create a master document that contains all of the recipe documents. After you combine the recipes, you can print the document in preparation for the big sale.

a. Create a new master document. Save the file as **chap4_mid1_recipes_solution**.

b. At the top of the page, add the title **Recipes for the Animals in Your Life** and format it using the Heading 1 style, then insert two blank lines.

c. Below the heading type the following categories on different lines: **Dogs**, **Cats**, **Birds**, and **Horses**. These category headings classify the type of recipes that follow. Format the category headings using the Heading 2 style.

d. Insert the following subdocuments into the master document below the appropriate category heading: *chap4_mid1_dogs*, *chap4_mid1_cats*, *chap4_mid1_birds*, *chap4_mid1_horses*.

e. Change the document properties and specify the following:

Title	Humane Society Animal Recipe Book
Author	Friends of the Humane Society
Comments	Distributed Fall 2008

f. Take appropriate actions so the recipes for each type of animal start on the top of a page. Remove any section breaks that create large gaps of white space within the group of recipes for a particular animal. If removal of breaks changes formatting of category headings, reapply the Heading 2 style.

g. Save and close the master document. If a window asks you to overwrite the original subdocuments, click No.

2 Sidewalk Café

Your friend Sue McCrory just purchased the Sidewalk Cafe restaurant. She prepared an information sheet to distribute to several office buildings within the neighborhood. As you review the information sheet, you annotate the document with comments. After you review your comments, you edit one comment and delete another comment. Later, you receive a revision of the document from Sue. With two different documents, you use the Compare and Combine features to consolidate the documents into one final copy that Sue will distribute.

a. Open the *chap4_mid2_cafe* document and save it as **chap4_mid2_cafe_solution**.

b. Position the insertion point at the end of the subtitle and type the comment **Placing the italicized slogan below the restaurant name is a good idea.** Position the insertion point after *Turkey Club* and type the comment **Adding some photos of lunch items will enhance the information sheet.** In the fourth paragraph below the list, select *Sunday brunch* and insert the comment **What's on this menu?**

c. Change the Track Changes options to view markup balloons on the left side of the screen and resize the markup balloons to 1.5" wide. Select the Track formatting check box, if necessary. Change the Formatting option to display double underline and, if necessary, change the formatting color to show **By Author**.

...continued on Next Page

d. Position the mouse pointer over the first comment markup balloon to see the comment with your name as the reviewer. Edit your second comment by adding **full-color** between *some* and *photos*. Delete the third comment.

e. Confirm the Track Changes option is toggled on. Delete the words *diverse and eclectic* on the second line of the first main paragraph and replace them with the word **wide**. In the second paragraph, delete *on a daily basis*, including the space before *on*, but do not delete the colon at the end of that line. Italicize all instances of *Sue McCrory* and *Ken McCrory*, or any variation of their names.

f. Change the Display for Review option to Final Showing Markup, if necessary. Make appropriate adjustments so that only your changes display onscreen. Accept all of your changes.

g. Display comments and changes by all reviewers. Accept the change to delete the words *restaurant, bar, and grill*, but reject the change to delete the words *is homey and*.

h. Open the original file, **chap4_mid2_cafe**, and view it side by side with the revised file you have edited. Close the *chap4_mid2_cafe* document when your review is complete.

i. Sue made revisions to another copy of the original, named *chap4_mid2_caferevision*, and sent a copy to you. Combine that document with the *chap4_mid2_cafe_solution* document and display the results in a new document named **chap4_mid2_caferevision_solution**.

j. View Sue's markups only and accept all of her changes. View all remaining markups; reject only the deletion of the phrase "is homey and" and accept all remaining changes.

k. Delete all comments.

l. Save and close all documents.

3 Web Design

You work as a Web designer at a local advertising agency and have been asked to provide some basic information to be used in a senior citizens workshop. You want to provide the basic elements of good Web design and format the document professionally. Use the basic information you have already, in a Word document, and revise it to include elements appropriate for a research-oriented paper.

a. Open the *chap4_mid3_web* document and save it as **chap4_mid3_web_solution**.

b. On the cover page, insert your name at the bottom.

c. Place the insertion point at the end of the *Proximity* paragraph on the page numbered 2. Insert the following text into an endnote: **Max Rebaza, <u>Effective Web Sites</u>, Chicago: Windy City Publishing, Inc. (2004): 44.**

d. Change all endnotes into footnotes.

e. In preparation for adding a Bibliography to your document, create a citation using the book source from Step c. If a selection from the citation displays in the document, delete it.

f. Select the Chicago style of writing and add a bibliography at the end of the document. Use the default format and settings for the bibliography. Type a heading on the page and format it using the Heading 2 style.

g. Add captions to each graphic that displays in the paper. Allow Word to number the captions sequentially and display the caption below the graphic. Add a caption to the table on page six and display the caption below the table.

h. Create a Table of Figures at the beginning of the document, on a separate page after the table of contents. If the Table 1 entry displays instead of figures, click the Caption label

...continued on Next Page

drop down list in the Table of Figures dialog box and select Figure. Give the page an appropriate heading and format the heading using the Heading 2 style.

i. Create bookmarks for the three major headings, *Proximity and Balance*, *Contrast and Focus*, and *Consistency*. The bookmarks should be named **proximity**, **contrast**, and **consistency**.

j. Insert a cross-reference at the end of the *Font Size and Attributes* paragraph on the seventh page. Type **See also**, then insert a **Heading** *reference type* for the **Contrast and Focus** heading. End the sentence with a period.

k. Display the Document Map and click on **Table of Contents**. Update the table and select the option to update the entire table. Close the Document Map.

l. Save and close the document.

4 Table of Authorities

As the junior partner in a growing law firm, you must proofread and update all legal briefs before they are submitted to the courts. You are in the final stage of completing a medical malpractice case, but the brief cannot be filed without a Table of Authorities.

a. Open the file *chap4_mid4_authorities* and save the file as **chap4_mid4_authorities_solution**.

b. Mark all references to legal cases throughout the document.

c. Insert a Table of Authorities at the beginning of the document. Insert an appropriate header at the top of the page and format it using Heading 1 style.

d. Change document properties, insert your name as Author, title the document **Bradford v Hillcrest**, and use **Medical malpractice** as the subject.

e. Save and close the document.

Capstone Exercise

You work in a medical office where many patients have been examined or screened for cancer. The disease is a huge threat to society and a major focus of the health care system. Because of the potential risk and consequences of this disease, you decide to perform research to learn more about it and the preventive measures you should undertake to avoid it. Your coworkers have similar concerns, and you discover they also have been researching the topic. After a few conversations, the staff of nurses and administrative assistants decide to create an informational document that can be distributed to patients. They offer to e-mail you the documents that contain information they found.

Combine Documents

You receive two documents from coworkers who searched for information about cancer on the Internet. The information is interesting and could be valuable to other people you know, so you decide to create a well-formatted document that you can distribute to anyone who expresses an interest in basic information about cancer.

a. Open the two files *chap4_cap_cancer1* and *chap4_cap_cancer2*, then view them side by side.

b. Combine the two documents into a new document. Show the source documents after you combine them into a new document.

c. The new document should contain all information from both files. Accept all insertions and reject any deletions.

d. Save the new file as **chap4_cap_cancer_solution**.

Credit Sources

You notice several places in the document where the source of the information is listed. Remembering the documentation features in Word 2007, you decide to create citations and add a bibliography to your document.

a. Insert a citation for each source posted in the document.

b. Create a footnote that displays at the end of the paragraph preceding the source listing. Cut each source listing and paste it into the footnote area. Make adjustments as necessary so the source information displays next to the number in the footnote.

c. You decide to include a bibliography as well. Use a page break to add a page to the end of the document and insert a bibliography there. Use the APA writing style for the bibliography, and provide a title formatted in the Heading 2 style. Remove any comments after creating the reference page.

Figure References

The graphics in the document are quite informative, and you want to add descriptive captions to them, and also list them on a reference page.

a. Select the first table and type the following caption: **Table 1. Cancer-related deaths from 1990–1998**. Display the captions above the graphics.

b. Select the second graphic and display the following caption above it: **Figure 1. Rate* of prostate cancer deaths, 1990–1998**.

c. Select the final graphic and display the following caption above it: **Figure 2. Rate* of female breast cancer deaths, 1990–1998**.

d. At the beginning of the document, insert a cover page using the Mod theme. Type **Cancer Information** as the document title and remove all other fields except the author name. If necessary, replace the existing author name with your own.

e. Create a blank page following the cover page and type **Table of Figures** at the top. Format the text with the Heading 2 style.

f. Below the heading insert a table of figures, using the Distinctive format. Change table of figure options so that it builds the table from captions (found in the Table of Figures Options dialog box).

Add Navigation

The document is becoming complex, and you decide to add a few bookmarks to help the reader find information quickly.

a. Display the Document Map. Click *Other primary causes of cancer include:* Place the insertion point at the left side of the heading, and then insert a bookmark named **causes**.

b. Use the Document Map to place the insertion point at the left side of the heading *What are the symptoms of cancer?* and insert a bookmark named **symptoms**.

c. Place the insertion point at the left side of the heading *Cancer treatment can take the following forms:* and insert a bookmark named **treatment**.

d. Click Go To and use the bookmarks to move the insertion point to the section about *causes*. Close the Document Map.

e. Place the insertion point to the left side of the line directly below the heading Cancer: Choosing a Treatment Program and insert a cross-reference to another paragraph heading in the document. The text for the cross-reference should begin **See also the section titled**. Allow the cross-reference to complete the statement by inserting the heading text *What are the treatments for cancer?*

f. Modify document properties and type your name in the Author field. In the Title text box, type **Cancer Information**.

g. Save and close all documents.

Mini Cases

Use the rubric following the case as a guide to evaluate your work, but keep in mind that your instructor may impose additional grading criteria or use a different standard to judge your work.

This case requires collaboration between members of a group. Two people in the group will open the *chap4_mc1_collaborate* document. Each member will turn on track changes and proceed to make corrections and add suggestions to the document. Each group member should save the modified file, adding their group number to the file name. Upon completion, the first two people will send the document to two additional group members who also will turn on Track Changes and make additional corrections and suggestions. It is acceptable to correct the previous member's corrections, but do not accept or reject changes at this time. After each member corrects the document, the group should meet together and combine the two documents using the Compare and Combine feature in Word. Combine the documents into a new document, accept and reject changes to the document, and save the final version as **chap4_mc1_collaborate_solution**. View the final version side by side with the original document.

Performance Elements	Exceeds Expectations	Meets Expectations	Below Expectations
Collaboration	Each member of the group participated by using the Track Changes feature while making modifications.	At least half of the members of the group participated.	Fewer than half of the members of the group participated.
Use of tools	Each member of the group used Changes feature at all times while making modifications.	The group used Track Changes at least half of the time while making modifications.	The group did not use the Track Changes feature while making modifications to the document.
Final product	The final version of the document contained proper spelling, punctuation, grammar, and well-written and complete thoughts.	The final version of the document requires additional edits to achieve proper spelling, punctuation, grammar, and well-written and complete thoughts.	The final version of the document requires vast improvements to achieve proper spelling, punctuation, grammar, and well-written and complete thoughts.

Do you know someone who has been the victim of identity theft? It occurs every day. But what exactly is involved in this growing crime? Use your research skills to locate information about identity theft. You should find at least one source from the Internet, at least one source from a book, and at least one source from a journal. Use your school's library or online library resources to help locate the information sources. After you find your sources, write a two-page report, double spaced, describing identity theft. Include information about the crime, statistics, government policies, and laws that have been passed because of this crime, and the effects on victims. Cite the sources in your paper, use footnotes where appropriate, and develop a bibliography for your paper based on the APA writing style. Save the report as **chap4_mc2_idtheft_solution**.

Performance Elements	Exceeds Expectations	Meets Expectations	Below Expectations
Research	Report cites more than one source each from a book, a journal, and an Internet site.	Report cites one source each from a book, a journal, and an Internet site.	Report cites fewer than three total sources.
Content	Report contains at least four categories of information about identity theft.	Report contains two or three topics of information about identity theft.	Report contains a minimum amount of information about identity theft.
Citations	Report includes citations, footnotes, and bibliography in APA style.	Report includes bibliography, but not in APA style. Some sources are included in footnotes, but not in bibliography.	Sources are not cited. Bibliography is missing.

Repairing
Bookmarks

DISASTER RECOVERY

You work in the city's Planning and Zoning department as an analyst. You begin to prepare the Guide to Planned Developments document for posting on the city's intranet. The administrative clerk who typed the document attempted to use bookmarks for navigation purposes, but he did not test the bookmarks after inserting them. You must review the document and repair the bookmarks. Additionally, several cross-reference statements are embedded in the document, but appear to be erroneous. The cross-references are highlighted in the document so you can locate them; the highlights should be removed when you have corrected the references. Open *chap4_mc3_bookmarks* and save your revised document as **chap4_mc3_bookmarks_solution**.

Performance Elements	Exceeds Expectations	Meets Expectations	Below Expectations
Bookmarks	All erroneous bookmarks were repaired, and links work properly.	At least half of the erroneous bookmarks were repaired, and links work properly.	Fewer than half of the erroneous bookmarks were repaired.
Cross-references	All erroneous cross-references were repaired, and links work properly.	At least half of the erroneous cross-references were repaired, and links work properly.	Fewer than half of the erroneous cross-references were repaired.

chapter 1 | Excel

Introduction to Excel

What Can I Do with a Spreadsheet?

Objectives

After you read this chapter, you will be able to:

1. Define worksheets and workbooks **(page 314)**.
2. Use spreadsheets across disciplines **(page 314)**.
3. Plan for good workbook and worksheet design **(page 315)**.
4. Identify Excel window components **(page 317)**.
5. Enter and edit data in cells **(page 322)**.
6. Describe and use symbols and the order of precedence **(page 328)**.
7. Display cell formulas **(page 330)**.
8. Insert and delete rows and columns **(page 331)**.
9. Use cell ranges; Excel move; copy, paste, paste special; and AutoFill **(page 332)**.
10. Manage worksheets **(page 340)**.
11. Format worksheets **(page 341)**.
12. Select page setup options for printing **(page 353)**.
13. Manage cell comments **(page 356)**.

Hands-On Exercises

Exercises	Skills Covered
1. INTRODUCTION TO MICROSOFT EXCEL (page 324) **Open:** none **Save as:** chap1_ho1_jake_solution.xlsx	• Plan Your Workbook • Start Microsoft Office Excel 2007 • Enter and Edit Data in Cells • Use the Save As Command and Explore the Worksheet
2. JAKE'S GYM CONTINUED (page 335) **Open:** chap1_ho2_jake.xlsx **Save as:** chap1_ho2_jake_solution.xlsx	• Open an Existing Workbook • Use Save As to Save an Existing Workbook • Insert a Row and Compute Totals • Copy the Formulas • Continue the Calculations • Insert a Column
3. FORMATTING JAKE'S GYM WORKSHEET (page 347) **Open:** chap1_ho2_jake_solution.xlsx (from Exercise 2) **Save as:** chap1_ho3_jake_solution (additional modifications)	• Manage the Workbook • Apply Number Formats • Apply Font Attributes and Borders • Change Alignment Attributes • Insert an Image
4. PRINTING JAKE'S GYM WORKSHEET (page 357) **Open:** chap1_ho3_jake_solution (from Exercise 3) **Save as:** chap1_ho4_jake_solution (additional modifications)	• Insert a Comment • Insert Custom Header and Footer • Format to Print the Worksheet

CASE STUDY

Weddings by Grace

Grace Galia is a wedding consultant who specializes in all aspects of wedding planning for her clients. Although more and more couples are striving to cut costs by handling most of the planning on their own, Grace is successfully growing her business based on a proven history of superbly run events resulting in many happy newlyweds. She offers her clients a complete wedding package that includes the cocktail hour, dinner, and beverage (including alcohol). The client chooses the type of dinner (e.g., chicken, salmon, filet mignon, or some combination), which determines the cost per guest, and specifies the number of guests, and then the cost of the reception is obtained by simple multiplication.

Case Study

Grace provides a detailed budget to all of her clients that divides the cost of a wedding into three major categories—the ceremony, the reception (based on the package selected), and other items such as music and photography. She asks each client for their total budget, and then works closely with the client to allocate that amount over the myriad items that will be necessary. Grace promises to take the stress out of planning, and she advertises a turnkey operation, from invitations to thank-you notes. She assures her clients that their needs will be met without the clients overextending themselves financially. Grace has asked you, her manager trainee, to complete her worksheet comparing the two wedding plans she offers her clients.

Your Assignment

- Read the chapter carefully, focusing on spreadsheet formulas and basic spreadsheet commands.
- Open *chap1_case_wedding*, which contains the partially completed worksheet, and save it as **chap1_case_wedding_solution**.
- Insert formulas to calculate the cost of the reception in both options.
- Use appropriate formulas to calculate the difference in cost for each item in the two options.
- Copy the total formula to the difference column.
- Format cells as currency with no decimals. Widen or narrow columns as necessary to conform to good design principles.
- Emphasize totals with borders and separate the categories with a complimentary fill color.
- Merge and center rows 1 and 2 so the headings are centered over the worksheet. Change the font, font color, and font size to match your design.
- Insert an appropriate image in the space indicated. You may have to resize to fit.
- Emphasize the category headings.
- Add your name and today's date to the worksheet.
- Choose the options you need to set from the Page Setup dialog box.

Introduction to Spreadsheets

After word processing, a spreadsheet program is the second most common software application in use. The most popular spreadsheet program used in businesses and organizations around the world is Microsoft Excel. A *spreadsheet*, is the computerized equivalent of a ledger. It is a grid of rows and columns enabling users to organize data, recalculate results for cells containing formulas when any data in input cells change, and make decisions based on quantitative data. A *spreadsheet program* is a computer application, such as Microsoft Excel, that you use to build and manipulate electronic spreadsheets. The spreadsheet has become a much more powerful tool since the first spreadsheet program, VisiCalc, was introduced in 1979.

Before the introduction of spreadsheet software, people used ledgers to track expenses and other quantitative data. Ledgers have been the basis of accounting for hundreds of years, but the accountant was always faced with the issue of making changes to correct errors or update values. The major issue, however, was the time and work involved in changing the ledger and manually calculating the results again. Figure 1.1 shows an edited ledger page that had to be recalculated. A spreadsheet makes these changes in a significantly shorter period of time and, if the data and formulas are correct, does not make errors. Any area that has numeric data is a potential area of application for a spreadsheet. Herein lies the advantage of the electronic spreadsheet: quicker, more accurate changes than were possible with a manual ledger. Further, the use of formulas and functions in Excel, along with the ability to easily copy these formulas, adds to the program's functionality and power. Figure 1.2 shows an electronic spreadsheet, and Figure 1.3 shows that the results are automatically recalculated after changing the unit price.

> A *spreadsheet*, the computerized equivalent of a ledger, contains rows and columns of data. A *spreadsheet program* is a computer application designed to build and manipulate spreadsheets.

> A spreadsheet makes these changes in a significantly shorter period of time and, if the data and formulas are correct, does not make errors.

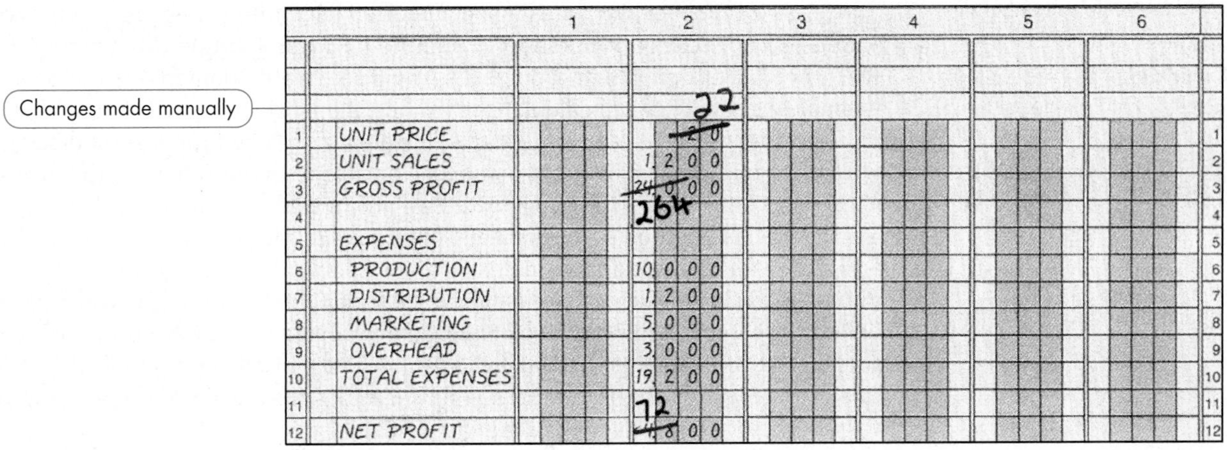

Figure 1.1 Ledger

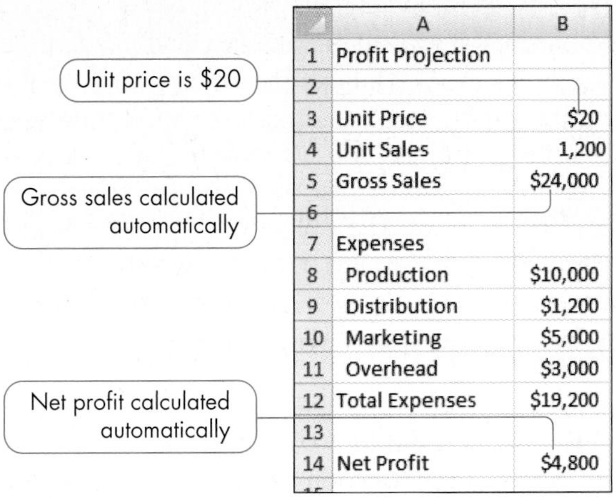

Figure 1.2 Original Spreadsheet

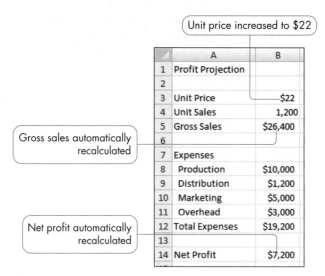

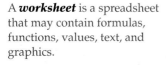

Figure 1.3 Modified Spreadsheet

In this section, you learn about workbooks and worksheets and how spreadsheets are used in various disciplines. You plan good workbook and worksheet design and identify Excel window components prior to creating a spreadsheet.

Defining Worksheets and Workbooks

A **worksheet** is a spreadsheet that may contain formulas, functions, values, text, and graphics.

A **workbook** is a file containing related worksheets.

A **worksheet** is a single spreadsheet consisting of a grid of columns and rows that often contain descriptive labels, numeric values, formulas, functions, and graphics. The terms worksheet and spreadsheet are often used interchangeably. A **workbook** is a collection of related worksheets contained within a single file. Storing multiple worksheets within one workbook helps organize related data in one file. In addition, it enables you to perform calculations among the worksheets within the workbook.

Managers often create workbooks to store an organization's annual budget. The workbook may consist of five worksheets, one for each quarter, with the fifth spreadsheet showing summary figures. Alternatively, individuals and families often create a budget workbook of 12 worksheets, one for each month, to store personal income and expenses. Instructors often create a workbook to store a grade book with individual worksheets for each class. On a personal level, you might want to list your DVD collection in one workbook in which you have a worksheet for each category, such as action, comedy, drama, etc. Within each worksheet, you list the DVD title, release date, purchase price, and so on. Regardless of the situation, you can use one workbook to contain many related worksheets.

> **TIP** The Workbook
>
> An Excel workbook is the electronic equivalent of the three-ring binder. A workbook contains one or more worksheets (or chart sheets), each of which is identified by a tab at the bottom of the workbook. The worksheets in a workbook are normally related to one another; for example, each worksheet may contain the sales for a specific division within a company. The advantage of a workbook is that all of its worksheets are stored in a single file, which is accessed as a unit.

Using Spreadsheets Across Disciplines

Students typically think spreadsheets are used solely for business applications. Spreadsheets are used for accounting and business planning using powerful "what-if" functions. These functions enable business planners to project different amounts of profit as other factors change. Even students can use basic "what if" analysis with a budget to determine if they can afford a particular payment or determine if they have sufficient income to buy a new car.

Spreadsheets are, however, used in many other areas. Because of the powerful graphing or charting feature of Excel, geologists and physical scientists use spreadsheets to store data about earthquakes or other physical phenomena, chart the data with a scatter chart, and then plot it on maps to predict where these phenomena might occur. Historians and social scientists have long used spreadsheets for predicting voting behavior or supporting or refuting theses such as Beard's Economic Interpretation of the Constitution. Figure 1.4 shows another use for spreadsheets—a summary of temperatures over time for several cities.

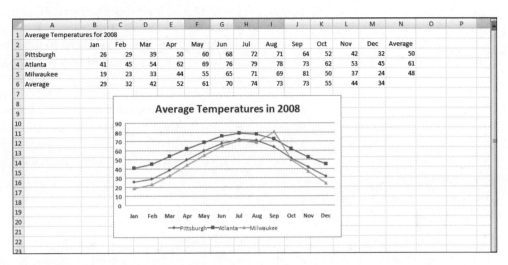

Figure 1.4 Temperatures over Time by City Example Spreadsheet

Educators at all levels—elementary school teachers through university professors—are increasing their use of electronic spreadsheets. Many Web sites now show literally thousands of examples of how educators are using spreadsheets in their classrooms. Once both students and teachers understand the basics of Excel, the possibilities are endless. As noted, spreadsheets are widely used in education. The most common use of Excel is in creating grade book spreadsheets.

Planning for Good Workbook and Worksheet Design

Figures 1.5, 1.6, and 1.7 show three views of a teacher's grade book. The first figure shows a grade book as a teacher might keep it with paper and pencil. The second figure shows the grade book in a spreadsheet program, and the third figure shows the grade book after some changes are made. The handwritten version of the grade book has the teacher writing in grades and calculating averages with a calculator or on paper. If changes are necessary, out comes the eraser and correction fluid. The second and third examples using the electronic spreadsheet show its simplicity. The teacher can easily enter grades, change grades, use weighted items, and recalculate—that is the power of the spreadsheet. For many teachers the spreadsheet grade book is such an integral part of their work that they have never seen or cannot remember a paper grade book.

You should plan the structure of the spreadsheet before you start entering data into a new worksheet. At times, it may be necessary for you to sit with paper and pencil and create the spreadsheet design on paper. See Figure 1.5 for an example of a handwritten grade book. The steps that are necessary for the design of a workbook and a worksheet include the following:

1. Figure out the purpose of the spreadsheet and how it will be constructed. For example, a professor's purpose is to create an electronic grade book to store student names and scores and to calculate student grades.

2. Make it obvious where data are to be entered. The teacher needs to store student first names, last names, and three test scores for all students in the class. See Figure 1.6 for a sample worksheet.

3. Enter data and set up formulas wherever possible. Never do manually what Excel can do automatically. You could, for example, calculate each student's class average. Furthermore, you can calculate the class average for each test to see if the tests are too easy or too difficult.

4. Test, test, and test again to make sure the results are what you expect. It is easy to make mistakes when entering data and when constructing formulas. Make whatever changes are necessary.

5. Format the worksheet so it is attractive but not so obtrusive that the purpose of the worksheet is lost. Include a title and column headings, and center the headings. Make sure decimal points align. Add bold to headings, increase the font size for readability, and use color to draw attention to important values or to trends.

6. Document the worksheet as thoroughly as possible. Include the current date, your name, class, and semester. Include cell comments describing the formulas so you know what values are used to produce the results.

7. Save and print the finished product. Auditors and teachers may require you to print a second time with cell formulas displayed so they can verify the formulas are correct. We will discuss cell formulas more thoroughly later in the chapter.

Student	Test 1	Test 2	Final	Average
Adams	100	90	81	90.3
Baker	90	76	87	84.3
Glassman	90	78	78	82.0
Moldof	60	60	40	53.3
Walker	80	80	90	83.3
Class Average	84.0	76.8	75.2	

Walker's average grade is 83.3

Walker's final exam grade is 90

Figure 1.5 The Professor's Grade Book

	A	B	C	D	E	F
1	Student	Test 1	Test 2	Final	Average	
2						
3	Adams	100	90	81	90.3	
4	Baker	90	76	87	84.3	
5	Glassman	90	78	78	82.0	
6	Moldof	60	60	40	53.3	
7	Walker	80	80	90	83.3	
8						
9	Class Average	84.0	76.8	75.2		
10						

Walker's final exam grade is 90

Figure 1.6 Original Grades

Formulas recalculate the results automatically

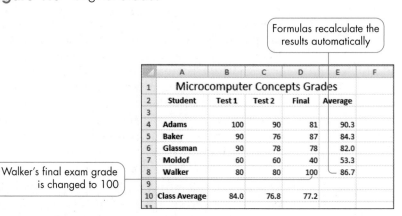

	A	B	C	D	E	F
1	Microcomputer Concepts Grades					
2	Student	Test 1	Test 2	Final	Average	
3						
4	Adams	100	90	81	90.3	
5	Baker	90	76	87	84.3	
6	Glassman	90	78	78	82.0	
7	Moldof	60	60	40	53.3	
8	Walker	80	80	100	86.7	
9						
10	Class Average	84.0	76.8	77.2		
11						

Walker's final exam grade is changed to 100

Figure 1.7 Modified Spreadsheet

Identifying Excel Window Components

Each window in Excel has its own Minimize, Maximize, and Close buttons. The title bar contains the name of the application (Excel) and the name of the workbook you are using. At the bottom and right of the document window are the vertical and horizontal scroll bars. The *active cell* is the cell you are working in, the cell where information or data will be input. Its cell reference appears in the name box, its contents in the formula bar, and it is surrounded by a dark black box. The active cell can be changed by clicking in a different cell or using the arrow keys to move to another cell.

The *active cell* is the cell you are working in, the cell where information or data will be input.

The Excel window includes items that are similar to other Office applications and items that are unique to the Excel application. See Figure 1.8, the Excel window, with the parts of the window identified. The following paragraphs name and describe items in the Excel window.

- **Ribbon**: The Ribbon is made of tabs, groups, and commands.
- **Tab**: Each tab is made up of several groups so that you can see all of its functions without opening menus. The contents of each tab are shown on the reference page. This defines the tabs, the groups they contain, and their general function. You will refer to this page frequently.
- **Office Menu**: The Office menu displays when you click the Office Button in the upper left of the Excel window and contains the following commands, all of which open dialog boxes: New, Open, Save, Save As, Finish, Share, Print, and Close. A list of recently used workbooks and an extensive Excel Options section displays. See Figure 1.9 for the contents of the Office menu.

The *formula bar* is used to enter or edit cell contents.

- **Formula Bar**: The formula bar appears below the Ribbon and above the workbook screen and shows the active cell's contents. The *formula bar* displays the contents of cells; you can enter or edit cell contents here or directly in the active cell.

The *name box* indicates the location or name for the active cell.

- **Name Box**: The *name box* is another name for the cell reference of the cell currently used in the worksheet. The name box appears to the left of the formula bar and displays the active cell's address (D4) or a name it has been assigned.

Sheet tabs tell the user what sheets of a workbook are available.

- **Sheet Tabs**: *Sheet tabs* are located at the bottom left of the Excel window and tell the user what sheets of a workbook are available. Three sheet tabs, initially named Sheet1, Sheet2, and Sheet3, are included when you open a new workbook in Excel. To move between sheets, click on the sheet you want to work with. You can even rename sheets with more meaningful names. If you create more sheets than can be displayed, you can use the sheet tab scroll buttons to scroll through all sheet tabs.
- **Status Bar**: The status bar is located at the bottom of the Excel window. It is below the sheet tabs and above the Windows taskbar and displays information about a selected command or operation in progress. For example, it displays CAPS when Caps Lock is active and the default setting is On.

The *Select All button* is clicked to select all elements of the worksheet.

- **Select All Button**: The *Select All button* is the square at the intersection of the rows and column headings, and you can use it to select all elements of the worksheet.

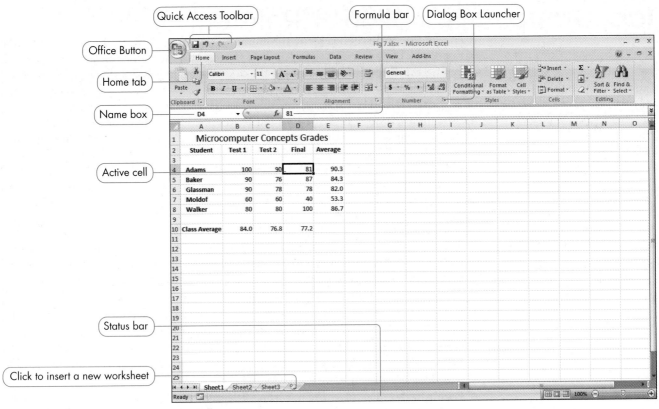

Figure 1.8 The Excel Window

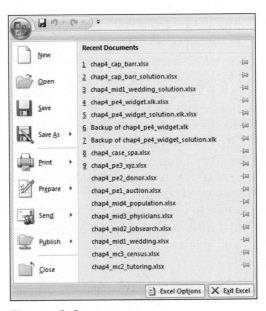

Figure 1.9 The Office Menu

Tab, Group, Description | Reference

Tab and Group	Description
Home Clipboard Font Alignment Number Style Cells Editing	The basic Excel tab. Contains basic editing functions such as cut and paste along with most formatting actions. As with all groups, pull-down areas are available and do increase functionality. Your Tabs may display differently depending on your screen resolution.

Insert Tables Illustrations Charts Links Text	Brings together all insert functions in one area. Includes ability to create graphs and add tables. Contains powerful picture functions. Headers and footers are inserted here.

Page Layout Themes Page Setup Scale to Fit Sheet Options Arrange	Contains all functions associated with page appearance, setup, and printing. Allows for many custom views.

Formulas Function Library Defined Names Formula Auditing Calculation	The area that contains the mathematical backbone of Excel. Includes basic areas (Function Library) as well as more advanced (Formula Auditing).

Data

Get External Data
Connections
Sort & Filter
Data Tools
Outline

The heart of the database portions of Excel. While not a true relational database, it has much power and includes Goal Seek and Scenario Manager.

Review

Proofing
Comments
Changes

Contains all reviewing tools in Excel, including such things as spelling, the use of comments, and sharing and protection.

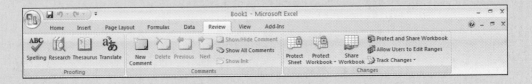

View

Workbook Views
Show/Hide
Zoom
Window
Macros

Contains basic and advanced view settings. Some of these options also appear below the horizontal and vertical scroll bars.

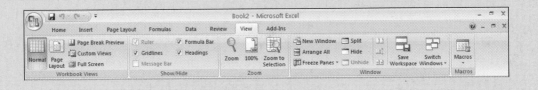

Navigate in Worksheets

Selecting cells to make them active and navigating from cell to cell are basic navigational skills in Excel. Using the mouse is probably the most convenient way to select a cell and navigate. To make a cell active, click on the desired cell. Making another cell active simply involves clicking on another cell. If the cell to be made active is not visible, use the vertical or horizontal scroll bars or the arrow keys to move so the desired cell is visible.

The other way is to use different keys to navigate through the worksheet. Table 1.1 shows keys that can be used to move in a worksheet.

Table 1.1   Keystrokes and Actions

Keystroke	Action
↑	Moves up one cell.
↓	Moves down one cell.
←	Moves left one cell.
→	Moves right one cell.
PgUp	Moves active cell up one screen.
PgDn	Moves active cell down one screen.
Home	Moves active cell to column A of current row.
Ctrl+Home	Moves active cell to cell A1.
Ctrl+End	Moves to the rightmost, lowermost active corner of the worksheet.
F5	Displays the GoTo dialog box to enter any cell address.

Identify Columns, Rows, and Cells

A spreadsheet is divided into columns and rows, with each column and row assigned a heading. Columns are assigned alphabetic headings from column A to Z, continue from AA to AZ, and then from BA to BZ until the last of the 18,278 columns is reached. Rows have numeric headings ranging from 1 to 1,048,576 (the maximum number of rows allowed).

A **cell** is the intersection of a column and row.

A **cell reference** is designated by a column letter and a row number.

The intersection of a column and row forms a *cell*, with the number of cells in a spreadsheet equal to the number of columns times the number of rows. Each cell has a unique *cell reference*, which is the intersection of a column and row designated by a column letter and a row number. For example, the cell at the intersection of column A and row 9 is known as cell A9. The column heading always precedes the row heading in the cell reference.

Start Excel and Create a New Worksheet

The first thing you should do is open Excel. You can do this by taking the following steps:

1. Click the Start button to display the Start menu. Position the mouse pointer over All Programs, select Microsoft Office, and then select Microsoft Office Excel 2007 from its location on the Programs menu.
2. Maximize the Excel program if necessary.

This opens a new Excel workbook with the default three-sheet worksheet tabs. When Excel is already open and you want to open a new workbook, complete the following steps:

1. Click the Office Button.
2. Select New, and then select Blank Workbook.

A new workbook is now open.

Entering and Editing Data in Cells

The three types of data that can be entered in a cell in an Excel worksheet are text, values, and formulas, which also include functions. You can create very sophisticated workbooks and simple worksheets with any combination of text, values, and formulas.

Enter Text

Text includes letters, numbers, symbols, and spaces.

Text is any combination of entries from the keyboard and includes letters, numbers, symbols, and spaces. Even though text entries may be used as data, they are most often used to identify and document the spreadsheet. Text is used to indicate the title of the spreadsheet. Typically text is used for row and column labels. When you need to enter text, click in the cell where the text is to appear, type the text, and either press Enter or click the ✓ on the formula bar.

Sometimes, you may have a long label that does not fit well in the cell. You can insert a line break to display the label on multiple lines within the cell. To insert a line break, press Alt+Enter where you want to start the next line of text within the cell.

Enter Values

A ***value*** is a number that represent a quantity, an amount, a date, or time.

Values are numbers entered in a cell that represent a quantity, an amount, a date, or time. As a general rule, Excel can recognize if you are entering text or values by what is typed. The biggest difference between text and value entries is that value entries can be the basis of calculation while text cannot.

Enter Formulas

A ***formula*** is a combination of numbers, cell references, operators, and/or functions.

Formulas (and their shorthand form, functions) are the combination of constants, cell references, arithmetic operations, and/or functions displayed in a calculation. For Excel to recognize a formula, it must always start with an equal sign (=). You learn about basic formulas in this chapter. Chapter 2 provides a detailed discussion of formulas and functions. At this point, it is sufficient to say that =A2+B2 is an example of a formula to perform addition.

> ### TIP   AutoComplete
>
> As soon as you begin typing a label into a cell, Excel searches for and (automatically) displays any other label in that column that matches the letters you typed. AutoComplete is helpful if you want to repeat a label, but it can be distracting if you want to enter a different label that begins with the same letter. To turn the feature on (or off), click the Office Button, click Excel Options, and click the Edit tab. Check (clear) the box to enable (disable) the AutoComplete feature.

Edit and Clear Cell Contents

You have several ways to edit the contents of a cell. You will probably select and stay with one technique that you find most convenient. The first method is to select the cell you want to edit, click in the formula bar, make changes, and then press Enter. The second method requires that you double-click in the cell to be edited, make the edits, and then press Enter. The third method is similar except that you select the cell, press the F2 key, and then make the edit.

You have two options to clear the contents of a cell. First, just click on a cell and press Delete. The second option involves clicking the Clear arrow in the Editing group on the Home tab. This gives you several options as to what will be cleared from the cell (see Figure 1.10).

Figure 1.10 Clear Pull-down List

Use Save and Save As

It is basic computer practice that files, including workbooks, should be saved often. If you are using a workbook and you do not want to change its name, the easiest way to save it is to click the Office Button and select Save. If you prefer keyboard short-cuts, press Ctrl+S. You also can click Save on the Quick Access Toolbar.

The first time you save a workbook, you can use the Save command or the Save As command that is located on the Office menu. For an unnamed file, either command displays the Save As dialog box. You can then assign a file name that is descriptive of the workbook (gradebook08, for example), determine the file location, and choose the file type. After selecting the appropriate options, click Save. When you use the Save command after initially saving a workbook, the subsequent changes are saved under the same workbook name and in the same location. If you want to assign a different name to a modified workbook so that you can preserve the original workbook, use the Save As command.

 TIP   File Management with Excel

Use the Office Button in the Open or Save As dialog box to perform basic file management within any Office application. You can select any existing file or folder, and delete it or rename it. You can also create a new folder, which is very useful when you begin to work with a large number of documents. You can also use the Views button to change the way the files are listed within the dialog box.

Hands-On Exercises

1 | Introduction to Microsoft Excel

Skills covered: 1. Plan Your Workbook **2.** Start Microsoft Office Excel 2007 **3.** Enter and Edit Data in Cells **4.** Use the Save As Command and Explore the Worksheet

---

Step 1
Plan Your Workbook

Refer to Figure 1.11 as you complete Step 1.

a. Prepare notes before beginning Excel.

Specify or define the problem. What statistics will be produced by your spreadsheet? Do you already have the statistics, or do you need to collect them from another source? Brainstorm about what formulas and functions will be required. Experiment with paper and pencil and a calculator. The first spreadsheet you create will be a sample showing membership sales in a gym. This sample worksheet includes monthly sales by region for both first and second quarters. Also included are the calculations to determine total monthly sales, average monthly sales, total and average sales by region, and increase or decrease in sales between the first and second quarters.

b. Simplify your Excel spreadsheet for those who will enter data.

You should treat your Excel workbook like a Microsoft Word document by doing such things as adding cell comments, giving instructions, and using attractive formatting.

c. Consider these layout suggestions when designing your Excel spreadsheets:

- Reserve the first row for a spreadsheet title.

- Reserve a row for column headings.

- Reserve a column at the left for row headings.

- Do not leave blank rows and columns for white space within the spreadsheet layout.

- Widen the columns and rows and use alignment instead of leaving blank rows or columns.

- Save your work often.

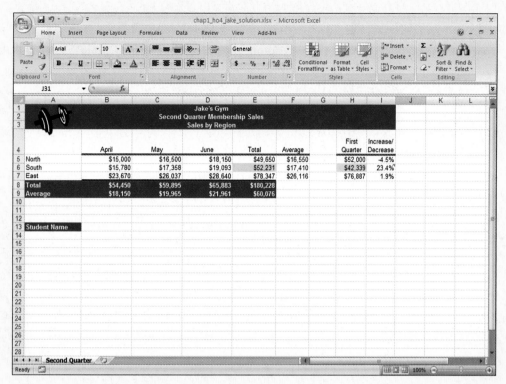

Figure 1.11 Well-Designed Spreadsheet

a. Click the **Start button** to display the Start menu. Click (or point to) **All Programs**, click **Microsoft Office**, and then click **Microsoft Office Excel 2007** to start the program.

You should be familiar with basic file management and very comfortable moving and copying files from one folder to another. If not, you may want to review the Help material for basic file management.

b. If necessary, click the **Maximize** button in the application window so that Excel takes the entire desktop, as shown in Figure 1.11. Click the **Maximize** button in the document window (if necessary) so that the workbook window is as large as possible.

Refer to Figure 1.12 as you complete Step 3.

a. Click **cell A1**, type **Jake's Gym**, and press **Enter**.

b. Click in **cell A2** and type **Second Quarter Membership Sales**.

c. Click **cell B3**, type the label **April**, and press the **right arrow**.

d. Click in **cell C3**, type the label **May**, and press the **right arrow**. Complete the typing for **cells D3** through **H3** as shown. Do not be concerned if the entire column label is not visible.

D3	June
E3	Total
F3	Average
G3	First Quarter
H3	Increase/Decrease

e. Enter the data for three regions as shown below:

Region	April	May	June	First Quarter
North	15000	16500	18150	31000
South	15780	17358	19093	42339
East	23670	26037	28640	76887

TROUBLESHOOTING: Data entry is important for good spreadsheet use. Verify values as you finish typing them. To change an entry, click on the cell and retype the value. To delete an entry, click on the cell and press Delete.

f. Type **Total** in **cell A7** and type **Average** in **cell A8**.

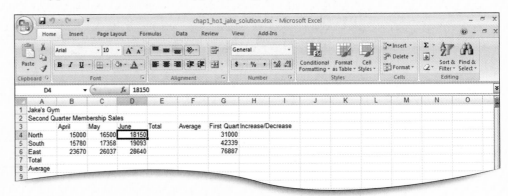

Figure 1.12 Jake's Gym Data

Step 4

Use the Save As Command and Explore the Worksheet

Refer to Figures 1.12 and 1.13 as you complete Step 4. Your Tab may not display exactly as shown because of different screen resolutions.

a. Click the **Office Button** and select **Save As** to display the Save As dialog box shown in Figure 1.13.

b. Type **chap1_ho1_jake_solution** as the name of the new workbook.

A file name may contain up to 255 characters. Spaces, underscores, and commas are allowed in the filename.

c. Navigate to the location of your data files and click the **Save button**.

You should see the workbook in Figure 1.12.

d. Click in **cell D4**, the cell containing 18150 or the North June sales.

Cell D4 is now the active cell and is surrounded by a heavy border. The name box indicates that cell D4 is the active cell, and its contents are displayed in the formula bar.

e. Click in **cell D5** (or press the down arrow key) to make it the active cell.

The name box indicates cell D5.

f. Refer to Table 1.1 as you move around the worksheet.

g. Close the *chap1_ho1_jake_solution* workbook.

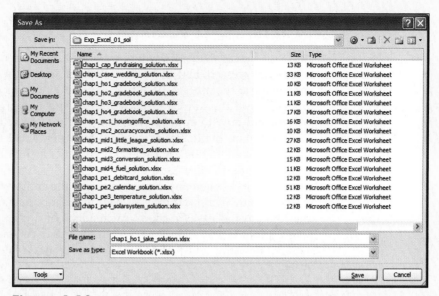

Figure 1.13 Save As Dialog Box

TIP Keyboard Shortcuts—The Dialog Box

Press Tab or Shift+Tab to move forward or backward between fields in a dialog box, or press Alt plus the underlined letter to move directly to an option. You will see underlined letters in words in dialog boxes. These are the letters you use in conjunction with the Alt key. Use the spacebar to toggle check boxes on or off and the up (or down) arrow keys to move between options in a list box. Press Enter to activate the highlighted command and Esc to exit the dialog box without accepting the changes. These are universal shortcuts and apply to any Windows application.

Mathematics and Formulas

You have used calculators where numbers are entered, the correct arithmetic function key is pressed, and the correct answer appears. What is missing though is the knowledge of the process, or how to arrive at the correct answer. These mathematical processes are the key to understanding and using Excel. Without knowing the process and how to apply it in Excel, you are left with just numbers, not answers. Arithmetic and mathematics produce answers by calculating numbers using Excel. You might want to think of Excel as a gigantic calculating program on the most powerful calculator of all, a computer.

With Excel, when any change is made, the entire worksheet is updated based on this new value. This fact brings us back to an important question: Why use Excel when one could just as easily perform calculations on a calculator or on paper? What happens if profit is 4% rather than 5%? In the pre-Excel days, answering these questions required rewriting and retyping the whole business plan using pencil, paper, and typewriter.

> Formulas can be as simple or as complex as necessary, but always begin with an = sign and contain mathematical operators.

In this section, you learn about the mathematical operations that are the backbone of Excel. You also will see that the order these mathematical operations are performed in can have a significant impact on the results. We touch briefly on the construction of mathematical expressions, called *formulas*, that direct Excel to perform mathematical operations and arrive at a calculated result. Whenever you want Excel to perform a calculation, you must enter an equal sign (=) in the cell where the answer is to appear. For example, if you wanted to calculate the sum of cells C2 and C3 in cell C4, you would do the following:

1. Click in cell C4 and type an = sign.
2. Click in cell C2 and type a + sign.
3. Click in cell C3 and press Enter.

This is an extremely simplified example but the principle holds true in all formulas. See Table 1.2 for examples of formulas. Formulas can be as simple or as complex as necessary, but always begin with an = sign and contain mathematical operators.

Table 1.2 Formula Examples

Operation	Formula
Addition	=C1+C2
Subtraction	=C2-C1
Multiplication	=C1*C2
Division	=C1/C2

Describing and Using Symbols and the Order of Precedence

The four mathematical functions—addition, subtraction, multiplication, and division—are the basis of all mathematical operations. Table 1.3 lists the arithmetic operators and their purposes.

Table 1.3 Arithmetic Operators and Symbols

Operation	Common Symbol	Symbol in Excel
Addition	+	+
Subtraction	–	–
Multiplication	X	*
Division	÷	/
Exponentiation	^	^

Enter Cell References in Formulas

If this were all there was to it, Excel would be effortless for all of us, but two other things need to be done if Excel is to perform mathematical functions as it was designed to do. First, rather than entering the numbers that are contained in the cells, Excel works at its full potential if cell references (C5, B2, etc.) are used rather than the numbers themselves. See Figure 1.14 for an example.

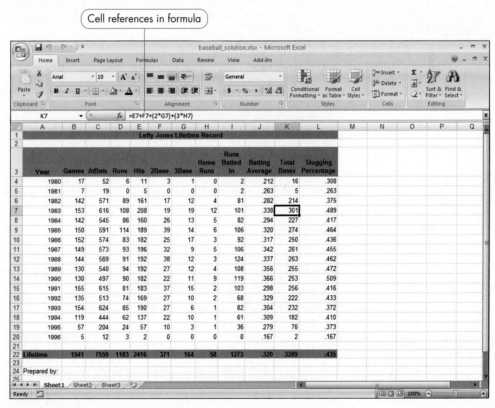

Figure 1.14 Baseball Statistics with Cell References

The first thing to consider is how Excel (or the computer) recognizes that you want to perform a mathematical operation. For example, you decide that you need to add the contents of cells C1 and C2 and place the sum in cell C3. In C1 you have the number 5, and in C2 you have the number 3. If you enter 5+3 and press Enter, the result you see will be "5+3." This is not the answer, however, that you are looking for. You want the result of 8. Anytime you want Excel to perform a mathematical calculation, you must begin by typing =. The equal sign tells Excel "get ready to do some math." One way to get the answer of 8 is by typing =5+3 and pressing Enter to see the sum, 8, in cell C3.

If you then change the number in cell C1 from 5 to 7, you must now change the 5 to a 7 in the formula in cell C3 to calculate the new result. Excel gives you an easier and much more efficient way to update results of calculations so you do not have to change the content of cell C3 every time the values in cells C1 or C2 change. This operation is done by using cell references. Rather than using the expression =5+3 in cell C3 to get a sum, you should enter the expression =C1+C2 in cell C3. This way, even if you change the values of cell C1 or C2, the value in cell C3 remains the sum of cells C1 and C2 because you are using cell references rather than the value in the cells.

Control the Results with the Order of Precedence

The **order of precedence** controls the sequence in which arithmetic operations are performed, which affects the result.

Before moving on to formulas, the final mathematics concept you need to know is order of precedence. The **order of precedence** are rules that control the order or sequence in which arithmetic operations are performed, which in turn, will change the result reported in Excel. Excel performs mathematical calculations left to right in this order: parentheses, exponentiation, multiplication or division, and finally addition or subtraction.

Review the expressions in Table 1.4 and notice how the parentheses change the value of the expression. In the second expression, the addition inside the parentheses is performed before the multiplication, changing the order of operations. Strictly following the order of mathematical operations eliminates many puzzling results when using Excel.

Table 1.4 Examples of Order of Precedence

Expression	Order to Perform Calculations	Output
= 6 + 6 * 2	Multiply first **and then** add.	18
= (6 + 6) * 2	Add the values inside the parentheses first **and then** multiply.	24
= 6 + 6 ^ 2	Simplify the exponent first: 36=6*6, **and then** add.	42
= 10/2 + 3	Divide first **and then** add.	8
= 10/(2+3)	Add first to simplify the parenthetical expression **and then** divide.	2
= 10 * 2 - 3 * 2	Multiply first **and then** subtract.	14

Displaying Cell Formulas

One of the tools that can be used to document an Excel worksheet is the ability to display cell formulas. When you display formulas, they will appear in the cells instead of the results of the calculation. See Figures 1.15 and 1.16. The quickest way to display cell formulas is to press Ctrl+~. The tilde (~) key is in the upper-left corner of the keyboard, under Esc. Note: you do not press the Shift key with the tilde key to make cell formulas visible in your worksheet.

	A	B	C	D	E	F
J9			f_x			
1	Microcomputer Concepts Grades					
2	Student	Test 1	Test 2	Final	Average	
3						
4	Adams	100	90	81	90.3	
5	Baker	90	76	87	84.3	
6	Glassman	90	78	78	82.0	
7	Moldof	60	60	40	53.3	
8	Walker	80	80	100	86.7	
9						
10	Class Average	84.0	76.8	77.2		

Figure 1.15 Spreadsheet with Values Displayed

	A	B	C	D	E
1	Microcomputer Concepts Grades				
2	Student	Test 1	Test 2	Final	Average
3					
4	Adams	100	90	81	=AVERAGE(B4:D4)
5	Baker	90	76	87	=AVERAGE(B5:D5)
6	Glassman	90	78	78	=AVERAGE(B6:D6)
7	Moldof	60	60	40	=AVERAGE(B7:D7)
8	Walker	80	80	100	=AVERAGE(B8:D8)
9					
10	Class Average	=AVERAGE(B4:B9)	=AVERAGE(C4:C9)	=AVERAGE(D4:D9)	
11					

Figure 1.16 Spreadsheet with Formulas Displayed

Inserting and Deleting Rows and Columns

After you construct a worksheet, it is often necessary to add or delete columns or rows of information. For example, in a grade book kept by a professor, names are constantly added or deleted. This process typically involves the use of the Insert command that adds cells, rows, or columns or the Delete command that deletes cells, rows, or columns. When you use either command, the cell references in existing cells are adjusted automatically to reflect the insertion or deletion. These commands also allow sheets to be added or deleted from the workbook.

To insert a row, click in the row below where you want a row inserted (rows are always inserted above, and columns are always inserted to the left of, the selected cell), and then click the Insert down arrow in the Cells group on the Home tab. You would then select Insert Sheet Rows. To insert a column, the user would select Insert Sheet Columns. For example, if the active cell is E4, row 4 is the current row. The row added is inserted above. If a column is inserted, it is inserted to the left of E4. The process is similar for deleting rows and columns, except you begin by choosing the Delete pull-down arrow in the Cells group. The row above the row selected is deleted, and the column to the left of the selected column is deleted.

TIP   Inserting and Deleting Individual Cells

In some situations, you may need to insert and delete individual cells instead of inserting or deleting an entire row or column. To insert a cell, click in the cell where you want the new cell, click the Insert pull-down arrow in the Cells group on the Cells tab, and then click Insert Cells to display the Insert dialog box. Click the appropriate option to shift cells right or down and click OK (see Figure 1.17). To delete a cell or cells, select the cell(s), click the Delete arrow in the Cells group on the Cells tab, and then click Delete Cells to display the Delete dialog box. Click the appropriate option to shift cells right or down and click OK (see Figure 1.18).

Figure 1.17 Insert Dialog Box

Figure 1.18 Delete Dialog Box

Using Cell Ranges; Excel Move; Copy, Paste, Paste Special; and AutoFill

Each of these topics is a basic editing function in Excel. They will be discussed in detail here, and you will be able to show your proficiency with them in Hands-On Exercise 2.

Select a Range

A ***range*** is a rectangular group of cells.

(A range may be as small as a single cell or as large as the entire worksheet.)

Every command in Excel applies to a rectangular group of cells known as a ***range***. A range may be as small as a single cell or as large as the entire worksheet. It may consist of a row or part of a row, a column or part of a column, or multiple rows or columns. The cells within a range are specified by indicating the diagonally opposite corners, typically the upper-left and lower-right corners of the rectangle. Many different ranges could be selected in conjunction with the worksheet shown in Figure 1.19. For example, the 1980 Player data is contained in the range B4:I4. The Lifetime Totals are found in the range B22:L22. The Batting Averages are found in the range J4:J20.

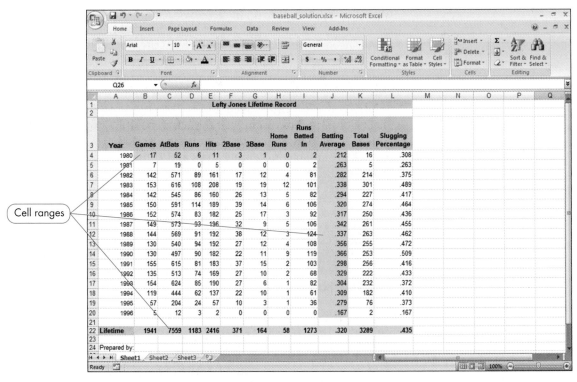

Figure 1.19 Defined Ranges

The easiest way to select a range is to click and drag—click at the beginning of the range and then press and hold the left mouse button as you drag the mouse to the end of the range, where you release the mouse. To select an entire column, click the column letter. To select an entire row, click the row number. Once selected, the range is highlighted, and its cells will be affected by any subsequent command. The range remains selected until another range is defined or until you click another cell anywhere on the worksheet.

Move a Cell's Contents

The ***move operation*** transfers the content of a cell or cell range from one location to another, with the cells where the move originated becoming empty.

The ***move operation*** transfers the content of a cell or cell range from one location in the worksheet to another, with the cells where the move originated becoming empty. The use of the move command can be confusing when you copy a cell containing a formula. The cell references within formulas are not changed when a cell containing a formula is moved. Excel does, however, adjust all of the cells making up the formula when a cell containing a formula is moved. You can use the drag-and-drop technique to move a range of cells or the cut and paste method. To use the cut and paste method:

1. Select the range of cells to be moved.
2. Pick Cut in the Clipboard group on the Home tab.
3. Select the range the cells will be moved to.
4. Click Paste in the Clipboard group on the Home tab.

The ***delete operation*** removes all content from a cell or from a selected cell range.

The ***delete operation*** removes all content from a cell or from a selected cell range. While there are several ways to execute the delete operation, the most simple is to select a cell or range of cells and press Delete to remove the information from the cell(s).

Copy, Paste, Paste Special

The Copy, Paste, and Paste Special operations are essential editing operations in any Microsoft Office 2007 application. The Copy command enables you to begin to duplicate information in a cell or range of cells into another cell or range of cells. In order to copy material, you select the cell(s) to be copied and click Copy in the Clipboard group on the Home tab. The Paste operation enables you to duplicate cell contents that you have copied to a new location. Once the contents of a cell or range of cells have been copied, select the location on the worksheet where the material is to be copied to and click Paste in the Clipboard group on the Home tab. The Paste Special operation provides several different options when pasting material (see Figure 1.20). The power of the Copy and Paste operation is enhanced with the use of Paste Special in Excel.

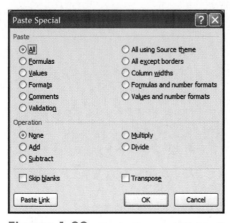

Figure 1.20 Paste Special Dialog Box

Use AutoFill

AutoFill enables you to copy the content of a cell or a range of cells by dragging the fill handle over an adjacent cell or range of cells.

The **fill handle** is a small black square appearing in the bottom-right corner of a cell.

AutoFill is an Excel operation that enables you to copy the content of a cell or a range of cells by dragging the *fill handle* (a small black square appearing in the bottom-right corner of a cell) over an adjacent cell or range of cells. AutoFill can be used in two different ways. First, you can use it to repetitively copy the contents of one cell. To do this, click the cell and use the fill handle to repeat the content. This operation is valuable for copying formulas, because the cell references are updated automatically during the AutoFill process. AutoFill also can be used to complete a sequence. For example, if you enter January in a cell, you can use AutoFill to enter the rest of the months of the year.

You can complete the quarters of a year by typing Qtr 1 in a cell and using AutoFill to fill in Qtr 2, Qtr 3, and Qtr 4 in sequence. Other sequences you can complete are weekdays and weekday abbreviations by typing the first item and using AutoFill to complete the other entries. For numeric values, however, you must specify the first two values in sequence. For example, if you want to fill in 5, 10, 15, and so on, you must enter the first two values in two cells, select the two cells, and then use AutoFill so that Excel knows to increment by 5.

TIP Two Different Clipboards

The Office Clipboard holds a total of up to 24 objects from multiple applications, as opposed to the Windows Clipboard, which stores only the results of the last Cut or Copy command. Thus, each time you execute a Cut or Copy command, the contents of the Windows Clipboard are replaced, whereas the copied object is added to the objects already in the Office Clipboard. To display the Office Clipboard, click the Home tab and click the arrow to the right of the word Clipboard. Leave the Clipboard open as you execute multiple cut and copy operations to observe what happens.

---

2 | Jake's Gym Continued

Skills covered: 1. Open an Existing Workbook **2.** Use Save As to Save an Existing Workbook **3.** Insert a Row and Compute Totals **4.** Copy the Formulas **5.** Continue the Calculations **6.** Insert a Column

Step 1	Refer to Figures 1.21 and 1.22 as you complete Step 1.
Open an Existing Workbook	

a. Click the **Office Button** and select **Open**.

You should see the Open dialog box, similar to Figure 1.21.

b. Click the **Views drop-down arrow**, and then select **Details**.

You changed the file list to a detailed list view, which shows more information.

c. Click the arrow on the **Look In** list box and click the appropriate drive depending on the location of your data.

You are navigating to the file you want to open.

d. Click the scroll arrow if necessary in order to select *chap1_ho2_jake*. Click **Open** to open the workbook shown in Figure 1.22.

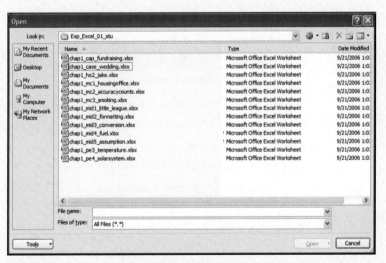

Figure 1.21 Open Dialog Box

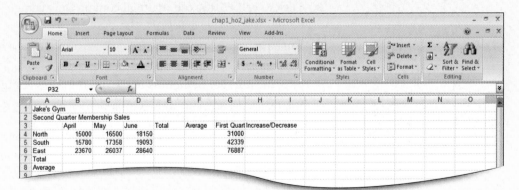

Figure 1.22 Original Jake's Gym Spreadsheet

a. Click the **Office Button** and select **Save As** to display the Save As dialog box.

b. Type **chap1_ho2_jake_solution** as the name of the new workbook.

A file name may contain up to 255 characters. Spaces, underscores, and commas are allowed in the file name.

c. Click the **Save** button.

Two identical copies of the file exist on disk, *chap1_ho2_jake* and *chap1_ho2_jake_solution*, which you just created. The title bar shows the latter name, which is the workbook currently in memory. You will work with *chap1_ho2_jake_solution* workbook but can always return to the original *chap1_ho2_jake* workbook if necessary.

TIP   Create a New Folder

Do you work with a large number of different workbooks? If so, it may be useful to store those workbooks in different folders, perhaps one folder for each subject you are taking. Click the Office Button, select Save As to display the Save As dialog box, and then click the Create New Folder button to display the associated dialog box. Enter the name of the folder, and then click OK. After you create the folder, use the *Look in* box to change to that folder the next time you open that workbook.

Refer to Figure 1.23 as you complete Step 3.

a. Select **row 3**, click the **Insert arrow** in the Cells group on the Home tab, and select **Insert Sheet Rows**.

You have inserted a new row between rows 2 and 3.

b. Click in **cell A3**. Type **Sales by Region** and press **Enter**.

c. Click in **cell E5**, the cell that will contain the quarterly sales total for the North region. Type **=B5+C5+D5** and press **Enter**.

The border appearing around cells B5, C5, and D5 indicates they are part of the formula you are creating. You entered the formula to compute a total.

d. Click in **cell E5**, check to make sure the formula matches the formula in the formula bar in Figure 1.23.

If necessary, click in the formula box in the formula bar and make the appropriate changes so that you have the correct formula in cell E5.

e. Click in **cell F5**, the cell that will contain the average sales for the North region for the second quarter. Type **=E5**.

You have begun to create the formula to calculate the average for the second quarter.

f. Type **=E5/3** to calculate the average for the second quarter by dividing the total by 3, the number of months in the quarter. Press **Enter**.

Total sales, 49650, is the second quarter total, and 16550 is the average quarterly sales.

TROUBLESHOOTING: If you type an extra arithmetic symbol at the end of a formula and press Enter, Excel will display an error message box suggesting a correction. Read the message carefully before selecting Yes or No.

g. Click in **cell F5** and verify that the formula **=E5/3** is correct.

h. Type your name in **cell A13** and click **Save** on the Quick Access Toolbar to save the workbook.

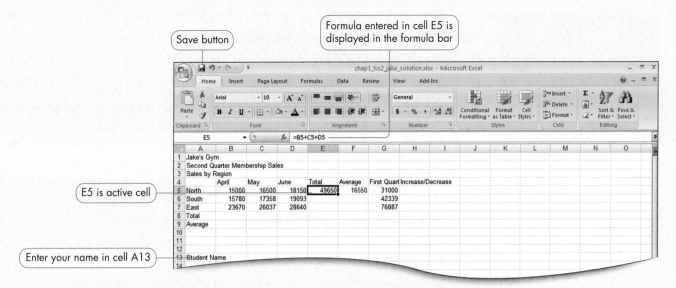

Figure 1.23 Insert Name and Compute Totals

Refer to Figure 1.24 as you complete Step 4.

a. Click **cell E5**.

Point to the fill handle in the lower-right corner of cell E5. The mouse pointer changes to a thin crosshair.

b. Drag the fill handle to **cell E7** (the last cell in the region total column).

A light gray color appears as you drag the fill handle, as shown in Figure 1.24.

c. Release the mouse to complete the copy operation.

The formulas for region totals have been copied to the corresponding rows for the other regions. When you click in cell E7, the cell displaying the total for the East region, you should see the formula: =B7+C7+D7.

d. Click **cell F5** and drag the fill handle to **cell F7** to copy the average sales formula down the column.

e. Save the workbook.

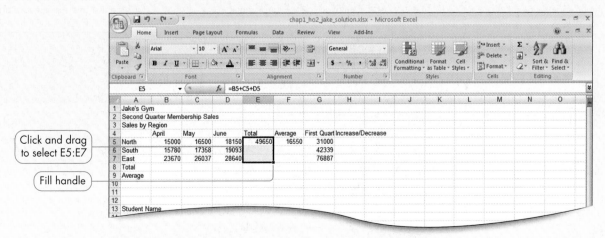

Figure 1.24 Copy the Formulas

Refer to Figure 1.25 as you complete Step 5.

a. Click **cell H5**, the cell that will contain the quarterly sales increase or decrease.

b. Type **=(E5–G5)/G5** and press **Enter**.

You should see 0.601613 as the increase in sales from the first quarter to the second quarter for the North region. If this result is not correct, click cell H5 and verify that the formula =(E5-G5)/G5 is correct. Correct it in the formula bar if necessary.

c. Click **cell H5** and use the fill handle to copy the formula down the column to **cell H7**.

d. Click in **cell B8**. Type **=B5+B6+B7** and press **Enter**.

e. Click in **cell B9** to begin the formula to calculate the average sales for April. Type **=(B5+B6+B7)/3** and press Enter.

If the formula is entered correctly, you will see 18150 in cell B9. This is an awkward method of creating a formula to determine an average of values, and you will learn to use another method in Chapter 2. However, this formula illustrates the use of parentheses to control the order of precedence.

TROUBLESHOOTING: The parentheses used in the formula force the addition before the division and must be used to calculate the correct value.

f. Click **cell B8** and drag through **cell B9** to select both cells. Drag the fill handle in the lower-right corner of cell B9 across through **cell E9** to copy the formulas.

You copied the formulas to calculate both the monthly sales totals and averages for columns B through E.

g. Click in **cell G5** and type **52000**, then press **Enter**. See Figure 1.25.

Updated information shows that the first-quarter earnings in the North region were misreported. The new number, 52000, represents a decrease in sales between the first and second quarters in the North region.

h. Save the workbook.

You entered the formulas to calculate the appropriate totals and averages for all regions for the second quarter. You also entered the formula to determine the increase or decrease in sales from the first quarter to the second quarter.

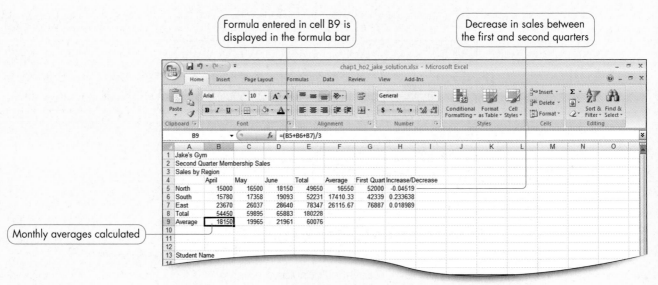

Figure 1.25 Continue the Calculations

Refer to Figure 1.26 as you complete Step 6.

a. Click the **column letter G**, the column to the left of where you want to insert a column.

When you insert a column, it appears to the left of your initial selection, and the columns are moved to the right.

b. Click on the **Insert down arrow** in the Cells group on the Home tab.

Figure 1.26 shows the Insert options in the Cells group.

c. Select **Insert Sheet Columns**.

You inserted a blank column to the left of the First Quarter column or column G.

d. Save the *chap1_ho2_jake_solution* workbook and keep it onscreen if you plan to continue to the next hands-on exercise. Close the workbook and exit Excel if you do not want to continue with the next exercise at this time.

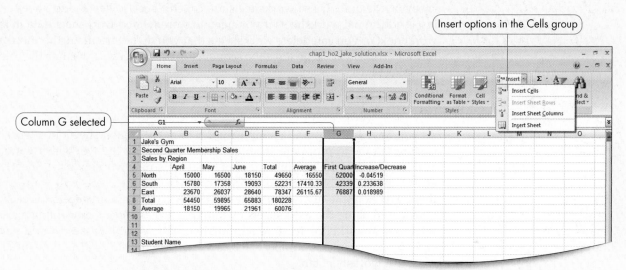

Figure 1.26 Insert a Column

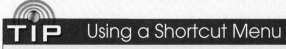

TIP   Using a Shortcut Menu

Another method to insert a row or column is to right-click anywhere on a row or column to show a shortcut menu. Click Insert to insert a row or a column and then select the appropriate option from the dialog box. Rows are inserted above the active cell, and columns are inserted to the left of the active cell.

Workbook and Worksheet Enhancements

At the beginning of this chapter, you learned that a worksheet or spreadsheet is a grid containing columns and rows to store numerical data. Further, you learned that a workbook is a single file that contains one or more related worksheets. So far, you have created one worksheet within a workbook. However, as you continue using Excel to develop workbooks for personal and professional use, you need to learn how to manage multiple worksheets.

In this section, you learn how to manage worksheets. Specifically, you rename worksheets and change worksheet tab colors. Furthermore, you learn how to insert, delete, add, and move worksheets.

Managing Worksheets

When you start a new blank workbook in Excel, the workbook contains three worksheets by default. These worksheets are called Sheet1, Sheet2, and Sheet3. You can insert additional worksheets if you need to store related worksheet data in the same workbook, or you can delete worksheets that you do not need. Furthermore, you can rename worksheets, rearrange the sequence of worksheets, or change the color of the worksheet tabs.

Rename Worksheets

As you have learned, it is a simple matter to move among sheets in a workbook by clicking on the appropriate sheet tab at the bottom of the worksheet window. You also learned that the default names of sheets in a new workbook are Sheet1, Sheet2, etc. To give workbook sheets more meaningful names, you will want to rename them. For example, if your budget workbook contains worksheets for each month, you should name the worksheets by month, such as *January* and *February*. A teacher who uses a workbook to store a grade book for several classes should name each sheet by class name or number, such as *MIS 1000* and *MIS 2450*. Follow these steps to rename a worksheet tab:

1. Right-click a sheet tab to show a shortcut menu.
2. Select Rename and the sheet tab name is highlighted.
3. Type the new sheet tab name and press Enter.

Change Worksheet Tab Color

The sheet tabs are blue in color by default. The active worksheet tab is white. When you use multiple worksheets, you might find it helpful to add a color to sheet tabs in order to make the tab stand out or to emphasize the difference between sheets. For example, you might want the January tab to be blue, the February tab to be red, and the March tab to be green in a workbook containing monthly worksheets. Changing the color of the tabs in workbooks when sheets have similar names helps to identify the tab you want to work with. Follow these steps to change the worksheet tab color:

1. Right-click the Sheet1 tab.
2. Select Tab Color.
3. You select Theme Colors, Standard Colors, No Color, or More Colors.

Move, Delete, Copy, and Add Worksheets

The fastest way to move a worksheet is to click and drag the worksheet tab. To delete a worksheet in a workbook, right-click on the sheet tab and select Delete from the shortcut menu. You can copy a worksheet in similar fashion by pressing and holding

Ctrl as you drag the worksheet tab. Move, Copy, and Delete worksheet operations also are accomplished by right-clicking the desired sheet tab and selecting the needed option from the shortcut menu.

To add a new blank worksheet, right-click any sheet tab, and select Worksheet from the Insert dialog box, and click OK.

You might want to move a worksheet to reorder existing sheets. For example, January is the first budget sheet, but at the end of January you move it after December so February is the sheet that opens first. If a professor is no longer teaching a course, she might delete a grade book sheet. Once a grade book sheet is created, it can be copied, modified, and used for another course.

> ### TIP   Moving, Copying, and Renaming Worksheets
>
> The fastest way to move a worksheet is to click and drag the worksheet tab. You can copy a worksheet in similar fashion by pressing and holding Ctrl as you drag the worksheet tab. To rename a worksheet, double-click its tab to select the current name, type the new name, and press Enter.

Formatting Worksheets

Formatting worksheets allows you to change or alter the way numbers and text are presented. You can change alignment, fonts, the style of text, and the format of values, and apply borders and shading to cells, for example. These formatting procedures allow you to prepare a more eye-appealing worksheet. You format to draw attention to important areas of the worksheet, and you can emphasize totals or summary area values.

(*. . . formatting procedures allow you to prepare a more eye-appealing worksheet.*)

Merge and Center Labels

You may want to place a title at the top of a worksheet and center it over the material contained in the worksheet. Centering helps to unify the information on the worksheet. The best way to do this is to *merge and center cells* into one cell across the top of the worksheet and center the content of the merged cell. See Figure 1.27, the before, and Figure 1.28, the after. The merged cells are treated as one single cell. This is a toggle command and can be undone by clicking Merge & Center a second time. To merge cells and center a title across columns A through L you would:

The *merge and center cells* option centers an entry across a range of selected cells.

1. Enter the title in cell A1.
2. Select cells A1:L1.
3. Click Merge & Center in the Alignment group on the Home tab.

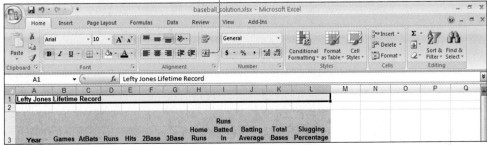

Figure 1.27   Merge and Center Title

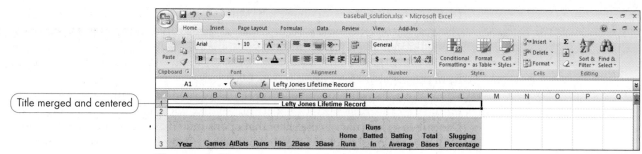

Title merged and centered

Figure 1.28 Merged and Centered Title

Adjust Cell Height and Width

It often is necessary to change the height and/or width of a cell so all of its contents are visible. When labels are longer than the cell width, they are displayed in the next cell if it is empty. If the adjacent cell is not empty, the label is truncated. Numbers appear as a series of pound signs (######) when the cell is not wide enough to display the complete number. To widen a column, drag the border between column headings to change the column width.

For example, to increase or decrease the width of column A, point to the border, and you will see a two-headed arrow. Drag the border between column headings A and B to the right or left. You also can double-click the right boundary of a column heading to change the column width to accommodate the widest entry in that column.

To increase or decrease the width of row 1, drag the border between row headings 1 and 2 up or down. You can also double-click the bottom boundary of a row heading to change the row height to accommodate entries in their entirety. Alternatively, right-click on the row number to show a shortcut menu and select Row Height. Enter an integer and click OK.

AutoFit automatically adjusts the height and width of cells.

AutoFit is an important command used when formatting a spreadsheet to automatically adjust the height and width of cells. You can choose from two types of AutoFit commands available in Format in the Cells group on the Home tab (see Figure 1.29). The AutoFit Column Width changes the column width of the selected columns to fit the contents of the column. AutoFit Row Height changes the row height of the selected row to fit the contents of the row.

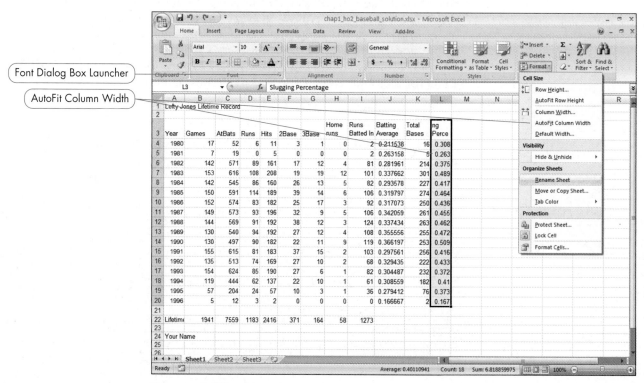

Font Dialog Box Launcher

AutoFit Column Width

Figure 1.29 AutoFit

To change the row height of many rows at one time, select the multiple rows and right-click to show the shortcut menu. Select Row Height and enter a number in the Row Height dialog box, as shown in Figure 1.30. Click OK. To change the column width of many columns at one time, select the multiple columns and right-click to show the shortcut menu. Select Column Width and enter a number in the Column Width dialog box. Click OK.

Figure 1.30 Row Height Dialog Box

Apply Borders and Shading

You have several options to choose from when adding borders to cells or applying a shade to cells. You can select a cell border from Borders in the Font group on the Home tab or you can use the Border tab in the Format Cells dialog box. Either way, you can create a border around a cell (or cells) for additional emphasis. Click the Font Dialog Box Launcher in the Font group on the Home tab (see Figure 1.29), and then click the Border tab. Figure 1.31 shows the Border tab in the Format Cells dialog box. Select (click) the line style at the left of the dialog box, and then click the left, right, top, and/or bottom border. It is possible to outline the entire cell or selected cells, or choose the specific side or sides; for example, thicker lines on the bottom and right sides produce a drop shadow, which can be very effective. Also, you can specify a different line style and/or a different color for the border, but a color printer is needed to see the effect on the printed output.

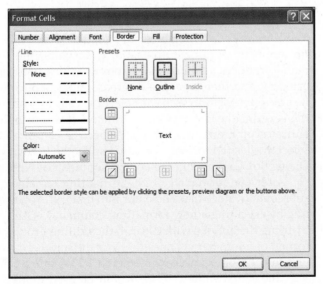

Figure 1.31 Border Tab on the Format Cells Dialog Box

You can add a shade to a cell from Fill Color in the Font group on the Home tab or you can use the Fill tab in the Format Cells dialog box. The Fill tab and Fill Color enable you to choose a different color in which to shade the cell and further emphasize its contents. The Pattern Style drop-down list lets you select an alternate pattern, such as dots or slanted lines. Click OK to accept the settings and close the dialog box. Figure 1.32 shows the Fill tab of the Format Cells dialog box.

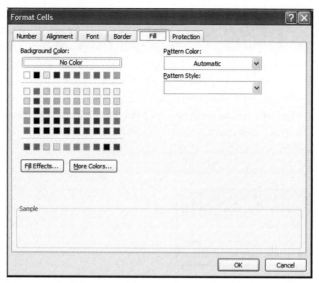

Figure 1.32 Fill Tab on the Format Cells Dialog Box

Insert Clip Art

A good way to enhance the appearance of a spreadsheet is to insert a clip art image. These images can represent the subject of the spreadsheet, the company preparing the spreadsheet, or even the personal interests of the person preparing the spreadsheet. You should use caution when inserting clip art because they can be distracting to the user of the spreadsheet or can take large amounts of disk space and slow operations on the spreadsheet. If you want to insert clip art, click Clip Art in the Illustrations group on the Insert tab to open the Clip Art task pane. Type a keyword in the Search for text box and click Go to begin the search for images matching your keyword. When you find an appropriate image, double-click it to place it in your spreadsheet. You can now move and resize the image as desired.

Format Cells

The **Format Cells** operation controls formatting for numbers, alignment, fonts, borders, colors, and patterns.

The *Format Cells* dialog box and commands on the Home tab control the formatting for numbers, alignment, fonts, borders, colors, and patterns. Execution of the command produces a tabbed dialog box in which you choose the particular formatting category, and then enter the desired options. All formatting is done within the context of select-then-do. You can select the cells to which the formatting is to apply and then execute the Format Cells command. If you want to apply the same formats to an entire column or row, click the respective column letter or row number, and then select the desired format. You can display the Format Cells dialog box by clicking the Dialog Box Launcher in the Font, Alignment, or Number group.

After you format a cell, the formatting remains in the cell and is applied to all subsequent values that you enter into that cell. You can, however, change the formatting by executing a new formatting command. Also, you can remove the formatting by using the options with Clear in the Editing group on the Home tab. Changing the format of a number changes the way the number is displayed, but does not change its value. If, for example, you entered 1.2345 into a cell, but displayed the number as 1.23, the actual value (1.2345) would be used in all calculations involving that cell. The numeric formats are shown and described in Table 1.5. They are accessed by clicking the Number Format down arrow in the Number group on the Home tab. The tabbed Format Cells dialog box is displayed by selecting More.

Table 1.5 Formatting Definitions

Format Style	Definition
General	The default format for numeric entries and displays a number according to the way it was originally entered. Numbers are shown as integers (e.g., 123), decimal fractions (e.g., 1.23), or in scientific notation (e.g., 1.23E+10) if the number exceeds 11 digits.
Number	Displays a number with or without the 1000 separator (e.g., a comma) and with any number of decimal places. Negative numbers can be displayed with parentheses and/or can be shown in red.
Currency	Displays a number with the 1000 separator and an optional dollar sign (which is placed immediately to the left of the number). Negative values can be preceded by a minus sign or displayed with parentheses, and/or can be shown in red.
Accounting	Displays a number with the 1000 separator, an optional dollar sign (at the left border of the cell, vertically aligned within a column), negative values in parentheses, and zero values as hyphens.
Date	Displays the date in different ways, such as March 14, 2009, 3/14/09, or 14-Mar-09.
Time	Displays the time in different formats, such as 10:50 PM or the equivalent 22:50 (24-hour time).
Percentage	Shows when the number is multiplied by 100 for display purposes only, a percent sign is included, and any number of decimal places can be specified.
Fraction	Displays a number as a fraction, and is appropriate when there is no exact decimal equivalent. A fraction is entered into a cell by preceding the fraction with an equal sign—for example, =1/3. If the cell is not formatted as a fraction, you will see the results of the formula.
Scientific	Displays a number as a decimal fraction followed by a whole number exponent of 10; for example, the number 12345 would appear as 1.2345E+04. The exponent, +04 in the example, is the number of places the decimal point is moved to the left (or right if the exponent is negative). Very small numbers have negative exponents.
Text	Left aligns the entry and is useful for numerical values that have leading zeros and should be treated as text, such as ZIP codes.
Special	Displays a number with editing characters, such as hyphens in a Social Security number.
Custom	Enables you to select a predefined customized number format or use special symbols to create your own customized number format.

Use Fonts

You can use the same fonts in Excel as you can in any other Windows application. All fonts are WYSIWYG (What You See Is What You Get), meaning that the worksheet you see on the monitor will match the printed worksheet.

Any entry in a worksheet may be displayed in any font, style, or point size, as indicated in the Font group on the Home tab, as shown in Figure 1.33. The example shows Arial, Bold, Italic, and 14 points. Special effects, such as subscripts or superscripts, are also possible. You can even select a different color, but you will need a color printer to see the effect on the printed page.

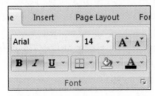

Figure 1.33 Font Group on the Home Tab

Alignment of Cell Contents

The Alignment tab in the Format Cells dialog box and the Alignment group on the Home tab together give you a wealth of options to choose from. Changing the orientation of cell contents is useful when labels are too long and widening columns is not an option. Wrapping text in a cell also reduces the need to widen a column when space is at a premium. Centering, right aligning, or left aligning text can be done for emphasis or to best display cell contents in columns. When the height of rows is changed, it is necessary to vertically adjust alignment for ease of reading. Figure 1.34 shows both the Alignment group and the Format Cells dialog box with the Alignment tab visible.

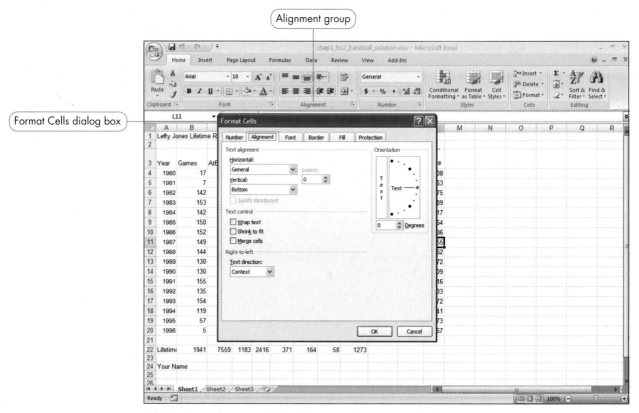

Figure 1.34 Alignment Group and Alignment Tab

TIP   Use Restraint

More is not better, especially in the case of too many typefaces and styles, which produce cluttered worksheets that impress no one. Limit yourself to a maximum of two typefaces per worksheet, but choose multiple sizes or styles within those typefaces. Use boldface or italics for emphasis, but do so in moderation, because if you emphasize too many elements, the effect is lost. Figure 1.37 shows locations of number format commands.

Hands-On Exercises

3 | Formatting Jake's Gym Worksheet

Skills covered: 1. Manage the Workbook **2.** Apply Number Formats **3.** Apply Font Attributes and Borders **4.** Change Alignment Attributes **5.** Insert an Image

---

Step 1
Manage the Workbook

Refer to Figure 1.35 as you complete Step 1.

a. If necessary, open the *chap1_ho2_jake_solution* workbook and save it as **chap1_ho3_jake_solution**.

b. Right-click **Sheet1 tab** at the bottom of the worksheet and select **Rename** from the shortcut menu.

   You selected the generic Sheet1 tab so you can give it a more meaningful name.

c. Type **Second Quarter** and press **Enter**.

d. Right-click on the **Second Quarter** sheet tab and select **Tab Color**.

e. Select **Accent 5** color from the Theme Colors gallery.

   You applied a color to the Second Quarter sheet tab to make it more distinctive.

f. Right-click the **Sheet2 tab** and click **Delete**.

g. Right-click the **Sheet3 tab** and click **Delete**.

   You have deleted the unused worksheets from the workbook.

h. Save the workbook.

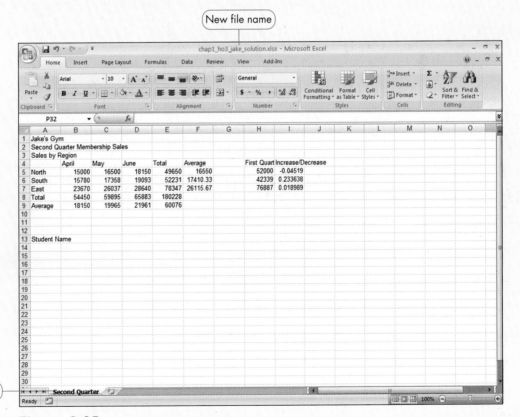

Figure 1.35 Workbook Management

Refer to Figure 1.36 as you complete Step 2.

a. Click in **cell I5** and then click and drag to select the **range I5:I7**.

You selected the range of cells to be formatted.

b. Click the **Home tab** and click the **Number Dialog Box Launcher** in the Number group.

The Format Cells dialog box shown in Figure 1.36 is now displayed on your screen.

c. Click the **Number tab** and select **Percentage** from the *Category* list.

d. Type **1** in the Decimal places box. Click **OK** to close the dialog box.

You formatted the increase or decrease in sales as a percentage with 1 decimal place.

e. Click and drag to select the **range B5:H9**.

f. Click the **Number Dialog Box Launcher** in the Number group.

g. Click the **Number tab** and select **Currency** from the *Category* list.

h. Type **0** for the Decimal places box. Click **OK** to close the dialog box.

You formatted the remaining values as currency with 0 decimal places.

i. Save the workbook.

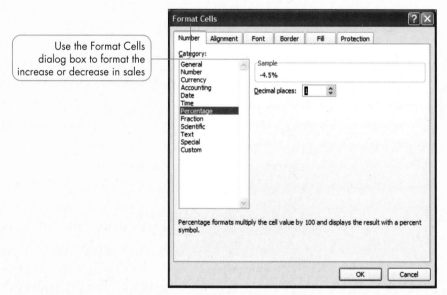

Use the Format Cells dialog box to format the increase or decrease in sales

Figure 1.36 Apply Number Format

TIP Number Formats

You can change some number formats in the Number group on the Home tab. For example, you can click Accounting Number Format to display dollar signs and align decimal points for monetary amounts. You can click the Number down arrow to select various number formats, such as Number, Accounting, Date, Percentage, and Fraction. The Number group also contains commands to increase or decrease the number of decimal points. Figure 1.37 shows locations of number format commands.

Refer to Figure 1.37 as you complete Step 3. Your screen display may be different depending on your screen resolution.

a. Click and drag to select the **range A1:I3**.

b. Press and hold **Ctrl** while selecting the **range A8:E9**. Continue to press and hold Ctrl while clicking **cell A13** to select it.

You selected several ranges of noncontiguous cells and you can now apply multiple formats to these ranges.

c. Click the **Fill Color** arrow in the Font group and select the color **Purple**.

d. Click the **Font Color** arrow in the Font group and select **White**.

> **TROUBLESHOOTING:** If you apply a format and change your mind, just apply another format or clear the formatting using Clear in the Editing group on the Home tab.

e. Click **Bold** in the Font group to make the text stand out.

You formatted parts of the worksheet by using a color fill, a font color, and a font enhancement. You want to draw attention to these areas of the worksheet.

f. Select the **range B4:F4**, then press and hold **Ctrl** while selecting the **ranges H4:I4** and **B7:E7**.

g. Click **More Borders** arrow in Font group and click **Bottom Double Border**.

You again selected noncontiguous ranges of cells and then applied a double border to the bottom of the cells.

h. Select **cell E6**, press and hold **Ctrl** while selecting **cell H6,** and select **Yellow** from **Fill Color** in the Font group.

This highlights the large increase in sales in the South region between the first and second quarter.

i. Save the workbook.

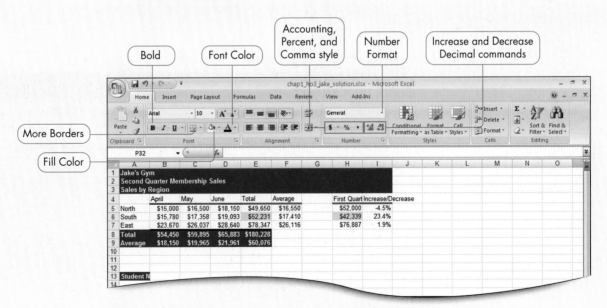

Figure 1.37 Continue Formatting Attributes and Borders

Step 4

Change Alignment Attributes

Refer to Figure 1.38 as you complete Step 4.

a. Click on the **Home tab** if it is not already active.

b. Click and drag to select the **range A1:I1**.

c. Click **Merge & Center** in the Alignment group on the Home tab.

d. Click and drag to select the **range A2:I2**.

e. Click **Merge & Center** in the Alignment group on the Home tab.

f. Click and drag to select the **range A3:I3**.

g. Click **Merge & Center** in the Alignment group on the Home tab.

You have now merged cells and centered the title and two subtitles in single cells. You cannot select more than one row and merge into a single cell.

h. Click and drag to select the **range A4:I4**.

i. Right-click on the selected cell range to display a shortcut menu, then select **Format Cells** to display the dialog box.

j. Click the **Alignment tab**, and then click the **Wrap text check box** in the *Text control* section.

k. Click the **Horizontal drop-down arrow** in the *Text alignment* section, select **Center**, and click **OK** to accept the settings and close the dialog box.

You used the shortcut menu to open the dialog box and made two enhancements to the selected text. It is more efficient to make multiple changes using a dialog box.

TROUBLESHOOTING: If your monitor is set for a high resolution or if you have a wide screen monitor, you may see text by some of the command icons. For example, you might see the words *Wrap Text* by the Wrap Text command in the Alignment group. If you want your screen to have the same resolution as the figures shown in this textbook, change your resolution to 1024 × 768.

 TIP Split a Cell

If you merge too many cells or decide you no longer want cells to be merged, you can split the merged cell into individual cells again. To do this, select the merged cell and click Merge & Center in the Alignment group or deselect Merge cells on the Alignment tab in the Format Cells dialog box.

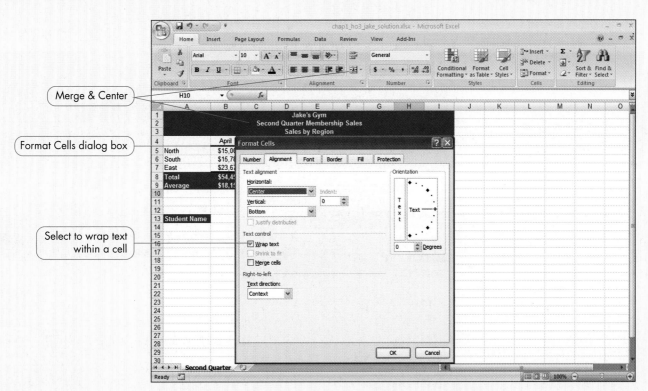

Figure 1.38 Change Alignment Attributes

Refer to Figure 1.39 as you complete Step 5.

a. Click in **cell A1**, click the **Insert tab**, and click **Clip Art** in the Illustrations group. A Clip Art task pane opens. Type **exercise** in the **Search for** box and click **Go**.

You are going to insert a clip art image in the worksheet but must first search for an appropriate image.

b. Click to insert the image shown in Figure 1.39. Click the image to select it and drag the lower-right sizing handle to resize the image to fit the worksheet.

When working with images, it is necessary to resize the images and widen columns or change row height.

c. Save the *chap1_ho3_jake_solution* workbook and keep it onscreen if you plan to continue to the next hands-on exercise. Close the workbook and exit Excel if you do not want to continue with the next exercise at this time.

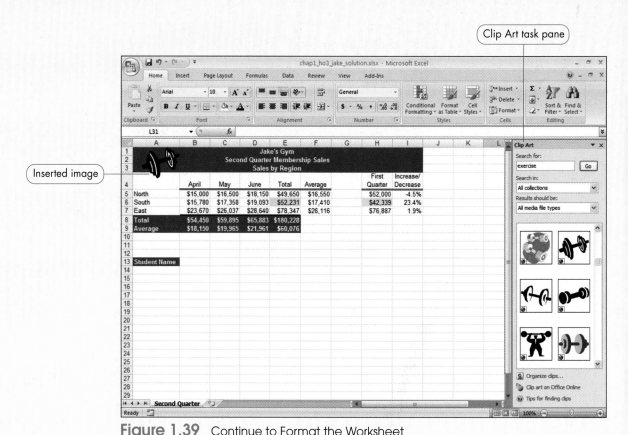

Figure 1.39 Continue to Format the Worksheet

Page Setup and Printing

The Page Setup command gives you complete control of the printed worksheet. Many of the options may not appear significant now, but you will appreciate them as

> The Page Setup command gives you complete control of the printed worksheet.

you develop larger and more complicated worksheets later in the text. Workbooks and worksheets become part of auditor's reports in organizations' annual reports and quarterly reports. Spreadsheets are part of dissertations and grade books, and are the basis for budgeting both for personal use and corporate use. As you can see, printing workbooks and worksheets is an important function.

In this section, you select options in the Page Setup dialog box that will help make your printouts look more professional.

Selecting Page Setup Options for Printing

The key to selecting correct settings to print lies within the Page Setup dialog box. This dialog box contains four tabs. You will make selections from each to indicate the printing settings for the worksheet you want to print. The Page Setup dialog box also contains the Print Preview button. This appears on each tab, and you will use the preview feature to view your selections from each tab. Print preview is a handy and efficient way to see how the printed output will appear without wasting paper. To launch the Print Dialog box, you click the Page Setup Dialog Box Launcher from the Page Setup group on the Page Layout tab. This dialog box is shown in Figure 1.40.

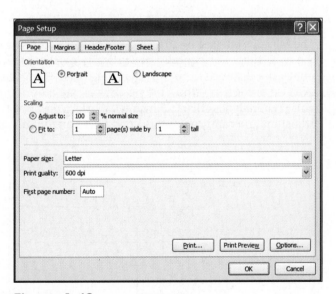

Figure 1.40 Page Setup Dialog Box

Specify Page Options with the Page Tab

The first tab that is open in the Page Setup dialog box is the Page tab, as shown in Figure 1.41. Note that you can use the Print Preview button from any of the Page Setup dialog box tabs and that the Options button takes the user to settings for the particular printer he or she is using. The Print Preview command shows you how the worksheet will appear when printed and saves you from having to rely on trial and error.

The Page orientation options determine the orientation and scaling of the printed page. ***Portrait orientation*** (8.5 × 11) prints vertically down the page. ***Landscape orientation*** (11 × 8.5) prints horizontally across the page and is used when the worksheet is too wide to fit on a portrait page. Changing the page orientation to landscape is often an acceptable solution to fit a worksheet on one page. The other option, scaling, can produce uneven results when you print a workbook consisting of multiple worksheets.

Portrait orientation prints vertically down the page.

Landscape orientation prints horizontally across the page.

Scaling option buttons are used to choose the scaling factor. You can reduce or enlarge the output by a designated scaling factor, or you can force the output to fit on a specified number of pages. The latter option is typically used to force a worksheet to fit on a single page. The Paper size and Print quality lists present several options for the size paper your printer is using and the dpi (Dots Per Inch) quality of the printer.

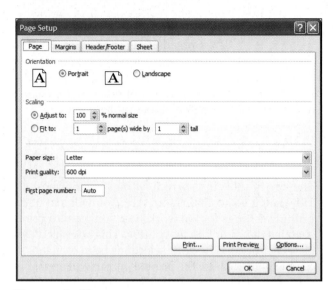

Figure 1.41 Page Tab

Use the Margins Tab to Set Margins

The Margins tab (see Figure 1.42) not only controls the margins, but is used to center the worksheet horizontally or vertically on the page. The Margins tab also determines the distance of the header and footer from the edge of the page. You must exercise caution in setting the margins as not all printers can accept very small margins (generally less than .25 inches). Worksheets appear more professional when you adjust margins and center the worksheet horizontally and vertically on a page.

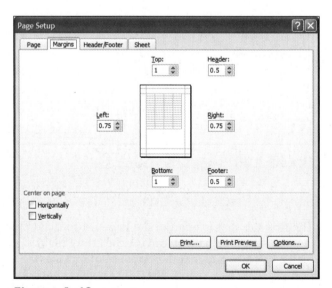

Figure 1.42 Margins

Create Headers and Footers with Header/Footer Tab

The Header/Footer tab, shown in Figure 1.43, lets you create a header and/or footer that appears at the top and/or bottom of every page. The pull-down list boxes let you choose from several preformatted entries, or alternatively, you can click the Custom Header or Custom Footer button, and then click the appropriate formatting button to customize either entry. Table 1.6 below shows a summary of the formatting buttons for headers and footers. You can use headers and footers to provide additional information about the worksheet. You can include your name, the date the worksheet was prepared, and page numbers, for example.

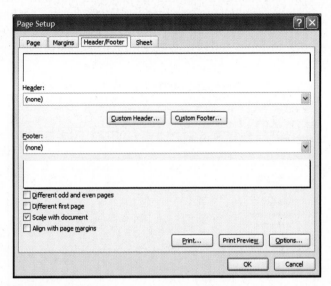

Figure 1.43 Headers and Footers

Table 1.6 Header/Footer Button Summary

Button	Name	Code Entered	Result
A	Format Text	None	Sets font, size, and text style.
	Insert Page Number	&(Page)	Inserts page number.
	Insert Number of Pages	&(Pages)	Indicates total number of pages.
	Insert Date	&(Date)	Inserts the current date.
	Insert Time	&(Time)	Inserts the current time.
	Insert File Path	&(Path)&(File)	Indicates path and file name.
	Insert File Name	&(File)	Indicates the file name.
	Insert Sheet Name	&(Tab)	Shows the name of the active worksheet.
	Insert Picture	&(Picture)	Inserts an image file.
	Format Picture	None	Opens the Format Picture dialog box.

Select Sheet Options from the Sheet Tab

The Sheet tab contains several additional options, as shown in Figure 1.44. The Gridlines option prints lines to separate the cells within the worksheet. The Row and Column Headings option displays the column letters and row numbers. Both options should be selected for most worksheets. Just because you see gridlines on the screen does not mean they print. You must intentionally select the options to print both gridlines and row and column headings if you want them to print.

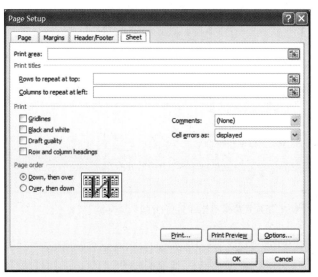

Figure 1.44 Sheet Tab

TIP Print Preview

The Print Preview button is on all tabs of the Page Setup dialog box. This button is used to verify options as you make your page setup choices. Print Preview is a paper-saving feature because you can preview before printing. The Print button is located on all tabs of the Page Setup dialog box.

Managing Cell Comments

*A **comment** adds documentation to a cell.*

The use of cell *comments* in Excel is an important yet simple way to provide documentation to others who may view the file. Comments add documentation to a cell and are inserted in a cell to explain the preparer's thoughts to or define formulas for those using the workbook. Often, the creator of a file will want to provide information about a cell or cells in a worksheet without them always being visible. Inserting comments will accomplish this result. A red triangle appears in the cell containing the comment, and the comment is visible when you point at the cell. See Figure 1.45. To create a cell comment:

1. Click the cell requiring a comment.
2. On the Review tab, in the Comments group, click New Comment.
3. Enter the comment.
4. Click any other cell to complete the process.
5. Or right-click on the cell requiring a comment and select Insert Comment from the shortcut menu.

Hands-On Exercises

4 | Printing Jake's Gym Worksheet

Skills covered: 1. Insert a Comment **2.** Insert Custom Header and Footer **3.** Format to Print the Worksheet

---

Step 1

Insert a Comment

Refer to Figure 1.45 as you complete Step 1.

a. Open the *chap1_ho3_jake_solution* workbook and save it as **chap1_ho4_jake_solution**.

b. Click in **cell I6**.

You will type a descriptive comment in the selected cell.

c. Click the **Review tab** and click **New Comment** in the Comments group.

The name in the comment box will be different depending on how the application was registered.

d. Type **The largest percent of increase**.

e. Click any other cell to complete the process.

You can right-click the cell requiring a comment and select Insert Comment from the shortcut menu.

TROUBLESHOOTING: You can print your comments by first clicking in the cell containing a comment, and then clicking Show All Comments in the Comments group of the Review tab. Then select As displayed on sheet from the Comments list in the Sheet tab of the Page Setup dialog box.

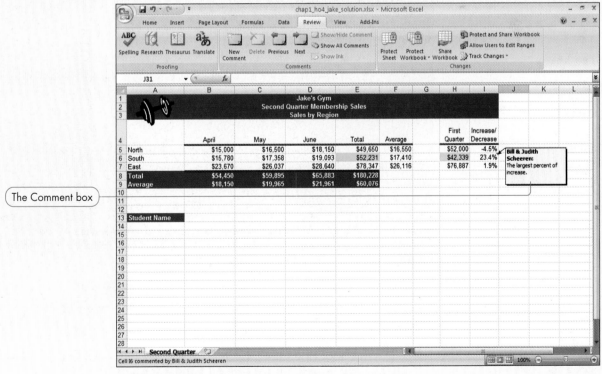

The Comment box

Figure 1.45 Insert a Comment

Step 2

Insert Custom Header and Footer

Refer to Figure 1.46 as you complete Step 2.

a. Click the **Page Layout tab** and click the **Page Setup Dialog Box Launcher** in the Page Setup group.

You opened the Page Setup box so you can make several selections at one time.

b. Click the **Header/Footer tab**.

c. Click **Custom Header** and type your name in the left section.

d. Click in the right section and click **Insert Page Number**. Click **OK**.

You created a header so your name and page number will display at the top of the spreadsheet page.

e. Click **Custom Footer** and click in the center section. Type your instructor's name.

f. Click in the right section, click **Insert Date**, and click **OK**.

You created a footer so your instructor's name and the date will print at the bottom of the spreadsheet page.

g. Click **Print Preview**.

You use the preview feature to verify the accuracy and placement of your header and footer information. You can also determine how much of the worksheet will print on a page. Close Print Preview when you are finished.

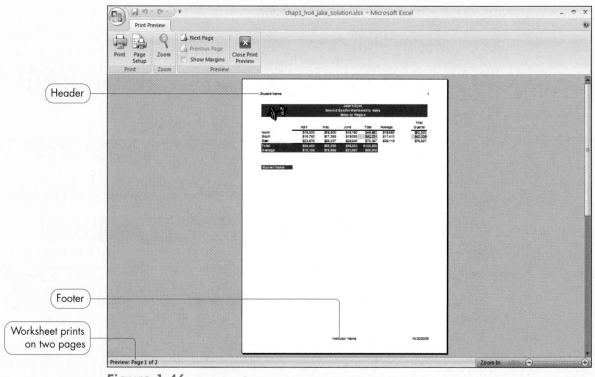

Figure 1.46 Insert a Custom Header and Footer

Step 3

Format to Print the Worksheet

Refer to Figure 1.47 as you complete Step 3.

a. Click the **Page Layout tab** if it is not the active tab. Click the **Orientation** arrow in the Page Setup group and select **Landscape**.

You changed from portrait to landscape as one method to make sure the worksheet prints on one page.

b. Click the **Size** arrow in the Page Setup group, select **More Paper Sizes**, and click the **Fit to 1 page option** in the *Scaling* section.

You opened the Page Setup dialog box and selected *Fit to 1 page* to force the worksheet to print on a single page, another method to print the worksheet on one page. You will continue to make selections from the Page Setup dialog box.

c. Click the **Margins tab** in the Page Setup dialog box and click the **Horizontally** and **Vertically check boxes** in the *Center on page* section.

Printing a worksheet that is centered both horizontally and vertically results in a Professional-appearing document.

d. Click the **Sheet tab** in the Page Setup dialog box and click the **Row and column headings** and **Gridlines check boxes** in the *Print* section. Click the **Print Preview button**.

Row and column headings and gridlines facilitate reading the data in a worksheet.

e. Click **Print** to print the worksheet.

f. Save the workbook and press **Ctrl+~** to show the cell formulas rather than the displayed values. See Figure 1.47. Adjust the column widths as necessary to print on one page and then print the worksheet a second time.

Displaying and printing cell formulas is one of the more important tasks associated with worksheet creation. Formulas are the basis of many values, and it is necessary to verify the accuracy of the values. Analyzing the formulas and perhaps manually calculating the formulas is one way to verify accuracy. Printing with formulas displayed is part of worksheet documentation.

g. Close the workbook. Do not save the changes unless your instructor tells you to save the worksheet.

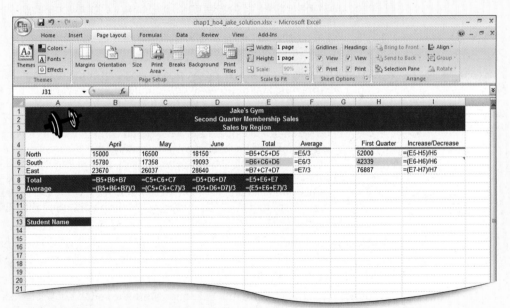

Figure 1.47 Displayed Cell Formulas

TIP Quit Without Saving

At times, you may not want to save the changes to a workbook—for example, when you have edited it beyond recognition and wish you had never started. Click the Office Button, click the Close command, and then click No in response to the message asking whether to save the changes. Click the Office Button, click the file's name at the right of the menu to reopen the file, and then begin all over.

Summary

1. **Define worksheets and workbooks.** A spreadsheet is the computerized equivalent of an accountant's ledger. It is divided into rows and columns, with each row and column assigned a heading. The intersection of a row and column forms a cell. Spreadsheet is a generic term. Workbook and worksheet are Excel specific. An Excel workbook contains one or more worksheets.

2. **Use spreadsheets across disciplines.** Spreadsheets are used in many areas other than business. Because of the powerful graphing or charting feature of Excel, geologists and physical scientists use spreadsheets to store data about earthquakes or other physical phenomena and then graph it. Historians and social scientists have long used the power of spreadsheets for such uses as predicting voting behavior.

3. **Plan for good workbook and worksheet design.** Planning a spreadsheet before entering data into it is a necessary activity. The more prior planning that is done, the better the spreadsheet will appear, and it also will ensure that the spreadsheet shows what it is supposed to.

4. **Identify Excel window components.** The elements of the Excel window include the ribbon, tabs, and groups. There are also quick buttons above the tabs to simplify some functions. The formula bar, sheet tabs, the status bar, and the Select All button are parts of the Excel window.

5. **Enter and edit data in cells.** You can enter three types of data in an Excel worksheet. They are text, values, and formulas. Each of these types of data has different uses in Excel.

6. **Describe and use symbols and the order of precedence.** Mathematical symbols are the base of all calculations in Excel. Understanding the order of precedence also helps clarify how mathematical calculations occur in Excel.

7. **Display cell formulas.** One of the tools that can be used to document an Excel worksheet is the ability to display cell formulas. When this tool is used, the formulas that appear in cells are shown rather than the results of the calculation.

8. **Insert and delete rows and columns.** This feature typically involves the use of the Insert command that adds cells, rows, or columns or the Delete command that deletes cells, rows, or columns. When either of these commands is used, the cell references in existing cells are automatically adjusted to reflect the insertion or deletion.

9. **Use cell ranges; Excel move; copy, paste, paste special; and AutoFill.** Each of these topics is a basic editing function in Excel. Every command in Excel applies to a rectangular group of cells known as a *range*. The Move operation transfers the content of a cell or cell range from one location on the worksheet to another with the cells where the move originated becoming empty. The Delete operation removes all content from a cell or from a selected cell range. The Copy command enables users to begin to duplicate information in a cell or range of cells into another cell or range of cells. The Paste operation enables the user to duplicate cell contents that have been copied to a new location. The Paste Special operation enables users several different options when pasting material. AutoFill is an Excel operation that enables users to copy the content of a cell or a range of cells by dragging the fill handle over another cell or range of cells.

10. **Manage worksheets.** These are operations that users of Excel should be familiar with in order to make worksheets more attractive and also to understand some basic operations that can assist in the construction of worksheets.

11. **Format worksheets.** Formatting is done within the context of select-then-do; that is, select the cell or range of cells, then execute the appropriate command. The Format Cells command controls the formatting for numbers, alignment, fonts, borders, and patterns (colors). The Formatting toolbar simplifies the formatting process. As you format a worksheet to improve its appearance, you might want to insert clip art as well.

12. **Select page setup options for printing.** The Page Setup command provides complete control over the printed page, enabling you to print a worksheet with or without gridlines or row and column headings. The Page Setup command also controls margins, headers and footers, centering the worksheet on a page, and orientation. The Print Preview command shows the worksheet as it will print and should be used prior to printing.

13. **Manage cell comments.** The use of comments in Excel is an important, yet simple, way to provide documentation to others who may view the file. Often the creator of a file will want to provide information about a cell or cells in a worksheet without them always being visible.

Key Terms

Multiple Choice

1. Which of the following is true?
   (a) A worksheet contains one or more workbooks.
   (b) A workbook contains one or more worksheets.
   (c) A spreadsheet contains one or more worksheets.
   (d) A worksheet contains one or more spreadsheets.

2. The cell at the intersection of the second column and third row is cell:
   (a) B3
   (b) 3B
   (c) C2
   (d) 2C

3. Which options are mutually exclusive in the Page Setup menu?
   (a) Portrait and landscape orientation
   (b) Cell gridlines and row and column headings
   (c) Left and right margins
   (d) Fit to page and Adjust to normal size

4. Which of the following is not a symbol for a mathematical operation in Excel?
   (a) +
   (b) –
   (c) C
   (d) *

5. Which command enables you to change the margins for a printed worksheet?
   (a) View
   (b) Edit
   (c) Page Setup
   (d) Options

6. What is the effect of typing F5+F6 into a cell without a beginning equal sign?
   (a) The entry is equivalent to the formula =F5+F6.
   (b) The cell will display the contents of cell F5 plus cell F6.
   (c) The entry will be treated as a text entry and display F5+F6 in the cell.
   (d) The entry will be rejected by Excel, which will signal an error message.

7. The Save command:
   (a) Brings a workbook from disk into memory.
   (b) Brings a workbook from disk into memory and then erases the workbook on disk.
   (c) Stores the workbook in memory on disk.
   (d) Stores the workbook in memory on disk and then erases the workbook from memory.

8. Which of the following is not a basic mathematical operation?
   (a) Parentheses
   (b) Division
   (c) Multiplication
   (d) Subtraction

9. Given the formula =B5*B6+C3/D4^2, which expression would be evaluated first?
   (a) B5*B6
   (b) D4^2
   (c) C3/D4
   (d) It is impossible to determine.

10. If you see the term "C3" used in relation to Excel, this refers to what?
    (a) Absolute reference
    (b) Cell reference
    (c) Worksheet reference
    (d) Mixed reference

11. Which of the following is the correct order of mathematical operations?
    (a) Parentheses, multiplication or division, addition or subtraction
    (b) Parentheses, exponents, multiplication or division, addition or subtraction
    (c) Parentheses, exponents, addition or subtraction, multiplication or division
    (d) Multiplication or division, addition or subtraction, parentheses, exponents

12. What is the answer to =10+4*3?
    (a) 42
    (b) 22
    (c) 34
    (d) 17

Multiple Choice Continued...

13. What is the answer to =(6*5)+4?
    (a) 34
    (b) 44
    (c) 26
    (d) 54

14. The fill handle is used to:
    (a) Copy
    (b) Paste
    (c) Cut
    (d) Select

15. The small black square in the bottom-right corner of a cell is called what?
    (a) Pointer
    (b) Fill handle
    (c) Cross hair
    (d) Select box

16. A red triangle in a cell indicates which of the following:
    (a) A cell is locked.
    (b) The cell contains an absolute reference.
    (c) The cell contains a comment.
    (d) The cell contains numeric data.

17. Which of the following is entered first when creating a formula?
    (a) The equal sign
    (b) A mathematical operator
    (c) A function
    (d) A value

18. What is the end result of clicking in a cell and then clicking Italic on the Home tab twice in a row?
    (a) The cell contents are displayed in italic.
    (b) The cell contents are not displayed in ordinary (non-italicized) type.
    (c) The cell contents are unchanged and appear exactly as they did prior to clicking the Italic button twice in a row.
    (d) Impossible to determine.

19. Which option is not available when creating a custom header or custom footer?
    (a) Format Text
    (b) Insert Formula
    (c) Insert Number of Pages
    (d) Format Picture

One of the more common challenges beginning college students face is keeping track of their finances. The worksheet in this problem is one that you could use to verify your weekly debit card expenditures. Failure to track your debit card correctly could lead to financial disaster, as you are charged for overdrafts and could get a bad credit rating. You will use the data shown in the table below to create the worksheet. Refer to Figure 1.48 as you complete this exercise.

a. Start Excel and select **New** to display a blank workbook. Save the workbook as **chap1_pe1_debitcard_solution**.

b. Click in **cell A1** and type **Your Name Debit Card**. Do not worry about formatting at this time. Enter the labels as shown in the table below:

Cell Address	Label
A2	Item #
B2	Date
C2	Description
D2	Amount
E2	Deposit
F2	Balance

c. Click in **cell F3** and type the initial balance of **1000**. You will format the values later. Use the table below to enter the data for the first item:

Cell Reference	Data
A4	100
B4	6/2
C4	Rent
D4	575

d. Click in **cell F4** and type the formula **=F3-D4+E4** to compute the balance. The formula is entered so that the balance is computed correctly. It does not matter if an amount or deposit is entered as the transaction because Excel treats the blank cells as zeros.

e. Enter data in rows 5 through 8, as shown in Figure 1.48. Type **Weekly Verification** in cell C8. Click in **cell F4** and use the fill handle to copy the formula to **cells F5:F7**.

f. Insert a new row above row 8 by right-clicking in row 8, selecting **Insert** from the shortcut menu, clicking **Entire row** in the Insert dialog box, and then clicking **OK**.

g. Click in **cell D9** to enter the formula to total your weekly expenditure amount. Type **= D4+D6+D7** and press **Enter**. If the formula is entered correctly, you will see 670.43 in cell D9.

h. Click in **cell E9** and type **=E5** to enter the formula to total your weekly deposit. If the formula is entered correctly, you will see 250 as the total first week deposit.

i. To verify your balance, click in **cell F9**, and type **=F3-D9+E9,** and press **Enter**. If you entered the formula correctly, you will see 579.57 as the balance.

j. Right-click **cell F9** and select **Insert Comment**. Type the following comment: **Balance is equal to the initial balance minus the amounts and ATM withdrawals plus the deposits.**

k. Format the completed worksheet, as shown in Figure 1.48. Click in **cell D3**, and then click and drag to select the **range D3:F9**. Click the **Home tab** and click the **Number Format down arrow** in the Number group. Click **Currency** from the Number Format gallery.

l. Click and drag to select the **range B4:B7**. Click the **Number Format down arrow** in the Number group. Click **Short Date** from the Number Format gallery. Select the **range**

...continued on Next Page

A4:A7; press and hold **Ctrl** while dragging to select the **range A2:F2**. Click **Center** in the Alignment group on the Home tab.

m. Click and drag to select the **range A1:F2**. Click the **Fill Color arrow** in the Font group and select the color **Orange**. Click the **Font Color arrow** in the Font group and select **Blue**. Click **Bold** in the Font group and **select 16** from **Font Size** list to make the text stand out. Click **More Borders** in the Font group and click **Top and Thick Bottom Border**.

n. Widen columns A through F so all text is visible by dragging the right border of each column to the right.

o. Click and drag to select the **range A1:F1**. Click **Merge & Center** in the Alignment group on the Home tab.

p. Click the **Page Layout tab** and click the **Page Setup Dialog Box Launcher** in the Page Setup group. Click the **Header/Footer tab**, click **Custom Header**, and type **Your Name** in the *Left section*. Click in the *Right section* and click **Insert Page Number**. Click **OK**.

q. Click **Custom Footer** and click in the *Center section*. Type **Your Instructor's Name**. Click in the *Right section*, click **Insert Date**, and click **OK**. Click **Print Preview**. Click **Page Setup** on the Print Preview tab.

r. Click the **Margins tab** in the Page Setup dialog box and click the **Horizontally** and **Vertically check boxes** in the *Center on page* section. Click the **Sheet tab** and click the **Row and column headings** and **Gridlines check boxes** in the *Print* section. Click **OK**. Click **Close Print Preview** on the Print Preview tab.

s. Click **Save** on the Quick Access Toolbar to save the workbook. Click the **Office Button**, select **Print**, and select **Quick Print** to print the worksheet.

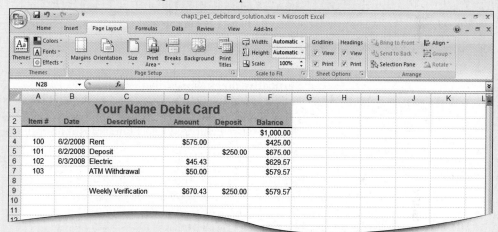

Figure 1.48 Verify Your Debit Card

---

2 Formatting—Create a Calendar

Excel is a spreadsheet application that gives you a row column table to work with. In this exercise, you will use the row column table to create a calendar worksheet that also demonstrates the formatting capabilities available in Excel. You will insert images representing a variety of activities in a particular month. Review Figure 1.49 to see a sample calendar page.

a. Start Excel to display a blank workbook and save it as **chap1_pe2_calendar_solution**.

b. In **cell D1**, enter the month for which you will create the calendar—July, for example. Click and drag to select **cells D1:F1**, then click **Merge & Center** in the Alignment group on the Home tab. Use the Font group to select **Comic Sans MS** font and **26** for the font size. Type **Your Name** in **cell D2** and press **Enter**. Click and drag to select **cells D2:F2** and merge and center as described above. Use the Font group to select **Comic Sans MS** font and **14** for the font size.

c. Right-click **row 1**, select **Row Height** from the shortcut menu, and type **39** in the Row Height dialog box to increase the row height. In similar fashion, right-click **row 2** and verify the row height is **21**.

d. Select **columns B** through **H**, right-click, select **Column Width** from the shortcut menu, and type **16** to change the width of the selected columns.

...continued on Next Page

e. Press and hold **Ctrl** while selecting the **ranges B1:H3**, **B4:B8**, and **H4:H8**. Click the **Fill Color** arrow in the Font group and select the color **Blue**. Click the **Font Color** arrow in the Font group and select **White**. Click **Bold** in the Font group to make the text stand out.

f. Click in **cell B3**, type **Sunday**, and press **Enter**. Click **cell B3** to make it the active cell. Click and drag the fill handle from **cell B3** to **H3** to automatically enter the remaining days of the week.

g. Keeping cells B3:H3 selected, click **Center** in the Alignment group on the Home tab. Increase the row height by right-clicking **row 3**, selecting **Row Height** and typing **23.25** in the Row Height dialog box, and then clicking **OK**.

h. Click **cell D4** and type **1** for the first day of the month. Type numbers for the remaining 30 days of the month in rows **4** through **8**. Increase the row height in rows 4 through 8 to **65**. Select rows **4** through **8**, and click **Top Align**, and click **Align Text Left** in the Alignment group on the Home tab. Click and drag to select **cells B4:G8**, then select **Arial**, **14 point**, and **Bold** in the Font group on the Home tab. Click and drag to select **cells B3:H8**, right-click the selected cells, select **Format Cells** to open the Format cells dialog box. Click **Border**, and then click both **Outline** and **Inside** in the *Presets section*. Click **OK**.

i. Click **Clip Art** in the Illustrations group on the Insert tab and type **Fourth of July** in the **Search for** text box. Insert and resize the images, as shown in Figure 1.49. Search for **Cardinal**, insert, and resize the image shown in Figure 1.49.

j. Right-click on the **Sheet1 tab**, select **Rename**, and type **July**. Right-click the July tab, select **Tab Color**, and select **Red**. Delete the remaining sheets by right-clicking the sheet tab and selecting **Delete**.

k. Click the **Page Layout tab** and click the **Page Setup Dialog Box Launcher** in the Page Setup group. Click the **Header/Footer tab**. Click **Custom Footer** and type **Your Name** in the *Left section*. Click in the *Right section* and type your instructor's name. Click **OK**.

l. Click the **Margins tab** in the Page Setup dialog box and click the **Horizontally** and **Vertically check boxes** in the *Center on page* section. Click the **Page tab**, click **Landscape** in the *Orientation section*, and click **OK**.

m. Click **Save** on the Quick Access Toolbar to save the workbook. Click the **Office Button**, select **Print**, and select **Quick Print** to print the worksheet.

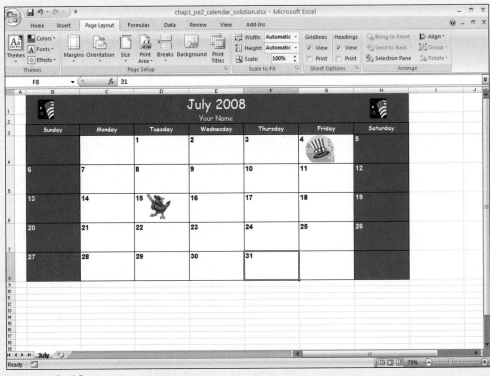

Figure 1.49 Create a Calendar

...continued on Next Page

Your hobby is collecting, recording, and monitoring metrological data to track trends in temperature. Figure 1.50 displays the average temperature for summer in three American cities. Working with the partially completed workbook, you will create formulas, copy and paste a portion of a spreadsheet, and format both worksheets in an attractive and readable manner.

a. Open the *chap1_pe3_temperature* workbook and save it as **chap1_pe3_temperature_ solution** so that you can return to the original workbook if necessary.

b. Click in **cell E3**, type **=(B3+C3+D3)/3**, and press **Enter**. You entered the formula to calculate the average summer temperature for Pittsburgh. Click in **cell E3** and use the fill handle to copy the formula to **cells E4:E5**.

c. Click in **cell A6** and type **Monthly Averages**. Enter the formula to calculate the average temperature for June by clicking in **cell B6** and typing **=(B3+B4+B5)/3**, then pressing **Enter**. Click in **cell B6** and use the fill handle to copy the formula to **cells C6:D6**.

d. Click in **cell E9** and type **=(B9+C9+D9)/3**, then press **Enter** to calculate the average temperature by city for the winter months. Click in **cell E9** and use the fill handle to copy the formula to **cells E10:E11**.

e. Click in **cell A12** and type **Monthly Averages**. Click in **cell B12** and type **=(B9+B10+B11)/3**, then pressing **Enter** to calculate the average temperature for December. Click in **cell B12** and use the fill handle to copy the formula to **cells C12:D12**.

f. Format numbers in column E and rows 6 and 12 with 2 decimals by pressing and holding **Ctrl** while selecting **cells E3:E5, E9:E11, B6:D6**, and **B12:D12**. Click the **Number Format arrow** in the Number group on the Home tab and select **Number**. Widen **column A** to **18**, and **columns B** through **E** to **11.**

g. Insert a blank row above row 1 by right-clicking the row number and selecting **Insert** from the shortcut menu. Type the title **Temperature Comparison** in **cell A1**.

h. Select **cells A1:E1** and click **Merge & Center** in the Alignment group. Repeat for cells **A2:E2** and cells **A8:E8**. Press and hold **Ctrl** while selecting **A1:E2** and **A8:E8**, and then select **Light Blue** from **Fill Color** and **White** from **Font Color** in the Font group. Change the title font and size by selecting **cells A1:E1** and then selecting **Comic Sans MS** from the **Font** drop-down list and **18** from the **Font Size** drop-down list in the Font group.

i. Press and hold **Ctrl** while selecting **cells B3:E3** and **B9:E9** and clicking **Center** in the Alignment group.

j. Press and hold **Ctrl** while selecting **cells A1:E3, A7:E9**, and **A13:E13** and click **Bold** in the Font group.

k. Press and hold **Ctrl** while selecting **A4:A6** and **A10:A12** and clicking **Increase Indent** in the Alignment group.

l. Type **Your Name** in **cell G1** to identify the worksheet as yours.

m. You will move your winter temperature data, as well as the title to a new sheet, and then rename and change the color of both sheet tabs and delete Sheet3. Select **cell A1** and click **Copy** in the Clipboard group on the Home tab.

n. Click the **Sheet2 tab**, make sure cell A1 is the active cell, and click the **Paste down arrow** in the Clipboard group, and select **Paste Special**. Select **All** from the *Paste* section of the Paste Special dialog box, and then click **OK** to paste the formatted title in cell A1. Immediately open the Paste Special dialog box again and select **Column Widths** from the *Paste* section. When you click **OK** to close, you will see the correct column widths.

o. Click the **Sheet1 tab**, press **Esc** to cancel the previous selected range, select **cells A8:E13**, and click **Copy** in the Clipboard group. Click the **Sheet2 tab**, make sure **cell A2** is the active cell, click the **Paste down arrow** in the Clipboard group, and select **Paste Special**. Select **All** from the *Paste* section of the Paste Special dialog box, and then click **OK** to paste the formatted portion of the worksheet in cell A2. Click **Sheet1** and delete the winter portion of the worksheet by right-clicking and selecting **Delete** from the shortcut menu. Select **Shift cells up** and click **OK**. Right-click the **Sheet1 tab**, select **Rename**, and type **Summer**. Right-click the **Sheet2 tab**, select **Rename**, and type **Winter**. Right-click the **Sheet3 tab,** and select **Delete**. Right-click the **Summer tab** and select **Red** from the **Tab color palette**. Repeat but choose **Blue** for the **Winter tab**.

...continued on Next Page

p. Click the **Page Layout tab** and click the **Page Setup Dialog Box Launcher** in the Page Setup group. Click the **Header/Footer tab**. Click **Custom Header** and type **Your Name** in the *Left section*. Click in the *Right section* and type your course name. Click **OK**.

q. Click the **Margins tab** in the Page Setup dialog box, click **Horizontally** and **Vertically check boxes** in the *Center on page* section, and click **OK**.

r. Print the worksheet two ways, to show both displayed values and cell formula. Save the workbook.

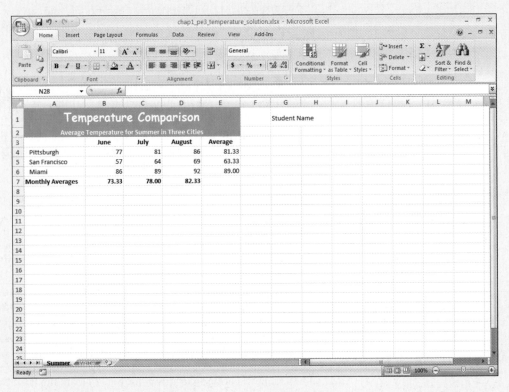

Figure 1.50 Temperature Data

4 Astronomy Lab

The potential uses of a spreadsheet are limited only by your imagination, as shown by Figure 1.51, which displays a spreadsheet with information about our solar system. Your astronomy professor asked you to complete the worksheet as part of your lab assignment. You will open the partially completed version of the workbook and complete the worksheet by developing the formulas for the first planet, copying those formulas to the remaining rows in the worksheet, and then formatting the worksheet for your professor.

a. Open the *chap1_pe4_solarsystem* workbook and save it as **chap1_pe4_solarsystem_ solution** so that you can return to the original workbook if necessary.

b. Click in **cell C15** and enter your weight in pounds on Earth. Click in cell **C16** and enter **Pi=3.141597**, which is the value of Pi for this worksheet.

c. Click in **cell D4** and enter the formula to compute the diameter of the first planet (Mercury). The diameter of a planet is equal to twice its radius. Type **Pi=2*B4** and press **Enter**.

d. Click in **cell E4** and enter the formula to compute the circumference of a planet. The circumference is equal to the diameter times Pi. Type **pi=3.141597*D4** and press enter.

e. Click in **cell F4** and enter the formula to compute the surface area, which is equal to four times Pi times the radius squared. This is the formula to compute the surface area of a sphere, which is different from the formula to compute the area of a circle. Type **Pi=4*pi=3.141597*B4^2** and press **Enter**.

...continued on Next Page

f. Click in **cell G4** and enter the formula to compute your weight on Mercury, which is your weight on Earth times the relative gravity of Mercury compared to that of Earth. Type **=150*C4** and press **Enter**. The weight in the example is 150, but you will enter your weight and the result will be different.

g. To copy the formulas, select **cells D4:G4** and use the **fill handle** to copy the formula to **cells D4:G11**.

h. Click in **cell E14** and type **Your Name**. Format the worksheet appropriately making sure to do the following:

- Merge and center the cells in **row 1**.

- Format numbers in columns **B, D, E,** and **F** as Number with 0 decimal places

- Last selection in custom list is a time format. This is not a good format for numbers. Format it with number, no decimal places.

- Widen columns as necessary.

- Bold rows **1, 3,** and **13**.

- Use **Green Navy** fill and **White** font color for cell ranges **A1:G3, A13:C13,** and **E13:F13**.

i. Use the Page Setup command to specify:

- **Landscape** orientation and appropriate **scaling** so that the entire worksheet fits on a single page.

- Create a custom header that includes the name of your institution and the current date.

- Display gridlines and row and column headings.

- **Center** the worksheet **horizontally** on the page.

j. Print the worksheet two ways in order to show both displayed values and cell formulas.

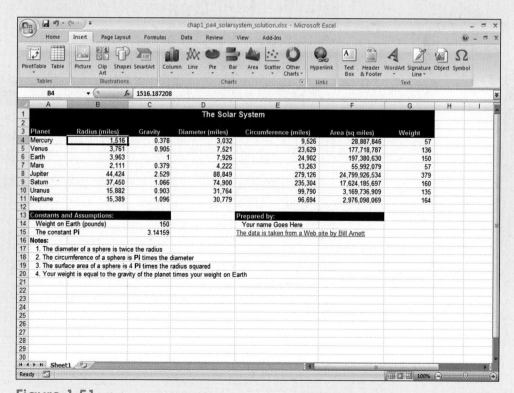

Figure 1.51 Astronomy Lab

Your mother has appointed you the family statistician for your siblings throughout their Little League career. Figure 1.52 displays the completed worksheet showing the statistical data from the last two seasons. Your task is to enter the formulas, format, and print the worksheet for your mother. You will calculate batting averages, totals for statistical data, and family totals.

a. Open the *chap1_mid1_little_league* workbook and save it as **chap1_mid1_little_league_solution** so that you can return to the original workbook if necessary.

b. Click in **cell B16** and type **Your Name**. Enter the formula to compute totals in cells **C7:I7** and **C14:I14**. Click in **cell J4** and enter a formula to compute batting average, Hits/At Bats.

c. Click and drag to select the formula in **cell J4** and copy the formula to **cells J5:J7**. Enter the formula to determine the Batting Average and copy it for the 2007 season.

d. Click in **cell A18** and type **Family Batting Average**. Enter a formula in **cell B18** to calculate the family batting average. Hint: Parentheses are important here.

e. Format the worksheet exactly as shown in Figure 1.52.

f. Print the worksheet twice, once to show displayed values and once to show the cell formulas. Use **landscape** orientation and be sure that the worksheet fits on one sheet of paper.

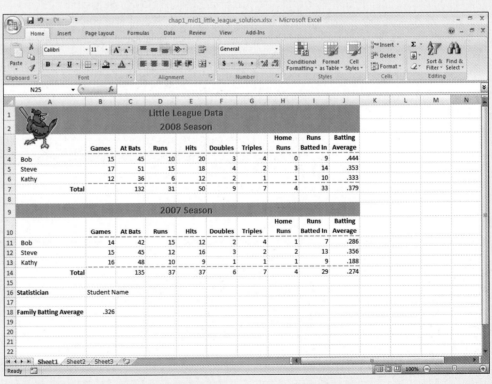

Figure 1.52 Little League Statistician

...continued on Next Page

Your computer professor has determined that you need more practice with basic formatting and cell operations in Excel. The workbook in Figure 1.53 offers this practice for you. Remember to start in cell A1 and work your way down the worksheet, using the instructions in each cell.

a. Open the *chap1_mid2_formatting* workbook and save it as **chap1_mid2_formatting_ solution** so that you can return to the original workbook if necessary. Click in **cell A1** and type your name, then change the formatting as indicated. Merge and center **cells A1** and **B1** into a single cell.

b. Change the width of column A to **53**.

c. Move to **cell A3** and format the text as indicated in the cell. Move to **cell B3** and double underline the text in Green.

d. Format **cells A4:B7** according to the instructions in the respective cells.

e. Follow the instructions in cells A8 to A14 to format the contents of cells **B8 to B14**. Click in **cell B4**, click the Format Painter tool, and then click and drag **cells A8:A14** to apply the formatting from **cell B4**.

f. Click in **cell A15**, then deselect the Merge & Center command to split the merged cell into two cells. Follow the instructions in the cell to wrap and center the text. Cell B15 should be blank when you are finished.

g. Right-click in **cell A16**, select Insert from the shortcut menu, click to shift cells down, and then click **OK**. You have inserted a new cell A16, but the contents in cell B16 should remain the same. Format **cell B16**.

h. Merge cells **A17** and **B17**, and then complete the indicated formatting.

i. Use the Page Setup command to display gridlines and row and column headings. Change to landscape orientation and center the worksheet horizontally on the page. Add a custom footer that contains your name and the date and time you completed the assignment. Print the completed workbook.

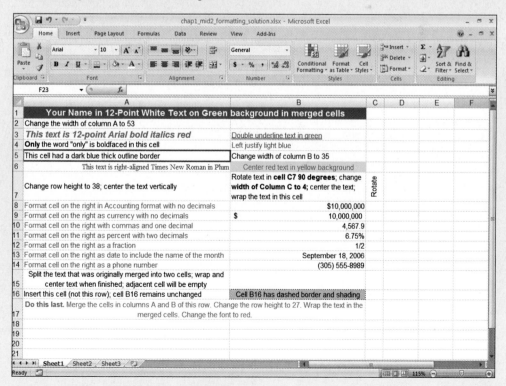

Figure 1.53 Exploring Formatting Options

...continued on Next Page

You work in a testing lab for a major industrial company, and your supervisor has asked you to prepare a table of conversion factors and a table of equivalencies. You will use this as a "crib sheet" during your work and in the preparation of reports, so you want to make it as complete and as accurate as possible. The workbook in Figure 1.54 provides practice with formulas, formatting, and basic cell operations. You do have to match the formatting exactly and you must enter the identical values into column G.

a. Open the *chap1_mid3_conversion* workbook and save it as **chap1_mid3_conversion_ solution** so that you can return to the original workbook if necessary. Click in **cell E8** and type the formula **=1/E7**. Cell E7 contains the value to convert inches to centimeters; the reciprocal of that value will convert centimeters to inches. Enter the appropriate formula into **cell E19** to convert kilograms to pounds.

b. A kilobyte is mistakenly thought of as 1,000 bytes, whereas it is actually 1,024 (2^{10}) bytes. In similar fashion, a megabyte and a gigabyte are 2^{20} and 2^{30} bytes. Use this information to enter the appropriate formulas to display the conversion factors in cells **E21**, **E22**, and **E23**.

c. Enter the formulas for the first conversion into row 7. Click in **cell H7** and type **=C7**. Click in **cell J7** and type **=E7*G7**. Click in **cell K7** and type **=D7**. Copy the formulas in row 7 to the remaining rows in the worksheet. The use of formulas for columns H through K builds flexibility into the worksheet; that is, you can change any of the conversion factors on the left side of the worksheet and the right side will be updated automatically.

d. Enter a set of values in column G for conversion; for example, type 12 in **cell G7** to convert 12 inches to centimeters. The result should appear automatically in **cell J7**.

e. Type your name in **cell G3**. Use Aqua as the fill color in **cells G7:G23** and other ranges of cells, as shown in Figure 1.54.

f. Use the Merge & Center command as necessary throughout the worksheet to approximate the formatting in Figure 1.54. Change the orientation in column B so that the various labels are displayed as indicated.

g. Display the border around the groups of cells, as shown in Figure 1.54.

h. Print the displayed values and the cell formulas. Be sure to show the row and column headings as well as the gridlines. Use landscape orientation to be sure the worksheet fits on a single sheet of paper.

...continued on Next Page

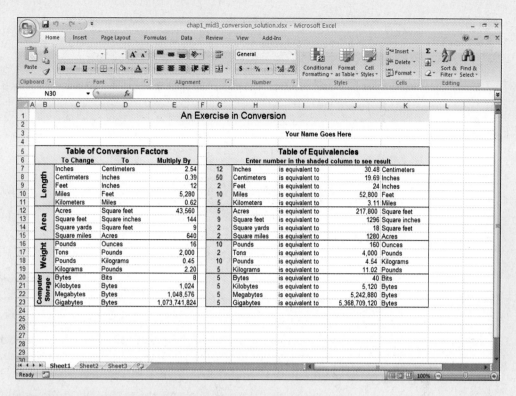

Figure 1.54 Measurement Conversions

4 Fuel Efficiency

Your summer vacation involved traveling through several states to visit relatives and to view the scenic attractions. While traveling, you kept a travel log of mileage and gasoline purchases. Now that the vacation is over, you want to determine the fuel efficiency of your automobile. The partially completed worksheet in Figure 1.55 includes the beginning mileage for the vacation trips and the amount of fuel purchased. This exercise provides practice with formulas, formatting, copying, and basic cell operations.

a. Open the *chap1_mid4_fuel* workbook and save it as **chap1_mid4_fuel_solution** so that you can return to the original workbook if necessary. Click in **cell C12** and change the gallons to **9.2** because you are correcting a typing error.

b. Insert a new column between columns B and C and type **Miles Driven** in **cell C3**.

c. Select **cells A5:A12**, copy the selected range, and paste it in **cells B4:B11**. This ensures that the ending mileage for one trip is the same as the beginning mileage for the next trip. Click **cell B12** and type **34525**, the mileage at the end of the last trip.

d. Use cell references and create the formula to calculate the miles driven for each trip. Use cell references and create the formula to calculate the miles per gallon for each trip.

e. Select **cells A1:E1** and apply the Dark Blue fill color. Apply the following formats to **cell A1**: Times New Roman, 16 point, Bold, White font color. Merge and center the title over columns A through E.

f. Word-wrap the contents of **cells C3** and **E3**. Bold and center horizontally the headings in row 3. Apply the following number formats to the values in columns A and B: whole numbers, no decimals, comma format.

...continued on Next Page

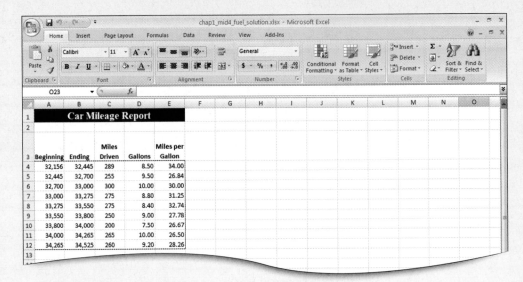

Figure 1.55 Fuel Efficiency

g. Format the last two columns of values as whole numbers with two decimals. Center the values in the third column. Display a border around **cells A4:E12**, as shown in Figure 1.55.

h. Use the Page Setup command to display gridlines and row and column headings. Change to landscape orientation and center the worksheet horizontally on the page. Add a custom footer that contains your name and the date and time you completed the assignment. Print the completed workbook.

5 Freshman Seminar Grade Book

Figure 1.56 displays your instructor's sample grade book complete with a grading scheme. Students take three exams worth 100 points each, submit a term paper and various homework assignments worth 50 points each, and then receive a grade for the semester based on their total points. The maximum number of points is 400. Your semester average is computed by dividing your total points by the maximum total points. You will complete the Freshman Seminar Grade Book worksheet so the displayed values match Figure 1.56.

a. Open the *chap1_mid5_assumption* workbook and save it as **chap1_mid5_assumption_solution** so that you can return to the original workbook if necessary.

b. Click in **cell A6** and type **Your Name**. Enter your test scores: **98, 87, and 99**. The term paper is worth **46** and the homework **24**. Insert a column between columns D and E. Type **Exam Total** in **cell E3**. Click in **cell E4** and enter a formula to compute Smith's exam total points. Click in **cell H4** and enter a formula that will compute Smith's total points for the semester. Click in **cell I4** and enter a formula to compute Smith's semester average.

c. Click and drag to select the formula in **cell E4**. Copy this formula through **E6**. Click and drag to select the formulas in **cells H4:I4** and copy the formulas through **I6**.

d. Click in **cell B7** and enter a formula that will compute the class average on the first exam. Copy this formula to cells **C7:H7**.

e. Insert a column between columns C and D and type **Percent Change in Exams** in **cell D3**. Click in **cell D4** and enter the formula to calculate the change in exam scores between the first and second exam.

f. Format the worksheet appropriately, as shown in Figure 1.56.

...continued on Next Page

g. Add your name as the grading assistant, then print the worksheet twice, once to show displayed values and once to show the cell formulas. Use landscape orientation and be sure that the worksheet fits on one sheet of paper.

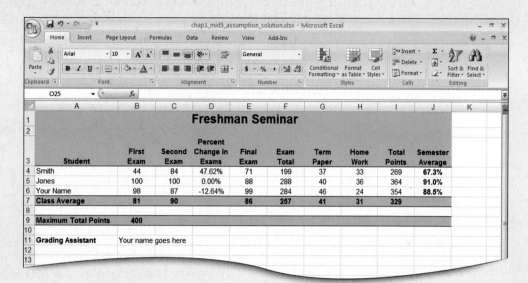

Figure 1.56 Freshman Seminar Grade Book

Capstone Exercise

You are the new assistant to the band director for the Upper Saddle River Marching Band and you must prepare a report showing the status of the marching band fund-raising event for the board of trustees. The report will summarize sales of all items and include the total profit to date with the amount remaining to reach the profit goal. You will open the partially completed workbook, create formulas, and format for presentation to the board of trustees.

Open and Save Worksheet

You must open a worksheet that has the fundraising sales information in it and complete the worksheet.

a. Open the *chap1_cap_fundraising* workbook.

b. Save it as **chap1_cap_fundraising_solution**.

c. Type your name in **cell A20**.

Calculate Values

You are to create the formulas used to calculate profit per item and profit based on the number of items sold. You create a formula to calculate total profit to date and the remaining profit needed to reach the goal.

a. Enter the profit per item formula in **column C**. The profit per item is 50% of the sales price.

b. Enter the profit formula in **column E**. The profit is the profit per item multiplied by the number items sold.

c. Copy all appropriate formulas.

d. Enter a formula to calculate the total profit to date in **cell E15**.

e. The formula for calculating the remaining profit to reach the goal is the goal minus the total profit to date. Enter the formula in **cell E16**.

Format the Worksheet

Now that you have finished the calculations, you must format the worksheet in a professional manner and suitable for presentation to the board of trustees of the college.

a. Insert a comment in **cell E16** and explain the formula in **cell E16**.

b. Format all money figures as currency with two decimals. Format the profit with no decimals.

c. Center and merge rows 1 and 2.

d. Change the font to Arial and increase font size in rows 1, 2, and 3, increasing row height as needed.

e. Change font color in rows 1, 2, 3, 5, 15, and 16.

f. Place borders at the top and bottom of **cells A4:E4**. Place a border at the bottom of **cells A14:E14**.

g. Change the fill color for **cells E4:E4**.

h. Search for the keyword **marching band** in the Clip Art task pane. Insert the bass drums image in **cell E2**, resizing as necessary.

Lay Out the Worksheet

Now that you have finished the major formatting, you must lay out the worksheet to further separate and define areas of the worksheet. This step makes the worksheet more aesthetically pleasing and easier to read.

a. Insert new rows above **row 4** and **row 16**.

b. Delete sheet tabs 2 and 3.

c. Change the color of Sheet1 to **purple**.

d. Rename Sheet1 as **Fundraising**.

Print the Report

Before printing the report, you see it is missing the standard headers and should be printed in landscape orientation to fit on one page. You also want to show and print the cell formulas.

a. Create a custom header with your name on the left and your instructor's name on the right.

b. Change the page orientation to landscape.

c. Print the worksheet with displayed values.

d. Print the worksheet again with cell formulas but make sure to fit the worksheet on one page.

e. Save your changes and exit Excel.

Mini Cases

Use the rubric following the case as a guide to evaluate your work, but keep in mind that your instructor may impose additional grading criteria or use a different standard to judge your work.

Housing Office

GENERAL CASE

Your supervisor in the student housing office has asked for your help in preparing a workbook for her annual budget. Open the partially completed *chap1_mc1_housingoffice* workbook and save it as **chap1_mc1_housingoffice_solution**. This workbook is intended to compute the revenue for the dorms on campus. The revenue includes the income from single rooms, double rooms, and the associated meal plans. Your assignment is to complete the workbook. If you do the assignment correctly, the total revenue for Douglass Hall should be $5,325,000. Note that each double room has two students, each of whom is required to pay for the meal plan. Format the completed worksheet as appropriate. Place your name somewhere in the worksheet and print the worksheet two ways in order to show both displayed values and cell formulas. Be sure to use the Page Setup command to specify landscape orientation and appropriate scaling so that the entire worksheet fits on a single page.

Performance Elements	Exceeds Expectations	Meets Expectations	Below Expectations
Create formulas	All formulas work and most efficiently stated.	Formulas are correct.	No formulas, numbers entered.
Attractive, appropriate format	Well formatted and easy to read.	Adequately formatted, difficult to read.	No formatting.
Print formulas and values	Prints both formulas and values.	Prints ether formulas or values.	No printout.

The Cost of Smoking

RESEARCH CASE

Smoking is hazardous to your health as well as your pocketbook. A one-pack-a-day habit, at $4.50/pack, will cost you more than $1,600 per year. Use the Web to find the current price for the items listed in the worksheet that you could purchase in one year. Open the partially completed *chap1_mc2_smoking* workbook, save it as **chap1_mc2_smoking_solution**, and compute the number of various items that you could buy over the course of a year in lieu of cigarettes. The approximate prices have been entered already, but you need not use these numbers and/or you can substitute additional items of your own. Place your name somewhere in the worksheet and print the worksheet two ways to show both displayed values and cell. Be sure to use the Page Setup command to specify landscape orientation and appropriate scaling so that the entire worksheet fits on a single page.

Performance Elements	Exceeds Expectations	Meets Expectations	Below Expectations
Research current prices	Prices current within 30 days.	Prices current within 3 months.	Prices more than 3 months old.
Create formulas	All formulas work and most efficiently stated.	Formulas are correct.	No formulas, numbers entered.
Format for one sheet	Formatted correctly and easy to read.	Adequately formatted, difficult to read.	Not formatted for one sheet.
Print values and cell formulas	Values and formulas both printed.	Values or formulas printed.	No print.

Accuracy Counts

The *chap1_mc3_accuracycounts* workbook was the last assignment completed by your predecessor prior to his unfortunate dismissal. The worksheet contains a significant error, which caused your company to underbid a contract and assume a subsequent loss of $200,000. As you look for the error, do not be distracted by the attractive formatting. The shading, lines, and other touches are nice, but accuracy is more important than anything else. Write a memo to your instructor describing the nature of the error. Include suggestions in the memo on how to avoid mistakes of this nature in the future. Open the *chap1_mc3_accuracycounts* workbook and save it as **chap1_mc3_accuracycounts_solution**.

Performance Elements	Exceeds Expectations	Meets Expectations	Below Expectations
Identify and correct the error	Error correctly identified within 10 minutes.	Error correctly identified within 20 minutes.	Error not identified.
Explain the error	Complete and correct explanation of the error.	Explanation is too brief to fully explain the error.	No explanation.
Describe how to prevent the error	Prevention description correct.	Prevention description too brief to be of any value.	No prevention description.

Formulas and Functions

Math Basics for Spreadsheet Use

bjectives

After you read this chapter, you will be able to:

1. Create and copy formulas **(page 381)**.

2. Use relative and absolute cell addresses **(page 382)**.

3. Use AutoSum **(page 389)**.

4. Insert basic statistical functions **(page 390)**.

5. Use date functions **(page 392)**.

6. Use the IF function **(page 399)**.

7. Use the VLOOKUP function **(page 400)**.

8. Use the PMT function **(page 408)**.

9. Use the FV function **(page 409)**.

Hands-On Exercises

Exercises	Skills Covered
1. SMITHTOWN HOSPITAL RADIOLOGY DEPARTMENT PAYROLL (PAGE 384) **Open:** chap2_ho1_payroll.xlsx **Save as:** chap2_ho1_payroll_solution.xlsx	• Compute the Gross Pay • Complete the Calculations • Copy the Formulas with the Fill Handle
2. COMPLETING THE SMITHTOWN HOSPITAL RADIOLOGY DEPARTMENT PAYROLL (PAGE 394) **Open:** chap2_ho1_payroll_solution.xlsx (from Exercise 1) **Save as:** chap2_ho2_payroll_solution.xlsx (additional modifications)	• Compute the Totals • Using Other General Functions • Apply Number Formatting • Apply Font and Alignment Formatting • Insert a Comment to Complete the Worksheet
3. ATHLETIC DEPARTMENT ELIGIBILITY GRADEBOOK (PAGE 403) **Open:** chap2_ho3_gradebook.xlsx **Save as:** chap2_ho3_gradebook_solution.xlsx	• Use the IF Function • Use the VLOOKUP Function • Copy the IF and VLOOKUP Functions • Apply Page Setup Options and Print the Worksheet
4. PURCHASING A VAN FOR THE SCHOOL FOR EXCEPTIONAL CHILDREN (PAGE 410) **Open:** New workbook **Save as:** chap2_ho4_van_solution.xlsx	• Create the Worksheet • Insert the PMT Function • Format the Worksheet • Complete the Worksheet

CASE STUDY

West Transylvania College Athletic Department

The athletic department of West Transylvania College has reached a fork in the road. A significant alumni contingent insists that the college upgrade its athletic program from NCAA Division II to Division I. This process will involve adding sports, funding athletic scholarships, expanding staff, and coordinating a variety of fundraising activities.

Tom Hunt, the athletic director, wants to determine if the funding support is available both inside and outside the college to accomplish this goal. You are helping Tom prepare the five-year projected budget based on current budget figures. The plan is to increase revenues at a rate of 10% per year for five years while handling an estimated 8% increase in expenses over the same five-year period. Tom feels that a 10% increase in revenue versus an 8% increase in expenses should make the upgrade viable. Tom wants to examine how increased alumni giving, increases in college fees, and grant monies will increase the revenue flow. The Transylvania College's Athletic Committee and its Alumni Association Board of Directors want Tom to present an analysis of funding and expenses to determine if the move to NCAA Division I is feasible. As Tom's student assistant this year, it is your responsibility to help him with special projects. Tom prepared the basic projected budget spreadsheet and has asked you to finish it for him.

Case Study

Your Assignment

- Read the chapter carefully and pay close attention to mathematical operations, formulas, and functions.
- Open *chap2_case_athletics*, which contains the partially completed, projected budget spreadsheet.
- Study the structure of the worksheet to determine what type of formulas you need to complete the financial calculations. Identify how you would perform calculations if you were using a calculator and make a list of formulas using regular language to determine if the financial goals will be met. As you read the chapter, identify formulas and functions that will help you complete the financial analysis. You will insert formulas in the revenue and expenditures sections for column C. Use appropriate cell references in formulas. Do not enter constant values within a formula; instead enter the 10% and 8% increases in an input area. Use appropriate functions for column totals in both the revenue and expenditures sections. Insert formulas for the Net Operating Margin and Net Margin rows. Copy the formulas.
- Review the spreadsheet and identify weaknesses in the formatting. Use your knowledge of good formatting design to improve the appearance of the spreadsheet so that it will be attractive to the Athletic Committee and the alumni board. You will format cells as currency with 0 decimals and widen columns as needed. Merge and center the title and use an attractive fill color. Emphasize the totals and margin rows with borders. Enter your name and current date. Create a custom footer that includes a page number and your instructor's name. Print the worksheet as displayed and again with cell formulas displayed. Save the workbook as **chap2_case_athletics_solution**.

Formula Basics

Mathematical operations are the backbone of Excel. The order in which these mathematical operations are performed has a significant impact on the answers that are arrived at. We touched briefly on the construction of mathematical expressions or *formulas* that direct Excel to perform mathematical operations and arrive at a calculated result. A formula also may be defined as the combination of constants, cell references, and arithmetic operations displayed in a calculation. Formulas can be as simple or as complex as necessary, but they always begin with an = sign and contain mathematical operators. In this section, you learn how to use the pointing method to create formulas and the fill handle to copy formulas. Finally, you learn how to prevent a cell reference from changing when you copy a formula to other cells.

A **formula** performs mathematical operations that produce a calculated result.

Formulas can be as simple or as complex as necessary, but they always begin with an = sign and contain mathematical operators.

Creating and Copying Formulas

As you recall, whenever you want Excel to perform a calculation, you must enter an equal sign (=) in the cell where the answer is to appear. The equal sign indicates within Excel that a mathematical calculation is about to begin. Previously, you created formulas by typing in the cell references. Here in Chapter 2, you enter cell references to create a formula in a more efficient, straightforward way.

Point to Create a Formula

Rather than typing a cell address . . . as you construct a formula, you can use an alternative method that involves *minimal* typing.

Pointing uses the mouse or arrow keys to select the cell directly when creating a formula.

As previously discussed, the creation of formulas in Excel is the mathematical basis for the program and the use of cell references is integral in the creation of formulas. However, rather than typing a cell address, such as C2, as you construct a formula, you can use an alternative method that involves *minimal* typing. *Pointing* uses the mouse or arrow keys to select the cell directly when creating a formula. To use the pointing technique to create a formula:

1. Click on the cell where the formula will be entered.
2. Type an equal sign (=) to start a formula.
3. Click on the cell with the value to be entered in the formula.
4. Type a mathematical operator.
5. Continue clicking on cells and typing operators to finish the formula.
6. Press Enter to complete the formula.

While the formulas may be more complex than indicated in this example, the steps are the same.

Copy Formulas with the Fill Handle

The **fill handle** is a small black square in the bottom-right corner of a selected cell.

Another powerful copying tool in Excel is the *fill handle*, which is a small black solid square in the bottom-right corner of a selected cell. Using the fill handle provides another, more clear-cut alternative method for copying the contents of a cell. You can use the fill handle to duplicate formulas. To copy and paste using the fill handle:

1. Click on the cell (or drag through the cells) to be copied.
2. Position the mouse pointer directly over the fill handle on the cell or cells to be copied. The pointer changes to a thin crosshair.
3. Click and hold down the left mouse button while dragging over the destination cells. Note that using the fill handle only works with contiguous or adjacent cells.

4. Release the mouse button. If the cell to be copied contained a formula, the formula is copied, the cell references are changed appropriately, and Excel performs the calculations.

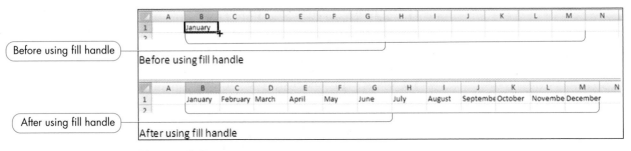

Before using fill handle

After using fill handle

Figure 2.1   Fill Handle

Using Relative and Absolute Cell Addresses

Excel uses three different ways to express a reference to a cell in a formula. These references are relative, absolute, and mixed, and each affects copying cell references in different ways.

A *relative cell reference* is a typical cell reference that changes when copied.

A *relative cell reference* within a formula is a cell reference that changes *relative to* the direction in which the formula is being copied. It is expressed in the form C13 (column letter, row number) and is adjusted or changed according to the direction and relative distance it is copied. When you copy a formula containing a relative cell reference over multiple columns, the column letter changes. When you copy a formula containing a relative cell reference down multiple rows, the row number changes. For example, if you copy the contents of cell C5, =C3+C4, to cell E5, the formula becomes =E3+E4. If you copy the contents of cell C5, =C3+C4, to cell E6, the formula becomes =E4+E5.

An *absolute cell reference*, indicated by dollar signs before the column letter and row number, stays the same regardless of where a formula is copied.

An *absolute cell reference* in a formula, on the other hand, is one that stays the same no matter where you copy a formula. An absolute cell reference appears with dollar signs before both the column letter and row number ($C$13). Absolute cell references are used when the value in the cell seldom changes but the formula containing the absolute cell reference is copied. An example would be in a payroll spreadsheet that includes a calculation for state income tax using a constant tax rate. The reference to the cell that contains the state income rate (C13) would therefore be expressed as an absolute cell reference when used in a formula (=$C$13*D26). The absolute address prevents the cell reference from changing when you copy the formula to calculate the amount of state income tax for the other employees. A benefit of an absolute cell reference is that if an input value changes, for example if the state income tax rate changes from 14% to 15.5% in this example, you

> A benefit of an absolute cell reference is that if an input value changes, . . . you type the new input value in only one cell and Excel recalculates . . . all the formulas. You do not have to individually edit cells containing formulas. . . .

type the new input value in only one cell and Excel recalculates the amount of state tax for all the formulas. You do not have to individually edit cells containing formulas to change the tax rate value because the formulas contain an absolute cell reference to the cell containing the state tax rate.

The third type of cell reference, the ***mixed cell reference***, occurs when you create a formula that combines an absolute reference with a relative reference ($C13 or C$13). As a result, either the row number or column letter does not change when the cell is copied. Using the relative cell reference C13, it would be expressed as a mixed reference either as $C13 or C$13. In the first case, the column C is absolute and the row number is relative; in the second case, the row 13 is absolute and the column C is relative.

The ***mixed cell reference*** combines an absolute reference with a relative reference.

TIP   The F4 Key

The F4 key toggles through relative, absolute, and mixed references. Click on any cell reference within a formula on the formula bar; for example, click on B4 in the formula =B4+B5. Press F4, and B4 changes to an absolute reference, $B$4. Press F4 a second time, and $B$4 becomes a mixed reference, B$4; press F4 again, and it is a different mixed reference, $B4. Press F4 a fourth time, and the cell reference returns to the original relative reference, B4.

In the first hands-on exercise, you calculate the gross pay for employees in the Smithtown Radiology Department using the pointing method. You perform other payroll calculations, and then use the fill handle to copy the formulas for the remaining employees.

Hands-On Exercises

1 | Smithtown Hospital Radiology Department Payroll

Skills covered: 1. Compute the Gross Pay **2.** Complete the Calculations **3.** Copy the Formulas with the Fill Handle

---

Step 1
Compute the Gross Pay

Refer to Figure 2.2 as you complete Step 1.

a. Start Excel. Open the *chap2_ho1_payroll* workbook to display the worksheet shown in Figure 2.2.

b. Save the workbook as **chap2_ho1_payroll_solution** so that you can return to the original workbook if necessary.

c. Click in **cell F4**, the cell that will contain gross pay for Dwyer. Press = on the keyboard to begin pointing, click **cell C4** (producing a moving border around the cell), press the **asterisk key** (*), and then click **cell D4**.

You have entered the first part of the formula to compute the gross pay.

d. Press the **plus sign** (+), click **cell E4**, press *, click **cell C4**, press *, click **cell D20**, press **F4** to change the cell reference to **$D$20**, and then press **Enter**.

The formula, =C4*D4+E4*C4*$D$20, calculates the gross pay for employee Dwyer by multiplying the $8 hourly wage by 40 regular hours. This amount is added to the 8 overtime hours, multiplied by the $8 hourly wage, multiplied by the 1.5 overtime rate. Note the use of the absolute address ($D$20) in the formula. You should see 416 as the displayed value in cell F4.

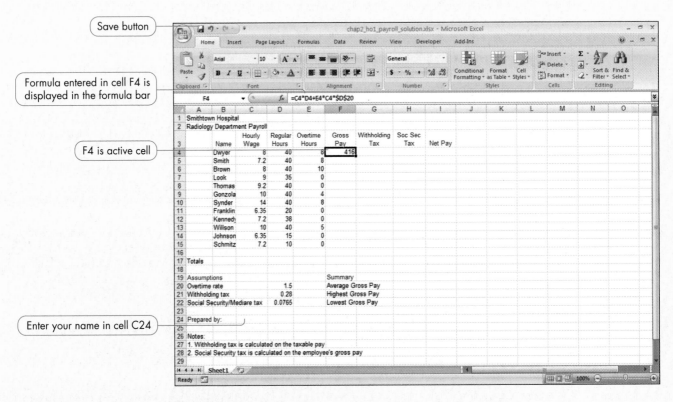

Figure 2.2 Compute the Gross Pay with Absolute Reference

e. Click in **cell F4** to be sure that the formula you entered matches the formula shown in the formula bar in Figure 2.2. If necessary, click in the formula bar and make the appropriate changes so the formula is correct in cell F4.

f. Enter your name in **cell C24** and save the workbook.

Step 2
Complete the Calculations

a. Click in **cell G4**, the cell that will contain the withholding tax for Dwyer. Press = to begin pointing, and then click **cell F4**, the cell containing the gross pay cell. Press the * and click **cell D21**, the withholding tax.

Cell G4 now contains the formula =F4*D21 that calculates Dwyer's withholding tax. However, if you were to copy the formula now, the copied formula would be =F5*D22, which is not quite correct. If a cell address is not made explicitly absolute, Excel's default relative address mode will automatically change a cell address when a formula is copied.

b. Verify that the insertion point is within or immediately behind cell reference D21 and press **F4**.

Pressing F4 changes the cell reference to $D$21 and explicitly makes the cell address an absolute reference. The formula can be copied and will calculate the desired result.

c. Press **Enter**.

The value in cell G4 should be 116.48. This amount is Dwyer's withholding tax.

d. Use the pointing method to enter the remaining formulas for Dwyer. Click in **cell H4** and enter the formula **=F4*$D$22**.

The formula calculates the employee's Social Security tax, which is 7.65% of the gross pay. The formula uses an absolute reference ($D$22) so the cell reference will not change when you copy the formula for the other employees. The value in cell H4 should be 31.824, and this is Dwyer's Social Security tax.

e. Click in **cell I4**, and enter the formula **=F4–(G4+H4)**. Press **Enter** when you finish.

The formula adds the withholding tax and Social Security tax, and then subtracts the total tax from the gross pay. The formula uses only relative cell addresses because you want the copied formulas to refer to the appropriate gross pay and tax cells for each respective employee. The value in cell I4 should be 267.696, and this amount is Dwyer's net pay.

f. Save the workbook.

Step 3
Copy the Formulas with the Fill Handle

Refer to Figure 2.3 as you complete Step 3.

a. Click and drag to select **cells F4:I4**, as shown in Figure 2.3. Point to the fill handle in the lower-right corner of **cell I4**. The mouse pointer changes to a thin crosshair.

You have selected the range containing formulas that you want to copy. Pointing to the fill handle triggers the display of the thin crosshair.

b. Drag the fill handle to **cell I15**, the lower-right cell in the range of employee calculations, and release the mouse to complete the copy operation.

The formulas for Dwyer have been copied to the corresponding rows. You can use Excel to calculate the gross pay, withholding tax, Social Security tax, and net pay for each employee.

c. Click in **cell F5**, the cell containing the gross pay for Smith.

You should see the formula =C5*D5+E5*C5*$D$20.

d. Click in **cell G5**, the cell containing the withholding tax for Smith.

You should see the formula =F5*$D$21, which contains a relative reference (F5) that is adjusted from one row to the next, and an absolute reference ($D$21) that remains constant from one employee to the next.

e. Save the *chap2_ho1_payroll_solution* workbook and keep it onscreen if you plan to continue to the next hands-on exercise. Save the workbook. Close the workbook and exit Excel if you do not want to continue with the next exercise at this time.

TROUBLESHOOTING: If you double-click a cell that contains a formula, Excel will display the formula, highlight the components, and allow for editing in the cell. If you double-click a cell that contains values or text, you can edit the data directly in the cell.

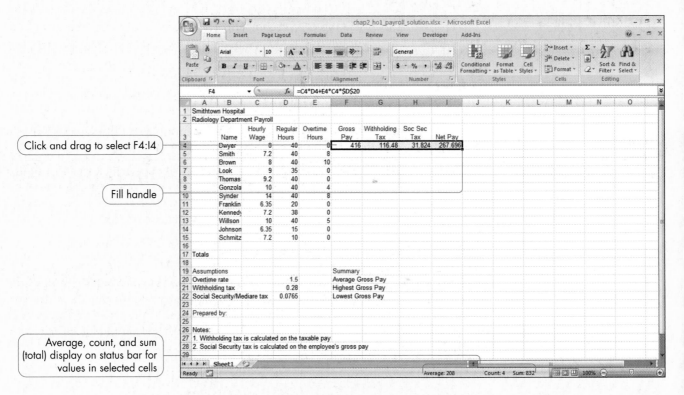

Figure 2.3 Copy the Formulas

 TIP Isolate Assumptions

The formulas in a worksheet should always be based on cell references rather than specific values—for example, C25 or $C$25 rather than .07. The cells containing the values are clearly labeled and set apart from the rest of the worksheet. You can vary the inputs (or assumptions on which the worksheet is based) to see the effect within the worksheet. The chance for error is minimized because you are changing the contents of just a single cell instead of multiple formulas that reference those values. Excel automatically recalculates formulas when values change.

Function Basics

SUM Function | Reference

SUM(number1,number2,. . .)

A **function** is a preconstructed formula that makes difficult computations less complicated.

The **SUM function**, represented by Σ or sigma, adds up or sums the numeric entries within a range of cells.

Syntax refers to the rules for constructing the function.

Arguments are values as input that perform an indicated calculation, and then return another value as output.

(Using Insert Function greatly simplifies the construction of functions. . . .)

You also can construct formulas by using a **function**, a preconstructed formula that makes difficult computations less complicated. But keep in mind that functions CANNOT replace all formulas. Functions take a value or values, perform an operation, and return a value or values. The most often used function in Excel is the **SUM function**, represented by Σ or sigma. It adds or sums numeric entries within a range of cells, and then displays the result in the cell containing the function. This function is so useful that the SUM function has its own command in the Function Library group on the Formulas tab. In all, Excel contains more than 325 functions, which are broken down into categories, as shown in Table 2.1.

When you want to use a function, keep two things in mind. The first is the *syntax* of the function or, more simply put, the rules for constructing the function. The second is the function's *arguments*, which are values as input that perform an indicated calculation, and then return another value as output or the data to be used in the function. While users often type functions such as =SUM(C7:C14), it also is possible to click Insert Function in the Function Library group on the Formulas tab to display the Insert Function dialog box. Using the Insert Function dialog box enables you to select the function to be used (such as MAX, SUM, etc.) from the complete list of functions and specify the arguments to be used in the function. Using Insert Function greatly simplifies the construction of functions by making it easier to select and construct functions. Clicking Insert Function in the Function Library group on the Formulas tab (see Figure 2.4) displays the Insert Function dialog box shown in Figure 2.5. Use the Insert Function dialog box to do the following:

Table 2.1 Function Category and Descriptions

Category Group	Description
Cube	Works with multi-dimensional data stored on an SQL server.
Database	Analyzes data stored in Excel.
Date and Time	Works with dates and time.
Financial	Works with financial-related data.
Information	Determines what type of data is in a cell.
Logical	Calculates yes/no answers.
Lookup and Reference	Provides answers after searching a table.
Math and Trigonometry	Performs standard math and trig functions.
Statistical	Calculates standard statistical functions.
Text	Analyzes labels.

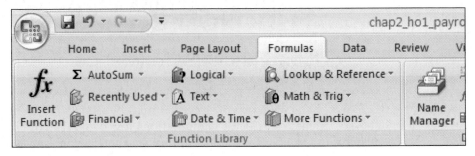

Figure 2.4 Function Library

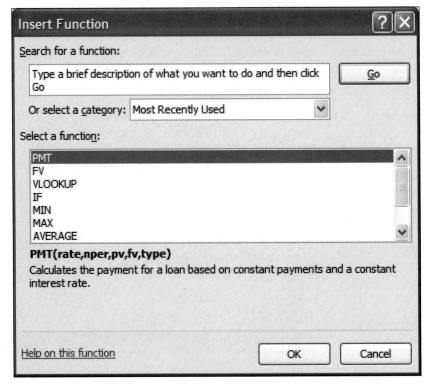

Figure 2.5 Insert Function Dialog Box

1. Search for a function by typing a brief description of what you want the function to do.
2. Select a function from the *Most Recently Used* list, by function category displayed in alphabetical order, or from an alphabetical list of *All* functions.
3. Click the function name to see the syntax and description or double-click the function name to see the function and the Function Arguments dialog box for help with adding the correct arguments. Figure 2.6 shows the Function Arguments dialog box for the SUM function.

If you know the category of the function you want to use, you can click the appropriate command in the Function Library group on the Formulas tab. Select the function and use the Function Arguments dialog box to add the arguments. See Figure 2.4 for the Function Library group.

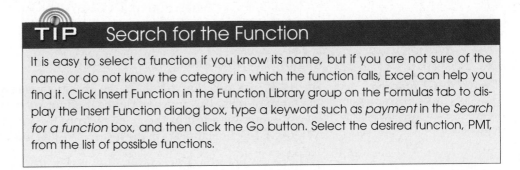

Figure 2.6 Function Arguments Box

In this section, you insert a variety of commonly used functions, such as the SUM function.

Using AutoSum

In this chapter, you will examine several different commonly used functions, beginning with the SUM function. You can create formulas in different ways. For example, if you want to add the contents of cells C4 through C10, the formula would be written =C4+C5+C6+C7+C8+C9+C10. However, creating this type of formula manually is time-consuming and increases the probability of entering an inaccurate cell address. This process would be especially problematic if you had to add values stored in several hundred cells. Using the SUM function simplifies this operation and improves the accuracy of the addition. To create the same formula using the SUM function, you can type **=SUM(C4:C10)**. The C4:C10 represents the cell range containing the values to be summed. Rather than typing this entire formula, you can also type **=SUM(**, and then click and drag to select the range of cells containing values to be summed, then type the closing parenthesis. Alternatively, you can click Σ (AutoSum) in the Function Library group on the Formulas tab. To use the AutoSum, click the cell where you want to see the results, and then click AutoSum. Drag to select the cell range or values to be summed and press Enter to see the total.

Inserting Basic Statistical Functions

The use of the SUM function, the most basic statistical function, already has been discussed. Now you will learn several other commonly used statistical functions. These functions perform a variety of calculations to identify key values to help people make decisions. For example, you can use functions to calculate how much you spend on average per month on DVD rentals, what your highest electric bill is to control spending, and what your lowest test score is so you know what you have to study for the final exam. You can use the statistical functions to create or monitor your budget. Climatologists use statistical functions to compare rainfall averages over time in specific geographic areas.

Calculate an Average with the AVERAGE Function

AVERAGE Function | Reference

AVERAGE(number1,number2,. . .)

The **AVERAGE function** calculates the arithmetic mean, or average, for the values in an argument list.

The *AVERAGE function* calculates the arithmetic mean, or average, for the values in a range of cells. This function can be used for such calculations as the average of several scores on a test or the average score for a number of rounds of golf. The AVERAGE function appears in the form =AVERAGE(C6:C24).

Identify the Lowest Value with the MIN Function

MIN Function | Reference

MIN(number1,number2,. . .)

The **MIN function** determines the smallest value of all cells in a list of arguments.

The *MIN function* determines the smallest value of all cells in a list of arguments. An application of the MIN might be to determine the lowest score on a test. The function typically appears as =MIN(C6:C24). Although you could manually inspect a range of values to identify the lowest value, doing so is inefficient, especially in large spreadsheets. The MIN function increases your efficiency by always identifying the lowest value in the range. If you change values in the range, the MIN function will identify the new lowest value and display this value in the cell containing the MIN function.

Identify the Highest Value with the MAX Function

MAX Function | Reference

MAX(number1,number2,. . .)

The **MAX function** determines the highest value of all cells in a list of arguments.

The *MAX function* is the opposite of the MIN function in that it analyzes an argument list to determine the highest value, as in the highest score on a test or the highest points a basketball player scored in a game in a season. This function appears as =MAX(C6:C24). Like the MIN function, when the values in the range change, the MAX function will display the new highest value within the range of cells. Generally the MIN and MAX statistical functions are discussed in concert with the AVERAGE function. These three functions are typically beginning statistical functions and are used together as a start point for more sophisticated analysis. They also are commonly used educational statistics in gradebooks and in analysis of test scores.

Identify the Total Number with the COUNT and COUNTA Functions

COUNT Function | Reference

COUNT(value1,value2,. . .)

COUNTA Function | Reference

COUNTA(value1,value2,. . .)

The **COUNT** *function* counts the number of cells in a range that contain numerical data.

The **COUNTA** *function* counts the number of cells in a range that are not blank.

The two basic count functions, COUNT and COUNTA, enable a user to count the cells in a range that meet a particular criterion. The **COUNT** *function* counts the number of cells in a range that contain numerical data. This function is expressed as =COUNT(C6:C24). The **COUNTA** *function* counts the number of cells in a range that are not blank. This function is expressed as =COUNTA(C6:C24). These functions might be used to verify data entry; for example, you may need to verify that the correct type of data has been entered into the appropriate number of cells. The COUNT function is used to verify that cells have numbers in them and the COUNTA function is used to make sure data are in every cell.

Determine the Midpoint Value with the MEDIAN Function

MEDIAN Function | Reference

MEDIAN(number1,number2,. . .)

The **MEDIAN** *function* finds the midpoint value in a set of values.

Another easy basic statistical function often overlooked is the **MEDIAN** *function* that finds the midpoint value in a set of values. It is helpful to identify at what value ½ of the population is above or below. The median shows that half of the sample data are above a particular value and half are below that value. The median is particularly useful because the AVERAGE function often is influenced by extreme numbers. For example, if 10 grades are between 90 and 100 and the eleventh grade is 0, the extreme value of 0 distorts the overall average as an indicator of the set of grades. See Table 2.2 for this example. Note that 86 is the average and 95 is the median.

Table 2.2 Compare Average and Median

Scores	
99	
98	
97	
96	
95	
95	**Midpoint Score (half the scores above and half the scores below this score)**
93	
92	
91	
90	
0	
86	**Average Score (Equal to the sum of the values divided by the number of values)**
95	**Median (midpoint) Score**

TIP | Average, Count, and Sum

When you select a range of cells containing values, Excel displays the average, count, and sum of those values on the status bar. See Figure 2.3 at the end of Hands-On Exercise 1 for an example.

Using Date Functions

Before electronic spreadsheets, you could spend hours trying to figure out pay dates for the next year or when a new employee's probation period was up. Excel enables you to increase your productivity by using date and time functions. These functions help in two ways: by efficiently handling time-consuming procedures and by helping you analyze data related to the passing of time. For example, you can use the date and time functions to calculate when employees are eligible for certain benefits or how many days it takes to complete a project. You also can use the date functions to help you calculate if an account is 30, 60, or more days past due. Excel converts and stores dates as numbers. Using date functions allows you to calculate the difference between dates, add or subtract days from a given date, and so on.

TODAY Function | Reference

TODAY( )

The *TODAY function* displays the current date in a cell.

The *TODAY function* is a date-related function that places the current date in a cell. The function is expressed as =TODAY(). This function is updated when the worksheet is calculated or the file is opened. Unlike the statistical functions you just learned about, some date functions like TODAY() do not require cell references or data as arguments. However, you must still include the parentheses for the function to work.

NOW Function | Reference

NOW( )

The *NOW function* uses the computer's clock to display the current date and time side by side in a cell.

The *NOW function* uses the computer's clock to display the current date and time side by side in a cell. It returns the time the workbook was last opened, so the value will change every time the workbook is opened. The Now function does the same thing as the Today function, except the result is formatted to display the current time as well as the current date. Both of these functions will display the current date/time when the spreadsheet file is opened. Thus, date/time is always current; it is not the date/time when the function was first entered in the cell. The NOW function is expressed as =NOW(). Note that failure to insert the parentheses will cause Excel to return an error message.

TIP | Function AutoComplete

Use Function AutoComplete to quickly create and edit functions, minimizing typing and syntax errors. Type an = and the beginning letters of the desired function, and Excel will display a drop-down list of valid functions, names, and text strings matching the letters. Double-click the appropriate function from the list to complete the function name automatically.

Functions Used | Reference

Name	Syntax	Definition
SUM	SUM(number1,number2, . . .)	The **SUM function**, represented by Σ or sigma, adds up or sums the numeric entries within a range of cells.
AVERAGE	AVERAGE(number1,number2, . . .)	The **AVERAGE function** calculates the arithmetic mean, or average, for the values in an argument list.
MIN	MIN(number1,number2, . . .)	The **MIN function** determines the smallest value of all cells in a list of arguments.
MAX	MAX(number1,number2, . . .)	The **MAX function** determines the highest value of all cells in a list of arguments.
COUNT	COUNT(value1,value2, . . .)	The **COUNT function** counts the number of cells in a range that contain numerical data.
COUNTA	COUNTA(value1,value2, . . .)	The **COUNTA function** counts the number of cells in a range that are not blank.
MEDIAN	MEDIAN(number1,number2, . . .)	The **MEDIAN function** finds the midpoint value in a set of values.
NOW	NOW( )	The **NOW function** uses the computer's clock to display the current date and time side by side in a cell.
TODAY	TODAY( )	The **TODAY function** displays the current date in a cell.
IF	IF(logical_test,value_if_true,value_if_false)	The **IF function** is the most basic logical function in that it returns one value when a condition is met and returns another value when the condition is not met.
VLOOKUP	VLOOKUP(lookup_value,table_array, col_index_num,range_lookup)	The **VLOOKUP function** allows the Excel user to look up an answer from a table of possible answers.
PMT	PMT(rate,nper,pv,fv,type)	The **PMT function** calculates the payment on a loan.
FV	FV(rate,nper,pmt,pv,type)	The **FV function** returns the future value of an investment

2 | Completing the Smithtown Hospital Radiology Department Payroll

Skills covered: 1. Compute the Totals **2.** Using Other General Functions **3.** Apply Number Formatting **4.** Apply Font and Alignment Formatting **5.** Insert a Comment to Complete the Worksheet

Step 1
Compute the Totals

Refer to Figure 2.7 as you complete Step 1.

a. Open the *chap2_ho1_payroll_solution* workbook if you closed it after the last hands-on exercise and save it as **chap2_ho2_payroll_solution**.

b. Click in **cell F17**, the cell that will contain the total gross pay for all employees. Click the **Formulas tab**, click **AutoSum** in the Function Library group, and click and drag over **cells F4:F15** to select the correct range.

c. Press **Enter** to complete the formula.

Cell F17 displays the value 4144.25 and if you click in **cell F17**, you will see the function =SUM(F4:F15) in the formula bar. You have entered the SUM function to calculate the total gross pay.

d. Click and drag the fill handle in **cell F17** to **cell I17**, the remaining cells in the row. Complete the copy operation by releasing the mouse.

Cell I17 now displays 2666.825, which is the total net pay for all employees.

e. Save the workbook.

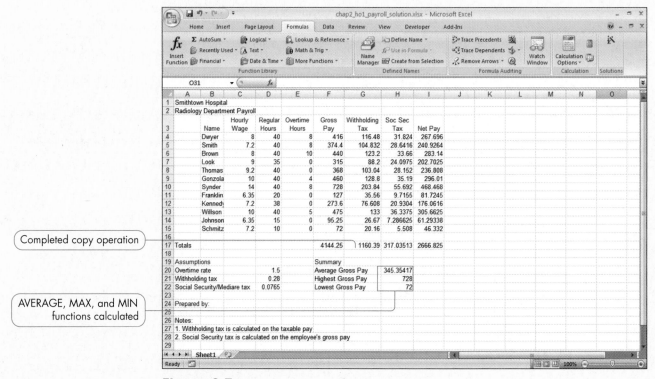

Figure 2.7 Using Functions

Step 2
Using Other General Functions

Refer to Figure 2.7 as you complete Step 2.

a. Click in **cell H20**. This cell will contain the average gross pay for all employees.

b. Type **=AVERAGE(F4:F15)** and press **Enter**.

Cell H20 displays 345.35417, which is the average gross pay for all radiology department employees.

c. Click in **cell H21**.

d. Type **=MAX(** and move the mouse pointer to cell **F4**. Click and drag to select **cells F4:F15**. The dashed line indicates the cells selected as you drag the mouse. Release the mouse, type **)**, and press **Enter**.

Cell H21 displays the value 728, which is the highest gross pay for any employee of the radiology department.

e. Click in **cell H22**.

This cell will display the lowest gross pay of any radiology department employee.

f. Type **=MIN(** and move the mouse pointer to **cell F4**. Click and drag to select **cells F4:F15**. Release the mouse, type **)**, and press **Enter**.

Cell H22 displays the value 72, which is the lowest gross pay for any employee of the radiology department.

g. Click in **cell F24**, type **=TODAY()**, and press **Enter**. The current date displays in cell F24. Widen the column if necessary. Save the workbook.

Step 3
Apply Number Formatting

Refer to Figure 2.7 as you complete Step 3.

a. Select **cells C4:C15**. Press and hold **Ctrl** as you click and drag to select **cells F4:I15**, **cells F17:I17**, and **cells H20:H22**. Click the **Home tab**, click the **Number Format arrow** in the Number group, and then click **Currency**.

b. Click and drag to select **cells D21:D22**. Click **Percent Style** in the Number group on the Home tab and click **Increase Decimal** twice in the Number group to format each number to two decimal places.

c. Save the workbook.

Step 4
Apply Font and Alignment Formatting

Refer to Figure 2.8 as you complete Step 4.

a. Select **cells A3:I3**. Press and hold **Ctrl** as you click and drag to select **cells A19:I19**. Continue to hold **Ctrl** as you click and drag to select **cells A24:I24**.

This action will produce three rows of non-adjacent selected cells.

b. Click the **Fill Color arrow** in the Font group and select **Black** as the fill color. Click the **Font Color arrow** in the Font group and select **White** as the text color. Click **Bold** in the Font group so the text stands out.

c. Click and drag to select **cells A3:I3**, which also will deselect the cells in rows 19 and 24. Click **Wrap Text** in the Alignment group on the Home tab.

The column heading text is now centered and wraps in cells.

TROUBLESHOOTING: Excel may not automatically increase row height after you wrap text. You may have to increase the height of row 3 manually if necessary. Click and drag the dividing line between rows 3 and 4 to increase the height of row 3.

d. Click and drag to select **cells A1:I1**.

- Click **Fill Color** in the Font group to apply the last fill color, which is black.
- Click **Font Color** in the Font group to apply the last font color, which is white.
- Click **Bold** in the Font group so the text stands out.
- Click **Merge and Center** in the Alignment group on the Home tab.

The title, *Smithtown Hospital*, is now bold, white, and centered in a black box over the nine columns in the worksheet.

e. Click and drag to select **cells A2:I2** and apply the same four formats that you did in Step 3d.

The subtitle, *Radiology Department Payroll*, is now bold, white, and centered in a black box over the columns in the worksheet.

f. Save the workbook.

TIP · The Format Painter

The Format Painter copies the formatting of the selected cell to other cells in the worksheet. Click the cell whose formatting you want to copy, then double-click Format Painter in the Clipboard group on the Home tab. The mouse pointer changes to a paintbrush to indicate that you can copy the current formatting; just click and drag the paintbrush over the cells that you want to assume the formatting of the original cell. Repeat the painting process as often as necessary, then click Format Painter a second time to return to normal editing.

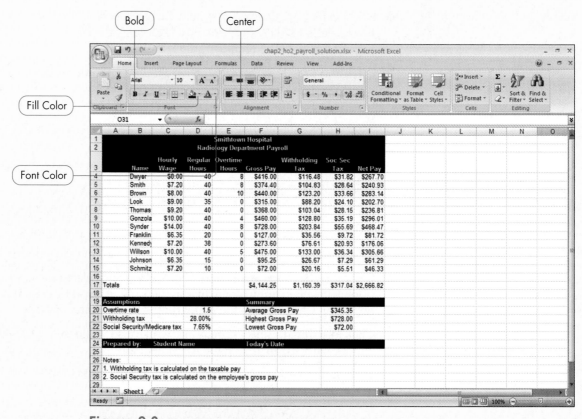

Figure 2.8 Complete the Formatting

Refer to Figure 2.9 as you complete Step 5.

a. Click in **cell D21**. Click the **Review tab**, click **New Comment** in the Comments group, and type **The exercise uses a constant value for simplicity's sake.**, as shown in Figure 2.9.

TROUBLESHOOTING: The name in the Comment box will be different on your system. The name or initials entered when registering the Microsoft Office 2007 software will appear in the comment box as the author of the comment. Use Help to learn how to change the name or initials for yourself.

b. Click any cell.

Clicking another cell after you finish entering the comment closes the comment box. The text of the comment is no longer visible, but a tiny triangle is visible in cell D21. When you point to cell D21, you will see the text of the comment.

c. Click the **Page Layout tab**, click **Orientation** in the Page Setup group, and click **Landscape**. Click **Size** and select **More Paper Sizes**.

Clicking More Paper Sizes displays the Page Setup dialog box.

TIP Displaying the Page Setup Dialog Box

You also can click the Page Setup Dialog Box Launcher in the lower-right corner of the Page Setup group to display the Page Setup dialog box.

d. Click the **Page tab**, if necessary, in the Page Setup dialog box and click **Fit to 1 page** in the *Scaling* section.

e. Click the **Margins tab** and click the **Horizontally check box** in the *Center on page* section.

This option centers worksheet data between the left and right margins.

f. Click the **Sheet tab**, click the **Row and column headings check box**, and click the **Gridlines check box** in the *Print* section. Click **OK**.

You changed the orientation of the spreadsheet for printing as well as selected the option to force the spreadsheet on one piece of paper. The spreadsheet also will be centered horizontally with row/column headings and gridlines printed.

g. Print the worksheet. Save the *chap2_ho2_payroll_solution* workbook.

h. Press **Ctrl + ~** (to the left of the number 1 key) to show the cell formulas rather than the displayed values. Adjust the column widths as necessary and print the worksheet a second time.

To view the underlying formulas in your worksheet, press and hold down Ctrl while pressing ~ (tilde). This key is located above Tab on the keyboard.

i. Close the workbook without saving the view of the formulas. Exit Excel if you do not want to continue with the next exercise at this time.

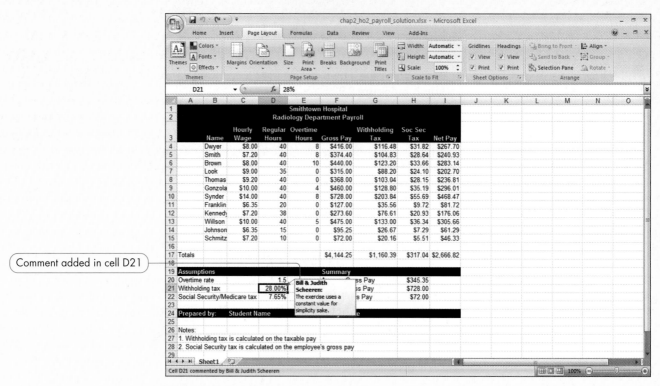

Comment added in cell D21

Figure 2.9 Comments and Formatting

Logical and Lookup Functions

(*. . . mathematics is the problem; thinking is the solution. . . .*)

Several functions in Excel are designed to return an answer when a particular condition is met. These logical functions are very useful for decision-making. Excel also contains functions that search for or "look up" information in a table. These lookup functions use a designated worksheet area or table and search row by row for a match. Just remember that mathematics is the problem; thinking is the solution as you work with these functions. In this section, you use one major logical function and one major lookup function.

Using the IF Function

IF Function | Reference

IF(logical_test,value_if_true,value_if_false)

The **IF function** returns one value when a condition is met and returns another value when the condition is not met.

In the set of logical functions, the **IF function** is the most basic in that it returns one value when a condition is met and returns another value when the condition is not met. For example, you may have a display of student GPAs and want to determine if the students are eligible for the Dean's List. If the range of student GPAs were C6 through C24, the IF function would appear in cell D6 as =IF(C6>3.5, "Dean's List", "No"). This function then would be copied to cells D7 through D24. The IF function supports the decision-making capability that is used in a worksheet. The IF function has three arguments:

1. a condition that is tested to determine if it is either true or false,
2. the resulting value if the condition is true, and
3. the resulting value if the condition is false.

This function can be illustrated as:

=IF(condition,value_if_true,value_if_false)

            Value when condition is false

        Value when condition is true

   Condition is true or false

An IF function returns either the second or third argument, depending if the condition is true or false. The value_if_true and value_if_false parameters can contain text, a value, a formula, or a nested function. For example, an IF function used in a gradebook might award a bonus for a student whose homework is "OK," while others do not get the bonus.

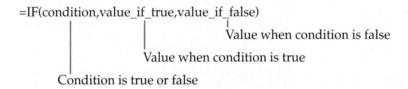

=IF(H4= "OK",G4=$H$19,G4)

          Value if condition is false

      Value if condition is true

   Condition is true or false

Note that when you want to compare the contents of a cell to specific text, you must enclose the comparison text in quotation marks. You also can return text in the value_if_true and value_if_false parameters by enclosing the text (but not the commas) in quotation marks.

The condition in the IF function includes one of the six comparison operators shown in Table 2.3.

Table 2.3 Comparison Operators

Operator	Description
=	Equal to
<>	Not equal to
<	Less than
>	Greater than
<=	Less than or equal to
>=	Greater than or equal to

The small sample worksheet, Figure 2.10, shows the data the IF function uses to create the examples in Table 2.4. Arguments may be numeric, cell references to display cells' contents, a formula, a function, or a text entry. Review Table 2.4 to see how Excel evaluates conditions and the results.

	A	B	C	D	E
1	10	15	April		
2	10	30	May		
3					

Figure 2.10 IF Data

Table 2.4 IF Function, Evaluation, and Result

IF Function	Evaluation	Result
=IF(A1=A2,1000,2000)	10 is equal to 10, TRUE	1000
=IF(A1<>A2,1000,2000)	10 is not equal to 10, FALSE	2000
=If(A1<>A2,B1,B2)	10 is not equal to10, FALSE	30
=IF(A1<B2,MAX(B1:B2),MIN(B1:B2))	10 is less than 30, TRUE	30
=IF(A1<A2,B1+10,B1−10)	10 is less than 10, FALSE	5
=IF(A1=A2,C1,C2)	10 is equal to 10, TRUE	April

Using the VLOOKUP Function

VLOOKUP Function | Reference

VLOOKUP(lookup_value,table_array,col_index_num,range_lookup)

When you order something on the Web or by catalog, you look up the shipping costs for your order. You find the information you want because you look up a specific piece of information (the total amount of your order) to find the associated information (the shipping cost). The VLOOKUP function works the same way. You can use the VLOOKUP function to find a company's specific tax rate from a table or look up your own tax rate. The *VLOOKUP function* evaluates a value and looks up this value in a vertical table to return a value, text, or formula. Use VLOOKUP to search for exact matches or for the nearest value that is less than or equal to the search value (such as assigning a shipping cost of $15.25 to an order of $300.87). Or use the VLOOKUP function to assign a B grade for an 87% class average.

The **VLOOKUP function** looks up an answer from a vertical table of possible answers.

Understand the VLOOKUP Function Syntax

The VLOOKUP function has three arguments:

1. a lookup value stored in a cell,
2. a range of cells containing a lookup table, and
3. the number of the column within the lookup table that contains the value to return.

One use of a VLOOKUP function is the assignment of letter grades in a gradebook based on numeric values. Figure 2.11 shows a portion of a worksheet with a Grading Criteria Table that associates letter grades with the numerical value earned by a student. The first student's overall class average is 76.3. You can use the VLOOKUP function to identify the cell containing the student's numerical average and use that value to look up the equivalent letter grade in a table. To determine the letter grade in cell J4 based on a numeric value in cell I4, you would use the following:

=VLOOKUP(I4,$I$20:$J$24,2)

          Column number with the grade

      Range of the table

   Value to lookup (semester average)

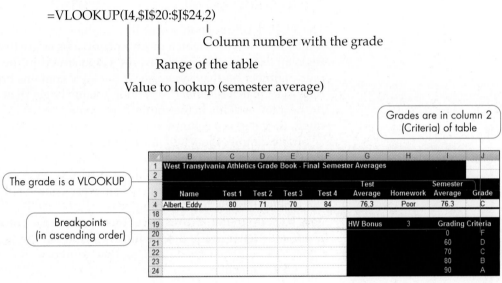

Figure 2.11   VLOOKUP Table Data

The **lookup value** is the value to look up in a reference table.

The **lookup table** is a range of cells containing the reference table.

The **column index number** is the column number in the lookup table that contains return values.

Cell I4 is the **lookup value** that represents the cell containing the value to look up in a table. In this example, the lookup value is 76.3. The table that Excel searches using a lookup function is called a **lookup table**. In this example, the lookup table is stored in the range $I$20:$J$24. Note that an absolute reference is used so the address is not changed when the formula is copied to other cells. The **column index number**, indicated by col_index_num in the function, refers to the number of the column in the lookup table that contains the return values. In the example, the col_index_num of 2 returns the value in the second column in the lookup table that corresponds to the value being looked up.

Structure the Lookup Table

The VLOOKUP function searches the left column of a table for a specific value and returns a corresponding value from the same row but a different column. You set up the table to include unique values in the left column (for example, ranges of total amounts or numeric ranges to assign letter grades), and then Excel retrieves the associated information (for example, shipping cost or letter grade) from another column. In Figure 2.11, the lookup table extends over two columns, I and J, and five rows, 20 through 24. The table is located in the range I20:J24.

You should set up the lookup table before using the VLOOKUP function. The left column, known as the lookup column, of the table includes the reference data used to look up information in the table, such as customer number, income, grade points, or the total amount range of the order. The other columns include information related to the first column, such as customer credit limit, tax rate, letter grades, or shipping cost. The values in the left or lookup column must be sorted in ascending order, from lowest to highest value. However, instead of typing an entire range, such as 80–89, for the range of B grades, you enter breakpoints only. The **breakpoint** is the lowest numeric value for a specific category or in a series of a lookup table to produce a corresponding result to return for a lookup function. Breakpoints are listed in ascending order in the first column of the lookup table. For example, the breakpoints in the gradebook lookup table represent the lowest numerical score to earn a particular letter grade. The breakpoints are listed in column I, and the corresponding letter grades are found in column J.

Understand How Excel Processes the Lookup

The VLOOKUP function works by searching in the left column of the lookup table until it finds an exact match or a number that is larger than the lookup value. If Excel finds an exact match, it returns the value stored in the column designated by the index number on that same row. If the table contains breakpoints for ranges rather than exact matches, when Excel finds a value larger than the lookup value, it returns the next lower value in the column designated by the col_index_num. To work accurately, the reference column must be in ascending order.

For example, the VLOOKUP function to assign letter grades works like this: Excel identifies the lookup value (76.3 stored in I4) and compares it to the values in the lookup table (stored in I20:J24). It tries to find an exact match; however, the table contains breakpoints rather than every conceivable numeric average. Because the lookup table is in ascending order, it notices that 76.3 is not equal to 80, so it goes back up to the 70 row. Excel then looks at the column index number of 2 and returns the letter grade of C, which is located in the second column of the lookup table. The returned grade of C is then stored in the cell J4, which contains the VLOOKUP function.

TIP   HLOOKUP Function

The VLOOKUP function is arranged vertically in a table, while its counterpart, the HLOOKUP function, is arranged horizontally. Use the HLOOKUP function when your comparison values are located in a row across the top of a table of data and you want to look down a specified number of rows.

Hands-On Exercises

3 | Athletic Department Eligibility Gradebook

Skills covered: 1. Use the IF Function **2.** Use the VLOOKUP Function **3.** Copy the IF and VLOOKUP Functions **4.** Apply Page Setup Options and Print the Worksheet

---

Step 1

Use the IF Function

Refer to Figure 2.12 as you complete Step 1.

a. Open the *chap2_ho3_gradebook* workbook and save it as **chap2_ho3_gradebook_ solution** so that you can return to the original workbook if necessary.

The partially completed gradebook contains student test scores and their respective test averages. You need to create an IF function to determine if students have completed their homework. If they did, they receive a 3-point bonus added to their semester average. Those students who did not complete homework receive no bonus, so their semester average is the same as their test average.

b. Click in **cell I4**. Click the **Formulas tab** and click **Insert Function** in the Function Library group. Select the **IF** function from the *Select a function* list. Click **OK** to close the Insert Function dialog box and display the Function Argument dialog box.

You will use the Function Arguments dialog box to build the IF function.

c. Click in the **Logical_test** box, keep the Function Arguments dialog box open but drag it down to see cell H4, click **cell H4** in the worksheet, and type **="OK"** to complete the logical test.

d. Click in the **Value_if_true** box, keep the Function Arguments dialog box open, click **cell G4** in the worksheet, type **+**, and click **cell H19**. Press **F4** to change H19 to an absolute cell reference.

e. Click in the **Value_if_false** box, keep the Function Arguments dialog box open, and click **cell G4** in the worksheet.

TROUBLESHOOTING: Text values used in arguments must be enclosed in quotes.

f. Click **OK** to insert the function into the worksheet. Save the workbook.

Because Eddy's homework was "Poor," he did not earn the 3-point bonus. His semester average is the same as his test average, which is 76.3 in cell I4.

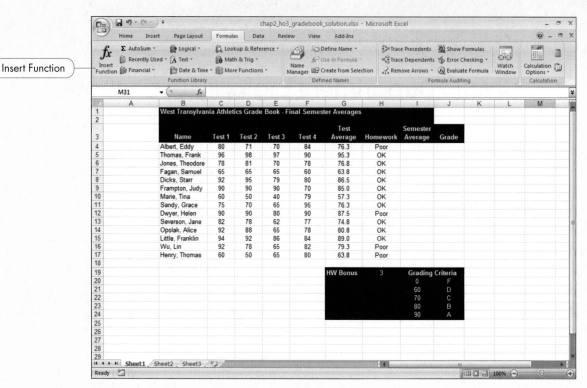

Insert Function

Figure 2.12 Athletics Gradebook

Refer to Figure 2.11 as you complete Step 2.

a. Click in **cell J4** and click the **Lookup & Reference arrow** in the Function Library group on the Formulas tab. Select **VLOOKUP**.

You will create a VLOOKUP function using the semester average stored in column I to determine the letter grade for each student.

b. Click in the **Lookup_value** box and click **cell I4** in the worksheet.

The first student's semester average, which is stored in cell I4, is the value to look up.

c. Click in the **Table_array** box. Click **cell I20** and drag to **cell J24**, and then press **F4** to convert the entire range reference to absolute ($I$20:$J$24).

The table containing the letter grade equivalents is stored in I20:J24. You made the reference absolute so that the cell addresses do not change when you copy the function for the remaining student athletes.

d. Click in the **Col_index_num** box and type **2**.

e. Click **OK** to insert the function into the worksheet and save the workbook.

The first student's letter grade is C because his semester average of 76.3 is over 70 but less than 80.

TROUBLESHOOTING: Make sure to use an absolute reference with the table in the VLOOKUP function. You will see inaccurate results if you forget to use absolute references.

Step 3
Copy the IF and VLOOKUP Functions

Refer to Figure 2.13 as you complete Step 3.

a. Copy the IF and VLOOKUP Functions by selecting **cells I4:J4**, point to the fill handle in the lower-right corner of **cell J4**, and drag the fill handle over cells **I5:J17**.

You just copied the original IF and VLOOKUP functions for the rest of the students.

b. Check that the semester averages are formatted to one decimal place.

c. Click **cell A19** and enter your name. Click **cell A1** and type **=TODAY()** to enter today's date.

d. Click **cell A1** and hold **Ctrl** as you click **cell A19**. Click the **Home tab** and click **Bold** in the Font group. Save the workbook.

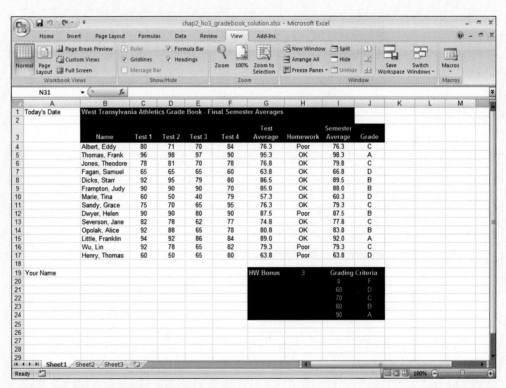

Figure 2.13 Athletics Gradebook

Step 4
Apply Page Setup Options and Print the Worksheets

a. Click the **Page Layout tab** and click **Margins** in the Page Setup group. Click **Custom Margins** to display the Margins tab in the Page Setup dialog box.

b. Click the **Horizontally check box** in the *Center on page* section to center the worksheet between the left and right margins.

c. Click the **Sheet tab**. Click the **Gridlines check box** and click the **Row and column headings check box** in the *Print* section.

d. Click **OK**. Save the workbook.

e. Click the **Office Button** and select **Print**. Click the **Preview button** to see how the workbook will print.

TROUBLESHOOTING: If the worksheet previews as two pages in the Print Preview window, close the Print Preview window, display the Page Setup dialog box, and decrease the scaling. Display the worksheet in Print Preview again to make sure the worksheet fits on one page.

f. Click the **Print button**, and then click **OK** to print the worksheet.

g. Press **Ctrl + ~** to show the cell formulas rather than the values. Adjust the column width as necessary and print the worksheet a second time. Close the workbook without saving.

Financial Functions

A spreadsheet is a tool used for decision-making. Many decisions typically involve financial situations: payments, investments, interest rates, and so on. Excel contains several financial functions to help you perform calculations with monetary values.

Review Figures 2.14, 2.15, 2.16, and 2.17 to see how a worksheet might be applied to the purchase of a car. You need to know the monthly payment, which depends on the price of the car, the down payment, and the terms of the loan. In other words:

> (**Can you afford the monthly payment on the car of your choice?**)

- Can you afford the monthly payment on the car of your choice?
- What if you settle for a less expensive car and receive a manufacturer's rebate?
- What if you work next summer to earn money for a down payment?
- What if you extend the life of the loan and receive a better interest rate?
- Have you accounted for additional items such as insurance, gas, and maintenance?

The answers to these and other questions determine whether you can afford a car, and if so, which car, and how you will pay for it. The decision is made easier by developing the worksheet in Figure 2.14, and then by changing the various input values as indicated.

The availability of the worksheet lets you consider several alternatives. You realize that the purchase of a $14,999 car, as shown in Figure 2.15, is prohibitive because the monthly payment is almost $476.96. Settling for a less expensive car, coming up with a substantial down payment, and obtaining a manufacturer's rebate in Figure 2.16 help, but the $317.97 monthly payment is still too high. Extending the loan to a fourth year

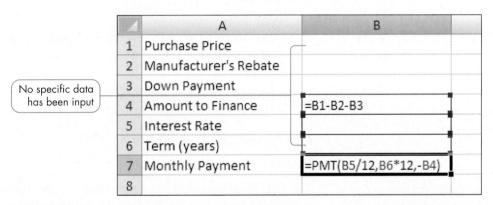

	A	B
1	Purchase Price	
2	Manufacturer's Rebate	
3	Down Payment	
4	Amount to Finance	=B1-B2-B3
5	Interest Rate	
6	Term (years)	
7	Monthly Payment	=PMT(B5/12,B6*12,-B4)
8		

No specific data has been input

Figure 2.14 Spreadsheets for Decision-Making

	A	B	C	D
1	Purchase Price	$14,999		
2	Manufacturer's Rebate			
3	Down Payment			
4	Amount to Finance	$14,999		
5	Interest Rate	9%		
6	Term (years)	3		
7	Monthly Payment	$476.96		
8				

Data entered

Figure 2.15 Spreadsheets for Decision-Making

	A	B	C	D
1	Purchase Price	$13,999		
2	Manufacturer's Rebate	$1,000		
3	Down Payment	$3,000		
4	Amount to Finance	$9,999		
5	Interest Rate	9%		
6	Term (years)	3		
7	Monthly Payment	$317.97		
8				

Rebate
Less expensive car
Down payment made

Figure 2.16 Spreadsheets for Decision-Making

	A	B	C	D
1	Purchase Price	$13,999		
2	Manufacturer's Rebate	$1,000		
3	Down Payment	$3,000		
4	Amount to Finance	$9,999		
5	Interest Rate	8%		
6	Term (years)	4		
7	Monthly Payment	$244.10		
8				

Lower interest rate
Longer term
Lower monthly payment

Figure 2.17 Spreadsheets for Decision-Making

at a lower interest rate, as in Figure 2.17, reduces the monthly payment to $244.10, which is closer to your budgeted amount.

Using the PMT Function

PMT Function | Reference

PMT(rate,nper,pv,fv,type)

The **PMT function** calculates
the payment on a loan.

The **PMT function** calculates payments for a loan that is paid off at a fixed amount at a periodic rate. The PMT function requires three arguments: the interest rate per period, the number of periods, and the amount of the loan, from which it computes the associated payment on a loan. The arguments are placed in parentheses and are separated by commas. Consider the PMT function as it might apply to Figure 2.15:

=PMT(.09/12,36,–14999)

Amount of loan (as a *negative* amount)

Number of periods (3 years × 12 months/year)

Interest rate per period (annual rate divided by 12)

Instead of using specific values, however, you should use cell references in the PMT function arguments, so that you can easily change the input values in the individual cells instead of editing the values in the function itself. The PMT function is entered as =PMT(B5/12,B6*12,–B4) to reflect the terms of a specific loan whose arguments are in cells B4, B5, and B6. You must divide the 9% annual percentage rate (APR) by 12 months to obtain the monthly *periodic* rate. Next, you must multiply the

3-year term by the number of payments per year. Because you will make monthly payments, you multiply 3 by 12 months to calculate the total number of months in the term, which is 36. The amount of the loan is a minus figure because it is a debt. The loan is considered a negative because it is an outflow of cash or an expense. The amount of the loan is entered as a negative amount so the worksheet will display a positive value after calculations.

Using the FV Function

FV Function | Reference

FV(rate,nper,pmt,pv,type)

The **FV function** returns the future value of an investment.

The **FV function** returns the future value of an investment if you know the interest rate, the term, and the periodic payment. You can use the FV function to determine how much an IRA would be worth in a particular period of time. This function would be expressed as =FV(rate,nper,payment).

Assume that you plan to contribute $3,000 a year to an IRA, that you expect to earn 7% annually, and that you will be contributing for 40 years. The future value of that investment—the amount you will have at age 65—would be $598,905! You would have contributed $120,000 ($3,000 a year for 40 years). The difference, more than $470,000, results from compound interest you will earn over the life of your investment of $120,000!

(. . . more than $470,000, results from compound interest you will earn over the life of your investment of $120,000!)

The FV function has three arguments—the interest rate (also called the rate of return), the number of periods (how long you will pay into the IRA), and the periodic investment (how much you will invest into the IRA per year). The FV function corresponding to the earlier example would be:

Amount at retirement =FV(Rate of return, Term, Periodic payment)

$3,000

40 years

7%

Computed value becomes $598,905

It is more practical, however, to enter the values into a worksheet and then use cell references within the FV function. If, for example, cells A1, A2, and A3 contained the rate of return, term, and annual contribution, respectively, the resulting FV function would be =FV(A1,A2,−A3). The periodic payment is preceded by a minus sign, just as the principal in the PMT function.

These financial functions as well as the other examples of functions provide you with the tools to perform sophisticated mathematical, statistical, and financial calculations.

Hands-On Exercises

4 | Purchasing a Van for the School for Exceptional Children

Skills covered: 1. Create the Worksheet **2.** Insert the PMT Function **3.** Format the Worksheet **4.** Complete the Worksheet

Step 1
Create the Worksheet

Refer to Figure 2.18 as you complete Step 1.

a. Start a new blank workbook. Click in **cell B1** and type the title **School for Exceptional Children**. Enter the remaining labels for column B, as shown in Figure 2.18.

As the transportation director, one of your responsibilities is to purchase vehicles for the school's use. You will create a worksheet, use the PMT function, and format a worksheet to show the proposed purchase price.

b. Increase the column widths to accommodate the widest entry, as necessary (other than cell B3). Enter the following as indicated below. Include the dollar sign and the percent sign as you enter the data to automatically format the cell.

Cell	Value
C4	$26,000
C5	$1,000
C6	$3,000
C8	9%
C9	3

The loan parameters have been entered into the worksheet, and you are ready to work with the PMT function.

c. Enter the formula to caculate the Amount to Finance in cell C7 by clicking in **cell C7** and typing **=C4−(C5+C6)**. Press **Enter**.

Although parentheses are not required for order of precedence, they may be used to help for understandability. You could also enter the formula **=C4−C5−C6** as an alternative.

d. Save the workbook as **chap2_ho4_van_solution**.

Step 2
Insert the PMT Function

a. Click the **Formulas tab**. Click **cell C10**, click **Financial** in the Function Library group, and click the **PMT** function. Click in the **Rate** box, click **cell C8** of the worksheet, then type **/12**.

The Rate box contains C8/12 because interest is calculated monthly.

b. Click in the **Nper** box, click **cell C9** of the worksheet, and type ***12**.

The Nper box contains C9*12 to calculate the total number of payment periods in the loan.

c. Click in the **Pv** box, type a minus sign (−), and click **cell C7**. Click **OK** to close the Function Arguments dialog box.

The monthly payment of $699.59 is now displayed in cell C10.

d. Save the workbook.

TROUBLESHOOTING: Divide the interest rate by 12 because the rate is requested as a percentage per period. Multiply the years by 12 because the term of the loan is stated in years.

Step 3
Format the Worksheet

a. Click the **Home tab**, select cells **B1** and **C1**, and click **Merge and Center** in the Alignment group.

b. Click the **Font size arrow** in the Font group and click **12**. Click **Bold** in the Font group to boldface the title.

c. Click **cell B3**, press and hold **Ctrl** as you click **cells B10:C10**, and click **Bold**.

d. Click and drag to select **cells B4:B9**. Click **Increase Indent** in the Alignment group to indent the labels.

e. Click in **cell A12** and enter your name. Click **cell A1** and use the **TODAY** function to enter today's date. Click **cell A1** and hold **Ctrl** as you click **cell A12**. Click **Bold**. Save the workbook.

Step 4
Complete the Worksheet

a. Click the **Page Layout tab** and click **Margins** in the Page Setup group. Click **Custom Margins** to display the Page Setup dialog box.

b. Click the **Horizontally check box** in the *Center on page* section.

c. Click the **Sheet tab**, click the **Gridlines check box**, and click the **Row and column headings check box** in the *Print* section.

You used the Page Layout options to print gridlines as well as row and column headings and centered the worksheet horizontally.

d. Click **OK**. Save the workbook.

e. Click the **Office Button**, select **Print**, and click **Preview** to see how the workbook will print. Click the **Print button**, and then **OK** to print the worksheet.

f. Press **Ctrl + ~** to show the cell formulas rather than the values. Adjust the column width as necessary and print the worksheet a second time. Close the workbook.

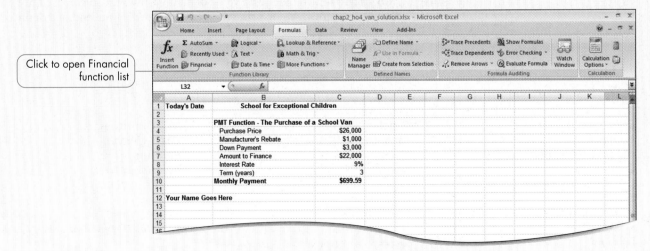

Figure 2.18 School for Exceptional Children Van

Summary

1. **Create and copy formulas.** When constructing formulas in Excel, it is more efficient to enter cell references in formulas rather than the cell contents. Entering cell references means that an addition formula should be stated as =A2+B2 rather than =1+2. By using cell references rather than cell contents, the formula does not have to be changed when the cell content changes. Pointing and using the fill handle are techniques that make the development of an Excel spreadsheet easier. The fill handle is a small black square at the lower-right corner of a selected cell(s). It is the efficient way to copy cell formulas to adjacent cells.

2. **Use relative and absolute cell addresses.** A relative reference (such as C4) changes both row and column when the cell containing the reference is copied to other worksheet cells. An absolute cell reference, such as $C$4, stays the same during the copy process. A mixed reference, such as $C4 or C$4, modifies the row or column during the copy. The use of relative and absolute references is common in the design and construction of most spreadsheets.

3. **Use AutoSum.** The AutoSum is the most often used statistical function in Excel. It is represented by the sigma and automatically sums values contained in a range of cells.

4. **Insert basic statistical functions.** Statistical functions discussed include SUM, which returns the sum of an argument list, and AVERAGE, MEDIAN, MAX, and MIN, which return the average value, the midpoint of a range of values, the highest value, and lowest value, respectively, in an argument list. The COUNT function displays the number of cells with numeric entries and the COUNTA function displays the number of cells with numeric and/or text entries.

5. **Use date functions.** The NOW function uses the computer's clock to display the current date and time side by side in a cell. The TODAY function is another date-related function that places the current date in a cell.

6. **Use the IF function.** In the set of logical functions, the IF is the most basic. It returns one value when a condition is met and returns another value when the condition is not met. The IF function allows decision-making to be used within a worksheet. IF functions have three arguments: the condition, the result when true, and the result when false.

7. **Use the VLOOKUP function.** You can use VLOOKUP to look up an answer from a table of possible answers. The table that Excel searches using a lookup function is called a lookup table, and the value being used to search the lookup table is called a lookup value.

8. **Use the PMT function.** You can use the PMT function to calculate payments for a loan that is paid off at a fixed amount at a periodic rate. The PMT function requires three arguments: the interest rate per period, the number of periods, and the amount of the loan, from which it computes the associated payment on a loan. The arguments are placed in parentheses and are separated by commas.

9. **Use the FV function.** If you know the interest rate, the term, and the periodic payment, then you can use the FV function to return the future value of an investment. You can use the FV function to determine how much an investment would be worth at the end of a defined period of time.

Key Terms

Multiple Choice

1. After entering numbers and using the SUM function to sum the numbers, when is the function updated if one of the numbers changes?

   (a) When the file is saved

   (b) When you refresh the worksheet

   (c) When you close the file

   (d) At once

2. Which of the following returns the system date?

   (a) The Date() function

   (b) The Today() function

   (c) Date arithmetic

   (d) The Insert Date command

3. If you see the term "C3" used in relation to Excel, it refers to what?

   (a) Absolute reference

   (b) Cell reference

   (c) Worksheet reference

   (d) Mixed reference

4. The entry =PMT(C5/12,C6*12,C7):

   (a) Is invalid because the cell reference C7 is not absolute

   (b) Computes an annual payment

   (c) Divides the interest rate in C5, multiplies the number of periods in C6, and C7 is the loan amount

   (d) Is invalid because the value in C7 is negative

5. Pointing is a technique to:

   (a) Select a single cell

   (b) Select a range of contiguous cells

   (c) Select ranges of noncontiguous cells

   (d) All of the above

6. The small black square in the bottom-right corner of a cell is called what?

   (a) Pointer

   (b) Fill handle

   (c) Crosshair

   (d) Select box

7. Given the function =VLOOKUP(C6,D12:F18,3):

   (a) The entries in cells D12 through D18 are in ascending order.

   (b) The entries in cells D12 through D18 are in descending order.

   (c) The entries in cells F12 through F18 are in ascending order.

   (d) The entries in cells F12 through F18 are in descending order.

8. Which of the following must be entered when creating a formula?

   (a) The equal sign

   (b) A mathematical operator

   (c) A function

   (d) Nothing special is required.

9. Which of the following is an example of an absolute cell reference?

   (a) C4

   (b) $C$4

   (c) =C4

   (d) $C4

10. If you wanted the contents of only a column to stay the same throughout the copy process, you would use which of the following?

    (a) Relative reference

    (b) Mixed reference

    (c) Absolute reference

    (d) This is not possible

11. Which of the following references would indicate that the column would not change during the copy process?

    (a) $C$4

    (b) =C4

    (c) $C4

    (d) C$4

12. The Σ indicates which of the following functions?

    (a) AVERAGE

    (b) MAX

    (c) MIN

    (d) SUM

13. Which function will return the number of nonempty cells in the range A2 through A6, when the cells contain text as well as numeric entries?

    (a) =COUNT(A2:A6)

    (b) =COUNTA(A2:A6)

    (c) =COUNT(A2,A6)

    (d) =COUNTA(A2,A6)

14. The MAX function is an example of what type of function?

    (a) Database

    (b) Statistical

    (c) Logical

    (d) Lookup

15. If you want to determine the future value of an investment, what function would you use?

    (a) PV

    (b) FV

    (c) VLOOKUP

    (d) IF

Practice Exercises

1 West Transylvania Women's Basketball Season Statistics

You are the statistician for the West Transylvania Women's basketball team. You have entered basic statistics into a worksheet for the 2007–08 season. The coach wants to expand the statistics so that she can compare production for different seasons. Complete the worksheet as directed using Figure 2.19 as a guide.

a. Open the *chap2_pe1_basketball* workbook and save it as **chap2_pe1_basketball_ solution** so that you can return to the original workbook if necessary.

b. The first calculation will be total points (TP). Click in **cell I5**, the cell that will contain the total points for Adams. Type = on the keyboard to begin pointing, then click **cell C5** to enter the first part of the formula to calculate total points.

c. Type **+(** and click **cell F5**, then type ***2)+(** and click **cell H5**. Type ***3)**. You should see 84 as the displayed value for cell I5. Enter your name in **cell I22**. Save the workbook.

d. Click in **cell D5**, the cell that contains Adams's free throw percentage (FT%). Type = and click **cell C5**. Type / and click **cell B5**. Press **Enter**. You should see .8 in cell D5.

e. To calculate two-point field goal percentage (2-Pt FG%), click in **cell G5**, type =, click **cell F5**, type /, and click **cell E5**. Press **Enter** to see .36364 in cell G5.

f. To calculate points per game (PPG), type =. Click **cell I5**, type /, and click **cell C22**. Press **F4** to set cell C22 as absolute ($C$22) and press **Enter**. You should see 7 in cell J5.

g. To calculate rebounds per game (RPG), click **cell L5** and type =. Click **cell K5**, type /, click **cell C22**, and press **F4** to make C22 an absolute reference ($C$22). Press **Enter** and you will see 4.58333 in cell L5. Save the workbook.

h. Click in **cell D5**. Point to the fill handle in the lower-right corner of cell D5; the mouse pointer changes to a thin crosshair. Drag the fill handle to **cell D14**.

i. Release the mouse to complete the copy operation. The formula for FT% has been copied to the corresponding rows for the other players. Repeat the above two steps for columns G, I, J, and L to complete all players' statistics.

j. Use statistical functions to complete the summary area below the player statistics. Click in **cell B18**, type **=AVERAGE(**, and click and drag **cells B5:B14**. Type **)** and press **Enter**. Click in **cell B19**, type **=MAX(**, and click and drag cells **B5:B14**. Type **)** and press **Enter**. Click in **cell B20**, type **=MIN(**, and click and drag cells **B5:B14**. Type **)** and press **Enter**.

k. To copy the formulas across the worksheet, click and drag over **cells B18:B20**. Point to the fill handle in the lower-right corner of cell B20; the mouse pointer changes to a thin crosshair. Drag the fill handle to **cell L20**.

l. To calculate totals in row 17, click in **cell B17**, click **AutoSum** in the Function Library group on the Formulas tab, and then click and drag **cells B5:B14**. Press **Enter** to finish the function. To copy, click **cell B17** and click **Copy** in the Clipboard group on the Home tab. Click in **cell C17** and click **Paste** in the Clipboard group on the Home tab. Click and **Paste** in **cells E17**, **F17**, **H17**, **I17**, and **K17** to paste the formula in the appropriate cells. Enter **=TODAY()** in **cell I23** for today's date. Verify your calculations and format the worksheet, as shown in Figure 2.19.

m. Format columns D and G as **Percent Style** with **1** decimal place. Format columns J and L as **Number** with **1** decimal place. Replace **Your Name** with your name in **cell I22** and use a **date function** to retrieve today's date in **cell I5**. Verify your calculations and format the worksheet, as shown in Figure 2.19.

n. Click the **Page Layout tab**. Click **Orientation** and click **Landscape** in the Page Setup group. Click **Size**, select **More Paper Sizes**, and click **Fit to 1 page** in the *Scaling* section. Click the **Margins tab** and then click the **Horizontally check box** in the *Center on page* section. Click the **Sheet tab**, click the **Gridlines check box**, and click the **Row and column headings check box** in the *Print* section. Click **OK**. Print the worksheet.

o. Save the workbook. Press **Ctrl + ~** to show the cell formulas rather than the displayed values. Adjust the column widths as necessary and print the worksheet a second time. Save and close the workbook.

...continued on Next Page

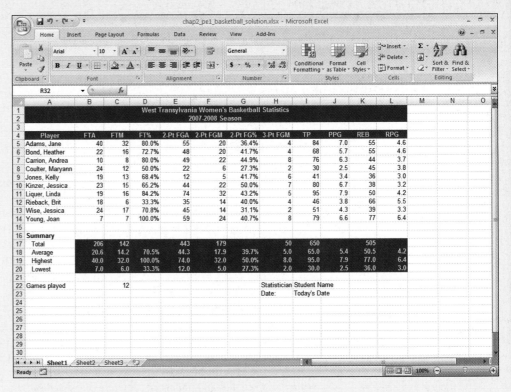

Figure 2.19 Women's Basketball Statistics

2 Predicting Retirement Income

Retirement might be years away, but it is never too soon to start planning. The Future Value function enables you to calculate the amount of money you will have at retirement, based on a series of uniform contributions. Once you reach retirement, you do not withdraw all of the money immediately, but withdraw it periodically, perhaps as a monthly pension. Your assignment is to create a new worksheet similar to the one in Figure 2.20.

a. In a new blank workbook, enter the data for the accrual phase as shown in the following table (begin in cell A3):

Annual salary	$60,000
Employee contribution	6.20%
Employer contribution	6.20%
Total contribution	
Interest rate	6%
Years contributing	45

b. The first calculation will be the total contribution per year. Click in **cell B7**, type =, click **cell B4**, and type * and (. Click **cell B5**, type +, and click **cell B6**. Type). The total contribution in **cell B7** is a formula based on a percentage of your annual salary, plus a matching contribution from your employer. The 6.2% in the figure corresponds to the percentages that are currently in effect for Social Security.

c. The future value of your contributions (i.e., the amount of your "nest egg") depends on the assumptions on the left side of the worksheet. The 6% interest rate is conservative and can be achieved by investing in bonds, as opposed to equities. The

...continued on Next Page

45 years of contributions corresponds to an individual entering the work force at age 22 and retiring at 67 (the age at which today's worker will begin to collect Social Security). To calculate the future value of your nest egg, type **Future Value** in **cell A10**. Click in **cell B10**, where the future value will be calculated. Enter the FV function as follows:

- Click the **Formulas tab**, click **Financial** in the Function Library group, and click **FV**.
- Click in the **Rate** box, and then click **cell B8**.
- Click in the **Nper** box and click **cell B9**.
- Click in the **Pmt** box, type a minus sign (–), and click **cell B7**.
- Click **OK** to close the Function Arguments dialog box. The future value of your nest egg is $1,582,812.

d. The pension phase uses the PMT function to determine the payments you will receive in retirement. The formula in cell E4 is a reference to the amount accumulated in cell B10. The formula in cell E7 uses the PMT function to compute your monthly pension based on your nest egg, the interest rate, and the years in retirement. Note that accrual phase uses an *annual* contribution in its calculations, whereas the pension phase determines a *monthly* pension.

- Click **cell D3** and type **Pension Phase**. Enter the data shown below beginning in cell D4

The size of your "nest egg"	=B10
Interest rate	6%
Years in retirement	25

- Click in **cell D7** and type **Monthly Pension**. Click in **cell E7** to begin to enter the PMT function.
- Click **Financial** in the Function Library group on the Formulas tab, and then click **PMT**.
- Click in the **Rate** box, click **cell E5**, and type **/12**.
- Click in the **Nper** box, click **cell E6**, and type ***12**.
- Click in the **Pv** box, type a minus sign (–), and click **cell E4**.
- Click **OK** to close the Function Arguments dialog box. The monthly pension is $10,198.

e. Click in **cell D10** and enter your name. Enter **=TODAY()** in **cell D11** for today's date. Verify your calculations and format the worksheet, as shown in Figure 2.20.

f. Click the **Page Layout tab**, click **Orientation** in the Page Setup group, and click **Landscape**. Click **Size**, click **More Paper Sizes**, and click **Fit to 1 page** in the *Scaling* section. Click the **Margins tab** and click the **Horizontally check box** in the *Center on page* section. Click the **Sheet tab**, click the **Gridlines check box**, and click the **Row and column headings check box** in the *Print* section. Click **OK**. Print the worksheet.

g. Save the workbook as **chap2_pe2_retirement_solution.xlsx**. Press **Ctrl + ~** to show the cell formulas rather than the displayed values. Adjust the column widths as necessary and print the worksheet a second time.

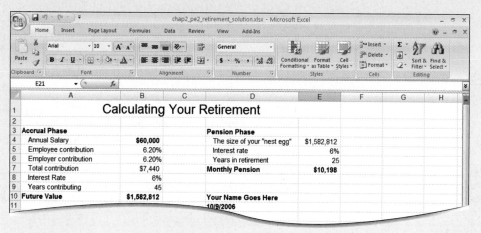

Figure 2.20 Predicting Retirement Income

...continued on Next Page

The presidential election has come and gone, but it is interesting to analyze the results of both the popular and electoral votes. You want to compare total votes and votes by state. You will find a partially completed version of the workbook shown in Figure 2.21 and enter functions to help identify election trends.

a. Open the *chap2_pe3_election* workbook and save it as **chap2_pe3_election_solution**.

b. Enter an appropriate IF function in cells D9 and F9 to determine the number of electoral votes for each candidate. The electoral votes are awarded on an all-or-nothing basis; that is, the candidate with the larger popular vote wins all of that state's electoral votes. The other candidate gets zero votes.

- Click in **cell D9** to begin the first IF function. Click the **Formulas tab** and click **Insert Function** in the Function Library group.
- Click **IF** to select the IF function.
- Click in the **Logical test** box in the Function Arguments dialog box and type **C9>E9**.
- Click in the **Value_if_true** box and click **cell B9**.
- Click in the **Value_if_false** box and **type ""** (quotes are needed to make empty cells).
- Click **OK** to finish the IF function and close the dialog box.
- Click **cell F9** to begin the second IF function.
- Click **Insert Function** in the Function Library on the Formulas tab and click **IF** to select the IF function.
- Click in the **Logical test** box, type **E9>C9**.
- Click in the **Value_if_true** box and click **cell B9**.
- Click in the **Value_if_false** box and **type ""** (quotes are needed to make empty cells).
- Click **OK** to finish the IF function and close the dialog box.

c. You will now copy the entries in cells D9 and F9 to the remaining rows in the respective columns. You also will format these columns to display red and blue values, for Mr. Bush and Mr. Kerry, respectively.

- Click in **cell D9** and drag the fill handle through **D59** to copy the formula.
- To format the columns select **cells C8:D59**. Click the **Home tab**, click the **Font Color arrow** in the Font group, and click **Red**.
- Adapt the previous two bulleted list instructions for columns E and F, substituting the appropriate column letters and applying **Blue** font color.

d. Enter a formula into cell G9 to determine the difference in the popular vote between the two candidates. The result will appear as a positive number and you will use an absolute value function. Copy this formula to the remaining rows in the column.

- Click in **cell G9** and type **=ABS(**.
- Click in **cell C9**, type minus (–), click in **cell E9**, type **)**, and press **Enter**.
- Click in **cell G9** and drag the fill handle through **G59** to copy the formula.

e. You will calculate the percentage differential in the popular vote. This differential is the difference in the number of votes, divided by the total number of votes.

- Click in **cell H9** and type **=G9/(**.
- Click in **cell C9**, type **+**, click **cell E9**, and type **)**.
- Click in **cell H9** and drag the fill handle through **H59** to copy the formula.

f. Enter the appropriate SUM functions in cells B4, B5, C4, and C5 to determine the electoral and popular vote totals for each candidate.

- To calculate the total in cell B4, click in **cell B4**, click **AutoSum** in the Function Library on the Formulas tab, click and drag **cells C9:C59**, and press **Enter**.
- To calculate the total in cell B5, click in **cell B5**, click **AutoSum** on the Formulas tab, click and drag **cells D9:D59**, and press **Enter**.
- Repeat the first two bulleted instructions in Step f for **cells C4** and **C5** using the appropriate cell ranges.

...continued on Next Page

g. Add your name as indicated. Click the **Page Layout tab**, click **Margins** in the Page Setup group, and click **Custom Margins**. Type **0.75** in the **Top** and **Bottom** boxes to ensure the worksheet fits on one page. Adjust the column widths as necessary. Create a custom footer that shows the **date** the worksheet was printed. Print the displayed values, and then print the worksheet a second time to show the cell formulas. Save and close the workbook.

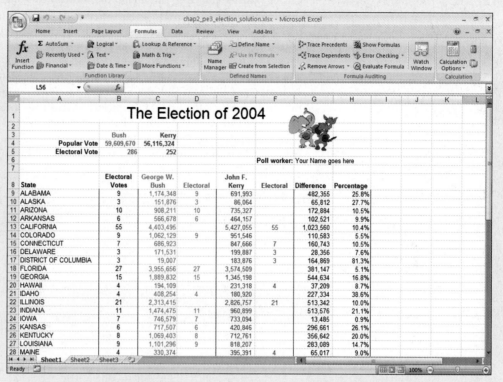

Figure 2.21 Election Trends

4 Expanded Payroll

You will revisit the payroll completed earlier in this chapter in the hands-on exercises but revise it to use a VLOOKUP function to determine the withholding tax amount based on a tax bracket, rather than a flat tax rate. Use Figure 2.22 for reference to complete the expanded payroll example. Be sure to use the appropriate combination of relative and absolute addresses so the formula in column G may be copied to the remaining rows in the worksheet.

a. Open the *chap2_pe4_exppayroll* workbook and save it as **chap2_pe4_exppayroll_ solution**.

b. Click in **cell G4**, click the **Formulas tab**, click **Insert Function** in the Function Library group, and click **VLOOKUP** from the *Select a function* list. Click **OK** to close the Insert Function dialog box and display the **Function Arguments** dialog box.
   - Click in the **Lookup_value** box and click **cell F4**.
   - Click in the **Table_array** box, drag through **cells J20:K24**, and press **F4** to make the table references absolute.
   - Click in the **Col_index_num** box and type **2**.
   - Click **OK** to finish the VLOOKUP function and close the Function Argument box.
   - Click after the closing parenthesis for the VLOOKUP function in the formula bar, type ***F4**, and press **Enter**.

c. Click in **cell G4** and drag the fill handle through **G15** to copy the formula.

...continued on Next Page

d. To calculate the Social Security withholding tax, click **cell H4**, and type **=F4***

e. Click **cell D21**, press **F4**, and then press **Enter**.

f. Click **cell H4** and drag the fill handle through **H15** to copy the formula.

g. Calculate the net pay by clicking **cell I4** and type **=F4–(**.

h. Click **cell G4**, type **+,** click **cell H4**, type **)**, and press **Enter**.

i. Click in **cell I4** and drag the fill handle through **I15** to copy the formula.

j. Format columns G, H, and I as **currency** with two decimal places. Replace **Your Name** with your name and use a **date function** to retrieve today's date. Verify your calculations and format the worksheet, as shown in Figure 2.22.

k. Click the **Page Layout tab**, click **Orientation** in the Page Setup group, and click **Landscape**. Click **Size**, select **More Paper Sizes**, and click **Fit to 1 page** in the *Scaling* section. Click the **Margins tab** and click the **Horizontally check box** in the *Center on page* section. Click the **Sheet tab**, click the **Gridlines check box**, and click the **Row and column headings check box** in the *Print* section. Click **OK**. Print the worksheet.

l. Save the workbook. Press **Ctrl + ~** to show the cell formulas rather than the displayed values. Adjust the column widths as necessary and print the worksheet a second time.

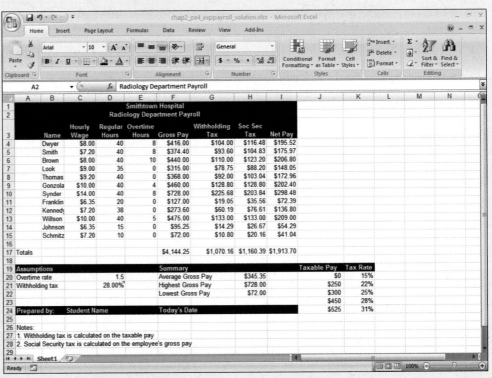

Figure 2.22 Expanded Payroll

Mid-Level Exercises

1 Banquet Room Inventory

Managing or tracking inventory is an important way for businesses to control operating costs. During semester breaks you work as an assistant to the manager of a banquet room facility and are responsible for updating the inventory workbook. You will create formulas and functions to illustrate how Excel is used for inventory control. Refer to Figure 2.23 as you complete the worksheet.

a. Open the *chap2_mid1_banquet* workbook. Save it as **chap2_mid1_banquet_ solution** so that you can return to the original workbook if necessary.

b. The cost is calculated by multiplying number purchased by purchase price (e.g., 200 chairs * $186.00). The total cost of inventoried items is the sum of all values. Use the **SUM function** to compute the total cost.

c. Enter the **MAX** and **MIN functions** where appropriate to determine the most and least expensive items in inventory. Use the **COUNTA function** to determine the number of categories of items in inventory.

d. Replace Student Name with Your Name. Add an appropriate Clip art image somewhere in the worksheet using the same technique as in any Microsoft Office 2007 application. Use an appropriate date function to get today's date in your worksheet and format it as **mm/dd/yyyy**.

e. Format the worksheet in an attractive fashion, making sure to format dollar figures as currency with two decimal places. Wrap the column heading text to increase readability.

f. Print the completed worksheet twice, once with displayed values, and once to show the cell formulas. Use Page Setup for the cell formulas to switch to landscape orientation and force the output onto one page. Print gridlines and row and column headings. Save and close the workbook.

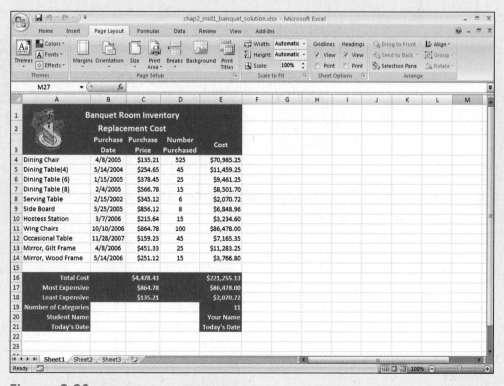

Figure 2.23   Banquet Room Inventory

...continued on Next Page

The real estate market is booming, and electronic methods are necessary to keep up with the rapidly changing field. As an intern with the Duke Real Estate company, you have prepared the worksheet shown in Figure 2.24. It shows how the Duke Real Estate company uses Excel to track monthly sales and sales commissions. You will complete the Real Estate worksheet so that the displayed values match Figure 2.24.

The price per square foot is calculated by dividing the selling price by size. The percent of list price is calculated by dividing the selling price by the list price. Use an absolute reference to determine sales commission so the formula can be copied to other rows.

a. Open the *chap2_mid2_rls* workbook and save it as **chap2_mid2_rls_solution** so that you can return to the original workbook if necessary.

b. Enter the **SUM function** in **cell B14** to compute the total square feet. Copy the formula to the remaining cells in the row. Use the appropriate functions to calculate the values in the summary area.

c. Format the worksheet in an attractive manner, making sure to display all dollar amounts with the currency symbol and no decimal places. Display percentages with the percent symbol and one decimal place. Use a date function to display the current date in the cell below the heading.

d. Enter Your Name in **cell A17** and print the worksheet twice, once with displayed values, and once to show cell formulas. Use the Page Setup command to switch to landscape orientation and force the output onto one page. Print gridlines and row and column headings. Save and close the workbook.

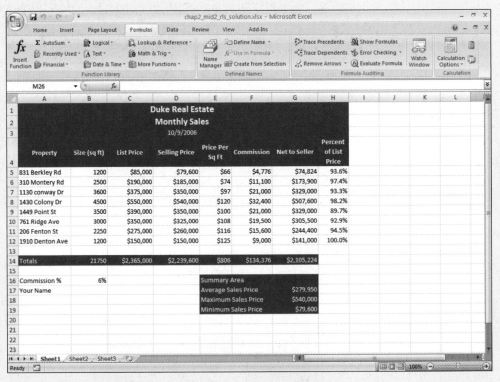

Figure 2.24 Real Estate Sales

...continued on Next Page

The Greater Latrobe School District is well known for its 70-year-old art collection. One of your duties as a summer intern is to help ready the collection for a traveling exhibition. You will use the IF function and the VLOOKUP function in Excel to determine costs associated with this art exhibition. You will complete the Greater Latrobe School District worksheet so that displayed values match Figure 2.25.

a. Open the *chap2_mid3_glsd* workbook and save it as **chap2_mid3_glsd_solution** so that you can return to the original workbook if necessary.

b. The cost of insurance is based on the value of the artwork. If the value is greater than $500, then the insurance is 25% of the value; otherwise, the insurance is 10% of the value of the painting. Enter an **IF function** in G6 to compute the cost of insurance and copy the formula to the remaining cells in the column.

c. Cubic footage is calculated by multiplying height by width and dividing by 144. Enter the formula in cell H6 and copy the formula to the remaining cells.

d. The cost of the box is determined by looking up the value in a lookup table. The shipping cost also is determined by looking up the value in a lookup table. Use the table at **cells H23:J28** with a **VLOOKUP function** to determine the cost of a box. Remember to use absolute references for the table and copy the formula to the remaining cells in the column.

e. Use the table at **cells H23:J28** with a **VLOOKUP function** to determine the shipping cost. Remember to use absolute references for the table and copy the formula to the remaining cells in the column. Save and close the workbook.

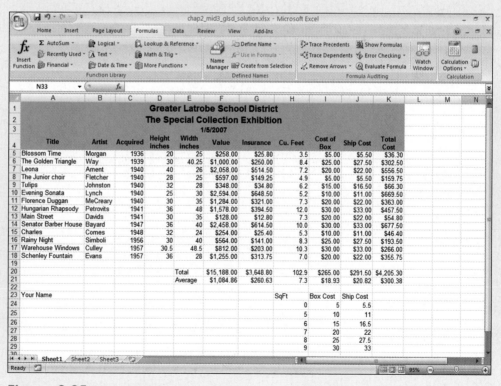

Figure 2.25 Art Collection

...continued on Next Page

f. Use the **SUM function** in **cell F20** to compute the total value of the art collection. Copy the formula to the remaining cells in the row. Use the **AVERAGE function** in **cell F21** to compute the average value of a painting. Copy the formula to the remaining cells in the row.

g. Format the worksheet in an attractive manner but similar to Figure 2.25, making sure to display all dollar amounts with the currency symbol and two decimal places. Display height, width, and cubic feet with one decimal place. Use a date function to display the current date in **cell A3**.

h. Enter **Your Name** in **cell A23** and print the worksheet twice, once with displayed values, and once to show cell formulas. Use the Page Setup command to switch to landscape orientation and force the output onto one page. Print gridlines and row and column headings. Save and close the workbook.

4 Financial Functions

Your accounting professor has asked you to create a worksheet that compares interest rates and monthly payments over different time periods. Figure 2.26 is an example of how Excel is used to compare interest rates and monthly payments over different time periods. You will create this worksheet and use financial functions with relative, absolute, and mixed references.

a. Begin a new workbook by typing the following in the cells indicated:

Cell	Value
A1	Amount Borrowed
A2	Starting Interest
A5	Interest
B5	30 Years
C5	15 Years
D5	Difference
D1	100000
D2	.075
A13	Assumptions
A14	30 years
A15	15 years
B14	30
B15	15
A16	Financial Consultant
A17	Your Name

b. Save the workbook as **chap2_mid4_financial_solution**.

c. To copy the interest rate and then use it in a formula, enter the formula =D2 in **cell A6** and enter the formula =A6+.01 in **cell A7**. Copy the formula into **cells A8:A11**.

d. Calculate the payment for 30 years in **cell B6**. Make sure to use an absolute reference for **B14**. Copy the formula down the column, **B7:B11**.

e. Calculate the payment for 15 years in **cell C6**. Remember to use an absolute reference for **B15** and copy the formula down the column, **C7:C11**. If any cell displays a series of #####, use AutoFit to quickly widen the selection.

...continued on Next Page

f. Calculate the difference between 15 years and 30 years and copy the formula down the column, **D7:D11**.

g. Format the worksheet in an attractive manner but similar to Figure 2.26, making sure to display all dollar amounts with the currency symbol and two decimal places. Use a date function to display the current date in **cell A19.**

h. Print the worksheet twice, once with displayed values, and once to show cell formulas. Use the Page Setup command to switch to landscape orientation and force the output onto one page. Print gridlines and row and column headings. Save the changes.

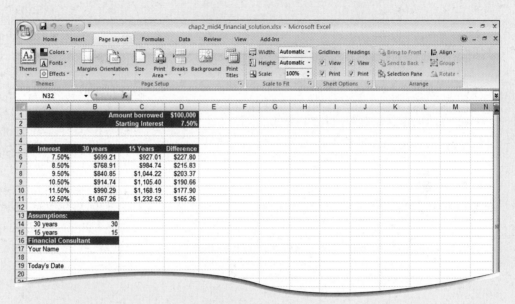

Figure 2.26 Financial Functions

Capstone Exercise

You are an intern at the First National Bank working in the loan department, and your boss has asked you to prepare the monthly "New Loan Report" for the Board of Directors. This analysis report will clearly list and summarize all new loans for residential housing in the past month. The summary area includes the loan statistics as labeled in the data file. The format of the report is appropriate for the Board of Directors for the First National Bank.

Open and Save Worksheet

You must open a worksheet that lists housing sales and finish it to complete the capstone exercise.

a. Open the file *chap2_cap_housing*.

b. Save it as **chap2_cap_housing_solution**.

c. Enter your name in **cell B28**.

Calculate Values

Functions are used to calculate the interest rate, down payment, monthly payment, and average selling price for each residential home in the worksheet. You need to create a formula to determine the down payment. Finish the calculations by using the appropriate functions to complete the Loan Statistics summary area of the worksheet.

a. Use a VLOOKUP function to determine the interest rates in column D.

b. Calculate the down payment by multiplying the results of a VLOOKUP function by the selling price. Enter the formula in column E.

c. Calculate the amount financed by subtracting the down payment from the selling price. Enter the formula in column F.

d. Use a PMT function to determine the monthly payment in column G.

e. Copy all formulas as appropriate.

f. Use an AVERAGE function to calculate the average selling price in **cell B13**.

g. Use appropriate functions to determine the statistics in **cells C22:C26**.

Format the Worksheet

Now that you have finished the calculations, you must format the worksheet in a professional manner and suitable for presentation to the Board of Directors of the bank.

a. Format all money figures as currency with two decimal places. Remember the Loan Statistics summary figures.

b. Format the interest rates in percent style with two decimal places. Format column D and the data table columns used in the VLOOKUP functions as percent with two decimals.

c. Insert an image appropriate for a bank and representative of the housing market.

d. Widen columns to display the headings but wrap the text in columns F and G. Center all column headings.

e. Merge and center the title of the report. Apply dark blue font color to the title and headings.

Print the Report

Before printing the report, you see it is missing the standard headers and should be printed in the landscape orientation to fit on one page.

a. Create a custom header with your name on the left and your instructor's name on the right.

b. Change the page orientation to landscape.

c. Print the worksheet with displayed values.

d. Print the worksheet again with cell formulas but make sure to fit the worksheet on one sheet.

e. Save your changes and close the workbook.

Mini Cases

Use the rubric following the case as a guide to evaluate your work, but keep in mind that your instructor may impose additional grading criteria or use a different standard to judge your work.

Corporate Salary Summary

GENERAL CASE

As a recent graduate and newly hired employee at the JAS Corporation, you are asked to complete the Annual Salary Summary Report. You are to open the *chap2_mc1_salary* workbook, save it as **chap2_mc1_salary_solution**, and complete the worksheet. You will AutoFill the months as headings, and calculate deductions, totals, and net salaries for each month. Format the worksheet for the corporate environment, making sure to use currency, no decimal places, and commas as well as percent symbols with two decimal places. Include your name in the worksheet and print displayed values and cell formulas.

Performance Elements	Exceeds Expectations	Meets Expectations	Below Expectations
Create formulas	All formulas work and most efficiently stated.	Formulas are correct.	No formulas, numbers entered.
Use functions	All functions entered correctly.	One function incorrectly used.	No functions used, numbers entered.
Attractive, appropriate format	Well formatted and easy to read.	Adequately formatted, difficult to read.	No formatting.
Printing	Printed correct range and widened columns for cell formulas.	Printed correct range but did not widen columns.	Printed once (missing formula copy or worksheet copy).

Investment Club

RESEARCH CASE

As treasurer of your investment club, you must update the monthly statement for the members. Open the *chap2_mc2_investment* workbook, save it as **chap2_mc2_investment_solution**, and use the Web to find the current price per share for each of the listed stocks. Complete the worksheet, formatting as appropriate to fit on one sheet. Enter your name as treasurer, the current date as a function formatted as mm/dd/yyyy, and print displayed values as well as cell formulas, making sure to fit on one page.

Performance Elements	Exceeds Expecations	Meets Expectations	Below Expectations
Research current price	All current stock prices found.	Missing two current prices.	No current prices.
Create formulas and functions	All formulas and functions correctly applied.	Two or more formulas and functions incorrectly applied.	No formulas or functions applied.
Format attractively for analysis use	Easy to read and analyze date on single sheet.	Difficult to read; lining up multiple sheets.	Lack of formatting hinders analysis.
Print values and cell formulas on one sheet	Printed correct range and widened columns for cell formulas.	Printed correct range but did not widen columns.	Printed once (missing formula copy or worksheet copy).

Peer Tutoring

DISASTER RECOVERY

As part of your service-learning project, you volunteered to tutor students in Excel. Open the spreadsheet *chap2_mc3_tutoring*, save it as **chap2_mc3_tutoring_solution**, and find five errors. Correct the errors and explain how the errors might have occurred and how they can be prevented. Include your explanation in the cells below the spreadsheet.

Performance Elements	Exceeds Expectations	Meets Expectations	Below Expectations
Identify five errors	Identified all five errors.	Identified four errors.	Identified three or fewer errors.
Correct five errors	Corrected all five errors.	Corrected four errors.	Corrected three or fewer errors.
Explain the error	Complete and correct explanation of each error.	Explanation is too brief to fully explain errors.	No explanations.
Prevention description	Prevention description correct and practical.	Prevention description but obtuse.	No prevention description.

Charts

Delivering a Message

bjectives

After you read this chapter, you will be able to:

1. Choose a chart type (**page 431**).

2. Create a chart (**page 438**).

3. Modify a chart (**page 450**).

4. Enhance charts with graphic shapes (**page 453**).

5. Embed charts (**page 459**).

6. Print charts (**page 460**).

Hands-On Exercises

Exercises	Skills Covered
1. **THE FIRST CHART (page 443)** **Open:** chap3_ho1_sales.xlsx **Save as:** chap3_ho1_sales_solution.xlsx	• Use AutoSum • Create the Chart • Complete the Chart • Move and Size the Chart • Change the Worksheet • Change the Chart Type • Create a Second Chart
2. **MULTIPLE DATA SERIES (page 454)** **Open:** chap3_ho1_sales_solution.xlsx (from Exercise 1) **Save as:** chap3_ho2_sales_solution.xlsx (additional modifications)	• Rename the Worksheet • Create Chart with Multiple Data Series • Copy the Chart • Change the Source Data • Change the Chart Type • Insert a Graphic Shape and Add a Text Box
3. **EMBEDDING, PRINTING, AND SAVING A CHART AS A WEB PAGE (page 462)** **Open:** chap3_ho2_sales_solution.xlsx (from Exercise 2), chap3_ho3_memo.docx **Save as:** chap3_ho3_sales.solution.xlsx (additional modifications), chap_ho3_memo_solution.docx	• Embed a Chart in Microsoft Word • Copy the Worksheet • Embed the Data • Copy the Chart • Embed the Chart • Modify the Worksheet • Update the Links • Print Worksheet and Chart • Save and View Chart as Web Page

CASE STUDY

The Changing Student Population

Congratulations! You have just been hired as a student intern in the Admissions Office. Helen Dwyer, the dean of admissions, has asked you to start tomorrow morning to help her prepare for an upcoming presentation with the Board of Trustees in which she will report on enrollment trends over the past four years. Daytime enrollments have been steady, whereas enrollments in evening and distance (online) learning are increasing significantly. Dean Dwyer has asked for a chart(s) to summarize the data. She also would like your thoughts on what impact (if any) the Internet and the trend toward lifelong learning have had on the college population. The dean has asked you to present the infor-

Case Study

mation in the form of a memo addressed to the Board of Trustees with the data and graph embedded onto that page.

Dean Dwyer will be presenting her findings on "The Changing Student Population" to the Board of Trustees in two weeks. She will speak briefly and then open the floor for questions and discussion among the group. She has invited you to the meeting to answer specific questions pertaining to these trends from a student's perspective. This is an outstanding opportunity for you to participate with a key group of individuals who support the university. Be prepared to present yourself appropriately!

Your Assignment

- Read the chapter carefully and pay close attention to sections that demonstrate chart creation, chart formatting, and chart printing.
- Open the workbook *chap3_case_enrollment*, which has the enrollment statistics partially completed. You will save your workbook as **chap3_case_enrollment_solution**.
- When you review the workbook, think about the mathematical operations, formulas, and functions you would use to complete the worksheet. You will create formulas and functions to calculate annual totals and type of course totals. You also will format cells appropriately: use numbers with commas, merge and center the title, use an attractive fill color, and increase font sizes for improved readability.
- As you read the chapter, pay particular attention to the types of charts that are discussed. Some are more appropriate for presenting enrollment data than others. You will use your understanding of chart methods to determine the most appropriate charts used with the enrollment data. You will create charts to emphasize enrollment data on separate sheets. Remember to format the charts for a professional presentation that includes titles, legends, and data labels.
- As part of your presentation, you also must consider the preparation of a memo describing the enrollment information presented both in the worksheet and in the chart. The worksheet and the charts will be embedded in the final memo. The memo in Microsoft Word will summarize your enrollment data findings and include the embedded worksheet and charts.
- Remember that you will present the information to the university Board of Trustees, and the trustees will expect a professional, polished report. Save the memo as **chap3_case_enrollment_solution** after creating custom footers that include the page number, your name, and your instructor's name. Print the memo, the worksheet, and the charts.

A Picture Is the Message

A **chart** is a graphic representation of data.

A picture really is worth a thousand words. Excel makes it easy to create a **chart**, which is a graphic or visual representation of data. Once data is displayed in a chart, the options to enhance the information for more visual appeal and ease of analysis are almost unlimited. Because large amounts of data are available, using graphical analysis is valuable to discover what messages are hidden in the data.

In this chapter, you learn the importance of determining the message to be conveyed by a chart. You select the type of chart that best presents your message. You create and modify a chart, enhance a chart with a shape, plot multiple sets of data, embed a chart in a worksheet, and create a chart in a separate chart sheet. You enhance a chart by creating lines, objects, and 3-D shapes. The second half of the chapter explains how to create a compound document, in which a chart and its associated worksheet are dynamically linked to a memo created in Word.

Choosing a Chart Type

Managers know that a graphic representation of data is an attractive, clear way to convey information. Business graphics are one of the most exciting Windows applications, where charts (graphs) are created in a straightforward manner from a worksheet with just a few keystrokes or mouse clicks.

In this section, you learn chart terminology and how to choose a chart type based on your needs. For example, you learn when to use a column chart and when to use a pie chart. You select the range of cells containing the numerical values and labels from which to create the chart, choose the chart type, insert the chart, and designate the chart's location.

A **data point** is a numeric value that describes a single item on a chart.

A **data series** is a group of related data points.

A **category label** describes a group of data points in a chart.

A chart is based on numeric values in the cells called **data points**. For example, a data point might be the database sales for Milwaukee. A group of related data points that appear in row(s) or column(s) in the worksheet create a **data series**. For example, a data series might be a collection of database data points for four different cities. In every data series, exactly one data point is connected to a numerical value contained in a cell. Textual information, such as column and row headings (cities, months, years, product names, etc.), are used for descriptive entries called **category labels**.

The worksheet in Figure 3.1 is used throughout the chapter as the basis for the charts you create. As you can see from the worksheet, the company sells different types of software programs, and it has sales in four cities. You believe that the sales numbers are more easily grasped when they are presented graphically instead of only relying on the numbers. You need to develop a series of charts to convey the sales numbers.

	Transylvania Software Sales				
	Milwaukee	Buffalo	Harrisburg	Pittsburgh	Total
Word Processing	$50,000	$67,500	$200,000	$141,000	$458,500
Spreadsheets	$44,000	$18,000	$11,500	$105,000	$178,500
Database	$12,000	$7,500	$6,000	$30,000	$55,500
Total	$106,000	$93,000	$217,500	$276,000	

Figure 3.1 Worksheet for Charts

The sales data in the worksheet can be presented several ways—for example, by city, by product, or by a combination of the two. Determine which type of chart is best suited to answer the following questions:

- What percentage of the total revenue comes from each city? What percentage comes from each product?

- How much revenue is produced by each city? What is the revenue for each product?

- What is the rank of each city with respect to sales?
- How much revenue does each product produce in each city?

> (. . . you cannot create an effective chart unless you are sure of what that message is.)

In every instance, realize that a chart exists only to deliver a message and that *you cannot create an effective chart unless you are sure of what that message is*. The next several pages discuss various types of charts, each of which is best suited to a particular type of message. After you understand how charts are used conceptually, you will create various charts in Excel.

Create Column Charts

A *column chart* displays data comparisons vertically in columns.

The *X or horizontal axis* depicts categorical labels.

The *Y or vertical axis* depicts numerical values.

The *plot area* contains graphical representation of values in data series.

The *chart area* contains the entire chart and all of its elements.

A *column chart* displays data vertically in a column formation and is used to compare values across different categories. Figure 3.2 shows total revenue by geographic area based on the worksheet data from Figure 3.1. The category labels represented by cities stored in cells B3:E3 are shown along the *X or horizontal axis*, whereas the data points representing total monthly sales stored in cells B7:E7 are shown along the *Y or vertical axis*. The height of each column represents the value of the individual data points. The *plot area* of a chart is the area containing the graphical representation of the values in a data series. The *chart area* contains the entire chart and all of its elements.

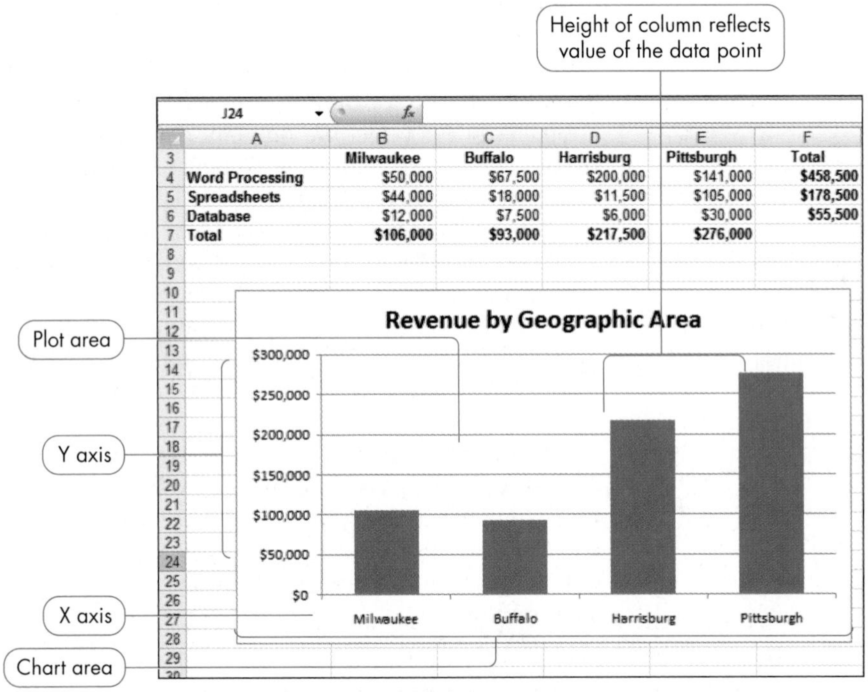

Figure 3.2 Column Chart Depicting Revenue by Geographic Area

Different types of column charts can be created to add interest or clarify the data representation. Figure 3.3 is an example of a three-dimensional (3-D) column chart. The 3-D charts present a more dynamic representation of data, as this chart demonstrates. However, the 3-D column chart is sometimes misleading. Professors often discourage students from using 3-D charts because the charts do not clearly communicate the data—the third dimension distorts data. In 3-D column charts, some columns appear taller than they really are because they are either somewhat behind or at an angle to other columns. See Figure 3.3 for an example of this.

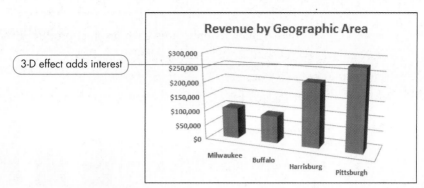

Figure 3.3 Three-Dimensional Column Chart

A ***multiple data series*** compares two or more sets of data in one chart.

Another example of the use of column charts is to compare *multiple data series*—two or more data series—on the same chart. The concept of charting multiple data series will be discussed at some length later in the chapter, but this concept involves the use of clustered column charts.

The choice of clustered versus stacked column charts depends on the intended message. If you want the audience to see the individual sales in each city or product category, the clustered column chart in Figure 3.4 is more appropriate. If, on the other hand, you want to emphasize the total sales for each city or product category, the stacked columns are preferable. The advantage of the stacked column is that the totals are shown clearly and can be compared easily. The disadvantage is that the segments within each column do not start at the same point, making it difficult to determine the actual sales for the individual categories. ***Clustered column charts*** group similar data together in columns making visual comparison of the data easier to determine. ***Stacked column charts*** place similar data in one column with each data series a different color. The effect emphasizes the total of the data series.

A ***clustered column chart*** groups similar data in columns, making visual comparison easier to determine.

A ***stacked column chart*** places (stacks) data in one column with each data series a different color for each category.

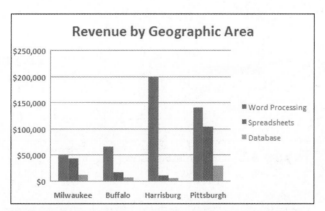

Figure 3.4 Clustered Column Chart

The scale on the Y axis is different for charts with clustered columns versus charts with stacked columns. The clustered columns in Figure 3.4 show the sales of each product category and so the Y axis goes to $250,000. The stacked columns in Figure 3.5 reflect the total sales for all products in each city, and thus the scale goes to $300,000. For a stacked column chart to make sense, its numbers must be additive. You would not convert a column chart that plots units and dollar sales side by side to a stacked column chart, because units and dollars are not additive, that is, you cannot add products and revenue. The chart in Figure 3.5 also displays a legend on the right side of the chart. A *legend* identifies the format or color of the data used for each series in a chart.

A ***legend*** identifies the format or color of each data series.

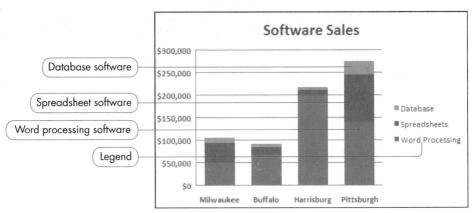

Figure 3.5 Stacked Columns

Column charts are most effective when they are limited to small numbers of categories—generally seven or fewer. If more categories exist, they end up being plotted so close together that reading and labeling become difficult or impossible.

Create a Bar Chart

A ***bar chart*** is a column chart that has been given a horizontal orientation.

A ***bar chart*** is basically a column chart that has a horizontal orientation, as shown in Figure 3.6. Many people prefer this representation because it emphasizes the difference between items. Further, long descriptive labels are easier to read in a bar chart than in a column chart. Sorting the data points either from lowest to highest or highest to lowest makes a bar chart even more effective. The most basic bar chart is a clustered bar chart.

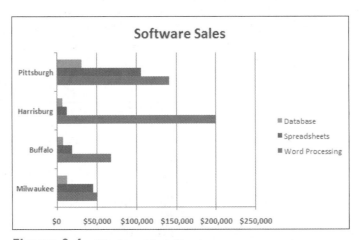

Figure 3.6 Clustered Bar Chart

TIP   Keep It Simple

This rule applies to both your message and the means of conveying that message. Excel makes it easy to change fonts, styles, the shape of columns, type sizes, and colors, but such changes often detract from rather than enhance a chart. More is not necessarily better, and you do not have to use a feature just because it is there. A chart must ultimately succeed based on content alone.

Create a Pie Chart

A ***pie chart*** displays proportional relationships.

A ***pie chart*** is the most effective way to display proportional relationships. It is the type of chart to select whenever words like *percentage* or *market share* appear in the message to be delivered. The pie, or complete circle, denotes the total amount. Each slice of the pie corresponds to its respective percentage of the total.

The pie chart in Figure 3.7 divides the pie representing total sales into four slices, one for each city. The size of each slice is proportional to the percentage of total sales in that city. The chart depicts a single data series, which appears in cells B7:E7 on the associated worksheet. The data series has four data points corresponding to the total sales in each city. The data labels are placed in the wedges if they fit. If they do not fit, they are placed outside the wedge with a line pointing to the appropriate wedge.

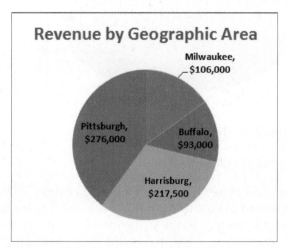

Figure 3.7 Pie Chart Showing Values

To create the pie chart, Excel computes the total sales ($692,000 in our example), calculates the percentage contributed by each city, and draws each slice of the pie in proportion to its computed percentage. Pittsburgh's sales of $276,000 account for 40% of the total, so this slice of the pie is allotted 40% of the area of the circle.

An *exploded pie chart* separates one or more slices of the pie for emphasis.

An *exploded pie chart*, shown in Figure 3.8, separates one or more slices of the pie for emphasis. Another way to achieve emphasis in a chart is to choose a title that reflects the message you are trying to deliver. The title in Figure 3.7, *Revenue by Geographic Area*, is neutral and leaves the reader to develop his or her own conclusion about the relative contribution of each area. In contrast, the title in Figure 3.8, *Buffalo Accounts for Only 13% of the Revenue*, is more suggestive and emphasizes the problems in this office. The title could be changed to *Pittsburgh Exceeds 40% of Total Revenue* if the intent were to emphasize the contribution of Pittsburgh.

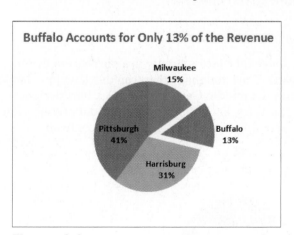

Figure 3.8 Pie Chart Showing Percentages

A *three-dimensional pie chart* is a pie chart that contains a three-dimensional view.

Three-dimensional pie charts may be created in exploded or unexploded format. See Figure 3.9 for an example of an unexploded pie chart. The 3-D chart is misleading because it appears as though the Harrisburg slice is larger than the Pittsburgh slice. This difference is why 3-D charts are seldom used. A pie chart is easiest to read when the number of slices is small (for example, not more than six or seven), and when small categories (percentages less than five) are grouped into a single category called *Other*.

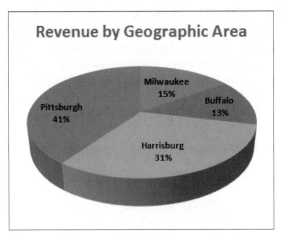

Figure 3.9   Three-Dimensional Pie Chart

Create a Line Chart

A line chart uses a line to connect data points in order to show trends over a long period of time.

A *line chart* shows trends over a period of time. A line connects data points. A line chart is used frequently to show stock market or economic trends. The X axis represents time, such as ten-year increments, whereas the vertical axis represents the value of a stock or quantity. The line chart enables a user to easily spot trends in the data. Figure 3.10 shows a line chart with yearly increments for four years.

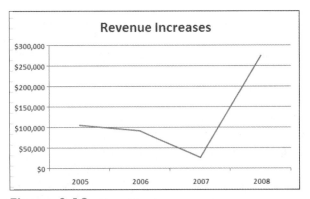

Figure 3.10   Line Chart

Create Other Chart Types

A doughnut chart displays values as percentages of the whole.

The *doughnut chart* is similar to a pie chart in that it shows relationship of parts to a whole, but the doughnut chart can display more than one series of data, and it has a hole in the middle (see Figure 3.11). Chart designers sometimes use the doughnut hole for titles. Each ring represents a data series. Note, however, the display of the data series in a doughnut chart can be confusing.

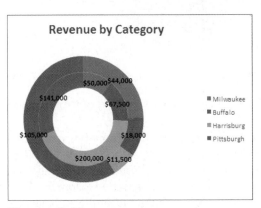

Figure 3.11   Doughnut Chart

A *scatter (XY) chart* shows a relationship between two variables.

A *scatter (XY) chart* shows a relationship between two variables. Scatter charts are used to represent the data from scientific or educational experiments that demonstrate relationships. A scatter chart is essentially the plotted dots without any connecting line. A scatter chart is used to determine if a relationship exists between two different sets of numerical data. If you plot people's wages and educational levels, you can see if a relationship between wages and education levels exists. Figure 3.12 shows a comparison of temperature over time. As the month of April passes, the temperatures rise. However, higher- and lower-than-normal temperatures affect the trend.

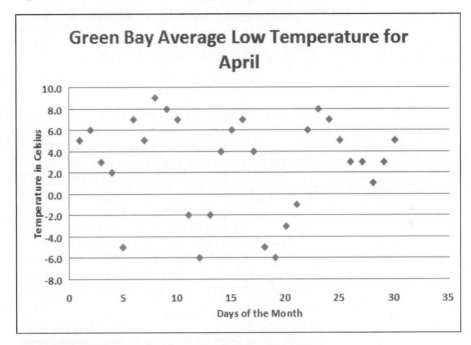

Figure 3.12 Scatter Chart

A *stock chart* shows the high, low, and close prices for individual stocks over a period of time.

Stock charts have only one major purpose: to show the high, low, and close prices for individual stocks over a period of time. While stock charts may have some other uses, such as showing a range of temperatures over a period of time, they usually are used to show stock prices. Figure 3.13 shows a stock chart that displays opening stock price, high stock price, low stock price, and closing stock price over time.

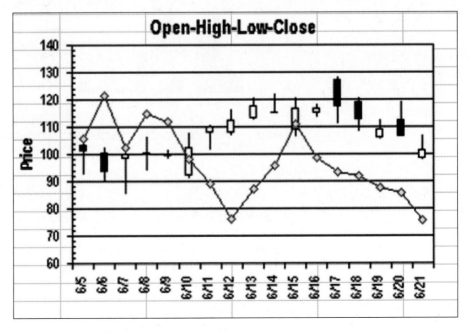

Figure 3.13 Stock Chart

Creating a Chart

Creating a chart in Excel is quick. Excel provides a variety of chart types that you can use when you create a chart. The main types of charts are described above. The six main steps to create a chart are the following:

1. Specify the data series.
2. Select the range of cells to chart.
3. Select the chart type.
4. Insert the chart and designate the chart location.
5. Choose chart options.
6. Change the chart location and size.

Specify the Data Series

For most charts, such as column and bar charts, you can plot the data in a chart that you have arranged in rows or columns on a worksheet. Some chart types, however, such as a pie chart, require a specific data arrangement. On the worksheet, arrange the data that you want to plot in a chart for the type of chart you will select.

The charts presented so far in the chapter displayed only a single data series, such as the total sales by location or the total sales by product category. Although such charts are useful, it is often more informative to view multiple data series, which are ranges of data values plotted as a unit in the same chart. Figure 3.14 displays the worksheet we have been using throughout the chapter. Figure 3.4 displays a clustered column chart that plots multiple data series that exist as rows (cells B4:E4, B5:E5, and B6:E6) within the worksheet. Figure 3.14 displays a chart based on the same data when the series are in columns (cells B4:B6, C4:C6, D4:D6, and E4:E6).

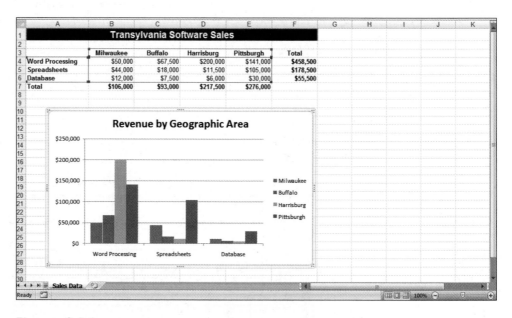

Figure 3.14 Clustered Column with Multiple Data Series as Columns

Both charts plot a total of 12 data points (three product categories for each of four locations), but they group the data differently. Figure 3.4 displays the data by city in which the sales of three product categories are shown for each of four cities. Figure 3.14 is the reverse and groups the data by product category. This time, the sales in the four cities are shown for each of three product categories. The choice between the two charts depends on your message and whether you want to emphasize revenue by city or by product category. You should create the chart according to your intended purpose.

Figure 3.15 shows two charts. The one on the left plots data series in the cells B4:E4, B5:E5, and B6:E6, whereas the chart on the right plots the same data series but

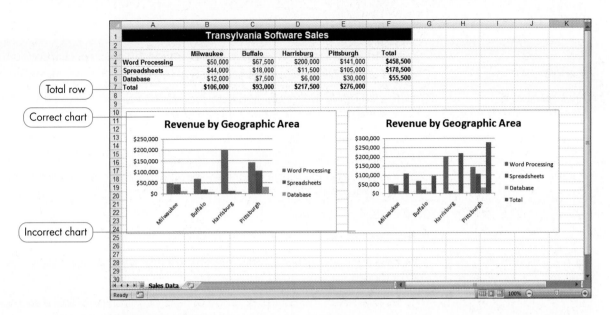

Figure 3.15

includes B7:E7, which is the total for all products. Including the total row figures (or column total figures) dramatically skews the chart, presents a misleading picture, and indicates you have selected an incorrect range for your chart. Do NOT include totals and individual data points on the same chart.

Select the Range to Chart

Too often Excel users do not put any thought into the data they select for a chart. Selecting the correct data goes hand-in-hand with having a plan for what a chart should display. For example, a user would not want to show totals in column totals that represent only several months. Even though it is a simple process to deselect cells once they have been selected, users should have a plan before selecting cells for a chart.

Table 3.1 describes different techniques for selecting cells.

Select the Chart Type

After you select the range of cells that you want to chart, your next step is to select the type of chart you want to create. Each type of chart is designed to visually illustrate a particular type of data. Table 3.2 lists the different types of charts and their purposes. Use this table as a guide for selecting the type of chart you want to use for the worksheet data.

In the Charts group on the Insert tab, do one of the following:

1. Click the chart type, and then click a chart subtype that you want to use.

2. To see all available chart types, click a chart type, and then click All Chart Types to display the Create Chart dialog box.

3. Click the arrows to scroll through all available chart types and chart subtypes, and then click the one that you want to use.

Insert the Chart and Designate the Chart Location

Excel places the chart as an embedded object on the current worksheet. You can leave the chart on the same worksheet as the worksheet data used to create the chart, or you can place the chart in a separate chart sheet. If you leave the chart in the same worksheet, you can print the worksheet and chart on the same page. If you want to print a full-sized chart, you can move the chart to its own chart sheet.

Table 3.1 Cell Selection Techniques

To Select	Do This
A single cell	Click the cell, or press the arrow keys to move to the cell.
A range of cells	Click the first cell in the range, and then drag to the last cell, or hold down Shift while you press the arrow keys to extend the selection. You also can select the first cell in the range, and then press F8 to extend the selection by using the arrow keys. To stop extending the selection, press F8 again.
A large range of cells	Click the first cell in the range, and then hold down Shift while you click the last cell in the range. You can scroll to make the last cell visible.
All cells on a worksheet	Click the Select All button. To select the entire worksheet, you also can press Ctrl+A.
Nonadjacent cells or cell ranges	Select the first cell or range of cells, and then hold down Ctrl while you select the other cells or ranges. You also can select the first cell or range of cells, and then press Shift+F8 to add another nonadjacent cell or range to the selection. To stop adding cells or ranges to the selection, press Shift+F8 again.
An entire row or column	Click the row or column heading. You also can select cells in a row or column by selecting the first cell and then pressing Ctrl+Shift+Arrow key (Right Arrow or Left Arrow for rows, Up Arrow or Down Arrow for columns).
Adjacent rows or columns	Drag across the row or column headings. Or select the first row or column, then hold down Shift while you select the last row or column.
Noncontiguous rows or columns	Click the column or row heading of the first row or column in your selection, then hold down Ctrl while you click the column or row headings of other rows or columns that you want to add to the selection.

Table 3.2 Chart Types and Purposes

Chart Type	Purpose
Column	Compares categories, shows changes over time.
Bar	Shows comparison between independent variables. Not used for time or dates.
Pie	Shows percentages of a whole. Exploded pie emphasizes a popular category.
Line	Shows change in a series over categories or time.
Doughnut	Compares how two or more series contribute to the whole.
Scatter	Shows correlation between two sets of values.
Stock	Shows high-low stock prices.

To change the location of a chart:

1. Click the embedded chart or the chart sheet to select it and to display the chart tools.
2. Click Move Chart in the Location group on the Design tab.
3. In the *Choose where you want the chart to be placed* section, do one of the following:
   - Click *New sheet* to display the chart in its own chart sheet.
   - Click *Object in*, click the drop-down arrow, and select a worksheet to move the chart to another worksheet.

Choose Chart Options

When you create a chart, the Chart Tools contextual tab is available. The Design, Layout, and Format tabs are displayed in Chart Tools. You can use the commands on these tabs to modify the chart. For example, use the Design tab to display the data series by row or by column, make changes to the source data of the chart, change the location of the chart, change the chart type, save a chart as a template, or select predefined layout and formatting options. Use the Layout tab to change the display of chart elements such as chart titles and data labels, use drawing tools, or add text boxes and pictures to the chart. Use the Format tab to add fill colors, change line styles, or apply special effects. Review the Reference Page for examples of the contextual chart tools tab with the Design, Layout, and Design tabs depicted.

Chart Tools | Reference

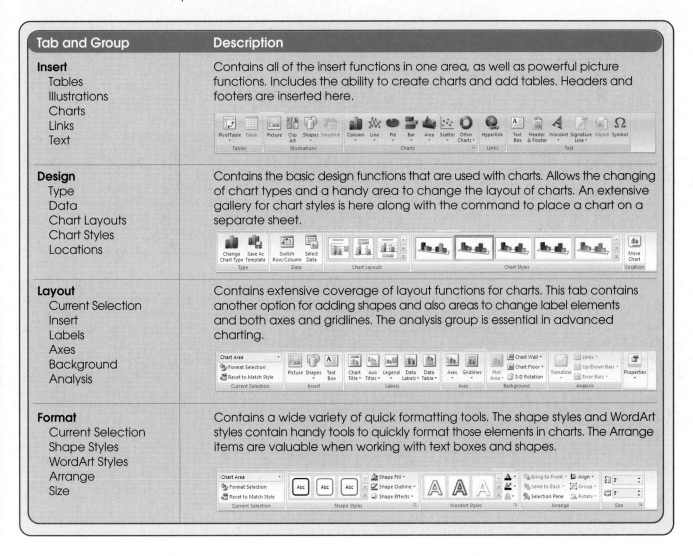

Tab and Group	Description
Insert Tables Illustrations Charts Links Text	Contains all of the insert functions in one area, as well as powerful picture functions. Includes the ability to create charts and add tables. Headers and footers are inserted here.
Design Type Data Chart Layouts Chart Styles Locations	Contains the basic design functions that are used with charts. Allows the changing of chart types and a handy area to change the layout of charts. An extensive gallery for chart styles is here along with the command to place a chart on a separate sheet.
Layout Current Selection Insert Labels Axes Background Analysis	Contains extensive coverage of layout functions for charts. This tab contains another option for adding shapes and also areas to change label elements and both axes and gridlines. The analysis group is essential in advanced charting.
Format Current Selection Shape Styles WordArt Styles Arrange Size	Contains a wide variety of quick formatting tools. The shape styles and WordArt styles contain handy tools to quickly format those elements in charts. The Arrange items are valuable when working with text boxes and shapes.

Add Graphics in Charts

You may want to add graphics, such as company logos or representative clip art, to charts to personalize the charts or make them more distinctive. In either case the procedure is simple. Again, this is a case where less is sometimes more. Be sparing in the use of graphics that can change the message being conveyed.

To add a graphic to a chart:

1. In the Illustrations section on the Insert tab, select the medium where the graphic will come from (Picture, Clip Art, or Smart Art).
2. Search for and insert the graphic.
3. Size and move the graphic on the chart as desired.

TIP   Set a Time Limit

You can customize virtually every aspect of every object within a chart. That is the good news. It is also bad news because you can spend inordinate amounts of time for little or no gain. It is fun to experiment, but set a time limit and stop when you reach the allocated time. The default settings are often adequate to convey your message, and further experimentation might prove counterproductive.

Change the Chart Location and Size

Whether the chart is embedded on the worksheet with the data or on a separate sheet, at times you will need to move a chart or to change its size. To move a chart on any sheet, click the chart to select it. When the pointer appears as a four-headed arrow while on the margin of the chart, click and drag the chart to another location on the sheet.

To change the size of a chart, select the chart. Sizing handles are located in the corners of the chart and at the middle of the edge borders. Clicking and dragging the middle left or right sizing handle of the edge borders adjusts the width of the chart. Drag the sizing handle away from the chart to stretch or widen the chart; drag the sizing handle within the chart to decrease the width of the chart. Clicking and dragging the top or bottom middle sizing handle adjusts the height of the chart. Drag the sizing handle away from the chart to increase its height; drag the sizing handle into the chart to decrease its height. Clicking and dragging a corner sizing handle increases or decreases the height and width of the chart proportionately.

Hands-On Exercises

1 | The First Chart

Skills covered: 1. Use AutoSum **2.** Create the Chart **3.** Complete the Chart **4.** Move and Size the Chart **5.** Change the Worksheet **6.** Change the Chart Type **7.** Create a Second Chart

Step 1
Use AutoSum

Use Figure 3.16 as a guide as you work through the steps in the exercise.

a. Start Excel. Open the *chap3_ho1_sales* workbook and save it as **chap3_ho1_sales_ solution**.

b. Click and drag to select **cells B7:E7** (the cells that will contain the total sales for each location). Click **AutoSum** in the Editing group on the Home tab to compute the total for each city.

c. Click and drag to select **cells F4:F6**, and then click **AutoSum**.

The SUM function is entered automatically into these cells to total the entries to the left of the selected cells.

d. Click and drag to select **cells B4:F7** and format these cells with the currency symbol and no decimal places.

e. Bold the row and column headings and the totals. Center the entries in **cells B3:F3**.

f. Save the workbook.

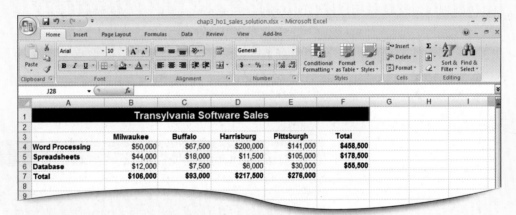

Figure 3.16 Formatted Worksheet with Totals

Step 2
Create the Chart

Refer to Figure 3.17 as you complete Step 2. Note that the colors displayed in figures may not match your screen display.

a. Select **cells B3:E3** to select the category labels (the names of the cities). Press and hold **Ctrl** as you drag the mouse over **cells B7:E7** to select the data series (the cells containing the total sales for the individual cities).

You have selected the cities that will become the X axis in your chart. You selected B7 through E7 as the values that will become the data series.

b. Check that **cells B3:E3** and **cells B7:E7** are selected. Click the **Insert tab** and click **Column** in the Chart group.

You should see the Column Chart palette, as shown in Figure 3.17. When the Column chart type and Clustered column subtype are selected, the chart appears on Sheet1. Note that your default colors may differ from those displayed in your textbook.

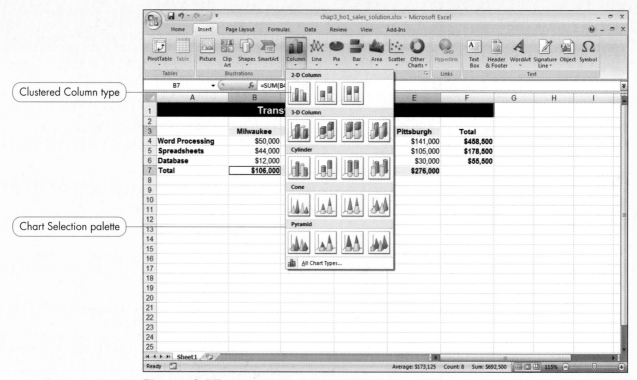

Clustered Column type

Chart Selection palette

Figure 3.17 Gallery of Chart Types

TROUBLESHOOTING: If you select too little or too much data for charting purposes, you can change your data ranges. Make the Design tab active, then click Edit Data Source to open the Edit Data Source dialog box. Click Edit and select the correct data range.

c. Click **Clustered Column** in the *2-D Column* section to insert a chart.

As you move the mouse over the palette, a ScreenTip appears that indicates the name of the chart type.

TIP | The F11 Key

The F11 key is the fastest way to create a chart in its own sheet. Select the worksheet data, including the legends and category labels, and then press F11 to create the chart. The chart displays according to the default format built into the Excel column chart. After you create the chart, you can use the Chart Tools tabs, Mini toolbars, or shortcut menus to choose a different chart type and customize the formatting.

Step 3
Complete the Chart

Refer to Figure 3.18 as you complete Step 3.

a. Click the chart object to make the chart active. Click the **Layout tab**, click **Chart Title** in the Labels group, and then click **Above Chart** to create a title for the chart.

You selected the chart, and then selected the placement of the chart title using the Chart Tools tabs.

b. Type **Revenue by Geographic Area** for the title and press **Enter**.

c. Click **Legend** in the Labels group of the Layout tab and select **None** to delete the legend.

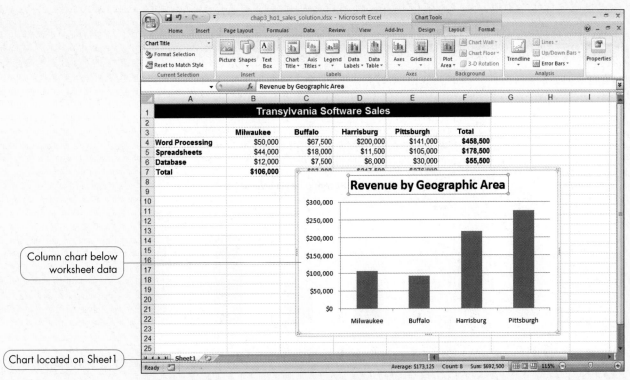

Figure 3.18 Column Chart with Title

Column chart below worksheet data

Chart located on Sheet1

Step 4
Move and Size the Chart

Refer to Figure 3.19 as you complete Step 4.

a. Move and size the chart just as you would any other Windows object.

You should see the completed chart in Figure 3.19. When you click the chart, the sizing handles indicate the chart is selected and will be affected by subsequent commands.

1. Click the chart border to select the chart, then click on the highlighted outline of the chart and drag (the mouse pointer changes to a four-sided arrow) to move the chart so that the top left side of the chart starts in **cell A9**.

2. Drag a corner handle (the mouse pointer changes to a double arrow) to change the length and width of the chart simultaneously so that the chart covers the **range A9:G29**.

b. Click outside the chart to deselect it. The sizing handle is no longer visible.

When working with any graphic object in Excel, you can resize it by making it active and dragging sizing handles that appear at the corners and on the perimeter of the object.

c. Save the workbook.

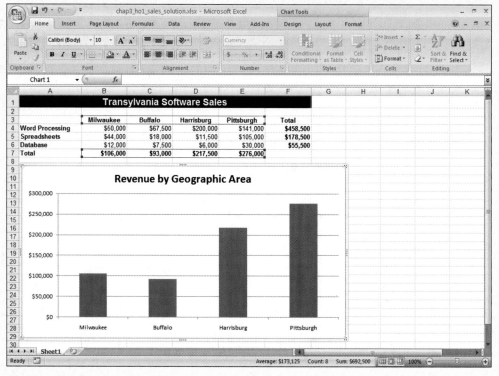

Figure 3.19 Chart Size and Location Changed

TIP Embedded Charts

An embedded chart is treated as an object that can be moved, sized, copied, or deleted just as any other Windows object. To move an embedded chart, click the border of the chart to select the chart and drag it to a new location in the worksheet. To size the chart, select it and then drag any of the eight sizing handles in the desired direction. To delete the chart, select it and press Delete. To copy the chart, select it, click Copy in the Clipboard group on the Home tab to copy the chart to the clipboard, click elsewhere in the workbook where you want the copied chart to go, and click Paste.

Step 5
Change the Worksheet

Refer to Figure 3.20 as you complete Step 5.

a. Click in **cell B4**. Change the entry to **$225,000** and press **Enter**.

Any changes in a worksheet are automatically reflected in the associated chart. The total sales for Milwaukee in cell B7 change automatically to reflect the increased sales for word processing. The column for Milwaukee also changes in the chart and is now larger than the column for Pittsburgh.

b. Click in **cell B3**. Change the entry to **Chicago** and press **Enter**.

The category label on the X axis changes automatically to reflect the new city name (see Figure 3.20).

c. Click **Undo** twice on the Quick Access Toolbar.

You changed the worksheet and chart back to Milwaukee and $50,000 by clicking Undo twice. The worksheet and chart are restored to their earlier values.

d. Save the workbook.

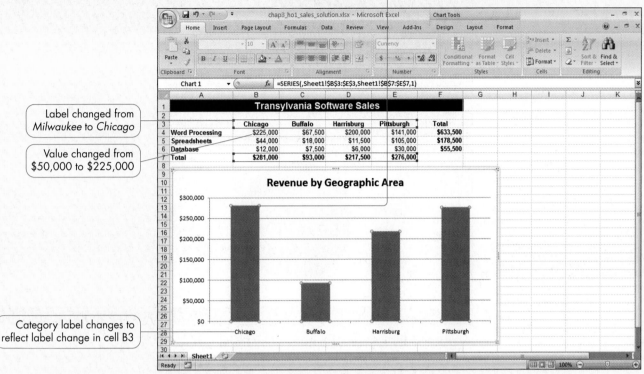

Figure 3.20 Temporary Data Changes Affect Chart

Annotations on figure:

Column height increases to reflect new total in cell B7 based on value change in cell B4

Label changed from *Milwaukee* to *Chicago*

Value changed from $50,000 to $225,000

Category label changes to reflect label change in cell B3

Step 6	Refer to Figure 3.21 as you complete Step 6.
Change the Chart Type	

a. Click the chart border area to select the chart, click **Change Chart Type** in the Type group on the Design tab, click the **Pie** type, and then click **Pie** (the first button in the Pie row). Click **OK**, and the chart changes to a pie chart.

You used the Design tab to change the type of chart. The following steps will guide you through adding data labels to the chart area, and formatting those data labels as percentages.

b. Point to any pie wedge, click the right mouse button to display a shortcut menu, and click **Add Data Labels**.

c. Right-click the mouse button on any pie wedge to display a shortcut menu and select **Format Data Labels** to display the Format Data Labels dialog box. Make sure **Label Options** in the left column is selected, and then click the **Category Name** and **Percentage** check boxes to format the data labels. Remove the checks from the **Value** and **Show Leader Lines** check boxes.

d. Change the values in the data labels to percentages by clicking **Number** below *Label Options* on the left side of the dialog box, click **Percentage** in *Category* list, type **0** in the **Decimal places** box, and click **Close** to accept the settings and close the dialog box.

The pie chart now displays data labels as percentages. The Number format is the default when initially inserting data labels.

e. Modify each component as necessary:

1. Click the plot area to select the chart. Click and drag the sizing handles to increase the size of the plot area within the embedded chart.

2. Click a label to select all data labels. Click the **Home tab**, click the **Font Size down arrow** in the Font group, and select **12**.

f. Save the workbook.

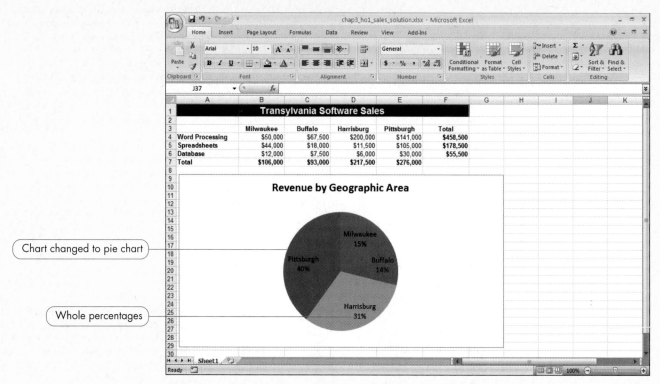

Figure 3.21 Chart Changed to Pie Chart

Labels on figure:
- Chart changed to pie chart
- Whole percentages

Step 7

Create a Second Chart

Refer to Figure 3.22 as you complete Step 7.

a. Click and drag to select **cells A4:A6** in the worksheet. Press and hold **Ctrl** as you drag the mouse to select **cells F4:F6**.

b. Click the **Insert tab**, click **Column** in the Chart group, and select **3-D Clustered Column**.

When the Column chart type and 3-D Clustered Column subtype are selected, the chart appears on Sheet1. The values (the data being plotted) are in cells F4:F6. The category labels for the X axis are in cells A4:A6.

c. Click **Chart Title** in the Labels group on the Layout tab and select **Centered Overlay Title.**

d. Type **Revenue by Product Category** for the title. Click **Legend** in the Labels group on the Layout tab and select **None** to delete the legend.

You have created a title for your 3-D clustered column chart. You deleted the legend because you have only one data series.

e. Click the **Design tab** and click **Move Chart** in the Location group. Click **New sheet**, and then click **OK** to display the chart on a new sheet and close the Move Chart dialog box.

The 3-D column chart has been created in the chart sheet labeled Chart1, as shown in Figure 3.22.

f. Save the workbook. Exit Excel if you do not want to continue with the next exercise at this time.

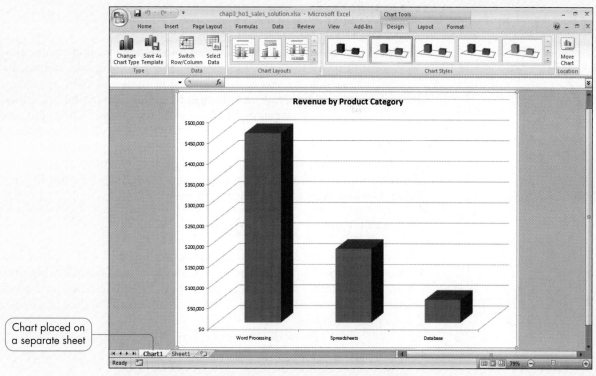

Chart placed on a separate sheet

Figure 3.22 Chart Moved to Chart1 Sheet

Chart Enhancements

Now that you already have created a chart by selecting the appropriate values and labels, you must improve the appearance of the chart. Adding and editing chart elements enhance the information value of a chart. For example, you can draw attention to a specific bar using an arrow shape that includes an appropriate text phrase. Charts are used to express information visually, and subtle visual enhancements improve comprehension while presenting a more powerful message.

> Charts are used to express information visually, and subtle visual enhancements improve comprehension while presenting a more powerful message.

In this section, you modify a chart. Specifically, you change and edit chart elements, format a chart, add data labels, and change the fill color for chart elements. Then you enhance charts by adding shapes.

Modifying a Chart

You can modify any chart element to enhance the chart and improve its appearance. Some of the most common chart modifications include the following properties: size, color, font, format, scale, or style just by selecting the element and choosing from a variety of options. Mini toolbars and shortcut menus appear as needed for you to make your selections.

TIP   Anatomy of a Chart

A chart is composed of multiple components (objects), each of which can be selected and changed separately. Point to any part of a chart to display a ScreenTip indicating the name of the component, then click the mouse to select that component and display the sizing handles. You can then click and drag the object within the chart and/or right-click the mouse to display a Mini toolbar and shortcut menu with commands pertaining to the selected object.

Change and Edit Chart Elements

It is often necessary to change chart elements such as titles and axes. For example, you might need to change the title of the chart or adjust the font size of the title to balance the title text and the chart size. You can change these elements to reflect different words or edit the elements to reflect formatting changes.

On a chart, do one of the following:

- To edit the contents of a title, click the chart or axis title that you want to change.
- To edit the contents of a data label, click twice on the data label that you want to change.
- Click again to place the title or data label in editing mode, drag to select the text that you want to change, type the new text or value, and then press Enter.

To format the text, select it, and then click the formatting options that you want on the Mini toolbar. You can also use the formatting buttons in the Font group on the Home tab. To format the entire title or data label, right-click the selected text, select Format Chart Title, Format Axis Title, or Format Data Labels on the shortcut menu, and then select the formatting options that you want.

Format a Chart

The options for formatting a chart may be approached in two ways, either by using the tabs or by selecting the chart and then right-clicking and using the various format commands on the shortcut menu. Table 3.3 shows the different tabs and the formatting capabilities available with each. Figures 3.23 through 3.26 show these tabs as defined in Table 3.3.

Table 3.3 Tab and Format Features

Tab	Format Features
Insert	Insert shapes, insert illustrations, create and edit WordArt and textboxes, insert symbols.
Design	Change chart type, edit the data sources, change the chart style and layout, and change the location of the chart.
Layout	Again allows the insertion of shapes, graphics, and text boxes. Add or change chart title, axis title, legend, data labels, and data table. Format axis and change the background.
Format	Deals with more sophisticated control of WordArt, shapes, and arrangement.

Figure 3.23 Insert Tab

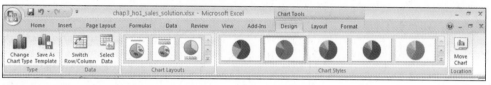

Figure 3.24 Design Tab

Figure 3.25 Layout Tab

Figure 3.26 Format Tab

Add Data Labels

A ***data label*** is the value or name of a data point.

One of the features of Excel charting that does much to enhance charts is the use of ***data labels***, which are the value or name of a data point. The exact values of data shown by charts are not always clear, particularly in 3-D charts, as well as scatter charts and some line charts. It assists the readers of your charts if you label the data points with text and their values. These labels amplify the data represented in the chart by providing their numerical values on the chart. To add data labels to a chart:

1. Select the chart that will have data labels added.

2. Click on the Data Labels list in the Labels group on the Layout tab.

3. Select the location for the data labels on the chart.

Change the Fill Color for Chart Elements

Another component you can change is the color or fill pattern of any element in the chart. Colors are used to accentuate data presented in chart form. Colors also are used to underplay data presented in chart form. Charts often are used in Microsoft PowerPoint for presentation, so you must pay attention to contrast and use appropriate colors for large screen display. Remember also that color blindness and other visual impairments can change how charts are viewed. To change the color of a data series in a column chart:

1. Right-click on any column to open the shortcut menu.
2. Select Format Data Series.
3. Select Fill from the Series Options and select a color from the Color list.
4. Click Close.

To change the color of the plot area, right-click on the plot area to open the shortcut menu and select Format Plot area. Repeat Steps 3 and 4 above.

Another unique feature you can use to enhance a chart and make the data more meaningful is to use an image in the data series. See Figure 3.27 for an example of a chart using an image of an apple to represent bushels of apples. To use an image as a data series, select the data series, click the Shape Fill down arrow in the Shape Styles group on the Format tab, and select Picture. From the Insert Picture dialog box, select the image and click Insert.

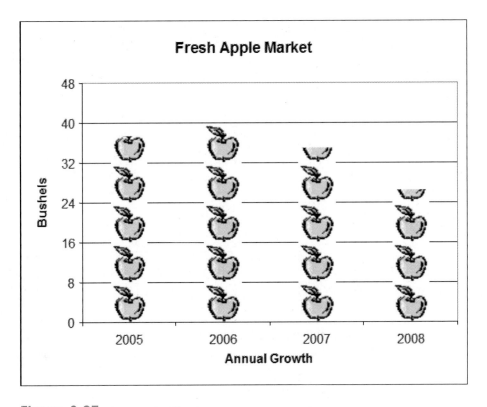

Figure 3.27 Images in Charts

TIP   Quick Layout

Excel enables you to instantly change the look of a chart. After creating a chart, quickly apply a predefined layout to the chart. Choose from a variety of useful predefined layouts and then manually customize the layout of individual chart elements if desired. Select the chart before formatting. This action displays Chart Tools tab, adding the Design, Layout, and Format tabs. On the Design tab, in the Quick Layout group, click the chart layout that you want to use. To see all available layouts, click More.

TIP   Shape Fill

As an alternative to right-clicking a chart element to change a fill color, you can select the specific chart element, such as one data series and click the Shape Fill down arrow in the Shape Styles group on the Format tab. You can choose specific colors, such as **Red, Accent 2, Lighter 60%** in the *Theme Colors* section, or you can select a regular color from the *Standard Colors* section.

Enhancing Charts with Graphic Shapes

Using shapes is a technique that lets you add pre-made graphics to a chart to emphasize the content of a part of a chart. Ready-made shapes come in forms such as rectangles, circles, arrows, lines, flowchart symbols, and callouts. Words also can be placed in shapes using text boxes.

Shapes can be inserted either from the Insert tab or from the Layout tab. You want to experiment with both techniques and decide which you prefer. To insert a shape using the Layout tab:

1. Click the Shapes pull-down menu on the Layout tab.

2. Click on the shape you want to insert.

3. Place the crosshair pointer over the location on the chart where the graphic is to be located and drag the pointer to place the shape. To constrain the drawing element to the proportion illustrated in the shapes palette, hold Shift while you drag the pointer to place the shape.

4. Release the mouse button.

5. To resize a shape, select the shape and use one of the nine selection handles to change its size.

6. Rotate the graphic by clicking the green rotation handle and dragging to rotate the shape.

7. Change the shape of the graphic by clicking the yellow diamond tool and dragging.

Hands-On Exercises

2 | Multiple Data Series

Skills covered: 1. Rename the Worksheet **2.** Create Chart with Multiple Data Series **3.** Copy the Chart **4.** Change the Source Data **5.** Change the Chart Type **6.** Insert a Graphic Shape and Add a Text Box

---

Step 1
Rename the Worksheet

Refer to Figure 3.28 as you complete Step 1.

a. Open the *chap3_ho1_sales_solution* workbook if you closed it at the end of the previous exercise. Save the workbook as **chap3_ho2_sales_solution**.

b. Point to the workbook tab labeled Sheet1, right-click the mouse to display a shortcut menu, and then click **Rename**.

The name of the worksheet (Sheet1) is selected.

c. Type **Sales Data** to change the name of the worksheet to the more descriptive name. Press **Enter**. Right-click the worksheet tab a second time, select **Tab Color**, then change the color to the **Blue, Accent 1** theme shade. Click **OK**.

You renamed the worksheet and will now change the color of the sheet tab.

d. Change the name of the Chart1 sheet to **Column Chart**. Change the tab color to the **Red, Accent 2** theme shade. Save the workbook.

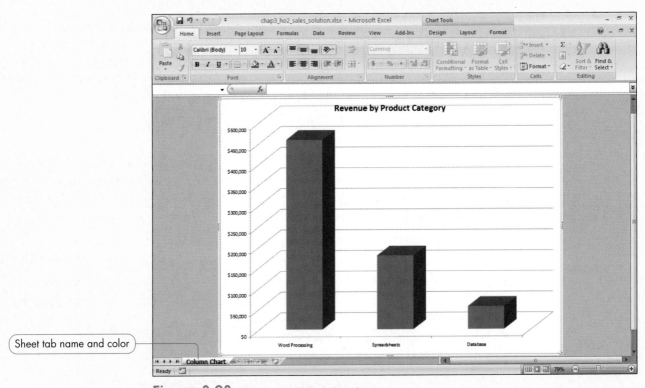

Figure 3.28 Renamed Worksheet

Refer to Figure 3.29 as you complete Step 2.

a. Click the **Sales Data tab**, then click and drag to select **cells A3:E6**.

b. Click the **Insert tab**, click the **Column** list in the Chart group, and select **Clustered Column** as the subtype from the gallery of column chart types.

This type of chart is best for displaying multiple data series.

c. Click **Chart Title** in the Labels group on the Layout tab and select **Above Chart** to create a title for the chart.

d. Type **Revenue by City** for the chart title and press **Enter**.

Using appropriate chart titles is essential as no chart should appear without a title. Viewers of your chart need to be able to quickly identify the subject of the chart.

e. Click **Move Chart** in the Location group on the Design tab. Click **New sheet**, and then click **OK**.

You have moved the chart from the Sales Data sheet to a new chart sheet.

f. Change the name of the Chart2 sheet to **Revenue by City**. Your sheet name for the chart may differ. Change the tab color to theme shade **Orange, Accent 6**. Save the workbook.

After changing both the tab name and tab color, your chart should be similar to Figure 3.29.

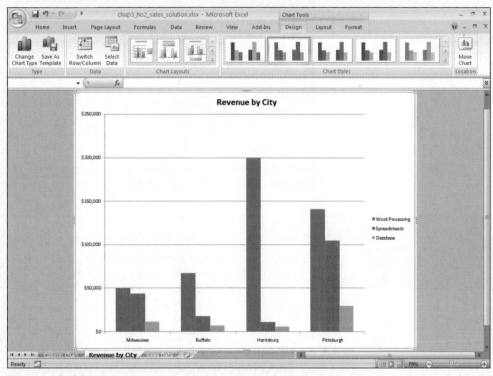

Figure 3.29 Multiple Data Series

Refer to Figure 3.30 as you complete Step 3.

a. Click anywhere in the chart title to select the title. Click the **Font Size** list box on the Home tab and change to **24-point** type to enlarge the title.

You changed the font size of the title to make it easier to read.

b. Point to the worksheet tab named **Revenue by City** and click to select it if it is not already selected. Then click **Format** in the Cells group of the Home tab. Click **Move or Copy sheet** to display the dialog box shown in Figure 3.30.

c. Click **Sales Data** in the Before Sheet list box. Check the box to **Create a copy**. Click **OK**.

d. A duplicate worksheet called Chart 4 (your sheet tab name may vary) is created and appears before or to the left of the Sales Data worksheet.

You have now created a copy of the original chart and can enhance it without having to replot the data.

TROUBLESHOOTING: The appearance of the Chart Tools tabs will change depending on the type of chart created and the location of the chart.

e. Double-click the newly created worksheet tab to select the name. Type **Revenue by Product** as the new name and save the workbook.

Figure 3.30 Move or Copy Dialog Box

Step 4

Change the Source Data

Refer to Figure 3.31 as you complete Step 4.

a. Click the **Revenue by Product tab** to make it the active sheet if it is not already active. Click anywhere in the title of the chart, select the word *City*, and then type **Product Category** to replace the selected text. Click outside the title to deselect it.

You edited the title of the chart to reflect the new data source.

b. Click the **Design tab** and click **Select Data** in the Data group to display the Select Data Source dialog box, as shown in Figure 3.31.

c. Click the **Switch Row/Column button**. Click **OK** to close the Select Data Source dialog box.

Your original chart plotted the data in rows. The chart originally contained three data series, one series for each product. Your new chart plots the data in columns. The chart contains four data series, one for each city.

d. Save the workbook.

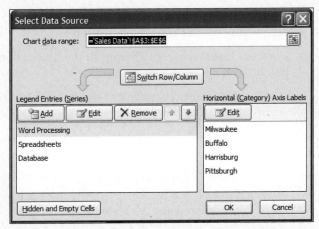

Figure 3.31 Edit Data Source Dialog Box

Step 5
Change the Chart Type

Refer to Figure 3.32 as you complete Step 5.

a. Click the chart border area to select the chart, click **Change Chart Type** in the Type group on the Design tab, and click the **Stacked Column** (the second from the left in the top row of the column chart gallery). Click **OK**.

The chart changes to a stacked column chart.

b. Right-click the legend and select 14 points font size from the Mini toolbar.

You increased the font size of the legend to make it more readable. Your chart should be similar to Figure 3.32.

c. Save the workbook.

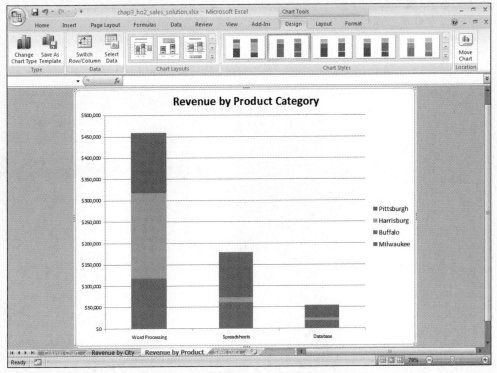

Figure 3.32 Stacked Column Chart

Refer to Figure 3.33 as you complete Step 6.

a. Click the **Insert tab**, click **Shapes** in the Illustrations group to view the Shapes palette, and click the **Left Arrow**.

The mouse pointer changes to a thin crosshair that you will drag to "draw" the arrow shape. The crosshair appears when you click in the chart.

b. Click and drag to create a thick arrow that points to the Word Processing column. Release the mouse. The arrow is selected, and you are viewing the **Format** tab.

c. Click **Text Box** in the Insert Shapes group on the Format tab to insert a text box. Click and drag a text box on top of the thick arrow. Release the mouse. Type **Word Processing Leads All Categories.**

You can use shapes to draw attention to significant trends or changes in date. The text in the shape describes the trend or change.

d. Select the text you just typed, then right-click to display a shortcut menu and Mini toolbar. Use the Mini toolbar to change the font to **12-point** bold white.

TROUBLESHOOTING: Should you have difficulty selecting the text box, right-click on the text itself to reshow the shortcut menu and Mini toolbar.

e. Click the title of the chart and you will see sizing handles around the title to indicate it has been selected. Click the **Font Size down arrow** on the Home tab. Click **24** to increase the size of the title. Your chart will be similar to Figure 3.33.

Increasing the size of the title enables your viewers to quickly see the subject of the chart.

f. Save the workbook, but do not print it. Exit Excel if you do not want to continue with the next exercise at this time.

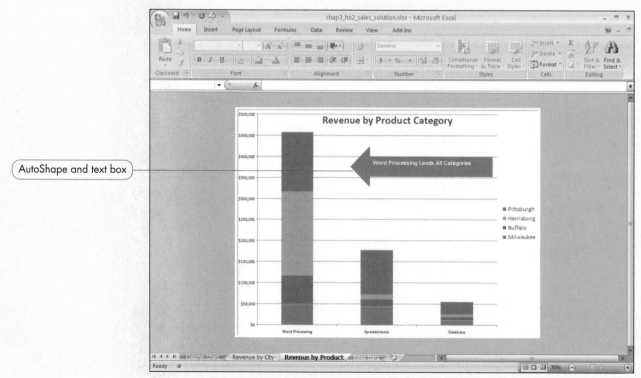

Figure 3.33 Chart with AutoShape and Text Box

Chart Distribution

You can create visual information masterpieces that could be shared with others.

You can create visual information masterpieces that could be shared with others. Charts are used as documentation in Web pages, memos, reports, research papers, books, and a variety of other types of documents. Therefore, it is important to experience how charts are transferred to these documents.

In this section, you embed Excel charts in other Microsoft Office applications. Then you learn how to print the chart within a worksheet or by itself. Finally, you learn how to save a chart as a Web file.

Embedding Charts

Microsoft Excel 2007 is just one application in the Microsoft Office 2007 suite. The applications are integrated and enable for data sharing. It is straightforward to copy worksheets and charts and paste in Word and PowerPoint. You can then format the objects in Word or PowerPoint.

Export to Other Applications

Microsoft Office 2007 enables you to create a file in one application that contains data (objects) from another application. The memo in Figure 3.34, for example, was created in Word, and it contains an object (a chart) that was developed in Excel. The Excel object is linked to the Word document, so that any changes to the Excel workbook data are automatically reflected in the Word document. Formatting of the object

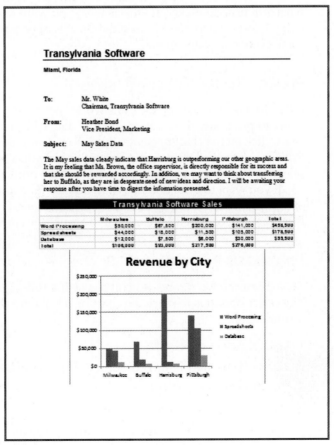

Figure 3.34 Memo in Microsoft Office Word

in Excel after it is placed in the Word document will not be seen in the Word document. The steps to embed a chart in a Word (or PowerPoint) document are:

1. Click on the chart in Excel to select it.
2. Click Copy in the Clipboard group on the Home tab.
3. Open the appropriate Word or PowerPoint document.
4. Click Paste in the Clipboard group on the Home tab.

Remember that changes to the worksheet data made in Excel will automatically update the chart in Excel and the other application, but changes in formatting will not be updated in the other application.

TIP Hiding and Unhiding a Worksheet

A chart delivers a message more effectively than the corresponding numeric data, and thus it may be convenient to hide the associated worksheet on which the chart is based. Click the Home tab. Then click Format in the Cells group, click Hide & Unhide, and then Hide Sheet the worksheet you want to hide. Repeat the selecting Unhide Sheet to make the worksheet visible again.

Printing Charts

Printing charts is a straightforward operation but requires that you closely observe the Print Preview window in the Print group on the Office menu. You have to see what will print to make sure this is what you want to print. Printing is an output that many Excel users prefer because the chart is often part of a report, research paper, or some other paper document.

Print an Object in a Worksheet

If the chart is contained on the same worksheet page as the data, you have two options, either to print only the chart or only the data table, or to print both. To print only the chart, click on the chart to ensure it is selected. You then select Print Preview from the Print group on the Office menu. Verify that only the chart is selected for printing. Then select the Page Setup options that best show the printed chart, and then print the chart.

If you want to print both the chart and the data table, the above steps are followed except you must ensure that the chart is deselected. This is a case where the use of the Print Preview command is essential to ensure the correct items are being printed.

Print a Full-Page Chart

The options above can be difficult to use if a full-page printing of a chart is desired. The easier option is to place the chart on a separate sheet in the workbook and print it from there.

1. Click to select the chart.
2. Click Move Chart in the Location group on the Design tab.
3. Click the New Sheet option.
4. Move to the sheet added in Step 3.
5. Use Print Preview to ensure the chart will be displayed properly when printed.
6. Select the appropriate Page Setup options and print the chart.

Save as a Web Page

Excel users can place an Excel chart (and sometimes entire workbooks) on the World Wide Web. The first step to placement on the Web is to save the worksheet as a Web page. To do this:

1. Click the Office Button and select Save As.
2. Select Web Page (*.htm; *.html) from the *Save as Type* menu.
3. Title the file appropriately and save it to the desired location.
4. You can preview the chart or workbook by opening your browser, navigating to the location of the Web page, and opening it.

Hands-On Exercises

3 | Embedding, Printing, and Saving a Chart as a Web Page

Skills covered: 1. Embed a Chart in Microsoft Word **2.** Copy the Worksheet **3.** Embed the Data **4.** Copy the Chart **5.** Embed the Chart **6.** Modify the Worksheet **7.** Update the Links **8.** Print Worksheet and Chart **9.** Save and View Chart as Web Page

Step 1
Embed a Chart in Microsoft Word
	Refer to Figure 3.35 as you complete Step 1.
	
	a. Start Word and if necessary, click the **Maximize** button in the application window so that Word takes up the entire screen.
	
	b. Click the **Office Button** and select **Open**.
	
	    1. Open the *chap3_ho3_memo* document.
	
	    2. Save the document as **chap3_ho3_memo_solution**.
	
	c. Click **Print Layout** on the status bar to change to the Print Layout view, and then set the **Zoom slider** to **100**%.
	
	    The software memo is open on your desktop.

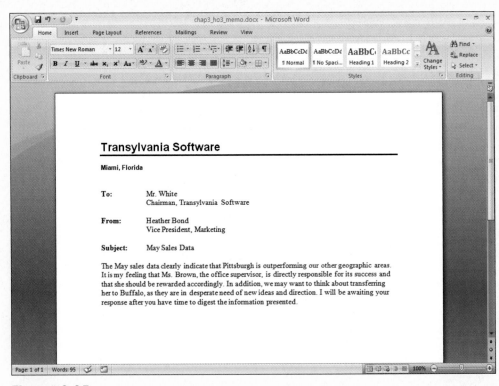

Figure 3.35 Memo in Word

Refer to Figure 3.36 as you complete Step 2.

a. Open the *chap3_ho2_sales_solution* workbook from the previous exercise.

- If you did not close Microsoft Excel at the end of the previous exercise, you will see its button on the taskbar. Click the **Microsoft Excel button** to return to the *chap3_ho2_sales_solution* workbook.

- If you closed Microsoft Excel, start Excel again, and then open the *chap3_ho2_sales_solution* workbook.

b. Save the workbook as **chap3_ho3_sales_solution**.

The taskbar contains a button for both Microsoft Word and Microsoft Excel. You can click either button to move back and forth between the open applications. End by clicking the Microsoft Excel button to make it the active application.

c. Click the **Sales Data tab**. Click and drag to select **cells A1:F7** to select the entire worksheet, as shown in Figure 3.36.

d. Right-click the selected area and select **Copy** from the shortcut menu.

A moving border appears around the entire worksheet, indicating that it has been copied to the clipboard.

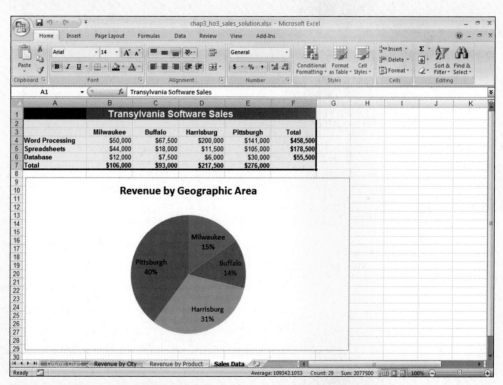

Figure 3.36 Worksheet Data to Copy

Refer to Figure 3.37 as you complete Step 3.

a. Click the **Microsoft Word button** on the taskbar to display the *chap3_ho3_memo_solution* document. Press **Ctrl+End** to move to the end of the memo, which is where you will insert the Excel worksheet.

Microsoft Word is the active window, and the insertion point is at the end of the Memo document.

b. Open the **Paste** list in the Clipboard group on the Home tab and select **Paste Special** to display the dialog box shown in Figure 3.37.

c. Click **Microsoft Office Excel Worksheet Object** in the As list. Click **Paste link**. Click **OK** to insert the worksheet into the document.

Using the Paste Special option gives you the opportunity to paste the object and establish the link for later data editing in Excel.

d. Right-click the worksheet, select **Format Object** on the shortcut menu to display the associated dialog box, and click the **Layout tab**.

TROUBLESHOOTING: If you paste the spreadsheet only, it becomes a table in Word, not an object. You cannot format it because it is not an object with a link to Excel. You must use the Paste Special option to make sure the worksheet link is created.

e. Choose **Square** in the *Wrapping Style* section and click **Center**. Click **OK** to accept the settings and close the dialog box. Click anywhere outside the table to deselect it. Save the *chap3_ho3_memo_solution* document.

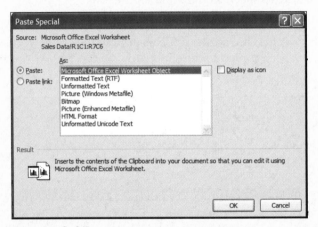

Figure 3.37 Paste Special Dialog Box

Step 4
Copy the Chart

a. Click the **Microsoft Excel button** on the taskbar to return to the worksheet.

b. Click outside the selected area to deselect the cells. Press **Esc** to remove the moving border.

c. Click the **Revenue by City tab** and click the chart area to select the chart.

The chart is selected when you see the sizing handles on the border of the chart area.

d. Click **Copy** in the Clipboard group on the Home tab.

Step 5
Embed the Chart

Refer to Figure 3.38 as you complete Step 5.

a. Switch to **Word** and click **Paste** in the Clipboard group on the Home tab.

b. Click the **Smart Tag** down arrow and verify that Chart (link to Excel data) is selected.

You pasted the chart object into your Memo. As an object, it will be updated when the spreadsheet data is updated. The object, created with the Paste Special option, permits chart formatting within the Word document.

TROUBLESHOOTING: If the object moves to another page, use the resize handles to shrink the object until it fits on the previous page.

c. Click **Center** in the Paragraph group on the Home tab to center the chart.

d. Click the **Office Button**, select **Print**, and then select **Print Preview**.

Your document should be similar to Figure 3.38. You use Print Preview to view your document to verify that the elements fit on one page.

e. Save the document.

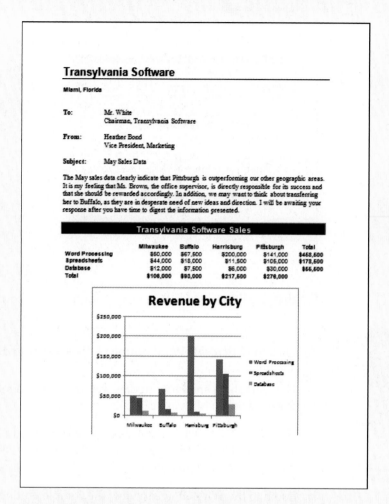

Figure 3.38 Chart Embedded in Memo

Refer to Figure 3.39 as you complete Step 6.

a. Working in the Word document, click anywhere in the worksheet to select the worksheet and display the sizing handles.

The status bar indicates that you can double-click to edit the worksheet.

b. Double-click the worksheet to start Excel so you can change the data.

Excel starts and reopens the *chap3_ho3_sales_solution* workbook.

c. Click **Maximize** to maximize the Excel window, if needed.

d. Click the **Sales Data tab** within the workbook, if needed. Click in **cell B4**. Type **$150,000** and press **Enter**.

The wedge for Milwaukee shows the increase in the chart.

e. Click the **Revenue by City tab** to select the chart sheet. Save the workbook.

The chart reflects the increased sales for Milwaukee.

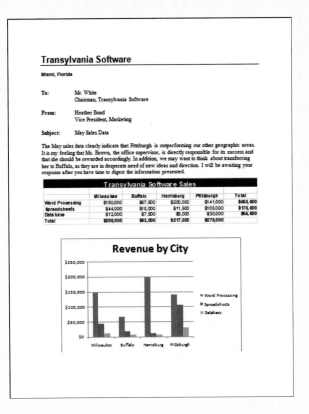

Figure 3.39 Modified Worksheet Changes Reflected in Word Document

---

Step 7
Update the Links

a. Click the **Microsoft Word button** on the taskbar to display the *chap3_ho3_solution* document.

The worksheet and chart update automatically to reflect $150,000 for word processing sales in Milwaukee.

TROUBLESHOOTING: If the worksheet and chart do not automatically update, then point to the sheet object and click the right mouse button. Select Update Link from the shortcut menu.

b. Zoom to the **Whole Page** to view the completed document. Click and drag the worksheet or the chart within the memo to make any last-minute changes.

c. Save the memo again and close Word.

Step 8
Print Worksheet and Chart

Refer to Figure 3.40 as you complete Step 8.

a. Click on the **Sales Data tab** to make the Sales Data sheet active. Click the chart area to select it. Click **Move Chart** on the Design tab to display the dialog box. Click **New Sheet** and click **OK** to close the dialog box.

The chart has been moved from below the spreadsheet to a new page and is displayed as full-screen view.

b. Click the **Office Button** and select **Print Preview** from the Print menu. Click **Show Margins** on the **Print Preview** toolbar to toggle the display of the margins on and off. Click **Close Print Preview** to return to the chart.

You used Print Preview and the Show Margins option to verify that the chart displays properly before printing.

c. Click **Page Setup** on the Page Layout tab. Click the **Page tab** in the Page Setup dialog box. Verify that **Landscape** is selected.

Changing the print option to Landscape enables you to see more of the chart.

d. Click the **Header/Footer tab** in the Page Setup dialog box, and then click **Custom Footer** to display the Footer dialog box.

e. Click the text box for the left section and enter your name. Click the text box for the center section and enter your instructor's name.

Headers and footers provide documentation on each page for any worksheet and chart.

f. Click the text box for the right section. Click the **Date** button, press **Spacebar**, and then click the **Time** button. Click **OK** to accept these settings and close the Footer dialog box. Click **OK** to close the Page Setup dialog box.

You used the Page Setup options to change to landscape mode and create a custom header and footer on the page with the chart.

g. Print the workbook. Close the workbook without saving.

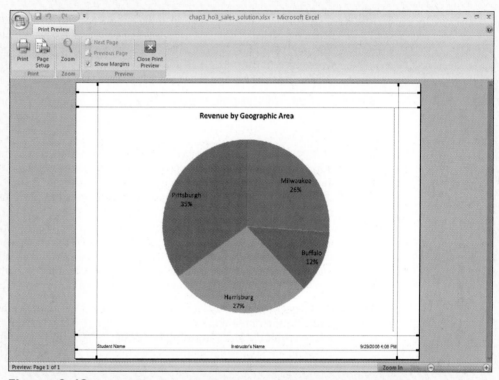

Figure 3.40 Print Preview of Chart with Custom Footers and Margin

---

Step 9
Save and View Chart as Web Page

a. Start Excel and open the *chap3_ho3_sales_solution* workbook.

b. Click on the **Revenue by Product tab** to make it the active sheet. Click the **Office Button** and select **Save As**.

c. Select **Web Page** from the *Save as type* list. Click **Selection: Chart**. Title the file appropriately and save it to the desired location.

d. You can preview the chart or workbook by opening your browser, navigating to the location of the Web page, and opening it.

Summary

1. **Choose a chart type.** A chart is a graphic representation of data in a worksheet. The type of chart chosen depends on the message to be conveyed. A pie chart is best for proportional relationships. A column or bar chart is used to show actual numbers rather than percentages. A line chart is preferable for time-related data. The choice between a clustered and a stacked column chart depends on the intended message. A clustered chart shows the contribution of each data point, but the total for each series is not as clear as with a stacked column chart. The stacked column chart, on the other hand, shows the totals clearly, but the contribution of the individual data points is obscured because the segments do not start at zero. It is important that charts are created accurately and that they do not mislead the reader. Stacked column charts should not add dissimilar quantities such as units and dollars.

2. **Create a chart.** Using the Insert tab is an effortless way to create charts. The title of a chart can help to convey the message. A neutral title such as "Revenue by City" leaves the reader to draw his or her own conclusion. Using a different title such as "Boston Leads All Cities" or "New York Is Trailing Badly" sends a very different message.

3. **Modify a chart.** Once created, a chart can be enhanced with arrows and text boxes. Multiple data series may be specified in either rows or columns. If the data are in rows, the first row is assumed to contain the category labels, and the first column is assumed to contain the legend. Conversely, if the data are in columns, the first column is assumed to contain the category labels, and the first row the legend.

4. **Enhance charts with graphic shapes.** These objects can be moved or sized and/or modified with respect to their color and other properties. The chart itself can also be modified using various tabs.

5. **Embed charts.** A chart may be embedded in a worksheet or created in a separate chart sheet. An embedded chart may be moved within a worksheet by selecting it and dragging it to its new location. An embedded chart may be sized by selecting it and dragging any of the sizing handles in the desired direction. Object embedding enables the creation of a compound document containing data from multiple applications. The essential difference between linking and embedding is whether the object is stored within the compound document (embedding) or in its own file (linking). An embedded object is stored in the compound document, which in turn becomes the only user (client) of that object. A linked object is stored in its own file, and the compound document is one of many potential users of that object. The same chart can be linked to a Word document and a PowerPoint presentation.

6. **Print charts.** Several options exist for printing charts. Users can print one chart, several charts, or a combination of the worksheet and the charts. Placing a chart on a separate sheet enables the user to print the chart in full-page format. Charts and worksheets can be saved as Web pages in HTML format and then be published to the World Wide Web (WWW).

Key Terms

Multiple Choice

1. Which type of chart is best to portray proportion or market share?
   (a) Pie chart
   (b) Line chart
   (c) Column chart
   (d) Combination chart

2. Which of the following chart types is *not* suitable to display multiple data series?
   (a) Pie chart
   (b) Horizontal bar chart
   (c) Column chart
   (d) All of the above are equally suitable.

3. Which of the following is best to display additive information from multiple data series?
   (a) A column chart with the data series stacked one on top of another
   (b) A column chart with the data series side by side
   (c) A scatter chart with two data series
   (d) A pie chart with five to ten wedges

4. A workbook can contain:
   (a) A separate chart sheet for every workbook
   (b) A separate workbook for every chart sheet
   (c) A sheet with both a workbook and chart
   (d) A separate chart sheet for every worksheet

5. Which of the following is true regarding an embedded chart?
   (a) It can be moved elsewhere within the worksheet.
   (b) It can be made larger or smaller.
   (c) Both (a) and (b).
   (d) Neither (a) nor (b).

6. Which of the following will produce a shortcut menu?
   (a) Pointing to a workbook tab and clicking the right mouse button
   (b) Pointing to an embedded chart and clicking the right mouse button
   (c) Pointing to a selected cell range and clicking the right mouse button
   (d) All of the above

7. Which of the following is done *prior* to beginning to create a chart?
   (a) The data series are selected.
   (b) The location of the embedded chart within the worksheet is specified.
   (c) The workbook is saved.
   (d) The worksheet is formatted.

8. Which of the following will display sizing handles when selected?
   (a) An embedded chart
   (b) The title of a chart
   (c) A text box or arrow
   (d) All of the above

9. How do you switch between open applications?
   (a) Click the appropriate button on the taskbar.
   (b) Click the Start button in the taskbar.
   (c) Use Shift+Tab to cycle through the applications.
   (d) Use Crtl+~ to cycle through the applications.

10. To represent multiple data series on the same chart:
    (a) The data series must be in rows, and the rows must be adjacent to one another on the worksheet.
    (b) The data series must be in columns, and the columns must be adjacent to one another on the worksheet.
    (c) The data series may be in rows or columns so long as they are adjacent to one another.
    (d) The data series may be in rows or columns with no requirement to be next to one another.

11. If multiple data series are selected and rows are specified:
    (a) The first row will be used for the category labels.
    (b) The first row will be used for the legend.
    (c) The first column will be used for the legend.
    (d) The first column will be used for the category labels.

12. If multiple data series are selected and columns are specified:

(a) The first column will be used for the category (X axis) labels.

(b) The first row will be used for the legend.

(c) Both (a) and (b).

(d) Neither (a) nor (b).

13. Which of the following is true about the scale on the Y axis in a column chart that plots multiple data series clustered versus one that stacks the values one on top of another?

(a) The scale for the stacked columns chart contains larger values than the clustered chart.

(b) The scale for the clustered columns contains larger values than the stacked columns.

(c) The values on the scale will be the same for both charts.

(d) The values will be different, but it is not possible to tell which chart has higher values.

14. A workbook includes a revenue worksheet with two embedded charts. The workbook also includes one chart in its own worksheet. How many files does it take to store this workbook?

(a) 1

(b) 2

(c) 3

(d) 4

15. You have created a Word document and embedded an Excel worksheet in that document. You make a change to the worksheet. What happens to the worksheet in the Word document?

(a) It will be updated when you select the Refresh Data command.

(b) It is unchanged.

(c) It is automatically updated to reflect the changes.

(d) You cannot change the worksheet because you have embedded it in a Word document.

16. You have selected cells B5:B10 as the data series for a chart and specified the data series are in columns. Which of the following is the legend text?

(a) Cells B5 through F5

(b) Cells C6 through F10

(c) Cells B5 through B10

(d) It is impossible to determine from the information given.

17. The same data range is used as the basis for an embedded pie chart, as well as a column chart in a chart sheet. Which chart(s) will change if you change the values in the data range?

(a) The column chart

(b) The pie chart

(c) Both the pie chart and the column chart

(d) Neither the pie chart nor the column chart

Practice Exercises

1 Vacation Park Admissions

Your summer job is with the professional organization representing theme parks across the country. You have gathered data on theme park admissions in four areas of the country. In this exercise you will finish the worksheet and create charts. The completed version of the worksheet is shown in Figure 3.41.

a. Open the *chap3_pe1_vacation* workbook and save it as **chap3_pe1_vacation_solution**.

b. Select **cells B8:E8**. Click **AutoSum** in the Editing group on the Home tab to compute the total for each quarter. Select **cells F4:F8**, and then click **AutoSum**.

c. Select **cells B4:F8** and format these cells as **Number with Commas**. Bold the row and column headings and the totals. Center the entries in **cells B3:F3**. Select **cells A1:F1**, then click **Merge and Center** in the Alignment group on the Home tab to center the title. With the same cells selected, choose the **Blue, Accent 1** theme color from the **Fill color** list. Increase the title font size to **14 points** and change the Font color to **white**. Select **cells B3:F3** and change the Font color to the same theme color used in row 1. Similarly, change **cell A8**. Save the workbook.

d. Complete the substeps to create a column chart that shows the number of admissions for each region and for each quarter within each region and insert the graphic, as shown in Figure 3.41:

   • Select **cells A3:E7**. Click the **Insert tab** and click **Column** in the Chart group. When the Column chart type and Clustered column subtype are selected, the chart appears on Admissions Data worksheet.

   • Click the outline of the chart to select it. Using the four-headed arrow, drag the chart into position under the worksheet.

   • Right-click the legend and select **Bold** and **Italic** to format the legend.

   • Click the **Insert tab** and click the left facing arrow in the Shapes group. Click and drag to create a thick arrow that points to the **1st Quarter South** column. Release the mouse. The arrow is selected, and you are viewing the Format tab.

   • Click **Text Box** in the Insert Shapes group on the Format tab to insert a text box. Click and drag a text box on top of the thick arrow. Release the mouse. Enter text by typing **South First-Quarter Admissions High**. Select the text you just typed and use the Mini toolbar to change the font to **9-point** bold white.

e. Complete the substeps to create a pie chart, in its own sheet, that shows the percentage of the total number of admissions in each region:

   • Select **cells A4:A7**, then press and hold **Ctrl** while selecting **cells F4:F7**.

   • Click the **Insert tab** to make it active. Click **Pie** in the Chart group and the pie chart appears on the Admissions Data sheet. Click **Move Chart** on the Design tab, click the **New Sheet** option, and click **OK**. Right-click the **Chart 1 tab** just created and select **Rename** from the shortcut menu. Type **Pie Chart** and press **Enter**.

   • Right-click any pie wedge and select **Add Data Labels** to add data labels to the chart area. Right-click any pie wedge and select **Format Data Labels** to display the Format Data Labels dialog box. Click **Label Options**, and then click the **Category Name** and **Percentage check boxes** to format the data labels. Remove the check from the **Value** check box.

   • Change the values in the data labels to percentages by clicking **Number** in Label options, click **Percentage** in **Category** options and click **Close** to accept the settings and close the dialog box. Right-click any data label and increase the font size to **14-point** italic.

...continued on Next Page

- Click **Legend** in the Labels group on the Layout tab and select **None** to delete the legend.
- Click **Chart Title** in the Labels group on the Layout tab and select **Centered Overlay Title**. Type **Vacation Park Admissions by Region**.

f. Complete the substeps to create a stacked column chart, in its own sheet, showing the number of admissions for each quarter and for each region within each quarter:

- Select **cells A3:E7**. Click the **Insert tab** and click **Column** in the Chart group. When the Column chart type and Stacked Column in 3-D subtype are selected, the chart appears on Sheet1.
- Click **Move Chart** on the Design tab, click the **New sheet** option, and click **OK**. Right-click the **Chart-2 tab** just created and select **Rename**. Type **Stacked Column** and press **Enter**.
- Click in the outline of the chart to select the entire chart. Click the **Data Labels** list in the Labels group on the Layout tab and select **Show**. Click **Chart Title** in the **Labels** group on the **Layout** tab and select **Centered Overlay Title**. Type **Admissions by Quarter and Region Within Quarter**. Change the color of each worksheet tab to **Accent 1**.

g. Click the **Stacked Column tab** to make it the active sheet. Click the **Office Button** and select **Save As**. Select **Web Page** from the *Save as type* list. Click **Selection: Chart**. Click **Change Title** and type **Vacation Web Page**, then click **OK** and save it. You can preview the chart by opening your Internet browser, navigating to the location of the Web page, and opening it.

h. Create a custom header for the worksheet that includes your name, your course, and your instructor's name. Create a custom footer for the worksheet that includes the name of the worksheet. Print the entire workbook, consisting of the worksheet in Figure 3.41, plus the additional sheets you created. Use portrait orientation for the **Admissions Data** worksheet and landscape orientation for the other worksheets. Save and close the workbook.

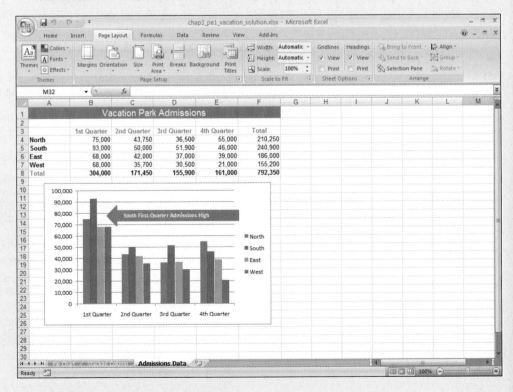

Figure 3.41 Vacation Park Charts

...continued on Next Page

The worksheet shown in Figure 3.42 shows third-quarter revenues for each salesperson at AnytimeTalk, Inc., the cellular company where you will do your internship this summer. One of your assigned duties is to complete the Fourth-Quarter Revenue worksheet and create a column chart showing a comparison of each salesperson's total sales for the fourth quarter. The chart is to be formatted for a professional presentation.

a. Open the *chap3_pe2_talk* workbook and save it as **chap3_pe2_talk_solution**.

b. Click and drag to select **cells E3:E7**. Click **AutoSum** in the Editing group on the Home tab to compute the total for each salesperson. Click and drag to select **cells B8:E8**, and then click **AutoSum** to compute the totals for each month and the total for the quarter.

c. Click and drag to select **cells B3:E8** and format these cells as **Currency with no decimals**. Bold the row and column headings and the totals. Center the entries in **cells B2:E2**.

d. Select **cells A1:E1**, then click **Merge and Center** in the Alignment group on the Home tab to center the title. With the same cells selected, choose **Orange, Accent 6** from the theme colors in the **Fill color** list. Increase the title font size to **18 points** and change the Font color to **Orange, Accent 6, Darker 50%**.

e. Increase the height of row 1 as necessary to display the title. Select **cells A2:E2** and change the Font color to the same theme color used in row 1.

f. Select **cells A4:E4** and use Fill color in the Font group on the Home tab to highlight the cells with a theme shade. Similarly, change **cell A8**. Save the workbook.

g. Select **cells A3:A7**, and while holding **Ctrl**, select **cells E3:E7**. Click the **Insert tab** and click **Column** in the Chart group. When the Column chart type and Clustered Cylinder column subtype are selected, the chart appears on the Sales Data sheet.

h. Click the white background of the chart to select it and using the four-headed arrow, drag the chart into position below the worksheet data. Right-click the legend and select **Delete** to delete the legend.

i. Right-click any cylinder and select **Add Data Labels** to add data labels to the chart area. Right-click any cylinder and select **Format Data Labels** to display the Format Data Labels dialog box.

j. Triple-click the second column to select just this column. Right-click the selected column, select **Format Data Point**, click the **Fill** option in the associated dialog box, click **Gradient Fill**, and then change the color of this column to the coordinating theme shade. Select **Close** to close the dialog box.

k. Click in **cell A4** and enter your name. The value on the X axis changes automatically to reflect the entry in cell A4. Open the **Chart Title** menu in the Labels group on the Layout tab. Click **Above Chart** and type **Fourth-Quarter Revenues** as the title of the chart.

l. Click the **Insert tab**. Click **Line Callout 1** in the Shapes group. Click and drag to create a callout that points to your cylinder. Release the mouse. The callout is selected, and you are viewing the Format tab. Change the Shape Fill color and the Shape Outline color by selecting appropriate theme colors from the **Shape Fill** list and the **Shape Outline** list in the Shape Styles group on the Format tab.

m. Click **Text Box** in the Insert Shapes group on the Format tab to insert a text box. Click and drag a text box on top of the callout. Release the mouse. Enter text by clicking **Text Fill** in the WordArt group of the Format tab and type the words **This Cylinder Represents My Data**. Select the text you just typed, right-click the selected text, and change the font to **10 point** from the Mini toolbar.

n. Right-click the border of the chart, select **Format Chart Area**, then change the border to include rounded corners with a shadow effect. Use the Border Styles and Shadow options to make the changes.

o. Save the workbook and print the completed worksheet. Close the workbook.

...continued on Next Page

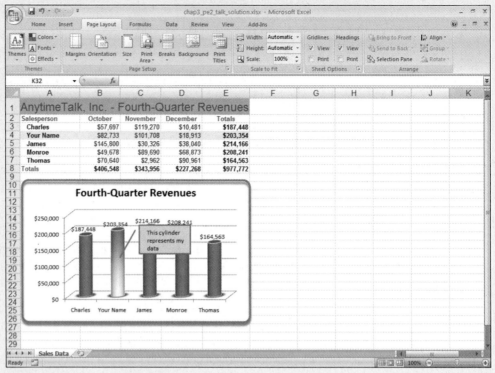

Figure 3.42 AnytimeTalk, Inc.

3 Printing Charts

Your sister asked you to chart weekly sales from her chain of mystery bookstores. As shown in Figure 3.43, stores are in four cities, and you must plot four product lines. You will create the charts as embedded objects on the worksheet. Do not be concerned about the placement of each chart until you have completed all four charts. The first chart is a clustered column and emphasizes the sales in each city (the data are in rows). The second chart is a stacked column version of the first chart. The third chart (that begins in column H of the worksheet) is a clustered column chart that emphasizes the sales in each product line (the data are in columns). The fourth chart is a stacked column version of the third chart. Figure 3.43 shows a reduced screen view of the four charts.

a. Open the *chap3_pe3_print* workbook and save it as **chap3_pe3_print_solution**.

b. Select **cells A2:E6** and click the **2-D Column** area of **Column** in the Charts group on the Insert tab to embed a clustered column chart. With the chart selected, click **Style 16** in the Chart Styles group on the Design tab. To add a chart title, click **Layout 1** in the Chart Layouts group on the Design tab. To change the default title, click the words *Chart Title* to select the words and type **Weekly Sales by Location and Product Line**. Right-click the already selected title and change the font size to 14 points. Drag the chart into position below the workbook. Save the workbook.

c. Select the chart, click the **Home tab**, click **Copy** in the Clipboard group to copy the chart, click in **cell A27**, and click **Paste** in the Clipboard group on the Home tab. With the chart selected, click the **Design tab** and click **Change Chart Type** in the Type group. Click **Stacked Column** in the Column area of the Change Chart Type dialog box and click **OK**. Save the workbook.

d. Select the **first** chart, click the **Home tab**, click in **cell H2**, and click **Paste**. With the chart selected, click the **Design tab** and click **Switch Row and Column** in the Data group. Save the workbook.

e. Select the chart, click the **Home tab**, click **Copy** to copy the chart, click in **cell H19**, and click **Paste** on the Home tab. With the chart selected, click the **Design tab** and click **Change Chart Type** in the Type group. Click the **Stacked Column** in the Column area of the Change Chart Type dialog box and click **OK**. Save the workbook.

...continued on Next Page

f. Click **Page Break Preview** in the Workbook Views group on the View tab. Your screen should be similar to Figure 3.43. You will see one or more dotted lines that show where the page breaks will occur. You will also see a message indicating that you can change the location of the page breaks. Click **OK** after you have read the message.

g. Remove any existing page breaks by clicking and dragging the solid blue line that indicates the break. (You can insert horizontal or vertical page breaks by clicking the appropriate cell, clicking **Breaks** in the Page Setup group on the Page Layout **tab**, and selecting **Page Break**.) To return to Normal view, click **Normal** in the Workbook Views group on the View tab.

h. Print the worksheet and four embedded charts on one page. Change to landscape orientation for a more attractive layout. Open the **Orientation** list in the Page Setup group on the Page Layout tab and select **Landscape**. Click the **Page Layout tab** and use the Page Setup dialog box to create a custom header with your name, your course, and your instructor's name. Create a custom footer that contains today's date, the name of the workbook, and the current time. Click **OK** to close the dialog box. Print the worksheet. Save and close the workbook.

i. Write a short note to your instructor that describes the differences between the charts. Suggest a different title for one or more charts that helps to convey a specific message.

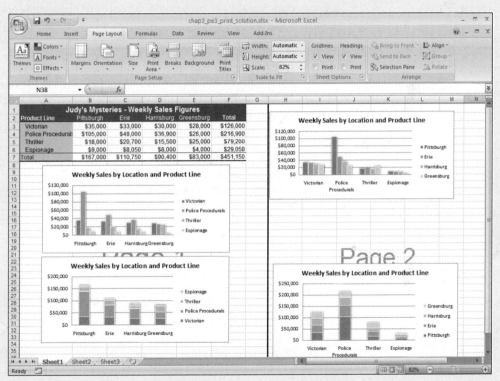

Figure 3.43 Printing Charts

4 Stock Price Comparisons

Figure 3.44 contains a combination chart to display different kinds of information on different scales for multiple data series. You start by creating a clustered column chart for the revenue and profits, and then you create a second data series to chart the stock prices as a line. Two different scales are necessary because the magnitudes of the numbers differ significantly. Your investment club asked you to make a recommendation about the purchase of the stock based on your analysis.

a. Open the *chap3_pe4_stock* workbook and save it as **chap3_pe4_stock_solution**.

b. Select **cells A1:F4**. Click the **Insert tab** and click **Column** in the Charts group. Then select **Clustered Column** from the 2-D Column row.

...continued on Next Page

c. Click chart outline to select the chart and using the four-headed arrow, drag the chart into position under the worksheet. Right-click the legend and select **Format Legend**. In the *Legend Options* section, click **Bottom** as the legend position and click **Close**.

You are now going to add a secondary vertical axis to display Stock Price because the size of the numbers differs significantly from Revenue and Profit.

d. Click the chart to make it active. Click the **Format tab**. Click the **Chart Elements down arrow** in the Current Selection group and select **Series "Stock Price"** as the data series to plot on the secondary axis.

e. Click **Format Selection** in the Current Selection group and click **Secondary Axis** in *Series Options* in the Format Data Series dialog box. Click **Close** to close the dialog box. Click the **Layout tab**, click **Axes** in the Axes group, select **Secondary Vertical Axis**, and select **Show Default Axis**.

f. Change the data series to a line chart to distinguish the secondary axis. Click the **Format tab**, click the **Chart Elements down arrow** in the Current Selection group, and select **Series "Stock Price."** Click the **Design tab**, click **Change Chart Type** in the Type group, select **Line** as the chart type, and then click the first example of a line chart. Click **OK** to view the combination chart.

g. Right-click on the chart but above the plot area, select **Format Chart Area**, click **Border Styles**, check **Rounded Corners** and increase the width to 1.5 pts, click **Border Color**, click **Solid Line**, and choose a coordinating theme color from the color selection menu. Click **Shadow** and select an appropriate shadow from the **Presets** list. Click **Close** to see the customized border around the chart.

h. Deselect the chart. Click the **Page Layout tab** and open the *Page Setup* dialog box. Click **Landscape** for orientation, click the **Margins tab**, and click the **Horizontally** and **Vertically check boxes** to center the worksheet and chart on the page. Click the **Header/Footer tab** create a custom header for the worksheet that includes **your name**, **your course name**, and **your instructor's name**. Create a custom footer that contains the name of the **file** in which the worksheet is contained, **today's date**, and the **current time**. Save the workbook and print your worksheet. Close the workbook.

i. What do you think should be the more important factor influencing a company's stock price, its revenue (sales) or its profit (net income)? Could the situation depicted in the worksheet occur in the real world? Summarize your thoughts in a brief note to your instructor. Print the document.

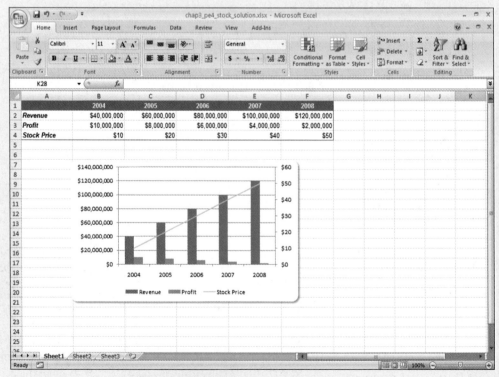

Figure 3.44 Stock Price Comparison

Mid-Level Exercises

1 The Next Car You Purchase

The Word document in Figure 3.45 displays descriptive information about a car you are interested in purchasing, a picture of the car, and a hyperlink to the Web site where the information was obtained. In addition, the document is linked to an Excel workbook that computes the car payment for you, based on the loan parameters that you provide. Your assignment is to create a similar document based on any car you choose.

a. Open the *chap3_mid1_auto* document and save it as **chap3_mid1_auto_solution**.

b. Locate a Web site that contains information about the car you are interested in. You can go to the Web site of the manufacturer, or you can go to a general site such as carpoint.msn.com, which contains information about all makes and models. Select the car you want and obtain the retail price of the car.

c. Enter the price of the car, a hypothetical down payment, the interest rate of the car loan, and the term of the loan in the indicated cells. The monthly payment will be determined automatically by the PMT function that is stored in the workbook. Use Help if needed to review the PMT function. Save the workbook.

d. Select **cells A3:B9** (the cells that contain the information you want to insert into the Word document) and copy the selected range to the Clipboard.

e. Open the partially completed *chap3_mid1_auto* Word document. Use the Paste Special option to paste the worksheet data. Save the Word document as **chap3_mid1_auto solution**.

f. Use the taskbar to return to the Excel workbook. Change the amount of the down payment to **$8,500** and the interest rate for your loan to **6%**. Save the workbook. Close Excel. Return to the Word document, which should reflect the updated loan information.

g. Return to the Web page that contains the information about your car. Right-click the picture of the car that appears within the Web page and select **Save As** to save the picture of the car to your computer. Use the **Insert** command to insert the picture that you just obtained.

h. Complete the Word document by inserting some descriptive information about your car. Print the completed document. Save and close the document.

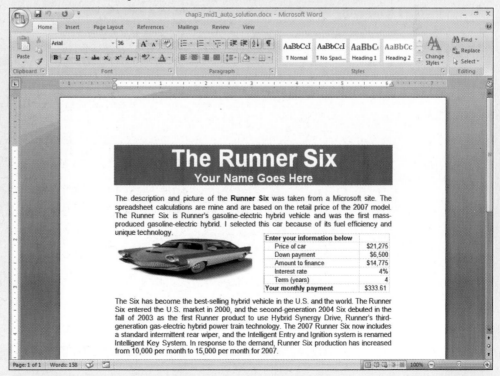

Figure 3.45 The Next Car You Purchase

...continued on Next Page

Figure 3.46 displays a worksheet with two similar charts detailing annual visits to different exhibits at the local Petting Zoo, one that plots data by rows and the other by columns. The distinction depends on the message you want to deliver. Both charts are correct. You collected the data at your summer job at the Petting Zoo and must now plot it for your intern supervisor as part of the analysis of the most popular animals at the zoo. You will create both charts shown and for comparison purposes create two more charts on a new sheet to determine the best presentation of data.

a. Open the *chap3_mid2_zoo* workbook and save it as **chap3_mid2_zoo_solution**.

b. Use **AutoSum** to compute the total number of visits for each animal category and each quarter. Rename the Sheet1 tab as **Side by Side Columns**. Format the worksheet in an attractive manner by matching the formatting shown in Figure 3.46.

c. Create each of the charts in Figure 3.46 as embedded charts on the current worksheet. The first chart specifies that the data series are in columns. The second chart specifies the data series are in rows.

d. Change to landscape orientation when the chart is printed. Create a custom header that includes your name, your course, and your instructor's name. Create a custom footer with the name of the worksheet, today's date, and the current time. Specify that the worksheet will be printed at 110% to create a more attractive printed page. Be sure, however, that the worksheet and associated charts fit on a single page.

e. Copy the worksheet and name the duplicate worksheet as **Stacked Columns**.

f. Select the first chart in the newly created Stacked Columns worksheet. Change the chart type to Stacked Columns. Change the chart type of the second chart to Stacked Columns as well. Repeat step d for the Stacked Columns worksheet.

g. Print the completed workbook (both worksheets). Add a short note that summarizes the difference between plotting data in rows versus columns and between clustered column charts and stacked column charts. Save and close the workbook.

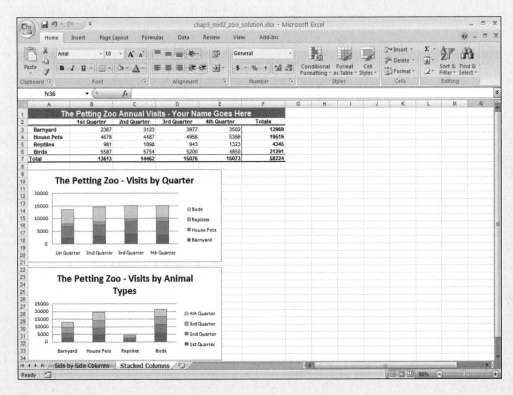

Figure 3.46 Comparison of Rows and Columns

...continued on Next Page

Your first job is as a management trainee at the Needlework Nook, a store specializing in home arts. The store manager has asked you to examine sales for the four quarters of the current year in five categories. She also has asked you to chart the sales figures. Complete the partially completed version of the spreadsheet in Figure 3.47 and create a chart that highlights quarterly product sales for the current year.

a. Open the *chap3_mid3_homearts* workbook and save it as **chap3_mid3_homearts_solution**.

b. Use the **AutoSum** command to compute the totals for the quarters and categories of products. Format the completed worksheet in an attractive manner duplicating the formatting exactly as shown. Rename sheet 1 as **Current Year**.

c. Create a stacked column chart based on the data in **cells A2:E7**. Specify that the data series are in rows so that each column represents total sales for each quarter. Display the legend on the right side of the chart. Save the chart in its own sheet called **Graphical Analysis**.

d. Experiment with variations of the chart created. Change the chart type from a stacked column to a clustered column and change the orientation of the data series from rows to columns. Choose the chart most appropriate to show the sales by quarter and category. Also experiment with the placement of the legend by moving to the bottom and the top. After experimenting with the placement of the legend, place it to the right of the chart.

e. Add data labels to the stacks on the Graphical Analysis sheet. Change the color of the worksheet tabs to **Aqua Accent 5** for the Current Year tab and **Aqua, Accent 5, Darker 50%** for the Graphical Analysis tab.

f. Use the Page Setup dialog box to display gridlines and row and column headings. Create a custom header that includes your name, your course, and your instructor's name. Create a custom footer with the name of the worksheet, today's date, and the current time.

g. Print the completed workbook consisting of two worksheets. Save and close the workbook.

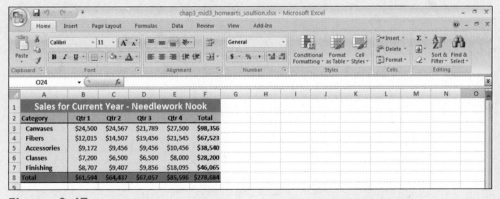

Figure 3.47 Home Arts

...continued on Next Page

Your sociology professor wants to know the correlation between time spent studying for quizzes and quiz scores, if any. You recorded the time spent studying for 10 quizzes and asked two friends to do the same thing. Now you must plot the data in a scatter chart and complete the analysis. Use the worksheet shown in Figure 3.48 and chart your data.

a. Open the *chap3_mid4_scatter* workbook and save it as **chap3_mid4_scatter_solution**.

b. Insert a row above the worksheet and type the title **Test Analysis**. Center the title above the worksheet. Format the completed worksheet in an attractive manner. You do not have to duplicate our formatting exactly.

c. Create a scatter chart based on the data in **cells A2:E12**. Display the legend to the right of the chart.

d. Insert a chart title **Study Time and Quiz Scores.** Add an X-axis title **Time in Hours** and a Y-axis title **Test Score**.

e. Change the chart type to **Scatter with Smooth Lines and Markers**. Change the chart style so the colors are more vibrant.

f. Remember to add your analysis of the correlation between study time and quiz scores below the chart.

g. Delete the Sheet2 and Sheet3 tabs and rename Sheet1 as **Test Scores**. Add a tab color, Red, to the Test Scores tab.

h. Use the Page Setup dialog box to display gridlines and row and column headings. Create a custom header that includes your name, your course, and your instructor's name. Create a custom footer with the name of the worksheet, today's date, and the current time.

i. Print the completed workbook making sure the worksheet, chart, and analysis fit on one page. Save and close the workbook.

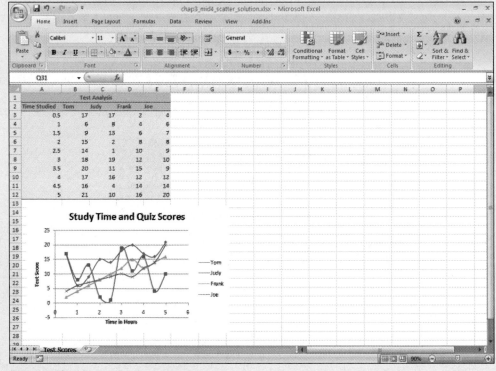

Figure 3.48 Study Analysis

...continued on Next Page

Your computer professor has asked you to provide a comparison of computer sales across the country. Complete the worksheet shown in Figure 3.49 but include three charts to show the sales in a variety of ways. Include a summary indicating the most effective chart and why you consider it the most effective for comparing sales data.

a. Open the *chap3_mid5_computer* workbook and save it as **chap3_mid5_computer_solution**.

b. Use **AutoSum** to compute the totals for the corporation in column F and row 6.

c. Format **cells B3:F6** as currency, zero decimal. Center the title above the worksheet. Format the completed worksheet in an attractive manner. You do not have to duplicate our formatting exactly.

d. Use the completed worksheet as the basis for a stacked column chart with the data plotted in rows.

e. Create a pie chart showing total sales by city, placing it on a separate sheet. Rename the sheet as **Sales by City**.

f. Make a cluster column chart, placing it on a separate sheet and renaming the sheet **Sales by Product**. Include a legend below the chart, a chart title, axes titles, and a shape to draw attention to the city with the highest notebook sales. Include an appropriate text message on the shape.

g. Use the Page Setup dialog box to display gridlines and row and column headings. Create a custom footer that contains your name, the name of the worksheet, and today's date. Print the entire workbook. Save and close the workbook.

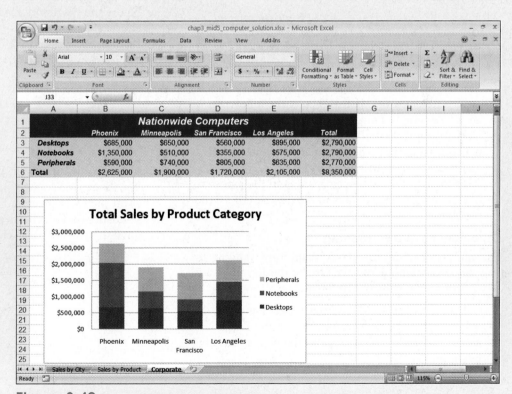

Figure 3.49 Computer Sales Analysis

Capstone Exercise

What if people split a dinner check using the principles of the progressive income tax that is central to our tax code? Five lifelong friends of various means meet once a week for dinner and split the $100 check according to their ability to pay. Tom, Dick, and Harry are of relatively modest means and pay $1, $4, and $9, respectively. Ben and Ken are far more prosperous and pay $18 and $68, respectively.

The friends were quite satisfied with the arrangement until the owner offered a rebate. "You are excellent customers, and I will reduce the cost of your meal by $15." The question became how to divide the $15 windfall to give everyone his fair share? The proprietor suggested that they allocate the savings according to the amount each contributed to the original check. He made a quick calculation, and then rounded each person's share to an integer. For example, Tom's new bill should have been 85 cents, but it was decided he would eat for free. In similar fashion, Dick now owes $3, Harry $7, Ben $15, and Ken $60. (Ken, the most prosperous individual, made up the difference with respect to the cents that were dropped.) The new total is $85, and everyone saves money.

Once outside the restaurant, the friends began to compare their savings. Tom and Dick each complained that they saved only $1. Harry grumbled that he saved only $2. Ben thought it unfair that Ken saved more than the other four friends combined. Everyone continued to pick on Ken. The next week, Ken felt so uncomfortable that he did not show up, so his former friends ate without him. But when the bill came, they were $60 short.

Create the Worksheet

You will create the worksheet that is the basis for the charts. The first sheet, which you will name Numerical Analysis, contains the labels and data described below.

a. Enter a title in row 1. In row 3 enter the following labels: **Person**, **% Paid**, **Amount**, **Projected Saving**, **New Amount**, **Actual Saving**, **% Saving**. Type **Total** in **cell A9** and type **The Original Total** in **cell A11** and **Reduction in Bill** in **cell A12**.

b. Type the names, the percent paid, and the amounts in **cells A4:C8**. This data is in the description of the problem.

Calculations and Formatting

The analysis includes calculations and formatting necessary for presentation. You will create the formulas and select appropriate formatting options.

a. Calculate the projected savings for each individual in column D, the new account in column E, the actual savings in column F, and the percent savings in column G.

b. Calculate appropriate totals in **cells B9:G9**.

c. Calculate the original total in **cell C11** and the reduction in bill in **cell C12**.

d. Format columns B through G as appropriate for the values displayed.

e. Format the remainder of the worksheet with appropriate colors, borders, fonts, and font size.

Create the Charts

You will create the charts based on the worksheet values. The charts provide information visually and help you to analyze that information. You will create three charts: a pie chart, a clustered column chart, and a combination chart.

a. Create a pie chart on a separate sheet that shows the percentage of the bill each individual pays before the refund. Include descriptive titles and labels.

b. Create a column chart on a separate sheet showing the amount each individual saves. Include data labels below the chart and an overlay showing the percentage of savings.

c. Add a shape with text box describing the results depicted on the chart. Include descriptive titles.

d. Create a clustered column chart on a separate sheet showing the new amount of the bill and the actual savings for each individual. Include data labels below the chart and a legend to the right of the chart.

e. Include a shape with a text box describing the data depicted in the chart. Include descriptive titles and labels.

Footers and Printing

Your instructor requires documentation for assignments. You will print the data sheet and the three chart sheets with your name, page numbers, and your instructor's name.

a. Create a custom footer that includes the page number, instructor's name, and your name.

b. Print the worksheet and charts in landscape format to ensure that all charts print on separate pages.

c. Save the workbook as **chap3_cap_dinner_solution**.

Mini Cases

Use the rubric following the case as a guide to evaluate your work, but keep in mind that your instructor may impose additional grading criteria or use a different standard to judge your work.

Designer Clothing

GENERAL CASE

This assignment asks you to complete a worksheet and create an associated chart for a designer clothing boutique, and then link these Excel objects to an appropriate memo. Open the partially completed *chap3_mc1_design* workbook; compute the sales totals for each individual salesperson as well as the totals for each quarter, then format the resulting worksheet in an attractive fashion. Include your name in the title of the worksheet (cell A1). We have started the memo for you and have saved the text in the *chap3_mc1_design* Word document. Open the Word document, and then link the Excel worksheet to the Word document. Repeat the process to link the Excel chart to the Word document. Print the completed document for your instructor. Save as **chap3_mc1_design_solution**.

Performance Elements	Exceeds Expectations	Meets Expectations	Below Expectations
Compute totals	Totals all correct.	Inconsistent use of SUM function.	Typed in the number.
Attractive, appropriate format	Very attractive.	Adequate.	Ugly.
Embed sheet	Sheet embedded correctly.	Sheet embedded but not in correct location.	No embedded sheet.
Embed chart	Chart embedded correctly.	Sheet embedded but not in correct location.	No embedded sheet.

The Convention Planner

RESEARCH CASE

Your first task as a convention planner is to evaluate the hotel capacity for the host city in order to make recommendations as to which hotels should host the convention. The data form can be found in the *chap3_mc2_convention* workbook, which contains a single worksheet. You are to select a city for the convention and research six different hotels in that city. For each hotel, determine the number of standard and deluxe rooms and the rate for each. Insert this information into the worksheet. Complete the worksheet by computing the total number of rooms in each category. Format the worksheet in an attractive way. Create a stacked column chart that shows the total capacity for each hotel. Create a second chart that shows the percentage of total capacity for each hotel. Store each chart in its own worksheet, and then print the entire workbook for your instructor. Save the workbook as **chap3_mc2_convention_solution**.

Performance Elements	Exceeds Expectations	Meets Expectations	Below Expectations
Research hotel information	Found six hotels and data.	Found six hotels but incomplete data.	Found fewer than six hotels with incomplete data.
Create totals	Totals all correct.	Inconsistent use of SUM function.	Typed in the number.
Format attractive	Very attractive.	Adequate.	Ugly.
Create stacked column chart	Chart created correctly.	Incorrect data used for chart.	No chart.
Create second chart	Chart created correctly.	Incorrect data used for chart.	No chart.
Charts on separate sheets	Both charts on separate sheets.	One chart on separate sheet.	No chart.
Printing	Three printed sheets.	Two printed sheets.	No printed output.

Peer Tutoring

DISASTER RECOVERY

As part of your service learning project you volunteer tutoring students in Excel, you will identify and correct six separate errors in the chart. Your biggest task will be selecting the correct type of chart to show the data most clearly. Open the spreadsheet *chap3_mc3_peer* and find six errors. Correct the errors and explain how the errors might have occurred and how they can be prevented. Include your explanation in the cells below the embedded chart. Save as **chap3_mc3_peer_solution**.

Performance Elements	Exceeds Expectations	Meets Expectations	Below Expectations
Identify six errors	Finds all six errors.	Finds four errors.	Finds three or fewer errors.
Explain the error	Complete and correct explanation of each error.	Explanation is too brief to fully explain error.	No explanations.
Prevention description	Prevention description correct and practical.	Prevention description but obtuse.	No prevention description.

Working with Large Worksheets and Tables

Manipulating Worksheets and Table Management

Objectives

After you read this chapter, you will be able to:

1. Freeze rows and columns **(page 488)**.

2. Hide and unhide rows, columns, and worksheets **(page 489)**.

3. Protect a cell, a worksheet, and a workbook **(page 490)**.

4. Control calculation **(page 493)**.

5. Print large worksheets **(page 493)**.

6. Explore basic table management **(page 505)**.

7. Sort data **(page 510)**.

8. Filter and total data **(page 514)**.

Hands-On Exercises

Exercises	Skills Covered
1. **MARCHING BAND ROSTER (page 497)** **Open:** chap4_ho1_band.xlsx **Save as:** chap4_ho1_band_solution.xlsx	• Freeze and Unfreeze Rows and Columns • Hide and Unhide Rows, Columns, and Worksheets • Protect a Worksheet and a Workbook and Control Calculations • Print a Large Worksheet
2. **MARCHING BAND ROSTER REVISITED (page 519)** **Open:** chap4_ho1_band_solution.xlsx (from Exercise 1) **Save as:** chap4_ho2_band_solution.xlsx (additional modifications)	• Create a Table • Add, Edit, or Delete Records, and Use Find and Replace • Format a Table • Sort a Table • Filter a Table • Create Column Totals and a Summary Report • Print the Completed Worksheet

CASE STUDY

The Spa Experts

You and Tim like to relax and went into business shortly after graduation selling spas and hot tubs. Business has been good, and your expansive showroom and wide selection appeal to a variety of customers. You and your business partner maintain a large inventory to attract the impulse buyer and currently have agreements with three manufacturers: Serenity Spas, The Original Hot Tub, and Port-a-Spa. Each manufacturer offers spas and hot tubs that appeal to different segments of the market with prices ranging from affordable to exorbitant.

The business has grown rapidly, and you need to analyze the sales data in order to increase future profits—for example, which vendor generates the most sales? Who is the leading salesperson? Do most customers purchase their spa or finance it? Are sales promotions nec-

Case Study

essary to promote business, or will customers pay the full price? You have created a simple worksheet that has sales data for the current month. Each transaction appears on a separate row and contains the name of the salesperson, the manufacturer, and the amount of the sale. You will see an indication of whether the spa was purchased or financed, and whether a promotion was in effect. You are preparing a worksheet for Tim to keep him updated on sales for the current month.

Your Assignment

- Read the chapter carefully and pay close attention to sections that demonstrate working with data tables, sorting information, filtering data, preparing summary reports, charting summary data, and printing large worksheets.

- Open the *chap4_case_spa* workbook, which contains the partially completed financial worksheet, and save it as **chap4_case_spa_solution**.

- Study the structure of the worksheet to determine what sorts will be required, perform the appropriate sort, and create a summary report showing total sales by salesperson.

- Identify how you would prepare a summary report and how you would then chart the data. Determine how you can format the worksheet to best print it and the chart. Convert the range to a data table and prepare a chart illustrating total sales by salesperson. Substitute your name for Jessica Benjamin throughout the worksheet.

- Create a custom footer, include gridlines and row and column headings, landscape the worksheet, and center it horizontally and vertically on the page. Repeat the first three rows on each sheet when printing. Print the worksheet and the chart. Adjust the page break so all sales for a salesperson appear on the same page.

- Filter the data table so you only see the spas that are financed. Change the page print area by adjusting the margins to print just the financed spas, not the totals. Print the filtered report.

Large Worksheet Preparation

Working with large worksheets, those that are too big to display within one monitor screen, can confuse users because they are not able to view the entire worksheet at one time. When this occurs, it is necessary for you to know how to view parts of the worksheet not visible, how to keep some parts of the worksheet always in view, and how to hide selected rows and columns. These ideas are illustrated in Figure 4.1, which shows a large worksheet with cell A1 the active cell. It shows columns A through H and rows 1 through 30. Items that begin in column I or row 31 are not visible in this view.

> Working with large worksheets . . . can confuse users because they are not able to view the entire worksheet at one time.

In order to view other columns, you can click the horizontal scroll bar to view one or more columns to the right. When the active cell is in the rightmost visible column (H1 for example), pressing the right arrow key does the same thing. Clicking the down arrow in the vertical scroll bar or pressing the down arrow key when the active cell is in the bottom visible row moves the screen down one row. This is known as scrolling, but it does not address the issue of rows and columns formerly visible becoming invisible as the scrolling occurs.

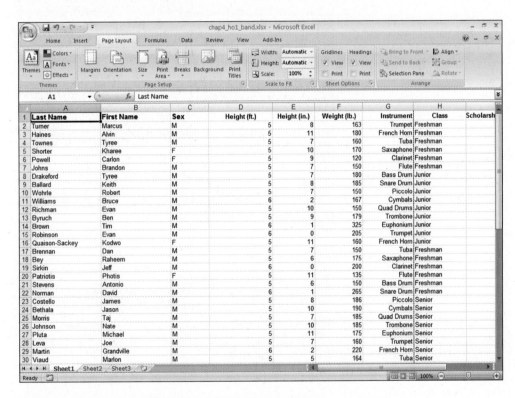

Figure 4.1 Large Worksheet

TIP Go to a Specific Cell

Pressing Ctrl+Home and Ctrl+End takes you to the upper-left and bottom-right cells within a worksheet, respectively. But how do you get to a specific cell? One way is to click the Find & Replace down arrow in the Editing group on the Home tab and select the Go To command (or press F5 or press Ctrl+G) to display the Go To dialog box, enter the address of the cell in the Reference text box, then press Enter to go directly to the cell.

Freezing Rows and Columns

When you scroll to parts of a worksheet not initially visible, some rows and columns disappear from view. It is sometimes valuable to be able to view row and column headings no matter where you scroll. This is done by *freezing*, which is the process that enables you to keep headings on the screen as you work with large worksheets, rows, and columns, as shown in Figure 4.2. Rows and columns that were not previously visible now are visible and so are the row and column headings. Figure 4.2 also shows a horizontal line and a vertical line after particular rows and columns, indicating they are frozen.

Freezing is the process of keeping headings on the screen at all times.

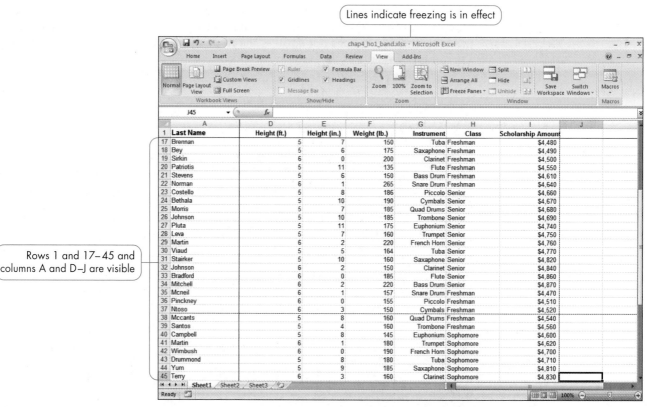

Lines indicate freezing is in effect

Rows 1 and 17–45 and columns A and D–J are visible

Figure 4.2   Visible Rows and Column Headings

To freeze columns and rows:

1. Select the cell below the row(s) and to the right of the column(s) you want to freeze.

2. Click the View tab and click Freeze Panes in the Window group. You can freeze both rows and columns or just the top row or the first column. After making your selection, you can unfreeze rows and columns by selecting Freeze Pane. You will notice that the *Freeze* option you previously selected now displays *Unfreeze*. Click that option to unfreeze rows and columns.

Hiding and Unhiding Rows, Columns, and Worksheets

Hidden is the state of rows, columns, and sheets being invisible.

Figure 4.3 shows a worksheet with rows, columns, and a worksheet *hidden*, which is the process of making rows, columns, and sheets invisible. The hiding of these items in a worksheet is a common practice and is done for a variety of reasons. Often, it is done to conceal nonessential information, or information not needed at a particular time. At other times, confidential information is contained in a workbook and rows, columns, or sheets must be hidden to allow nonauthorized users to view a workbook. You might also hide rows or columns to make other rows or columns visible. Row and columns containing sensitive data or data that uniquely identifies an individual or product are hidden from colleagues or competitors. Social Security Numbers, salary, or rate of pay, pricing data, and trade secret information are some examples of data used in worksheets that might be hidden. Large workbooks might include worksheets that not all employees are authorized to view because of the classified nature of the data contained in the worksheet. Trade secret information or information specifically classified by the federal government are just two examples of why worksheets may be hidden.

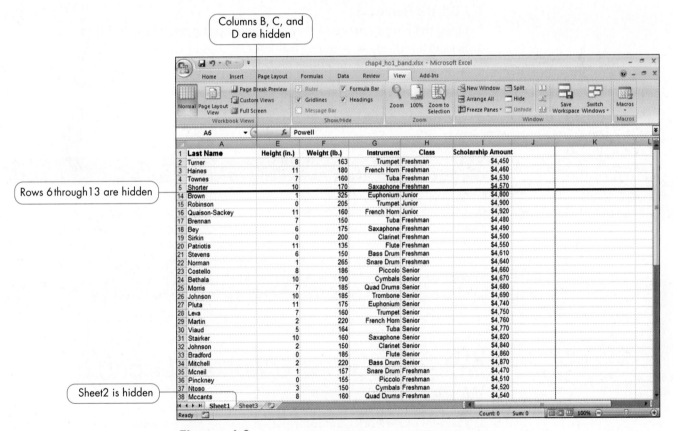

Figure 4.3 Hidden Rows, Columns, and Worksheet

Keep in mind that Hide is not a delete command. Hiding an element of a worksheet does not affect the data in that element, nor does it affect any other visible cell that might reference data in the hidden element. Formulas will still display correct results even when the references used in the formulas are hidden. To hide a particular row or column in a worksheet:

1. Select the row or column to be hidden.
2. Click the Home tab.
3. Open the Format menu in the Cells group and select Hide & Unhide.
4. Select the appropriate hide option.

To unhide rows or columns, repeat the above steps, except the rows or columns on either side of the hidden row or column must be selected and the appropriate unhide option is selected.

To hide a worksheet:

1. Make active the sheet to be hidden.
2. Click the Home tab.
3. Open the Format menu in the Cells group and select Hide & Unhide.
4. Select Hide Sheet.

To unhide a worksheet:

1. Click the Home tab.
2. Open the Format menu in the cells group and select Hide & Unhide.
3. Select Unhide Sheet. A dialog box appears asking which sheet is to be unhidden. Click the sheet to be unhidden and click OK.

TIP   Unhiding Rows and Columns

Hiding a row or column is easy: You select the row(s) or column(s) you want to hide, click the right mouse button, then select the Hide command from the shortcut menu. Unhiding a row or column is more challenging because you cannot see the target cells. To unhide a column, for example, you need to select the columns on either side. For example, select columns A and C if you are trying to unhide column B. To unhide column A, click in the Name box and type A1. Click Format in the Cells group on the Home tab, point to Hide & Unhide, and click Unhide Columns.

Protecting a Cell, a Worksheet, and a Workbook

The advent of networks and information sharing also introduced the need to protect data from being altered and from falling into the hands of the wrong person. When you post a spreadsheet on the company network, it becomes available to any user of the network. Network users can make any change to any worksheet in the workbook file. Excel has protection controls that, used with the proper restrictions, can ensure that the right people see only the right data. Unauthorized users will not be able to get into the spreadsheet. Authorized users can edit only those areas you give them access to. The formulas that calculate the visible values are confidential unless you choose to make them visible. The issue of protecting cells, worksheets, or workbooks is an important one because it can determine if users can change an element of a workbook. Generally, when a workbook is protected, the creator of the workbook controls if changes can be made to a file.

Lock and Unlock Cells

All cells in a workbook have a locked property that determines if changes can be made to a cell. This concept has no effect if a worksheet is not protected. On the other hand, once a worksheet is protected, if the locked property is on, all cells are locked, and no data can be entered. Locking cells allows you to prevent viewers of your worksheet from making any changes to the cells. You can unlock just those cells you permit others to change. For example, if you are working in a payroll department and have created an employee salary worksheet that lists pay rates, you may want to lock this data to prevent unauthorized users from changing their own pay rate. Similarly, you would want to lock the formulas for calculating gross pay. Table 4.1 illustrates the protect sheet and locked property. You can see that the Protect Sheet command must be on along with the Locked Property in order to prevent data from being entered. It is possible to allow data to be entered in some cells but not all.

1. Select the cells where entering or changing data will be allowed.
2. Click the Home tab, open the Format menu in the Cells group, and select Format Cells to open the Format Cells dialog box.
3. Select the Protection tab, clear the Locked check box, and click OK.
4. Click the Home tab, open the Format menu in the Cells group, and click Protect Sheet.
5. Select a password if desired and clear the *Select locked cells* check box.
6. Click OK.

To unprotect the sheet and unlock all cells, click the Home tab, open the Format menu in the Cells group, and select Unprotect Sheet.

Table 4.1 Protect/Lock Sheet Property

Protect Sheet	Locked Property On	Locked Property Off
Yes	No data can be entered.	Data can be entered.
No	Data can be entered.	Data can be entered.

Protect and Unprotect a Worksheet

The process of protecting a worksheet can be a two-step process, because the protection can allow users to only perform certain functions in the spreadsheet or allow users to only perform certain functions in certain cells. To protect a worksheet, follow this general procedure:

1. Click the Home tab and open the Format menu in the Cells group.
2. Click Protect Sheet.
3. Select a password if desired and click the options that users will be permitted in the worksheet. See Figure 4.4 for a display of the protect options.
4. Click OK.

It is recommended that you only use a protection password in cases requiring very tight security and that the password be placed in a safe location. Passwords can be up to 255 characters including letters, numbers, and symbols and are case sensitive. It is up to you to choose a suitably difficult password but not one that uses all 255 characters. If you should forget the password, it is gone; you cannot get into the locked file any more than the people you were trying to block in the first place.

To unprotect a worksheet:

1. Click the Home tab and open the Format menu in the Cells group.
2. Select Unprotect Sheet.

Figure 4.4 Protect Sheet Dialog Box

Protect a Workbook

Even though protecting a worksheet provides a relatively high level of protection, it does not prevent a criminal or vandal from changing the structure or windows of a workbook. This could include such things as deleting or renaming sheets. Protected workbooks prevent anyone from viewing hidden worksheets; moving, deleting, hiding, or changing the names of worksheets; and moving or copying worksheets to another workbook. The general procedure you use for protecting a workbook is as follows:

1. Click the Review tab and click Protect Workbook in the Changes group.
2. Click the boxes for the protection desired, as shown in Figure 4.5.
3. Click Protect Structure and Windows.
4. Enter a password, if desired, in the Protect Workbook dialog box.
5. Click OK.

Figure 4.5 Protect Workbook Dialog Box

TIP   Protect the Formulas

The formulas in a well-designed worksheet should be based on a set of assumptions and initial conditions that are grouped together for ease of change. The user can change any of the initial values and see the effect ripple throughout the spreadsheet. The user need not, however, have access to the formulas and thus, the formulas should be protected. Remember, protection is a two-step process. First, you unlock the cells that you want to be able to change after the worksheet has been protected, and then you protect the worksheet.

Controlling Calculation

Calculation is the computing of formulas and the display of the results or values in the cells that contain the formulas. In Excel, the default recalculation takes place when the cells formulas refer to change. This default recalculation can be changed as circumstances warrant. Table 4.2 illustrates different recalculation schemes. These schemes all begin by clicking the Office Button, clicking Excel Options, and then clicking the Formulas category.

Table 4.2 Formula Recalculation Schemes

Recalculation Action	Steps
All dependent formulas every time a change is made to a value, formula, or name.	Click Automatically under Calculate options in the Calculate performance section.
All dependent formulas except data tables every time a change is made to a value, formula, or name.	Click Automatically except for data tables under Calculate options in the Calculate performance section.
Turn off automatic recalculation and recalculate open workbooks only when desired.	Click Manually under Calculate in the Calculate performance section.
Manually recalculate.	In the Calculation group on the Formulas tab, click Calculate Now in the Calculate group or press F9.

Printing Large Worksheets

Printing all or parts of a large worksheet presents special challenges to even veteran users of Excel. It is easy for you to make erroneous assumptions about what will print and be unpleasantly surprised. You must consider such things as Page Breaks, Page Orientation, Printing a selection, and the order in which pages print when printing all or part of a large worksheet. Figure 4.6 shows a worksheet that prints on six pieces of paper with just one column printing on page 3 and one row printing on pages 4, 5, and 6. You can adjust column widths, margins, and page orientation before printing and wasting paper.

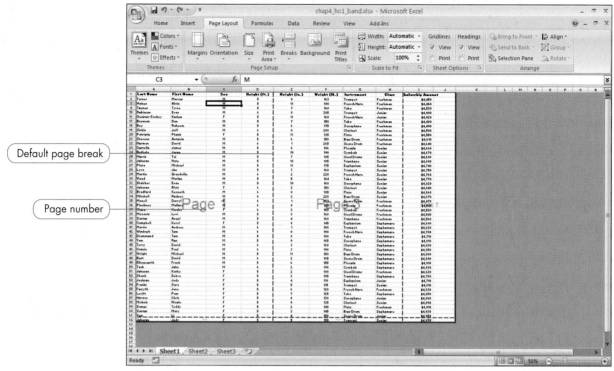

Figure 4.6 Page Break Preview

Manage Page Breaks

The **Page Break Preview** shows where page breaks occur and gives you the opportunity to change where the page breaks.

The **Page Break Preview** command shows you where page breaks currently occur and gives you the opportunity to change where the page breaks occur when a worksheet is printed. Figure 4.6 displays a Page Break Preview. The dashed blue line indicates where the default page breaks occur. To use the Page Break Preview command and adjust page breaks:

1. Click the Page Break Preview button on the status bar. If the Welcome to Page Break Preview dialog box appears, check the *Do not show this dialog again* box and click OK.
2. A watermark shows the page numbers.
3. Move the dashed blue lines as appropriate to adjust the page breaks.

Change Page Orientation

Printing an entire worksheet on a single piece of paper is more efficient in terms of paper use and provides the reader with the whole picture. The reader does not have to shuffle pages in order to get to the totals or perhaps the summary portion of the spreadsheet. One of the more efficient ways to have more of a worksheet printed on a page is to change the page orientation. Page orientation can be either Portrait (tall) or Landscape (wide). To change page orientation to print more of a worksheet on a page:

1. Click Orientation in the Page Setup group the Page Layout tab.
2. Select Portrait or Landscape.

Print a Selection

Excel users working with large spreadsheets sometimes want to print only a portion of a worksheet. Printing a portion of a worksheet involves selecting an area to print prior to actually printing. Figure 4.7 shows a selected area of a worksheet and the Print dialog box with Selection as the print range. Complete the following steps to print a selection or range of a worksheet:

1. Select the portion of the worksheet you want to print.
2. Click the Page Layout tab, and then click the Page Setup Dialog Box Launcher in the Page Setup group.
3. Click Print, and then click Selection in the *Print what* section.
4. Verify the selection using Preview.

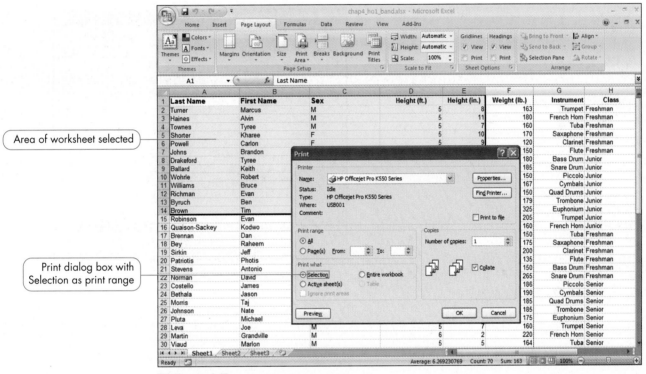

Figure 4.7 Printing a Selection

Control Print Page Order

The complexity of large spreadsheets sometimes makes it necessary for you to change the order that pages will print. The print order may be changed because the data will make more sense if the order of pages printed is changed or to keep like data together. When you have four pages to print, you can print left to right, 1–2 and then 3–4, or you can print top to bottom, 1–3 and then 2–4. You choose which order to print based on your worksheet; data may be arranged wider than it is tall. You control the order in which pages are numbered and printed. To change the order of the printing of pages:

1. Click the Page Setup Dialog Box Launcher of the Page Layout tab.
2. Click the Sheet tab.
3. Change the *Page order* options, as appropriate, as shown in Figure 4.8.

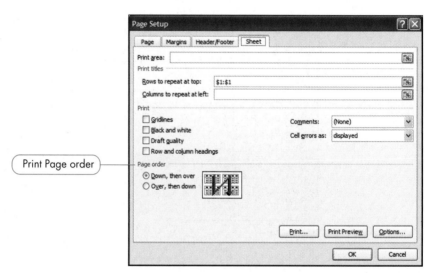

Figure 4.8 Page Setup Dialog Box

Hands-On Exercises

1 | Marching Band Roster

Skills covered: 1. Freeze and Unfreeze Rows and Columns **2.** Hide and Unhide Rows, Columns, and Worksheets **3.** Protect a Worksheet and a Workbook and Control Calculations **4.** Print a Large Worksheet

---

Step 1
Freeze and Unfreeze Rows and Columns

Refer to Figure 4.9 as you complete Step 1.

a. Start Excel. Open the *chap4_ho1_band* workbook and save it as **chap4_ho1_band_solution** so that you can return to the original workbook if necessary.

As you use the horizontal scroll bar to view the worksheet, note that some columns disappear. Rows also disappear when you use the vertical scroll bar. The worksheet is too large to fit on one screen and you must use Freeze Panes to keep parts of the worksheet in constant view.

b. Click **cell B2**, the cell below the row you will freeze. Click the **View tab**, click **Freeze Panes** in the Window group, and select **Freeze Top Row**.

Use the vertical scroll bar to see that the row data becomes visible while the row data labels remain constant.

c. Click **cell B2**, the cell to the right of the column you will freeze. Click the **View tab**, click **Freeze Panes** in the Window group, and select **Freeze First Column**.

Use the horizontal scroll bar to see that the first column data are always visible as columns become visible.

d. Click the **Freeze Panes** in the Window group and select **Unfreeze Panes**.

Now that the panes are no longer frozen, use either scroll bar to see that the worksheet is again too large to view on one screen.

TROUBLESHOOTING: Your screen definition settings may change your view of the spreadsheet and make freezing more or less important.

e. Enter and format a heading:

- Select **row 1**, click the **Home tab**, click **Insert** in the Cells group, and click **Insert Sheet Rows**.

- Click in **cell A1** and type **State University Marching Band Roster**.

- Select **cells A1:I1** and click **Merge & Center** in the Alignment group on the Home tab.

- Point to the title and right-click the mouse to display the Mini toolbar. Click the **Bold** button and select a font size of **14**.

- Click **Font Color** in the Font group and select **Dark Blue** from Standard Colors; similarly, open **Fill Color** and select the complement, **Accent 1, Lighter 80%** from the blue theme colors.

f. Save the workbook.

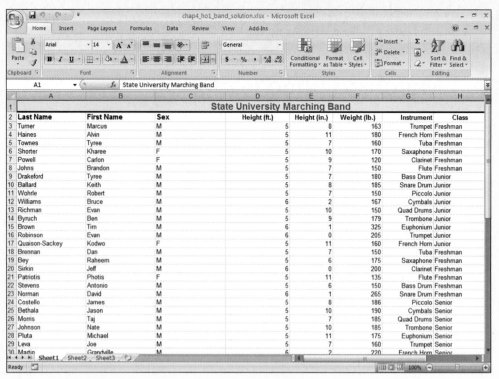

Figure 4.9 Freeze and Unfreeze Rows and Columns

Refer to Figure 4.10 as you complete Step 2.

a. Select **column F**. Click the **Home tab**, click **Format** in the Cells group, select **Hide & Unhide**, and click **Hide Columns**.

Column F is hidden and a thick black line appears between columns E and G, indicating the location of the hidden column. When you begin the next step, the line disappears.

b. Select **row 6** and open **Format** in the Cells group, select **Hide & Unhide**, and click **Hide Rows**.

Row 6 is hidden and a thick black line appears between rows 5 and 7, indicating the location of the hidden row.

c. Right-click the **Sheet2 tab** and select **Hide** to hide the sheet.

When a sheet is hidden, the sheet and sheet tab disappear, and there is no indication that a sheet is hidden, unlike a hidden row or column. Refer to Figure 4.10 and note the hidden row, column, and sheet.

d. Select **columns E** and **G**, click **Format** menu in the Cells group, select **Hide & Unhide**, and click **Unhide Columns** to display the column again.

TROUBLESHOOTING: Note that the columns on either side of the hidden columns must be selected prior to unhiding. Rows above and below hidden rows must be selected prior to unhiding.

e. Selecting **rows 5** and **7**, click the **Home tab**, click **Format** in the Cells group, select **Hide & Unhide**, and click **Unhide Rows** to display row 6 again.

f. Click **Format** in the Cells group, select **Hide & Unhide**, click **Unhide Sheet** to see the Unhide dialog box, select **Sheet2**, and click **OK** to display Sheet2 again. Save the workbook.

Figure 4.10 Hiding Rows, Columns, and Worksheets

Refer to Figure 4.11 as you complete Step 3.

Step 3
Protect a Worksheet and a Workbook and Control Calculations

a. Select **Sheet1** and select **cells G3:G63**, the cells that you want to edit.
   - Click **Format** in the Cells group, and then click **Format Cells** to open the Format Cells dialog box.
   - Click the **Protection tab**, click the **Locked check box** to deselect it, and click **OK**.
   - Click the **Home tab** and select **Protect Sheet** from **Format** in the Cells group to see the Protect Sheet dialog box.
   - Check the **Select unlocked cells** option if necessary, uncheck the **Select locked cells**, and click **OK**.
   - You unlocked cells for editing purposes, and then protected or locked all other cells. The only data that you can change is a band member's instrument. Try to change any player's name or other statistic except their instrument and you will see the Microsoft Office Excel warning box.

You must unprotect the worksheet in order to unlock the cells you previously protected and before continuing with this exercise.

b. Click **Format** in the Cells group and click **Unprotect Sheet** to unprotect the worksheet again.

c. Click the **Review tab** and click **Protect Workbook** in the Changes group. Then click **Protect Structure and Windows**. The Protect Workbook dialog box is opened. Verify that a check mark appears in the **Structure** box and click **OK** to protect the workbook.

Remember, you are the creator of the workbook and can make any changes. You have protected the workbook so that others cannot make changes.

TROUBLESHOOTING: If you enter a password in any dialog box, only those who know the password will be able to change data or perhaps open the workbook. If you forget the password, you cannot edit or perhaps cannot even open the workbook.

d. To unprotect the workbook, click **Protect Workbook** in the Changes group. Click **Protect Structure and Windows** to deselect it. Save the workbook. Close the workbook and exit Excel if you do not want to continue with the next exercise at this time.

e. Click the **Office Button**, click **Excel Options**, and then click **Formulas**.

Calculation options are displayed at the top of the Excel Options dialog box. You can use these options to change how and when Excel calculates formulas.

f. Click **Cancel** to close the Excel Options dialog box.

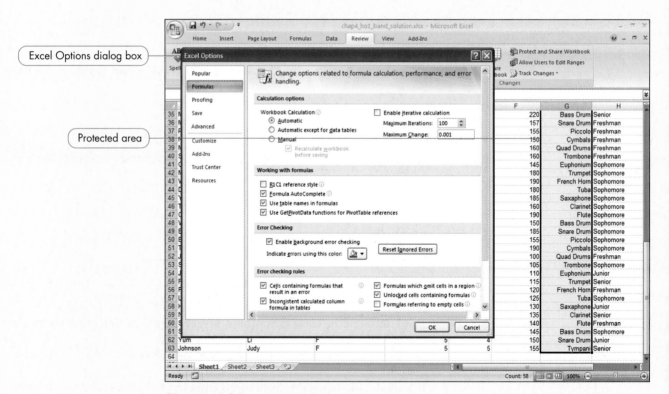

Figure 4.11 Protected Area of Worksheet

Refer to Figure 4.12 as you complete Step 4.

a. Click the **Page Break Preview** button on the status bar in the lower-right area of the window. If you see the Welcome to Page Break Preview dialog box, click **OK**.

You will use the Page Break Preview command to adjust the page breaks in a large spreadsheet.

b. Move the **blue dashed line** that separates pages 1 and 3 as well as pages 2 and 4 to the right to eliminate the page break.

c. Move the **blue dashed line** that now separates pages 1 and 2 down to eliminate the page break.

You will now see just page 1, as all page breaks have been eliminated.

d. Click the **Normal** button on the status bar to return to Normal view.

e. Click the **Page Layout tab**, click **Orientation**, and select **Landscape** to change the page orientation.

- Click the **Page Setup Dialog Box Launcher** on the Page Layout tab to launch the Page Setup dialog box.
- Click the **Print Preview** button and verify that the worksheet will print on one page.
- Click **Print** to print the worksheet.
- Click the **Close Print Preview** button to return to the worksheet.

Changing to landscape orientation enables more of the worksheet to fit on one page. You used the Print Preview feature to view how much now fits on one page before printing and then printed the worksheet.

f. Select **cells A4:H10**, then click **Print Area** in the **Page Setup** group on the Page Layout tab.

- Click **Set Print Area**.
- Click the **Page Setup Dialog Box Launcher** on the Page Layout tab to launch the Page Setup dialog box.
- Click **Print Preview** and verify that your selection is correct.
- Click the **Print** button to print your selection.
- Click **Close Print Preview** and click **Cancel** to close the Page Setup dialog box.
- Click **Print Area** in the Page Setup group on the Page Layout tab and select **Clear Print Area**.

You selected just a specific portion or area of the worksheet and verified that the selection you wanted to print was correct. You then printed the selection and after printing, cleared the selection.

g. Click in **cell A28**, click **Breaks** on the Page Setup tab, and select **Insert Page Break**.

h. Select **column G**, click **Breaks** on the Page Setup tab, and select **Insert Page Break**. Click the **Page Break** preview button on the status bar.

You placed page breaks above cell A28 and after Column F to print the worksheet on four pages.

i. Click the **Page Setup Dialog Box Launcher** on the Page Layout tab, click the **Sheet tab**, click **Over, then down button** in the *Page order* section, and then click **OK**.

j. Click the **Page Setup Dialog Box Launcher** on the Page Layout tab, click the **Print Preview** button to verify that you will print four pages, click **Print**, and then close the Print Preview window.

Before printing the four-page worksheet you changed the order in which the pages will print. (See Figure 4.12 and note that the Rows to repeat at top: box contains the default rows to print on each page.)

k. Save the workbook. Close the workbook and exit Excel if you do not want to continue with the next exercise at this time.

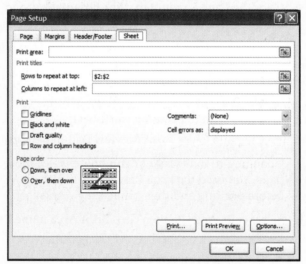

Figure 4.12 Print a Large Worksheet

Excel Data Tables

All enterprises, be they business, educational, or governmental, maintain data in the form of lists. Companies have lists of employees. Educational institutions maintain lists of students and faculty members. Governmental entities, such as the military, maintain extensive inventory lists. In this part of the chapter, we will present the fundamentals of table management, which is how Excel presents lists of data so that it can be manipulated by the program. This section begins with definitions of basic terms, such as *table*, *field*, and *record*, and then discusses the creation of tables; how to add, edit, or delete records in a table; and how to use the Find and Replace feature to change recurring data in a table. Formatting tables will be presented.

> All enterprises . . . maintain data in the form of lists.

In the first part of this section, you learn how to distinguish between information and data and describe how one is converted into another. Sorting of data in tables will be explored, both in simple sorts and in multiple-level sorts. In the second part of this section, you will filter records in a table and insert column totals and summary reports with charts.

The concepts associated with tables in Excel are database concepts. These can be difficult concepts to understand in the abstract, so the following example may help to clarify things. As the Director of Human Resources at State University, you manually maintain employee data for the members of the university faculty. You maintain specifics about each employee such as name, salary, and faculty rank in an individual manila file folder that is stored in a file cabinet. The file folders have the faculty member's name on the tab, and they are sorted alphabetically by last name in the filing cabinet.

This example shows the basics of manual database management. Each item can be equated to a database term. The set of manila file folders corresponds to a file. Each folder can be equated to a record. Each item within the file folder equates to a field in a record. See Figure 4.13 for an example of a file cabinet analogy.

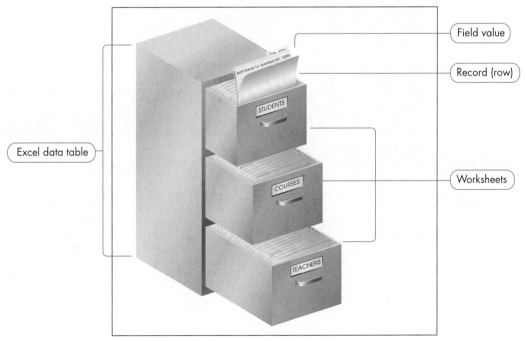

Figure 4.13   File Cabinet Analogy

A **_table_** is an area in the worksheet that contains rows and
columns of similar or related
information.

Excel maintains lists of data in the form of a table. A **_table_** is an area in the worksheet that contains rows and columns of similar or related information. A table can
be used as part of a database or organized collection of related information, where
the worksheet rows represent the records and the worksheet columns represent the
fields in a record. The first row contains the column labels or field names. This identifies the data that will be entered in the columns. Each row in the table contains a
record. Every cell in the table area, except the field names, contains a specific value
for a specific field in a specific record. Every record (row) contains the same fields
(columns) in the same order as every other record.

Figure 4.14 contains a college marching band roster. This roster contains nine
fields in every record: Last Name, First Name, Sex, Height (ft.), Height (in.), Weight,
Instrument, Class, and Scholarship Amount. Assigned field names should be meaningful and unique. Field names may contain up to 255 characters, but they should be
kept short so the column does not become too wide and unwieldy to work with.
How the fields are arranged is consistent from record to record. Last Name was chosen as the key so the records are in alphabetical order by that label.

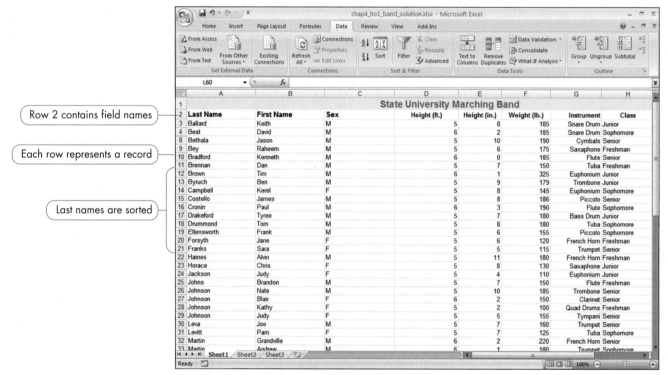

Row 2 contains field names

Each row represents a record

Last names are sorted

Figure 4.14 Marching Band Roster

Exploring Basic Table Management

Creating tables is a relatively straightforward task to complete in Excel. You choose the area in the worksheet that will contain the list, create the table, and then indicate that the table has labels or field names. Each field name must be unique to prevent confusion. Data for individual records are entered in the rows below the row of field names.

Once you have created a table, any field in any record can be edited, just as entries can be changed in a regular worksheet. The Insert Rows command allows additional rows (records); the Insert Columns command allows additional columns (fields); the Delete command allows deletion of rows or columns. Shortcut menus streamline many of these operations, and formatting can be accomplished from the contextual tab. The contents of the contextual tab are shown in the reference table. The table defines the Design tab, the groups it contains, and their general function.

Create and Use Tables

As described, the process for creating a table is clear-cut. Tables can be created either from data already in a spreadsheet, or a table may be created and then the data added. The steps for creating a table with or without data are similar. To create a table without data:

1. Select a range of cells on a sheet.
2. Click the Insert tab and click Table in the Tables group. The Create Table dialog box appears asking for the range of data for the table. Users should place a check mark in the box My table has headers. See Figure 4.15.
3. Click OK; a contextual Design tab becomes active once the table is created.

To create a table from already existing data on a sheet:

1. Select the range of cells on the sheet that contains the data.
2. Click the Insert tab and click Table in the Tables group. The Create Table dialog box described previously appears. Changes should be made as appropriate.
3. Click OK to complete the table creation and display the contextual Design tab. You will see that Excel automatically applied the default Table Style Medium 9 banded rows to your table. The contextual Table Tools tab is also the active tab, and each cell in the header row has sort arrows. See Figure 4.16 for the style, tab, and arrows.

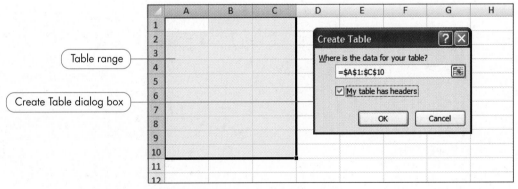

Figure 4.15 Define Table Area

Table Tools Design Groups and Description | Reference

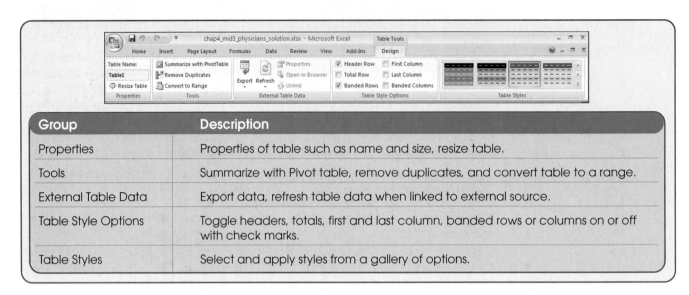

Group	Description
Properties	Properties of table such as name and size, resize table.
Tools	Summarize with Pivot table, remove duplicates, and convert table to a range.
External Table Data	Export data, refresh table data when linked to external source.
Table Style Options	Toggle headers, totals, first and last column, banded rows or columns on or off with check marks.
Table Styles	Select and apply styles from a gallery of options.

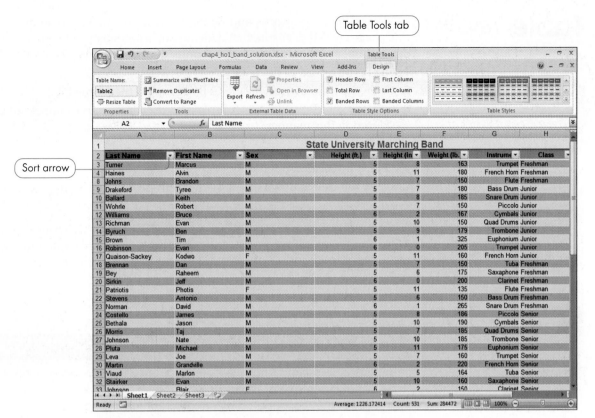

Figure 4.16 Data Table

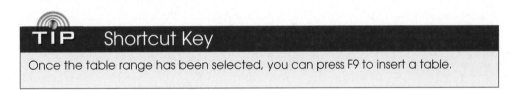

TIP   Shortcut Key

Once the table range has been selected, you can press F9 to insert a table.

Add, Edit, or Delete Records and Fields

Once you have created a table, you will add, edit, or delete records. You will use previously learned Excel commands. It is possible to edit any field in any record in the same way you change entries in a spreadsheet.

1. Click the field (cell) of the data to be edited.
2. Edit the data as desired.
3. Accept the change by pressing Enter.

To add or delete records as your data table expands or contracts, several techniques are available. To add a record:

1. Select a cell in the record below where you want the new record inserted and open the Insert drop-down list in the Cells group on the Home tab.
2. Select Insert Table Rows Above.

If you wanted to insert a field (column) in a table, you would make active the field to the right of where the field is to be inserted and repeat the previous steps, except that the selection from the Insert drop-down list is Insert Table Columns to the Left.

While deleting records and fields is physically an easy operation, extreme care must be exercised to ensure that data are not erroneously deleted. If you accidentally delete data, use the Undo command immediately. To delete a record from a table:

1. Select the record to be deleted.
2. Open the Delete arrow in the Cells group on the Home tab.
3. Select Delete Table Rows. Multiple records, contiguous or noncontiguous, may be deleted in this manner.

To delete one or more fields from a table:

1. Select the column or columns to be deleted.
2. Open the Delete down arrow in the Cells group on the Home tab.
3. Select Delete Table Columns.

Again, extreme caution must be exercised when deleting records or fields. Make sure you have selected the desired row or column before initiating the delete procedures.

 TIP Edit Clear Versus Edit Delete

The Delete command in the Cells group on the Home tab deletes the selected cell, row, or column from the worksheet, and thus, its execution will adjust cell references throughout the worksheet. It is very different from Clear Contents in the shortcut menu, which erases the contents (and/or formatting) of the selected cells, but does not delete the cells from the worksheet and hence has no effect on the cell references in formulas that reference those cells. Pressing Delete erases the contents of a cell and thus corresponds to the Clear Contents command.

Use Find and Replace

The Find and Replace command can be valuable when some part of the data in a table changes and there are multiple occurrences of the data. Rather than editing the data individually in each record, Find and Replace allows global editing of data. For example, Figure 4.17 shows a school marching band roster. The field shown in column H is each player's class. Rather than going to each record to edit the class, Find and Replace is used to advance the class level at the end of each school year.

1. Select the field that is to be edited.
2. Select Replace from the Find & Select down arrow in the Editing group on the Home tab.
3. Enter the data to be changed in the *Find what* box.
4. Enter the data that will replace the changed data in the *Replace with* box.
5. The user can either look at each occurrence of the data to determine if the change is appropriate or click Replace All to replace all occurrences at one time.

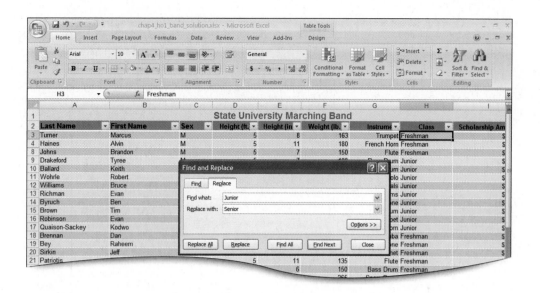

Figure 4.17 Find and Replace Data

TIP Garbage In, Garbage Out (GIGO)

The information produced by a system is only as good as the data on which it is based. It is absolutely critical, therefore, that you validate the data that goes into a system, or else the associated information will not be correct. No system, no matter how sophisticated, can produce valid output from invalid input. In other words, garbage in—garbage out.

Format the Table

Formatting tables can make them more attractive and easier to read, and you can emphasize data. The standard types of formatting available in worksheets are available for you to use with tables. Some of these format options, such as cell height and width, are available in the Format down arrow of the Cells group on the Home tab. Other formatting options are available in the Cell Styles gallery of the Styles group on the Home tab (see Figure 4.18). Other formatting options are present in the Number, Alignment, and Font groups of the Home tab.

The Design contextual tab provides a variety of formatting options for tables. The Table Styles group presents a selection of predefined table styles. You can see the effect of each style on a table by pointing to the style. Your table will display the style as you move the mouse across the Table Style gallery.

The Table Style Options group, shown in Figure 4.19, contains a set of boxes to select specific format actions in a table. Table 4.3 lists the options and the effect when each is selected. Whatever formatting and formatting effects you choose to use, remember that oftentimes less is more. It is not good to apply so many formatting effects that the message you want to present with the data is obscured or lost.

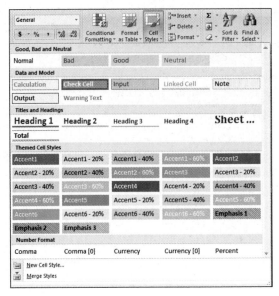

Figure 4.18 Cell Styles Gallery

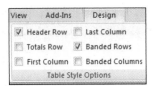

Figure 4.19 Table Style Options Group

Table 4.3 Table Style Options

Check Box Options	Action
Header Row	Turns on or off the header or top row of a table.
Totals Row	Turns on or off the totals or last row of a table.
First Column	Shows special formatting for the first column of a table.
Last Column	Shows special formatting for the last column of a table.
Banded Rows	Displays banded rows where even rows are differently formatted than odd rows.
Banded Columns	Displays banded columns where even columns are differently formatted than odd columns.

Sorting Data

The data in a table are easier to understand and work with if they are in some meaningful order. The marching band roster shown in Figure 4.20 is in no particular order, and it is difficult to locate individual band members. Parents would like the roster in alphabetical order so they can easily locate their children. Announcers and members of the media would like it arranged by name also. Instrument teachers would want it arranged by instrument so they can quickly identify the students they teach. University administrators want it arranged by scholarship amount so that they know who has been awarded how much.

Sorting arranges records in a table by the value in field(s) within a table.

The **sort command** puts lists in ascending or descending order according to specified keys.

Keys are the fields that records are sorted on.

Sorting arranges records in a table by the value of one or more fields within a table. The **sort command** puts lists in ascending or descending order according to specified keys. The most basic types of sorts are ascending, or low to high, and descending high to low, sequence. Putting a table in alphabetical order is considered an ascending sort. It is also possible to sort on more than one field at a time. An example of this with the marching band roster would be sorting alphabetically by class and then alphabetically by last name. The field or fields that you use to sort the table on are called keys. **Keys** are the fields that records are sorted on. Keys dictate the sequence of the records in the table; for example, if you want to put the marching band table in order by instrument, then instrument is the key field in the sort process.

Figures 4.21, 4.22, and 4.23 show the marching band roster worksheet sorted using three different keys. Figure 4.21 shows the roster sorted by last name. Note that the four Johnsons in the roster are not sorted in order. Figure 4.22 shows the same roster sorted by instrument. Finally, Figure 4.23 shows the roster sorted alphabetically by class in descending order.

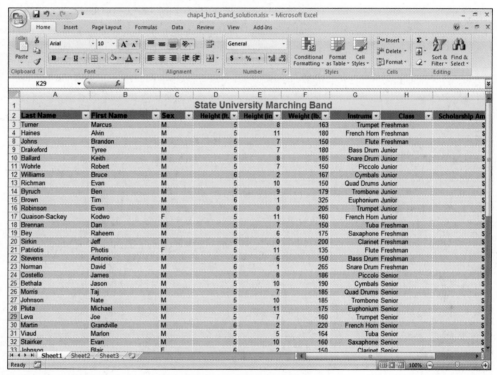

Figure 4.20 Data in No Particular Order

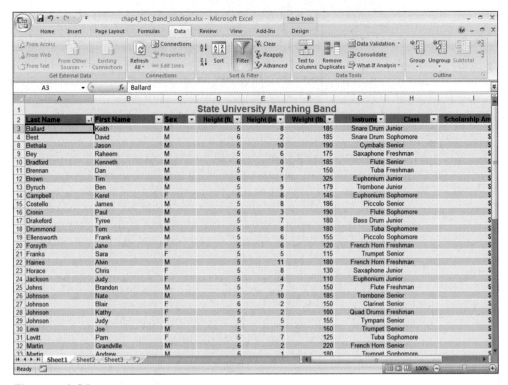

Figure 4.21 Sorted by Last Name

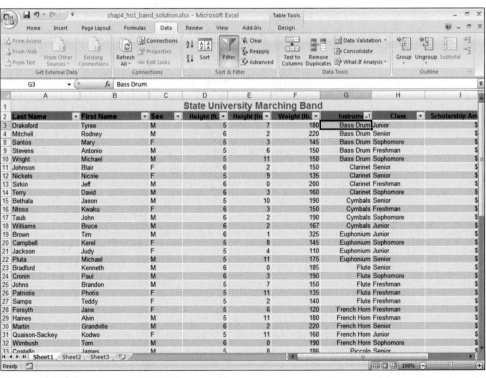

Figure 4.22 Sorted by Instrument

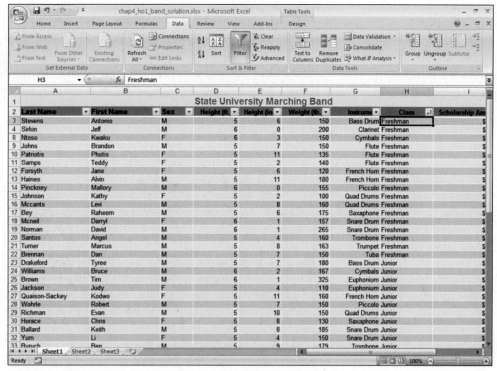

Figure 4.23 Alphabetically by Class in Descending Order

Sort in Ascending or Descending Order

The most basic sorts are those done in ascending or descending order. An ascending order sort will sort text data alphabetically from A to Z, and numeric data in increasing order, or 1 to 100, for example. The descending order sort will sort text data in reverse alphabetical order from Z to A, and the numeric data in decreasing order, or 100 to 1. To accomplish this:

1. Click in any cell in the column to be sorted.
2. Click either Sort A to Z or Sort Z to A in the Sort & Filter group on the Data tab.

Perform a Multiple Level Sort

At times, sorting on only one field yields several records that have the same information—for example the same last name or the same class. Refer to Figure 4.21 for multiple Johnsons and Figure 4.23 for multiple members of the same class. The single key does not uniquely identify a record. You might need both last name and first name to uniquely identify an individual. Using multiple level sorts allows differentiation among records with the same data in the first key. For example, university administrators might sort on Class, Last Name, and First Name to see an alphabetical list of band members by class. Excel allows sorts on 64 different keys. To perform a multiple level sort:

1. Click in any cell in the table.
2. Click Sort in the Sort & Filter group on the Data tab. This opens the Sort dialog box.
3. Click the Add Level button and choose the first key from the Sort by drop-down list. Verify that the results are correct.
4. Continue to click the Add Level button and add keys until you have entered all desired sort keys. See Figure 4.24.
5. Click OK.

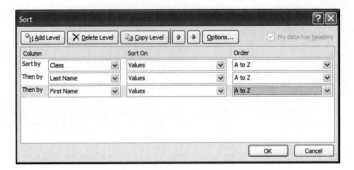

Figure 4.24 Sort Dialog Box

TIP   Choose a Custom Sort Sequence

Alphabetic fields normally are arranged in strict alphabetical order. You can, however, choose a custom sort sequence such as the days of the week or the months of the year. Click Sort in the Sort & Filter group on the Data tab. Select Custom List. . . from the Order drop-down list, choose a sequence other than the alphabetic, and then close the Custom Lists dialog box.

Filtering and Totaling Data

Data refer to facts about a specific record or sets of records.

Information is data that have been arranged in some form and are viewed as useful.

Data and **information** are not the same thing, although you often hear the two terms used interchangeably. Data refer to facts about a specific record or sets of records, such as a band member's name, his instrument, or his weight as reflected in the marching band roster you have been using. Information is data that have been arranged in some form and is viewed as useful. With the marching band roster, an example of data would be the entire list, but information is a list of members who play the flute. In other words, data are the raw material, and information is the final product selected based on that data.

Decisions in any organization, from businesses to marching bands, are based not just on raw data but on information. The military intelligence-gathering process is an analogy to the decision making process. Many pieces of intelligence data are gathered and analyzed prior to the preparation and dissemination of intelligence information. Similarly, a band director gathers data about such things as his members and their past performances before determining how many members who play which instruments need to be recruited.

In today's world, all organizations gather data that lead to information. The maintenance of data was discussed in some detail in the previous section. This final section of the chapter focuses on using data to create information.

Use AutoFilters

Filtering data using AutoFilter is a quick way to display a subset of data from a table. The filtered data display only the records that meet the criteria you, the Excel user, specify. Records that do not meet the specified criteria are hidden: Hidden records are not deleted; they are just not displayed. Figure 4.16 depicts the marching band roster we have been using, and Figure 4.25 shows the same roster filtered to show only those members in the band who are juniors. When you created a data table, Filter in the Sort & Filter group on the Data tab was highlighted. This default option indicates that the Filter command is available. To apply a simple AutoFilter to a data table, click the arrow in the column header. Either Text Filters or Number Filters will display according to the type of data in the column; see Figure 4.25. Remove the check mark from the Select All box, select the filter conditions(s) to be imposed, and click OK.

If the header column arrows are not visible:

1. Select the data table.
2. Click Sort & Filter in the Editing group on the Home tab.
3. Click Filter to show the arrows in each column header.

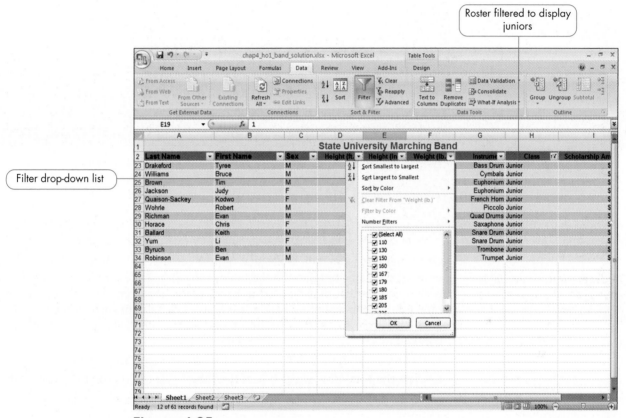

Figure 4.25 Filtered Roster

Use Multiple AutoFilters

Often, Excel users need to filter on more than one criteria to display the exact information required. Multiple AutoFilters can be used to return a more specific result. With AutoFilter, you can filter more than one criteria. Filters are additive, which means that each additional filter is based on the current filtered data and further reduces a data subset. To apply multiple AutoFilters you would repeat the steps described above until the subset of data is exactly what is desired. Figure 4.26 shows the marching band roster filtered to show only Snare Drum members who are also Juniors. Typically, you will filter from gross to fine. For example, if you wanted to identify the freshman female flute players, you would filter first by class (freshman), then by sex (F), and finally by instrument (flute).

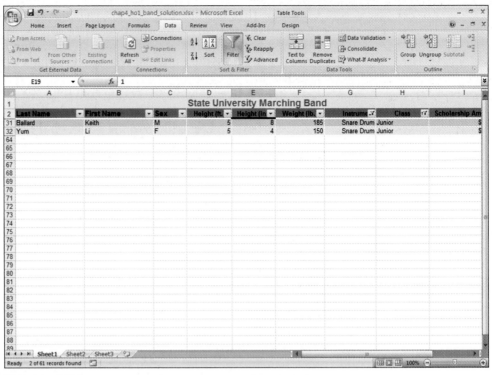

Figure 4.26 The Members Who Are Juniors and Play the Snare Drum

Insert Column Totals

Often, fields exist in data tables that require calculation in order to best display some or all of the data contained in the table. You can use Help to learn more about database functions that may be used in Excel. Here, however, you will find a simple column total. In the marching band roster, there is a field for each member's scholarship amount. Figure 4.27 shows a column total for the scholarships awarded to marching band members. To insert column totals:

1. Ensure a cell in the table is selected so the Design Tab is available.
2. Click the Total Row check box of the Table Style options on the Design tab.

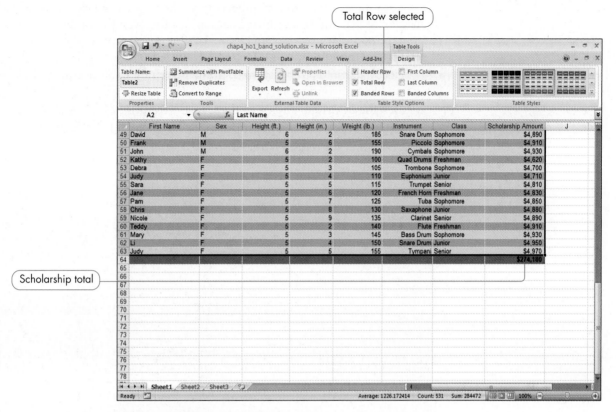

Scholarship total

Figure 4.27 Scholarship Total

Create a Summary Report with a Chart

Creating a summary report computes subtotals for groups of records within a list. It is imperative you remember that the subtotals command will not function with data in tables. The records in the list are grouped according to value in a specific field such as Class. The subtotals command inserts a subtotal row into the list when the value of a designated field such as Class changes from one record to the next. Automatic row insertions are not permitted in a data table.

A grand total is displayed after the last record. The list must be in sequence by the field on which the subtotals will be grouped prior to executing the subtotals command. The list can be sorted while it is a data table or when it is a list. Figure 4.28 shows a summary report for scholarship amounts by class for the marching band. To create a summary report:

1. To make sure the data are a list and not a table, click Convert to Range in the Tools group on the Design tab as necessary, and click Yes in the warning box.
2. Click in the list and then click Subtotal in the Outline group on the Data tab.
3. Select the criteria and the Add subtotal categories as appropriate.
4. Click OK.

Creating a chart of the summary data follows the principles used in the previous chapter. A chart of the summary data is an ideal way to graphically depict the data from the summary report. See Figure 4.29 for an example of a pie chart showing the scholarship amount by class. To create a summary chart:

1. Select data fields to be charted. In the marching band example, it was necessary to select noncontiguous cells.
2. Click the Insert tab and open the Charts group.
3. Select the type of chart appropriate for the data and click OK.
4. Format and move the chart as appropriate.

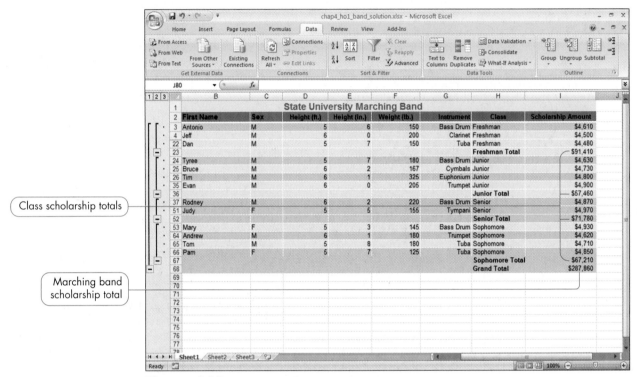

Figure 4.28 Scholarship Summary Report

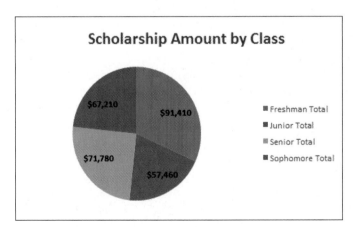

Figure 4.29 Chart of Summary Report

Hands-On Exercises

2 | Marching Band Roster Revisited

Skills covered: **1.** Create a Table **2.** Add, Edit, or Delete Records, and Use Find and Replace **3.** Format a Table
4. Sort a Table **5.** Filter a Table **6.** Create Column Totals and a Summary Report **7.** Print the Completed Worksheet

Step 1 **Create a Table**	Refer to Figure 4.30 as you complete Step 1.

a. Open a new blank workbook.

b. Select **cells D2:G13**.

> You have selected the area that will be defined as a table.

c. With the Insert tab active, click **Table** in the Tables group to display the Create Table dialog box.

d. Verify that the range of cells in the **Where is the data for your table?** box is correct, click in the box for **My table has headers**, and click **OK**.

> You selected a blank area of the worksheet and formally defined it as a table. The contextual Design tab becomes active once the table is created. Refer to the reference table to see the Table Tools Design contextual tab and groups. Also note the default style is applied to the header row with banded rows.

e. Close Book1 without saving it.

f. Open the *chap4_ho1_band_solution* workbook. Save it as **chap4_ho2_band_solution**.

g. Select **cells A2:I63**, click the **Insert tab**, and click **Table**. Verify the range in the **Where is the data for your table?** box, make sure the **My table has headers** box is checked, and click **OK**.

> The data in the selected range are converted to a table with a clearly identifiable header row. Each column header cell contains an arrow that will be used later. The default table style is applied with banded rows. You will change the style later in the hands-on exercise.

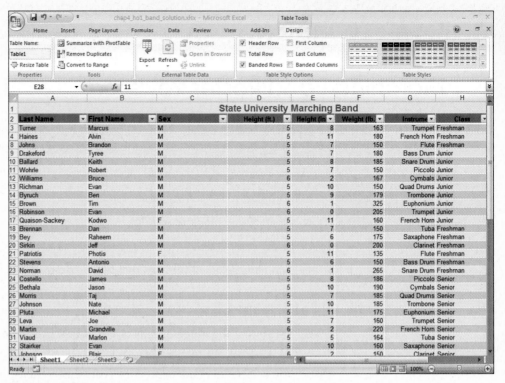

Figure 4.30 Table Created

Refer to Figure 4.31 as you complete Step 2.

a. Click in **cell F28**, type **195**, and press **Enter**.

You changed Michael Pluta's weight to 195 from 175. Editing a single field is done in this manner everywhere in the table. Click the cell and type the change.

b. Click **cell A11**, click the **Home tab**, and click the **Insert** down arrow in the **Cells** group. Select **Insert Table Rows Above**. Type the following data for the new record:

Cell address	Data
A11	Thomas
B11	Joe
C11	M
D11	6
E11	3
F11	167
G11	Tuba
H11	Sophomore
I11	4550

You inserted a blank record for row 11 and entered all the data for that record.

---

c. Save the workbook with the new record.

d. Select **cells A11:I11**, open the **Delete** down arrow in the Cells group, and select **Delete Table Rows.**

You deleted Joe Thomas from the data table and now see that Robert Wohrle is record 11.

TROUBLESHOOTING: If you accidently press Delete, the entire record is deleted.

e. Select **cells H3:H63**, open the **Find and Select** down arrow in the Editing group, and select **Replace**.

f. In the **Find what** box, type **Sophomore**; in the **Replace with** box, type **Junior**.

g. Click the **Replace All** button and a Microsoft Office Excel message box appears, indicating the number of replacements made.

h. Click **OK**, and then click **Close** to close the Replace box.

You replaced all sophomores with juniors and would repeat this step for each class after graduation. Because this is a fictitious scenario, you will not replace other text.

TROUBLESHOOTING: If no replacements were made, verify the spelling in the Find text box. Remember that using Replace All allows Excel to make the decision to replace all occurrences automatically. You must click the Replace button to manually approve the replace if you do not want all replaced automatically.

i. Click **Undo** on the Quick Access Toolbar to undo the replace. Save the workbook.

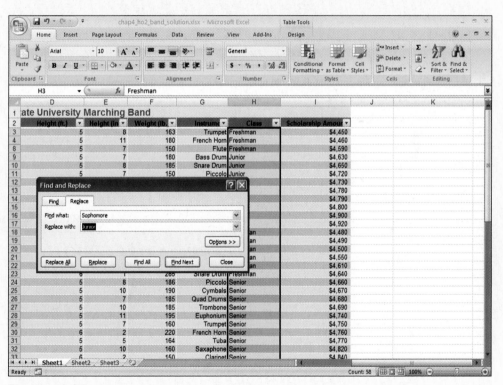

Figure 4.31 Edited Records

Step 3
Format a Table

You will explore the table style options group in this exercise by first changing the banding from rows to columns and then changing the style of the whole table. Refer to Figure 4.32 as you complete Step 3.

a. Click anywhere in the defined table, click the **Design tab**, and select **Banded Columns** in the Table Style Options group.

b. Remove the check mark from **Banded Rows** in the Table Style Options group.

c. Click the **More Command** in the Table Style group choose a visual style for the table from the **Gallery**.

Move the mouse over various table styles to preview the results. The live update is designed to provide you with a preview before making your final selection.

d. Click **Table Style Medium 7** (the last style in the first row of the Medium section).

e. Save the workbook.

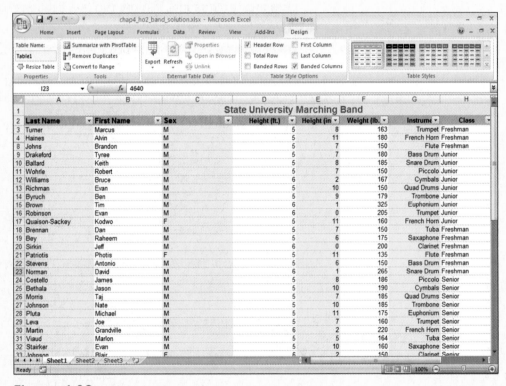

Figure 4.32 Formatting a Table

Step 4
Sort a Table

Refer to Figure 4.33 as you complete Step 4.

a. Click in any cell in **column H**, click the **Data tab**, and click **Sort A to Z** in the **Sort & Filter** group.

You have sorted the marching band roster alphabetically by Class (Freshman, Junior, Senior, Sophomore). Note this is an alphabetical sort, and there are several occurrences of the same last name in the roster.

b. Click **Sort** in the Sort & Filter group on the Data tab to open the Sort dialog box.

The Sort by Class option already exists because you last sorted using this key.

c. Click **Add Level**, open the **Then by** drop-down list, and select **Last name**.

d. Click **Add Level** again, open the **Then by** drop-down list, and select **First Name**. Click **OK** to perform the sort.

You sorted the marching band roster using multiple keys: alphabetically by Class, then by Last Name, and finally, by First Name.

e. Save the workbook.

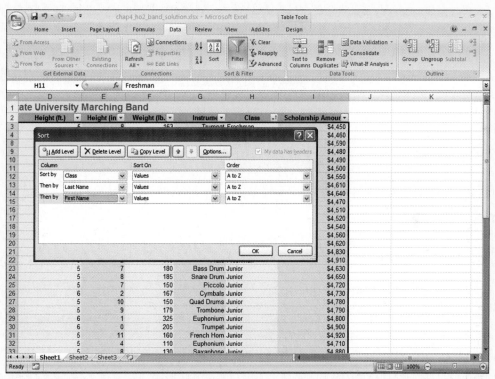

Figure 4.33 Multiple Level Sort

Refer to Figure 4.34 as you complete Step 5.

a. Click the column arrow for the **Class column** (column H). Remove the check mark from the **Select all** check box. Put a check in the **Junior** box and click **OK**.

This filter selected just the Junior members of the band and these are now the only data rows visible.

TROUBLESHOOTING: If the column headers do not display the Filter column arrows, click **Sort & Filter** in the Editing group on the Home tab and select **Filter**. Or you can click **Filter** in the Sort & Filter group on the Data tab. Either way, you will make the drop-down list visible in each column header.

b. Open the **Instrument** column arrow (column G) and **remove the check mark** for **Select all**. Place a check in the **Euphonium** box and click **OK**.

You have now reduced the Junior members to just those who play the Euphonium.

c. Click the **Home tab**, open the **Sort & Filter** down arrow in the Editing group, and select **Clear**. Save the workbook.

The Clear command removes all filters and all rows are now displayed.

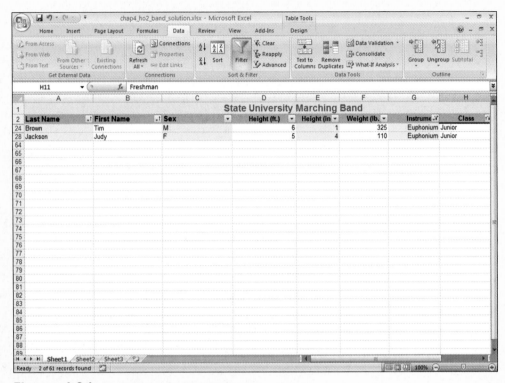

Figure 4.34 Multiple Level AutoFilter

Step 6
Create Column Totals and a Summary Report

Make sure that any cell in the table is selected and that the table is sorted by Class. Refer to Figure 4.35 as you complete Step 6. Note, some rows are hidden so you can see all subtotals.

a. Click the **Design tab**, check **Total Row** in the Table Style Options group. Save the workbook.

Scroll to see that you now have a total scholarship amount in cell I64 with a row label in A64.

b. Click **Convert to Range** in the Tools group on the Design tab. Click **Yes** in the Microsoft Office Excel warning box.

TROUBLESHOOTING: You must convert the data table to a range or list to create a summary report of the data. Also note that the Table Tools contextual tab has disappeared now that you have converted the table to a list.

c. Click the **Data tab**, and then click **Subtotal** in the Outline group to open the Subtotal dialog box.
 • Open the drop-down list for the **At each change in** label and select **Class**.
 • Open the drop-down list **Use function** and select **Sum**.
Make sure there is a check in Scholarship Amount. If necessary, check Replace current subtotals and Summary below data.
 • Click **OK**.
Scroll through your list to see the Summary Report totals for Scholarships for each Class.

d. Select **cells H23:I23**, **H36:I36**, **H52:I52**, and **H67:I67**. Click the **Insert tab**, click **Pie** in the Charts group, and select **Pie**.

You made a pie chart because this best shows the proportion of scholarship money by class.

e. Click the **Design tab** and click **Move Chart** in Location group to open the Move Chart dialog box. Click **New sheet** and click **OK**.

f. Click the **Layout tab**, click **Data Labels** in the Labels group, and select **Inside End**.

- Click **Chart** title in the Labels group on the Layout tab and select **Above Chart**.

- Type **Scholarship Distribution** as the title of the chart.

You selected just the summary report data and made a pie chart for a visual analysis of the data. You further enhanced the chart to highlight the charted data.

g. Save the workbook.

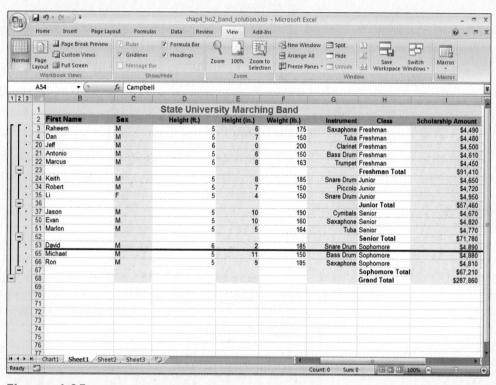

Figure 4.35 Summary Report

Step 7
Print the Completed Worksheet

You will format the worksheet for printing by adding a custom header and footer. You will position page breaks and select page printing order. Refer to Figure 4.36, the completed worksheet, as you complete Step 7.

a. Click the **Sheet1 tab**, click **Page Layout View** on the status bar, and then reduce the Zoom view to about **70%** and scroll to view four pages.

b. Click the **Page Layout tab** and click the **Page Setup Dialog Box Launcher** to view the Page Setup dialog box.

- Click the **Header/Footer tab**, click **Custom Header**, and type **Your Name** in the Left section, **Marching Band Roster** in the Center section, and your instructor's name in the Right section and click **OK**.

- Click the **Custom Footer** and use the icons to insert the date in the Left section and the page number in the Right section. Click **OK**.

- Click the **Margins tab** and select **Horizontally** and **Vertically** in the *Center on page* section.

- Click the **Sheet tab** and select **Over, then down** in the *Page order* section. Also check **Gridlines** in the *Print* section.

- Click **Print Preview** to make sure you have entered or selected the correct options.

- Click **Close Print Preview**.

It is important to view your worksheet before printing to verify your selections for headers and footers, page numbers, orientation, gridlines, and any other choices you make in the page setup dialog box.

c. Click **Page Break Preview** on the status bar and click **OK** in the Welcome message box.

d. Drag the vertical page break blue dashed line to the left so the page break is between columns E and F.

e. Drag the horizontal page break blue dashed line so it is between rows 36 and 37.

f. Click **Page Layout** view on the status bar and click **Page Setup Dialog Box Launcher** in the Page Layout tab.

g. Click **Print Preview** in the Page Layout dialog box to preview your spreadsheet.

h. Click **Print** and click **OK** to print your worksheet. Save the workbook and exit Excel.

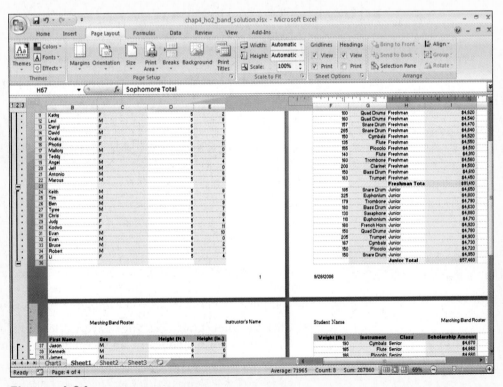

Figure 4.36 Page Layout View

Summary

1. **Freeze rows and columns.** Working with large worksheets, those that are too big for one monitor screen, can confuse users because they are not able to view the entire worksheet at one time. When working with a large worksheet, it is necessary to know how to view parts of the worksheet not visible, how to keep some parts of the worksheet always in view, and how to hide selected rows and columns. When a user is scrolling to parts of a worksheet not initially visible, some rows and columns disappear from view. It is sometimes valuable to be able to view row and column headings no matter where you scroll to, and this is done by freezing rows and columns.

2. **Hide and unhide rows, columns, and worksheets.** The hiding of rows and columns in a worksheet is a common practice and is done for a variety of reasons. It is done to conceal nonessential information, or information not needed at a particular time. There may be times when confidential information is contained in a worksheet, and rows, columns, or sheets must be hidden to allow nonauthorized users to view the worksheet.

3. **Protect a cell, a worksheet, and a workbook.** With the advent of networks and information sharing, the need evolved to protect data from change and from the wrong person. When you post a spreadsheet on the company network, it becomes available to any user of the network. They can make any change to any worksheet in the workbook file. Microsoft Excel 2007 has protection controls that, used with the proper restrictions, can ensure that the right people see only the right data.

4. **Control calculation.** Calculation is the computing of formulas and the display of the results or values in the cells that contain the formulas. In Excel, the default recalculation occurs when the cells that formulas refer to change. This default recalculation can be changed as circumstances warrant.

5. **Print large worksheets.** Printing all or parts of a large worksheet presents special challenges to even the veteran user of Excel. It is easy to make erroneous assumptions about what will print and be unpleasantly surprised. Users must consider such things as page breaks, page orientation, printing a selection, and the order in which pages will print when printing all or part of a large workbook.

6. **Explore basic table management.** Creating tables is a relatively straightforward task to complete in Excel. You choose the area in the worksheet that will contain the list, create the table, and then indicate that the table has labels or field names. Each field name must be unique to prevent confusion. Data for individual records are entered in the rows below the row of field names.

7. **Sort data.** The data in a table are often easier to understand and work with if they are in some meaningful order. Sorting arranges records in a table by the value of one or more fields within the table.

8. **Filter and total data.** Data and information are not the same thing, although you often hear the two terms used interchangeably. Data refer to facts about a specific record, such as a band member's name, his instrument, or his weight as reflected in the marching band roster you have been using. Information is data that have been arranged in some form viewed as useful. Creating a summary report computes subtotals for groups of records within a list. It is imperative that you remember that the subtotals command will not function with data in tables.

Key Terms

Multiple Choice

1. Which of the following lets you see and/or modify page breaks that will occur when the worksheet is printed?

    (a) The Page Break Preview command

    (b) The Page Setup command

    (c) The Page Breaks command

    (d) The Print Preview command

2. You are working with a large worksheet. Your row headings are in column A. Which command(s) should be used to see the row headings and the distant information in columns X, Y, and Z?

    (a) The Freeze Panes command

    (b) The Hide Rows command

    (c) The New Window command and cascade the windows

    (d) The Split Rows command

3. The command that lets you specify the order in which rows in a table appear is:

    (a) AutoFilter command

    (b) AutoFill command

    (c) Hide Rows command

    (d) Sort command

4. Columns A and B contain row headings, columns C through T contain the results of individual measurements you have taken, and columns U, V, and W contain summary and statistical information based on those measurements. What can you do to display and/or print only the row headings and the summary information?

    (a) Apply the outline feature.

    (b) Freeze rows and columns.

    (c) Hide columns C through T.

    (d) Hide columns A and B.

5. Which of the following options enables you to increase the number of columns that will be displayed on a printed worksheet?

    (a) Freezing panes

    (b) Changing from portrait to landscape orientation

    (c) Hiding columns

    (d) Using the Split command

6. You have used the AutoFilter command to display only certain rows. The other rows are not displayed. What has happened to them?

    (a) Nothing; the filtered rows are displayed in a new worksheet.

    (b) They have been written to a new worksheet.

    (c) They have been hidden.

    (d) They have been deleted.

7. All of the following statements regarding fields are true except:

    (a) Field names must be entered in the first row of the list.

    (b) Field names will change from record to record.

    (c) Field name must be unique.

    (d) Fields will be in the same order in every record.

8. Which of the following statements is true?

    (a) The Delete command can be used to delete a field, but not a record.

    (b) The Delete command can be used to delete a record, but not a field.

    (c) The Delete command erases the contents of the selected area, but does not delete it.

    (d) The Delete command can be used to delete either a record or a field.

9. You have a list of all the members of a club that you belong to. The worksheet contains other data as well. How can you be sure Excel recognizes the boundaries of the list?

    (a) Insert a comment in the upper-left corner of the list.

    (b) Insert a blank row between the field names and the data.

    (c) Insert a blank row and a blank column between the list and other data in the worksheet.

    (d) Type a row of dashes (- - -) after the last row of the list.

10. You have a list of all the employees in your organization. The list contains employee name, office, title, and salary. You want to list all employees in each office branch. The branches should be listed alphabetically, with the employee earning the highest salary listed first in each office. Which is true of your sort order?

(a) Branch office is the primary sort and should be in ascending order.

(b) Salary is the primary sort and should be in descending order.

(c) Salary is the primary sort and should be in ascending order.

(d) Branch office is the primary sort and should be in descending order.

11. You have a list of all the employees in your organization. The list contains employee name, location, title, and salary. You want to list all employees in each location. The locations should be listed alphabetically, with the highest-paid employees listed first for each location. Which is true of your sort order?

(a) Sort by location ascending, then by salary ascending.

(b) Sort by location ascending, then by salary descending.

(c) Sort by salary descending, then by location ascending.

(d) Sort by location descending, then by salary ascending.

12. You have a list containing all the employees in your organization. You select the AutoFilter command, and then select New York from the location field. What is the result?

(a) The list is sorted by city, with New York first.

(b) The rows where the location is New York are written to another worksheet.

(c) The rows where the location is not New York are deleted.

(d) The rows where the location is not New York are hidden.

13. Which of the following statements about the AutoFilter command is true?

(a) Records that do not meet the criteria are deleted.

(b) If two criteria are entered, records must meet both conditions to be selected.

(c) Records that meet the selected criteria are copied to another worksheet.

(d) All of these statements are true.

14. How must the data be arranged before creating a summary report?

(a) In a table

(b) In a list

(c) In either a table or a list

(d) In a range

15. Which of the following will compute a summary function for groups of records within a list?

(a) The Advanced Filter command

(b) The Subtotals command

(c) The AutoFilter command

(d) The Totals command

16. You want to show total sales for each location. What should you do before executing the Subtotals command?

(a) Sort by Sales, in ascending order.

(b) Sort by Sales, in descending order.

(c) Sort by Sales, in either ascending or descending order, then by Location.

(d) Sort by Location, in either ascending or descending order.

Practice Exercises

1 West Transylvania Education Foundation Silent Auction

You are assisting the director of the Education Foundation as she prepares for the Chef's Table fundraising event. Your task is to record silent auction donations as they are delivered and prepare the printed report for the director. The completed worksheet is shown in Figure 4.37, and you will use this as a guide as you practice freezing panes, editing titles, protecting the worksheet, and hiding rows and columns.

a. Open the *chap4_pe1_auction* workbook and save it as **chap4_pe1_auction_solution** so that you can return to the original workbook if necessary. Use the horizontal scroll bar to view the worksheet, noting that some column headings disappear. Rows also disappear when you use the vertical scroll bar because the worksheet is too large to fit on one screen. You must use Freeze Panes to keep parts of the worksheet in constant view.

b. Click in **cell B3**, the cell below the row and the column to the right of the column you will freeze. Click the **View tab**, click **Freeze Panes** in the Window group, and click **Freeze Panes**. Use the vertical and horizontal scroll bars to see that the row and column data becomes visible while the row and column data labels remain constant.

c. Click **Freeze Panes** in the Window group and select **Unfreeze Panes**. Now that the panes are no longer frozen, use either scroll bar to see that the worksheet is again too large to view on one screen.

d. Edit and format a heading:
   - Click **cell A1**, select the words **Silent Auction Donor Listing** in the Formula Bar, click the **Home tab**, and then click **Cut** in the Clipboard group.
   - Right-click **row 2**, then select **Insert** from the shortcut menu to insert a new row.
   - Right-click **cell A2** and select **Paste** from the shortcut menu.
   - Select **cells A2:L2** and click **Merge & Center** in the Alignment group on the Home tab.
   - Select **cells A1:A2**, click the **Fill Color down arrow** to open the Theme Colors palette in the Font group on the Home tab, and choose **Blue**.
   - Open the **Font Color palette** in the Font group on the Home tab and choose **White** for the title text.

e. Select **cells J4:J28**, the cells that you want to edit or protect.
   - Click **Format** in the Cells group on the Home tab and click **Format Cells** to open the Format Cells dialog box.
   - Select the **Protection tab** and clear the check mark from the **Locked box**. Click **OK**.
   - Select **Protect Sheet** in the Format drop-down list in the Cells group on the Home tab to see the Protect Sheet dialog box.
   - Check the **Select unlocked cells** option if necessary, and uncheck the Select locked cells. You unlocked cells for editing purposes and then protected or locked all other cells. The only data that you can change are Item Values in column J. Try to change any donor's name or other personal information.

f. Click **Format** in the Cells group and select **Unprotect Sheet**. Click **Format** in the Cells group and click **Protect Sheet**. Clear all check marks from the *Allow all users of this worksheet to* area and click **OK**. You must unprotect the worksheet in order to unlock the cells you previously protected and before continuing with this exercise.

g. Click **Format** in the Cells group and click **Unprotect Sheet**. Click the **Review tab**, and then click **Protect Workbook** in the Changes group. Click **Protect Structure and Windows** to open the Protect Structure and Windows dialog box. Place a check mark in the **structure** check box and click **OK**.

h. Click **Protect Workbook** in the Changes group and click **Protect Structure and Windows** to deselect it. Select **columns D** through **H** and click the **Home tab**. Open **Format** in the Cells group, select **Hide & Unhide**, and click **Hide Columns**. Columns D through H are hidden and a thick black line appears between columns C and I indicating the location of the hidden columns.

...continued on Next Page

i. Select **rows 6** through **12** and click **Format** in the Cells group, select **Hide & Unhide**, and click **Hide Rows**. Rows 6 through 12 are hidden, and a thick black line appears between rows 5 and 13, indicating the location of the hidden rows.

j. Click the **Sheet2 tab** to make it active, click the **Home tab**, and click **Format** in the Cells group. Select **Hide & Unhide**, then click **Hide Sheet** to hide Sheet2.

k. Add your name in **cell A30**. Click the **Page Layout tab**, click **Orientation**, and select **Landscape**. Click **Size**, select **More Paper sizes**, and pick **Fit to** 1 page. Click the **Margins tab**, then check to center the worksheet **horizontally**. Click the **Sheet tab**. Check the **Row and Column Headings** and **Gridlines**. Click **OK**. Print the worksheet, save the workbook, and exit Excel.

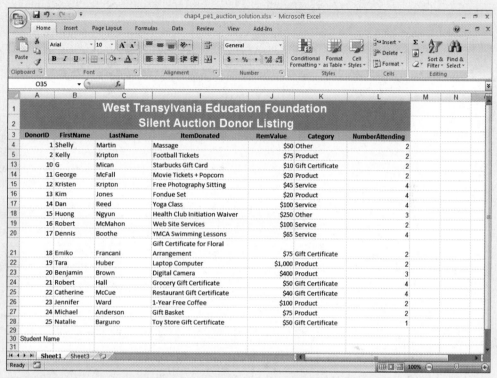

Figure 4.37 Silent Auction

2 West Transylvania Education Foundation Donor List

You are assisting the director of the Education Foundation as she prepares for the major funding event of the year. Your task is to format for printing and print the list of donors and their personal information so that they can receive an acknowledgement for income tax purposes. The completed worksheet is shown in Figure 4.38, and you will use this figure as a guide as you work with page breaks, page orientation, and control print order.

a. Open the *chap4_pe2_donor* workbook and save it as **chap4_pe2_donor_solution** so that you can return to the original workbook if necessary. You will use the Page Break Preview command to adjust the page breaks in a large spreadsheet.

b. Click the **Page Break Preview** button on the status bar in the lower-right area of the window. If you see the Welcome to Page Break Preview dialog box, click **OK**.

c. Move the **blue dashed line** that separates pages 1, and 2 to the right to eliminate the page break. You will now see just page 1 as all page breaks have been eliminated. Click the **Normal** button on the status bar to return to normal view.

d. Change the **Page Orientation** by clicking the **Page Layout tab** and click **Orientation**. Click **Landscape**.

...continued on Next Page

- Click the **Page Setup Dialog Box Launcher** on the Page Layout tab to launch the Page Setup dialog box.
- Click the **Header/Footer tab** and create a custom footer with **Your Name** in the center position.
- Click **Print Preview** and verify that the worksheet will print on one page.
- Click **Print** to print the worksheet.
- Click **Close Print Preview** to return to the worksheet.

e. Click in **cell A16**, open **Breaks** on the Page Setup tab, and select **Insert Page Break**. Select **column H**, open **Breaks** on the Page Setup tab, and select **Insert Page Break**. Click the **Page Break** Preview button on the status bar.

f. Click the **Page Setup Dialog Box Launcher** on the Page Layout tab.
- Click the **Sheet tab** and click the **Over, then down button** in the Page order section and verify that Gridlines and Row and column headings are selected.
- Click **Print Preview** and verify that you will print four pages.
- Click **Print** and then close the Print Preview dialog box.

g. Save the workbook and exit Excel.

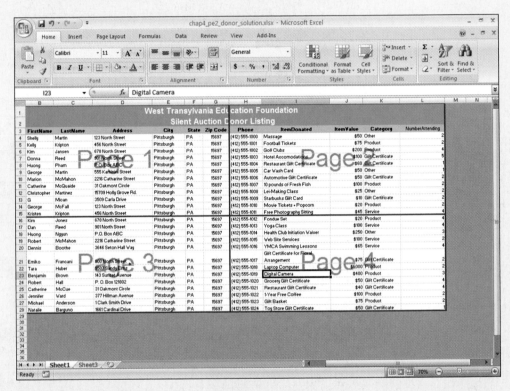

Figure 4.38 Education Foundation Donor List

3 XYZ Corporation Employee List

Your summer internship in the XYZ Corporation human resources department gives you the opportunity to practice your Excel skills. You are tasked with preparing a series of employee reports. You will use Excel and the data table feature to sort and filter the data into reports required by management. The data table you will work with is shown in Figure 4.39, and you will use this as a guide as you work with sorts and filters, but you will print several different pages.

a. Open the *chap4_pe3_xyz* workbook and save it as **chap4_pe3_xyz_solution** so that you can return to the original workbook if necessary. Select **cells A1:H156**, click the **Insert tab**, and click **Table**. Verify the range in the Where is the data for your table? text box, check **My table has headers**, and click **OK**. You defined the worksheet data as a table.

...continued on Next Page

b. Click anywhere in the defined table, click the **Design tab**, and then click **Banded Columns** in the Table Style Options group. Remove the check mark from **Banded Rows** in the Table Style Options group on the Design tab. Click the **More Command** button in the Table Styles group on the Design tab and select **Table Style Medium 12**.

c. Insert a new row above row 1 and type: **XYZ Corporation Employee List** in **cell A1**. Merge and center the title in **cells A1** through **H1**, and format the titles as **Comic Sans, 16, Bold**. Fill the title area with **Purple** color, and change the font color to **White**. Select **cells F3:F157** and format as currency, no decimals.

d. Select **cell A11** and click the Insert down arrow in the Cells group. Select **Insert Table Rows Above**. Type the following data for the new record:

Cell address	Data
A11	12378
B11	Your Last Name
C11	Your First Name
D11	Your Gender
E11	Trainee
F11	37800
G11	Kansas City
H11	Excellent

e. Select **cells A17:H17**, open the **Delete** down arrow in the Cells group on the Home tab, and select **Delete Table Rows**. You deleted Maylou Sampieri from the data table.

f. Select **cells G3:G157**, click the **Find and Select** drop-down list in the Editing group on the Home tab, and select **Replace**. In the **Find what** box, type **Atlanta**; in the **Replace with** box, type **Miami**. The company moved its branch office. Click the **Replace All** button and a Microsoft Office Excel message box appears indicating the number of replacements made. Click **OK**, and then click **Close** to close the Replace box.

g. Select **cells A4:H11**, then open **Print Area** in the Page Setup group on the Page Layout tab. Click **Set Print Area**.
   - Click the **Page Setup Dialog Box Launcher** on the Page Layout tab to launch the Page Setup dialog box.
   - Click **Print Preview** and verify that your selection is correct. Click the **Print** button to print your selection.
   - Click **Print Area** in the Page Setup group on the Page Layout tab and select **Clear Print Area**.

h. Click in any cell in column G, click the **Data** tab, and click **Sort A to Z** in the Sort & Filter group. The table is sorted by branch office location.
   - Click **Sort** in the Sort & Filter group on the Data tab to open the Sort dialog box. Click **Add Level**, open the **Then by** drop-down list, and select **Last name**.
   - Click **Add Level** again, open the **Then by** drop-down list, and select **First Name**. Click **OK** to perform the sort. You sorted the employee list by location, last name, and finally by first name.

i. Select **cells A22:H39**, then open **Print Area** in the Page Setup group on the Page Layout tab. Click **Set Print Area**. Click the **Page Setup Dialog Box Launcher** on the Page Layout tab to launch the Page Setup dialog box. Click Sheet tab and select Row and column headings, then click **Print Preview** and verify that your selection is correct. Click the **Print** button to print your selection.

j. Click **Close Print Preview** and click cancel to close the Page Setup dialog box. Click **Print Area** in the Page Setup group on the Page Layout tab and select **Clear Print Area**. Click the column arrow for **Title** (column E). **Remove the check mark** from the **Select all** check box. Put a check in the **Trainee** box and click **OK**. This filter selected just the Trainees in the corporation, and these are now the only data rows visible.

...continued on Next Page

k. Open the **Performance** column arrow (column H) and remove the check mark for **Select all**. Place a check in the **Excellent** box and click **OK**. You have reduced the Trainees to just those whose performance has been rated Excellent.

l. Click the **Page Setup Dialog Box Launcher** on the Page Layout tab to launch the Page Setup dialog box. Click the **Page tab** and select **Landscape** as well as **Fit to 1 page**. Click the **Header/Footer tab** and insert a custom footer with your name in the center section. Click the **Sheet** tab and select **Gridlines** and **Row and columns** headings, then click **Print Preview** and verify your changes. Click the **Print** button to print your filtered table.

m. Save and close the workbook.

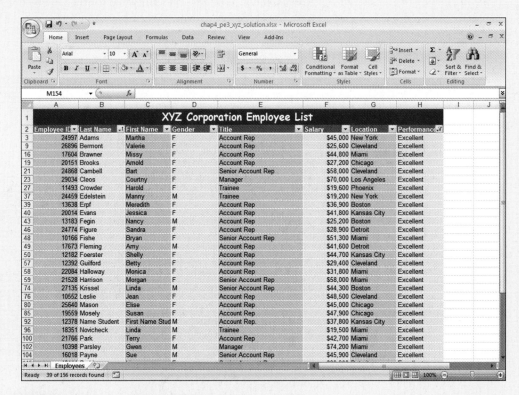

Figure 4.39 XYZ Corporation Employee List

4 Widget Employee List

As the director of Human Resources for the Widget Group, you will complete a worksheet that will show a total of salaries paid and further break down salaries by employee title. In addition, you will create a chart that shows salaries by job title. The worksheet and chart will help you assess salary outlays. The data table you will work with is shown in Figure 4.40, and you will use this as a guide as you work with sorts, summary reporting, and charting.

a. Open the *chap4_pe4_widget* workbook and save it as **chap4_pe4_widget_solution** so that you can return to the original workbook if necessary.

b. Click in any cell in column E, click the **Data tab**, and click **Sort A to Z** in the Sort & Filter group. The table is sorted by job title.

   • Click **Sort** in the Sort & Filter group on the Data tab to open the Sort dialog box. Click **Add Level**, open the **Then by** drop-down list, and select **Last Name**.

   • Click **Add Level** again, open the **Then by** drop-down list, and select **First Name**. Click **OK** to perform the sort. You sorted the employee list by job title, last name, and finally, by first name. The sort was the necessary first step in the creation of the summary report.

c. Click in any cell in column H, click the **Design tab**, and then check **Total Row** in the **Table Style Options** group. Scroll to see that you now have a total in cell H158 with a row label in A158. Make sure that any cell in the table is selected and that the table is

...continued on Next Page

sorted by Title before continuing. Click **Convert to Range** in the **Tools** group on the Design tab. Click **Yes** in the Microsoft Office Excel warning box.

d. Click the **Data tab**, and then click **Subtotal** in the Outline group to open the Subtotal dialog box. Open the drop-down list for the *At each change in* label and select **Title**. Open the drop-down list for *Use function* and select **Sum**. Make sure there is a check in **Salary**. If necessary, check **Replace current subtotals** and **Summary below data**. Click **OK**. Scroll through your list to see the Summary Report totals for Salaries for each Title group.

e. Select **cells A102** through **H108**, click the **Page Layout tab**, and then click **Print Area** in the Page Setup group. Click **Set Print Area**. Click the **Page Setup Dialog Box Launcher** on the Page Layout tab to launch the Page Setup dialog box. Click **Sheet tab** and select Row and columns headings, then click **Print Preview** and verify that your selection is correct. Click the **Print** button to print your selection.

f. Select **cells E101**, **H101**, **E108**, **H108**, **E143**, **H143**, **E161**, and **H161**. Remember to use Ctrl while selecting noncontiguous cells.

- Click the **Insert tab**, open the **Column** drop-down list in the Charts group, and select **Clustered Column**.
- Click the **Move Chart** button in the Location group on the **Design** tab to open the Move Chart dialog box. Click **New sheet** and click **OK**.

g. Click **Data Labels** in the Labels group on the Layout tab and select **Outside End**. Click **Chart** title on the Labels group on the Layout tab and select **Above Chart**. Type **Salary by Job Type** as the title of the chart. Save the file.

h. You will format the worksheet for printing by adding a custom header and footer. Click **Page Layout View** on the status bar, reduce the **Zoom** view to about **70%**, and scroll to view 10 pages. Click the **Page Setup Dialog Box Launcher** on the Page Layout tab to view the Page Setup dialog box. Select **Landscape**, and on the Header/Footer tab, click Custom header and type your name in the Left section, **The Widget Group** in the Center section, and your **Instructor's Name** in the Right section. Click **OK**.

i. Click the **Custom** footer button and use the icons to insert the date in the Left section and the page number in the Right section. Click **OK**. Click the **Margins tab** and select **Horizontally** and **Vertically** in the *Center on page* section. Make left and right margins .25". Click the **Sheet tab** and select check **Gridlines** in the **Print** section. Click **Print Preview** to make sure you have entered or selected the correct options.

j. Click Close Print Preview. Click **Print**, and then click **OK** to print your worksheet. Save and close the workbook.

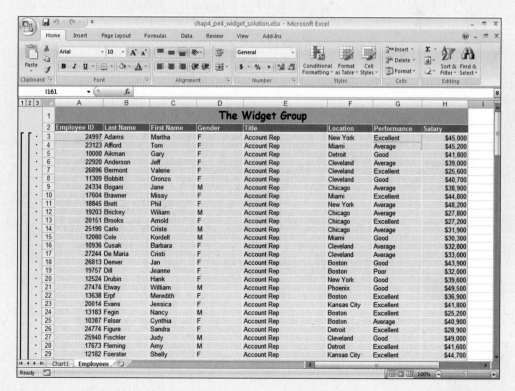

Figure 4.40 Widget Salary Analysis

Mid-Level Exercises

1 The Wedding Planner

Weddings by Grace is in the final stages of a wedding plan, your task as Grace's assistant is to group the guests attending the wedding by table number. The guests already have been assigned to a table based on their reception card returns. In addition, you will prepare a summary report showing how many guests will be seated at each table. You will print a report for Grace. Figure 4.41 shows the completed worksheet. Use this figure as a guide as you complete your worksheet, which will include subtotals, sorting, hiding columns, and printing a large worksheet.

a. Open the *chap4_mid1_wedding* workbook and save it as **chap4_mid1_wedding_solution** so that you can return to the original workbook if necessary.

b. Freeze rows 1 and 2 so that they are always visible. In cell A80, which is the first blank cell at the bottom of the list of guests, add your name and that of your guest in the appropriate columns. Type **2** as the number attending; you will be sitting at Table 01. Click in **cell A81** and enter your instructor's name and guest. Your instructor will be sitting at Table 02 and **2** will attend.

c. Combine the Names in Column E, Guest Names. Use the formal forms of Address, for example; Mr. and Mrs. Joe Sutherland, Ms. Nancy Miles and Mr. Jack Wadsworth, Drs. Sam and Judy Grauer.

d. Click and drag to select the column headings for columns A, B, C, and D so that all four columns are selected. Right-click in any cell in the four selected columns and click **Hide** in the shortcut menu.

e. Click in **cell F3**. Sort the guests by table number in sequential order then last name and first name ascending.

f. Use the Subtotal command to display the associated subtotal dialog box. The subtotals should be calculated at each change in table; that is, use the Sum function to add the total to the Number field. Check the boxes to replace current subtotals and to place the summary below data.

g. Add a yellow fill color to highlight the cells that contain your name and your instructor's name. Merge and center the text in **cells E1:G1**. Increase the font size in the worksheet title to 48, change the font to Comic Sans MS, bold the title, and then Align Right. Add a clip art image and resize columns and rows as appropriate.

h. The worksheet looks better if it is centered and printed on two pages. Display the worksheet in Page Break Preview and adjust the break so that the guests at Table 08 start the second page. Use the Page Setup dialog box to repeat rows 1 and 2 on both pages and preview the pages to be sure that two pages will print. Adjust top and bottom margins if necessary. Print the completed worksheet.

i. Save and close the workbook.

...continued on Next Page

Figure 4.41 Weddings by Grace

2 The Job Search

As the personnel director, you maintain a list of applicants. You are searching for applicants for two different positions. For the first, the position requires people who are bilingual, do not require relocation, and are judged to be experienced. The second position is a directorship requiring no relocation. You will print a report of the qualified applicants for consideration by the vice president for Human Resources. Figure 4.42 shows the completed worksheet results of the second filter, and you will use the figure as a guide as you complete your worksheet. Your work will include converting data to a table, sorting the data, applying multiple filters, formatting the table, and formatting for printing.

a. Open the *chap4_mid2_jobsearch* workbook and save it as **chap4_mid2_ jobsearch_solution** so that you can return to the original workbook if necessary.

b. Select **cells A2:H176** and convert the range of data to a data table. Sort by last name, and then by first name.

c. Click the **Bilingual** column arrow and select only those who are bilingual. Click the **Relocation** column arrow and select only those who do not have to be relocated. Finally, click the **Experience** column arrow and select only those who are judged to be experienced.

d. Format the title as shown in Figure 4.42.

e. You will format the worksheet in an attractive fashion. Use the Page Setup command to create a custom footer with your name, the date, and the name of the class you are taking. Display gridlines and row and column headings. Be sure the worksheet fits on one page. Print the worksheet.

f. Clear the three filters from the worksheet in order to initiate a second search for applicants who are applying for the position of "Director" and do not require relocation. Print this worksheet for your instructor and hand in both worksheets.

g. Save and close the workbook.

...continued on Next Page

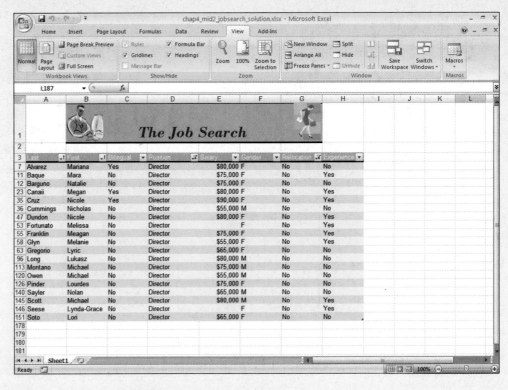

Figure 4.42 Job Search

3 Searching for a Doctor

You have just moved to Florida with your family and are searching for a doctor or doctors who can satisfy your family medical needs. You have obtained a list of more than 80 board-certified physicians from the state licensing agency. In this exercise, you will narrow the list using filters to a particular specialty, the city they practice in, and whether they take new patients. Furthermore, you will sort, format, and print the results for your family. Figure 4.43 shows the completed worksheet results. Use the figure as a guide as you complete your worksheet. You work will include converting data to a table, sorting the data, applying multiple filters, formatting, and formatting for printing.

a. Open the *chap4_mid3_physicians* workbook and save it as **chap4_mid3_physicians_solution** so that you can return to the original workbook if necessary.

b. Select **cells A1:H83** and convert the range of data to a data table.

c. Click the **City** column arrow and select only those who practice in Fort Lauderdale. Click the **Specialty** column arrow and select **Cardiology** and **Internal Medicine**. Finally, click the **New Patients** column arrow and select only those who accept new patients (TRUE).

d. Sort by specialty, last name, and then by first name.

e. Use the Page Setup command to create a custom header with your name, the date, and the name of the class you are taking. Display gridlines and row and column headings. Be sure the worksheet fits on one page. Print the worksheet.

f. Save and close the workbook.

...continued on Next Page

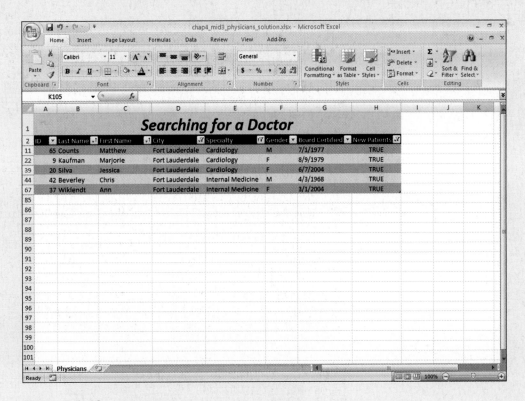

Figure 4.43 Searching for a Doctor

4 Population Analysis

Your geography professor has given you an assignment to analyze population data of the 50 states in the United States. In this exercise, you will determine the population density of each state, sort the states by geographic region, prepare a summary report showing the population by region, and prepare a chart illustrating the region populations. Finally, you will filter the list to show only those states in a particular geographic region and print both the chart and the filtered report. Figure 4.44 shows the filtered worksheet results with chart; use the figure as a guide as you complete your worksheet. The work you perform will include converting data to a table, sorting the data, applying multiple filters, creating a chart, formatting, and formatting for printing.

a. Open the *chap4_mid4_population* workbook and save it as **chap4_mid4_population_ solution** so that you can return to the original workbook if necessary.

b. Click in **cell F2** and enter the formula to calculate population density (population divided by area). Copy the formula for all states. Format the population as number with 1 decimal.

c. Sort the range by region and then by state.

d. Create a summary report showing population subtotals by region. Use the Subtotal command to display the associated subtotal dialog box. The subtotals should be calculated at each change in region. Use the **Sum** function to add the total to the Population field. Check the boxes to replace current subtotals and to place the summary below data.

e. Add a fill color to highlight the cells that contain the region name and the region's total population. Create a clustered column chart on a separate sheet that shows total population by region. Be sure to format the chart in an aesthetically pleasing manner, include a descriptive title. Rename the Chart1 tab **Region Chart**.

...continued on Next Page

f. Insert a row on Sheet1, then type the title **Population Statistics**. Select **cells A2:F60** and convert the list of data to a data table. Format the table using one of the table styles and format the title of the worksheet to match.

g. Filter the table by clicking the Region column arrow and select only Middle Atlantic, Middle Atlantic Total, New England, New England Total, South Atlantic, South Atlantic Total.

h. Create a pie chart as an object on the worksheet showing total population by the three geographic regions. Format the chart so it is color coordinated with your data table.

i. Use the Page Setup command to create a custom footer with your name, the date, and the name of the class you are taking. Display gridlines and row and column headings. Be sure the worksheet and chart fit on one page. Print the worksheet and the region chart.

j. Save and close the workbook.

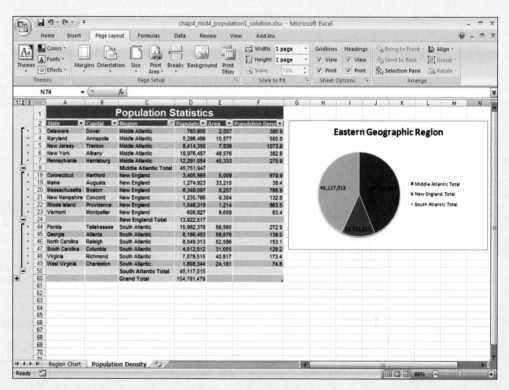

Figure 4.44 Population Analysis

Capstone Exercise

You are an intern with the Regional Realty Association and are analyzing the claim made by Alice Barr Realty that "we get your price." You have prepared a spreadsheet that shows data relating to three months' sales by Alice Barr Realty. You are going to determine the percent of asking price for each home sold that month. Determine which sales people have the most total sales and determine how many sales are made within the city of Miami. You will prepare an attractively formatted summary report for your boss and a chart showing the total sales by sales person.

Open and Save Worksheet

You must open a worksheet that lists home sales for three months.

a. Open the file *chap4_cap_barr*.

b. Save it as **chap4_cap_barr_solution**.

Calculate Percent of Asking Price and Format the Data

A formula is used to calculate the percent of asking price, and this formula is applied to all listed sales. You will format the list in an attractive and useful manner.

a. The percent of asking price is calculated by dividing the selling price by asking price. Enter the formula in column F.

b. Format columns D and E as currency, no decimals. Format columns G and H as dates so just the day and month (for example, 5-May) are visible. Change column F to a percentage with one decimal.

c. Widen columns to make all data and headings visible. Format titles as appropriate for the Regional Realty Association. Bold and center the column headings.

Sort the Data and Prepare the Summary Report and Chart

In order to sort the data by asking price and sales person, you must first convert the list to a data table. Once the data

are sorted, in order to prepare the summary report, you must convert the data table back into a range.

a. Convert the range to a data table.

b. Sort the data by asking price and then by selling agent.

c. Format the data table attractively.

d. Convert the data table back to a range.

e. Prepare a summary report showing total asking price and selling price by agent.

f. Use a fill color to highlight each sales person's total asking price and selling price.

g. Prepare a chart on a separate chart sheet that shows each sales person's total asking price and selling price. Include a title and a legend, and format the chart to compliment the worksheet. Rename the chart sheet tab Sales Analysis.

h. Print the chart.

Filter the Data Table and Print the Report

Your report should list just those properties sold in Miami by agent Carey, and you will use a filter to extract this data. Further, you must format before printing to make sure the report is documented and fits on one page.

a. Convert the range to a data table and filter the data table to show only those properties sold in Miami by agent Carey. Delete the Summary Total and Grand Total from the bottom of the filtered list.

b. Create a custom header with your name on the left and your instructor's name on the right. Change the orientation to landscape, center horizontally and vertically, and print gridlines and row and column headings. Preview your worksheet and make any necessary adjustments to print on one page. Save your changes, print the worksheet, and print the Sales Analysis chart.

Mini Cases

Use the rubric following the case as a guide to evaluate your work, but keep in mind that your instructor may impose additional grading criteria or use a different standard to judge your work.

Night on the Nile

GENERAL CASE

The University Museum is celebrating the 30th anniversary of founding with a glamorous "evening along the Nile River" theme that includes fine art, fine food, and lively entertainment featuring Egyptian dance and music. As a recent graduate and newly hired employee at the University Museum, you are tasked with maintaining the guest list, assigning guests to tables, and tracking payments for the fundraising dinner. Open the *chap4_mc1_nile* workbook and save it as **chap4_mc1_nile_solution**. You will convert the list to a data table and sort the data table. You will create a formula to calculate the total amount of revenue; the cost per person is $125. You will create a summary report to determine revenue by table and highlight the table totals. Format the completed worksheet as appropriate. Place your name somewhere in the worksheet. Be sure to use the Page Setup dialog box and tabs to create a custom header with the current date and page number, repeat the title rows on all pages, and center vertically and horizontally. Print the report. You will filter the report to determine who has not yet paid and then print this report as well.

Performance Elements	Exceeds Expectations	Meets Expectations	Below Expectations
Create and sort table	Table created correctly with headings.	Table created without headings.	No table created.
Create formula	Formula entered correctly.	Formula incorrectly used.	No formulas, numbers entered.
Summary report	Well formatted and easy to find totals.	Adequately formatted, difficult to identify totals.	No summary report.
Appropriate format for printing	All print format requirements met.	All but one print format requirement met.	Two or more print formats missing.

Census Data

RESEARCH CASE

Your geography professor has given you an assignment to analyze population data for the last three censuses. In this exercise, you use the census Web site to research the last three censuses, 1980, 1990, and 2000, to find the population for each of the 50 states. Once you determine the population of each state, you will sort the states by geographic region, prepare a summary report showing the population for all three censuses by region, and print the report. Finally, you will filter the list to show only those states in your geographic region. Prepare a chart illustrating the region populations and print both the chart and the filtered report. Open the *chap4_mc2_census* workbook and save it as **chap4_mc2_census_solution**.

Performance Elements	Exceeds Expectations	Meets Expectations	Below Expectations
Research census statistics	All three censuses found.	Missing 2 censuses.	No census data.
Create and sort table	Table created correctly with headings.	Table created without headings.	No table created.
Summary report	Well formatted and easy to find totals.	Adequately formatted, difficult to identify totals.	No summary report.
Chart	Chart correctly prepared and attractively formatted.	Chart correctly prepared with no formatting.	No chart.
Printed formatted report	Both summary report and chart printed.	Either summary report or chart printed.	Nothing printed.

Your service-learning project, tutoring students, is coming to an end, but you must provide assistance with data tables, summary reports, and summary charting in your final session. The assignment your tutoring student is working to complete is for a Political Science course that is analyzing the 2004 Presidential Election. Open the spreadsheet *chap4_mc3_tutoring* and save it as **chap4_mc3_tutoring_solution**, then find three errors. Correct the errors and explain how the errors might have occurred and how they can be prevented. Include your explanation in the cells below the spreadsheet. Review formula creation, summary report creation, and chart creation.

Performance Elements	Exceeds Expectations	Meets Expectations	Below Expectations
Identify 3 errors	Identified all 3 errors.	Identified 2 errors.	Identified 0 errors.
Correct 3 errors	Corrected all 3 errors.	Corrected 2 errors.	Corrected 1 or fewer errors.
Explain the error	Complete and correct explanation of each error.	Explanation is too brief to fully explain error.	No explanations.
Prevention description	Prevention description correct and practical.	Prevention description but obtuse.	No prevention description.

Data to Information

Data Tables, Conditional Formatting,
PivotTables, and PivotCharts

bjectives

After you read this chapter, you will be able to:

1. Design tables based on data table theory **(page 547)**.

2. Import data from text files and other sources **(page 548)**.

3. Apply conditional formatting **(page 551)**.

4. Apply advanced filtering and sorting methods **(page 561)**.

5. Create and use range names **(page 566)**.

6. Use database functions **(page 569)**.

7. Create and delete PivotTables and PivotCharts **(page 583)**.

8. Format, sort, filter, subtotal, and refresh a PivotTable **(page 587)**.

Hands-On Exercises

Exercises	Skills Covered
1. **GEE AIRLINES HUMAN RESOURCES DEPARTMENT** (page 556) **Open:** chap5_ho1_hremployee.txt and chap3_ho1_hremployee.accdb **Save as:** chap5_ho1_hremployee_solution.xlsx	• Use the Text Import Wizard • Apply and Clear Conditional Formatting • Import Access Data • Apply Color Scales and Icon Sets Conditional Formatting
2. **GEE AIRLINES HUMAN RESOURCES DEPARTMENT REVISITED** (page 574) **Open:** chap5_ho1_hremployee_solution.xlsx (from Exercise 1) **Save as:** chap5_ho2_hremployee_solution.xlsx (additional modifications)	• Use Date Arithmetic • Sort and Filter with Conditional Formatting • Use Custom AutoFilter • Create a Criteria Range and Use an Advanced Filter • Define a Named Range • Set Up a Summary Area and Use DAVERAGE • Use DMAX, DMIN, DSUM, and DCOUNT Functions • Change the Criteria
3. **EYE FIRST ADVERTISING DEPARTMENT SALES** (page 592) **Open:** chap5_ho3_salesrep.xlsx **Save as:** chap5_ho3_salesrep_solution.xlsx	• Create a PivotTable • Complete the PivotTable • Modify the Source Data and Refresh the PivotTable • Pivot the Table • Create a PivotChart • Change and Enhance the PivotChart • Complete the PivotChart • Create a Web Page from a PivotTable • Change Underlying Data

CASE STUDY

Legal Specialties

Your proficiency with Excel and data analysis has landed you an internship with a new national law firm with headquarters in Pennsylvania. The partners in the firm are in the process of recruiting lawyers to join their firm, although the real recruiting will start next month. The practice has just gotten started and fewer than 100 lawyers have signed on.

Before proceeding further, however, the partners want to analyze the lawyers already in the firm to be sure that they recruit the right specialties in the right geographic areas. Accordingly, the founder of the practice has provided you with the *chap5_case_law* file, Legal Specialties workbook containing existing data. The record for each lawyer in the workbook contains seven fields: the lawyer's first name and last name; the city in which he or she practices; the lawyer's specialty, gender, and date

of passing the bar; and an indication of whether the lawyer is accepting new clients. The founder believes an analysis of this data will provide the information he is seeking to make the necessary regional hires.

The multiple fields provide the potential for detailed analysis, for example, identifying the female lawyers in a designated specialty in a particular city or who passed the bar after a specific date. Perhaps the founder wants to locate all the criminal lawyers in the firm working in Erie for a client living in Erie. Another analysis might be to determine if any divorce lawyers who passed the bar after 2004 are accepting new cases.

Your Assignment

- Read the chapter carefully and pay close attention to sections that demonstrate creating and using data and information as well as the creation and use of PivotTable reports and PivotChart reports. Open the *chap5_case_law* file, which contains the collected data for the law firm.
- Examine the list of lawyers to determine which specialties and/or which cities are underrepresented. How would you display the data for analysis? Is a simple PivotTable report embedded on the worksheet the solution? Or is this best accomplished by creating a simple PivotTable, on its own worksheet, with the specialty in the row area and the city in the column area? What range name would you create when you are searching the data table? Consider how you would sort the data. Would you sort by last name plus first name plus city? How many levels of sort would be appropriate? Is it better to display the data using a filter with one or more filters applied?
- Count the number of lawyers for each combination of city and specialty. The founder of the practice is visually oriented and has requested a chart, as opposed to a table of numerical data. As you review the chapter, consider if conditional formatting might be used to enhance the information for the founder of the practice.
- Determine who the most experienced lawyers are in the firm. Use conditional formatting to indicate the most experienced lawyers. The head of the law firm would like to know which member most recently passed the bar exam and which member first passed the bar. Use appropriate database functions to determine the most experienced and least experienced lawyers.
- Print the completed workbook. The workbook should contain three worksheets: the complete list of participating lawyers, the PivotTable report, and the corresponding PivotChart report. Print the PivotChart in landscape orientation. Be sure that all of the fields for each lawyer fit on one page; this worksheet will still require a second page, and thus the first several rows with the column headings and descriptive information should appear on both pages.
- Create a custom footer that includes your name, a page number, and your instructor's name. Print the worksheet as displayed. Save the workbook as **chap5_case_law_solution**.

Table Management

People often refer to data and information as if the words refer to the same thing. In fact, however, data and information are different. If the terms were put on a continuum, it would be easy to say that you start with data and end with information. Data are facts about a specific record. Information is data put into a useful form by a user.

A series of names is data, but sorting the list alphabetically and adding the title *Class Roster* to the list of names transforms data into useful information. Another example, the date July 4, 1776, is data; stating that the Declaration of Independence was signed on July 4, 1776, becomes information.

> All organizations maintain data in order to produce information that is used to make informed decisions.

All organizations maintain data in order to produce information that is used to make informed decisions. Data are converted to information through a combination of database functions and commands discussed in this chapter. You can prepare many reports from a data table in Excel using database functions and commands such as custom sorts, advanced filters, and other specialized reporting techniques. In this section, you design tables based on data table theory, import text files, and apply conditional formatting.

Designing Tables Based on Data Table Theory

Often data tables are created from existing files, and little or no thought is put into the creation of a data table that will be used for complex data analysis. A poorly designed table may result in flawed analysis or make it impossible to generate the information a company requires. Just as you spent time planning a spreadsheet, you should plan the elements of a data table. You should think about who will use the data table, what types of reports will be produced, and what types of searches might be done. As a general rule, the more thorough your planning process is, the fewer changes will be needed to the table after it is created and in use. Though it is not always necessary, it can be helpful to set up a small table with your field names and sample data. You can then create field names that are descriptive of their function in your table.

Below are some guidelines that can make the construction of a data table more efficient:

- The top row should contain the field names for the data table.
- Field names should be short, descriptive, and easy to remember.
- Formatting the field names makes them easy for users to identify.
- Each column should contain the same type of information for each row in the table.
- Though a table can be just part of a worksheet, it helps to separate it from other elements of the spreadsheet.

Importing Data from Text Files and Other Sources

Importing is the process of inserting data from another application. As you work in an organization, you will probably need to import data created in another format or in another application into an Excel table. This often occurs when data are stored on a mainframe computer, an Access database table, or another source and are then analyzed on a PC. Though it is possible to import text files as an external data range where the data remains outside Excel, generally, you will want to import a text file by opening it, forgoing the conversion that is necessary when importing a file as an external data range.

Depending on your future needs, you may want to import files using the Open dialog box. Doing so imports the original data but does not maintain a connection to the original data. Changes in the original data do not update in Excel. If you want to maintain a connection to the original data, use the commands in the Get External Data group on the Data tab to import data from several supported source formats, such as text files, Access database tables, Web data, and other sources. When you want to maintain a connection to the data source, use the Data Connection Wizard to create the connection. To see existing data connections, click Existing Connections in the Get External Data group on the Data tab. You will want to maintain a connection to live data when using a just-in-time inventory system. Just-in-time inventory systems are commonly found in retail establishments and hospital pharmacies. If you use Excel with library circulation systems, you might maintain a live data connection. Maintaining the connection is a way to use current data without repeating the copy-and-paste or import steps each time you analyze the data.

Import a Text File

Text files, distinguished by the .txt file extension, contain ordinary textual characters with no formatting, graphical characters, or sound and video data. Text files are made up of letters, digits, and punctuation, including spaces. Comma Separated Value (CSV) files contain fields separated by commas and rows separated by a new-line character. Both text and CSV-formatted files are used to exchange data between different applications. The CSV format is the standard for moving data between applications.

Text file data are often imported into Excel for use in a spreadsheet. Individual data elements are separated by a delimiter. A *delimiter* is a character used to separate one column from another in the text file. Fields are arranged in rows, and when imported into Excel fields become columns. The most common delimiters in a text file are commas or tabs. Figure 5.1 shows a comma-delimited text file and the Excel workbook created when the text file is imported.

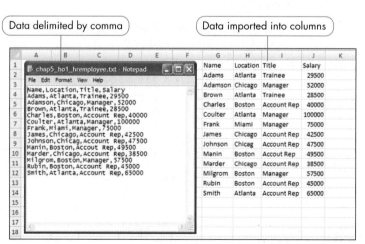

Figure 5.1 Comma-Delimited Text File and Data Imported into Excel

You can import and convert a text file created in another application into an Excel workbook. To import a text file, display the Open dialog box, select Text Files from the *Files of type* drop-down list, and then double-click the text file that contains data you want to import. If the file is a .csv file, Excel automatically converts the file and opens it. If the file is a .txt file, the Text Import Wizard appears, prompting you for information about the external data, and then converts the data into an Excel workbook during these three major steps:

1. Select *Delimited* or *Fixed width* based on how the text is formatted and set the *Start import at row* value to where you want the data to begin (see Figure 5.2). If the text file contains a title or extraneous data extending across multiple columns, you would not import from row 1; you would start importing from the row that contains the actual data. A fixed-width text file is one where fields are aligned and spaces are used to separate the fields. Click Next at the bottom of the Text Import Wizard – Step 1 of 3 dialog box.

2. Do one of the following in the Text Import Wizard – Step 2 of 3 dialog box, and then click Next.

   • If the text file is delimited, check the appropriate delimiter symbol, such as Tab (see Figure 5.3).

   • If the text file is fixed-width, move the column break lines to where the columns begin and end.

3. Select a *Column data format* for the columns to be imported, then click the *Do not import column* option to skip a specific column in the Text Import Wizard – Step 3 of 3 dialog box (see Figure 5.4). Click Finish.

TIP   Connecting to a Text File

If you click From Text in the Get External Data group on the Data tab, you import the text file with a connection to the original text file. This approach, in contrast to the previous method, enables you to refresh the data in Excel to match any changes made to the original text file, as long as the text file is in the same location.

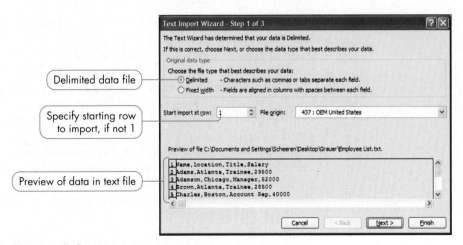

Figure 5.2 Step 1 Text Import Wizard

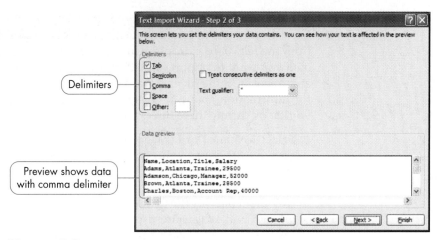

Figure 5.3 Step 2 Text Import Wizard

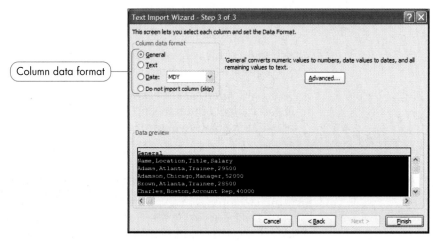

Figure 5.4 Step 3 Import Text Wizard

Import an Access Database Table

Excel and Access are two programs in the Microsoft Office 2007 Suite. As you work with Microsoft Office 2007, often you will need to import an Access database into Excel to analyze the data in more detail. Access databases may be imported in three ways: as a table, as a PivotTable Report, or as a PivotChart and Pivot Table Report.

Car dealerships maintain a database of cars in inventory and cars sold, but may use Excel to analyze weekly or monthly car sales data. The ability to import the Access database into a PivotTable Report or PivotChart and PivotTable Report gives you unprecedented power to analyze the data. When importing an Access database into Excel, you can maintain a live connection to the data. This way when cars are sold or added to inventory, in the above example, the Excel spreadsheet automatically updates. Furthermore, maintaining a connection to the Access database eliminates the need to continually copy and paste data from Access to Excel.

To import an Access database into Excel:

1. Click From Access in the Get External Data group on the Data tab.
2. In the Select Data Source dialog box, locate the Access file to be imported, select it, and click open.
3. Choose a table from the list of Access tables and click OK.
4. In the Import Data dialog box (see Figure 5.5), select how you want to view the data in your workbook and where you want to put the data, and click OK.

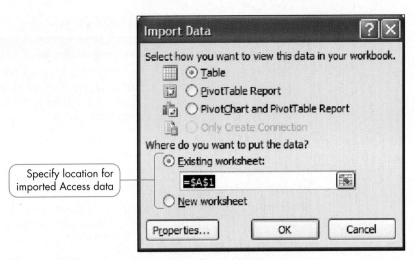

Figure 5.5 Import Access Data Dialog Box

Specify location for imported Access data

Import Data from Other Sources

Data can be imported from sources other than text files and Access databases. The From Other Sources command in the Get External Data group lists several types of sources. The other sources are listed and summarized in Table 5.1.

Table 5.1 Importing Data from Other Sources

Source	Definition
SQL Server	Create a connection to a SQL Server Table and import data as a table or PivotTable report.
Analysis Services	Create a connection to a SQL Server Analysis Services cube. Import data as a table or PivotTable report.
XML Data Import	Open or map an XML file into Excel.
Data Connection Wizard	Import data for an unlisted format by using the Data Connection Wizard or OLEDB.
Microsoft Query	Import data for an unlisted format by using the Microsoft Query Wizard and ODBC.

Applying Conditional Formatting

Conditional formatting applies specific formats to cells that contain particular values.

When the data in a cell meet specified conditions, the formatting that appears in that cell is referred to as conditional formatting. *Conditional formatting* is used to apply specific formats automatically to cells that contain particular values or content. For example, you might want to identify cells containing the year 2009 by applying a different fill color to those cells. You would use conditional formatting for this task. Conditional formatting makes it easy to highlight interesting cells or ranges of cells, emphasize unusual or duplicate values, or visualize data using data bars, color scales, or icon sets. For example, you might have every cell that contains a test score below 60% turn red. A baseball coach might want to highlight cells with batting averages above 300 in green. Conditional formatting is another way to visualize data. In conditional formatting, if the condition is true, the cell is formatted automatically based on that condition. If it is false, the cell is not formatted based on that condition. If you change a value in a conditionally formatted cell, Excel examines the new value to see if it should apply the conditional formatting. Table 5.2 lists and describes a number of different conditional formats that you can apply.

Table 5.2 Conditional Formatting Options

Conditional Formatting	Display Description
Highlight Cell Rules	Formats cells if values are greater than, less than, between two values, or equal to a value. Formats text that contains particular letters, a specific date, or duplicate values.
Top/Bottom Rules	Formats the top 10 items, the top 10%, bottom 10 items, bottom 10%, values above the average, or values below the average. This is used in education and economics statistics.
Data Bars	Displays gradient-filled horizontal bars in which the bar length represents the value in relation to other values in the column.
Color Scales	Formats different cells with different colors, assigns one color to the lowest value, another color to the highest value, and a blend of these colors to all other values.
Icon Sets	Uses an icon from the icon palette to indicate values. Sometimes used to show progress in contests. Only Excel's predefined icon set is used.

Data bars are gradient-colored bars that help you visualize the value of a cell relative to other cells.

Data bars help you visualize the value of a cell relative to other cells, as shown in Figure 5.6. The width of the gradient data bar represents the value in a cell, with a wider bar representing a higher value and a shorter bar a lower value. Data bar conditional formatting is used when identifying high and low values in large amounts of data. Excel locates the largest value and makes it the widest data bar. Excel then finds the smallest value and makes it the smallest data bar. If you change the values in your worksheet, Excel automatically updates the widths of the data bars. Data bars are used to view large values in relation to small values, are most useful when working with a big range of values, and are more effective with wider columns than narrow columns.

	A	B	C	D	E	F
1				WCCC Challenge		
2		Monday	Tuesday	Wednesd:	Thursday	Friday
3	Joe Smith	14	16	19	45	36
4	Frank Thomas	4	22	54	110	90
5	Tom Jones	30	45	44	25	20
6	Leona Riley	8	6	6	17	1
7	Jane Doe	12	13	10	6	15
8	Kathy Bena	74	7	16	19	25
9	Anna Genwich	33	26	20	35	35
10	Tom Albaugh	4	29	6	10	10

Figure 5.6 Data Bars Conditional Formatting

Color scales format cells with colors based on the relative value of a cell compared to other cells.

Color scales format cells with different colors based on the relative value of a cell compared to other adjacent cells. Cells may be formatted using a two-color scale. This scale assists in comparing a range of cells using gradations of two colors. The shade of the color represents higher or lower values. Cells may also be formatted with a three-color scale. This scale helps you compare a range of cells by using gradations of three colors. The shade of the color represents the high, middle, or lower values. Figure 5.7 shows an example of color scales conditional formatting. The color scale, unlike data bars, uses shading to visualize relative values. Use color scales to understand variation in the data to identify trends, for example to view good stock returns and weak stock returns.

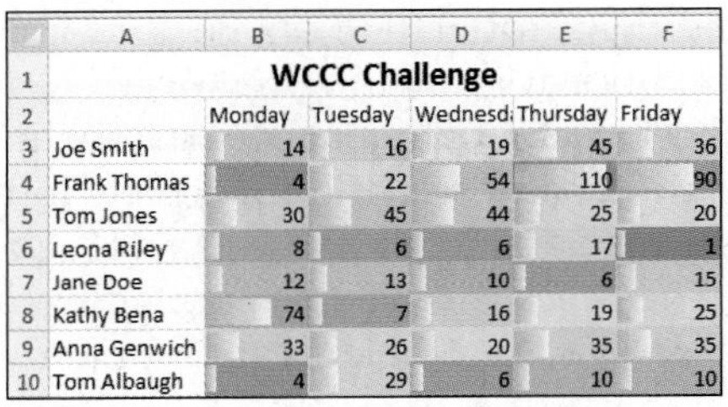

Figure 5.7   Color Scales Conditional Formatting

Icon sets are little graphics or symbols that display in cells based on the cell contents.

Icon sets are little graphics or symbols that display in cells and are used to classify data into three to five categories, based on the contents of the cells. The categories are separated by a threshold value. Each icon represents a range of values. The category range is assigned an icon that displays in a cell. The icons are effective when you want to annotate or present data that are quickly readable and understandable. Figure 5.8 shows a worksheet formatted with a variety of icon sets. In most worksheets, however, you would limit the icon sets to only one or two to avoid overwhelming the reader.

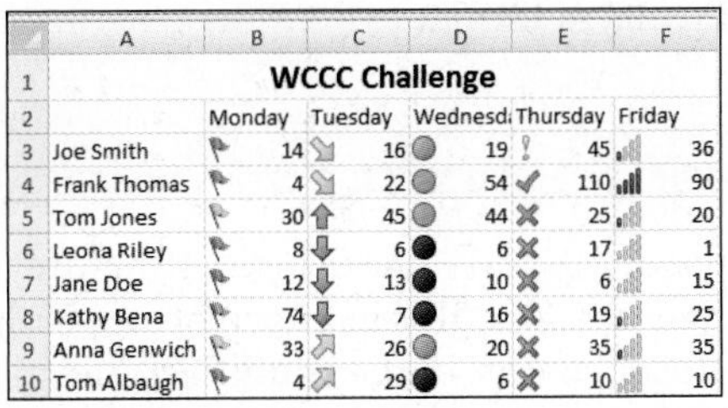

Figure 5.8   Icon Sets Conditional Formatting

To apply a conditional format, select the cells, click Conditional Formatting in the Styles group on the Home tab, and select the specific conditional formatting style you want to apply. For example, a weather tracker may have a spreadsheet containing the temperatures for each day of a month. She might want to conditionally format cells that contain temperatures between 70 and 75 degrees. To apply this conditional formatting, she would select Highlight Cells Rules, and then select Between. In the Between dialog box, she would type 70 in the *Format cells that are BETWEEN* and 75 in the *and* box. She would then select the type of conditional formatting.

Table 5.3 describes why you would use conditional formatting for particular types of cells.

Table 5.3   Why format?

Format What	Why
Cells that contain text, number, or date or time values	This type of formatting easily finds specific cells based on a comparison operator. This is a powerful conditional format with many options.
Only top- or bottom-ranked values	You can find the highest and lowest values in a range of cells based on a specified cutoff point and then apply formatting.
Only values above or below average	You can find and conditionally format a range of cells above or below an average or a standard deviation.
Only unique or duplicate values	This applies conditional formatting to cells that have a value that appears only once or cells that have a value that appears more than once.
Using a formula to determine which cells to format	In more complex conditional formatting, you can use logical formulas to specify the formatting criteria.

Clearing conditional formatting can be done in two ways, depending on where you want the conditional formatting removed. To remove conditional formatting from an entire sheet, click Conditional Formatting in the Styles group on the Home tab, select Clear Rules, and select Entire Sheet. To remove conditional formatting from a range of cells, a table, or a PivotTable, select the range of cells, table, or PivotTable first. Then click Conditional Formatting, select Clear Rules, and Selected Cells, This Table, or This PivotTable, as appropriate.

Create Conditional Formatting Rules

You can apply conditional formatting with either Quick Formatting or Advanced Formatting using the Conditional Formatting Rules Manager dialog box. Quick Formatting uses the options in Conditional Formatting in the Styles group on the Home tab. To apply Quick Formatting, select a range of cells or ensure that the active cell is in a table or PivotTable report. Then select the appropriate command from the Conditional Formatting drop-down list based on Table 5.2. Quick Formatting is a speedy way to apply formatting, but you cannot use it when a formula is used to determine which cells to format.

Use Advanced Formatting

The principles used with advanced formatting are similar to those used in Quick Formatting but use the Conditional Formatting Rules Manager dialog box, which provides much closer control of the conditional formatting (see Figure 5.9). To apply advanced formatting:

1. Select a range of cells or ensure the active cell is in a table or PivotTable report.
2. Click Conditional Formatting in the Styles group on the Home tab and select Manage to display the Conditional Formatting Rules Manager dialog box (see Figure 5.9).
3. Click New Rule to display the New Formatting Rule dialog box (see Figure 5.10).
4. Select a new rule in the *Select a Rule Type* section.
5. Use the *Format Style* list box in the *Edit the Rule Description* section, which changes based on the general rule you select in Step 4.
6. Make appropriate choices to complete the conditional formatting.

Figure 5.9 Conditional Formatting Rules Manager

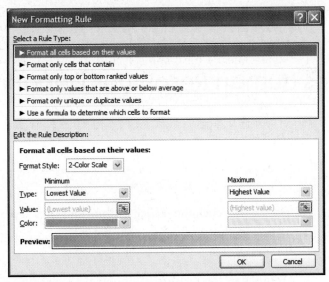

Figure 5.10 New Formatting Rule Dialog Box

Use Formulas in Conditional Formatting

Excel provides a vast number of conditional formatting options. If you need to create a complex conditional formatting rule, you can select a rule that uses a formula to format cells. For example, you might want to format gross pay cells for individuals who earn more than $10 an hour **and** who worked 5 or more overtime hours in a week to analyze your payroll budget. Figure 5.11 shows the conditional formatting applied to the gross pay column.

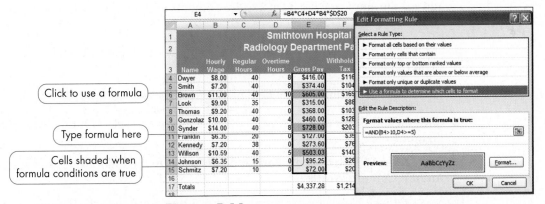

Figure 5.11 Formula-Based Conditional Formatting

To create a formula-based conditional formatting rule, select the data, click Conditional Formatting, and then select New Rule. In the New Formatting Rule dialog box, select *Use a formula to determine which cells to format* and then type the formula in the *Format values where this formula is true* box. In the previous example, the AND function requires that the hourly wage in column B be more than $10 and the overtime hours in column D be equal to or greater than 5. When both conditions are true, the cells are formatted with the fill color.

Hands-On Exercises

1 | Gee Airlines Human Resources Department

Skills covered: 1. Use the Text Import Wizard **2.** Apply and Clear Conditional Formatting **3.** Import Access Data **4.** Apply Color Scales and Icon Sets Conditional Formatting

Step 1 Use the Text Import Wizard	Refer to Figure 5.12 as you complete Step 1.

a. Start Excel, click the **Office Button**, and click **Open**.

b. Select **Text Files** from the *Files of type* drop-down list and open the *chap5_ho1_hremployee* file.

You began the process of importing a text file. The Text Import Wizard opens automatically. The wizard recognizes that the file is in delimited format.

c. Click **Next**.

d. Click the **Tab check box** to deselect this delimiter and click the **Comma check box**.

Each field is now shown in a separate column.

e. Click **Next**.

You do not need to change the default format (general) of any of the fields.

f. Click **Finish**.

You see the employee list in an Excel workbook, and the sheet tab is now named *chap5_ho1_hremployee*.

g. Select **cells A1:E1**, click **Bold** in the Font group on the Home tab, and click **Center** in the Alignment group.

These formats distinguish the field names from the data records.

h. Click the **Fill Color down arrow** in the Font group and select **Orange Accent 6, Lighter 60%**.

i. Select **cells A1:E14**, click the **Format down arrow** in the Cells group, and select **AutoFit Column Width**.

j. Select **cells E2:E14**, click the **Number Format down arrow** in the Number group, and select **Currency**. Click **Decrease Decimal** twice in the Number group.

You formatted the salary values as currency with no decimals (see Figure 5.12).

k. Save the workbook as **chap5_ho1_hremplyee_solution**. Click the **Save as type drop-down arrow** and select **Excel workbook**. Click **Save**.

TROUBLESHOOTING: You opened a text file and it is assumed you will save a text file. If you use the Save As dialog box, you must use the *Save as type* drop-down arrow to select the Excel workbook file type. You can also point to Save As after clicking the Office Button, and then select Excel Workbook to save.

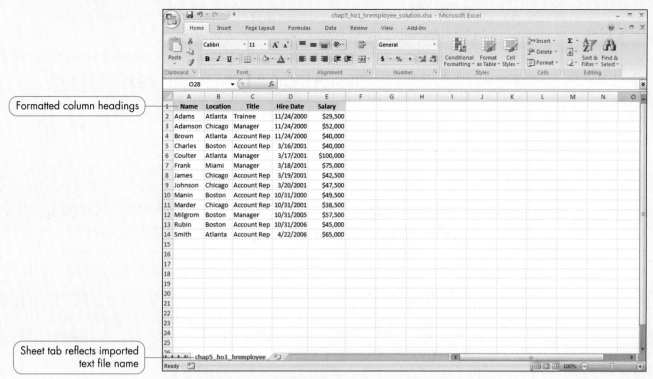

Formatted column headings

Sheet tab reflects imported text file name

Figure 5.12 Import Text File

TIP   Exporting Data from Excel

You began the exercise by importing data from a text file into an Excel workbook. You can also go in the opposite direction; that is, you can export the data in an Excel worksheet into a CSV, comma-separated value or text file, or an XML document. Click the Office Button, select Save As, and select Other Formats. Then specify the file type, e.g., a text file, by selecting the type of file you want from the *Save as type* drop-down list.

Step 2
Apply and Clear Conditional Formatting

Refer to Figure 5.13 as you complete Step 2.

a. Select **cells E2:E14** and click **Conditional Formatting** in the Styles group on the Home tab.

Conditional Formatting enables you to analyze your data. In this case, you want to select and highlight those employees whose salary is above $60,000.

b. Point to **Highlight Cells Rules** and select **Greater Than** to open the Greater Than dialog box.

c. Type **$60,000** in the **Format cells that are GREATER THAN** box.

d. Click the **with drop-down arrow**, select **Light Red Fill**, and click **OK**.

You highlighted with light red fill color those salaries greater than $60,000 in the entire data table.

e. Click **Conditional Formatting** in the Styles group, point to **Clear Rules**, and select **Clear Rules from Entire Sheet**.

You cleared all conditional formatting from the data table so it is not brought into the next exercise.

f. Save the workbook.

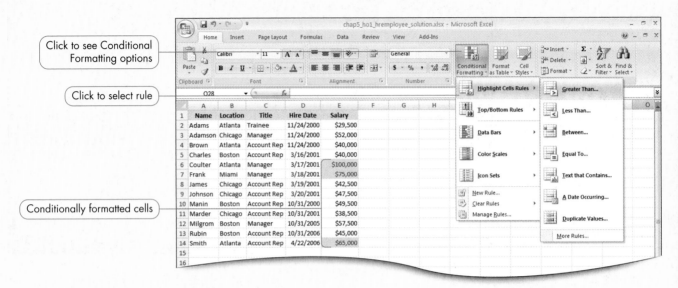

Figure 5.13 Conditional Formatting

Step 3
Import Access Data

Refer to Figure 5.14 as you complete Step 3.

a. Click **From Access** in the Get External Data group on the Data tab and open the *chap5_ho1_hremployee* file.

The Import Data dialog box opens so you can select how you want to view the data and where they are placed.

b. Verify that Table is selected, click **New worksheet** to place the data on a new worksheet, and click **OK**.

The data are imported as a table and display the Excel table characteristics. The table contains banded rows and a header row.

c. Double-click the **Sheet2 tab** and type **Access Data** to rename the tab.

d. Click **Table Style Medium 7** in the Table Styles group on the Table Tools Design tab.

The data are formatted with the Table Style Medium 7 style. This style applies a dark orange fill and white font color to the column headings. Every other row is formatted with a light orange color.

e. Save the workbook.

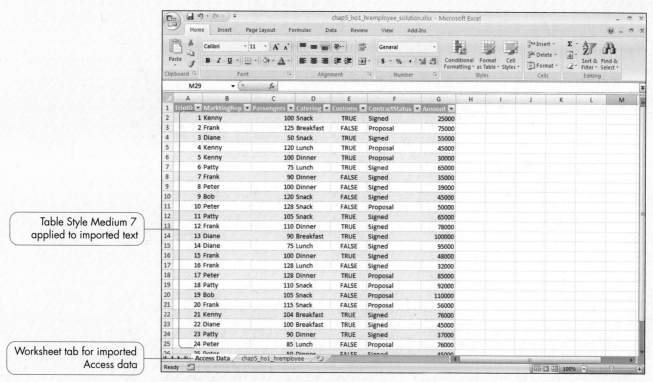

Table Style Medium 7 applied to imported text

Worksheet tab for imported Access data

Figure 5.14 Imported Access Data

Refer to Figure 5.15 as you complete Step 4.

Step 4

Apply Color Scales and Icon Sets Conditional Formatting

a. Select **cells C2:C28** and click **Conditional Formatting** in the Styles group on the Home tab.

You will now apply conditional formatting to the Access data you previously imported.

b. Select **Color Scales** and click **Blue – Yellow – Red Color Scale**

You applied the Color Scales to the number of passengers column and now see which Marketing Reps booked the most passengers and which Marketing Reps booked the fewest passengers.

c. Select **cells G2:G28** and click **Conditional Formatting** in the Style group.

d. Select **Icon Sets** and click **3 Flags**.

You can now clearly see that green flags highlight the flights generating the most revenue and the red flags highlight the flights generating the least revenue.

e. Save the *chap5_ho1_hremployee_solution* workbook and keep it onscreen if you plan to continue to the next hands-on exercise. Close the workbook and exit Excel if you do not want to continue with the next exercise at this time.

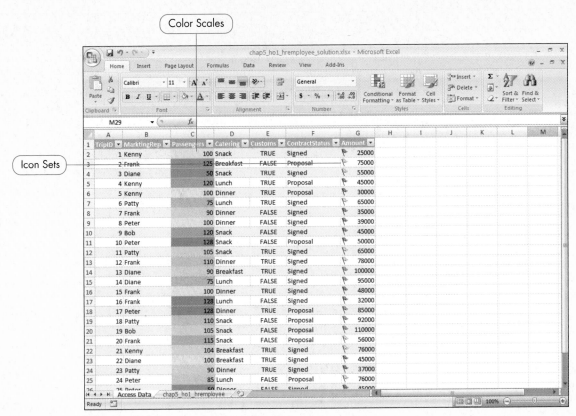

Figure 5.15   Conditional Formatting

Data Management

Once information has been placed in a range and the range converted to a data table, you can perform more complex data management analyses, such as using advanced data filters with defined criteria ranges, database functions to perform calculations on the information in the data table, and defined names to make the use of database functions more efficient. The items discussed are sequential; in other words, to better understand the concepts of data management the steps will work best if completed in the order presented.

In this section, you learn how to apply specialized sorting and filtering, extract specific data using advanced filtering techniques, define and use range names, and use database functions.

Applying Advanced Filtering and Sorting Methods

Data become more useful and important when they are organized or sorted and they can be reduced in volume by selecting a subset of data that meets specific conditions. For example, a teacher wants to know which students earned an "A," which students earned a "B," and so on in her sections of College Writing. A production manager wants an alphabetical list of employees working first, second, and third shifts arranged by shift. A bank manager wants a list of customers with CDs maturing in December. These are examples of information used to make decisions. It is data that are sorted and extracted using specific conditions to make them meaningful.

You have previous experience in simple filtering and sorting. However, you may need more complex sorting and filtering conditions. For example, you may want to filter records based on conditional formatting you applied, or you may want to create an advanced filter and place these extracted records together in a different location.

Sort and Filter Using Conditional Formatting

Excel provides several useful ways to organize and extract data using filters and conditional formatting. Once data are conditionally formatted, you can sort or filter the data to match the conditional formatting. For example, you might want to sort a table that has been conditionally formatted with a fill color based on ranges of housing costs. Sorting by color places all the records with the same color together for easy reference. To sort by color, click the filter drop-down arrow for the field that you want to sort, select Sort by Color, and select the formatting color or icon set. Cells containing that color are displayed at the top of the list. The Sort dialog box enables you to sort with more than one color at a time.

You can also set a filter based on conditional formatting. For example, assume that you applied the flags icon set. You can filter the records to show only records that have a particular flag color. To filter by conditional formatting, click the filter drop-down arrow for the field that you want to filter, select Filter by Color, and select the conditional formatting color or icon set. Figure 5.16 shows the Gee Airlines flights generating the most revenue. The filter displays only those amounts containing the green flags.

Sort and Filter by Cell Attributes

Another way you can visually present data is to sort by a cell attribute, such as cell color or font color. To sort by cell attributes, display the Sort dialog box, select the column for sorting, specify the cell attribute, such as Cell Color from the *Sort On* drop-down list, and select the order. You can filter records based on cell attributes. For example, Figure 5.17 depicts a worksheet filtered to show only the cells that are red. These cells also represent the flights with the fewest passengers.

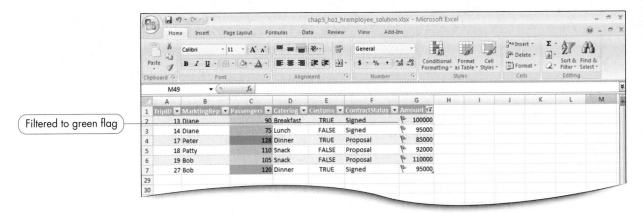

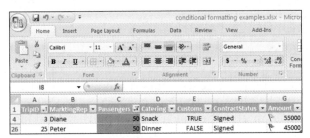

Figure 5.16 Filter by Conditional Formatting—Icon Set

Filtered to green flag

Figure 5.17 Filter by Conditional Formatting—Cell Color

Filter Data with Number Filters

Data can be filtered by using predefined number filters. Figure 5.18 shows the menu of options you can use to apply to numeric data. If you want a list of all flights carrying more than 50 passengers, you would use a number filter to obtain the data. If you want a list of flights producing less than $25,000 in revenue, you would use a number format.

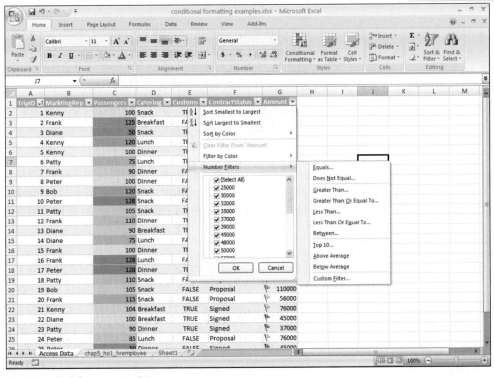

Figure 5.18 Number Filters

You can create custom filters by using a combination of different number filters. For example, if you want to see all the flights with more than 75 passengers but fewer than 100 passengers, you would create a custom filter.

Define a Criteria Range

A ***criteria range*** is an area separate from the data table and specifies the conditions used to filter the table.

Although the AutoFilter provides a variety of ways to filter data, you may need to create an advanced filter with more complex criteria. Before you can use Excel's advanced filtering capability, you must define a criteria range. A ***criteria range*** is an area that specifies the conditions to filter the table. A criteria range is independent of the table and exists as a separate area on a worksheet, typically above or below the main table. A criteria range must be at least two rows deep and one column wide.

The most basic criteria range you use has two rows and as many columns as in the table. The first row contains the field names as they appear in the table, and the second row contains the conditions (e.g., values) you are looking for. See Figure 5.19 for an example of a basic criteria range. The database is filtered to show only records in which the location is Atlanta.

(A criteria range is independent of the table and exists as a separate area on a worksheet.)

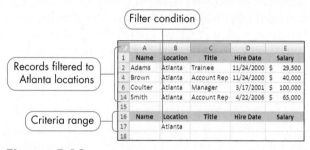

Figure 5.19 Criteria Range

Multiple values in the second row create an AND condition, which requires that records selected meet both conditions. Spelling is particularly important because variations in spelling or misspelled words will not meet the criteria. If you want to select those employees named Smith AND who have a pay period of 10, you would enter Name and PayPeriod in the first criteria row and Smith and 10 immediately below the respective labels in the second criteria row. Figure 5.20 shows multiple criteria that filter the records to display all Account Reps located in Atlanta. Note that *both* conditions must be met. Account Reps in other cities are not listed and other job titles in Atlanta are not listed.

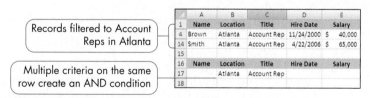

Figure 5.20 Criteria Range

When values are entered in multiple rows, an OR condition is created. Returned records are those meeting either condition. Figure 5.21 shows an OR condition with Atlanta listed on one row and Account Reps listed on a different row. Running the advanced filter displays all Atlanta employees (regardless of job titles) and all Account Reps (regardless of location), compared to the previous AND condition that required that both conditions be met.

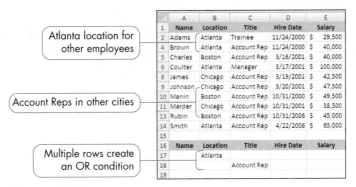

Figure 5.21 Criteria Range

You can combine AND and OR conditions for more specific filters. For example, you might want to show Account Reps in Atlanta *or* any employee in Boston. The Account Reps and Atlanta create an AND condition and are placed on one row. Boston is placed on the next row to form an OR condition.

Relational operators are symbols used to compare cell contents to another cell or specific value. Relational operators include <, >, <=, >=, <>, and =. They may be used with date or numeric fields to return records within a designated range. Recall that you used relational or comparison operators in the conditional test argument of an IF function, such as = IF(B10<B1,B10*.05,B10*.10), in which the value of cell B10 is compared to see if it is less than the value of cell B1.

Figure 5.22 shows three sets of criteria ranges. The first criteria range shows the less than relational operator used with a date. This condition displays records in which the date is *before* 3/16/2001. The second criteria range shows the greater than relational operator used with numerical data. This condition displays records in which the salary is greater than $40,000. The third criteria range establishes a boundary for the same field by repeating the field within the criteria range. This condition identifies salaries that are greater than or equal to $40,000 and less than or equal to $60,000.

A *relational operator* is a symbol used to compare cell contents to another cell or value.

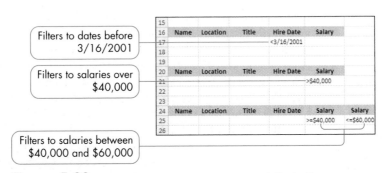

Figure 5.22 Relational Operators Used in Criteria Ranges

Using equal (=) and unequal (<>) symbols selects records with empty and non-empty fields, respectively. An equal with nothing after it will return all records with no entry in the designated field (see Figure 5.23). An unequal (<>) with nothing after it will select all records with an entry in the field. An empty row in the criteria range returns every record in the list.

Figure 5.23 Criteria Range

Apply the Advanced Filter

After you create the criteria range, you are ready to apply the advanced filter. Instead of displaying the AutoFilter drop-down arrows, the Advanced command displays the Advanced Filter dialog box. This dialog box enables you to filter the table in place or copy the selected records to another area in the worksheet, specify the list range, specify the criteria range, or display unique records only. Excel uses the separate criteria range in the Advanced Filter dialog box as the source for the advanced criteria.

To set an advanced filter:

1. Create a criteria range.
2. Click a cell in the data table.
3. Click Advanced in the Sort & Filter group on the Data tab.
4. Click *Filter the list, in-place* to filter the range by hiding rows that do not match your criteria. If you want to copy the rows that match your criteria to another area of the worksheet, click *Copy to another location*, click in the Copy to box, and then click the upper-left corner cell where you want to paste.
5. Enter the criteria range, including the criteria labels, in the *Criteria range* box, and then click OK. Figure 5.24 shows the Advanced Filter dialog box with an example advanced command setup.

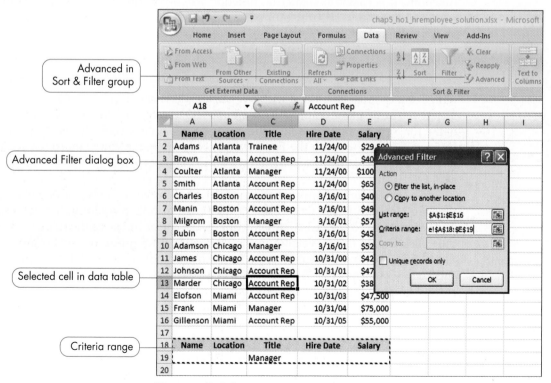

Figure 5.24 Advanced Filter

TIP Filter the List in Place

Use the Advanced Filter command to filter the list in place and display the records that meet the current criteria. Click anywhere in the list, click the Data down arrow, select the Filter command, and then choose Advanced Filter to display the Advanced Filter dialog box. Click the option to filter the list in place, and then click OK to display the selected records. You have to execute this command each time the criteria change.

Creating and Using Range Names

A **range name** is a word or string of characters that represents a cell, range of cells, or constant value.

In previous sections, you used a range of cells such as A1:E15 in formulas, functions, and data tables. You can create a **range name**, a word or string of characters, to represent a cell, range of cells, or constant value. For example, the name EmployeeList represents a cell or range of cells such as A1:E15. After assigning a name to a range of cells, you can use that name to reference cells in formulas and functions. A range name can be up to 255 characters long but must begin with a letter or underscore. It can be a mixture of upper or lowercase letters, numbers, periods, and underscores, but a range name cannot have blank spaces or special characters. Furthermore, a range name should not look like a cell address, such as B15.

Once you define a range name, it automatically adjusts for insertions or deletions within a range. For example, if you assign the name EmployeeList to the range A1:E15 and delete a row in the range, the definition changes to A1:E14. In a similar fashion, if a column is added the definition would change to A1:F15. Names are used in formulas and serve as documentation while helping to clarify formula components. A name can be used in any formula or function instead of cell addresses. This is of particular value when using database functions but is useful for all functions. A range name can represent a single cell; B15, for example, is state sales tax and in the formula = stax*B2, stax is used to document the worksheet. When using database functions, it is easier to create the function when you can use range names for the required arguments. It is also important to note that names used in formulas are absolute references.

Create a Range Name

Range names must be unique within a workbook. When a name is created for use in Sheet1 the same name cannot be used in Sheet2 to refer to different cells. To create a name for a range of cells, select the range to be named, click Define Name in the Defined Names group on the Formula tab, type the name you want to use for your reference in the Name box in the New Name dialog box (see Figure 5.25), and then click OK.

You can create multiple range names at once instead of creating one name at a time. To create multiple names, select the range of cells containing the names you want to create and the cells that will contain the formulas using the names. You can then click Create from Selection in the Defined Names group on the Formulas tab. Figure 5.26 shows the Create Names from Selection dialog box with the *Left column* checked. This means that the range names—Average, Highest, and Lowest—will be created because they are in the left column.

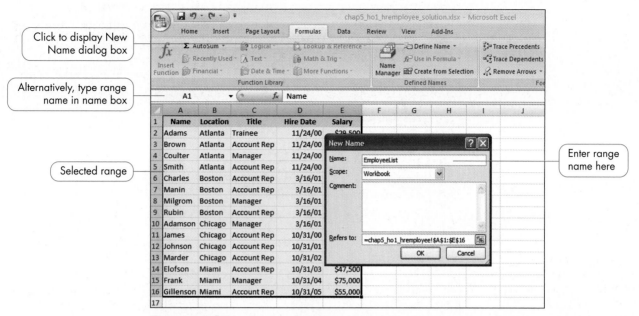

Figure 5.25 Naming a Range

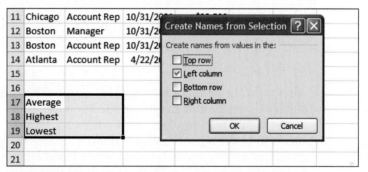

Figure 5.26 Create Range Names from Selection

TIP   Name Range Shortcuts

Excel provides several other methods when you want to name a range. You can select the range, click in the Name box (left side of the Formula Bar), type the name, and press Enter. You can right-click the selected range, select *Name range* from the shortcut menu, and fill in the New Name dialog box entries. Or you can click Name Manager in the Defined Names group on the Formulas tab and click New. Fill in the New Name dialog box entries as above.

Modify and Delete a Range Name

How often do you type something and discover that you made a mistake? Maybe the word is incorrect or more often the name does not represent the data in the cells. You can use the Name Manager dialog box to edit existing range names, delete existing range names, and create new range names. Figure 5.27 shows the Name Manager dialog box that displays when you click Name Manager in the Defined Names group on the Formulas tab. If you want to edit or delete an existing name, click the name and click either Edit or Delete, respectively. When you click Edit, another dialog box opens so you can type the correct name and change the cell reference, if necessary.

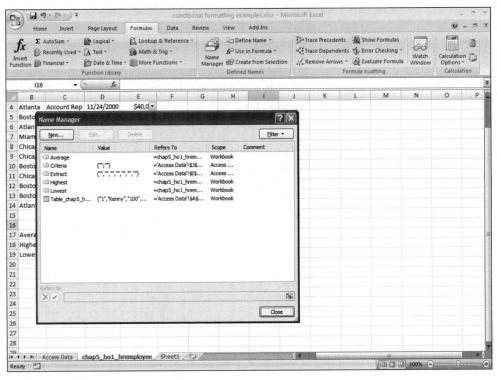

Figure 5.27 Edit or Delete a Range Name

Insert a Table of Range Names

After creating several range names in a workbook, you might want to display an alphabetical list of the range names. A good location for an alphabetical list of range names would be a separate sheet within the workbook, such as the documentation sheet. To insert a list of range names, click Use in Formula in the Defined Names group on the Formulas tab, and select Paste Names. Figure 5.28 shows the Paste Name dialog box. Click Paste List. Excel then pastes an alphabetical list of range names starting in the active cell (see Figure 5.29). The first column displays the range names, and the second column displays the worksheet name and cell reference. Note that this is not a linked operation. If you add or change any of the listed range names, you must Paste Names again to update the list.

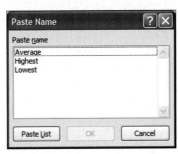

Figure 5.28 Paste Name Dialog Box

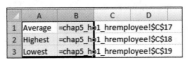

Figure 5.29 List of Range Names

Use Range Names in Formulas

After you create a range name, you can use that range name instead of cell references in formulas. For example, assume that cell C15 contains a purchase amount and cell C5 contains the sales tax amount. Instead of typing =C15*C5 to calculate the sales tax, you can type =C15*stax, assuming that cell C5 has been named *stax*. The *stax* range name is an absolute reference to cell C5. If you need to copy the formula down the column for other purchases, you do not have to worry about creating an absolute reference like you would by typing =C15*$C$5. When you copy the formula =C15*stax, the copied formula for the next row is =C16*stax. Furthermore, as you build a formula and click a cell that is range-named, Excel will automatically substitute the range name for the cell address in the formula.

TIP   AutoComplete Formulas with Range Names

When you start typing a range name within a formula, the Formula AutoComplete feature displays a list of possible functions or range names. For example, if you type =C15*s, you will see a list of functions that start with s. As you continue typing, you will see the appropriate range name. You can then double-click the range name to enter it in the formula.

Using range names in formulas is helpful when you need to create formulas that reference a cell or a range of cells on a different worksheet. Instead of typing the worksheet name and cell references, you can use the range name. Because the range name creates an absolute reference to a cell or range of cells, the range-name reference in a formula is absolute. The Formula Bar in Figure 5.30 displays the database function DAVERAGE with one range name for an argument. EmployeeList is the name used for the database.

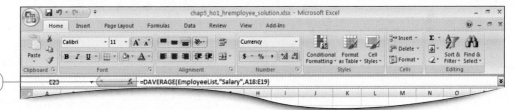

Formula using named range

Figure 5.30 Range Names in a Formula

If you create range names after creating formulas, you can update the formulas to use range names rather than cell references. Select the cells that contain formulas that you want to update and click the Define Name down arrow in the Defined Names group on the Formulas tab. In the Apply Names dialog box, select the applicable range names for the formulas you have selected, select appropriate options, and click OK. Use Help to learn about the other options in the Apply Names dialog box.

Using Database Functions

The ***database functions*** analyze data for selected records in a table.

The ***database functions*** analyze data only for selected records in a table. These functions are similar to statistical functions (SUM, AVERAGE, MAX, MIN, COUNT) except that database functions are exclusively used for database tables; these functions affect only records that satisfy the specified criteria. Data not meeting the specified criteria are filtered out and are not included in the function calculations. Database functions, as with all functions, return a value and save you time because you do not have to construct the underlying mathematical formula. All database functions use a criteria range that defines the search parameters. Using range names can simplify the construction of database functions.

Database functions have three arguments:

1. **Database**. The database range is the entire table, including column headings and all columns, on which the function operates. The database reference may be represented by a range name. In the DAVERAGE function shown in Figure 5.30, the database range is EmployeeList, which refers to cells A1:E16.
2. **Field**. The field is the column in the database that contains the values operated on by the function. You can enter the name of the column heading in quotation marks, such as "Salary" in the DAVERAGE function shown in Figure 5.30. Alternatively, you can enter the number that represents the location of that column within the table. For example, if the Salary column is the sixth column in the table, you can enter a 6 for the Field.
3. **Criteria**. The criteria range defines the conditions to be met by the function. This range must contain at least one column label and a cell below the label that specifies the condition. The criteria range is A18:E19 in the DAVERAGE function shown in Figure 5.30. The criteria range may include more than one column with conditions for each column label. The criteria may be defined by a range address or by a range name.

The summary shown in Figure 5.31 is based on the salaries for only the managers, not all employees. Each database function includes the criteria range in cells A18:F19 as the third argument. The criteria range limits the calculations to just the managers.

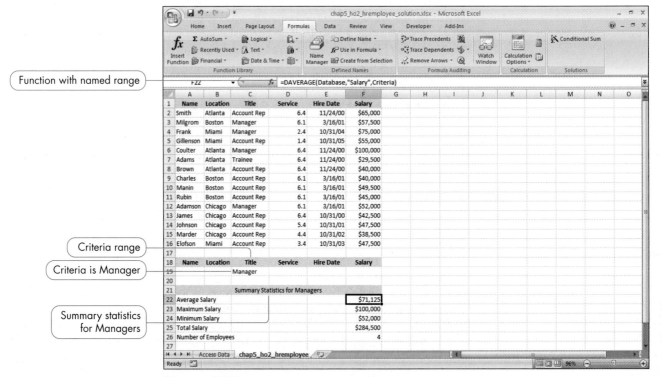

Figure 5.31 Database Functions

To insert a database function, you can click Insert Function between the name box and the Formula Bar, click the *Or select a category* drop-down arrow, select Database, and then click the desired database function in the *Select a function* list box. Figure 5.32 shows the database functions in the Insert Function dialog box.

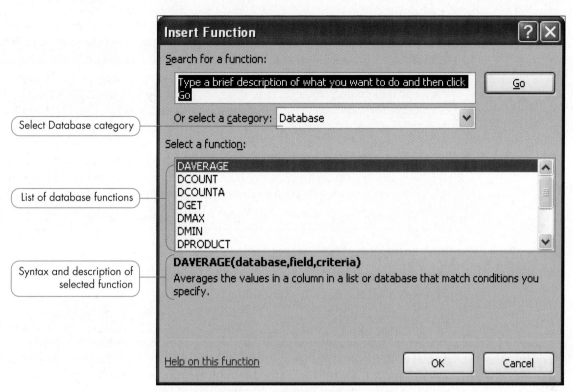

Figure 5.32 Database Functions

Alternatively, you can type =D in a cell and then select the appropriate database function from the Formula AutoComplete list. The reference box on page 332 lists and describes some common database functions.

Calculate a SUM with the DSUM Function
DSUM Function | Reference

DSUM(database,field,criteria)

The **DSUM function** sums the numeric entries in a field in a database that match specified conditions.

The **DSUM function** adds up or sums the numeric entries in a field of records in a list or database that match conditions you specify. For example, you might want to calculate the total amount that one specific employee was paid over 32 pay periods, or you might want to find the total salaries paid for employees in Boston. In Figure 5.31, the DSUM function is used to calculate the total salary of all managers.

Calculate an Average with the DAVERAGE Function
DAVERAGE Function | Reference

DAVERAGE(database,field,criteria)

The **DAVERAGE function** determines the average of numeric entries in a field of records in a database that match specified conditions.

The **DAVERAGE function** determines the arithmetic mean, or average, of numeric entries in a field of records in a list or database that match conditions you specify. For example, you might want to use DAVERAGE to determine the average number of hours that interns worked during a pay period or the average GPA of psychology majors. In Figure 5.31, the DAVERAGE function is used to calculate the average salary of all managers.

Identify the Highest Value with the DMAX Function
DMAX Function | Reference

DMAX(database,field,criteria)

The **DMAX *function*** determines the highest value in a field of records in a database that match specified conditions.

The **DMAX** *function* returns the highest value of numeric entries in a field of records in a list or database that match conditions you specify. For example, you can use the DMAX function to determine the maximum number of hours worked during pay period 10 or the highest number of points scored by a basketball player in a particular game. In Figure 5.31, the DMAX function is used to calculate the highest salary within the list of all managers.

Identify the Lowest Value with the DMIN Function
DMIN Function | Reference

DMIN(database,field,criteria)

The **DMIN *function*** returns the lowest value of numeric entries in a field of records in a database that match specified conditions.

The **DMIN** *function* returns the lowest value of numeric entries in a field of records in a list or database that match conditions you specify. For example, you can use the DMIN function to determine the lowest number of patients in a hospital during April or the lowest score on a statistics test for male students. In Figure 5.31, the DMIN function is used to calculate the lowest salary of all managers.

Identify the Total Number with the DCOUNT Function
DCOUNT Function | Reference

DCOUNT(database,field,criteria)

The **DCOUNT *function*** counts the cells that contain numbers in a field of records in a database that match specified conditions.

The **DCOUNT** *function* counts the cells that contain numbers in a field of records in a list or database that match conditions you specify. For example, you can use the DCOUNT function to count the number of pay periods where the hours are greater than 8 but less than 6 or count the number of females who participated in a market research study. In Figure 5.31, the DCOUNT function is used to count the number of managers in the database.

Database Functions | Reference

Name	Syntax	Definition
DSUM	DSUM(database,field,criteria)	Calculates the total of values in a field that meets the specified condition(s).
DAVERAGE	DAVERAGE(database,field,criteria)	Determines the mathematical average of values in a field that meets the specified condition(s).
DMAX	DMAX(database,field,criteria)	Identifies the largest value in a field that meets the specified condition(s).
DMIN	DMIN(database,field,criteria)	Identifies the smallest value in a field that meets the specified condition(s).
DCOUNT	DCOUNT(database,field,criteria)	Counts the number of records for a field that meets the specified condition(s).
DCOUNTA	DCOUNTA(database,field,criteria)	Counts the number of records that contain values (nonblank) in a field that meets the specified condition(s).
DPRODUCT	DPRODUCT(database,field,criteria)	Multiplies the values within a field that meets the specified condition(s).
DSTDEV	DSTDEV(database,field,criteria)	Calculates the standard deviation for values in a field that meets the specified condition(s).
DVAR	DVAR(database,field,criteria)	Estimates the sample population variance for values in a field that meets the specified condition(s).
DVARP	DVARP(database,field,criteria)	Estimates the entire population variance for values in a field that meets the specified condition(s).

Hands-On Exercises

2 | Gee Airlines Human Resources Department Revisited

Skills covered: 1. Use Date Arithmetic **2.** Sort and Filter with Conditional Formatting **3.** Use Custom AutoFilter **4.** Create a Criteria Range and Use an Advanced Filter **5.** Define a Named Range **6.** Set Up Summary Area and Use DAVERAGE **7.** Use DMAX, DMIN, DSUM, and DCOUNT Functions **8.** Change the Criteria

---

Step 1
Use Date Arithmetic

Refer to Figure 5.33 as you complete Step 1.

a. Open the *chap5_ho1_hremployee_solution* workbook, save it as **chap5_ho2_hremployee_solution**, and rename the chap5_ho1_hremployee sheet tab as **chap5_ho2_hremployee**.

b. Right-click the **column D heading** and select **Insert** from the shortcut menu.

The column of hire dates has been moved to column E and a new empty column is inserted.

c. Click **cell D1**, type **Service**, and press **Enter**.

d. Click **cell D2** and type **=(Today()-E2)/365**, as shown in Figure 5.33, and press **Enter**.

The years of service for Adams, the first employee, are displayed in cell D2.

e. Click **cell D2**, then click **Decrease Decimal** in the Number group on the Home tab several times to display the length of service with only one decimal.

f. Drag the fill handle in **cell D2** to the remaining cells in that column, **cells D3:D16**.

You copied the formula to compute the length of service for the remaining employees. You do not have to format the cells because you copied the format with the formula.

TROUBLESHOOTING: Your results will differ because the TODAY function returns the current date when Excel calculates the function. Figure 5.33 displays the result based on a previous date.

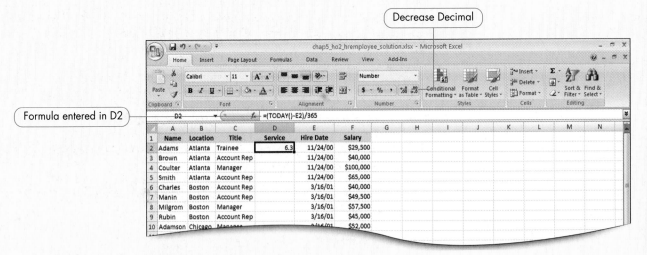

Figure 5.33 Calculate Years of Service

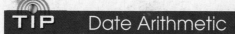

TIP   Date Arithmetic

Excel stores a date as an integer or serial number, starting with January 1, 1900; that is, January 1, 1900, is stored as the number 1, January 2, 1900, as the number 2, and so on. This enables you to use dates in an arithmetic computation. An employee's service, for example, is computed by subtracting the hire date from the Today() function and dividing the result by 365. For greater precision in dealing with leap years, divide the result by 365.25.

Step 2
Sort and Filter with Conditional Formatting

Refer to Figure 5.34 as you complete Step 2.

a. Click any cell in the list and click **Filter** in the Sort & Filter group on the Data tab.

You now see the down arrows to the right of each field name. These are used with all Filters.

b. Select **cells F2:F16**, click **Conditional Formatting** in the Styles group on the Home tab, and select **Icon Sets**, as shown in Figure 5.34.

You will apply conditional formatting to the Salary field. This represents the first step in the sort and filter process.

c. Click **3 Traffic Lights** (unrimmed) on the Icon Sets palette.

You applied conditional formatting to the salaries, with green representing the highest and red representing the lowest.

d. Click the **Salary drop-down arrow**, select **Sort by Color**, and click the yellow **Traffic Light Cell Icon**.

You sorted your data table by yellow, the middle salary group.

e. Click the **Salary drop-down arrow** a second time, click **Filter by Color**, and select **Red** in the Filter by Cell Icon list.

The display changes to show only those employees who meet the filter. The row numbers for the visible records are blue, showing that some records are ignored. The pull-down for Salary now displays the filter symbol, indicating it is part of the filter condition.

f. Click the **Salary drop-down arrow** a third time, click **(Select All)** to remove the filter condition on location, and click **OK**.

You removed the filters so all data are again displayed.

g. Click **Conditional Formatting** in the Styles group, select **Clear Rules**, and click **Clear Rules from Selected Cells**.

You removed the filter and the conditional formatting rules so you can proceed to the next hands-on step.

h. Save the workbook.

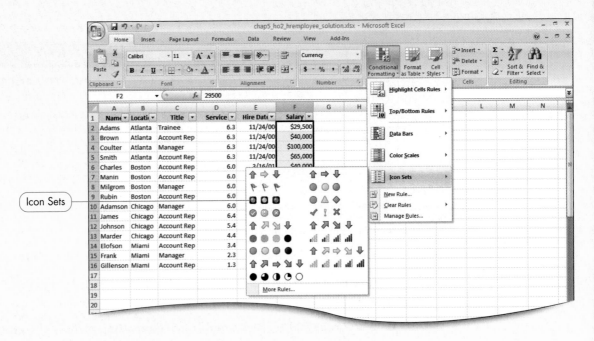

Figure 5.34 Conditional Formatting Icon Sets

Step 3
Use Custom AutoFilter

Refer to Figure 5.35 as you complete Step 3.

a. Click the **Salary drop-down arrow** and click **Custom Filter** from the Number Filters list.

The Custom AutoFilter dialog box is displayed, as shown in Figure 5.35, and you can create a custom AutoFilter.

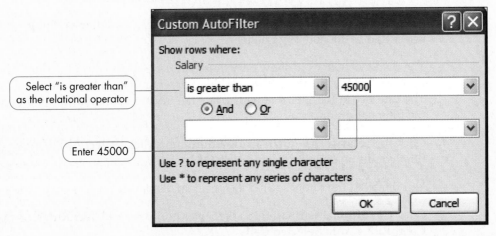

Select "is greater than" as the relational operator

Enter 45000

Figure 5.35 Custom AutoFilter

b. Click **is greater than** as the relation operator in the drop-down in the left box for **Salary**.

c. Type **45000** in the text box for the salary amount and click **OK**.

The list changes to display only those employees whose title is Account Rep and who earn more than $45,000.

d. Click **Filter** in the Sort & Filter group on the Data tab.

You toggled the AutoFilter command off and removed the arrows next to the field names to cancel all filter conditions. All of the records in the list are now visible.

e. Save the workbook.

Step 4
Create a Criteria Range and Use an Advanced Filter

Refer to Figure 5.36 as you complete Step 4.

a. Click and drag to select **cells A1:F1**, then click **Copy** in the Clipboard group on the Home tab.

A moving border appears around the selected cells.

b. Click **cell A18**, click **Paste** in the Clipboard group, and press **Esc** to cancel the moving border.

TROUBLESHOOTING: The field names in the criteria range must be spelled exactly the same way as in the associated list. The best way to ensure the names are identical is to copy the entries from the list to the criteria range.

c. Click **cell C19** and type **Manager**.

d. Click anywhere in the employee list, then click **Advanced** in the Sort & Filter group on the Data tab to display the Advanced Filter dialog box shown in Figure 5.36.

The list range is already entered because you selected a cell in the list before executing the command.

e. Click in the **Criteria Range** text box, and then click and drag **cells A18:F19**.

A moving border appears around the cells in the worksheet, and the corresponding cell reference is entered in the dialog box, as shown in Figure 5.36.

f. Check to make sure **Filter the list, in-place** is selected and click **OK**.

The display changes to show just the managers. Now only rows 3, 4, 6, and 12 are visible.

g. Click **cell B19**, type **Atlanta**, and press **Enter**.

h. Click **Advanced** in the Sort & Filter group.

The Advanced Filter dialog box already displays the cell references for the list and criteria range.

i. Click **OK**.

The display changes to show just the manager in Atlanta. Only row 6 is visible because it is the only row meeting the criteria.

j. Click **Clear** in the Sort & Filter group.

You have removed all filter conditions and the entire list is visible.

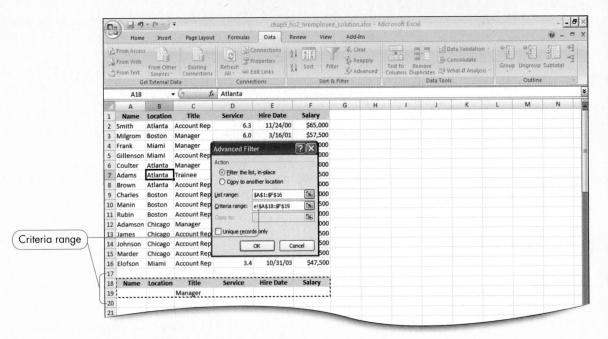

Criteria range

Figure 5.36 Advanced AutoFilter

Step 5
Define a Named Range

Refer to Figure 5.37 as you complete Step 5.

a. Click and drag to select **cells A1:F16**.

b. Click **Name Manager** in the Defined Names group on the Formulas tab to open the Name Manager dialog box, and then click **New** to show the New Name dialog box.

c. Type **Database** in the name box and click **OK** to display the Name Manager dialog box again.

The Name Manager dialog box contains two range names: Database, which you just defined, and Criteria, which was defined automatically when you specified the criteria range in Step 4.

d. Click **Close** in the Name Manager dialog box.

e. Click **cell I1**, type **Range Names**, and press **Enter**.

f. Click **Use in Formula** in the Defined Names group on the Formulas tab and select Paste Name.

g. Click **Paste List**.

You pasted the list of range names in your worksheet for future reference.

h. Save the workbook.

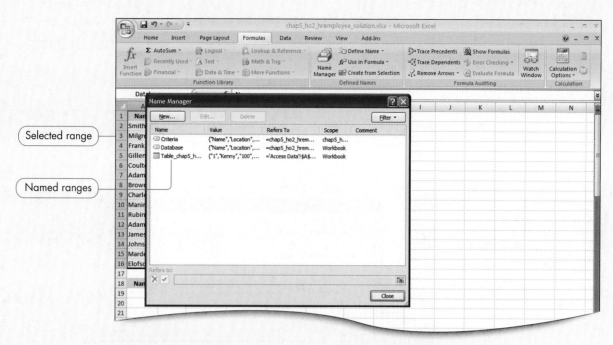

Selected range

Named ranges

Figure 5.37 Name a Range in the Name Manager Dialog Box

Step 6
Set Up a Summary Area and Use DAVERAGE

Refer to Figure 5.38 as you complete Step 6.

a. Click **cell A21**, type **Summary Statistics for Managers**, press **Enter**, and then select **cells A21:F21**.

b. Click **Merge & Center** in the Alignment group on the Home tab.

c. Click **Fill Color** in the Font group and select **Orange Accent 6, Lighter 60%** from the Theme Colors palette.

d. Enter the labels for **cells A22:A26** as shown in Figure 5.38.

You created and formatted an area in your worksheet for summary statistics from your database.

e. Click **cell B19** and press **Delete**.

The criteria range is now set to select only managers.

f. Click **cell F22** and click **Insert Function** in the Function Library group on the Formulas tab to display the Insert Function dialog box.

g. Select **Database** from the Category list, select **DAVERAGE** as the function name, and then click **OK** to open the Function Arguments dialog box shown in Figure 5.38.

You selected the DAVERAGE function and are now ready to enter the arguments for the function.

h. Enter the function arguments as shown below:

Argument	Type Text:
Database	Database
Field	Salary
Criteria	Criteria

TROUBLESHOOTING: Database and Criteria are range names you previously created and are typed exactly as you created them. Salary will appear in quotes in the Formula Bar and must be typed within quotes when typing the formula because it is a text field name and is also typed exactly as it appears in the column heading.

i. Click **OK** to enter the DAVERAGE function into the worksheet.

If the function was entered correctly, you will see 71125 in cell F22.

j. Save the workbook.

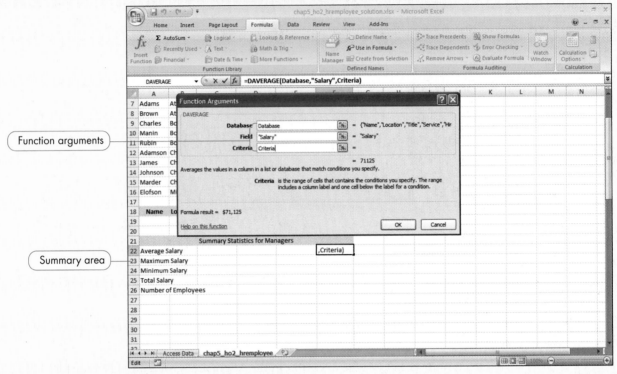

Figure 5.38 Summary Area

Refer to Figure 5.39 as you complete Step 7.

a. Enter the DMAX, DMIN, DSUM, and DCOUNT functions in **cells F23:F26**. Use **Insert Function** in the Function Library group on the Formulas tab to enter each function individually as shown below.

Cell	Function
F23	=DMAX(Database,"Salary",Criteria)
F24	=DMIN(Database,"Salary",Criteria)
F25	=DSUM(Database,"Salary",Criteria)
F26	=DCOUNT(Database,"Salary",Criteria)

The computed values are shown in Figure 5.39.

b. Format **cells F22:F25** as **currency** with **zero** decimals.

c. Click and drag the border between **columns F and G** to widen column F if necessary. Save the workbook.

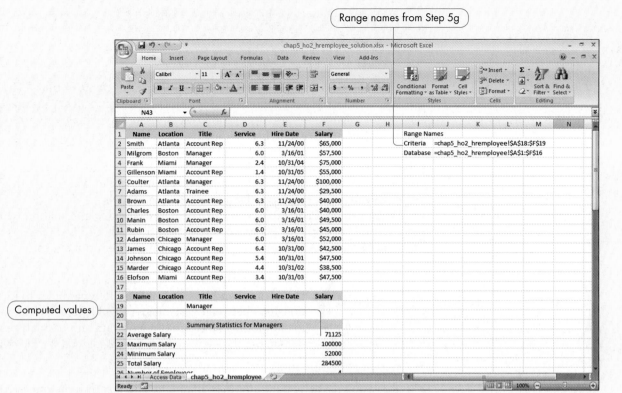

Computed values

Figure 5.39 Database Functions

Step 8
Change the Criteria

Refer to Figure 5.40 as you complete Step 8.

a. Click in the **Name box**, type **B19**, and press **Enter** to make cell B19 the active cell.

b. Type **Chicago** to change the criteria to Chicago managers and press **Enter**.

The values displayed by the DAVERAGE, DMIN, DMAX, and DSUM functions change to $52,000, reflecting the one employee, Adamson, who meets the current criteria, a manager in Chicago. The value displayed by the DCOUNT function changes to 1 to indicate one employee, as shown in Figure 5.40.

c. Click **cell C19** and press **Delete**.

The average salary changes to $45,125, reflecting all employees in Chicago.

d. Click **cell B19** and press **Delete**.

The criteria range is now empty. The DAVERAGE function displays $52,300, which is the average salary of all employees in the database.

e. Click **cell C19**, type **Manager**, and press **Enter**.

The average salary is $71,125, the average salary for all managers.

f. Save and close the workbook.

Criteria changed

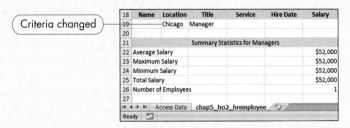

Figure 5.40 Change the Criteria

Data Analysis with PivotTables and PivotCharts

A ***PivotTable*** is a way to quickly summarize large amounts of data.

A ***PivotTable*** is a powerful, interactive data mining feature that enables you to quickly summarize and analyze large amounts of data in tables. You can also specify the type of calculations you need to analyze the data. PivotTables give you the ability to quickly summarize long lists of data by categories. The concept that led to today's pivot table came from Lotus Development Corporation with a spreadsheet program called Lotus Improv. Improv was envisioned in 1986 by Pito Salas. Salas realized that spreadsheets have patterns of data and by designing a tool that could recognize these patterns, you could quickly build advanced data models.

When using a PivotTable, you can calculate summary information without writing a formula or copying a single cell. The best thing about PivotTables is their flexibility in data analysis: They enable you to arrange them dynamically as your data

> The best thing about PivotTables is their flexibility in data analysis . . .

needs require. This dynamic process of rearranging a PivotTable is known as "pivoting" your table. You turn the same information around and look at it from different angles to identify relationships between variables. A PivotTable is an interactive way to summarize large amounts of data and to analyze numerical data in depth. They are especially designed for the following:

- Querying large amounts of data in user-friendly ways.
- Subtotaling numeric data, summarizing data, and creating custom calculations.
- Expanding and collapsing levels of data to facilitate focusing.
- Pivoting or moving rows to columns or columns to rows to see different summaries of data.

If you were working for a marketing company, you would create a PivotTable using census data to summarize the data based on gender, ethnic groups, or geographic location. This is particularly valuable with marketing companies' increased emphasis on data mining for target advertising.

Figure 5.41 shows the relationship between the data tools and the PivotTable. In a PivotTable, each column or field in the source data becomes a PivotTable field that summarizes multiple rows of information. A value field provides the values to be summarized, and a grand total is calculated.

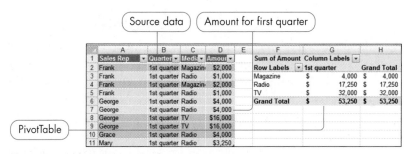

Figure 5.41   Data Table with PivotTable

A ***PivotChart*** is a graphical representation of data in a PivotTable.

A ***PivotChart*** is an interactive graphical representation of the data in a PivotTable. A PivotChart enables you to visually present the data in a report. A PivotChart always has an associated PivotTable that has a corresponding layout. Both reports have fields that correspond to each other, and when you change the position of a field in one report, the corresponding field in the other report also moves. Both PivotTables and PivotCharts enable you to make informed decisions based on the data. Figure 5.42 shows the specialized elements in a PivotChart that correspond to the PivotTable.

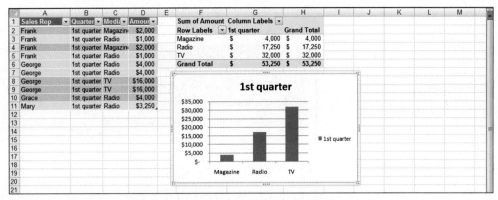

Figure 5.42 PivotTable and PivotChart

Creating and Deleting PivotTables and PivotCharts

The PivotTable command displays the Create PivotTable dialog box, and the PivotChart report command displays the Create PivotTable with PivotChart dialog box. Both commands are in Insert PivotTable in the Tables group on the Insert tab. Both dialog boxes have similar interfaces, but the difference is that the Create PivotTable dialog box creates a PivotTable only, whereas the Create PivotTable with PivotChart dialog box creates a PivotChart and an associated PivotTable.

Create a PivotTable or PivotChart

Before creating a PivotTable, you must think about the design of the data table itself. Make sure to use meaningful column headings, accurate data, and most importantly, do not leave any blank rows in your data table. One column must have duplicate values, such as names of cities, states, or departments. The duplicate values are used to create categories for organizing and summarizing data. Another column must have numeric values to produce quantitative summaries, such as averages or sums. To create a PivotTable or PivotChart, you need to connect to a data source and specify the report's location. To create the report:

1. Select a cell in a named range of cells or in an Excel table. Make sure the range of cells has column headings.
2. To create a PivotTable, click Insert PivotTable in the Tables group on the Insert tab to display the Create PivotTable dialog box. To create a PivotTable and PivotChart, click PivotChart in the Insert PivotTable list, in the Tables group on the Insert tab, to display the Create PivotTable with PivotChart dialog box.
3. Choose the data to be analyzed by clicking *Select a table or range*. If you selected a cell in a range or table, the range of cells or table name reference shows in the Table/Range box (see Figure 5.43). Otherwise, you will have to type a range of cells or a table name reference in the Table/Range box.
4. To place a PivotTable in a new worksheet, click New Worksheet. To place it on an existing worksheet, select Existing Worksheet and type the first cell in the range where the PivotTable will be located. Generally, it is beneficial to place PivotTables and PivotCharts on new sheets so that the original data source is separated from the manipulated data in the PivotTable or PivotChart.
5. Click OK. An empty PivotTable appears on the left side of the worksheet, and the PivotTable Field List window appears on the right side of the window so that you can add fields, create a layout, and customize the PivotTable.

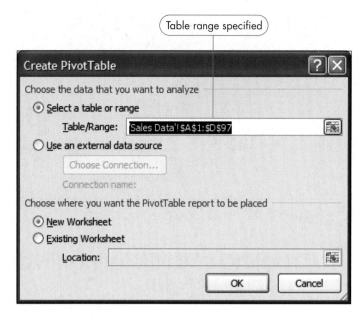

Figure 5.43 Create PivotTable Dialog Box

To create a PivotChart report from an existing PivotTable report:

1. Click the PivotTable.
2. Click a chart type in the Charts group on the Insert tab. You may select any type of chart, except a scatter, bubble, or stock chart.

Delete a PivotTable or PivotChart

If you no longer need a PivotTable or PivotChart, you can delete it. Deleting PivotTables and PivotCharts requires only a few steps. To delete a PivotTable, click the PivotTable. Click Select in the Actions group on the Options tab, select Entire PivotTable, and then press Delete. To delete a PivotChart, select the PivotChart and press Delete. Deleting the PivotChart does not delete the associated PivotTable.

> **TIP** Customize the PivotTable
>
> Right-click anywhere in a PivotTable to display a shortcut menu and select PivotTable Options to display the PivotTable Options dialog box. The default settings work well for most tables, but you can customize the table in a variety of ways. You can, for example, suppress the row or column totals or display a specific value in a blank cell. You can also change the formatting for any field within the table by right-clicking the field and selecting the Format Cells button from the resulting menu.

Add Fields to a PivotTable or PivotChart

The PivotTable Field List window (see Figure 5.44) is used to add fields to a PivotTable or a PivotChart. It is also used to remove and rearrange fields. The PivotTable Field List window displays two sections:

1. A field section at the top shows fields from an external data source. You use this section to add and remove fields.
2. A layout section at the bottom is used to arrange and reposition fields as Report Filter, Row Labels, Column Labels, and Values.

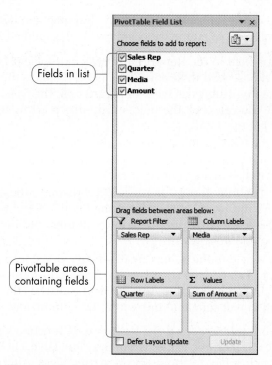

Fields in list

PivotTable areas containing fields

Figure 5.44 PivotTable Field List

To create a quick PivotTable, check the fields in the *Choose fields to add to report* section of the PivotTable Field List window. Excel arranges the fields based on their data types. Text fields are typically used for row labels, and numeric fields are typically used for column labels. Although the default layout might be acceptable in some situations, you might want to control where fields appear in the PivotTable. Table 5.5 lists and describes the areas of a PivotTable, and Table 5.6 lists and describes the areas of a PivotChart.

Table 5.5 Areas of a PivotTable Report

Area	Description
Values	Display summary numeric data.
Row Labels	Display fields on the left side of the report to organize data into categories, with each row summarizing one particular category.
Column Labels	Display fields as columns at the top of the report to organize data into categories, with each column summarizing one particular category.
Report Filter	Filters the entire report based on the selected item in the report filter.

Table 5.6 Adding Fields to PivotChart Reports

PivotChart Report	Description
Valued	Displays summary numeric data.
Axis Field (categories)	Displays fields in an axis on the chart.
Legend Fields (series) Labels	Displays fields in the legend for the chart.
Report Filter	Filters the entire report based on the selected item in the report filter.

You can organize PivotTables by dragging and dropping data fields to different rows, columns, or summary positions. To design the PivotTable, do the following:

1. Drag a field to the Report Filter area in the Field List or right-click a field name and choose Add to Report Filter. Excel displays the field in the Report Filter area in the PivotTables as well. In Figure 5.44, the Sales Rep field is used to filter the data. You can click the field's drop-down arrow to select a particular value for filtering the data.

2. Drag a field to the Column Labels or right-click a field and choose Add to Column Labels to organize data into columns. Drag a field to the Row Labels area of the Field List or right-click a field and choose Add to Row Labels to organize data into groups on rows. Excel displays the field in the respective Column Labels and Row Labels area of the PivotTable as well. In Figure 5.44, the Media field is used to organize data into columns, and the Quarter field is used to organize data into rows.

3. Drag a field to the Values area in the Field List or right-click a field and choose Add to Values. Excel displays the field in the Values area of the PivotTable as well. In Figure 5.44, the Amount field is used as the Values field. The default function will sum amounts within the column and row categories.

If you want to use a different summary function instead of SUM, you can change it. To do so, click in a value within the PivotTable, click the PivotTable Tools Options tab, and click Field Settings in the Active Field. Alternatively, you can right-click a value in the PivotTable to display the Value Field Settings dialog box. The dialog box enables you to select other calculation types, such as Count, Average, Max, and Min. Furthermore, you can create your own custom calculations, such as percentage differences or running totals. You should explore the different options in the Value Field Settings and experiment with the available options.

In addition to selecting different summary functions and customizing calculations, you can create a calculated field. Similar to a calculated field in Access, a calculated field is a user-defined field that does not exist in the original data source. It derives its values based on performing calculations on other original data source fields. To create a calculated field, select a cell within the PivotTable, click the PivotTable Tools Options tab, and click Formulas in the Tools group. Then select Calculated Field to display the Insert Calculated Field dialog box. Use Excel Help to learn more about creating calculated fields in PivotTables.

TIP   The Page Field

A page field adds a third dimension to a PivotTable. Unlike items in the row and column fields, however, the items in a page field are displayed one at a time. Creating a page field on Quarter, for example, lets you view the data for each quarter separately, by clicking the down arrow on the Page field list box, then clicking the appropriate quarter.

You can rearrange or reposition existing fields in both PivotTables and PivotCharts by using one of the four areas at the bottom of the layout section. To rearrange fields, click and drag the field between the field and layout sections and between the different areas or click the field name in one of the areas, and then select one of the commands from Table 5.7.

Table 5.7 Rearrange Fields in PivotTables and PivotCharts

Command	Moves the Field . . .
Move Up	up one position in the area
Move Down	down one position in the area
Move to Beginning	to the beginning of the area
Move to End	to the end of the area
Move to Report Filter	to the Report Filter area
Move to Row Labels	to the Row Labels area
Move to Column Labels	to the Column Labels area
Move to Values	to the Values area

To remove a field, click the field name in the layout section, and then click Remove Field or clear the check box next to each field name in the field section. Alternatively, you can click and hold a field name in the layout section and drag it outside the PivotTable Field List.

Formatting, Sorting, Filtering, Subtotaling, and Refreshing a PivotTable

After you create a PivotTable, you will format it to enhance its information value. You will sort and filter your table to best analyze the data. Because PivotTables contain numeric data, you will generally subtotal and total the values. It is important to note that when your original data table data change, the PivotTable does not. PivotTables and PivotCharts are NOT dynamic; you must refresh the reports.

Format the PivotTable

Formatting PivotTables is primarily done in the PivotTable Tools Design tab. The dynamic Design palette shown in Figure 5.45 displays a wide variety of preset formats that are used to format PivotTables. In addition, the PivotTable Style Options group provides several other tools such as Banded rows and Banded columns for further formatting of the PivotTable.

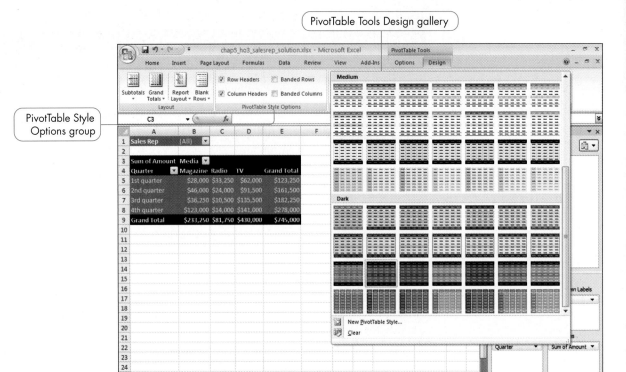

Figure 5.45 Tools for Formatting PivotTables

TIP   Design and Design Time

Excel provides a wide variety of design options in tools, galleries, and styles, but you must remember that less can be better. You do not have to choose all options, all colors, or all styles for all elements in your PivotTable or PivotChart. Further, some visually impaired people have difficulty distinguishing red and green colors. Use these colors sparingly.

Sort and Filter the PivotTable

PivotTables can be as complicated as the original data on which the PivotTable is based. Sorting and filtering the PivotTable make the data more manageable and easier to analyze. This simplifies the data analysis in the PivotTable. To sort or filter a PivotTable, click the drop-down arrow for a particular column heading. Figure 5.46 shows the Sort and Filter option lists available for PivotTables. The sorting and filtering options are similar to how you sort regular data tables.

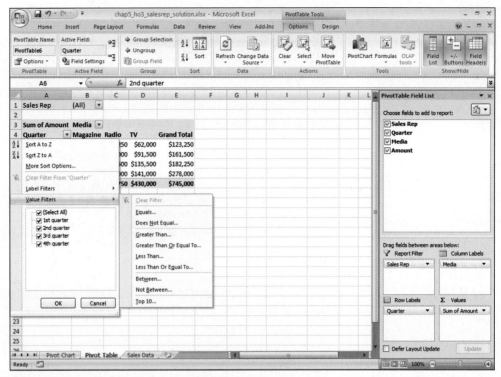

Figure 5.46 PivotTable Sort and Filter Options

Subtotal the PivotTable

By default, the values area consolidates data by showing subtotals for each category. You can customize PivotTable subtotals using the Subtotals command in the Layout group on the Design tab. Figure 5.47 displays the three subtotal options. When your PivotTable is large, displaying the subtotals at the top of the group draws attention to the totals and enables you to scroll to view all of the supporting data if necessary.

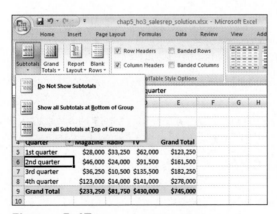

Figure 5.47 PivotTable Subtotals

Refresh the PivotTable and PivotChart

Excel does not update PivotTables and PivotCharts automatically when you change the source data. To refresh a PivotTable or PivotChart, right-click any cell in a PivotTable and select Refresh. Alternatively, with the PivotTable Tools contextual tab displayed, click the Options tab and click Refresh in the Data group (see Figure 5.48).

If you want to make sure your PivotTable is up-to-date when you open the workbook, click the PivotTable Tools Option tab, click the Options down arrow in the PivotTable group, and select Options. In the PivotTable Options dialog box, click the Data tab, select *Refresh data when opening the file,* and click OK.

Figure 5.48 PivotTable Tools

TIP Format the Data Series

Why settle for a traditional bar chart when you can change the color, pattern, and shape of its components? Right-click any column to select a data series and display a shortcut menu, then select Format Data Series to display a dialog box in which you can customize the appearance of the vertical columns. We warn you that it is addictive and that you can spend much more time than you intended initially. Set a time limit and stop when you reach it.

PivotTable/PivotChart Tools | Reference

PivotTable Tools Tab and Group	Description
Options PivotTable Active Field Group Sort Data Actions Tools Show/Hide	The basic PivotTable tab. Contains basic editing functions for PivotTables. As with all groups, pull-down areas are available and do increase functionality.
	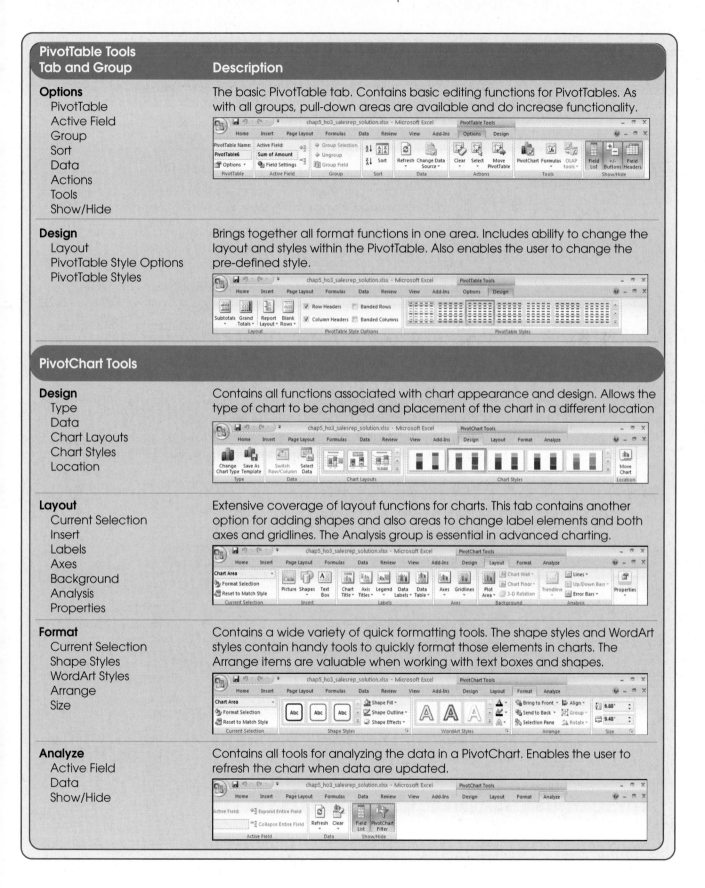
Design Layout PivotTable Style Options PivotTable Styles	Brings together all format functions in one area. Includes ability to change the layout and styles within the PivotTable. Also enables the user to change the pre-defined style.

PivotChart Tools

Design Type Data Chart Layouts Chart Styles Location	Contains all functions associated with chart appearance and design. Allows the type of chart to be changed and placement of the chart in a different location
Layout Current Selection Insert Labels Axes Background Analysis Properties	Extensive coverage of layout functions for charts. This tab contains another option for adding shapes and also areas to change label elements and both axes and gridlines. The Analysis group is essential in advanced charting.
Format Current Selection Shape Styles WordArt Styles Arrange Size	Contains a wide variety of quick formatting tools. The shape styles and WordArt styles contain handy tools to quickly format those elements in charts. The Arrange items are valuable when working with text boxes and shapes.
Analyze Active Field Data Show/Hide	Contains all tools for analyzing the data in a PivotChart. Enables the user to refresh the chart when data are updated.

Hands-On Exercises

3 | Eye First Advertising Department Sales

Skills covered: 1. Create a PivotTable **2.** Complete the PivotTable **3.** Modify the Source Data and Refresh the PivotTable **4.** Pivot the Table **5.** Create a PivotChart **6.** Change and Enhance the PivotChart **7.** Complete the PivotChart **8.** Create a Web Page from a PivotTable **9.** Change Underlying Data

---

Step 1
Create a PivotTable

Refer to Figure 5.43 and Figure 5.49 as you complete Step 1.

a. Start Excel and open the *chap5_ho3_salesrep* workbook and save it as **chap5_ho3_salesrep_solution** so that you will be able to return to the original workbook.

The workbook contains a list of sales records for an advertising agency. Each record displays the name of the sales representative, the quarter in which the sale was recorded, the media type, and the amount of the sale.

b. Click anywhere in the list of sales data and click **PivotTable** in the Tables group on the Insert tab to open the Create PivotTable dialog box, as shown in Figure 5.43.

c. Verify that the **Select a table or range** is selected and that the **Table/Range** is Sheet1!$A$1:$D$97.

The Table/Range is the range for your data table and will be the basis for your PivotTable.

d. Verify that **New Worksheet** is selected and click **OK**. You will see Sheet1 (the PivotTable sheet) and the PivotTable Field List pane.

The option to put the PivotTable into a new worksheet was already selected. One additional sheet has been added to the workbook, but the PivotTable is not yet complete.

e. Save the workbook.

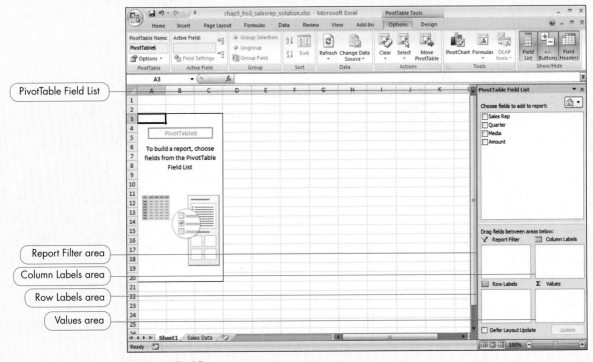

Figure 5.49 New PivotTable Placeholder

Step 2	a.	Verify that the **Sheet1 tab** is selected and complete the PivotTable as follows: Drag the **Media** field to the Row Labels area.

Step 2
Complete the PivotTable

a. Verify that the **Sheet1 tab** is selected and complete the PivotTable as follows: Drag the **Media** field to the Row Labels area.

- The Media field box is checked and the field is simultaneously moved to the Row Label area in the PivotTable.
- Drag the **Sales Rep** field to the Column Labels area.
- The Sales Rep field box is checked and the field is simultaneously moved to the Column Labels area in the PivotTable.
- Drag the **Quarter** field to the Report Filter area.
- The Quarter field box is checked and the field is simultaneously moved to the Report Filter area in the PivotTable.
- Drag the **Amount** field to the Σ Values area.

The Amount field box is checked and the field is simultaneously moved to the Values area in the PivotTable, where it changes to the Sum of the Amount. You should see the total sales for each sales representative for each type of media within the PivotTable.

b. Double-click the **Sheet1 tab** (the worksheet that contains the PivotTable), type **PivotTable** as the new name, and press **Enter**.

You renamed the worksheet so it is more descriptive of its contents.

c. Click **cell B3**, type **Sales Rep**, and press **Enter**.

d. Click **cell A4**, type **Media**, and press **Enter**.

You changed the headings in the PivotTable to reflect the data labels in the data table.

e. Select the PivotTable by clicking and dragging **A1:J8**. Click **Format** in the Cells group on the Home tab and select **AutoFit Column Width**.

You changed the width of the columns to best display the report data.

TROUBLESHOOTING: If you click in a cell not in the PivotTable, the PivotTable Field List pane closes and the PivotTable tools are no longer available. Click anywhere in the PivotTable to redisplay the PivotTable Field List pane and the PivotTable tools.

f. Save the workbook.

Step 3
Modify the Source Data and Refresh the PivotTable

Refer to Figure 5.50 as you complete Step 3.

a. Click the **Sales Data sheet tab**, click **Find & Select** in the Editing group on the Home tab, and then click **Replace** to display the Find and Replace dialog box.

You will replace Peter's name within the list of transactions with your own name.

b. Type **Peter** in the *Find what* box and type **Your First Name and First Initial** in the *Replace with* box.

c. Click **Replace All**, click **OK** after the replacements have been made, and close the Find and Replace dialog box.

You used Find and Replace to replace all occurrences of Peter with your own name.

d. Click the **Pivot Table tab** to return to the PivotTable.

The name change is not yet reflected in the pivot table because the table must be manually refreshed whenever the underlying data changes.

e. Click anywhere in the PivotTable, click **Refresh** in the Data group on the Options tab, and then click **Refresh All** to update the PivotTable.

TROUBLESHOOTING: You must click Refresh All to update the PivotTable whenever the underlying data changes.

You should see your name as one of the sales representatives.

f. Save the workbook.

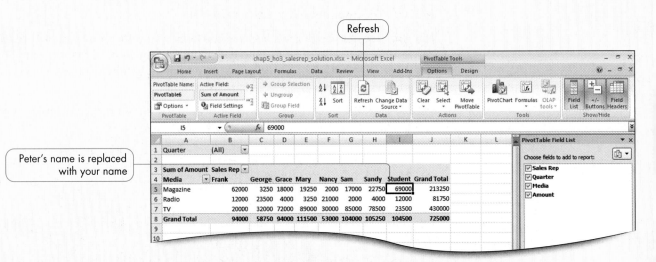

Figure 5.50 Modified Sales Data

Step 4
Pivot the Table

Refer to Figure 5.51 as you complete Step 4.

a. Click and drag the **Quarter** field to the **Row Labels area**.

You can change the arrangement of a PivotTable by dragging fields from one area to another. After moving the Quarter field, the Report Filter area is now empty and you can see the breakdown of sales by quarter and media type.

b. Click and drag the **Media** field to the **Column Labels area**, and then drag the **Sales Rep** field to the **Report Filter area**.

c. Click **cell A4**, type **Quarter**, and press **Enter**.

d. Click **cell B3**, type **Media**, and press **Enter**.

Your PivotTable should match the one in Figure 5.51. You pivoted the table by dragging the Media and Sales Rep fields. You then manually changed the labels.

e. Click anywhere in the PivotTable, click the **Sum of Amount drop-down arrow**, and select **Value Field Settings** to display the Value Field Settings dialog box.

The Value Field Settings dialog box enables you to select a different calculation function, such as Average. In addition, you use this dialog box to specify the number format.

f. Click **Number Format** in the Value Field Settings dialog box, and then choose **Currency** and **zero** decimal places.

g. Click **OK** to close the Format Cells dialog box and click **OK** a second time to close the Value Field Settings dialog box.

h. Save the workbook.

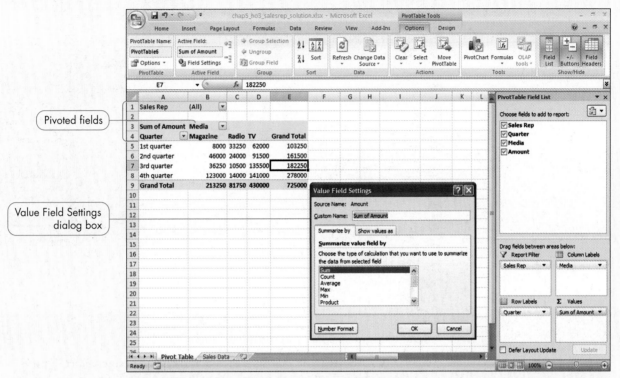

Figure 5.51 Pivoted Table

Refer to Figure 5.52 as you complete Step 5.

a. Click anywhere in the PivotTable and click **PivotChart** in the Tools group on the Options tab.

TROUBLESHOOTING: You must make sure the PivotTable is active before you can create a PivotChart report.

b. Click **Clustered Column**, the first chart in the first row, in the Insert Chart dialog box and click **OK**.

You created a PivotChart that is displayed on the PivotTable sheet. The PivotChart shows total sales for all sales reps by media for each quarter. The PivotChart Filter pane displays the active fields on the PivotChart. The PivotChart Tools context tab displays four tools tabs you will use to enhance the appearance of the chart and to analyze your data.

c. Save the workbook.

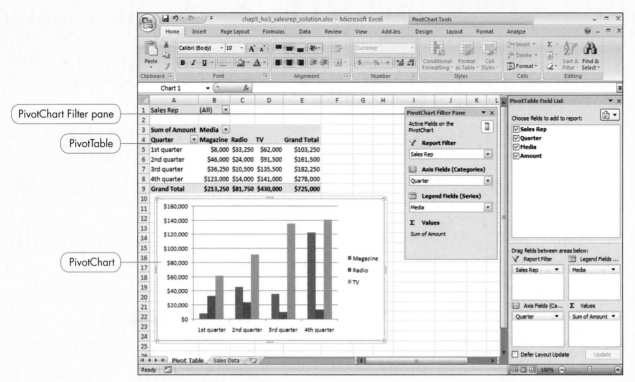

Figure 5.52 PivotChart

Refer to Figure 5.53 as you complete Step 6.

a. Verify that the PivotChart is selected and click **Change Chart Type** in the Type group on the Design tab to open the Change Chart Type dialog box.

b. Click **Stacked Column** and click **OK**.

You changed the chart type to better show total media sales by quarter.

c. Click **Move Chart** in the Location group on the Design tab to open the Move Chart dialog box.

d. Click **New sheet**, type **Pivot Chart** in the text box, and click **OK**.

You placed the PivotChart on a separate sheet and simultaneously renamed the sheet tab. Moving the chart expands the visible chart area for effective analysis.

e. Close the PivotTable Field List pane if necessary and close the PivotChart Filter pane.

f. Click **Chart Title** in the Labels group on the Layout tab and select **Above Chart**.

g. Type **Advertising Revenue by Quarter and Media Type**.

h. Click **Axis Titles** in the Labels group on the Layout tab and select **Primary Vertical Axis Title** and **Rotated Title**.

i. Type **Total Revenue**.

You added a title and labeled the Y axis to better identify the data.

j. Save the workbook.

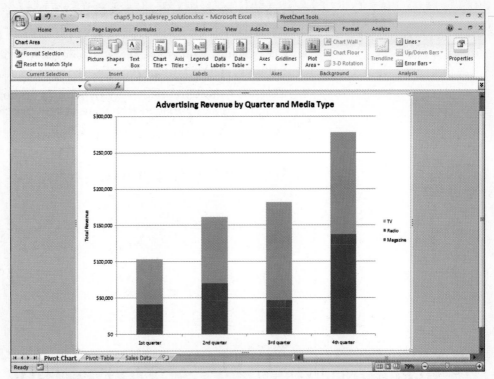

Figure 5.53 PivotChart on New Sheet

Step 7
Complete the PivotChart

a. Click the **Pivot Table sheet tab**, press and hold **Ctrl**, and click the **Sales Data sheet tab**.

You selected the Sales Data sheet and the Pivot Table sheet. Both worksheets are selected and both will be affected by the next command.

b. Click **Margins** in the Page Setup group on the Page Layout tab, select **Custom Margins**, and click the **Horizontally check box** in the *Center on page* section.

c. Click the **Header/Footer tab**, click **Custom Footer**, type **Your Name** in the Left section, click in the Right section, click **Insert Page Number**, and click **OK**.

d. Click the **Sheet tab**, click the **Gridlines check box**, and click the **Row and column headings check box** in the *Print* section.

e. Click **Print Preview** to verify that the PivotTable and the Sales Data will print correctly.

f. Save the workbook.

Step 8
Create a Web Page from a PivotTable

Refer to Figure 5.54 as you complete Step 8.

a. Click the **Sales Data sheet tab** to deselect the two tabs and click the **PivotTable tab**.

b. Click and drag to select the entire PivotTable.

If you have difficulty selecting the table, click and drag from the bottom-right cell to the top-left cell.

c. Click the **Office Button** and select **Save As** to open the Save As dialog box.

d. Click the **Save as type drop-down arrow** and select **Web Page (*.htm; *.html)**. Click **Publish: PivotTable**, and then click **Publish** to open the Publish as Web Page dialog box.

The selected PivotTable is going to be saved as a Web page, but first, you must enter a title and make the Web page interactive.

e. Click **Change** to open the Set Title dialog box, type **Advertising Agency Solution**, and then click **OK**.

f. Click the **AutoRepublish every time this workbook is saved check box** and click the **Open published web page in browser check box**.

g. Check that your settings match those in Figure 5.54 and click **Publish** to publish the PivotTable.

h. View the Web page in your browser and leave the browser open as you continue to Step 9.

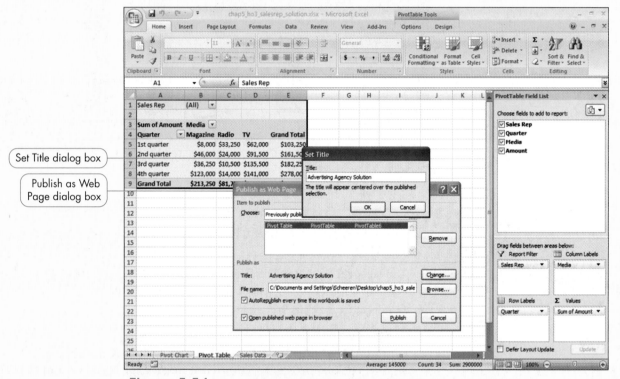

Figure 5.54 Create Web Page from PivotTable

| **Step 9**
Change
Underlying Data | Refer to Figure 5.55 as you complete Step 9. |

a. Click the Excel button on the Windows taskbar to return to Excel and click the **Sales Data worksheet**.

b. Click **cell D18**, type **22000**, and press **Enter**.

You changed your magazine sales in the first quarter from $2,000 to $22,000.

c. Click the **Pivot Table sheet tab**, click anywhere in the PivotTable, click **Refresh** in the Data group on the Options tab, and select **Refresh All**.

The magazine sales in the 1st quarter increase to $28,000, and the grand total changes to $123,250.

d. Save the workbook, click **Enable the AutoPublish**, and then click **OK** in the Microsoft Office dialog box.

e. Return to Internet Explorer, then click **Refresh** on the browser toolbar to update the Web page (see Figure 5.55).

The numbers within the Web PivotTable change to reflect the change in magazine sales. If the numbers do not refresh, close Internet Explorer, reopen it, and then reopen the Web page from the Exploring Excel folder.

f. Click **PivotTable Tools Option tab**, click the **Options down arrow** in the PivotTable group, and select **Options**.

g. Click the **Data tab** in the PivotTable Options dialog box, select **Refresh data when opening the file**, and click **OK**.

Your PivotTable will automatically refresh when the workbook is opened and the PivotTable will display accurate results.

h. Close Internet Explorer. Close Excel. Click **Yes** if prompted to save the changes.

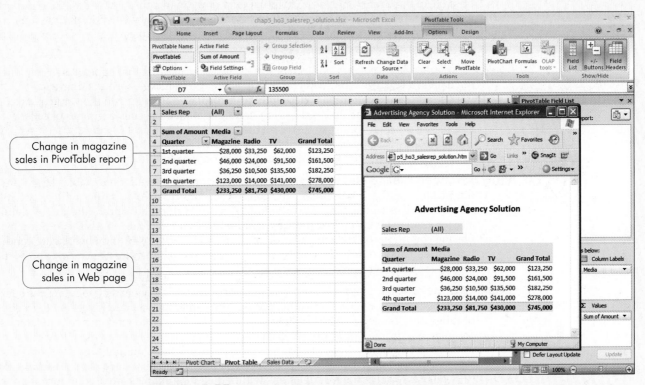

Figure 5.55 Updated PivotTable and Web Page

Summary

1. **Design tables based on data table theory.** Often, data tables are created from existing files and little or no thought is put into the creation of a data table that will be used for complex data analysis. Just as you spent time planning a spreadsheet, you should plan the elements of a data table. You should think about who will use the data table, what types of reports will be produced, and what types of searches might be done. As a general rule, the more thorough your planning process, the fewer changes will be needed to the table after it is created and in use.

2. **Import data from text files and other sources.** You have some options for importing data created in another format or in another application into an Excel table. This often occurs when data are collected on a mainframe computer and are then analyzed on a PC. Whereas it is possible to import text files as an external data range, generally, you will want to import a text file by opening it, forgoing the conversion that is necessary when importing a file as an external data range. You can import data from Access data tables and from sources such as the World Wide Web.

3. **Apply conditional formatting.** Conditional formatting is formatting that appears in a cell when the data in a cell meet specified conditions or are the result of a formula. It is used to impose additional conditions with alternative formats depending on the value of a cell. Conditional formatting makes it easy to highlight interesting cells or ranges of cells, emphasize unusual values, or visualize data using data bars, color scales, or icon sets. In conditional formatting, if the condition is true, the cell formatting is based on that condition. If it is false, the cell is not formatted based on that condition.

4. **Apply advanced filtering and sorting methods.** You can sort and filter data tables based on conditional formatting. For example, you can filter records to display values with a particular icon set, such as a green flag. Furthermore, you can perform advanced filtering by defining a criteria range for specifying multiple conditions. You can create an AND condition by placing conditions on the same row or you can create an OR condition by placing conditions on separate rows in the criteria range. Use relational operators, such as < and >, to restrict the filtered records.

5. **Create and use range names.** Creating a name, a word or string of characters representing a cell, range of cells, or constant value, equates the name, such as EmployeeList, to a cell or range of cells such as A1:E15. This name can then be used to reference cells in later commands. A name can be up to 255 characters long but must begin with a letter or underscore. It can be a mixture of upper or lowercase letters, numbers, periods, and underscores, but cannot have blank spaces. Once you have defined a range name, it automatically adjusts for insertions or deletions within the range. Names are used in formulas and serve as documentation while helping to clarify formula components. After creating range names, you can paste an alphabetical list of range names into a documentation worksheet for reference.

6. **Use database functions.** The database functions operate only on the selected records in a table. Their functions are similar to statistical functions (SUM, AVERAGE, MAX, MIN, COUNT) except that they only affect records that satisfy the criteria.

7. **Create and delete PivotTables and PivotCharts.** A PivotTable provides the most flexibility in data analysis. A PivotTable divides records in a list into categories and computes statistics for those categories. A PivotTable summarizes, analyzes, explores, and presents summary data. A PivotChart enables you to visually present the data in a report. Both PivotTable and PivotChart enable you to make informed decisions based on the data.

8. **Format, sort, filter, subtotal, and refresh a PivotTable.** Once you make a PivotTable, you format it to enhance its information value. You sort and filter your table to best analyze the data. You can even change subtotal options and select other summary functions, such as Average. Because PivotTables contain numeric data, you will often have to subtotal and total the values. It is important to note that when your original data changes, the PivotTable does not. PivotTables and PivotCharts are NOT dynamic; you must refresh the reports.

Key Terms

Multiple Choice

1. All of the following statements regarding fields are true except:

   (a) The field names must be entered in the first row of the list.

   (b) The field names will change from record to record.

   (c) Each field name must be unique.

   (d) The fields will be in the same order in every record.

2. You have a list of all the members of a club you belong to. The worksheet contains other data as well. How can you be sure Excel recognizes the boundaries of the list?

   (a) Insert a comment in the upper-left corner of the list.

   (b) Insert a blank row between the field names and the data.

   (c) Insert a blank row and a blank column between the list and other data in the worksheet.

   (d) Type a row of dashes (- - -) after the last row of the list.

3. You have a list of all the employees in your organization. The list contains employee name, office, title, and salary. You want to list all employees in each office branch. The branches should be listed alphabetically, with the employee earning the highest salary listed first in each office. Which is true of your sort order?

   (a) Branch office is the primary key and should be in ascending order.

   (b) Salary is the primary key and should be in descending order.

   (c) Salary is the primary key and should be in ascending order.

   (d) Branch office is the primary key and should be in descending order.

4. You have a list of all the employees in your organization. The list contains employee name, location, title, and salary. You want to list all employees in each location. The locations should be listed alphabetically, with the highest-paid employees listed first for each location. Which is true of your sort order?

   (a) Sort by location ascending, then by salary ascending.

   (b) Sort by location ascending, then by salary descending.

   (c) Sort by salary descending, then by location ascending.

   (d) Sort by location descending, then by salary ascending.

5. The maximum number of keys you can sort by is:

   (a) One

   (b) Two

   (c) Three

   (d) Unlimited

6. The Text Import Wizard can be used to import data from what type of files?

   (a) HTML files

   (b) Database files

   (c) ASCII files

   (d) Graphic files

7. You have a list of all employees in your organization. You want to use the Sort Ascending button to list them by location, then by title, then by last name alphabetically. How do you do this?

   (a) Sort by location first, then by title, then by last name.

   (b) Sort by location first, then either by title or by last name.

   (c) Sort by last name first, then by title, then by location.

   (d) This is impossible; the Sort Ascending button can only sort by one field.

8. You have a list containing all the employees in your organization. You select the AutoFilter command, and then select New York from the location field. What is the result?

   (a) The list is sorted by city, with New York first.

   (b) The rows where the location is New York are written to another worksheet.

   (c) The rows where the location is not New York are deleted.

   (d) The rows where the location is not New York are hidden.

9. You have a list containing all the employees in the organization. You want to display all rows where employees earn more than $50,000, but less than $75,000. How should you set up your criteria range?

   (a) Have one column entry for the salary field, with >50000 in one row and <75000 in another row.

   (b) Have two column entries for the salary field, with >50000 in one column and <75000 in another column, on the same line.

   (c) Have two column entries for the salary field, with >50000 in one column and <75000 in another column, on different lines.

   (d) It is not possible to set up the criteria range to enable this.

10. You have a list containing all the employees in your organization. You have a criteria range that shows Manager in the Title field in row 18 and New York in the Location field in row 19. Which rows will be displayed?

(a) All managers in New York

(b) All managers regardless of location and all employees in New York

(c) All managers except those in New York

(d) All managers except those in New York and all New York employees

11. You have a criteria range that you thought would select marketing reps with sales greater than $1,000,000. When you apply the filter, all rows are displayed. What is the most likely reason for this?

(a) You used an OR instead of an AND in your criteria range.

(b) You have a blank row in the criteria range.

(c) You have a blank row in the list.

(d) You mistyped the field names in the criteria range.

12. To open a dialog box showing all the range names you have defined, use the:

(a) Edit Names command

(b) Go To command

(c) View Names command

(d) List Names command

13. You want to show total sales for each location. What should you do before executing the Subtotals command?

(a) Sort by Sales, in ascending order.

(b) Sort by Sales, in descending order.

(c) Sort by Sales, in either ascending or descending order, then by Location.

(d) Sort by Location, in either ascending or descending order.

14. You use the DAVERAGE function. No rows match your criteria. What is the result of the function?

(a) ###########

(b) The #REF! error message

(c) A circular reference

(d) The #DIV/0 error message

15. Which method will correctly import data from an Access database into Excel?

(a) Use the Query Wizard.

(b) Use the Text Import Wizard.

(c) Use the Import External Data command.

(d) You cannot import data from Access into Excel.

16. You have a list containing all the employees in your organization. You want to generate two sets of subtotals: the number of employees in each office, and within each office, the number of employees by job title. How can you accomplish this?

(a) You cannot accomplish what the question asks.

(b) Sort the list by office, generate subtotals, resort by title, and then generate subtotals again. Use the COUNT summary function for both subtotals.

(c) Sort the list by office, then by title and generate subtotals on both fields. Use the COUNT summary function for both fields.

(d) Sort the list by office, then by title. Generate subtotals on the office field using the COUNT function. Generate subtotals on the title field using the COUNT field and then clearing the check box to replace the current subtotals.

17. You have created a PivotTable and make some changes to the cells underlying the PivotTable. How can you update the information in the PivotTable?

(a) Click the cell(s) you changed, and then use the Refresh PivotTable command.

(b) Click the PivotTable, and then use the Refresh command.

(c) PivotTables are automatically updated once you alter the data.

(d) Once created, PivotTables cannot be updated.

18. You have created a PivotChart showing sales by quarter by sales rep. Before presenting it to management, you notice the name of a rep who has since been fired. How do you delete this rep from the chart without deleting the data?

(a) Click the arrow next to the Sales Rep field and remove the employee's name.

(b) Make the employee's data points and axis titles invisible.

(c) You can't delete the rep from the chart without first deleting the data.

(d) Hide that rep's row(s) in the underlying list, which automatically removes that rep from the chart.

Practice Exercises

1 XYZ Restaurant Corporation Charitable Trust Fundraiser

Your work with the XYZ Restaurant Corporation Charitable Trust, which allows you to demonstrate your expertise with Excel. The workbook shown in Figure 5.56 is the completed list of attendees, addresses, and the items they have donated to the fundraiser. You will import a text file, add donors, sort the data, format the worksheet for professional presentation, and use conditional formatting.

a. Start Excel, click the **Office Button**, click **Open**, click the **Files of type drop-down arrow**, select **Text Files**, and open the *chap5_pe1_trust* workbook. Click **Next**, clear the **Tab Delimiter check box**, click the **Comma Delimiter check box**, click **Next**, and click **Finish**.

b. Format the worksheet with these specifications:

- Click and drag to select **cells A1:L1**, then click **Bold** in the Font group on the Home tab.

- Click **Center** in the Alignment group.

- Click the **Fill Color down arrow** in the Font group, select **Aqua Accent 5, Darker 50%**, and select **White** as the font color.

- Select **cells A1:L26**, click the **Format down arrow** in the Cells group, and select **AutoFit Column Width**.

c. Save the workbook as **chap5_pe1_trust_solution**. Click the **Save as type drop-down arrow** and select **Excel workbook**. Click **Save**.

d. Click **cell A27** and enter the data for **Ciafre**, as shown in the table below, pressing **Tab** to move from field to field.

Cell Reference	Data
A27	26
B27	Eugene
C27	Ciafre
D27	456 Franklin Way
E27	Pittsburgh
F27	PA
G27	15697
H27	(412) 555-1025
I27	Michelle Wie Autographed Photo, COA
J27	$200
K27	Product
L27	2

e. Click **cell L15** (Reed's record) and change the number attending to **3** and the value of the Yoga class to **$150**. Select **cells A11:L11** (Mican's record), right-click the selected cells, and select **Delete**. Click **Entire row** in the Delete dialog box, and then click **OK**.

f. Click **Spelling** in the Proofing group on the Review tab, click **Change** to accept the suggested correction for **Pittsburgh**, continue checking the document, and click **OK** to return to the worksheet.

g. Click a cell anywhere in the attendee list and click Sort in the Sort & Filter group on the Data tab. Click the **Sort by drop-down arrow**, select **LastName**, and then click **Add Level**. Click the **Then by drop-down arrow** and select **FirstName**. Click **OK** to sort alphabetically by alumni name.

continued on Next Page

...continued on Next Page

h. Apply Conditional Formatting based on these specifications:

- Select **cells J2:J26**.

- Click **Conditional Formatting** in the Styles group on the Home tab.

- Point to **Highlight Cells Rules** and select **Greater Than** to open the Greater Than dialog box.

- Type **$300** in **Format Cells that are GREATER THAN:**.

- Select **Yellow Fill with Dark Yellow Text** from the **with drop-down** list and click **OK**.

i. Save the workbook. You will create a custom footer that contains your name and today's date.

- Click **Page Layout** on the status bar and click **Footer** in the Header & Footer group on the Header & Footer Tools Design tab.

- Click in the left footer area and type your name.

- Click in the center footer area and click **Current Date** in the Header & Footer Elements group.

- Click in the right footer area and type your instructor's name.

- Click **Normal** on the status bar and click the **Page Setup Dialog Box Launcher**.

- Click the **Page tab** and click **Fit to 1 page**.

- Click the **Sheet tab** and check the boxes to show gridlines and row and column headings. Print the entire workbook, and then close it.

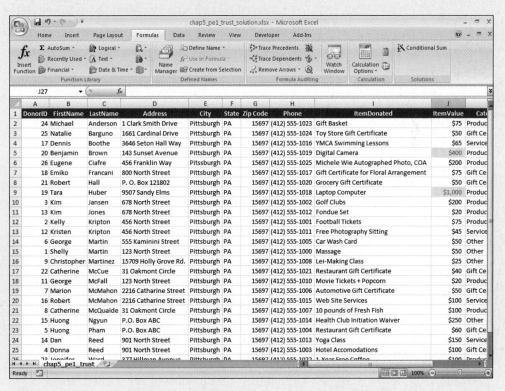

Figure 5.56 XYZ Restaurant Corporation Charitable Trust

...continued on Next Page

Your work at an advertising agency allows you to put your statistical analysis skills to good use. Your advertising agency is launching a campaign for the U.S. Mint's collection of 13 quarters that depict and honor the traditions of the original 13 states. Therefore, your company will first target residents of the original 13 states. The workbook shown in Figure 5.57 contains three worksheets with different views of the same data about the United States. You are going to calculate population density and format the workbook. Further, you will copy worksheets and create a data table for sorting and filtering. Complete the workbook as directed, using Figure 5.57 as a guide.

a. Open the *chap5_pe2_filter* workbook and save it as **chap5_pe2_filter_solution** so that you can return to the original workbook if necessary.

b. Click **cell F5** and enter the formula **=D5/E5** to compute the population density for the first state in the list.

c. Format the cells with these specifications:

   • Click the **Number Format down arrow** and select **More Number Formats** to open the Format Cells dialog box.

   • Click **Number** in the Category list, then type **0** for the number of decimal places.

   • Click **OK**.

   • Use the Fill handle to copy the formula to the remaining rows in the list.

d. Select **cells A1:F1**, merge and center the title, apply bold, and change the font to 16.

   • Click **cell A2** and type **The Most Densely Populated States (People/Square Mile)**.

   • **Merge & Center**, then change the **Font Size** to **12, Bold**.

   • Select **cells A4:F4**, click **Bold** in the Font group, click **Wrap Text** in the Alignment group, and then click **Center**.

e. Right-click the worksheet tab, select **Move or Copy** to copy the worksheet, check the box to create a copy, and click **OK**.

   • Right-click the worksheet tab for the copied worksheet and select Rename.

   • Type **Population Density**.

   • Copy the original data worksheet a second time, renaming the copied worksheet **13 Original States**.

f. Use AutoFilter based on these specifications:

   • Click the **Population Density worksheet tab**.
   • Select **cells A4:F54**, click the **Insert tab**, and then click **Table** in the Tables group.

   • Verify that the table range is correct in the Create Table dialog box and make sure the **My table has headers box** is checked, then click **OK**.

   • Click the **Population Density arrow**, click **Number Filters** to display the Number Filters list, and select **Top 10**.

   • Verify that you have the appropriate entries in each of the three list boxes—that is, Top, 10 for the number of entries, and Items.

   • Click **OK** to display the filtered list. Click in **column F**, click the **Data tab**, and click **Sort Largest to Smallest** in the Sort & Filter group.

   • Type a new subtitle in **cell A2**, **The Ten Most Densely Populated States (People/Square Mile)**.

...continued on Next Page

g. Click the worksheet tab for the 13 Original States and create a filtered list to display the first 13 states admitted to the Union based on these specifications:

- Select **cells A4:F54**, click the **Insert tab**, and then click **Table** in the Tables group.

- Verify that the table range is correct in the Create Table dialog box and make sure the **My table has headers check box** is checked, then click **OK**.

- Click the **Year Admitted arrow**, click **Number Filters** to display the Number Filters list, and select **Top 10**.

- Select **Bottom**, type **13**, and select **Items** as the appropriate entries in each of the three list boxes.

- Click **OK** to display the filtered list. Click in **column C**, click the **Data tab**, and click **Sort Smallest to Largest** in the Sort & Filter group.

- Type a new subtitle in **cell A2**, **Population Density for the First 13 States**.

h. Save the workbook. Press and hold **Ctrl** as you select all three worksheets. You will create a custom footer that contains your name, the worksheet tab, and today's date.

- Click the **Page Layout tab**, click the **Page Setup Dialog Box Launcher**, click the **Header/Footer tab**, click **Custom Footer**, and type your name in the Left section.

- Click in the Center section and click **Insert Sheet Name**.

- Click in the Right section, click **Insert Date**, and click **OK**.

- Click the **Page tab** and click **Fit to 1 page**.

- Click **Sheet tab** and check the boxes to show gridlines and row and column headings.

i. Print the entire workbook, and then close it.

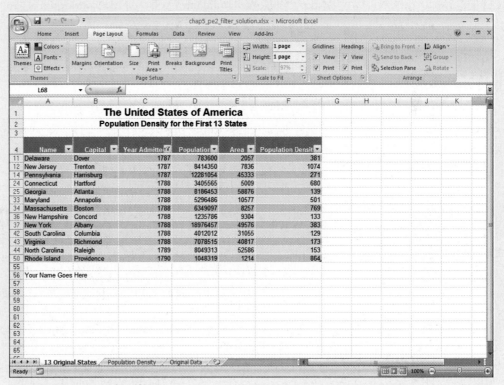

Figure 5.57 Top 10 Filters

...continued on Next Page

The director of your local service organization asked for your help. She wants to award scholarship money based on students achieving Dean's List status. You will find a partially completed version of the workbook shown in Figure 5.58. You will enter functions to help identify students making the Dean's List and their year in school.

a. Open the *chap5_pe3_scholarship* workbook and save it as **chap5_pe3_scholarship_ solution**.

b. Add a transfer student by right-clicking **row 18** and selecting **Insert** from the context menu to insert a blank row. **Kathy Lucente**, majoring in **Engineering**, has completed **14** credits and has **45** quality points. Enter the data. (Kathy's record can be seen in Figure 5.58, but it is not in the workbook that opened.)

c. Enter the appropriate formula in **cell F4** to compute the GPA for the first student (the quality points divided by the number of credits). Copy the formula to the other cells in the column.

d. Select **cells B25:E26**, click the **Formulas tab**, and then click **Define Name** in the Defined Names group. Verify that the Name is **Credits** and the *Refers to* box contains the selected range and click **OK**.

e. Click cell **E4**, click **Lookup & Reference** in the Function Library, and select **HLOOKUP**. Click cell **E4** for the Lookup_value, type **Credits** in the Table_array box, type **2** in the Row_index_num box, and click **OK**. Copy the formula to the other cells in the column.

f. Format the worksheet based on these specifications:

   • Select **cells A1:G3** and press and hold **Ctrl** while selecting **A22:G22**, **A25:E25**, and **A28**.

   • Click the **Home tab**, click the **Fill Color down arrow** in the Font group, and select **Dark Blue**.

   • Click the **Font Color down arrow** and select **White**.

   • Click **Bold** in the Font group. Select **cells A1:G1** and click **Merge & Center** in the Alignment group.

   • Click the **Font Size down arrow** and select **20**.

   • Select **cells A3:G3**, press and hold **Ctrl** while selecting **A22:G22** and **A25:E25**, and click **Center** in the Alignment group.

   • Select **cells F4:F19** and click **Increase Decimal** in the Number group to show GPA with two decimal places.

g. Select **cells A3:G19**, click the **Insert tab**, and click **table**. Verify the range in the **Where is the data for your table? box** and make sure the **My table has headers check box** is selected. Click **OK**. Click the **Last name arrow** and select **Sort A to Z**.

h. Filter the data based on these conditions:

   • Click **cell F23**, the criteria range, and type **>3.2**, the qualifying minimum for the Dean's List.

   • Click any cell in the data table, click the **Data tab**, and click **Advanced** in the Sort & Filter group.

   • Verify that **Filter the list, in-place** is selected and the **List range** is your table area.

   • Click in the **Criteria range** box, select **cell A22:G23**, and click **OK**. You used the Advanced Filter command to filter the list in place so that the only visible students are those on the Dean's List with a GPA greater than 3.2, as shown in Figure 5.58.

i. Save the workbook. You will create a custom footer that contains your name and today's date based on these specifications:

...continued on Next Page

- Click **Page Layout** on the status bar and click **Footer** in the Header & Footer group on the Header & Footer Tools Design tab.

- Click in the left footer area and type your name.

- Click in the center footer area and click **Current Date** in the Header & Footer Elements group.

- Click in the right footer area and type your instructor's name.

- Click **Normal** on the status bar and click the **Page Setup Dialog Box Launcher**.

- Click the **Sheet tab** and check the boxes to show gridlines and row and column headings. Print the entire workbook, and then close it.

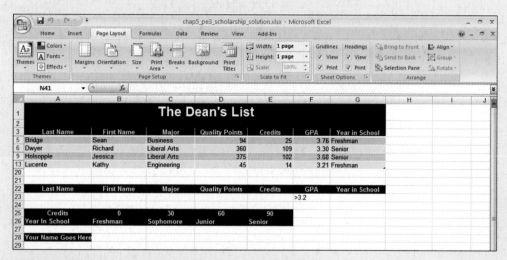

Figure 5.58 Service Organization Scholarship List

4 Service Organization Scholarship PivotTable and PivotChart

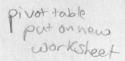

You will revisit the service organization workbook completed earlier in the exercises but revise it to use a PivotTable and a PivotChart to analyze grade point average by major and year in school. Use Figure 5.59 for reference to complete the expanded scholarship example. You will select the option to create a PivotTable and a PivotChart. You will also specify the range of the PivotTable and select the option to put the PivotTable on a new worksheet. Rename the resulting worksheets, Sheet1 and Chart1, to PivotTable and PivotChart, as shown in Figure 5.59.

a. Open the *chap5_pe4_exscholarship* workbook and save it as **chap5_pe4_exscholarship_solution**.

b. Select **cells A3:G19**, click the **Insert tab**, and click **PivotTable** in the Tables group to open the Create PivotTable dialog box. Verify that **Table1** is the Table/Range name in the *Select a table or range* box. Also make sure that **New Worksheet** is the choice in *Choose where you want the PivotTable report to be placed* and click **OK**.

c. Click **Major** in the PivotTable Field List and make sure that it appears in the Row Labels section. Drag the **Year in School** field to the **Columns Labels section**. Drag **GPA** to the Σ **Values section**.

d. You used GPA as the value field, but will specify the average GPA rather than the sum. Click the **Sum of GPA arrow** and select **Value Field Settings** to open the Value Field Settings dialog box. Then do the following:

- Click in **Custom Name** and type **Average of GPA**.

- With the Summarize by tab active, click **Average** in the *Summarize value field by* list box.

...continued on Next Page

- Click **Number Format**.
- Click **Number** in the Category list and make sure Decimal places is 2.
- Click **OK** twice to close the Format Cells dialog box and the Value Field Settings dialog box.

e. Click **cell B3**, type **Year in School**, and press **Enter**. Click **cell A4**, type **Major**, and press **Enter**. Click **cell F4**, type **Average GPA**, and press **Enter**. Click **cell A8**, type **Average GPA**, and press **Enter**.

f. Select **cells A4:F4**, click the **Home tab**, and click **Wrap Text** in the Alignment group. Click **Center** in the Alignment group. Right-click the **Sheet1 tab**, select **Rename**, type **PivotTable**, and press **Enter**.

g. Select **cells E4:E8** and drag the selection between columns B and C to manually sort the classes. Widen column C to make Sophomore visible, if necessary. Save the workbook.

h. Click anywhere in the PivotTable, click the PivotTable Tools **Options tab**, and click **PivotChart** in the Tools group. Click **Clustered Column**, the first chart in the first row in the Insert Chart dialog box, and click **OK**.

i. Click the **Design tab**, then click **Move Chart** in the Location group to open the Move Chart dialog box. Click **New sheet**, type **PivotChart** in the text box, and click **OK**. Close the PivotTable Field List pane if necessary and close the PivotChart Filter pane.

j. Click the **Design tab**, then click **Layout 1** in the Chart Layouts group. Click **Chart Title**, type **GPA by Major by Year**, and press **Enter**.

k. Press and hold **Ctrl** while clicking the **PivotTable tab** and the **Student List tab**. Click the **Page Setup Dialog Box Launcher** in the Page Setup group on the Page Layout tab to open the Page Setup dialog box.

l. Click the **Header/Footer tab**, click **Custom Header**, type your name in the Left section, click in the Right section, click **Insert Page Number**, and click **OK**. Click **Print Preview** to verify that the PivotTable and the Student List will print correctly. Save, print, and close the workbook.

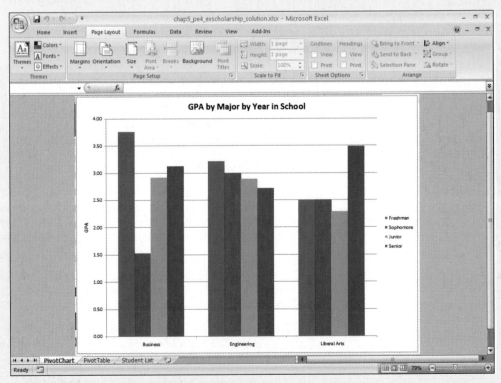

Figure 5.59 Dean's List Revisited

Mid-Level Exercises

1 Compensation Analysis for Hotel Management

Your supervisor has assigned you the task of analyzing the compensation for several employees in the national hotel management chain. Your assignment is to open the partially completed workbook and complete the workbook to match Figure 5.60. The workbook in Figure 5.60 is used to analyze employee compensation with respect to the dollar amount and percentage of their latest salary increase.

a. Open the *chap5_mid1_compensation* workbook and save it as **chap5_mid1_compensation_solution**, so you can return to the original workbook if necessary. Enter the formula to compute the dollar increase for the first employee in **cell G4**. Note, however, that not every employee has a previous salary, and thus the formula requires an IF function. Copy this formula to the remaining rows in column G.

b. Enter the formula to compute the percentage increase for the first employee in **cell H4**. The percentage increase is found by dividing the amount of the increase by the previous salary. Again, not every employee has a previous salary and the formula requires an IF function to avoid dividing by zero when there is no previous salary. Copy this formula to the remaining rows in column H.

c. Name the database and the criteria range. Enter the DAVERAGE function in **cell C21** and the DMIN function in **cell C22** to reflect only those employees who have received a raise. Be sure to include the greater-than-zero entry under Previous Salary in the criteria row. Enter a function in **cell D21** to calculate the average percentage increase in salary. Enter a function in **cell D22** to calculate the minimum percentage increase in salary.

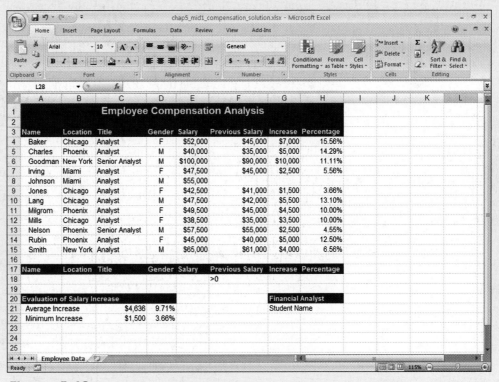

Figure 5.60 Compensation Analysis

...continued on Next Page

d. Format the worksheet in an attractive fashion by duplicating as closely as possible the formatting shown in Figure 5.60. Note, too, that you should suppress the display of zero values. (If necessary, click the **Home** tab, click **Format** in the Cells group, and then click **Format Cells**. Click **Custom** in the Category list, and then type **0;-0;;@** in the Type box.)

e. Create a custom footer for both worksheets that includes your name and today's date. Print the worksheet with both displayed values and cell formulas. Use landscape orientation as necessary to be sure that the worksheet fits on a single sheet of paper. Save the workbook.

f. Apply conditional formatting to the range of salaries using Icon Sets and print the worksheet again.

g. Print the worksheet in at least one other sequence—for example, by the smallest (or largest) percentage increase, and apply conditional formatting to the percentage using data bars. Close the workbook.

2 Compensation Analysis for Hotel Management PivotTables

Your supervisor at the hotel management company liked the work you did in the previous exercise and now wants you to create a PivotTable report using the same data table. The PivotTable shown in Figure 5.61 is based on the compensation analysis in the worksheet from the previous exercise.

a. Open the *chap5_mid2_pivottable* workbook and save it as **chap5_mid2_pivottable_ solution**.

b. Click anywhere within the Employee table and create a PivotTable using **cell A3:H15** on a new worksheet. You will need to specify two data fields, the salary increase and the percent of salary increase, and choose the average function for each.

c. Format the PivotTable in an attractive fashion for professional presentation matching Figure 5.61 as closely as possible. Use the currency and percent symbols as appropriate, as well as two decimal places for the percentage figures.

d. Use the same style of formatting for the text in your PivotTable as in the previous exercise, so that your workbook has a uniform look. Use Custom Format as described in the previous exercise to suppress the display of zero values.

e. Use Page Layout on the status bar to create a custom footer containing your name, the name of the worksheet, and today's date. Verify that the worksheet prints on one page.

f. Print the completed workbook to show the displayed values for each worksheet. Print the Employee Data worksheet a second time to show the cell formulas.

g. Save the worksheet, then experiment with pivoting the table by changing the row, column, and/or page fields and/or the function associated with the data fields. PivotTables are one of the best-kept secrets in Excel even though they have been available in the last several releases of the program. Close the workbook.

...continued on Next Page

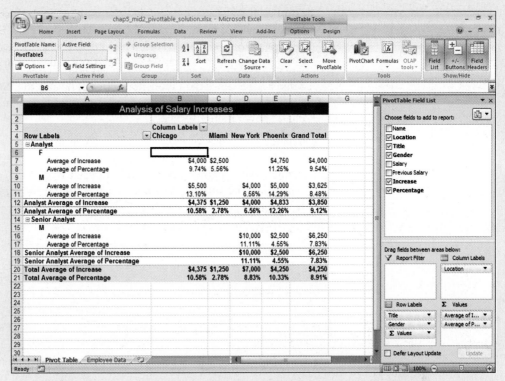

Figure 5.61 Compensation Analysis for Hotel Management PivotTable

3 The Golf Trader

Your father, the owner of The Golf Shoppe, asked for your help with his analysis of his sales staff. He has data indicating what the staff sold on a particular date and the amount of each order. You will assist him by showing the sales by category both in a PivotTable report and showing the data graphically in a PivotChart report. The PivotChart report in Figure 5.62 is based on the associated PivotTable report, which in turn is derived from the source data worksheet. PivotTables can help analyze the data and discern trends that are not otherwise visible.

a. Open the *chap5_mid3_golf* workbook and save it as **chap5_mid3_golf_solution**.

b. Click Find & Select in the Editing group on the Home tab and select Replace. Type **Moldof** as the **Find What** string and **your last name** as the **Replace with** string. Click the **Replace All button**, and then click **OK** when you see the dialog box indicating 111 replacements. Close the Find and Replace box.

c. Click **cell A2**. Click PivotTable in the Tables group on the Insert tab and verify that the Table/Range is **$A$1:$D$788** and that the PivotTable will be placed on a new sheet. The PivotTable should have two fields, Category and Salesperson, which serve as the row and column fields, respectively. The Order Amount goes in the Values area.

d. Click the worksheet tab for Sheet1, which contains the newly created PivotTable. Right-click any numeric entry within the body of the PivotTable, click Value Field Settings to display the Value Field Settings dialog box, and then click Number Format to display the Format Cells dialog box. Change the formatting to Currency with no decimals. Close all open dialog boxes.

...continued on Next Page

e. Sort the PivotTable so the category with the highest sales total appears first. To do this, click anywhere in the Grand Total column, then click Sort Largest to Smallest in the Sort group on the Options tab. The category with the highest sales total appears first.

f. Create a PivotChart using a Stacked Column chart type. Move the chart to a new sheet titled Chart. Close the PivotChart Filter pane and the PivotTable Field List pane. Click Data Table in the Labels group on the Layout tab and select Show Data Table. Add the chart shown in Figure 5.62.

g. Change the names of the worksheet tabs to match those in Figure 5.62, then print the completed PivotChart. Use Page Layout to create an appropriate custom footer, which includes your name and the name of each worksheet. Do not print the Source Data worksheet, because it runs many pages due to the large quantity of data. Save and close the workbook.

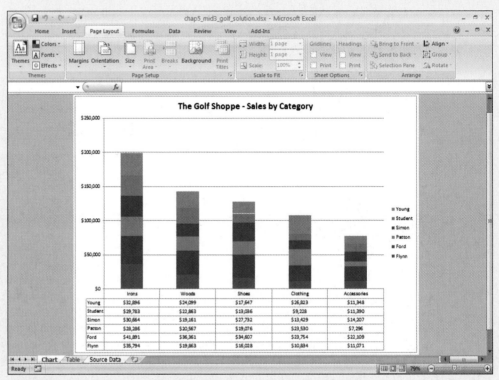

Figure 5.62 The Golf Shoppe Salesperson Analysis

4 JAS Bank Consumer Loans

Your first assignment for the JAS Bank is to analyze the data shown in Figure 5.63. It displays selected loans, those with a loan type of "A," from a comprehensive set of loan records. Your immediate supervisor asked you to analyze this data before the end of the business day. You are to open the partially completed workbook and complete the worksheet and associated PivotTable report shown in Figure 5.63.

a. Open the *chap5_mid4_consumerloans* workbook and save it as **chap5_mid4_consumerloans_solution**.

...continued on Next Page

b. Click **cell H4**, the cell containing the ending date for the first loan. Enter the formula to compute the ending date, based on the starting date and the term of the loan. For the sake of simplicity, you do not have to account for leap year. To compute the ending date, multiply the term of the loan by 365 and add that result to the starting date. Be sure to format the starting and ending dates to show a date format and widen columns as necessary.

c. Click **cell I4** and enter the PMT function to compute the monthly payment for the first loan. Copy the formulas in **cells H4** and **I4** to the remaining rows in the worksheet.

d. Enter the indicated criteria in **cell D29**, then enter the indicated database functions toward the bottom of the worksheet, as shown in Figure 5.63.

e. Use the Advanced Filter command to filter the list in place to display only those loans that satisfy the indicated criteria, as shown in Figure 5.63.

f. Format the list in an attractive fashion, duplicating as closely as possible Figure 5.63.

g. Look closely at the bottom of Figure 5.63 and note the presence of a PivotTable Report worksheet. You are to create a PivotTable that has the loan type and branch location in the row and column fields, respectively. Your PivotTable is to contain two data fields, the total amount of the loans, and the average interest rate. Format the PivotTable report as currency with 2 decimals and percentage with 2 decimals. Add **Summary Loan Statistics** and the title of the report. Rename the Sheet2 tab **PivotTable**.

h. Print the entire workbook. Print both the displayed values and cell formulas for the loans worksheet, but only the displayed values for the PivotTable. Use the Page Setup command to create a custom footer containing your name, the name of the worksheet, and today's date. Be sure to print the gridlines and row and column headings, making sure the Loans worksheet and PivotTable print on one page. Save and close the workbook.

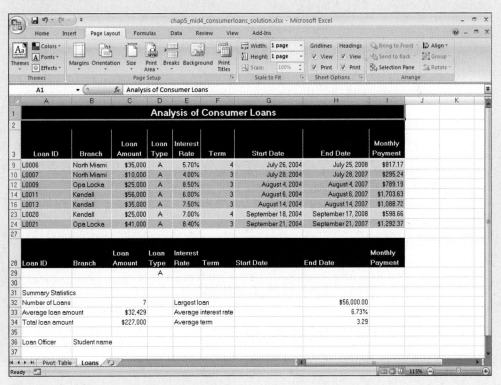

Figure 5.63 Consumer Loan Analysis

Capstone Exercise

You are a data-entry specialist at Fly First Airways, an independent airline offering charters and special tours. The airline has several independent agents, each of whom books trips for the airline. The data for all trips are maintained in a text file exported from the reservations database on the mainframe and will be imported into Excel. Your assignment is to open a new Excel workbook and import the data you will use to create a PivotTable report and a PivotChart report for data analysis.

Import Data, Save, and Format Worksheet

You must open a workbook import a text file, and use the data to complete the capstone exercise. The data are in text format and you will have to format the data in Excel.

a. Open Excel and import the file *chap5_cap_airlines*.
b. Save it as **chap5_cap_airlines_solution**.
c. Add the title **Airline Trip Status** to your worksheet, format it for a professional presentation, **Dark Blue** fill with **White** font color, and widen columns as needed.

Name a Range and Apply Conditional Formatting

Conditional formatting is used to identify records meeting specified criteria or a range of criteria. You want to identify the records of all trips that sell for more than $85,000. As part of your profitability analysis, you want to know how many flights are close to capacity. You want to identify the number of records for flights booked with more than 100 passengers.

a. Construct a criteria range below the data table with the criteria amount greater than $85,000.
b. Name the data table **database**, Passengers criteria range **passengers**, and the criteria range **criteria**.
c. Generate a list of range names on the *chap5_cap_airlines* sheet beginning in **cell I1**.
d. Use conditional formatting to select and highlight amounts greater than $85,000.
e. Use custom formatting to select the same dark blue fill and white font color as the title.
f. Apply conditional formatting using an Icon Set of your choice to passengers.

Use Database Functions

You must provide a financial summary and will use several database functions in a summary area for your analysis data. The financial summary will be placed at the bottom of your worksheet.

a. Enter the title **Financial Summary** in **cell B34**.
b. Enter the label **Sum of Trip Cost** in **cell B35** and the database function to calculate the cost in **cell E35**.
c. Enter the label **Average of Trip Cost** in **cell B36** and the database function to calculate the average cost in **cell E36**.

d. Enter the label **Highest Trip Cost** in **cell B37** and the database function to calculate the highest cost in **cell E37**.
e. Enter the label **Lowest Trip Cost** in **cell B38** and the database function to calculate the lowest cost in **cell E38**.
f. Format the values as currency with 2 decimals.
g. Enter the label **Trips more than 100 passengers** in **cell B39** and the database function to calculate the number of these trips in **cell E39**.

Create a PivotTable Report and a PivotChart

Your PivotTable should show the number of contracts by marketing representative and contract status and whether the trip is still in the proposal stage or whether it has already been signed. The table should also have the flexibility to show all trips and trips that do or do not require passage through customs.

a. Create a PivotTable, then verify that the table range is correct and placed on a new worksheet.
b. Place the **Customs** field in the Report Filter area.
c. Place the **ContractStatus** field in the Column Labels area.
d. Place the **MarketingRep** field in the Row Labels area.
e. Place the **Amount** field in the Values area.
f. Format the values as currency with no decimals.
g. Format the PivotTable in an attractive and readable manner.
h. Rename the PivotTable sheet tab as PivotTable.
i. Create a PivotChart based on the PivotTable data, placing it on a new sheet.
j. Rename the Chart1 sheet tab as PivotChart.

Print the PivotTables and PivotCharts

You must document your work before printing the reports, and you see that they are missing the standard footers. Use the Page Setup command to create a custom footer that contains your name and the name of the worksheet. Print the completed reports.

a. Select both the PivotTable and *chap5_cap_airlines* sheet tabs and create a custom footer with your name on the left, the sheet name in the middle, and your instructor's name on the right.
b. Select the PivotChart sheet tab and create a custom footer with the same information.
c. Change the page orientation to landscape.
d. Print the worksheet with displayed values.
e. Save your changes and close the workbook.

Mini Cases

Use the rubric following the case as a guide to evaluate your work, but keep in mind that your instructor may impose additional grading criteria or use a different standard to judge your work.

Asset Allocation

GENERAL CASE

It is several years in the future and you find you are happily married and financially prosperous. You and your partner have accumulated substantial assets in a variety of accounts. Some of the money is in a regular account for use today, and other funds are in retirement accounts for later use. Much of the money, both regular and retirement, is invested in equities (i.e., the stock market), but a portion of your funds is also in nonequity funds such as money-market checking accounts and bank certificates of deposit. Your accounts are also in different places such as banks and brokerage houses. Open the *chap5_mc1_allocation* workbook and save it as **chap5_mc1_allocation_solution**. A summary of your accounts can be found in the Family Assets worksheet. Your assignment is to open the workbook and develop a PivotTable that will enable you and your spouse to keep track of your investments.

Performance Elements	Exceeds Expectations	Meets Expectations	Below Expectations
PivotTable report	Created on same sheet.	Created on different sheet.	No PivotTable report.
PivotTable field List	All fields entered correctly.	One field incorrectly used.	No fields used.
Attractive, appropriate format	Well formatted and easy to read.	Adequately formatted, difficult to read.	No formatting.
Printing	Printed correct range on one sheet with custom footer.	Printed correct range but did not include footer.	Printed on multiple pages with no footer.

Job Title Analysis

RESEARCH CASE

As you approach graduation and enter into the workforce, you must research different jobs to determine what factors influence salary. The factors might include gender, experience, ability to relocate, and bilingual skills. Use the Web and tools such as the *Occupation Outlook Handbook* or Monster.com to identify six job titles and at least four factors that could influence salary. Import the data into an Excel workbook and create a PivotTable report analyzing job titles and the factors influencing salary. Save your workbook as **chap5_mc2_jobtitle_solution.** Complete the worksheet, formatting as appropriate to fit on one sheet.

Performance Elements	Exceeds Expectations	Meets Expectations	Below Expectations
Research current salary for six job titles	Identified six job titles.	Missing two job titles.	No job titles.
Identify factors influencing salary	Four or more identified.	Two identified.	No factors identified.
PivotTable report created	Correct data used and identified.	Incorrect data used.	No PivotTable.
PivotTable report formatted	Easy to read and analyze data.	Difficult to read and interpret data.	No formatting.
Identify sources	Two sources identified and correctly cited.	One source identified and correctly cited.	No sources identified or sources not cited.

Your volunteer service learning project involves tutoring students in Excel. Open the spreadsheet *chap5_mc3_donor*, save it as **chap5_mc3_donor_solution**, and find five errors. Correct the errors and explain how the errors might have occurred and how they can be prevented. Use Excel Help to locate information about possible errors and to assist you in the explanation of the error. Use Help to find the correct steps used to prevent the error. Include your explanation in the cells below the spreadsheet.

Performance Elements	Exceeds Expectations	Meets Expectations	Below Expectations
Identify and correct five errors	Identified and corrected all five errors.	Identified and corrected four errors.	Identified and corrected three or fewer errors.
Explain the errors	Complete and correct explanation of each error.	Explanation is too brief to fully explain error.	No explanations.
Prevention description	Prevention description correct and practical.	Prevention description present but obtuse.	No prevention description.
PivotTable created	Correct data used and identified.	Incorrect data used.	No PivotTable.
PivotTable formatted	Easy to read and analyze data.	Difficult to read and interpret data.	No formatting.
Identify sources	Two sources identified and correctly cited.	One source identified and correctly cited.	No sources identified or sources not cited.

Data Tables and Amortization Tables

Revisiting Data Tables and Amortizing

Objectives

After you read this chapter, you will be able to:

1. Separate and combine text **(page 621)**.

2. Manipulate text with functions **(page 623)**.

3. Identify and remove duplicate rows **(page 629)**.

4. Group and subtotal data **(page 630)**.

5. Work with windows **(page 633)**.

6. Use conditional functions **(page 641)**.

7. Create nested IF functions **(page 643)**.

8. Use AND, OR, NOT, and IFERROR functions **(page 644)**.

9. Define the amortization table **(page 651)**.

10. Use functions in amortization tables **(page 652)**.

Hands-On Exercises

Exercises	Skills Covered
1. IT DEPARTMENT STRING MANIPULATION (page 625) **Open:** chap6_ho1_textstrings.xlsx **Save as:** chap6_ho1_textstrings_solution.xlsx, chap6_ho1_textstrings_solution.txt, and chap6_ho1_textstrings2_solution.xlsx	• Convert Text to Columns • Use PROPER and CONCATENATE Functions to Create a User ID List • Use LOWER and CONCATENATE Functions to Create E-Mail Addresses • Use SUBSTITUTE Function to change E-Mail Addresses
2. AJAX COLLEGE BAND (page 636) **Open:** chap6_ho2_band.xlsx **Save as:** chap6_ho2_band_solution.xlsx	• Convert Text to Columns • Identify and Remove Duplicate Rows • Subtotal the Data • Group and Ungroup Data • Use Multiple Windows
3. CLASSIC CARS AND SECURITY (page 646) **Open:** chap6_ho3_classiccars.xlsx **Save as:** chap6_ho3_classiccars_solution.xlsx	• Use SUMIF, AVERAGEIF, and COUNTIF Functions • Use SUMIFS, AVERAGEIFS, and COUNTIFS Functions • Nest the AND Function in an IF Function • Nest the OR Function in an IF Function • Nest the IF Function
4. PURCHASE A NEW HOUSE (page 655) **Open:** chap6_ho4_amortization.xlsx **Save as:** chap6_ho4_amortization_solution.xlsx	• Enter the Loan Parameters • Enter Formulas for the First Payment • Name a Cell • Add the IF Functions • Enter the Formulas for the Second Payment • Complete the Payment Schedule • Complete the Summary Area and Print

CASE STUDY

Refinance Your Home

You purchased your first home three years ago. It is in a good neighborhood, your neighbors are friendly, you have a large yard for your dog, and you are at home. You took out a 30-year mortgage for $300,000 at 7.5%, which resulted in a monthly payment of just under $2,100. You have paid approximately $75,000 to the bank (principal and interest) during the three years you have lived in the house, but are shocked to learn that you still owe approximately $291,000 on the mortgage. In other words, you have paid approximately $65,000 in interest and only $10,000 in principal.

The good news is that interest rates are at or near their lowest level in 40 years. You have been approached by multiple mortgage brokers about the benefits of refinancing, yet you still have doubts about whether you should refinance. You know that your monthly payment will go down, but you will incur additional closing costs of 4% to obtain the new loan on the remaining principal of $291,000. You plan to roll the closing costs into the new mortgage to avoid an out-of-pocket

expense. You can obtain either a 15- or 30-year mortgage and you want to explore the advantages of each. Is it possible that the lower interest rates on a new 15-year loan could keep your payments at the same level as your existing 30-year mortgage? Further, you will pay an extra amount each month in order to pay the loan off sooner. What impact will the extra payments have on the term of your mortgage? What is your payment for a 20-year mortgage or a 40-year mortgage?

Your Assignment

- Read the chapter carefully and pay close attention to information on how to create and use a loan amortization workbook. Your workbook will enable you to enter an additional payment each month, reducing the total time of your mortgage.

- Open the *chap6_case_house* file and save it as **chap6_case_house_solution**. You notice that the column headings are combined in cell A12. Convert the text into columns, splitting text at the appropriate delimiter.

- Look at the Rate Comparison worksheet, which displays various financial institutions, rates, and points. However, the table contains duplicate information. Remove duplicate rows. As you build the amortization table, try out different terms and rates based on the data in the Rate Comparison worksheet.

- Compare your existing mortgage to a new 15-year mortgage at 5%. It should show the monthly payment, the savings per month, and the total interest over the life of each loan. It should also determine the number of months to break even on the new 15-year mortgage. Incorporate nested IF functions and date functions to perform the calculations.

- Use the completed workbook to enter extra payments each month to reduce the term of the mortgage.

- Experiment with different interest rates to see the impact each has on the mortgage. Test your work for both a 20- and 40-year mortgage, extending the workbook if necessary.

- Split the worksheet windows to view the top five and last five payments.

- Create a custom footer that includes your name, a page number, and your instructor's name. Print the worksheet as displayed and with formulas visible. Save the completed workbook.

Tables

All enterprises—business, education, health care, or government—maintain data in the form of lists. Companies have lists of employees. Educational institutions maintain lists of students and faculty members. Governmental entities, such as the military, maintain extensive inventory lists. The concepts associated with tables in Excel are database concepts.

Excel maintains lists of data in the form of a table. A table is an area in the worksheet that contains rows and columns of similar or related information. A table can be used as part of a database or organized collection of related information, where the worksheet rows represent the records, and the worksheet columns represent the fields in a record. The first row contains the column labels or field names, such as *First Name*, *Last Name*, *Address*, *City*, *State*, and *Zip Code*. This identifies the data that will be entered in the columns. Each row in the table contains a record. Every cell in the table area, except the field names, contains a specific value for a specific field in a specific record. Every record (row) contains the same fields (columns) in the same order as the other records. For example, if cell A1 contains *First Name* as the column heading, all records contain first names in the first column.

Tables and table theory were introduced in a previous chapter, and in this chapter you will continue to explore tables and manipulate table data. In this section you will convert text to columns and remove duplicate rows from tables. You will work with separating and combining text, features that are sometimes necessary to work with data in tables. You will use a function to join text and use functions to convert text from one case to another. These actions will yield more accurate and meaningful data.

Separating and Combining Text

Often colleagues share data files with each other in organizations. Sharing Excel workbooks helps others update budgets and prepare financial reports. Although you might receive a workbook that contains data you need, it might not be formatted the way you need it. Specifically, you might need to convert text to columns, combine text entries, or remove duplicate rows.

Convert Text to Columns

You previously learned how to import text files into a workbook using the Text Import Wizard. As you completed the wizard, you had to select the delimiter type to separate data into columns as they were imported. After you import the text file data, you might find that data are combined into one column when they should be separated into two columns. In other situations, a colleague might send you an Excel workbook in which data are combined into one column but need to be separated so that you can manipulate them.

> You can use the Text to Columns command to ... separate *Sam Jones* into two columns—one column for first name and one column for last name.

For example, a column might combine first and last names, such as Sam Jones. You need to sort the list alphabetically by last name, but you cannot do that as long as the first and last names are combined. You can use the Text to Columns command to split the contents in one column into separate columns. For example, you can use Text to Columns to separate *Sam Jones* in two columns— one column for first name and one column for last name. Figure 6.1 shows first and last names combined in Column A and the results after converting text into two columns.

The Convert Text to Columns Wizard is very similar to the Text Import Wizard. To place the first and last names in different cells:

1. Select the column containing the text you want to split.
2. Click Text to Columns in the Data Tools group on the Data tab.
3. Use the Convert Text to Columns Wizard to distribute the data (see Figure 6.2). As with the Import Text Wizard, you must specify the file type and click Next.

4. Specify the delimiters, such as a Tab or Space, in the Convert Text to Columns Wizard – Step 2 of 3. The data shown in Figure 6.2 are delimited by spaces. The wizard can use the space to separate the first and last names in this example. Click Next.

5. Select the type of data, such as General, in the Convert Text to Columns Wizard – Step 3 of 3 and click Finish.

It is important to allow enough columns to the right of the column to be split so data are not overwritten. If you have a first name, middle name, and last name all in one column and you separate to get a first name column, middle name column, and last name column, you must have three empty columns. If your columns are not empty, Excel will overwrite existing data.

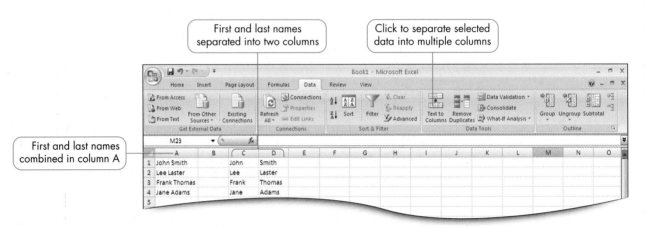

Figure 6.1 Combined Names and Separated Names

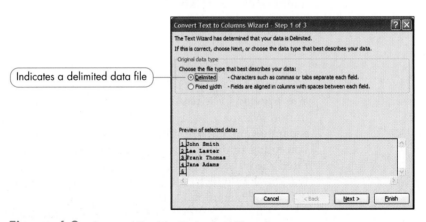

Figure 6.2 Convert Text to Columns Wizard

Combine Text into One Cell
CONCATENATE Function | Reference

CONCATENATE(text1,text2, . . .)

Text labels are often referred to as text strings. A text string is any entry in a cell that is not used for calculation. Both 2008 and 3/15/2008 are text strings when used as labels. Name is a label but the cell contents might be Jane Doe, and both are text strings. Often, you want to combine two or more text strings located in two or more cells into just one string in one cell. For example, you must make an account name and want to combine last name with first name. Perhaps you would even include a comma and a space after the comma. The *CONCATENATE function* joins two or

The **CONCATENATE function** joins two or more text strings into one text string.

more text strings into one text string and permits you to include the comma or space separators in the text string. If first name is in cell A4, last name in cell B4, and the result in cell C4, you would enter =CONCATENATE(B4,", ",A4) in cell C4. Note the comma and space included inside the quotes to produce *Doe, Jane*. When constructing a CONCATENATE function, be careful to place any commas and spaces correctly so that you get the desired result. See Figure 6.3 for an example of the CONCATENATE function. The text items can be strings of text, numbers, or single-cell references, but Excel enables you to join up to only 255 text items into a single text item.

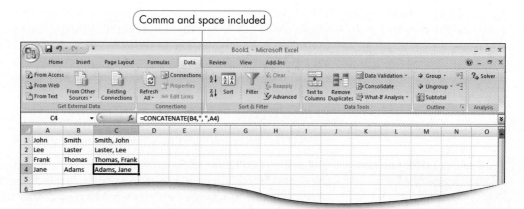

Figure 6.3 Concatenation—Join Text Strings

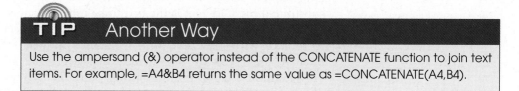

TIP Another Way

Use the ampersand (&) operator instead of the CONCATENATE function to join text items. For example, =A4&B4 returns the same value as =CONCATENATE(A4,B4).

Manipulating Text with Functions
PROPER Function | Reference

PROPER(text)

The **PROPER function** capitalizes the first letter in a text string and any other letters in text that follow any character other than a letter.

Excel has several functions that are specifically designed to enable you to change or manipulate text strings. Often, a spreadsheet is created with names typed in all lowercase letters, all uppercase letters, or some combination. The **PROPER function** capitalizes the first letter of a text string and any other letters in a text string that follow any character other than a letter and converts all uppercase or all lowercase so just the first letter of a string is uppercase. The PROPER function converts all other letters to lowercase. The syntax for the PROPER function is PROPER(text). The text argument is a text string that must be enclosed in quotation marks, a formula that returns text, or a reference to a cell that contains text that you want to partially capitalize. For example, if you receive a spreadsheet with song titles including the song "hello I must be going" you could use the PROPER function to convert the text string to "Hello I Must Be Going."

UPPER Function | Reference

UPPER(text)

The **UPPER function** converts text to uppercase letters.

The **UPPER function** converts text strings to uppercase letters. The syntax for the UPPER function is UPPER(text). The text argument is the text to be converted to uppercase and can be a reference or text string. You use this function when a cell or range contains text in lowercase letters and you need the text to be formatted in all uppercase letters. Often you will want to standardize your text strings to be all uppercase and will use the UPPER function to convert columns of text to all uppercase. When searching a table, you will get skewed results if your search criteria include uppercase text but your data are in lower or mixed case.

LOWER Function | Reference

LOWER(text)

The **LOWER function** converts all uppercase letters to lowercase.

The *LOWER function* converts all uppercase letters in a text string to lowercase. The syntax for the LOWER function is LOWER(text). The text argument is text you want to convert to lowercase. The LOWER function does not change characters in text that are not letters. E-mail addresses and computer user IDs are typically used in lowercase. You can use the LOWER function to convert text not already in lowercase.

SUBSTITUTE Function | Reference

SUBSTITUTE(text,old_text,new_text,instance_num)

The **SUBSTITUTE function** substitutes new text for old text in a text string.

The *SUBSTITUTE function* substitutes new text for old text in a text string. You use the SUBSTITUTE function when you want to replace specific text in a text string. You would use this function when you want to replace any text in a specific location in a text string. For example, colleges that become universities can use the SUBSTITUTE function to substitute the string "college" with "university" in the title of all workbooks. The syntax for the SUBSTITUTE function is SUBSTITUTE(text, old_text,new_text,instance_num). Text is the text or reference to a cell that is to be substituted for. Old_text is the text to be replaced, new_text is the text you want to replace old_text with. Instance_num specifies which occurrence of old_text you want to replace with new text. When instance_num is specified, only that instance is changed. If you do not include instance_num, all occurrences are changed. For example, if your text string was February 1, 2011, you could use =SUBSTITUTE(A4,"1","2",3) to produce February 1, 2012. Excel will replace the third instance of "1" with a "2." Review Figure 6.4 for examples of the text functions in row 6.

Nested functions are functions within another function.

The text functions are often used in combination or as nested functions. Nesting is a technique that lets you put one function inside another. *Nested functions* are functions within another function. For example, you can nest a CONCATENATE function inside an UPPER function argument. For example, =UPPER(CONCATE-NATE(B4,", ",A4)) concatenates the contents of cells B4, a comma and a space, and the contents of cell A4. The concatenated result is then converted to uppercase.

	A	B	C	D	E	F	G	H	I	J	K	L	M
1	John	Smith	Smith, John	SMITH, JOHN	smith, john	February 1, 2011		February 1, 2012					
2	Lee	Laster	Laster, Lee	LASTER, LEE	laster, lee								
3	Frank	Thomas	Thomas, Frank	THOMAS, FRANK	thomas, frank								
4	Jane	Adams	Adams, Jane	ADAMS, JANE	adams, jane								
5													
6	Function Used			=UPPER(C1)	=LOWER(C1)			=SUBSTITUTE(F1,"1","2",3)					
7													

Figure 6.4 Text Functions

Hands-On Exercises

1 | IT Department String Manipulation

Skills covered: 1. Convert Text to Columns **2.** Use PROPER and CONCATENATE Functions to Create a User ID List **3.** Use LOWER and CONCATENATE Functions to Create E-Mail Addresses **4.** Use SUBSTITUTE Function to Change E-Mail Addresses

---

Step 1
Convert Text to Columns

Refer to Figure 6.5 as you complete Step 1.

a. Open the *chap6_ho1_textstrings* workbook and save it as **chap6_ho1_textstrings_ solution** so you can return to the original workbook if necessary.

You notice that the names of students in the IT department are in one cell in first name, last name order. You must convert the text into columns.

b. Select **cells A3:A76** and click **Text to Columns** in the Data Tools group on the Data tab.

You selected the names of all students.

c. Verify that **Delimited** is selected in the *Original data type* section in the Convert Text to Columns Wizard – Step 1 of 3 dialog box and click **Next**.

d. Click the **Space check box**, remove the check from the **Tab check box** in the *Delimiters* section in the Convert Text to Columns Wizard – Step 2 of 3 dialog box, and click **Next**.

The combined data are separated by a space; therefore, you must use the space to delimit the data.

e. Verify that the **General** option is selected in the *Column data format* section, the **Destination** box contains **$A$3**, the *Data preview* is correct, and then click **Finish**.

f. Click **OK** when prompted *Do you want to replace the contents of the destination cells?*

You will see that Excel separated the name data into columns A and B.

g. Type **First Name** in **cell A2** and press **Enter**.

h. Save the workbook.

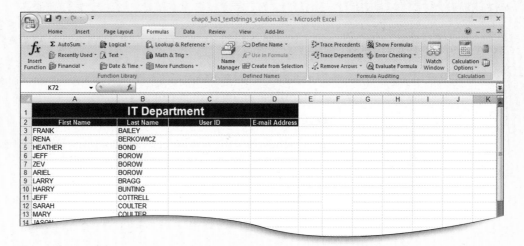

Figure 6.5 Separated First and Last Names

Refer to Figure 6.6 as you complete Step 2.

a. Click in **cell C3**.

b. Type =**PROPER(CONCATENATE(B3,".",A3))**.

You created a nested function that will first join last name and first name with a period separating the two. Excel then converted the uppercase text to proper case.

TROUBLESHOOTING: Make sure your parentheses match before pressing Enter.

c. Press **Enter**.

d. Click in **cell C3** and copy through **cell C76**.

Excel created a list of User IDs for all employees in the IT Department.

e. Save the workbook.

TROUBLESHOOTING: If you reverse the nested functions, use the PROPER function twice: =CONCATENATE(PROPER(B3),".",PROPER(A3)).

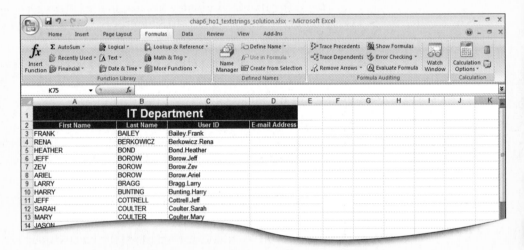

Figure 6.6 User ID List

Refer to Figure 6.7 as you complete Step 3.

a. Click in **cell D3**. Type =**LOWER(CONCATENATE(A3,"_",B3,"@myschool.edu"))** and press **Enter**.

You used the LOWER and CONCATENATE functions to create e-mail addresses for those in the IT department.

b. Click in **cell D3** and copy the formula through **cell D76**.

c. Double-click the border between columns D and E to AutoFit the contents of column D.

You used functions to manipulate text to produce the results shown in Figure 6.7. The results in columns C and D are functions and not text.

d. Click the **Office Button** and select **Save As**.

e. Click the **Save as type drop-down arrow**, select **Text (Tab delimited) (*.txt)**, and click **Save**.

If you want to use the results of your text manipulation in another application, you must convert the function produced results to text data. When you save your workbook as a text file, Excel automatically converts the contents of cells to text and formatted numbers and removes all worksheet formatting. You could use the Paste Special Values to convert small amounts of function-produced data to text.

TROUBLESHOOTING: You will see a Microsoft Excel warning box when you save the file as a text file. You are warned that you could lose some functions when converting to a text file. The warning box is shown in Figure 6.7.

f. Click **Yes**.

g. Close the text file.

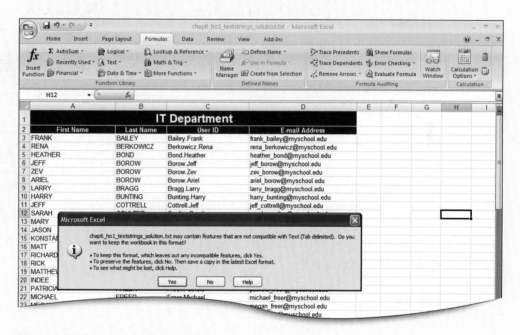

Figure 6.7 E-Mail Addresses

Step 4
Use SUBSTITUTE Function to Change E-Mail Addresses

Refer to Figure 6.8 as you complete Step 4.

a. Open the file **chap6_ho1_textstrings_solution.txt** you just created.

The Text Import Wizard automatically opens.

b. Verify that **Delimited** is selected in the *Original data type* section and click **Next**.

c. Click the **Tab check box** in the *Delimiters* section, remove the check from the **Space check box**, and click **Next**.

d. Verify that **General** is selected in the *Column data format* section and click **Finish**.

You imported a text file into Excel.

e. Click the **Office Button**, select **Save As**, click the **Save as type drop-down arrow**, select **Excel Workbook (*.xlsx)**, and save the file as **chap6_ho1_textstrings2_solution**.

f. Click in **cell E2**, type **New E-mail Address**, and press **Enter**.

This is the column where you will use the SUBSTITUTE function to convert all e-mail addresses to the new e-mail address.

g. Format the worksheet as shown in Figure 6.8.

h. Click in **cell E3**, type **=SUBSTITUTE(D3,"myschool.edu","mynewschool.com")**, and press **Enter**.

i. Click in **cell E3** and copy the formula through **cell E76**.

j. Double-click the border between columns E and F to AutoFit the text.

Using the SUBSTITUTE function you were able to have Excel replace the old school e-mail address with a new address.

k. Save and close the workbook.

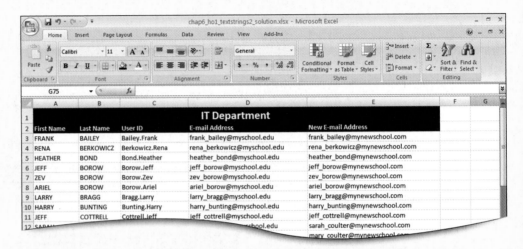

Figure 6.8 New E-Mail Addresses

Data Analysis and Windows

Previously, you learned the difference between data and information and will continue to learn new techniques to help you analyze data. Data analysis is the process of methodically applying statistical and logical techniques to describe, summarize, and compare data.

In this section, you learn how to identify and remove duplicate rows, group and subtotal data, and manipulate windows. These techniques individually and collectively are used to prepare and present data for analysis.

Identifying and Removing Duplicate Rows

Despite the best efforts to check data, duplicate values can slip into data tables. Often, you can see duplicate values if the table is small. However, if the table is large, it may involve considerable scrolling to identify these duplicates. For example, assume you are hosting a formal dinner for your organization. You believe that your assistant entered duplicates for some of your guests. You need to identify the duplicate rows so that you do not assign the same guests to multiple tables. Review Figure 6.9 to see how it is possible to assign the same two people to two different tables.

Using conditional formatting techniques, discussed previously, it is possible to identify duplicates.

1. Select the column in a table that is to be checked for duplicates.
2. Click the Home tab, and then click Conditional Formatting in the Styles group.
3. Point to Highlight Cell Rules, and then Select Duplicate Values to open the Duplicate Values dialog box. You then choose the formatting that will show duplicate values and click OK.

Excel highlights all values that are duplicated in the selected column(s). This is a dynamic option and continues to work even as records with duplicated values are added. Figure 6.9 shows duplicate rows. Excel 2007 automates the removal of duplicate rows.

1. Click any cell in a table.
2. Click Remove Duplicates in the Data Tools group on the Data tab.
3. The Remove Duplicates dialog box prompts you to select the columns that may contain duplicates.
4. Click OK. A report of the number of duplicates found and deleted is shown in the dialog box in Figure 6.10.

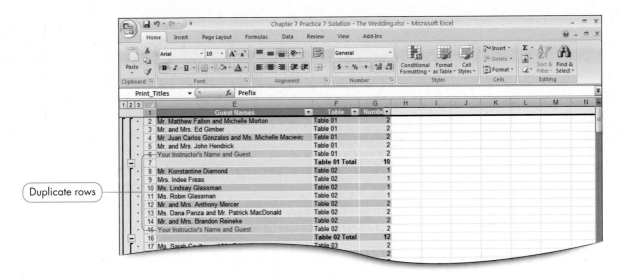

Figure 6.9 Worksheet with Duplicate Rows

Figure 6.10 Remove Duplicates Dialog Box

Grouping and Subtotaling Data

Grouping is often used to compress data for presentation or analysis by different groups of people. For example, in the manufacturing process, production managers are primarily concerned with daily production figures. The production reports are detailed, showing the finest granularity of items produced. The next level of supervisor is not concerned with the finer details of daily production, but instead, uses the monthly production figures. The president of the company is interested in viewing the quarterly production figures. Excel's grouping feature enables you to create the reports used by various people in the organization.

Group and Ungroup Data

A way to simplify complex worksheets containing formulas is to group data. Grouping enables you to consolidate related rows or columns into single units. Once you have consolidated the rows or columns into a group, you can collapse the group to make it easier to view only what you want to see. Figure 6.11 shows the details and three groups for quarterly, monthly, and daily sales by salesperson for a clothing store.

To group data, select the rows or columns to be grouped. Then click Group in the Outline group on the Data tab. It is now possible to collapse the group by clicking the minus sign in the margin area.

To ungroup this data and expand the group, select all columns or rows that were grouped and click Ungroup in the Outline group on the Data tab. Excel will not create an outline or group data if no formulas exist in the worksheet. Grouping data in a worksheet with no formulas produces one level, not a detailed outline.

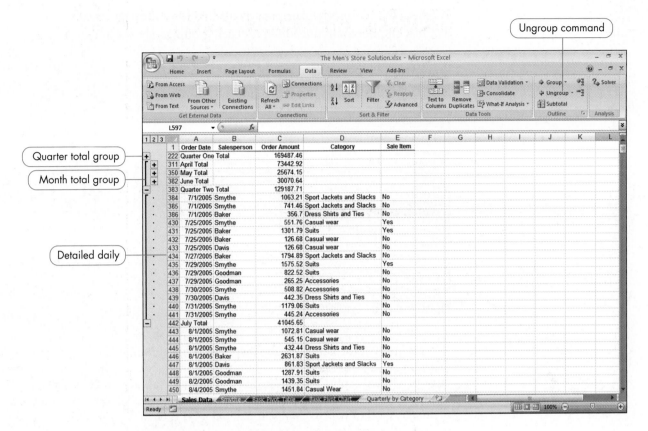

Figure 6.11 Grouped Data

Subtotal Data

The **Subtotal command** inserts a subtotal row where the value of the designated field changes.

The **Subtotal command** uses a summary function such as SUM, AVERAGE, or COUNT to compute subtotals within a sorted data table. The records are grouped according to the value of a specific field, such as location, and the Subtotal command inserts a subtotal row where the value of the designated field changes. A grand total is displayed after the last record. The records must be in sequence by the field on which the subtotals will be grouped prior to executing the Subtotal command. Referred to as control break reports, the subtotals provide summary totals used in data analysis. For example, a multinational organization will compare several data from individual countries. The organization will review the data from just one country. Figures 6.13, 6.14, and 6.15 show all data, city totaled data, and a grand total, respectively. The data are grouped and totaled.

To add automatic subtotals:

1. Sort the data in the group field. Do this by selecting a cell in the column and clicking Sort A to Z in the Sort & Filter group on the Data tab. The subtotal option in Excel will produce erroneous or not useful results if the data are not sorted first.

2. Select a cell containing data.

3. Click Subtotal in the Outline group of the Data tab to open the Subtotal dialog box.

4. Click the *At each change in* drop-down arrow and select the column heading for the column used as the group field. If you select the incorrect field for the change, Excel will produce a total in every cell.

5. Click the *Use function* drop-down arrow and select the function you want to apply to the data.

6. Check the appropriate field in the *Add subtotal to* list for each field you want to total, as shown in Figure 6.12. You can use all functions for columns that contain numerical data. For text fields, you can only count the number of rows within the group.

7. Select *Page break between groups* as needed for your page breaks.
8. Click OK. Subtotals are added for each group, as shown in Figure 6.12.

Figure 6.12 Subtotal Dialog Box

Summary information can be displayed with different levels of detail, as shown in Figures 6.13, 6.14, and 6.15. A minus sign indicates that the group has been collapsed, while the plus sign indicates that more detail is available. You can click the symbol (1, 2, 3, etc.) above the plus or minus signs to collapse or expand the amount of detail. Another way to change the detail level is to click Show Detail or Hide Detail in the Outline group of the Data tab.

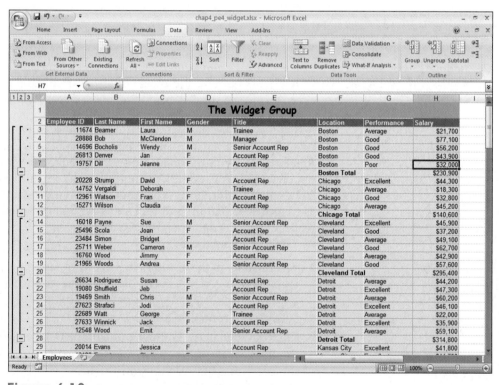

Figure 6.13 Table with All Data Visible

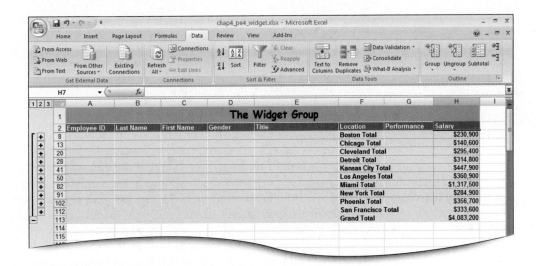

Figure 6.14 Table with Summary Totals—Less Data Visible

Figure 6.15 Table with Least Data Visible

Working with Windows

Often, you will have multiple workbooks open at one time. When you want to compare data from one workbook to another or when you want to combine data from several individual workbooks in one comprehensive workbook, you will need to have several workbooks open at one time. Maybe you have first-quarter sales open to compare to last year's first-quarter sales. It is easy to compare the data when you can view these worksheets side by side on your screen. You can work with multiple workbooks visible in multiple windows on your screen. Refer to the View tab shown in Figure 6.16.

Figure 6.16 The View Tab

Open and Arrange Windows

When you have several Excel windows open at the same time, you might have an occasion when you want to see more than one window at a time. Accountants, for example, will compare your last year's tax return to this year's tax return in separate windows and on the screen at the same time. Teachers will have your research paper open and their grade book open at the same time and visible in separate windows on the screen.

To open and arrange windows, click Arrange All in the Window group on the View tab. Select one of the options from the Arrange Windows dialog box, and then click OK. The arrangement of windows can be changed as often as necessary to view the data with which you must work.

Split a Window

When you work with very large, complex worksheets, you may need to view different sections at the same time. For example, you may need to look at input data on rows 5 and 6 and see how changing the data affects overall results on row 150. To see these different worksheet sections at the same time, you can split the worksheet window. *Splitting a window* is the process of dividing a worksheet window into two or four resizable panes so you can view widely separated parts of a worksheet at the same time. All window panes are part of the one worksheet. Any changes you make to one window affect the entire worksheet.

To do this, click Split in the Window group on the View tab. To resize these split panes, you can drag the horizontal or vertical splitter controls. A *splitter control* is the two-headed arrow at the top of the vertical scroll bar and at the right of the horizontal scroll bar and it is used to divide a window into panes. As you drag the splitter control, you see a gray bar that shows where the window pane will be divided. You drag the horizontal splitter bar to divide the window pane into upper and lower (horizontal) panes. You can drag the vertical splitter bar to split the window pane into left and right (vertical) window panes. Within each window pane, you can scroll to the desired area you wish to see. When you split the worksheet vertically, synchronized scrolling is on. If you scroll any pane, the cells in the other panes move. If you have different worksheets visible in the panes, you can use the Synchronous Scrolling command in the Window group on the View tab to turn off synchronous scrolling and scroll just one pane at a time. Figure 6.17 shows both the beginning summary area and bottom of a large worksheet.

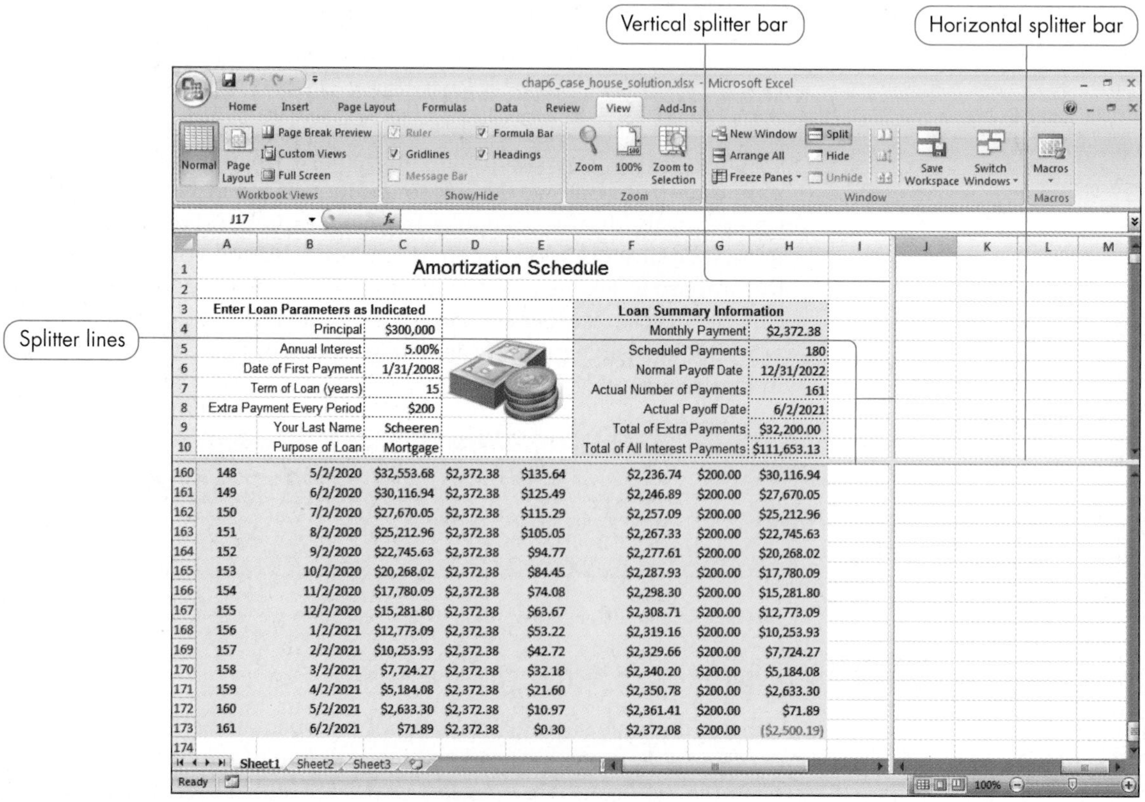

Splitting a window is the process of dividing a worksheet window.

A *splitter control* is the two-headed arrow in the scroll bar used to divide a window into panes.

Figure 6.17 Split Window

Change the View in a Single Window

You can view multiple worksheets or multiple workbooks in the same window. To do this, either arrange the windows so all are visible and click one to make it active or click a sheet tab to make it active. Then you may click many of the view options on the View tab, as shown in Figure 6.16. The options you select are only in effect for the active window. Figure 6.18 shows multiple views of the same workbook.

If your job requires you to open the same workbooks all the time and you always arrange the workbook windows the same way, you will find the custom workspace feature beneficial. To use the feature, you will first open and arrange the windows for your needs. Click Save Workspace in the Window group on the View tab, enter a file name, and click Save. The file is saved with the .XLW extension to distinguish the file from workbook files.

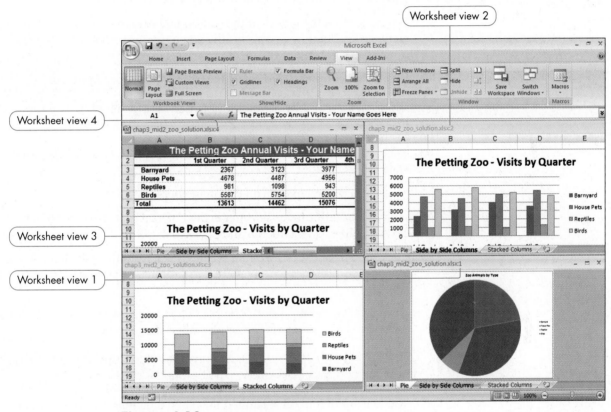

Figure 6.18 Multiple Views

Hands-On Exercises

2 | Ajax College Band

Skills covered: 1. Convert Text to Columns **2.** Identify and Remove Duplicate Rows **3.** Subtotal the Data **4.** Group and Ungroup Data **5.** Use Multiple Windows

---

Step 1
Convert Text to Columns

Refer to Figure 6.19 as you complete Step 1.

a. Open the *chap6_ho2_band* workbook and save it as **chap6_ho2_band_solution** so you can return to the original workbook if necessary.

You notice that the names of the band members are in one cell in first name, last name order. Before you can sort the names in any order except by first name, it is necessary to convert the text to columns.

b. Right-click **column B** and select **Insert** from the shortcut menu.

TROUBLESHOOTING: If you do not insert new columns for the separated data, existing data will be overwritten.

c. Select **cells A2:A65** and click **Text to Columns** in the Data Tools group on the **Data tab**.

You selected the names of all band members.

d. Verify that **Delimited** is selected in the *Original data type* section in the Convert Text to Columns Wizard box and click **Next**.

e. Click the **Space check box**, remove the check from the **Tab check box** in the *Delimiter* section in the Convert Text to Columns Wizard dialog box, and click **Next**.

f. Verify that **General** is selected in the *Column data format* section, **Destination** is **$A$2**, and *Data preview* is correct, and then click **Finish**.

TROUBLESHOOTING: If you make an error in the Convert Text to Columns Wizard box, you can click Back at any time before clicking Finish.

You will see that Excel separated the name data into columns A and B.

g. Type **First Name** in **cell A1** and **Last Name** in **cell B1**.

h. Save the workbook.

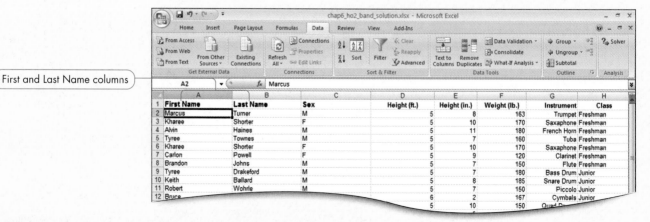

Figure 6.19 Convert Text to Columns

Refer to Figure 6.20 as you complete Step 2.

a. Click **column B** to select it.

The selected column is used to identify duplicate last names.

b. Click the **Home tab** and click **Conditional Formatting** in the Styles group.

c. Point to **Highlight Cells Rules** and click **Duplicate Values** to open the Duplicate Values dialog box.

d. Select **Red Border** from the values with drop-down list and click **OK**.

You highlighted the duplicate last names by placing a red border around the cells. Before actually deleting the identified duplicate rows, review the highlighted rows to verify that they are actually duplicated rows.

e. Deselect column B, click the **Data tab**, and click **Remove Duplicates** in the Data Tools group.

f. Click **Unselect All**, click the **First Name** and **Last Name check boxes**, verify that the **My data has header check box** is selected, and click **OK**.

Last name and first name were selected so individuals with the same last name but different first name are not inadvertently deleted.

g. Click **OK** to verify the deletion of the rows.

h. Click **Conditional Formatting** in the Styles group on the Home tab, point to Clear Rules, and click **Clear Rules from Entire Sheet**.

You removed all conditional formatting from your worksheet.

i. Save the workbook.

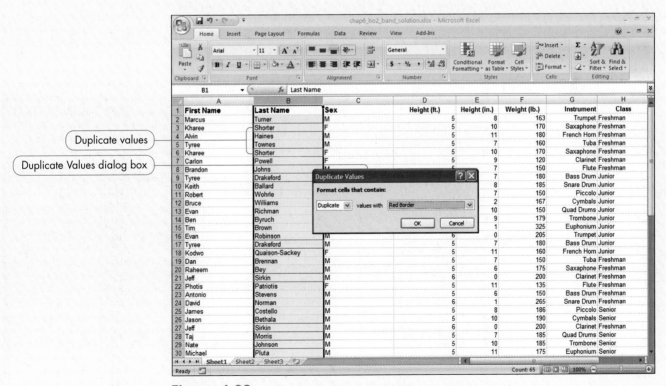

Figure 6.20   Identify Duplicate Last Names

Refer to Figure 6.21 as you complete Step 3.

a. Click the **Select All** box to select the entire worksheet, click **Format** in the Cells group on the Home tab, and click **AutoFit Column Width**.

You changed column widths so the data optimally fit the cells and to make the entire worksheet visible on the screen.

b. Click in **column H**, then click **Sort A to Z** in the Sort & Filter group on the Data tab.

You sorted the data by class and are now ready to subtotal the scholarship amount data by class.

c. Click **cell I2** and click **Subtotal** in the Outline group to open the Subtotal dialog box.

d. Select **Class** from the **At each change in drop-down list** and verify the following:

- The *Use function* is **Sum**.
- The **Scholarship Amount check box** is checked in the *Add subtotal to* section.
- The **Replace current subtotals check box** is checked.
- The **Summary below data check box** is checked.

e. Click **OK**.

You created a subtotal for the scholarship amounts by class.

f. Save the workbook.

TROUBLESHOOTING: Subtotaling data is impossible if the data are in a table. Data must be in a range. If you are working with a data table, click in the table and click Convert to Range in the Tools group on the Table Tools Design tab.

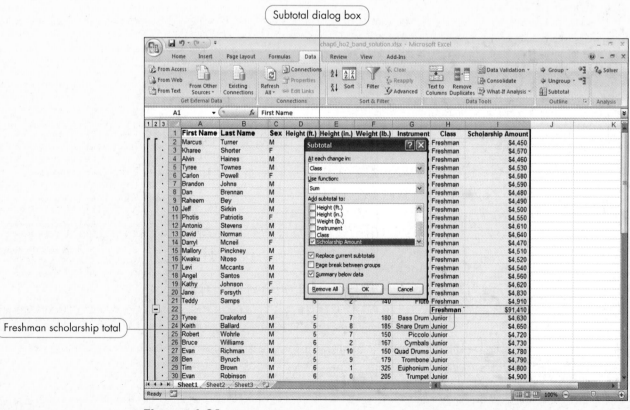

Figure 6.21 Subtotals

Refer to Figure 6.22 as you complete Step 4.

a. Click the **minus symbol** to the left of **rows 22, 35, 51,** and **66**.

You now see the scholarship subtotals for each class as well as the grand total for all scholarship amounts.

b. Click the **minus symbol** to the left of **row 67**.

You now see only the grand total for all scholarship amounts, as shown in Figure 6.22.

c. Click the **plus symbol** to the left of **row 67** and click each of the four **plus symbols**.

You used the plus symbols to reveal the details for each class and are now viewing the entire worksheet with subtotals by class.

d. Save the workbook.

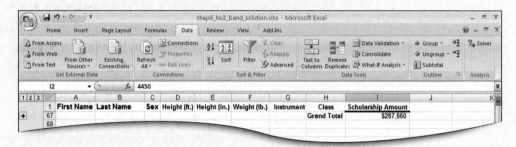

Figure 6.22 Scholarship Grand Total

Refer to Figure 6.23 as you complete Step 5.

a. Click **cell I6**, click **Split** in the Window group on the View tab, and drag the **vertical splitter** to the left until it disappears.

b. Drag the **horizontal splitter** to just below row 1.

You split the window into two panes so you can view the header information while scrolling to the bottom of the worksheet.

c. Click **Split** again to return to the original single window.

d. Click the **minus symbol** to the left of **rows 22, 35, 51,** and **66**.

e. Select **cells H22:I66**, click **Pie** in the Chart group on the **Insert tab**, and click **Pie**.

f. To enhance the pie chart:

- Click **Layout 3** in the Chart Layouts group on the Design tab.
- Click **Layout tab**, click **Chart Title** in the Labels group, and select **Above Chart**.
- Type **Scholarship Totals** and press **Enter**.
- Click **Move Chart** in the Location group on the Design tab, select **New sheet** in the Move Chart dialog box, type **Graph**, and click **OK**.

You created a pie chart to visually show scholarship totals for each class.

g. While viewing the pie chart, click **New Window** in the Window group on the View tab.

You have opened a second window.

h. Click **Arrange All** in the Window group, click **Horizontal** in the Arrange Windows dialog box, and click **OK**.

i. Click the **Sheet1 tab** in the top window to view the worksheet.

You have two windows visible on the screen. One displays the chart and one shows the grouped sheet.

j. Save and close the workbook.

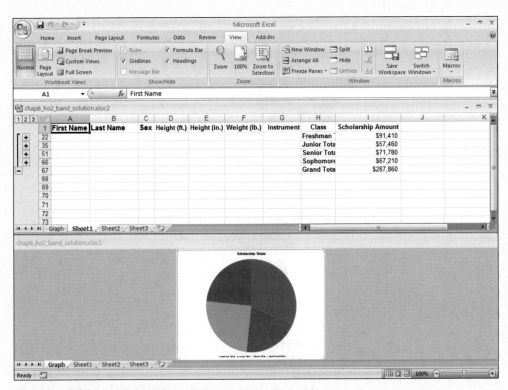

Figure 6.23 Multiple Windows

TIP Print Preview Versus Page Break Preview

The Print Preview command displays a worksheet as it will be printed including the header and/or the footer. The Page Break Preview, however, lets you see and/or modify the page breaks by dragging the breaks, which are indicated by a solid or dashed blue line, to allow more or less on any given page. Click Page Break Preview in the status bar to see the worksheet with the intended page breaks. Click Normal to return to the familiar view of a spreadsheet.

Conditional and Logical Functions

Functions are powerful tools that are built-in formulas you do not have to create yourself. This section will discuss the use of more complex functions. You will use conditional functions to SUM, AVERAGE, or COUNT data based on particular conditions or criteria. In the payment tables, you will use functions that include nested IF and the use of AND, OR, and NOT. The IFERROR function that is used primarily with error checking will be introduced, as well as several text-manipulation functions. Logical functions are a category of function in Excel and are one of the workhorses in workbook use. Accountants, teachers, statisticians, and managers use logical functions on a regular basis. In this section, you use conditional and logical functions.

> (. . . use conditional functions to SUM, AVERAGE, or COUNT data based on particular conditions or criteria.)

Using Conditional Functions

When you created formulas with SUM, COUNT, and AVERAGE functions, you summed, counted, or averaged all values in a range of cells. Two sets of three functions expand the power of the SUM, COUNT, and AVERAGE functions. The first set is SUMIF, COUNTIF, and AVERAGEIF, which return the total, count, or average for one criterion. For example, you might want the total sales for just one particular salesperson from the whole sales force, or you might want to know the number of blue bicycles manufactured last year from a rainbow of colors produced. The second set of functions is SUMIFS, COUNTIFS, and AVERAGEIFS. These functions return a total, count, or average based on two criteria. For example, you can use the SUMIFS function to determine the total sales for a salesperson for the weeks in the first quarter, or you might want the total of blue bicycles manufactured the first two weeks of this month.

Use SUMIF, COUNTIF, and AVERAGEIF Functions
SUMIF Function | Reference

SUMIF(range,criteria,sum_range)

The **SUMIF function** adds the cells specified by a given criterion.

The **SUMIF function** is similar to the SUM function except that it enables you to calculate a sum of values in a range that satisfies a specific condition you specify instead of calculating the sum of an entire range. SUMIF is often called a conditional sum because it sums the values that meet a particular condition. In the syntax for the SUMIF function, the range is the range of cells that are evaluated by criteria. Cells in the range must be numbers, range names, arrays, or references that contain numbers. The criteria are expressed in the form of a number, expression, or text that defines which cells will be added. The sum_range argument includes the actual cells to add if their corresponding cells in the range match the criteria.

COUNTIF Function | Reference

COUNTIF(range,criteria)

The **COUNTIF function** counts the number of cells within a range that meet the given criterion.

The **COUNTIF function** calculates the number of cells in a range that match the specified criteria rather than the number of all cells in a range that would be calculated using the COUNT function. The COUNTIF function is often referred to as a conditional count. In the syntax for COUNTIF the range is one or more cells to count, and can include numbers or range names, arrays, or references that contain numbers. The criteria are expressed in the form of a number, expression, cell reference, or references that contain numbers. When using criteria, you can test if:

- a cell matches a specific value.
- a cell is greater than (>) or less than (<) a specific number.
- a cell matches, or is greater or less than, a number in another cell.
- the text in a cell matches a pattern.

AVERAGEIF Function | Reference

AVERAGEIF(range,criteria,average_range)

The **AVERAGEIF function** returns the average of all the cells in a range that meet a given criterion.

The third function in the group of functions is the **AVERAGEIF function**. This function calculates the average, or arithmetic mean, of all cells in a range that meet criteria you specify. The range in the syntax for AVERAGEIF is one or more cells to average and may include names, arrays, or references that contain numbers. The criteria are expressed in the form of a number, expression, cell reference, or text that defines which cells are averaged. The average range is the set of cells to average. Review cells B22, B26, and B30 shown in Figure 6.24 to see examples of the SUMIF, AVERAGEIF, and COUNTIF functions, respectively.

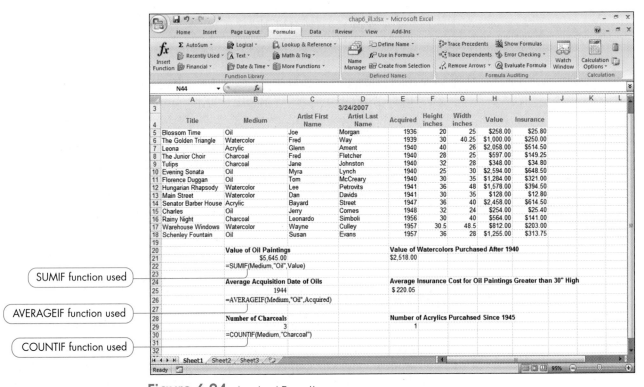

Figure 6.24 Logical Functions

Use SUMIFS, COUNTIFS, and AVERAGEIFS Functions
SUMIFS Function | Reference

SUMIFS(sum_range,criteria_range1,criteria1,criteria_range2,criteria2. . .)

COUNTIFS Function | Reference

COUNTIFS(range1,criteria1,range2,criteria2. . .)

AVERAGEIFS Function | Reference

AVERAGEIFS(average_range,criteria_range1,criteria1,criteria_range2,criteria2. . .)

The three functions described in this section are the logical outgrowth of the SUM, COUNT, and AVERAGE, and SUMIF, COUNTIF, and AVERAGEIF functions. The actions for the functions are the same as their counterparts except that you can use

The **SUMIFS function** adds the cells in a range that meet multiple criteria.

The **COUNTIFS function** counts the number of cells within a range that meet multiple criteria.

The **AVERAGEIFS function** returns the average of all the cells that meet multiple criteria.

multiple conditions. The SUMIFS function sums cells in a range that meet multiple criteria. The sum_range in the syntax is the first argument in the *SUMIFS function* but the last argument in the SUMIF function. This function allows up to 127 criteria to be evaluated. The *COUNTIFS function* counts the number of cells in a range that meet multiple criteria. Up to 127 criteria can be evaluated with the function. The *AVERAGEIFS function* calculates the average of all cells meeting up to 127 criteria. These functions are useful when you want to answer such questions as: What is the total value of the watercolors in the collection that were acquired before 1940? Perhaps you want to know the average insurance cost for oil paintings that are larger than 30 inches or how many acrylic paintings were acquired before 1945. Review cells E22, E26, and E30 shown in Figure 6.25 to see examples of the SUMIFS, AVERAGEIFS, and COUNTIFS functions, respectively.

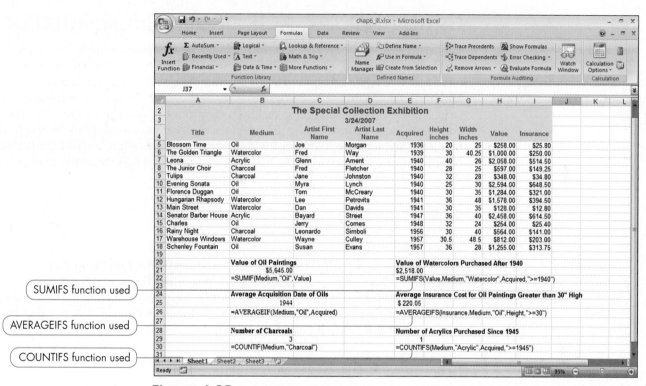

Figure 6.25 Logical Functions

Creating Nested IF Functions

The IF function enables two possible formulas: The logical text is true and the first formula is used or the logical test if false and the second formula is used. You can expand the power of the IF by choosing more than two options, by nesting multiple IF statements in one formula. Nesting is done by placing one function within another. Excel permits up to 64 IF statements in one formula. As previously stated, nesting functions is a technique that permits you to place one function inside another. A nested IF can be used to calculate taxable earnings, for example, IF year-to-date pay minus total earnings is less than the FICA limit, then zero taxable earnings, else IF year-to-date pay is greater than the FICA limit, then FICA limit minus the total of (year-to-date pay minus total earnings), else total earnings.

The following formula is another example of nested IFs: =IF(A20<500,A20*2%, IF(A20>10000,A20*5%,A20*3%)). In this case, the formula calculates commission when the total sales value is in cell A20. If the sales are less than $500, the commission is 2%; if sales are above $10,000, the commission is 5%; the commission is 3% in all other instances. If the first condition is met, Excel carries out the calculation. If the first condition is not met, Excel moves on to the second condition, which is actually a second IF statement. The use of multiple IF statements can be very confusing and you should exercise care when using them.

TIP Creating Nested Functions

You cannot use the Insert Function dialog box when creating nested functions because it does not allow for the use of multiple functions within the same formula (function within a function). When you get an error message after typing a nested function, you can delete the equal sign (=), making your formula a text string that will display in a cell. It is now convenient to view and edit the formula. Remember that parentheses must match, that is you must have an equal number of left and right parentheses in the formula.

Using AND, OR, NOT, and IFERROR Functions

The AND, OR, NOT, and IFERROR functions are examples of logical functions that expand the power of Excel. They are often used with conditional functions. You would use the AND function to test when more than one condition is met. For example, if a salesperson earns a $10 bonus for each snow blower sold on Sunday you would use the AND function to test both conditions. The OR function tests whether any of the arguments are true. Using the same example, a salesperson earns a $10 bonus for selling snow blowers any day of the week or selling anything on Sunday. NOT functions reverse the logic; true becomes false and false becomes true. It is not recommended that you use the NOT function.

AND Function | Reference

AND(logical1,logical2,. . .)

The *AND function* returns true when all arguments are true and returns false when one or more arguments are false.

The *AND function* accepts two or more conditions and returns true if all conditions are true and false if any of the conditions are false. The syntax of the function is AND(logical1,logical2,. . .). If an array or reference argument contains text or empty cells, those values are ignored. If there are no logical values in the specified range, AND returns the #VALUE! Error.

OR Function | Reference

OR(logical1,logical2,. . .)

The *OR function* returns true if any argument is true and returns false if all arguments are false.

The *OR function* also accepts two or more conditions and returns true if any of the conditions are met. It returns a false only if all conditions are false. The syntax for the OR function is OR(logical1,logical2,. . .). Up to 255 conditions can be tested that can be either true or false. Table 6.1 shows examples of OR functions:

Table 6.1 Examples of OR Functions

Formula	Result
=OR(TRUE)	One argument is true, returns true.
=OR(1+1=1,2+2=5)	All arguments are false, returns false.
=OR(TRUE,FALSE,TRUE)	At least one argument is true, returns true.

NOT Function | Reference

NOT(logical)

The **NOT function** reverses the value of its argument.

The **NOT function** reverses the value of its argument. You would use NOT when you want to make sure a value is not equal to a particular value. The syntax of the NOT function is NOT(logical). If logical is false, not returns true, and if the logical is true, NOT returns false. Table 6.2 shows examples of NOT functions.

Table 6.2 Examples of NOT Functions

Formula	Result
=NOT(FALSE)	Returns true, the reverse of false.
=NOT(1+1=2)	Returns false as the reverse of an equation that returns true.

IFERROR Function | Reference

IFERROR(value,value_if_error)

The **IFERROR function** returns a value you specify if a formula evaluates to an error.

The **IFERROR function** is a function used in error checking. IFERROR checks an indicated cell and displays a value specified if a formula evaluates to an error. If there is no error, the IFERROR function returns the value of the formula. This function is used to trap and handle errors in formulas. The syntax of the IFERROR function is IFERROR(value,value_if_error). In the syntax, value is the argument that is checked for an error, and value_if_error is the value to return if the formula evaluates to an error. #N/A, #VALUE!, #REF!, #DIV/0!, #NUM!, #NAME?, and #NULL! are the types of errors evaluated.

Hands-On Exercises

3 | Classic Cars and Security

Skills covered: 1. Use SUMIF, AVERAGEIF, and COUNTIF Functions **2.** Use SUMIFS, AVERAGEIFS, and COUNTIFS Functions **3.** Nest the AND Function in an IF Function **4.** Nest the OR Function in an IF Function **5.** Nest the IF Function

Step 1 Use SUMIF, AVERAGEIF, and COUNTIF Functions	Refer to Figure 6.26 as you complete Step 1.

a. Open the *chap6_ho3_classiccars* workbook and save it as **chap6_ho3_classiccars_solution** so that you will be able to return to the original workbook.

Note that names have been assigned to ranges to facilitate your work. The workbook contains a Classic Cars worksheet where you will use conditional functions and a Security worksheet where you will use nested IF, AND, and OR functions.

b. Click the **Classic Cars tab**, click **cell C18**, click the **Formulas tab**, and click **Insert Function** in the Function Library group to open the Insert Function dialog box.

c. Type **SUMIF** in the *Search for a function* section and click **OK**.

d. Ensure that SUMIF is highlighted in the *Select a function* section and click **OK** to open the Function Arguments dialog box.

e. Select **cells C4:C15** and the range name *Model* appears in the Range text box.

f. Click in the **Criteria** text box and type **Convertible**.

Excel encloses text strings in the Criteria box automatically.

g. Click in the **Sum_range** text box and select **cells H4:H15**.

The range name *Value* appears in the Sum_range text box.

h. Click **OK**.

i. Use Insert Function to create the AVERAGEIF and COUNTIF functions, as shown in the table below:

Cell	Function
C22	=AVERAGEIF(Model,"Hardtop",Acquired)
C26	=COUNTIF(Model,"Hardtop")

Using the SUMIF, AVERAGEIF, and COUNTIF functions demonstrates the use of one-variable conditional functions. You were able to answer the following questions: What is the value of all convertibles in the collection? What is the average acquisition date of hardtops? How many hardtops are in the collection?

j. Save the workbook.

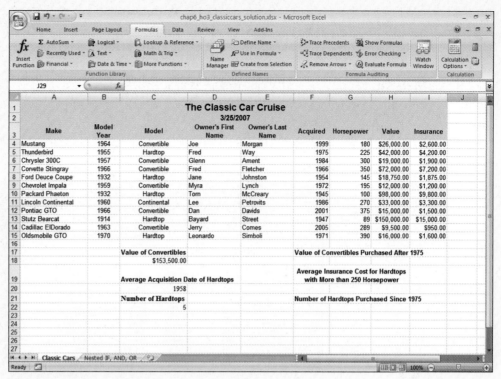

Figure 6.26 One-Variable Conditional Functions

Refer to Figure 6.27 as you complete Step 2.

a. Verify that the **Classic Cars tab** is selected, click **cell F18**, click the **Formulas tab**, and click **Insert Function** in the Function Library group to open the Insert Function dialog box.

b. Type **SUMIFS** in the *Search for a function:* section and click **OK**.

c. Ensure that SUMIFS is highlighted in the *Select a function* section and click **OK** to open the Function Arguments dialog box.

d. Select **cells H4:H15** and the range name *Value* appears in the Sum_range text box.

e. Click in the **Criteria_range1** text box and type the range name **Model**.

f. Click in the **Criteria1** text box and type **Convertible**.

TROUBLESHOOTING: Text strings and conditional operations entered in the Criteria text boxes are automatically enclosed in quotes when you use Insert Function. If you type the function, you must remember to enclose text strings and conditional operations in quotes.

g. Click in the **Criteria_range2** text box and type the range name **Acquired**.

h. Click in the **Criteria2** text box. Type **>=1975** and click **OK**. Then widen column F if necessary.

i. Use Insert Function to create the AVERAGEIFS and COUNTIFS functions, as shown in the table below:

Cell	Function
H22	=AVERAGEIFS(Insurance,Model,"Hardtop",Horsepower,>250)
H26	=COUNTIFS(Model,"Hardtop",Acquired,">=1975")

Using the SUMIFS, AVERAGEIFS, and COUNTIFS functions demonstrates the use of two variable conditional functions. You were able to answer the following questions: What is the value of all convertibles purchased after 1975? What is the average insurance cost for hardtops with more than 250 horsepower? How many hardtops were purchased since 1975?

j. Save the workbook.

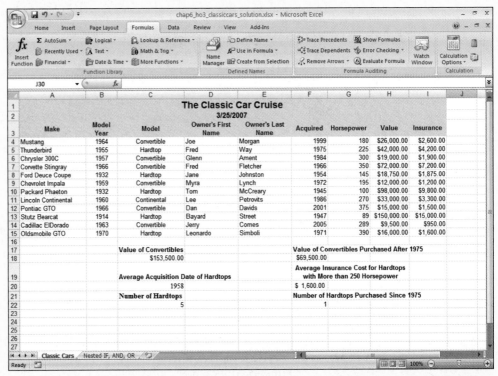

Figure 6.27 Two-Variable Conditional Functions

Step 3
Nest the AND Function in an IF Function

Refer to Figure 6.28 as you complete Step 3.

a. Click the **Nested IF, AND, OR** sheet tab, click **cell E5**, type
=IF((AND(D5>7,C5>30000)),3,2), and press **Enter**.

In this example, salespeople who have worked for XYZ Security Systems more than seven years **AND** have annual sales more than $30,000 will be assigned a job classification of 3. All others have a job classification code of 2.

In the above nested IF function, the AND function is calculated first because it is in the innermost set of parentheses. The value returned by the AND function is TRUE; therefore, the value 3 is the result of the IF function.

b. Click and drag to copy the formula through **cell E12**.

Only two people meet the conditions and now have a job classification of 3.

c. Save the workbook.

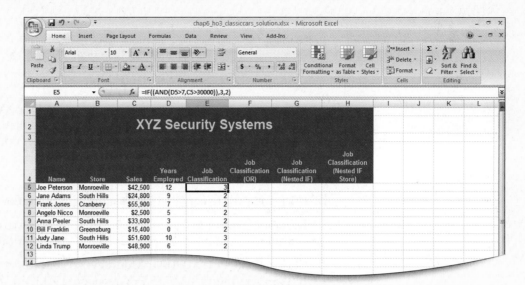

Figure 6.28 Nested AND in an IF Function

Refer to Figure 6.29 as you complete Step 4.

a. Click **cell F5**. Type **=IF((OR(D5>7,C5>30000)),3,2)** and press **Enter**.

In this example, salespeople who have worked for XYZ Security Systems more than seven years **OR** have annual sales of more than $30,000 will be assigned a job classification of 3. An employee meeting either criterion receives a job classification of 2.

b. Click and drag to copy the formula through **cell F12**.

Only two employees meet neither criterion, and six employees meet one or the other criterion.

c. Save the workbook.

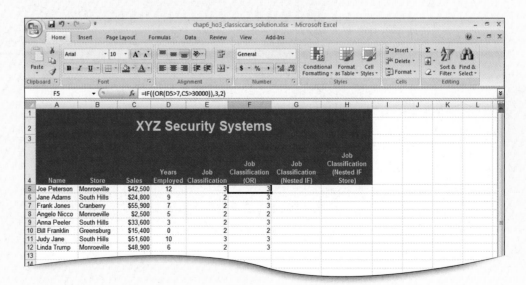

Figure 6.29 Nested OR in an IF Function

Refer to Figure 6.30 as you complete Step 5.

a. Click **cell G5**. Type **=IF((AND(D5>7,C5>30000)),3, (IF((OR(D5>7,C5>30000)),2,1)))** and press **Enter**.

In this example, salespeople who have worked for XYZ Security Systems more than seven years **AND** have annual sales of more than $30,000 will be assigned a job classification of 3. An employee meeting either criterion receives a job classification of 2, and an employee meeting NO criteria is assigned a job classification code of 1.

b. Click and drag to copy the formula through **cell G12**.

Four employees now have a job classification of 2, two employees have a job classification of 3, and two employees have a job classification of 1.

c. Click **cell H5**, type **=IF((B5="Monroeville"),4,IF((B5="South Hills"),3, IF((B5="Cranberry"),2,IF((B5="Greensburg"),1,"")))),** and press **Enter**.

Another example of a nested IF assigns job classification based on store location. If employees of XYZ Security Systems work in the Monroeville store, they are assigned classification 4; if employees work in South Hills, they are assigned classification 3; if employees work in Cranberry, they are assigned classification 2; and any employee working in Greensburg is assigned a classification of 1.

d. Click and drag to copy the formula through **cell H12**.

e. Save and close the workbook.

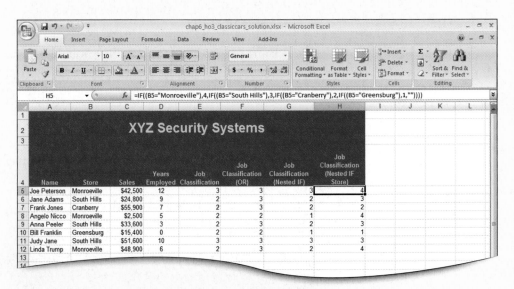

Figure 6.30 Nested IF Functions

Amortization Table

One of the most commonly used applications for Excel is to determine a payment or *amortization* schedule for a loan. As we moved later into the twentieth century, it became easier for consumers to borrow money for major purchases such as a car or a house. It is now common for the cost of a car to be many times what our parents or grandparents paid for a house. The price of new houses today is just beyond many of our parents' or grandparents' comprehension. This payment or amortization schedule becomes all-important. Excel makes it easier for you to quickly determine your payment schedule for a variety of purchases. This section introduces you to the amortization table, its components, and results.

> (... the cost of a car to be many times what our parents or grandparents paid for a house.)

Amortization is the payment schedule for a loan.

Defining the Amortization Table

The amortization schedule shows the date of each loan payment, the amount of each payment that goes to principal and interest, and the remaining balance, which eventually reaches zero. Figures 6.31 and 6.32 show the amortization schedules for an automobile loan and for a house mortgage, respectively. The parameters for the loans are entered in the upper-left portion of the worksheets and the other values are calculated automatically.

The car loan in Figure 6.31 is for $30,000 for four years, resulting in a monthly payment of $732.39. The payments begin February 1, 2008, and continue for 48 months until January 1, 2012, when the loan is paid off. The borrower pays a total of $35,154.61 (48 payments of $732.39 each). These payments equal the principal of $30,000 plus $5,154.61 in interest during the life of the loan.

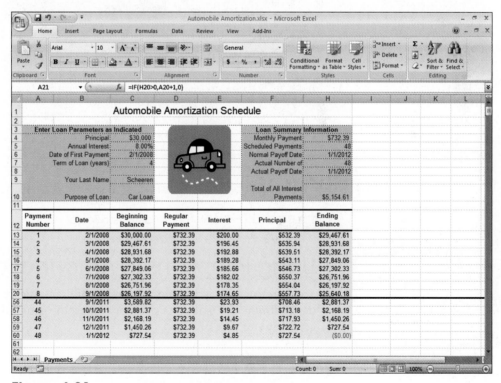

Figure 6.31 The Car Loan Amortization Table

The body of the worksheet shows how principal and interest comprise each payment. The balance of the loan at the beginning or the first period is $30,000. The interest rate for the entire first year would be $2,400, which represents 8% of $30,000. Payments are made monthly, so the interest is also computed monthly (8%/12). The interest payment for the first month is, therefore, $200. The interest for the second period is less than for the previous period because the beginning balance is less. Remember that interest is paid on the remaining balance. As each month's beginning balance decreases, so does the monthly interest. The payment remains the same with less payment going toward interest and more toward principal. This process continues until the loan is paid off.

Figure 6.32 shows the amortization worksheet for a home mortgage of $300,000 at 6.25% for 30 years. This loan has one other parameter: an optional extra payment of $100 per month. Paying an extra $100 per month enables the borrower to pay off the loan in 313 rather than 360 payments. Making an extra payment is a good strategy if you can afford it. Many home buyers choose a 30-year mortgage to keep the monthly payment low but opt to make extra payments to reduce the length of the mortgage and the interest paid.

This reduction in interest can be substantial—in our case, over $50,000 over the life of the mortgage. The borrower will pay $31,300 or 313 payments of $100 each, in early payments. This is money that the borrower would have paid during the life of the mortgage but elected to pay early to reduce the total amount of interest.

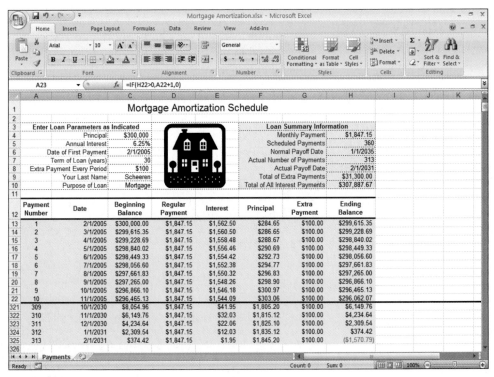

Figure 6.32 The House Amortization Table

Using Functions in Amortization Tables

You can use several functions to help build an amortization table. These functions deal with the calculation of payment dates, the actual number of payments, and the actual payoff date of a loan.

Use YEAR, MONTH, and DAY Functions

Calculating payment dates in Excel is more complicated than you might expect because Excel stores dates as integers (serial numbers) that are equivalent to the number of days that have elapsed since January 1, 1900. Stated another way, January 1, 1900, is stored as day one, January 2, 1900, is stored as day two, and so on. This makes it possible to determine a past or future date by adding or subtracting the number of days to your date. Excel, in these calculations, also accounts for differing numbers of days in months, such as 31 days in March, 30 days in April, or 28 days in February, except in leap year.

Your paycheck is issued weekly, biweekly, or perhaps monthly. You can use Excel to calculate your pay dates for the entire year if you use date functions. These functions work with serial numbers and you can easily add numbers to a date to produce a new date. For example, if your first paycheck is dated January 13, 2008, and you add 14, you will find that your next biweekly pay date is January 27, 2008. Figure 6.33 shows the serial number 42265 in cell A1, formatted as a date in cell B1, and the results of the YEAR, MONTH, and DAY functions in cells B2 through B4.

YEAR Function | Reference

YEAR(serial_number)

MONTH Function | Reference

MONTH(serial_number)

DAY Function | Reference

DAY(serial_number)

The *YEAR function* returns the year corresponding to a date.

The *MONTH function* returns the month represented by a serial number.

The *DAY function* returns the day of a date represented by a serial number.

The functions DAY, MONTH, and YEAR return the numeric day, month, and year. The *YEAR function* returns the year corresponding to a date. The *MONTH function* returns the month represented by a serial number, and the *DAY function* returns the day of a date represented by a serial number. For example, if you have a date in cell B1, the function =MONTH(B1) returns the numeric month of the date in cell B1. Similarly, =MONTH(B1)+1 will add one to the numeric month shown in cell B1. The reference box on page 424 summarizes these functions.

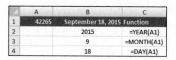

	A	B	C
1	42265	September 18, 2015	Function
2		2015	=YEAR(A1)
3		9	=MONTH(A1)
4		18	=DAY(A1)

Figure 6.33 YEAR, MONTH, and DAY Functions

Use Match and Index Functions
MATCH Function | Reference

MATCH(lookup_value,lookup_array,match_type)

The *MATCH function* returns the relative position of an item in an array that matches a specified value in a specified order.

The MATCH and INDEX functions are functions commonly used with amortization tables showing payment schedules for loans. The *MATCH function* returns the relative position of an item in an array that matches a specified value in a specified order. The MATCH function returns the position in the list where the match occurs, which is the actual payment number where the zero balance is reached. A MATCH function has three arguments:

1. The value being looked up, typically a zero ending balance.
2. An associated cell range, the cells containing the balance at the end of each period.
3. The type of match; is it an exact match or not? The type of match is 1, 0, or -1.

INDEX Function | Reference

INDEX(array,row_num,column_num)

The **INDEX function** returns a value or the reference to a value within a table or range.

The **INDEX function** returns a value or the reference to a value within a table or range. If a borrower wants to know the actual number of payments required when extra payments are made, the MATCH function is used. The INDEX function shows the actual payoff date of the loan. Review Figure 6.34 to see how the MATCH and INDEX functions are used in the Loan Summary Information area. The INDEX function uses the result of the MATCH function to determine the payoff date for the loan. The INDEX function has three arguments:

1. A cell range in the form of a table.
2. A row number in the table, which is the value returned by the MATCH function.
3. A column number in the table, which has the date of the payment. The INDEX function returns a value in the specified cell.

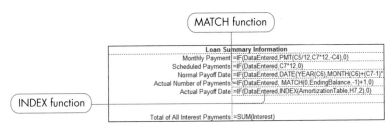

Figure 6.34 MATCH and INDEX Functions

Use ROUND Function
ROUND Function | Reference

ROUND(number, num_digits)

The **ROUND function** rounds a value to a specified number of digits.

The **ROUND function** rounds a value to a specified number of digits. In other words, it enables you to adjust fractional or decimal numbers such as 67.889 so that they are more manageable. Unfortunately, using the ROUND function instead of rounding by modifying the number format gives you less precision. Figure 6.35 shows values in column A that are formatted as Currency with 2 decimals in column B. Column C shows the same values rounded with the ROUND function. Columns D and E display the results of column B and column C multiplied by 56. Note the loss of precision between column D and E. Accountants typically use rounding for more accuracy when working with currency.

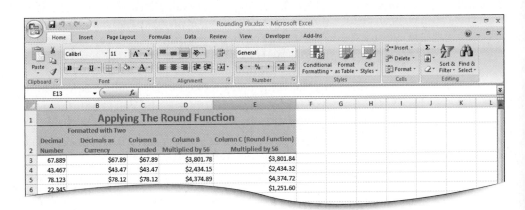

Figure 6.35 Values and the ROUND Function

Hands-On Exercises

4 | Purchase a New House

Skills covered: 1. Enter the Loan Parameters **2.** Enter Formulas for the First Payment **3.** Name a Cell **4.** Add the IF Functions **5.** Enter the Formulas for the Second Payment **6.** Complete the Payment Schedule **7.** Complete the Summary Area and Print

---

Step 1
Enter the Loan Parameters

Refer to Figure 6.36 as you complete Step 1.

a. Start Excel, open the *chap6_ho4_amortization* workbook, and save it as **chap6_ho4_amortization_solution** so that you will be able to return to the original workbook.

Some areas of the workbook are preformatted and represent summary areas you will complete as you work through the hands-on exercise.

b. Click in **cell C4**. Enter **$400,000** as the principal (the amount you are going to borrow).

c. Enter **6.25%**, **2/1/2008**, and **30** into **cells C5:C7**, respectively.

d. Click in **cell H4** and type the formula **=PMT(C5/12,C7*12,−C4)**.

The formula you entered is used to calculate the periodic payment. You should see $2,462.87, as shown in Figure 6.36.

e. Click in **cell H5** and type the formula **=C7*12**.

The formula you entered is used to calculate the number of scheduled payments. You should see 360; that is, there will be 360 monthly payments.

f. Save the workbook.

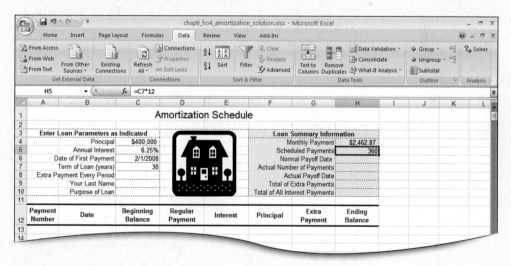

Figure 6.36 Loan Parameters

TIP · The PMT function

The PMT (payment) function has three required arguments; the interest rate per period, the number of periods, and the principal (amount that you are borrowing). The interest rate is typically entered on an annual basis, whereas the payments are made monthly; thus, the interest rate is divided by 12 within the PMT function. In similar fashion, the number of periods is multiplied by 12 to convert the number of years to the equivalent number of months. The principal is equal to the present value of the future sum of periodic payments; it is normally entered with a minus sign so that the calculated payment appears as a positive number within the worksheet.

Step 2

Enter Formulas for the First Payment

Refer to Figure 6.37 as you complete Step 2.

a. Click in **cell A13** and type **1**.

This represents the payment number.

b. Click in **cell B13** and type the formula **=C6**.

You copied the date of the first payment from the input area.

c. Click in **cell C13** and type **=C4** to obtain the beginning balance.

d. Click in **cell D13** and type **=$H$4** to get the regular payment.

> **TROUBLESHOOTING:** This entry must be absolute because the entries in the remaining rows should always reflect this amount.

e. Click in **cell E13** and type the formula **=($C$5/12)∗C13**.

The interest is charged on the unpaid balance at the beginning of the period (cell C13). The interest rate is the annual rate (cell C5) divided by 12.

f. Click in **cell F13** and type the formula **=D13–E13**.

The amount of the payment that goes toward principal is the amount left after paying the interest. The regular payment is divided into two parts, one for the interest and the remainder for principal.

g. Click in **cell G13** and type **=$C$8** to copy the extra payment (if any).

h. Click in **cell H13** and type the formula **=C13–F13–G13**.

The formula is used to calculate the remaining balance. You should see $399,620.46, as shown in Figure 6.37.

i. Save the workbook.

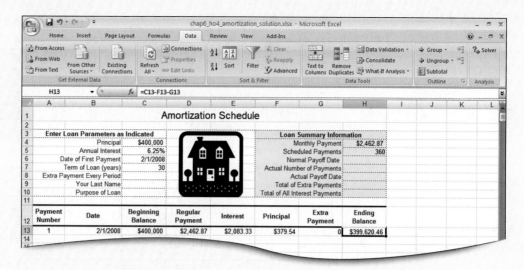

Figure 6.37 The First Payment

Step 3
Name a Cell

a. Click **cell D6**.

b. Click in the **name box**.

c. Type **DataEntered** and press **Enter**.

You have named the cell D6 and can now use DataEntered in formulas.

d. Save the workbook.

Step 4
Add the IF Functions

Refer to Figure 6.38 as you complete Step 4.

a. Click and drag the clip art image so you can see the contents of cell D6.

The value is currently TRUE because all of the loan parameters have been entered.

b. Click in **cell C7** and press **Delete**.

The value in cell D6 is now FALSE because a loan parameter is missing. In addition, the worksheet now contains several "Division by zero" error messages because the PMT function is unable to compute a value when the term of the loan is missing.

c. Click in **cell A13** and type =IF(DataEntered,1,0).

The errors can be hidden by including an IF function to ensure that all of the loan parameters have been entered. The value of the cell is 1 if cell D6 is true and 0 otherwise. The name DataEntered has been assigned to cell D6.

d. Click in **cell B13** and type a new formula: =IF(A13>0,C6,0).

There will be a nonzero payment date only if there is a payment. You will see 1/0/1900, which is the number 0 formatted as a date.

e. Click in **cell C13** and change the formula to =IF(A13>0,C4,0). Modify the remaining formulas in row 13 to test the value in cell A13 as well.

f. Click in **cell H4** and type =IF(DataEntered,PMT(C5/12,C7∗12,–C4),0).

g. Click in **cell H5** and type the formula =IF(DataEntered,C7∗12,0).

The error messages are gone.

h. Click in **cell C7** and type 30.

The values for the first payment reappear.

i. Drag the clip art back to its original position and save the workbook.

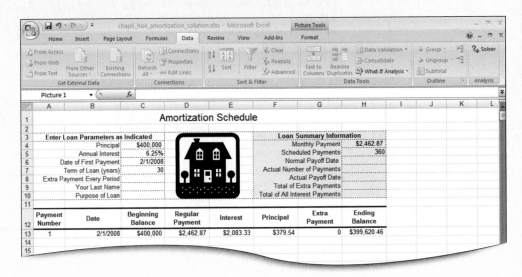

Figure 6.38 Division by Zero

Step 5
Enter the Formulas for the Second Payment

Refer to Figure 6.39 as you complete Step 5.

a. Click in **cell A14** and type the formula **=IF(H13>0,A13+1,0)**.

A second payment is necessary only if there is a balance after the first payment.

b. Click in **cell B14** and type
=IF(A14>0,DATE(YEAR(B13),MONTH(B13)+1,DAY(B13)),0).

The date is shown as 39508 because it is not yet formatted.

c. Click the **General down arrow** and select **Short Date** in the Number group, as shown in Figure 6.39.

d. Click in **cell C14** and type the formula **=IF(A14>0,H13,0)**.

The beginning balance for the second period is equal to the ending balance from the first period.

e. Format using **Currency** from the **General down arrow** in the Number group.

f. Select **cells D13:H13** and drag the fill handle to copy the formulas into **row 14**.

You should see $399,238.95 in cell H14. The formulas in cells D14:H14 are the same as those in row 13 but are adjusted through the relative references in these cells.

TROUBLESHOOTING: The formula in cell D14 must contain an absolute reference to H4 because the monthly payment does not change.

g. Save the workbook.

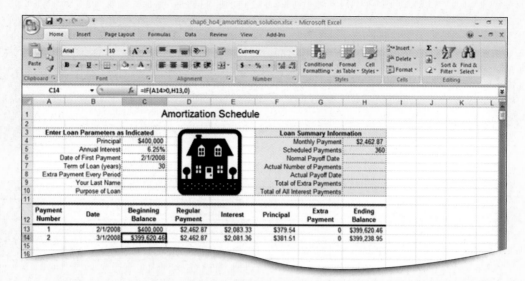

Figure 6.39 The Second Payment

TIP   The IPMT and PPMT Functions

The IPMT and PPMT functions compute the portion of a monthly payment that goes toward interest and principal, respectively. These functions refer to the original principal and cannot accommodate extra payments toward principal and are not used in this worksheet. They could be used with simpler amortization tables and/or to verify the calculations of this worksheet in the absence of extra payments. See Help for additional information.

Step 6
Complete the Payment Schedule

Refer to Figure 6.40 as you complete Step 6.

a. Click in **cell C7** and temporarily change the term to **45**.

The completed spreadsheet is to be as general as possible, capable of creating amortization tables that run to 45 years and are for use with conventional mortgages. The monthly payment is reduced to $2,217.48.

b. Select **A14:H14**, then drag the fill handle to row 552. This takes you to the 540th payment, at which point the balance goes to zero.

c. Click in **cell C7** and reset the term of the loan to 30 years to restore the monthly payment to $2,462.87.

Scroll down column H until you come to an ending balance of zero. This will occur in the 360th payment.

d. Click the **Office Button**, click **Excel Options**, and click **Advanced** to view Advanced Options for Working with Excel.

e. Scroll through the options to see *Display options for this worksheet* (payments), remove the check from **Show a zero in cells that have zero value**, and click **OK**.

Your spreadsheet contained many rows of superfluous zeros and the Excel Options enabled you to hide them. The zeros are no longer visible, but the formulas are still there.

f. Save the workbook.

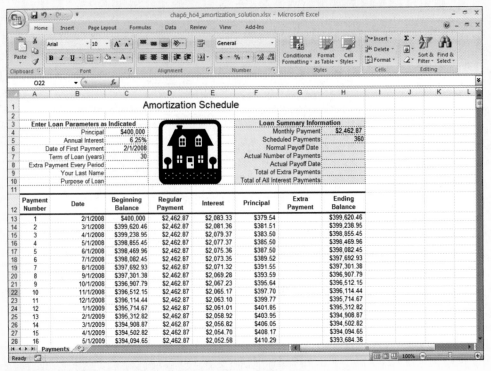

Figure 6.40 The Payment Schedule

Refer to Figure 6.41 as you complete Step 7.

a. Click in **cell C8** and type **$200** as the optional extra payment that will be made each period.

You elected to pay $200 per month because the total of the extra payments for the year is the approximate amount due per month. The displayed values change, as shown in Figure 6.41.

b. Click in **cell H6** and type
=IF(DataEntered,DATE(YEAR(C6),MONTH(C6)+(C7–1)*12+11,DAY(C6)),0)
and Format as Short Date.

The formula you entered is used to determine the normal payoff date for the loan. You should see 1/1/2038.

c. Name the ranges as indicated below:

- Cells **H13:H306** named **EndingBalance**.
- Cells **A13:A306** named **AmortizationTable**.
- Cells **G13:G306** named **ExtraPayment**.
- Cells **E13:E306** named **Interest**.

d. Click in **cell H7** and type **=IF(DataEntered,MATCH(0,EndingBalance,–1)+1,0)**.

The MATCH function is used to search the range name EndingBalance for the smallest value that is greater than or equal to zero. The balance never goes exactly to zero because of a rounding error; thus, the row below the match corresponds to the number of actual payments.

e. Click in **cell H8** and type **=IF(DataEntered,INDEX(AmortizationTable,H7,2),0)**.

This formula returns the date from column 2 of the row within the table that was returned by the MATCH function.

f. Click in **cell H9** and type **=SUM(ExtraPayment)**.

The SUM function is used to determine the total amount of the extra payments over the life of the mortgage.

g. Click in **cell H10** and type **=SUM(Interest)**.

This SUM function is used to determine the total amount paid in interest over the life of the mortgage. You should see the values in Figure 6.41.

h. Format **cell H8** as **Short Date** and **cells H9:H10** and **cells H13:H306** as **Currency**.

i. Type your name in **cell C9** and type **Mortgage** in **cell C10**.

j. Print the first page of the worksheet. Save and close the workbook.

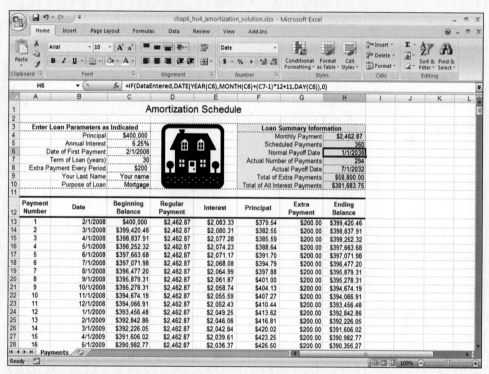

Figure 6.41 The Completed Payment Schedule

Functions Used | Reference

Name	Syntax	Definition
CONCATENATE	CONCATENATE(text1,text2,...)	Joins two or more text strings into one text string.
PROPER	PROPER(text)	Capitalizes the first letter in a text string.
UPPER	UPPER(text)	Converts text to uppercase letters.
LOWER	LOWER(text)	Converts all uppercase letters to lowercase.
SUBSTITUTE	SUBSTITUTE(text,old_text,new_text, instance_num)	Substitutes new_text for old_text in a text string.
SUMIF	SUMIF(range,criteria,sum_range)	Adds the cells specified by a given criterion.
COUNTIF	COUNTIF(range,criteria)	Counts the number of cells within a range that meet the given criterion.
AVERAGEIF	AVERAGEIF(range,criteria, average_range)	Returns the average of all the cells in a range that meet a given criterion.
SUMIFS	SUMIFS(sum_range,criteria_range1, criteria1,criteria_range2, criteria2...)	Adds the cells in a range that meet multiple criteria.
COUNTIFS	COUNTIFS(range1,criteria1,range2, criteria2...)	Counts the number of cells within a range that meet multiple criteria.
AVERAGEIFS	AVERAGEIFS(average_range, criteria_range1,criteria1, criteria_range2,criteria2...)	Returns the average of all the cells that meet multiple criteria.
AND	AND(logical1,logical2,...)	Returns true when all arguments are true and returns false when one or more arguments are false.
OR	OR (logical1,logical2,...)	Returns true if any argument is true and returns false if all arguments are false.
NOT	NOT(logical)	Reverses the value of its argument.
IFERROR	IFERROR(value,value_if_error)	Returns a value you specify if a formula evaluates to an error.
YEAR	YEAR(serial_number)	Returns the year of a date. The year is shown as an integer from 1900 to 9999.
MONTH	MONTH(serial_number)	Returns the month of a date as a serial number. The month is shown as an integer from 1 (January) to 12 (December).
DAY	DAY(serial_number)	Returns the day of a date as a serial number. The day is shown as an integer from 1 to 31.
MATCH	MATCH(lookup_value, lookup_array,match_type)	Returns the relative position of an item in an array that matches a specified value in a specified order.
INDEX	INDEX(array,row_num, column_num)	Returns a value or the reference to a value within a table or range.
ROUND	ROUND(number, num_digits)	Rounds a value to a specified number of digits.

Summary

1. **Separate and combine text.** Converting text to columns enables you to convert information in a single column, such as a name, into two columns so the names could be sorted by both first and last name. On the other hand, if data are stored in multiple cells, you can use the CONCATENATE function to join the text strings together.

2. **Manipulate text with functions.** Functions can be used to change the case of text strings. The PROPER function capitalizes the first letter in a text string and converts remaining characters to lowercase. The UPPER function converts all letters in a text string to uppercase. The LOWER function converts all letters in a text string to lowercase. The SUBSTITUTE function substitutes new text for existing text in a text string.

3. **Identify and remove duplicate rows.** Large lists or tables might contain duplicate records. The duplicate data can cause inaccurate statistical analysis. To ensure that only unique records are contained in the table, you can remove duplicate rows. The process deletes records that are exact duplicates, yet leaves the original record.

4. **Group and subtotal data.** Grouping is a way to simplify complex worksheets. Grouping enables you to consolidate related rows or columns into single units. After you consolidate the rows or columns into a group, you can collapse the group to make it easier to view only what you want to see. The Subtotal command uses a summary function such as SUM, AVERAGE, or COUNT to compute subtotals within the data table. The records are grouped according to the value of a specific field, such as location, and the Subtotal command inserts a subtotal row where the value of the designated field changes. A grand total is displayed after the last record. The records must be in sequence by the field on which the subtotals will be grouped prior to executing the Subtotal command.

5. **Work with windows.** Often, you will have multiple workbooks open at one time. It is easy to compare the data when you can view these worksheets side by side on your screen. You can even split a large worksheet into multiple panes to view different parts of the worksheet at the same time.

6. **Use conditional functions.** When you created formulas with SUM, COUNT, and AVERAGE functions, you summed, counted, or averaged all values in a range of cells. Two sets of three functions expand the power of the SUM, COUNT, and AVERAGE functions. The first set is SUMIF, COUNTIF, and AVERAGEIF, which return the total, count, or average for one criterion. The second set of functions is SUMIFS, COUNTIFS, and AVERAGEIFS. These functions return a total, count, or average based on two criteria.

7. **Create nested IF functions.** When multiple conditions need to be evaluated to determine the correct action, you can nest functions within an IF statement. A nested IF function can include a second IF function to help evaluate multiple conditions. Other functions can also be nested in an IF function.

8. **Use AND, OR, NOT, and IFERROR functions.** These logical functions are used with conditional expressions. The AND function determines if both conditions are true, while the OR function determines if either condition is true. The NOT function reverses the value of true and false conditions, and the IFERROR function is used in error checking.

9. **Define the amortization table.** One of the most commonly used applications for Excel is to determine a payment or amortization schedule for a loan. The amortization schedule shows the date of each loan payment, the amount of each payment that goes to principal and interest, and the remaining balance, which eventually reaches zero.

10. **Use functions in amortization tables.** Several functions are available to help create amortization tables. The YEAR function returns the year for a date, the MONTH function returns the month represented by a serial number, and the DAY function returns the day represented by a serial number. You can use the MATCH function to return the relative position of an item in an array, and the INDEX function returns a value within a table. Finally, the ROUND function rounds a value to a specified number of digits.

Key Terms

Multiple Choice

1. A(n) _____ is used to display how a loan is being repaid, and displays the date, amount of principal, and amount of interest for each payment.

   (a) Template
   (b) Amortization schedule
   (c) MATCH function
   (d) AND function

2. The _____ function returns True if all its arguments are true.

   (a) MATCH
   (b) IF
   (c) INDEX
   (d) AND

3. All of the following are required arguments to the DATE function except:

   (a) The cell containing the date
   (b) The year portion of the date
   (c) The month portion of the date
   (d) The day portion of the date

4. All of the following are required arguments for the MATCH function except:

   (a) The value you are looking up
   (b) The cell range you are looking in
   (c) The number of rows in the cell range you are looking in
   (d) The type of match

5. Cell G12 contains the date 12/19/2008. Which of the following will return the date 1/19/2009?

   (a) =DATE(YEAR(G12),MONTH(G12)+1,DAY(G12))
   (b) =DATE(YEAR(G12)+1,MONTH(G12)+1,DAY(G12))
   (c) =G12 + MONTH(1)
   (d) =MONTH(G12)+1

6. The INDEX function returns:

   (a) The position in a list where a match occurs
   (b) The number of cells in the list
   (c) The cell in the list that contains the desired value
   (d) The value in the cell being looked up

7. The MATCH function returns:

   (a) The cell in the list where a match occurs
   (b) The number of cells in the list
   (c) The position in a list where a match occurs
   (d) The column in the list that contains the desired value

8. The _____ function shows the amount of a loan payment that is applied towards principal repayment.

   (a) PMT
   (b) PPMT
   (c) MATCH
   (d) IPMT

9. Assume that cell E12 contains the date February 26, 2008. Which of the following will display the date February 25, 2008?

   (a) =DATE(E12) – 1
   (b) =DATE(YEAR(E12), MONTH(E12), DAY(E12)–1)
   (c) =DATE(YEAR(E12), MONTH(E12), DAY(E12–1))
   (d) =DATE(YEAR(E12)–1, MONTH(E12)–1, DAY(E12)–1)

10. You created a workbook on December 12, 2007, and entered the Today() function in cell B5. You modified and saved the workbook on December 19, 2007. On January 3, 2008, you opened the workbook again. What is displayed in cell B5?

    (a) December 19, 2007
    (b) December 12, 2007
    (c) January 3, 2008
    (d) It depends on how you created the Today() function.

11. The IPMT function returns the amount of a(n):

    (a) Periodic payment
    (b) Periodic payment that is applied towards principal
    (c) Periodic payment that is applied towards interest
    (d) Extra payment

12. The primary benefit of using the ROUND function rather than formatting values as currency is:

    (a) Ease of working with fractional numbers
    (b) Increases precision in numbers
    (c) Easier to use than the number format
    (d) Gives you less control when copying values

13. Which of the following statements is true?

(a) The Delete command can be used to delete a record, but not a field.

(b) The Delete command erases the contents of the selected area, but does not delete it.

(c) The Delete command can be used to delete either a record or a field.

(d) The Delete command can be used to delete a field, but not a record.

14. You have created a named range called MyCDs that is equivalent to the range A1:E19. What is the extent of the range if you subsequently delete row 1 and delete column C?

(a) A1:D18

(b) A1:E19

(c) A1:E18

(d) A1:D19

15. Which of the following causes a named range to be adjusted automatically?

(a) Inserting a row within the range

(b) Deleting a row within the range

(c) Either inserting or deleting a row within the range

(d) Neither inserting nor deleting a row within the range

16. Which of the following enables you to create several named ranges at once?

(a) The Insert Name Define command

(b) The Insert Name Create command

(c) The Name Box

(d) The Go To command

Your work as Event Coordinator with the state medical society enables you to demonstrate your expertise with Excel. The workbook shown in Figure 6.42 is the completed list of donors to the medical society major fund-raising event. You will convert name text to columns, remove duplicate records, use conditional functions, subtotal data, create a chart, and view the results in several different window arrangements.

a. Open the *chap6_pe1_donations* workbook and save it as **chap6_pe1_donations_ solution** so that you can return to the original workbook if necessary.

b. Convert text to columns for column B by completing the following tasks:

- Right-click **column C** and select **Insert** to insert a new column.

- Select **cells B3:B31** and click **Text to Columns** in the Data Tools group on the Data tab to start the Convert Text to Columns Wizard.

- Verify that **Delimited** is selected in the *Original data type* section and click **Next**.

- Click the **Space check box**, remove the check from the **Tab check box** in the *Delimiter* section, and click **Next**.

- Verify that **General** is selected in the *Column Data Format* section, that **Destination is $B$3**, that Data Preview is correct, and then click **Finish**.

- Type **First Name** in cell B2 and type **Last Name** in **cell C2**.

c. Convert text to columns for column E using the following specifications:

- Right-click **column F** and select **Insert** from the menu to insert a new column. Repeat the step to insert a second column.

- Select **cells E3:E31** and click **Text to Columns** in the Data Tools group on the Data tab to launch the Convert Text to Columns Wizard.

- Verify that **Delimited** is selected in the *Original data type* section and click **Next**.

- Click the **Space check box** and click **Next**.

- Verify that **General** is selected in the *Column Data Format* section, that **Destination** is **$E$3**, that Data Preview is correct, and then click **Finish**.

- Type **State** in **cell F2** and type **Zip Code** in **cell G2**.

- Click the **Select All** box to select the entire worksheet, click **Format** in the Cells group on the Home tab, and click **AutoFit Column Width**.

d. Remove duplicate rows by completing the following tasks:

- Click **column B** to select it.

- Click **Remove Duplicates** in the Data Tools group of the Data tab.

- Verify that **Expand the selection** is selected in the Remove Duplicates Warning box and click **Remove Duplicates**.

- Click **Unselect All**, click the **DonorID check box**, verify that the **My data has headers check box** is selected, and click **OK**.

- Click **OK** to verify the deletion of 4 rows with 26 unique remaining.

...continued on Next Page

e. Create a SUMIF function that determines the total of product contributions by completing the following tasks:

- Click in **cell B35**, then click **Insert Function** in the Functions group on the Formulas tab to open the Insert function dialog box.

- Type **SUMIF** in the **Search for a function** text box, click **Go**, click **SUMIF** in the **Select a function** list, and click **OK** to display the Function Arguments dialog box.

- Type **J30** in the **Range** box, **Product** in the **Criteria**, and **K3:K30** in the **Sum_range** box. Click **OK**.

f. Create a SUMIFS function to determine the total of product contributions greater than $400 by completing the following:

- Click in **cell E35**, then click **Insert Function** in the Functions group to open the Insert Function dialog box.

- Type **SUMIFS** in the **Search for a function** text box, click **Go**, click **SUMIFS** in **the Select a function** list, and click **OK**.

- Enter the following in the Function Arguments dialog box: **K3:K30** in the **Sum_range** box, **J3:J30** in the **Criteria_range1** box, **Product** in the **Criteria1** box, **K3:K30** in the **Criteria_range2** box, and **>400** in the **Criteria2** box. Click **OK**.

- Format **cell E35** as **Currency** with **0** decimal places.

g. Create an AVERAGEIFS function to determine the average value of the restaurant gift certificates by completing the following tasks:

- Click in **cell B38** and click **Insert Function** in the Functions group on the Formulas tab to open the Insert function dialog box.

- Type **AVERAGEIFS** in the **Search for a function** text box, click **Go**, click **AVERAGEIFS** in the **Select a function list**, and click **OK**.

- Enter the following in the Function Arguments dialog box: **K3:K30** in the **Average_range** box, **J3:J30** in the **Criteria_range1** box, **Gift Certificate** in the **Criteria1** box, **I3:I30** in the **Criteria_range2** box, and **Restaurant Gift Certificate** in the **Criteria2** box. Click **OK**.

h. Create an AVERAGEIF function to determine the average value of the service donations by completing the following tasks:

- Click in **cell E38**, then click **Insert Function** in the Functions group to open the Insert function dialog box.

- Type **AVERAGEIF** in the **Search for a function** text box, click **Go**, click **AVERAGEIF** in the **Select a function** list, and click **OK**.

- Enter the following in the Function Arguments dialog box: **J3:J30** in the **Range** box, **Service** in the **Criteria** box, and **K3:K30** in the **Average_range** box. Click **OK**.

- Format **cell E38** as **Currency** with **0** decimal places.

i. Create a COUNTIF function to determine the number of service items donated by completing the following tasks:

- Click in **cell B41**, then click **Insert Function** in the Functions group on the Formulas tab to open the Insert function dialog box.

- Type **COUNTIF** in the **Search for a function** text box, click **Go**, click **COUNTIF** in the **Select a function** list, and click **OK**.

- Enter the following in the Function Arguments dialog box: **J3:J30** in the **Range** box and **Service** in the **Criteria** box. Click **OK** and format **cells B35** and **B38** as **Currency**.

…continued on Next Page

j. Create a COUNTIFS function to determine the number of gift certificates valued at more than $50 by completing the following tasks:

- Click in **cell E41** and click **Insert Function** in the Functions group to open the Insert Function dialog box.

- Type **COUNTIFS** in the **Search for a function** text box, click **Go**, click **COUNTIFS** in the **Select a function** list, and click **OK**.

- Enter the following in the Function Arguments dialog box: **J3:J30** in the **Criteria_range1** box, **Gift Certificate** in the **Criteria1** box, **K3:K30** in the **Criteria_range2** box, and **>50** in the **Criteria2** box. Click **OK**.

k. Subtotal the data using the following specifications:

- Click in **column J**, click the **Data tab**, and click **Sort A to Z** in the Sort & Filter group.

- Click **cell K3** and click **Subtotal** in the Outline group to open the Subtotal dialog box.

- Click the **At a change in drop-down arrow**, then select **Category**.

- Verify that the **Use function** is set to **Sum**.

- Uncheck **Category** and check **ItemValue** in the *Add subtotal to* section.

- Verify that the **Replace current subtotals check box** is checked.

- Verify that the **Summary below data check box** is checked.

- Click **OK**.

l. Split the worksheet window by completing the following tasks:

- Click **Split** in the Window group on the View tab and drag the vertical splitter to the left until it disappears.

- Drag the **horizontal splitter** to just below **row 2**.

- Click **Split** again to return to the original single window.

m. Group and ungroup data by completing the following tasks:

- Click the **minus symbol** to the left of **rows 11**, **16**, **26**, and **31**.

- Click the **minus symbol** to the left of **row 32**.

n. Create a chart:

- Click the **plus symbol** to the left of row 32.

- Select **cells J11:K31**, click **Bar** in the Chart group on the Insert tab, and click **Clustered Bar** from the Chart Gallery.

o. To enhance the bar chart:

- Click **Style 14** in the Chart Styles group on the Design tab.

- Click **Layout tab**, click **Chart Title** in the Labels group, and select **Above Chart**.

- Type **Donations** and press **Enter**.

- Click **Legend** and select **None** to remove the legend.

p. Click **Move Chart** in the Location group on the Design tab, select **New sheet** in the Move Chart dialog box, type **Graph**, and click **OK**.

...continued on Next Page

q. View multiple windows by completing the following tasks:

- While viewing the bar chart, click **New Window** in the Window group on the View tab.

- Click **Arrange All** in the Window group, click **Horizontal** in the Arrange Windows dialog box, and click **OK**.

- Click the **Sheet1 tab** in the top window to view the worksheet in that window with the chart in the second window below.

r. Create a custom footer that includes your name, a page number, and your instructor's name. Print the worksheet as displayed and with formulas visible. Save, print, and close the workbook.

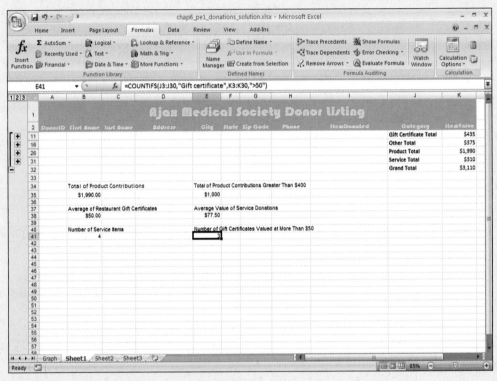

Figure 6.42 Medical Society Fundraiser

2 Finding the Month and Day

The workbook in Figure 6.43 illustrates the table lookup function in conjunction with date functions. You will create the workbook and use functions to determine the month and day of the week for a given birth date.

a. Create a new workbook:

- Open a blank workbook.

- Click in cell **A1**, type **Finding the Month and Day**, and merge and center the title over **cells A1:D1**.

- Click in cell **A3** and type your birth date.

- Click in cell **A4** and type **You were born on a**.

- Click in cell **C4** and type **in the month of**.

...continued on Next Page

- Click in **cell B3** and type your birth date in the form **MM/DD/YYYY** to test your formulas.

- Click in **cell A9**, type **1**, press **Enter**, type **2**, and then use AutoFill to enter the numbers shown in Figure 6.43.

- Click in **cell B9**, type **Sunday**, press **Enter**, and use AutoFill enter the days of the week.

- Click in **cell C9**, type **1**, press **Enter**, type **2**, and then use AutoFill to enter the numbers shown in Figure 6.43.

- Click in **cell D9**, type **January**, press **Enter**, and use AutoFill enter the months of the year.

b. Name the ranges:

- Click in **cell B3**, click **Name Manager** in **the Defined Names** group on the Formulas tab, and click **New** in the Name Manager dialog box.

- Type **birthdate** in the **Name** text box, verify that Workbook appears in **Scope** and that =Sheet1!$B$3 appears in **Refers to**, and click **OK** to return to the Name Manager dialog box.

- Click **New**, type **DayofWeek**, click in the **Refers to** box, select **cells A9:B15**, and click **OK** to return to the Name Manager dialog box.

- Click **New**, type **MonthofYear**, click in the **Refers to** box, select **cells C9:D20**, and click **OK** to return to the Name Manager dialog box.

- Click **Close** to close Name Manager dialog box.

c. Click in **cell B8** and type the formula **=IF(Birthdate<>"",WEEKDAY(B3),"")**. You used an IF function with a variation of the DAY function to determine the day of the week on which you were born.

d. Click in **cell D8** and type the formula **=IF(Birthdate<>"",MONTH(B3),"")**. You used an IF function with a variation of the MONTH function to determine the month in which you were born.

e. Click in **cell B4** and type the formula **=IF(Birthdate<>"",VLOOKUP(B8,DayofWeek,2),"")**.

f. Click in **cell D4** and type **=IF(Birthdate<>"",VLOOKUP(D8,MonthofYear,2),"")**.

g. Create a custom footer that includes your name, today's date, and your instructor's name. Print the worksheet as displayed and with formulas visible. Save and close the workbook.

...continued on Next Page

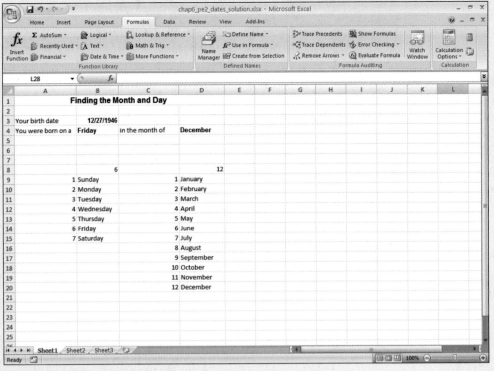

Figure 6.43 Display Birth Day and Month

3 Pay Off Your Credit Card

You have found that during your college years you have run up considerable credit card debt. In an effort to discharge this debt, you have resolved to pay it all off. The workbook in Figure 6.44 resembles the amortization table completed in Hands-On Exercise 4 except the interest is much higher. Refer to Figure 6.44 as you complete the exercise.

a. Open the *chap6_pe3_debt* workbook and save it as **chap6_pe3_debt_solution**.

b. Drag the clip art out of the way, click in **cell D7** and type =AND(C5>0,C6>0,C7>0,OR(C4>0,C8>0)). Drag the clip art back into place.

c. Type the parameters shown in Figure 6.44 into **cells C4:C7**.

d. Click **Name Manager** in the **Defined Names** group on the **Formulas tab** to see the ranges that are already named in the workbook. You will use these in your formulas. Close the dialog box.

e. Create the formulas for the first payment beginning in row 14:

- Click in **cell A14** and type =IF(DataEntered,1,0).

- Click in **cell B14** and type =IF(A14>0,C6,0). Format **cell B14** as Short Date.

- Click in **cell C14** and type =IF(A14>0,C4,0).

- Click in **cell D14** and type =IF(A14>0,($C$5/12)*C14,0). The interest is charged on the unpaid balance at the beginning of the period.

- Click in **cell E14** and type =IF(A14>0,$C$8,0).

- Click in **cell F14** and type =IF(A14>0,D14+$C$7*(C14+E14),0). The minimum payment is the interest due plus the minimum percent required by the credit card company, which is computed on the initial balance plus the new charges.

- Click in **cell G14** and type =IF(A14>0,$C$9,0).

...continued on Next Page

- Click in cell **H14** and type **=IF(A14>0,C14+D14+E14-F14-G14,0)**.

- Format **cells C14:H14** as Currency and verify that your results match Figure 6.44.

f. Create the formulas for the second payment:

- Click in **cell A15** and type **=IF(H14>0,A14+1,0)**.

- Click in **cell B15** and type **=IF(A15>0,DATE(YEAR(B14),MONTH(B14)+1,DAY(B14)),0)** to compute the date of the next payment. Format **cell B15** as Short Date.

- Click in **cell C15** and type **=IF(A15>0,H14,0)**. Format **cell C15** as Currency.

- Copy the formulas from **cells D14:H14** to **cells D15:H15**.

- Copy **cells A15:H15** to the remaining payments (through row 193, where you see payment 180).

g. Click the **Office Button**, click **Excel Options**, and click **Advanced** to view Advanced Options for Working with Excel.

h. Scroll through the options to see *Display options for this worksheet* and remove the check from **Show a zero in cells that have zero value**, then click **OK**.

i. Create a custom footer that includes your name, today's date, and your instructor's name. Select **cells A1:H19** and print the selection as displayed with formulas visible. Save and close the workbook.

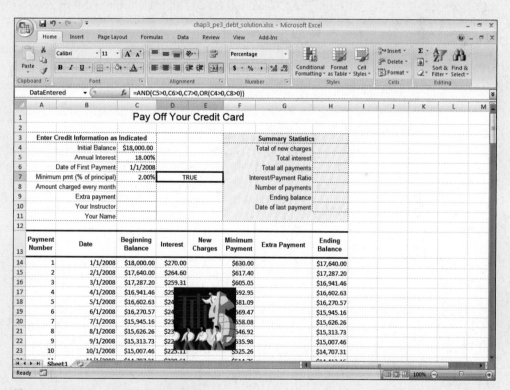

Figure 6.44 Credit Card Debt

...continued on Next Page

This exercise continues the development of the credit card worksheet by computing the summary information. Figure 6.45 shows the completed summary information which you will use for reference.

a. Open the completed workbook, *chap6_pe3_debt_solution*, from the previous exercise and save it as **chap6_pe4_debt_solution**.

b. Select **cell G13**, click **Unmerge Cells** in the Alignment group, type **Extra Payment** in **cell G13**, and type **Ending Balance** in **cell H13**.

c. Click in **cell C9** and type **$25.00** for the extra payment you feel you can make to pay the debt off early.

d. Type the following formulas in the summary area beginning with **cell H4**:

- Click in **cell H4** and type **=SUM(NewCharges)**. The range name has already been defined in the workbook. An IF statement is not required in the formula because zero values are suppressed.

- Click in **cell H5** and type **=SUM(Interest)**.

- Click in **cell H6** and type **=SUM(MinimumPayment,ExtraPayment)**.

- Click in **cell H7** and type **=IF(H6>0,H5/H6,0)**.

- Click in **cell H8** and type the formula shown in Figure 6.45 to compute the number of payments. The nested IF calculates the number of payments only if all of the data have been entered. The range name EndingBalance refers to the balance after the 180th payment when the table ends; that is, if a zero balance is not reached at this point, there are 180 payments.

- Click in **cell H9** and type **=IF(H8>0,INDEX(PaymentTable,H8,8),0)**.

- Click in **cell H10** and type **=IF(H8>0,INDEX(PaymentTable,H8,2),"")**.

e. Click in **cell H11** and type a formula to determine if you are still in debt, or are debt free: **=IF(DataEntered,IF(H9<=0,"Congratulations, you are debt free!","You are still in debt!"),"")**. You should see the values in Figure 6.45.

f. Create a custom footer that includes your name, a page number, and your instructor's name. Print the worksheet as displayed and with formulas visible.

g. Save and close the workbook.

...continued on Next Page

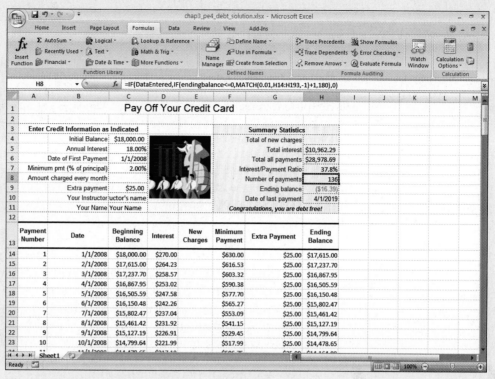

Figure 6.45 Credit Card Debt Continued

Mid-Level Exercises

1 Nix Mortgage Corporation Salary Analysis

Congratulations, you have been awarded a summer internship position with the Nix Mortgage Corporation. Your summer internship assignment is to open the partially completed workbook and complete it to match Figure 6.46. The workbook in Figure 6.46 is used to analyze employee salary with respect to job title. The corporation is considering downsizing, and your boss asked you to prepare a summary showing the total salaries of the managers and account reps. He wants to know the total salary of the account reps working in Miami and the total salary of the managers working in Boston. He also wants to know how many employees might be affected in Chicago and Atlanta. Further, he wants a report of the average salary by location and a chart to show visually the average salary for the job titles.

a. Open the *chap6_mid1_salary* workbook and save it as **chap6_mid1_salary_solution** so you can return to the original workbook if necessary. Sort the data by job title. This is the first step required to prepare the summary report. Create range names for all columns of data in the worksheet.

b. Use conditional functions to determine the total salary of all managers, the average salary of the account reps, the number of employees working in Chicago, the total salary of the account reps working in Miami, the average salary of the managers working in Boston, and the number of trainees working in Atlanta. Format appropriate values as Currency with 2 decimal places.

c. Click anywhere in the data and create a subtotal report showing the salary totals for each job title. Make sure you subtotal when Title changes, use the SUM function, and subtotal on Salary. The resulting summary report did not give you the data required by your boss.

d. Sort the data by city, and then create a subtotal that shows average salary by city. Make sure you subtotal when Location changes, use the AVERAGE function, and subtotal on Salary.

e. Reduce the report displayed to display just the city average salaries. Use this data to create a pie chart displayed on a separate sheet. Make sure you include a title, data labels, and a legend on your chart.

f. Make all the data visible on Sheet1 and create a new window for this data. Arrange your windows vertically.

g. Create a custom footer that includes your name, today's date, and your instructor's name. Print the worksheet as displayed and with formulas visible. Close the workbook.

...continued on Next Page

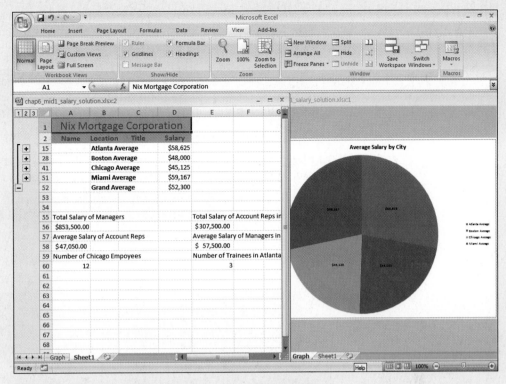

Figure 6.46 NIX Mortgage Corporation Salary Analysis

2 Nested IFs and Other Functions

As a graduate assistant, you are tasked with maintaining your professor's grade book. Dr. Smith decided to drop the lowest test grade if the student has taken all five exams. Students are allowed to take the course for credit only and, thus, the formula to compute the semester grade must determine whether the student elected this option, and if so, whether the student has passed. Figure 6.47 shows the completed version of a grade book that uses a variety of Excel functions. These functions are used individually and in conjunction with one another. This challenging exercise provides you with the opportunity to practice and apply your skill with the text-to-columns operation, concatenate functions, nested IFs, and other functions.

a. Open the *chap6_mid2_gradebook* workbook and save it as **chap6_mid2_gradebook_solution**.

b. Click in **cell A4** and freeze panes.

c. Join students' names—last name, comma, first name—in column A, and then delete column B.

d. Use the appropriate command to separate the test scores in column C to columns C through G and suppress the zeros in the columns.

e. Click in **cell G4** and type the formula to compute the student's test average, and drop the lowest grade if the student has taken all five exams.

The professor also wants you to round the calculated average. Alex Pons, for example, would get a C rather than a B if his average were not rounded. Click in **cell H4** and enter the function that rounds the student's score to zero decimal places. The zero indicates the number of decimal places in the rounded number.

...continued on Next Page

f. Create a formula in cells J3 through J18 that calculates the students' grade and displays the word *Pass* when students are taking the course for credit only and pass.

g. Use the Rank function to determine each student's rank in class according to the computed value of his or her semester average. Use Help to learn how to enter the Rank function.

h. Copy the formulas in row 4 to the remaining rows in the worksheet.

i. Calculate the summary statistics for each exam, as shown in rows 21 through 25.

j. Use the COUNTIF function to determine the grade distribution. The entry in cell K22, for example, is COUNTIF($J$4:$J$19,"=F").

k. Format the worksheet in attractive fashion, as shown in Figure 6.47. You are required to use conditional formatting to display grades of A and F in blue and red, respectively.

l. Create a custom footer that includes your name, today's date, and your instructor's name. Print the worksheet as displayed and with formulas visible. Close the workbook.

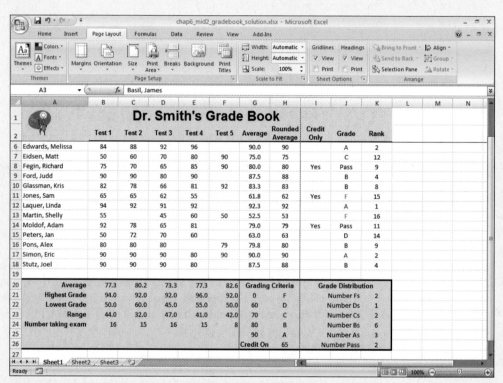

Figure 6.47 Professor's Grade Book

...continued on Next Page

Your father, the owner of The Golf Shoppe, asked for your help with Excel. He recently purchased a new dump truck and wants to create an amortization schedule to see what his monthly payments will be for the life of the loan. The final amortization table is shown in Figure 6.48 and should be used as you complete this exercise.

a. Open the *chap6_mid3_dumptruck* workbook and save it as **chap6_mid3_dumptruck_solution**. Enter the loan parameters, as shown in the table below:

Principal	50000
Annual Interest	8%
Date of First Payment	2/1/2008
Term of Loan (years)	4
Your Last Name	Your name
Purpose of Loan	Truck Loan

b. Enter formulas in **cell G4** and **cell G5** to calculate the monthly payment and the total number of monthly payments. Enter formulas in row 13 for the first payment.

c. Create and type IF functions in **cell C7**, **cell A13**, **cell B13**, **cell C13**, **cell G4**, and **cell G5**. These IF formulas prevent an error message from displaying before all data is entered in the worksheet.

d. Type the formulas in row 14 for the second payment. Hint: These are IF functions that show second payment information only if there is a balance after the first payment.

e. Complete the payment schedule for the life of the loan or when there is a zero balance.

f. Change the annual interest rate and the term of the loan to see the changes made to the amortization schedule.

g. Create a custom footer that includes your name, a page number, and your instructor's name. Select the first 20 rows of the worksheet and print the selection as displayed and with formulas visible. Close the workbook.

...continued on Next Page

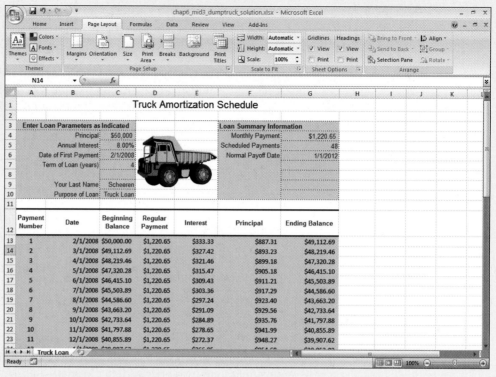

Figure 6.48 The Golf Shoppe Dump Truck Amortization

4 Planning for Retirement

Compound interest is called the eighth wonder of the world. It can work against you, as in the case of credit card and other debt. It works in your favor if you are able to save periodically toward retirement, especially when you begin saving at an early age. The best time to start is when you begin your first job, because the longer your money is invested, the more time it has to grow. Assume, for example, that you begin saving $25 a week at age 22 and that you continue to save for 45 years until you reach age 67, the regular retirement age under Social Security. Let us further assume that you earn an annual return of 8%, which is the historic rate of return for a broad-based investment in the stock market. When you retire, you will have contributed a total of $58,500, but your money will have grown to more than $540,000. The compound interest you earned on your money accounts for almost 90% of your nest egg. Let us say that you delay for 10 years and that all other parameters are the same. Your total contribution is $45,500 ($13,000 less), but your nest egg will be only $241,000, less than half of what you would have had if you had contributed the additional 10 years. Use Figure 6.49 for reference as you complete the retirement worksheet. The summary portion of the worksheet is complete; all of the formulas have already been entered. You will enter the parameters in the blue-shaded input area, **cells C4:C8**, to see your retirement projection.

a. Open the *chap6_mid4_retirement* workbook and save it as **chap6_mid4_retirement_solution**. Enter the required data in **cells C4:C8**, as shown in Figure 6.49.

b. Enter the appropriate formulas to complete the amortization schedule for **cells C11:G55**. Hint: Some formulas involve the use of functions while others are simple formulas.

...continued on Next Page

c. Format values as **Currency** with zero decimals, **Percentages** with two decimals, and dates as **Short Dates** where appropriate.

d. Create a custom footer that includes your name, a page number, and your instructor's name. Select the first 20 rows of the worksheet and print the selection as displayed and with formulas visible. Close the workbook.

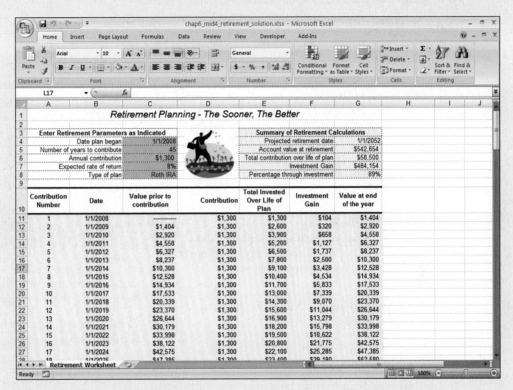

Figure 6.49 Retirement Planning

Capstone Exercise

As the owner of the JAS Bakery, you are a jack of all trades. You develop the recipes, make the recipes, market your baked goods, and manage the business. Your business has been very successful, and you are now considering an expansion of your business. In this exercise, you are going to modify your customer list, analyze your sales totals for the past year, and prepare an amortization schedule for the loan you are applying for that will allow you to expand.

Open and Save the Worksheet

You must open a workbook that contains three worksheets: customers, product sales, and a sheet that will contain the amortization schedule.

a. Open the file *chap6_cap_bakery*.

b. Save it as **chap6_cap_bakery_solution**.

Manipulate the Customer List

You have collected data about your customers, but the data is not in a form that you can sort or search in any meaningful way. You have duplicate records and must sort on last name as well as zip code.

a. Use the Excel feature to help you identify and remove duplicate records.

b. Use the appropriate feature to separate the first and last names into two columns.

c. Use the appropriate feature to separate the city, state, and zip code in column D into separate columns. Remember to insert columns to accommodate the expanded data.

d. Sort the customer list by last name in alphabetical order.

e. Insert a title for your customer list, add column headings, and format the worksheet in a professional fashion. Create a custom footer that includes your name, a page number, and your instructor's name.

Summarize Sales Data

You must provide a financial summary and will create a summary report of your sales for the year. Your goal is to determine which month has the best sales.

a. Click the Product Sales sheet tab to review your sales data. Insert an appropriate title at the top of the worksheet.

b. Use the Subtotal command to average annual product sales.

c. Use the Subtotal command to total sales by month.

d. Format the worksheet to highlight the monthly totals.

e. Create a custom footer that includes your name, a page number, and your instructor's name.

Create a Loan Amortization

The bakery is doing well and you want to expand your facility to better serve your customers and to increase profits. To do this, you want to secure a small business loan to expand the bakery facility. You will use the BusinessLoan sheet to complete the amortization schedule to see what your monthly payment will be, how many monthly payments you must make, the date of the final payment, and total of all interest payments.

a. Create the formulas to determine Monthly Payment, the number of Scheduled Payments, and the Payoff Date. These formulas involve the use of nested IFs.

b. Create a formula in **cell D6** to suppress zeros throughout the worksheet.

c. Create the appropriate formulas in **cells A13:G13** for the first payment.

d. Create the appropriate formulas in **cells A14:G14** for the second payment. Hint: You cannot copy all formulas.

e. Copy **cells A14:G14** through **cells A72:G72**.

f. Format all cells with the appropriate format for dates, percents, and currency.

Print the Workbook

Before printing the reports, you see they are missing the standard footers. Create a custom footer that contains your name, page number, and your instructor's name. Print the completed workbook.

a. Select the CustomerList, ProductSales, and BusinessLoan sheet tabs and create a custom footer with your name on the left, the page number in the middle, and your instructor's name on the right.

b. Change the page orientation to landscape.

c. Print the workbook with displayed values.

d. Save your changes and close the workbook.

Mini Cases

Use the rubric following the case as a guide to evaluate your work, but keep in mind that your instructor may impose additional grading criteria or use a different standard to judge your work.

Upper Saddle River Gallery

GENERAL CASE

As the owner of the Upper Saddle River Gallery, you must calculate information about the collection. Specifically, you need the value of all oil paintings, the average acquisition data of all paintings, the number of charcoal works, the value of watercolor pieces purchased after 1940, the insurance value of oil paintings greater than 30 inches in height, and the number of acrylic paintings purchased since 1945. You also want to divide the artist names into two columns so you can search on last name only. Open the *chap6_mc1_art* workbook and save it as **chap6_mc1_art_solution**. Your assignment is to open the workbook and use appropriate conditional functions to calculate the required information.

Performance Elements	Exceeds Expectations	Meets Expectations	Below Expectations
Text manipulation	Labeled names in two columns.	Names in two columns.	Names not separated.
Conditional functions	Three completed.	Two completed.	One or none completed.
Conditional functions with more than one criterion	Three completed.	Two completed.	One or none completed.

Celebrity Birthdays

RESEARCH CASE

You will use the workbook *chap6_mc2_celebrities* to compare your age to that of several celebrities. The finished workbook will be a sophisticated spreadsheet using a nested IF function and conditional formatting. Open the partially completed version, *chap6_mc2_celebrities*, and use the Web to locate the birth date of the listed celebrities. You may want to begin your search at birthdays.celebehoo.com. Row C will contain the formula to calculate the amount the celebrity is older or younger than you. Column D will contain a formula to determine the difference in your ages. Column E will have a formula that produces the word *years*. Save your workbook as **chap6_mc2_celebrities_solution**.

Performance Elements	Exceeds Expectations	Meets Expectations	Below Expectations
Research birth dates for celebrities	Identified 17 birth dates.	Identified 14 birth dates.	Identified fewer than 14 birth dates.
Correct function in column C	Yes.	Yes.	No.
Correct formula in column D	Yes.	Yes.	No.
Calculation of your age	Completed using a formula.	Typed age (no formula used).	No entry.

Your volunteer service learning project involves tutoring students in Excel. Open the spreadsheet *chap6_mc3_sales* and save it as **chap6_mc3_sales_solution**. You will find four major errors in subtotals, duplicate names, and page break anomalies. Correct the errors and explain how the errors might have occurred and how they can be prevented. Include your explanation in the cells below the spreadsheet.

Performance Elements	Exceeds Expectations	Meets Expectations	Below Expectations
Identify four errors	Identified all four errors.	Identified three errors.	Identified two or fewer errors.
Correct four errors	Corrected all four errors.	Corrected three errors.	Corrected two or fewer errors.
Explain the error	Complete and correct explanation of each error.	Explanation is too brief to fully explain error.	No explanations.
Prevention description	Prevention description correct and practical.	Prevention description but obtuse.	No prevention description.

Data Consolidation, Links, and Formula Auditing

Worksheet References, File Linking, and Auditing Formulas

bjectives

After you read this chapter, you will be able to:

1. Consolidate data from multiple worksheets **(page 687)**.

2. Define the three-dimensional workbook **(page 688)**.

3. Create three-dimensional formulas **(page 692)**.

4. Link workbooks **(page 704)**.

5. Create the documentation worksheet **(page 706)**.

6. Restrict values to a drop-down list **(page 716)**.

7. Validate data **(page 717)**.

8. Audit formulas **(page 719)**.

9. Set up a Watch Window **(page 722)**.

Hands-On Exercises

Exercises	Skills Covered
1. CONSOLIDATING BEST RESTAURANT CORPORATE SALES (page 696) **Open:** chap7_ho1_new_york.xlsx, chap7_ho1_chicago.xlsx, and chap7_ho1_philadelphia.xlsx **Save as:** chap7_ho1_summary_solution.xlsx	• Begin a New Workbook and Open Individual Workbooks • Copy Workbook Data • Verify the Copy Procedure • Insert a Worksheet • Create a 3-D Formula • Arrange Windows and Change Data • Edit Grouped Worksheets • Format Grouped Worksheets
2. CONSOLIDATING WORKBOOKS FOR CORPORATE SALES AND ADDING DOCUMENTATION (page 710) **Open:** chap7_ho2_new_york.xlsx, chap7_ho2_chicago.xlsx, and chap7_ho2_philadelphia.xlsx **Save as:** chap7_ho2_linking_solution.xlsx	• Open the Workbooks and Use AutoFill • Link Files and Copy Cell Formulas • Change the Data • Work with Comments and Documentation Worksheets
3. JAS MANUFACTURING (page 723) **Open:** chap7_ho3_jas.xlsx **Save as:** chap7_ho3_jas_solution.xlsx	• Trace Precedents • Audit a Region's Quarterly Sales and Remove Cell Error Indicators • Correct a Cell Formula and Trace a Cell's Dependents • Use Error Checking • Create a Watch Window • Validate Data

CASE STUDY

Judy's Luxury Ice Cream Shoppe

Judy's Luxury Ice Cream Shoppe offers old-fashioned, homemade ice cream in a comfortable setting that has a strong appeal to young families. The first store was opened three years ago in Madison, Wisconsin. Everyone loves ice cream, and the store was an instant hit. Two other stores in other Wisconsin communities quickly followed, both with similar success.

Judy Scheeren, the owner of Judy's Luxury Ice Cream Shoppe, has received an unsolicited offer to sell the three stores. Judy has bigger plans, however, and wants to expand further before selling out at what she hopes will be a much better price. She knows that she needs

Case Study

to evaluate the overall performance of the chain before opening additional stores, and thus she is especially interested in the comparative results of the various ice cream products she sells. Each store in the three cities sells the same variety of ice cream products, and each store maintains its own spreadsheet reflecting store sales by quarter.

Each store manager has entered the sales data for last year in a separate workbook. Because of your experience as an Excel consultant, Judy hired you to consolidate sales data to assist her in making an informed decision.

Your Assignment

- Read the chapter carefully and pay close attention to data consolidation, workbook linking, and formula auditing topics that demonstrate the techniques you will use to complete the case study.

- Consolidate the data into a single workbook that shows the total sales for each quarter and each ice cream category. The information should be shown in spreadsheet form as well as in graphical form. Create a drop-down list to choose from three cities, and include an appropriate input message and error message. You will create a summary workbook with multiple worksheets, one for each store location, a summary, a chart, and a documentation sheet. After consolidating the data, determine which store has the highest quarterly sales and which store has the lowest quarterly sales.

- Use the Formula Auditing tools on the Formulas tab to verify all of your formulas. Accurate financial information is a major concern to Judy as she will use your results to expand her business. Verify and change any formatting to make a consistent appearance among all worksheets and the chart.

- Begin by opening and reviewing the completed workbooks for the individual stores: *chap7_case_madison*, *chap7_case_milwaukee*, and *chap7_case_greenbay*. The *chap7_case_summary* workbook is partially complete and will become the final workbook.

- Print the completed summary workbook for Judy, your supervisor, to show both displayed values and cell formulas. Print the associated chart as well as the documentation sheet. Save the workbook as **chap7_case_summary_solution**.

Data Consolidation

Some of the most powerful tools in Excel are those that enable you to consolidate data from more than one workbook or more than one worksheet within a workbook into either a summary workbook or a summary worksheet. If you are the marketing manager for a national corporation and want each branch manager to report to you on a quarterly basis, you would need to consolidate the data received in some meaningful way, such as on a consolidated spreadsheet. You would then analyze the data, perhaps comparing product sales from each city. Which city has the greatest or lowest sales? Which product is the best-selling product? This situation is depicted graphically in Figure 7.1. This figure shows separate reports for Chicago, Philadelphia, and New York, all leading to a summary report for the corporation. Once a workbook is consolidated, you have the summary as well as the detailed spreadsheets available in one workbook.

(Which city has the greatest or lowest sales? Which product is the best-selling product?)

In this section, you consolidate data from multiple worksheets into one workbook, work with three-dimensional references, and control calculations in workbooks.

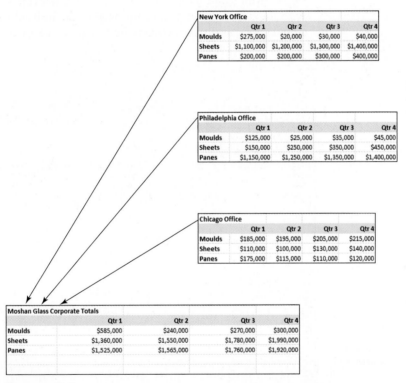

Figure 7.1 Consolidating Data from Multiple Worksheets

Consolidating Data from Multiple Worksheets

You are able to reconcile corporate totals for each product in each quarter with the amounts provided by each branch office. For example, consider the sales of moulds in the first quarter. The Chicago office sold $185,000, the Philadelphia office $125,000, and the New York office $275,000. The corporation sold a total of $585,000 worth of moulds during the first quarter ($185,000 + $125,000 + $275,000 = $585,000). The New York, Philadelphia, and Chicago offices sold $1,100,000, $150,000, and $110,000 worth of sheets in the first quarter, for a corporation total of $1,360,000.

Another example of the value of data consolidation would be in the creation of an extensive grade book for a professor. Each class would have a separate workbook and each student would have a separate worksheet within the workbook. The professor then creates a summary worksheet that summarizes the entire class's performance during the course. In this case, the professor might use averages rather than sums in the consolidated worksheet. Businesses with 5 to 10 employees use data consolidation for payroll, with each sheet representing one employee. Collectively, the workbook is the payroll workbook.

Chapter 7 presents two ways to consolidate the Moshan Glass corporate totals data shown in Figure 7.1. One way is to use the three-dimensional capabilities of Excel, where one workbook contains multiple worksheets. The workbook contains a separate worksheet for each branch and a summary worksheet that holds the consolidated corporate data. Another way to accomplish this is to maintain the data for each branch office in separate workbooks and create a summary workbook that uses file linking to reference cells in the other workbooks. Advantages and disadvantages for each technique are discussed in the chapter.

Defining the Three-Dimensional Workbook

The workbook shown in Figure 7.2 contains four worksheets. The title bar displays the name of the workbook, Corporate Sales, and the four tabs at the bottom of the workbook window display the names of each worksheet: Summary, New York, Philadelphia, and Chicago. The drill-down concept begins with the Summary sheet, with the details behind the summary in the individual sheets. This is a three-dimensional effect, and when you create formulas, you will reference specific worksheets.

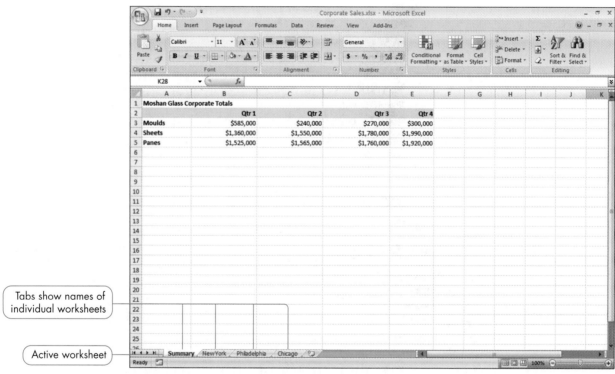

Figure 7.2 Worksheets Used in Consolidation

The Summary worksheet shows the total amount of each product sold during each quarter. The data in this worksheet reflect the amounts shown in Figure 7.1. Each entry in the Summary worksheet is the sum of the corresponding entries in the worksheets of the individual cities. Because the worksheets for the individual cities are not visible in the example in Figure 7.2, it may be useful and convenient to open multiple windows to see the individual city worksheets while you view the Summary worksheet.

Figure 7.3 shows the four worksheets in the Corporate Sales workbook. A different sheet is displayed in each window. The sheet tab indicates the worksheet displayed in the tiled view. The individual windows are smaller than the view in Figure 7.2, but the view does show how the Summary worksheet consolidates the data from each worksheet. The New Window command is used to open each additional window in

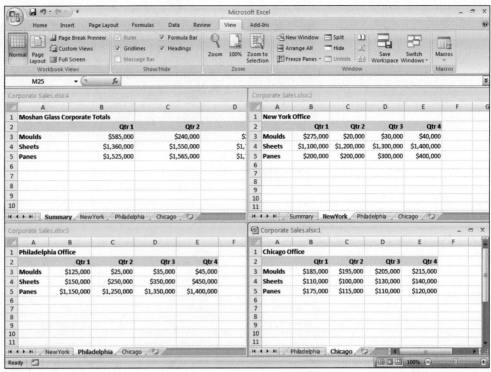

Figure 7.3 All Workbook Worksheets Open and Tiled

the same workbook. After all desired windows are open, you use the Arrange All command to tile or cascade all open windows.

Just one window is active at a time, and all commands apply only to the active window. To make a different window active, click in that window.

Copy Worksheets

Figure 7.3 shows a workbook that summarizes the data in individual worksheets. Placing the data in each worksheet can be accomplished in several ways. You could type the data in each worksheet as you receive the workbooks from each branch office. This is the most inefficient way to accomplish the task, however. It is more effective to enter the data by using one of two copy techniques. The first copy technique is to copy the data from the individual workbooks received from the branches into the appropriate sheets of the Corporate Sales workbook.

Another way to copy data is to copy worksheets from one workbook into another. To do this:

1. Select the sheets you want to move or copy.

2. Click Format in the Cells group on the Home tab.

3. Click Move or Copy Sheet in the Organize Sheets section.

4. Click the workbook to which you want to copy the selected sheets in the *To book* list.

5. In the *Before sheet* list, either click the sheet before which you want to insert the copied list or click Move to end to insert the copied sheet after the last sheet in the workbook.

6. Select the *Create a copy* check box.

TIP The Horizontal Scrollbar

The horizontal scrollbar contains four scrolling buttons to scroll through the worksheet tabs in a workbook as shown in Figure 7.4. The default workbook has three worksheets. Click ▶ or ◀ to scroll one tab to the left or right. Click |◀ or ▶| to scroll to the first or last tab in the workbook. Once the desired tab is visible, click the tab to select it. The number of tabs that are visible simultaneously depends on the setting of the horizontal scroll bar; that is, you can drag the tab split bar to change the number of tabs that can be seen at one time.

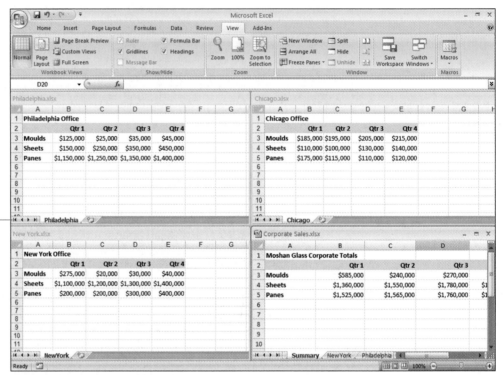

Figure 7.4 Multiple Workbooks

Use Multiple Workbooks

At first glance, Figure 7.4 is the same as Figure 7.3, but with one major difference. Figure 7.3 shows four different worksheets from the same workbook, but Figure 7.4 shows four different workbooks. Three workbooks contain only one worksheet; each worksheet has the sales data for the branch city. The fourth workbook contains four worksheets and is the workbook displayed in Figure 7.3.

Each technique has advantages and disadvantages. The single workbook shown in Figure 7.3 is easier for the manager to use as all of the data are in one file. The disadvantage is that the worksheets have to be maintained in remote locations and that several people have to have access to the same workbook. The multiple workbooks shown in Figure 7.4 make it easier to maintain the data, but four separate files are required for summary data.

Change Formula Recalculation, Iteration, or Precision

Calculation is the process of computing formulas and then displaying the results as values in the cells that contain the formulas. As calculation goes on, you can perform other actions in Excel. The program interrupts calculation to perform these actions, and then continues to calculate. Calculation can take more time if any of the following conditions exist:

- The workbook has a large number of formulas.
- The worksheets contain data tables or functions that automatically recalculate each time you enter data and the workbook is recalculated.
- The worksheets contain links to other worksheets or workbooks, and those data are updated.

To change when a worksheet or workbook recalculates, click the Office Button, click Excel Options, and click the Formulas category. In the *Calculation options* section, choose a Workbook Calculation option. Table 7.1 lists the Workbook Calculation options.

Table 7.1 Recalculation Options

To	Click
Recalculate all dependent formulas each time you make a change to a value, formula, or name.	Automatic
Recalculate all dependent formulas, except data tables, each time you make a change to a value, formula, or name.	Automatic except for data tables
Turn off automatic recalculation and recalculate open workbooks only when you do so explicitly.	Manual

TIP Manual Calculation

When manual calculation is enabled, you can recalculate either the workbook or the worksheet. Click Calculate Now in the Calculate group on the Formulas tab to calculate the entire workbook. Click Calculate Sheet in the Calculate group on the Formulas tab to calculate the current worksheet.

Iteration is the repeated recalculation of a worksheet until a specific numeric condition is met.

Iteration is the repeated recalculation of a worksheet until a specific numeric condition is met. Iteration entries determine how long Solver works to solve a problem, and you will learn more about this topic later. To change the number of times Excel iterates a formula, click the Office Button, click Excel Options, and click the Formulas category (see Figure 7.5). Select the Enable iterative calculation check box in the *Calculation options* section. Type the number of iterations in the Maximum Iterations box. The higher the number, the more times Excel needs to recalculate the worksheet. To set the maximum amount of change you will accept between recalculation results, type the amount in the Maximum Change box.

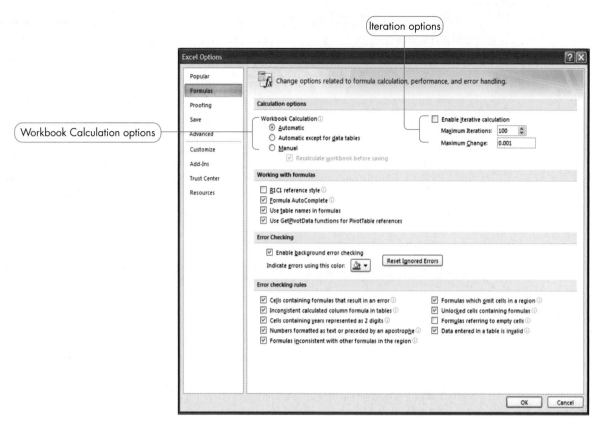

Figure 7.5 Formulas Section of Excel Options Dialog Box

Precision is a measure of the degree of accuracy for a calculation.

Precision is a measure of the degree of accuracy for a calculation. Excel stores and calculates 15 significant digits of precision. Precision defines how exact the calculation needs to be. The smaller the number (the more zeros after the decimal), the greater the precision. You will learn more about precision and iteration in a later chapter. To change the Precision settings, click the Office Button, click Excel Options, and then click the Advanced category. Select the workbook you want in the *When calculating this workbook* section. Select the Set precision as displayed check box.

Creating Three-Dimensional Formulas

You have read about and used cell references in earlier chapters where you refer to a particular cell in a worksheet by its cell reference or cell address. Cell B3 is cell B3 no matter what worksheet or workbook you work with; people who work with spreadsheets understand this cell reference naming convention. This issue becomes more complicated when you work the multiple worksheets in the same workbook. Each worksheet contains a cell B3, and if you want to reference a cell in another worksheet, a naming scheme must exist.

A **worksheet reference** is a reference to a cell in a worksheet not currently active.

If you want to reference a cell or cell range in a worksheet that is not active, you need to begin the cell address with a *worksheet reference*. A worksheet reference is a reference to a cell in a worksheet not currently active. An example of a worksheet reference is Philadelphia!B3, which references cell B3 in the Philadelphia worksheet. Worksheet references may also be used with cell ranges to simplify functions and formulas. The worksheet reference NewYork!B2:E5 references cells B2 through E5 in the NewYork worksheet. Failure to include a worksheet reference defaults to the cell reference in the active worksheet. In the following examples, note that the name of the worksheet is NewYork, not New York.

Review Figure 7.6 for an example of how worksheet references are used on the Summary worksheet. Each entry on the Summary worksheet calculates the sum of the corresponding cells in the NewYork, Philadelphia, and Chicago worksheets. The following formulas would be entered in cell B3:

=NewYork!B3+Philadelphia!B3+Chicago!B3

|Chicago is the worksheet reference

Philadelphia is the worksheet reference

NewYork is the worksheet reference

In a worksheet reference, an exclamation point separates the worksheet reference from the cell reference. Worksheet references are always absolute references; however, the cell reference may be either relative (NewYork!B3), absolute (NewYork!$B$3), or mixed (NewYork!$B3 or NewYork!B$3).

This combination of relative cell references and constant worksheet references enables you to enter the formula once (in cell B3), and then copy it to the remaining cells in the worksheet. You enter the formula in cell B3 to calculate total sales for moulds in the first quarter, and then you copy that formula to the other cells in row 3, C3 through E3, to obtain the totals for moulds in the second, third, and fourth quarters. Similarly, you then copy the entire row, cells B3 through E3, to rows 4 and 5 to generate totals for Products 2 and 3 in all four quarters.

The correct use of relative and absolute references in the original formula in cell B3 is what makes it possible to copy the cell formulas. Look at the formula that was copied from cell B3 into cell C3:

=NewYork!C3+Philadelphia!C3+Chicago!C3

|Chicago is the worksheet reference

Philadelphia is the worksheet reference

NewYork is the worksheet reference

The worksheet references, such as NewYork!, remain absolute, but the cell references adjust for the new location of the formula, cell C3. The same kind of adjustment is made in all of the other copied formulas.

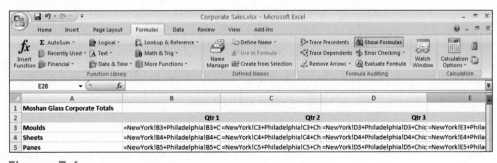

Figure 7.6 Worksheet References

Define a Three-Dimensional Formula

A *three-dimensional (3-D) formula* is a formula that refers to the same cell or range in multiple worksheets.

A formula or function that refers to the same cell or range in multiple worksheets is called a *three-dimensional (3-D) formula*. The individual reference to a cell on multiple worksheets is called a 3-D cell reference. It is a convenient way to reference several identically structured worksheets in which the cells in each worksheet contain the same type of data, such as when you consolidate sales information from different branches into the Summary worksheet. You can type a 3-D reference directly into a cell formula or function, but using the point-and-click method is more efficient. To enter a 3-D reference in a cell formula, type = in the cell that will contain the cell reference. To reference a cell in another worksheet, click the tab for that worksheet and then click the cell or range of cells to be referenced.

An example of a 3-D formula is =SUM(Philadelphia:Chicago!B3) that sums cell B3 in the Philadelphia, NewYork, and Chicago worksheets. The sheet range is specified with a colon between the beginning and ending worksheets. An exclamation point follows the last worksheet, before the cell reference. Worksheet references are constant and do not change when a formula is copied. Cell references may be relative or absolute.

Three-dimensional references used in the Summary worksheet are an alternative method to compute totals for each product-quarter combination. To calculate the corporate sales for Product 1 in quarter 1 in cell B3, you would create the following function:

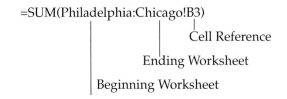

The 3-D formula includes all worksheets starting with Philadelphia and ending with Chicago, including in-between worksheets, such as NewYork. The reference automatically adds any worksheets that are subsequently added between Philadelphia and Chicago and similarly adjusts for worksheets that are deleted. The cell reference is relative so that the formula can be copied from cell B3 in the Summary worksheet to the remaining cells in row 3. The formulas can then be copied to the appropriate cells in rows 4 and 5.

You can also create 3-D formulas using functions, such as SUM or AVERAGE. To create a 3-D formula using a function:

1. Click the cell where you will enter the function.

2. Type =, type the name of the function, such as SUM, and then type an opening parenthesis.

3. Click the tab for the first worksheet to be referenced, such as Philadelphia.

4. Hold down Shift and click the tab for the last worksheet to be referenced, such as Chicago.

5. Select the cell or range of cells that you want to reference, such as cell C3.

6. Complete the formula and press Enter.

Group Worksheets

Worksheets in a workbook are often similar to one another in content or formatting. The formatting in the four worksheets shown in Figure 7.3 is identical. Although you can format worksheets individually, it is more efficient to format a group of worksheets than it is to format the worksheets individually.

Excel is capable of grouping worksheets to format or enter data in multiple worksheets at the same time. After worksheets are grouped, anything you do in one worksheet is done to the other worksheets in the group. Examples of what you can do to grouped worksheets might include:

• Entering row and column labels

• Formatting data

• Entering formulas to compute row and column totals

• Setting identical headers and footers, margins, and other layout options

You must remember to ungroup worksheets to enter data in a specific worksheet. To group worksheets in a workbook:

1. Click a worksheet tab.
2. Press and hold Ctrl as you click the worksheet tab for each worksheet to be included in the group. The grouped worksheet tabs display as white and the word *Group* appears in the title bar.
3. To ungroup, click any worksheet tab.

TIP Selecting Text

You can use Shift to select contiguous sheets and use Ctrl to select non-contiguous sheets. Remember also that you can use Shift to select contiguous cells and use Ctrl to select non-contiguous cells.

Hands-On Exercises

1 | Consolidating Best Restaurant Corporate Sales

Skills covered: 1. Begin a New Workbook and Open Individual Workbooks **2.** Copy Workbook Data **3.** Verify the Copy Procedure **4.** Insert a Worksheet **5.** Create a 3-D Formula **6.** Arrange Windows and Change Data **7.** Edit Grouped Worksheets **8.** Format Grouped Worksheets

Step 1
Begin a New Workbook and Open Individual Workbooks
	Refer to Figure 7.7 as you complete Step 1.
	
	a. Start Excel and delete all worksheets except Sheet1 and:
	
	   • Click the **Sheet2 tab** and press **Shift** as you click the **Sheet3 tab**.
	   • Right-click the **Sheet3 tab** and select **Delete**.
	
	You grouped and then deleted Sheet2 and Sheet3 from the workbook. The workbook should contain only Sheet1.
	
	b. Save the workbook as **chap7_ho1_summary_solution**.
	
	c. Click the **Office Button** and click **Open** to display the Open dialog box.
	
	d. Click the *chap7_ho1_new_york* workbook, then press and hold **Ctrl** as you click the *chap7_ho1_chicago* and *chap7_ho1_philadelphia* workbooks.
	
	You used Ctrl to select all three workbooks at the same time.
	
	e. Click **Open** to open the selected workbooks.
	
	The selected workbooks are open in individual windows.
	
	f. Click the **View tab** and click **Arrange All** in the Window group to display the Arrange Windows dialog box. Make sure **Tiled** is selected in the dialog box, and then click **OK**.
	
	You should see four open workbooks, as shown in Figure 7.7. Your workbooks may be arranged differently.

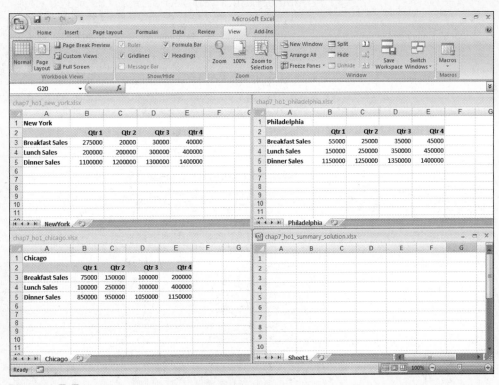

Figure 7.7 Opening Individual Workbooks

Step 2
Copy Workbook Data

Refer to Figure 7.8 as you complete Step 2.

a. Click the **chap7_ho1_new_york** workbook and select **cells A1:E5**.

b. Click **Copy** in the Clipboard group on the Home tab and click **cell A1** of the Summary workbook.

c. Click **Paste** in the Clipboard group on the Home tab.

You copied the New York office financial data and pasted it in the Summary workbook.

d. Right-click the **Sheet1 tab** in the Summary worksheet window and select **Rename**.

e. Type **New York** and press **Enter**.

You changed the worksheet tab from Sheet1 to New York.

f. Click in the **chap7_ho1_philadelphia** workbook to make it active.

g. Click the **Philadelphia tab**, then press and hold **Ctrl** as you drag the tab to the right of the New York tab in the Summary workbook.

You will see a tiny spreadsheet with a plus sign as you drag the tab. The plus sign indicates that the worksheet is being copied; the ▼ symbol indicates where the worksheet will be placed.

h. Release the mouse, and then release Ctrl.

The worksheet from the Philadelphia workbook should have been copied to the Summary workbook and appears as Philadelphia in that workbook.

TROUBLESHOOTING: The Philadelphia workbook should still be open; if it is not, it means that you did not press Ctrl as you were dragging the tab to copy the worksheet. If this is the case, click the Office Button and reopen the Philadelphia workbook, and, if necessary, tile the open windows.

The Philadelphia worksheet should appear to the right of the New York worksheet. If the worksheet appears to the left of New York, click and drag the tab to its desired position. The ▼ symbol indicates where the worksheet will be placed.

i. Repeat steps f through h to copy the Chicago data to the Summary workbook, placing the new sheet to the right of the Philadelphia sheet.

j. Save the Summary workbook.

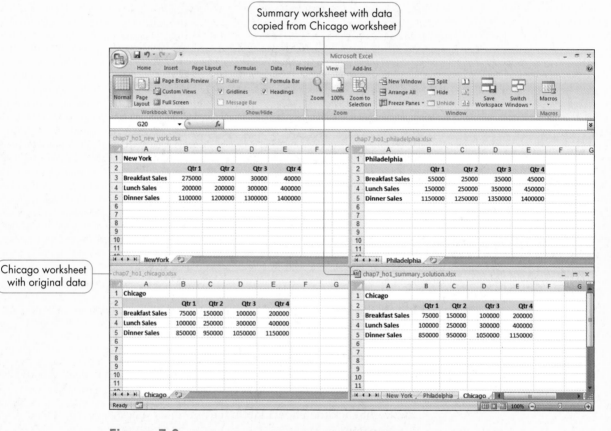

Figure 7.8 Consolidated Data from Multiple Workbooks

Step 3
Verify the Copy Procedure

a. Verify that the **Summary** workbook is the active workbook. Click the **Maximize button** so that this workbook fills the entire screen.

You are going to verify that your copy procedure worked by clicking to view the data on each of the worksheets.

b. Click the **New York tab** to display the worksheet for New York.

c. Click the **Philadelphia tab** to display the worksheet for Philadelphia.

d. Click the **Chicago tab** to display the worksheet for Chicago.

e. Close the *chap7_ho1_new_york*, *chap7_ho1_philadelphia*, and *chap7_ho1_chicago* workbooks, saving changes if prompted.

Step 4
Insert a Worksheet

Refer to Figure 7.9 as you complete Step 4.

a. With the *chap7_ho1_summary_solution* workbook open, click the **New York tab** to select this worksheet, then click the **Insert down arrow** in the Cells group on the Home tab and select **Insert Sheet**.

You should see a new worksheet.

b. Double-click the tab of the newly inserted worksheet to select the name, type **Summary**, and press **Enter**.

The name of the new worksheet has been changed.

c. Click **cell A1** of the Summary worksheet and type **Best Restaurant Corporate Sales**.

d. Click cell **B2**, type **Qtr 1**, and copy through **cell E2**.

e. Right-align the column labels.

f. Click **cell A3**, type **Breakfast Sales**, click **cell A4**, type **Lunch Sales**, click **cell A5**, and type **Dinner Sales**.

g. Save the workbook.

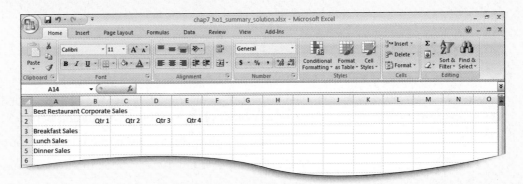

Figure 7.9 Newly Inserted Worksheet

Step 5
Create a 3-D Formula

Refer to Figure 7.10 as you complete Step 5.

a. Click **cell B3** of the Summary worksheet and type **=SUM(**.

- Click the **New York tab** to begin the pointing operation.
- Press and hold **Shift**, click the **Chicago tab**, then release Shift and click **cell B3**.

The Formula Bar should now contain =SUM('NewYork:Chicago'!B3.

- Press **Enter** to complete the function.

Pressing Enter automatically enters the closing right parenthesis and returns you to the Summary worksheet.

b. Click **cell B3** and drag the fill handle over **cells C3:E3**.

You have copied the formula and obtained the total sales for Product 1 in all four quarters.

c. With **cells B3:E3** still selected, drag the fill handle to **cell E5**.

You should see the total sales for all products in all quarters.

d. Click **cell E5** to examine the formula in the cell and note that the worksheet references are constant (they remained the same), whereas the cell references are relative (they were adjusted).

e. Click in other cells to review their formulas in similar fashion.

f. Save the workbook.

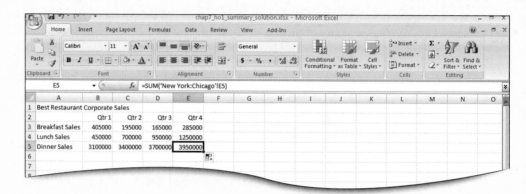

Figure 7.10 Summing the Worksheets

Step 6
Arrange Windows and Change Data

Refer to Figure 7.11 as you complete Step 6.

a. The *chap7_ho1_summary_solution* workbook should be the only open workbook. Close any other open workbooks, including Book1.

b. Click **New Window** three times in the Window group on the View tab.

You opened the Summary workbook three additional times in new windows.

c. Click **Arrange All** to display the Arrange Windows dialog box. If necessary, select the **Tiled option** and click **OK**.

You should see four tiled windows.

d. Click in the upper-right window and click the **New York tab** to display the New York worksheet in this window.

e. Click the lower-left window and click the **Philadelphia tab** to display the Philadelphia worksheet in this window.

f. Click in the lower-right window, click the **Tab scrolling button** until you can see the Chicago tab, and click the **Chicago tab**.

Cell B3 in the Summary worksheet displays the value 405000, which reflects the total Breakfast sales in Quarter 1 for New York, Philadelphia, and Chicago (275000, 55000, and 75000, respectively).

g. Click **cell B3** of the Chicago worksheet, type **95000**, and press **Enter**.

The value of cell B3 in the Summary worksheet changes to 425000 to reflect the increased sales in Chicago, as shown in Figure 7.11.

h. Click **Undo** on the Quick Access Toolbar to see that the Breakfast sales for Chicago revert to 75000 and the Summary total is again 405000.

i. Save the workbook.

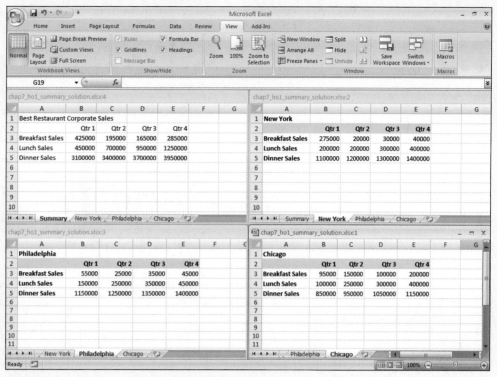

Figure 7.11 Changing Data

Refer to Figure 7.12 as you complete Step 7.

a. Click the **Summary tab**, and press and hold **Shift** as you click the **Chicago tab**.

All four tabs should be selected and are displayed in white. You should also see [Group] in the title bar.

TROUBLESHOOTING: Click in the window where the Summary worksheet is active. Point to the split box separating the tab-scrolling buttons from the horizontal scroll bar, and the pointer becomes a two-headed arrow. Click and drag to the right until you can see all four tabs at the same time.

b. Click cell **A6**, click **Center** in the Alignment group on the Home tab, and type **Total**. Press **Enter**.

The text is centered in cell A6 of all four worksheets.

c. Click cell **B6** and type **=SUM(B3:B5)**.

Note that the formula is entered in all four sheets simultaneously because of group editing.

d. Copy the formula to **cells C6:E6**.

e. Type **Total** in **cell F2**, click **cell F3**, and type **=SUM(B3:E3)**.

f. Copy this formula to **cells F4:F6**.

You just totaled the Breakfast, Lunch, and Dinner sales for each quarter; summed the quarterly sales; and calculated the grand total of all sales.

g. Save the workbook.

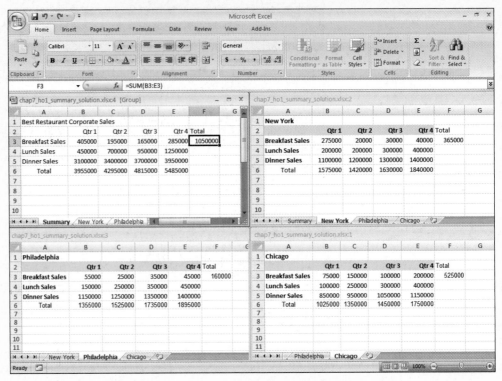

Figure 7.12 Group Editing

Refer to Figure 7.13 as you complete Step 8 and make sure that all four tabs are still selected so that group editing is still in effect.

a. Format the Summary worksheet, as shown in Figure 7.13.

- The Fill Color for all text cells is **Dark Blue**.
- A merged and centered title is **20 point**, **Bold**, and **White**.
- All other labels are **14 point**, **Bold**, and **White**.

The format is applied to all four selected sheets. You can see the effects in the worksheet visible in the four windows. Click on any tab in any window to see the formatting.

b. Select **cells B3:F6**, click the **Number down arrow** in the Number group on the Home tab, and select **Currency**.

c. Click **Decrease Decimal** two times to remove the decimal places.

d. Change the width of **columns B through F** as necessary to accommodate the additional formatting.

It is easiest to select all of the columns at the same time, then click and drag the border between any two of the selected columns to change the width of all selected columns.

e. Click the **New York tab** to ungroup the worksheets. Save the workbook. Close all four windows. Exit Excel if you do not want to continue with the next exercise at this time.

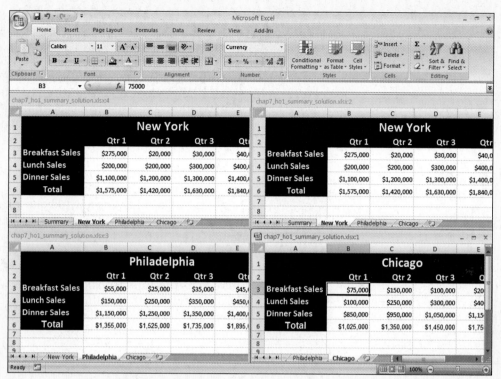

Figure 7.13 Group Formatting

Workbook Linking and Documentation

Workbook linking is another way to consolidate data. Earlier, you worked with worksheet references that consolidate data within one workbook. When you link workbooks, you consolidate the data from several workbooks into another workbook. External references can be used effectively when you want to merge data from several workbooks, when you want to create different views of your data, or when you want to streamline large, complex models.

> External references can be used effectively when you want to merge data from several workbooks . . .

Documenting a workbook means that you include such elements as the author, subject, and location of the workbook, and you define formulas used in the workbook. These and other elements used to document a workbook become essential when large, complex workbooks are created and accessed by several people. Though you know what is in a workbook, others who work with it may not. Auditors use documentation when they verify accuracy of formulas. These are examples of the value of workbook documentation.

In this section, you learn how to link workbooks and create a documentation worksheet.

TIP   Pointing to Cells in Other Worksheets

A worksheet reference can be typed directly into a cell formula, but it is easier to enter the reference by pointing. Click in the cell that is to contain the reference, then enter an equal sign to begin the formula. To reference a cell in another worksheet, click the tab for the worksheet you want to reference and click the cell or cell range you want to include in the formula. Complete the formula as usual, continuing to first click the tab whenever you want to reference a cell in another worksheet.

Linking Workbooks

Linking uses formulas that reference cells in other workbooks.

Linking in Excel uses formulas that reference cells in other workbooks. Linking in Excel and the other Office applications enables you to paste a copy of an object so that it keeps its connection to the original object. Linking is established by the creation of external references that refer to a cell or range of cells in another workbook. Linking enables you to make a change in one workbook and see the change in another workbook. You use a dependent workbook that contains the external references and reflects data in the source workbooks. Linking is used to update workbooks so that the data are consistent across the application. The dependent workbook, the Linking Worksheet in Figure 7.14, contains the external references and reflects, or is dependent on, the data in one or more source workbooks. The source workbooks—Philadelphia, New York, and Chicago—contain data that are referenced by the dependent workbook.

Figure 7.15 shows the use of linking in the example you have been working with. You have four separate workbooks; each contains one open worksheet. The Linking Worksheet is the dependent workbook and uses external references to obtain summary totals. The Philadelphia, New York, and Chicago workbooks are the source workbooks. Cell B3 is the active cell in the Linking Worksheet. The contents are displayed in the Formula Bar. Corporate sales for the first quarter are calculated by summing the corresponding values in the source workbooks. Workbook names are displayed in square brackets to indicate that they are external references.

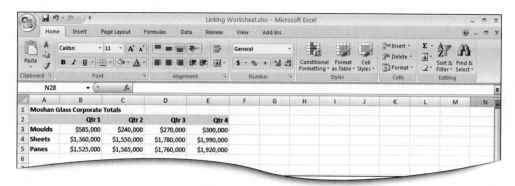

Figure 7.14 Summary Linking Workbook

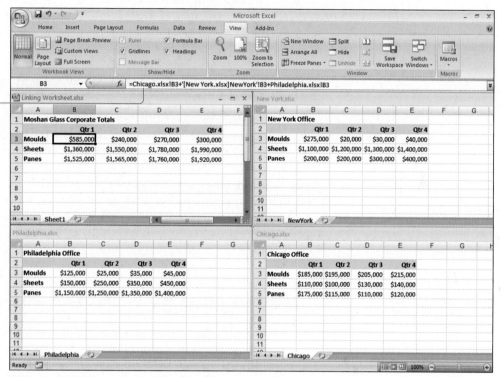

External references

Figure 7.15 Tiled Linking Workbooks

The formulas to compute corporate totals for moulds in the second, third, and fourth quarters contain similar external references. Workbook references, like sheet references, are absolute, but cell references may be relative or absolute. This enables the formula to be copied to remaining cells in the row to calculate the totals for moulds in the remaining rows after the formula is completed in cell B3.

Formulas with external references are displayed in two ways, depending whether the source workbook is open or closed. When the source is open, the external reference includes the workbook name in square brackets, the worksheet name, an exclamation point, and the cells on which the formula depends.

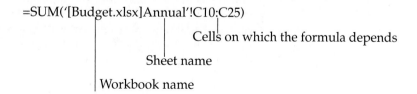

=SUM('[Budget.xlsx]Annual'!C10:C25)

Cells on which the formula depends

Sheet name

Workbook name

When the source is not open, the external reference includes the entire path to the workbook file as shown in the following example.

=SUM('C:\Reports\[Budget.xlsx]Annual'!C10:C25)

| Complete path

To create an external reference between cells in different workbooks:

1. Open the destination workbook and all source workbooks.
2. Select the cell or cells to hold the external reference.
3. Type =. If you want to perform calculations or functions on the external references, type the operator or function.
4. Switch to the source workbook and click the worksheet that contains the cells you want to link to.
5. Select the cells you want to link to.
6. Return to the destination workbook and press Enter.

TIP   Drive and Folder Reference

An external reference is updated regardless of whether the source workbook is open. The reference is displayed differently depending on whether or not the source workbook is open. The references include the path, the drive, and folder if the source workbook is closed; the path is not shown if the source workbook is open. The external workbooks must be available to update the summary workbook. If the location of the workbooks changes, as may happen if you copy the workbooks to a different folder, click Edit Links in the Connections group on the Data tab.

Creating the Documentation Worksheet

A ***documentation worksheet*** describes the contents of each worksheet within the workbook.

This Excel textbook emphasizes design of worksheets through the isolation of assumptions and initial conditions on which the worksheet is based. A *documentation worksheet* describes the contents of each worksheet within the workbook. Documenting a workbook and the worksheets in the workbook is important because spreadsheets are very often used by individuals other than the person who created them. You, the author, know what is in the workbook, but others may not. Everyone who works with a workbook, including anyone who has never seen it before, needs to be able to recognize the purpose and the structure of the workbook. Even if you do not share the workbook with others, you may forget some aspects of it as time passes and will appreciate documentation.

The best way of documenting a workbook is by creating a documentation worksheet that describes the contents of each worksheet within a workbook. Figure 7.16 shows a sample documentation worksheet created for some of the examples in this chapter. A documentation worksheet may contain some or all of the following information: author, date of creation, date of last modification, description of the workbook, list of sheets in the workbook, and description of each sheet.

A documentation worksheet should be attractively formatted and take advantage of color and font size to call attention to the title of the workbook. Remember, though, not to format to the point that the message is lost. Other users appreciate clear, concise, and attractive documentation.

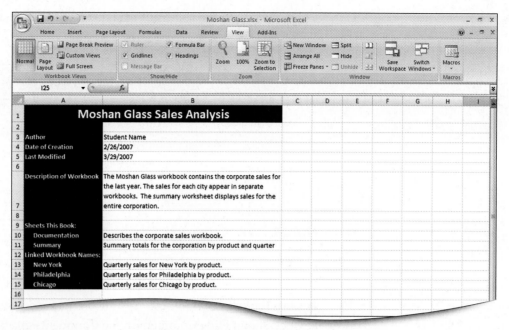

Figure 7.16 Documentation Worksheet

TIP   Workbook Properties

A documentation worksheet is one way to describe the author and other properties of a workbook. Excel also documents various properties automatically, but gives you the opportunity to modify and add to that information. Click the Office Button, select Prepare, and select Properties to display the workbook properties. Some properties are entered for you, such as the author in the Author text box. Select Advanced Properties from the Document Properties drop-down arrow to see the worksheet names on the Contents tab and the date on which the worksheet was created and last modified in the Statistics tab. Other properties can be modified as necessary, especially in the Custom tab.

Insert, Edit, and Delete Comments

Using comments is one of the easiest ways for Excel users to share or collaborate in their work and to provide additional documentation beyond that contained in the documentation worksheet. Comments, which appear as yellow boxes, can be used to indicate a possible error, ask a question, or make a suggestion. Comments are frequently used to clarify formulas, describe cell contents, or indicate any assumptions. When you are using comments, you are not changing the worksheet itself, even though the comments do become part of the worksheet. Excel does not limit the number of comments that can be placed in a workbook; however, a cell may have only one comment. To create a new comment:

1. Click the cell to which you want to add a comment.
2. Click New Comment in the Comments group on the Review tab.
3. Type the comment.
4. Click the cell again after you have typed the comment to finish the insert comment process.

The cell with the comment contains a red triangle in the upper-right corner, as shown in Figure 7.17.

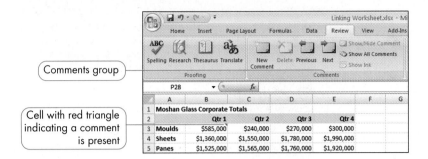

Figure 7.17 Comments

You can use either the Comments group on the Review tab or the shortcut menu to edit an existing comment (see Figure 7.18). To edit a comment:

1. Click the cell containing the comment.
2. Click Show/Hide Comment in the Comments group on the Review tab.
3. Click in the comment and edit it as desired.
4. Right-click on the comment and select Exit Edit Text or click in the cell containing the comment.

Alternatively,

1. Click in the cell containing the comment to finish the edit process.
2. Click Show/Hide Comment in the Comments group of the Review tab to hide the comment.

Note that you can format comment text by selecting Format Comment from the shortcut menu associated with the comment. To delete a comment, click Delete in the Comments group of the Review tab after clicking in the cell with the comment or right-click the cell and select Delete Comment.

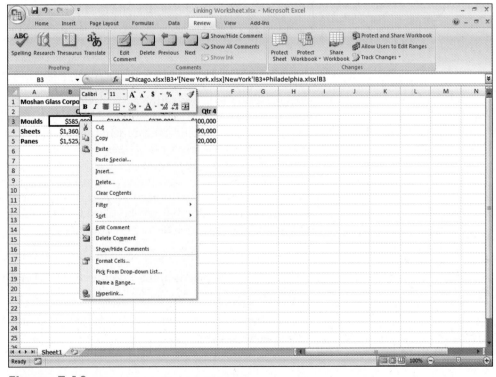

Figure 7.18 Comments Shortcut Menu

Print Comments

When you print a worksheet, comments do not print by default. You do have two options when you choose to print comments. The first option is that they may be printed if they are not hidden on the worksheet itself. This option would cause parts of the worksheet to be covered or hidden by the visible comments. The second option is to print the comments on a separate sheet.

To print comments, click the Page Setup Dialog Box Launcher on the Page Layout tab. Click the Sheet tab and select either *At end of sheet* or *As displayed on sheet* from the Comments drop-down arrow, as shown in Figure 7.19. Click OK.

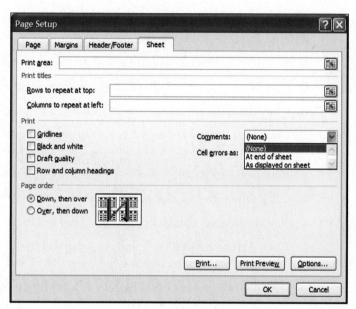

Figure 7.19 Page Setup Dialog Box with Comments Print Choices

Hands-On Exercises

2 | Consolidating Workbooks for Corporate Sales and Adding Documentation

Skills covered: 1. Open the Workbooks and Use AutoFill **2.** Link Files and Copy Cell Formulas **3.** Change the Data **4.** Work with Comments and Documentation Worksheets

<table>
<tr>
<td>

Step 1

Open the Workbooks and Use AutoFill

</td>
<td>

Refer to Figure 7.20 as you complete Step 1.

a. In a new workbook, delete all worksheets except **Sheet1**.

b. Save the workbook as **chap7_ho2_linking_solution**.

c. Click the **Office Button** and click **Open** to display the Open dialog box.

d. Click the *chap7_ho2_new_york* workbook, then press and hold **Ctrl** as you click the *chap7_ho2_chicago* and *chap7_ho2_philadelphia* workbooks.

You used Ctrl to select all three workbooks at the same time.

e. Click **Open** to open the selected workbooks.

The workbooks will be opened one after another.

f. Click **Arrange All** in the Window group on the View tab to display the Arrange Windows dialog box. If necessary, select the **Tiled option**, and then click **OK**.

You should see four open workbooks as shown in Figure 7.20. Your workbooks may be arranged differently.

g. Click **cell A1** in the *chap7_ho2_linking_solution* workbook to make this the active cell in the active workbook and type **Best Restaurant Corporate Sales**.

h. Click **cell B2**, type **Qtr 1**, click **cell B2**, and drag the fill handle over **cells C2:E2**.

A border appears to indicate the destination range. Cells C2 through E2 now contain the labels Qtr 2, Qtr 3, and Qtr 4, respectively.

i. Right-align the entries in **cells B2:E2** and reduce the column widths so you can see the entire worksheet in the window.

j. Click **cell A3**, type **Breakfast Sales**, and use AutoFill to enter the labels **Lunch Sales** and **Dinner Sales** in **cells A4:A5**.

</td>
</tr>
</table>

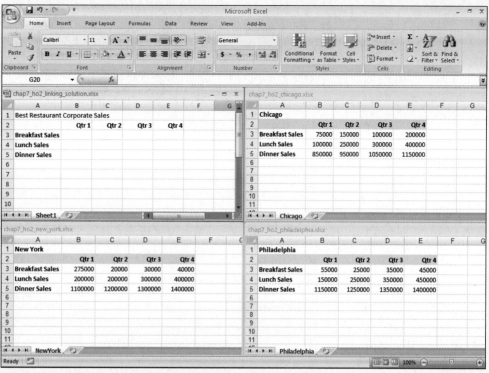

Figure 7.20 Setup for Linking

Refer to Figure 7.21 as you complete Step 2.

a. Click **cell B3** of the *chap7_ho2_linking_solution* workbook and type =.

You will now create the formula by pointing.

b. Click in the window for the New York workbook and click **cell B3**.

The Formula Bar should display =[chap7_ho2_new_york.xlsx]NewYork!$B$3. But you must make the cell reference relative.

c. Press **F4** until the cell reference changes to B3.

d. Type +, click in the window for the Philadelphia workbook, and click **cell B3**.

The formula expands to include:
+[chap7_ho2_philadelphia.xlsx]Philadelphia!$B$3.

e. Press **F4** until the cell reference changes to B3.

f. Type +, click in the window for the Chicago workbook, and click **cell B3**.

The formula expands to include +[chap7_ho2_chicago.xlsx]Chicago!$B$3.

g. Press **F4** until the cell reference changes to B3.

h. Press **Enter**.

The formula is complete, and you should see 405000 in cell B3 of the *chap7_ho2_linking_solution* workbook.

i. Click **cell B3**.

The entry on the Formula Bar should match the entry in Figure 7.21.

j. Drag the fill handle over **cells C3:E3** to copy this formula to the remaining cells in row 3.

k. Make sure that **cells B3:E3** are still selected and drag the fill handle to **cell E5**.

You should see the total sales for all products in all quarters, as shown in Figure 7.21. Click cell E5 to view the copied formula. Note that the workbook and sheet references are the same but that the cell references have adjusted.

l. Save the workbook.

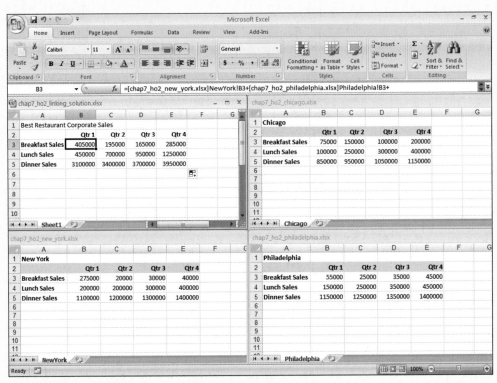

Figure 7.21 Linked Files and Copied Formulas

Step 3
Change the Data

Refer to Figure 7.22 as you complete Step 3.

a. Click **cell B3** in the *chap7_ho2_linking_solution* workbook to make it the active cell.

Note that the value displayed in the cell is 405000.

b. Close the *chap7_ho2_linking_solution* workbook and click **Yes** if asked whether to save the changes.

c. Click in the window containing the Chicago workbook, click **cell B3**, type **95000**, and press **Enter** and close the workbook.

Click **Yes** if asked whether to save the changes. Only two workbooks, *chap7_ho2_new_york* and *chap7_ho2_philadelphia* are now open.

d. Open the *chap7_ho2_linking_solution* workbook.

When you click Options after the Security Warning message shown in Figure 7.22 displays, you will see the dialog box also shown in Figure 7.22, asking whether to enable the content. Note that cell B3 still displays 405000 because you have not yet updated the link.

e. Select **Enable this content** and click **OK** to update the links.

TROUBLESHOOTING: Excel displays a security warning dialog box asking whether external content should be enabled or disabled. You should enable the external content if you are sure that it is from a trustworthy source.

The value in cell B3 of the *chap7_ho2_linking_solution* workbook changes to 425000 to reflect the change in the Chicago workbook, even though the latter is closed.

f. Click cell **B3** in the *chap7_ho2_linking_solution* workbook to view the Formula Bar that displays the contents of the cell. It includes the drive and folder reference for the Chicago workbook because the workbook is closed.

g. Close the *chap7_ho2_new_york* and *chap7_ho2_philadelphia* workbooks.

Saving the source workbook(s) before the dependent workbook ensures that the formulas in the source workbooks are calculated, and that all external references in the dependent workbook reflect current values.

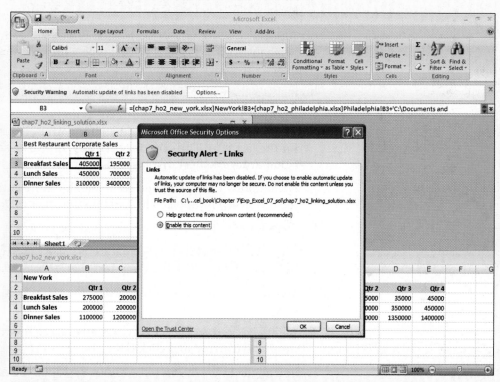

Figure 7.22 Microsoft Office Security Options Dialog Box

Step 4
Work with Comments and Documentation Worksheets

Refer to Figure 7.23 as you complete Step 4.

a. Maximize the *chap7_ho2_linking_solution* workbook if necessary. Click **cell B3**, click the **Review tab**, click **New Comment** in the Comments group, and type **This is the summary total breakfast sales for the three cities**.

TROUBLESHOOTING: The name in the Comment box will be different on your system. The name or initials entered when registering the Microsoft Office 2007 software will appear in the comment box as the author of the comment. Use Help to learn how to change the name or initials.

b. Click in any cell.

Clicking in another cell after you finish entering the comment closes the comment box. The text of the comment is no longer visible, but a tiny red triangle is visible in cell B3. When you point to cell B3, you will see the text of the comment.

c. Click **cell B3**, click **Edit Comment** in the Comments group, delete the word **four** and type **three**, and click in any cell.

You realize that just three cities have sales and edited the comment appropriately. The following steps will add the documentation worksheet.

d. Click the **Home tab**, click the **Insert down arrow** in the Cells group, and select **Insert Sheet**.

e. Double-click the new worksheet tab, type **Documentation**, and press **Enter**.

You inserted a new worksheet and named it Documentation.

f. Double-click the **Sheet1 tab**, type **Summary** to rename the sheet, and press **Enter**.

g. Type the descriptive entries in column A as shown in Figure 7.23, type your name in **cell B3**, click **cell B5** and type **=Today()**, and press **Enter**. Left-align the date.

h. Increase the width of column B as shown in Figure 7.23, click **cell B7**, and type the descriptive entry shown below:

The Best Restaurants Corporate Sales workbook contains the corporate sales for the last year. The sales for each city appear in separate workbooks. The summary worksheet displays sales for the entire corporation.

Do not press Enter until you complete the entire entry. Do not be concerned if the text in cell B7 appears to spill into the other cells in row 7.

i. Press **Enter** when you have completed the entry.

j. Right-click **cell B7**, select **Format Cells**, click the **Alignment** tab in the Format Cells dialog box, click the **Wrap text check box**, and click **OK**.

You wrapped the descriptive text to the cell width, making the text more readable.

k. Right-click **cell A7**, select **Format Cells**, select **Top** from the Vertical alignment drop-down arrow, and click **OK**.

You aligned the label in cell A7 with the top of the cell to facilitate readability.

l. The following will format the Documentation sheet to enhance its appearance:

- Click **cell A1**, type **Best Restaurants Corporate Sales Analysis**, and change the font size to **20 point**.
- Click and drag to select **cells A1:B1**, then click **Merge & Center** in the Alignment group.
- Check that cells A1:B1 are still selected and press and hold while you select **A2:A15**.
- Click **Dark Blue** from the Fill Color down arrow and click **Bold** in the Font group.
- With cells A1:B1 and A2:A15 selected, click **White** from the Font Color down arrow.
- Click outside the selected cells to see the effects of the formatting change. You should see white letters on a dark blue background.
- Widen column A as necessary.

Refer to Figure 7.23 as you complete the text entries in cells B10 through B15.

m. Save and close the workbook. Exit Excel if you do not want to continue with the next exercise at this time.

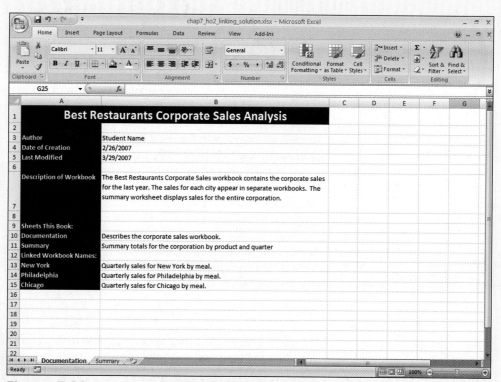

Figure 7.23   The Documentation Worksheet

Workbook Auditing

Errors can occur in a worksheet in several ways, and different forms of errors will occur in a worksheet. Sometimes, it is just an incorrectly entered formula that causes an error value to be returned in Excel. More difficult to detect are errors that appear correct but are not because an incorrect formula has been entered. A **syntax error** is an error that occurs because a formula or function violates correct construction, such as a misspelled function name or illegal use of an operator. Syntax errors typically occur prior to the execution of a procedure and must be corrected for the procedure to continue. An example of a syntax error is a run-time error; a program halts until the error is corrected. In Excel consider the divide by zero error a syntax error. Attempting to divide a value by zero violates basic mathematical syntax.

> More difficult to detect are errors that appear correct but are not because an incorrect formula has been entered.

A **syntax error** is an error that violates correct construction of a formula.

A **logic error** is an error that produces inaccurate results.

Logic errors are the result of a syntactically correct formula but logically incorrect construction, which produces inaccurate results. Logic errors occur when the wrong operator or cell reference is used in a formula. An example of a logic error is one in which a formula divides when it should multiply two cells.

This section discusses validating data, which enables you to set rules to guide data entry in particular cells, and formula auditing, which enables you to review the way your formulas are constructed and how they behave in a spreadsheet.

Restricting Values to a Drop-Down List

To make data entry a bit easier or to limit spreadsheet items to certain defined items and thereby be more accurate, you can create a drop-down list of valid entries. The drop-down list is assembled from cells in other parts of the workbook. When you create a drop-down list, it displays an arrow in the cell, and information is entered by clicking the down arrow and then clicking the desired entry. You can choose from just those entries provided. You cannot enter invalid data. To create a drop-down list:

1. Create a list of valid entries in a single column or row without blank cells.
2. Click Data Validation in the Data Tools group on the Data tab to show the Data Validation dialog box.
3. Click the Settings tab, click the Allow drop-down arrow, and select List.
4. Enter a reference to the list in the source box. See Figure 7.24.
5. Make sure that the In-cell dropdown check box is selected and that the Ignore blank check box is clear or selected.

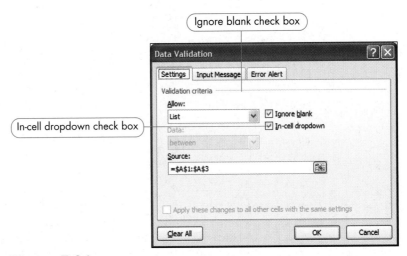

Figure 7.24 Data Validation Dialog Box

Validating Data

Data validation enables you to restrict values that can be entered into a cell.

Data validation enables you to restrict values that can be entered into a cell. It warns and prevents people other than you from entering "wrong" data in a cell. Data validation enables you to specify and correct the kind of data that can be entered, specify an input message warning people when they click a cell that only specific types of data can be entered in that cell, and specify error messages that appear when others persist and attempt to enter incorrect data. All of these tasks are accomplished using the Data Validation dialog box. You access this dialog box by clicking Data Validation in the Data Tools group on the Data tab.

Specify Data Validation Criteria

In the Settings tab of the Data Validation dialog box, you set the values that are permitted in a cell. In the Allow list box, you specify the type of data permitted in a cell. These types include Any value, Whole number, Decimal, Date, Time, and Text length. For example, if you specify Decimal and you enter a whole number, Excel will not permit you to enter a whole number and will display an error message.

You then set the data range in the Data list box. The data range is not available if you select List from the Allow drop-down arrow in the dialog box. You will set the parameters and then specify the Minimum and Maximum values permitted. You would create a drop-down list if the valid grades were A, B, or C, or valid zip codes were 15601, 15697, or 15146. Figure 7.25 shows a validation rule in which the cell contents must be (a) a whole number and (b) between a minimum and maximum value, which are stored respectively in cells F4 and F6.

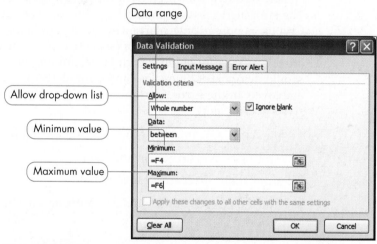

Figure 7.25 Settings Tab of the Data Validation Dialog Box

TIP **Circle Text**

The Data Validation down arrow list contains an item called Circle Invalid Data. When this item is clicked, circles appear around cells that contain invalid data. When the data are corrected, the circles disappear. Data Validation rules must be defined for the cells before the Circle Invalid Data option can be invoked.

Create an Input Message

An **input message** is descriptive text or instructions for data entry.

Input messages are descriptive text or instructions for data entry. You add input messages to cells, and they are displayed when a user moves to a cell that has some data entry restriction. Input messages consist of two parts: a title and an input message (see Figure 7.26). Generally, input messages should be a bit more than just a description of the data validation settings and should explain or show something about the data that can be entered in the cell. For example, an input message might be *Enter hire date in the form: mm/dd/yyyy.* or *Enter Employee name: last name, first name.*

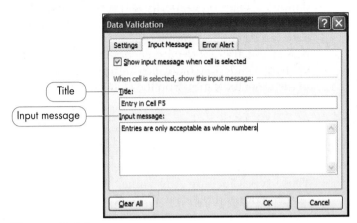

Figure 7.26 Input Message Tab of the Data Validation Dialog Box

Create an Error Alert

Sometimes, no matter how descriptive you are, users will attempt to enter invalid data in a cell. Instead of using Excel's default error message, you have the ability to create your own user-friendly message using the Error Alert tab (see Figure 7.27). The error alert message should be polite and should clearly state what the error is. Cryptic, nondescriptive alert messages do not help users understand the data entry problem. You are creating a worksheet that someone else will use. Data entry people are not necessarily familiar with Excel, nor are they familiar with the business. You should design input messages and error alerts for the novice Excel user and the new employee. In the Error Alert tab in the Data Validation dialog box, you have three styles of error alert:

1. Stop—Prevents the user from entering invalid data.

2. Warnings—Will accept invalid data.

3. Information—Will accept invalid data.

You then create a title and descriptive message to complete the Error Alert.

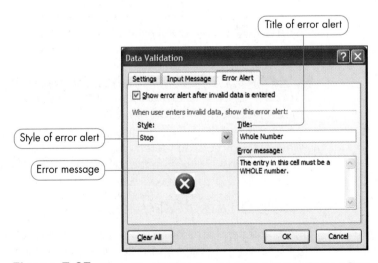

Figure 7.27 Error Alert Tab in the Data Validation Dialog Box

Auditing Formulas

To this point, you have reviewed material pertaining to invalid entry of new data. However, a worksheet might contain instances where formulas have been entered incorrectly and Excel returns error messages. Even harder to detect are instances where the formula is correct but it is the wrong formula for the application. This is a common logic error. If Excel cannot perform the calculations called for by a formula in a cell, an error value is displayed in the cell. *Formula auditing* enables you to display or trace relationships between cells and formulas. Table 7.2 displays Excel error values and the source of the error. In Excel 2007, all auditing of formulas is done using commands in the Formula Auditing group on the Formulas tab, as shown in Figure 7.28.

Formula auditing enables you to display or trace relationships between cells and formulas.

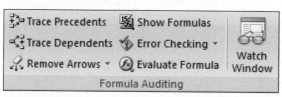

Figure 7.28 The Formula Auditing Group

Table 7.2 Excel Errors and Source of Error

Error Value	Source
#DIV!0!	Formula contains a number divided by zero.
#NAME?	Failure to recognize text in a function, such as misspelling a function name or range name.
#N/A	Value not available to the formula.
#NULL!	Formula requires cell ranges to intersect and they do not.
#NUM!	Invalid numbers used in a formula.
#REF!	Cell reference in a formula no longer valid.
#VALUE!	Incorrect type of argument used in formula.

Trace Precedents and Dependents

Often when auditing formulas, it is difficult to locate the source of an error in a formula when the formula uses precedent or dependent cells. *Precedent cells* are cells that are referred to by a formula in another cell, such as hourly wage and regular hours being referred to by a formula to calculate gross pay. *Dependent cells* contain formulas that refer to other cells such as the formula for gross pay depending on the hourly wage and regular hours. You use the Trace Precedents and Trace Dependents commands to graphically display, using tracer arrows, the relationship between these cells and formulas (see Figure 7.29). The tracer arrows help you identify cells that are causes of errors. An error message icon may also display with an explanation of the possible error, and the down arrow list contains possible fixes. To trace precedents:

Precedent cells are cells referred to by a formula in another cell.
Dependent cells contain formulas that refer to other cells.

1. Select the cell that contains the formula for which you will find precedent cells.
2. Click Trace Precedents in the Formula Auditing group of the Formulas tab.

Blue arrows show cells with no errors. Red arrows show cells that cause errors. To remove tracer arrows, click Remove Precedent Arrows in the Formula Auditing group on the Formulas tab. To trace dependent cells:

1. Click the cell for which you will find dependents.
2. Click Trace Dependents in the Formula Auditing group on the Formulas tab.

Again, blue arrows show cells with no errors and red arrows show cells that cause errors.

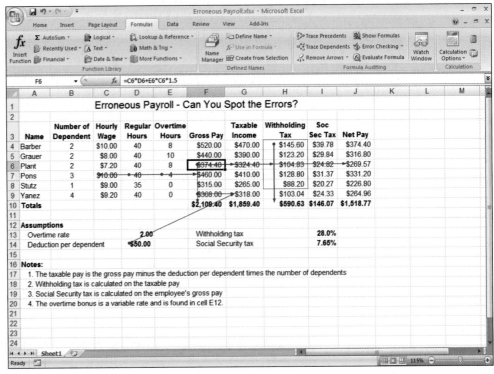

Figure 7.29 Trace Precedents

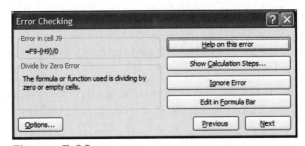

> **TIP** Remove Tracer Arrows
>
> Click Remove Arrows from the down arrow in the Formula Auditing group on the Formulas tab. You may remove all tracer arrows or just precedent or dependent tracer arrows.

Check For and Repair Errors

When the tracing of precedents or dependents shows errors in formulas, or if you want to check for errors that have occurred in formulas anywhere in a spreadsheet, you can use the Error Checking command in the Formula Auditing group on the Formulas tab. When an error is identified in a cell by the Error Checking command, the Error Checking dialog box appears, as shown in Figure 7.30.

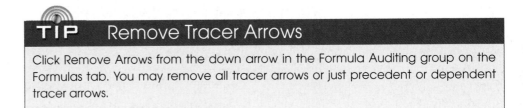

Figure 7.30 Error Checking Dialog Box

This identifies the cell with an error and describes the error. When you click the Help on this error button, Excel transfers you to the section of Excel Help that describes the error. Clicking Show Calculation Steps opens the Evaluate Formula dialog box, as shown in Figure 7.31. This dialog box graphically displays an evaluation of the formula and shows which part of the evaluation will result in an error.

Clicking Ignore Error either moves to the next error or indicates that Error Check is complete. When you click Edit in the Formula Bar, you can correct the formula in the Formula Bar.

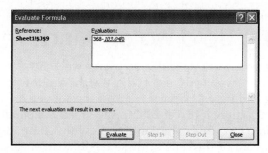

Figure 7.31 Evaluate Formula Dialog Box

> **TIP** The Formulas Are Color-Coded
>
> The fastest way to change the contents of a cell is to double-click in the cell and make the changes directly in the cell rather than to change the entries on the Formula Bar. Note, too, that if the cell contains a formula as opposed to a literal entry, Excel will display each cell reference in the formula in a different color that corresponds to the border color of the referenced cells elsewhere in the worksheet. This makes it easy to see which cell or cell range is referenced by the formula. You can also click and drag the colored border to a different cell to change the cell formula.

Evaluate a Formula

Using nested formulas can make it difficult to understand the evaluation of the formula. Understanding how a nested formula calculates is hard because there are intermediate calculations and logical tests. You can use the Evaluate Formula dialog box to view different parts of a nested formula and view how they are evaluated in the order the formula is calculated. To use the Evaluate Formula dialog box:

1. Select the cell to be evaluated.
2. Click Evaluate Formula in the Formula Auditing group on the Formulas tab to see the Evaluate Formula dialog box, as shown in Figure 7.31.
3. Click Evaluate to examine the value of the reference that is underlined.
4. If the underlined part of the formula is a reference to another formula, click Step In to display the other formula in the Evaluation box.
5. Click Step Out to return to the previous cell and formula.
6. Continue until the entire formula has been evaluated.
7. Click Close to end the evaluation.

Avoid Circular References

A ***circular reference*** is a formula that contains a cell reference that relies on its own value.

A ***circular reference*** happens when you create a formula that relies on its own value. The reliance can be either direct or indirect. For example, if you enter the formula =A3+10 in cell A3, you create a circular reference. For this formula to work, Excel needs to add 10 to the current value of cell A3. This formula, however, changes the value of A3 and means Excel needs to recalculate the formula. Without correction this process creates an endless loop, never producing a value. Circular references inevitably lead to invalid data. The most common way you will inadvertently create a circular reference is to begin your formula with the active cell, the cell that contains a value, rather than an empty cell that will display the result.

Setting Up a Watch Window

When you are working with a very large worksheet, formulas in cells that are not visible can be "watched" using the Watch Window box. You do not need to keep scrolling to different parts of the worksheet if you are using Watch Window. Among the new features in Excel 2007 is the greatly expanded worksheet; you now have many more rows and columns to work with. Computer screens are not large enough to display all of the cells of these larger worksheets. The Watch Window feature enables you create a small window so you can view the formula calculation. You can conveniently inspect, audit, or confirm formula calculations involving cells that are not displayed on the screen. You can double-click a cell in the Watch Window to quickly jump to that cell. To add cells to the Watch Window:

1. Select the cell or cells you want to watch.
2. Click Watch Window in the Formula Auditing group on the Formulas tab.
3. Click Add Watch in the Watch Window toolbar.
4. Select the cells to be watched in the Add Watch dialog box and click Add Watch.
5. The Watch Window dialog box shows the watch, as shown in Figure 7.32.

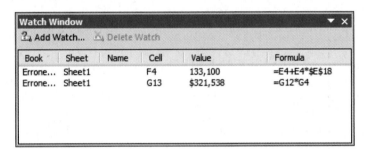

Figure 7.32 The Watch Window

TIP Changes to Watched Cells

Anytime you make a change to the watched cell, the Watch Window dialog box shows you the current value of the watched cell or cells.

Comments and Auditing Commands | Reference

Icon	Command	Description
	New Comment	Inserts a new comment in the active cell
	Edit Comment	Opens comment for active cell so that you can edit the comment
	Delete	Deletes the comment for the active cell
	Previous	Navigates to and displays the previous comment in the worksheet
	Next	Navigates to and displays the next comment in the worksheet
	Show/Hide Comment	Shows (or hides) the comment for the active cell
	Show All Comments	Displays all comments in the worksheet
	Trace Precedents	Displays arrows to show what cells have an impact on the current cell's value
	Trace Dependents	Displays arrows to show what cells are affected by (dependent upon) the current cell's value
	Remove Arrows	Removes the arrows that trace precedents and/or dependents
	Show Formulas	Displays formulas in the worksheet
	Error Checking	Checks worksheet for common errors within formulas
	Evaluate Formula	Launches the Evaluate Formula dialog box to evaluate each part of a specific formula to debug it
	Watch Window	Monitors values of particular cells while changes are made to the worksheet

Hands-On Exercises

3 | JAS Manufacturing

Skills covered: 1. Trace Precedents **2.** Audit a Region's Quarterly Sales and Remove Cell Error Indicators **3.** Correct a Cell Formula and Trace a Cell's Dependents **4.** Use Error Checking **5.** Create a Watch Window **6.** Validate Data

<table>
<tr><td>

Step 1

Trace Precedents

</td><td>

Refer to Figure 7.33 as you complete Step 1.

a. Open the *chap7_ho3_jas* workbook and save it as **chap7_ho3_jas_solution** so that you can return to the original workbook if necessary.

The partially completed workbook contains errors that you will identify and correct.

b. Click the **Quarterly Summary tab**.

You will see the seven regions for the JAS Manufacturing Company and Quarterly Sales Summary totals.

c. Click **Formulas tab**, click **cell C12**, and click **Trace Precedents** in the Formula Auditing group.

Tracer arrows are displayed and a box encompasses the range of cells included in the formula. An error alert is displayed because the range is incorrect.

d. Verify that cell C12 is selected, click the Formula Bar to edit the formula as **=SUM(C4:C10)**, and press **Enter**.

e. Save the workbook.

</td></tr>
</table>

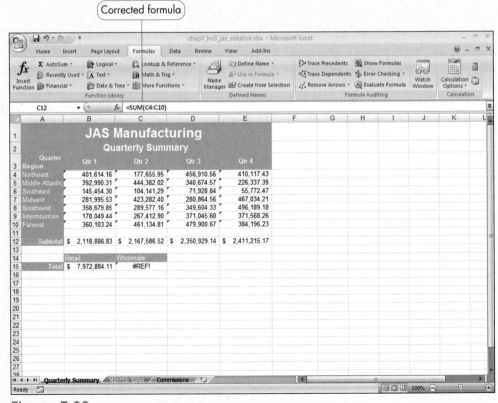

Figure 7.33 Identify and Correct Errors

Step 2
Audit a Region's Quarterly Sales and Remove Cell Error Indicators

a. Click **cell B10** and click **Trace Precedents** in the Formula Auditing group.

The tracer arrow points to a worksheet icon indicating that the cell refers to another worksheet.

b. Double-click the **tracer arrow** to view the Go To dialog box.

The dialog box displays the cell references on which the formula may depend.

c. Click the first cell reference listed in the dialog box and click **OK**.

The Monthly sales worksheet opens and one of the cell ranges is highlighted. This shows the relationship between the quarterly worksheet and the summary worksheet.

d. Click the **Quarterly Summary tab**, point to the Error message box, and click the drop-down arrow to display options for resolving the error.

You can review the options available for correcting errors in the list. Excel anticipates what you might do and in this case, the formula is correct as entered.

e. Click and drag to select **cells B4:E10**, click the down arrow for the Error message box, and select **Ignore Error**.

f. Click any cell to deselect the cell range and click **Remove Arrows** from the Formulas Auditing group.

You removed the green triangles which indicated possible errors in cells.

g. Save the workbook.

TROUBLESHOOTING: Double-clicking a tracer arrow is an efficient way to locate dependent or precedent cells on either the current worksheet or another worksheet.

Step 3
Correct a Cell Formula and Trace a Cell's Dependents

Refer to Figure 7.34 as you complete Step 3.

a. Click **cell C9** in the **Monthly Sales** worksheet.

b. Click the **Error message box drop-down arrow**.

The error message Number Stored as Text means that cell C9 contains text instead of a value. The formula in the Formula Bar begins with an apostrophe ('). You will correct the formula after tracing the cell's dependents.

c. Click **Trace Dependents** in the Formula Auditing group.

d. Double-click the **tracer arrow**, click the first item in the list, and click **OK** in the Go To dialog box.

e. Verify that **cell C9** on the **Quarterly Summary** sheet is selected and click **Trace Dependents** in the Formula Auditing group.

By tracing dependents on both worksheets, you see the relationship between the data on the Monthly Sales worksheet and the Quarterly Summary worksheet.

f. Click the **Monthly Sales tab** and click **Remove Arrows** in the Formula Auditing group.

g. Click **cell C10**, click the **Error message drop-down arrow**, and select **Convert to Number**.

Excel converted the text string to a value.

h. Save the workbook.

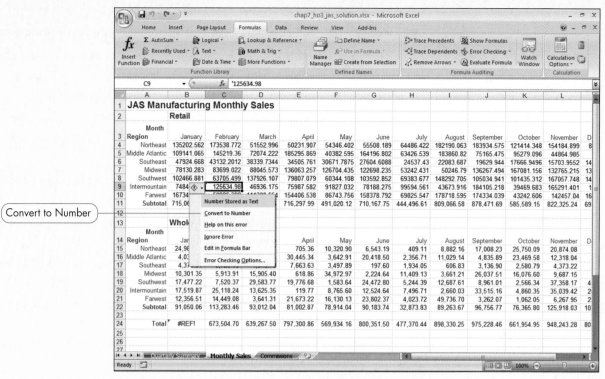

Figure 7.34 Error Message Shortcut Menu

Step 4
Use Error Checking

Refer to Figure 7.35 as you complete Step 4.

a. Click **cell C15** on the **Quarterly Summary tab**.

b. Click **Error Checking** in the Formula Auditing Group to open the Error Checking dialog box.

c. Click **Help on this error** to open Excel Help to display possible solutions to the error, as shown in Figure 7.35.

d. Close the Help window, click **Next**, and then click **OK** to acknowledge that the error check of the entire sheet is complete.

e. Click the **Error Checking down arrow** on the Formula Auditing group and select **Trace Error**.

The tracer error points to a worksheet icon indicating that the error source is on another worksheet.

f. Double-click the **tracer arrow**, click the first item in the Go to list, and click **OK**.

Cell N24 on the Monthly Sales worksheet becomes the active cell.

g. Click the **Error Checking down arrow** in the Formula Auditing group and select **Trace Error**.

A red tracer arrow leads from cell B24 through and including cell N24. The arrow indicates that the root of the error is in cell B24.

h. Verify that cell B24 is selected and type **=B11+B22** and press **Enter**.

The red tracer arrow becomes a blue tracer arrow and the dependent formulas are correct.

i. Click **Remove Arrows** in the Formula Auditing group.

j. Format the worksheets as **Currency** with **2** decimal places.

k. Save the workbook.

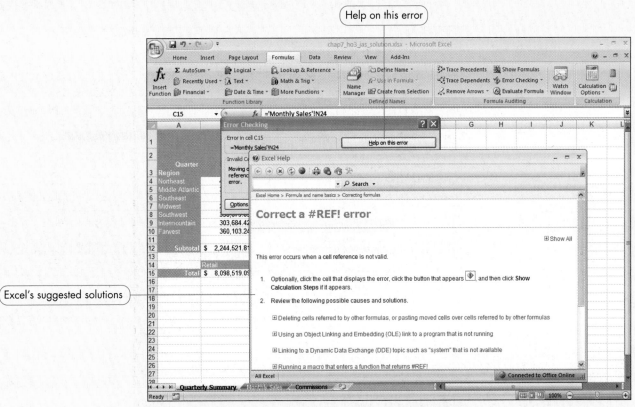

Figure 7.35 Error Checking Dialog Box with Excel Help

Refer to Figure 7.36 as you complete Step 5.

Step 5
Create a Watch Window

a. Click **cell N11** on the Monthly Sales sheet, then press and hold **Ctrl** while clicking **cell N25**.

These cells are not visible without scrolling through the worksheet and to view them, you will set up a Watch Window.

b. Click **Formulas tab** and click **Watch Window** in the Formula Auditing group.

c. Click **Add Watch** in the Watch Window dialog box and verify that **cells N11** and **N24** are displayed in the Add Watch dialog box. See Figure 7.36.

d. Click **Add**.

The Add Watch box closes but the Watch Window box remains open so you can easily jump to any of the cells in the Watch Window box.

e. Click **cell B10**, type **170000**, and press **Enter**.

Cells N11 and N24 were not visible, but you viewed the changes to these cells when you entered a new value in B10.

f. Close the Watch Window box, click **Undo** on the Quick Access Toolbar, and save the workbook.

TROUBLESHOOTING: Anytime you click Watch Window in the Formula Auditing group, the Watch Window dialog box appears with cells N11 and N24 listed.

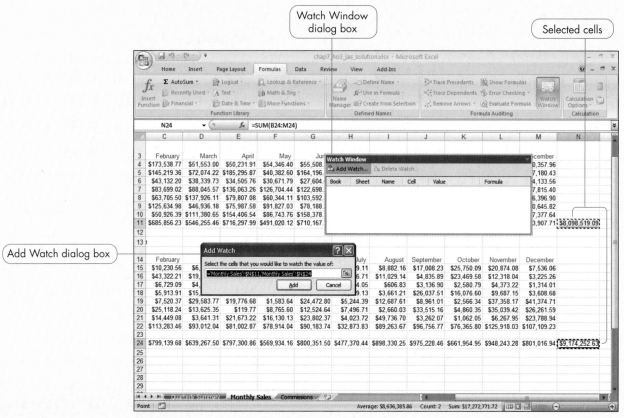

Figure 7.36 Watching Cells

Refer to Figure 7.37 as you complete Step 6.

a. Click the Commissions sheet tab to make it the active worksheet.

b. Click **cell F3**, type **18%**, and press **Enter**. Excel displays the error message "Value too high or too low!!"

c. Click **Cancel**.

You are not able to enter a value above 15% into cell F3 because the error type previously defined was specified as "Stop" rather than a warning. You will now create your data validation rules.

d. Click and drag to select **cells F4:F24**.

e. Click the **Data tab**, click **Data Validation** in the Data Tools group, open the Data Validation dialog box, and do the following:

- Click the **Settings tab** and select **Whole number** from the Allow drop-down arrow list.
- Verify that **between** is selected in the Data drop-down arrow list.
- Type **4** in the Minimum text box and **15** in the Maximum text box.
- Click the **Input Message** tab and type **Invalid Data** in the Title text box.
- Type **Commission rates are between 4% and 15% at JAS.** in the Input message text box.

- Click the **Error Alert** tab and verify that Stop is the Style list box.
- Type **INVALID DATA** in the Title text box.
- Type **You have entered an invalid commission amount** in the Error message text box.

f. Click **OK** and test your validation rule by typing **25%** in **cell F6**.

g. Click **Cancel** and type a value between **4%** and **15%**.

h. Save the workbook and Exit Excel.

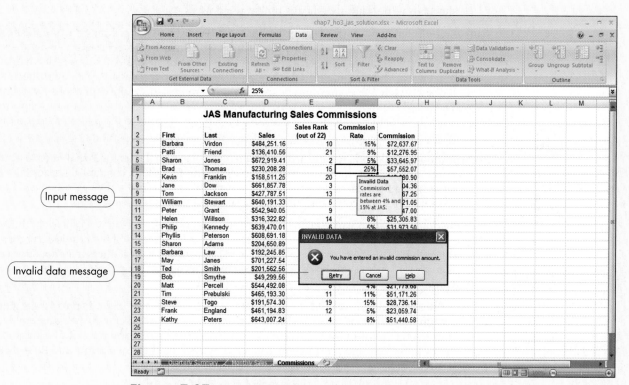

Figure 7.37 Validation Rules

Summary

1. **Consolidate data from multiple worksheets.** One way is to use the three-dimensional capabilities of Excel, where one workbook contains multiple worksheets. The workbook contains a separate worksheet for each of the branches and a summary worksheet that holds the consolidated corporate data. Another way to accomplish this is to maintain the data for each branch office in separate workbooks and create a summary workbook that uses file linking to reference cells in the other workbooks.

2. **Define the three-dimensional workbook.** Excel workbooks are often said to be the electronic version of a filing cabinet. They may contain one or more worksheets that are identified by a worksheet tab at the bottom of the document window.

3. **Create three-dimensional formulas.** If you want to reference a cell or cell range in a worksheet that is not active, you need to begin the cell address with a worksheet reference. A worksheet reference is a reference to a cell on a worksheet not currently active. An example of a worksheet reference is Philadelphia!B3, which references cell B3 on the Philadelphia worksheet. Worksheet references may also be used with cell ranges to simplify functions and formulas. The worksheet reference NewYork!B2:E5 references cells B2 through E5 on the New York worksheet. Failure to include a worksheet reference defaults to the cell reference on the active worksheet.

4. **Link workbooks.** Linking is established by the creation of external references that refer to a cell or range of cells in another workbook. The dependent workbook contains the external references and reflects, or is dependent on, the data in one or more source workbooks. The source workbooks contain data that are referenced by the dependent workbook.

5. **Create the documentation worksheet.** Documenting a workbook and the worksheets in the workbook itself is important because spreadsheets are very often used by individuals other than the author. You, the author, know what is in the workbook, but others may not. Everyone who works with a workbook needs to be able to recognize the purpose and structure of the workbook.

6. **Restrict values to a drop-down list.** To make data entry a bit easier or to limit spreadsheet items to certain defined items, you can create a drop-down list of valid entries that is assembled from cells in other parts of the workbook. When you create a drop-down list, it displays a down arrow in the cell, and information is entered by clicking the down arrow and then clicking the desired entry.

7. **Validate data.** Data validation warns and prevents people other than you from entering "wrong" data in a cell. It enables you to specify and correct the kind of data that can be entered, specify an input message that warns people when they click a cell that only specific types of data can be entered in that cell, and specify error messages appear when others persist and attempt to enter incorrect data.

8. **Audit formulas.** In some instances when formulas have been entered incorrectly and Excel returns error messages. Even harder to detect are instances where the formula is correct but it is the wrong formula for the application. If Excel cannot perform the calculations called for by a formula in a cell, an error value is displayed in the cell.

9. **Set up a Watch Window.** When you are working with a very large worksheet, formulas in cells that are not visible can be "watched" using the Watch Window box. You do not need to keep scrolling to different parts of the worksheet if you are using a Watch Window.

Key Terms

Multiple Choice

1. What is the easiest way to change the active worksheet to another worksheet in the same workbook?

   (a) Click the workbook tab to change to the desired workbook, and then click the worksheet in the resulting window.

   (b) Open the View menu, and then click the desired worksheet from the list at the bottom of the menu.

   (c) Select Tile from the Window menu, and then click the desired worksheet.

   (d) Click the worksheet tab of the desired worksheet at the bottom of the current workbook.

2. Which of the following opens a new window within the same workbook?

   (a) The Arrange All command in the Window group

   (b) The New Window command in the Window group

   (c) The Tiled command in the Arrange Windows dialog box

   (d) The New command on the Office menu

3. You have four windows open, each displaying a different worksheet. To display all open windows in one screen, select the:

   (a) Arrange command in the File group, then choose Show All

   (b) Arrange All command in the Window group, then choose Tiled

   (c) Tile Windows command in the Window group

   (d) Arrange All command in the Window group

4. To change the number of worksheet tabs that can be seen at one time:

   (a) Select Cascade from the Window group.

   (b) Change the Tabs option in Excel Options.

   (c) Drag the splitter bar.

   (d) Resize the tabs.

5. References to another worksheet in the same workbook are called:

   (a) Worksheet references

   (b) Cell references

   (c) 3-D cell references

   (d) Linked references

6. In the reference Sales!E5:G12, the worksheet reference (Sales!) is considered:

   (a) Mixed

   (b) Absolute

   (c) Relative

   (d) Impossible to determine

7. In the formula =January!$B$1+February!$B$1+ March!$B$1:

   (a) The worksheet references are absolute and the cell references are relative.

   (b) The worksheet references are relative and the cell references are absolute.

   (c) Both the worksheet and the cell references are absolute.

   (d) Both the worksheet and the cell references are relative.

8. You have grouped the following worksheets in a workbook: Q1Sales, Q2Sales, and Q3Sales. Q2 is the active worksheet. You enter the formula =SUM(C12:E14) into cell F17. What is the result of this action?

   (a) The formula =SUM(C12:E14) is entered into cell F17 on all three worksheets.

   (b) The sum of cells C12:C14 is entered into cell F17 on all three worksheets, but the formula is not copied to any of the cells.

   (c) The formula =SUM(Q2Sales!C12:Q2Sales!E14) is entered into cell F17 on all three worksheets.

   (d) The formula =SUM(C12:E14) is entered into cell F17 on the Q2 worksheet.

9. You have a workbook with three sheets named January, February, and March, arranged in that order. The formula =SUM(January:March!C10:E15) refers to the sum of:

   (a) Cell C10 on January and E15 on March

   (b) All cells between C10 on January and E15 on March

   (c) Cell ranges C10:E15 on January and March

   (d) Cell ranges C10:E15 on January, February, and March

10. Which of the following is NOT normally included in a documentation worksheet?

    (a) The name of the person who created the workbook

    (b) The initial conditions and assumptions on which a worksheet is based

    (c) The name and description of each worksheet in the workbook

    (d) The date the workbook was last modified

11. You have three workbooks named AREA1.XLS, AREA2.XLS, and AREA3.XLS. They contain data that are to be consolidated using file linking in a summary workbook. Which of the following statements is true?

    (a) The summary workbook will contain external references to the area workbooks.

    (b) The summary workbook must contain a separate worksheet for each district.

    (c) The district workbooks should be grouped prior to creating the summary worksheet.

    (d) Updates to any of the area workbooks will not be reflected in the summary workbook.

12. You have three workbooks named Atlanta, Boston, and Chicago. A summary workbook named Summary contains links to all three workbooks. Which of the following statements is true?

    (a) Atlanta, Boston, and Chicago are considered dependent workbooks.

    (b) Summary is considered the dependent workbook.

    (c) Summary is considered the source workbook.

    (d) A change in Summary is automatically updated in the appropriate workbook.

13. If cell B5 contains the formula =B3+B4, B5 is:

    (a) A dependent of cell B3, but not B4

    (b) A precedent of cells B3 and B4

    (c) A dependent of cells B3 and B4

    (d) Both a dependent and a precedent of cells B3 and B4

14. A dependent cell is one which:

    (a) Derives its value from one or more dependent cells

    (b) Derives its value from one or more precedent cells

    (c) Is independent and not necessary for any relationship

    (d) Is required for a precedent cell

15. Which tool enables a user to stipulate the values that can be entered into a cell?

    (a) The Garbage In/Garbage Out command

    (b) The Auditing toolbar

    (c) The Data Validation command

    (d) The Reviewing toolbar

16. You have a worksheet designed to calculate a salesperson's commission each month. Cell B5 contains sales dollars for the month, whereas cell B6 contains the commission percentage. Cell B8 contains the formula =B5*B6. You want to ensure that commissions are always based on a positive sales amount, so you have decided to use data validation. Which cell should contain the validation?

    (a) B6

    (b) B8

    (c) B5

    (d) It is impossible to determine from the information given.

17. You have entered data validation into a cell, with a maximum value of 10% and a warning alert. What happens if a user enters 12% into that cell?

    (a) The user will get a message forcing him or her to enter a new value.

    (b) The user will get an error message and Excel will shut down.

    (c) The user will get a message stating that the maximum value of that cell is 10% and giving him or her the option of accepting the entered value or entering a new one.

    (d) The user will get a message stating that the maximum value of that cell is 10%, but Excel will accept the value.

18. What is the easiest way to edit or delete an existing comment?

    (a) Click on the context-sensitive menu and select the appropriate command.

    (b) Right-click on the cell, use the context-sensitive menu, and select the appropriate command.

    (c) Point to the cell, highlight the comment, and click on Edit Clear.

    (d) Point to the cell, highlight the comment, and click on Edit Delete.

19. A small green triangle in the upper-left corner of a cell indicates that:

    (a) The cell contains a comment.

    (b) The cell has been changed by a user.

    (c) The cell contains a circular reference.

    (d) The cell may contain an error.

Practice Exercises

1 Range Free Foods Corporation

The Range Free Foods Corporation began operation last year in Pittsburgh by opening three stores in different areas of the city. The manager of each store has prepared a workbook that summarizes the results for last year. As the assistant to the general manager, your task is to combine the results from the three individual workbooks into a corporate summary, as shown in Figure 7.38.

a. Open the *chap7_pe1_rangefreecorporate* workbook and save it as **chap7_pe1_rangefree corporate_solution**, which consists of a single worksheet that will be used to hold the summary data.

b. Open the three workbooks for the individual stores: *chap7_pe1_rangefreebloomfield*, *chap7_pe1_rangefreeshadyside*, and *chap7_pe1_rangefreesouthside*. You are not saving these workbooks because you will not make any changes.

c. Click **Arrange All** in the Window group on the View tab, ensure that **Tiled** is selected from the Arrange Windows dialog box, and click **OK**.

d. Click in the window containing the corporate workbook, then click **cell B3** to make it the active cell. The formula looks complicated, but you can enter it through pointing:

   - Type =, click in the window containing the **South Side** workbook, click **cell B3**, use **F4** to change to a relative reference (B3 instead of $B$3), and type +.
   - Click in the window containing the **Shady Side** workbook, click **cell B3**, change to a relative reference, and type +.
   - Click in the window containing the **Bloomfield** workbook, click **cell B3**, change to a relative reference, and press **Enter** to complete the formula.
   - Close the workbooks for the three individual stores and maximize the corporate workbook.

e. Copy and complete the formulas:

   - Use the fill handle to copy the formula in cell B3 to cells B3:E3.
   - Copy the formulas in row 3 to rows 4–8.
   - Enter the appropriate Sum functions in cells F3:F8 and cells B9:F9.
   - Cell F9 should display the value 1501937.

f. Format the completed worksheet using these specifications:

   - Values are formatted as **Currency**, with **0** decimal places.
   - **Merge & Center** the title and use a fill color of **Orange, Accent 6, Darker 25%**. Font size is 18, and font color is **Dark Blue**.
   - Using the same theme, format Category labels and column headings.
   - Indent the Category labels, resizing column A if necessary, and center column headings.

g. Create a Stacked column chart by product category in its own sheet with the data series in columns, as shown in Figure 7.38. Change the name of the worksheet tab as shown.

h. Create a custom footer for both sheets containing your name, today's date, and your instructor's name. Use landscape orientation for both worksheets. Print the completed workbook. Save and close the workbook.

...continued on Next Page

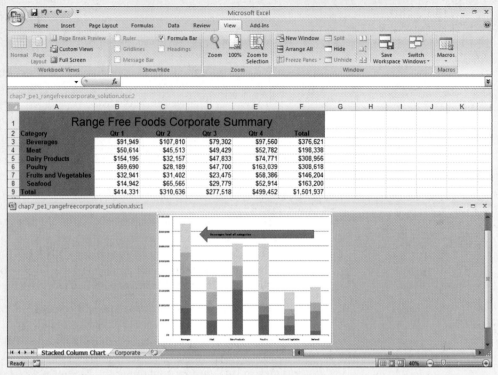

Figure 7.38 Range Free Foods—Workbook References

2 SARA Apartment Rentals Corporation

Although using separate workbooks to create a summary workbook is a good way to summarize and display information, it is not the only way. As the assistant to the general manager for the SARA Apartment Rentals Corporation, you will use a single workbook that contains worksheets for the individual rental locations, as opposed to referencing external workbooks as in the previous exercise. Use Figure 7.39 for reference as you complete the workbook.

a. Open the *chap7_pe2_apartment* workbook and save it as **chap7_pe2_apartment_solution**, which consists of a single worksheet that will be used to hold the summary data.

b. Open the three workbooks for the individual rental locations: *chap7_pe2_saraoakland*, *chap7_pe2_sarahill*, and *chap7_pe2_saracarlow*. You do not need to save these workbooks because you will not change them.

c. Click **Arrange All** in the Window group on the View tab, ensure that Tiled is selected from the Arrange Windows dialog box, and click **OK**.

d. Copy the individual rental location workbooks to the corporate workbook:

- Click the window containing the Carlow workbook.
- Click and drag the worksheet tab to the corporate workbook and the Carlow workbook closes automatically.
- Click and drag the worksheet tabs for the Oakland and Hill worksheets in the same way.
- The Corporate workbook now contains three more worksheets.
- Click **New Window** three times in the Window group on the View tab.
- Tile the windows and click a different sheet tab in each window so that the three rental locations and the corporate sheet are all visible.

e. Create and copy formulas:

- Click in the window containing the corporate worksheet, click **cell B3**, and type =.
- Click in the window containing the Carlow worksheet, click **cell B3**, and type +.
- Click in the window containing the Hill worksheet, click **cell B3**, and type +.

...continued on Next Page

- Click in the window containing the Oakland worksheet, click **cell B3**, and press **Enter** to complete the formula.
- Use the fill handle to copy the formula in **cell B3** to **cells B3:E3** and copy the formulas in row 3 to **rows 4** through **8**.

f. Group the four worksheets:

- Click the **corporate worksheet tab**, then press and hold **Shift** while you click the **Hill** tab. This is the right-most sheet tab.
- Enter the appropriate Sum functions in **cells F3:F8** and **cells B9:F9** on the corporate sheet. The formulas appear on the individual sheets because they are all grouped.
- Cell F9 of the corporate worksheet should display the value 1501937.

g. Format the completed worksheet:

- Values are formatted as **Currency** with **0** decimal places.
- **Merge & Center** the title and use a fill color of **Blue**. Font size is **16**, and Font color is **Yellow**.
- Using the same color scheme, format Category labels and column headings.
- Indent the Category labels, resizing column A if necessary, and center column headings.

h. Create a custom footer for all sheets containing your name, today's date, and your instructor's name. Use landscape orientation for all worksheets. Print the completed workbook. Save and close the workbook.

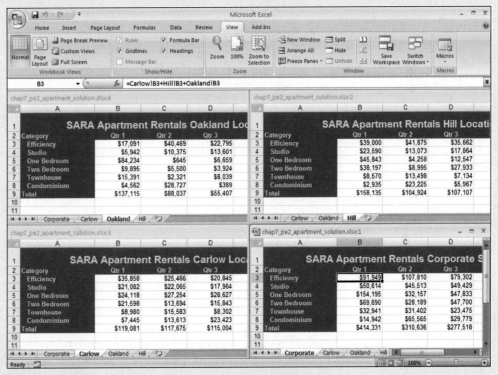

Figure 7.39 SARA Apartment Rentals—Worksheet References

...continued on Next Page

Retirement is a long way off, but it is never too soon to think about saving money. The worksheet shown in Figure 7.40 will calculate the value of your retirement, based on a set of uniform annual contributions to a retirement account. In effect, you contribute a fixed amount of money each year, $3,000, and the money accumulates at an estimated rate of return of 8%. You indicate the age when you start to contribute, your projected retirement age, the number of years in retirement, and the rate of return you expect to earn on your money when you retire. The worksheet determines the total amount you will have contributed, the amount of money you will have accumulated, and the value of your monthly pension. The numbers are impressive, and the sooner you begin to save, the better. The calculations use the Future Value (FV) and Payment (Pmt) functions, respectively. You will calculate the future value of your retirement, validate the date entered in the workbook, and protect the workbook to prevent users from entering unrealistic data.

a. Open the *chap7_pe3_validity* workbook and save it as **chap7_pe3_validity_solution** so you can open the workbook again.

b. Enter the appropriate formulas:
   - Click cell **B11**, type **=B3*(B5-B4)**, and press **Enter.**
   - Click cell **B12**, type **=FV(B6,(B5-B4),-B3)**, and press **Enter**.
   - Click cell **B13**, type **=PMT(B8/12,B7*12,-B12)**, and press **Enter**.

c. Format **cells B11:B13** as Currency, zero decimals.

d. Create the first validity check to verify that retirement age is greater than 59.5:
   - Click cell **B5**, then click **Data Validation** in the Data Tools group on the Data tab to open the Data Validation dialog box.
   - Click the **Settings tab**, then choose **Decimal** from the Allow down arrow list.
   - Choose **greater than or equal to** from the Data down arrow list.
   - Type **59.5** in the Minimum text box.
   - Click the **Input Message** tab and type **Retirement Age** in the Title text box.
   - Type **Federal Law does not permit pension payout prior to 59.5** in the Input message text box.
   - Click the **Error Alert** tab and select **Warning** from the Style down arrow list.
   - Type **Invalid Data** in the Title text box
   - Type **Age must be greater than 59.5** in the Error message text box, and click **OK**.

e. The second and third validity checks verify that the rate of return will not exceed 8% during the period you are investing money, and the rate of return during retirement cannot exceed 7%. You are to display a warning message if the user violates either of these conditions. The warning will allow the user to override the assumptions. Create the required validity checks in **cells B6** and **B8**. Remember to enter your values as decimal values.

f. Enter the parameters that are displayed in Figure 7.40, including the invalid entry of .08 in cell B8, by overriding the warning message. Click **Yes** in the Excel warning box.

g. Select **Circle Invalid Data** from the down arrow list in the Data Tools group to circle invalid data with a red circle.

h. Create a custom footer containing your name, a page number, and your instructor's name. Print the completed workbook to show both displayed values and cell formulas. Save and close the workbook.

...continued on Next Page

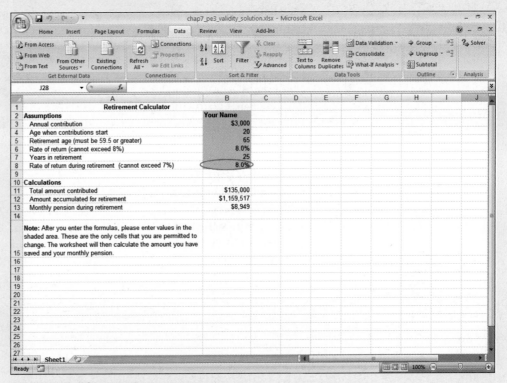

Figure 7.40 Retirement Calculator

4 Employee Profit Sharing—Circular References

A circular reference usually indicates a logic error, but there are times when it can be valid. Figure 7.41 displays a worksheet for an employee profit-sharing plan, in which the company contributes 25% of its net income to profit sharing. The net income is determined by subtracting expenses from revenue, but one of those expenses is profit sharing, which in turn creates the circular reference. In other words, the formula in cell B7 depends on the formula in cell B6, which depends on the formula in cell B7.

a. Open the *chap7_pe4_profitsharing* workbook and save it as **chap7_pe4_profitsharing_solution**.

b. Click **cell B7** and type the formula to compute the net income after profit sharing, **=B4-B5-B6**. Excel indicates that there is a circular reference. Click **OK** and close the Help screen if it appears. The Trace Precedents and Trace Dependents arrows appear in cells B6 and B7 to indicate a circular reference. The status bar shows a circular reference in cell B6.

c. Create a Watch Window:

• Click **Watch Window** in the Formula Auditing group on the **Formulas** tab to open the Watch Window dialog box.

• Click **Add Watch**, click **cell B6** to display =Sheet1!$B$6 in the **Select the cells that you would like to watch the value of:** in the Add Watch dialog box, and click **OK**.

• Click **Add Watch**, verify that =Sheet1!$B$7 is in the **Select the cells that you would like to watch the value of:** in the Add Watch dialog box, and click **OK**.

d. Click the **Office Button**, select **Excel Options**, click **Formulas**, select **Manual** in the Calculation options section, check **Enable iterative calculations**, select **1** in the Maximum Iterations box, and click **OK**. You can now recalculate the spreadsheet manually to see the effects of the circular reference.

...continued on Next Page

e. Click **Calculate Sheet** in the Calculation group continually or press **F9** (recalculate) continually to see the spreadsheet go through multiple iterations, eventually settling on steady state values of $400,000 and $1,600,000 for the profit sharing and net income, respectively. Note that the profit sharing value of $400,000 is 25% of the net income value of $1,600,000.

f. Close the Watch Window and create a custom footer containing your name, today's date, and your instructor's name.

g. Print the completed workbook. Save and close the workbook.

h. Restore Calculation Settings:

- Open a blank workbook.
- Click the **Office Button**.
- Select **Excel Options**.
- Click **Formulas**.
- Select **Automatic** in the Calculation options section.
- Remove the check from **Enable iterative calculations**.
- Type **100** in the Maximum Iterations box and click **OK**.

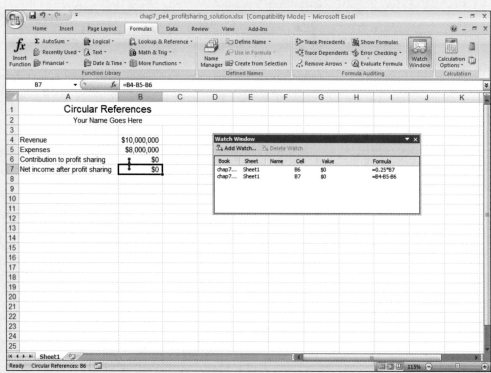

Figure 7.41   Circular Reference

The workbook shown in Figure 7.42 displays a summary worksheet that includes exam results for multiple sections of an introductory computer course. It also contains an individual worksheet for each section of the course. Your assignment as the professor's teaching assistant is to open the partially completed workbook, compute the test averages for each section, and then create the summary worksheet.

a. Open the *chap7_mid1_linkprofessor* workbook and save it as **chap7_mid1_link professor_solution** so that you can return to the original workbook if necessary.

b. Group the worksheets.

c. Create a formula to calculate the average on the first test for the students in Section 1. Copy the formula to **cells C10** and **D10**. The sections have different numbers of students, but the last student in every section appears in row 8 or before. The Average function ignores empty cells within the designated range, and you can use the same function for all four worksheets.

d. Check that the worksheets are still grouped and apply the same formatting to each worksheet.

e. Merge and center the name of the section in the first row and use bold text and a fill color. Change the color of the worksheet tab to match the formatting in the worksheet. You will not see the color change until you ungroup the worksheets.

f. Ungroup the worksheets and insert a blank worksheet for the summary, as shown in Figure 7.42. Enter the title and column headings as shown in rows 1 and 2.

g. Click **cell A3** of the summary worksheet and use a formula to display the section names in **cells A3:A6**.

h. Click **cell B3** of the summary worksheet and use a formula to display the average test score for Test 1 in Section 1. Copy the formula in **cell B3** to **cells C3** and **D3** of the summary worksheet. Enter the test grades for the other sections in similar fashion.

i. Format the summary worksheet using the same colors, fonts, and font sizes as the section sheets.

j. Insert a new sheet and create a documentation worksheet, making sure to include: Your Name as Author, Date of creation, Date of last modification, Description of the workbook, List of sheets in the workbook, and Description of each sheet.

k. Create a custom footer containing your name, a page number, and your instructor's name. Print the completed workbook. Save and close the workbook.

...continued on Next Page

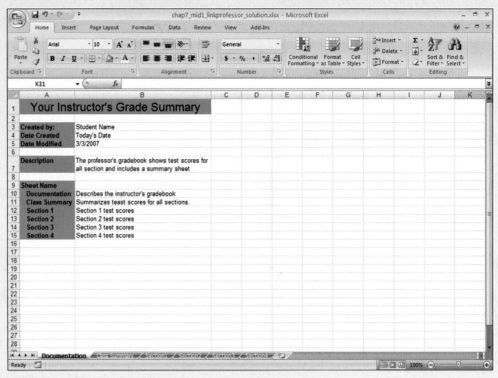

Figure 7.42 Linking Professor's Grade Sheets

2 The Plumber Corporation—Grouping Sheets

Your new job with The Plumber Corporation allows you to demonstrate your expertise with Excel. The workbook shown in Figure 7.43 contains a separate worksheet for each month of the year as well as a summary worksheet for the entire year. Each monthly worksheet tallies the expenses for five divisions in each of four categories to compute a monthly total for each division. The summary worksheet is designed to display the total expense for each division. However, only the months of January, February, and March are complete. Your assignment is to open the partially completed workbook and complete it as indicated below.

a. Open the *chap7_mid2_plumbercorp* workbook and save it as **chap7_mid2_plumber corp_solution**.

b. Insert a new worksheet for April to the right of the March worksheet and enter the appropriate row and column headings. Assume that Division 1 spends $100 in each category, Division 2 spends $200 in each category, Division 3 spends $300 in each category, and so on. Change the worksheet tab to April.

c. Group the sheets for January through April and calculate the expense total by division and by category.

d. Format the worksheet in an attractive fashion, making sure you include bold text, borders, and shaded cells as appropriate. Values are Currency with **0** decimal places. Change the color of the worksheet tab. Ungroup the worksheets and view the various monthly worksheets to verify that the formulas and formatting appear in each worksheet.

e. Click the worksheet tab for the summary worksheet. Insert a column for April to the right of the column for March. Click **cell B3**, type **=**, click in the January worksheet, click **cell F3** (the cell that contains the January total for Division 1), and press **Enter**. Enter the formulas for the remaining months for Division 1 in similar fashion.

...continued on Next Page

f. Create formulas to calculate year-to-date totals by division and totals by month. Copy the formulas in **cells B3:F3** to the remaining rows in the summary worksheet. Format the summary worksheet in the same manner as the monthly worksheets.

g. Use Page Setup to create a custom footer for all worksheets that includes your name, the name on the worksheet tab, and your instructor's name. Print the worksheet for April and the summary worksheet for your instructor as displayed and with formulas visible. Save and close the workbook.

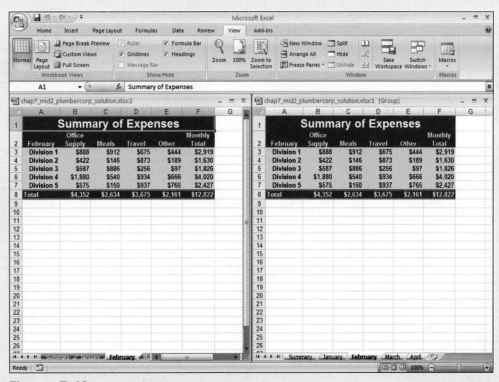

Figure 7.43 The Plumber Corporation

3 The Golf Shoppe Payroll

Your father, the owner of The Golf Shoppe, asked for your help with Excel. The worksheet shown in Figure 7.44 displays an erroneous version of a worksheet that computes the payroll for The Golf Shoppe. The worksheet is nicely formatted but your father wants you to make it more eye-catching. Several calculations are in error, and your assignment is to find the errors and correct the worksheet. You can "eyeball" the worksheet to find the mistakes, but you will use Formula Auditing techniques. Follow the guidelines below to correct the worksheet.

a. Open the *chap7_mid3_golfpayroll* workbook, save it as **chap7_mid3_golfpayroll_solution**, and print the worksheet prior to making any corrections.

b. Calculate the pay. The gross pay is the regular pay, hourly wage times regular hours, plus the overtime pay, hourly wage times the overtime hours times the overtime rate. The overtime rate is entered as an assumption within the worksheet.

c. Calculate the net pay, which is the gross pay minus the deductions, the withholding tax, and the Social Security tax.

d. Calculate the taxable income, which is the gross pay minus the deduction per dependent multiplied by the number of dependents.

e. Calculate the withholding tax, which is based on the individual's taxable income. The Social Security tax is based on the individual's gross pay.

...continued on Next Page

f. Format the worksheet in an attractive manner using fill colors, font colors, font sizes, and alignment.

g. Insert comments to describe the gross pay, taxable income, withholding tax, net pay, and total gross pay.

h. Create a custom footer that includes your name, today's date, and your instructor's name. Print the corrected worksheet with displayed values, comments, and cell formulas. Save and close the workbook.

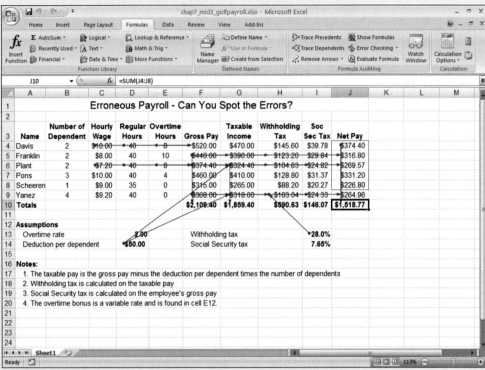

Figure 7.44 The Golf Shoppe Payroll

4 J&W Bank Mortgage Calculator

As the manager trainee of the J&W Bank, you must create a Mortgage Calculator in Excel. The worksheet shown in Figure 7.45 should be completely flexible in that it accepts the user's input in the shaded cells, and then it computes the associated monthly payments in the body of the worksheet. It also introduces the Evaluate Formula tool in the Formula Auditing group on the Formulas tab. The Evaluate Formula tool enables you to step through the calculation of any formula within a worksheet. Your assignment is to create the worksheet, as shown in Figure 7.45. This worksheet is protected so users can change only the shaded input values. You may want to review material on the PMT function, mixed references, and protecting worksheets.

a. Open the *chap7_mid4_jwbank* workbook and save it as **chap7_mid4_jwbank_solution**.

b. Click in **cell B8** and enter the formula =E4; the initial interest rate in the body of the spreadsheet is taken from the user's input in cell E4. Click in **cell C8** and enter the formula to calculate the incremental increases in interest rates, and copy the formula to the remaining cells in this row. Enter parallel formulas in **cells A9** to **A19** to compute the values for the principal amounts that will appear in the table. Check that your formulas

...continued on Next Page

are correct by changing the input parameters in rows 4 and 5. Any changes to the input parameters should be reflected in row 8 and/or column A.

c. Develop an appropriate PMT function for cells B9:G19. Remember to use mixed references in cell B9.

d. Use Evaluate Formula to evaluate formulas within the workbook to see how this tool can help you to understand how a formula works.

e. Format the completed worksheet to include eye-appealing fill color, font size, and font color, and values as Percent with 2 decimals or Currency with 2 decimals. You do not have to match the formatting shown exactly, but you are to shade the input parameters.

f. Unlock **cells B4:B6** and **cells E4:E5**, and then protect the completed worksheet. DO NOT USE a password for your worksheet.

g. Create a custom footer that includes your name, a page number, and your instructor's name.

h. Print the worksheet two ways, once with displayed values and once with the cell formulas. Use landscape orientation. Save and close the workbook.

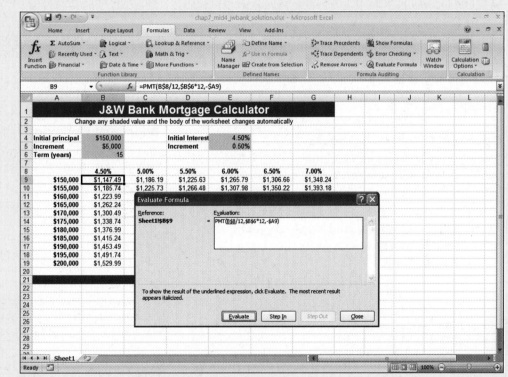

Figure 7.45 Mortgage Calculator

Capstone Exercise

Bruno's Pizza offers a tasty pizza at a "steal" of a price, with a strong appeal to the college and family crowds. Their pizzas are generously proportioned and made with a homemade spicy pizza sauce to create a unique zesty flavor, and their list of toppings includes some of the most off-the-wall but healthy selections around. This tried-and-true proven product offering, combined with great customer service, keeps their pizzas flying out the door! Bruno's Pizza has expanded from its initial restaurant downtown to two additional sites elsewhere in the city.

The owner, Joe Bruno, wants to evaluate the overall performance of the chain before expanding further. He is especially interested in the comparative results of three dining categories: dine-in, pickup, and delivery. Joe knows you are studying Excel at the local college and asked for your help in return for a small stipend and all the pizza you can eat. You have already prepared a template and distributed it to each restaurant manager, who has entered the sales data for last year. Your next task is to consolidate the data into a single workbook that shows the total sales for each quarter and each dining category. The information should be shown in tabular as well as graphical form. You will also create a documentation sheet so that Joe will know exactly what you have created. Make sure you audit all formulas, trace precedents and dependents, and evaluate the formulas for accuracy.

Open and Save the Workbooks

You must open four workbooks: the partially completed Summary and the completed Westside, Eastside, and Downtown workbooks.

a. Open the files: *chap7_cap_summary*, *chap7_cap_westside*, *chap7_cap_eastside*, and *chap7_cap_downtown*.

b. Save the Summary workbook as **chap7_cap_summary_solution**.

Copy and Arrange the Worksheets

You have collected quarterly sales data for three modes of dining from the managers and want to summarize them on one worksheet.

a. Copy the Eastside, Westside, and Downtown worksheets into the Summary workbook.

b. Tile the four worksheets so you can see all of the data.

Summarizing Dining Categories by Quarter

You must provide a summary report of the dining category sales by quarter for the year so Joe Bruno knows exactly what each location is doing.

a. Create formulas to calculate sales by dining category and quarter for all locations on the Summary sheet.

b. Calculate grand totals by quarter and by dining category.

Audit Formulas

Before giving your financial report to Joe Bruno, you must verify the accuracy of your formulas and results. You will use the tools in the Formula Auditing group on the Formulas tab to verify your results.

a. Trace Precedents and Dependents on the Summary worksheet.

b. Use Error Checking to determine if there are errors in your formulas and to trace any errors.

c. Use Evaluate Formula to verify the results of your formula.

Create Chart

Joe Bruno is more of a visual person, and you want to present your data in an alternate way. You will create a chart visualizing your summary data.

a. Create a chart on a separate sheet.

b. Include a title, legend, and data labels on your chart.

c. Format the chart to coordinate with your summary chart using the same colors, fonts, font sizes, and clip art.

Document Workbook

You must document your workbook with a professional-looking documentation sheet before Joe Bruno can reimburse you for your work.

a. Insert a new sheet and rename the sheet tab Documentation.

b. Include the following on your documentation worksheet: Your Name as Author, Date of creation, Date of last modification, Description of the workbook, List of sheets in the workbook, and Description of each sheet.

c. Format your documentation worksheet using the same colors and font as used in the other worksheets and chart.

d. Hide the gridlines on the documentation sheet.

Print the Workbook

As part of the documentation process, you recognize that each worksheet in the workbook must include standard footers. Create a custom footer that contains your name, page number, and your instructor's name. Print the completed workbook.

a. Group the worksheets and create a custom footer with your name on the left, the page number in the middle, and your instructor's name on the right.

b. Add the custom footer to the chart sheet.

c. Print the workbook as displayed, and print the Summary worksheet with formulas displayed. Save and close the workbook.

Mini Cases

Use the rubric following the case as a guide to evaluate your work, but keep in mind that your instructor may impose additional grading criteria or use a different standard to judge your work.

Leason International Security Sales Summary

GENERAL CASE

Each branch manager of Leason International Security creates an identically formatted workbook with the sales information for his or her branch office. Your job as marketing manager is to consolidate the regional quarterly sales information into a single workbook, and then graph the results appropriately. The branch data are to remain in the individual workbooks; that is, the formulas in your workbook are to contain external references to the sales information workbooks. Begin by opening the individual workbooks: *chap7_mc1_foreign*, *chap7_mc1_eastern*, and *chap7_mc1_western* and saving them as: **chap7_mc1_foreign_solution**, **chap7_mc1_eastern_solution**, and **chap7_mc1_western_solution**. Enter the appropriate formulas to total the data for each product and each quarter. Begin a new workbook and save it as **chap7_mc1_summary_solution**. You will use the summary workbook to reflect the quarterly totals for each branch through external references to the individual workbooks. Any change in the individual workbooks should be automatically reflected in the consolidated workbook. Be sure to include a documentation worksheet in your summary workbook.

Performance Elements	Exceeds Expectations	Meets Expectations	Below Expectations
Consolidate with accurate formulas	All formulas correct.	One formula incorrect.	Two or more formulas incorrect.
Chart	Chart accurate, includes title and legend.	Chart accurate but missing either title or legend.	No chart.
Documentation worksheet	Four or more major documentation items included.	Two or more major documentation items included.	No documentation worksheet.

Watch Window

RESEARCH CASE

Use Excel Help to research the concept of Watch Windows. You are specifically looking for information about when they are used and what their purpose is. You want to know where they are most effectively and efficiently used. You will open and use the *chap7_mc2_mines* workbook to practice what you learn about Watch Windows. Save the workbook as **chap7_mc2_mines_solution**. Your final workbook will include a Watch Window with watches on three cells containing formulas. Include a brief paragraph summarizing the use of Watch Windows. Print the workbook.

Performance Elements	Exceeds Expectations	Meets Expectations	Below Expectations
Watch Window	Watching three or more cells.	Watching two cells.	No Watch Window.
Summary	Complete and inclusive.	Either incomplete or not inclusive.	No summary.
Print	Includes standard footer data.	No footer included.	No printout.

Find and Fix the Errors

DISASTER RECOVERY

A friend of yours has asked for your help. He has created a grade book to use with his student teaching experience. The grade book is well formatted and easy to read, but it contains some fundamental errors. You are to correct the errors and complete any additional processing requirements for your colleague. Use the tools in the Formula Auditing tools to identify and correct the errors. Open the workbook *chap7_mc3_studentteaching* and save it as **chap7_mc3_student teaching_solution.** You will create a VLOOKUP function and find three major errors. Correct the errors and explain how the errors might have occurred and how they can be prevented. Include your explanation in the form of comments in the appropriate cells in the spreadsheet.

Performance Elements	Exceeds Expectations	Meets Expectations	Below Expectations
VLOOKUP function	Correct with accurate results.	Formula incorrectly applied.	No VLOOKUP.
Identify and correct errors	Identified and corrected all three errors.	Identified and corrected two errors.	Identified and corrected one or no errors.
Explain the error	Complete and correct explanation of each error.	Explanation is too brief to fully explain error.	No explanations.
Prevention description	Prevention description correct and practical.	Prevention description, but obtuse.	No prevention description.

Introduction to Access

Finding Your Way Through a Database

bjectives

After you read this chapter, you will be able to:

1. Explore, describe, and navigate among the objects in an Access database **(page 749)**.

2. Understand the difference between working in storage and memory **(page 756)**.

3. Practice good file management **(page 757)**.

4. Back up, compact, and repair Access files **(page 758)**.

5. Create filters **(page 767)**.

6. Sort table data on one or more fields **(page 770)**.

7. Know when to use Access or Excel to manage data **(page 772)**.

8. Use the Relationship window **(page 780)**.

9. Understand relational power **(page 781)**.

Hands-On Exercises

Exercises	Skills Covered
1. INTRODUCTION TO DATABASES (page 759) **Open:** chap1_ho1-3_traders.accdb **Copy, rename, and back up as:** chap1_ho1-3_traders_solution.accdb and chap1_ho1_traders_solution.accdb	• Create a Production Folder and Copy an Access File • Open an Access File • Edit a Record • Navigate an Access Form and Add Records • Recognize the Table and Form Connectivity and Delete a Record • Back Up and Compact the Database
2. DATA MANIPULATION: FILTERS AND SORTS (page 774) **Open:** chap1_ho1-3_traders_soution.accdb (from Exercise 1) **Copy, rename, and back up as:** chap1_ho1-3_traders_solution.accdb (additional modifications), chap1_ho2_traders_solution.docx, and chap1_ho2_traders_solution.accdb	• Use Filter by Selection with an Equal Setting • Use Filter by Selection with a Contains Setting • Use Filter by Form with an Inequity Setting • Sort a Table
3. INTRODUCTION TO RELATIONSHIPS (page 783) **Open:** chap1_ho1-3_traders_solution.accdb (from Exercise 2) **Copy, rename, and back up as:** chap1_ho1-3_traders_solution.accdb (additional modifications)	• Examine the Relationships Window • Discover That Changes in Table Data Affect Queries • Use Filter by Form with an Inequity Setting and Reapply a Saved Filter • Filter a Report • Remove an Advanced Filter

CASE STUDY

Medical Research—The Lifelong Learning Physicians Association

Today is the first day of your information technology internship appointment with the *Lifelong Learning Physicians Association*. This medical association selected you for the internship because your résumé indicates that you are proficient with Access. Bonnie Clinton, M.D., founded the organization with the purpose of keeping doctors informed about current research and to help physicians identify quali-

Case Study

fied study participants. Dr. Clinton worries that physicians do not inform their patients about study participation opportunities. She expressed further concerns that the physicians in one field, e.g., cardiology, are unfamiliar with research studies conducted in other fields, such as obstetrics.

Because the association is new, you have very little data to manage. However, the system was designed to accommodate additional data. You will need to talk to Dr. Clinton on a regular basis to determine the association's changing information needs. You may need to guide her in this process. Your responsibilities as the association's IT intern include many items.

Your Assignment

- Read the chapter, paying special attention to learning the vocabulary of database software.
- Copy the *chap1_case_physicians.accdb* file to your production folder, rename it **chap1_case_physicians_solution.accdb**, and enable the content.
- Open the Relationships window and examine the relationships among the tables and the fields contained within each of the tables to become acquainted with this database.
- Open the Volunteers table. Add yourself as a study participant by replacing record **22** with your own information. You should invent data about your height, weight, blood pressure, and your cholesterol. Examine the values in the other records and enter a realistic value. Do not change the stored birthday.
- Identify all of the volunteers who might be college freshmen (18- and 19-year-olds). After you identify them, print the table listing their names and addresses. Use a filter by form with an appropriately set date criterion to identify the correctly aged participants.
- Identify all of the physicians participating in a study involving cholesterol management.
- Open the *Studies and Volunteers Report*. Print it.
- Compact and repair the database file.
- Create a backup of the database. Name the backup **chap1_case_physicians_backup.accdb**.

Data and Files Everywhere!

You probably use databases often. Each time you download an MP3 file, you enter a database via the Internet. There, you find searchable data identifying files by artist's name, music style, most frequently requested files, first lines, publication companies, and song titles. If you know the name of the song but not the recording artist or record label, you generally can find it. The software supporting the Web site helps you locate the information you need. The server for the Web site provides access to a major database that contains a lot of data about available MP3 files.

> Each time you download an MP3 file, you enter a database via the internet.

You are exposed to other databases on a regular basis. For example, your university uses a database to support the registration process. When you registered for this course, you entered a database. It probably told you how many seats remained but not the names of the other students. In addition, Web-based job and dating boards are based on database software. Organizations rely on data to conduct daily operations, regardless of whether the organization exists as a profit or not-for-profit environment. The organization maintains data about employees, volunteers, customers, activities, and facilities. Every keystroke and mouse click creates data about the organization that needs to be stored, organized, and analyzed. Microsoft Access provides the organizational decision-maker a valuable tool facilitating data retrieval and use.

In this section, you explore Access database objects and work with table views. You also learn the difference between working in storage and memory to understand how changes to database objects are saved. Finally, you practice good file management techniques by backing up, compacting, and repairing databases.

Exploring, Describing, and Navigating Among the Objects in an Access Database

A **field** is a basic entity or data element, such as the name of a book or the telephone number of a publisher.

A **record** is a complete set of all of the data (fields) about one person, place, event, or idea.

A **table** is a collection of records. Every record in a table contains the same fields in the same order.

A **database** consists of one or more tables and the supporting objects used to get data into and out of the tables.

To understand database management effectively and to use Access productively, you should first learn the vocabulary. A **field** is a basic entity, data element, or category, such as book titles or telephone numbers. The field does not necessarily need to contain a value. For example, a field might store fax numbers for a firm's customers. However, some of the customers may not have a fax machine so the Fax field is blank for that record. A **record** is a complete set of all of the data (fields) about one person, place, event, or idea. For example, your name, homework, and test scores constitute your record in your instructor's grade book. A **table**, the foundation of every database, is a collection of related records that contain fields to organize data. If you have used Excel, you will see the similarities between a spreadsheet and an Access table. Each column represents a field, and each row represents a record. Every record in a table contains the same fields in the same order. An instructor's grade book for one class is a table containing records of all students in one structure. A **database** consists of one or more tables and the supporting objects used to get data into and out of the tables.

Prior to the advent of database management software, organizations managed their data manually. They placed papers in file folders and organized the folders in multiple drawer filing cabinets. You can think of the filing cabinet in the manual system as a database. Each drawer full of folders in the filing cabinet corresponds to a table within the database. Figure 1.1 shows a college's database system from before the information age. File drawers (tables) contain student data. Each folder (record) contains facts (fields) about that student. The cabinet also contains drawers (tables) full of data about the faculty and the courses offered. Together, the tables combine to form a database system.

TIP   Data Versus Information

Data and information are not synonymous, although, the terms often are used interchangeably. Data is the raw material and consists of the table (or tables) that comprise a database. Information is the finished product. Data is converted to information by selecting (filtering) records, by sequencing (sorting) the selected records, or by summarizing data from multiple records. Decisions in an organization are based on information compiled from multiple records, as opposed to raw data.

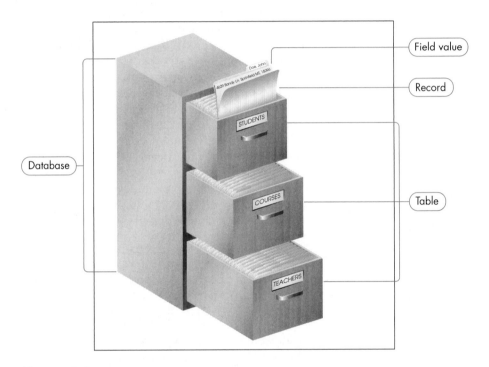

Figure 1.1   Primitive Database

Identify Access Interface Elements

Figure 1.2 shows how Microsoft Access appears onscreen. It contains two open windows—an application window for Microsoft Access and a document (database) window for the open database. Each window has its own title bar and icons. The title bar in the application window contains the name of the application (Microsoft Access) and the Minimize and Maximize (or Restore) icons. The title bar in the document (database) window contains the name of the object that is currently open (Employees table). Should more than one object be open at a time, the top of the document window will display tabs for each open object. The Access application window is maximized; therefore, Restore is visible.

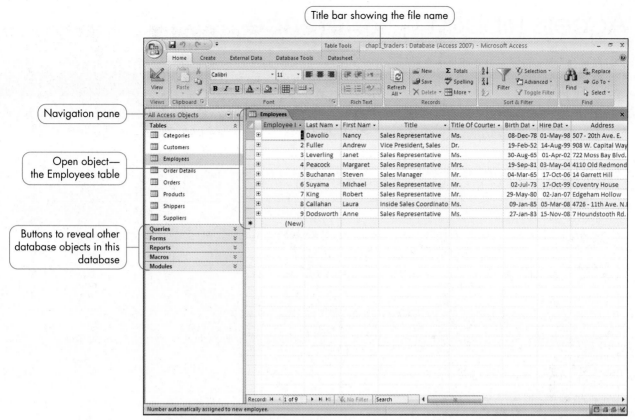

Figure 1.2 An Access Database

Let us look at an example of a database for an international food distribution company—The Northwind Traders. This firm sells specialty food items to restaurants and food shops around the world. It also purchases the products it sells from diversely located firms. The Northwind Traders Company database contains eight tables: Categories, Customers, Employees, Order Details, Orders, Products, Shippers, and Suppliers. Each table, in turn, consists of multiple records, corresponding to the folders in the file cabinet. The Employees table, for example, contains a record for every employee. Each record in the Employees table contains 17 fields—where data about the employee's education, address, photograph, position, and so on are stored. Occasionally, a field does not contain a value for a particular record. One of the employees, Margaret Peacock, did not provide a picture. The value of that field is missing. Access provides a placeholder to store the data when it is available. The Suppliers table has a record for each vendor from whom the firm purchases products, just as the Orders table has a record for each order. The real power of Access is derived from a database with multiple tables and the relationships that connect the tables.

The database window displays the various objects in an Access database. An
*An Access **object** contains the basic elements of the database.*
Access **object** stores the basic elements of the database. Access uses six types of objects—tables, queries, forms, reports, macros, and modules. Every database must contain at least one table, and it may contain any, all, or none of the other objects. Each object type is accessed through the appropriate tab within the database window. Because of the interrelationships among objects, you may either view all of the objects of a type in a single place or view all of the related objects in a way that demonstrates their inner-connectivity. You select an object for viewing using the Navigation pane. The Navigation pane on the left side groups related objects.

The Reference page describes the tabs and groups on the Ribbon in Access 2007. You do not need to memorize most of these tabs and groups now. You will learn where things are located as you explore using the features.

Access Ribbon | Reference

Tab and Group	Description
Home Views Clipboard Font Rich Text Records Sort & Filter Find	The basic Access tab. Contains basic editing functions such as cut and paste along with most formatting actions. As with all groups, Dialog Box Launchers are available and do increase functionality.
Create Tables Forms Reports Other	Brings together all create operations in one area. Includes ability to create queries through the wizard or in Design view.
External Data Import Export Collect Data SharePoint Lists	Contains all of the operations to facilitate collaboration and data exchange.
Database Tools Macro Show/Hide Analyze Move Data	The area that contains the operational backbone of Access. Here, you create and maintain the relationships of the database. You also analyze the file performance and perform routine maintenance.

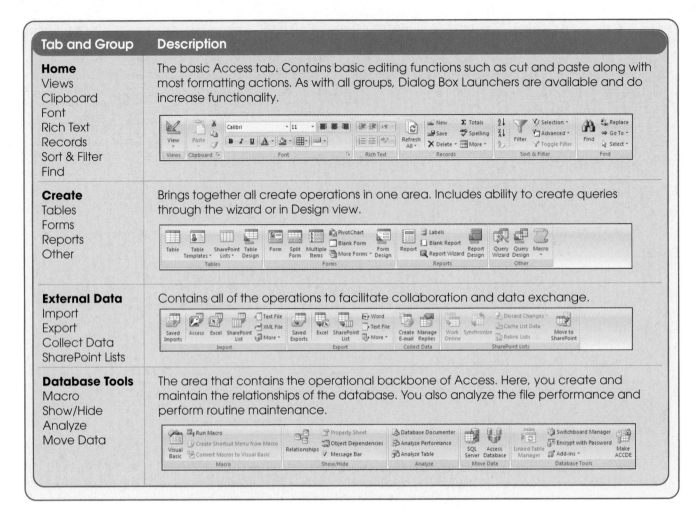

Work with Table Views

The **Datasheet view** is a grid where you add, edit, and delete the records of a table.

The **Design view** is a different grid where you create and modify the properties of the table.

Access provides different ways in which to view a table and most other objects. The **Datasheet view** is a grid containing columns (fields) and rows (records). You can view, add, edit, and delete records of a table in the Datasheet view. You can use the **Design view** to create and modify the table by specifying the fields it will contain and their associated properties. The field type (for example, text or numeric data) and the field length are examples of field properties. If you need the values stored in a particular field to display as currency, you would modify the property of that field to ensure all values display appropriately.

Figure 1.3 shows the Datasheet view for the Customers table. The first row in the table displays the field names. Each additional row contains a record (the data for a specific customer). Each column represents a field (one fact about a customer). Every record in the table contains the same fields in the same order.

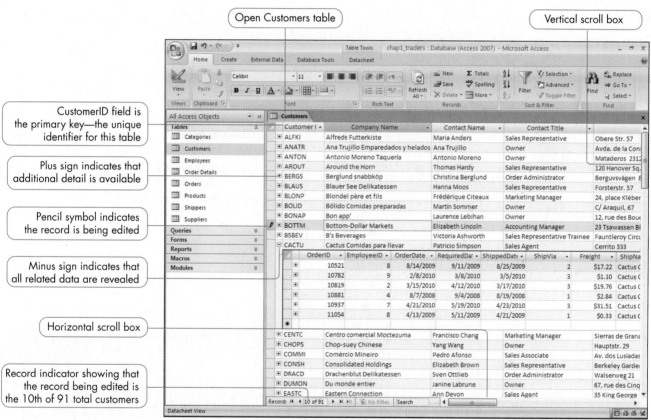

Figure 1.3 The Customers Table and Related Order Information

The **primary key** is the field that makes each record in a table unique.

The **primary key** is the field (or combination of fields) that makes each record in a table unique. The CustomerID is the primary key in the Customers table; it ensures that every record in a table is different from every other record, and it prevents the occurrence of duplicate records. Primary key fields may be numbers, letters, or a combination of both. In this case the primary key is text (letters).

The Navigation bar at the bottom of Figure 1.3 shows a table with 91 records and record number 10 as the current record. You can work on only one record at a time. The vertical scroll bar at the right of the window shows that more records exist in the table than you can see at one time. The horizontal scroll bar at the bottom of the window indicates that you cannot see an entire record.

The pencil icon at the left of the record indicates that the data in the current record are being edited and that the changes have not yet been saved. The pencil icon disappears after you complete the data entry and move to another record, because Access saves data automatically as soon as you move from one record to the next.

Figure 1.4 displays the navigation buttons that you use to move within most Access objects. You may navigate using commands to go to the last and first records, advance and go back one record, and add a new record.

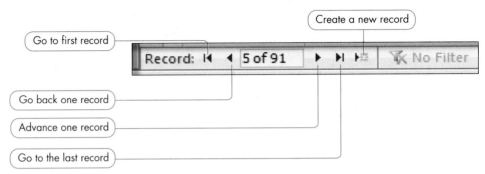

Figure 1.4 Navigation Buttons

Use Forms, Queries, and Reports

As previously indicated, an Access database is made up of different types of objects together with the tables and the data they contain. A table (or set of tables) is at the heart of any database because it contains the actual data. The other objects in a database—such as forms, queries, and reports—are based on an underlying table. Figure 1.5 displays a form based on the Customers table shown earlier.

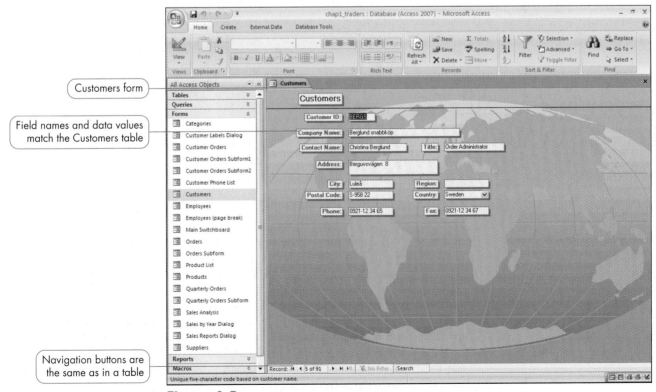

Figure 1.5 Customers Form

A **form** is an interface that enables you to enter or modify record data.

A **query** provides information that answers a question.

A **criterion** (**criteria**, pl) is a rule or norm that is the basis for making judgments.

A **form** is an interface that enables you to enter or modify record data. Commands may appear in the form to add a new record, print a record, or close the form. The form provides access to all of the data maintenance operations that are available through a table. The status bar and navigation buttons at the bottom of the form are similar to those that appear at the bottom of a table. You use the form in Datasheet view, but create and edit the form structure in Design view.

Figure 1.6 displays a query that lists the products that the firm purchases from a particular supplier. A **query** provides information that answers a question based on the data within an underlying table or tables. The Suppliers table, for example, contains records for many vendors, but the query in Figure 1.6 shows only the products that were supplied by a specific supplier. If you want to know the details about a specific supplier, you establish a criterion to specify which supplier you need to know about. A **criterion** (**criteria**, pl) is a rule or norm that is the basis for making judgments. If you need the names of all the suppliers in New York, you set a criterion to identify the New York suppliers. The results would yield only those suppliers from New York. Query results are similar in appearance to the underlying table, except that the query contains selected records and/or selected fields for those records. The query also may list the records in a different sequence from that of the table. (You also can use a query to add new records and modify existing records.) If you have a query open and notice an error in an address field, you can edit the record, and the edited value would immediately and permanently transfer to the table storing that record. Queries may be opened in Datasheet view or Design view. You use the Datasheet view to examine the query output and use the Design view to specify which fields and records to include in the query.

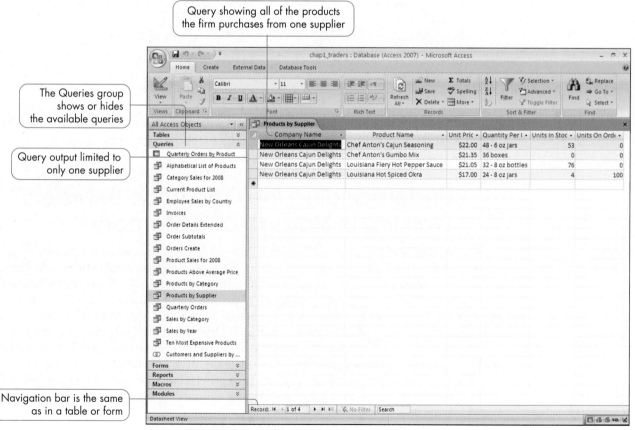

Figure 1.6 Results of a Query Shown in Datasheet View

Figure 1.7 displays a report that contains the same information as the query in Figure 1.6. A *report* contains professionally formatted information from underlying tables or queries. Because the report information contains a more enhanced format than a query or table, you place database output in a report to print. Access provides different views for designing, modifying, and running reports. Most Access users use only the Print Preview, Print Layout, and Report views of a report.

A *report* presents database information professionally.

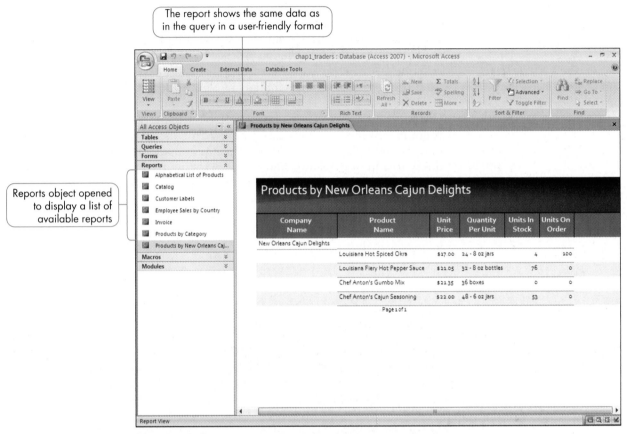

Figure 1.7 Report Displaying the Query Information from Figure 1.6

Understanding the Difference Between Working in Storage and Memory

Access is different from the other Microsoft Office applications. Word, Excel, and PowerPoint all work primarily from memory. In those applications you can easily reverse mistakes by using Undo. You make a change, discover that you dislike it, and click Undo to restore the original. These actions are possible because you work in memory (RAM) most of the time while in the other Microsoft Office applications; changes are not saved automatically to the file immediately after you make the changes. These actions are also possible because, generally, you are the only user of your file. If you work on a group project, you might e-mail the PowerPoint file to the others in the group, but you are the primary owner and user of that file. Access is *different*.

Access is different from the other Microsoft Office applications.

Access works primarily from storage. When you make a change to a field's content in an Access table (for example, changing a customer's area code), Access saves your changes as soon as you move the insertion point to a different record; you do not need to click Save. You can click Undo to reverse several editing changes (such as changing an area code and a contact name) for a single record **immediately** after making the changes to that record. However, unlike other Office programs that let you continue

Undoing actions, you cannot use Undo to reverse edits to more than the last record you edited or to restore a field if you delete it.

Multiple users can work on the database simultaneously. As long as no two users attempt to interact with the same record at the same time, the system updates as it goes. This also means that any reports extracting the information from the database contain the most up-to-date data. The only time you need to click Save is when you are creating or changing a structural element, such as a table, query, form, or report.

TIP Save Edits While Keeping a Record Active

When you want to save changes to a record you are editing while staying on the same record, press Shift+Enter. The pencil icon, indicating an editing mode, disappears, indicating that the change is saved.

Be careful to avoid accidentally typing something in a record and pressing Enter. Doing so saves the change, and you can retrieve the original data if you are lucky enough to remember to click Undo immediately before making or editing other records. Because Access is a relational database, several other related objects (queries, reports, or forms) could also be permanently changed. In Access, one file holds everything. All of the objects—tables, forms, queries, and reports—are saved both individually and as part of the Access collection.

TIP Data Validation

No system, no matter how sophisticated, can produce valid output from invalid input. Thus, good systems are built to anticipate errors in data entry and to reject those errors prior to saving a record. Access will automatically prevent you from adding records with a duplicate primary key or entering invalid data into a numeric or date field. The database developer has the choice whether to require other types of validation, such as requiring the author's name.

Practicing Good File Management

You must exercise methodical and deliberate file management techniques to avoid damaging data. Every time you need to open a file, this book will direct you to copy the file to your production folder and rename the copied file. Name the production folder with **Your Name Access Production**. You would not copy a real database and work in the copy often. However, as you learn, you will probably make mistakes. Following the practice of working in a copied file will facilitate mistake recovery during the learning process.

Further, it matters to which type of media you save your files. Access does not work from some media. Access runs best from a hard or network drive because those drives have sufficient access speed to support the software. Access speed measures the time it takes for the storage device to make the file content available for use. If you work from your own computer, create the production folder in the My Documents folder on the hard drive. Most schools lock their hard drives so that students cannot permanently save files there. If your school provides you with storage space on the school's network, store your production folder there. The advantage to using the network is that the network administration staff backs up files regularly. If you have no storage on the school network, your next best storage option is a thumb drive, also known as USB jump drive, flash drive, Pen drive, or stick drive.

Access speed measures the time it takes for the storage device to make the file content available for use.

All of the objects in an Access database are stored in a single file. You can open a database from within Windows Explorer by double-clicking the file name. You also can open the database from within Access through the Recent Documents list or by clicking the Microsoft Office Button (noted as Office Button only in this textbook) and selecting Open from the Office menu. The individual objects within a database are opened from the database window.

Backing Up, Compacting, and Repairing Access Files

Data is the lifeblood of any organization. Imagine what would happen to a firm that loses the records of the orders placed but not shipped or the charity that loses the list of donor contribution records or the hospital that loses the digital records of patient X-rays. What would happen to the employee who "accidentally" deleted mission-critical data? What would happen to the other employees who did not lose the mission-critical data? Fortunately, Access recognizes how critical backup procedures are to organizations and makes backing up the database files easy.

Back Up a Database

You back up an Access file (and all of the objects it contains) with just a few mouse clicks. To back up files, click the Office Button and select Manage from the Office menu. When you select Back Up Database, the Save As dialog box opens. You may use controls in the Save As dialog box to specify storage location and file name. Access provides a default file name that is the original file name followed by the date. In most organizations, this step is useful because the Information Technology department backs up every database each day.

Compact and Repair a Database

All databases have a tendency to expand with use. This expansion will occur without new information being added. Simply using the database, creating queries and running them, or applying and removing filters may cause the file to store inefficiently. Because the files tend to be rather large to start with, any growth creates problems. Access provides another utility, Compact and Repair, under the Manage submenu in the Office menu that addresses this issue. The Compact and Repair utility acts much like a disk defragmenter utility. It finds related file sectors and reassembles them in one location if they become scattered from database use. You should compact and repair your database each day when you close the file. This step often will decrease file size by 50% or more. Access closes any open objects during the compact and repair procedure, so it is a good idea to close any objects in the database prior to compacting so that you will control if any design changes will be saved or not.

In the next hands-on exercise, you will work with a database from an international gourmet food distributor, the Northwind Traders. This firm purchases food items from suppliers and sells them to restaurants and specialty food shops. It depends on the data stored in the Access database to make daily decisions.

Hands-On Exercises

1 | Introduction to Databases

Skills covered: 1. Create a Production Folder and Copy an Access File **2.** Open an Access File **3**. Edit a Record **4.** Navigate an Access Form and Add Records **5.** Recognize the Table and Form Connectivity and Delete a Record **6.** Back Up and Compact the Database

---

Step 1
Create a Production Folder and Copy an Access File

Refer to Figure 1.8 as you complete Step 1.

a. Right-click **My Computer** on the desktop and select **Explore** from the shortcut menu.

This step opens the Explore utility in a two-pane view that facilitates transferring materials between folders.

b. Determine where your production folder will reside and double-click that location. For example, double-click the **My Documents** folder if that is where your files will reside.

For the remainder of this book, it is assumed that your production folder resides in the My Document folder on the hard drive. Your folder may actually exist on another drive. What is important is that you (1) create and use the folder and (2) remember where it is.

c. Right-click anywhere on a blank spot in the right pane of the Exploring window. Select **New**, and then select **Folder** from the shortcut menu.

A new folder is created with the default name, New Folder, selected and ready to be renamed.

d. Type **Your Name Access Production** and press **Enter**.

e. Open the folder that contains the student data files that accompany this textbook.

f. Find the file named *chap1_ho1-3_traders.accdb*, right-click the file, and select **Copy** from the shortcut menu.

g. Go to the newly created production folder named with your name. Right-click a blank area in the right side of the Exploring window and select **Paste**.

You have created a copy of the original *chap1_ho1-3_traders.accdb* file. You will work with the copy. In the event that you make mistakes, the original remains intact in the student data folder. You can recopy it and rework the exercise if necessary.

h. Rename the newly copied file **your_name_chap1_ho1-3_traders_solution.accdb**.

You need to remember to rename all of the solution files with your name. If your instructor requests that you submit your work for evaluation using a shared folder on the campus network, each file must have a unique name. You risk overwriting another student's work (or having someone overwrite your work) if you do not name your files with your name and the file designation.

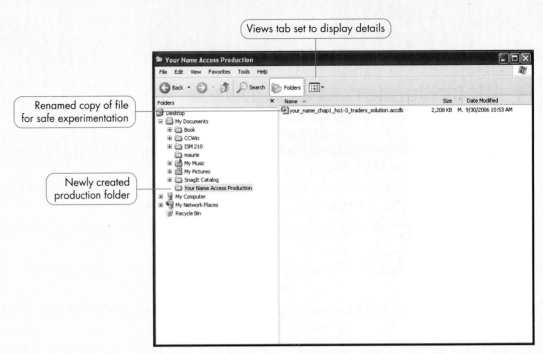

Figure 1.8 Production Folder Created Showing Copied and Renamed File

Step 2

Open an Access File

Refer to Figure 1.9 as you complete Step 2.

a. Double-click the *your_name_chap1_ho1-3_traders_solution* file to open it.

This step launches Access and opens the Explore file. From now on, this book will refer to the files without the *your_name* prefix.

b. Click **Options** on the Security Warning toolbar. See Figure 1.9.

Each time you open an Access file for the remainder of the class, you will need to enable the content. Several viruses and worms may be transmitted via Access files. You may be reasonably confident of the trustworthiness of the files in this book. However, if an Access file arrives as an attachment from an unsolicited e-mail message, you should not open it. Microsoft warns all users of Access files that a potential threat exists every time the file is opened.

c. Click **Enable this content**, and then click **OK**.

The Microsoft Office Security Options dialog box closes and the Security Warning toolbar disappears.

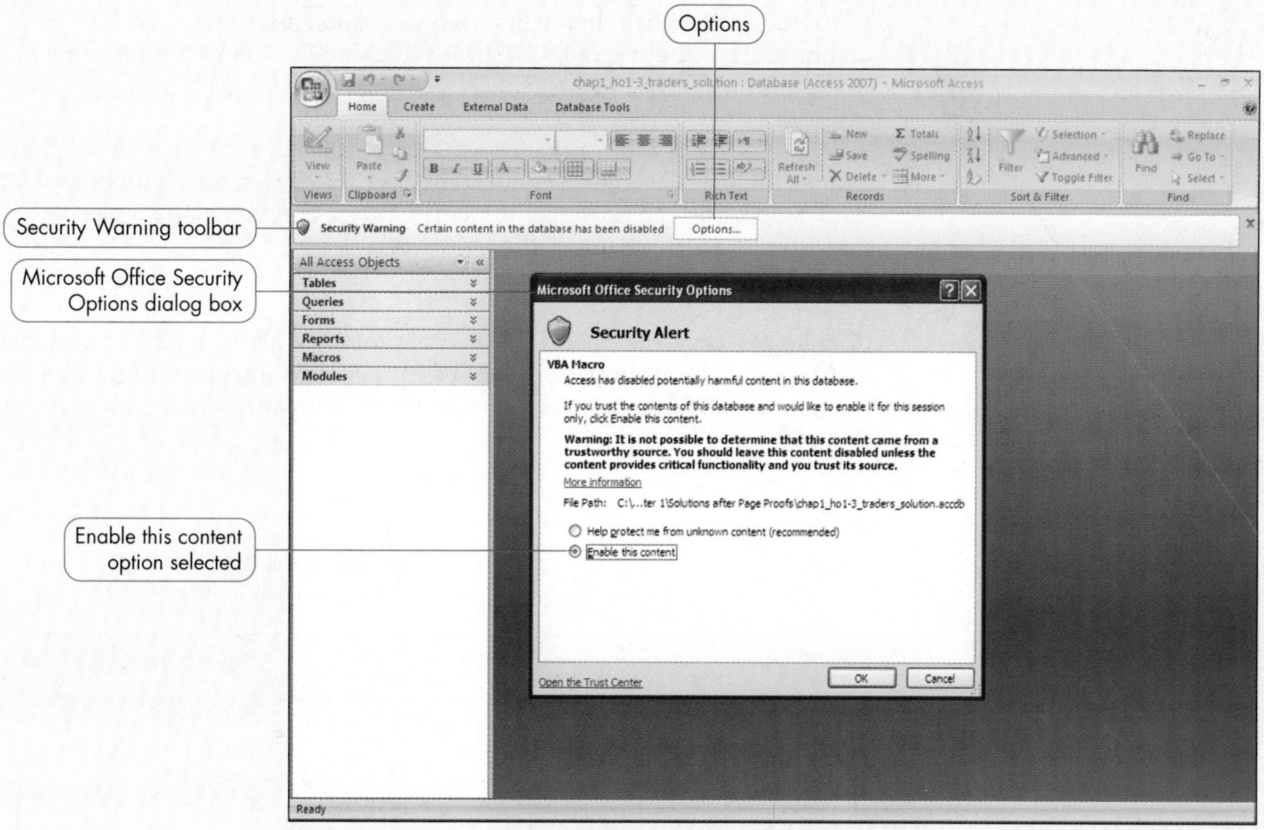
Options
Security Warning toolbar
Microsoft Office Security Options dialog box
Enable this content option selected
chap1_ho1-3_traders_solution : Database (Access 2007) - Microsoft Access
Home
Create
External Data
Database Tools
Security Warning
Certain content in the database has been disabled
Options...
All Access Objects
Tables
Queries
Forms
Reports
Macros
Modules
Microsoft Office Security Options
Security Alert
VBA Macro
Access has disabled potentially harmful content in this database.
If you trust the contents of this database and would like to enable it for this session only, click Enable this content.
Warning: It is not possible to determine that this content came from a trustworthy source. You should leave this content disabled unless the content provides critical functionality and you trust its source.
More information
File Path: C:\...ter 1\Solutions after Page Proofs\chap1_ho1-3_traders_solution.accdb
Help protect me from unknown content (recommended)
Enable this content
Open the Trust Center
OK
Cancel
Ready

Figure 1.9 Microsoft Office Security Options Dialog Box

Step 3
Edit a Record

Refer to Figure 1.10 as you complete Step 3.

a. Click **Tables** in the Navigation pane to expand the list of available tables.

   The list of tables contained in the database file opens.

b. Double-click the **Employees table** to open it. See Figure 1.10.

c. Click the insertion point in the fourth row. Double-click *Peacock* in the LastName field. The entire name highlights. Type **your last name** to replace *Peacock*.

d. Press **Tab** to move to the next field in the fourth row. Replace *Margaret* with **your first name**.

   You have made changes to two fields in the same record (row); the pencil displays in the row selector box.

e. Click **Undo** on the Quick Access Toolbar.

   Your first name reverts back to Margaret because you have not yet left the record.

f. Type your name again to replace *Margaret* with **your first name**. Press **Enter**.

   You should now be in the Title field and your title, *Sales Representative*, is selected. The pencil icon still displays in the row selector.

g. Click anywhere in the third row where Janet Leverling's data are stored.

   The pencil icon disappears; your changes to the table have been saved.

h. Click the address field in the first record, the one for Nancy Davolio. Select the entire address and type **4004 East Morningside Dr**. Click your insertion point into Andrew Fuller's name field.

i. Click **Undo**.

Nancy's address changes back to *20th Ave. E.* However, the Undo command is now faded. You can no longer undo the change that you made replacing Margaret Peacock's name with your own.

j. Click **Close** to close the Employees table.

The Employees table closes. You are not prompted about saving your changes, because they have already been saved for you. If you reopen the Employees table, you will find your name, not Margaret's, because Access works in storage, not memory.

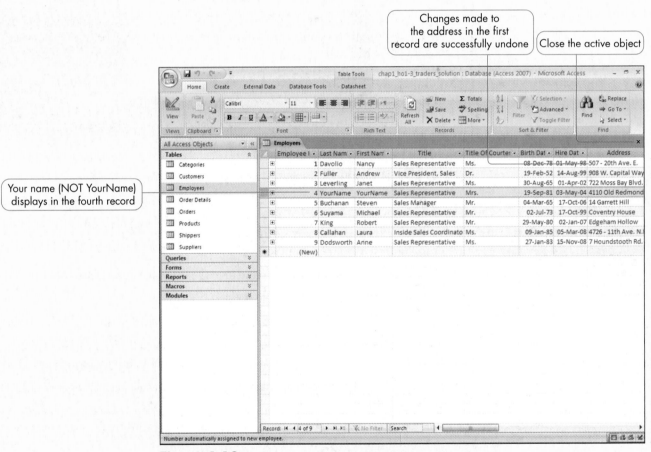

Figure 1.10 The Edited Employees Table

Step 4

Navigate an Access Form and Add Records

Refer to Figure 1.11 as you complete Step 4.

a. Click **Tables** in the Navigation pane to close it.

The list of available tables collapses.

b. Click **Forms** in the Navigation pane to expand it.

c. Double-click the **Products form** to open it.

d. Practice with the navigation buttons above the status bar to move from one record to the next. Click **Next record**, and then click **Last record**.

e. Click **Find** in the Find group on the Home tab.

The Find command is an ideal way to search for specific records within a table, form, or query. You can search a single field or the entire record, match all or part of the selected field(s), move forward or back in a table, or specify a case-sensitive search. The Replace command can be used to substitute one value for another. Be careful, however, about using the Replace All option for global replacement because unintended replacements are far too common.

f. Type **ikura** in the *Find What* section of the Find and Replace dialog box. Check to make sure that the *Look In* option is set to **Product Name** and the *Match* option is set to **Whole Field**. The *Search* option should be set to **All**. Click **Find Next**.

You should see the information about *ikura*, a seafood supplied by Tokyo Traders.

g. Type **Grandma** in the *Find What* box, click the **Match drop-down arrow**, and select **Any Part of Field**. Click **Find Next**.

You should see information about Grandma's Boysenberry Spread. Setting the match option to any part of the field will return a match even if it is contained in the middle of a word.

h. Close the Find and Replace dialog box.

i. Click **New (blank) record** located on the Navigation bar.

j. Enter the following information for a new product. Press **Tab** to navigate the form.

Field Name	Value to Type
Product Name	Your Name Pecan Pie
Supplier	Grandma Kelly's Homestead (Note, display the drop-down list to enter this information quickly)
Category	Confections (Use the drop-down box here, too)
Quantity Per Unit	1
Unit Price	25.00
Units in Stock	18
Units on Order	50
Reorder Level	20

As soon as you begin typing in the product name box, Access assigns a Product ID, in this case 78, to the record. The Product ID is used as the primary key in the Products table.

k. Close the Products form.

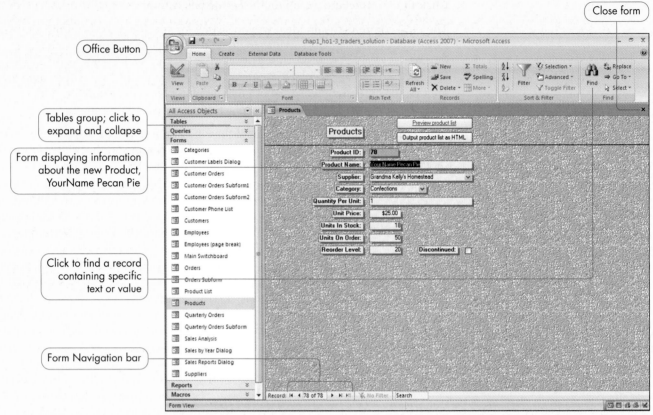

Office Button

Close form

Tables group; click to expand and collapse

Form displaying information about the new Product, YourName Pecan Pie

Click to find a record containing specific text or value

Form Navigation bar

Figure 1.11 The Newly Created Record in the Products Form

Step 5

Recognize the Table and Form Connectivity and Delete a Record

Refer to Figure 1.12 as you complete Step 5.

a. Click **Forms** in the Navigation pane to close it.

The list of available forms collapses.

b. Click **Tables** in the Navigation pane to expand it.

The list of available tables expands. You need to assure yourself that the change you made to the Products form will transfer to the Products table.

c. Double-click the **Products table** to open it.

d. Click **Last record** on the Navigation bar.

The Products form was designed to make data entry easier. It is linked to the Products table. Your newly created record about the Pecan Pie product name is stored in the Products table even though you created it in the form.

e. Navigate to the fifth record in the table, *Chef Anton's Gumbo Mix*.

f. Use the horizontal scroll bar to scroll right until you see the *Discontinued* field.

The check mark in the Discontinued check box tells you that this product has been discontinued.

g. Click the row selector box at the left of the window (see Figure 1.12).

The row highlights with a gold-colored border.

h. Press **Delete**.

An error message appears. It tells you that you cannot delete this record because the table, Order Details, has related records. Even though the product is now discontinued and none of it is in stock, it cannot be deleted from the table because related records are connected to it. A customer in the past ordered this product. If you first deleted all of the orders in the Order Details table that referenced this product, you would be permitted to delete the product from the Products table.

i. Read the error message. Click **OK**.

j. Navigate to the last record. Click the *row selector* to highlight the entire row.

k. Press **Delete**. STOP. Read the error message.

A warning box appears. It tells you that this action cannot be undone. This product can be deleted because it was just created. No customers have ever ordered it so no related records are in the system.

l. Click **No**. You do not want to delete this record.

TROUBLESHOOTING: If you clicked Yes and deleted the record, return to Step 4j. Reenter the information for this record. You will need it later in the lesson.

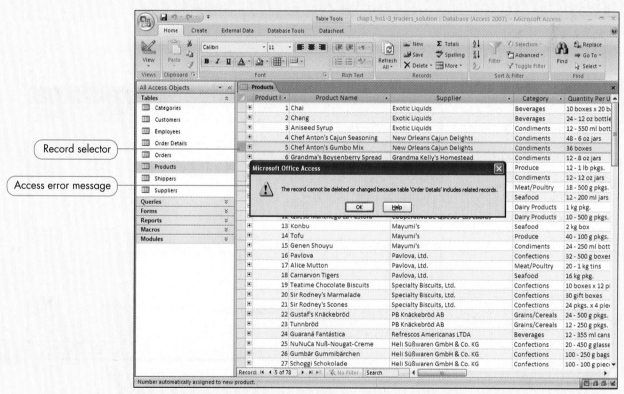

Figure 1.12 How Databases Work to Protect Data

Step 6
Back Up and Compact the Database

Refer to Figure 1.13 as you complete Step 6.

a. Click the **Office Button** and select **Manage**.

The Manage menu gives you access to three critically important tools.

b. Select **Compact and Repair Database**.

Databases tend to get larger and larger as you use them. This feature acts as a defragmenter and eliminates wasted space. As it runs, it closes any open objects in the database.

c. Click the **Office Button**, select **Manage**, and then select **Back Up Database**.

The Save As dialog box opens. The backup utility assigns a default name by adding a date to your file name.

d. Type **chap1_ho1_traders_solution** and click **Save**.

You just created a backup of the database after completing the first hands-on exercise. The original database *chap1_ho1-3_traders_solution* remains onscreen. If you ruin the original database as you complete the second hands-on exercise, you can use the backup file you just created.

e. Close the file and exit Access if you do not want to continue with the next exercise at this time.

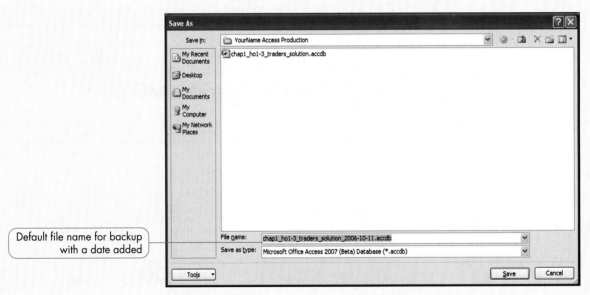

Default file name for backup with a date added

Figure 1.13 Save As Dialog Box to Back Up a Database

Filters, Sorts, and Access Versus Excel

Microsoft Office provides you with many tools that you may use to identify and extract only the records needed at the moment. For example, you might need to know which suppliers are located in New Orleans or which customers have not ordered any products in the last 60 days. You might use that information to identify possible disruptions to product deliveries or customers who may need a telephone call to see if all is well. Both Access and Excel contain powerful tools that enable you to sift through data and extract the information you need and arrange it in a way that makes sense to you. An important part of becoming a proficient computer user is recognizing when to use which tool to accomplish a task.

In this section, you learn how to create filters to examine records and organize these records by sorting table data. You also will examine the logic of Access and Excel in more detail. You will investigate when to use which application to complete a given task.

Creating Filters

A *filter* lets you find a subset of data meeting your specifications.

In the first hands-on exercise, you used data from an existing table to obtain information from the database. You created new records and saw that the changes made in a form update data in the associated table data. You found the pecan pie, but you also saw lots of other products. When all of the information needed is contained in a single table, form, report, or query, you can open the object in the Datasheet view, and then apply a filter to display only the records of interest to you. A *filter* displays a subset of records; from the object according to specified criteria. You use filters to examine data. Applying a filter does not delete any records; it simply hides extraneous records from your view.

Figure 1.14 displays a Customers table with 91 records. The records in the table are displayed in sequence according to the CustomerID, which is also the primary key (the field or combination of fields that uniquely identifies a record). The status bar indicates that the active record is the sixth in the table. Let's explore how you would retrieve a partial list of those records, such as records of customers in Germany only.

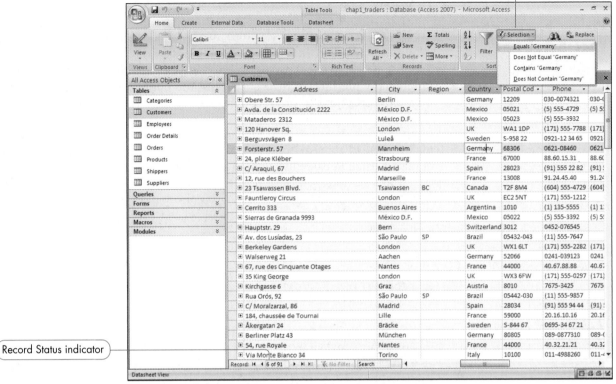

Sort & Filter group with Filter by Selection options displayed

Record Status indicator

Figure 1.14 Unfiltered Table with Appropriate Sort Options Selected

Figure 1.15 displays a filtered view of the same table in which we see only the customers in Germany. The Navigation bar shows that this is a filtered list and that the filter found 11 records satisfying the criteria. (The Customers table still contains the original 91 records, but only 11 records are visible with the filter applied.)

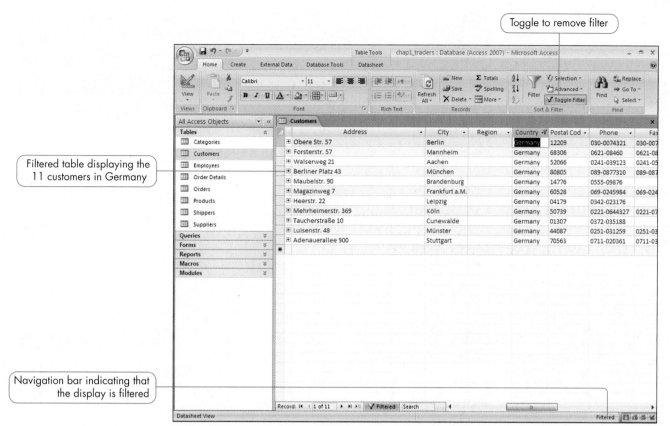

Toggle to remove filter

Filtered table displaying the 11 customers in Germany

Navigation bar indicating that the display is filtered

Figure 1.15 Filtered Table with Appropriate Sort Options Selected

TIP Use Quick Keyboard Shortcuts

Look for underlined letters in Access menus. They indicate the letters to use for the keyboard shortcuts. For example, when you click in a field and click the Selection down arrow in the Sort & Filter group, you can click the Equals "London" menu selection or simply type the letter e because the letter E in Equals is underlined, indicating a shortcut key.

Filter by Selection selects only the records that match the pre-selected criteria.

Filter by Form permits selecting criteria from a drop-down list or applying multiple criteria.

An **inequity** examines a mathematical relationship such as equals, not equals, greater than, less than, greater than or equal to, or less than or equal to.

The easiest way to implement a filter is to click in any cell that contains the value of the desired criterion (such as any cell that contains *Account Rep* in the Title field), then click Filter by Selection in the Sort & Filter group. **Filter by Selection** selects only the records that match the pre-selected criteria.

Figure 1.16 illustrates an alternate and more powerful way to apply a filter. **Filter by Form** permits selecting the criteria from a drop-down list and/or applying multiple criteria simultaneously. However, the real advantage of the Filter by Form command extends beyond these conveniences to two additional capabilities. First, you can specify relationships within a criterion; for example, you can use an inequity setting to select products with an inventory level greater than (or less than) 30. An **inequity** examines a mathematical relationship such as equals, not equals, greater than, less than, greater than or equal to, or less than or equal to. Filter by Selection, on the other hand, requires you to specify criteria equal to an existing value. Figure 1.16 shows the filtered query setup to select Beverages with more than 30 units in stock.

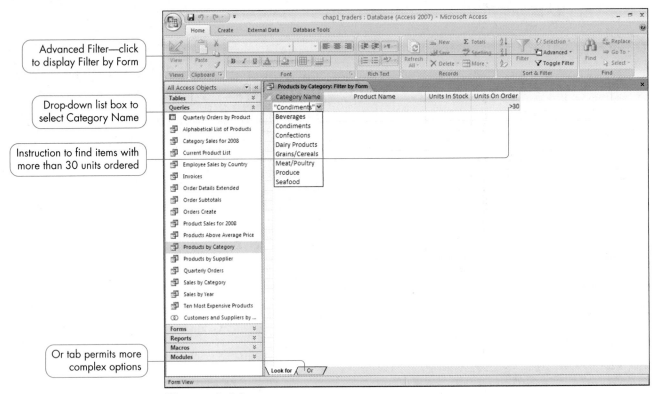

Figure 1.16 Filter by Form Design Grid

The following labels appear to the left of the figure:

- Advanced Filter—click to display Filter by Form
- Drop-down list box to select Category Name
- Instruction to find items with more than 30 units ordered
- Or tab permits more complex options

A second advantage of the Filter by Form command is that you can specify alternative criteria (such as customers in Germany or orders for over 30 units) by clicking the Or tab. (The latter capability is not implemented in Figure 1.16.) However, the availability of the various filter and sort commands enables you to obtain information from a database quickly and easily without creating a query or report.

Sorting Table Data on One or More Fields

You also can change the order of the information by sorting by one or more fields. A *sort* lists those records in a specific sequence, such as alphabetically by last name or by EmployeeID. To sort the table, click in the field on which you want to sequence the records (the LastName field in this example), then click Sort Ascending in the Sort & Filter group on the Home tab. *Sort Ascending* provides an alphabetical list of text data or a small to large list of numeric data. *Sort Descending* is appropriate for numeric fields such as salary, if you want to display the records with the highest value listed first. Figure 1.17 shows the Customers table sorted in alphabetical order by country. You may apply both filters and sorts to table or query information to select and order the data in the way that you need to make decisions.

A *sort* lists those records in a specific sequence, such as alphabetically by last name.

Sort Ascending provides an alphabetical list of text data or a small to large list of numeric data.

Sort Descending displays records with the highest value listed first.

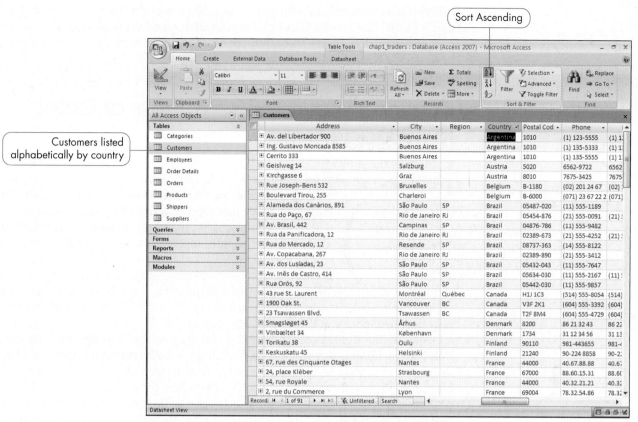

Figure 1.17 Customers Table Sorted by Country

The operations can be done in any order; that is, you can filter a table to show only selected records, then you can sort the filtered table to display the records in a different order. Conversely, you can sort a table, and then apply a filter. It does not matter which operation is performed first, and indeed, you can go back and forth between the two. You can also filter the table further, by applying a second (or third) criterion; for example, click in a cell containing *USA* and apply a Filter by Selection. Then click in a record for Oregon (OR) and apply a Filter by Selection a second time to display the customers from Oregon. You also can click Toggle Filter at any time to display all of the records in the table. Filters are a temporary method for examining subsets of data. If you close the filtered table or query and reopen it, all of the records display.

> ### TIP   The Sort or Filter—Which Is First?
>
> It doesn't matter whether you sort a table, and then apply a filter or filter first, and then sort. The operations are cumulative. Thus, after you sort a table, any subsequent display of filtered records for that table will be in the specified sequence. Alternatively, you can apply a filter, and then sort the filtered table by clicking in the desired field and clicking the appropriate sort command. Remember, too, that all filter commands are cumulative and hence, you must remove the filter to see the original table.

You may be familiar with applying a filter, sorting data, or designing a form using Excel. The fact is, Excel can accomplish all of these activities. You need to examine your data needs and think about what your future data requirements may be to decide whether to use Access or Excel.

Knowing When to Use Access or Excel to Manage Data

If you have the ability to control data and turn it into useful information, you possess a marketable skill. It does not matter whether you are planning to become a social worker, a teacher, an engineer, an entrepreneur, a radiologist, a marketer, a day care worker, a musician, or an accountant. You will need to collect, store, maintain, manage, and protect data as well as convert it into information used to make strategic decisions. A widely used program that you probably already know is Excel. This course will help you become familiar with Access. You can accomplish many of the same things in either software. Although the two packages have much in common, they each have advantages. So, how do you choose whether to use Access or Excel?

> If you have the ability to control data and turn it into useful information, you possess a marketable skill.

Making the right choice is critical if you want to find and update your information with maximum performance and accuracy. Ideally, your data needs and the type and amount of data used will determine how to pick the program that will work best. Sometimes organizations use Access when they probably would be better served with Excel and vice versa. The answer to the question of which to use may depend on who you ask. An accountant probably will use Excel. The information technology professional probably will use a more sophisticated database software like Oracle, but not Access. The middle manager in the marketing or manufacturing department will probably use Access. The question remains.

Select the Software to Use

A contacts list is an example of flat data. Each column of data (names, addresses, and phone numbers) is logically related to the others. If you can store your data logically in a single table or worksheet, then do. Update your data in the same type of file. Data contained in a single page or sheet (not multiple) are called *flat or non-relational data*. You would never store your friend's last name on a different sheet from the sheet containing the friend's cell phone number.

> Data contained in a single page or sheet (not multiple) are called *flat or non-relational data*.

Suppose you had a spreadsheet of club members' names and contact information. Your club decides to sell cookies as a fundraiser. You might create a new worksheet listing how many boxes of which type of cookie each member picked up to sell. Your third worksheet might show how much money each member has turned in from the cookie sales. These data are different. They are not flat. Can you imagine needing to know someone's phone number or how many cookie boxes he or she promised to sell while looking at the worksheet of data about how much money has been turned in? These data are multi-dimensional and need to be stored in more than one worksheet or table. This describes relational data. Each table holds a particular type of data (number of boxes collected, contact information, funds turned in). Relational data are best stored in Access. In this example, you would create a database with three tables. You need to adhere to the following rules about assigning data to the appropriate table.

Assign table data so that each table:

- Represents only a single subject
- Has a field(s) that uniquely identifies each record
- Does not contain duplicate fields
- Has no repetition of the same type of value
- Has no fields belonging in other tables

As the quantity and complexity of data increase, the need to organize it efficiently also increases. Access affords better data organization than Excel. Access accomplishes the organization through a system of linkages among the tables. Each record (row) should be designated with a primary key—a unique identifier that sets it apart from all of the other records in the table. The primary key might be an account number, a student identification number, or an employee access code. All data in Excel have a unique identifier—the cell address. In life, you have a Social Security Number. It is the best unique identifier you have. Ever notice how, when at the doctor's office or applying for college admission, you are asked for your Social Security Number as well as your name? Your record in its database system probably uses your Social Security Number as a unique identifier.

You still need to answer the question of when to use Access and when to use Excel.

Use Access

You should use Access to manage data when you:

- Require a relational database (multiple tables or multi-dimensional tables) to store your data or anticipate adding more tables in the future.

  For example, you may set your club membership contact list in either software, but if you believe that you also will need to keep track of the cookie sales and fund collection, use Access.

- Have a large amount of data.

- Rely on external databases to derive and analyze the data you need.

  If you frequently need to have Excel exchange data to or from Access, use Access. Even though the programs are compatible, it makes sense to work in Access to minimize compatibility issues.

- Need to maintain constant connectivity to a large external database, such as one built with Microsoft SQL Server or your organization's Enterprise Resource Planning system.

- Need to regroup data from different tables in a single place through complex queries.

  You might need to create output showing how many boxes of cookies each club member picked up and how much money they turned in along with the club member's name and phone number.

- Have many people working in the database and need strong options to update the data.

  For example, five different clerks at an auto parts store might wait on five different customers. Each clerk connects to the inventory table to find out if the needed part is in stock and where in the warehouse it is located. When the customer says, "Yes, I want that," the inventory list is instantly updated and that product is no longer available to be purchased by the other four customers.

Use Excel

You should use Excel to manage data when you:

- Require a flat or non-relational view of your data (you do not need a relational database with multiple tables).

  This idea is especially true if that data is mostly numeric—for example, if you need to maintain an expense statement.

- Want to run primarily calculations and statistical comparisons on your data.

- Know your dataset is manageable in size (no more than 15,000 rows).

In the next exercise, you will create and apply filters, perform sorts, and develop skills to customize the data presentation to answer your questions.

Hands-On Exercises

2 | Data Manipulation: Filters and Sorts

Skills covered: 1. Use Filter by Selection with an Equal Setting **2.** Use Filter by Selection with a Contains Setting **3.** Use Filter by Form with an Inequity Setting **4.** Sort a Table

---

Step 1
Use Filter by Selection with an Equal Setting

Refer to Figure 1.18 as you complete Step 1.

a. Open the *chap1_ho1-3_traders_solution* file if necessary, and click **Options** on the Security Warning toolbar, click the **Enable this content option** in the Microsoft Office Security Options dialog box, and click **OK**.

> **TROUBLESHOOTING:** If you create unrecoverable errors while completing this hands-on exercise, you can delete the *chap1_ho1-3_traders_solution* file, copy the *chap1_ho1_traders_solution* backup database you created at the end of the first hands-on exercise, and open the copy of the backup database to start the second hands-on exercise again.

b. Open the **Customers table**; navigate to record 4 and replace *Thomas Hardy's* name with **your name** in the **Contact Name field**.

c. Scroll right until the **City field** is visible. Look through the record values of the field form until you locate a customer in **London**, for example, the fourth record. Click in the field box to select it.

The word *"London"* will have a gold colored border around it to let you know that it is active.

d. Click **Selection** in the Sort & Filter group on the Home tab.

e. Choose **Equals "London"** from the menu.

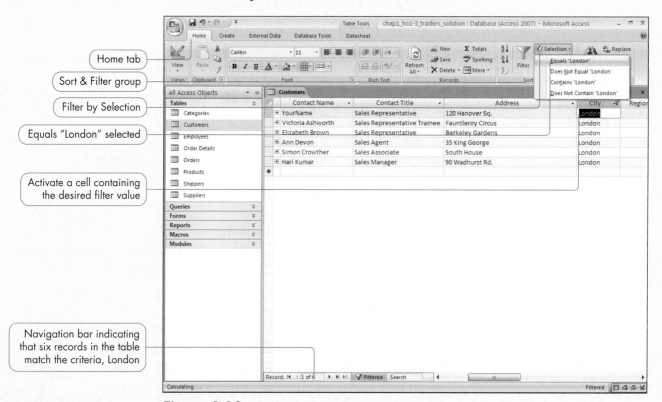

Figure 1.18 Customers Table Filtered to Display London Records Only

Refer to Figure 1.19 as you complete Step 2.

a. Find a record with the value **Sales Representative** in the **Contact Title field**. Click your insertion point to activate that field. The first record has a value of *Sales Representative* for the Contact Title field.

Sales Representative will have a gold colored border around it to let you know that it is activated.

b. Click **Selection** on the Sort & Filter group located on the Home tab.

c. Click **Contains "Sales Representative"** (or type t).

You have applied a second layer of filtering to the customers in London. The second layer further restricts the display to only those customers who have the words Sales Representative contained in their title.

d. Scroll left until you see your name. Compare your results to those shown in Figure 1.19.

e. Click the **Office Button**, position the mouse pointer over **Print**, and then select **Quick Print**.

f. Click **Toggle Filter** in the Sort & Filter group to remove the filters.

g. Close the Customers table. Click **No** if a dialog box asks if you want to save the design changes to the Customers table.

TIP Removing Versus Deleting a Filter

Removing a filter displays all of the records that are in a table, but it does not delete the filter because the filter is stored permanently with the table. To delete the filter entirely is more complicated than simply removing it. Click Advanced on the Sort & Filter group and select the Clear All Filters option from the drop-down list box. Deleting unnecessary filters may reduce the load on the CPU and will allow the database manager to optimize the database performance.

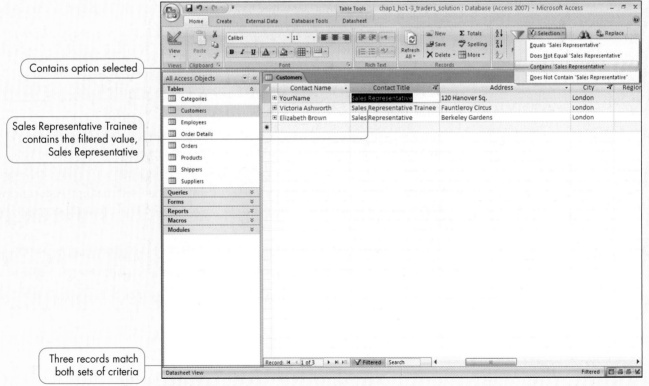

Figure 1.19 Customers Table Filtered to Display London and Sales Representative Job Titles

Refer to Figure 1.20 as you complete Step 3.

a. Click **Tables** in the Navigation pane to collapse the listed tables.

b. Click **Queries** in the Navigation pane to expand the lists of available queries.

c. Locate and double-click the **Order Details Extended** query to open it.

This query contains information about orders. It has fields containing information about the salesperson, the Order ID, the product name, the unit price, quantity ordered, the discount given, and an extended price. The extended price is a term used to total order information.

d. Click **Advanced** in the Sort & Filter group on the Home tab.

The process to apply a filter by form is identical in a table or a query.

e. Select **Filter By Form** from the list.

All of the records seem to vanish and you see only a list of field names.

f. Click in the **first row** under the **First Name** field.

A down arrow appears at the right of the box.

g. Click the **First Name down arrow**. A list of all available first names appears.

Your name should be on the list. It may be in a different location than that shown in Figure 1.20 because the list is in alphabetical order.

TROUBLESHOOTING: If you do not see your name and you do see Margaret on the list, you probably skipped Steps 3c and 3d in Hands-On Exercise 1. Close the query without saving changes, turn back to the first hands-on exercise, and rework it, making sure not to omit any steps. Then you can return to this spot and work the remainder of this hands-on exercise.

h. Select **your first name** from the list.

i. Click in the *first row* under the *Last Name field* to turn on the drop-down arrow. Locate and select **your last name** by clicking it.

j. Scroll right until you see the Extended Price field. Click in the *first row* under the Extended Price field and type **<50**.

This will select all of the items ordered where the total was under $50. You ignore the drop-down arrow and type the expression needed.

k. Click **Toggle Filter** in the Sort & Filter group.

You have specified which records to include and have executed the filtering by clicking Toggle Filter. You should have 31 records that match the criteria you specified.

l. Click the **Office Button**, and then select **Print**. In the Print dialog box, locate the **Pages** control in the *Print Range* section. Type **1** in the *From* box and again in the *To* box. Click **OK**.

You have instructed Access to print the first page of the filtered query results.

m. Close the query. Click **No** when asked if you want to save the design changes.

TIP   Deleting Filter by Form Criterion

The Filter by Form command has all of the capabilities of the Filter by Selection command and provides two additional capabilities. First, you can use relational operators such as >, >=, <, or <= as opposed to searching for an exact value. Second, you can search for records that meet one of several conditions (the equivalent of an "Or" operation). Enter the first criterion as you normally would, then click the Or tab at the bottom of the window to display a second form in which you enter the alternate criteria. (To delete an alternate criterion, click the associated tab, and then click Delete on the toolbar.)

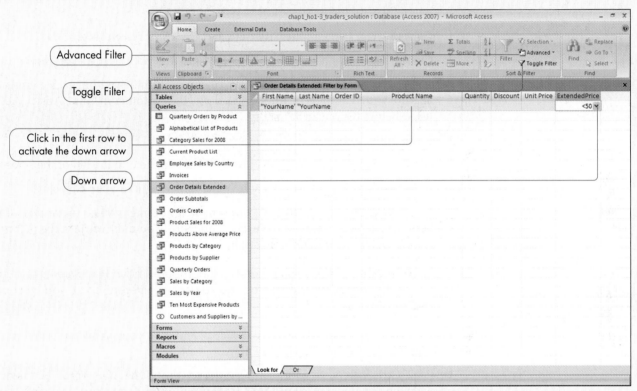

Figure 1.20   Filter by Selection Criteria Settings

Step 4
Sort a Table

Refer to Figure 1.21 as you complete Step 4.

a. Click **Queries** in the Navigation pane to collapse the listed queries.

b. Click **Tables** in the Navigation pane to expand the lists of available tables.

c. Locate and double-click the **Customers table** to open it.

This table contains information about customers. It is sorted in ascending order by the Customer ID field. Because this field contains text, the table is sorted in alphabetical order.

d. Click any value in the **Customer ID field**. Click **Sort Descending** in the Sort & Filter group on the Home tab.

Sorting in descending order on a character field produces a reverse alphabetical order.

e. Scroll right until you can see both the **Country** the **City fields**.

You will sort the customers by country and then by city within the countries. You can sort on more than one field as long as you sort on the primary field (in this case the country) last.

f. Click the field name for **Country**.

The entire column selects.

g. Click the **Country field name box** and hold the left mouse down.

A thick dark blue line displays on the left edge of the Country field column.

h. Check to make sure that you see the thick blue line. When you do, drag the country field to the **left**. When the thick black line moves to between the *Address and City* fields, release the mouse and the Country field position moves to the left of the City field.

i. Click any city name in the **City field** and click **Sort Ascending**.

j. Click any country name in the **Country field** and click **Sort Ascending**.

The countries are sorted in alphabetical order. The cities within each country also are sorted alphabetically. For example, the customer in Graz, Austria, is listed before the one in Saltzburg.

k. Scroll down until you see the *UK* customers listed.

l. Scroll to the left until the *Contact Name* is the first field in the left of the screen.

m. Press **PrntScrn** located somewhere in the upper right of your keyboard.

You have captured a picture of your screen. If nothing seemed to happen, it is because the picture was saved to the Clipboard. You must retrieve the picture from the Clipboard in order to see it.

TROUBLESHOOTING: Some notebook computers have Print Screen as a function. If the words Print Screen on the key are a different color, you must press **Fn+Print Screen**.

n. Launch Word, open a *new blank document*, and type **your name and section number** on the first line. Press **Enter**.

o. Press **Ctrl+V** to paste your picture of the screenshot into the Word document. Save the document as **chap1_ho2_traders_solution.docx**. Print the Word document. Close Word.

p. Close the **Customers table**. Do not save the changes.

q. Click the **Office Button**, select **Manage**, and then select **Compact and Repair Database**.

r. Click the **Office Button** again, select **Manage**, and then select **Back Up Database**. Type **chap1_ho2_traders_solution** as the file name and click **Save**.

You just created a backup of the database after completing the second hands-on exercise. The original database *chap1_ho1-3_traders_solution* remains onscreen. If you ruin the original database as you complete the third hands-on exercise, you can use the backup file you just created.

s. Close the file and exit Access if you do not want to continue with the next exercise at this time.

The Cowes customer lists before the London customers

Figure 1.21 The Customers Table Sorted by Country and Then by City in Word

The Relational Database

A ***relational database management system*** is one in which data are grouped into similar collections, called tables, and the relationships between tables are formed by using a common field.

The power of a relational database lies in the software's ability to organize data and combine items in different ways to obtain a complete picture of the events the data describe.

In the previous section you read that you should use Access when you have multidimensional data. Access derives power from multiple tables and the relationships among those tables. A ***relational database management system*** is one in which data are grouped into similar collections called tables, and the relationships between tables are formed by using a common field. The design of a relational database system is illustrated in Figure 1.22. The power of a relational database lies in the software's ability to organize data and combine items in different ways to obtain a complete picture of the events the data describe. Good database design connects the data in different tables through a system of linkages. These links are the relationships that give relational databases the name. Look at Figure 1.1. The student record (folder) contains information about the student, but also contains cross-references to data stored in other cabinet drawers, such as the advisor's name or a list of courses completed. If you need to know the advisor's phone number, you can open the faculty drawer, find the advisor's record, and then locate the field containing the phone number. The cross-reference from the student file to the faculty file illustrates how a relationship works in a database. Figure 1.22 displays the cross-references between the tables as a series of lines connecting the common fields. When the database is set up properly, the users of the data can be confident that if they search a specific customer identification number, they will be given accurate information about that customer's order history and payment balances, and his/her product or shipping preferences.

In this section, you will explore the relationships among tables, learn about the power of relational integrity, and discover how the software protects the organization's data.

Using the Relationship Window

The relationship (the lines between the tables in Figure 1.22) is like a piece of electronic string that travels throughout the database, searching every record of every table until it finds the data satisfying the user's request. Once identified, the fields and records of interest will be tied to the end of the string, pulled through the computer and reassembled in a way that makes the data easy to understand. The first end of the string was created when the primary key was established in the Customers table. The primary key is a unique identifier for each table record. The other end of the string will be tied to a field in a different table. If you examine Figure 1.22, you will see that the CustomerID is a foreign field in the Orders table. A ***foreign key*** is a field in one table that also is stored in a different table as a primary key. Each value of the CustomerID can occur only once in the Customers table because it is a primary key. However, the CustomerID may appear multiple times in the Orders table because one customer may make many different purchases. The CustomerID field is a foreign key in the Orders table but the primary key in the Customers table.

A ***foreign key*** is a field in one table that also is stored in a different table as a primary key.

Examine Referential Integrity

Referential integrity is the set of rules that ensure that data stored in related tables remain consistent as the data are updated.

The relationships connecting the tables will be created using an Access feature that uses referential integrity. Integrity means truthful or reliable. When ***referential integrity*** is enforced, the user can trust the "threads" running through the database and "tying" related items together. The sales manager can use the database to find the names and phone numbers of all the customers who have ordered Teatime Chocolate Biscuits (a specific product). Because referential integrity has been enforced, it will not matter that the order information is in a different table from the customer data. The invisible threads will keep the information accurately connected. The threads also provide a method of ensuring data accuracy. You cannot enter a record in the Orders table that references a ProductID or a CustomerID that does not exist elsewhere in the system. Nor can you easily delete a record in one table if it has related records in related tables.

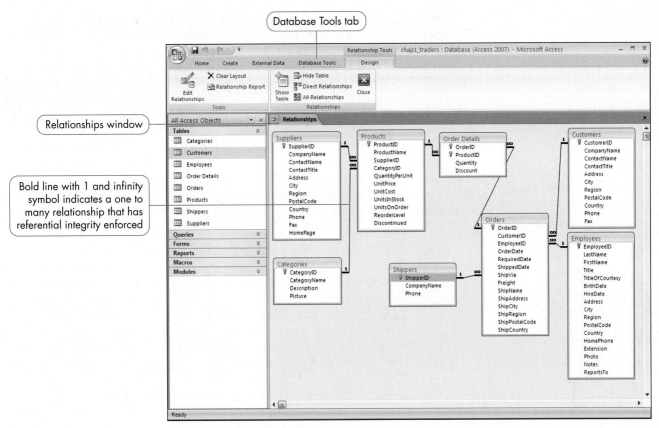

Database Tools tab

Relationships window

Bold line with 1 and infinity symbol indicates a one to many relationship that has referential integrity enforced

Figure 1.22 The Relationships Window Displaying Table Connections

If this were a real organization's data system, the files would be much, much larger and the data more sophisticated. When learning database skills, you should start with smaller, more manageable files. The same design principles apply regardless of the database size. A small file gives you the ability to check the tables and see if your results are correct. Even though the data amounts are small, you need to develop the work practices needed to manage large amounts of data. With only a handful of records, you can easily count the number of employees at the Washington state office. In addition to learning how to accomplish a task, you also should begin to learn to anticipate the computer's response to an instruction. As you work, ask yourself what the anticipated results should be and then verify. When you become skilled at anticipating output correctly, you are surprised less often.

> As you work, ask yourself what the anticipated results should be and then verify. When you become skilled at anticipating output correctly, you are surprised less often.

Understanding Relational Power

In the previous section, you read that you should use Access when you have multi-dimensional data. Access derives power from multiple tables and the relationships between those tables. This type of database is known as a relational database and is illustrated in Figure 1.22. This figure describes the database structure. Examine some of the connections. The EmployeeID is a foreign field in the Orders table. For example, you can produce a document displaying the history of each order a customer had placed and the employee's name (from the Employees table) that entered the order. The Orders table references the Order Details table where the OrderID is a foreign field. The ProductID relates to the Products table (where it is the primary key). The CategoryID is the primary key in the Categories table, but shows up as a foreign field in the Products table. The table connections, even when more than one table is involved, provide the decision-maker power. This feature gives the manager the ability to find out sales by category. How many different beverages were shipped last week? What was the total revenue generated from seafood orders last year?

Suppose a customer called to complain that his orders were arriving late. Because the ShipperID is a foreign field in the Orders table, you could look up which shipper delivered that customer's merchandise, and then find out what other customers received deliveries from that shipper the same month. Are the other orders also late? Does the firm need to reconsider its shipping options? The design of a relational database enables us to extract information from multiple tables in a single query or report. Equally important, it simplifies the way data are changed in that modifications are made in only one place.

In the previous hands-on exercises, you have made modifications to table data. You created a new product, you changed an employee and customer name to your name, and you sorted data. You will trace through some of those changes in the next hands-on exercise to help you understand the power of relationships and how a change made to one object travels throughout the database file structure.

Hands-On Exercises

3 | Introduction to Relationships

Skills covered: 1. Examine the Relationships Window **2.** Discover That Changes in Table Data Affect Queries **3.** Use Filter by Form with an Inequity Setting and Reapply a Saved Filter **4.** Filter a Report **5.** Remove an Advanced Filter

Step 1 Examine the Relationships Window	Refer to Figure 1.23 as you complete Step 1. **a.** Open the *chap1_ho1-3_traders_solution* file if necessary, click **Options** on the *security warning* toolbar, click the **Enable this content option** in the Microsoft Office Security Options dialog box, and click **OK**. **TROUBLESHOOTING:** If you create unrecoverable errors while completing this hands-on exercise, you can delete the *chap1_ho1-3_traders_solution* file, copy the *chap1_ho2_traders_solution* database you created at the end of the second hands-on exercise, and open the copy of the backup database to start the third hands-on exercise again. **b.** Click the **Database Tools tab** and click **Relationships** in the Show/Hide group. Examine the relationships that connect the various tables. For example, the Products table is connected to the Suppliers, Categories, and Order Details tables. **c.** Click **Show Table**. The Show Table dialog box opens. It tells you that there are eight available tables in the database. If you look in the Relationship window, you will see that all eight tables are in the relationship diagram. **d.** Click the **Queries tab** in the Show Table dialog box. You could add all of the queries to the Relationships window. Things might become cluttered, but you could tell at a glance where the queries get their information. **e.** Close the Show Table dialog box. **f.** Click the **down arrow** in the All Access Objects bar of the Navigation pane. **g.** Click **Tables and Related Views**. You can now see not only the tables, but also the queries, forms, and reports that connect to the table data. If a query is sourced on more than one table, it will appear multiple times in the Navigation pane. This view provides an alternate method of viewing the relationships connecting the tables. **h.** Close the Relationships window. Save the changes.

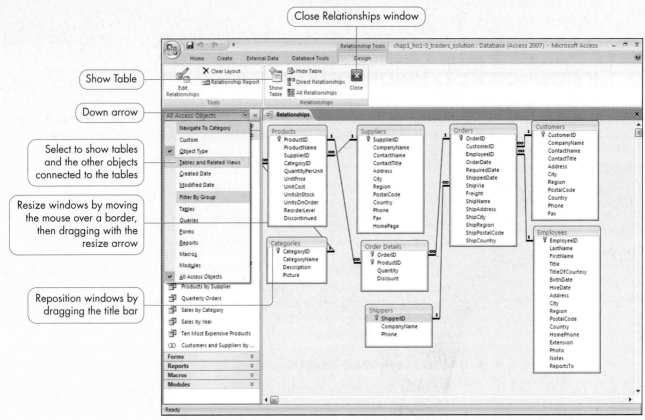

Figure 1.23 The Relationships Window Displaying the Northwind Table Relationships

Labels in the figure:

- Close Relationships window
- Show Table
- Down arrow
- Select to show tables and the other objects connected to the tables
- Resize windows by moving the mouse over a border, then dragging with the resize arrow
- Reposition windows by dragging the title bar

Step 2
Discover That Changes in Table Data Affect Queries

Refer to Figure 1.24 as you complete Step 2.

a. Scroll in the Navigation pane until you see the *Products table and Related Objects*. Locate and double-click the **Order Details Extended query**.

b. Examine the icons on the left edge of the Navigation pane. Figure 1.24 identifies the object type for each of the objects.

c. Find an occurrence of *your last name* anywhere in the query (record 7 should show your name) and click it to make it active.

The query contains your name because in Hands-On Exercise 1 you replaced Margaret Peacock's name in the Employees table with your name. The Employees table is related to the Orders table, the Orders table to the Order Details table, and the Order Details table to the Products table. Therefore, any change you make to the Employees table is carried throughout the database via the relationships.

d. Click **Filter by Selection** in the Sort & Filter group. Select **Equals "YourName"** from the selection menu.

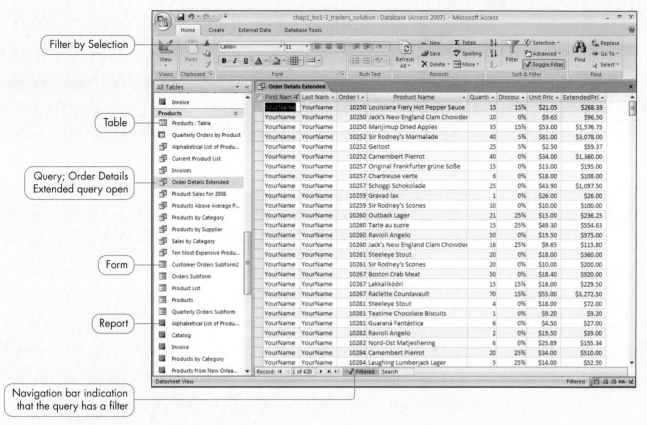

Filter by Selection

Table

Query; Order Details
Extended query open

Form

Report

Navigation bar indication
that the query has a filter

Figure 1.24 Filtered Query Results

Step 3

Use Filter by Form with an Inequity Setting and Reapply a Saved Filter

Refer to Figure 1.25 as you complete Step 3.

a. Click **Advanced Filter options**.

b. Select **Filter By Form** from the drop-down list.

Because you already applied a filter to these data, the Filter By Form design sheet opens with one criterion already filled in. Your name displays in the selection box under the Last Name field.

c. Scroll right (or press **Tab**) until the Extended Price field is visible. Click the insertion point in the **first row** under the Extended Price field.

d. Type **>2000**.

The Extended Price field shows the purchased amount for each item ordered. If an item sold for $15 and a customer ordered 10, the Extended Price would display $150.

e. Click **Toggle Filter** in the Sort & Filter group. Examine the filtered results.

Your inequity instruction, >2000, identified the items ordered where the extended price exceeded $2,000.

f. Press **Ctrl+S** to save the query. Close the query by clicking the X in the object window.

g. Open the **Order Details Extended query**.

The filter disengages when you close and reopen the object. However, your filtering directions have been stored with the query design. You may reapply the filter at any time by clicking the Toggle Filter command.

h. Click **Toggle Filter** in the Sort & Filter group.

i. Compare your work to Figure 1.25. If it is correct, close the query.

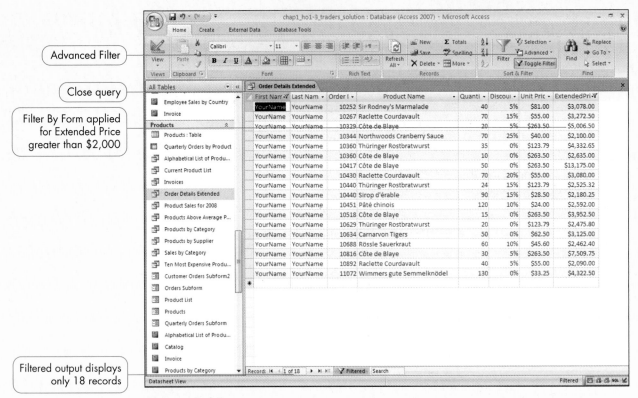

Advanced Filter

Close query

Filter By Form applied
for Extended Price
greater than $2,000

Filtered output displays
only 18 records

Figure 1.25 Filtered Query Results After Limiting Output to Extended Prices over $2,000

Step 4
Filter a Report

Refer to Figure 1.26 as you complete Step 4.

a. Open the **Products by Category report** located in the Navigation pane under the Products group. You may need to scroll down to locate it.

The report should open in Print Preview with a gray stripe highlighting the report title. The Print Preview displays the report exactly as it will print. This report was formatted to display in three columns.

TROUBLESHOOTING: If you do not see the gray stripe and three columns, you probably opened the wrong object. The database also contains a Product by Category query. It is the source for the Products by Category report. Make sure you open the report (shown with the green report icon) and not the query. Close the query and open the report.

b. Examine the Confections category products. You should see **Your Name Pecan Pie**.

You created this product by entering data in a form in Hands-On Exercise 1. You later discovered that changes made to a form affect the related table. Now you see that other related objects also change when the source data changes.

c. Right-click the **gold report tab**. Select **Report View** from the shortcut menu.

The Report view displays the information a little differently. It no longer shows three columns. If you clicked the Print command while in Report view, the columns would print even though you do not see them. The Report view permits limited data interaction (for example, filtering).

d. Scroll down in the report until you see the title *Category: Confections*. **Right-click** the word **Confections** in the title. Select **Equals "Confections"** from the shortcut menu.

Right-clicking a selected data value in an Access table, query, form, or report activates a shortcut to a Filter by Selection menu. Alternatively you can click the selected value, in this case, Confections, and then click the Filter by Selection command in the Sort & Filter group.

e. Right-click the **gold report tab**. Select **Print Preview** from the shortcut menu.

You need to print this report. Always view your reports in Print Preview prior to printing.

f. Click the **Office Button**, position the mouse pointer over **Print**, and then select **Quick Print** to produce a printed copy of the filtered report. Click **OK**.

The Quick Print command sends your work to the default printer as soon as you click it. You can use this safely when you have already viewed your work in Print Preview.

g. Save and close the report.

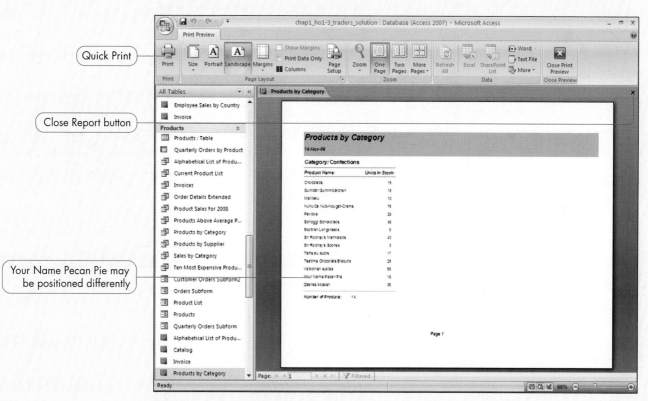

Figure 1.26 Filtered Report Results

Refer to Figure 1.27 as you complete Step 5.

Step 5
Remove an Advanced Filter

a. Open the **Order Details Extended query**.

All 2,155 records should display in the query. You have unfiltered the data. However, the filter still exists.

b. Click **Toggle Filter** in the Sort & Filter group.

You will see the same 18 filtered records that you printed in Step 3.

c. Click **Advanced** in the Sort & Filter group and click **Clear All Filters**.

d. Close the query. A dialog box opens asking if you want to save changes. Click **Yes**.

e. Open the **Order Details Extended query**.

f. Click **Advanced Filter Options** in the Sort & Filter group.

g. Check to ensure the *Clear All Filters* option is dim. Save and close the query.

h. Click the **Office Button**, select **Manage**, and select **Compact and Repair Database**. Close the file and exit Access.

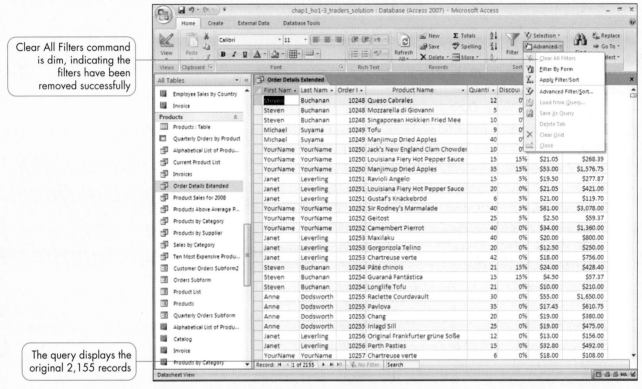

Clear All Filters command is dim, indicating the filters have been removed successfully

The query displays the original 2,155 records

Figure 1.27 Query Results with Filters Removed

Summary

1. **Explore, describe, and navigate among objects in an Access database.** An Access database has six types of objects: tables, forms, queries, reports, macros, and modules. The database window displays these objects and enables you to open an existing object or create new objects. You may arrange these objects by type or by relationship views. The relationship view provides a listing of each table and all other objects in the database that use that table as a source. Thus, one query or report may appear several times, listed once under each table from which it derives information. Each table in the database is composed of records, and each record is in turn composed of fields. Every record in a given table has the same fields in the same order. The primary key is the field (or combination of fields) that makes every record in a table unique.

2. **Understand the difference between working in storage and memory.** Access automatically saves any changes in the current record as soon as you move to the next record or when you close the table. The Undo Current Record command cancels (undoes) the changes to the previously saved record.

3. **Practice good file management.** Because organizations depend on the data stored in databases, database users need to be intentional about exercising good file management practices. You need to be intentional about where you save your files. As you learn new Access skills, you need to make a copy of the database file and practice on the copy. This practice provides a recovery point should you make data-damaging errors.

4. **Back up, compact, and repair Access files.** Because using a database tends to increase the size of the file, you should always close any database objects and compact the database prior to closing the file. This step may reduce the storage requirement by half. Adequate backup is essential when working with an Access database (or any other Office application). A duplicate copy of the database should be created at the end of every session and stored off-site (away from the computer).

5. **Create filters.** A filter is a set of criteria that is applied to a table to display a subset of the records in that table. Microsoft Access lets you Filter by Selection or Filter by Form. The application of a filter does not remove the records from the table, but simply suppresses them from view.

6. **Sort table data on one or more fields.** The records in a table can be displayed in ascending or descending order by clicking the appropriate command on the Home tab.

7. **Know when to use Access or Excel to manage data.** Excel data typically is flat. All of the needed information easily presents in a one-dimensional spreadsheet. Use Excel when the data are primarily numeric. Access handles multi-dimensional data more effectively. Use Access when you need to exchange data with other databases, for large amounts of data, or if your data needs are likely to expand.

8. **Use the Relationship window.** The Relationships window provides a summarizing overview of the database design. Use it to discover which fields are stored in what table. It displays the system of linkages among the table data. The Relationships window provides an excellent tool for you to become acquainted with a new database quickly.

9. **Understand relational power.** A relational database contains multiple tables and enables you to extract information from those tables in a single query. The related tables must be consistent with one another, a concept known as referential integrity. Thus, Access automatically implements additional data validation to ensure the integrity of a database. No system, no matter how sophisticated, can produce valid output from invalid input. Changes made in one object travel through the database and affect other, related objects. The relationships are based on linking primary and foreign key fields between tables.

Key Terms

Multiple Choice

1. Which sequence represents the hierarchy of terms, from smallest to largest?

   (a) Database, table, record, field
   (b) Field, record, table, database
   (c) Record, field, table, database
   (d) Field, record, database, table

2. Which of the following is not true regarding movement within a record (assuming you are not in the first or last field of that record)?

   (a) Press Tab or the right arrow key to move to the next field.
   (b) Press Spacebar to move to the next field to the right.
   (c) Press Shift+Tab or the left arrow key to return to the previous field.
   (d) Press the Enter key and move to the next record.

3. You are performing routine maintenance on a table within an Access database. When should you execute the Save command?

   (a) Immediately after you add, edit, or delete a record
   (b) Periodically during a session—for example, after every fifth change
   (c) Once at the end of a session
   (d) None of the above since Access automatically saves the changes as they are made

4. Which of the following objects are not contained within an Access database?

   (a) Tables and forms
   (b) Queries and reports
   (c) Macros and modules
   (d) Web sites and worksheets

5. You have opened an Access file. The left pane displays a table with forms, queries, and reports listed under the table. Then another table and its objects display. You notice some of the object names are repeated under different tables. Why?

   (a) The database has been set to Object Type View. The object names repeat because a query or report is frequently based on multiple tables.
   (b) The database has been set to Tables and Related View. The object names repeat because a query or report is frequently based on multiple tables.
   (c) The database has been set to Most Recently Used View. The object names repeat because an object has been used frequently.
   (d) The database objects have been alphabetized.

6. Which of the following is not true of an Access database?

   (a) Every record in a table has the same fields as every other record. The fields are in the same order in each record.
   (b) Every table contains the same number of records as every other table.
   (c) Every record in a table has the same fields as every other record. The fields may be ordered differently depending on the record.
   (d) All records contain the same data as all other records.

7. Which of the following is true regarding the record selector symbol?

   (a) A pencil indicates that the current record already has been saved.
   (b) An empty square indicates that the current record has not changed.
   (c) An asterisk indicates the first record in the table.
   (d) A gold border surrounds the active record.

8. You have finished an Access assignment and wish to turn it in to your instructor for evaluation. As you prepare to transfer the file, you discover that it has grown in size. It is now more than double the original size. You should:

   (a) Zip the database file prior to transmitting it to the instructor.
   (b) Turn it in; the size does not matter.
   (c) Compact and repair the database file prior to transmitting it to the instructor.
   (d) Delete extra tables or reports or fields to make the file smaller.

9. Which of the following will be accepted as valid during data entry?

   (a) Adding a record with a duplicate primary key
   (b) Entering text into a numeric field
   (c) Entering numbers into a text field
   (d) Omitting an entry in a required field

10. In a Replace command, the values for the Find and Replace commands must be:

    (a) The same length
    (b) The same case
    (c) Any part of a word
    (d) Either the same or a different length and case

11. Which of the following capabilities is available through Filter by Selection?

    (a) The imposition of a relational condition

    (b) The imposition of an alternate (OR) condition

    (c) The imposition of an Equal condition

    (d) The imposition of a delete condition

12. You open an Access form and use it to update an address for customer Lee Fong. You exited the record and closed the form. Later you open a report that generates mailing labels. What will the address label for Lee Fong show?

    (a) The new address

    (b) The old address

    (c) The new address if you remembered to save the changes made to the form

    (d) The old address until you remember to update it in the report

13. You have created a Filter by Form in an Order Total field. You set the criterion to >25. Which of the following accurately reflects the instruction given to Access?

    (a) All orders with an Order Total of at least 25

    (b) All orders with an Order Total of less than 25

    (c) All orders with an Order Total over 25

    (d) All orders with an Order Total of 25 or less

14. You have used Find and Replace to find all occurrences of the word "his" with "his/her." You typed only his in the Find box and only his/her in the Replace box. What will the result be?

    (a) History will become His/Herstory

    (b) This will become This/Her

    (c) His will become His/Her

    (d) All of the above

    (e) None of the above

15. You are looking at an Employees table in Datasheet view. You want the names sorted alphabetically by last name and then by first name, e.g., Smith, Andrea is listed before Smith, William. To accomplish this, you must:

    (a) First sort ascending on first name, and then on last name

    (b) First sort descending on first name, and then on last name

    (c) First sort ascending on last name, and then on first name

    (d) First sort ascending on last name, and then on first name

Practice Exercises

1 Comfort Insurance

The Comfort Insurance Agency is a midsized company with offices located across the country. You are the human resource director for the company. Your office is located in the home office in Miami. Each employee receives an annual performance review. The review determines employee eligibility for salary increases and the performance bonus. The employee data are stored in an Access database. This database is used by the Human Resource department to monitor and maintain employee records. Your task is to identify the employees who have a performance rating of excellent and a salary under $40,000 per year (if any). Once you identify the appropriate records, you need to sort them alphabetically by the employee's last name. Verify your work by examining Figure 1.28.

a. Copy the partially completed file in *chap1_pe1_insurance.accdb* from the Exploring Access folder to your production folder. Rename it **chap1_pe1_insurance_solution**. Double-click the file name to open it. Enable the security content by clicking the **Options** command in the Security Warning bar. Select **Enable this content**, and then click **OK**.

b. Click the **Database Tools tab** and click **Relationships** in the Show/Hide group. Examine the table structure, relationships, and fields. Once you are familiar with the database, close the Relationships window.

c. Double-click the **Raises and Bonuses query** in the Navigation pane to open it. Find *Debbie Johnson*'s name in the seventh record. Double-click *Debbie* and type your **first name**. Double-click *Johnson* and type your **last name**. Click a different record to save your change.

d. Examine the number of records in the query and remember it for future reference.

e. Find a record that has a value of *Excellent* in the *Performance field*. The record for Johnny Park (sixth record) is one. Click your insertion point in that field on the word **Excellent**.

f. Activate the **Filter by Selection** in the Sort & Filter group. Select **Equals "Excellent"** from the menu. Examine the number of records in the query and remember it for future reference.

g. Click **Advanced Filter** in the Sort & Filter group and select **Filter By Form**.

h. Position the insertion point in the first row in the *Salary field*. Type **<40000**. (Make sure you apply this number to the Salary field and not the NewSalary field.)

i. Click **Toggle Filter** in the Sort & Filter group. Examine the number of records in the query and remember it for future reference. As you add additional criteria, the number of filtered results should decrease.

j. Click the **first record** in the *LastName* field. Click **Sort Ascending** in the Sort & Filter group on the Home tab to sort the filtered output by the employee's last name alphabetically.

k. Compare your results with Figure 1.28. Your name will be sorted into the list so your results may not match exactly. The number of records should exactly match.

l. Click the **Office Button** and position the mouse pointer over **Print**. Select **Quick Print** and click **OK**. Save the query.

m. Click the **Office Button**, select **Manage**, and select **Compact and Repair Database**. Close the file.

...continued on Next Page

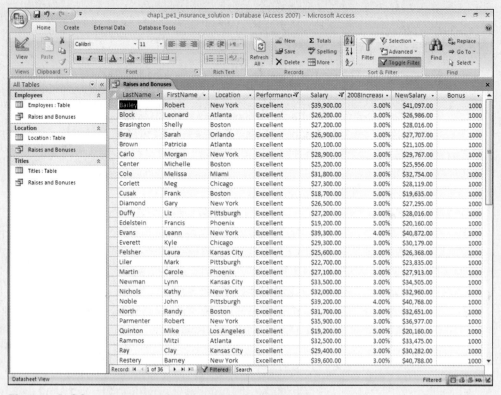

Figure 1.28 Sorted and Filtered Query Results

2 Member Rewards

The Prestige Hotel chain caters to upscale business travelers and provides state of the art conference, meeting, and reception facilities. It prides itself on its international, four-star cuisines. Last year, it began a member rewards club to help the marketing department track the purchasing patterns of its most loyal customers. All of the hotel transactions are stored in the database. Your task is to update a customer record and identify the customers who had weddings in St. Paul. Verify your work by examining Figure 1.29.

a. Copy the partially completed file in *chap1_pe2_memrewards.accdb* from the Exploring Access folder to your production folder. Rename it **chap1_pe2_memrewards_solution**. Double-click the file name to open it. Enable the security content by clicking the **Options** command in the Security Warning bar. Select **Enable this content** and then click **OK**.

b. Open the **Members Form form** and click **New (blank) record** in the Navigation bar. (It has a yellow asterisk.)

c. Enter the information below in the form. Press **Tab** to move from field to field.

Field Name	Value
MemNumber	1718
LastName	Your Last Name
FirstName	Your First Name
JoinDate	7/30/2008
Address	124 West Elm Apt 12
City	Your hometown
State	Your state (2 character code)
Zip	00001

...continued on Next Page

Phone	9995551234
Email	Your e-mail
OrderID	9325
ServiceDate	8/1/2008
ServiceID	3
NoInParty	2
Location	20

d. Click **Close form** in the database window (X) to close the form.

e. Double-click the **Members table** in the Navigation pane. Find Boyd Pegel in the first and last name field and replace his name with **your name**.

f. Double-click the **Member Service by City query** in the Navigation pane. Find a record that displays **St Paul** as the value in the *City field*. Click **St Paul** to select that data entry.

g. Select **Filter by Selection** in the Sort & Filter group on the Home tab. Click **Equals "St Paul"**.

h. Find a record that displays **Wedding** as the value in the *ServiceName* field. Click **Wedding** to select that data entry.

i. Select **Filter by Selection** in the Sort & Filter group on the Home tab. Click **Equals "Wedding"**.

j. Click any value in the **FirstName** field. Click **Sort Ascending** in the Sort & Filter group on the Home tab. Click any value in the **LastName** field. Click **Sort Ascending** in the Sort & Filter group on the Home tab.

k. Click the **Office Button**, select **Print**, and click **OK** to print the sorted and filtered query.

l. Save and close the query.

m. Click the **Office Button**, select **Manage**, and then select **Compact and Repair Database**. Close the file.

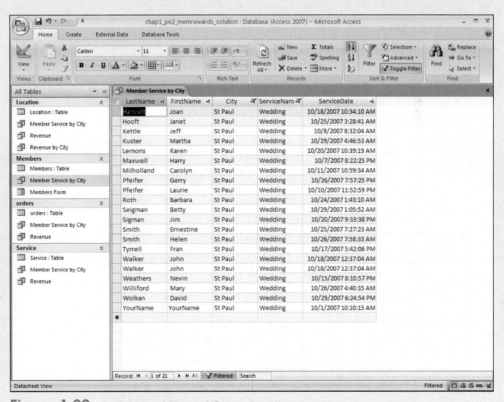

Figure 1.29 Sorted and Filtered Query Results

...continued on Next Page

The Vancouver Preschool is a dynamic and exciting educational environment for young children. It launches each school year with a fundraiser that helps provide classroom supplies. Patrons are asked to donate goods and services, which are auctioned at a welcome-back-to-school dinner for students, parents, grandparents, and friends. All of the data about the donations are contained in an Access file. Your task is to make some modifications to the data and print a form and a report. Verify your work by comparing it to Figure 1.30. The report in the figure is displayed at a higher zoom percentage so that you can read the report easily. Your report may appear as a full page.

a. Copy the partially completed file *chap1_pe3_preschool.accdb* from the Exploring Access folder to your production folder. Rename it **chap1_pe3_preschool_solution.accdb**. Double-click the file name to open it. Click **Options** on the Security Warning bar, click **Enable this content**, and then click **OK**.

b. Open the **Donors form**. Navigate to a **new blank record** by clicking the navigation button with the yellow asterisk on it.

c. Enter the information below in the form.

Field Name	Value
DonorID	(New)
FirstName	Your First Name
LastName	Your Last Name
Address	124 West Elm Apt 12
City	Your hometown
State	Your state
Zip	00001
Phone	9995551234
Notes	Your e-mail
Item Donated	Car wash and hand wax
Number Attending	2
Item Value	100
Category	Service

d. Click **Print Record**. Close the form.

e. Open the **Items for Auction** report. Check to ensure that the *car wash and hand wax* donation is listed. If it is, print the report. Close Print preview.

f. Click the **Office Button**, select **Manage**, and select **Compact and Repair Database**.

g. Click the **Office Button**, select **Manage**, and select **Back Up Database**. Use the default backup file name.

h. Close the file.

...continued on Next Page

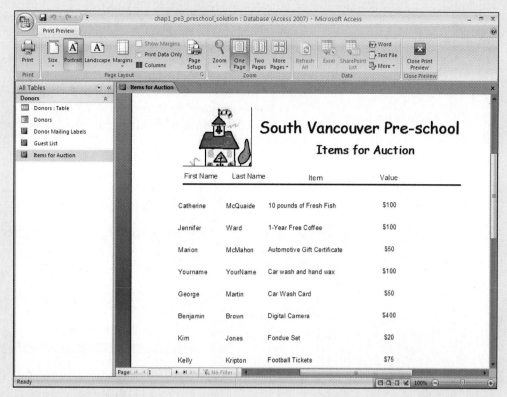

Figure 1.30 Report

4 Custom Coffee

The Custom Coffee Company is a small service organization that provides coffee, tea, and snacks to offices. Custom Coffee also provides and maintains the equipment for brewing the beverages. Although the firm is small, its excellent reputation for providing outstanding customer service has helped it grow. Part of the customer service is determined through a database the firm owner set up to organize and keep track of customer purchases. Verify your work by comparing it to Figure 1.31. The report in the figure is displayed at a higher zoom percentage so that you can read the report easily. Your report may appear as a full page.

a. Copy the partially completed file *chap1_pe4_coffee.accdb* from the Exploring Access folder to your production folder. Rename it **chap1_pe4_coffee_solution.accdb**. Double-click the file name to open the file. Click **Options** in the Security Warning bar, click **Enable this content**, and then click **OK**.

b. Click the **Navigation pane down arrow** to change the object view from Tables and Related Views to **Object Type**.

c. Examine the other objects, reports, forms, and queries in the database. Click the **Navigation pane down arrow** and restore the **Tables and Related Views** method of looking at the objects.

d. Double-click the **Sales Reps table** to open it. Replace *YourName* with **your name**. Close the table by clicking Close in the database window.

e. Double-click the **Customers Form** to open it. Navigate to a **new blank record** by clicking the navigation button with the yellow asterisk on it. Use **your name** for the *Customer* and *Contact* fields. Invent an address, phone, and e-mail. Type **Miami** for the city and **FL** for the state fields. The *Service Start Date* is **01/17/2005**. The *Credit Rating* is **A**. Type a **2** for the *Sales Rep ID*. It will convert to *S002* automatically.

f. Close the Customers Form.

g. Double-click the **Orders form** to open it. Navigate to a new blank record by clicking the navigation button with the yellow asterisk on it.

h. Type **16** as the *Customer ID*. The database will convert it to *C0016*. In the *Payment Type*, type **Cash**.

...continued on Next Page

i. Type **4** in the *Product ID box* and **2** in *Quantity*. In the next row, type **6** and **1** for *Product ID* and *Quantity*. The Product IDs will convert to P0004 and P0006. Close the form, saving changes if requested.

j. Open the **Order Details Report**. Scroll down to verify that your name appears both as a customer and as a sales rep. Right-click **your name** in the SalesRep field and select **Equals "Your Name"** from the shortcut menu. Right click **Miami** in the City field and select **Equals "Miami"** from the shortcut menu.

k. Click the **Office Button**, position the mouse pointer over **Print**, and select **Print Preview**. Click **Print**.

l. Click the **Office Button**, select **Manage**, and then select **Compact and Repair Database**.

m. Click the **Office Button**, select **Manage**, and then select **Back Up Database**. Use the default backup file name. Close the file.

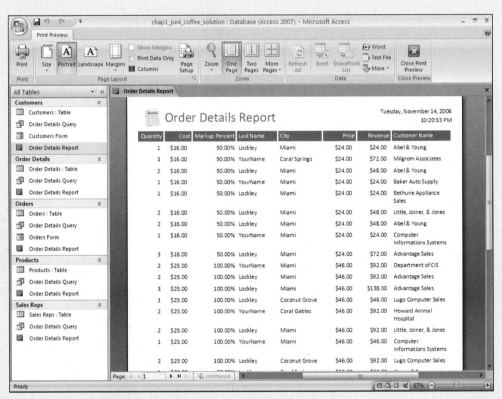

Figure 1.31 Report Showing Changes Made to Forms

Mid-Level Exercises

1 Object Navigation, Data Entry, and Printing Database Objects

Your little sister lives to play soccer. She told her coach that you have become a computer expert. Coach (who is also the league director) called you to ask for help with the Access database file containing all of the league information. You agreed, and he promptly delivered a disc containing a copy of the league's database. The file contains information on the players, the coaches, and the teams. Players are classified by skill and experience level, with the best players described as "A." The Coaches table classifies coaching status as level 1 (head coaches) or 2 (assistant coaches). Coach asks that you add new players to the database and then identify all of the players not yet assigned to teams. He also needs you to identify the teams without coaches, the unassigned coaches, and asks that you assign each team a head and an assistant coach. Finally, Coach convinces you to volunteer as a coach in the league. Verify your work by looking at Figure 1.32.

a. Locate the file named *chap1_mid1_soccer.accdb*, copy it to your working folder, and rename it **chap1_mid1_soccer_solution.accdb**. Open the file and enable the content.

b. Open the Relationships window and examine the tables, the relationships, and the fields located in each table. Close the Relationships window.

c. Examine all of the objects in the database and think about the work Coach asked you to do. Identify which objects will assist you in accomplishing the assigned tasks.

d. Open the **Players form** and create a new record. Use your name, but you may invent the data about your address and phone. You are classified as an "A" player. Print the form containing your record. Close the form.

e. Open the **Coaches table**. Replace record 13 with **your instructor's name**. Add **yourself** as a new record. You are a *coach status* **1**.

f. Identify the players not assigned to teams. Assign each player to a team while balancing skill levels. (You would not want one team in the league to have all of the "A" skill level players because they would always win.)

g. Identify the teams without coaches and the coaches not assigned to teams. Assign a head coach and an assistant coach to each team. You may need to assign a person with head coaching qualifications to an assistant position. If you do, change his or her *status* to **2**.

h. After you assign all of the players and coaches to teams, open and print the **Master Coaching List report**.

i. After you assign all of the players and coaches to teams, open and print the **Team Rosters report**. Close the database.

...continued on Next Page

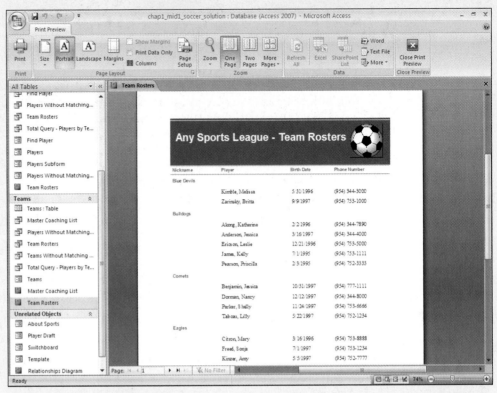

Figure 1.32 Team Roster Report

2 Sorting and Filtering Table Data Using Advanced Filters

You are the senior partner in a large, independent real estate firm that specializes in home sales. Although you still represent buyers and sellers in real estate transactions, you find that most of your time is spent supervising the agents who work for your firm. This fact distresses you because you like helping people buy and sell homes. There is a database containing all of the information on the properties your firm has listed. You believe that by using the data in the database more effectively, you can spend less time supervising the other agents and spend more time doing the part of your job that you like doing the best. Your task is to determine how many three-bedroom, two-bathroom, and garage properties your firm has listed for sale with a listing price under $400,000. Finally, you need to sort the data by list price in descending order. Refer to Figure 1.33 to verify that your results match the results shown.

a. Locate the file named *chap1_mid2_realestate.accdb*; copy it to your working folder and rename it **chap1_mid2_realestate_solution.accdb**. Open the file and enable the content. Open the *Agents* table. Find and replace *YourName* with **your name** in the first and last name fields.

b. Create a filter by form on the data stored in the *Under 400K query*. Set the criteria to identify **three or more bedrooms**, **two or more bathrooms**, and **garage** properties you have listed for sale with a listing price **under $400,000**.

c. Sort the filtered results in **descending** order by the **ListPrice** field.

d. After you are sure that your results are correct, save the query.

e. Capture a screenshot of the sorted and filtered Under 400K query. With the sorted and filtered table open on your computer, press **PrintScrn**. Open Word; launch a new blank document, type **your name and section number**, and press **Enter**. Press **Ctrl+V** or

...continued on Next Page

click Paste. Print the word document. Save it as **chap1_mid2_realestate_solution. docx.** Close the Word document.

f. Compact, repair, and back up the database. Name the backup **chap1_mid2_ realestate_backup.accdb.** Close the database.

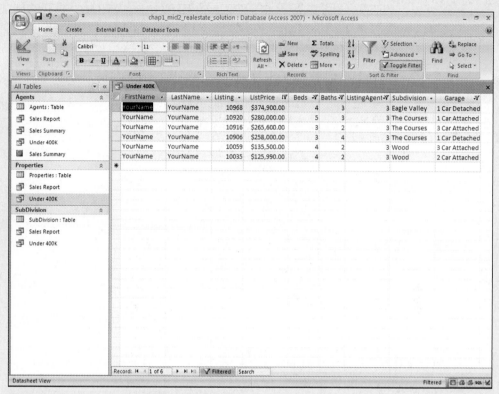

Figure 1.33   Sorted, Filtered Table

3 Sorting and Filtering Table Data Using Advanced Filters, Printing a Report

You work for the Office of Residence Life at your university as a work/study employee. The dean of student affairs, Martha Sink, Ph.D., placed you in this position because your transcript noted that you were enrolled in a computing class covering Microsoft Access. Dr. Sink has a special project for you. Each year, the Association of Higher Education hosts a national conference to share new ideas and best practices. Next year, the conference will be held on your campus, and the Office of Residence life has the responsibility of planning and organizing the events, speakers, and physical meeting spaces. To facilitate the work, the IT department has created a database containing information on the rooms, speakers, and sessions. Dr. Sink needs your assistance with extracting information from the database. Examine Figure 1.34 to verify your work.

a. Locate the file named *chap1_mid3_natconf.accdb*; copy it to your working folder and rename it **chap1_mid3_natconf_solution.accdb.** Open the file and enable the content. Open the **Speakers table.** Find and replace *YourName* with **your name.** Close the Speakers table.

...continued on Next Page

b. Open the **Speaker - Session Query** and apply a filter to identify the sessions where you or Holly Davis are the speakers. Use Filter by Form and engage the Or tab.

c. Sort the filtered results in descending order by the RoomID field.

d. Capture a screenshot of the sorted and filtered Speaker Session query. With the sorted and filtered query open on your computer press **PrintScrn**. Open Word, launch a new blank document, type **your name and section number**, and press **Enter**. Press **Ctrl+V** or click **Paste**. Print the Word document. Save it as **chap1_mid3_natconf_solution.docx**. Close the Word document.

e. Open the **Master List – Sessions and Speakers report** in Report View. Apply a filter that limits the report to sessions where you are the speaker. Print the report.

f. Compact, repair, and back up the database. Name the backup **chap1_mid3_natconf_backup.accdb**. Close the database.

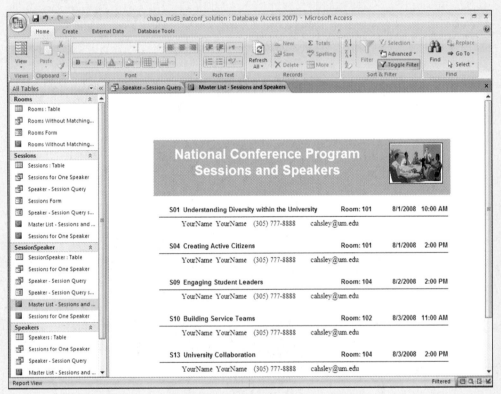

Figure 1.34 Master Sessions and Speakers Report

Capstone Exercise

Your boss expressed a concern about the accuracy of the inventory reports in the bookstore. He needs you to open the inventory database, make modifications to some records, and determine if the changes you make carry through to the other objects in the database. You will make changes to a form and then visit those changes in a table, a query, and a report. When you have verified that the changes update automatically, you will compact and repair the database and make a backup of it.

Database File Setup

You need to copy an original database file, rename the copied file, and then open the copied database to complete this capstone exercise. After you open the copied database, you will replace an existing employee's name with your name.

a. Locate the file named *chap1_cap_bookstore.accdb* and copy it to your working folder.

b. Rename the copied file as **chap1_cap_bookstore_solution.accdb**.

c. Open the *chap1_cap_bookstore_solution.accdb* file and enable the content.

d. Open the **Author Form** form.

e. Navigate to record 7 and replace *YourName* with **your name**.

f. Add a new *Title*, **Computer Wisdom II**. The *ISBN* is **0-684-80416-5**, the *PubID* is **SS**, the *PublDate* is **2007**, the *Price* is **$28.00** (just type 28, no $, period, or zeros), and *StockAmt* is **27** *units*.

g. Navigate to record 6 (or any other record). Close the form.

h. Open the **Author Form** again and navigate to record 7. The changes are there because Access works from storage, not memory. Close the form.

Sort a Query and Apply a Filter by Selection

You need to reorder a detail query so that the results are sorted alphabetically by the publisher name.

a. Open the **Publishers, Books, and Authors Query**.

b. Click in any record in the PubName field and sort the field in alphabetical order.

c. Check to make sure that two books list you as the author.

d. Click *your name* in the Author field and filter the records to show your books.

e. Close the query without saving the changes.

View a Report

You need to examine the Publishers, Books, and Authors report to determine if the changes you made to the Author form carried through to the report.

a. Open the **Publishers, Books, and Authors Report**.

b. Check to make sure that the report shows two books listing you as the author.

c. Print the report.

d. Close the report.

Filter a Table

You need to examine the Books table to determine if the changes you made to the Author form carried through to the related table. You also will filter the table to display books published after 2004 with fewer than 30 copies in inventory.

a. Open the **Books** table.

b. Click **Advanced** in the Sort & Filter group and then select **Filter by Form** from the drop-down list.

c. Create the criteria that will identify all records with fewer than 30 items in stock.

d. Apply the filter.

e. Print the filtered table.

f. Close the table. Do not save the design changes.

Compact, Repair, and Back Up a Database

Now that you are satisfied that any changes made to a form, table, or query carry through the database, you are ready to compact, repair, and back up your file.

a. Select the option to compact and repair your database.

b. Select the option to create a backup copy of your database, accept the default file name, and save it.

c. Close the file.

Mini Cases

Use the rubric following the case as a guide to evaluate your work, but keep in mind that your instructor may impose additional grading criteria or use a different standard to judge your work.

Applying Filters, Printing, and File Management

The *chap1_mc1_safebank.accdb* file contains data from a small bank. Copy the *chap1_mc1_safebank.accdb* file to your working storage folder, name it **chap1_mc1_safebank_solution.accdb**, and open the copied file. Use the skills from this chapter to perform several tasks. Open the Customer table, replace YourName with your name, and sort the data in alphabetical order by LastName. Print the Customer table. Open the Branch table and make yourself the manager of the Campus branch. Close both tables. Open the Branch Customers query and filter it to show only the accounts at the Campus branch with balances over $1,500.00. Print the filtered query results. Compact, repair, and backup your work.

GENERAL CASE

Performance Elements	Exceeds Expectations	Meets Expectations	Below Expectations
Sort and print table data	Printout displays data sorted in requested order.	The table was successfully printed, but the order is incorrect.	Output missing or corrupted.
Apply filters and print query data	Appropriate filters successfully created and printed.	One of the requested filters but not both work correctly. Output created.	Output missing or corrupted.
Data entry	Data were entered correctly.	Some but not all of the requested data were entered correctly, or other data were overwritten.	Output missing or corrupted.
File management	Database was correctly compacted, repaired, and backed up.	The database was successfully compacted but not backed up or vice versa.	Files not submitted.

Combining Name Fields

This chapter introduced you to the power of using Access filters and setting criteria, but you have much more to explore. Copy the file named *chap1_mc2_traders.accdb* to your production folder and rename it **chap1_mc2_traders_solution.accdb**. Open the file and enable the content. Open the Employees table and replace YourName with your first and last names. Open the Revenue report and switch to the appropriate view. Use the tools that you have learned in this chapter to filter the report. You wish to limit the output to only your sales of Seafood. You may need to use Access Help to get the filters to work. Once the report is filtered, print it. Write your instructor a letter explaining how you accomplished this step. Use a letter template in Word, your most professional writing style, and clear directions that someone could follow in order to accomplish this task. Attach the printout of the name list to the letter. Turn the printouts in to the instructor if instructed to do so. Back up, compact, and repair your database.

RESEARCH CASE

Performance Elements	Exceeds Expectations	Meets Expectations	Below Expectations
Use online help	Appropriate articles located, and letter indicates comprehension.	Appropriate articles located, but letter did not demonstrate comprehension.	Articles not found.
Report filtered to display only your sales of seafood	Printed list attached to letter in requested format.	Printed list is attached, but the filter failed to screen one or more salespeople or categories.	List missing or incomprehensible.
Summarize and communicate	Letter clearly written and could be used as directions.	Letter text indicates some understanding but also weaknesses.	Letter missing or incomprehensible.
File management	Database was correctly compacted, repaired, and backed up.	Database was successfully compacted but not backed up or vice versa.	Files not submitted.
Esthetics	Letter template correctly employed.	Template employed but signed in the wrong place or improperly used.	Letter missing or incomprehensible.

Coffee Revenue Queries

DISASTER RECOVERY

A co-worker called you into his office and explained that he was having difficulty with Access 2007 and asked you to look at his work. Copy the *chap1_mc3_coffee.accdb* file to your working storage folder, rename it **chap1_mc3_coffee_solution.accdb**, and open the file. Your co-worker explains that the report is incorrect. It shows that Lockley is the sales representative for "Coulter Office Supplies" and the "Little, Joiner, and Jones" customers, when in fact, you are those customers' sales representative. Make sure your name replaces YourName in the Sales Reps table. Find the source of the error and correct it. Run and print the report and turn the printout and file in to your instructor if instructed to do so. Compact, repair, and backup your database.

Performance Elements	Exceeds Expectations	Meets Expectations	Below Expectations
Error identification	Correct identification and correction of all errors.	Correct identification of all errors and correction of some errors.	Errors neither located nor corrected.
Reporting	Report opened, run, and printed successfully.	Printout submitted, but with errors.	No printout submitted for evaluation.
File management	Database was correctly compacted, repaired, and backed up.	Database was successfully compacted but not backed up or vice versa.	Files not submitted.

Relational Databases
and Multi-Table Queries

Designing Databases and Using Related Data

bjectives

After you read this chapter, you will be able to:

1. Design data **(page 809)**.

2. Create tables **(page 814)**.

3. Understand table relationships **(page 827)**.

4. Share data with Excel **(page 828)**.

5. Establish table relationships **(page 832)**.

6. Create a query **(page 844)**.

7. Specify criteria for different data types **(page 847)**.

8. Copy and run a query **(page 851)**.

9. Use the Query Wizard **(page 851)**.

10. Understand large database differences **(page 855)**.

Hands-On Exercises

Exercises	Skills Covered
1. TABLE DESIGN, PROPERTIES, VIEWS, AND WIZARDS (page 820) **Open:** a new blank database **Save as:** chap2_ho1-3_safebank_solution.accdb **Back up as:** chap2_ho1_safebank_solution.accdb	• Create a New Database • Create a Table by Entering Data • Change the Primary Key, Modify Field Properties, and Delete a Field • Modify Table Fields in Design View • Create a New Field in Design View • Switch Between the Table Design and the Table Datasheet Views
2. IMPORTS AND RELATIONSHIPS (page 837) **Open:** chap2_ho1-3_safebank_solution.accdb (from Exercise 1) and chap2_ho2_safebank.xlsx **Save as:** chap2_ho1-3_safebank_solution.accdb (additional modifications) **Back up as:** chap2_ho2_safebank_solution. accdb	• Import Excel Data into an Access Table • Import Additional Excel Data • Modify an Imported Table's Design • Add Data to an Imported Table • Establish Table Relationships • Understand How Referential Integrity Protects Data
3. MULTIPLE-TABLE QUERY (page 856) **Open:** chap2_ho1-3_safebank_solution.accdb (from Exercise 2) **Save as:** chap2_ho1-3_safebank_solution.accdb (additional modifications)	• Create a Query Using a Wizard • Specify Simple Query Criteria • Change Query Data • Add a Table to a Query Using Design View and Sort a Query

CASE STUDY

National Conference

You received a work-study assignment to the Office of Student Life at your school. This morning, the dean of Student Affairs, Jackie Cole, invited you to come to her office. Dr. Cole returned from the National Conference of Student Service Providers yesterday. Thousands of educators participate in this conference annually. She volunteered your school to host the event next year. She explained that this is a wonderful opportunity to showcase your school to the rest of the education world, but that the conference details need to be planned carefully so that the scheduled events execute flawlessly. Then Dr. Cole explained that she selected you as the work-study student because of your Access skills. She explained that no one else in the office knew anything about Access. She noted that a project of this magnitude required a database to efficiently manage the data. Then she said, "We are depending on you to create and manage the database and make our school look good."

Dr. Cole asked the IT department to help you design the database. The IT staff has created a small database with a table for the speakers and a table that joins the speakers and sessions together. An Excel spreadsheet contains information about the sessions. You will need to import the Excel data into the Access file, connect it with the rest of the database, and update the data.

Case Study

The IT staff did not think about the conference participants when they designed the database. You need to design a table that will hold the information about the conference participants. Think carefully about what information might be needed about each registrant. Then think about how to connect the registration information to the rest of the database. You need to establish the primary and foreign keys for the Registrant table as you plan the other fields in that table.

Your Assignment

- Copy the file named *chap2_case_natconf.accdb* to your production folder. Name the copy **chap2_case_natconf_solution.accdb**.
- Open each table and familiarize yourself with the data.
- Open the Relationships window and acquaint yourself with the tables, fields, and relationships among the tables in the database.
- Import the data contained in the Excel file, *chap2_case_sessions.xlsx*. As you create the import, think about which field will be the primary key and establish appropriate properties.
- Establish a relationship between the Sessions table and the other tables in the database. Remember that a relationship may only be formed on data of like type and size.
- Replace the first record in the Speakers table with information about you.
- Create a new record in the Speakers table. Add yourself as a speaker. Your area of expertise is Student Life.
- Create a new Session. Title it **Undergraduate Challenges**. Examine the session times and rooms and schedule this session so that it does not conflict with the other sessions.
- Create a query that will show the speaker's name, the session title, and the room number. Add parameters to limit the output to sessions conducted by **Davis**, **Kline**, and **you**. Print the query results.
- Create a table for conference participant's registrations. Carefully anticipate which fields need to be included. Participants must pay a $500 registration fee.
- Create a new record in the registration table. Add yourself as a participant.
- Capture a screenshot of the Relationships window. Paste the screenshot into a Word file. Save the file as **chap2_case_natconf_solution.docx**.
- Compact and repair your file. Back up the database as **chap2_case_natconf_solution_backup.accdb**.

Table Design, Properties, Views, and Wizards

Good database design provides the architectural framework supporting the work the database accomplishes. If the framework is flawed, the resulting work will always have flaws, too. You may remember the period leading to New Year's Eve in 1999, Y2K. Many people stocked up on groceries, withdrew cash from their checking accounts, and filled their gas tanks because they believed that the computer-operated grocery checkouts, automatic banking machines, and gasoline pumps would not function properly (if at all) on New Year's Day, 2000. These frightened people had legitimate reasons due to poor database design. Electronic data storage was (and remains) relatively expensive. Principles of good design dictate saving storage space when possible. As a space-saving measure, most dates in most computers prior to the mid-1990s stored the year as a two-digit number. For example, 1993 was stored as 93. The Information Systems and Computer Science professionals responsible for managing the databases in the world failed to anticipate the consequences of flawed database design.

Computers perform relatively simple arithmetic computations to measure time lapses. When subtracting 1993 from 1995, the computer knows that two years have passed. The results do not change when the dates are stored as 93 and 95. However, what would happen when the computer subtracted 99 from 01? You know that a two-year period has passed. But, the computer would believe that a *negative* 98 years had passed! Before New Year's Day, 2000, IS professionals worked extra hours correcting the design flaws in the way their systems handled and processed dates. On January 1, 2000, computerized grocery stores, ATMs, and gas pumps virtually all worked. The overtime hours combined with the new hardware and software required cost an estimated $21 billion globally to fix.

This chapter introduces the Safebank database case study to present the basic principles of table and query design. You use tables and forms to input data, and you create queries and reports to extract information from the database in a useful and organized way. The value of that information depends entirely on the quality of the underlying data, which must be both complete and accurate.

In this section, you learn about the importance of proper design and essential guidelines that are used throughout the book. After developing the design, you implement that design in Access. You create a table, and then refine its design by changing the properties of various fields. You will gain an understanding of the importance of data validation during data entry.

Designing Data

As a consumer of financial services, you know that your bank or credit union maintains data about you. Your bank has your name, address, phone number, and Social Security number. It knows if you have a credit card and what your balances are. Additionally, your bank keeps information about its branches. Think about the information your bank generates and then make a list of the data needed to produce that information. The key to the design process is to visualize the output required to determine the input needed to produce that output. Think of the specific fields you need and characterize each field according to the type of data it contains (such as text, numbers, or dates) as well as its size (length). Figure 2.1 shows one sample list of fields. Your list may vary. The order of the fields within the table and the specific field names are not significant. What is important is that the tables contain all necessary fields so that the system can perform as intended.

Customer's Last Name–Text
Customer's First Name–Text
Customer's Identification Number–Either text or number
Address–Text
City–Text
State–Text
Postal Code–Number
Phone–Text
Branch Identification–Either text or number
Branch Manager's Name–Text
Branch Manager's Start Date–Number date formatted
Branch Location–Text
Account Number–Either text or number
Balance–Number formatted as currency

Figure 2.1 Data Needed for a Bank Database

Figure 2.1 reflects the results of a careful design process based on six essential guidelines:

1. Include the necessary data.
2. Design for the next 100 years.
3. Design in compliance with Sarbanes Oxley.
4. Design in compliance with PNPI Regulations.
5. Store data in its smallest parts.
6. Avoid calculated fields in table data.
7. Design to accommodate date arithmetic.

The following paragraphs discuss these guidelines. As you proceed through the text, you will begin developing the experience necessary to design your own systems. Design is an important skill. You also must understand how to design a database and its tables to use Access effectively.

Include the Necessary Data

(. . . ask yourself what information will be expected from the system, and then determine the data required to produce that information.)

The best way to determine what data are necessary is to create a rough draft of the reports you will need, and then design tables that contain the fields necessary to create those reports. In other words, ask yourself what information will be expected from the system, and then determine the data required to produce that information. Consider, for example, the type of information that can and cannot be produced from the table in Figure 2.1:

- You can determine which branch a customer uses. You cannot, however, tell the customer with multiple accounts at different locations what the total balance of all accounts might be.

- You can calculate a total of all account balances by adding individual account balances together. You could also calculate the sum of all deposits at a branch. You cannot tell when a deposit was made because this small exercise does not store that data.

- You can determine who manages a particular branch and which accounts are located there. You cannot determine how long the customer has banked with the branch because the date that he or she opened the account is not in the table.

Whether these omissions are important depends on the objectives of the system. Of course, the data stored in a real bank's database is far more complex and much larger than the data you will use. This case has been simplified.

Design for the Next 100 Years

A fundamental law of information technology states that systems evolve continually and that information requirements change. Try to anticipate the future needs of the system, and then build in the flexibility to satisfy those demands. Include the necessary data at the outset, and be sure that the field sizes are large enough to accommodate future expansion. The *field size property* defines how many characters to reserve for a specific field.

The *field size property* defines how much space to reserve for each field.

When you include all possible elements of data that anyone might ever need, you drive up the cost of the database. Each element costs employee time to enter and maintain the data and consumes storage space. Computers have a finite amount of space. Good database design must balance the current and future needs of the system against the cost of recording and storing unnecessary data elements. Even with using data warehouses, the amount of data that we can store is limited.

> Good database design must balance the current and future needs of the system against the cost of recording and storing unnecessary data elements.

Suppose you are designing a database for your college. You would need to include students' on-campus and permanent addresses. It might be useful for someone to know other places a student might have lived or even visited during their lives. A worker in the Student Life office could help an international student connect with someone who used to live in or at least visited the international student's homeland. A student who had moved often or traveled extensively might need an extra page on his or her application form. Completing the application might take so long that the student might apply to a different college. A worker in the admissions office would need extra time to enter all the places of residence and travel into the database. The school's database file would grow and require additional storage space on the university computer system. The benefits provided to the international student from connecting him to someone who had been in his country may not justify the cost of entering, maintaining, and storing the additional data.

The data will prove useful only if they are accurate. You need to anticipate possible errors a data entry operator might commit. Access provides tools to protect data from user error. A *validation rule* restricts data entry in a field to ensure the correct type of data is entered or that the data does not violate other enforced properties, such as exceed a size limitation. The validation rule checks the authenticity of the data entered when the user exits the field. If the data entry violates the validation rule, an error message appears and prevents the invalid data from being stored in the field.

A *validation rule* checks the authenticity of the data entered in a field.

Design in Compliance with Sarbanes Oxley

Following the financial and accounting scandals involving Enron and World Com in 2002, the U.S. Congress passed the *Sarbanes Oxley Act (SOX)*. Its intent is to protect the general public and companies' shareholders against fraudulent practices and accounting errors. The Securities and Exchange Commission (SEC) enforces the act. Although primarily focused on the accounting practices followed by publicly traded companies, SOX permeates corporate Information Technology policies and practices. The act requires that all business records, including electronic messages, be saved for a period of five years and be made available to the SEC on request. Penalties for

Sarbanes Oxley Act (SOX) protects the general public and companies' shareholders against fraudulent practices and accounting errors.

non-compliance include fines, imprisonment, or both. The IT department faces the challenge of archiving all the required information in a cost-effective and efficient way.

Design in Compliance with PNPI Regulations

Federal laws and regulations govern the safeguarding of personal, non-public information (**PNPI**), such as Social Security Numbers (SSNs), credit or bank account numbers, medical or educational records, or other sensitive, confidential or protected data (i.e., grades used in context with personally identifiable information such as name, address, or other easily traceable identifiers). Organizations must store your personal information in computer systems. For example, without your Social Security Number, the financial aid office cannot release scholarship money to pay your tuition. Your employer cannot cut a paycheck without knowing your Social Security Number. Your doctor cannot tell the student health service at your school whether you have been immunized against the measles without your written permission. The data must be stored with protected and restricted access. Congress has passed several laws to protect you from identity theft or other misuse of your private, personal information. The most important of these laws include the following:

- Family Educational Rights and Privacy Act (FERPA) [educational records]
- Gramm-Leach-Bliley Act (GLBA) [financial institution and customer data]
- Health Insurance Portability and Accountability Act (HIPAA) [health information]

Store Data in Their Smallest Parts

The design in Figure 2.1 divides a customer's name into two fields (first and last name) to reference each field individually. You might think it easier to use a single field consisting of both the first and last name, but that approach is inadequate. Consider this list in which the customer's name is stored as a single field:

- Allison Foster
- Brit Reback
- Carrie Graber
- Danielle Ferrarro
- Evelyn Adams
- Frances Coulter

The first problem in this approach is lack of flexibility: You could not easily create a salutation of the form *Dear Allison* or *Dear Ms. Foster* because the first and last names are not accessible individually. In actuality you could write a procedure to divide the name field in two, but that is beyond the capability of the Access novice.

A second difficulty is that the list of customers cannot be put into alphabetical order by last name very easily because the last name begins in the middle of the field. The names are already alphabetized by first name because sorting always begins with the left position in a field. Thus the "A" in Allison comes before the "B" in Brit, and so on. The proper way to sort the data is on the last name, which can be done more efficiently if the last name is stored as a separate field.

Think of how an address might be used. The city, state, and postal code should always be stored as separate fields. Any type of mass mailing requires you to sort on postal codes to take advantage of bulk mail. Other applications may require you to select records from a particular state or postal code, which can be done more efficiently if you store the data as separate fields. Often, database users enter the postal code, and the database automatically retrieves the city and state information. You may need to direct a mailing to only a neighborhood or to a single street. The guideline is simple: Store data in their smallest parts.

Avoid Calculated Fields in Table Data

A ***calculated field*** is a field that derives its value from a formula that references one or more existing fields.

A ***calculated field*** produces a value from an expression—a formula or function that references an existing field or combination of fields. Although the information derived from calculations can be incredibly valuable to the decision maker, it is useful only at the moment the calculation is made. It makes no sense to store outdated data when recalculating; it will provide the decision maker with fresh, accurate information. Calculated fields should not be stored in a table because they are subject to change and waste space.

The total account balance for a customer with multiple accounts is an example of a calculated field because it is computed by adding the balances in all of the customer's accounts together. It is unnecessary to store the calculated sum of account balances in the Account table, because the table contains the fields on which the sum is based. In other words, Access is able to calculate the sum from these fields whenever it is needed, which is much more efficient than doing it manually.

Design to Accommodate Date Arithmetic

A ***constant*** is an unchanging value, like a birth date.

Date arithmetic is the process of subtracting one date from another.

A ***date/time field*** is a field that facilitates calculations for dates and times.

A person's age and date of birth provide equivalent information, as one is calculated from the other. It might seem easier, therefore, to store the age rather than the birth date to avoid the calculation. That would be a mistake because age changes continually and needs to be updated continually, but the date of birth remains *constant*—an unchanging value. Similar reasoning applies to an employee's length of service versus date of hire. Like Excel, Access stores all dates as a serial integer. You can use *date arithmetic* to subtract one date from another to find out the number of days, months, or years that have lapsed between them. Access provides a special data definition for *date/time fields* to facilitate calculations.

Design Multiple Tables

After listing all of the data items that you want to include in the database, you need to group them into similar items. Group the customer information into one table, the branch information into another, and the account information into a third table. A well-designed database provides a means of recombining the data when needed. When the design is sound, the **referential integrity** rules ensure that consistent data is stored in a related table. For example, the Customers and Account tables are linked by relationship. Referential integrity ensures that only valid customer IDs that exist in the Customers table are used in the Account table; it prevents you from entering an invalid customer ID in the Account table.

Data redundancy occurs when unnecessary duplicate information exists in a database.

Avoid ***data redundancy***, which is the unnecessary inclusion of duplicate data among tables. You should never store duplicate information in multiple tables in a database. The information about a customer's address should only exist in a single table, the Customers table. It would be poor database design to also include the customer's address in the Account table. When duplicate information exists in a database, errors may result. Suppose the address data were stored in both the Customers and Account tables. You need to anticipate the consequences that may result when a customer moves. A likely outcome would be that the address would be updated in one but not both tables. The result would be unreliable data. Depending on which table served as the source for the output, either the new or the old address might be provided to the manager requesting the information. It is a much stronger design to have the address stored in only one table but tied to the rest of the database through the power of the relationships. See Figure 2.2.

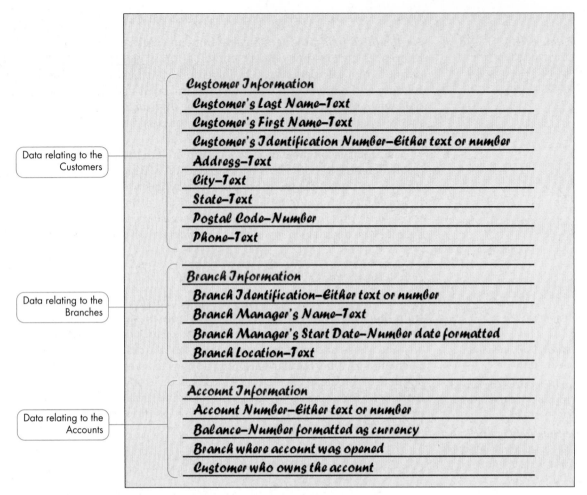

Figure 2.2 Bank's Database Data Grouped to Form a Table

Creating Tables

A table and all Access objects must be created within an Access file. To create a table, you must first create the file that will house it. Access works from storage, not memory. The other Microsoft Office programs work from memory: You create first and then save. With Access you must save a file first, and then create its contents. You will open a new blank database and save it to a specific storage location before you can begin creating your tables.

Access provides several ways to create a table. You can create a table by entering the table data into a field. You also can import table data from another database or application, for example, Excel. Regardless of how a table is created, you can modify it to include a new field or to delete an existing field.

Every field has a field name to identify the data that is entered into the field. The field name should be descriptive of the data and can be up to 64 characters in length, including letters, numbers, and spaces. Actual databases employ *CamelCase notation* for fields, objects, and file names. Instead of spaces in multi-word field names, use uppercase letters to distinguish the first letter of each new word, for example, ProductCost or LastName. Access is used frequently as a user-friendly means to connect to large databases stored on mainframes. Using Access, the manager can enter the organization's databases without needing courses in specialized computer languages. The manager then can find the data needed to make a decision and convert it to information. Most large databases and most mainframe computer systems will not accept spaces in field names.

CamelCase notation uses no spaces in multi-word field names, but uses uppercase letters to distinguish the first letter of each new word.

Every field also has a *data type* that determines the type of data that can be entered and the operations that can be performed on that data. Access recognizes nine data types.

A *data type* determines the type of data that can be entered and the operations that can be performed on that data.

Illustrations of Data Types and Uses | Reference

Data Type	Description	Example
Number	A **Number** field contains a value that can be used in a calculation, such as the number of credits a student has earned. The contents of a number field are restricted to numbers, a decimal point, and a plus or minus sign.	Height
Text	A **Text** field stores alphanumeric data, such as a student's name or address. It can contain alphabetic characters, numbers, and/or special characters (i.e., an apostrophe in O'Malley). Fields that contain only numbers but are not used in a calculation (i.e., Social Security Number, telephone number, or postal code) should be designated as text fields. A text field can hold up to 255 characters.	City
Memo	A **Memo** field can be up to 65,536 characters long. Memo fields are used to hold descriptive data (several sentences or paragraphs).	Library databases that store research papers
Date/Time	A **Date/Time** field holds formatted dates or times (i.e., mm/dd/yyyy) and allows the values to be used in date or time arithmetic.	March 31, 2008
Currency	A **Currency** field can be used in a calculation and is used for fields that contain monetary values.	Your checking account balance
Yes/No	A **Yes/No** field (also known as a Boolean or Logical field) assumes one of two values, such as Yes or No, True or False, or On or Off.	Dean's list
OLE	An **OLE** Object field contains an object created by another application. OLE objects include pictures, sounds, or graphics.	Excel workbook
AutoNumber	An **AutoNumber** field is a special data type that Access uses to assign the next consecutive number each time you add a record. The value of an AutoNumber field is unique for each record in the file, and thus, AutoNumber fields are frequently used as the primary key. The numbering may be sequential or random.	Customer account number
Hyperlink	A **Hyperlink** field stores a Web address (URL). All Office documents are Web-enabled so that you can click a hyperlink and display the associated Web page.	www.UNCG.edu

Establish a Primary Key

The **primary key** is a unique field (or combination of fields) that identifies each record in a table. Access does not require that each table have a primary key. Good database design strongly recommends the inclusion of a primary key in each table. You should select infrequently changing data for the primary key. For example, a complete address (street, city, state, and postal code) may be unique but would not make a good primary key because it is subject to change when someone moves.

You probably would not use a person's name as the primary key because many people have the same name. A Customer Identification Number, on the other hand, is unique and is a frequent choice for the primary key, as in the Customers table in this chapter. The primary key emerges naturally in many applications, such as a part number in an inventory system, or the ISBN in the Books table of a bookstore or library. At your school, you have a Student ID that uniquely identifies you. No other student has the same Student ID. When no primary key occurs naturally, you can create a new field with the *AutoNumber field* type, and Access will assign a unique identifying number to each new record. Figure 2.3 illustrates two types of table data. In the table shown at the top of the figure, the book's ISBN is the natural primary key because no two book titles have the same ISBN. It uniquely identifies the records in the table. The lower table depicts a table where no unique identifier emerged naturally from the data, so Access automatically numbered the records in order to distinguish them.

> The *AutoNumber field* type assigns a unique identifying number to each record.

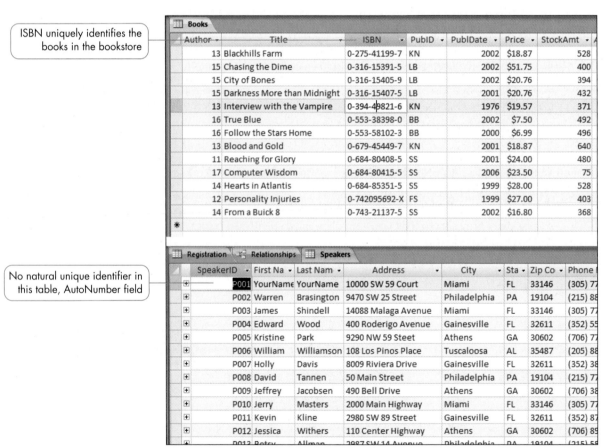

ISBN uniquely identifies the books in the bookstore

No natural unique identifier in this table, AutoNumber field

Figure 2.3 Tables Illustrating AutoNumbered and Naturally Emerging Primary Keys

Explore Foreign Key

A **foreign key** is a primary key from one table that is used in a different table as the basis for the relationship between the tables. The Customer ID may be the primary key in the Customers table. It serves to uniquely identify each customer. It often will appear as a foreign key in a related table. For example, the Order table may contain a field establishing which customer placed an individual order. Although a single Customer Identification Number can appear only one time in the Customers table, it may appear repeatedly in the Order table. A single customer may place multiple orders.

If you were the database administrator for the Youth Soccer League, you would assign a primary key to each player in the Players table and to each team in the Teams table. The Players table would have a field to show for which team the players play. The primary key in the Players table would uniquely identify the child with a PlayerID and also would show which team he or she played on using a TeamID (foreign key). Because each team has several players, you will find the TeamID repeated frequently in the Players table. Figure 2.4 depicts portions of the Players and Teams tables.

TeamID is the primary key in the Teams table

TeamID is a foreign key in the Players table; one team has several different players

Figure 2.4 Tables Illustrating Primary and Foreign Keys

Use Table Views

You may view your table in different ways. For example, you work in Datasheet view to add, edit, and delete records. The Datasheet view of an Access table resembles an Excel spreadsheet and displays data in rows (records) and columns (fields). In this chapter, you will use the Design view to create and modify a table's structure, properties, and appearance. The *PivotTable view* provides a convenient way to summarize and organize data about groups of records. The *PivotChart view* displays a chart of the associated PivotTable view. Figure 2.5 displays a table in Datasheet view that corresponds to the table you saw in Figure 2.1. The Datasheet view displays the record selector symbol for the current record. It displays an asterisk in the record selector column next to the blank record at the end of the table.

The *PivotTable view* provides a convenient way to summarize and organize data about groups of records.

The *PivotChart view* displays a chart of the associated PivotTable View.

Field names

First record

Figure 2.5 Customers Table in Datasheet View

Work with Properties

A **_property_** is a characteristic or attribute of an object that determines how the object looks and behaves.

A **_property_** is a characteristic or attribute of an object that determines how the object looks and behaves. Every Access object (tables, forms, queries, and reports) has a set of properties that determine the behavior of that object. The properties for an object are displayed or changed in a property sheet. Each field has its own set of properties that determine how the data in the field are stored and displayed. The properties are set to default values according to the data type, but you can modify if necessary. The properties are displayed in the Design view and described briefly in the following paragraphs.

Exclusively using CamelCase notation provides a consistent method to name your fields, but it may make the information difficult to read and understand. Therefore, you can use the **_caption property_** to create a more readable label that appears at the top of a column in Datasheet view and in forms and reports. For example, a field named ProductCostPerUnit can have the caption _Per Unit Product Cost_. The caption displays at the top of a table or query column in Datasheet view and when the field is used in a report or form. You use the formal field name, ProductCostPerUnit, in any expressions.

A **_caption property_** specifies a label other than the field name that appears at the top of a column in Datasheet view, forms, and reports.

In the following hands-on exercise, you begin by creating a database and entering data into a table. Then you switch to the Design view to add additional fields and modify selected properties of various fields within the table.

Before launching Access, use Windows Explorer to verify that you have a folder named **Your Name Access Production** on your storage device. Remember that you cannot run Access from a floppy or a Zip disk or a CD, even a CD-RW. The access speed of most USB thumb drives is adequate. Access runs best from the My Documents folder or a network drive.

Access Table Property Types and Descriptions | Reference

Property Type	Description
Field Size	The **Field Size** property adjusts the size of a text field or limits the allowable value in a number field. Microsoft Access uses only the amount of space it needs even if the field size allows a greater number. However, Access often connects to other database programs that reserve space for the specified field length. Good practice limits the field size to reduce system storage requirements.
Format	The **Format** property changes the way a field is displayed or printed, but does not affect the stored value.
Input Mask	The **Input Mask** property facilitates data entry by displaying literal characters that are displayed but not stored, such as hyphens in a Social Security Number or slashes in a date. It also imposes data validation by ensuring that the data entered by the user fits within the mask (i.e., it prevents typing an additional digit in a phone number).
Caption	The **Caption** property specifies a label other than the field name for forms and reports. It also displays on the table's Datasheet view. It permits a more user-friendly way to View the data.
Default Value	The **Default Value** property automatically enters a designated (default) value for the field in each record that is added to the table. If 90 percent of your customers lived in North Carolina, you might consider setting the default value for the State field to NC in order to save data entry time.
Validation Rule	The **Validation Rule** property rejects any record in which the data entered does not conform to the specified rules for data entry.
Validation Text	The **Validation Text** property specifies the error message that is displayed when the validation rule is violated.
Required	The **Required** property rejects any record that does not have a value entered for this field.
Allow Zero Length	The **Allow Zero Length** property enables text or memo strings of zero length.
Indexed	The **Indexed** property increases the efficiency of a search on the designated field. (The primary key in a table is always indexed.)
Unicode Compression	The **Unicode Compression** property is set to "Yes" by default for Text, Memo, and Hyperlink fields to store the data more efficiently.
IME Mode IME Sentence Mode	The **IME Mode and IME Sentence Mode** properties refer to the Input Method Editor for East Asian languages.
Smart Tags	The properties permit advanced users to add action buttons to a field. If you were using a database offering products for sale, a Smart Tag button embedded in a product name might open an inventory file and tell the database user what products are in stock.

Hands-On Exercises

1 | Table Design, Properties, Views, and Wizards

Skills covered: 1. Create a New Database **2.** Create a Table by Entering Data **3.** Change the Primary Key, Modify Field Properties, and Delete a Field **4.** Modify Table Fields in Design View **5.** Create a New Field in Design View **6.** Switch Between the Table Design and the Table Datasheet Views

Step 1 **Create a New** **Database**	Refer to Figure 2.6 as you complete Step 1.

a. Start Microsoft Access.

You should see the Welcome Window.

b. Click **Blank Database** in the New Blank Database section of the *Getting Started with Microsoft Office Access* window.

The lower right corner of the window displays the Blank Database section with file management tools.

c. Click **Browse**—the little yellow folder.

d. Click the **Save in drop-down arrow** and select the appropriate drive. Double-click the **Your Name Access Production** folder.

You need to be intentional about where you save your database file. Otherwise, you may have difficulty finding it again.

e. Click in the **File name** box and select *Database1.accdb*. Type **chap2_ho1-3_safebank_solution.accdb** to name your database and click **OK**. Click the **Create command** in the Blank Database section of the *Getting Started with Microsoft Office Access* window.

The Database window for the *chap2_ho1-3_safebank_solution.accdb* should appear.

TROUBLESHOOTING: If you skipped the instructions in Step 1d, you may have problems finding your file. From the desktop, right-click My Computer and select Explore from the shortcut menu. Click the Search tool. Select All Files or Folders. In the box, type **chap2_ho1-3_safebank_solution.accdb**. When the search results return, copy the file, and then paste it into the appropriate folder. Open and work the remainder of the hands-on exercises from the appropriate folder.

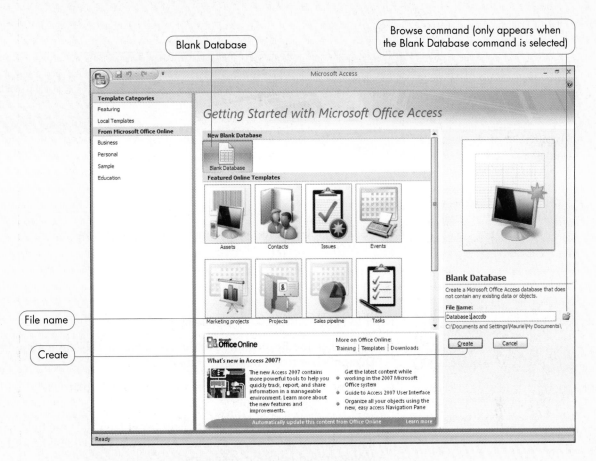

Blank Database

Browse command (only appears when the Blank Database command is selected)

File name

Create

Figure 2.6 Welcome to Microsoft Office Access

Refer to Figure 2.7 as you complete Step 2.

a. Type **B1** in the gold bordered cell and press **Enter**. The insertion point moves to the right. You also may navigate between the cells in the table by pressing **Tab** or the **arrow keys**.

b. Type **Lockley** in the first row of the third column. Press **Enter** and type **Uptown** in the next column.

c. Click in the cell below B1 and type **B2**, **Weeks**, and **Eastern**.

If your ID numbers do not match those shown in Figure 2.7, do not be concerned. You will be deleting that field in a later step.

d. Enter the additional data for the new table, as shown in Figure 2.7. Replace YourName with your first and last names.

e. Click **Save** on the Quick Access Toolbar. Type **Branch** in the Save As dialog box and click **OK**.

Entering data provides an easy way to create the table initially. You can now modify the table in Design view as described in the next several steps.

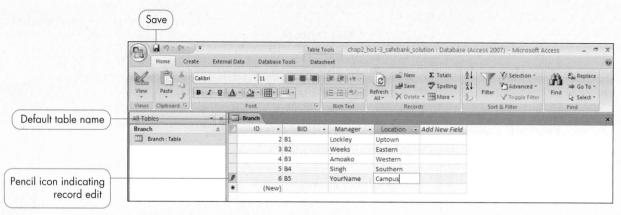

Save

Default table name

Pencil icon indicating record edit

Figure 2.7 Table Data for the (Unnamed) Branch Table

Step 3
Change the Primary Key, Modify Field Properties, and Delete a Field

Refer to Figure 2.8 as you complete Step 3.

a. Right-click the **Branch table** under All Tables in the Navigation Pane and select **Design View** from the shortcut menu.

b. Click and Drag *Field1* to select it and type **BID**. Replace *Field2* with **Manager** and *Field3* with **Location**.

The fields are named ID, Field1, Field2, and Field3. These field names are not descriptive of the data, so you need to change Field1, Field2, and Field3 to BID, Manager, and Location, respectively.

c. Click the **row selector** to the left of the *BID* field. The entire row selects, as shown in Figure 2.8.

d. Click **Primary Key** in the Tools group on the Design tab.

You changed the primary key in this table from the automatically generated one that Access created for you to the one you intended, the BID. As soon as you identified BID as the primary key, the Indexed property updated to Yes (No Duplicates). The primary key must be a unique identifier for each record.

TROUBLESHOOTING: A primary key must be a unique identifier for each record in the table. If you had trouble here, check to make sure the Indexed property is set to Indexed, Yes (No Duplicates). Return to Datasheet view and examine your data entry to ensure that you typed the correct values in the BID field.

e. Right-click the row selector to the left of the ID field. Select **Delete Rows** from the shortcut menu. Click **Yes** in the warning box instructing Access to permanently delete the selected field.

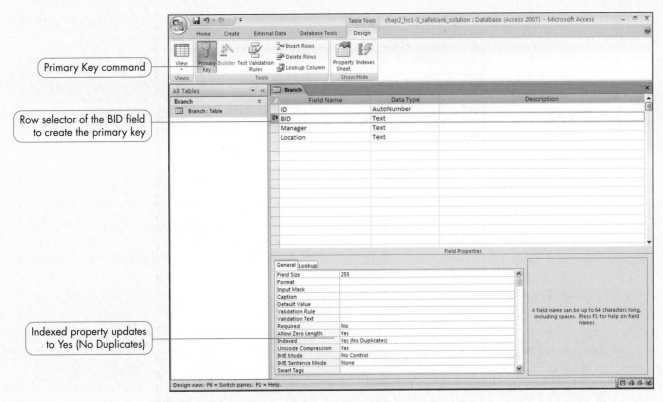

Primary Key command

Row selector of the BID field
to create the primary key

Indexed property updates
to Yes (No Duplicates)

Figure 2.8 Branch Table in Design View

Step 4

**Modify Table Fields in
Design View**

Refer to Figures 2.8 and 2.9 as you complete Step 4.

a. Modify some of the properties of the **BID** field.

1. Click in the **BID** field in the top section of the design window.

2. Click in the **Field Size** property box in the Field Properties section and type **10**.

3. Click in the **Caption** property box and type **Branch ID**.

4. Check the **Indexed** property box to make sure it is **Yes (No Duplicates)**.

If you need to change it, click in the Indexed property box. A drop-down arrow displays on the right side of the box. Scroll to select **Yes (No Duplicates)**, as shown in Figure 2.8.

For the next several tasks, you will toggle between the top of the design screen and the Field Property box on the bottom of the design screen.

b. Click the **Manager** field name at the top of the window. Look in the Field Properties section. In the **Field Size** property box, replace *255* with **30**. In the **Caption** property box, type **Manager's Name**.

A caption provides a more descriptive field name. It will head the column in Datasheet view and describe data in other database objects, such as reports, forms, and queries.

c. Click the **Location** field name at the top of the window. In the **Field Size** property box, change *255* to **30**. In the **Caption** property, type **Branch Location**.

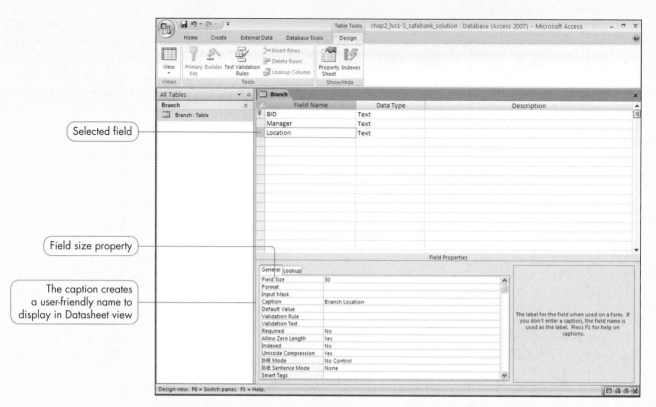

Figure 2.9 Change Field Properties to Increase Efficiency

Labels on figure:
- Selected field
- Field size property
- The caption creates a user-friendly name to display in Datasheet view

Step 5

Create a New Field in Design View

Refer to Figure 2.10 as you complete Step 5.

a. Click the blank cell below the *Location* field name. Create a new field by typing the field name named **StartDate**.

b. Press **Tab** to move to the *Data Type* column. Click the **Data Type drop-down arrow** and select **Date/Time**.

c. Press **Tab** to move to the *Description* column and type **This date is the date the manager started working at this location.**

d. Click in the **Caption** property box and type **Manager's Start Date**.

e. Click the **Format property drop-down arrow** and select **Short Date** from the list of Date formats.

f. Click **Save** on the Quick Access Toolbar to save the Branch table within the *chap2_ho1-3_safebank_solution* database.

A warning dialog box opens to indicate that the size of the BID, Manager, and Location field properties were shortened. It asks if you want to continue anyway. Always read the Access warnings! In this case, you are OK. You changed the size of the BID field from 255 to 10 in Step 4a. You did not need 255 characters to identify the BID. Your bank only has five locations. You changed the other two field sizes in Steps 4b and 4c.

g. Click **Yes** in the warning box.

The table Design view is useful to modify the structure of fields or to add fields to an existing table. However, tables cannot be populated in the Design view. The Datasheet view must be used to add data to a table.

TIP Keyboard Shortcut for Data Types

You also can type the first letter of the field type such as D for Date/Time, T for Text, or N for number. Click into the data type column in the field's row and, using the keyboard, type the first letter of the field type.

> Click in the Data Type column to reveal a hidden drop-down list of data types

> Click to toggle between Design View and Datasheet View

> Right-click to switch and select Datasheet View

> Click in the first blank Field Name column to create a new field

> Click to reveal a hidden drop-down list of data formats

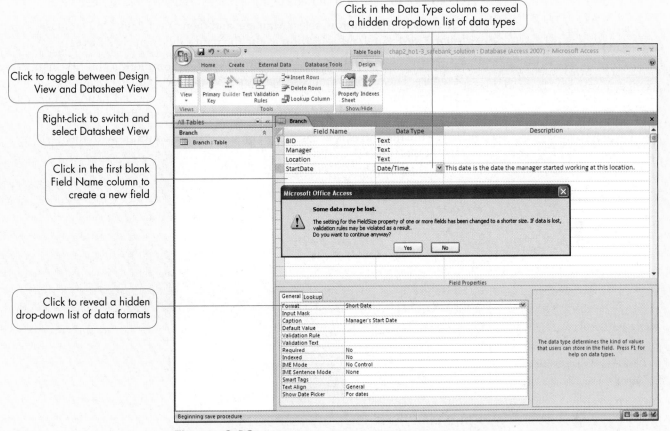

Figure 2.10 Change Field Properties to Increase Efficiency

Step 6

Switch Between the Table Design and the Table Datasheet Views

Refer to Figure 2.11 as you complete Step 6.

a. Right-click the gold tab shown in Figure 2.10 and select **Datasheet View** from the shortcut menu. (To return to the Design view, right-click the tab in Datasheet view and select Design View or click **View** in the Views group on the Design tab.)

b. Enter the dates each manager started work, as shown in Figure 2.11.

After entering the date for yourself, you remember that you started work on October 11.

c. Click the **calendar command** and click the **October 11** date on the calendar.

d. Click the table's **Close command**. **Do not save the changes**.

e. Double-click the **Branch table** in the Navigation Pane to open the table. Check the start dates.

You did not save any changes you made; you closed the table without saving changes. The dates are correct because Access works from storage, not memory.

f. Click the **Office Button**, position the mouse pointer over **Print**, and then select **Quick Print**.

Most users do not print Access table data. Tables store and organize data and rarely generate output. People do not spend time formatting table data. Check with your instructor to see if you should submit a printed Branch table for feedback.

g. Click the **Office Button**, select **Manage**, and then select **Back Up Database**. Type **chap2_ho1_safebank_solution** as the file name and then click **Save**.

You just created a backup of the database after completing the first hands-on exercise. The original database *chap2_ho1-3_safebank_solution* remains onscreen. If you ruin the original database as you complete the second hands-on exercise, you can use the backup file you just created and rework the second exercise.

h. Close the file and exit Access if you do not want to continue with the next exercise at this time.

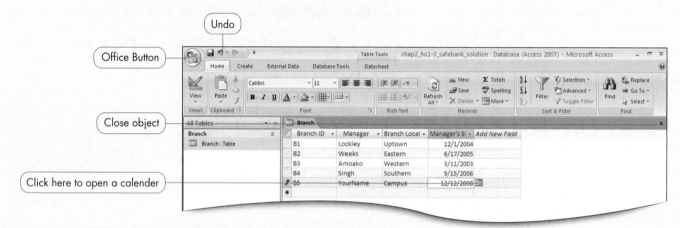

Figure 2.11 Calendar Facilitates Data Entry

Multiple Table Database

Earlier, you designed a database and combined similar data items into groupings called tables. You have completed the first table in the database, the Branch table. If you re-examine your design notes and Figure 2.2, recall that you planned for two additional tables in the Safebank database. The power of a relational database lies in its ability to organize and combine data in different ways to obtain a complete picture of the events the data describe. Good database design connects the data in different tables through links. These links are the relationships that give relational databases the name. In your Safebank database, one customer can have many accounts or can bank at any of the bank locations. That is, the customer's ID may be listed for many account numbers in the Accounts table, but the customer's ID is listed only one time in the Customers table. When the database is set up properly, database users can be confident that if they search for a specific customer identification number, they will be given accurate information about that customer's account balances, address, or branch preferences.

In this section, you learn about table relationships, referential integrity, indexing, and importing data from Excel.

Understanding Table Relationships

The relationship is like a piece of electronic string that travels throughout the database, searching every record of every table until it finds the events of interest. Once identified, the fields and records of interest will be tied to the end of the string, pulled through the computer, and reassembled in a way that makes the data easy to understand. The first end of the string was created when the primary key was established in the Branch table. The primary key is a unique identifier for each table record. The other end of the string ties to a field in a different table. You will include the Branch ID as a foreign field in the Accounts table. A foreign key is a field in one table that is also stored in a different table as a primary key. Each value of the Branch ID (BID) can occur only once in the Branch table because it is a primary key. However, the BID may appear multiple times in the account table because many different accounts are at the same branch.

Establish Referential Integrity

The relationships will be created using an Access feature that enforces referential integrity. Integrity means truthful or reliable. When referential integrity is enforced, the user can trust the threads running through the database and tying related items together. The Campus branch manager can use the database to find the names and phone numbers of all the customers with accounts at the Campus branch. Because referential integrity has been enforced, it will not matter that the branch information is in a different table from the customer data. The invisible threads keep the information accurately connected. Managers need organized and dependable data upon which they base decisions. The threads also provide a method of ensuring data accuracy. You cannot enter a record in the Account table that references a Branch ID or a Customer ID that does not exist in the system. Nor can you delete a record in one table if it has related records in other tables.

> Ask yourself what the anticipated results should be, and then verify. When you become skilled at anticipating output correctly, you are surprised less often.

If this were a real bank's data system, the files would be much larger and the data more sophisticated. However, the same design principles apply regardless of the database size. A small file gives you the ability to check the tables and see if your results are correct. Even though the data amounts are small, you need to develop the work practices to manage large amounts of data. With only a handful of records, you can easily count the number of accounts at the Campus branch. In addition to learning HOW to accomplish a task, you should learn to anticipate the computer's response to an instruction. Ask yourself what the anticipated results should be, and then verify. When you become skilled at anticipating output correctly, you are surprised less often.

Identify Cascades

Cascades are an Access feature that helps update related data across tables. In databases, *cascades* permit data changes to travel from one table to another. The database designer may establish cascades to update or delete related records. The string tying related items together can also make global changes to the data. If one bank branch closed and the accounts were not transferred to a different branch, the *cascade delete* feature would search the database and delete all of the accounts and customers who banked solely at the closed branch. (This may not be an optimal business practice, but it explains how the cascade delete feature works.) If a customer with an account at one branch opens a new account at a different branch, the *cascade update* will travel through the databases and connect the new account to the customer's address in the Customers table and the new account balance in the Accounts table.

As a general rule, you do not want changes cascading through the database. An inattentive data entry clerk could, with the click of a mouse, delete hundreds of records in various tables throughout the database. However, you need the power of a cascade occasionally. Suppose your company and another firm merged. Your firm has always stored customer account numbers as a five-digit number. The other firm has always used a three-digit account number. In this case, you would turn the cascade update feature on, open the Customers table, and change all of the three digit numbers to five digit ones. The new account numbers would cascade through the database to any records in any table related to the Customers table—for example, the Payments or Orders tables.

Cascades permit data changes to travel from one table to another.

Cascade delete searches the database and deletes all of the related records.

Cascade update connects any primary key changes to the tables in which it is a foreign key.

Retrieve Data Rapidly by Indexing

In Hands-On Exercise 1, you created the Branch table and established the BID as the primary key. Access changed the *indexed property* to Yes (No Duplicates). Access uses indexing exactly like you would read a book on U.S. history. If you need to know who succeeded Van Buren as president, you could start on page 1 and read the book in order page by page. Alternatively, you could go to the index and discover where the information about Van Buren may be found and open directly to that page. Using the index in a book makes finding (retrieving) information quicker. Indexing a database field has the same effect; it greatly reduces retrieval time. The actual index is a list that relates the field values to the records that contain the field value. Without an index, each row in the database would need to be scanned sequentially, an inefficient search method. The increased search time would adversely affect the performance of the database. All primary keys must be indexed. Additional table fields also may be indexed.

The *indexed property* is a list that relates the field values to the records that contain the field value.

Sharing Data with Excel

Many Access and Excel tasks overlap. Although you are learning the highly valuable skill of using Access, more people know how to use Excel than Access. Therefore, a lot of data resides within Excel spreadsheets. Often, the data stored in those spreadsheets fits well into an Access database design. Therefore, you need to be able to integrate existing Excel spreadsheet data into the organization's database. Fortunately, Access provides you with wizards that facilitate data sharing with Excel. Access can both import data from Excel and export data to Excel easily.

Figures 2.12–2.18 show how to use the Get External Data – Excel Spreadsheet wizard. You launch the wizard by clicking the External Data tab. Table 2.1 lists and describes the four groups on the External Data tab.

Table 2.1 Access and Other Applications Share Data

Process	When Used
Get External Data	Used to bring data into an Access database. The data sources include Excel, other Access files, XML, SharePoint Lists, and Text files.
Export Data	Used to send a portion of a database to other applications. You might use this to create a Mail Merge letter and envelopes in Word. You could create an Excel file for a co-worker who does not know how to use (or does not have) Access, or could share your data over the Internet via a SharePoint List.
Collect and Update	You could create an e-mail mail merge to send e-mails to your clients, and then use Access to manage the clients' responses.
Offline SharePoint Lists	This process might be used when traveling, if an immediate Internet connection is not available.

Launch the wizard by clicking the Excel command in the Get External Data Group.

Figure 2.12 shows the External Data tab that contains the Import Excel command. After you specify the data storage location, you can use the imported data to create a new table in Access, to *append* new records to an existing Access table, or to create a link between the Excel file and the Access table. When linked, any changes made to the Excel file will be updated automatically in the database, too.

You *append* records to an existing table by adding new records to the end of the table.

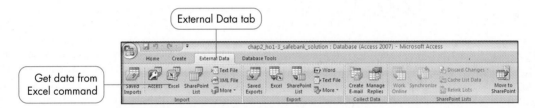

Figure 2.12 Select the Source and Destination for the Data

Figure 2.13 shows the Get External Data – Excel Spreadsheet dialog box. This feature controls where you find the data to import. It asks you to choose among three options governing what to do with the data in Access: place it in a new table, append the data to an existing table, or link the Access table to the Excel source.

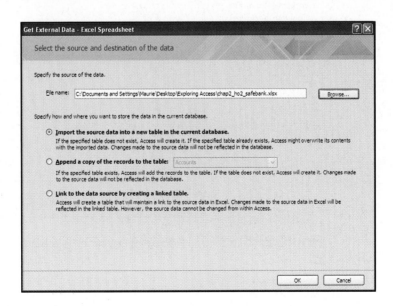

Figure 2.13 Select the Source and Destination of the Data

After you select the Excel workbook, you see the Import Spreadsheet Wizard dialog box, which displays a list of the worksheets in the specified workbook (see Figure 2.14). Use the options to specify a worksheet, in this case, the Customers worksheet. The bottom of the Import Spreadsheet Wizard dialog box displays a preview of the data stored in the specified worksheet.

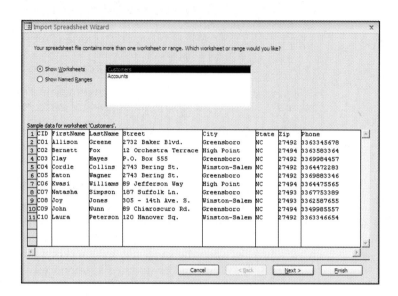

Figure 2.14 Show Available Worksheets and Preview Data

Although well-designed spreadsheets include descriptive labels, not all Excel users practice good spreadsheet design. The second window of the Import Spreadsheet Wizard dialog box contains a check box that gives you a chance to describe the data to Access (see Figure 2.15). When you find a label row in a spreadsheet, check the box. Access will use the Excel labels to generate the Access field names. When you find unlabeled data, do not check the box, and the data will import using Field1, Field2, and so on as field names.

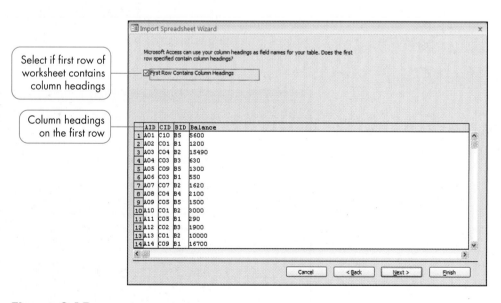

Figure 2.15 Column Headings Become Field Names

The third window of the Import Spreadsheet Wizard dialog box enables you to stipulate field properties (see Figure 2.16). The AID field is shown in the figure. Because it will become this table's primary key, you need to set the Index Property to Yes (No Duplicates). Use the Field Name box to select other fields (columns) in the worksheet and establish their properties. Not all Access table properties are supported by the wizard. You will need to open the table in Design view after importing it and make some additional property changes.

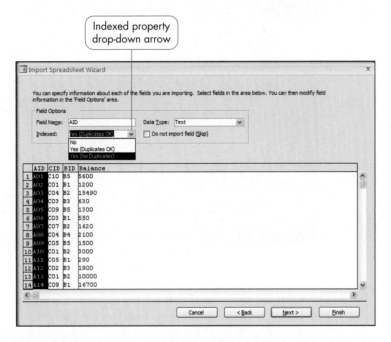

Figure 2.16 Field Options for Importing the Spreadsheet

The fourth window of the Import Spreadsheet Wizard dialog box enables you to establish the primary key before the import takes place (see Figure 2.17). If the option for *Let Access add primary key* is selected, Access will generate an AutoNumber field and designate it as the primary key. In the import described in the figure, the Excel data has a unique identifier that will become the table's primary key on import.

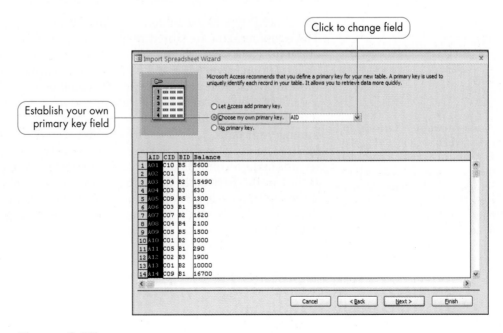

Figure 2.17 Primary Key Designation

Use the final window of the Import Spreadsheet Wizard dialog box prompts you to name the Access table. If the worksheet in the Excel workbook was named, Access uses the worksheet name as the table name (see Figure 2.18).

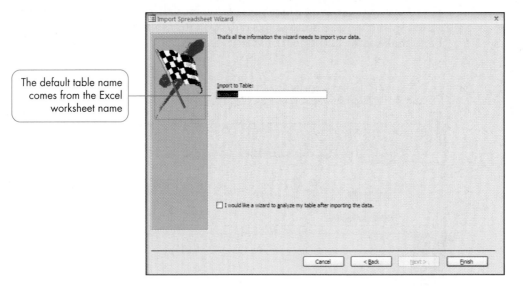

The default table name comes from the Excel worksheet name

Figure 2.18 Table Name for Import Spreadsheet

Finally, the wizard will ask if you wish to save the import steps. Frequently, data is shared between Access and Excel on a recurrent basis. At the close of a day or week or month, data from Excel are routinely imported and updated in Access. Saving the import steps expedites the data re-importation the next time it is needed. The imported data become a permanent part of the Access file. Access will open a final dialog box asking if you want to save the import specifications. In your hands-on exercise, the data import is a one-time only event so you do not need to save the import parameters.

Establishing Table Relationships

You should store like data items together using a logical file management structure. The customer data are stored in the Customers table. The Branch table stores data about the bank's branch, management, and location. The Accounts table stores data about account ownership and balances. You learned earlier that relationships form the strings that tie the related table data together. When you tie something, you use a knot. Any scout or sailor uses different knots for different purposes. Just as you use different knots for differing tasks, Access provides several differing relationships for joining your data. You have already discovered that a *one-to-many relationship* exists when each record in the first table may match one, more than one, or no records in the second table. Each record in the second table matches one and only one record in the first table to establish a powerful knot or relationship. In a well-designed database, you use this type of relationship most frequently. Table 2.2 lists and describes the different types of relationships you can form between Access tables.

A *one-to-many relationship* exists when each record in the first table may match one, more than one, or no records in the second table. Each record in the second table matches one and only one record in the first table.

Table 2.2 Relationship Types

Relationship Name	Definition
One-To-Many	This relationship is between a primary key in the first table and a foreign key in the second table. The first table must have only one occurrence of each value. That is: Each customer must have a unique identification number in the Customers table or each employee must have a unique employee identification number in the Employee table. The foreign key field in the second table may have recurrent values. For example, one customer may have many different account numbers, or one employee can provide service to many customers.
One-To-One	Two different tables use the same primary key. Sometimes security reasons require a table to be split into two related tables. For example, anyone in the company can look in the Employee table and find the employee's office number, department assignment, or telephone extension. However, only a few people need to have access to the employee's salary, Social Security Number, performance review, or marital status. Both tables use the same unique identifier to identify each employee.
Many-To-Many	This is an artificially constructed relationship giving many matching records in each direction between tables. It requires construction of a third table called a juncture table. For example, a database might have a table for employees and one for projects. Several employees might be assigned to one project, but one employee might also be assigned to many different projects. When Access connects to databases using Oracle or other software, you find this relationship type. When using Access as a stand-alone software, you would specify a Multivalue field and record multiple items as legitimate entries in a single field.

Establish a One-To-Many Relationship

When you click the Database Tools tab, you see the Show/Hide group (see Figure 2.19). The first command is the tool that opens the Relationship window. If this were a long established database, the Relationship window would be populated with the related tables in the database.

Figure 2.19 The Show/Hide Group and Show Table Dialog Box

Because the first time you will use the Relationship window you will be working in a newly created database, you must first use the Show Table dialog box to add the necessary tables to the Relationship window (see Figure 2.19). Select the tables you want to use in relation to other tables and add them to the Relationship window by clicking Add.

> ### TIP   Navigation Between the Relationship Window and a Table's Design
>
> When you right-click the table title bar in the Relationship window, the shortcut menu offers you a chance to open the table in Design view. Because relationships may be established only between data with the same definition, you have a chance to check how the data in different tables have been defined.

When possible, expand the table windows to display the complete list of field names shown in the table (see Figure 2.20). You may rearrange the tables by clicking and dragging the table window title bar.

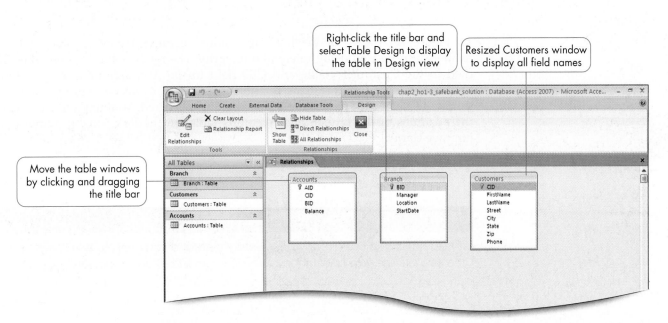

Figure 2.20 The Relationship Window with Resized Tables

Establish the relationships by clicking and dragging the field name from one table to the field name in the related table. When you release the mouse, the Edit Relationships dialog box opens (see Figure 2.21). Prior to establishing a relationship, Access runs through the table data to ensure that the rules you attempt to establish in the relationship can be met. For example, it checks to make sure that the branch identification number in the Accounts table (foreign key) exactly matches a Branch ID in the Branch table where it is the primary key. If all of the Branch IDs do not match exactly between the tables, Access cannot establish the relationship with referential integrity enforced. It will attempt to make a connection, but it will warn you that a problem exists with the data.

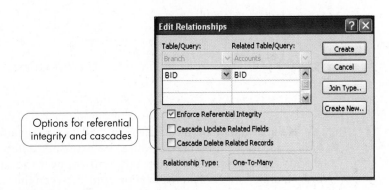

Figure 2.21 The Edit Relationships Dialog Box

Figure 2.22 shows the Relationship window for the Safebank database with all relationships created using referential integrity. The relationship between the CID field in the Customers table and CID field in the Accounts table runs behind the Branch table window. This relationship does not affect the Branch table; it simply displays with part of the connecting line obscured. You may want to switch the positions of the Branch and Accounts tables in the Relationship window to improve clarity.

TIP   Editing a Relationship

If the relationship has already been established and you need to edit it, right-click the juncture line. You also right-click the juncture line to delete a relationship.

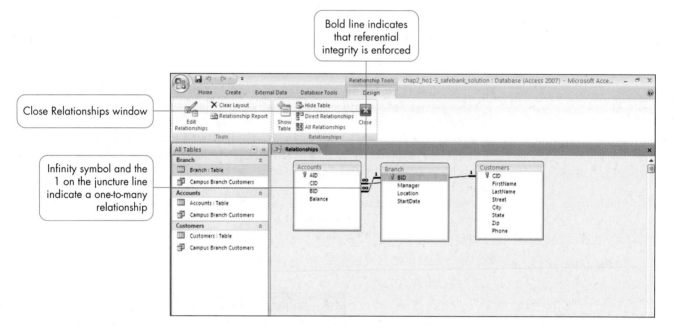

Figure 2.22   The Relationship Window Displaying One-to-Many Relationships

In the next hands-on exercise, you will create two additional tables by importing data from Excel spreadsheets into the Safebank database. You will establish and modify field properties. Then you will connect the newly imported data to the Branch table by establishing relationships between the tables.

Hands-On Exercises

2 | Imports and Relationships

Skills covered: 1. Import Excel Data into an Access Table **2.** Import Additional Excel Data **3.** Modify an Imported Table's Design **4.** Add Data to an Imported Table **5.** Establish Table Relationships **6.** Understand How Referential Integrity Protects Data

Step 1	Refer to Figure 2.23 and Figures 2.13 through 2.18 as you complete Step 1.
Import Excel Data into an Access Table	

a. Open the *chap2_ho1-3_safebank_solution.accdb* file if necessary, then click **Options** on the Security Warning toolbar, click the **Enable this content option** in the Microsoft Office Security Options dialog box, and click **OK**.

> **TROUBLESHOOTING:** If you create unrecoverable errors while completing this hands-on exercise, you can delete the *chap2_ho1-3_safebank_solution* file, copy the *chap2_ho1_safebank_solution* database you created at the end of the first hands-on exercise, and open the copy of the backup database to start the second hands-on exercise again.

b. Click the **External Data tab** (see Figure 2.12). Click **Import Excel Spreadsheet** in the Import group to launch the Get External Data – Excel Spreadsheet wizard. Select the **Import the source data into a new table in the current database option**, if necessary, as shown in Figure 2.13.

c. Click **Browse** and go to your **Exploring Access folder**. Select the *chap2_ho2_safebank.xlsx* workbook. Click **Open**, and then click **OK**.

The Import Spreadsheet Wizard activates. The first window shows all of the worksheets in the workbook. This particular workbook contains only two worksheets: Accounts and Customers. The Customers worksheet is active, and a list of the data contained in the Customers worksheet displays in the Wizard.

d. Click the **Customers worksheet** to preview the customer data. Return to the **Accounts worksheet** and click **Next** (see Figure 2.14).

e. Click in the **First Row Contains Column Headings check box** to tell Access that column heads exist in the Excel file (see Figure 2.15).

The field names, AID, CID, BID, and Balance will import from Excel along with the data stored in the rows in the worksheet.

f. Click **Next**.

The AID (Account ID) will become the primary key in this table. It needs to be a unique identifier, so we must change the properties to disallow duplicates.

g. Click the **Indexed Property drop-down arrow** and select **Indexed Yes (No Duplicates)**. Click **Next** (see Figure 2.16).

h. Click the **Choose my own primary key** option. Make sure that the **AID** field is selected. Click **Next** (see Figure 2.17).

The final screen of the Import Spreadsheet Wizard asks you to name your table. The name of the Excel worksheet was Accounts and Access defaults to the worksheet name. It is an acceptable name (see Figure 2.18).

i. Click **Finish**.

A dialog box opens asking if you wish to save the parameters of this import to use again. If this were sales data that were collected in Excel and updated to the database on a weekly basis, saving the import would save time.

j. Click **Close**.

Saving these import parameters is not necessary. The new table displays in Datasheet view and resides in the Safebank database (see Figure 2.18).

k. Open the newly imported **Accounts table** in Datasheet view.

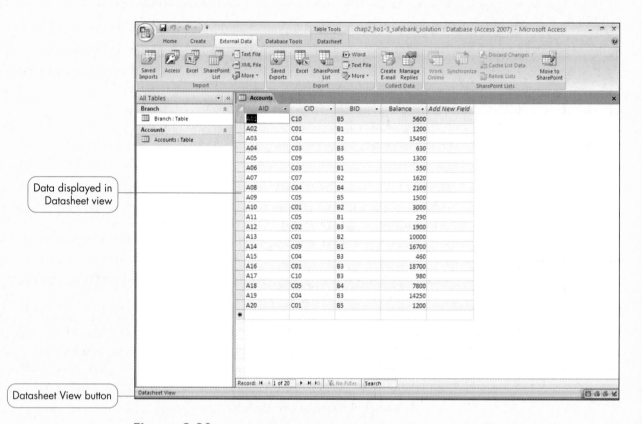

Figure 2.23 The Newly Imported Accounts Table

Step 2
Import Additional Excel Data

Refer to Figure 2.24 and Figures 2.13 through 2.18 as you complete Step 2.

a. Turn back to the beginning of Step 1 and repeat the instructions a through k.

b. Click on the **Customers worksheet** in Step 1d.

c. Change the index property of the **CID** field to **Yes (No Duplicates)** in Step 1f.

d. Identify the **CID** (Customer ID) as the primary key in Step 1g.

The default table name will be the Customers table. This is a good name so accept it.

e. Click **Finish** and click **Close**. The All Tables view will display three tables: Branch, Accounts, and Customers.

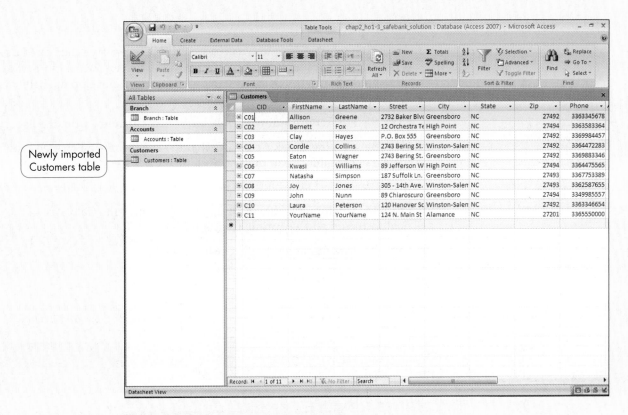

Figure 2.24 The Newly Imported Customers Table

Step 3

Modify an Imported Table's Design

Refer to Figure 2.25 as you complete Step 3.

a. Open the **Accounts table** in Design view and click the **AID** field if necessary.

b. Change the **AID** field size to **10**. Look at the bottom of the window in the Field Properties box.

   The field size was set at 255. Importing data from Excel saves typing but does not always create an efficiently designed database.

c. Type **Account ID** in the **Caption** property box for the AID field.

d. Click the **CID** field in the top of the Design view window to activate the *Properties* for the CID field.

e. Type **10** in the **Field Size** property box for the CID field using the Field Properties box in the bottom of the window.

f. Type **Customer ID** in the **Caption** property for the CID field.

g. Click the **BID** field in the top of the Design View window to activate the Properties for the BID field.

h. Type **10** in the **Field Size** property box for the BID field in the Field properties box at the bottom of the window.

i. Type **Branch ID** in the **Caption** property box for the BID field.

j. Click the **Balance** field in the top of the Design view window to activate the Properties for the Balance field.

k. Click in the **Format** property box to see a drop-down arrow.

Access often hides drop-down arrows until the property is activated. As you become more familiar with the software, you will learn which properties contain these hidden drop-down arrows. In the meanwhile, develop the habit of clicking around each new screen.

l. Click the **Format drop-down arrow** and select **Currency** from the list.

m. Click **Save** on the Quick Access Toolbar to save the design changes you made to the Accounts table. **Read the Warning Box!** Click **Yes**.

In this case, it is OK to click Yes because the size of three fields were shortened.

n. Open the **Customers table** in Design view. Change the **field size** of the **CID** field to **10** and add a **caption**, **Customer ID**.

o. Save the design changes to the Customers table.

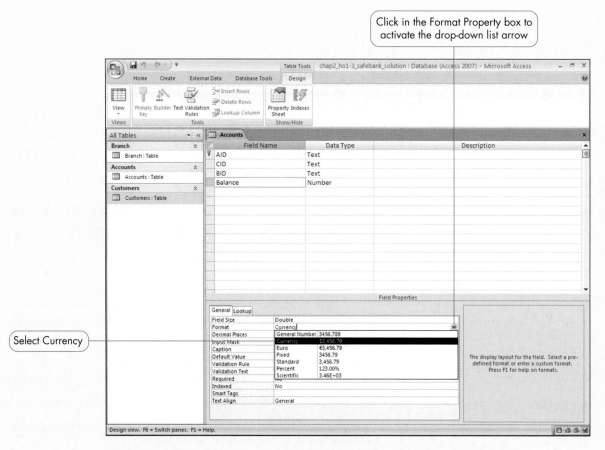

Figure 2.25 The Format Property of the Balance Field Set to Currency.

Refer to Figure 2.26 as you complete Step 4.

a. Open the **Customers table** in Datasheet view.

The asterisk in the row selector area is the indicator of a place to enter a new record.

b. Click the **Customer ID** field in the record after C10. Type **C11**. Fill in the rest of the data using your information as the customer. You may use a fictitious address and phone number.

c. Open **Accounts table** in Datasheet view. Create a new account ID A21. Enter **C11** as the Customer ID and **B5** as the Branch ID. Use your course number and section for the Balance field value.

If you were a student in section 04 of ISM 210, you would enter 21004 as the Balance.

d. Close all of the tables; keep the database open.

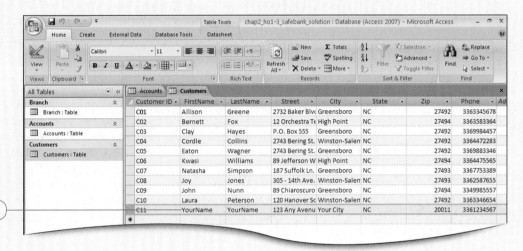

Add data about yourself

Figure 2.26 The Customers Table Displaying the New Account

Refer to Figures 2.27 and 2.21 as you complete Step 5.

a. Click the **Database Tools tab**. Click **Relationships**.

The Relationship window opens to the Show Table dialog box.

TROUBLESHOOTING: If the Show Table dialog box does not open, click Show Table in the Relationships group on the Design tab.

b. Double-click each of the three tables to add them to the Relationship window. (Alternatively, click a table, and then click **Add**.) Click **Close** in the Show Table dialog box.

The Accounts and Branch table boxes are large enough to display all of the field names. The Customers table has a scroll bar because it has too many fields to display in the small space.

TROUBLESHOOTING: If you duplicate a table, you may have gotten carried away clicking and adding. The duplicate table will display in the Relationship window with a number after its name, i.e. Branch1 or Customer2. Close the Show Table dialog box. Click the title bar of the duplicated table and press Delete. This procedure also works if you add the same table twice to a Query's design grid.

c. Run your mouse over the **blue line** at the bottom of the Customers table box until its shape changes to the **resize arrow**. With the double-headed arrow showing, click the left mouse button and drag down until all the field names display and the scroll bar disappears.

d. Click the **BID** field in the **Branch table**. Drag to the **BID** field in the **Accounts table** and release the mouse. The Edit Relationships dialog box opens. Check the **Enforce Referential Integrity** box. Click **Create**.

A thick black line displays joining the two tables. It has a 1 on the end near the Branch table signifying that it is connecting the primary key (unique identifier) to an infinity symbol on the end next to the Accounts table. You have established a one-to-many relationship between the Branch and Accounts tables.

e. Click the **CID** field in the **Customers table** to select it. Drag to the **CID** field in the **Accounts table** and release the mouse. The Edit Relationships dialog box opens. Check the **Enforce Referential Integrity** box. Click **Create**.

You have established a one-to-many relationship between the Customers and Accounts tables. A customer will have only a single Customer ID number. The same customer may have many different accounts: Savings, Checking, CDs, etc.

TROUBLESHOOTING: If you get an error message when you click Create, you possibly did not get all the field properties established correctly in Steps 3 and 4 of Hands-On Exercise 2. Relationships may be created only between like data types and sizes. Right-click the blue title bar of the Accounts window in the Relationship window and select Table Design from the shortcut menu. Click on the CID field and examine the size property. It should be set to 10. Click the BID field. It should be set to 10. Change the size property of one or both fields. Save your changes to the table design. Try to establish the relationship again. If it still does not work, check the size of the CID field in the Customers table. It should also be 10.

f. Click **Save** on the Quick Access Toolbar to save the changes to the Relationships. Close the Relationships window.

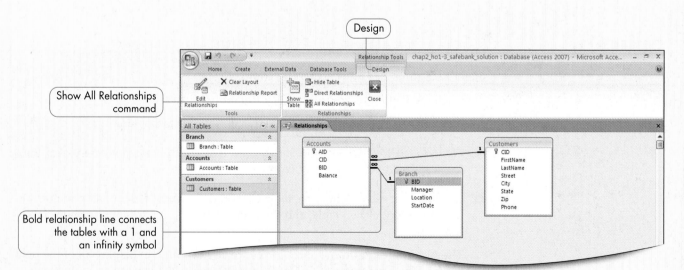

Figure 2.27 Properly Constructed Relationships Among the Tables

Refer to Figure 2.28 as you complete Step 6.

a. Open the **Accounts table** in Datasheet view. Add a new record: Account ID – A22; Customer ID – **C03** (Note, that is a zero, not a letter O); Branch ID – **B6**; Balance – **4000**. Press **Enter**.

A warning box appears. This bank has five branches. A sixth branch does not exist. In this case, the warning message is telling exactly what is wrong. There is no related record for B6 in the Branch table. Access does not permit data entry of unconnected data. Referential integrity was enforced between the Branch ID in the Branch table and the Branch ID in the Accounts table. Access prevents the entry of an invalid Branch ID.

b. Click **OK**. Replace *B6* with **B5** and press **Enter**. As soon as you move to a different record, the pencil symbol disappears and your data are saved.

You successfully identified a Branch ID that Access recognizes. Because referential integrity between the Accounts and Branch tables has been enforced, Access looks at each data entry item in a foreign key and matches it to a corresponding value in the table where it is the primary key. In Step 6a, you attempted to enter a nonexistent Branch ID and were not allowed to make that error. In Step 6b, you entered a valid Branch ID. Access examined the index for the Branch ID in the Branch table and found a corresponding value for B5.

c. Close the Accounts table. Reopen the **Accounts table** and you will find that the record you just entered for A22 has been saved.

d. Click the **Office Button**, select **Manage**, and then select **Back Up Database**. Type **chap2_ho2_safebank_solution** as the file name and click **Save**.

You just created a backup of the database after completing the second hands-on exercise. The original database *chap2_ho1-3_safebank_solution* remains onscreen. If you ruin the original database as you complete the third hands-on exercise, you can use the backup file you just created and rework the third exercise.

e. Close the file and exit Access if you do not want to continue with the next exercise at this time.

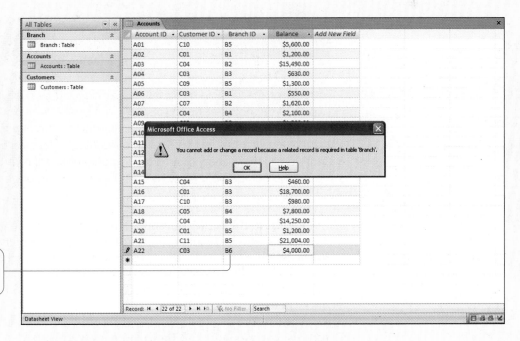

Invalid data entry generates an error when referential integrity is enforced

Figure 2.28 How Referential Integrity Works to Protect Data Accuracy

Queries

What if you wanted to see just the customers who bank at a specific branch or who have accounts with balances over $5,000? Perhaps you need to know the customers who have accounts at multiple branches. Maybe you will need a list of all the customers who bank with the branch managed by a specific manager. The manager's name is stored in the Branch table and the customer's name in the Customers table. In this small database, you could open both tables and mentally trace through the strings of the relationships and extract the information. But in a real world database with thousands of records, you would be unable to do this accurately. A query provides the ability to ask questions based on the data or a smaller grouping of data and to find the answers to those questions.

A **query** enables you to ask questions about the data stored in a database and returns the answers from the records in the order that matches your instructions.

A **query** permits you to see the data you want arranged in the sequence that you need. It enables you to select specific records from a table (or from several tables) and show some or all of the fields for the selected records. You can perform calculations to display data that are not explicitly stored in the underlying table(s), such as the amount of interest each bank account earned during the previous month.

In this section, you use the Query Wizard to create a query. You set specific conditions to display only records that meet the condition. Finally, you learn about large databases.

Creating a Query

The **Query Wizard** is an Access tool that facilitates new query development.

A **dataset**, which contains the records that satisfy the criteria specified in the query, provides the answers to the user's questions.

Create a query either by using the **Query Wizard** or specifying the tables and fields directly in Design view. Like all of the Microsoft wizards, the Query Wizard is a method to automate your work. It facilitates new query development. The results of the query display in a **dataset**, which contains the records that satisfy the criteria specified in the query.

A dataset looks and acts like a table, but it is not a table; it is a dynamic subset of a table that selects, sorts, and calculates records as specified in the query. A dataset is similar to a table in appearance and, like a table, it enables you to enter a new record or modify or delete an existing record. Any changes made in the dataset are reflected automatically in the underlying table.

 TIP   Changes Made to Query Results Overwrite Table Data

The connection between a query result and the underlying table data may create problems. On the one hand, it is to your advantage that you can correct an error in data if you should happen to spot it in a query result. You save time by not having to close the query, open the table, find the record in error, fix it, and run the query again to get robust results. On the other hand, you must be careful not to accidentally click into a query record and type something. If you press Enter or Tab, whatever you accidentally typed is stored forever in the underlying table.

The **query design grid** displays when you select a query's Design view; it divides the window into two parts.

Return to the earlier question. How would you identify the names of all of the customers who have an account at the Campus branch? Figure 2.29 contains the **query design grid** used to select customers who have accounts at the Campus Branch and further, to list those customers and their account balances alphabetically. (The design grid is explained in the next section.) Figure 2.30 displays the answer to the query in the form of a dataset.

The Customers table contains 21 records. The dataset in Figure 2.30 has only six records, corresponding to the customers who have Campus branch accounts. The records in the table are ordered by the Customer ID (the primary key), whereas the records in the dataset are in alphabetical order by last name. Changing the order of data displayed in a query has no effect on the underlying table data.

 TIP Examine the Record Number

An experienced Access user always examines the number of records returned in a query's results. As you add additional criteria, the number of records returned should decrease.

Create a Select Query

A **select query** searches the underlying tables to retrieve the data that satisfy the query parameters.

The query in Figures 2.29 and 2.30 is an example of a select query, which is the most common type of query. A **select query** searches the underlying tables to retrieve the data that satisfy the query parameters. The data display in a dataset (see Figure 2.30), which can be modified to update the data in the underlying table(s). The specifications for selecting records and determining which fields will be displayed for the selected records, as well as the sequence of the selected records, are established within the design grid of Figure 2.29. The select query is one of many different query operations Access supports.

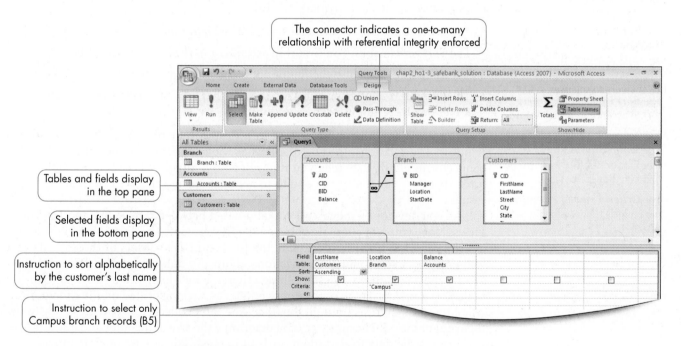

Figure 2.29 The Query Design View

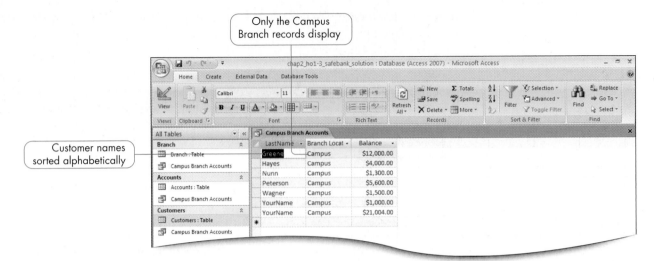

Figure 2.30 The Query Datasheet View

Use the Query Design Grid

The query design grid consists of two panes. The lower pane contains columns and rows. Each field in the query has its own column and contains multiple rows. The rows permit you to control query results.

The **Table row** displays the data source.

The **Field row** displays the field name.

The **Sort row** enables you to sort in ascending or descending sequence.

The **Show row** controls whether or not the field will be displayed in the dataset.

The **Criteria row(s)** determines the records that will be selected.

- The **Table row** displays the data source. The **Field row** displays the field name.
- The **Sort row** enables you to sort in ascending or descending sequence.
- The **Show row** controls whether or not the field will be displayed in the dataset.
- The **Criteria row(s)** determines the records that will be selected, such as customers with a Campus branch account.

The top pane contains table names in a design that resembles the relationship window. The relationship type displays as the connector between the tables. The connector in Figure 2.29 tells you that referential integrity between the tables is in force, that the relationship is a one-to-many relation, and that we can trust the query results.

As you developed the tables, you alternated between the Design and Datasheet views. Now, you will alternate between the Design view and Datasheet view as you develop queries. Use it to designate the fields and the subsets of those fields that will empower you to answer questions about the data and make decisions. You specify the data subsets by establishing criteria, which are rules or tests you can use to make a decision. Think of the query criteria as a sophisticated oil filter in your car. All of the car's oil runs through the filter. The filter collects dirt particles and strains them out of the oil. The query criteria determine the size of the filter and allow you to sift through the data to find the records of interest. The criteria operate much like a filter in a table. The difference between a filter and a query is that the query becomes a permanent part of the database. A filter gives you a temporary method to view the data.

Specifying Criteria for Different Data Types

The field data type determines how the criteria are specified for that field. You need to enter criteria for a text field enclosed in quotation marks. To find only the records of customers with accounts at the Campus branch, you would enter "Campus" as the criteria under the Location field. You enter the criteria for number, *currency* (e.g., $3.00 in the United States), and counter fields as digits with or without a decimal point and/or a minus sign. (Commas and dollar signs are not allowed.) When the criterion is in a date field, you enclose the criterion in pound signs. You should enter date criteria in the mm/dd/yyyy format, such as #10/14/2008#. You enter criteria for a Yes/No field as Yes (or True) or No (or False).

A *currency* is the medium of exchange; in the United States, currency formatted values display with a dollar sign.

Access accepts values for text and date fields in the design grid in multiple formats. You can enter the text with or without quotation marks, such as *Campus* or *"Campus."* You can enter a date with or without the pound signs, such as *1/1/2008* or *#1/1/2008#*. Access will enter the quotation marks or pound signs, respectively, for you when you move to the next cell in the design grid. Thus, text entries are always shown in quotation marks and dates in pound signs.

Use Wildcards

Select queries recognize the question mark and asterisk wildcards that enable you to search for a pattern within a text field. A question mark stands for a single character in the same position as the question mark; thus *H?ll* will return *Hall*, *Hill*, and *Hull*. An asterisk stands for any number of characters in the same position as the asterisk; for example, *S*nd* will return *Sand*, *Stand*, and *Strand*. If you search a two-letter state code field for *?C*, Access will return *NC*, *SC*, and *DC*. If you search the same field with either **C* or *C**, Access will return *CA*, *CO*, *CT*, *DC*, *NC*, and *SC*.

Use Operands in Queries

An *operator* is a mathematical symbol, such as +, -, *, and /.

An *operand* is the portion of the mathematical expression that is being operated on.

A numeric field may be limited through standard numeric operators; *operators* such as plus, minus, equals, greater than, less than, multiply (*), divide (/), and not equals (<>). An *operand* is a portion of the mathematical expression that is being operated on, such as the value stored in a field. In Access, you use the field name as an operand, such as Date() - 30. Both the Date() field and 30 are operands. Table 2.4 shows sample expressions and discusses their results.

Table 2.4 Criteria Operands

Expression	Result
>10	For a Price field, items with a price over $10.00
<10	For a Price field, items with a price under $10.00
>=10	For a Price field, items with a price of at least $10.00
<=10	For a Price field, items with a price of $10.00 or less
=10	For a Price field, items with a price of exactly $10.00
<> 10	For a Price field, items with a price not equal to $10.00
!=10	For a Price field, items with a price not equal to $10.00
#2/2/2008#	For a ShippedDate field, orders shipped on February 2, 2008
'2/2/2008'	For a ShippedDate field, orders shipped on February 2, 2008
Date()	For an OrderDate field, orders for today's date
Between 1/1/2007 and 3/31/2007	For a specified interval between a start and end date
Between Date( ) And DateAdd ("M", 3, Date( ))	For a RequiredDate field, orders required between today's date and three months from today's date
< Date( ) – 30	For an OrderDate field, orders more than 30 days old
Year((OrderDate)) = 2005	For an OrderDate field, orders with order dates in 2005
DatePart("q", (OrderDate)) = 4	For an OrderDate field, orders for the fourth calendar quarter
DateSerial(Year ((OrderDate)), Month ((OrderDate)) + 1, 1) – 1	For an OrderDate field, orders for the last day of each month
Year((OrderDate)) = Year(Now()) And Month((OrderDate)) = Month(Now())	For an OrderDate field, orders for the current year and month

Work with Null and Zero-Length Strings

Sometimes finding what is *not* known is an important part of making a decision. For example, which orders have been accepted but not shipped? Are we missing phone numbers or addresses for some of our customers? The computer term for a missing value is *null*. Table 2.5 gives the following illustrations on how to use the Null criterion in a query.

A *null* value is the formal, computer term for a missing value.

Table 2.5 Establishing Null Criteria Expressions

Expression	Result
Is Null	For an Employee field in the Customers table when the customer has not been assigned a sales representative. (Some fields, such as primary key fields, can't contain Null.)
Is Not Null	For a ShipDate field, orders already shipped to customers.
" "	For an E-mail field for customers who don't have an email address. This is indicated by a zero-length string. This is different from a Null value. Use this only when you know a customer has no e-mail, not when he or she has e-mail but you do not know what it is. You enter a zero-length string by typing two double quotation marks with no space between them (" ").

Understand Query Sort Order

The *query sort order* determines the order of items in the query Datasheet View.

The *query sort order* determines the order of items in the query Datasheet view. You can change the sort order of a query by specifying the sort order in the design grid. The sorts work from left to right. The leftmost field with a sort order specified will be the primary sort field; the next sort specified field to the right will be the secondary sort field, and so forth. Change the order of the query fields in the design grid to change the sort order of the query result. Alter the field order within the design grid by clicking in the Table row (the second row) of the design grid and specifying the table and then in the Field row and selecting a different field name. The table must be specified first because each field row drop-down list shows only the names of the fields in the specified table. You also may insert additional columns in the design grid by selecting the column, right-clicking the selection, and choosing Insert column from the shortcut menu. The inserted column will insert to the right of the highlighted column.

> **TIP Reorder Query Fields**
>
> With a query open in Design view, move your mouse above a field name. The mouse pointer will change shape to a bold black arrow. When you see the bold black arrow, click the mouse. The field's column selects. Move your mouse slowly over the top of the selected area until the pointer shape changes to the move shape (a thick white arrow). When the white arrow shape shows, click and drag the field to a new position on the design grid. A thick black border moves with your mouse to tell you where the field will move. Release the mouse when the border moves to the desired position.

Establish And, Or, and Not Criteria

Until now, all of the questions that you have asked the database to answer through queries have been relatively simple. Access adapts to more complex query specifications. What if you need a list of all of the customers who bank at the Campus branch and do not have accounts at any other branches? Which customers bank only at the Campus or Uptown branches? Are there customers of the Campus branch with deposits over $5,000? These questions involve multiple field interaction. The moment you specify criteria in multiple fields, Access combines the fields using the And or the Or operator. When the expressions are in the same row of the query design grid, Access uses the *And operator*. This means that only the records that meet *all* criteria in all of the fields will be returned. If the criteria are positioned in different rows of the design grid, Access uses the *Or operator* and will return records meeting *any* of the specified criteria. The *Not operator* returns the *opposite* of the specification.

The *And operator* returns only records that meet all criteria.

The *Or operator* returns records meeting any of the specified criteria.

The *Not operator* returns the opposite of the specified criteria.

Figure 2.31 shows a query in Design view that specifies an And operator. It will return all of the Campus branch accounts with balances over $5,000. Both conditions must be met for the record to be included. Figure 2.32 shows a query in Design view that specifies an Or operator. It will return all of the Campus branch accounts with any balance plus all accounts at any branch with balances over $5,000. Either condition may be met for a record to be included. Figure 2.33 shows a query in Design view that specifies a Not operator. It will return all of the accounts at all of the branches excluding the Campus branch. You may combine And, Or, and Not operators to achieve the desired result. If you need a list of the accounts with balances over $5,000 at the Campus and Uptown branches, you set the criteria so that the >5000 expression is duplicated for each location specified (see Figure 2.34).

Field:	LastName	Location	Balance
Table:	Customer	Branch	Account
Sort:	Ascending		
Show:	☑	☑	☑
Criteria:		"Campus"	>5000
or:			

Figure 2.31 And Criterion—Only Records Satisfying Both Conditions Will Return

Field:	LastName	Location	Balance
Table:	Customer	Branch	Account
Sort:	Ascending		
Show:	☑	☑	☑
Criteria:		"Campus"	
or:			>5000

Figure 2.32 Or Criterion—Records Meeting Either Condition Will Return

Field:	LastName	Location	Balance
Table:	Customer	Branch	Account
Sort:	Ascending		
Show:	☑	☑	☑
Criteria:		Not "Campus"	
or:			>5000

Figure 2.33 Not Criterion—Any Record Except the Matching Will Return

Field:	LastName	Location	Balance
Table:	Customer	Branch	Account
Sort:	Ascending		
Show:	☑	☑	☑
Criteria:		"Campus"	>5000
or:		"Uptown"	>5000

Figure 2.34 And and Or Criteria—Records Meeting Both Conditions at Both Branches Return

Copying and Running a Query

After you create a query, you may want to duplicate it to use as the basis for creating similar queries. Duplicating a query saves time in selecting tables and fields for queries that need the same structure but different criteria. After you create and save one or more queries, you can execute them whenever you need them to produce up-to-date results.

Copy a Query

Sometimes, you have one-of-a-kind questions about your data. Then you create and run the query, find the answer and close it. If you create the query with the wizard, you save and name it in the last step. If you create the query in Design view, it is possible for you to exit the query without saving changes. Most queries answer recurrent questions. What were sales last week in Houston, in Dallas, in Chicago? In cases like this, you set up the query for the dates and places of interest one time, then copy it, rename the copy and establish the parameters for a different city or date.

Frequently, you will need to examine multiple subsets of the data. In Hands-On Exercise 3, you will create a query displaying the names and account balances of the customers who have accounts at the Campus branch. Should you need to know the same information about the customers who have Uptown accounts, you would select the query in the Navigation pane, and then copy and paste it to a blank space at the bottom pane. Right-click the copy and rename it Uptown. Open the newly created Uptown query in Design view and replace the Campus criterion with Uptown. When you run and save the query, the resulting dataset displays customers and account balances from the Uptown branch. Using this method takes you a few minutes to create branch specific queries for all five locations.

Run a Query

When you **run a query**, Access processes the query instructions and displays records that meet the conditions.

After you create the query by specifying criteria and save it, you are ready to run it. You **run a query** by clicking the Run command (the red exclamation point) to direct Access to process the instructions specified by the query. In our databases, the queries run quickly. Even in the largest database you will use in the end of chapter exercises, no query will take more than a few seconds to run. As you learn how to work with these databases, keep in mind that real-world databases can be massive. Think through the query design carefully. Include all necessary fields and tables, but do not include fields or tables that are not necessary to answer the question. Unnecessary fields slow the query's run time.

Using the Query Wizard

You may create a query directly in Design view or by using the Query Wizard. Even if you initiate the query with a wizard, you will need to learn how to modify it in Design view. Often, it is much faster to copy an existing query and make slight modifications to its design than it would be to start at the beginning of the wizard. You also will need to know how to add additional tables and fields to an existing query in case you failed to think through the design thoroughly and you omitted a necessary field. To launch the Query Wizard, click the Create tab and click Query Wizard in the Other group (see Figure 2.35).

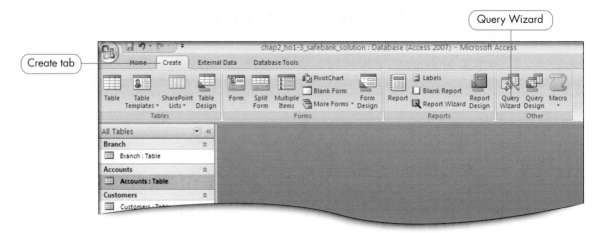

Figure 2.35 Launching the Query Wizard

Access produces many different kinds of queries. Here we will work with the most common query type, the select query. This is a powerful and sophisticated tool. Select the Simple Query Wizard in the first dialog box of the Query Wizard, as shown in Figure 2.36.

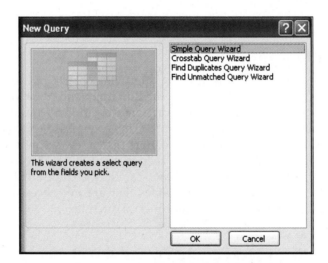

Figure 2.36 The Simple Query Wizard Step 1

In the second step of the Simple Query Wizard dialog box, you specify the tables and fields needed in your query. As soon as you click on the table in the Tables/Queries drop-down box, a list of that table's fields display in the Available fields box. See Figures 2.37 and 2.38.

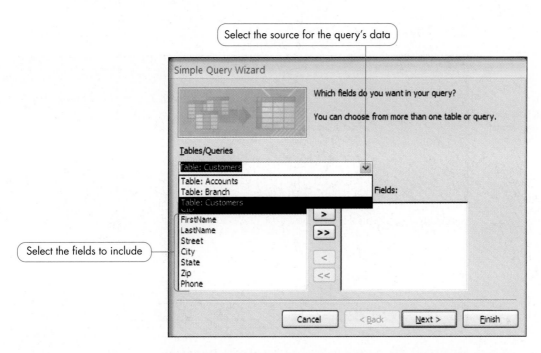

Figure 2.37   Specify Which Tables or Queries to Use as Input

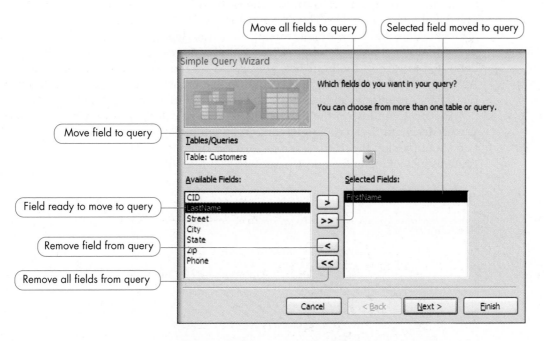

Figure 2.38   Specify the Fields for the Query

Select the necessary fields by clicking them to highlight, and then using the navigation arrows described in Figure 2.39.

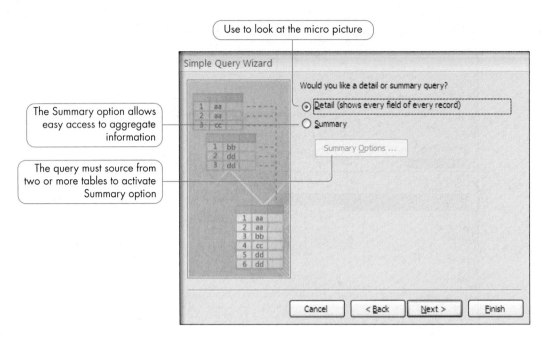

Figure 2.39 Select to Display Detail or to Summarize the Data

In the Simple Query Wizard, you choose between a detailed or a summary query. The detail query provides every record of every field. The summary enables you to aggregate data and View only summary statistics. *Aggregate* means the collection of individual items into a total. If you were only interested in the total of the funds deposited at each of the branches, you would set the query to a summary and ask Access to sum the balances of all accounts in that branch. Some Access users summarize data in the queries and others do so in reports. Either approach is acceptable.

Aggregate means the collection of individual items into a total.

The final window in the Simple Query Wizard directs you to name the query. A well-designed database might contain only 5 tables and 500 queries. Therefore, you should assign descriptive names for your queries so that you know what each contains by looking at the query name. See Figure 2.40.

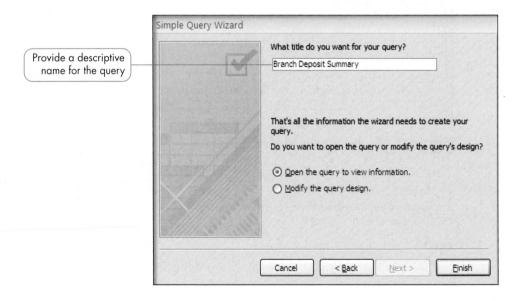

Figure 2.40 Name the Query Descriptively

Understanding Large Database Differences

Suppose you work for a large university. You need to identify all of the students at your university who are business majors, their advisor's names, and their specific majors. The Student table contains student names, identification numbers, majors, faculty advisor's identification number, class standing, addresses, and so on. The Faculty table contains faculty names, departmental affiliation, identification number, and rank. Your query needs to include fields for the student's name, major, and the advisor's name. You would not need the student's address or the faculty member's ID because those fields are unnecessary to answer the question. You need to establish criteria to select business majors: Accounting, Finance, Information Systems, Management, Marketing, and Economics.

Even if your computer is state-of-the-art, fast, powerful, and loaded with memory, this query might take up to 15 minutes to run. If you include unnecessary fields or tables, the run time increases. At the author's university, each additional table roughly doubles the query run time. As an Access beginner, your queries might contain too much or too little information. You will make frequent modifications to the query design as you learn. As you apply your database skills to work with large databases, you will learn to carefully design queries prior to running them to minimize the time to run the queries.

In addition to the earlier mentioned size difference between real world databases and those you will use in the class, real world databases involve multiple users. Typically, the organization stores the database file on the network. Multiple people may simultaneously log into the database. Each user makes changes to tables or forms. At your school, thousands of users can extract data from the university's database. Prior to meeting your advisor, you check your transcript online. You enter a database to find out how many hours you have completed and whether or not you have met the prerequisites. You have permission to view your transcript but you do not have the necessary permission to change what is recorded there. Several hundred other users have more extensive privileges in your school's database. Your Access professor can enter and probably change your grade in this class. If the securities are appropriately set on the database, your Access professor is not able to change the grade that you earned in other courses.

Most large organizations employ database administrators and managers that ensure data security, efficacy, and integrity. These professionals are well paid to make sure that no one inside or outside the firm has access to classified data or can corrupt the data resident in the system. Additionally, SOX rules mandate backup and security measures.

These positions involve a great deal of responsibility. How does someone charged with this vital role do it? One common method involves splitting the database into front and back ends. Typically, the *front end* of a database contains the objects, like queries, reports, and forms, needed to interact with data, but not the tables where the record values reside. The tables are safely stored in the *back end* system where users cannot inadvertently destroy or corrupt data. Most often, the front and back ends of the database are stored on different systems placed in different locations to provide an extra security measure. Users within the organization are divided into groups by their data needs. Then the groups are assigned rights and privileges. For example, a professor has privileges to record grades for students registered in his or her classes but not for other professors' classes. The financial aid officer may look at student grades and financial records, but may not alter either. The dean may look at student grades, but probably not their financial records. The student health center physician may view a student's immunization records and update it when necessary, but cannot see the student's grades.

The next hands-on exercise introduces queries as a more useful way to examine data. You use the Query Wizard to create a basic query, and then modify that query by adding an additional field and an additional table, and performing simple query criteria specifications.

The *front end* of a database contains the objects, like queries, reports, and forms, needed to interact with data, but not the tables where the record values reside.

The *back end* of the system protects and stores data so that users cannot inadvertently destroy or corrupt the organization's vital data.

Hands-On Exercises

3 | Multiple-Table Query

Skills covered: 1. Create a Query Using a Wizard **2.** Specify Simple Query Criteria **3.** Change Query Data **4.** Add a Table to a Query Using Design View and Sort a Query

Step 1 **Create a Query Using a Wizard**	Refer to Figure 2.41 as you complete Step 1.

a. Open the *chap2_ho1-3_safebank_solution.accdb* database from Hands-On Exercise 2 (if necessary), click **Options** on the Security Warning toolbar, click the **Enable this content option** in the Microsoft Office Security Options dialog box, and click **OK**.

TROUBLESHOOTING: If you create unrecoverable errors while completing this hands-on exercise, you can delete the *chap2_ho1-3_safebank_solution* file, copy the *chap2_ho2_safebank_solution* database you created at the end of the second hands-on exercise, and open the copy of the backup database to start the third hands-on exercise again.

b. Click the **Create tab** and click **Query Wizard** in the Other group to launch the wizard.

The New Query Dialog box opens.

c. Select **Simple Query Wizard** and click **OK**.

d. Click the **Tables/Queries drop-down arrow** and select **Table: Customers**.

This step asks you to specify the tables and fields needed in the query. A list of the fields in the Customers table displays in the Available Fields box.

e. Double-click the **FirstName** field.

The FirstName field moves from the Available Fields box to the Selected Fields box. You can also double-click a field in the Selected Fields box to move it back to the Available box.

f. Click the **LastName** field and click the **Move Field to Query command** (see Figure 2.38).

g. Click the **Tables/Queries drop-down arrow** and select **Table: Accounts**.

h. From the list of fields in the Accounts table, select **BID** and **Balance** and move them one at a time to the Fields in Query box. Click **Next**.

Your query should have four fields: first and last names, BID, and Balance.

i. Select **Detail**, if necessary, to choose between a Detail and Summary Query. Click **Next**.

j. Name your query **Campus Branch Customers**. Click **Finish**.

This name describes the data that will eventually populate the query. The default name, Customers Query, comes from the first table selected when you started the query wizard.

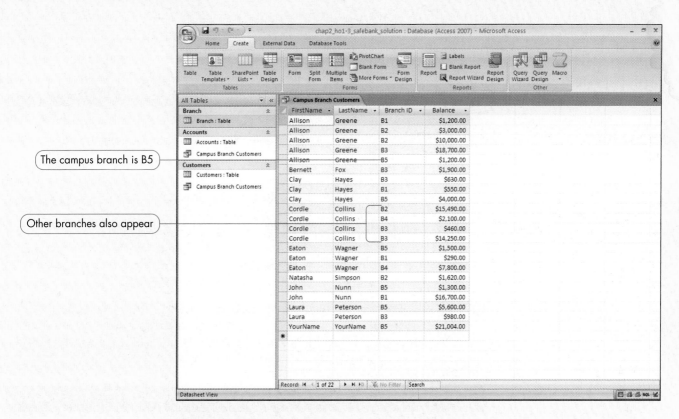

The campus branch is B5

Other branches also appear

Figure 2.41 Criteria Have Not Been Applied

Step 2
Specify Simple Query Criteria

Refer to Figure 2.42 as you complete Step 2.

a. Right-click the **Campus Branch Customers tab** and select **Design View** from the shortcut menu.

You have created the Campus Branch Customers query to view only those customers who have accounts at the Campus branch. However, other branch's accounts also display. You need to limit the query results to only the records of interest.

b. Click in the fifth row (the **criteria row**) under the **BID** field and type **b5**.

Access is not case sensitive but is frequently used to connect to larger databases for which case matters.

c. Click in the **Sort row** (third row) under the **LastName field** to activate the drop-down arrow. (This is another of the hidden arrows that only provides selections when the cell is active.) Select **Ascending** from the drop-down list.

d. Click **Run** in the Results group on the Design tab.

e. Save your query.

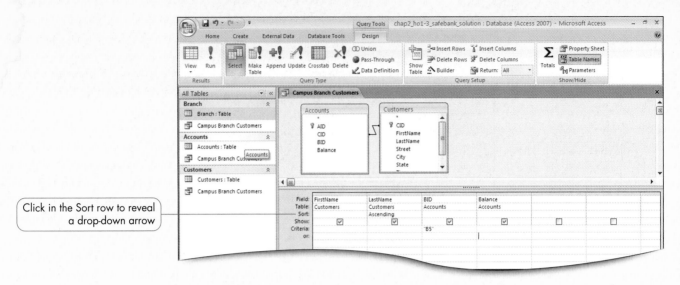

Click in the Sort row to reveal a drop-down arrow

Figure 2.42 Establishing Select Criteria and Sort Order

Step 3
Change Query Data

Refer to Figure 2.43 as you complete Step 3.

a. Click on the **Balance** field in the record for *Allison Greene's* account. Change **$1200** to **$12,000**. Press **Enter**. Close the query. Do *not* save your changes.

b. Open the **Accounts table**.

Only one account shows a $12,000 balance. The Customer ID is C01.

c. Open the **Customers table**. Find the name of the customer whose Customer ID is **C01**.

Allison Green's CID number is C01. The change you made in the query datasheet has permanently changed the data stored in the underlying table.

TROUBLESHOOTING: Changes in query data change table data! As soon as you pressed Enter in Step 3a, the balance for Allison's account saved. (Remember Access works in storage, not memory.) A wise Access user is extremely careful about the position of the cursor and about typing stray characters while a table or query is open. As soon as you move to a different record, any edits are saved automatically, whether you intend the save or not!

d. Add a new record to the **Accounts table**. The Accounts table should be open. If not, open it now.

e. Type **A23**, **C11**, **B5**, and **1000**. Press **Enter**.

f. Open the **Campus Branch Customers query**. Click **Run** on the Design tab.

You (as a bank customer) now show two accounts, one with a balance that matches your course and section number and one with a balance of $1,000.

Because you closed and reopened the query, it re-ran prior to opening. Access reruns queries to ensure that the data the query returns is the most recent in the database.

g. Close the **Accounts table**.

You successfully created a multi-table query. It does almost everything that you intended. Because this bank is so small, everybody who works there (and probably most of the customers) knows that the Campus branch is B5. But what if this were the database for a real bank? How many thousands of branches does it have? (Remember you are designing your database for 100 years.) You decide that you want to display the branch name, not the ID number. The branch name is a field in the Branch table. The Campus Branch Customers query was based on the Accounts and Customers tables. In order to display the branch name, you need to connect the Branch table to the query.

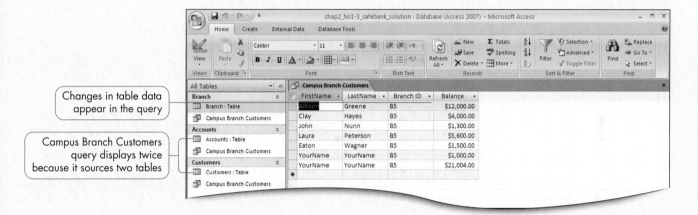

Changes in table data appear in the query

Campus Branch Customers query displays twice because it sources two tables

Figure 2.43 Campus Branch Customers Query Following Data Modifications

Step 4
Add a Table to a Query Using Design View and Sort a Query

Refer to Figure 2.44 as you complete Step 4.

a. Open the *Campus Branch Customers Query* if necessary. Right-click the query tab and select **Design View** from the shortcut menu.

b. Click the **Branch: table** under the **All Tables list** on the left-most window pane.

It will turn gold to indicate that it is selected.

c. Click and drag the selected **Branch table** to the **top pane** of the Query design grid.

Your mouse pointer shape will change to a Table as you drag.

d. Drop the **Branch table** next to the **Accounts table**.

The one-to-many relationship lines automatically connect the Branch table to the Accounts table. The query inherits the relationship specifications from the database design.

e. Click the **Location** field name in the Branch table and **drag** it down to the **first empty column**. It should be to the right of the Balance column.

f. Click the **Show row check box** under the **BID** field to hide this field.

The BID field is no longer needed because we have a more descriptive and easily understood name.

g. Remove the **b5** criterion by highlighting, and then deleting it.

h. Type **Campus** as a criterion in the **Location** field.

The syntax actually requires that you enter text criteria within quotation marks, such as "Campus". Access will enter these quotes for you if you forget. If you use Access to get into large databases, you may need to remember the quotation marks while setting parameters for character fields.

i. Click the word *Location*. As soon as you leave the criteria row, Access adds the missing quotes for you.

j. Click in the **Sort row** of the **Balance** field to activate the drop-down list. Select **Descending**.

The query will still be sorted alphabetically by the customer's last name because that is the left-most sort field in the design grid. You have added an additional, or secondary, sort. Customers with multiple accounts will have their accounts sorted from the largest to smallest balances.

k. Run and save your query.

l. Close the file and exit Access.

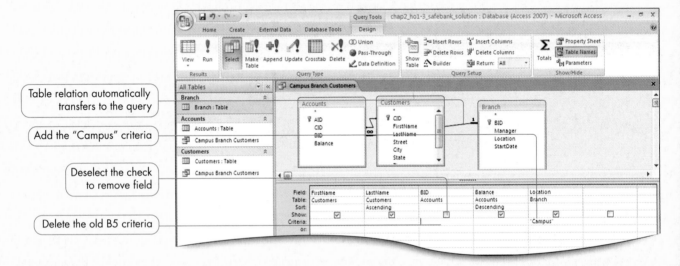

Figure 2.44 Drag and Drop the Branch Table to Add to the Query Design Grid

Summary

1. **Design data.** The architectural infrastructure that supports the database needs to be driven by the output the database will need to generate. You learned that good database design requires that you anticipate how the data will be used, both now and for a long time to come. Creating a database adds costs to the firm, and the designer must balance the costs of including data against the costs of needing it at some point in the future and not having it available. The Sarbanes Oxley Act governs how, where, and when publicly traded firms must store data. You learned that good design principles avoid making calculations in table data, that data should be stored in their smallest parts, and that like data should be grouped together to form tables.

2. **Create tables.** Access employs several ways to create a table. You can create a table yourself by entering the table data into a field. You also can import table data from another database or application, for example, Excel. You learned that each field needs a unique and descriptive name and were introduced to the CamelCase notation naming convention. Access accommodates many different types of data including: text, number, Date/Time, Yes/No, Memo, and others.

3. **Understand table relationships.** Data stored in different tables may be linked using the powerful tool of referential integrity enforcement. Typically, the primary key from one table (unique identifier) resides as a foreign key in another table. This becomes the means of creating the link.

4. **Share data with Excel.** Access facilitates data exchanges with Excel through imports and exports. You used the Import Wizard to import an Excel worksheet into an Access database table. The settings of the Import Wizard may be saved and reused when the import is recurrent.

5. **Establish table relationships.** You created links between tables in the database and attempted to enter an invalid branch number in a related table. You discovered that the enforcement of referential integrity prevented you from creating an account in a non-existent branch. Cascades give the database manager a powerful tool that facilitates updating or deleting multiple records in different tables simultaneously.

6. **Create a query.** You manipulated the data to display only those records of interest by creating a select query. Later, you learned to add additional fields or tables to an existing query.

7. **Specify criteria for different data types.** Establishing criteria empowers you to see only the records that meet the criteria. Different data types require different criteria specifications. Date fields are enclosed in pound signs (#) and text fields with quote marks (""). Additionally, you learned that there are powerful operators, And, Or, and Not, that return the results needed to answer complex questions. You established a sort order for arranging the query results. The Primary sort field needs to be in the left-most position in the query design grid. You may specify additional sort fields; their priority is determined by their left-to-right positions in the grid.

8. **Copy and run a query.** After specifying tables, fields, and conditions for one query, you can copy the query and modify only the criteria in the duplicate query. Copying queries saves time so that you do not have to select tables and fields again for queries that need the same structure but different criteria. After saving queries, you can run them whenever you need to display up-to-date results based on the query conditions.

9. **Use the Query Wizard.** An alternative to creating a select query is to use the Query Wizard. The wizard enables you to select tables and fields from lists. The last step of the wizard prompts you to save the query.

10. **Understand large database differences.** Large database queries may take a long time to run. Therefore, you should think carefully about what fields and tables to include in the query prior to executing it. You learned that database administrators often split the database into front and back ends. Different users of a large database have different levels of access and privilege in order to protect the data validity.

Key Terms

Multiple Choice

1. When entering, deleting or editing table data:

   (a) The table must be in Design view.
   (b) The table must be in Datasheet view.
   (c) The table may be in either Datasheet or Design view.
   (d) Data may be entered only in a form.

2. Which of the following is implemented automatically by Access?

   (a) Rejecting misspelled field entries in a record
   (b) Rejecting redundant field specifications among tables
   (c) Rejecting a record of a foreign key without a matching value in a related table
   (d) Rejecting a record in a primary key without a matching value in a related table

3. Social Security Number, phone number, and postal code should be designated as:

   (a) Number fields
   (b) Text fields
   (c) Yes/No fields
   (d) Any of the above, depending on the application

4. Which of the following is true of the primary key?

   (a) Its values must be unique.
   (b) It must be defined as a text field.
   (c) It must be the first field in a table.
   (d) It can never be changed.

5. Social Security Number should not be used as a primary key because:

   (a) The Social Security Number is numeric, and primary key fields should be text.
   (b) The Social Security Number is not unique.
   (c) The Social Security Number is too long.
   (d) Using the Social Security Number may expose employees or customers to identity theft.

6. An illustration of a one-to-many relationship would be:

   (a) A unique city name relates to a single postal code.
   (b) A customer ID may be related to multiple account numbers.
   (c) A branch location may contain many branch identification numbers.
   (d) A balance field may contain many values.

7. Which of the following was not a suggested guideline for designing a table?

   (a) Include all necessary data
   (b) Store data in its smallest parts
   (c) Avoid calculated fields
   (d) Designate at least two primary keys

8. A query's specifications providing instructions about which fields to include must be entered:

   (a) On the Show row of the query design grid
   (b) On the Sort row of the query design grid
   (c) On the Criteria row of the query design grid
   (d) On the Table Row of the query design grid

9. Which view is used to modify field properties in a table?

   (a) Datasheet view
   (b) Design view
   (c) PivotTable view
   (d) PivotChart view

10. Which of the following is true?

    (a) Additional tables may be added to a query only by restarting the Query Wizard.
    (b) Additional tables or fields may be added to a query by clicking and dragging in the query design grid.
    (c) Access does not permit the addition of additional tables or fields to an existing query.
    (d) Additional tables may be added by copying and pasting the fields from the table to the query.

11. In which view will you see the record selector symbols of a pencil and a triangle?

    (a) Only the Datasheet view of a table
    (b) Only the Datasheet view of a query
    (c) Neither the Datasheet view of a table nor query
    (d) Both the Datasheet view of a table nor query

12. You attempt to make a data edit in the Datasheet view of a query by changing an account balance, and then pressing Enter.

    (a) The change also must be made to the underlying table for it to be a permanent part of the database.
    (b) The change must be saved for it to be a permanent part of the database.
    (c) An error message will display because queries are used only to view data, not edit.
    (d) The change is saved, and the underlying table immediately reflects the change.

13. Data in a Name field is stored as Janice Zook, Zachariah Allen, Tom Jones, and Nancy Allen. If the field was sorted in ascending order, which name would be last?

(a) Janice Zook

(b) Zachariah Allen

(c) Tom Jones

(d) Nancy Allen

14. Which data type appears as a check box in a table?

(a) Text field

(b) Number field

(c) Yes/No field

(d) Name field

15. Which properties would you use to provide the database user with "user-friendly" column headings in the Datasheet View of a table?

(a) Field Size and Format

(b) Input Mask, Validation Rule, and Default Value

(c) Caption

(d) Required

16. Which of the following is true with respect to an individual's hire date and years of service, both of which appear on a query that is based on an employee table?

(a) Hire date should be a calculated field; years of service should be a stored field.

(b) Hire date should be a stored field; years of service should be a calculated field.

(c) Both should be stored fields.

(d) Both should be calculated fields.

17. What is the best way to store an individual's name in a table?

(a) As a single field consisting of the last name, first name, and middle initial, in that order.

(b) As a single field consisting of the first name, last name, and middle initial, in that order.

(c) As three separate fields for first name, last name, and middle initial.

(d) All of the above are equally suitable.

18. Which of the following would not be a good primary key?

(a) Student Number

(b) Social Security Number

(c) An e-mail address

(d) A branch identification number

19. A difference between student database files and "real world" files is not:

(a) Split between front and back end storage.

(b) Many users add, delete, and change records in "real world" files.

(c) Student files tend to much smaller than "real world" files.

(d) Students work in live databases but "real world" files have multiple copies of the database on all user's desktops.

20. Your query has a date field. If you wanted the records for the month of March 2007 returned, how would you set the criteria?

(a) <3/31/2007

(b) between 3/1/2007 and 3/31/2007

(c) >3/31/2007

(d) = March 2007

Practice Exercises

1 Martha's Vineyard Bookstore—Creation

One of your aunt's friends, Jennifer Frew, owns and operates a tiny bookstore during the tourist season on Martha's Vineyard. Jennifer asked you to help her after your aunt bragged that you are becoming quite the computer whiz because of this class. You believe that you can help Jennifer by creating a small database. She has stored information about the publication companies and the books that she sells in Excel spreadsheets. You, in consultation with Jennifer, determine that a third table—an author table— also is required. Your task is to design and populate the three tables, establish appropriate linkages between them, and enforce referential integrity. This project follows the same set of skills as used in Hands-On Exercises 1 and 2 in this chapter. If you have problems, reread the detailed directions presented in the chapter. Refer to Figure 2.45 as you complete your work.

a. Start Access and click **Blank Database** in the New Blank Database section of the *Getting Started with Microsoft Office Access* window. Click **Browse**, navigate to the Your Name Access Production folder, type **chap2_pe1_bookstore_solution.accdb**, and click **OK**. Then click **Create** in the Blank Database section of the *Getting Started with Microsoft Office Access* window.

b. Create a new table by entering data into what will become the Author table. Enter the following data.

Field1	Field2	Field3
11	Benchloss	Michael R.
12	Turow	Scott
13	Rice	Anne
14	King	Stephen
15	Connelly	Michael
16	Rice	Luanne

c. Click **Save** on the Quick Access Toolbar. Type **Author** in the Save As dialog box and click **OK**.

d. Right-click the **Author table** under All Tables in the Navigation Pane and select **Design View**. Access will automatically create a primary key; however, it is not the correct field for the primary key.

e. Click the row selector for the second row (Field1) and click **Primary Key** in the Tools group on the Design tab.

f. Check the properties of **Field1** to ensure that the *Indexed* property has been set to **Yes (No Duplicates)**, which is appropriate for a primary key. Select *Field1* and type **AuthorID** to rename the field, type **Author ID** as the caption, and select **Long Integer** as the field size.

g. Rename *Field2* as **LastName**, type **Author's Last Name** as the caption, and type **20** as the field size. Rename *Field3* as **FirstName**, type **Author's First Name** as the caption, and type **15** as the field size.

h. Click the **ID field row selector** to select the row and press **Delete**. Click **Yes**.

i. Click **Save** on the Quick Access toolbar to save the design changes. It is safe to ignore the lost data warning because you did shorten the field sizes.

j. Click the **External Data tab** and click **Import Excel Spreadsheet** in the Import Group to launch the Get External Data Wizard – Get External Spreadsheet Wizard. Select the **Import the source data into a new table in the current database option**, click **Browse**, and go to your Exploring Access folder. Select the *chap2_pe1_bookstore.xlsx* workbook and click **OK**. This workbook contains two worksheets.

k. Select the **Publishers worksheet**. Use the **PubID** field as the primary key. Set the *Indexed Field Options* property box to **Yes (No Duplicates)**. In the next wizard screen, select the **PubID** as your primary key. Name the table **Publishers**. Do not save the import steps.

...continued on Next Page

l. Repeat the Import Wizard to import the **Books worksheet** from the same file into the Access database as a table named **Books**. Set the *Indexed Field Options* property box for the ISBN to **Yes (No Duplicates)**. Set the **ISBN** as the primary field. Do not save the import steps.

m. Open the **Books table** in Design view. Make sure the **PubID** field is selected, click in the *Field Size* property box, and type **2**. Change the **ISBN** *Field size* property to **15**. Change the **Price** field *Format* property to **Currency**. Change the **AuthorCode** field *Field Size* property to **Long Integer** to create the relationship later. Click **Save** on the Quick Access toolbar to save the design changes to the **Books table**.

n. Open the **Publishers table** in Design view. Make sure the **PubID** field is selected, click in the *Field Size* property box and type **2**, and click in the *Caption* property box and type **Publisher's ID**. For each of the following fields, click in the *Field Size* property box and type **50**: **PubName, PubAddress**, and **PubCity** fields. Set the *Field Size* property for **PubState** field to **2**. Change the *Pub Address* field name to **PubAddress** and change the *Pub ZIP* field name to **PubZIP** (without the spaces to be consistent with the other field names). Click **Save** on the Quick Access Toolbar to save the design changes to the **Publishers table**. Close all open tables.

o. Click the **Database Tools tab** and click **Relationships** in the Show/Hide group. Double-click each table name to add it to the Relationship window. Click and drag the **AuthorID** field from the **Author table** to the **AuthorCode** field in the **Books table**. Click the **Enforce Referential Integrity check box** in the Create Relationships dialog box. Then click **Create** to create a one-to-many relationship between the Author and Books tables.

p. Click and drag the **PubID** field from the **Publishers table** to the **PubID** field in the **Books table**. Click the three check boxes in the Create Relationships dialog box and click **Create** to establish a one-to-many relationship between the Publishers and Books tables.

q. Click **Save** on the Quick Access Toolbar to save the changes to the Relationship window. Press **PrintScreen** to capture a screenshot. Nothing seems to happen because the screenshot is saved to the Clipboard. Launch Microsoft Word. Type **your name and section number** and press **Enter**. Paste the screenshot into the Word file, save the file as **chap2_pe1_bookstore_solution.docx**, and print it. Close Word. The Access file should still be open.

r. Close the Relationship window. Click the **Office Button**, select **Manage**, and then select **Back Up Database**. Name the backup **chap2_pe1_bookstore_solution_backup.accdb**. Close the database.

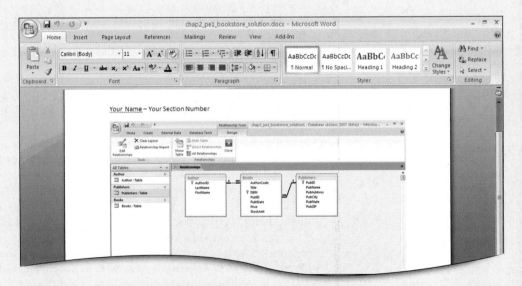

Figure 2.45 Word Screen Showing Capture of the Access Relationship Window

...continued on Next Page

Your mother's friend is thrilled with the work that you have completed on the bookstore's database. She has received additional stock and asks you to update the file with the new information. Once updated she wants you to provide a printout of all of the books in stock that were published by Simon & Shuster. **You must work Exercise 1 before you can start this one.** This project follows the same set of skills as used in Hands-On Exercise 3 in this chapter. If you have problems, reread the detailed directions presented in the chapter. Refer to Figure 2.46 as you complete your work.

a. Use Windows to copy the *chap2_pe1_bookstore_solution.accdb* database. Rename the copied database as **chap2_pe2_bookstore_solution.accdb**. Open the *chap2_pe2_ bookstore_solution* file. Click **Options** in the Security Warning bar, click **Enable this content** in the Microsoft Office Security Options dialog box, and click **OK.**

b. Double-click the **Author table** in the All Tables pane to open the table in Datasheet view. Locate the new record indicator (the one with the * in the row selector) and click the first field. Enter data for the new record using **17** as Author ID and **your name** as the first and last names. Press **Enter.**

c. Open the **Books table** and click the **New (blank) record command**. Type **17** in the AuthorCode field, **Computer Wisdom** in the Title field, **0-684-80415-5** in the ISBN field, **KN** in the PubID field, **2006** in the PubDate field, **23.50** in the Price field, and **75** in the StockAmt field. Press **Enter.**

d. Click the **Create tab** and click **Query Wizard** in the Other group. Choose the **Simple Query Wizard**. From the **Author table**, select the Author's **LastName** and **FirstName** fields. From the **Books table**, select **Title**. Select the **PubName** field from the **Publishers table**. Name the query **Your Name Publishers, Books, and Authors**.

e. Open the query in Design view. Click in the criteria row of the PubName field. Type Knopf to create a criterion to limit the output to only books published by **Knopf**. Click **Run** in the Results group on the Design tab.

f. Return to Design view. Click the Sort row in the **LastName** field and select **Ascending**.

g. Move your mouse over the top of the **Title** field until the mouse pointer shape changes to a bold down arrow, and then click. With the Title column selected, click and drag it to the left of the **LastName** field. Click the Sort row in the **Title** field and select **Ascending**. You will see sort commands on both the Title and LastName fields.

h. Click **Run** in the Results group on the Design tab. Save the query. Click the **Office Button**, position the mouse pointer over **Print**, and select **Quick Print**.

i. Click the **Office Button**, select **Manage**, and then select **Compact and Repair Database**.

...continued on Next Page

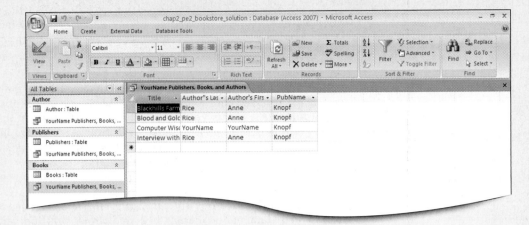

Figure 2.46 Sorted Query Results

3 Combs Insurance

The Comb's Insurance Company offers a full range of insurance services in four locations: Miami, Boston, Chicago, and Atlanta. Until now, they have stored all of the firm's Human Resource data in Excel spreadsheets. These files contain information on employee performance, salary, and education. Some of the files contain information on each of the company's job classifications, including education requirements and the salary range for that position. The firm is converting from Excel to Access to store this important data. There already is a database file containing two of the tables. You need to import the data for the third table from Excel. Once imported, you will need to modify field properties and connect the new table to the rest of the database. The Human Resources vice president is concerned that the Atlanta office ignores the salary guidelines published by the home office. He asks that you create a query to investigate the salary practices of the Atlanta office. This project follows the same set of skills as used in Hands-On Exercises 2 and 3 in this chapter. If you have problems, reread the detailed directions presented in the chapter. Refer to Figure 2.47 as you complete your work.

    a. Copy the *chap2_pe3_insurance.accdb* file and rename it **chap2_pe3_insurance_solution**. Open the *chap2_pe3_insurance_solution* database, then open and examine the data stored in the **Location** and **Titles** tables. Become familiar with the field names and the type of information stored in each table. Pay particular attention to the number of different Position titles.

    b. Click the **External Data tab** and click **Import Excel Spreadsheet** in the Import group to import the *chap2_pe3_employees.xlsx* file. Select the **Employees worksheet** and click the **First Row Contains Column Headings check box**. Set the *Indexed Field Options box* for the **EmployeeID** field to **Yes (No Duplicates)**. In the next wizard screen, select the **EmployeeID** as your primary key. Name the table **Employees**.

    c. Open the **Employees table** in Design view. In the top of the design window, position the insertion point on the **Location ID** field. Locate the *Field Size property* in the lower portion of the table Design view window and change the Field Size for the *Location ID* to **3**. Click in the *Caption* property box and type **Location ID**. In the top of the Design view

...continued on Next Page

window, position the insertion point on the **TitleID** field. Click in the *Field Size* property box in the lower portion of the table Design view window and type **3**. Click in the *Caption* property box and type **Title ID**. Save the design changes.

d. Switch the **Employees table** to the Datasheet view and examine the data. Click any record in the Title ID field and click **Descending** in the Sort & Filter group on the Home tab. How many different position titles are in the table? Does this match the number in the Titles table?

e. Locate the new record row, the one with the * in the row selector box. Click the first field. Add yourself as a new record. Your EmployeeID is **27201**. You are a **Trainee** (T03) in the **Atlanta** (L01) office earning **$27,350** and your performance rating is **Good**. Press **Enter**.

f. Open the **Titles table** in Datasheet view and add the missing title. The *TitleID* is **T04**; the *Title* is **Senior Account Rep**. The rest of the record is **A marketing position requiring a technical background and at least three years of experience.** It requires a **Four year degree**. The minimum salary is **$45,000**. The maximum is **$75,000**. Do not type the dollar sign or comma as you enter the salary data. Close all open tables.

g. Click **Relationships** in the Show/Hide group on the Database Tools tab. Add the three tables to the Relationship window by double-clicking them one at a time (You may have to click the Show Table button to bring up the Show Table dialog box.) Close the Add Table dialog box.

h. Click the **LocationID** in the Location table and drag it to the **LocationID** in the Employees table. Drop it. In the Relationship dialog box, click the **Enforce referential integrity check box**. Click the **TitleID** in the **Titles** table and drag it to the **TitleID** in the **Employees** table and drop it. In the Relationship dialog box, click the **Enforce Referential Integrity check box**. Save the changes to the relationships and close the Relationship window.

i. Click **Query Wizard** in the Other group on the Create tab. In the first screen of the Query Wizard, select **Simple Query Wizard**. Select **Table: Location** in the Tables/Queries list. Double-click **Location** to move it to the *Selected Fields* list. Select the **Employees table** in the Tables/Queries list. Double-click **LastName**, **FirstName**, and **Salary**. Select the **Titles** table in the Tables/Queries list. Double-click **MinimumSalary** and **MaximumSalary**. Click **Next**. Select the **Detail (shows every field of every record)** option and click **Next**. Type **Your Name Atlanta** as the query title and click **Finish**.

j. Open the **Your Name Atlanta query** in Design view. Click in the criteria row in the Location field. Type **Atlanta**. Click **Run** in the Results group on the Design tab. Check to ensure that the results display only Atlanta employees. Save and close the query.

k. Right-click the **Your Name Atlanta query** in the Navigation pane and select **Copy**. Right-click a white space in the All Objects pane and select **Paste**. In the Paste As window, type **Your Name Boston** for the query name. Click OK.

l. Open the **Your Name Boston query** in Design view. Click in the criteria row in the Location field. Type **Boston**. Click **Run** in the Results group on the Design Tab. Check to ensure that the results display only Boston employees. Save and close the query.

m. Open the **Your Name Atlanta** query and the **Your Name Boston** query. *Your screen should appear similar to Figure 2.47.* Print both queries.

n. Click the **Office Button**, select **Manage**, and then select **Compact and Repair Database**.

...continued on Next Page

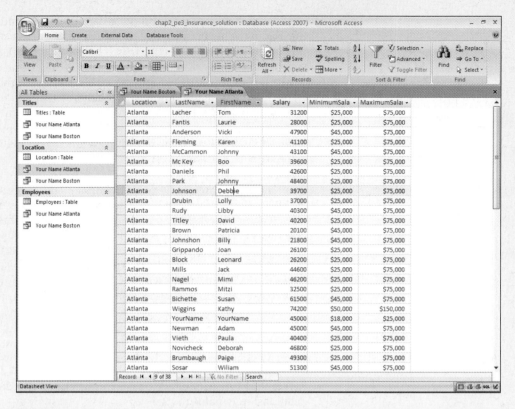

Figure 2.47 Atlanta Query Results

4 Coffee Service Company

The Coffee Service Company provides high-quality coffee, tea, snacks, and paper products to its customers. Most of the customers are offices in the area: IT firms, insurance offices, financial services. Coffee Service employees go to the customer location and restock the coffee, tea, and snacks supplied daily. A few accounts elect to pick up the merchandise at the Coffee Service Office. You have been asked to help convert the Excel files to an Access database. Once the database is set up, you need to use queries to help the owner do some market analysis. This project follows the same set of skills as used in Hands-On Exercises 2 and 3 in this chapter. The instructions are less detailed to give you a chance to practice your skills. If you have problems, reread the detailed directions presented in the chapter. Refer to Figure 2.48 as you complete your work.

a. Copy the *chap2_pe4_coffee.accdb* file. Rename the copy **chap2_pe4_coffee_solution. accdb**. Open the copied file, then open, enable the content, and examine the data stored in the tables. Become familiar with the field names and the type of information stored in each table.

b. Click the **External Data tab** and click **Import Excel Spreadsheet** in the Import group. Select the **Import the source data into a new table in the current database** option. Click **Browse**, select the *chap2_pe4_products.xlsx* workbook, click **Open**, then click **OK**. Select the **Products worksheet** and click **Next**. Click the **First Row Contains Column Headings check box**, and then click **Next**. Click the **Indexed property drop-down arrow** and select to **Yes** (No Duplicates). Make sure the ProductID field is active. Click **Next**. Click the **Choose my own primary** key **option** and select the **ProductID**. Click **Next**, type **Products** as the table name, and then click **Finish**.

c. Open the **Products table** in Design view. In the top of the design grid, click the **ProductID** field to select it. In the bottom portion of the window, change the *Field size* property to **Long Integer**. Click in the *Caption* property box and type **Product ID**. Save the changes to the Products table. Close the Products table.

...continued on Next Page

d. Click the **Database Tools tab**, and then click **Relationships** in the Show/Hide group. Click **Show Table** to open the Show Table dialog box. Double-click the **Products table** to add it to the Relationships window, if it is not already shown. Close the Show Table dialog box.

e. Click the **ProductID** in the **Products table** and drag and drop it on the **ProductID** in the **Order Details table**. The Edit Relationships dialog box opens. Click the **Enforce Referential Integrity check box**. Click **Create**. Save the changes to the Relationship window and close it.

f. Open the **Sales Reps table** and replace YourName in the *FirstName* and *LastName* fields with **YourName**.

g. Launch the **Query Wizard** in the Other group on the Create tab. Create a **Simple Select Query**. Select the **Sales Reps table** in the Tables/Queries list. Double-click the **LastName** and **FirstName** fields to move them to the Selected Fields list. Select the **Order Details table** in the Tables/Queries list. Double-click the **Quantity** field to move it to the query. Select the **Customers table** and double-click the **CustomerName** field. Select the **Products table** in the Tables/Queries list. Double-click the **ProductName**, **RefrigerationNeeded**, and **YearIntroduced** fields to move them to the query. This is a detail query. Name the query **Product Introduction**.

h. Open the **Product Information query** in Design view. Click in the sort row in the **YearIntroduced** field and select **Ascending**. Click the sort row of the **ProductName** field and select **Ascending**.

i. Click the criteria row in the LastName field and type **Your Last Name**. Click the criteria row in the FirstName field and type **YourName**. Click the criteria row in the YearIntroduced field and type **2004**. Click into the or row (the next row down) and type **2005**. Reenter your first and last name in the or criteria row for the FirstName and LastName fields. This establishes criteria so that only sales by you on products introduced in 2004 and 2005 display.

j. Click the **Design tab** and click **Run** in the Results group. Save the design changes to the query and close it. Right-click the query name in the Navigation pane and select **Rename**. Rename the query **2004–5 Product Introduction by YourName**. Print the query results.

k. Click the **Office Button**, select **Manage**, and then select **Compact and Repair Database**.

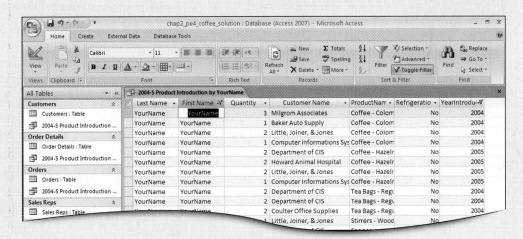

Figure 2.48 Sorted Product Introduction Query Results

You are an intern in a large, independent real estate firm that specializes in home sales. A database contains all of the information on the properties marketed by your firm. Most real estate transactions involve two agents—one representing the seller (the listing agent) and the other the buyer (the selling agent). The firm owner has asked that you examine the records of recent listings (real estate is listed when the home owner signs a contract with an agent that offers the property for sale) and sort them by subdivision (neighborhood) and the listing agent's name. The results need to include only the sold properties and be sorted by subdivision and the listing agent's last name. Refer to Figure 2.49 as you complete your work.

a. Locate the file named *chap2_mid1_realestate.accdb*, copy it to your working folder, and rename it **chap2_mid1_realestate_solution.accdb**. Open the file and enable the content. Open the **Agents table**. Find and replace *Kia Hart*'s name with your name. Close the **Agents** table.

b. Create a detail query. You need the following fields: **LastName**, **FirstName**, **DateListed**, **DateSold**, **ListPrice**, **SellingAgent**, and **Subdivision**. Name the query **YourName Sold Property by Subdivision and Agent**. Run the query and examine the number of records.

c. In Design view, enter the criteria that will remove all of the properties from the Water Valley Subdivision. Run the query and examine the number of records. It should be a smaller number than in Step b.

d. Rearrange the fields in the query so that the Subdivision field is in the leftmost column and the LastName field is the second from the left. Add the appropriate sort commands to the design grid to sort first by subdivision, and then by LastName.

e. Add a criterion that will limit the results to the properties sold after October 31, 2008.

f. Capture a screenshot of the Sales Summary query results. Have it open on your computer and press **PrnScrn**. to copy a picture of what is on the monitor to the clipboard. Open Word, type your name and section number in a new blank document, press **Enter**, paste the screenshot in Word, and press **Enter** again.

g. Return to Design view and capture a screenshot of the query in Design view. Paste this screenshot below the first in the Word document. Save the Word document as **chap2_mid1_realestate_solution.docx**. Print the document.

...continued on Next Page

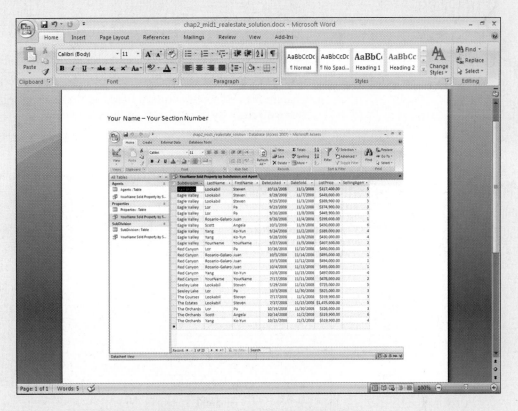

Figure 2.49 Sorted Product Introduction Query Results

2 Importing Excel Data, Creating, and Sorting a Query

The Prestige Hotel chain caters to upscale business travelers and provides state-of-the-art conference, meeting, and reception facilities. It prides itself on its international, four-star cuisines. Last year, it began a member rewards club to help the marketing department track the purchasing patterns of their most loyal customers. All of the hotel transactions are stored in the database. Your task is to help the manager of the Boston hotel identify the customers who used suites last year and who had more than two persons in their party. Refer to Figure 2.50 as you complete your work.

a. Copy the *chap2_mid2_memrewards.accdb* database and name the copy **chap2_mid2_ memrewards_solution.accdb.** Open and tour the newly copied file. Gain an understanding of the relationships and the data contained in the different tables. Specifically look for the tables and fields containing the information you need: dates of stays in Boston suites, the member's name, and the number in the party.

b. Import the Excel file *chap2_mid2_location.xlsx* into your database as a new table. Name the table as **Location**. Use the LocationID field as the primary key. Set the field size to Double.

c. Establish a relationship between the LocationID field in the **Location table** and the Location field in the **Orders table**. Enforce referential integrity.

d. Open the **Members table** and find Fred White's name. Replace Fred's name with your own first and last name. Now find *Karen Korte*'s name and replace it with your name.

e. Create a query that contains the fields you identified in Step a. Set a condition to limit the output to Boston, service from August–December 2007, and private parties greater than 2. Run the query and **sort** the results in descending order by the Service Date.

...continued on Next Page

Name the query **Your Name Boston Suites**. See Figure 2.50 if you need help figuring out which fields to select.

f. Examine the number of records in the status bar at the bottom of the query. It should display 23. If your number of records is different, examine the criteria.

g. Change the order of the query fields so that they display as **FirstName**, **LastName**, **ServiceDate**, **City**, **NoInParty**, and **ServiceName**.

h. Save and close the query. Copy it and in the Paste As dialog box, name the new query **YourName Miami Suites**.

i. Open the Miami Suites query in Design view and replace the Boston criterion with Miami. Run and save the changes.

j. Print your queries if directed to do so by your instructor. Compact, repair, and back up your file.

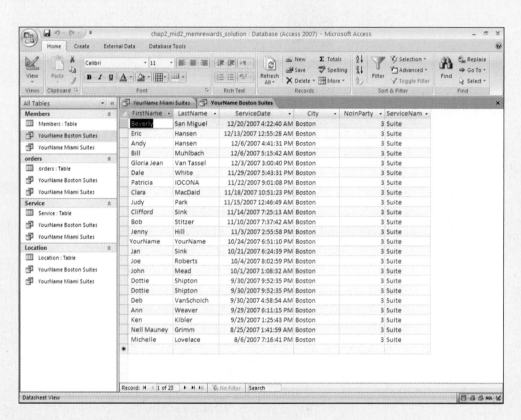

Figure 2.50 Boston Query Results

3 Creating and Using Queries

Northwind Traders is a small, international, specialty food company. It sells products in eight different divisions: Beverages, Confections (candy), Condiments, Dairy Products, Grains and Cereals, Meat and Poultry, Produce, and Seafood. Although most of its customers are restaurants and gourmet food shops, it has a few retail customers, too. It purchases the merchandise from a variety of suppliers. All of the order information is stored in the company's database. The marketing department uses this database to monitor and maintain sales records. You are the marketing

...continued on Next Page

manager. Your task is to identify which customers purchase Chai (tea) and Chang (Chinese Beer) in 2007. It would be valuable for you to discover the order quantities and the countries where the orders ship. After you complete the query, you will copy it and add the salesperson's name field to the copy. Refer to Figure 2.51 as you complete your work.

a. Copy the *chap2_mid3_traders.accdb* file and rename the copy **chap2_mid3_traders_solution.accdb**. Open the newly copied file and enable the content. Tour the database Relationship window to gain an understanding of the relationships and the data contained in the different tables. As you tour, specifically look for the tables and fields containing the information you need, that is, orders shipped in **2007** for the **beverages Chai** and **Chang**, the quantities purchased, the date the order shipped, and the countries the purchases were shipped to. You are interested in all of the countries *excluding* the United States.

b. After you identify the necessary fields, create a query that includes the fields of interest. Name this query **YourName Shipping for Chai and Chang**.

c. Set the query criteria to select the records of interest—2007 orders of Chai and Chang shipped to all of the world except for the United States.

d. Sort the query results by the Company name (alphabetically), and then by the quantity ordered. (If the same company is listed twice, the largest quantity should be listed first.)

e. Print the query results. Save and close the query.

f. Copy the query and name the copy **YourName Chai and Chang Sales by Employee**.

g. Open the **Employees table** and replace *Andrew* Fuller's name with your own name.

h. Add the employee's First and Last Name fields to the newly copied query.

i. Rearrange the fields so that the employee last name field is the first in the design grid and the Employee's FirstName is the second. Sort the results by the Employee's LastName.

j. Run, save, and print the query. Compact, repair, and back up your file.

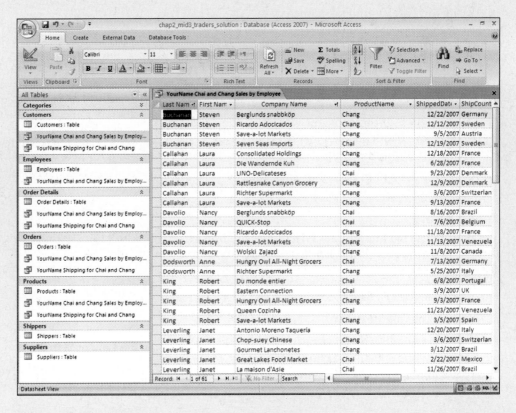

Figure 2.51 *2007 Chai and Chang Sales by Employee*

Capstone Exercise

The JC Raulston Arboretum at NC State University staff have been carefully saving their data in Excel for years. One particular workbook contains a worksheet that lists the names of all the Arboretum's "friends." This not-for-profit organization solicits contributions in the form of cash gifts, volunteer service, and "in-kind" gifts. An in-kind gift is a gift of a plant to the arboretum. Each year, one of the major fundraising events is the Gala. This is a formal event held on a delightful spring afternoon with cocktails, gourmet hors d'oeuvres, live music, and a silent auction featuring a plethora of unique plants and an eclectic array of many other distinctive items. As friends contribute service or funds to the Arboretum, another reward they receive are connoisseur plants. Connoisseur plants are rare new plants or hard-to-find old favorites, and they are part of the annual appeal and membership drive to benefit the Arboretum's many fine programs and its day-to-day operational expenses. These wonderful plants are sent to those who join the Friends of JC Raulston Arboretum at the Sponsor, Patron, Benefactor, or Philanthropist levels. The organization has grown. The files are too large to handle easily in Excel. Your task will be to begin the conversion of the files from Excel to Access.

Database File Setup

You need to open an Excel workbook that contains data on four named worksheets. Examine the data in the worksheets, paying attention to which fields will become the primary keys in each table and where those fields will appear as foreign keys in other tables in order to form the relationships.

a. Locate the Excel workbook named *chap2_cap_friends.xlsx* and open it.

b. Locate the Excel workbook named *chap2_cap_connplants.xlsx* and open it.

c. Examine the data, identify what will become the primary field in each table, and look for that field to reappear in other tables so that you can form relationships.

d. Launch Access, browse to your working folder, and create a new, blank database named **chap2_cap_arboretum_solution.accdb**.

e. Enable the content in *chap2_cap_arboretum_solution.accdb*.

Import Wizard

You need to use the Import Data Wizard twice to import each of the worksheets in the workbook from Excel into Access. You need to select the worksheets, specify the primary keys, set the indexing option, and name the newly imported tables (see Figures 2.12 through 2.18).

a. Activate the Import Wizard.

b. In the first window of the wizard, identify the source of your data. Browse to the Exploring Access folder and select the *chap2_cap_friends.xlsx* file.

c. The FriendID field will become the primary key. Set its indexing option to **Yes (No Duplicates)**.

d. When prompted, select the **FriendID** as the primary key.

e. Name the table **Friends**.

f. Import the *chap2_cap_connoisseur.xlsx* file, set the ID field as the primary key, and name the table as **Connoisseur**.

g. In Datasheet view, examine the newly imported tables.

Create Relationships

You need to create the relationship between the tables. Identify the primary fields in each table and, using the Relationships window, connect them with their foreign key counterparts in other tables. Enforce referential integrity.

a. Close any open tables, and then display the Relationships window.

b. Add the two tables to the Relationship window with the Show Table dialog box. Then, close the Show Tables dialog box.

c. Drag the FriendID from the **Friends table** to the FriendNumber field in the **Connoisseur table**. Enforce Referential Integrity.

d. Print the Relationships window.

e. Close the Relationship window and save your changes.

Create, Add Criteria to, and Sort a Query

You need to create a query that identifies the people who have received at least one connoisseur plant and who are not attending the Gala. Use the Query Wizard to identify the tables, Friends and Connoisseur, and fields necessary. Establish criteria that will limit the results to only records where one or more plant has been sent and there is no Gala reservation. This query will need to be sorted by the last name field.

a. Launch the Query Wizard.

b. From the **Friends table** select the NameFirst, NameLast, and the Gala fields. From the **Connoisseur table**, select the SendPlant field.

c. Name the query as **YourName Gala No, Conn Plant Yes**.

d. Open the query in Design view and set criteria in the Gala field to **No** and in the SentPlants field to **>0**.

e. Sort the query by the NameLast field in alphabetical order.

f. Print the results. Compact, repair, and back up the file.

Mini Cases

Use the rubric following the case as a guide to evaluate your work, but keep in mind that your instructor may impose additional grading criteria or use a different standard to judge your work.

Employee Performance Review

GENERAL CASE

The *chap2_mc1_insurance.accdb* file contains data from a large insurance agency. Copy the *chap2_mc1_insurance.accdb* file, name it **chap2_mc1_insurance_solution.accdb**, and open the copied file. Use the skills from this chapter to perform several tasks. The firm's employee policy states that an employee needs to maintain a performance rating of good or excellent to maintain employment. If an employee receives an average or poor performance rating, she receives a letter reminding her of this policy and advising her to improve or suffer the consequences. You are the manager of the Atlanta office. You need to identify the employees who need a letter of reprimand. Once the query has been completed, it will be used to generate a form letter to be sent to the employees. You need to include fields for the letter that contain the employees' first and last names, their position titles, and their salary. You do not need to write the letter, only assemble the data for the letter to be written. The results need to be alphabetized by the employee's names. As you work, consider the order that the fields will need to be used in the letter and order the query fields accordingly.

Performance Elements	Exceeds Expectations	Meets Expectations	Below Expectations
Create query	All necessary and no unneeded fields included.	All necessary fields included but also unnecessary fields.	Not all necessary fields were included in the query.
Establish criteria	The query results correctly identified and selected records.	The query results correctly identified and selected records.	Incorrect criteria specifications.
Sorting	Query fields were logically ordered and appropriately sorted.	Query fields were appropriately sorted but not logically ordered.	Both the order and the sort were incorrect.
Query name	The query name described the content.	The query name partially described the content.	The query employed the default name.

Database Administrator Position

RESEARCH CASE

This chapter introduced you to the idea that employees who administer and manage databases receive high pay, but you have much more to explore. Use the Internet to search for information about database management. One useful site is published by the federal government's Bureau of Labor Statistics. It compiles an Occupational Outlook Handbook describing various positions, the type of working environment, the education necessity, salary information, and the projected growth. The Web site is **http://www.bls.gov/oco**. Your challenge is to investigate the position of Database Administrator. Use the BLS Web site and at least one other source. Write your instructor a memo describing this position. Use a memo template in Word, your most professional writing style, and specify the data sources.

Performance Elements	Exceeds Expectations	Meets Expectations	Below Expectations
Use online resources	Appropriate articles located and memo indicates comprehension.	Appropriate articles located but memo did not demonstrate comprehension.	Articles not found.
Extract useful information from the resources	Most major components of the position described accurately.	Many elements of the position described.	Many elements of the position missing or the description incomprehensible.
Summarize and communicate	Memo clearly written and free of misspellings.	Memo text indicates some understanding but also weaknesses.	Memo missing or incomprehensible.
Esthetics	Memo template correctly employed.	Template employed but signed in the wrong place or improperly used.	Memo missing or incomprehensible.

May and Beverage Queries

A co-worker called you into his office and explained that he was having difficulty with Access 2007 and asked you to look at his work. Copy the *chap2_mc3_traders.accdb* file to your working storage folder, name it **chap2_mc3_traders_solution.accdb**, and open the file. It contains two queries, May 2007 Orders of Beverages and Confections and 2007 Beverage Sales by Ship Country. The May 2007 Orders of Beverages and Confections query is supposed to only have information from May. You find other dates included in the results. Your challenge is to find and correct the error(s). The 2007 Beverage Sales by Ship Country returns no results. It needs to be ordered by country. It needs to be repaired and resorted. Print the Datasheet View of both queries.

Performance Elements	Exceeds Expectations	Meets Expectations	Below Expectations
Error identification	Correct identification and correction of all errors.	Correct identification of all errors and correction of some errors.	Errors neither located nor corrected.
May query	Correct criteria and sorted logically.	Correct criteria but inadequately sorted.	Incorrect criteria.
Beverage query	Correct criteria and sorted logically.	Correct criteria but inadequately sorted.	Incorrect criteria.

Customize, Analyze, and Summarize Query Data

Creating and Using Queries to Make Decisions

bjectives

After you read this chapter, you will be able to:

1. Understand the order of precedence **(page 881)**.
2. Create a calculated field in a query **(page 881)**.
3. Create expressions with the Expression Builder **(page 891)**.
4. Create and edit Access functions **(page 892)**.
5. Perform date arithmetic **(page 896)**.
6. Create and work with data aggregates **(page 906)**.

Hands-On Exercises

Exercises	Skills Covered
1. **CALCULATED QUERY FIELDS (page 885)** **Open:** chap3_ho1-3_realestate.accdb **Save as:** chap3_ho1-3_realestate_solution.accdb **Back up as:** chap3_ho1_realestate_solution.accdb	• Copy a Database and Start the Query • Select the Fields, Save, and Open the Query • Create a Calculated Field and Run the Query • Verify the Calculated Results • Recover from a Common Error
2. **EXPRESSION BUILDER, FUNCTIONS, AND DATE ARITHMETIC (page 897)** **Open:** chap3_ho1-3_realestate.accdb (from Exercise 1) **Save as:** chap3_ho1-3_realestate_solution.accdb (additional modifications) **Back up as:** chap3_ho2_realestate_solution.accdb	• Create a Select Query • Use the Expression Builder • Create Calculations Using Input Stored in a Different Query or Table • Edit Expressions Using the Expression Builder • Use Functions • Work with Date Arithmetic
3. **DATA AGGREGATES (page 909)** **Open:** chap3_ho1-3_realestate.accdb (from Exercise 2) **Save as:** chap3_ho1-3_realestate_solution.accdb (additional modifications)	• Add a Total Row • Create a Totals Query Based on a Select Query • Add Fields to the Design Grid • Add Grouping Options and Specify Summary Statistics

CASE STUDY

Replacements, Ltd.

(Replacements, Ltd exists. The data in the case file are actual data. The customer and employee information have been changed to ensure privacy. However, the inventory and sales records reflect actual transactions.)

Today is the first day in your new position as associate marketing manager at Replacements, Ltd. In preparation for your first day on the job you have spent hours browsing the Replacements Web site, www.replacements.com. There you learned that Replacements, Ltd. (located in Greensboro, N.C.) has the world's largest selection of old and new dinnerware, including china, stoneware, crystal, glassware, silver, stainless, and collectibles. Its 300,000-square-foot facilities (the size of five football fields!) house an incredible inventory of 10 million pieces in 200,000 patterns, some more than 100 years old. While interviewing for the position, you toured the show room and warehouses. You learned that Replacements provides its customers with pieces that exactly match their existing patterns of china, silver, crystal, etc. People who break a cup or accidentally drop a spoon in the disposal purchase replacement treasures.

Case Study

You have been given responsibility for managing several different patterns of merchandise. You need to maintain adequate inventory levels. On the one hand you need to have merchandise available so that when a customer wishes to purchase a fork in a specific pattern, the customer service representatives can find it and box it for shipment. To accomplish this task, you need to closely monitor past sales in the various patterns in order to understand purchasing habits and product demand. On the other hand, the firm cannot afford to stock inventory of patterns no one wishes to purchase. You exchange information with the customer service representatives and monitor their performance. If you discover that one of the patterns you manage has excess inventory, you will need to direct the buyers to stop purchasing additional pieces in that pattern and encourage the customer service representatives to suggest the pattern to customers. You will determine if and when a pattern should be discounted or if an incentive program or contest should be implemented to reward the sales associates for successfully selling the overstocked merchandise.

Your Assignment

- Copy the *chap3_case_replacement.accdb* file to your production folder. Name the copy **chap3_case_replacement_solution.accdb**.
- Open the Relationships window and acquaint yourself with the tables, fields, and relationships among the tables in the database.
- You need to convert the data into useful information. To accomplish this task, you will need to create a query that identifies the revenue generated from sales in each of the patterns you manage.
- You also must determine which patterns customers purchase most often.
- Replacements encourages the customer service representatives by paying them bonuses based on the orders that they fill. You will calculate each customer service representative's total sales and calculate their bonuses. The bonus will be calculated based on ½% of the representative's total sales.
- Finally, you need to compare the inventory levels of each pattern piece with its sales volume. Careful monitoring of stock levels will prevent excessive inventory. For each item calculate the percent of the inventory level that was sold in the past month. For example, if there were 100 cups in a specific pattern in inventory at the beginning of the month and 18 of them were sold during the month, the sales-inventory ratio would be 18%. Set criteria so that the zero OnHandQuantity items are excluded from the calculation.

Data Summary and Analysis

Practicing good database design discourages storing calculations as table data. Although storing calculated results in a table is not a good idea, Access *can* perform arithmetic calculations using formulae and functions much like Excel. However, the calculated results do not belong in tables. Instead, calculations needed to summarize and analyze data are found in three places: queries, forms, and reports. Professionals who use Access to develop applications within organizations have very different opinions about the most appropriate placement of calculations in Access. One group assembles and manipulates data inside a query. After you establish the calculations and criteria, the data are sent to an Access report to be cosmetically enhanced. (This is the practice that you will employ throughout the exercises in this book.) The other group does all of the calculations inside of forms and reports. This group uses fewer queries but creates far more sophisticated reports and forms.

In this section, you learn about the order of precedence and create a calculated field in a query.

Understanding the Order of Precedence

The **order of precedence** establishes the sequence by which values are calculated.

The **order of precedence** establishes the sequence by which values are calculated in an expression. Evaluate parenthetically expressed values, then exponents, multiplication and division, and, finally, addition and subtraction. Access calculates exactly what you tell it to calculate—even if your formulae are incorrect! Table 3.1 shows some examples of arithmetic order. You must have a solid understanding of these rules in order to "teach" the computer to generate the required output. Access, like Excel, uses the following symbols:

- Addition   +
- Subtraction   −
- Multiplication   *
- Division   /
- Exponentiation   ^

Creating a Calculated Field in a Query

You instruct Access to perform calculations in the Design view of the query. Create the calculated values in the first row of a blank column. You may scroll, if necessary, to find a blank column in the design grid or insert a blank column where you want

Table 3.1 Examples of Order of Precedence

Expression	Order to Perform Calculations	Output
= 2 + 3 * 3	Multiply first, and then add.	11
= (2 + 3) * 3	Add the values inside the parenthesis first, and then multiply.	15
= 2 + 2 ^ 3	Simplify the exponent first. $2^3 = 2*2*2$ or 8. Then add.	10
= (2 + 2) ^3	Add the parenthetical values first (2 + 2 = 4), and then raise the result to the 3rd power. $4^3 = 4*4*4$.	64
= 10/2 + 3	Divide first, and then add.	8
= 10/(2+3)	Add first to simplify the parenthetical expression, and then divide.	2
= 10 * 2 − 3 * 2	Multiply first, and then subtract.	14

An **expression** is a formula used to calculate new fields from the values in existing fields.

the calculated value to appear. A formula used to calculate new fields from the values in existing fields is also known as an **expression**. An expression consists of a number of different items to produce the answers needed. The items used in an expression may include the following:

- Identifiers (the names of fields, controls or properties)
- Operators (arithmetic instructions about what to do with the identifiers like + or –)
- Functions (as in Excel, Access has built-in functions to perform routine calculations, like SUM or Average)

A **constant** refers to a value that does not change.

- *Constants* and values (numbers that may be used as a part of a calculation but are unlikely to change)

You may use the expression to perform calculations, retrieve a value from a field, set query criteria, verify data created, calculate fields or controls, and set grouping levels in reports. Access not only organizes and protects a firm's valuable data but also enables you to summarize, understand, and make decisions based on the data. Your value to an organization dramatically increases when you master the skills that surround expression building in Access.

Build Expressions with Correct Syntax

Syntax is the set of rules by which the words and symbols of an expression are correctly combined.

Enter the expression in the first row of the column. Using simple *syntax* rules, you instruct the software to calculate the necessary values. You can create expressions to perform calculations using either field values or constants. You must correctly spell the field names for Access to find the appropriate values. You should assign descriptive names to the calculated fields. Access ignores spaces in calculations. The general syntax follows:

CalculatedFieldName: [InputField1] operand operator [InputField2] operand

Although this is the most appropriate format, Access enters the brackets for you if it recognizes the field name. Remember that an **operator** is a symbol, such as *, that performs some operation, such as multiplication. An **operand** is the value that is being manipulated or operated on. In calculated fields in Access, the operand is either a literal value or a field name. Figure 3.1 shows a calculated field named Interest. The calculated field first calculates the monthly interest rate by dividing the 3.5% (0.035) annual rate by 12. The monthly interest rate is then multiplied by the value in the Balance field to determine the amount of interest owed.

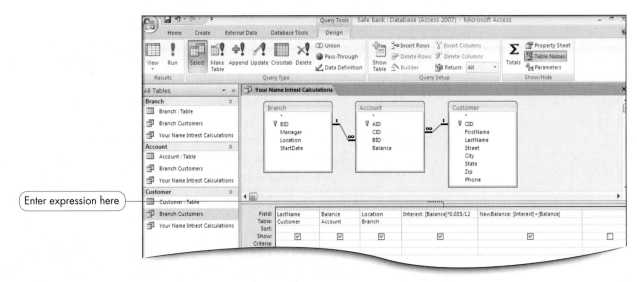

Figure 3.1 The Correct Location for a Calculated Query Expression

To help reinforce how calculated fields work, suppose you need to calculate the revenue from a purchase order. Revenue is the name of the calculated field. The following expression generates the calculated field by multiplying the unit price by the quantity ordered:

Revenue:Price*Quantity

Access enters the brackets for you and converts the expression to the following:

Revenue: [Price]*[Quantity]

For a final example of calculated fields, suppose you need to calculate a 10% price increase on all products you sell. NewPrice is the name of the calculated field. The following expression multiplies the old price by 110%:

NewPrice:Price*1.1

Access enters the brackets for you and converts the expression to the following:

NewPrice: [Price]*1.1

When you run the query, the calculated results display in the query's Datasheet view. Using the above example, Access goes to the table(s) where the prices and order quantities are stored, extracts the current data, loads it into the query, and uses the data to perform the calculation. When you direct Access to collect fields that are stored in related tables, Access uses the "strings" that form the relationship to collect the appropriate records and deliver them to the query. For example, suppose you create a query that retrieves customers' names from the customer table and the dates that the orders were placed from the Order table. The Customers table might contain 50,000 customer records. The query will return only those customers who ordered something because the relationship integrity will limit the output to only the records of interest. After the data are assembled, you can manipulate the data in each record by entering expressions. After you run the query, you need to examine the calculated results to verify that the output is what you need. Access has the ability to process a lot of numbers very quickly. Unfortunately, Access can also return incorrectly calculated results equally quickly if the formula you create is incorrect. Remember and avoid GIGO—Garbage In; Garbage Out!

(GIGO—Garbage In; Garbage Out!)

Verify Calculated Results

After your query runs, look at the values of the input field and then look at the calculated results returned. Ask yourself, "Does this answer make sense?" Use a pocket calculator or the Windows calculator to perform the same calculation using the same inputs and compare the answers. Alternatively, you can use Excel to check your calculated results. Copy and paste a few records into Excel. Repeat all of the calculations and compare the answers. The Access calculated field, the calculator, and the Excel calculations should return identical results.

After verifying the calculated results, you should save the query to run the next time you need to perform the same calculations.

Save a Query Containing Calculated Fields

Saving a query does *not* save the data. It saves only your instructions about what data to select and what to do with it once it is selected. Think of a query as a set of instructions directing Access to deliver data and the form the data are to assume at delivery. Writing a query is like placing an order with a restaurant server. You may order a medium rare steak, a baked potato, and tossed salad with blue cheese dressing. Your server writes the order and any special instructions and delivers it to the kitchen. In the kitchen the cook fills the order based on your instructions. Then the server delivers the ordered food to you. The data in a database is like the raw food in the kitchen. It is stored in the freezer or refrigerator or the cupboard (the tables). Data from the query (server's order) are assembled and "cooked." The big difference is that in the restaurant, once your steak is delivered to you, it is no longer available to other diners to order. The data in a database are *never* consumed. Data can be ordered simultaneously by multiple queries in a multiple user database environment. The data physically reside in the tables and never move from their storage location. Running the query collects the field values in the records of interest. The query contains only the instructions governing how Access selects and interacts with the data. If you type over a data item in a query table view, the new value automatically replaces the old one in the table.

After you run, verify, and save the query, you can use the newly created calculated fields in subsequent calculations. You may use a calculated field as input for other calculated fields. However, you must first save the query so that the calculation's results will be available.

In the first hands-on exercise, you will create calculated expressions, practice verification techniques, and generate and recover from a common error.

Hands-On Exercises

1 | Calculated Query Fields

Skills covered: 1. Copy a Database and Start the Query **2.** Select the Fields, Save, and Open the Query **3.** Create a Calculated Field and Run the Query **4.** Verify the Calculated Results **5.** Recover from a Common Error

---

Step 1
Copy a Database and Start the Query

Refer to Figure 3.2 as you complete Step 1.

a. Use Windows Explorer to locate the file named *chap3_ho1-3_realestate.accdb*. Copy the file to your production folder and rename the copied file as **chap3_ho1-3_realestate_solution.accdb**.

b. Open the *chap3_ho1-3_realestate_solution.accdb* file.

c. Click **Options** on the Security Warning toolbar, and then click **Enable this content** in the Microsoft Office Security Options dialog box and click **OK**.

d. Click the **Create tab**, and then click **Query Wizard** in the Other group.

e. Select **Simple Query Wizard** in the New Query dialog box. Click **OK**.

The Simple Query Wizard dialog box displays so that you can specify the table(s) and fields to include in the query design.

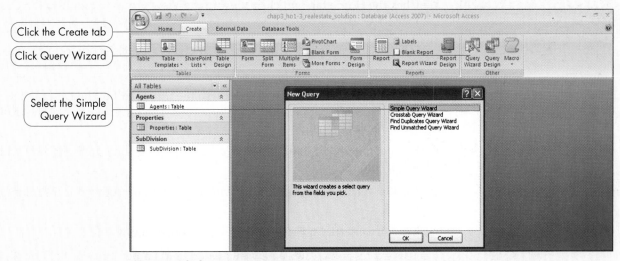

Figure 3.2 New Query Dialog Box

Step 2
Select the Fields, Save, and Open the Query

Refer to Figure 3.3 as you complete Step 2.

a. Click the **Tables/Queries drop-down arrow** and select **Table: Agents**. Double-click the **FirstName** and **LastName** fields in the **Available Fields list** to select them.

b. Click the **Tables/Queries drop-down arrow** and select **Table: Properties**. Double-click the following fields to select them: **DateListed**, **DateSold**, **ListPrice**, **SalePrice**, **SqFeet**, and **Sold**.

c. Compare your selected fields to those shown in Figure 3.3, and then click **Next**.

d. Verify that the **Detail (shows every field of every record) option** is selected in the *Would you like a detail or summary query?* screen in the Simple Query Wizard dialog box. Click **Next**.

e. Type **YourName Sale Price per SqFt** for the query title. Click **Finish**.

The results of the query appear in the Datasheet view.

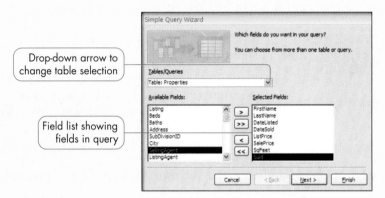

Figure 3.3 Select Fields for the Query

Step 3
Create a Calculated Field and Run the Query

Refer to Figure 3.4 as you complete Step 3.

a. Click the **Home tab** and click **View** in the View group to toggle to the Design view.

TROUBLESHOOTING: If you click View and Access does not toggle to the Design view, click the View arrow and select Design View.

This query was based on two tables, so the upper half of the Design view displays the two tables, Agents and Properties. The lower portion of the Design view displays the fields currently in the query.

b. Use the horizontal scroll bar to scroll the design grid to the right until you see a blank column.

c. Click in the first row of the first blank column to position your insertion point there.

d. Type **PricePerSqFt: SalePrice/SqFeet** and press **Enter**.

This expression creates a new calculated field named PricePerSqFt by dividing the values in the SalePrice field by the values in the SqFeet field. In this calculated field, the operator is the division symbol (/) and the operands are the SalePrice and SqFeet fields. Look at Figure 3.4 if you need help with the syntax for the expression.

TIP Increasing Width of Columns

To increase the column width so that you can see the entire calculated field expression, double-click the vertical line in the gray area above the field names between the calculated field column and the blank column.

e. Right-click the field text box in the design grid that contains the PricePerSqFt calculated field. Select **Properties** from the shortcut menu. Click the **Format drop-down arrow** in the Property Sheet window and select **Currency**. Click the X to close the Property Sheet window.

f. Click the **Design tab**, if needed, and then click **Run** in the Results group.

When you run the query, Access performs all of the calculations and opens in the table view to display the results.

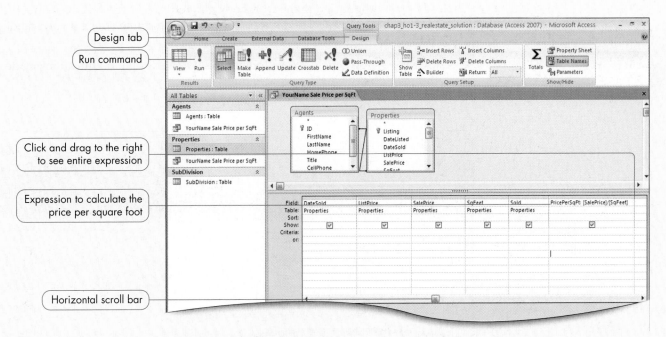

Figure 3.4 Expression Syntax

Step 4
Verify the Calculated Results

Refer to Figure 3.5 as you complete Step 4.

a. Examine the results of the calculation. Ask yourself if the numbers make sense to you.

TROUBLESHOOTING: Are you having a problem? You may wish to read Step 5 now. Often, a typo entered in a calculated field will result in a parameter box opening. Step 5 discusses how to recover from this error.

Look at the fourth record. The sale price is $155,000, and the number of square feet is 1,552. You can probably verify these results by dividing the values in your head. The result is about $100. The PricePerSqFt field in Figure 3.5 displays $99.87.

b. Use the row selectors to select the first four records by clicking and dragging. After you select the four records, right-click them and select **Copy** from the shortcut menu.

c. Launch Excel, activate **cell A1** of a blank workbook and paste the Access records into Excel.

The field names appear in the first row, and the four records appear in the next four rows. The fields are located in Columns A–I. The calculated field results are pasted in Column I as values rather than as a formula.

TROUBLESHOOTING: If you see pound signs (#####) instead of numbers in an Excel column, that means the column is too narrow to display the values. Position the mouse pointer on the vertical line between the column letters, such as between D and E, and double-click the vertical line to increase the width of column D.

d. In **cell J2**, type **=F2/G2** and press **Enter**.

The formula divides the sale price by the square feet. Compare the results in the I and J columns. The numbers should be the same. If the numbers are the same, close Excel without saving the workbook and return to Access. If the values differ, look at both the Excel and Access formulae. Determine which is correct and then find and fix the error in the incorrect formula.

e. Click **Save** on the Quick Access Toolbar to save the design modifications made to the *Your_Name Sale Price per SqFt* query.

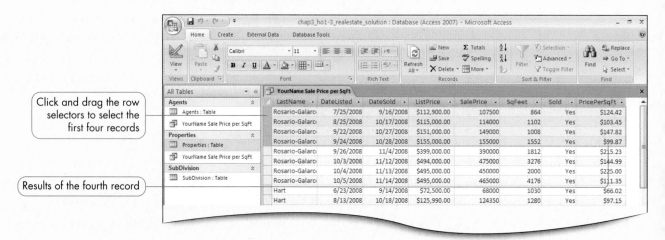

Figure 3.5 Examine Calculated Results

Refer to Figure 3.6 as you complete Step 5.

Step 5
Recover from a Common Error

a. In the *YourName Sale Price per SqFt* query, click **View** in the Views group to switch to Design view. Scroll to the first empty column and click in the first row to position the insertion point.

Because Access users occasionally make a typing error when creating an expression, it is useful to learn how to recover from this type of error. You will intentionally misspell a field name used in a calculation by typing the field name SalePrice as SaleSPrice and SqFeet as SqRFeet.

b. Type **WrongPricePerSqFt: SaleSPrice/SqRFeet**.

Be sure that you added the extra *S* and *R* to the field names. You are making intentional errors to learn how Access will respond.

c. Click the **Design tab** and click **Run** in the Results group.

You should see the Enter Parameter Value dialog box. Examine the dialog box. What is it asking you to do? The dialog box indicates that Access could not find a value for SaleSPrice in the first record. This error occurs because the table does not contain a SaleSPrice field. Because Access is asking you to supply a value, you will type in a value.

d. Type **100000** in the parameter box. Before you click OK, try to anticipate what the software will do next. You intentionally misspelled *two* field names. Press **Enter** or click **OK**.

Another Enter Parameter Value dialog box displays, asking that you supply a value for SqRFeet. This error occurs because the table does not contain a SqRFeet field.

e. Type **1000** and press **Enter**.

The query has the necessary information to run and returns the results in Datasheet view.

f. Scroll right and examine the results of the calculation for WrongPricePerSqFt.

All of the records show 100. This result occurs because you entered the values 100000 and 1000, respectively, in the Enter Parameter Value dialog boxes, which used those literal values in the expression. The result of 100 appears for all records.

g. Return to Design view and correct the errors in the WrongPricePerSqFt field by changing the formula to **WrongPricePerSqFt: SalePrice/SqFeet**.

h. Right-click the field text box in the design grid that contains the WrongPricePerSqFt calculated field. Select **Properties** from the shortcut menu. Click the **Format drop-down arrow** in the Property Sheet window and select **Currency**. Click the X to close the Property Sheet window.

i. Run and save the query again.

The calculated values in the last two columns should be the same.

j. Click the **Office Button**, select **Manage**, and then select **Back Up Database**. Enter the file name **chap3_ho1_realestate_solution** (note *ho1* instead of *ho1-3*) and click **Save**.

You just created a backup of the database after completing the first hands-on exercise. The original database *chap3_ho1-3_realestate_solution* remains onscreen. If you ruin the original database as you complete the second hands-on exercise, you can use the backup file you just created.

k. Close the file and exit Access if you do not want to continue with the next exercise at this time.

TIP Learning Software

Following step-by-step instructions is a way to begin learning application software. If you want to become proficient in software, you must learn how to recover from errors. As you work through the rest of the Hands-On Exercises in this book, follow the instructions as presented and save your work. Then go back a few steps and make an intentional error just to see how Access responds. Read the error messages (if any) and learn from your mistakes in a safe environment.

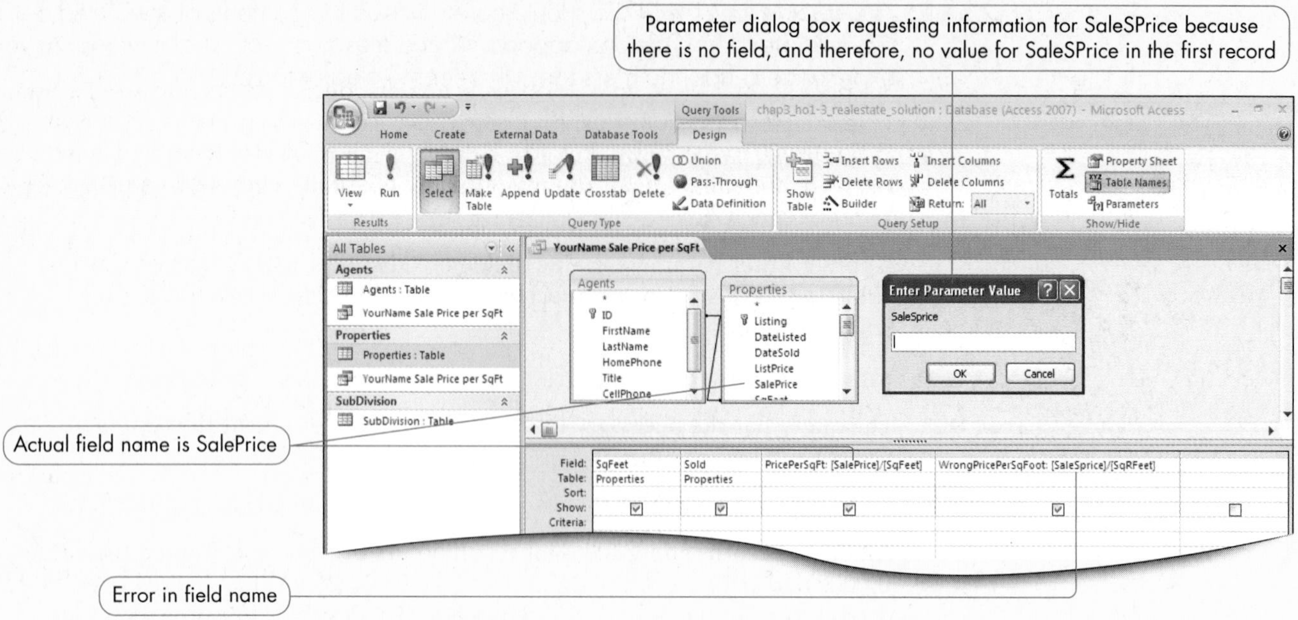
Parameter dialog box requesting information for SaleSPrice because there is no field, and therefore, no value for SaleSPrice in the first record
Actual field name is SalePrice
Error in field name
Enter Parameter Value
SaleSprice
OK
Cancel
PricePerSqFt: [SalePrice]/[SqFeet]
WrongPricePerSqFoot: [SaleSprice]/[SqRFeet]

Figure 3.6 Error Recovery

Expression Builder

Before people used electronic database programs, decision makers were hampered because they could not find valid, timely, and accurate data to base decisions on. In today's world, data remains a problem for decision makers; however, the nature of the problem has changed. The data are current, accurate, and authentic. But because so much data are available, managers can become overwhelmed. In the last hands-on exercise, you calculated a price per square foot for real estate listings. That simple calculation can assist a decision maker to ascribe value to a property. It is a useful way to examine a complex transaction in a simplified fashion. Access enables you to calculate the value, but typing (and spelling correctly) all of those field names in the calculation is a lot of work. Fortunately, you can use the *Expression Builder* as an alternative, easier method to perform calculations. When you create an expression in the field text box, you must scroll to see the entire expression. The Expression Builder's size permits you to see even long, complex formulae and functions in their entirety.

The ***Expression Builder*** is a tool to help you create a formula that performs calculations easily.

In this section, you learn how to create expressions with the Expression Builder. You then learn how to create and edit functions. Finally, you perform date arithmetic.

Creating Expressions with the Expression Builder

You can use the Expression Builder in a query design grid to assist you in properly crafting the appropriate syntax. It is a blend of a calculator and a spreadsheet. You also can use the Expression Builder in other Access objects where calculations are needed. These objects include the control properties in forms and reports and table field properties. The Expression Builder requires some practice for you to learn how to use it effectively. Once you master the Expression Builder, you may use it to create a formula from scratch, or you can use it to select some pre-built expressions or functions. Additionally, the Expression Builder enables you to include useful items such as page numbers and the current date or time.

> The Expression Builder . . . is a blend of a calculator and a spreadsheet.

Access automatically assigns placeholder names to all expressions created with the Expression Builder as Expr1, Expr2, Expr3. You need to develop the habit of running the query, verifying the calculation results and then returning to the design grid and replacing Exp1 with a descriptive field name. Good work habits will save you hours and hours when you return to your calculations in six weeks or six months.

After you save the query, the newly calculated field and descriptively named field are available to use in subsequent calculations.

Launch the Expression Builder

Open the query in Design view and display the Design tab. The Builder command is found in the Query Setup group. Figure 3.7 shows the components of the Expression Builder. The middle column contains a list of fields available in the current query. Occasionally, you may need to use a field as a calculation input that is not contained in the current query. Everything in the database is available to you through the builder. If you click the plus sign to the right of the Tables or Queries folder in the left column, the folder will open and reveal the other tables and fields in the database. This is a wonderful feature for someone who forgot to include a needed field in a query.

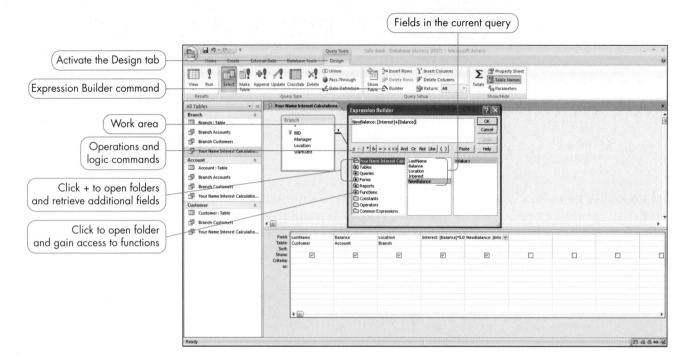

Figure 3.7 Expression Builder

The work area is the large rectangle at the top of the dialog box. Just as in Excel, an Access expression created using the Expression Builder begins with an equal sign. You may either type it or click the equal sign in the logic and operands area under the work area. When you need a field entered, find the field (look first in the middle column) and double-click it to add it to the expression. The field is added with the syntactically appropriate brackets inserted. Type or click operands (+, −, *, /) as needed and add additional fields to complete the expression. When you finish the expression, click OK.

Creating and Editing Access Functions

An **_Access function_** performs an operation using input supplied as arguments and returns a value.

An **_argument_** is a necessary input component required to produce the output for a function.

An _Access function_ calculates commonly used expressions using "canned" instructions and input values to return a calculated value. You must know the function's name and provide it arguments in order to use it. Access functions work much like Excel functions. You identify the function by its name (e.g., Average, Sum, PMT) and enter the required **_arguments_**—what input values should be averaged, added, or calculated as a payment. They are grouped into categories of similar functions: Math, Financial, Date/Time, General, etc.

Calculate Payments with the PMT Function

The **_PMT function_** calculates a periodic loan payment given a constant interest rate, term, and original value.

Figure 3.8 shows the **_PMT function_**, which calculates a periodic loan payment given a constant interest rate, specific term of the loan, and the original value of the loan. To use this function, you need to fill in values from data stored in fields from underlying tables or supply constants in the formula.

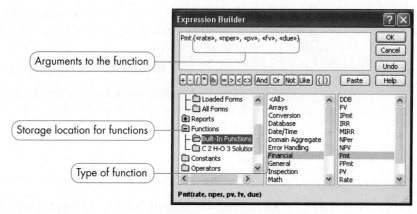

Arguments to the function

Storage location for functions

Type of function

Figure 3.8 Access Function Shown in Expression Builder

The following syntax is required for the PMT function. Table 3.2 lists and describes the arguments for the PMT function.

$$\text{Pmt}(\textit{rate, nper, pv, fv, type})$$

$$\text{Pmt}(.065/12, 4*12, 12500,0,0)$$

Table 3.2

Part	Description
( )	Everything inside the parentheses is an argument to the function. The arguments are separated by commas. This function requires three arguments.
rate	Required. Expression or value specifying interest rate per period. (The period is the term of the loan payment, such as monthly or quarterly. For example, a car loan at an annual percentage rate (APR) of 6.5% with monthly payments gives the rate per period (month) of 0.065/12, or 0.005417).
nper	Required. Expression or Integer value specifying total number of payment periods in the annuity. For example, monthly payments on a four-year car loan gives a total of 4 * 12 (or 48) payment periods.
pv	Required. Expression or value specifying present value (or how much you borrow) that a series of payments to be paid in the future is worth now. For example, the loan amount is the present value to the lender of the monthly car payments.
fv	Optional. Value specifying future value or cash balance you want after you've made the final payment. For example, most loans have a future value of $0 because that's what is owed after the final payment. However, if you want to save $50,000 over 18 years for your child's education, then $50,000 is the future value.
type	Optional. Value (0 or 1) identifying when payments are due. Use 0 if payments are due at the end of the payment period (the norm), or 1 if payments are due at the beginning of the period.

Execute Actions with the IIf Function

The **IIf function** evaluates a condition and executes one action when the condition is true and an alternate action when the condition is false.

Another useful function is the **IIf function**, which evaluates a condition and executes one action when the expression is true and an alternate action when the condition is false. The condition must evaluate as true or false only. For example, if balance >=10,000 or if City = "Chicago" illustrate appropriate conditions. Access evaluates the expression, determines whether it is true or false, and performs alternative actions based on the determination. For example, accounts with balances over

$10,000 earn a 3.5% interest rate, while accounts with balances below $10,000 earn only 2.75% interest. The following syntax is required for the IIf function:
IIf(expr,truepart,falsepart)

$$\text{IIf(Balance} >= 10000, .035, .0275)$$

Suppose you want to calculate the number of vacation weeks an employee is eligible to receive. The firm gives two weeks of vacation to employees with five or fewer years of employment and three weeks to employees who have worked more than five years for the firm. Your query has a field showing the number of years worked, YearsWorked. The proper syntax to calculate vacation weeks is the following:

$$\text{WksVacation:IIf([YearsWorked]>5, 3,2)}$$

This expression evaluates each record and determines if the number of years worked is more than five. When the number of years is greater than 5 (true), the expression returns the number 3 in the WksVacation field, indicating that the employee receives three weeks of vacation. If the years worked are not greater than 5 (false), the expression returns 2 in the WksVacation field, indicating that the employee receives two weeks of vacation. It is important that you write the expression so that it returns only a value of True or False for every record because Access cannot deal with ambiguities. The expression always evaluates both the true and false parts for each record. When the expression, the truepart, or the falsepart references a character string (words instead of numbers), you must type the return string (the true or false parts) inside of quotation marks.

TIP   Structure IIf Logic Carefully

Even experienced Access users get surprised sometimes when using IIf functions because the false part is evaluated even when the expression is true. Occasionally, this false part evaluation will result in a *divide by zero* error. You can prevent this error by rewriting the expression and reversing the inequity. For example, change > to <=. You also must reverse the truepart and falsepart actions.

When you complete the expression, click OK. The Expression Builder dialog box closes, but nothing seems to happen. You have written the instruction in a form the computer understands, but you have not yet given the command to the computer to execute your instructions. The next step is to force an execution of your command by clicking Run. Your newly calculated result displays in the Datasheet view of the table. The column heading shows the default name, Expr1. Examine and verify the results of the calculation. When you are satisfied that the results are correct, return to Design view. In the design grid, double-click <Expr1> to select it, type over <Expr1> with a descriptive field name, run, and save the query.

TIP   Calculated Field Availability

A calculated query field will not be available to use in subsequent calculations until after you save the query. When you need to make multiple-step calculations, you must author the steps one at a time, then run, verify, and save after each step.

Using the Expression Builder Steps | Reference

1.	Open the query in Design view.
2.	Position the insertion point in a blank column.
3.	Select the Design tab.
4.	Click the Builder icon to launch the Expression Builder.
5.	When entering a formula, type (or click) an equal sign, =.
6.	Double-click field names to add to the expression.
7.	Type or click the icons for operators.
8.	Double-click the Functions folder and select the type of function needed, then from the right column, select the individual function.
9.	Click OK to exit the Builder box.
10.	Run the query.
11.	Examine and verify the output.
12.	Return to the Design view.
13.	Highlight <Expr1> in the design grid and rename the field with a descriptive field name.
14.	Run the query and save it.

Performing Date Arithmetic

Because dates are stored as sequential numbers, you can calculate an age . . . or . . . how many days past due an invoice is.

Access, like Excel, stores all dates as serial numbers. You may format the stored dates with a format that makes sense to you. In Europe, the date *November 20, 2008*, might be formatted as *20-11-2008* or *20.11.2008*. In the United States, the same date might be formatted as *11/20/2008*, and in South Asia, the date might be formatted as *20/11/2008*. ***Date formatting*** affects the date's display without changing the serial value. All dates and times in Access are stored as the number of days that have elapsed since December 31, 1899. For example, January 1, 1900, is stored as 1, indicating one day after December 31, 1899. If the time were 9:00 PM on November 20, 2008, no matter how the date or time is formatted, Access stores it as 39772.857. The 39772 represents the number of days elapsed since December 31, 1899, and the .857 reflects the fraction of the 24-hour day that has passed at 9:00 PM. This storage method may seem complicated, but it affords an Access user power and flexibility when working with date values. For example, because dates are stored as sequential numbers, you can calculate the total numbers of hours worked in a week if you record the starting and ending times for each day. Using ***date arithmetic***, you can create expressions to calculate an age in years from a birth date or tell a business owner how many days past due an invoice is.

Date formatting affects the date's display without changing the serial value.

Using **date arithmetic** you can create expressions to calculate lapsed time.

Identify Partial Dates with the DatePart Function

You can look at entire dates or simply a portion of the date that is of interest. If your company increases the number of weeks of annual vacation from two weeks to three weeks after an employee has worked for five or more years, then the only part of the date of interest is the time lapsed in years. Access has a function, the ***DatePart function***, to facilitate this. Table 3.3 shows the DatePart function parameters.

The **DatePart function** enables users to identify a specific part of a date, such as only the year.

DatePart("yyyy",[Employees]![HireDate])

Do not let the syntax intimidate you. After you practice using the DatePart function, the syntax will get much easier to understand.

Useful date functions are:

- **Date**—Inserts the current date into an expression.
- **DatePart**—Examines a date and returns only the portion of interest.
- **DateDiff**—Measures the amount of time elapsed between two dates. This is most often today's date as determined by the date function and a date stored in a field. For example, you might calculate the number of days a payment is past due by comparing today's date with the payment DueDate.

Table 3.3 Using the DatePart Function

Function Portion	Explanation
DatePart	An Access function that examines a date and focuses on a portion of interest.
"yyyy"	The first argument, the interval, describes the portion of the date of interest. We specified the years. It could also be "dd" or "mmm".
(Employees)!(HireDate)	The second argument, the date, tells Access where to find the information. In this case, it is stored in the Employee Table in a field named HireDate.

2 | Expression Builder, Functions, and Date Arithmetic

Skills covered: 1. Create a Select Query **2.** Use the Expression Builder **3.** Create Calculations Using Input Stored in a Different Query or Table **4.** Edit Expressions Using the Expression Builder **5.** Use Functions **6.** Work with Date Arithmetic

---

Step 1
Create a Select Query

Refer to Figure 3.9 as you complete Step 1.

a. Open the *chap3_ho1-3_realestate_solution* file if necessary, click **Options** on the Security Warning toolbar, click the **Enable this content option** in the Microsoft Office Security Options dialog box, and click **OK**.

TROUBLESHOOTING: If you create unrecoverable errors while completing this hands-on exercise, you can delete the *chap3_ho1-3_realestate_solution* file, copy the *chap3_ho1_realestate_solution* backup database you created at the end of the first hands-on exercise, and open the copy of the backup database to start the second hands-on exercise again.

b. Open the **Agents table** and replace **Angela Scott's** name with your name. Close the Agents table.

c. Click the **Create tab** and click **Query Wizard** in the Other group. Select **Simple Query Wizard** and click **OK**.

d. Select the fields (in this order) from the Agents table: **LastName** and **FirstName**. From the Properties table, select **DateListed**, **DateSold**, **ListPrice**, **SalePrice**, and **SqFeet**. From the SubDivision table, select the **Subdivision** field. Click **Next**.

You have selected fields from three related tables. Because relationships exist among the tables, you can trust that the agent's name that returns when the query runs will be the agent associated with the property.

e. Check to make sure that the option for a detail query is selected and click **Next**.

f. Name this query **YourName Commissions** and click **Finish**.

The query should run and open in Datasheet view. An experienced Access user always checks the number of records when a query finishes running and opens. This query should have 54 records. See Figure 3.9.

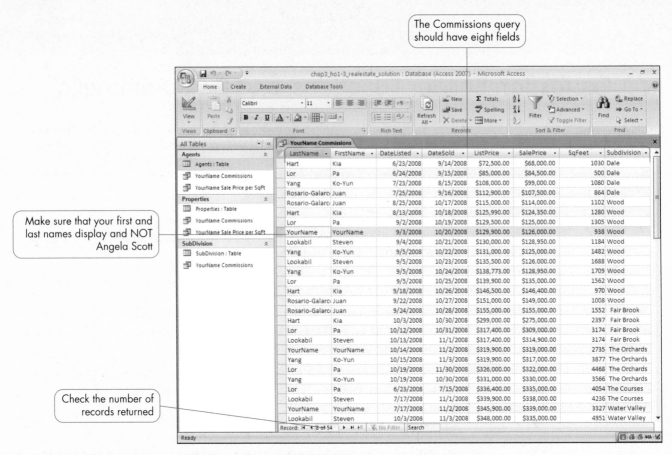

The Commissions query should have eight fields

Make sure that your first and last names display and NOT Angela Scott

Check the number of records returned

Figure 3.9 Datasheet View of the YourName Commissions Query

Step 2
Use the Expression Builder

Refer to Figure 3.10 as you complete Step 2.

a. Click the **Home tab** and switch to Design view. Scroll to the right to locate the first empty column in the design grid and position your insertion point in the first row.

b. Verify that the Design tab is selected and click **Builder** in the Query Setup group.

The Expression Builder dialog box opens. You may click the title bar and reposition it to a more convenient location if necessary.

c. Repeat the PricePerSqFt calculation from Hands-On Exercise 1 by using the Expression Builder. Click or type =.

d. Locate the list of fields in the Commissions query in the middle column and double-click the **SalePrice** field.

The work area of the Expression Builder dialog box should now display = **[SalePrice]**. The Expression Builder adds the **brackets** and always spells the field names correctly.

e. Click or type the divide operator (the forward slash, /), and then double-click the **SqFeet** field name in the middle column.

Now, the work area of the expression builder will display = **[SalePrice] / [SqFeet]**.

f. Click **OK**. Run the query. Scroll right in the Datasheet view to find the newly calculated field, which is named Expr1.

g. Verify the results of the calculation.

The fifth record has values that can be rounded more easily in your head—$114,000 and 1102 Sq. Ft. That should return a result slightly higher than $100. The actual result is 0103.44. Once you are satisfied with the accuracy of the calculation, continue with the next step.

h. Activate the **Home tab** (if necessary) and change the view to Design view.

TIP Switching Between Design and Datasheet Views

An easy way to alternate views for an Access object is to right-click the object window's title bar and select the appropriate view from the shortcut menu. You can also click the views buttons in the bottom-right corner of the Access window. In this case, the object title bar says YourName Commissions. See Figure 3.10 for instructions on where to right-click.

i. Double-click **Expr1** in the field row of the right column. Type **PricePerSqFt**.

j. Right-click the field text box in the design grid that contains the PricePerSqFt calculated field. Select **Properties** from the shortcut menu. Click the **Format drop-down arrow** in the Property Sheet window and select **Currency**. Click the X to close the Property Sheet window.

k. Run the query. Click **Save** (or press **Ctrl + S**) and return to Design view.

l. Click the insertion point in the Field row of the first empty column and activate the Expression Builder. Look in the middle column that shows the list of available fields in this query. The last listed field should be the newly saved PricePerSqFt.

TROUBLESHOOTING: Sometimes, you need to edit an expression created using the Expression Builder. When you open the Expression Builder to make the edits, you will find that Access adds <Expr1> to any unsaved expressions. Locate and double-click the <Expr1> to select it and delete it prior to making the necessary edits to the expression.

Figure 3.10   Working with the Expression Builder

Step 3

Create Calculations Using Input Stored in a Different Query or Table

Refer to Figure 3.11 as you complete Step 3.

a. Type = (equal sign) in the work area of the Expression Builder. Double-click **SalePrice** in the middle column to add it to the expression. Type or click / (divide symbol). Your formula in the work area should be = **[SalePrice]/**.

In addition to calculating the price per square foot, you decide that it would be helpful if you knew the price of the sold properties per bedroom, but you did not include a field for the number of bedrooms in the query. You have two options. One, you can cancel the expression, add the missing field to the query, and then restart the expression. Two, you also can use a field in a calculation that is not resident in the query. You need only tell Access where the field is stored.

b. Double-click the **Tables folder** in the left column of the Expression Builder.

The Tables folder expands to reveal the table objects in the database. Because you have not yet selected a table, the middle and right columns of the Expression Builder dialog box are empty.

c. Click the **Properties table**.

The middle column is populated with the names of the fields available from the Properties table. You will use this data to calculate the per bedroom sale price of the homes in the database.

d. Double-click the **Beds field**. Your expression will look like this:

= **[SalePrice] / [Properties]![Beds]**

This expression gives Access the instruction to go to the Properties table, locate the values of the number of bedrooms for each of the records in the Commissions query, and use that value to calculate a price per bedroom value. The appropriate number of bedrooms will be returned in each calculation because relationships exist between the tables. The query will inherit the referential integrity from the tables it sources.

e. Click **OK**. Click **Run**. Verify the calculated results.

f. Return to Design view. Double-click **Expr1** in the design grid to select it and type **PricePerBR**.

You have renamed Expr1, but the name change does not become permanent until you save the query design.

g. Right-click the PricePerBR calculated field. Select **Properties** from the shortcut menu. Click the **Format drop-down arrow** in the Property Sheet window and select **Currency**. Click the X to close the Property Sheet window.

h. Save the query.

i. Position the insertion point anywhere in the Field row in the PricePerBR column.

j. Click **Builder** in the Query Setup group on the Design tab.

The Expression Builder dialog box displays the renamed calculated field, PricePerBR, and a colon at the beginning of the expression without the equal sign (see Figure 3.11).

k. Click **OK** to close the Expression Builder dialog box.

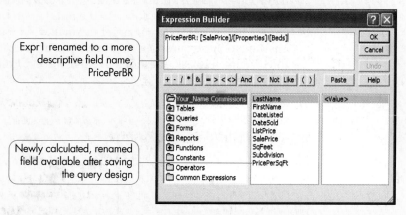

Figure 3.11 A Completed Expression

Refer to Figure 3.12 as you complete Step 4.

Step 4
Edit Expressions Using the Expression Builder

a. Click and drag to select the entire **PricePerBR** expression in the design grid. Right-click the selected expression and select **Copy**.

Be careful that you select and copy the entire expression. You need the new field name, all of the input fields, and the operands.

TROUBLESHOOTING: You cannot click into the next field in the design grid while the Expression Builder dialog box is open. Generally, any open dialog box in a Microsoft product is assigned top priority, and you must first deal with the dialog box before you can do anything anywhere else in the file. Close the Expression Builder dialog box if it is open.

b. Right-click in the field box of the first blank column and select **Paste**.

Your next task is to edit the copied formula so that it reflects the price per bathroom.

c. Position the insertion point anywhere in the copied formula and click **Builder**.

d. Move the I-beam pointer over any portion of the word *Beds* in the formula. Double-click.

The entire portion of the formula, [Properties]![Beds], should highlight.

e. Double-click the **Tables folder** in the left column, and then click the **Properties table** to open the folder and table, respectively.

Make sure that the middle column displays the field names of the available fields in the Properties table.

f. Double-click the **Baths field**.

The edited expression now displays **PricePerBR: [SalePrice] / [Properties]! [Baths]**.

g. Drag to select the **BR** in the *PricePerBR*. Replace BR with **Bath**.

The edited expression is **PricePerBath: [SalePrice] / [Properties]! [Baths]**.

h. Click **OK**. Click **Run**. Click **Save**, and then return to Design view.

i. Right-click the PricePerBath calculated field. Select **Properties** from the shortcut menu. Click the **Format drop-down arrow** in the Property Sheet window and select **Currency**. Click the X to close the Property Sheet window.

j. Run the query. Examine the calculated results in the Datasheet view.

Do your results make sense? Which field has larger numbers in it, the price per bedroom or the price per bathroom? Do most houses have more bedrooms or bathrooms? Which number would you expect to be larger? Remember, you are dividing in these calculations. As the number on the bottom of a fraction gets larger, does the answer get larger or smaller? You do not need to write the answers to these questions on paper. You do need to develop a critical eye and force yourself to ask questions like these every time you calculate a value.

k. Click **Save**.

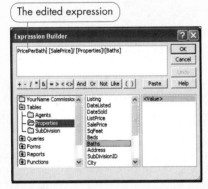

Figure 3.12 The Correctly Edited Formula

Step 5

Use Functions

Refer to Figures 3.13 and 3.14 as you complete Step 5.

a. Position the insertion point in the field row of the first blank column of the query in Design view.

You are going to use a financial function to calculate an estimated house payment for each of the sold properties. You make the following assumptions: 90% of the sale price financed, a 30-year period, monthly payments, and a fixed 6.5% annual interest rate. The first task is to calculate the amount financed. Assume a 10% down payment means that there will be 90% of the purchase price remaining to finance.

b. Right-click in the field box of the first blank column and select **Build** from the shortcut menu to display the Expression Builder dialog box. Type the formula = **[SalePrice] * .9** and click **OK**.

You will need to use this calculated value in subsequent calculations.

c. Run and save the query, return to Design view, double-click **Expr1**, and type **AmountFinanced**. Save the query.

d. Position the insertion point in the field row of the next available column. Launch the Expression Builder.

e. Double-click the **Functions folder** in the left column. Click **Built-In Functions folder**.

f. Look in the middle column. Click the **Financial** function category.

g. Look in the right column. Double-click the **Pmt function**.

The builder work area displays

Pmt(<<rate>>,<<nper>>,<<pv>>,<<fv>>,<<due>>)

We are assuming monthly payments at a 6½% interest rate over 30 years with no balloon payment at the end of the 30-year period and that the finance charges are calculated at the end of each period.

h. Double-click each formula argument to select it. Substitute the appropriate information:

Argument	Replacement Value
<<rate>>	0.065/12
<<nper>>	30*12
<<pv>>	(AmountFinanced)—Click the YourName Commissions folder to display a list of field names available to use in the query.
<<fv>>	0
<<due>>	0

TROUBLESHOOTING: If you do not see the AmountFinanced field in the list of available field names, you probably forgot to save the query after running it. Press Esc to close the Expression Builder dialog box. Click Save or press Ctrl+S to save the query design changes and re-work steps d through h.

i. Examine Figure 3.13 to make sure that you have entered the correct arguments. Click **OK**. Run the query.

The payments are all negative numbers. That is normal. You will edit the formula to return positive values.

j. Return to Design view. Click in the Payment calculated field and open the Expression Builder. Position the insertion point to the left of the left bracket, [, and type a hyphen, –. Double-click **Expr1** and type **Payment**. The expression will now be:

Payment: Pmt(0.065/12, 30*12, –[AmountFinanced], 0,0). Click **OK**.

k. Right-click the Payment calculated field. Select **Properties** from the shortcut menu. Click the **Format drop-down arrow** in the Property Sheet window and select **Currency**. Click the **X** to close the Property Sheet window.

l. Run and save the query.

The calculated field values now appear as positive, rather than negative, values.

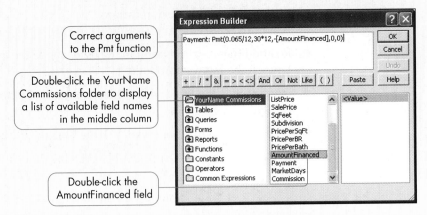

Correct arguments to the Pmt function

Double-click the YourName Commissions folder to display a list of available field names in the middle column

Double-click the AmountFinanced field

Figure 3.13 The Payment Function Arguments

Step 6
Work with Date Arithmetic

Refer to Figure 3.14 as you complete Step 6.

a. Position the insertion point in the field row of the first blank column of the query in Design view. Launch the Expression Builder.

You are going to calculate the number of days that each property was on the market prior to its sale.

b. Enter the formula = **[DateSold] – [DateListed]**. Run the query. Return to Design view and replace Expr1 with **MarketDays**. Save the query. Open the Property Sheet window and *format* the field as **Fixed** and set the *Decimal Places* to **0**.

Because Access stores all dates as serial numbers, the query returns the number of days on the market. The first property was placed on the market on June 23, and it sold on September 14. Look at your query result. This property was for sale all of July, all of August, and for parts of June and September. This is about three months. Does the query result reflect about three months?

c. Create a new field. Use the Expression Builder to multiply the SalePrice field by the commission rate of 7%. The formula in the Expression Builder is = **[SalePrice] * .07**. Run the query and replace Expr1 with **Commission**. Save the query.

The Commission calculated field calculates the total commission. The agent earns 7% of the sale price. The first agent's commission is 4760.

d. Right-click the Commission calculated field. Select **Properties** from the shortcut menu. Click the **Format drop-down arrow** in the Property Sheet window and select **Currency**. Click the **X** to close the Property Sheet window.

The values in the Commission calculated field now appear in Currency format. The first agent's commission displays as $4,760.00.

e. Click the **Office Button**, select **Manage**, and then select **Back Up Database**. Enter the file name **chap3_ho2_realestate_solution** (note *ho2* instead of *ho1-3*) and click **Save** on the Quick Access Toolbar.

You just created a backup of the database after completing the second hands-on exercise. The original database *chap3_ho1-3_realestate_solution* remains onscreen. If you ruin the original database as you complete the third hands-on exercise, you can use the backup file you just created.

f. Close the file and exit Access if you do not want to continue with the next exercise at this time.

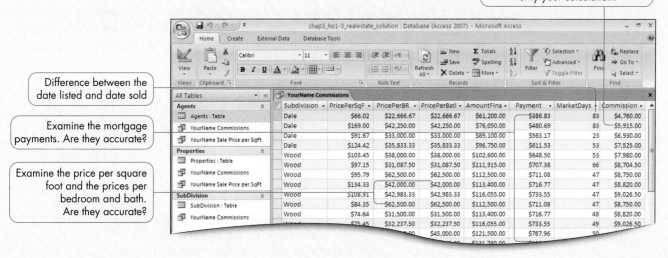

Figure 3.14 Verify, Verify, Verify!

Callouts in figure:

This property sold for $84,500. The commission rate is 7%. Does $5,915 reflect 7% of the sale price? Did you use a calculator or Excel to verify your calculation?

Difference between the date listed and date sold

Examine the mortgage payments. Are they accurate?

Examine the price per square foot and the prices per bedroom and bath. Are they accurate?

Table — YourName Commissions:

Subdivision	PricePerSqFt	PricePerBR	PricePerBath	AmountFina	Payment	MarketDays	Commission
Dale	$66.02	$22,666.67	$22,666.67	$61,200.00	$386.83	83	$4,760.00
Dale	$169.00	$42,250.00	$42,250.00	$76,050.00	$480.69	83	$5,915.00
Dale	$91.67	$33,000.00	$33,000.00	$89,100.00	$563.17	23	$6,930.00
Dale	$124.42	$35,833.33	$35,833.33	$96,750.00	$611.53	53	$7,525.00
Wood	$103.45	$38,000.00	$38,000.00	$102,600.00	$648.50	53	$7,980.00
Wood	$97.15	$31,087.50	$31,087.50	$111,915.00	$707.38	66	$8,704.50
Wood	$95.79	$62,500.00	$62,500.00	$112,500.00	$711.08	47	$8,750.00
Wood	$134.33	$42,000.00	$42,000.00	$113,400.00	$716.77	47	$8,820.00
Wood	$108.91	$42,983.33	$42,983.33	$116,055.00	$733.55	47	$9,026.50
Wood	$84.35	$62,500.00	$62,500.00	$112,500.00	$711.08	47	$8,750.00
Wood	$74.64	$31,500.00	$31,500.00	$113,400.00	$716.77	48	$8,820.00
Wood	$75.45	$32,237.50	$32,237.50	$116,055.00	$733.55	49	$9,026.50
				$45,000.00	$121,500.00	$767.96	50

Data Aggregates

Assume that you have an old-fashioned bank that still sends paper statements at the end of the month through the mail. Your statement arrives at your mailbox, and you open it. What is the first thing that you examine? If you are like most people, you first look at the balance for each account. The checking account information lists each transaction during the last month, whether it is a deposit or withdrawal, and the transaction method—ATM or paper check. These records provide vitally important data. But, the information contained in the account balances gives you a summarized snapshot of your financial health. You may then use the balance information to make decisions. "Yes, I can buy those concert tickets!" or "No, I better buy nothing but gas and groceries until payday." Your bank statement provides you with summary information. Your account balances are data aggregates.

A ***data aggregate*** is a collection of many parts that come together from different sources and are considered a whole. Commonly employed aggregating calculations include sum, average, minimum, maximum, standard deviation, and variance. Access provides you with many methods of summarizing or aggregating data. Decision makers use the methods to help make sense of an array of choices.

In this section, you learn how to create and work with data aggregates. Specifically, you learn how to use the totals row and create a totals query.

A ***data aggregate*** is a collection of many parts that come together from different sources and are considered a whole.

Creating and Working with Data Aggregates

Aggregates may be used in a query, table, form, or report. Access provides two methods of adding aggregate functions to a query. A ***total row*** displays as the last row in the Datasheet view of a table or query and provides a variety of summary statistics. The first method enables you to add a total row from the Datasheet view. This method is quick and easy, works in the Datasheet view of a table, and has the additional advantage that it provides the total information without altering the object design. You will recall that some databases are split into front and back end portions. Different users have different levels of privileges when interacting with the database. Adding a total row to a query or table can be accomplished by the lowest-privilege-level employee because it does not alter the structure of the object. The second method enables you to alter the query design and create a totals query. This method has the advantage of permitting you to group your data into relevant subcategories. For example, you can subtotal all houses sold in a specific subdivision or by each salesperson. After the summary statistics are assembled, you can employ them to make decisions. Who is the leading salesperson? In which neighborhood do houses sell most often or least often? This method requires that the user have rights to alter the design of a query. In a large, split database, a front-end user may not be afforded the rights to create or alter a query design. The query design is generally restricted to back-end users—the IT professionals only.

A ***total row*** displays as the last row in the Datasheet view of a table or query and provides a variety of summary statistics.

Data aggregation gives the decision maker a powerful and important tool. The ability to summarize and consolidate mountains of data into a distilled and digestible format makes the Access software a popular choice for managerial users. You already have learned that data aggregates may be created in queries. Access also permits aggregation in reports. In the first section, you learned that some users calculate all of their expressions in queries, whereas others perform needed calculations in forms and reports. The positioning of data aggregates also may be accomplished in a variety of ways. Some users aggregate and calculate summary statistics in queries, others in reports. You will need to learn both methods of aggregation because the practices and procedures governing database use differ among firms. Some firms allow users relatively free access to both the front and rear ends of the database; other firms grant extremely limited front-end rights only.

Create a Total Row in a Query or Table

Figure 3.15 illustrates adding a total row to the Datasheet view. Access can total or average numeric fields only. Begin by positioning your insertion point in a numeric or currency field of any record. Then click Totals in the Records group on the Home tab. The word Total is added below the new record row of the query. The highlighted numeric field shows a box with an arrow in the Total row. You may choose from several different aggregate functions by clicking the arrow. This method works in the same way if you want to add a total row to a numeric field in a table.

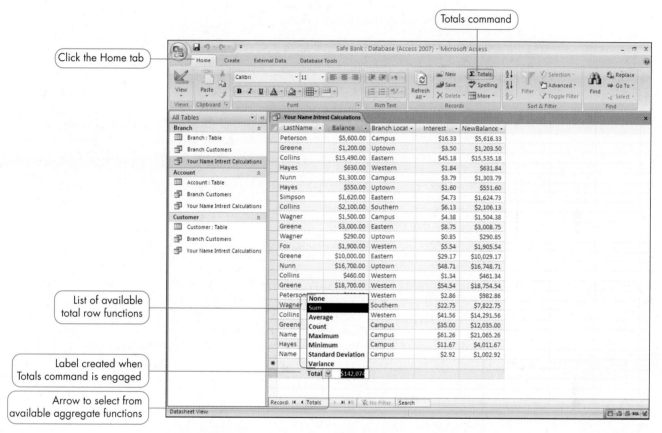

Figure 3.15 Adding a Total Row to a Query in Datasheet View

Group Totals in a Totals Query

The Total row, when added to a query, provides the decision maker with useful information. However, it does not provide any method of subtotaling the data. The total row is useful when a decision maker needs to know the totals or averages of all the data in a query or table. Sometimes knowing only the total is insufficient. The decision maker needs to know more detail. For example, knowing the total sales of houses during a period is good information. Knowing subtotals by salespeople would be more useful. Knowing subtotals by subdivision also would be useful information. Instead of using a total row, you can create a *totals query* to organize the results of a query into groups to perform aggregate calculations. It contains a minimum of two fields. The first field is the grouping field, such as the salesperson's last name. The second field is the numeric field that the decision maker wishes to summarize, such as the sale price of the homes. You may add other numeric fields to a totals query to provide additional information. The totals query in Access helps you provide a more detailed snapshot of the data.

A *totals query* organizes query results into groups by including a grouping field and a numeric field for aggregate calculations.

The SafeBank database that you created in Chapter 2 has five branch locations. If you need to know the total deposits by location, you would create a totals query. The two fields necessary would be the Location field in the Branch table and the Account

$\Bigg($ ... a totals query can only include the field or fields that you want to total and the grouping field. $\Bigg)$

Balance field in the Accounts table. After you create and run the query, you may add parameters to limit the totals query to a specific data subset. The process of adding criteria in a totals query is identical to any other query. Remember that a totals query can include only the field or fields that you want to total and the grouping field. No additional descriptive fields are allowed in the totals query. If you need to see the salesperson's last name, the sale price of the house, *and* the salesperson's first name, you would need to create two queries. The first query would be the totals query summarizing the sales data by last name. Then you would need to create a second query based on the totals query and add the additional descriptive field (the first name) to the new query. Figure 3.16 shows the setup for a totals query.

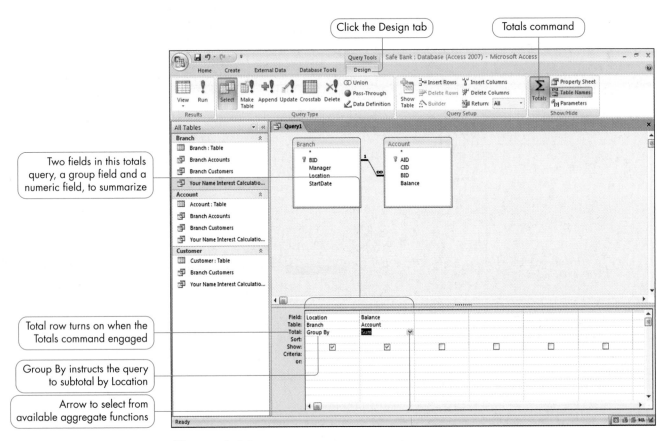

Figure 3.16 Constructing a Totals Query

Hands-On Exercises

3 | Data Aggregates

Skills covered: 1. Add a Total Row **2.** Create a Totals Query Based on a Select Query **3.** Add Fields to the Design Grid **4.** Add Grouping Options and Specify Summary Statistics

---

Step 1	Refer to Figure 3.17 as you complete Step 1.
Add a Total Row	

Refer to Figure 3.17 as you complete Step 1.

a. Open the *chap3_ho1-3_realestate_solution* file if necessary, click **Options** on the Security Warning toolbar, click the **Enable this content option** in the Microsoft Office Security Options dialog box, and click **OK**.

TROUBLESHOOTING: If you create unrecoverable errors while completing this hands-on exercise, you can delete the *chap3_ho1-3_realestate_solution* file, copy the *chap3_ho2_realestate_solution* backup database you created at the end of the second hands-on exercise, and open the copy of the backup database to start the third hands-on exercise again.

b. Open the **YourName Commissions query** in the Datasheet view.

c. Click the **Home tab** and click **Totals** in the Records group.

Look at the last row of the query. The Totals command is a toggle: Click it once to display the Total row. Click it again to hide the Total row. You need the Total row turned on to work the next steps.

d. Click in the cell that intersects the **Total row** and the **SalePrice** column.

This is another place in Access that when selected, a drop-down list becomes available. Nothing indicates that the drop-down menu exists until the cell or control is active. You need to remember that this is one of those places in order to aggregate the data.

e. Click the **drop-down arrow** and select **Sum** to calculate the total of all the properties sold. Widen the SalePrice field if you can't see the entire total value.

The total value of the properties sold is $19,936,549.00.

f. Scroll right, locate the **Subdivision field**, and click in the Total row to activate the drop-down list.

The choices from the total list are different. You may have the summary statistics set to None or Count. Subdivision is a character field. Access recognizes that it cannot add or average words and automatically limits your options to only tasks that Access is able to do with words.

g. Select **Count** from the drop-down list in the Total row for the Subdivision field.

h. Click in the **Total row** in the **PricePerSqFt** field. Click the **drop-down arrow** and select **Average**.

i. Click in any record of any field. Close the query.

A dialog box opens that asks if you wish to save the changes to the *layout* of the YourName Commissions query. It does NOT ask if you wish to save the changes made to the design. Toggling a Total row on and off is a layout (cosmetic) change only and does not affect the architectural structure of the query or table design.

j. Click **Yes**. The query saves the layout changes and closes.

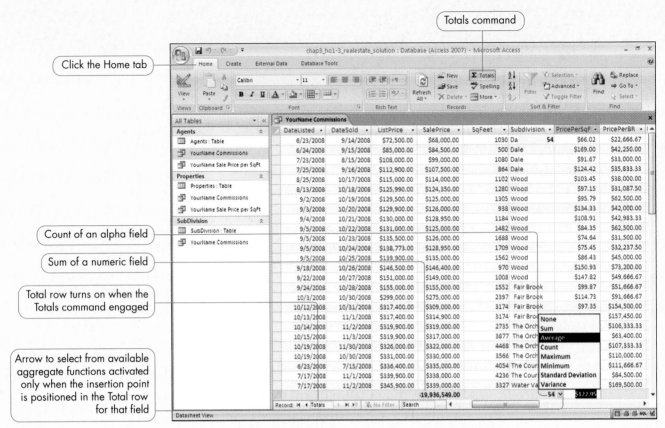

Callout labels (left to right / top to bottom):
- Totals command
- Click the Home tab
- Count of an alpha field
- Sum of a numeric field
- Total row turns on when the Totals command engaged
- Arrow to select from available aggregate functions activated only when the insertion point is positioned in the Total row for that field

Figure 3.17 Add a Total Row to the Query Datasheet View

Step 2
Create a Totals Query Based on a Select Query

Refer to Figure 3.18 as you complete Step 2.

a. Click the **Create tab** and click **Query Design** in the Other group.

The Show Table dialog box opens. You could source this query on the tables. However, because you already have made many useful calculations in the Commissions query, it will save you time to source the Totals query on the Commissions query.

b. Click the **Queries tab** in the Show Table dialog box.

c. Select the **YourName Commissions query** and click **Add**.

d. Click **Close**.

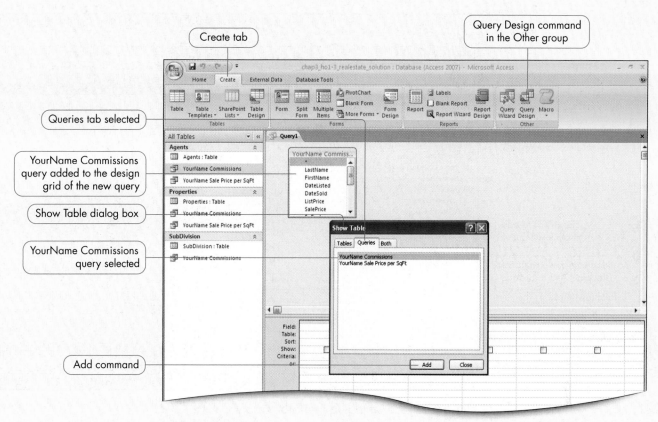

Figure 3.18 Create a Totals Query

Step 3

Add Fields to the Design Grid

Refer to Figure 3.19 as you complete Step 3.

a. Locate the **LastName** field in the YourName Commissions field list box.

You may add fields from the YourName Commissions query to the new query by clicking and dragging them to the design grid or by double-clicking.

b. Double-click the **LastName** field to add it to the grid.

You will create summary statistics based on each salesperson's activities. The LastName field is the grouping field in this totals query.

TROUBLESHOOTING: If you attempt to double-click a field name and the computer "beeps" at you, you probably forgot to close the Show Table dialog box.

c. Double-click the **SalePrice** field to add it to the grid.

d. Scroll down in the list of available fields box and double-click **MarketDays** to add it to the new query.

e. Add the **Commission** field to the new query.

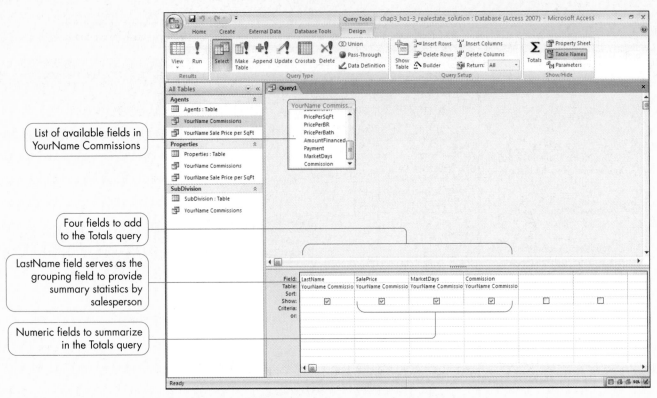

Figure 3.19 Setting Up the Totals Query

Labels pointing to the figure:
- List of available fields in YourName Commissions
- Four fields to add to the Totals query
- LastName field serves as the grouping field to provide summary statistics by salesperson
- Numeric fields to summarize in the Totals query

Step 4
Add Grouping Options and Specify Summary Statistics

Refer to Figures 3.20 and 3.21 as you complete Step 4.

a. Click **Totals** in the Show/Hide group on the Design tab.

Look at the lower part of the design grid. The Totals command toggles a new row between the Table and Sort rows of the design grid. When the Totals command is activated, all fields are set to Group by. You only want one Group by field, the LastName field.

b. Click in the **Total row** for the **SalePrice** field. Click the **drop-down arrow** and select **Sum** from the list.

Here is another of those hidden drop-down lists. As you gain experience, you will learn where to look for them. For now, simply memorize that one will show up in the Total row.

c. Click in the **Total row** of the **MarketDays** field. Click the **drop-down arrow** and select **Avg**.

d. Click the **Total row** in the **Commission** field and select **Sum**.

e. Run the query. Return to Design view and set the properties of the SalePrice and Commission fields as **Currency**. Set the Format property of the MarketDays field to **Fixed**. Set the Decimal Places property to **0**.

f. Verify results of the calculated summaries. Save the query as **YourName Commission Summary**.

g. Close the *chap3_ho1-3_realestate_solution* file.

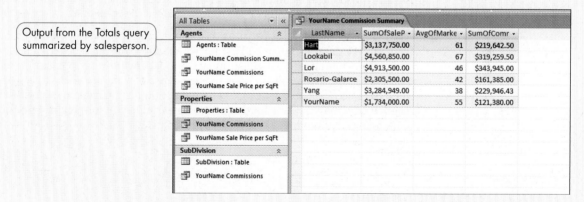

Totals command located in the
Show/Hide group on the Design tab

Specify the first field in the
query as the grouping field.
Results will be summarized
by salesperson's last name

Total row toggles on when the
Totals command is selected

Summary statistics will be
calculated on three different
numeric fields. Both Sums and
Averages will be produced.

Figure 3.20 Specify Grouping Field and Summary Statistics

Output from the Totals query
summarized by salesperson.

LastName	SumOfSaleP	AvgOfMarke	SumOfComr
Hart	$3,137,750.00	61	$219,642.50
Lookabil	$4,560,850.00	67	$319,259.50
Lor	$4,913,500.00	46	$343,945.00
Rosario-Galarce	$2,305,500.00	42	$161,385.00
Yang	$3,284,949.00	38	$229,946.43
YourName	$1,734,000.00	55	$121,380.00

Figure 3.21 Specify Grouping Field and Summary Statistics

Summary

1. **Understand the order of precedence.** Decision makers are overwhelmed with data. They need information that they may employ to make sound decisions. Access provides many powerful tools that expedite the process of converting raw data into useful information. The Access tools employ the standard rules of order in arithmetic calculations: parentheses, exponents, multiplication and division, and addition and subtraction.

2. **Create a calculated field in a query.** Access, like all computer software, must be instructed in what calculations to perform and how to do the work. The formal name for those instructions is an expression. You must "speak the language" of the software in order to accurately communicate with the computer. Syntax refers to the set of rules by which the words and symbols of an expression are correctly combined. You learned that you can write a syntactically correct expression that contains logic flaws. You also developed the practice of critically examining and verifying your data to avoid costly errors.

3. **Create expressions with the Expression Builder.** The chapter introduced powerful tools that facilitate converting data to information. The Expression Builder makes the logistics of formula creation easier. It also offers easy access to a number of pre-built formulae, called functions, which perform complex calculations relatively painlessly. Using Access functions requires the user to know the function's name and arguments. The arguments appear in the Expression Builder enclosed in symbols (<<XXX>>) as a visual cue that you need to substitute a constant or a field name. Access can use the output of earlier calculations as input to subsequent calculations, but the expression must be renamed and the query saved prior to subsequent use.

4. **Create and edit Access functions.** You learned that Access, like Excel, has a variety of functions that can perform complex tasks in an automated fashion. You employ the functions by identifying the function by name (IIf, Avg, Sum, Pmt), and then entering the arguments in the appropriate order. Arguments are the input data Access uses to create the output. They may be field names or values.

5. **Perform date arithmetic.** Dates in Access are stored as serial numbers based on the number of days that have elapsed from an arbitrarily chosen base date, December 31, 1899. Access provides several functions to facilitate date handling. Additionally, you can simply subtract one date from another or add a number to a date to create a different date.

6. **Create and work with data aggregates.** Data aggregates provide powerful means to summarize and analyze data. You may add a Total row to the Datasheet view of a table or query and select from a number of useful summary options including count, sum, average, minimum, and maximum. These calculations require only a few mouse clicks to create. Additionally, they have no effect on the design of the table or query. When a more robust summary is needed, you may create a Totals query. This permits you to establish grouping levels for the data to make summaries more meaningful.

Key Terms

Multiple Choice

1. Which statement most accurately describes the differences between a table field and a calculated field?

   (a) All data entries to a table field are permanently stored, but calculated field data do not exist in the database. They appear in the datasheet, form, or report but are not a part of the dataset.

   (b) A calculated field is permanently stored in the dataset when the query, table, form, or report design is saved. Only the properties governing the data are saved when a table is saved.

   (c) Query data and Table data are dynamic, and no data are permanently stored.

   (d) None of the above.

2. Which of the following correctly identify the rules of order of arithmetic operations?

   (a) Exponentiation, Parenthesis, Addition, Subtraction, Multiplication, Division

   (b) Parenthesis, Exponentiation, Addition, Subtraction, Multiplication, Division

   (c) Parenthesis, Exponentiation, Multiplication, Division, Addition, Subtraction

   (d) Addition, Subtraction, Multiplication, Division, Exponentiation, Parenthesis

3. Which set of parentheses is unnecessary in the following expression?

   = (3 * 5) + (7 / 2) − (6^2) * (36 *2)

   (a) (3 * 5)

   (b) (7 / 2)

   (c) (6^2)

   (d) (36 *2)

   (e) All of the above

4. Which statement about saving a query is true?

   (a) Data are extracted from the source table and saved in query form.

   (b) Data are duplicated from the source table and saved in query form.

   (c) Data created using expressions are saved when the query is saved, but the source data stays in the original table.

   (d) No data are saved in a query.

5. The Expression Builder icon may be found in the:

   (a) Manage group on the Databases Tools tab

   (b) Query Setup group on the Design tab

   (c) Database Management group on the Design tab

   (d) Design group on the Query Setup tab

6. Your database contains a Price field stored in the Products table and a Quantity field stored in the Orders table. You have created a query but forgot to add the Price field in the design. Now, you need to use the price field to calculate the total for the order. The correct syntax is:

   (a) OrderTotal:(Quantity)*(Products)!(Price)

   (b) OrderTotal=(Quantity)*(Products)!(Price)

   (c) OrderTotal:[Quantity]*[Products]![Price]

   (d) OrderTotal=[Quantity]*[Products]![Price]

7. Which of the following is true about a select query?

   (a) It may reference fields from more than one table or query.

   (b) It may reference fields from a table, but not a query.

   (c) It may reference fields from either a table or a query but not both.

   (d) It may reference fields from a form.

8. You correctly calculated a value for the OrderAmount using an expression. Now, you need to use the newly calculated value in another expression calculating sales tax. The most efficient method is to:

   (a) Run and save the query to make OrderAmount available as input to subsequent expressions.

   (b) Create a new query based on the query containing the calculated Order amount, and then calculate the sales tax in the new query.

   (c) Close the Access file, saving the changes when asked; reopen the file and reopen the query; calculate the sales tax.

   (d) Create a backup of the database, open the backup and the query, then calculate the sales tax.

9. If state law requires that wait staff be over age 21 to serve alcohol and you have a database that stores each employee's birthdate in the Employee table, which of the following is the proper syntax to identify the employees' year of birth.

   (a) Age:DatePart("yyyy",[Employee]![BirthDate])

   (b) Age=DatePart("yyyy",[Employee]![BirthDate])

   (c) Age:DatePart("yyyy",[BirthDate]![Employee])

   (d) Age=DatePart("yyyy",[BirthDate]![Employee])

10. You want to add a Totals row in a query Datasheet view. Where will you find the Totals command?

  (a) In the Data group on the Home tab

  (b) In the Home group on the Data tab

  (c) In the Records group on the Home tab

  (d) In the Home group on the Records tab

11. Which statement about a Totals query is true?

  (a) A Totals query may contain only one descriptive field but several aggregating fields.

  (b) A Totals query may contain several descriptive fields but only one aggregating field.

  (c) A Totals query has a limit of only two fields, one descriptive field, and one aggregating field.

  (d) A Totals query can aggregate data, but to find a grand total, you must create a new query based on the Totals query and turn on the Total row in the new query.

12. You built a query expression and clicked Run. A parameter dialog box pops up on your screen. Which of the following actions is the most appropriate if you expected results to display and do not want to enter an individual value?

  (a) Click OK to make the parameter box go away.

  (b) Read the field name specified in the parameter box and look for that spelling in the calculated expression.

  (c) Type numbers in the parameter box and click OK.

  (d) Close the query without saving changes. Re-open it and try running the query again.

13. A query contains fields for StudentName and Address. You have created and run a query and are in Datasheet view examining the output. You notice a spelling error on one of the student's names. You correct the error in the query Datasheet view.

  (a) The name is correctly spelled in this query but will be misspelled in the table and all other queries based on the table.

  (b) The name is correctly spelled in the table and in all queries based on the table.

  (c) The name is correctly spelled in this query and any other queries, but will remain misspelled in the table.

  (d) You cannot edit data in a query.

14. Which of the following is not available as an aggregate function within a query?

  (a) Sum

  (b) Min

  (c) Division

  (d) Avg

15. Which of the following is not true about the rows in the query design grid?

  (a) The Total row can contain different functions for different fields.

  (b) The Total row can source fields stored in different tables.

  (c) The Total row is located between the Table and Sort rows.

  (d) The Total row can be applied only to numeric fields.

Practice Exercises

1 Comfort Insurance—Salaries and Bonuses

The Comfort Insurance Agency is a midsized company with offices located across the country. Each employee receives a performance review annually. The review determines employee eligibility for salary increases and the annual performance bonus. The employee data are stored in an Access database, which is used by the human resource department to monitor and maintain employee records. Your task is to calculate the salary increase for each employee and his or her performance bonuses (if any). You are the human resource department manager. If you correctly calculate the employee salaries and bonuses, you will receive a bonus. Work carefully and check the accuracy of the calculations. This project follows the same set of skills as used in Hands-On Exercises 1 and 2 in this chapter. The instructions are less detailed to give you a chance to practice your skills. If you have problems, reread the detailed directions presented in the chapter. Compare your results to Figure 3.22.

a. Copy the partially completed file *chap3_pe1_insurance* to your production folder. Rename it **chap3_pe1_insurance_solution**, open the file, and enable security.

b. Click the **Database Tools tab**, and then click **Relationships** in the Show/Hide group. Examine the table structure, relationships, and fields. Once you are familiar with the database, close the Relationships window.

c. Click the **Create tab** and click **Query Wizard** in the Other group. Select **Simple Query Wizard** in the first screen of the dialog box. Click **OK**.

d. From the **Employees table** select the **LastName**, **FirstName**, **Performance**, and **Salary** fields to add fields to the query. From the **Titles table** select the **2008Increase** field. Click **Next**. This needs to be a detail query. Name the query **YourName Raises and Bonuses**. Click **Finish**.

e. Right-click the query window title bar or the Query tab and select **Design View** from the shortcut menu to switch to Design view.

f. Position the insertion point in the first blank column in the Field row. Type **NewSalary:[Salary]*[2008Increase]+[Salary]** to create an expression.

g. Click **Run** in the Results group on the Design tab to run the query. (If you receive the Enter Parameter Value dialog box, check your expression carefully for typos.) Look at the output in the Datasheet view. Verify that your answers are correct. If they are, use the Property Sheet window to format the **NewSalary** field as **Currency** and save the query.

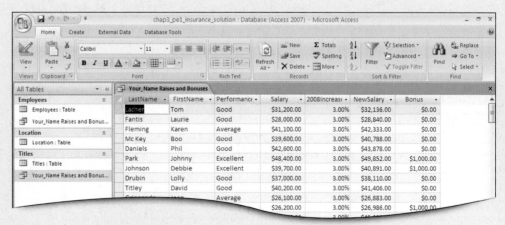

Figure 3.22 Raises and Bonuses

...continued on Next Page

h. Return to Design view. Position the insertion point in the first blank column in the Field row. Click **Builder** in the Query Setup group on the Design tab. In the **left column**, open the folder for **functions**. Open the **Built-In Functions** folder. Scroll the **right column** to locate the **IIf function**. Double-click to insert the function.

i. Double-click **<<expr>>** and replace it with **[Performance] = "Excellent"**; double-click **<<truepart>>** and replace it with **1000**; double-click **<<falsepart>>** and replace it with **0**. (That is zero, not the letter O.)

j. Run the query. Return to the Design view and double-click **Expr1** in the field row of the last column. Type **Bonus**. Run and save the query. Close the database.

2 Comfort Insurance—Vacation

The Comfort Insurance Agency is a midsized company with offices located across the country. The human resource office is located in the home office in Miami. Each year, each employee receives a performance review. The review determines employee eligibility for salary increases and the annual performance bonus. The employee data are stored in an Access database. This database is used by the human resource department to monitor and maintain employee records. Your task is to calculate the salary increase for each employee, the number of years they have worked for the firm, and the number of vacation days they are eligible to receive. You are the human resource department manager. If you correctly calculate the employee salaries and vacations, you will receive a bonus. Work carefully and check the accuracy of the calculations. This project follows the same set of skills as used in Hands-On Exercises 1 and 2 in this chapter. The instructions are less detailed to give you a chance to practice your skills. If you have problems, feel free to reread the detailed directions presented in the chapter. Compare your results to Figure 3.23.

a. Copy the partially completed file *chap3_pe2_insurance.accdb* to your production folder. Rename it **chap3_pe2_insurance_solution.accdb**, open the copied file, and enable the security content.

b. Click the **Database Tools tab**, and then click **Relationships** in the Show/Hide group. Examine the table structure, relationships, and fields. Once you are familiar with the database, close the Relationships window.

c. Create a new query using the Query Wizard. Click the **Create tab** and click **Query Wizard** in the Other group. Select **Simple Query Wizard** in the first screen of the dialog box. Click **OK**.

d. Add fields to the query. From the **Employees table** select the **LastName, FirstName, HireDate**, and **Salary** fields. From the **Titles table**, select the **2008Increase** field. Click **Next**. This needs to be a detail query. Name the query **Your_Name Raises and Tenure**. Click **Finish**.

e. Switch to Design view by right-clicking the query window tab and selecting **Design View** from the shortcut menu.

f. Position the insertion point in the first blank column in the Field row. Create an expression by typing **2008Raise:[Salary]*[2008Increase]**. Format it as **Currency**.

...continued on Next Page

g. Click **Run** in the Results group on the Design tab. Look at the output in the Datasheet view. Verify that your answers are correct. If they are, save the query.

h. Return to Design view. Position the insertion point in the first blank column in the Field row. Click **Builder** in the Query Setup group on the Design tab. In the left column, open the folder for functions. Open the Built-In Functions folder. Scroll the right column to locate the **DatePart** function. Double-click to insert the function to the work area.

i. Double-click <<*interval*>> in the function in the work area of the Expression Builder dialog box. Type **"yyyy"**. Double-click <<*date*>> and replace it with **[HireDate]**. Delete the rest of the arguments and commas but do not delete the closing parenthesis. Your expression should look like this:

DatePart ("yyyy", [HireDate])

j. Run and verify the output. Return to Design view and replace Expr1 in the field row of the last column with **YearHired**. Save the query.

k. Use the Expression Builder or type to create an expression that measures how long each employee has worked. Assume that this year is 2008. The finished expression will look like this:

YearsWorked:2008 – [YearHire]

l. Run and save the query. Sort the output in descending order by the YearsWorked field. Close the database.

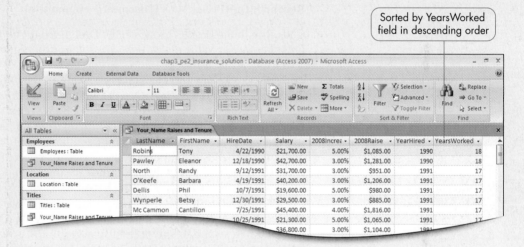

Figure 3.23   Raises and Tenure

3 Northwind Traders

Northwind Traders is a small, international, specialty food company. It sells products in eight different divisions: beverages, confections (candy), condiments, dairy products, grains and cereals, meat and poultry, produce, and seafood. The company offers discounts to some customers. Different customers receive differing discount amounts. The firm purchases merchandise from a variety of suppliers. All of the order and inventory information is stored in the company's database. This database is used by the marketing department to monitor and maintain sales records. You are the marketing manager. Your task is to determine the revenue from each order and to summarize the revenue figures by product category. This project follows the same set of skills as used in Hands-On Exercises 2 and 3 in this chapter. The instructions are less detailed to give you a chance to practice your skills. If you have problems, feel free to reread the detailed directions presented in the chapter. Compare your results to Figure 3.24.

...continued on Next Page

a. Copy the partially completed file *chap3_pe3_traders.accdb* to your production folder. Rename it **chap3_pe3_traders_solution.accdb**, open the file, and enable the content.

b. Click the **Database Tools tab**, and then click **Relationships** in the Show/Hide group. Examine the table structure, relationships, and fields. After you are familiar with the database, close the Relationships window.

c. Click the **Create tab** and click **Query Wizard** in the Other group. Select **Simple Query Wizard** in the first screen of the dialog box. Click **OK**.

d. From the **Order Details table**, select the **Quantity** and **Discount** fields to add the fields to the query. From the **Products table**, select the **UnitPrice** and **ProductCost** fields. From the **Categories table**, select the **CategoryName** Field. Click **Next**. This needs to be a detail query. Name the query **Your_Name Revenue**. Click **Finish**.

The UnitPrice field contains data on what customers pay to purchase the products. The ProductCost field contains data on what the company pays suppliers to purchase the products.

e. Right-click the query window tab and select **Design View** from the shortcut menu to switch to Design view.

f. Position the insertion point in the first blank column in the Field row. Create an expression that calculates revenue. Some customers receive discounts on their orders so you need to calculate the discounted price in the expression that calculates revenue.

Revenue:[UnitPrice] * (1 – [Discount]) * [Quantity]

g. Click **Run** in the Results group on the Design tab to run the query. (If you receive the Enter Parameter Value dialog box, check your expression carefully for typos.) Look at the output in the Datasheet view. Verify that your answers are correct.

h. Click the **Create tab** and click **Query Design** in the Other group. Click the **Queries Tab** in the Show Table dialog box. Double-click the **Your_Name Revenue** query to add it to the design grid. Click **Close** in the Show Table dialog box.

i. Position the insertion point in the first blank column in the Field row. Double-click the **CategoryName** field in the list of available fields in the Your_Name Revenue query. Click the insertion point in the next available column in the field row. Double-click **Revenue** to add it to the grid. Click the insertion point in the next available column in the field row. Double-click **Discount** to add it to the grid.

j. Click **Totals** in the Show/Hide group on the Design tab. The Total row will turn on in the design grid. This query should be grouped by the **CategoryName** field. Click in the Total row of the **Revenue** field to activate the drop down list and select **Sum**. Select **Avg** for the summary statistic in the **Discount** column.

k. Right-click the **Revenue** field name and select **Properties**. Click the box in the Property Sheet window to the right of **Format**. Select **Currency** from the drop down list to format the Revenue field as currency. With the Property Sheet Window still open, click the **Discount** field in the design grid. Click the box in the Property Sheet window to the right of **Format**. Select **Percent** from the drop-down list. Close the Property Sheet window by clicking the **X**.

l. Run the query. Verify the results. Name this query **Your_Name Revenue by Category**.

m. Close the database.

...continued on Next Page

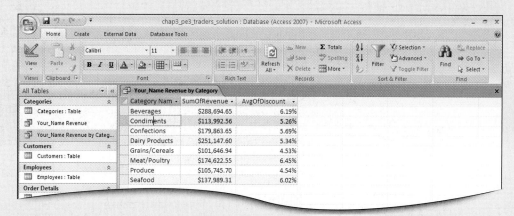

Figure 3.24 Revenue by Category

4 Member Rewards

The Prestige Hotel chain caters to upscale business travelers and provides state-of-the-art conference, meeting, and reception facilities. It prides itself on its international, four-star cuisines. Last year the chain began a member rewards club to help the marketing department track the purchasing patterns of its most loyal customers. All of the hotel transactions are stored in the database. Your task is to determine the revenue from each order and to summarize the revenue figures by location. This project follows the same set of skills as used in Hands-On Exercises 2 and 3 in this chapter. The instructions are less detailed to give you a chance to practice your skills. If you have problems, feel free to reread the detailed directions presented in the chapter. Compare your results to Figure 3.25.

a. Copy the partially completed file *chap3_pe4_memrewards.accdb* to your production folder. Rename it **chap3_pe4_memrewards_solution.accdb**, open the file, and enable the security content.

b. Click the **Database Tools tab**, and then click **Relationships** in the Show/Hide group. Examine the table structure, relationships, and fields. After you are familiar with the database, close the Relationships window.

c. Create a new query using the Query Wizard. Click the **Create tab** and click **Query Wizard** in the Other group. Select **Simple Query Wizard** in the first screen of the dialog box. Click **OK**.

d. Add fields to the query. From the **Location table**, select the **City**. From the **Orders table**, select the **NoInParty** Field. From the **Service table**, select the **PerPersonCharge** field. Click **Next**. This needs to be a detail query. Name the query **Your_Name Revenue**. Click **Finish**.

e. Right-click the query window tab and select **Design View** from the shortcut menu to Switch to Design view. Right-click **PerPersonCharge** and select **Properties** from the shortcut menu. Click the box to the right of **Format** in the Property Sheet. Select **Currency** from the drop-down. Click **X** to close the Property Sheet window.

f. Position the insertion point in the first blank column in the Field row. Create an expression that calculates revenue and format the field as **Currency**.

Revenue:[NoInParty] * [PerPersonCharge]

...continued on Next Page

g. Click **Run** in the Results group on the Design tab. (If you receive the parameter dialog box, check your expression carefully for typos.) Look at the output in the Datasheet view. Verify that your answers are correct. If they are, return to Design view and format the **PerPersonCharge** and **Revenue** fields as **Currency** by setting the appropriate properties. Save and close the query.

h. Click the **Create tab** and click **Query Design** in the Other group. Click the **Queries tab** in the Show Table dialog box. Double-click the **Your_Name Revenue** query to add it to the design grid. Click **Close** in the Show Table dialog box.

i. Position the insertion point in the first blank column in the Field row. Double-click the **City** field in the list of available fields in the Your_Name Revenue query. Click the insertion point in the next available column in the field row. Double-click **Revenue** to add it to the grid.

j. Click **Totals** in the Show/Hide group on the Design tab. The Total row will turn on in the design grid. This query should be grouped by the **City** field. Click in the Total row of the **Revenue** field to activate the drop-down list and select **Sum**.

k. Right-click **Revenue** and select **Properties** from the shortcut menu. Click the box to the right of **Format** in the Property Sheet. From the drop down menu select **Currency**. Click **X** to close the Property Sheet window. Run the query.

l. Click the **Home tab** in Datasheet view. Click **Totals** in the Records group to turn on the Totals row. Click the **SumOfRevenue** column in the Total row. Click the drop-down arrow and select **Sum**.

m. Save this query as **Your_Name Revenue by City**.

n. Run and save the query. Close the database.

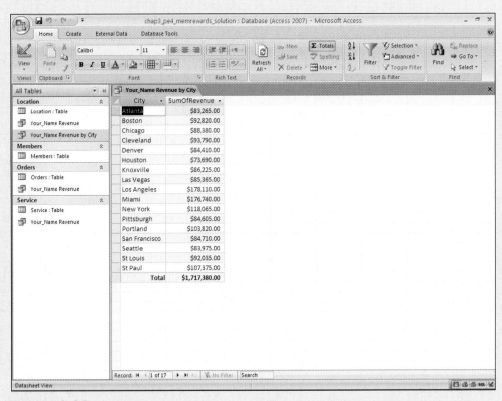

Figure 3.25 Revenue by City

Northwind Traders is a small, international, specialty food company. It sells products in eight different divisions: beverages, confections (candy), condiments, dairy products, grains and cereals, meat and poultry, produce, and seafood. Although most of its customers are restaurants and gourmet food shops, it has a few retail customers, too. The company offers discounts to some customers. Different customers receive differing discount amounts. The firm purchases merchandise from a variety of suppliers. All of the order information is stored in the company's database. This database is used by the finance department to monitor and maintain sales records. You are the finance manager. Your task is to determine the revenue and profit from each order and to summarize the revenue, profit, and discount figures by salesperson. *Revenue* is the money the firm takes in. *Profit* is the difference between revenue and costs. The salespeople may offer discounts to customers to reward loyal purchasing or to appease an angry customer when a shipment is late. Occasionally the sales people discount so deeply that the company loses money on an order, that is, the costs exceed the revenue. It is important that your calculations are correct. If the firm's profitability figures do not accurately reflect the firm's financial health, the employee's paychecks (including yours) might be returned as insufficient funds. Compare your results to Figure 3.26.

a. Locate the file named *chap3_mid1_traders.accdb*, copy it to your working folder, and rename it **chap3_mid1_traders_solution.accdb**. Open the file and enable the content. Open the **Employee table**. Find and replace **Margaret Peacock**'s name with **your name**.

b. Create a detail query that you will use to calculate profits for each product ordered. You will need the **LastName** field from the **Employees table**. You will also need the fields for **Quantity**, **Discount**, **OrderDate**, **ShippedDate**, **UnitPrice**, and **ProductCost**. Save the query as **Your_Name Profit**.

c. In Design view, calculate **Revenue** and **Profit**. Because the discounts vary, some (not all) of the profit numbers will be negative. You must factor the discount into the price as you calculate revenue. If a product price is $100 and is sold with a 20% discount, the discounted price would be $80. Calculate **revenue** by multiplying the discounted price by the quantity sold. Calculate **total costs** by multiplying the product cost by quantity. Calculate **profit** by subtracting total cost from revenue. UnitPrice is the price for which the company sells merchandise. ProductCost is what the company pays to purchase the merchandise.

d. In the Datasheet view, add a Total row. Use it to calculate the **average discount** and the **sums** for **Revenue** and **Profit**.

e. Create a **Totals query** based on **Your_Name Profit**. Group by **LastName** and summarize the fields for **Discount (average)**, **Revenue**, and **Profit (sums)**.

f. Format the **Discount** field as a percentage and the **SumOfRevenue** and **SumOfProfit** fields as currency.

g. Add a Total row to the Datasheet view. Average the discount field and sum the **SumOfRevenue** and **SumOfProfit** fields.

h. Save the totals query as **Your_Name Profit by Employee**.

i. Capture a screenshot of the Your_Name Profit by Employee query. Have it open on your computer and press **PrintScrn**. Open Word and press **Ctrl+V** or click **Paste** in the Clipboard group. Save the Word document as **chap3_mid1_solution**. Print the Word document. Close the Word document and close the database.

...continued on Next Page

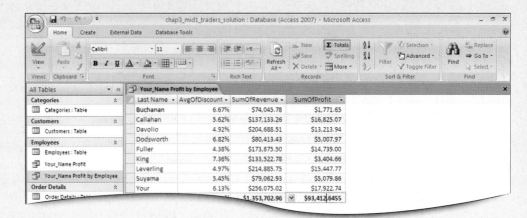

Figure 3.26 Profit by Employee

2 Calculating and Summarizing Bank Data in a Query

You are the manager of the loan department of the National Bank. Several customers have multiple loans with your institution. A single customer might have a mortgage loan, one or more car loans, and a home improvement loan. You need to monitor the total indebtedness of your customers to help them manage their debt load. Your task is to use the information stored in the database to calculate the loan payments for each loan and then to summarize the loans by customer. The PMT function requires five arguments. The first is the interest rate per period. The interest rates in the table are annual rates, so you will need to convert them to monthly rates in the function. The second argument is the number of periods (in years). Because the payments are monthly, you also need to convert the years for each loan to months in the function. The next argument is the PV, the present value of the loan—what the loan is worth today. It tells you how much each customer has borrowed. You generally supply zeros for the last two arguments, FV, and Type. FV shows the amount the borrower will owe after the last payment has been made—the future value of the monies borrowed. Generally, this is zero. The type argument tells Access whether the payment is made at the beginning or the end of the period (month). Most loans accept payments and charge interest on the unpaid balance throughout the period. Use zero as the argument for this function. See Table 3.2 for more information about the arguments to the PMT function. Compare your results to Figure 3.27.

a. Locate the file named *chap3_mid2_nationalbank.accdb*, copy it to your working folder, and rename it **chap3_mid2_nationalbank_solution.accdb**. Open the file and enable the content. Open the **Customers table**. Find and replace **Michelle Zacco**'s name with your name.

b. Create a detail query that you will use to calculate the payments for each loan. You will need the following fields: **LastName**, **Amount**, **InterestRate**, **Term**, and **Type**. Save the query as **Your_Name Payment**.

...continued on Next Page

c. In Design view, use the **Pmt** function to calculate the loan payment on each loan. Divide the annual interest rate by 12 and multiply the loan's term by 12 because every year has 12 months. Include a minus sign in front of the loan amount in the expression so the result returns a positive value. The last two arguments will be zero.

d. In the Datasheet view, add a Total row. Use it to calculate the **average** interest rate and the **sum** for the **payment**.

e. Create a Totals query based on Your_Name Loan Payment. **Group by LastName** and summarize the **sum** of the **Payment** field.

f. Format the **SumOfPayment** field as currency.

g. Add a total row to the Datasheet view that will sum the Payments. Save this query as **Your_Name Payment Summary**.

h. Capture a screenshot of the Payment Summary query. Have it open on your computer and press **PrintScrn**. Open Word and press **Ctrl+V** or click **Paste** in the Clipboard group. Save the Word document as **chap3_mid2_solution**. Print the Word document displaying the screenshot. Close the Word document and close the database.

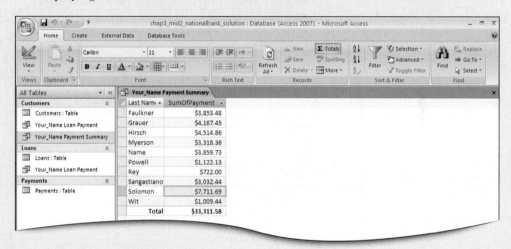

Figure 3.27 Payment Summary

3 Calculating and Summarizing Data in a Query, Working with Dates

You are the senior partner in a large, independent real estate firm that specializes in home sales. Although you still represent buyers and sellers in real estate transactions, you find that most of your time is spent supervising the agents who work for your firm. This fact distresses you because you like helping people buy and sell homes. Your firm has a database containing all of the information on the properties your firm has listed. You believe that by using the data in the database more effectively, you can spend less time supervising the other agents and spend more time doing the part of your job that you like doing the best. Your task is to determine the length of time each sold property was on the market prior to sale. Then calculate the commission from each property sale. Most real estate transactions involve two agents—one representing the seller (the listing agent) and the other the buyer (the selling agent). The two agents share the commission. Finally, you need to summarize the sales data by employee and calculate the average number of days each employee's sales were on the market prior to selling and the total commission earned by the employees. Compare your results to Figure 3.28.

a. Locate the file named *chap3_mid3_realestate.accdb*, copy it to your working folder, and rename it **chap3_mid3_realestate_solution.accdb**. Open the file and enable the content. Open the **Agents table**. Find and replace **Pa Lor**'s name with your name.

...continued on Next Page

b. Create a detail query that you will use to calculate the number of days each sold property has been on the market prior to sale. You will need the following fields: **LastName**, **DateListed**, **DateSold**, **SalePrice**, **SellingAgent**, **ListingAgent**, and **Subdivision**. Save the query as **Your_Name Sales Report**.

c. In Design view, build an expression, **DaysOnMarket**, to calculate the number of days each sold property has been on the market prior to sale. Subtract the **DateListed** field from the **DateSold** field. [Hint: The answers will *never* be negative numbers!]

d. Calculate the **Commission** for the selling and listing agents. Multiply the **SalePrice** by the Commission rate of **3.5%**. Name the newly created fields **SellComm** and **ListComm**. Both fields contain the same expression. They need to be named differently so that the proper agent—the listing agent or the selling agent—gets paid.

e. After you are sure that your calculations are correct, save the query. In Datasheet view, add a total row. Use it to calculate the average number of days on the market and the sums for the **SalePrice**, **SellComm**, and **ListComm** fields. Format the **SellComm**, **ListComm**, and **SalePrice** fields as **Currency**.

f. Create a Totals query based on **Your_Name Sales Report**. Group by **LastName** and summarize the **DaysOnMarket** field with an **average**. Summarize the **SalePrice**, **SellComm**, and **ListComm** fields as **sums**.

g. Add a Total row to the Datasheet view that will sum the price and commission fields and average the number of days on the market. Save this query as **Your_Name Sales Summary**.

h. Format the **AveOfDaysOnMkt** field so that it displays only two decimal places. Format the remaining numeric fields as Currency.

i. Capture a screenshot of the Sales Summary query. Have it open on your computer and press **PrintScrn**. Open Word and press **Ctrl+V** or click **Paste** in the Clipboard group. Save the Word document as **chap3_mid3_solution**. Print the Word document. Close the Word document and close the database.

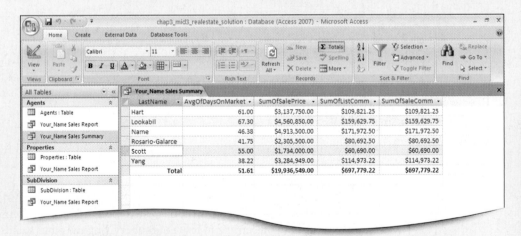

Figure 3.28 Sales Summary

Capstone Exercise

Your boss expressed a concern about shipping delays. She believes that customers are not receiving the products they order in a timely fashion. Because your firm's reputation as a provider of high-quality customer service is at risk, she asks that you investigate the sales and shipping records for the last six months and report what you have discovered. In addition, the sales staff is permitted to discount the prices for some customers. Your boss is worried that the discounting erodes profits. She wants you to identify the sales staff who discount the most deeply.

Database File Setup

You need to copy an original database file, rename the copied file, and then open the copied database to complete this capstone exercise. After you open the copied database, you will replace an existing employee's name with your name.

a. Locate the file named *chap3_cap_traders.accdb* and copy it to your production folder.
b. Rename the copied file as **chap3_cap_traders_solution.accdb**.
c. Open the *chap3_cap_traders_solution.accdb* file and enable the content.
d. Open the **Employees table**.
e. Find and replace *Margaret Peacock's* name with your name.

Sales Report Query

You need to create a detail query to calculate the number of days between the date an order was placed and the date the order was shipped for each order. You also need the query to determine the amount of a discount, calculate the revenue, calculate the total cost, and calculate the profit. Furthermore, the query should calculate the employee's commission on the sale.

a. Set a criterion that limits the query to only the most recent six months' worth of shipped orders.
b. Sort the records in the datasheet view by order date to determine the most recent order, if you want.
c. Include the following fields: **LastName** (from the Employee Table), **OrderDate**, **ShippedDate**, **UnitPrice**, **ProductCost**, **Quantity**, and **Discount**.
d. Save the query as **Your_Name Sales Report**.
e. In Design view, build an expression, DaysToShip, to calculate the number of days taken to fill each order. Subtract the OrderDate field from the ShippedDate field. (Hint: The answers will never be negative numbers.)
f. Calculate the profit for each product ordered. Multiply the UnitPrice by the Discount to

determine the amount of the discount. Then subtract the Discount amount from the UnitPrice and multiply the result by Quantity to calculate Revenue. Calculate TotalCost for each item ordered by multiplying ProductCost by Quantity. Subtract TotalCost from Revenue to calculate Profit.
g. Calculate the Commission for each profitable order. When the profit on the ordered item is positive, calculate Commission by multiplying profit by the commission rate of 3.5%. If the profit on the ordered item is negative (a loss), the salesperson receives no commission. Name the newly created field Commission.
h. Verify that the query calculations are correct and save the query.
i. In Datasheet view, add a total row to calculate the average number of DaysToShip and the sums for the Revenue, TotalCost, Profit, and Commission fields. Format the Revenue, TotalCost, Profit, and Commission fields as currency.

Totals Query

You need to create a totals query based on the Your_Name Sales Report query. You will group the totals query by last name to provide aggregate statistics that summarize each salesperson's performance and income. It also will provide the average number of days each salesperson's orders take to ship. Compare your results to Figure 3.28.

a. Create a **Totals** query based on Your_Name Sales Report. Group by **LastName** and summarize the **DaysToShip** field with an average. Summarize the **Revenue**, **TotalCost**, **Profit**, and **Commission** fields as sums. Format the Revenue, TotalCost, Profit, and Commission fields as currency.
b. Add a Total row to the Datasheet view that will sum the Revenue, TotalCost, Profit, and Commission fields and average the DaysToShip field.
c. Save this query as **Your_Name Shipping and Commission Summary**.
d. Capture a screenshot of the Sales Summary query. Open the query on your computer and press **PrintScrn**. Open Microsoft Word and press **Ctrl+V** or click **Paste**. Save the Word document as **chap3_cap_solution**. Print the Word document.
e. Close the Word document and close the database.

Mini Cases

Use the rubric following the case as a guide to evaluate your work, but keep in mind that your instructor may impose additional grading criteria or use a different standard to judge your work.

Vacation Time for Bank Employees

GENERAL CASE

The *chap3_mc1_safebank.accdb* file contains data from a small bank. Copy the *chap3_mc1_safebank.accdb* file to your working storage folder, name it **chap3_mc1_safebank_solution.accdb**, and open the copied file. Use the skills from this chapter to perform several tasks. The bank's employee policy states that an employee is eligible for three weeks of vacation after two years of employment. Before two full years, the employee may take two weeks of vacation. The Branch table stores the start date of each manager. You need to figure out how long each manager has worked for the bank. Once you have done that, you need to calculate the number of weeks of vacation the manager is eligible to enjoy. Set these calculations up so that when the query is opened in the future (for example, tomorrow, a month, or two years from now), the length of service and vacation values will update automatically. Summarize each customer's account balances. This summary should list the customer's name and a total of all account balances.

Performance Elements	Exceeds Expectations	Meets Expectations	Below Expectations
Create query	All necessary and no unneeded fields included.	All necessary fields included but also unnecessary fields.	Not all necessary fields were included in the query.
Compute length of service	Calculations and methods correct.	Calculations correct but method inefficient.	Calculations incorrect and methods inefficient.
Compute vacation entitlement	Calculations and methods correct, updates automatically.	Calculations and methods correct but fail to update.	Calculations incorrect, methods inefficient, no updates.
Summarize balances	Correct method, correct totals.	Correct totals but inefficient method.	Totals incorrect or missing.

Combining Name Fields

RESEARCH CASE

This chapter introduced you to the power of using Access Expressions, but you have much more to explore. Use Access help to search for Expressions. Open and read the articles titled *Create an expression* and *A guide to expression syntax*. Put your new knowledge to the test. Copy any of the database files that you used in this chapter and rename the copy with the prefix, **chap3_mc2**. For example, if you copy the safebank database, the file name should be **chap3_mc2_description_solution.accdb**. Open the file. Find a table that stores names in two fields: FirstName and LastName. Add your name to the table. Your challenge is to figure a way of combining the last and first name fields into one field that prints the last name, a comma, a space, and then the first name. Once you successfully combine the fields somewhere, alphabetize the list. Print it. Write your instructor a memo explaining how you accomplished this. Use a memo template in Word, your most professional writing style, and clear directions that someone could follow in order to accomplish this task. Attach the printout of the name list to the memo. Save the Word document as **chap3_mc2_solution**.

Performance Elements	Exceeds Expectations	Meets Expectations	Below Expectations
Use online help	Appropriate articles located and memo indicates comprehension.	Appropriate articles located but memo did not demonstrate comprehension.	Articles not found.
Prepare list of names	Printed list attached to memo in requested format.	Printed list is attached but the formatting has minor flaws.	List missing or incomprehensible.
Summarize and communicate	Memo clearly written and could be used as directions.	Memo text indicates some understanding but also weaknesses.	Memo missing or incomprehensible.
Aesthetics	Memo template correctly employed.	Template employed but signed in the wrong place or improperly used.	Memo missing or incomprehensible.

Coffee Revenue Queries

DISASTER RECOVERY

A co-worker called you into his office and explained that he was having difficulty with Access 2007 and asked you to look at his work. Copy the *chap3_mc3_coffee.accdb* file to your working storage folder, name it **chap3_mc3_coffee_solution.accdb**, and open the file. It contains two queries, Your_Name Revenue and Your_Name Revenue by City. The Revenue query is supposed to calculate product Price (based on a markup percentage on Cost) and Revenue (the product of Price and Quantity). Something is wrong with the Revenue query. Your challenge is to find and correct the error(s). Your co-worker also tried to use the Revenue query as input for a Totals query that should show revenue by city. Of course, since the Revenue query doesn't work correctly, nothing based upon it will work, either. After correcting the Revenue query, open, locate the errors in, and fix the Totals query. Run the queries. Display all of the Balance values as currency. Save the queries with your name and descriptive titles. Print the Datasheet view of the Totals query and turn the printout and file in to your instructor if instructed to do so.

Performance Elements	Exceeds Expectations	Meets Expectations	Below Expectations
Error identification	Correct identification and correction of all errors.	Correct identification of all errors and correction of some errors.	Errors neither located nor corrected.
Summary query	Correct grouping options and summarization selected.	Correct grouping but some summaries incorrectly selected.	Incorrect group by option selection.
Naming	Descriptive query name selected and employed.	Query name is only partially descriptive.	Query missing or default names used.

Create, Edit, and Perform Calculations in Reports

Creating Professional and Useful Reports

bjectives

After you read this chapter, you will be able to:

1. Plan a report **(page 933)**.

2. Use different report views **(page 935)**.

3. Create and edit a report **(page 939)**.

4. Identify report elements, sections, and controls **(page 949)**.

5. Add grouping levels in Layout view **(page 952)**.

6. Add fields to a report **(page 957)**.

7. Use the Report Wizard **(page 967)**.

Hands-On Exercises

Exercises	Skills Covered
1. **INTRODUCTION TO ACCESS REPORTS (page 941)** **Open:** chap4_ho1-3_coffee.accdb and chap4_ho1-3_coffee.gif **Save as:** chap4_ho1-3_coffee_solution.accdb **Back up as:** chap4_ho1_coffee_solution.accdb	• Create a Report Using the Report Tool • Create and Apply a Filter in a Report • Remove Fields from a Report and Adjust Column Widths • Reposition Report Objects and Insert Graphic Elements in a Report • Use AutoFormat and Format Report Elements
2. **CREATE, SORT, EDIT, NEST, AND REMOVE GROUPS FROM REPORTS (page 959)** **Open:** chap4_ho1-3_coffee_solution.accdb (from Exercise 1) **Save as:** chap4_ho1-3_coffee_solution.accdb (additional modifications) **Back up as:** chap4_ho2_coffee_solution.accdb	• Sort a Report • Create a Grouped Report and Sort It • Add Additional Grouping Levels and Calculate Summary Statistics • Remove Grouping Levels • Reorder Grouping Levels
3. **REPORT WIZARD (page 972)** **Open:** chap4_ho1-3_coffee_solution.accdb (from Exercise 2) **Save as:** chap4_ho1-3_coffee_solution.accdb (additional modifications)	• Assemble the Report Data • Create a Query-Based Report and Add Grouping • Create Summary Statistics • Select Layout and AutoFormatting • Modify the Report

CASE STUDY

Northwind Traders

Northwind Traders is a small, international, specialty food company. It sells products in eight different divisions: beverages, confections (candy), condiments, dairy products, grains and cereals, meat and poultry, produce, and seafood. Although most of its customers are restaurants and gourmet food shops, it has a few retail customers, too. All of the order information is stored in the company's database. This database is used by the finance department to monitor and maintain sales records. You are the finance manager. Your task is to determine

Case Study

the revenue from each order and to summarize the first-quarter revenue for each month and by each category. You need only report on gross revenue—the total amount the firm receives. This report does not need to calculate any costs or expenses. It is important that you report accurately. Figure 4.1 presents a rough layout of the report. You must identify the source data, prepare a report, and group it to match the layout.

Your Assignment

- Copy the file named *chap4_case_traders.accdb*. Rename the copy **chap4_case_traders_solution.accdb**. Open the copied file and enable the content.
- Locate and rename the Your Name Revenue query with your first and last name. Use this query as the source for your report. It contains all the needed fields for the report plus several fields you do not need.
- Create a report based on the Your Name Revenue query. Use any report creation method you learned about in the chapter.
- Add appropriate grouping levels to produce the output shown in Figure 4.1. Name the report **Your Name First Quarter Sales by Month and Category**. You may select formatting as you want, but the grouping layout should match the design shown.
- Print the completed report.
- Compact and repair the file.
- Back up the database.

Appearances Matter

By now, you know how to plan a database, create a table, establish relationships among table data, and extract, manipulate, and summarize data using queries. You generated output by printing table or query datasheets. If you look back at your earlier work, you will see that the information exists, but it is bland. You probably have worked in other application software sufficiently to wonder if Access can enhance the print files. Access provides a powerful tool, giving you the ability to organize and present selected data clearly. Most of the printed output generated by Access users comes from reports.

Enhanced data improves the functionality of database information. Just as in the other Microsoft Office applications, you can change the size, style, and placement of printed matter. You may highlight portions of output to call attention to them. You may also add graphs, pictures, or charts to help the report reader more easily convert the database data into useful information. Designing and producing clear, functional, and organized reports facilitates decision-making. Report production begins with planning the report's design.

In this section, you plan reports. First, you create reports using the Report Tool, and then you edit the report by using the Layout view.

Planning a Report

A **report** is a printed document that displays information from a database.

A **report** is a printed document that displays information from a database in a manner that provides clear information to managers. You can design a report to create a catalog, a telephone directory, a financial statement, a graph showing sales by month, a shipping label, or a letter to customers reminding them about a past due payment. All documents you create using table data are Access reports. You should carefully consider what information you need and how you can optimally present it.

Access provides powerful tools to help you accomplish this goal. However, if you do not take the time to plan the report in advance, the power of the tools may impede the report process. You should think through what elements you need and how they should be arranged on the printed page prior to launching the software. The time invested planning the report's appearance at the start of the process leads to fewer surprises with the end result. The report plan helps you take charge of the computer instead of the computer controlling you.

(The report plan helps you take charge of the computer instead of the computer controlling you.)

Draw a Paper Design

The most important tool you use to create an Access report may be a pencil. If you sketch your desired output before touching the mouse, you will be happier with the results. As you sketch, you must ask a number of questions.

- What is the purpose of the report?
- Who uses this report?
- What elements, including labels and calculations, need to be included? What formulae will produce accurate results?
- Will the results be sensitive or confidential? If so, does there need to be a warning printed on the report?
- How will the report be distributed? Will users pull the information directly from Access or will they receive it through e-mail, a fax, the Internet, Word, or Excel?

Sketch the report layout on paper. Identify the field names, their locations, their placement on the page, and other design elements as you sketch. Figure 4.1 provides a sample report layout.

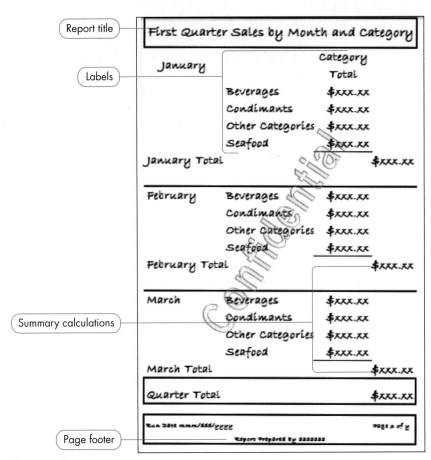

Figure 4.1 Report Plan

Identify Data Sources

In the next step of planning your report, you need to identify the data source(s) of each report element. You may use one or more tables, queries, or a combination of tables and queries as the report's source. Occasionally, a single table or query contains all of the records you need for the report. Typically, however, you need to specify several tables. When multiple tables are needed to create a report, you may assemble all necessary data in a single query, and then base the report on that query. Reports frequently contain graphics as well as data. As you identify the sources of report input, you also need to specify the graphic source. Frequently, a company logo on an invoice or a watermark, indicating that the material is confidential or proprietary, is printed on the report.

Select a Reporting Tool

Access gives you several tools to facilitate report creation. Which one you select depends on the data source and complexity of the report design. Table 4.1 summarizes the available tools and their usage.

Table 4.1 Report Tools, Location, and Usage

Report Tool	Location	Data Source	Output Complexity
Report Tool	Create Tab, Reports Group, Reports command	Single table or query	Limited. This creates a report showing all of the fields in the data source.
Report Wizard	Create Tab, Reports Group, Report Wizard command	Single or multiple tables or queries or a mixture of tables and queries	More sophisticated. Include (or exclude) fields. Add grouping and sorting instructions. Choose between detailed or summary data presentation.
Label Wizard	Create Tab, Reports Group, Labels command	Single or multiple tables or queries or a mixture of tables and queries	Limited. This feature only produces mailing labels (or name badges) but does so formatted to fit a variety of commercially available mailing labels. The output displays in multiple columns only in Print Preview. Filterable to exclude records.
Blank Report	Create Tab, Reports Group, Blank Report command	Single or multiple tables or queries or a mixture of tables and queries	Limited and extremely complex. Use to quickly assemble a few fields from multiple tables without stepping through the wizard. Alternatively, use to customize the most sophisticated reports with complex grouping levels and sorts.

Using Different Report Views

You have worked with Datasheet and Design views of tables and queries to perform different tasks. For example, you cannot perform data entry in an Access table in Design view, nor can you establish query criteria in Datasheet view. Similarly, Access 2007 provides different views of your report. You view and edit the report using different views depending on what you need to accomplish. Because Access reports may be more sophisticated than queries or tables, you have more views available. Each view accommodates different actions.

Use Print Preview

The **Print Preview** displays the report as it will be printed.

The **Print Preview** displays the report exactly as it will appear on the printed output. You may look at or print your reports in this view, but you cannot edit the report data. You may specify which pages to print in the Print dialog box. The default value will print all pages in the report. Figure 4.2 shows an Access report in Print Preview.

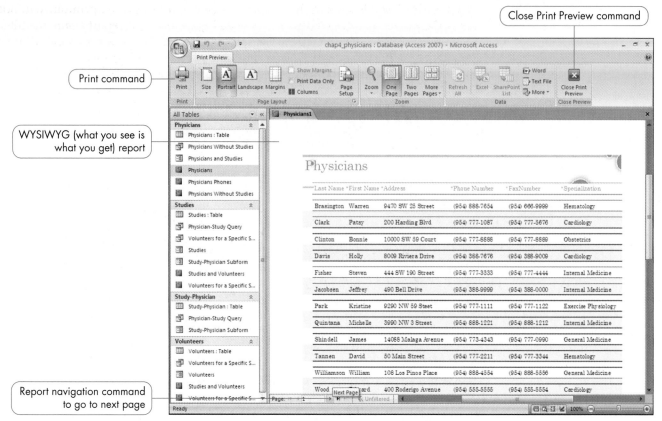

Close Print Preview command

Print command

WYSIWYG (what you see is what you get) report

Report navigation command to go to next page

Figure 4.2 Print Preview of an Access Report

TIP Always Preview Access Reports Prior to Printing

Because databases contain a great deal of information, Access reports may become very long and may require many pages to print. Experienced Access users **always** preview their work and go to the last page of the report by using the navigation commands. Although some reports require hundreds of pages to print, many that have multiple pages may be reformatted to print on one or a few pages. The rule is preview before printing.

View and Interact with Data in Report View

Use the **Report view** to make temporary changes to data while viewing it as it will print.

The second way to view Access reports, the **Report view**, provides you the ability to see what the printed report will look like and to make temporary changes to how the data are viewed. You can identify portions of the output by applying a filter. For example, if you need a list of physicians practicing Internal Medicine, you can right-click the record value and select the appropriate filtering option, *equals Internal Medicine*, from the shortcut menu. All of the other types of physicians are hidden temporarily (see Figure 4.3). If you print the filtered report, the printout will not show the hidden records. When you close and open a filtered report again, the filter disappears and all records appear in Report view. You may reapply the filter to reproduce the filtered results. The Report view permits you to copy selected formatted records to the Clipboard and paste them in other applications. Even when the security controls on the report have been tightly set by the database administrator, this view gives the report user a measure of customization and interactivity with the data.

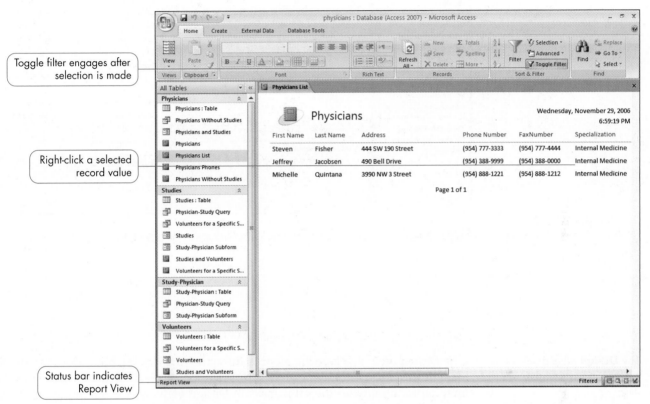

Toggle filter engages after selection is made

Right-click a selected record value

Status bar indicates Report View

Figure 4.3 Filtered Report Output Shown in Report View

Modify Reports in Layout View

Use the **Layout view** to alter the report design while viewing the data.

The third (and perhaps the most useful) report view is the Layout view. Use the **Layout view** to alter the report design while viewing the data. You should use Layout view to add or delete fields to the report, modify field control properties, change the column widths or row height to ensure that the entire field displays without truncation, add grouping and sorting levels to a report, or to filter reported data to extract only specific records. Although the display appears as what you see is what you get (WYSIWYG), you will find sufficient variations between the Layout and Print Preview views that you will need to use Print Preview. You do most of the report's modification using Layout view. Figure 4.4 shows a report in Layout view.

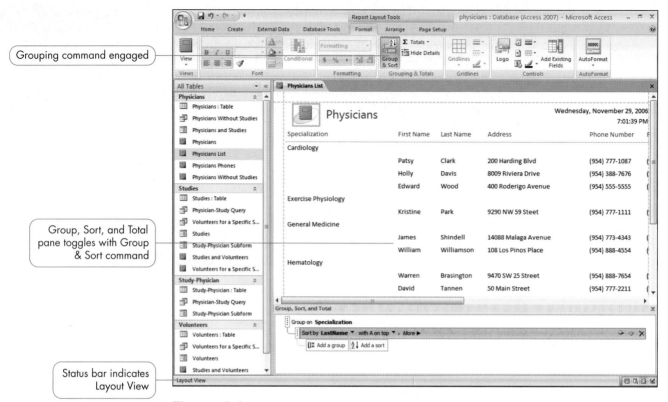

Grouping command engaged

Group, Sort, and Total pane toggles with Group & Sort command

Status bar indicates Layout View

Figure 4.4 Report in Layout View with Grouping and Sorting

Perfect a Report in Design View

The ***Design view*** displays the report's infrastructure but no data.

The ***Design view*** displays the report's infrastructure design, but it does not display data. It provides you the most powerful method of viewing an Access report. You may perform many of the same tasks in Design view as you can in Layout view—add and delete fields, add and remove sorting and grouping layers, rearrange data elements, adjust column widths, and customize report elements. You do not see any of the report's data while in this view. When the report is very lengthy, hiding the data as you alter the design may be an advantage because you save time by not scrolling. However, the Design view looks so different from the final output, it may be confusing. You need to experiment with using both the Layout and Design views and decide which view fits your style. Figure 4.5 displays the Physicians report in Design view. The next section provides explanations for all of the little boxes and stripes.

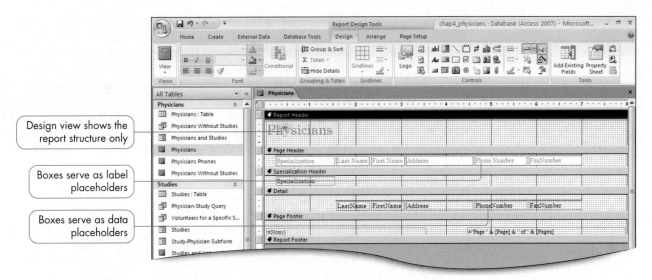

Design view shows the report structure only

Boxes serve as label placeholders

Boxes serve as data placeholders

Figure 4.5 Reports Shown in Design View Do Not Display Record Values

Create and Edit a Report

Access gives you several different methods to generate a report. You will first learn how to use the Report tool. Start by determining all of the fields needed for the report. To use the Report tool, you need to assemble all of the necessary data in one place. This tool is extremely easy to use and will adequately serve your needs much of the time. Occasionally, a table contains all of the fields for a report. More often, you will need to create or open a query containing the necessary fields. If an existing query has all of the fields needed for the report but also some unneeded fields, you will probably use the existing query. You can delete the extraneous fields.

Create a Report with the Report Tool

First, you need to determine the record source for the report. Open the record source in Datasheet view. Click the Create tab and click Report in the Reports group. Access creates the report and displays it in Layout view (see Figure 4.6). If you like the look of the report, you may print, save, and close it from the Layout view. When you reopen the saved report file, Access automatically returns to the record source and loads the most recent data into the report.

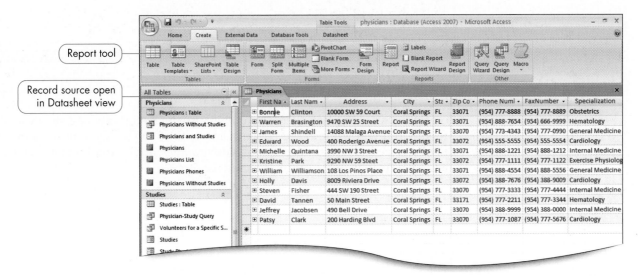

Report tool

Record source open in Datasheet view

Figure 4.6 Set Up for Using Report Tool

Edit a Report in Layout View

The report-editing functions in Layout view provide you with powerful and easy-to-use editing capabilities. If you have unnecessary fields in a report, simply click a value in the unneeded column and press Delete. Not only does the unneeded field go away, the remaining field's spacing adjusts to cover the gap where the deleted data had been. Change the column widths by clicking a value in the column, and then moving your mouse over the right column boundary. When the mouse pointer shape changes to a horizontal, double-headed arrow, click and drag the boundary to adjust the column width. You may move an object by selecting it, positioning your mouse in the middle of the selection, waiting until the pointer shape changes to the move shape (the four-headed arrow), and then clicking and dragging to reposition.

Use the select-and-do method of changing font, size, color, and effects in the same way as you would in Word or Excel. Add graphic elements by clicking Logo in the Controls group on the Format tab. Then browse to the storage location of the graphic file in the Insert Picture dialog box. The editing skills you already know from working in other software applications work is essentially the same way when you edit an Access report in the Layout view. Access provides many predefined formats that you may apply to the report. Figure 4.7 shows a report in Layout view.

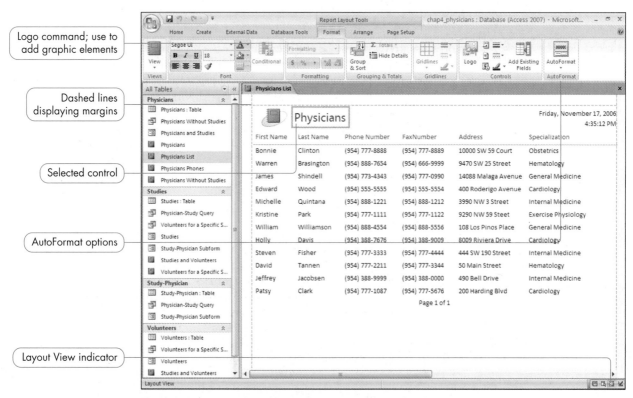

Figure 4.7 Report Layout View Elements

In the first hands-on exercise, you will use the Report tool to generate an Access report. You will work in the Layout view to filter the report, remove unnecessary fields, resize and reposition columns, add graphics, apply AutoFormats to the report, and then customize the AutoFormatted results.

Hands-On Exercises

1 | Introduction to Access Reports

Skills covered: 1. Create a Report Using the Report Tool **2.** Create and Apply a Filter in a Report **3.** Remove Fields from a Report and Adjust Column Widths **4.** Reposition Report Objects and Insert Graphic Elements in a Report **5.** Use AutoFormat and Format Report Elements

Step 1 Create a Report Using the Report Tool	Refer to Figure 4.8 as you complete Step 1. **a.** Use Windows Explorer to locate the file named *chap4_ho1-3_coffee.accdb*. Copy the file and rename it as **chap4_ho1-3_coffee_solution.accdb**. **b.** Open the *chap4_ho1-3_coffee_solution.accdb* file. **c.** Click **Options** on the Security Warning toolbar, click **Enable this content** in the Microsoft Office Security Options dialog box, and then click **OK**. **d.** Open the **Sales Reps table** and replace *Your Name* with your first and last names. Close the Sales Reps table. **e.** Right-click the **Your Name Revenue** query in the *All Tables window* and select **Rename**. Replace *Your Name* with your first and last names. **f.** Open the **Your Name Revenue query** in Datasheet view. **g.** Click the **Create tab**, and then click **Report** in the Reports group. Access creates the report and opens it in the Layout view. The report opens with the Format tab active because you almost always need to modify the format of a newly generated report.

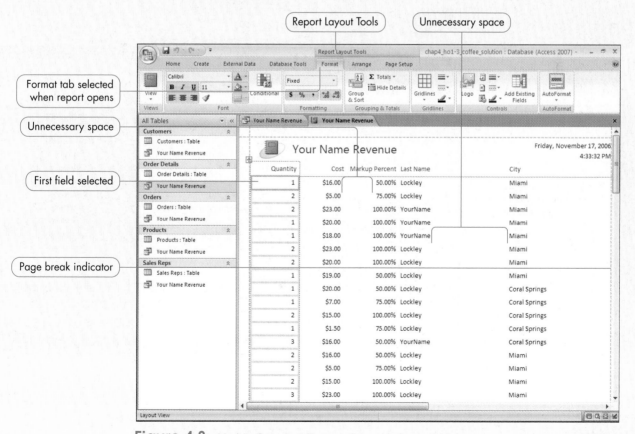

Figure 4.8 Newly Created Report Opens in Layout View

Refer to Figure 4.9 as you complete Step 2.

a. Right-click **Your Name** in the LastName field and select **Equals "Your Name"** from the shortcut menu.

You have created and applied a filter that displays only your orders. The status bar in the lower-right corner of the window tells you that the report has a filter applied. Only your records should display.

b. Right-click the word *Miami* and select **Does Not Equal "Miami"** from the shortcut menu.

Additional records are filtered out of the report, and a total for the Revenue field moves into view. Note that the total did not inherit the currency format from the source data. You may need to scroll right to see the total of the Revenue column.

c. Compare your selected fields to those shown in Figure 4.9 and then click **Save**.

The Save As dialog box opens with the default name (inherited from the source query) highlighted.

d. Type **Your Name Sales Outside of Miami**. Click **OK**.

e. Close the report and close the query.

You saved the report based on the query, so it no longer needs to be open. Although this is a small database, working with unnecessary objects open may slow your computer's response time. You should always close unnecessary objects.

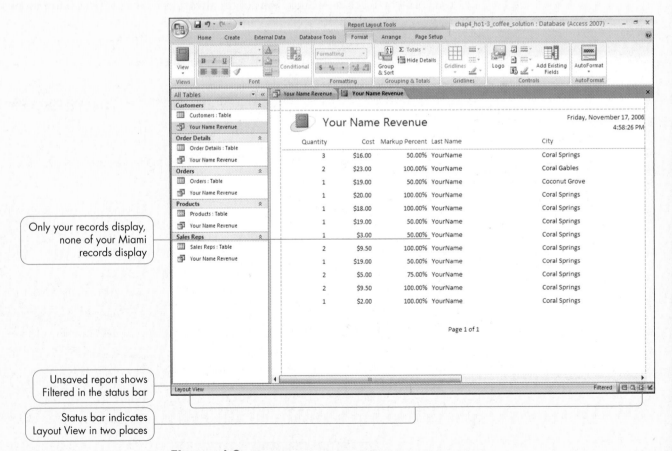

Figure 4.9 Filtered, Totaled Report

Refer to Figure 4.10 as you complete Step 3.

a. Open the **Your Name Sales Outside of Miami report**. Look at the right side of the status bar. It displays *Report View*. The status bar no longer indicates that the report is filtered.

When you reopen an existing report, it opens in Report view. This view lets you look at the report and permits limited filtering capabilities. Because this view provides limited editing interaction, you need to change to Layout view.

b. Right-click the **Your Name Sales Outside of Miami tab** and select **Layout View** from the shortcut menu.

c. Click the label **Quantity**.

A gold box surrounds the selected field name, and a dotted border surrounds the record values in the field.

TROUBLESHOOTING: The gold box should only be around the word Quantity. If it surrounds the entire label row, you are still in Report view. Switch to Layout view and then click Quantity again.

d. Press **Delete**.

The column disappears from the report. The remaining columns move left to fill the empty space.

e. Click **your name** in any record. Move your mouse to the right boundary of the gold border and, when the pointer shape changes to a double-headed arrow, click and drag the boundary to the left to decrease the column width.

f. Click a **city name** in any record. Move your mouse to the right boundary of the gold border and, when the pointer shape changes to a double-headed arrow, click and drag the boundary to the left to decrease the column width.

The report should fit on a single page now. You notice that the column heading for the Markup Percent column is much wider than the values in the column.

g. Click the **Markup Percent** column label to activate the gold border. Single-click **Markup Percent** again to edit the label.

You know you are in edit mode because the border color changes to black, and a flashing insertion point appears inside the border.

h. Position the insertion point to the left of the *P* in *Percent*. Press **Ctrl+Enter**. Click anywhere on the report to exit edit mode. Save the report.

The Ctrl+Enter command forces a line break. The word *Percent* moves below the word *Markup*.

TIP Forced Line Break

A similar command, Alt+Enter, may be used in Excel to force a line break, when the width of the column name greatly exceeds the width of the data displayed in the column. Although word wrapping may achieve the same effect, you can more precisely control which word prints on what line by forcing the break yourself.

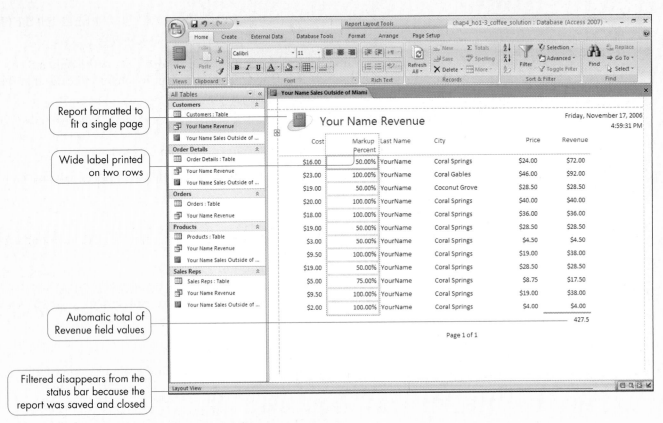

Report formatted to fit a single page

Wide label printed on two rows

Automatic total of Revenue field values

Filtered disappears from the status bar because the report was saved and closed

Figure 4.10 Resized Report

Step 4
Reposition Report Objects and Insert Graphic Elements in a Report

Refer to Figure 4.11 as you complete Step 4.

a. Click any record in the **City** column to select it. Move the mouse to the middle of the selected column. When the pointer shape changes to a *four-headed arrow*, click and drag to the left until the vertical gold line is on the left edge of the report. Release the mouse.

As you drag past other columns in the report, a gold line moves to tell you the column's current position. When you release the mouse, the City column moves to the first position.

TROUBLESHOOTING: When you begin to drag while located in a record, Access assumes that you want to change the height of the row until you move out of the column. While the mouse is inside the selected cell, a black boundary forms across the entire row. Keep dragging left. As soon as the mouse moves outside the original boundaries, the gold line will appear.

b. Click any record in the **Last Name** column to select it. Move the mouse to the middle of the selected column. When the pointer shape changes to a *four-headed arrow*, click and drag right. Continue the drag until the vertical gold line is on the right edge of the report. Release the mouse.

The Last Name column is the last column in the report.

c. Click the report title, *Your Name Revenue*, to select it, and then click it again to edit it. Type **Your Name Non–Miami Sales**.

d. Click the picture of the **report binder** to select it.

e. Click **Logo** in the Controls group on the Format tab.

The Insert Picture dialog box opens to the default folder, My Pictures, but the file you need is stored in the folder with the rest of the Access files.

f. Browse to your file storage folder; locate and open the file named *chap4_ho1-3_coffee.gif*. Click **OK**.

g. Move your mouse over the lower right corner of the picture until the pointer shape changes to a diagonal, double-headed arrow. Click and drag the lower-right picture corner until the picture's size roughly doubles.

The picture enlarges, but now it covers part of your name.

TIP Use the Properties Sheet to Exactly Size an Object

If you right-click the picture and select Properties from the shortcut menu, you may use measurements to exactly size the picture. You also may add special effects, like stretch or zoom.

h. Click the report's title, *Your Name Non–Miami Sales*, to select it. Position the mouse pointer in the middle of the box. When the pointer shape changes to the four-headed move arrow, click and drag the report title right and down (see Figure 4.11).

i. Click **Save** on the Quick Access Toolbar to save the design changes to the report.

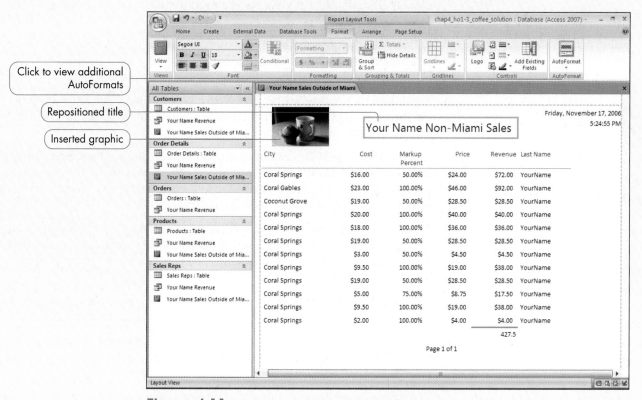

Figure 4.11 Graphic and Title Repositioned

Refer to Figure 4.12 as you complete Step 5.

a. Check to ensure the *Your Name Non–Miami Sales report* remains in Layout view. Right-click the **Revenue Total cell** (427.5) to select it and open the shortcut menu.

b. Select **Properties** from the shortcut menu.

The Property Sheet opens in the task pane.

c. Click the **Format tab** (if necessary), and then click the **drop-down arrow** in the *Format Property box* and select **Currency**.

You should see the value of the Revenue field total change to $427.50. Close the Property Sheet.

d. Click **AutoFormat** in the AutoFormat group on the Format tab (see Figure 4.12).

The AutoFormat list expands to display several formats. The last choice activates the AutoFormat Wizard.

e. Select the **Median AutoFormat** (2nd column, 3rd row) and click it.

The AutoFormat applies to the entire report. It does not matter what portion of the report you selected when you applied the AutoFormat. Every element of the report gets a format change. This effect may create problems.

f. Examine the results. Identify problems.

Although the Layout view gives you powerful editing capabilities, it does not perfectly duplicate the printed output. You need to use Print Preview to determine if the problem needs action.

g. Right-click the report tab and change to **Print Preview**. Examine the report's date and time. You should check the Report view, also. Right-click the report tab and change to **Report View**. Often, reports get copied and pasted or e-mailed directly from the Report view, so you need to make sure everything works there, too.

Fortunately, the date and time display correctly in Print Preview. You decide that you do not like the font color looks in the Revenue total. You think it would look better if it matched the other numbers in size, font, and color.

h. Right-click the report tab and change to **Layout View**. Click any record in the **Revenue** field. Click **Format Painter** in the Font group on the Format tab. Move to the **Revenue total** value and click it.

Clicking the format command instructs Access to save the source format. The mouse pointer has a paintbrush attached to it as you move to remind you that you will paint the stored format wherever you next click. When you reach the destination and click, the defined formats transfer.

i. Right-click the **brown area** at the top of the report and select **Properties** on the shortcut menu. Check to make sure the *Format tab* is open. Look in the *Back Color Property box*. The brown background color is color number **#775F55**. Select and **copy** the number or remember it.

You need to match the heading color to replace the blue background of the column headings. By looking up the property, you may make an exact color match.

j. Click the blue background for the **Cost heading**. Find the Back color property on the Format sheet. Click and drag to select its contents and press **Ctrl + V** to paste the brown color number in the box. Press **Enter**.

The color change does not take effect until you move to the next row. You like the new color but decide the type font will look better larger, centered, and boldfaced.

k. Click the **Font Size arrow** in the Font group and select **12**. Click **Bold**. Click the **Center text** command.

l. Scroll in the Property Sheet for the *Cost Heading* until you locate the Top Margin property. Type **0.1**.

m. Duplicate the format changes to the cost heading to the other headings by double-clicking **Format Painter** located in the Font group. Click the headings for *Markup Percent*, *Last Name*, *City*, *Price*, and *Revenue*. Press **Esc**.

Double-clicking the Format Painter permits painting a format to multiple areas without redefining the source after each painting. Pressing Esc or clicking the Format Painter again turns the Format Painter off.

n. Right-click the *Markup Percent* heading and change its Top Margin property in the Property Sheet to **0** (zero).

Because this heading is two lines, it needs to start higher up than the one line heading beside it.

o. Close the Property Sheet. Widen each column about a quarter inch so the entire page is filled (see Figure 4.12). Refer to Step 3e for instructions if necessary, except drag to widen rather than to narrow the column. Save your report.

TROUBLESHOOTING: Be sure to look at the report in Print Preview. Remember, the Layout view is not perfectly WYSIWYG. It is easy to make the right column a little too wide and push the report to an extra page. Check to make sure your report is still a single page. If it is not, make the columns a little narrower.

p. Click the **Office Button**, select **Manage**, and then select **Back Up Database**. Type **chap4_ho1_coffee_solution** (note *ho1* instead of *ho1-3*) and click **Save**.

You just created a backup of the database after completing the first hands-on exercise. The original database *chap4_ho1-3_coffee_solution* remains onscreen. If you ruin the original database as you complete the second hands-on exercise, you can use the backup file you just created.

q. Close the file and exit Access if you do not want to continue with the next exercise at this time.

T I P Learning Software

Following step-by-step instructions is a way to begin learning application software. If you want to become proficient in software, you must explore on your own. The properties sheet contains dozens of features that you did not cover in this lesson. You have finished Hands-On Exercise 1 and saved your file. You should experiment a little. Make a copy of the report and experiment on the copy. Activate the Property Sheet for a field and change properties to see the results.

Font Size selector

Format Painter command

Center command

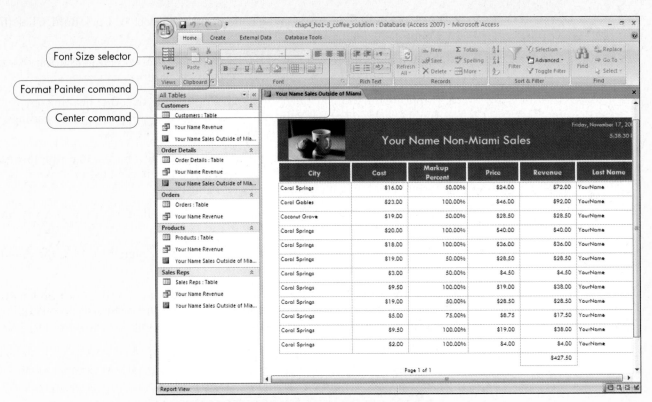

Figure 4.12 The Complete Single-Page Report

The Anatomy of a Report

You have produced reasonable, sophisticated output. Look at the report design depicted in Figure 4.13. It, too, contains summary statistics but on multiple levels. The desired layout contains indents to visually classify the differing elements. The finished report will likely require several pages. It would be much easier to read if the headings repeated at the start of each new page. Access can accomplish all of this, and more.

In this section, you will learn more about a report's sections and controls. You will also learn how to group an Access report into nested sections.

Identifying Report Elements, Sections, and Controls

Access divides all reports into sections, although you only see the sectional boundaries when you display the report in Design view. You need to become familiar with the sectional areas so that you can control report output completely. For example, if you place an instruction to add field values together in the detail section, the resulting calculation will duplicate each record's value for that field. The field in the detail section contains a single value from a single record.

Understand Sectional Divisions

The ***detail section*** repeats once for each record in the underlying record source.

The ***report header section*** prints once at the beginning of each report.

The ***report footer section*** prints once at the conclusion of each report.

The ***group header section(s)*** appear once at the start of each new grouping level in the report.

The ***group footer section(s)*** appear at the end of each grouping level.

The ***detail section*** repeats once for each record in the underlying record source. If you copied the calculation and placed it in a report header or footer, the result would display the sum of all that field's values for the entire report. The ***report header section*** prints once at the beginning of each report. The ***report footer section*** prints once at the conclusion of each report. Should you find all the stripes and little boxes confusing, you still must learn something about them to accurately produce the output you desire. You will begin by learning about the stripes—the sectional boundaries.

In Figure 4.13, each blue stripe marks the upper boundary of a report area. The top stripe denotes the upper boundary of the report header. The bottom stripe displays the top boundary of the report's footer. The gray, grid-patterned area beneath the stripes shows the space allotted to that element. Notice that the report has no space allocated to the report footer. You may change the space between areas by moving your mouse over the stripe's bottom. When the pointer shape changes to a double-headed arrow, click and drag to move the boundary. Use this method if you decide to add a footer to the report. A gray, grid-patterned work space appears as your mouse drags down. If you expand or contract the space allotment for a middle sectional boundary, the lower boundaries all move also. The ***group header section(s)*** appear once at the start of each new grouping level in the report. The ***group footer section(s)*** appear at the end of each grouping level.

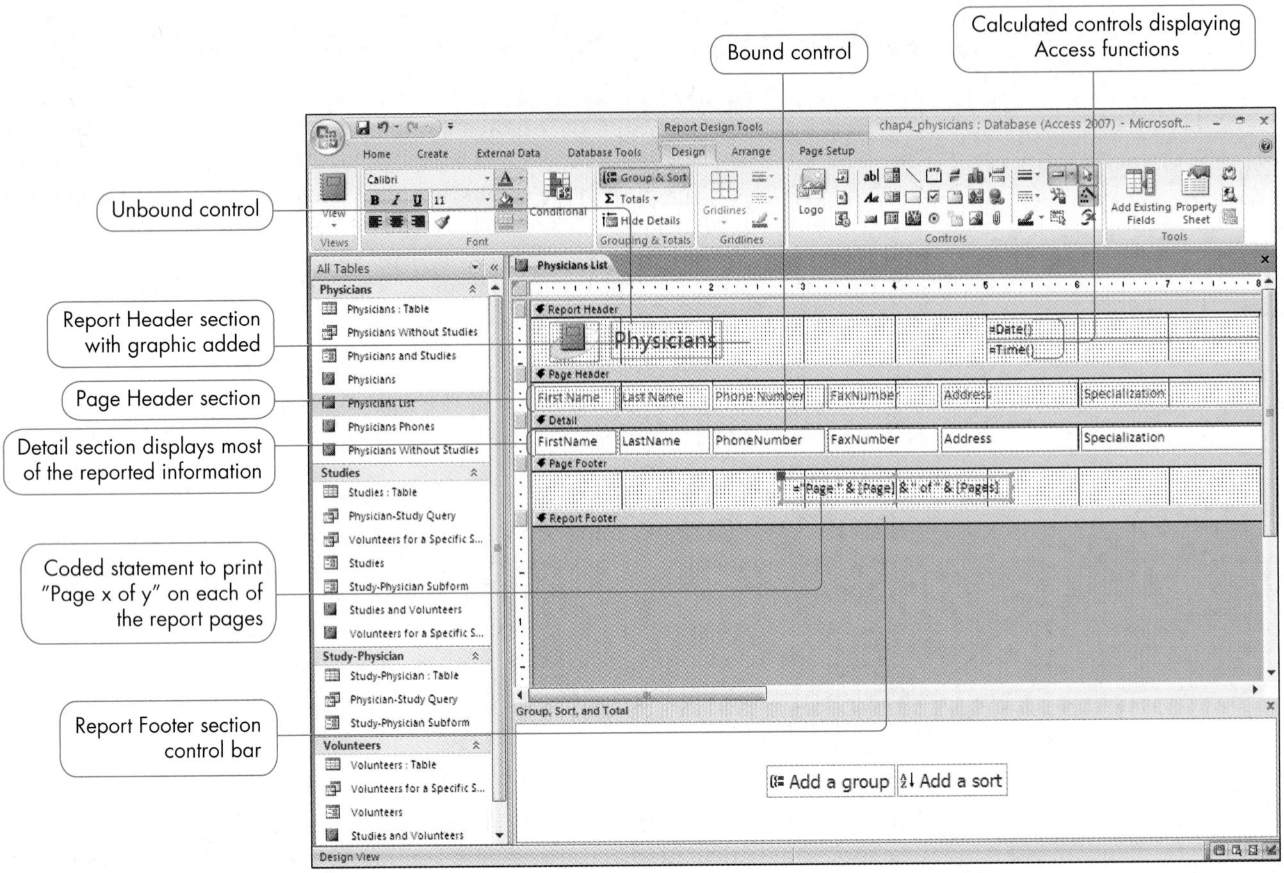
Calculated controls displaying Access functions
Bound control
Unbound control
Report Header section with graphic added
Page Header section
Detail section displays most of the reported information
Coded statement to print "Page x of y" on each of the report pages
Report Footer section control bar
Physicians
=Date()
=Time()
="Page " & [Page] & " of " & [Pages]
Add a group
Add a sort

Figure 4.13 Reports Shown in Design View Do Not Display Record Values

Page headers and ***page footers*** appear once for each page in the report at the top and bottom of the pages.

If you decide that the allotted space for a particular section is not needed, you may reposition the top of the next sectional boundary so that the boundary stripes touch. The element will remain in the report's design but will consume no space on the printed output and will not show in any other report view. Use the page header section to repeat column headings on the top of each new page. You will place information like page numbers in the page footer. ***Page headers*** and ***page footers*** appear once for each page in the report at the top and bottom of the report's pages, respectively.

All reports contain several different sections; see the reference page for more information about their placement and usage.

Report Tools, Location, and Usage | Reference

Design Element	Location	Frequency	Usage	Required
Report Header	Top of the report	Once	Think of the report header as the title page. It includes information like the organization's name, the report's name, and the run date.	Yes
Page Header	Top of each page	One per page	Page headers generally contain the column headings. In a multi-page report, the labels repeat at the top of each page to provide clarity	Yes
Group Header	At the start of each new group	One at the start of each new group (up to 10)	This element begins and identifies each new group. It generally contains the group name, i.e., in a report grouped by state, the state name would be the header. Any aggregating functions in a group header will summarize the group records, e.g., a SUM function will add all of the record values within the group.	No
Detail	Middle	Once per record reported	This element is repeated once for each selected record in the data source. If there were 500 records in the data source for the report, the report would have 500 detail lines. In a grouped report, there may be multiple detail sections—one per group. Often, you omit the detail section entirely. You might show state total without population information showing the population per county. You might do this even when the state population was calculated by adding the county figures.	No
Group Footer	At the end of each group	Once at the end of each group (up to 10)	This element generally repeats the group name, e.g., in a report grouped by state, the state name would repeat in the footer along with a descriptor of aggregating information. An annual sales report might group by month, and one group's footer may display the Total Revenue in May. Any aggregating functions in a group's footer will summarize the group records, e.g., a SUM function will add all of the record values within the group.	No
Page Footer	Bottom of the page	Once per page in the report	Use this feature to print page numbers, page summary statistics, contact information, or report preparation/run date.	Yes, but it need not contain any data
Report Footer	End of the report	One per report	You would use this feature to print grand totals or other summary information for entire project. Often, the date, authorship, or contact information displays here.	Yes

Work with Controls

The position and instructions about what to do with the data once retrieved from the table or query come through the use of controls (the little boxes in Design view). You use *controls* to position, display, format, and calculate the report data. Access reports use different types of controls for different purposes.

Use *controls* to position, display, format, and calculate the report data.

You use *bound controls* most frequently in preparing an Access report. These controls enable you to pull information from the underlying table or query data. Like the source data, the value of a bound control may be text, dates, numbers, pictures, graphs, or Yes/No values. The latter typically displays as a check box. The binding means that the control inherits most properties—size, formatting, and relationships—from the source table. For example, a text box may display a product's price in currency format. It is bound (tied) to the UnitPrice field in the Products table, which is also set to currency format. Most bound controls display with two small boxes in the report's Design view. The left box is the control's label, the right box or text box displays the record value. A bound control's label automatically comes from the field name or caption (if one exists).

Bound controls enable you to pull information from the underlying table or query data.

Unbound controls do not have any record source for their contents. The values contained there exist only in the report and nowhere else in the database. You use them to display information (the report's title), cosmetic elements (borders or lines to visually separate report sections), boxes, and pictures.

Unbound controls do not have any record source for their contents.

A *calculated control* uses an expression as opposed to a record value as its data source. The expression usually is bound to the record values of the fields referenced. A report expression, like a query expression, combines field names, operators, constants, and functions to instruct Access on how to perform a calculation. For example, you might use an expression to calculate a discounted price in a sales report. For example:

A *calculated control* uses an expression as opposed to a record value as its data source.

=[UnitPrice] * (1-[Discount] * [Quantity])

This expression would likely retrieve the UnitPrice data from the Products table, and the Discount and Quantity values from the Order Details table if you are using a retail store database that contains records for products, including unit price, selling price, and quantity.

Adding Grouping Levels in Layout View

Access provides you with several methods of creating data summaries.

- Create a Totals query by specifying a group by field and the field or fields to summarize.
- Create a grouped report using the Layout view's Sorting and Grouping tool.
- Create a grouped report using the Report Wizard and specifying the group layers within the Wizard.

Reports provide you with the same power as a Totals query and provide the added advantage of enhanced appearance. This section explores grouping and sorting in the Layout view method. The next section introduces you to the Report Wizard.

Engage the Group & Sort Tool

Open the report in Layout view. The report shown in Figure 4.14 contains over 2,000 records. Imagine that you must use this data to make decisions about your firm's operations. You would not easily identify trends and patterns by examining 50 or more printed pages. This data needs to be summarized. Begin summarizing by clicking Group & Sort in the Grouping & Totals group on the Format tab. The Group, Sort, and Total pane displays in the bottom of the report.

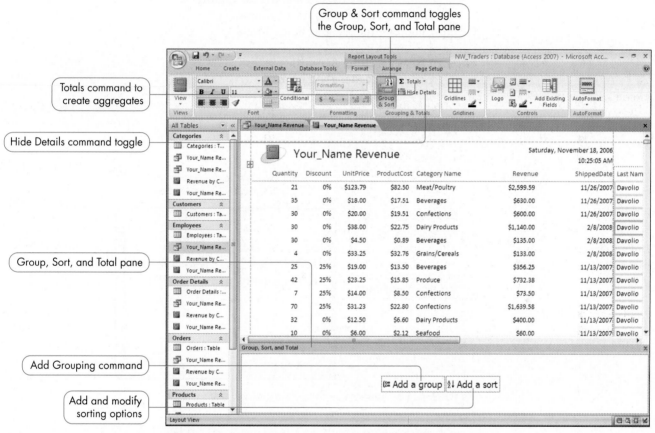

Figure 4.14 Display the Group, Sort, and Total Pane

Select the Primary Grouping Field

Nested groups provide a power-layering tool to organize information.

You may nest groups in different levels—up to 10. **Nested groups** provide a powerful layering tool to organize information. In this report, you need the sales figures summarized by the categories of products offered. Once created, each group contains introductory and summary information as well as the record values. Generally, the group header provides identification information, for example the name of the category. You use the group footer to present summary information for the group. Figure 4.15 depicts the Add a Group command engaged with the categories field selected as the primary grouping level.

After you establish the primary group, you may add additional levels. This feature works much like an outline. Suppose you needed a sales report grouped by salesperson, and then by quarter. Each successive grouping layer gets tucked between the header and footer of the previous layer.

Group 1 Header — Joe Adams' Sales
    Group 2 Header—Quarter 1
        Many Rows of Details for Quarter 1
    Group 2 Footer—Quarter 1 Summary

    Group 2 Header—Quarter 2
        Many Rows of Details for Quarter 2
    Group 2 Footer—Quarter 2 Summary

    Group 2 Header—Quarter 3
        Many Rows of Details for Quarter 3
    Group 2 Footer—Quarter 3 Summary

    Group 2 Header—Quarter 4
        Many Rows of Details for Quarter 4
    Group 2 Footer—Quarter 4 Summary
Group 1 Footer—Joe Adams' Sales Totals

Group 2 Header—Brenda Smith's Sales
    Group 2 Header—Quarter 1
        Many Rows of Details for Quarter 1
    Group 2 Footer—Quarter 1 Summary
The pattern repeats.

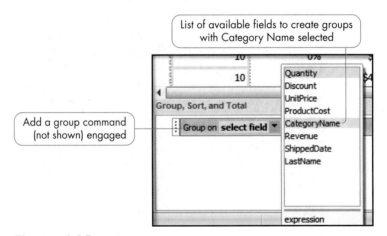

Figure 4.15 Select a Primary Grouping Level

Hide or Display Details

You must decide if the details—the values stored in each record that report used as a source—need to be displayed in the report. Many reports only display data summaries. How you decide to display details will depend on how the report will be used. Most Access report writers follow the general rule that the less detail and more summarizing information included, the more useful the report. Access makes it easy for you to add and remove detail levels. If you omit the detail and later discover that you need it, you can easily add it back. Engage the Hide Detail command to hide or display report details (see Figure 4.16).

> *. . . the less detail and more summarizing information included, the more useful the report.*

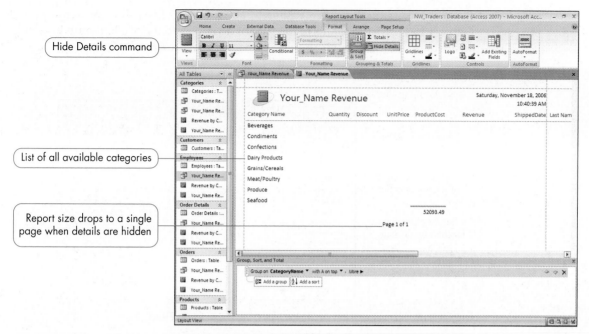

Figure 4.16 Summary Report with Details Hidden

Calculate Summary Statistics

The report in Figure 4.17 displays a list of the names of the categories of merchandise sold by the firm. The Totals command in the Grouping & Totals group helps you summarize data. First, select the control label for the data you want summarized. Then click Totals and select the necessary aggregating function from the drop-down list.

Decision-makers may wish to examine the same data using different aggregating functions to answer different questions. For example, a sum of all revenue generated by each product category will tell the manager important total sales information. Changing the report to display the maximum revenue will provide the decision-maker with information about which products generated the largest revenue. After you establish the grouping levels, Access makes it easy for you to examine the output in a variety of ways.

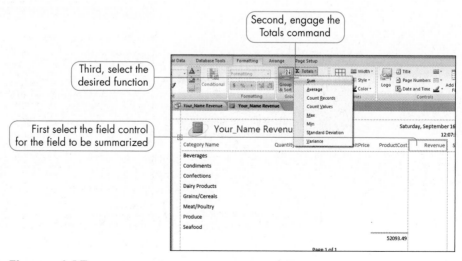

Figure 4.17 Creating a Sum of the Revenue Field

You may add summary values to additional fields using the same process. Figure 4.18 shows the results of the sum of revenue and the needed setup to calculate an average of the discounts provided customers in each product category.

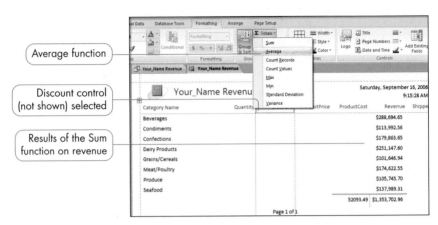

Figure 4.18 Creating an Average of the Discount Field

Add Additional Grouping Levels

You decide that having the report grouped by category is useful, but you also want to know who sells each category's products. You can add additional grouping levels to an existing report in Layout view by selecting the control that you need to group on and then clicking the Add a Group command in the Group, Sort, and Total pane. In the report displayed in Figure 4.19, you would first select the control for LastName field and then click the Add a group command. The figure displays the results of adding an additional grouping level to the report. The More command controlling the Category name group expands when selected, granting you access to additional features. The figure displays the settings necessary to display the totals (averages) for the categories below the salesperson totals.

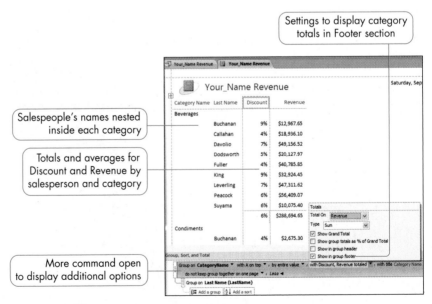

Figure 4.19 Nested Group Report with Totals Moved to Footer

Sort a Report

While working in the Layout view, you can interact with the sort order of the report's fields. Figure 4.20 shows a report with two sorting levels applied. The primary sort is the area of specialization. The secondary sort is by the physician's last name. This order groups the cardiologists together with Clark preceding Davis in the alphabetical listing.

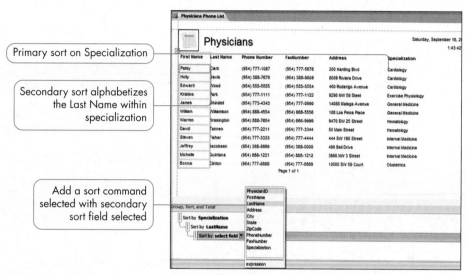

Figure 4.20 Sorted Report

Adding Fields to a Report

It is possible to omit a necessary field when designing a report. Even if a report has no errors, data needs change with time. You may need to add a new field to an existing report. Access provides an easy way to do that.

The **Field List pane** displays a list of all of the tables and fields in the database.

Open the report in Layout view. Activate the Format tab. Click Add Existing Fields in the Controls group. The Field List pane opens on the right side of the screen. The **Field List pane** displays a list of all of the tables and fields in the database. Once you locate the needed field in the Field List pane, drag and drop it on the report in the position that you want it to occupy. (Alternatively, you can double-click it.) Access creates the needed control to hold the new field, for example, a text box, and then binds the field to the newly created control (see Figure 4.21). Occasionally, you might want a different control type than the one Access creates for you. You may edit the newly created control's properties to get exactly the control you want. But, you cannot use Layout view to do so. You cannot change the control type property in Layout view. This change must be accomplished in Design view. Of course, you may only specify a control that is appropriate to that data type. For example, a Yes/No field might display as a check box, but you would rather have the words, Yes or No, display.

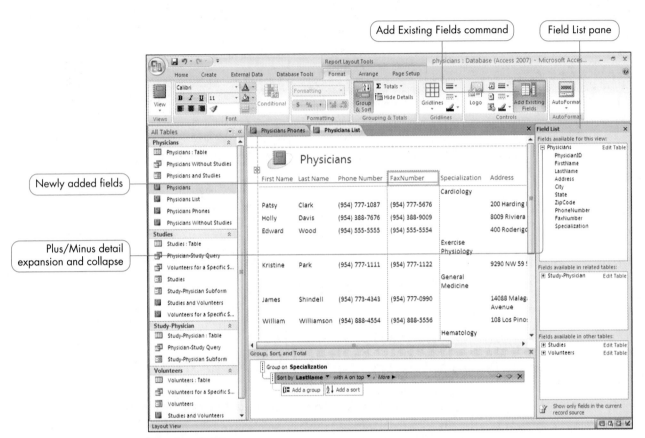

Figure 4.21 Sorted Report

In the next hands-on exercise, you will create a report, add sorting and grouping to refine the content, work with data aggregates, and add a new field to the report.

Hands-On Exercises

2 | Create, Sort, Edit, Nest, and Remove Groups from Reports

Skills covered: 1. Sort a Report **2.** Create a Grouped Report and Sort It. **3.** Add Additional Grouping Levels and Calculate Summary Statistics **4.** Remove Grouping Levels **5.** Reorder Grouping Levels

Step 1 Sort a Report	Refer to Figure 4.22 as you complete Step 1.

a. Open the *chap4_ho1-3_coffee_solution* file if necessary, click **Options** on the Security Warning toolbar, click the **Enable this content option** in the Microsoft Office Security Options dialog box, and click **OK**.

TROUBLESHOOTING: If you create unrecoverable errors while completing this hands-on exercise, you can delete the *chap4_ho1-3_coffee_solution* file, copy the *chap4_ho1_coffee_solution* backup database you created at the end of the first hands-on exercise, and open the copy of the backup database to start the second hands-on exercise again.

b. Open the **Your Name Revenue query** in Datasheet view. Click the **Create tab** and click **Report**.

c. Click **Group & Sort** in the Grouping & Totals group to turn on the Group, Sort, and Total pane at the bottom of the screen.

TROUBLESHOOTING: The Group & Sort command is a toggle. If you do not see the Group, Sort, and Total pane, click the Group & Sort command again. It may have been on, and you turned it off.

d. Click **Add a sort** in the Group, Sort, and Total pane.

A list box opens displaying the names of all the reports fields.

e. Click **LastName** from the list and select it.

Scroll through the list to see two names: Lockley and your name. If your name comes before Lockley alphabetically, your sales are reported first. If your name comes after Lockley alphabetically, Lockley's sales will be first. In the next step, you will sort the list so that your name is on the top—ascending or descending, depending on what letter your name begins with.

f. Find the **Sort with A on top drop-down arrow** in the Group, Sort, and Total pane. Click it to reveal two choices—with A on top and with Z on top. Click the choice that will position your name at the top of the list.

If your name is not on top, sort again, and select the other option.

g. Click the **Office Button**, choose **Save As**, and type **Sales by Employee and City**. Click **OK**.

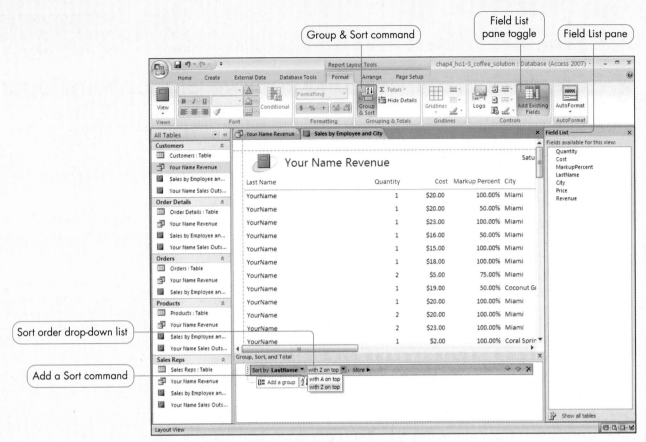

Figure 4.22 Correctly Sorted Report

Step 2

Create a Grouped Report and Sort It

Refer to Figure 4.23 as you complete Step 2.

a. Click **Add a group** in the Group, Sort, and Total pane.

A list box pops up asking you to select the field name that you want to group by.

b. Select the **LastName** field in the list box.

> **TROUBLESHOOTING:** If your screen does not look like Figure 4.23, it may be because you selected a different group by value. Click close on the gold Group on LastName bar in the Group, Sort, and Total pane to remove the incorrect grouping. Then rework Steps 2a and 2b.

c. Scroll right until you can see the label control box for the **Revenue** field. (It is blue.) Click to select it.

d. Click the **Format tab** and click **Totals** in the Grouping & Totals group.

A drop-down list providing function options appears.

e. Click **Sum**.

f. Save the report.

A sum has been added to the Revenue field after each group. You probably cannot see it because it is scrolled off-screen. Use the scrollbar to see that your revenue is 1599.125.

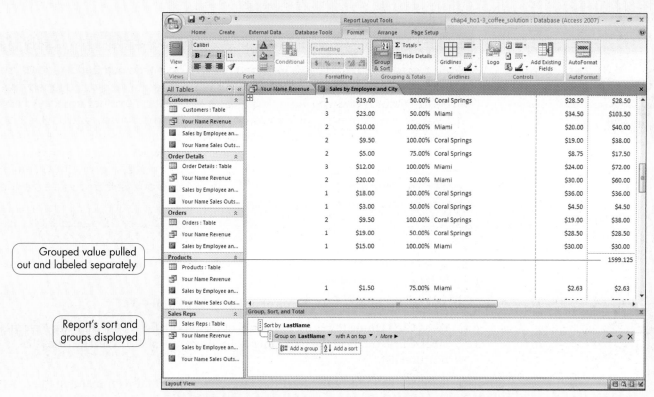

Grouped value pulled out and labeled separately

Report's sort and groups displayed

Figure 4.23 Correctly Sorted Report with Primary Group

<table>
<tr>
<td rowspan="5">

Step 3

Add Additional
Grouping Levels and
Calculate Summary
Statistics

</td>
</tr>
</table>

Refer to Figure 4.24 as you complete Step 3.

a. Ensure that you are still in Layout view. Click **Add a group** in the Group, Sort, and Total pane.

b. Scroll left to locate and select the **City** field in the Field List box.

The Primary grouping level is still the salesperson's last name. Now the customer's city is grouped together nested inside the LastName field. During this period, you sold one order to a customer in Coconut Grove, once to a customer in Coral Gables, 10 orders to customers in Coral Springs, and the rest of your orders came from Miami-based customers. You decide to create summary statistics by city and salesperson to analyze the sales information.

c. Click the **Cost** label to select it. Click **Totals** in the Grouping & Totals group. Select **Average** from the function list.

Scroll down until you see the average cost for the orders to Coral Springs displayed. You will see the average cost of an order from a Coral Springs customer was only $12.10, while the average costs of orders to Coral Gables and Coconut Grove were much higher.

d. Scroll up and click the **City** label to select it. Click **Totals** in the Grouping & Totals group. Select **Count Records** from the function list.

The City field is defined as a text field. Access presents different functions depending on whether the field contains text or numbers.

TIP Counting Records

If you create a report in Layout view and need to count the number of records, be sure to select a field that contains a non-null value for each record. If a report contained 20 records and you instructed Access to count a field that contained two null values, the resulting count would display 18. The missing values would not be included in the count. An easy way to fix this situation is to count only fields that have their Required property set to Yes. Alternatively, you can edit the field's control property. Select the text box containing the Count value, right-click, and select Properties. Click the Data tab. In the Control Source box, select and delete the expression and type =count(*).

e. Scroll to the last of the records from your customers (that is just above the name of the other salesperson, Lockley).

You see the number of records of orders sold by you—39.

f. Press **Ctrl+Home** to return to the top of the report. Select the **Markup Percent** label. Click **Totals** in the Grouping & Totals group. Select **Average** from the function list.

g. Scroll to the right. Select the **Price** label. Click the **Totals** command in the Grouping & Totals group. Select **Average** from the function list. Format as currency.

Like the Cost field, the Price field records a per-unit cost, so it does not make sense to sum it.

h. Scroll to the right. Select the **Revenue** label. Click **Totals** in the Grouping & Totals group. Select **Sum** from the function list. Check to make sure the value is formatted as currency.

TROUBLESHOOTING: A group summary statistic should automatically inherit its formatting properties from the field's format. Occasionally, the group total or average calculates correctly, but it is incorrectly formatted. To correct the format, right-click the incorrectly formatted value in the Layout view of the report and select Properties from the shortcut menu. Set the Format property to the correct value, e.g., currency, and close the Property Sheet. This action forces a format correction.

i. Narrow the first two columns so that the report fits on one page horizontally. Refer to Hands-On Exercise 1, Step 3e, if you do not remember how to do this step.

j. Save the report.

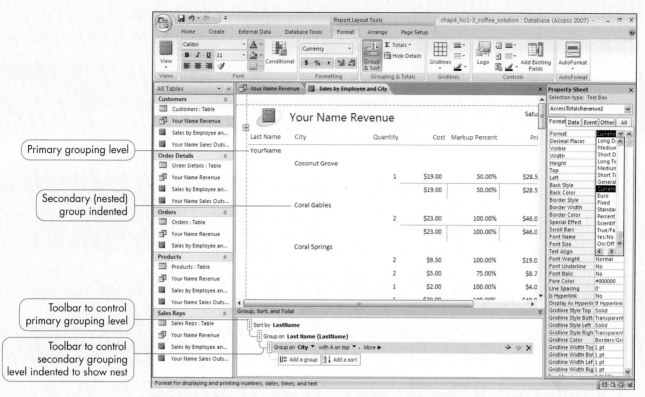

Primary grouping level

Secondary (nested) group indented

Toolbar to control primary grouping level

Toolbar to control secondary grouping level indented to show nest

Figure 4.24 Report with Two Grouping Levels Added

Step 4

Remove Grouping Levels

Refer to Figure 4.25 as you complete Step 4.

a. Save and close the Sales by Employee and City report.

You need practice deleting grouping levels, but you need to preserve the work from Step 3. You will copy the report and delete the group levels in the copy.

b. Right-click the **Sales by Employee and City report** in the All Tables pane. Select **Copy** from the shortcut menu. Move your mouse to a white space in the All Tables pane, right-click, and select **Paste**.

c. Name the copy **Sales by Employee**. Click **OK**.

d. Move your mouse to a white space in the All Tables pane. (Do this a second time.) Right-click and select **Paste**.

e. Name the copy **Sales by City**.

TROUBLESHOOTING: If your monitor resolution is set low, you may have trouble finding white space in which to paste. This file was set to display tables and related objects in the All Tables pane. That view repeats multi-table query and report names. A view that uses less space is the Objects view. Click the All Tables pane title bar and select Object Type. That should free up some white space for you to paste the copied report. After your copied report is pasted and renamed, switch back to the Tables and related view.

f. Open the **Sales by Employee report** in Layout view.

g. Click **Group & Sort** in the Grouping & Totals group on the Format tab to display the Group, Sort, and Total pane (if necessary).

h. Click the **Group on City bar** to select it.

The entire bar turns gold when selected.

i. Click **Delete** on the far right of the bar (it looks like an X).

A warning box tells you that the group has a header or footer section and the controls there also will be deleted.

j. Click **Yes**.

The City grouping disappears, but the employee grouping remains.

k. Click **Save**. Close your report.

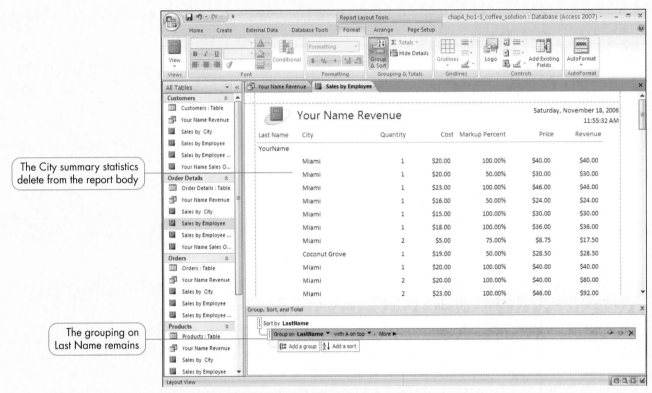

The City summary statistics delete from the report body

The grouping on Last Name remains

Figure 4.25 Sales by Employee

Step 5
Reorder Grouping Levels

Refer to Figure 4.26 as you complete Step 5.

a. Open the **Sales by City report** in Layout view.

You are going to change the order of the grouping fields so that the primary group will be the City and the secondary group the employee.

b. Click **Group & Sort** in the Grouping & Totals group on the Format tab to display the grouping pane (if necessary).

c. Click the **Group on LastName bar** in the Group, Sort, and Total pane to select it.

d. Click the **down arrow** in the right side of the Group on Last Name bar one time.

You might have expected that the report would now be grouped by city and then by your sales and Lockley's sales grouped within each city. Your sales are together in the top of the report, Lockley's in the bottom of the report. Examine the grouping window more carefully. There is a sort in effect. It receives the top priority. So the employee sales will not group in each city.

e. Click the **Sort by LastName bar** to select it.

f. Click **Delete** (X) on the right of the Sort by Last Name bar.

When you delete the sort, the grouping prioritization changes; now, the employees are sorted within the cities as expected.

g. Check to make sure the formats of the group totals and grand totals are appropriately formatted. If not, apply the Currency format.

h. Click the text box containing the report title, *Your Name Revenue*. Click it again to edit it. Change the report name to **Your Name City Revenue**. Save the report.

i. Click **Group & Sort** in the Grouping & Totals group on the Format tab.

j. Click the **Office Button**, select **Manage**, and then select **Back Up Database**. Enter the file name **chap4_ho2_coffee_solution** (*note ho2 instead of ho1-3*) and click **Save**.

You just created a backup of the database after completing the second hands-on exercise. The original database *chap4_ho1-3_coffee_solution* remains onscreen. If you ruin the original database as you complete the third hands-on exercise, you can use the backup file you just created.

k. Close the file and exit Access if you do not want to continue with the next exercise at this time.

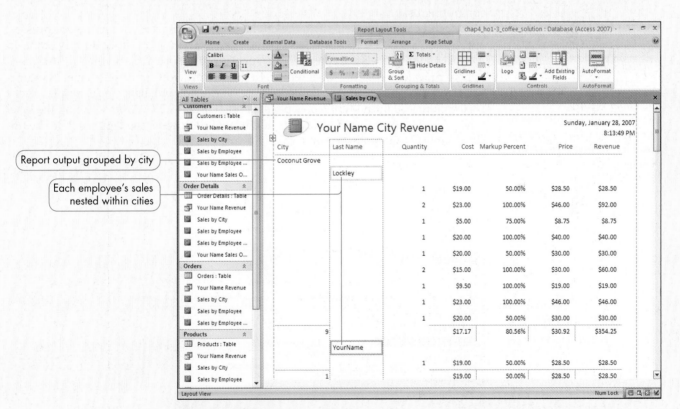

Figure 4.26 The City Report

The Report and Label Wizards

Earlier in this chapter, you created a polished, professional report with grouping levels, sorts, and summary statistics by using the Report tool. You edited the report through a GUI interface and immediately saw the effect on the output. You may recall that Access provides four ways of creating a report (see Table 4.1). In this section, you will create a report using the Report Wizard and edit it using both the Layout and Design views.

> The **Report Wizard** asks you questions and then, depending on how you answer, generates the report.

The **Report Wizard** asks you questions and then, depending on how you answer, generates the report. Many of the wizard's dialog boxes contain commands that lead you to further levels of options. As you read this section and work through the hands-on exercise, you should explore the additional options and think about how and when you might use them. Access provides so many methods of report generation because Access users require so many differing types of reports. As you gain experience, you will learn which tool is most appropriate for your tasks.

If no query exists that assembles the necessary fields for a report, the Report Wizard is probably the best option. It enables you to pull fields from multiple sources relatively easily. Access reports generated by using the Report Wizard sometimes require extensive revision to make them intelligible. Occasionally, the necessary revision time greatly exceeds the time needed to assemble the needed fields in a query in order to use the Report tool. You will need to experiment with the differing methods of report generation to discover which works most effectively with your data and computing usage style.

> **Mailing labels** are self-stick, die-cut labels that you print with names, addresses, and postal barcodes.

Mailing labels are self-stick, die-cut labels that you print with names, addresses, and postal barcodes. You purchase name-brand labels at an office supply store. In Access, mailing labels are considered a specialized report. You use the **Label Wizard** to help produce a mailing label report. In the wizard, you specify the label manufacturer and the label product number shown on the box of labels. For example, Avery 5660 contains 30 individual labels per sheet that are 1" x 2⅝". After selecting the label type, you place and format the fields in the label prototype (see Figure 4.27). The finished report is shown in Figure 4.28.

> The **Label Wizard** asks you questions and then, depending on how you answer, generates the report formatted to print on mailing labels.

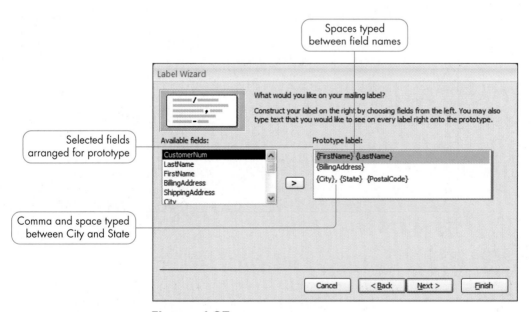

Figure 4.27 Label Prototype

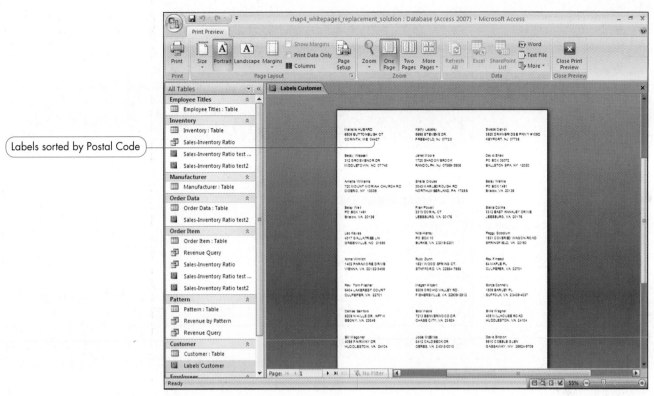

Figure 4.28 Completed Labels

Labels sorted by Postal Code

Using the Report Wizard

Even when using a wizard to guide your report formation, you need to pre-plan the desired output. Suppose you needed a monthly sales report that grouped the products by category and provided summary statistics monitoring the average discounts offered to customers and the revenue generated from product sales. This report would require one grouping level and two summary calculations—one for total revenue and the other for average discount rate. Next, you need to identify the report's record source. For this illustration, you may assume that all necessary records exist in a query. In actual practice, you may need to first create the query assembling the needed records. Some Access users source reports directly from table data. After thinking through the design and record source, you launch the wizard.

> Even when using a wizard to guide your report formation, you need to pre-plan the desired output.

Start the Report Wizard

You do not need to have the report record source open to launch the Report Wizard like you do when using the Report tool. You may wish to close any open objects in your database before launching the wizard. Find the Report Wizard on the Create tab in the Reports group. The first dialog box asks you to specify the record source (see Figure 4.29).

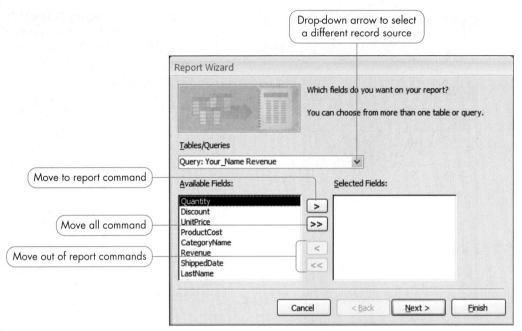

Figure 4.29 Select Records

Group Records

Grouping lets you organize and consolidate your data. You also can calculate aggregating information. In this report, you need the data grouped by the Category Name field, so in the wizard's box under "Do you want to add any grouping levels?" you would identify and double-click the Category Name field. If you needed additional grouping levels, you would double-click those field names also. The order in which you select the groups dictates the order of nesting in the report (see Figure 4.30). The Priority commands let you change your mind and restructure the nest levels. If you select a date/time field to group by, click Grouping Options to find an interval specification box. Use it to designate the grouping interval, such as week, month, or quarter.

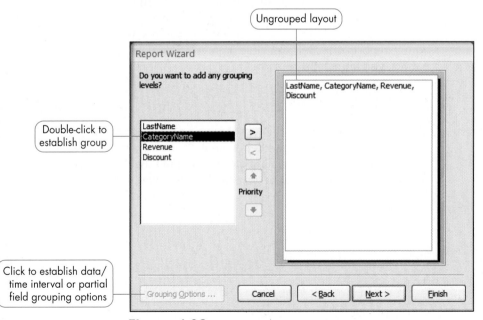

Figure 4.30 Specify Grouping Options

Figure 4.31 shows the grouping options set to group on Category Name. Once the group is established, the Grouping Options command activates. If the group field was a date/time field, you would establish the interval in the Grouping Intervals dialog box. Because this grouping field is a text field, the intervals displayed contain portions of the field name, i.e. the first two letters. You might use this feature if you were grouping an inventory list and the inventory IDs within a category started with the same letters. For example, FJW123, FJR123, FJB123 might be inventory numbers for the fine jewelry department for watches, rings, and bracelets. If you set the grouping interval option to the two initial letters, you would include the fine jewelry department's entire inventory.

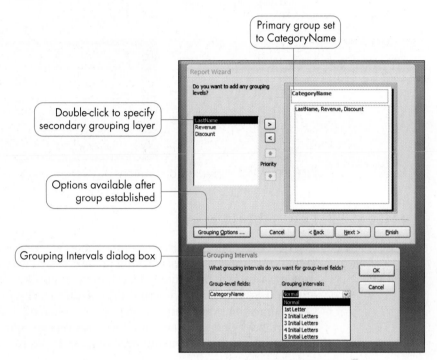

Figure 4.31 Grouping Options Set on Category

Add Sorts and Summary Instructions

The next dialog box asks "What sort order and summary information do you want for detail records?" Notice that the sorts apply only to a detail record. Some reports omit the detail, making the sort order moot. If this were a detail report, you might specify that the details be sorted first by category in ascending order, and then by revenue in descending order. Because you have decided to create a summary report, you need to click the Summary Options command. This step takes you to a screen where you may choose summary statistics (sum, average, minimum, and maximum), and whether or not you want the details presented (see Figure 4.32). Clicking either OK or Cancel returns you to the wizard.

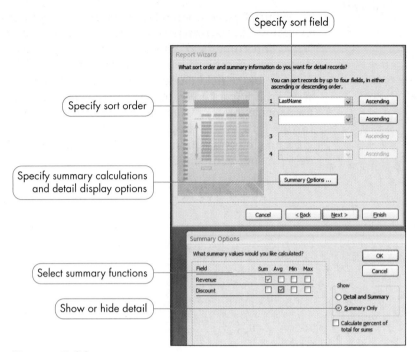

Specify sort field

Specify sort order

Specify summary calculations
and detail display options

Select summary functions

Show or hide detail

Figure 4.32 Specify Sort Options

Design the Report

The next two dialog boxes control the report's appearance. In the first, you select the layout from three options. Clicking an option will give you a general preview in the preview area. The final dialog box offers you options among the AutoFormats available (see Figure 4.33). In actual organizations, the Public Relations and Graphic Communications departments dictate the design of all printed output. The organization will have one template for all internal reports and one or two others for reports generated for external consumption (e.g., an invoice).

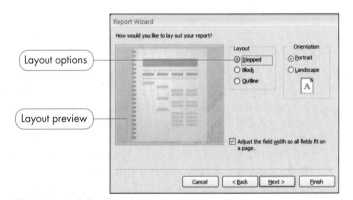

Layout options

Layout preview

Figure 4.33 Specify Layout Options

Ironically, the design selection variety makes life more difficult for students than for real-world practitioners. On the job, you typically employ fewer than five templates. You use them all day, every day. You become intimately acquainted with all of their quirks. You develop functional work-arounds. A *work-around* acknowledges that a problem exists and develops a sufficing solution. In a course, you use a variety of differing templates and never fully understand any of them. Figure 4.34 shows AutoFormat choices.

A *work-around* acknowledges that a problem exists, and develops a sufficing solution.

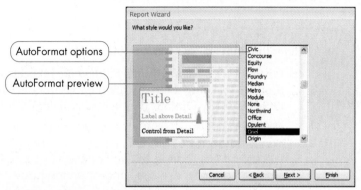

Figure 4.34 AutoFormat

Save and Name the Report

A well-designed database may contain only a few tables, but it may have many queries and reports. You should name all report objects descriptively to save you time and minimize frustration. Always name your report something that not only makes sense to you today, but also will communicate the report's contents to a co-worker or to you in six months (see Figure 4.35).

In the next hands-on exercise, you will create a report using the Report Wizard and edit it using the Layout view.

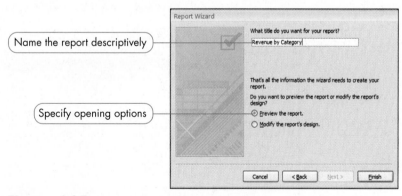

Figure 4.35 Use Descriptive Report Names

Hands-On Exercises

3 | Report Wizard

Skills covered: 1. Assemble the Report Data **2.** Create a Query-Based Report and Add Grouping **3.** Create Summary Statistics **4.** Select Layout and AutoFormatting **5.** Modify the Report

---

Step 1
Assemble the Report Data

Refer to Figure 4.36 as you complete Step 1.

a. Open the *chap4_ho1-3_coffee_solution* file if necessary, click **Options** on the Security Warning toolbar, click the **Enable this content option** in the Microsoft Office Security Options dialog box, and click **OK**.

TROUBLESHOOTING: If you create unrecoverable errors while completing this hands-on exercise, you can delete the *chap4_ho1-3_coffee_solution* file, copy the *chap4_ho2_coffee_solution* backup database you created at the end of the second hands-on exercise, and open the copy of the backup database to start the third hands-on exercise again.

b. Open the **Your Name Revenue query** in Design view.

c. Add the **OrderDate** field located in the *Orders* table to the design grid by double-clicking it.

d. Add the **ProductName** field located in the *Products* table to the design grid by double-clicking it.

e. Click **Run** in the Results group on the Design tab to run the query. Scroll right to ensure that the newly added fields exist.

f. Save the changes. Close the query. Check to make sure the query name is selected in the Navigation pane.

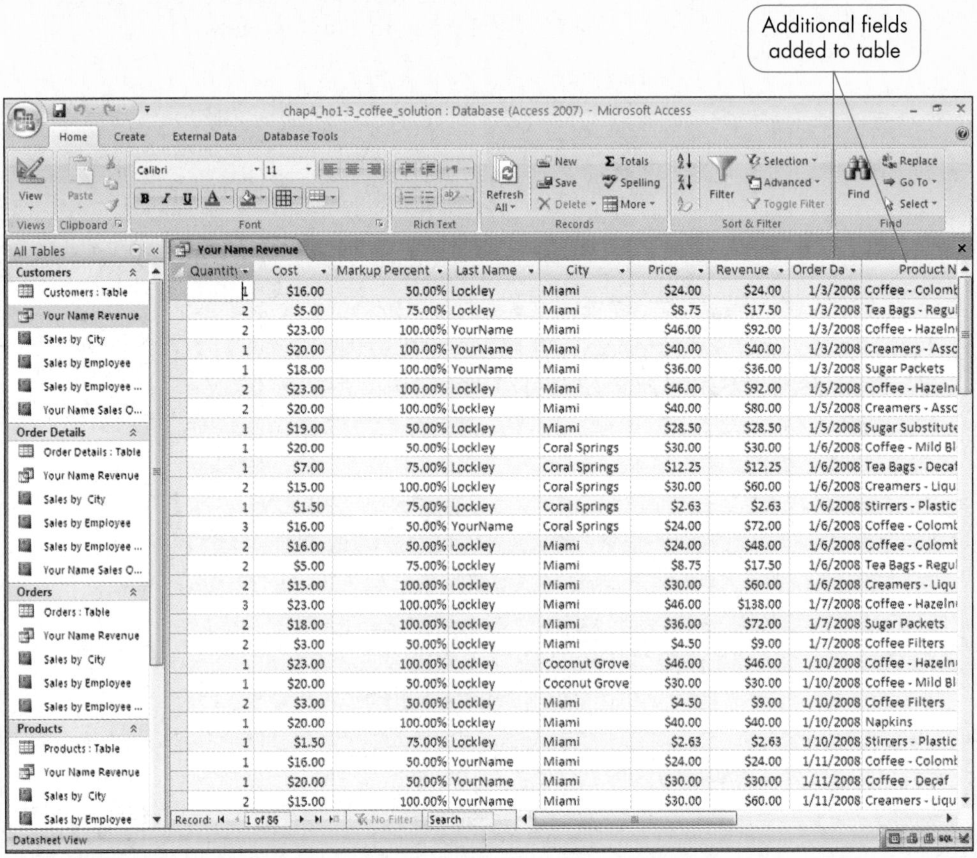

Figure 4.36 Assemble the Record Source

Step 2

Create a Query-Based Report and Add Grouping

Refer to Figure 4.37 as you complete Step 2.

a. Click the **Create tab** and click **Report Wizard** in the Reports group.

The wizard launches, and the Your Name Revenue query selects as the record source because it was highlighted when you started the wizard.

b. Click the **Move All command (>>)** to move all of the query fields to the Selected Fields box. Click **Next**.

c. Double-click **OrderDate** in the grouping level box.

The right box displays the default date grouping, OrderDate by Month. In this case, you want a monthly report so you do not need to change the grouping options command.

d. Double-click the **LastName** field in the left box to add it as a grouping level.

e. Compare your grouping levels to those shown in Figure 4.37. If they match, click **Next**.

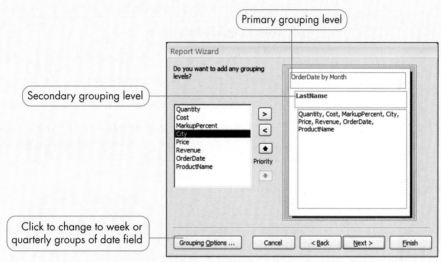

Figure 4.37 Create Groups

Step 3

Create Summary Statistics

Refer to Figure 4.38 as you complete Step 3.

a. Click the drop-down arrow beside the first sort box. Select **City** as the primary sort field.

b. Click **Summary Options**.

TROUBLESHOOTING: As long as the Report Wizard dialog box remains open, you can click Back and revisit your work.

c. Click the **Sum** check box for the **Revenue** field.

d. Click the **Calculate percent of total for sums** check box.

e. Compare your Summary Options to those shown in Figure 4.38. If they match, click **OK**, and then click **Next**.

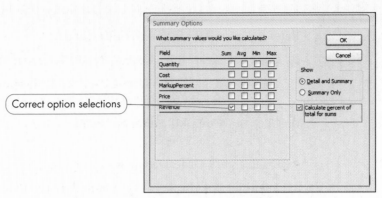

Figure 4.38 Summary Calculation Specifications

<table>
<tr><td>**Step 4**
Select Layout and
AutoFormatting</td></tr>
</table>

Refer to Figures 4.39 as you complete Step 4.

a. Select a **Stepped** layout and a **Portrait** orientation.

b. Click **Next**.

Spend some time exploring in the Report AutoFormats of the wizard.

c. Select the **Module** style.

d. Click **Next**.

e. Name the report **Your Name Monthly Revenue by Salesperson**.

f. Make sure the **Preview the report** option is selected. Click **Finish**.

You successfully generated output, but it has flaws. Examine your work critically, and then compare the problems you spot to those highlighted in Figure 4.39.

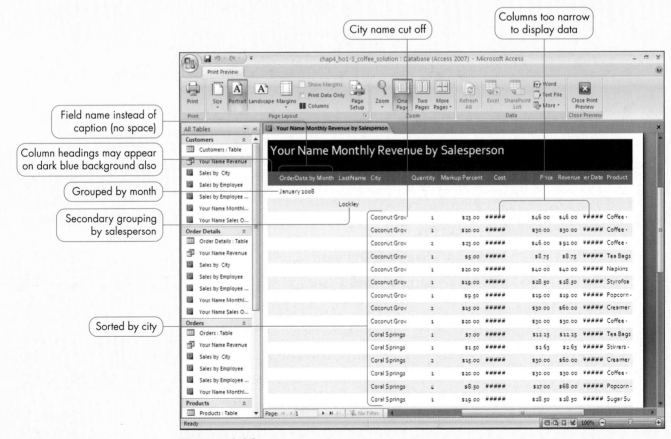

Figure 4.39 Create Groups

Refer to Figure 4.40 as you complete Step 4.

a. Right-click the report tab and select **Layout View**.

b. Select the text box for the OrderDate by Month control. Click it again to edit the text to **Order Month**. Press **Enter**.

Ideally, you should save and close the report, open the Orders table, switch to Design view and add a caption for the OrderDate field. Save the design change to the table and close it. Reopen the report. The caption will replace the field name in the text box in this and all other reports and forms that source on OrderDate. Because you also changed from OrderDate by Month to Order Month, it is excusable to make this a one-time change.

c. Ensure the **Order Month** control is still selected. Move your mouse over the right boundary and when the mouse pointer shape changes to the double-headed arrow, click and drag left about a quarter of an inch.

d. Select the text box for the **LastName** control. Click it again to edit the text. Type a **space** between Last and Name.

e. Select the **City** control text box and widen the column using the click and drag technique presented in Step 5c. Make sure the entire city name, Coconut Grove, displays.

You determine that the report is too crowded and that several fields do not need to be displayed. You decide to delete the Quantity, Markup Percent, Cost, and Price fields.

f. Click the **Quantity** field control text box and press **Delete**.

g. Delete the **Markup Percent**, **Cost**, and **Price** fields.

h. Widen the **Product Name** and **Order Date** fields.

i. Click the **Format tab**. Click **Hide Details** in the Grouping & Totals group.

The details of the report hide. This result makes it easier for you to find and edit the summary statistics.

j. Find the words, *Summary for 'LastName' = Lockley 47 detail records*. On the line below in blue, it says Sum. Look right. You should see a small text box with some numbers or pound signs in it. The control box is too small to display the value. Click the too-small control.

k. Mouse over the control's right boundary, get the double-headed resize arrows, and then click and drag to the **right** to widen the control.

When the box is large enough, you will see that the value of Lockley's total revenue is 1836.5. It is not formatted as currency.

l. Enlarge the controls for **Sum Grand Total**. Check to see that the text boxes are large enough to display the percent values, too. Enlarge those text boxes if necessary.

m. Click the **Sum** value for Lockley, 1836.5. **Right-click** and select **Properties** from the shortcut menu. Set the **Format** property to **Currency**. With the Properties Sheet still open, click the grand total and format it as **Currency**.

All of the sums should display in Currency format. Because there are two grouping levels, the Report Wizard repeats the grand total twice. You want to keep the bottom one because it is in the report footer along with the words, *Grand Total*.

n. Find the repeated Grand Total value (the one labeled Sum). Select it and press **Delete**. Select and delete the word *Sum*.

o. Click **Hide Details** in the Grouping & Totals group on the Format tab to return the details to the report.

You hid the details to format the totals. It moves them out of the way and makes it easier to format the total information.

p. Move the **Sum** and **Standard** control boxes left and position them under the Summary for 'LastName' = Your name. Align the total with the Revenue column. You also need to move the grand total controls.

q. Move the **percent** control boxes left under the Order Date column. Make the boxes wide enough to display the values. the control box containing **100%** and the **label**.

r. Locate the text box containing the **page number**. If necessary, move the right boundary left so that it no longer crosses the dotted line indicating the page break.

s. Right-click the report tab and select **Print Preview**.

t. Click **Two Pages** in the Zoom group. Use the navigation commands to preview the last page. Print the report. Save the report.

u. Click the **Office Button**, select **Manage**, and then select **Compact and Repair Database**.

v. Close the file and exit Access.

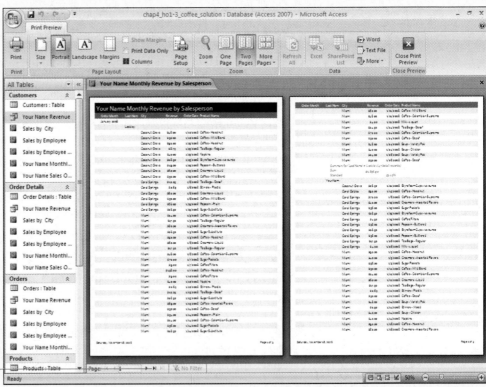

Figure 4.40 The Report in Print Preview

Summary

1. **Plan a report.** A report is a printed document that displays information from a database. Telephone directories, financial statements, shipping labels, and receipts are examples of reports. You should carefully consider what information you need and how you can optimally present it. A paper and pencil may be the best tools for planning. Develop a series of questions to ask to determine what the report should answer. Identify the data sources for the report. Select a reporting tool.

2. **Use different report views.** Access provides different views of your report depending on the operation you need to accomplish. Print Preview is an invaluable tool while designing reports. Use it liberally to preview your reports. Report view enables you to organize the data for the report by sorting and filtering it. Layout view enables you to alter the report design. This is the most powerful view and where you will spend most of your time. Design view displays the report's infrastructure design, but no data. This view has its advantages in large reports, but may be more difficult to use to make exact tweaks to the formatting.

3. **Create and edit a report.** To use the Report tool, you need to assemble all of the necessary data in one place. Occasionally, a table contains all of the necessary fields for a report. More often, you will need to create or open a query containing the necessary fields. If an existing query has all of the fields needed for the report but also some unneeded fields, you probably will use the existing query. You can delete the extraneous fields in Layout view. Access does a lot of the cosmetic work in your reports for you, by adjusting column widths as you add and remove columns. You can do the rest in Layout view.

4. **Identify report elements, sections, and controls.** Access divides all reports into sections, although you only see the sectional boundaries when you display the report in the Design view. Detail Section is the body of the report, containing each record. The Report Header (Footer) Section prints at the beginning (end) of each report. Group headers and footers appear at the tops and bottoms of each report group. Page headers and footers display at the top and bottom of each report page. You can edit these areas in the Design or Layout views. Controls display, position, format, and calculate the report data. You will use bound controls, those that are bound or tied to a source table or query, most frequently. Unbound controls have no record source in the underlying data. An example of an unbound control would be the report's title. A calculated control uses an expression as opposed to a record value as its data source. The expression usually is bound to record values of the fields referenced.

5. **Add grouping levels in Layout view.** Access provides several methods of grouping and summarizing data. You can create (1) a Totals query by specifying a group by field and the field or fields to summarize, (2) a grouped report using the Layout view's Sorting and Grouping tools, and (3) a grouped report using the Report Wizard and specifying the group layers within the wizard. Since most reports will have many thousands of records, you should sort them using the Group Sort tool. Nested groups make the report look similar to an outline. You also can hide and display details in reports and calculate summary statistics. You can add sub-groupings as needed.

6. **Add fields to a report.** Inevitably, after a report has been used, someone will say, "It would be nice to have this in the report, too." Use the Layout view to add additional fields to a report.

7. **Use the Report Wizard.** Access contains several wizards that will print common repeatedly used reports such as mailing labels. It is important that you organize your desired output for wizards just as you would if you designed the report from scratch. Unlike the Report tool, when using a Report Wizard, you should close any open objects in the data source. Like in the Report tool, you can customize the reports from the Report Wizard with groups, sorts, and summaries to tweak the overall design to best present your data. A well-designed database may only have a few tables, but dozens of queries and reports. Chances are good that they will be reused, so they should be saved and descriptively named.

Key Terms

Multiple Choice

1. Which statement most accurately describes the appropriate time to use a report in Access?

   (a) Entering data

   (b) Printing output for presentation

   (c) Querying data

   (d) Sorting records based on preset criteria

2. Which of the following is true?

   (I) You can edit the appearance of reports by changing fonts and styles.

   (II) You can add graphs, pictures, and charts to reports.

   (a) I but not II

   (b) II but not I

   (c) Neither I nor II

   (d) Both I and II

3. Which is an example of a report from a database?

   (a) A shipping label

   (b) A telephone directory

   (c) A sales receipt

   (d) All of the above

4. Which statement about saving a report is true?

   (a) Saved reports are static, and the data represented in a report will be the same every time you run a saved report.

   (b) Saving reports is generally not done in the real world because people rarely need the same information repeatedly.

   (c) You can edit a saved report to add additional fields at a later time.

   (d) Using a saved report can be costly and time-consuming.

5. The most important tool to create an Access report may be:

   (a) The Report Grid tool

   (b) A calculator

   (c) A pencil

   (d) The Report Creator tool

6. It is always best to ask _____ questions about what the report should look like and do.

   (a) the programmer

   (b) the end user

   (c) the customer

   (d) your manager

7. Which of the following are important things to know as you create an Access report?

   (a) Access cannot calculate data in a report.

   (b) Reports can be summarized, but the summaries have to be designed in the underlying query.

   (c) Reports cannot draw data from multiple tables.

   (d) What type of delivery mechanism will be used, fax, e-mail Word, Excel, PowerPoint, Internet, or printer, and what type and size of paper will be used for the report.

8. If you want to create mailing labels from your Customers table, the fastest and easiest tool would be Access':

   (a) Report Tool

   (b) Report Wizard

   (c) Label Wizard

   (d) Mailing Wizard

9. Which of the following is the most sophisticated and flexible tool for report generation?

   (a) Report Wizard

   (b) Report Tool

   (c) Free form report

   (d) WYSIWYG report

10. Use the _____ to see what the printed report will look like before printing. This step helps with the overall layout and makes the report easy to read and understand.

    (a) Report Tool

    (b) Report Wizard

    (c) Group Wizard

    (d) Print Preview

11. You should modify column widths and row heights for a report in:

    (a) Layout view

    (b) Print Preview

    (c) Group view

    (d) Report view

12. Which of the following is true?

    (I) Access can create a report from multiple tables.

    (II) You will usually have to create a new query to create a report.

    (a) I but not II

    (b) II but not I

    (c) Both I and II

    (d) Neither I nor II

13. What happens if you click a value in Layout view and press Delete?

    (a) The entire column is deleted from the report, and column widths are adjusted to use the empty space.

    (b) Nothing; you cannot change data in Layout view.

    (c) The record is deleted from the report but remains in the database.

    (d) An error message appears, saying that you should not attempt to manipulate records in a report.

14. Your pointer shape should be a _____ to widen or narrow a column in Layout view.

    (a) single arrow

    (b) hand

    (c) two-headed arrow

    (d) dashed-tail arrow

15. Which of these is not a sectional division used in Access?

    (a) Detail section

    (b) Report header and footer sections

    (c) Group header and footer sections

    (d) Summary section

16. Bound controls are so called because they are bound or attached to:

    (I) source data

    (II) the report's margins

    (a) I but not II

    (b) II but not I

    (c) Both I and II

    (d) Neither I nor II

17. Which of the following is true?

    (a) Unbound controls are used infrequently within reports.

    (b) Unbound controls are used to display cosmetic elements in a report.

    (c) Unbound controls must be saved separately because they are not part of a record.

    (d) Unbound controls cannot be used with bound controls in the same report.

18. To organize your data in a highly usable and readable report, you may use:

    (a) Nested tables

    (b) Nested groups

    (c) Nested queries

    (d) Calculated fields

Practice Exercises

1 Comfort Insurance Raises and Bonuses Report

The Comfort Insurance Agency is a midsized company with offices located across the country. The Human Resource office is located in the home office in Miami. Each year, each employee receives a performance review. The review determines employee eligibility for salary increases and the annual performance bonus. The employee data are stored in an Access database, which is used by the Human Resource department to monitor and maintain employee records. Your task is to prepare a report showing the salary increase for each employee and his or her performance bonuses (if any). You are the Human Resource department manager. If you correctly report the employee salaries and bonuses, you will receive a bonus. Work carefully and check the accuracy of the calculations. This project follows the same set of skills as used in Hands-On Exercises 1 and 2 in this chapter. If you have problems, reread the detailed directions presented in the chapter. Compare your results to Figure 4.41.

a. Copy the partially completed file *chap4_pe1_insurance* to your production folder. Rename it **chap4_pe1_insurance_solution**, open the file, and enable the security content.

b. Click the **Database Tools tab** and click **Relationships** in the Show/Hide group. Examine the table structure, relationships, and fields. After you are familiar with the database, close the Relationships window.

c. Rename the query with **your name**. Open the **Your Name Raises and Bonus query**.

d. Click the **Create tab** and click **Report** in the Reports group.

e. Click **Group & Sort** in the Grouping & Totals group, if necessary. Click **Add a sort** in the Group, Sort, and Total pane and select **LastName**.

f. Click the **LastName** label. Click it again to edit it and add a **space** between *Last* and *Name*. Click outside the text box to turn off editing. Move the mouse to the **right** control boundary and when the pointer shape changes to the double-headed arrow, click and drag the boundary about a half-inch to the left to make the column narrower.

g. Repeat Step f to add a space to the *FirstName* control and decrease its width. Also reduce the width for the *Performance* column. The report should only be one page wide. Add spaces to the *2008Increase* and *NewSalary* controls.

h. Click the **Report Graphic** (the picture in the upper left) to select it. Click **Logo** in the Controls group on the Format tab. Browse to and locate the file named *chap4_pe1_confident.jpg*. Click **OK** in the Insert Picture dialog box.

i. Click the report title *Your Name Raises and Bonuses* to select it. Point the mouse at the middle of the control box and when the pointer shape changes to the four-headed move arrow, move the report title right.

j. Click the **Confidential graphic** and drag the **right** boundary right to enlarge the warning.

k. Right-click any number in the **New Salary** field and select **Properties** from the shortcut menu. Set the Format property in the Property Sheet to **Currency** and close the Property Sheet.

l. Right-click any number in the **Bonus** field and select **Properties**. Set the **Format property** to **Currency**. Close the Property Sheet.

m. Right-click the report tab and switch to **Print Preview**. If your report looks like the one in the figure, save the report as **Your Name Raises and Bonuses**.

n. Close the database.

...continued on Next Page

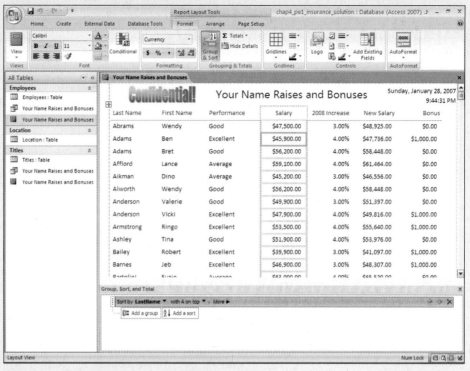

Figure 4.41 Raises and Bonuses Report

2 Comfort Insurance Raises by Location

The Comfort Insurance Agency is a midsized company with offices located across the country. The Human Resource office is located in the home office in Miami. Each year, each employee receives a performance review. The review determines employee eligibility for salary increases and the annual performance bonus. The employee data are stored in an Access database. This database is used by the Human Resource department to monitor and maintain employee records. Your task is to prepare a report showing employee raises and bonuses by city. You will need to total the payroll and bonus data for each city. You are the Human Resource department manager. If you correctly prepare the report, you will receive a bonus. This project follows the same set of skills as used in Hands-On Exercises 1 and 2 in this chapter. If you have problems, reread the detailed directions presented in the chapter. Compare your results to Figure 4.42.

a. Copy the partially completed file *chap4_pe2_insurance.accdb* to your production folder. Rename it **chap4_pe2_insurance_solution.accdb**, open the copied file, and enable the security content.

b. Click the **Database Tools tab** and click **Relationships** in the Show/Hide group. Examine the table structure, relationships, and fields. After you are familiar with the database, close the Relationships window.

c. Open the **Employees Query** in Datasheet view. Click the **Create tab** and click **Report** in the Reports group.

d. Click **Add Existing Fields** in the Controls group on the Format tab. The Field List pane opens on the right. In the bottom of the Field List pane is the *Fields available in related tables pane*. Click the **Show all tables** link. The Location table is listed with a plus sign next to it. Click the **plus sign** to reveal the hidden fields available in the Location table.

e. Double-click the **Location** field (not the LocationID field) to add it to the report. Because this field is in a table not in the original record source, Access asks if it is OK to create a new query that contains the Location field. Click **Yes**. The city names add to the report. The new field is selected. Close the Field List pane.

f. Click the **Location** text box at the top of the field. Move the mouse to the middle of the selected Location field and when the mouse pointer assumes the four-headed move shape, click and drag the field to the **leftmost** position in the report.

...continued on Next Page

g. Click the **LastName** text box at the top of the field to select it. Click it a second time to edit it. Type a **space** between Last and Name. Add spaces to **FirstName**, **HireDate**, **2008Increase**, **2008Raise**, **YearHired**, and **YearsWorked**.

h. Select the **Last Name** field. Move the mouse pointer over the right boundary and when the pointer shape changes to a double-headed arrow, click and drag **left** to narrow the column. Repeat this step for the **First Name** field.

i. Right-click any record in the **2008 Raise** field and select **Properties**. In the Properties Sheet, set the Format property to **Currency**. Close the Property Sheet.

j. Select the **Year Hired** field and delete it. Adjust any field column widths as necessary to make sure all the columns fit on one page.

k. Click **Group & Sort** in the Grouping & Totals group to turn on the Group, Sort, and Total pane (if necessary). Click **Add a group** in the Group, Sort, and Total pane. Click **Location** in the Group on Select field box.

l. Click the **More Options** command on the Group on Location bar. Click the drop-down arrow beside "with LastName totaled." Click the drop-down arrow in the Total On box and select **2008Raise**. Click the **Show Grand Total** and **Show in group footer** check boxes. Click anywhere outside the Total by box.

m. Click the report title and change it to **Your Name**.

n. Click the **Office Button**. Position the mouse pointer over **Print** and click **Print Preview**. Print the report.

o. Save the report as **Your Name Raises by Location**. Close the database.

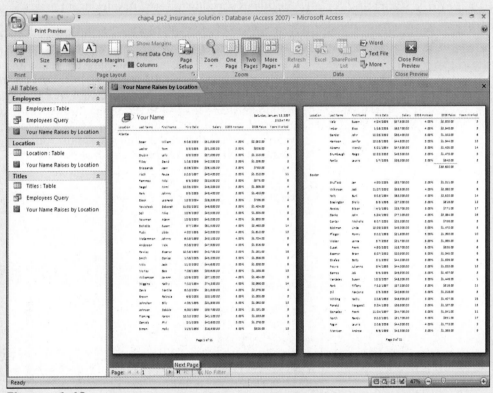

Figure 4.42 Raises by Location Shown in Print Preview

3 Northwind Traders

Northwind Traders is a small, international, specialty food company. It sells products in eight different divisions: beverages, confections (candy), condiments, dairy products, grains and cereals, meat and poultry, produce, and seafood. Although most of its customers are restaurants and gourmet food shops, it has a few retail customers, too. The firm purchases merchandise from a variety of suppliers. All of the order and inventory information is stored in the company's database. This database is used by the management to monitor and maintain records. You are the marketing manager. Your task is to prepare a report showing the profitability of the products in your inventory. You need to group the products by their categories. You also need to average the profit

...continued on Next Page

margin by category. (A profit margin is the profit divided by the price.) This project follows the same set of skills as used in Hands-On Exercises 1, 2, and 3. If you have problems, reread the detailed directions presented in the chapter. Compare your results to Figure 4.43.

a. Copy the partially completed file *chap4_pe3_traders.accdb* to your production folder. Rename it **chap4_pe3_traders_solution.accdb**, open the file, and enable the security content.

b. Click the **Database Tools tab** and click **Relationships** in the Show/Hide group. Examine the table structure, relationships, and fields. After you are familiar with the database, close the Relationships window.

c. Click the **Create tab** and click **Report Wizard** in the Reports group. Select the **Profit Margin query** in the first screen of the dialog box. Click the **Move all to Report command (>>)** to move all of the fields in the query to the report. Click **Next**.

d. Select **by Categories** to answer the "How do you want to view your data?" question. This step creates the necessary grouping level. Click **Next**. You already have established the grouping level so click **Next**, again two times.

e. Click **Summary Options** and indicate that you would like the **Avg** for the *PerUnitProfit* field. Click **OK**, and then **Next**.

f. Ensure that **Stepped** layout and **Portrait** orientation are selected and click **Next**.

g. Select the **Aspect** style and click **Next**. Name the report **Your Name Profit Margin**. Set it to open to **Preview**. Click **Finish**.

h. Right-click the report tab and select Layout View.

i. Click the report title to select it. Click again to edit it. Change the title to **Your Name Category Profit Margins**.

j. Click the **UnitsInStock** text box and click it again to edit it. Insert a **space** between Units and In. Position the insertion point left of the **S** in Stock and type **Ctrl+Enter** to force a line break. Click the **Profit Margin** text box and click it again to edit it. Position the insertion point left of the **M** in Margin and type **Ctrl+Enter** to force a line break.

k. Click the text box for **Per Unit Profit**. Move the mouse over the **right boundary**. When the pointer shape changes to the double-headed arrow, click and drag the right boundary **left** to make the column narrower. Make the Product Name and Category columns wider to display the record contents. Adjust the widths of the remaining columns as necessary to fit all on one page.

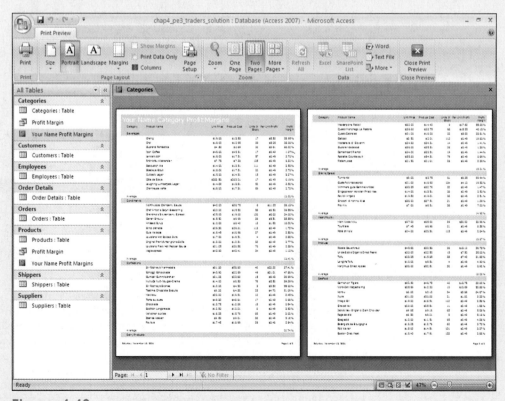

Figure 4.43 Profit Margin by Category

...continued on Next Page

l. Select the **Summary for Category Name . . .** and press **Delete**. Select **Ave** and replace it with **Average**.

m. Save the report. Print the report. Close the database.

4 Member Rewards

The Prestige Hotel chain caters to upscale business travelers and provides state-of-the-art conference, meeting, and reception facilities. It prides itself on its international, four-star cuisines. Last year, it began a member rewards club to help the marketing department track the purchasing patterns of its most loyal customers. All of the hotel transactions are stored in the database. Your task is to determine the revenue from each order and to summarize the revenue figures by location and service type. This project follows the same set of skills as used in Hands-On Exercises 2 and 3. If you have problems, reread the detailed directions presented in the chapter. Compare your results to Figure 4.44.

a. Copy the partially completed file *chap4_pe4_memrewards.accdb* to your production folder. Rename it **chap4_pe4_memrewards_solution.accdb**, open the file, and enable the security content.

b. Click the **Database Tools tab** and click **Relationships** in the Show/Hide group. Examine the table structure, relationships, and fields. After you are familiar with the database, close the Relationships window. Rename the **Your Name Revenue** query with **your name**.

c. Open the **Your Name Revenue** query in Datasheet view.

d. Click the **Create tab** and click **Report** in the Reports group.

e. Click **Group & Sort** in the Grouping & Totals group to turn on the Group, Sort, and Total pane (if necessary). Click **Add a group** in the Group, Sort, and Total pane. Click **City** in the Group on list box. Click **Add a group** and select **ServiceName** in the Group on list box.

f. Click **Hide Details** in the Grouping & Totals group.

g. Click **Group on ServiceName** in the Group, Sort, and Total pane to activate the group bar. Click the **More** command. Click the **with City totaled drop-down arrow**. In the **Total On** box, select **NoInParty**. In the **Type** box, select **Average**. Click the **Show in group header** check box.

h. Return to the Totals dialog box, click the drop-down arrow, and click **PerPersonCharge**. Set **Type** to **Average** and check **Show in group footer**.

i. Return to the **Totals** dialog box, click the drop-down arrow, and click **Revenue**. Set **Type** to **Sum** and check **Show in group header**.

j. Click **Group on City** to activate the group bar. Click **More**. Locate and click the **with City totaled drop-down arrow**. In the **Total On** box, select **NoInParty**. In the **Type** box, select **Average**. Click the **Show in group footer check box**.

k. Return to the Totals dialog box, click the drop-down arrow, and click **PerPersonCharge**. Set **Type** to **Average** and check **Show in group footer**.

l. Return to the Totals dialog box, click the drop-down arrow, and click **Revenue**. Set **Type** to **Sum** and check **Show in group footer** and **Show Grand Total**.

m. Click the **ServiceName** text box and click it again to edit it. Insert a **space** between Service and Name. Click NoInParty to select and type **Number In Party**. Position the insertion point right of the **r** in Number and type **Ctrl+Enter** to force a line break. Click the **PerPerson Charge** text box and click it again to edit it. Add a space between Per and Person. Position the insertion point left of the **C** in Charge and type **Ctrl+Enter** to force a line break.

...continued on Next Page

n. Click the text box for **City**. Move the mouse over the **right boundary**. When the pointer shape changes to the double-headed arrow, click and drag the right boundary **left** to make the column narrower. Adjust the widths of the remaining columns as necessary to fit all on one page.

o. Right-click a value in the **Number in Party** field. Select **Properties** from the shortcut menu. Set the **Format** property to **Fixed**. Click the **Decimal Place** property and select **1**. Click a value in the Per Person Charge field. Set the **Format property** to **Currency**. Click a value in the Revenue field to set the **Format property** to **Currency**. Examine the formats of the city and grand totals and adjust their formats if necessary.

p. Right-click the report tab and select **Print Preview**. Save the report as **Your Name Revenue by City and Service**. Close the database.

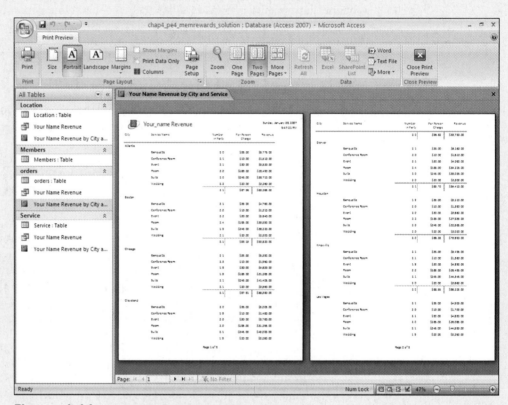

Figure 4.44 Revenue by City and Service

(Replacements, Ltd is a real company located in Greensboro, North Carolina. The data in the case file are actual data. The customer and employee information have been changed to ensure privacy. However, the inventory and sales records reflect actual transactions.)

Today is the first day in your new position as associate marketing manager at Replacements, Ltd., which has the world's largest selection of old and new dinnerware, including china, stoneware, crystal, glassware, silver, stainless, and collectibles. In preparation for your first day on the job, you have spent hours browsing the Replacements Web site, www.replacements.com. You classify the merchandise by category number where 1 is dinnerware, 2 is crystal/glassware, and 3 is flatware (knives and forks). You are responsible for managing several different patterns of merchandise. To accomplish this task, you need to closely monitor past sales in the various patterns to understand purchasing habits and product demand. You exchange information with the customer service representatives and monitor their performance. You need to create a report that summarizes sales by pattern for the merchandise in Product Category 1, dinnerware. Compare your work to Figure 4.45.

a. Locate the file named *chap4_mid1_replacement.accdb*, copy it to your working folder, and rename it **chap4_mid1_replacement_solution.accdb**. Open the file and enable the content.

b. Open the **Revenue query**. It contains information about all three product classifications. Today, you are interested only in dinnerware. Create a report and set a filter to select only product category 1.

c. Group the report on the **LongPatName** field. Click the **More Options** command on the group bar in the Group, Sort, and Total pane. Locate the Totals drop-down arrow and select Revenue. Eventually you will hide the details, so set the total to display in the group header.

d. Hide the details. Remove all of the fields except for the LongPatName and Revenue from the report. Replace the label, *LongPatName*, with **Pattern Name**.

e. Save the report as **Your Name Revenue by Dinnerware Pattern**. Title the report appropriately.

f. Insert the *chap4_mid1_replacement.jpg* picture in the logo area. This image depicts the Spode pattern. It is copyrighted by Replacements, Ltd., and is used with permission.

g. Select the **Wide** margin choice. **Enlarge** the picture and **move the controls** in the Report Header and Footer sections to make the report a single page and attractive.

h. Capture a screenshot of the report. Have it open on your computer and press **PrintScrn**. Open Word, type **Your Name and Section Number** and press **Enter**. Press **Ctrl+V**. Save the Word document as **chap4_mid1_replacement_solution**. Print the Word document. Close the Word document and close the database.

...continued on Next Page

Figure 4.45 Dinnerware Revenue by Pattern

2 Calculating and Summarizing Bank Data in a Query

You are the manager of the loan department of the National Bank. Several customers have multiple loans with your institution. A single customer might have a mortgage loan, one or more car loans, and a home improvement loan. The loan department's database contains the records of all of the customer indebtedness. Your task is to use the information stored in the database to summarize the loan payments by month. Compare your results to Figure 4.46.

a. Locate the file named *chap4_mid2_nationalbank.accdb*, copy it to your working folder, and rename it **chap4_mid2_nationalbank_solution.accdb**. Open the file and enable the content. Open the **Customers table**. Find and replace **Michelle Zacco's** name with your name.

b. Open the **Payments Received** query. Use it to create a report.

c. In Report Layout view, use the Group, Sort, and Total pane to add a group. Group these data on the **Payment Date** field.

d. Click the **More** command on the Group on PaymentDate bar in the Group, Sort, and Total pane and set the grouping interval to **Month**.

e. Click the drop-down arrow beside with Amount Received totaled to launch the Totals box. Select **AmountReceived** as the value for Totals on. Show this total in the **group footer**. Also show a **grand total**.

f. Make the name fields narrower. Save the report as **Your Name Payments Received**.

...continued on Next Page

g. Add spaces as needed to the boxes controlling the report labels. Examine the report in Print Preview. Click and drag the Zoom slider to 75%.

h. Capture a screenshot of the Payment Summary query. Have it open on your computer and press **PrintScrn**. Open Word, then type **your name and section number**. Press **Enter**, and then press **Ctrl+V** or click **Paste** in the Clipboard group. Save the Word document as **chap4_mid2_nationalbank_solution.docx**. Print the Word document displaying the screenshot. Close the Word document and close the database.

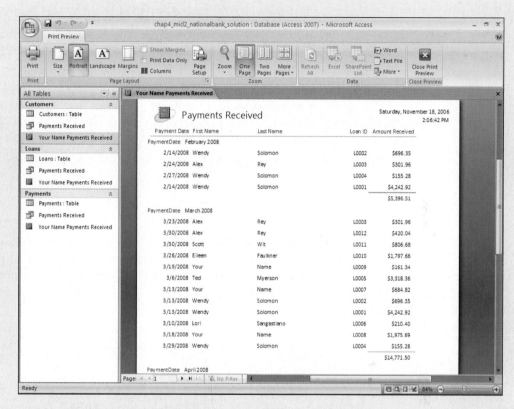

Figure 4.46 Payment Summary

3 Real Estate Report by Month and Salesperson

You are the senior partner in a large, independent real estate firm that specializes in home sales. Although you still represent buyers and sellers in real estate transactions, you find that most of your time is spent supervising the agents who work for your firm. This fact distresses you because you like helping people buy and sell homes. Your firm has a database containing all of the information on the properties your firm has for sale. You believe that by using the data in the database more effectively, you can spend less time supervising the other agents and spend more time doing the part of your job that you like doing the best. Your task is to prepare a sales report listing all recent transactions by month and salesperson. Finally, you need to summarize the sales and commission data by employee and calculate the average number of days each employee's sales were on the market prior to selling. Compare your results to Figure 4.47.

...continued on Next Page

a. Locate the file named *chap4_mid3_realestate.accdb*; copy and rename it **chap4_mid3_realestate_solution.accdb**. Open the file and enable the content. Open the **Agents** table. Find and replace **Pa Lor's** name with your name.

b. Rename the **Your Name Sales Report query** with **your name**. Open it. Create a report. Save the report as **Your Name Sales Report**. Open it in Layout view.

c. Add **spaces** as needed in the labels in the report header. Use **Ctrl + Enter** to force a line break between *On* and *Market* in *DaysOnMarket*. Make the **Subdivision** and **LastName** fields narrower so the report fits on a single page.

d. Activate the Group, Sort, and Total pane. Add a group to group the data monthly by the DateSold. Add another group to group by Last Name.

e. Add totals to the **SalePrice** and **SaleComm** fields that sum. Calculate the Average of the DaysOn Market field. Calculate grand totals for all three summary fields. Display all values in the group footers.

f. Use the Property Sheet to format the **DaysOnMarket** field as fixed with zero decimal places displayed. Format the **SalePrice** and **SaleComm** fields as Currency. Scroll through the complete report to ensure that all of the totals display fully and totals are formatted correctly. Adjust the text box widths if they do not.

g. Insert a picture of a house as the logo. Set the margins to wide.

h. Click the AutoFormat drop-down arrow and select the **AutoFormat Wizard** option. In the AutoFormat box select the Oriel format (3rd column, 4th row). View your report as two pages in Print Preview.

i. Capture a screenshot of the Sales Summary report. Have it open on your computer and press **PrintScrn**. Open Word and press **Ctrl+V** or click **Paste** in the Clipboard group. Save the Word document as **chap4_mid3_realestate_solution**. Print the screen. Close the Word document and close the database.

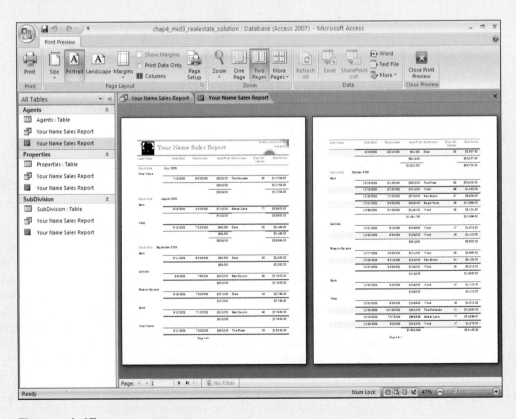

Figure 4.47 Sales Summary

Capstone Exercise

Your boss asked you to prepare a schedule for each speaker for the national conference being hosted next year on your campus. She wants to mail the schedules to the speakers so that they may provide feedback on the schedule prior to its publication. She believes that each speaker will find it easier to review his or her schedule if each speaker's schedule was printed in the same place. You assure her that you (and Access) can accomplish this task.

Database File Setup

You need to copy an original database file, rename the copied file, and then open the copied database to complete this capstone exercise. After you open the copied database, you will replace an existing employee's name with your name.

a. Locate the file named *chap4_cap_natconf.accdb* and copy it to a different folder.

b. Rename the copied file as **chap4_cap_natconf_ solution.accdb**.

c. Open the *chap4_cap_natconf_solution.accdb* file and enable the content.

d. Open the **Speakers table**.

e. Find and replace **Your Name** with your name.

Report Wizard

You need to create a report based on the Speakers and Sessions with Rooms query. You decide to use the Report Wizard to accomplish this task.

a. Activate the **Report Wizard**.

b. Select **Query: Speakers and Sessions with Rooms** as the data source for the report.

c. Move all fields to the report.

d. You want to view your data by speakers. Select **by speakers** if necessary.

e. You want the **LastName** and **FirstName** fields established as the primary grouping level. If they are not already moved into a box at the top of the report, double-click LastName and then FirstName to group by them.

f. Click the drop-down arrow for the first box and select **Date** as the primary sort field. Click **Next**.

g. Select the **Stepped** and **Portrait** options.

h. Choose the **Flow** style.

i. Name the report **Your Name Speaker Schedule**.

Report Edits

The report opens in the Print Preview. You need to examine the report and look for problems. Once they are identified, you will need to switch to Layout view and correct them.

a. Switch to the two-page view.

b. Right-click the report tab and select **Layout View**.

c. Click the **Page Setup tab**. Click **Margins** in the Page Layout group. Select **Wide** from the drop-down menu.

d. Click the text box for **SessionTitle**. Insert a **space** between the words. Add a space to **RoomID**.

e. Move the **Date** field to the right of the Room ID column.

f. Resize the **FirstName** field by making it more narrow. Widen the **Session Title** field. Make the **RoomID** and **Date** fields more narrow.

g. Move the **Speakers** title right. Set the font size to **28 point**.

h. Click the **Logo command** in the Controls group. Insert a picture of a campus. Resize to about the same width as the Speakers title.

Additional Field

You realize the session times were not included in the query and you need them added to the report.

a. Click the Add Existing Fields Command in the Controls group.

b. Click **Show All Tables** in the bottom of the **Field List pane**. Find and **double-click** the **StartingTime** field in the Sessions table on the top of the Field List pane.

c. Click **Yes** in the warning box. Close the Field List pane. Add a **space** between Starting and Time. Adjust columns as needed to fit all columns on one page.

d. Scroll to the end of the page. Find and select the text box for the page number and move it left so the page number prints under the Starting Time field.

e. Change the view to Print Preview, two-page view.

f. Capture a screenshot of the Sales Summary query. Open the query on your computer and press **PrintScrn**. Open Microsoft Word and press **Ctrl+V** or click **Paste**. Save the Word document as **chap4_ cap_natconf_solution**. Print the screenshot file. Close the Word document and close the database.

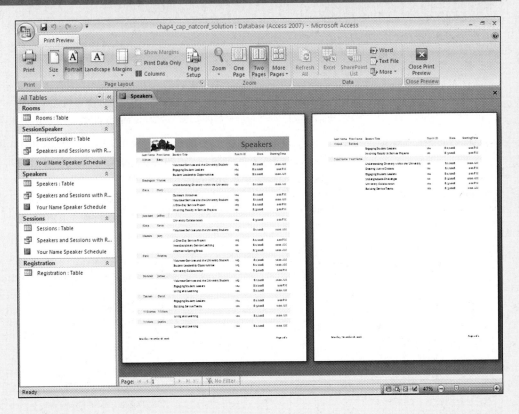

Figure 4.48 Speaker Schedule Report

Mini Cases

Use the rubric following the case as a guide to evaluate your work, but keep in mind that your instructor may impose additional grading criteria or use a different standard to judge your work.

Inventory Value

GENERAL CASE

The owner of a small bookstore called and asked for your help. Her insurance company requires that she provide the company with a report on the values of the inventory she stocks. Copy the *chap4_mc1_bookstore.accdb* file to your working storage folder, name it **chap4_mc1_bookstore_solution.accdb**, and open the copied file. Use the skills from this chapter to perform several tasks. Create a report that shows the publisher's name, the author's first and last names, the book title, the book price, the number in stock, and the value of the stock. The report needs to be grouped by publisher with appropriate summary statistics calculated. The books within each publisher's group should be listed in alphabetical order by the author's last name. The report needs to contain an appropriate graphic and a grand total. The file contains a query that you may use to create the report.

Performance Elements	Exceeds Expectations	Meets Expectations	Below Expectations
Create report	All necessary and no unneeded fields included.	All necessary fields included but also unnecessary fields.	Not all necessary fields were included.
Appropriate grouping and sorting	The grouping and sorting were correctly identified and executed.	Grouping correct but sorting incorrect or vice-versa.	Neither grouping nor sorting properly employed.
Summary statistics	Correct group aggregating information selected and appropriately displayed.	Correct group aggregating information selected, but the display had problems.	Group aggregating information not selected and/or inappropriately displayed.
Summarize balances	Correct method, correct totals.	Correct totals but inefficient method.	Totals incorrect or missing.

Producing Mailing Labels

RESEARCH CASE

This chapter introduced you to the power of using reports, but you have much more to explore. Use Access Help to search for mailing labels. Open and read the articles titled, *Use Access to Create and Print Labels* and *Learn Tips and Tricks for Creating Labels*. Put your new knowledge to the test. Copy the *chap4_mc2_arboretum.accdb* file and rename the copy as **chap4_mc2_arboretum_solution.accdb**. Open the file. It contains a query identifying volunteers who need to be invited to this year's gala. Your challenge is to figure out how to print the names and addresses as mailing labels. You have purchased Avery product number 5260 labels to print on. They are 1½" x 2⅝" with three columns of labels on each page. The mailing will be sent bulk rate, so the labels need to print sorted by postal code. After you successfully produce the report, print it on plain paper. Write your instructor a memo explaining how you accomplished this task. Use a memo template in Word, your most professional writing style, and clear directions that someone could follow in order to accomplish this task. Attach the printout of the labels to the memo. Save the Word document as **chap4_mc2_arboretum_solution**.

Each label should be set up in this fashion:

Mr. (Dr., Ms., Mrs.,) John Doe, Jr.
Street Address
City, State Postal Code

Performance Elements	Exceeds Expectations	Meets Expectations	Below Expectations
Use online help	Appropriate articles located and memo indicates comprehension.	Appropriate articles located, but memo did not demonstrate comprehension.	Articles not found.
Prepare labels	Printed list attached to memo in requested format.	Printed list is attached, but the formatting has minor flaws.	List missing or incomprehensible.
Summarize and communicate	Memo clearly written and could be used as directions.	Memo text indicates some understanding but also weaknesses.	Memo missing or incomprehensible.
Aesthetics	Memo template correctly employed.	Template employed but signed in the wrong place or improperly used.	Memo missing or incomprehensible.

Real Estate Development Report

DISASTER CASE

A co-worker called you into her office, explained that she was having difficulty with Access 2007 and asked you to look at her work. Copy the *chap4_mc3_realestate.accdb* file to your working storage folder, name it **chap4_mc3_realestate_solution.accdb**, and open the file. It contains a query, Your Name Sales Report. It also contains a report based on the query. The report is supposed to show each agent's total sales with each development listed under the agent's name. There should be totals for the sales and commissions columns for each salesperson and each development. Your challenge is to find and correct the error(s) and then to produce an attractive, easy-to-read report.

Performance Elements	Exceeds Expectations	Meets Expectations	Below Expectations
Error identification	Correct identification and correction of all errors.	Correct identification of all errors and correction of some errors.	Errors neither located nor corrected.
Grouping order	Correct grouping options and summarization selected.	Correct grouping, but some summaries incorrectly selected.	Incorrect group by option selection.
Aesthetics	Report design aids reader.	Inconsistent formatting, but all necessary data displays.	Controls improperly sized. Information obscured.

PivotTables and PivotCharts

Data Mining

bjectives

After you read this chapter, you will be able to:

1. Create a PivotTable view **(page 997)**.
2. Calculate aggregate statistics **(page 1002)**.
3. Modify a PivotTable **(page 1004)**.
4. Select an appropriate chart type **(page 1014)**.
5. Identify chart elements **(page 1015)**.
6. Edit a PivotChart **(page 1017)**.
7. Create calculations in a PivotTable **(page 1029)**.

Hands-On Exercises

Exercises	Skills Covered
1. CREATE AND USE A PIVOTTABLE (page 1007) **Open:** chap5_ho1-3_insurance.accdb **Save as:** chap5_ho1-3_insurance_solution.accdb **Back up as:** chap5_ho1_insurance_solution.accdb	• Create a PivotTable from a Query • Add Fields Using the Design Grid • Remove Fields Using the Design Grid • Calculate Summary Statistics and Alter Formats and Captions • Add and Rearrange PivotTable Fields • Remove a Field and Modify Summary Calculations
2. PIVOTCHARTS AND MODIFICATIONS (page 1023) **Open:** chap5_ho1-3_insurance_solution.accdb (from Exercise 1) **Save as:** chap5_ho1-3_insurance_solution.accdb (additional modifications) and chap5_ho2_insurance_solution.docx **Back up as:** chap5_ho2_insurance_solution.accdb	• Remove a PivotChart Field • Add a PivotChart Field • Change AutoCalc Calculation and Set PivotChart Properties and Captions • Edit Series Colors and Patterns
3. CALCULATING FIELD VALUES IN PIVOTTABLES (page 1033) **Open:** chap5_ho1-3_insurance_solution.accdb (from Exercise 2) **Save as:** chap5_ho1-3_insurance_solution.accdb (additional modifications)	• Add a Field to a PivotTable • Identify and Add Fields Needed for Calculations • Create a PivotTable Calculation and Apply Formatting • Total a Calculated Field and Change Formatting • Set Captions

CASE STUDY
Encouraging Volunteerism

You find that your internship at the JC Ralston Arboretum in Raleigh, North Carolina, has a new challenge each day. Today you will work with a group of dedicated volunteers and board members who want to share their love of gardening. They are dedicated to the mission of enriching urban landscapes by promoting a greater diversity of creative, environmentally sound landscapes. The organization enjoys the labor of hundreds of volunteers who donate thousands of hours of service each year. The volunteers enjoy the companionship and the creativity of the arboretum. The group you have been assigned to assist believes that they can increase volunteer participation by tracking

Case Study

involvement by community. Volunteers come from Raleigh and nearby communities such as Cary, Wake Forest, and Chapel Hill. You need to help track which communities the volunteers come from and how many total hours of volunteer time may be attributed to each local community.

Your supervisor tells you that the volunteer hours and city names are stored in the database. You suggest that a chart might be an easy way to communicate these data. The chart could have the city names along the bottom of the chart and different bar heights depicting the total number of volunteer hours for each city. Your supervisor thinks your chart idea is wonderful and asks that you show her your work.

Your Assignment

- Read the chapter, paying special attention to learning the vocabulary of PivotTables and PivotCharts.
- Copy the *chap5_case_arboretum.accdb* file to your production folder, rename it **chap5_case_arboretum_solution.accdb**, and enable the content.
- Open the Relationships window and examine the relationships among the tables and the fields contained within each of the tables to become acquainted with this database.
- Open the Vol + Gala Invite query and then switch to PivotTable view.
- Aggregate the volunteer hours (named Volwork) by summing across the cities.
- Create a PivotChart that displays the total volunteer hours by city.
- Print the table and chart.
- Compact and repair the database file.

Data Mining

At the grocery store's checkout, the cashier asks for your customer membership card and scans it. Many major grocery, bookstore, and electronics store chains employ some form of customer purchase tracking through memberships. You happily provide your membership card because it entitles you to discounts and special prices. You probably filled out a short form to enroll in the frequent buyer or important customer membership program. On the form, you answered questions about your age, education, income, race, and hobbies. The store provides you with a card containing a bar code (a unique identifier) that links your purchases to the promised discounts as well as to the demographic information stored about you from the questions you answered on the application form. *Demographics* are data describing population segments broken down by age, race, education, and so on by geographic regions.

The store analyzes the data describing you and your purchase habits and uses it to decide where to position merchandise in the store and what items to promote. For example, a major electronics retailer might use a frequent-buyer program to identify your purchase patterns and sends you an e-mail containing information on related products. If you purchase several movies of the same genre, you might receive an announcement of a new movie that has a similar theme. Most grocery chains sell the data about customer purchases to food manufacturing, health, and beauty aid companies; advertising firms; and marketing consulting firms. The data sold probably do not contain any of your personal information, such as your name or checking account number. The data are sold as aggregates. For example, the sold data might indicate the total number of 15-ounce boxes of Brand X cereal purchased by single, white females between the ages of 18 and 24 years who do not have a dog or a cat living with them.

Companies perform data mining to analyze consumer purchasing patterns and habits. *Data mining* is the process of analyzing large volumes of data and using advanced statistical techniques to identify patterns and relationships to assist managers in making informed decisions and help predict future customer behavior. Some data mining software is extraordinarily sophisticated and will, once a pattern has been identified, drill more deeply into the data to test further combinations of data without receiving additional instructions. Access provides two tools to help you perform limited data mining—PivotTables and PivotCharts.

PivotTables and PivotCharts enable the managerial decision maker to summarize and organize data with a variety of arrangements and multiple groupings. With the ability to collapse and expand groups and perform a range of calculations, PivotTables and PivotCharts empower the decision maker with the ability to discern patterns and trends in historical data in an attempt to predict and control the future.

In this section, you explore PivotTables and PivotCharts and work with query views. You also learn the specialized vocabulary that relates to PivotTables and PivotCharts. You will create a PivotTable based on a query and edit the result.

Creating a PivotTable View

The PivotTable views provide you with another method of summarizing and aggregating data. You have already worked with summary queries and grouped reports, which provide similar abilities. Sometimes managers need database reports on a regular basis. For example, a manager might need a weekly report summarizing payroll and overtime authorization by department. Often, the IT staff that manages the database generates that type of report and distributes it to the departmental managers who need the information. Routine and recurrent reports provide the decision maker with information to make routine and recurrent decisions. However, managerial information needs change when the decision is not routine. Opportunities arise and managers need the tools to adjust to changed circumstances. Even absent a surprise, decision makers sometimes have single-use data needs.

> Opportunities arise and managers need the tools to adjust to changed circumstances.

PivotTables and PivotCharts provide powerful aggregation and summarization tools. You can construct a PivotTable very quickly. Because of that, decision makers employ them to answer single-use questions. It would be an expensive use of IT staff time to assemble a report for one person to view only once. Because the PivotTables and PivotCharts can be constructed easily, the person who needs the single-use information may organize it without involving the IT staff. After a PivotTable is constructed, you can alter it easily to examine additional aspects.

Create a Query PivotTable View

You may employ PivotTable and PivotChart views to forms, tables, and queries. However, a PivotTable works with only one table or query at a time. Because the power of PivotTables and PivotCharts lies in their ability to combine complex data in different ways to discover patterns, you will primarily use query data to construct PivotTables and PivotCharts. The elements of good database table design that group only similar items in a table make table and form data less suitable for PivotTable analysis. For example, the human resource (HR) manager may wish to examine the pay raise percentage throughout the organization to ensure that employees receive equitable raises. The HR manager may need to examine raises by office location (from the Location table), by job classification (the Position table), or by employee performance rating (the Employee table). Complex data analysis tools need complex data to realize their potential. Therefore, you will create PivotTables and PivotCharts based on queries.

The first step in analysis of data using PivotTables and PivotCharts requires that you assemble your source data in a single object. Often, the database will contain a query containing the necessary data. If no query exists that contains the appropriate data, you need to create it or modify an existing query. After you assemble the source data, open the query and switch to PivotTable view. Figure 5.1 illustrates the PivotTable design grid.

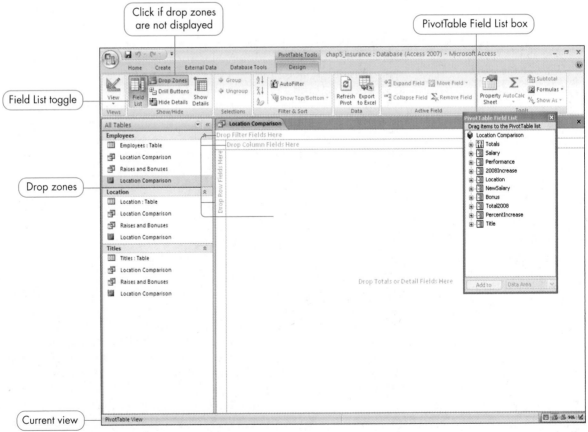

Figure 5.1 PivotTable Design Grid

Add Fields to the PivotTable View

A **_drop zone_** is an area in a PivotTable or PivotChart design grid where you drop fields to organize the data.

The **_row field_** is the field that you assign to group data horizontally into rows.

The PivotTable view appears blank when initiated because Access is waiting for your instructions on how to display the data. The light blue rectangles identify the drop zones. **_Drop zones_** are areas in the PivotTable or PivotChart design grid where you drop fields to organize the data. The primary drop zones are row field, column field, totals or detail field, and filter field. You use the row, column, and filter fields to define how to organize the data for analysis. The **_row field_** is the data source field that you use to group data horizontally into rows. Row fields are generally created by fields containing text, such as states or cities. In Figure 5.2, the Location field is selected. Notice the Drop Row Fields Here drop zone border is blue, indicating that the contents of the Location field are appropriate for a row field. After you click and drag the Location field to the Drop Row Fields Here drop zone, the PivotTable displays an alphabetical list of cities where the firm has offices.

Figure 5.2 Field Selected for Row Field

The **_detail field_** contains individual values to be summarized.

The largest drop zone contains the **_detail field_**, which is the location where you position the field or fields that contain data to be analyzed. Generally, the detail field is a field that contains individual numerical data, such as quantities, monetary values, or percentages. In Figure 5.3, the PercentIncrease field was added to the Drop Totals or Data Fields Here drop zone. This instructs Access to summarize the PercentIncrease field by city, the field used to organize data into rows. Dropping the PercentIncrease field in the detail field helps you analyze the data to see if pay raises across locations and positions are equitable. These data from the PercentIncrease field are averaged instead of totaled because the underlying values are percentages. For example, the average increase for Phoenix managers is 5.93%.

Figure 5.3 Average Increase (Detail Field) by City (Row Field)

You should notice a couple of things after adding fields to the drop zones. First, field names are bold in the PivotTable Field List window after you add them to the PivotTable. In Figure 5.3, the Location and PercentIncrease fields are bold after adding them to the drop zones. Second, you see *drill buttons*, the little plus (+) and minus (–) signs to the right of individual groups, such as Location in the current PivotTable. Click the + drill button to display additional details for a particular group, or click the – drill button to collapse a group that is currently expanded. These buttons are useful as you experiment with the PivotTable to get the right amount of detail to analyze the data properly. If the drill buttons do not appear in the PivotTable, click Drill Buttons in the Show/Hide group on the Design tab.

The *column field* is the data source field that you use to assign to group data vertically in columns in a PivotTable. Figure 5.4 shows the Title field dropped in the Drop Column Fields Here drop zone to display each job title as an analysis specification to determine percentage increase equity. Now, you can compare the average percent increase in each city by every position title: account rep, manager, senior rep, and trainee.

A *drill button* is the plus (+) or minus (–) sign that enables you to show or collapse details.

The *column field* is the field that you assign to group data vertically into columns.

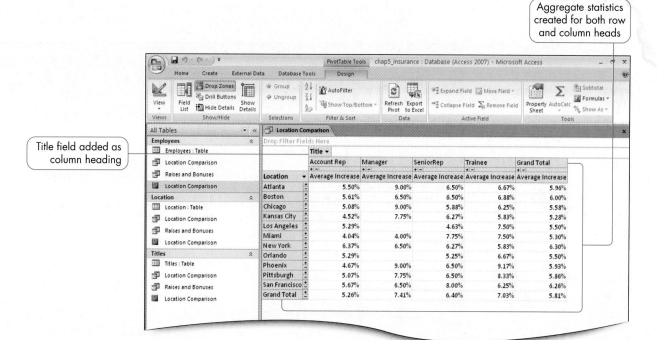

Aggregate statistics created for both row and column heads

Title field added as column heading

Figure 5.4 Title Field Added to Column Field Drop Zone

A ***filter field*** is the field that you use to filter data based on specified criteria.

A ***filter field*** is the data source field that you use to create specific criteria to filter data in a PivotTable. You use a filter to analyze data based on a particular condition; all other data are excluded from the analysis. For example, you can set a filter to display data for a particular state, department, job position, and so on. Figure 5.5 displays the Performance field added to the Drop Filter Fields Here drop zone. The filter is set to Good so that you can analyze data for all sales representatives who received a Good performance rating. The HR manager can then examine the results to determine if this year's salary increases are equitable for all of the employees with a good performance rating across locations and position titles. In this case, the raises are remarkably consistent. Good managers in Kansas City and New York received the same percentage increase in their salaries.

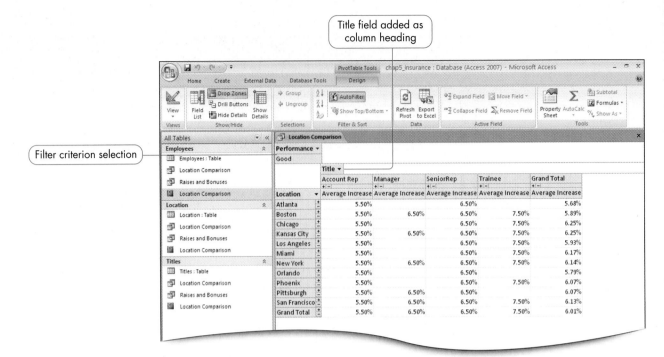

Title field added as
column heading

Filter criterion selection

Figure 5.5 Completed PivotTable with a Filtered Field Permits Easy Analysis

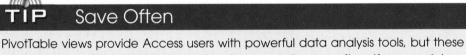

TIP   Save Often

PivotTable views provide Access users with powerful data analysis tools, but these views require some practice to master. As you work, save often. If you run into a problem or make a mistake, you can close the query, reopen it, and switch to PivotTable view to try again.

Calculating Aggregate Statistics

A **data aggregate** is a collection of parts from different sources to form a whole.

After you assemble data in the PivotTable, you can use Access tools to help analyze and extract the information. The PivotTable view provides the same aggregating functions as found in reports and other query views. A **data aggregate** is a collection of many parts that come together from different sources and are considered a whole. Commonly employed aggregating calculations include sum, average, minimum, maximum, standard deviation, and variance. Table 5.1 describes the aggregating functional usage. Access provides you with many methods of summarizing or aggregating data. Decision makers use the methods to help make sense of an array of choices.

Table 5.1 Aggregate Functions

Aggregate Name	Definition	Example
Sum	Adds values together.	Total contributions for a political campaign by state.
Count	Counts the non-null items.	The number of students who earned an A in a computer class.
Min	Returns the smallest value.	The employee with the smallest percent increase.
Max	Returns the highest value.	The employee with the largest salary increase.
Average	Calculates the arithmetic mean—the mean obtained by adding several quantities together and dividing the sum by the number of quantities. It ignores null values.	The average cost of a three-bedroom house in Tulsa.
Standard Deviation	Measures how widely spread the values are from the average when the data describe a sample of the population instead of the entire population.	If the average percent increase were 3 and the standard deviation were 5, these pay increases differ more than if the average were 3 and the standard deviation were 2. The range is more varied in the sample distribution.
Standard Deviation Population	Measures how widely spread the values are from the average when the data describe an entire population.	If the average percent increase were 3 and the standard deviation were 5, these pay increases differ more than if the average were 3 and the standard deviation were 2. The range is more varied in a population distribution.
Variance Population	Measures the square of the population standard deviation.	Spread or dispersion of salaries for employees in similar positions in an organization.

When the field is a text or a yes/no value, you may count its values. You may also count numeric fields and also calculate the sum, count, minimum value, maximum value, average, standard deviation, variance, standard deviation population, and population variance from the data fields in the data area. You must activate a data point in the Drop Totals or Detail Fields zone (the large center box) prior to performing any aggregating calculations. For example, the Bonus field displayed in Figure 5.6 shows the detail for the Atlanta location. Before you use the AutoCalc tool, you must first activate any detail (here the fourth record in the AccountRep column) before you click AutoCalc. The AutoCalc feature generates a drop-down list for you to select the necessary function.

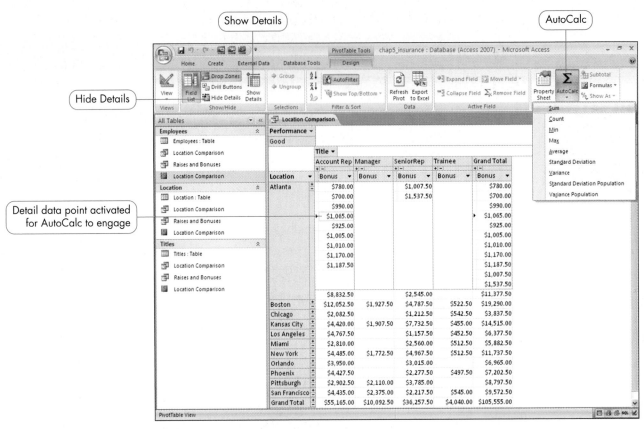

Figure 5.6 Calculating Summary Statistics

Modifying a PivotTable

After you create a PivotTable, you may want to modify the structure or format of the PivotTable. For example, you may decide to reorganize the PivotTable by rearranging fields from rows to columns, select other fields for displaying details, or remove a filter and set a different filter. In addition, you might want to change the format of the PivotTable to be easier to read.

Add and Remove PivotTable Fields

Data mining uses statistical tools to analyze patterns and relationships in data. Once the original PivotTable has been constructed, the decision maker can use the existing form to examine other fields. For example, after the HR manager examines the percent increase across locations, position titles, and good performance rating to ensure equity, he or she may wish to examine the annual bonuses to validate them. You can add additional data items to the drop zone by clicking them in the Field List Box to select them and dragging them to the Drop Totals or Detail Fields drop zone. Figure 5.7 demonstrates the Bonus field added to the PivotTable view. It displays totals for the Bonus field and averages for the PercentIncrease field. The summary shows the information needed by the HR manager, but it is presented in a rather cluttered format.

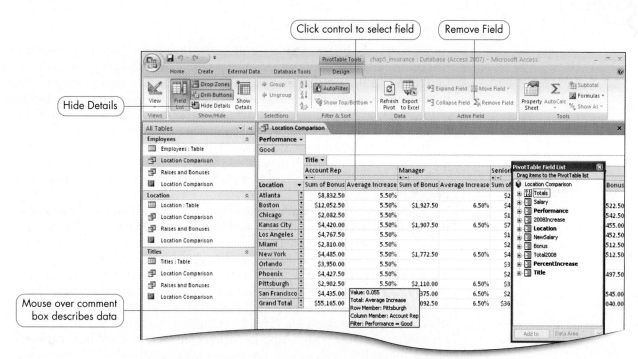

Figure 5.7 Bonus Field Added to an Existing Pivot

After establishing the PivotTable grid, you can easily add and remove data fields to analyze the data. Should you decide that displaying both the average percent increase and the bonus fields makes the information too cluttered to be useful, you can remove the PercentIncrease field data from the grid by clicking the field control button, and then clicking Remove Field in the Active Field group (shown in Figure 5.7). The resulting PivotTable demonstrates an important accounting concept, crossfooting. Accountants use *crossfooting* by summing the rows, summing the columns, and making sure the totals match. It provides an important check figure—a way to verify the accuracy of your data. See Figure 5.8.

Crossfooting sums the rows, sums the columns, and compares the totals.

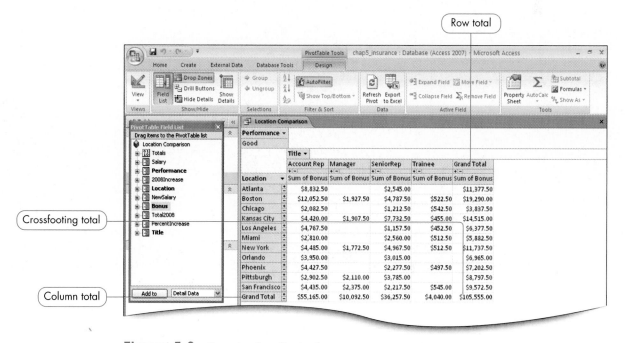

Figure 5.8 Crossfooting Illustration

Change Properties

Access stores the information controlling the data in the Data Properties dialog box. You can control the data's appearance by changing the data's background color or font color and size. It is generally a good idea to visually separate aggregating statistics from data points. You can do so by changing the font color or background color of the total row. This makes PivotTable output easier to understand. To change a format property, right-click the value or values to format and select Properties from the shortcut menu. Make sure the Format tab is active and select the appropriate formats. After formatting the first field, use the arrow in the Select box to define the next field you want to format. In addition to changing formats, you can also sort or delete PivotTable fields.

The Captions tab in the Properties dialog box sheet helps you customize the data presentation. Access uses default names for aggregating statistics. Sometimes the defaults are not easy to understand. They might say AverageofDaysOnMarket. This field name describes the data, but is too long to be easily understood. You can change the way it displays in the PivotTable view by establishing a caption. Click the Caption tab and select the field you wish to caption in the select box. Then type the name you want to display on the PivotTable, for example, Ave Market Days. You may only apply or modify a PivotTable caption by using the field properties if the caption was created with a caption in PivotTable view. If the field caption was created in the table's Design view, you cannot override it with a different caption.

In the following hands-on exercise, you will create a PivotTable, add and remove fields, calculate summary statistics, and display or hide detail.

Hands-On Exercises

1 | Create and Use a PivotTable

Skills covered: 1. Create a PivotTable from a Query **2.** Add Fields Using the Design Grid **3.** Remove Fields Using the Design Grid. **4.** Calculate Summary Statistics and Alter Formats and Captions **5.** Add and Rearrange PivotTable Fields **6.** Remove a Field and Modify Summary Calculations

---

Step 1

Create a PivotTable from a Query

Refer to Figure 5.9 as you complete Step 1.

a. Use Windows Explorer to locate the file named *chap5_ho1-3_insurance.accdb*. Copy the file and rename the copied file as **chap5_ho1-3_insurance_solution.accdb**.

b. Open *chap5_ho1-3_insurance_solution.accdb*. Click **Options** on the Security Warning toolbar, click **Enable this content** in the Microsoft Office Security Options dialog box, and click **OK**.

c. Rename the *Your_Name Raises and Bonuses* query with your name.

d. Copy the *Your_Name Raises and Bonuses* query and name the copy **Copy Of Your_Name Raises and Bonuses**.

You created a copy of the query in which to practice. If all goes well, you can delete the original and rename the copy by deleting the words *Copy Of*. If you run into problems, delete the copied query, recopy the original, and start the exercise again.

e. Open the **Copy Of Your_Name Raises and Bonuses** query. Click the **View down arrow** in the Views group on the Design tab and select **PivotTable View** from the menu.

f. Compare your screen to Figure 5.9.

The Drop Filter Fields Here, Drop Column Fields Here, Drop Row Fields Here, and Drop Totals or Detail Fields Here drop zones appear in the main part of the window. The PivotTable Field List box shows on the right side of the window.

TROUBLESHOOTING: If the drop zones do not appear, click Drop Zones in the Show/Hide group on the Design tab to display the drop zones. If the PivotTable Field List box does not appear, click Field List in the Show/Hide group to display the PivotTable Field List box.

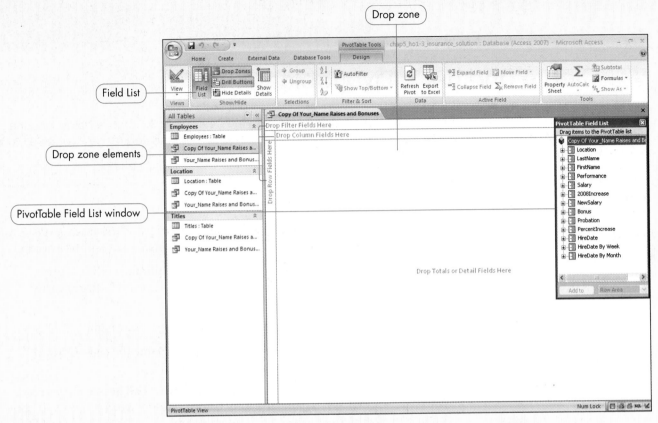

Figure 5.9 PivotTable Workspace

Refer to Figure 5.10 as you complete Step 2.

a. Click the **Location** field in the PivotTable Field List box and drag it to the **Drop Row Fields Here** drop zone.

Alternatively, click the **arrow** beside the Add to button on the bottom of the PivotTable Field List box. Select **Row Area** and click **Add to**.

TROUBLESHOOTING: PivotTables and PivotCharts consume system resources. They require huge amounts of memory and CPU time to run. Be patient. It may take a second or two for your command to execute.

b. Click and drag the **Performance field** from the PivotTable Field List box to the **Drop Column Fields Here drop zone**.

c. Click the **PercentIncrease** field in the PivotTable Field List Pane. Click the **Drop Zone location arrow**, select **Detail Data**, and click **Add to**.

d. Activate a data point by clicking *3.00%* in the Atlanta row and the Average column. Save your query.

Because you set the data to display details, a scroll bar turns on to let you scroll to view other data points.

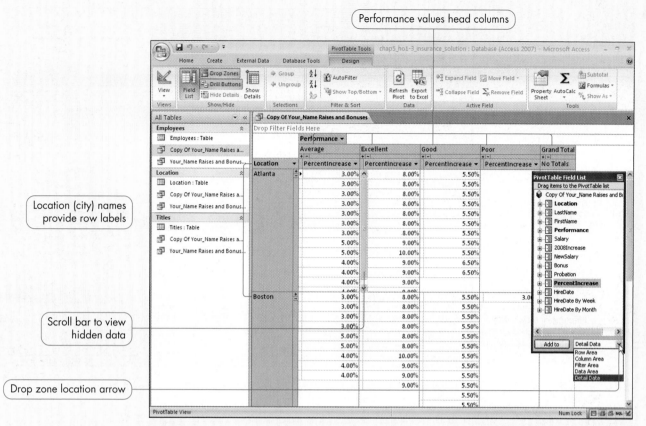

Performance values head columns

Location (city) names provide row labels

Scroll bar to view hidden data

Drop zone location arrow

Figure 5.10 A PivotTable Showing Detail

Refer to Figure 5.11 as you complete Step 3.

Step 3
Remove Fields Using the Design Grid

a. Click any of the **PercentIncrease** labels (look for the gray background) to select the values.

All of the detail values select and turn blue.

b. Check to make sure that **Detail Data** displays as the choice in the Drop Zone location box. Then click the **Bonus** field in the PivotTable Field List box. Click **Add to**.

c. Click any of the **Bonus** labels (look for the gray background) to select the values.

d. Click **Remove Field** in the Active Field group on the Design tab.

The Bonus field data disappear from the PivotTable, and the space it consumed is reallocated to the remaining fields.

e. Click **Save** on the Quick Access Toolbar.

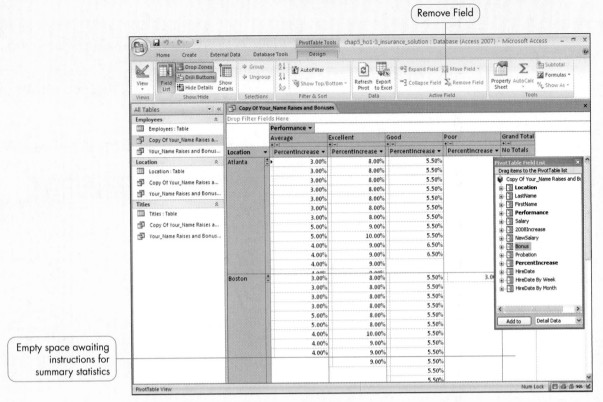

Remove Field

Figure 5.11 Bonus Field Added and Removed

Empty space awaiting instructions for summary statistics

Step 4
Calculate Summary Statistics and Alter Formats and Captions

Refer to Figure 5.12 as you complete Step 4.

a. Click the **PercentIncrease** column head to select it.

All of the values turn blue.

b. Click **AutoCalc** in the Tools group on the Design tab. Select **Average** from the drop-down menu.

The Grand Total column is no longer empty. It displays 5.96% for the Average of PercentIncrease summary statistic for the Atlanta location. You decide that viewing this level of detail is not helpful and decide to collapse the details.

c. Click **Hide Details** in the Show/Hide group on the Design tab.

The details collapse, and the columns get wider because the column labels change to Average of PercentIncrease. The longer title needs a wider column to display.

d. Right-click the **Average of PercentIncrease** column label and select **Properties** from the shortcut menu.

The Properties window for a pivoted field differs from the properties for table or query fields in that fewer options are available for PivotTable fields.

e. Click the **Captions tab** and position your insertion point in the box beside the word *Caption*. It should say *Average of PercentIncrease*. Click or type to change the caption property to **Average Increase**. Click the **red close button** in the top-right corner of the Properties window.

Not only do the column headings change but also the columns get more narrow to fit the smaller labels.

f. Right-click the **Performance** label, select **Properties**, and click the **Format tab**. In the *Cell format* section, click the **Background Color drop-down arrow** and select **White** (first column, last row). With the Properties window still open, click the **Location** label and set its background color to **White**.

TROUBLESHOOTING: If your colors did not come out as expected, use the arrow in the *Select box* of the Properties box and reapply the color change.

g. Close the Properties window. Save the changes made to the PivotTable view.

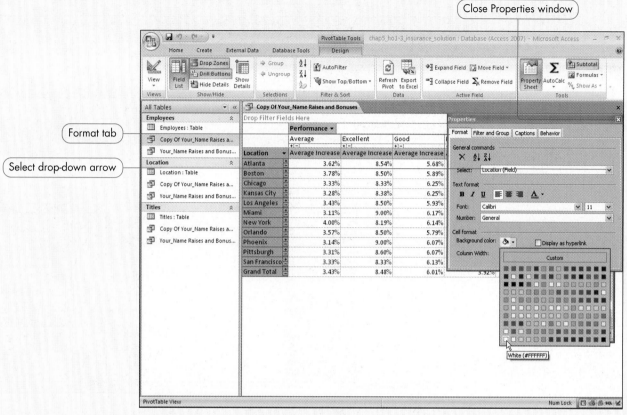

Figure 5.12 Applying Fill Property

Refer to Figure 5.13 as you complete Step 5.

Step 5
Add and Rearrange PivotTable Fields

a. Click **Field List** in the Show/Hide group on the Design tab to display the PivotTable Field List pane. Scroll down if necessary to find the HireDate By Month field in the PivotTable Field List pane.

b. Click and drag **HireDate By Month** to the left of the city names. When the thick blue line displays to the left of the Location column, release the mouse.

You added a second row field. The dates are grouped by year and then by location within each year. When you scroll, you see that only two locations, Atlanta and Miami, have employees that have worked for the company since 1990. If you scroll through the PivotTable data, you will discover that many locations have employees that started working in the years since 2000.

c. Click the **Years** label to select the column.

You know the column is selected because it highlights.

d. Click **Years** and drag it to the right. When the thick blue line is between *Location* and *Average Increase*, release the mouse.

You have exchanged the positions of the two row fields. Now, each location name appears only once in the report, but the years display over and over. Both displays could meet a managerial decision maker's needs. If the question that is most important is "Are the percent increases equitable between locations?," then you would display the location information first. If the question is "Are the percent increases equitable among employees with similar lengths of service?," you would present the data with the years in the left position.

e. Position your mouse over the first record in the **Excellent** column (8.00%). The box that appears drills the data and explains about the underlying data. Save the changes made to the PivotTable view.

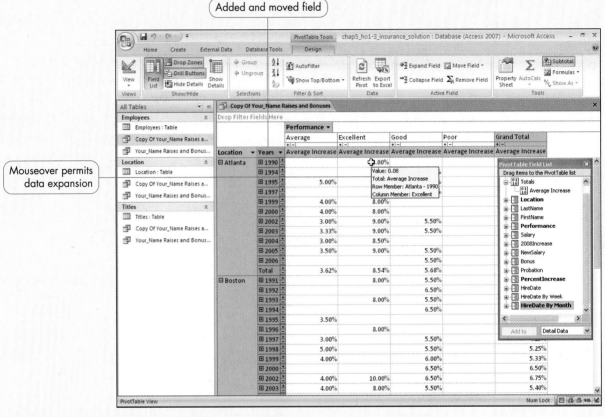

Figure 5.13 Expanded Information

Step 6
Remove a Field and Modify Summary Calculations

Refer to Figure 5.14 as you complete Step 6.

a. Click the **Performance** label. Click **Show Details** in the Show/Hide group.

The table expands to display the hidden detail.

b. Click any **PercentIncrease** label, and then click **Remove Field** in the Active Field group.

The PivotTable frame remains, but the detail data no longer appear.

TROUBLESHOOTING: If your Remove Field tool is dim, it is probably because you did not have a detail active when you attempted to use the Remove Field feature. You must not only have details displayed, but you must also have one active for the Remove Field tool to be available.

c. Click the **Average Increase** label below the Grand Total label, and then click **Remove Field** in the Active Field group to remove this data.

d. Click **Field List**, if needed, in the Show/Hide group to display the PivotTable Field List window, and then click the **Bonus** field to select it and drag it to the Detail area of the PivotTable.

Do not be concerned if no bonus values display in the Average or Poor.

e. Click any value in the detail area of the Bonus field to select it. Click **AutoCalc** in the Tools group. Select **Sum**.

TROUBLESHOOTING: If your AutoCalc tool is dim, it is probably because you did not have a detail active when you attempted to use the AutoCalc feature. You must not only have details displayed, you must also have one active for the AutoCalc tool to be available.

f. Click a **Bonus** label to select it. All of the Bonus values should highlight. Click **Hide Details** in the Show/Hide group.

g. Compare your work to Figure 5.14. If your work matches, continue following the steps. If your work does not match, close the query without saving changes, reopen the query, and rework Steps 6a through 6e.

h. Save and close your query.

i. Select and delete the original *Your_Name Raises and Bonuses* query. Rename the *Copy Of Your_Name Raises and Bonuses* query by deleting the words *Copy Of*.

j. Click the **Office Button**, select **Manage**, and select **Compact and Repair Database**.

k. Click the **Office Button**, select **Manage**, and select **Back Up Database**. Type **chap5_ho1_insurance_solution** and click **Save**.

You just created a backup of the database after completing the first hands-on exercise. The original database *chap5_ho1-3_insurance_solution* remains onscreen. If you ruin the original database as you complete the second hands-on exercise, you can use the backup file you just created.

l. Close the file and exit Access if you do not want to continue with the next exercise at this time.

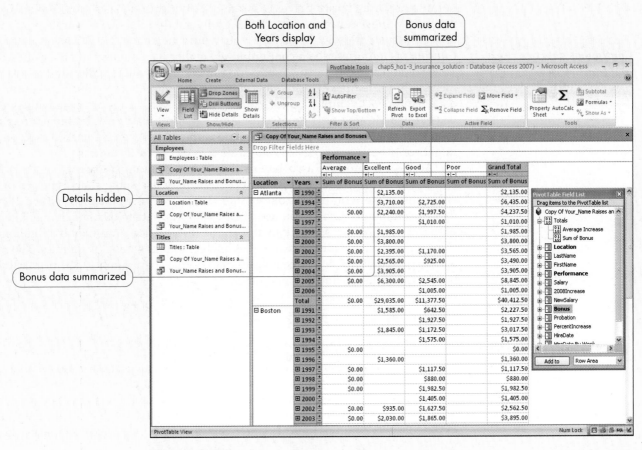

Figure 5.14 Analyzed Data Changed to Bonus

Charts Convey Information

Microsoft Office provides many tools to help you identify and extract only the records needed at the moment. After these records are identified, the decision maker needs to convert the data into information to make it useful. One of the best methods of distilling and summarizing data is to present it in a pictorial form—a chart. Well-designed charts facilitate data interpretation because charts make information clear graphically. You can present a chart differently to emphasize different data aspects. For example, if the proportion of patients receiving emergency room care differs dramatically on different days of the week, you might optimally express this difference with a pie chart. In most hospitals, the pie slices for emergency room care on Monday through Thursday will be about the same size, but the slices representing Friday, Saturday, and Sunday patient care will be much larger. An administrator in charge of scheduling can tell at a glance that more nurses need to be scheduled on the weekends. The same information could be presented in a bar or column chart, but those types of charts would not convey the same visual impact. If the old adage that a picture is worth a thousand words is true, then a well-designed chart is worth 10,000 words.

In this section, you learn about discrete and continuous data and the basics of good chart design. You will learn to create a PivotChart from PivotTable data. Finally, you will learn how to edit the chart to improve its readability.

Selecting an Appropriate Chart Type

Discrete data describe classifications and are measured and quantified in increments.

Before you can create a chart, you need to understand a little about data. You will use two different types of data to create Access charts, discrete and continuous. *Discrete data* describe classifications or categories, such as names of the countries that a company ships orders to, or quantifiable data, such as the number of male and female volunteers for a charity drive. Discrete data typically measure in integer (whole number) values and cannot be meaningfully subdivided. For example, you might have 250 customers in Texas, but you would not have 250.7 Texan customers. *Continuous data* describe a continuum of smaller increments and are easily scaled. These data may be logically subdivided into smaller and smaller units. Measurements of time, temperature, money, volume, size, and distance illustrate continuous data values. For example, manufactured products very rarely are exactly the weight or volume indicated on a container. Slight variances may exist. Manufacturers may randomly sample products to measure the variance. A beverage marked as 32 ounces might really be in any range of values, such as 31.7 or 32.25 ounces.

Continuous data describe a continuum of values.

Access can produce a variety of chart types. You must learn what chart type appropriately expresses each data type. You may use some chart types to depict either discrete or continuous data; other charts are more suited for either discrete data or continuous data. If you use a chart inappropriate to the data, it may interfere with the chart reader's ability to absorb the information. You may distill all of the chart types available into a few families and generalize across the families. The reference page at the end of this section summarizes the chart families. The primary chart families are column, line, pie, and other.

Create Column and Bar Charts

A *column chart* displays quantitative data vertically to compare values across categories.

The default chart type is the *column chart*, which displays quantitative data vertically in columns to compare values across different categories for a particular time frame. You might use it to depict the number of volunteers by city or the value of orders by product category for the first, second, third, and fourth budget quarters in 2009. The height of the columns indicates the relative value of the data being depicted. Taller columns indicate larger values, and shorter columns indicate smaller values.

A **bar chart** displays quantitative data horizontally to compare values across categories.

A **bar chart** also displays quantitative data to compare values across different categories. The width of the bars indicates the relative value of the data being depicted. Wider bars indicate larger values, and smaller bars indicate smaller values. Column and bar charts differ only in orientation. A column chart displays data series vertically in columns, whereas a bar chart displays data series horizontally, left to right. You may be able to use either a column or a bar chart to depict the same data; however, one chart may optimize comprehension of the data better. A bar chart may be preferable when the categorical labels are too wide to fit easily on the horizontal axis of a column chart. By plotting the data on a bar chart, the longer categorical labels might be easier to read.

Create Line Charts

A **line chart** plots data points to compare trends over time.

The **line chart** family, including the area and scatter plot chart types, describes continuously distributed data and should only be used to plot continuous data. You may use this chart family with all time series data. The basic line chart shows trends over time. For example, a line chart is appropriate to depict the number of college graduates over the last 25 years at a particular institution or the number of cellular phones in the United States over the last 10 years.

A **scatter plot chart** shows relationships between two variables.

Another member of the line chart family is the scatter plot chart. The **scatter plot chart** shows relationships between two variables. For example, you might use a scatter plot chart to examine average monthly temperatures and ice cream sales. Presumably, that chart would show lots of data points clustered during the warmest months and fewer data points during the colder months of the year. Scatter plot charts would also be appropriate to compare ACT scores and grade point averages, to compare number of hours of exercise per week and body fat percentage, or to compare number of hours practicing the piano and ratings at a music contest.

Create Pie and Donut Charts

A **pie chart** shows proportion to the whole for a single data series.

A **pie chart** describes parts in relation to a whole. Instead of showing values, the values are converted to percentages of the total value. The larger the slice of the pie, the larger the percentage a category represents of the total. For example, you can use a pie chart type to depict the proportion each product category contributes to the total revenue for a year. A pie chart is also appropriate to depict the proportion of undergraduate male students by class: seniors, juniors, sophomores, and freshmen. A **donut chart** also shows proportions in relationship to a whole, but a donut chart can also display more than one series of data. For example, a donut chart could use one ring to show the proportion of male students by class and the second ring to show the proportion of female students by class.

A **donut chart** shows proportion to the whole for multiple data series.

The other chart family compares values across categories and is most often used in the social sciences. For example, a psychologist might compare the results of an individual's personality attribute test to a population's normal test results.

Identifying Chart Elements

Figure 5.15 shows a PivotChart view of an Access PivotTable. Each PivotTable created also generates a PivotChart. When you created a PivotTable in Hands-On Exercise 1, you also created a PivotChart, even if you have not looked at it yet. Because the two views are linked, any changes you make to the chart will affect the table and any changes made to the table will change the chart. You may already know some of the terminology for a PivotChart because it is the same as in the other chart applications in Microsoft Office 2007. Some of the terms differ slightly. The plot area, title, and legend remain the same.

The **legend** tells which color represents the data for each data series.

The **axes** are the vertical and horizontal scales displaying the information to be plotted.

The **gridlines** are the lines that extend across the chart.

The **chart title** displays a name describing the data depicted in a chart.

The *legend* tells which color represents the data for each data series, such as blue for Product A, green for Product B, and red for Product C. The legend may display anywhere in the chart area. The *axes* are the vertical and horizontal scales displaying the information to be plotted. The axis may be edited to more correctly display the information that you wish to describe. In a column or line chart, the vertical axis, known as the Y-axis, typically displays quantitative values, and the horizontal axis, known as the X-axis, typically displays categories or time periods. The *gridlines* are the lines that extend across the chart. Use them as placeholders to make data interpretation easy. The *chart title* displays a name describing the data depicted in the chart. The other chart elements derive their names from the data used to create them. For example, in the chart shown in Figure 5.15, the field buttons are named Performance, Location, and Title because those are the names of the fields employed for row, filter, and column drop zones. (Here the word Title refers to the field name used in the table, not the chart title.) Figure 5.16 shows the PivotTable view of the same data.

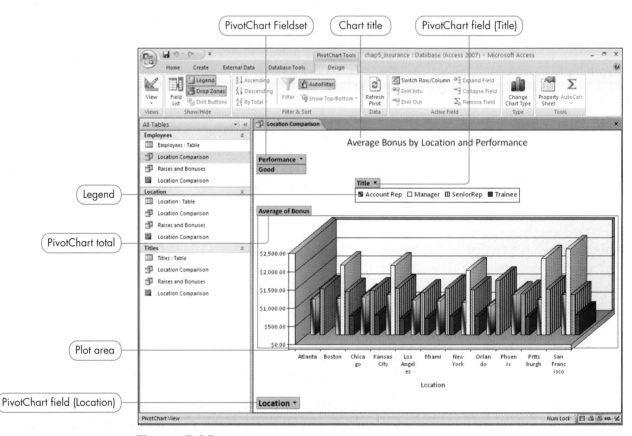

Figure 5.15 PivotChart: Average Bonus by Title and Location

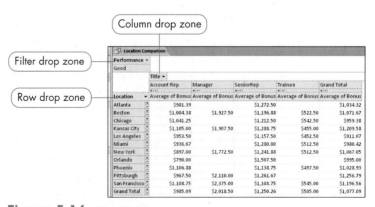

Figure 5.16 PivotTable

Figure 5.17 displays a filtered view of the same chart in which you see only the Account Rep data being plotted. All of the PivotChart fields contain arrows that will produce a filterable drop setting when clicked. If you apply a filter to display only a single position title in the chart, the underlying table also changes. Figure 5.18 displays the changes to the PivotTable after its associated chart was changed. The PivotTable and PivotChart views are locked together. Although you only see one of them at a time, any changes made to one also change the other.

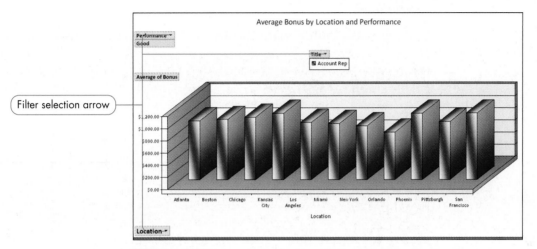

Filter selection arrow

Figure 5.17 PivotChart Filtered to Account Reps by Location

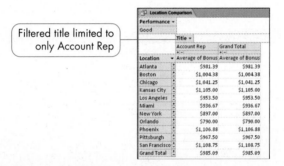

Filtered title limited to only Account Rep

Figure 5.18 Changes in a PivotChart Change the PivotTable

TIP   PivotTables and PivotCharts Locked

Remember that the PivotTables and PivotCharts change together. You will spend time editing a chart to make it display perfectly, make a change in the PivotTable view, and discover that the chart has changed, too. Remember, these are *views* of the object. You may make changes to either view, but the change will automatically update the other.

Editing a PivotChart

Once you realize the power of the PivotTables and PivotCharts, you may be tempted to add more and more data to the drop zones. Figures 5.15–5.18 show only a single performance classification at a time. If you need to examine the pay equity among different locations, you will also need to know if the pay raises are equitable inside performance classifications. For example, a sales representative in Chicago with a good rating should receive about the same bonus as a good Account Rep in Miami or

Boston. It is easy to drag the Performance field from the filter area to the row area of the PivotTable design grid. The table data become slightly more complex, but remain intelligible (see Figure 5.19). However, the PivotChart gives so much information that it no longer functions. Charts have a purpose: They help readers extract complex information from complex data quickly and easily. Figure 5.20 shows a chart that is so complex that readers cannot decipher it.

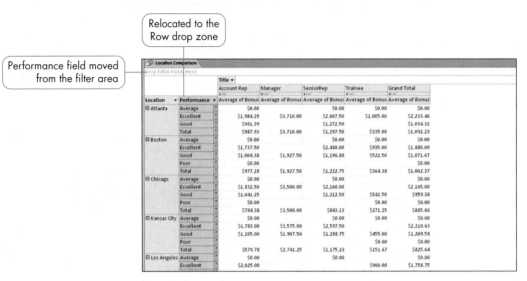

Figure 5.19 Moved Performance Field

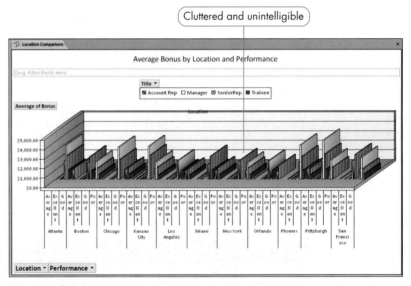

Figure 5.20 Unusable Chart

Change General Chart Properties

Editing an Access PivotChart is similar to editing a chart in Excel. First, you must select the element you wish to edit and then perform needed edits. The big difference is that you select the element through using the Properties window instead of double-clicking it. For example, let us say that you do not like the gray bars reflecting the managerial bonuses and you wish to change them. If you click an individual gray bar, you may edit it, but the edits will not automatically apply to all of the manager bars. To change all of a data series at the same time, you must first select the series. Click Property Sheet in the Tools group on the Design tab. The Properties window (shown in Figure 5.21) contains several tabs. You use the General tab to select the area of the chart for editing. In this illustration, the selected Manager field highlights all of the chart data points. These data points reflect manager bonuses. The selected objects display with a blue highlighted border.

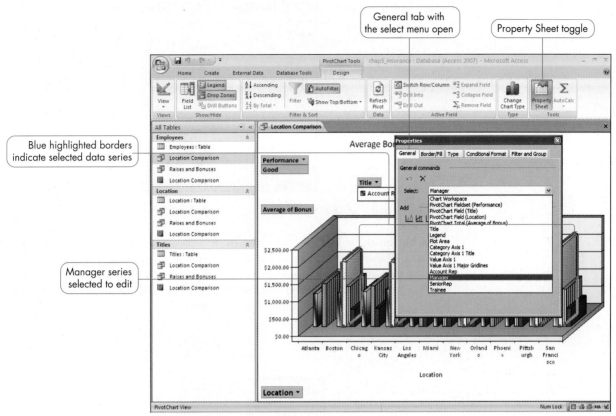

Figure 5.21 Selected Manager Data Series

Change Border and Fill Properties

The Border/Fill tab contains the editing tools you need to control the border or line surrounding the chart object's size and color. You can also define the object's internal color and pattern. You may specify fill types by clicking the Fill Type drop-down arrow in the *Fill* section and selecting from the available types (see Figure 5.22). For example, you may want to change from a solid color to a pattern or picture fill. In addition to changing the fill type, you can change the fill color by clicking the Color drop-down arrow in the *Fill* section (see Figure 5.23). Limit the number of colors you use on your charts. Too many colors may detract from your chart's aesthetics and interfere with the chart's ability to communicate. You need to remember that not everybody sees colors in the same way. Color discernment problems may make your chart unintelligible to some readers. Experiment and have fun, but produce your final chart by limiting the number of colors to only one or two.

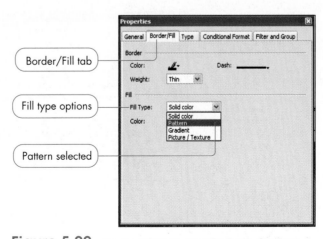

Figure 5.22 Border/Fill Tab and Fill Type Options

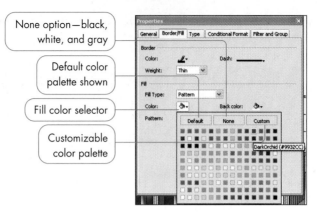

Figure 5.23 Fill Color Options

After establishing fill and color options, you will specify the pattern options. Figure 5.24 shows the range of patterns available. All patterns require you to specify two colors, a foreground color and a back color. Just as with color selection, limit the number and type of patterns you use in your charts. Readers may become confused looking at a chart with too many bold patterns.

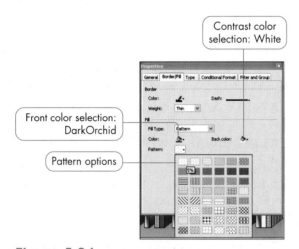

Figure 5.24 Pattern Options

Change Chart Workspace Options

Once the data series have been formatted to your liking, you may experiment with some of the other chart design features. From the General tab, select Chart Workspace to investigate options available for the chart in its entirety. The 3D View tab contains several options governing the appearance of your chart. Figure 5.25

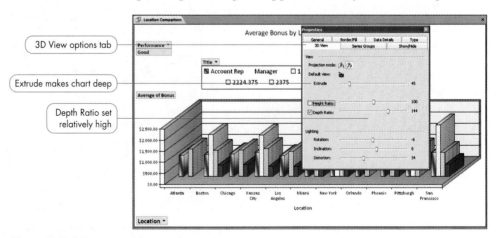

Figure 5.25 3D Adjustments

shows the option set selected to produce the chart displayed in this section. Some of the options have been modified to produce the chart shown in Figure 5.26.

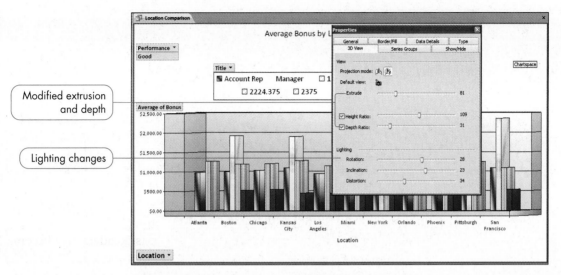

Figure 5.26 Lighting and Depth Options Varied

Adapt to Changes in Data Needs

You assembled the data necessary for PivotTable and PivotChart creation in a query to make your analysis work easier. However, data needs change. You may easily add fields to the PivotTable or PivotChart views. Activate the Field List pane by clicking the Field List in the Show/Hide group. The Field List window opens. Locate the needed field and drag it from the Field List window to the desired position on the PivotTable design grid. If you realize that you need to analyze data that you did not include in the original query design, you must switch to the design view of the query and add the field. Then when you change to the PivotTable view, the newly added field will display in the Field List window. To remove a PivotTable field, you must first display the details of the field you wish to remove. When the details display, click the field's gray title box and press Delete. If the field you wish to remove is a total field, you can delete it either by pressing Delete or with the Remove Field tool in the Active Field group on the Design tab.

In the next hands-on exercise, you will examine the PivotChart, edit it, modify it in design and structure, and save the changes.

Chart Families | Reference

Family Name	Chart Types	Use	Example	Illustration
Column	Column, Bar, Stock in two and three dimensions	Compares values across categories.	Plot number of students enrolled in pre-nursing programs, pre-med, pre-accounting, and pre-information systems courses.	
Line	Area and Line in two and three dimensions, XY Scatter	May only be used with continuously distributed data to show trends over time. Place time measurements on the X axis.	Plot volunteer hours donated by month. Display sales data by quarter.	
Pie	Pie and Donut	May be used only with discrete data to show proportions to the whole. Further, you must know the whole prior to using. If one observation is missing, you cannot draw a pie chart.	Show proportion of last week's revenue generated by product line.	
Other	Radar	Compare criteria. Several axes (one axis per criteria) radiate outward from a common center. Grid lines circle a uniform distance from the center. The purpose of the radar chart is to look at the "whole" of the object, rather than an individual piece. Radar charts are popular in the Eastern cultures, like Japan, because they look at a total picture.	Evaluate a car. Each criterion has a spoke from the middle. One spoke is labeled fuel economy, one handling, one acceleration, one styling, and one ride. The gridlines are at 2, 4, 6, 8, and 10. People were asked to rate the car in each of these areas and the average rating is plotted on the spoke for its criteria.	
Other	Polar	Plots data points as a function of distance from the center and angle around a circular grid.	Time series, directional, or scientific data needing a different analytical perspective.	
Other	Bubble	A variation of a scatter chart to show how sets of things compare according to various factors. The size of the bubbles show the relative size of the data being plotted.	Salaries by job title with the size of the bubble representing the percentage of the total salary budget.	

Hands-On Exercises

2 | PivotCharts and Modifications

Skills covered: 1. Remove a PivotChart Field **2.** Add a PivotChart Field **3.** Change AutoCalc Calculation and Set PivotChart Properties and Captions **4.** Edit Series Colors and Patterns

---

Step 1 Remove a PivotChart Field	Refer to Figure 5.27 as you complete Step 1. **a.** Open the *chap5_ho1-3_insurance_solution* file if necessary and click **Options** on the Security Warning toolbar. Then click the **Enable this content option** in the Microsoft Office Security Options dialog box and click **OK**. **TROUBLESHOOTING:** If you create unrecoverable errors while completing this hands-on exercise, you can delete the *chap5_ho1-3_insurance_solution* file, copy the *chap5_ho1_insurance_solution* backup database you created at the end of the first hands-on exercise, and open the copy of the backup database to start the second hands-on exercise again. **b.** Select the **Your_Name Raises and Bonuses query**, copy it, and paste the copy in a blank space in the All Tables pane. Accept the default name for the copy. You want to practice editing a PivotChart, but do not want to destroy your work from Hands-On Exercise 1. You may practice safely in the copy. **c.** Open the **Copy Of Your_Name Raises and Bonuses query**. Click the **View down arrow** in the Results group on the Design tab and select **PivotChart View** from the shortcut menu. Remember all PivotTables create PivotCharts. You have a chart, but it is not useful in its current form. You need to identify the element that clutters your chart. The Sum of Bonus displays on the Y-axis and the Locations display along the X-axis. That is what you would like. You determine the problem with the chart comes from trying to display the year each employee was hired. **d.** Click the **Years** control (the gray box) in the lower-left corner and drag it off the chart into the All Tables pane. As you drag, your mouse pointer changes shape by adding a red X to the pointer. Drop the **Years field control** anywhere you see the red X. Your chart now displays two series, red and green. However, the chart needs a legend to indicate what red means or what green represents. **e.** Click **Legend** in the Show/Hide group on the Design tab. The chart legend appears on the right side. It tells you that red bars indicate an Excellent review performance, and green bars indicate Good. You should wonder where the poor and average data series are in the chart. Why are there no blue or purple bars? The legend indicates that they exist. You need to examine the data to determine why there are missing bars. **TROUBLESHOOTING:** You never want to waste your time editing a chart that contains flawed or missing data. You might end up making a pretty picture of garbage. It is attractive, but it remains useless to the decision maker. **f.** Save your changes. Click **View** in the Views group on the Design tab and select **Design View** from the shortcut menu.

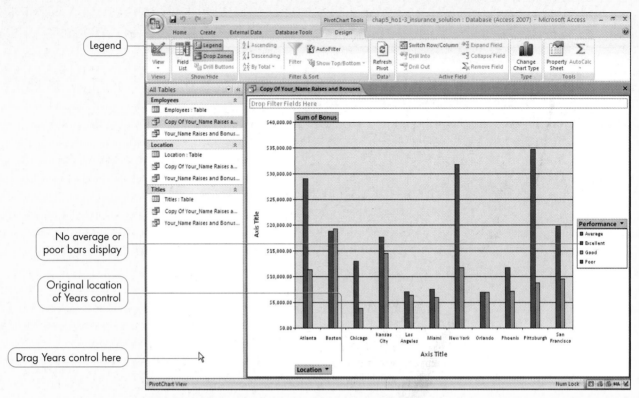

Figure 5.27 Bonus Chart After Year Field Removed

<table>
<tr><td>**Step 2**
Add a PivotChart Field</td><td>Refer to Figure 5.28 as you complete Step 2.</td></tr>
</table>

a. Scroll right in the Design view and click in the Bonus field. Click **Builder** in the Query Setup group on the Design tab.

   The Expression Builder dialog box opens to reveal the formula used to compute employee bonuses. Careful examination reveals that employees with an excellent rating receive bonuses of 5% of last year's salary and good-rated employees receive 2½% of last year's salary as a bonus. Employees with a performance rating of poor or average receive no bonus; therefore, no colored columns appear for these two data series in the chart.

b. Click **Cancel** in the Expression Builder dialog box to exit without changing anything.

c. Click the **View down arrow** in the Results group and select **PivotChart View** from the shortcut menu.

d. Click **Sum of Bonus** in the top-left corner of the chart. Drag it off the chart until you see that the mouse pointer has a red X. Release the mouse button.

   The bars disappear from the chart, but the chart structure—the names of the locations and the currency format on the Y-axis—remains.

e. Activate the Chart Field List pane by clicking **Field List** in the Show/Hide group if necessary.

   The Chart Field List window displays.

f. Click the **PercentIncrease** field and drag it to the top of the chart. When a blue-outlined row appears on the top of the chart, a ScreenTip by your mouse pointer displays *Drop Data Fields Here*. Release the mouse button to drop the PercentIncrease field.

   Your chart should now display the *Sum of PercentIncrease*.

g. Save your PivotChart.

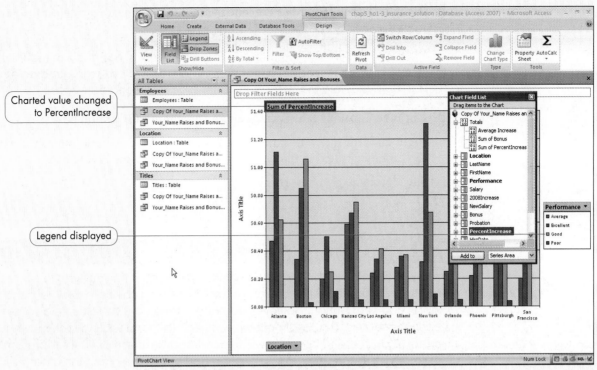

Charted value changed to PercentIncrease

Legend displayed

Figure 5.28 PercentIncrease Chart

TIP PivotTable Power

Once the PivotTable or PivotChart framework has been constructed, you can add and subtract fields to reassess the data. This power gives you an ability to dissect and reassemble data to obtain a complete picture of the activities they depict.

Step 3
Change AutoCalc Calculation and Set PivotChart Properties and Captions

Refer to Figure 5.29 as you complete Step 3.

a. Right-click the **Sum of PercentIncrease** field button, select **AutoCalc**, and then select **Average** from the shortcut menu.

You know that summing a percentage field is generally a bad idea, but believe that displaying the average increase by performance category will contain useful information. You realize that the Y-axis labels have retained the currency format. You need to change them to display percentages.

b. Right-click **any number in the Y-axis** and select **Properties** from the shortcut menu.

All of the numbers on the Y-axis highlight with a blue border.

c. Click the **Format tab** in the Properties window.

d. Click the **Number drop-down arrow**.

e. Select **Percent** on the drop-down menu.

You notice that the field button label, Average of PercentIncrease, is awkward and want it to display *Average Increase*. Unfortunately, you cannot set a field caption in PivotChart view. However, you remember that any changes made to a PivotTable affect the chart. You decide to change the field caption in the PivotTable view.

f. Right-click the query tab and select **PivotTable View**.

Notice that the PivotTable now displays the Average of PercentIncrease by location. It no longer has the year of hire field displayed.

g. Right-click the **Average of PercentIncrease** column head and select **Properties** from the shortcut menu.

> **TROUBLESHOOTING:** Remember that your work is in a copy of the PivotTable and PivotChart you created in Hands-On Exercise 1. If you run into problems, you can always delete the copy of the query, recopy it, and start again.

h. Click the **Captions tab**. Type **Average Percent** in the Caption box.

i. Right-click the query tab and select **PivotChart View**. Check to make sure that the caption applied in the PivotTable view changed the PivotChart.

j. Save the changes to the query.

TIP   Keep Looking

As you work in PivotTables and PivotCharts more frequently, you learn to appreciate their power and their limitations. Access does not provide a way to caption a PivotChart field button. However, you *can* caption a PivotTable field. When you cannot accomplish a task in one view, switch to the other and look for what you need to do there. Often you will find it. Because the two views represent two perspectives of the data, any changes made one place affect the other view.

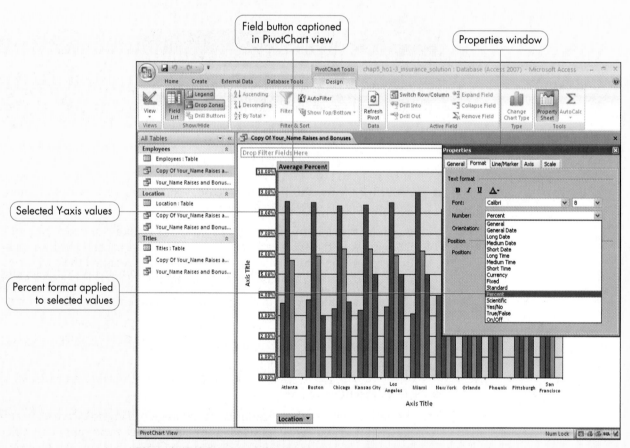

Figure 5.29 Caption and Format Changes Applied

Refer to Figure 5.30 as you complete Step 4.

a. Click the **General tab** in the Properties window, and then click the **Select drop-down arrow**. Click **Average** near the bottom of the list.

The blue bars that represent the Average data series all highlight.

b. Click the **Border/Fill tab**. Click the **Fill Color drop-down arrow** and click **BlueViolet** (fifth column, first row on the palette).

The first series of data color changes to BlueViolet.

c. Click the **General tab** in the Properties window and then click the **Select drop-down arrow**. Click the **Excellent** series near the bottom of the list.

The red bars that represent the Excellent data series all highlight.

d. Click the **Border/Fill tab**. Click the **Fill Color drop-down arrow** and click **Medium Turquoise** (sixth column, fourth row on the palette).

e. Click the **Fill Type drop-down arrow** and select **Pattern**.

f. Click the **Pattern drop-down arrow** and select **Dark Horizontal**.

g. Click the **Back Color drop-down arrow** and select **BlueViolet** (fifth column, first row).

h. Click the **General tab** in the Properties window, and then click the **Select drop-down arrow**. Click the **Good** series near the bottom of the list. Click the **Border/Fill tab**. Click the **Fill Color drop-down arrow** and click **Medium Turquoise** (sixth column, fourth row).

i. Click the **General tab** in the Properties window, and then click the **Select drop-down arrow**. Click the **Poor** series near the bottom of the list. Click the **Border/Fill tab**, click the **Fill drop-down arrow**, and click **Medium Turquoise** (sixth column, fourth row). Click the **Fill Color drop-down arrow** and select **Pattern** and set the Back color to **BlueViolet** (fifth column, first row). Click the **Pattern drop-down arrow** and select **Dotted Diamond** (last column, fourth row). Close the Properties window.

j. Capture a screenshot by pressing **Prnt Scrn**. Launch Word, type your name and section number, and paste your screenshot into a Word document. Save the Word file as **chap5_h02_insurance_solution.docx**.

TROUBLESHOOTING: Some notebook computers have Print Screen as a function. If the words Print Screen on the key are a different color, you must press **Fn+Print Screen**.

k. Return to Access. Click the **Performance field button arrow** on the legend. Click the **All check box** to deselect all the check marks. Click the **Poor check box**. Click **OK**.

You have filtered the chart to focus attention on the pay increases awarded poor performers in the company. You see a wide variation among the locations.

l. Right-click the **Axis Title label** on the bottom of the chart and select **Properties** from the shortcut menu. Click the **Format tab** and type **Poor Performance** in the Captions box.

m. Click the axis title along the Y-axis and press **Delete** to remove it. Close the Properties window. Click **Legend** in the Show/Hide group to turn it off. Capture a screenshot and paste it in the same Word file as the earlier one. Print the Word document.

n. Close the *Copy Of Your_Name Raises and Bonuses query*. Save the changes. Rename the query **Your_Name Poor Performance**.

o. Click the **Office Button**, select **Manage**, and then select **Compact and Repair Database**.

p. Click the **Office Button** again, select **Manage**, and then select **Back Up Database**. Type **chap5_ho2_insurance_solution** as the file name and click **Save**.

You just created a backup of the database after completing the second hands-on exercise. The original database *chap5_ho1-3_insurance_solution* remains onscreen. If you ruin the original database as you complete the third hands-on exercise, you can use the backup file you just created.

q. Close the file and exit Access if you do not want to continue with the next exercise at this time.

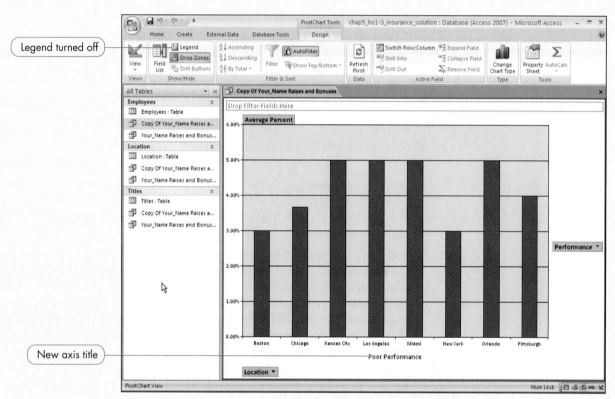

Figure 5.30 Average Increase of Employees Classified as Poor Performers

Calculations in PivotTables and PivotCharts

(The power of a relational database lies in the software's ability to organize data and combine items in different ways to obtain a complete picture of the events the data describe.)

As you learn about the more advanced features available in Microsoft Access 2007, you may wonder, who uses this stuff? Most organizations have two groups of people who use these sophisticated tools. The first group is the Information Technology (IT) staff. They may be classified as the professional query writers and data guardians. The second group may be classified as the data users in the organization—those who work in Finance, Marketing, or Human Resources and who use the data to make decisions about the organizational operation. The power of a relational database lies in the software's ability to organize data and combine items in different ways to obtain a complete picture of the events the data describe. But that power will only be realized when the data are delivered to the decision maker in the appropriate form. The PivotTable and PivotChart views may appeal more to these users because these objects more closely resemble the spreadsheet software they are familiar with.

In this section, you will learn how to perform calculations in a PivotTable. You learn how to create a calculated detail field and a calculated total field.

Creating Calculations in a PivotTable

Access provides several ways of calculating values. You have already created calculated fields in a query using the Expression Builder. You may also calculate values within the PivotTable structure. Performing calculations differs from aggregating, although you often use the two operations in the same query. You perform calculations at the detail level. The *calculated detail field* generates a new field that performs the stipulated calculation on all of the detail records. For example, suppose you had detail information in a query that communicated the number of units in stock and the unit cost for each product in your firm's inventory. Your insurance company or bank may need to know the value of the inventory. You could calculate it by multiplying the number of units by the unit cost values. A *calculated total field* would be used to customize aggregated data. When the sum, average, minimum, and so forth do not satisfy your data analysis needs, you may generate custom total calculations. This is most often used to calculate a percent of the total. You might use a sum aggregate to add the detail calculations for the value of inventory to determine the total value of the inventoried items. You might then create a calculated total field to calculate the percent of the total inventory value for each item.

Return to the earlier value of inventory illustration. Figure 5.31 shows a PivotTable ready to have a calculation performed. In this case, you would need to know the value of all of the inventory items, so you would select a calculated detail field. Figure 5.32 displays the Properties window where you enter the calculated formula. The syntax will be familiar to you. Do not begin the calculation with an equal sign; enclose all field names in brackets; and use standard operands, +, -, *, /, and ^. After typing your formula, click Change.

The *calculated detail field* generates a new field that performs the stipulated calculation on all of the detail records.

The *calculated total field* would be used to customize aggregating data.

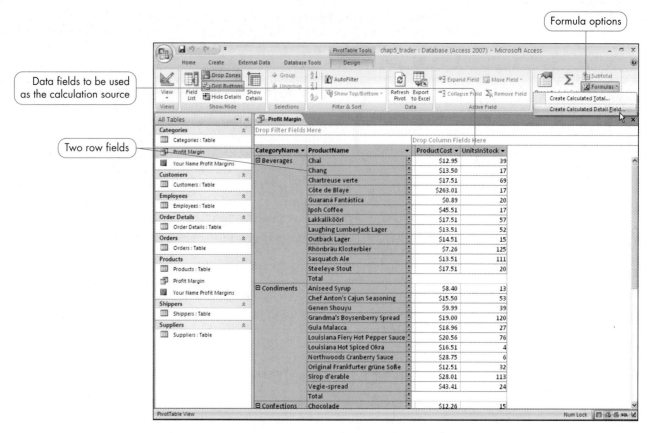

Figure 5.31 Setup for Calculated Fields

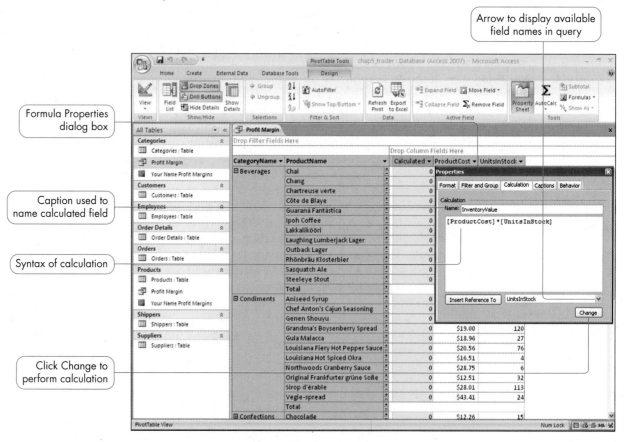

Figure 5.32 Syntax for Calculated Fields

After the calculation executes, you may treat the calculated PivotTable field like any other. You may use it as a source for summary calculations. Figure 5.33 shows the newly calculated field highlighted and ready to serve as input for a sum aggregate that will calculate total inventory values by product category. Figure 5.34 displays currency-formatted results of the Sum function, and Figure 5.35 displays only the category totals. Although the individual product names needed to be displayed to calculate the value of the inventory, after you complete the calculation, you may drag the (now extraneous) detail off the PivotTable design grid.

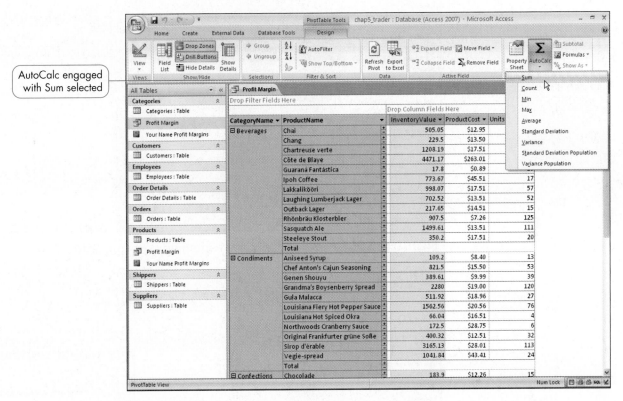

Figure 5.33 Setup for Summarizing a Calculated Field

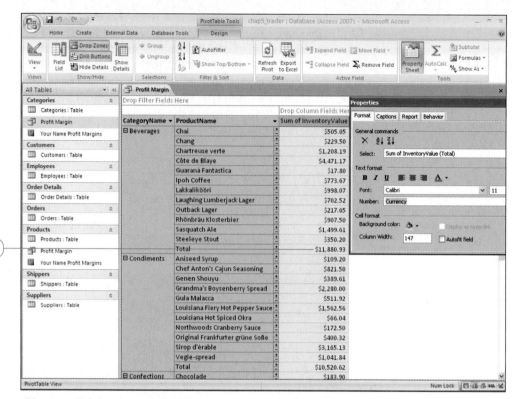

Sum displayed in Total row

Figure 5.34 Summary Calculation Performed on a Calculated Field

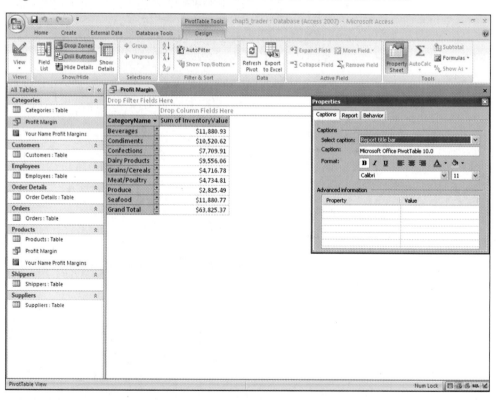

Figure 5.35 Details Removed

In the next hands-on exercise, you will calculate employee pay raises by using a Cost of Living Index. Because this organization employs workers in locations across the country, you will need to make adjustments to worker salaries to compensate them for cost of living differences. It is more expensive to live in New York City than it is in Pittsburgh or Phoenix. Your company recognizes this difference in cost of living and adjusts employee salaries to compensate them for the increased living expenses incurred in some places.

Hands-On Exercises

3 | Calculating Field Values in PivotTables

Skills covered: 1. Add a Field to a PivotTable **2.** Identify and Add Fields Needed for Calculations **3.** Create a PivotTable Calculation and Apply Formatting **4.** Total a Calculated Field and Change Formatting **5.** Set Captions

---

Step 1
Add a Field to a PivotTable

Refer to Figure 5.36 as you complete Step 1.

a. Open the *chap5_ho1-3_insurance_solution* file if necessary, click **Enable this Content** on the Security Alert toolbar, click the **Enable this content option** in the Microsoft Office Security Options dialog box, and click **OK**.

TROUBLESHOOTING: If you create unrecoverable errors while completing this hands-on exercise, you can delete the *chap5_ho1-3_insurance_solution* file, copy the *chap5_ho2_insurance_solution* database you created at the end of the second hands-on exercise, and open the copy of the backup database to start the third hands-on exercise again.

b. Open the **Location table**. Examine the values in the CostOfLiving field.

It reflects that a market basket of goods and services purchased in Phoenix costs about $1.00, whereas the same items purchased in San Francisco cost $1.71. You need to apply the cost of living factor to the NewSalary field. The data in the CostOfLiving field may be found in the Statistical Abstract at: http://www.census.gov/compendia/statab/prices/consumer_price_indexes_cost_of_living_index.

c. Copy the *Your_Name Raises and Bonuses* query and paste it using the **default name**. Open the **Copy Of Your_Name Raises and Bonuses** query in Design view.

You need the CostOfLiving field added to this query.

d. Double-click the **CostOfLiving** field in the Location table to add it to the query design grid. Click **Run** in the Results group on the Design tab to run the query. Scroll right to make sure the CostOfLiving field is successfully added.

You cannot add new fields to the PivotTable view. The field must be in the query before you use a PivotTable to examine it.

e. Save the query. Right-click the query tab and select **PivotTable View** from the shortcut menu.

f. Click the **Years** column head and drag it off the grid to remove it from the PivotTable view. Click the **Performance** column head and drag it off the grid. Click the **Sum Of Bonus** column head and drag it off the grid.

g. Click **Show Details** in the Show/Hide group.

The details of the Bonus field display. You removed the summary statistic, but now you need to remove the details also.

h. Click the **Bonus** detail field and drag it off the grid. Save the changes.

You have removed the fields that you do not need from the drop zones.

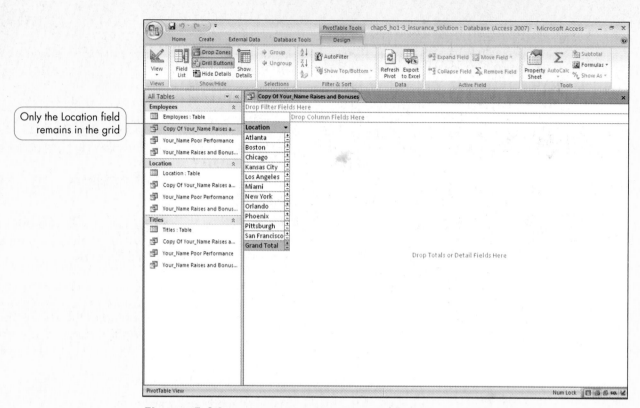

Figure 5.36 Unnecessary Fields Removed

Refer to Figure 5.37 as you complete Step 2.

Step 2
Identify and Add Fields Needed for Calculations

a. Click **Field List** in the Show/Hide group. Click the **LastName** field in the Field List pane and drag it to the right of the Location field in the **Drop Row Fields Here zone**.

Your query should now display the names of the employees in each city. You need to add the fields necessary to calculate the cost of living increase. You will need to multiply each employee's NewSalary by the CostOfLiving field.

b. Click the **NewSalary** field in the Field List pane and drag it to the **Drop Totals or Detail Fields Here zone** in the PivotTable grid.

c. Click the **CostOfLiving** field in the Field List pane and drag it to the **Drop Totals or Detail Fields Here zone** in the PivotTable grid.

Examine Figure 5.37. If your work matches, save the query. If not, remove fields from the drop zones and try again.

d. Save your query.

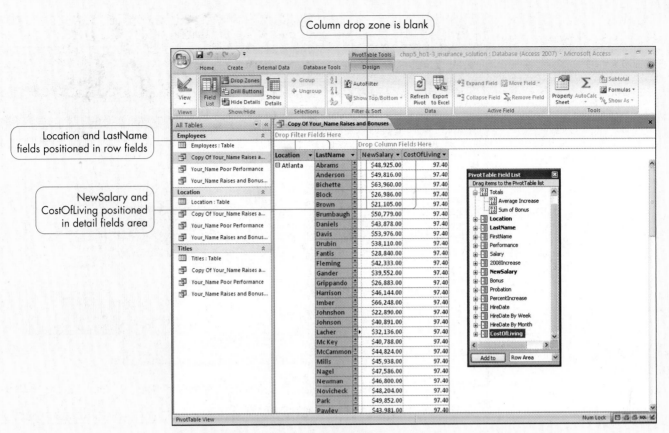

Figure 5.37 Filtered Query Results

Location and LastName fields positioned in row fields

NewSalary and CostOfLiving positioned in detail fields area

Step 3
Create a PivotTable Calculation and Apply Formatting

Refer to Figure 5.38 as you complete Step 3.

a. Click **Formulas** in the Tools group. Select **Create Calculated Detail Field**.

The Formula Properties window opens.

b. Ensure that the Calculation tab is selected. Type **AdjustedSalary** in the Name box.

You have instructed Access to name the newly calculated field AdjustedSalary.

c. Press **Tab**.

A new column is added to the Detail area named Calculated. The value of each record is zero.

d. Type **[NewSalary]*[CostOfLiving]/100**.

You need to divide by 100 because the recorded cost of living figures actually are percentages stored as integers. You do not need to divide all calculated PivotTable fields by 100. This calculation is unique to this circumstance.

e. Click **Change** in the Properties window. Examine the results.

The first Atlanta employee's adjusted salary dropped from $48,925 to $47,652.95. The cost of living in Atlanta is lower than that in the rest of the country. Atlanta employees' salaries get lowered to adjust for the cost of living. Your calculated answer does not yet have a currency format.

f. Scroll down until you see the Boston employees.

The cost of living in Boston is higher than in the rest of the country. The first Boston employee's salary increased from $58,448 to $79,138.59 after the cost of living adjustment.

g. Compare your work to Figure 5.38. If it is correct, save the query.

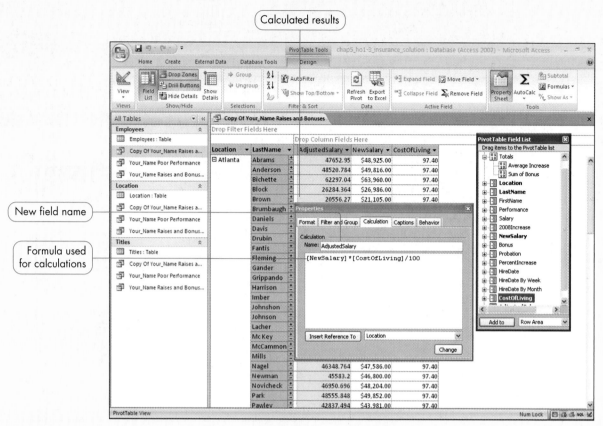

Figure 5.38 Custom Calculation

Refer to Figure 5.39 as you complete Step 4.

a. With the AdjustedSalary field active, click the **Format tab** in the Properties window. Click the **Number drop-down arrow** and select **Currency**.

> **TROUBLESHOOTING:** If your AdjustedSalary field is not highlighted with a blue background, you can reactivate it by clicking its column heading.

b. Click the **Captions tab** in the Properties window. Insert a space between *Adjusted* and *Salary* in the Caption box. The column head now has a space.

If you scroll the Field List box, you will see that the actual field name is still AdjustedSalary (without the space). The caption is a method of making the database data more user-friendly.

c. Close the Properties window.

d. With the Adjusted Salary still active, click **AutoCalc** in the Tools group. Select **Sum** from the menu.

Each employee's data are summed. This looks like it is simply repeating the information. You need to know the total salaries for each city.

e. Activate the **NewSalary** field by clicking the column head. Click **AutoCalc** and **Sum**.

f. Activate the **CostOfLiving** field by clicking the column head. Click **AutoCalc** and **Average**.

g. Click **Hide Details** in the Show/Hide group.

h. Drag the **LastName** field off the grid.

With details hidden and the LastName field removed, the PivotTable collapses to display the total of all salaries in each city.

i. Save the query.

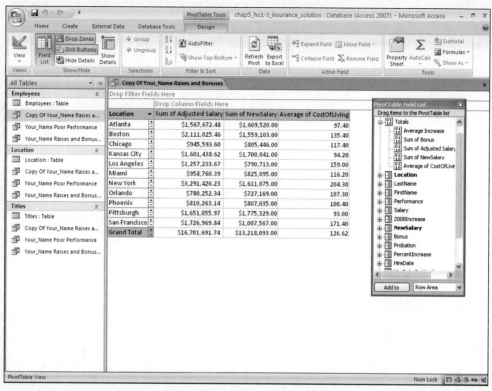

Figure 5.39 Totaled PivotTable with Details Collapsed

Step 5
Set Captions

Refer to Figure 5.40 as you complete Step 5.

a. Click the column head to select the **Sum of AdjustedSalary** field. Click **Property Sheet** in the Tools group.

b. Click the **Captions tab** (if necessary). Type **Total Adjusted Salary** in the Caption box.

c. Select the **Sum of NewSalary** field. Type **Total New Salary** in the Caption box.

When you selected a different field in the PivotTable, the Caption box updates to reflect the selected field.

d. Select the **Average of CostOfLiving** field. Type **Cost of Living** in the Caption box.

e. Examine Figure 5.40. If your results match, save the query.

f. Close the query.

g. Rename the *Copy of Your_Name Raises and Bonuses* query as **Your_Name Total Location Cost of Living**.

h. Click the **Office Button**, select **Manage**, and select **Compact and Repair**. Close the file and exit Access.

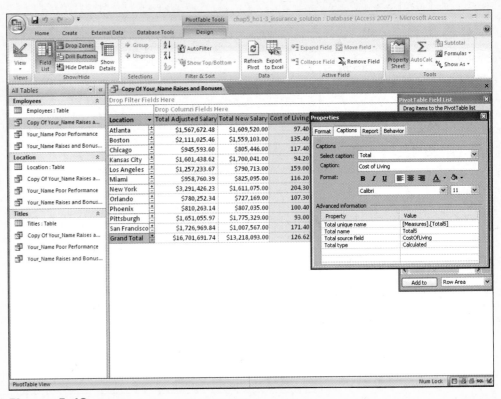

Figure 5.40 Query Results with Details Removed

Summary

1. **Create a PivotTable view.** The PivotTable view provides a method of summarizing and aggregating data. For example, an organization might need a weekly report summarizing payroll and overtime authorization by department. Because only one data source may be used for a PivotTable, you will typically use a query as the source for constructing a PivotTable, as queries may be based on multiple tables. Once the source data are assembled in a query, switch to PivotTable view. The PivotTable view is a GUI device that lets you arrange your data visually by dragging and dropping different fields into the appropriate drop zones: row, detail, column, and filter. The power of a PivotTable is its flexibility. Experienced users tend to put the field with the most possible choices in the row area and shorter ones in columns.

2. **Calculate aggregate statistics.** After you assemble data in the PivotTable view, Access provides tools to help analyze and extract the information. The PivotTable view provides the same aggregating functions as found in reports and other query views. The types of calculations available depend on the data types. The primary aggregate statistics include sum, count, min, max, average, standard deviation, standard deviation population, and variance population.

3. **Modify a PivotTable.** You add fields to a drop zone by clicking them in the PivotTable Field List window and dragging them to the appropriate drop zones. Once the PivotTable grid has been established, you can easily add and remove data fields to analyze. Should you decide that displaying certain fields makes the information too cluttered to be useful, you can remove them from the grid. Accountants use crossfooting by summing the rows, summing the columns, and making sure the totals match. It provides an important check figure. You can also modify a PivotTable by changing its properties. The Properties sheet enables you to add captions and format data in the PivotTable.

4. **Select an appropriate chart type.** One of the best methods of distilling and summarizing data is to present it in a pictorial form—a chart. Well-designed charts facilitate data interpretation. You can create PivotCharts from your PivotTable. Before you create a chart, you identify data types. Discrete data describe classifications and cannot be meaningfully subdivided. Continuous data describe a continuum of smaller increments and are easily scaled. Access can produce a variety of chart types. Column and bar charts are the most common and can be used to compare data across different categories. Line and scatter charts are used to depict data on a time line. Pie and donut charts depict percentages of a whole most effectively. Each PivotTable created also generates a PivotChart. Because the two views are linked, any changes you make to the chart will affect the table and any changes made to the table will change the chart.

5. **Identify chart elements.** The chart title describes the chart and its purpose. The legend provides a color-coded mapping of the data series in the chart. The axes in column, bar, line, and scatter charts typically indicate quantities and descriptions.

6. **Edit a PivotChart.** You edit an Access PivotChart similarly to editing a chart in Excel. First you must select the element you wish to edit and then perform needed edits. The big difference is that you select the element through using the Property sheet instead of double-clicking it. Be careful to add data that enhances the chart. You can overdo a PivotTable or PivotChart easily by putting too much data in it.

7. **Create calculations in a PivotTable.** Access provides several ways of calculating values. You have already created calculated fields in a query using the Expression Builder. You may also use the Expression Builder to create calculated fields in PivotTables.

Key Terms

Multiple Choice

1. When creating a PivotTable or PivotChart, in what order should fields be dragged to the drop zone?

   (a) Outside (Row, Column, Filter, or Page), then inside (Detail).

   (b) Inside (Detail) and then outside (Row, Column, Filter, or Page).

   (c) The order of the outside (Row, Column, Filter, or Page) is not important.

   (d) Both A and C.

2. You have a database query containing fields for donor's city and contribution type. If you want to find out which cities donors of volunteer hours live in, what order should the row fields be dropped in?

   (a) Contribution needs to be to the right of city.

   (b) Contribution needs to be to the left of city.

   (c) You may only drop one field into a row drop zone.

   (d) Drop order is unimportant.

3. You have a PivotTable that calculates an aggregate sum for each volunteer's city. How do you remove the city field from the PivotTable?

   (a) Click the Hide Detail tool if the details are hidden; activate a detail and press Delete.

   (b) Click the Hide Detail tool if the details are hidden; activate a detail and click the Remove Field tool.

   (c) Click the Hide Detail tool to hide the details; then click the gray column header and press Delete.

   (d) Both A and B.

4. You want to draw a chart that shows last month's sales by product line. The chart needs to show which product line sold the greatest proportion of total sales. Which chart type would most appropriately express these data?

   (a) Line chart

   (b) Column chart

   (c) Bubble chart

   (d) Pie chart

5. You want to draw a chart that shows donations over the past five years. Which chart type would most appropriately express these data?

   (a) Line chart

   (b) Column chart

   (c) Radar chart

   (d) Pie chart

6. You have created a 3D column chart that shows physician specialties in five different hospitals. The specialties are listed along the X-axis and the legend displays different colors for each of the hospitals. How do you change the color of one of the hospital's bars for each of the specialties?

   (a) Open the Properties window and select the series using the Select box on the General tab. Then change the series color using the Fill Color box on the Border/Fill tab of the Properties window.

   (b) Double-click any data point in the series to select the series. Then change the series color by right-clicking and selecting the Fill Color box.

   (c) Double-click any data point in the series to select the series. Then change the series color using the Fill Color box on the Border/Fill tab of the Properties window.

   (d) Open the Properties window and select the series using the Select box on the General tab. Then change the series color using the Fill Color box on the Filter and Group tab of the Properties window.

7. You have a PivotChart that summarizes employee bonuses by performance category and city. You have multiple series with different colors to indicate the different performance categories in each city. The little box that should tell the reader that the blue bars represent the excellent performance category is missing. What is the name of the box?

   (a) Property

   (b) Plot area

   (c) Legend

   (d) Series selector

8. You have a saved PivotTable that summarizes employee bonuses by performance category and city. You change to PivotChart view and decide that you need to filter for only the excellent performance category. What will happen to the PivotTable?

   (a) Nothing, it is saved.

   (b) The PivotTable will also be filtered for the excellent performance category.

   (c) You must return to the PivotTable view and filter the PivotTable to change the chart.

   (d) All of the aggregating statistics will be unchanged in the PivotTable but the details will disappear.

9. The practice of using advanced statistical techniques to analyze patterns and relationships and to examine data in large databases is called:

   (a) Database management

   (b) Data drilling

   (c) Market analysis

   (d) Data mining

10. You have a query with fields for OrderTotal, TaxRate, and Shipping. You want to create a calculated detail field that calculates the appropriate sales tab and then adds it to the Shipping and OrderTotal fields. Which of the following expressions uses proper syntax and will correctly calculate the answer?

    (a) [OrderTotal]*[TaxRate]+[OrderTotal]+[Shipping]

    (b) [TaxRate]+[OrderTotal]+[Shipping]

    (c) [OrderTotal]*([TaxRate]+[OrderTotal]+[Shipping])

    (d) [OrderTotal]+[TaxRate]+[OrderTotal]*[Shipping]

11. You have a field in a PivotTable or PivotChart that should display with a currency format but does not. How do you change a field's format in a PivotTable or PivotChart?

    (a) Activate the field, right-click it, and select Properties. In the Properties window, select the Format tab and set the Number format to currency.

    (b) Activate the field and click the Property Sheet tool. In the Properties window, select the Format tab and set the Number format to currency.

    (c) Neither A nor B are correct.

    (d) Both A and B are correct.

12. You need to calculate an average of the PercentIncrease field in a query that shows each employee's base salaries. To do this you would:

    (a) Use the Formulas tool.

    (b) Right-click into the first blank row in the design grid and select Average from the shortcut menu.

    (c) Use the AutoCalc tool.

    (d) Use the Formulas tool and select Average.

13. You need to remove a field from a PivotTable. How do you do this?

    (a) Activate the field and press Delete.

    (b) Activate the field and drag it. When the mouse pointer shape changes to a small gray rectangle, drop it.

    (c) Activate the field and drag it. When the mouse pointer shape changes to a red X, drop it.

    (d) Select the field's column head and press Backspace.

14. You have applied a filter to display only the job titles for the Sales Representatives. You enter the filter drop-down arrow and deselect the check box beside Sales Representative. What will happen to the PivotTable when you close the filter window?

    (a) Nothing.

    (b) All of the data disappear.

    (c) The PivotTable will display all of the job title's data because there is no applied filter.

    (d) You have insufficient information to answer this question.

15. You have created a PivotChart that displays hundreds of tiny, multi-colored bars. You cannot understand it. What is the most likely cause?

    (a) You selected an inappropriate chart type.

    (b) You forgot to group the bars.

    (c) You created the chart from complex, unfiltered PivotTable data.

    (d) You selected a text field for the Data Fields drop zone.

Practice Exercises

1 Miles Real Estate Sales Analysis

Nancy Miles offered you a position as the Data Manager of a small real estate firm that specializes in the sale of residential housing. Your firm sells homes in several different communities. For the last several months, the employees have been recording their activities in an Access database. Nancy asked for you to mine the data and produce a summary of the sales activities by community. Refer to Figure 5.41 to verify your work.

a. Copy the partially completed file in *chap5_pe1_realestate.accdb* from the Exploring Access folder to your production folder. Rename it **chap5_pe1_realestate_solution**. Double-click the file name to open it. Click **Options** on the Security Warning toolbar, click **Enable this content** in the Microsoft Office Security Options dialog box, and then click **OK**.

b. Click the **Database Tools tab** and click **Relationships** in the Show/Hide group. Examine the table structure, relationships, and fields. Once you are familiar with the database, close the Relationships window.

c. Open the **Agents table** and replace *Your_Name* with your name in the first and last name fields. Close the Agents table. Rename the **Your_Name Sales** query and open it in Datasheet view.

d. Right-click the **Your_Name Sales query tab** and select **PivotTable View** from the shortcut menu.

e. If necessary, click **Field List** in the Show/Hide group on the Design tab to turn on the PivotTable Field List pane.

f. Drag the **LastName** field from the PivotTable Field List to the **Drop Column Fields Here** zone. Drag the **Subdivision** field from the PivotTable Field List to the **Drop Row Fields Here** zone. Drag the **SalePrice** field from the PivotTable Field List to the **Drop Totals or Detail Fields Here** zone.

g. Click any of the **SalePrice** column heads to activate all of the SalePrice data points. Click **AutoCalc** in the Tools group and select **Sum** from the list.

h. Click **Property Sheet** in the Tools group. Click the **Format tab** (if necessary) and set the *Number* format to **Currency**.

i. Click **Hide Details** in the Show/Hide group.

j. Click the **Office Button**, select **Print**, and then select **Print Preview**.

k. Click **Landscape** in the Page Layout group. Click **Margins** in the Page Layout group and select **Wide**.

l. Click the **Office Button** and select **Print**. Select **Quick Print** and click **OK**. Save and close the query.

m. Click the **Office Button**, select **Manage**, and select **Compact and Repair Database**. Close the file.

...continued on Next Page

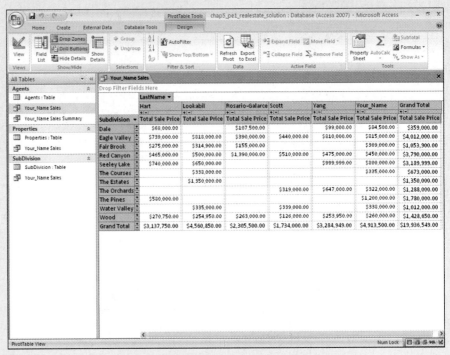

Figure 5.41 Sorted and Filtered Query Results

2 Real Estate City Analysis

Ms. Miles asks that you examine all of the listed properties by community. Your firm offers properties for sale in several cities. Each city may be divided into one or more subdivisions. Some of the houses are located in formal subdivisions that have community pools, tennis courts, and bike trails. You need to group the listed properties by city and then by the subdivision. You also need to indicate which agent listed each property. Finally, you need to summarize the value of the listed properties. Ms. Miles asks that you present the information in both tabular and graphical form. Refer to Figures 5.42 and 5.43 to verify your work.

a. Copy the partially completed file in *chap5_pe2_realestate.accdb* from the Exploring Access folder to your production folder. Rename it **chap5_pe2_realestate_solution**. Double-click the file name to open it. Click **Options** on the Security Warning toolbar, click **Enable this content** in the Microsoft Office Security Options dialog box, and then click **OK**.

b. Copy the **City Listings** query, then paste it as **Your_Name City Listings** in the Navigation Pane.

c. Open the **Agents table** and replace *Your_Name* with your name in the first and last name fields. Close the Agents table.

d. Open the **Your_Name City Listings** query, right-click the query tab, and select **PivotTable View** from the shortcut menu.

e. If necessary, click **Field List** in the Show/Hide group to turn on the PivotTable Field List pane. Drag the **City** field from the PivotTable Field List and drop it in the **Drop Row Field** zone.

f. Drag the **Subdivision** field from the PivotTable Field List and drop it in the **Drop Row Field** zone to the right of the City field.

g. Drag the **LastName** field from the PivotTable Field List and drop it in the **Drop Column Field** zone.

h. Drag the **ListPrice** field from the PivotTable Field List and drop it in the **Drop Totals or Detail Field** zone.

i. Click any of the ListPrice column heads to select. Click **AutoCalc** in the Tool group and select **Sum** from the list.

...continued on Next Page

j. Capture a screenshot of the first page of the PivotTable by pressing **Prnt Scrn**. Launch Word and type your name and section number at the top of the page. Press **Enter**. Paste the screenshot into the Word document and save the file as **chap5_pe2_realestate_solution.docx**. Keep the Word document open.

k. Right-click the query tab and select **PivotChart**. Close the PivotTable Field List window.

l. Click the **LastName Field Button** arrow. Click the **All** check box to clear it. Click the **Your_Name** box to select it. Keep the selection list of the agent's name open.

m. Capture a screenshot of the first page of the PivotChart by pressing **Prnt Scrn**. Switch to the Word document. Press **Enter**. Paste the screenshot into the Word document and save the file as **chap5_pe2_realestate_solution.docx**. Print the Word document.

n. Save and close the query. Click the **Office Button**, select **Manage**, and then select **Compact and Repair Database**. Close the file.

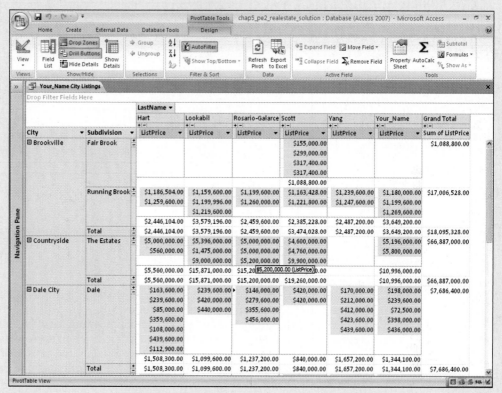

Figure 5.42 PivotTable

...continued on Next Page

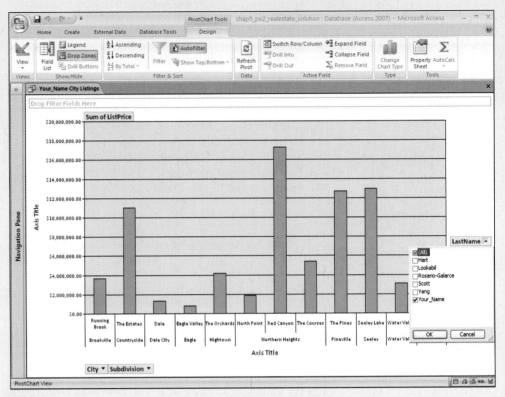

Figure 5.43 PivotChart

3 Bank Loans

You are interning in a bank. Each day you work with different employees and help them with their computer applications questions. Today, you work with Robert Wigman, one of the directors of the bank. Mr. Wigman asked you to help him summarize the sums of all the loan payments by type and interest rate. Mr. Wigman explains that different borrowers pay differing rates of interest. The bank needs to know how many loans are outstanding at each of the different interest rates. He also needs you to prepare a chart that shows total mortgage loan payments by interest rate. Refer to Figures 5.44 and 5.45 to verify your work.

a. Copy the partially completed file *chap5_pe3_nationalbank.accdb* from the Exploring Access folder to your production folder. Rename it **chap5_pe3_nationalbank_solution.accdb**. Double-click the file name to open it. Click **Options** on the Security Warning toolbar, click **Enable this content** in the Microsoft Office Security Options dialog box, and then click **OK**.

b. Rename the *Your_Name Loan Payment query* with your name. Open the query; right-click the query tab and select **PivotTable View**.

c. If necessary, click **Field List** in the Show/Hide group to turn on the PivotTable Field List window. Drag the **InterestRate** field from the PivotTable Field List and drop it in the **Drop Row Field Here Field** zone. Drag the Type field from the PivotTable Field List and drop it in the **Drop Column Field Here** zone. Drag the **Payment** field from the PivotTable Field List and drop it in the **Drop Detail Field Here** zone.

d. Click a **Payment Column head** to select the payments. Click **AutoCalc** in the Tools group and select **Sum** from the list.

e. Click **Hide Details** in the Show/Hide group.

f. Capture a screenshot of the PivotTable by pressing **Prnt Scrn**. Launch Word, then type your name and section number at the top of the page. Press **Enter**. Paste the screenshot into the Word document and save the file as **chap5_pe3_nationalbank_solution.docx**. Keep the Word document open.

...continued on Next Page

g. Return to Access. Right-click the query tab and switch to **PivotChart View**. Click the plot area to select the chart and click **Change Chart Type** in the Type group. In the Properties box, select the 3D Stacked Column Type (second row, third column).

h. Click the **General tab** in the Properties window. Click the **Select arrow** and select **C**. Click the **Border/Fill tab**. Click the **Color arrow** and change the color to **MediumBlue** (second row, fourth column from the right).

i. Click the **General tab** in the Properties window. Click the **Select arrow** and select **M**. Click the **Fill Type arrow** and select Gradient. Click the **Color arrow** and select **Yellow** (sixth row, fourth column). Click the **Border/Fill tab**. Click **Two Color**. Click the **Back color arrow** and change the color to **MediumBlue** (second row, fourth column from the right). Click **Style** and select **Horizontal End** (first row, second column).

j. Click the **General tab** in the Properties window. Click the **Select arrow** and select **O**. Click the **Border/Fill tab**. Click the **Color arrow** and change the color to **Yellow** (sixth row, fourth from the right).

k. Click **Legend** in the Show/Hide group.

l. Close the Properties sheet and the PivotTable Field List window. Capture a screenshot of the PivotChart by pressing **Prnt Scrn**. Return to Word, then type **Enter** after the screenshot of the PivotTable. Paste the screenshot into the Word document and save the document as **chap5_pe3_nationalbank_solution.docx**. Print and close the Word document.

m. Save and close the query. Click the **Office Button**, select **Manage**, and select **Compact and Repair Database**.

n. Close the file.

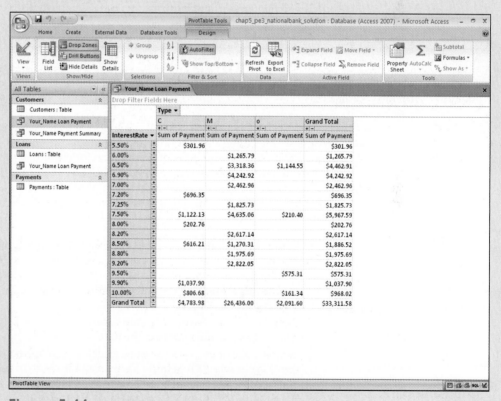

Figure 5.44 PivotTable

...continued on Next Page

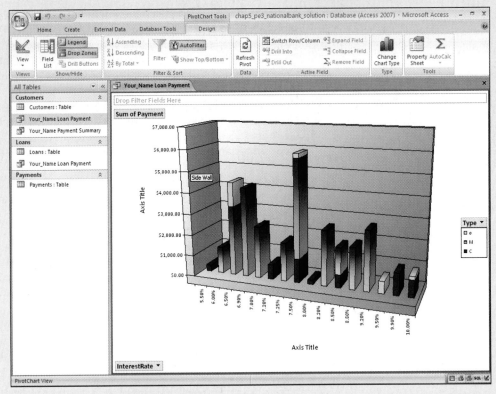

Figure 5.45 PivotChart

4 Custom Coffee

The Custom Coffee Company is a small service organization that provides coffee, tea, and snacks to offices. Custom Coffee also provides and maintains the equipment for brewing the beverages. Although the firm is small, its excellent reputation for providing outstanding customer service has helped it grow. Part of this customer service is because the firm owner set up a database to organize and keep track of customer purchases. You need to use the data mining techniques from the chapter to help convert the data into information. You need to calculate order profits and produce a chart that shows weekly sales by salesperson. Refer to Figures 5.46 and 5.47 to verify your work.

a. Copy the partially completed file *chap5_pe4_coffee.accdb* from the Exploring Access folder to your production folder. Rename it **chap5_pe4_coffee_solution.accdb**. Double-click the file name to open the file. Click **Options** on the Security Warning toolbar, click **Enable this content** in the Microsoft Office Security Options dialog box, and then click **OK**.

b. Double-click the **Sales Rep table** to open it. Replace *Your_Name* with your name. Close the table by clicking Close in the database window.

c. Rename the *Your_Name Revenue* query with your name. Open it and right-click the *query tab* to select **PivotTable View** from the shortcut menu.

d. If necessary, click **Field List** in the Show/Hide group to turn on the PivotTable Field List window. Drag the **OrderDate by Week** field from the PivotTable Field List and drop it in the **Drop Row Field Here** zone. Drag the **LastName** field from the PivotTable Field List and drop it in the **Drop Column Field Here** zone. Drag the **Revenue** and **TotalCost** fields from the PivotTable Field List and drop them in the **Drop Totals or Detail Fields Here** zone.

e. Click the **Year 2008 drill button** to expand to display the weeks.

f. Click **Formulas** in the Tools group, and then select **Create Calculated Detail Field**. In the Calculation Properties box, click in the Name box and type **Profit**. In the Calculation box, delete the zero and type **[Revenue] – [TotalCost]**. Click **Change**.

...continued on Next Page

g. Click the **Profit column head** to select the column, click **AutoCalc** in the Tools group, and select **Sum**. Use the same method to calculate totals for the Revenue and Total cost fields.

h. Click the **Profit column head** to select the column and click the **Format tab** in the Properties box. Click the **Number arrow** and select **Currency**. Click the **Sum of Profit column head** to select the column and click the **Format tab** in the Properties box. Click the **Number arrow** and select **Currency**.

i. Click **Hide Details** in the Show/Hide group. Close the Properties window and the PivotTable Field List. Capture a screenshot of the PivotTable by pressing **Prnt Scrn**. Launch Word, and then type your name and section number at the top of the page. Press **Enter**. Paste the screenshot into the Word document and save the document as **chap5_pe4_coffee_solution.docx**. Keep the Word document open.

j. Return to Access. Right-click the query tab and select **PivotChart View** from the short-cut menu.

k. Click the plot area to select the chart, then click **Change Chart Type** in the Type group. Choose a **line chart** and the first sub-chart option.

l. Click the **field button** for the **Sum of Revenue** field and drag it off the chart. Drop it when you see the red X attached to the mouse pointer. Drag the **Sum of Cost** field off the chart.

m. Click the X-axis Axis Title box and select the Format tab in the Properties sheet. Click in the Caption box, delete *Axis Title,* and type **January Weeks**. Click the Y-axis Axis Title box and press **Delete**.

n. Close the Properties window and the PivotTable Field List window. Click **Legend** to display the legend. Capture a screenshot of the PivotChart by pressing **Prnt Scrn**. Return to Word, press **Enter** after the screenshot of the PivotTable, and paste the screenshot. Save the Word document as **chap5_pe4_coffee_solution.docx**. Print and close the Word document.

o. Save the query. Click the **Office Button**, select **Manage**, and then select **Compact and Repair**. Close the file.

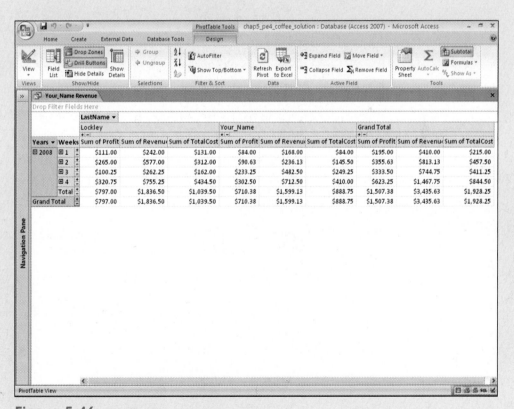

Figure 5.46 PivotTable

...continued on Next Page

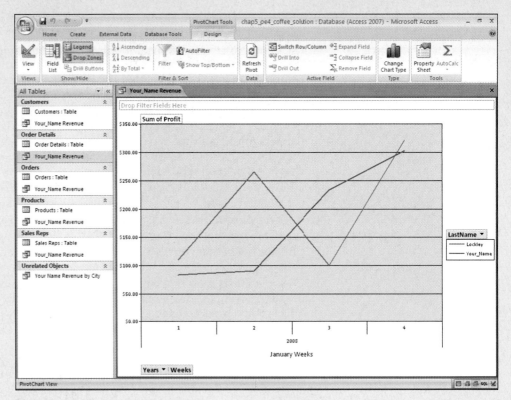

Figure 5.47 PivotChart of January Weekly Sales

The Northwinds Traders is a small, international specialty foods distribution firm. It sells products in a variety of different categories, including beverages and condiments. The Sales Manager has asked you to provide her with a chart that shows beverage sales by month for 2007. She will use the chart to review each salesperson's performance in the annual review meeting. Refer to Figure 5.48 to verify your work.

a. Locate the file named *chap5_mid1_traders.accdb*, copy it to your production folder, and rename it **chap5_mid1_traders_solution.accdb**. Open the file and enable the content.

b. Rename the *Your_Name Revenue* query with **your name**. Open the Employees table and replace *Your_name* in the first and last name fields with your name.

c. Open the *Your_Name Revenue* query and switch to PivotTable view.

d. Add the **ShippedDate By Month** field to the row drop zone. Expand the 2007 values to display the months. Deselect the 2008 values.

e. Remove the **Quarters** field from the PivotTable.

f. Add the **CategoryName** field to the filter zone. Uncheck the All box and select **Beverages.** Add the **LastName** field to the column drop zone. Uncheck the All box and select the **Your_Name** box.

g. Use the Properties window to enter **Total Revenue** as the Sum of Revenue caption.

h. Switch to **PivotChart view**. Change the chart type to Line and the subtype to 3D line (first column, third row). Display the legend.

i. Change the series line color to DarkGreen (fifth row, last column). Change the plot area color to Violet (first row, fourth column). Change the Y-axis title to **Revenue** and change the X-axis title to **Beverages**.

j. Print the chart. Compact and repair the database. Close the database.

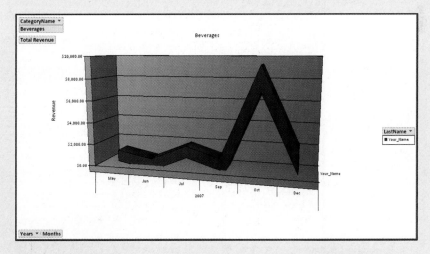

Figure 5.48 PivotChart Displaying Your Sales of Beverages

...continued on Next Page

You are the general manager of a large hotel chain. Your establishment provides a variety of guest services ranging from rooms and conferences to weddings. You need to calculate the total revenue generated by service type and city. You want a chart that provides quickly interpretable information. Finally, you need to sort the data by total revenue in descending order. Refer to Figure 5.49 to verify your work.

a. Locate the file named *chap5_mid2_memrewards.accdb*, copy it to your production folder, and rename it **chap5_mid2_memrewards_solution.accdb**. Open the file and enable the content. Rename the *Revenue* query as **Your_Name Revenue**. Open it in PivotTable view.

b. Use the *City* field for the **Row Field**, the *ServiceName* field for the **Column Field**, and the *NoInParty* and *PerPersonCharge* fields for the **Detail Fields**.

c. Create a *Calculated Detail Formula Field* that calculates **Revenue** by multiplying PerPersonCharge by NoInParty.

d. Use the AutoCalc tool to **Sum** the Revenue field. Format it as currency.

e. Hide the details of the PivotTable.

f. Create a PivotChart. Use a stacked 3D column chart (second row, third column). Caption the *X-axis title* with **your_name**. Caption the *Y-axis title* with the **Total Revenue**. Display a legend.

g. Modify the Rotation and Inclination options of the 3D View Properties to approximate Figure 5.49.

h. Capture a screenshot of the PivotChart. Open Word, launch a new blank document, type **your name and section number**, and press **Enter**. Press **Ctrl+V** or click Paste. Print the Word document. Save it as **chap5_mid2_memrewards_solution.docx**. Close the Word document.

i. Compact, repair, and close the database.

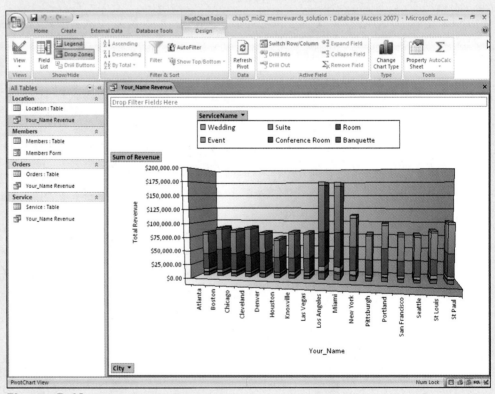

Figure 5.49 Stacked Column Chart

...continued on Next Page

3 Nesting Pivoted Data for a Hotel Chain

You are the general manager of a large hotel chain. Your establishment provides a variety of guest services ranging from rooms and conferences to weddings. You need to examine the total revenue generated by service type in each city and quarter. Refer to Figures 5.50 and 5.51 to verify your work.

a. Locate the file named *chap5_mid3_memrewards.accdb*, copy it to your production folder, and rename it **chap5_mid3_memrewards_solution.accdb**. Open the file and enable the content. Rename the *Revenue query* as **Your_Name Revenue**. Open the query and switch to the PivotTable view.

b. Drag the **City** and **ServiceName** fields to the row drop zone. Nest the service names inside each city. Drag the **ServiceDate By Month** field to the column drop zone. Limit the dates to only 2007 and display them by **quarter**. Display only the third- and fourth-quarter data.

c. Add the **Revenue** field to the detail drop zone and sum it.

d. Capture a screenshot of the PivotTable. Open Word, launch a new blank document, type your name and section number, and press **Enter**. Press **Ctrl+V** or click Paste. Save the document as **chap5_mid3_memrewards_solution.docx**. Press **Enter**. Keep the Word document open and return to Access.

e. Save the changes and close your query. Rename the query **Your_Name Revenue by City**.

f. Copy the query and name the copy as **Your_Name Revenue by Service**. Open the Revenue by Service query and modify the PivotTable so that the services are the primary group, and the city names nest within each service.

g. Capture a screenshot of the PivotTable. Return to Word and paste your second PivotTable below the first. Save the Word document as as **chap5_mid3_memrewards_solution.docx**. Close the Word document and return to Access.

h. Save your query. Compact, repair, and close the database.

...continued on Next Page

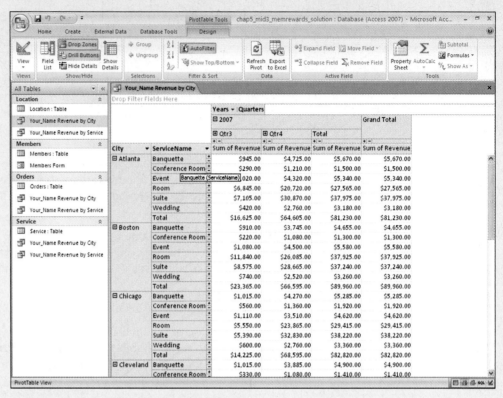

Figure 5.50 Revenue by City PivotTable

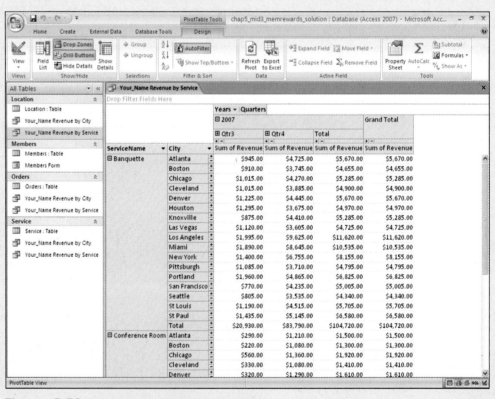

Figure 5.51 Revenue by Service PivotTable

Capstone Exercise

(Replacements, Ltd., is a real company. The data in the case file are actual data. The customer and employee information has been changed to ensure privacy. However, the inventory and sales records reflect actual transactions.)

You work as an associate marketing manager at Replacements, Ltd. Your responsibilities include browsing the Replacements Web site, www.replacements.com. There you learned that Replacements, Ltd. (located in Greensboro, NC) has the world's largest selection of old and new dinnerware, including china, stoneware, crystal, glassware, silver, stainless, and collectibles. You need to oversee the marketing of some of the patterns in the inventory. You need to discover which patterns produce the most revenue. You want to create a chart that displays the revenue generated from the sale of the patterns for which you are responsible. After you complete the work, you will compact and repair the database and make a backup of it.

Database File Setup

You need to copy an original database file, rename the copied file, and then open the copied database to complete this capstone exercise. After you open the copied database, you will replace an existing employee's name with your name.

a. Locate the file named *chap5_cap_replacements.accdb* and copy it to your working folder.

b. Rename the copied file as **chap5_cap_ replacements.accdb_solution**.

c. Open the *chap5_cap_replacements_solution.accdb* file and enable the content.

d. Open the **Employees Table** form.

e. Navigate to record 55 and replace *Carmen Thomas*'s name with your name. Press **Enter** and close the table.

f. Rename the Revenue query as **Your_Name Revenue**. Open the query.

Switch to PivotTable View and Lay Out the PivotTable Zones

You need to create a PivotTable to display sales information by pattern name. You will need to filter it to display only the sale of the patterns for which you are responsible.

a. Open the query in **PivotTable view**.

b. Place the **LongPatName** field in the row drop zone and the **LastName** field in the column drop zone.

c. Filter the **LastName** field so that only **Your_Name** displays.

d. Place the **Qty** and **Price** fields in the detail fields drop zone.

e. Save the query.

Create a Calculated Field

You need to create a field that calculates revenue as the product of price and quantity.

a. Highlight the **Price** field.

b. Click the Formula tool and use it to create a calculated detail field.

c. Name the field **Revenue**.

d. Multiply Price by Qty to perform the calculation.

Calculate Totals and Format the Results

You need to calculate totals for each pattern.

a. Make sure the Revenue field is still selected.

b. Apply the **Sum** function to the Revenue field.

c. Click the **Format tab** in the Properties window.

d. Apply the **Currency** for the **Revenue** field.

e. Apply the **Currency Format** for the **Sum of Revenue** field.

f. Hide the details.

g. Save your PivotTable changes.

Create and Format a PivotChart

Now that you are satisfied that the data summary is complete, graphically depict it.

a. Switch to PivotChart View and select a **3D Bar chart**.

b. From the General tab of the Properties sheet select **Your_Name** to select all of the chart bars.

c. Select the Border/Fill tab, then select the **Gradient** Fill Type and *Preset*: **Ocean** color scheme.

d. Print the chart. Save and close the query.

e. Compact and restore the database.

f. Close the file.

Mini Cases

Use the rubric following the case as a guide to evaluate your work, but keep in mind that your instructor may impose additional grading criteria or use a different standard to judge your work.

Determining Row and Column Data for PivotTables and PivotCharts

GENERAL CASE

The *chap5_mc1_traders.accdb* file contains data from an international specialty foods distribution firm. You have a query that assembles the necessary fields but need to mine these data to determine profits by item for each salesperson and country to which the goods were shipped. You will use this information to reward sales performance and to analyze where your customers are using the products you sell. Copy the *chap5_mc1_traders.accdb* file, rename the copied file as **chap5_mc1_traders_solution.accdb**, open the copied file, and enable the content. Use the skills from this chapter to perform several tasks. Open the Employees table and replace Your_Name with your name. Rename the Your_Name Revenue query with your name. Use the PivotTable view to calculate profits by subtracting total costs from revenue. Summarize and total the cost, revenue, and profit data by salesperson and the country of shipment. Draw a chart that displays your profits by country. Print the chart. Compact, repair, and back up your database.

Performance Elements	Exceeds Expectations	Meets Expectations	Below Expectations
Profit calculation	Calculated fields accurate.	Calculated fields accurate.	Output missing or incorrect.
Data summaries	Appropriate summaries and aggregating calculations performed.	Most of the requested summaries and aggregates present and accurate.	Output missing or inaccurate.
Detail manipulation	Appropriate levels of details displayed and formatted correctly.	Appropriate levels of details displayed with some formatting problems.	Insufficient understanding of detail manipulation.
Chart construction	Data are presented in an easy-to-interpret, aesthetically pleasing chart.	Data are presented in a chart with some aesthetic issues or minor clarity problems.	Chart is illegible or incomprehensible.

Combining Name Fields

RESEARCH CASE

This chapter introduced you to the power of using Access PivotTables and PivotCharts, but you have much more to explore. Copy the *chap5_mc2_coffee.accdb* file, rename the copied file as **chap5_mc2_coffee_solution.accdb**, open the file, and enable the content. Open the Your_Name Revenue query and set it to PivotTable view. You need to share these data with a coworker who does not have Access on her computer. She has Word, Excel, and PowerPoint. Use Help to research how to share this information with your coworker. After you successfully get the file into a usable form for your coworker, write your instructor explaining how you accomplished this step. Save and print the output that you generated for your coworker and name it **chap5_mc2_coffee_solution**, using the appropriate extension for the software that you used. Compact, repair, and back up your database.

Performance Elements	Exceeds Expectations	Meets Expectations	Below Expectations
Use online Help	Appropriate articles located, and instructions indicate comprehension.	Appropriate articles located, but instructions did not demonstrate comprehension.	Articles not found.
Data successfully transferred to another application	A Word or Excel file and printout submitted demonstrating file sharing.	A Word or Excel file and printout submitted with some minor problems from file sharing.	Files missing or incomprehensible.
Summarize and communicate	Instructions clearly written and could be used as directions.	Instruction text indicates some understanding but also weaknesses.	Instructions missing or incomprehensible.
File management	Database was correctly compacted, repaired, and backed up.	Database was successfully compacted but not backed up or vice versa.	Files not submitted.

Coffee Revenue Queries

DISASTER RECOVERY

A coworker called you into her office and explained that she was having difficulty with Access 2007 and asked you to look at her work. You are employed by the Human Resources Department of a large insurance company with offices and employees nationwide. Your coworker is trying to analyze the year-end salary adjustments for all of the positions and offices in the country to ensure pay equity. Copy the *chap5_mc3_insurance.accdb* file, rename the copied file as **chap5_mc3_insurance_solution.accdb**, open the file, and enable the content. Your coworker explains she cannot understand the chart. She intended that it should show the average new salary for each position title and performance rating. She needs to examine this information to determine if the excellently rated workers in all positions earn higher average salaries than do good-, average-, or poor-rated workers. Find the source of the error and correct it. Run and print the chart or charts. Compact, repair, and back up your database.

Performance Elements	Exceeds Expectations	Meets Expectations	Below Expectations
Error identification	Correct identification and correction of all errors.	Correct identification of all errors and correction of some errors.	Errors neither located nor corrected.
Reporting	Chart(s) designed and printed successfully.	Printout submitted, but with errors.	No printout submitted for evaluation.

Data Protection

Integrity, Validation, and Reliability

bjectives

After you read this chapter, you will be able to:

1. Establish data validity **(page 1061)**.

2. Create and modify a lookup field **(page 1064)**.

3. Create and modify a multivalued lookup field **(page 1067)**.

4. Work with input masks **(page 1068)**.

5. Create forms by using the Form Tool **(page 1078)**.

6. Create custom forms in Design view **(page 1091)**.

7. Create subforms **(page 1094)**.

8. Design functional formats **(page 1095)**.

Hands-On Exercises

Exercises	Skills Covered
1. DATA PROTECTION (page 1072) **Open:** chap6_ho1-3_nationalbank.accdb **Save as:** chap6_ho1-3_nationalbank_solution.accdb **Back up as:** chap6_ho1_nationalbank_solution.accdb	• Establish Required and Default Field Properties • Create and Test Validation Rules and Text • Create a Lookup Field • Modify a Lookup Field Value • Create a Multivalued Lookup Field • Create and Edit Input Masks
2. FORM CREATION TOOLS (page 1085) **Open:** chap6_ho1-3_nationalbank_solution.accdb (from Exercise 1) **Save as:** chap6_ho1-3_nationalbank_solution.accdb (additional modifications) **Back up as:** chap6_ho2_nationalbank_solution.accdb	• Use the Form Tool and Identify Form Controls • Create a Split Form • Create a Multiple Items Form • Create a Datasheet Form • Create PivotTable and PivotChart Forms
3. CUSTOMIZING FORMS (page 1099) **Open:** chap6_ho1-3_nationalbank_solution.accdb (from Exercise 2) **Save as:** chap6_ho1-3_nationalbank_solution.accdb (additional modifications)	• Use the Blank Form Tool to Create a Form • Create a Form in Design View • Add Action Buttons and Controls • Create and Edit a Form with a Subform • Customize a Form by Moving Controls and Adding a Theme

CASE STUDY

Simplify Data Entry

You work as an office manager at the Real Estate Agency. Your firm helps people buy and sell homes. The office has several agents who work with clients to help them find a match between their housing needs and what they can afford. The agents may work with home buyers, sellers, or both. The properties for sale are located in a variety of communities. Your agency maintains a database containing information about the homes, the agents, and the subdivisions in which the properties are located. The agents do not take prospective purchasers into a home unless the homeowner knows they are coming. Sometimes a prospective home purchaser needs to visit a property with very little notice. The agent needs to find the homeowner quickly and obtain permission to show the property. The agency owner asked you to add a new database table that will contain information about the clients the agents assist. You need to design a customer contact table, design a form, and make the form easy for the nontechnical staff in the firm to use. You will need to think through the design of the table carefully. Some of the fields you will need are obvious, such as customers' first and last names. Other fields need to serve the unique needs of the real estate agents.

Case Study

How can you help them reach a client quickly and easily? A prospective home purchaser has strong opinions about which subdivision he or she wants to live in. You need to consider how to capture the customer's preferences and enable the agents to use their time and the customer's time efficiently. For example, a customer who must have at least four bedrooms and two bathrooms would not want to spend an hour looking at a two-bedroom, one-bath house. An agent would not want to spend time showing a $750,000 house to a customer who qualifies for a $200,000 mortgage. When properly designed, your table will help your firm provide better customer service and make more efficient use of the agent's time. After you determine what fields to store in the table, you need to design a form based on the table. All of the agents need to use this table and its data. Therefore, your form must be designed in a way that will accommodate the least skilled agents in the firm. You should consider how to design the form to facilitate accurate data entry.

Your Assignment

- Read the chapter, paying special attention to the tools described that help protect data integrity and validity.
- Copy the *chap6_case_realestate.accdb* file to your production folder, rename it **chap6_case_realestate_solution.accdb**, and enable the content.
- Open the Relationships window and examine the relationships among the tables and the fields contained within each of the tables to become acquainted with this database.
- Create a new Customers table. Include fields for contact information, assuming that many of the customers are couples, so the information about names and cell phone numbers needs to be listed separately for each individual. Include fields to record the minimum number of bedrooms and bathrooms the couple wants. Finally, include information about which communities the couple wants to live in.
- Determine which fields should be required, how large each field should be, and what type of data you should define.
- Create a multivalued lookup for the subdivision.
- Create input masks for the phone numbers.
- Create a form that will facilitate data entry. Arrange the form logically and attractively. Add at least two action buttons to simplify the form's use. Test the form by populating at least one record.
- Submit your file to your instructor for evaluation. Compact and repair the database file.

Data Validity

Your friend e-mailed you a fun Web quiz that claims to measure your love of chocolate. After answering all of the questions, you submit your answers. Before you can learn your score, a pop-up window opens that asks you to log in or join as a new user of the free service. Because you have no account, you click the new-user link. A form containing many questions appears, requiring you to type answers in little boxes. You fill out your name, e-mail, password, birth date, gender, and education. As you enter your birth date, you receive an error message telling you that you need to format your birth date as MMDDYYYY. You fix the birth date and click the Submit button. The boxes return with the daytime phone box (which you missed) and an error message saying, "We're sorry, you need to provide your daytime phone number." You type your phone number, resubmit, and wonder if you will ever find out your chocolate love score. Perhaps you receive another error message about neglecting to provide your state. Eventually, you create an account, log in to it, and receive your score.

In completing the new-user information profile, you interacted with a database form over the Internet. The form refused to accept any answers until you answered all of the required questions and submitted your answers in a predetermined format. The software provided you with hints about what you did wrong and instructions about how to fix your data. Eventually, you and everyone else taking the chocolate lovers quiz provide the Web site with organized data. All of the records contain a daytime phone number; all of the birth dates are formatted identically. You found out how much you love chocolate, and the Web site owner collected demographic and psychographic information about you.

In this section, you explore establishing safeguards on table data to protect it from data-entry and user error. As you acquire these skills you shift from being the data user to becoming the individual in the organization who administers, manages, and protects the organization's data.

Establishing Data Validity

You already know about GIGO—Garbage In Garbage Out. No organization's management can make decisions unless they are able to trust the source data. Good data management practices include data validation as a critical component of the data systems. *Data validation* is a set of constraints or rules that help control the type and accuracy of the data entered into a field. Access provides some data validation automatically. For example, you cannot enter text into a numerically defined field or type a primary key value that duplicates another record's primary key value. Access supports the following data validation methods that help ensure the integrity of data by defending the data against user errors:

Data validation is a set of constraints or rules that help control the type and accuracy of the data entered into a field.

- **Required**—Sets the required property of a field to force data entry, such as a daytime phone number.

- **Default Values**—Specifies the default property of a field to automatically enter a specific value. For example, if most of your organization's donors live in North Carolina, you can set the default value of the state field to NC. The data entry operator can overwrite the default value with a different state abbreviation when needed.

- **Validation Rule**—Limits the type of text a user can enter into a field. For example, if all of your school's course numbers are larger than 100, then you could establish a validation rule to prohibit values under 100 on a registration form.

- **Validation Text**—Provides the error message telling users what they did wrong and gives them instructions on what they need to do to fix it. For example, the validation text for the rule violation above might be, "You have entered an invalid course number. Please recheck the number and enter a value greater than 100."

- **Lookup Lists**—Specifies the field values be limited to a predefined drop-down list of values. For example, class status in a university's database might be Freshman, Sophomore, Junior, Senior, Graduate, or Other.

- **Multiple Value Fields**—Accepts several different field values in a single record. For example, a single employee might be assigned to work on several different projects concurrently.
- **Input Masks**—Uses non-stored characters to force conformity on the data entered. For Example, a Social Security number (SSN) field might be entered and stored as 123456789. However, what the data entry operator sees on the screen is 123-45-6789. The hyphens do not need to be typed, nor are they stored with the entered data.
- **Logical**—Compares values in two fields and establishes rules governing their interaction. For example, a university database might have fields storing the enrollment and graduation dates for each student. To help prevent data entry errors, you might create a rule that the graduation date value must be larger than the enrollment date value.

Establish Required and Default Field Values

A required field is one that cannot be blank when you create a new record. You have already learned about setting the required property of a field. All primary keys must be required fields for the relational power of the database to work. The default Required setting is No for all the remaining fields, which enables you to create a record with missing data in those fields. However, to ensure the integrity of a database table, you should require that data be entered for critical fields. With the table open in Design view, click in the top half of the grid to select the field you need to require. Then switch to the Field Properties grid in the lower section of the Design view, click the Required property drop-down arrow, and select Yes (see Figure 6.1). When you create a new record or modify an existing record, you must enter data into the required field.

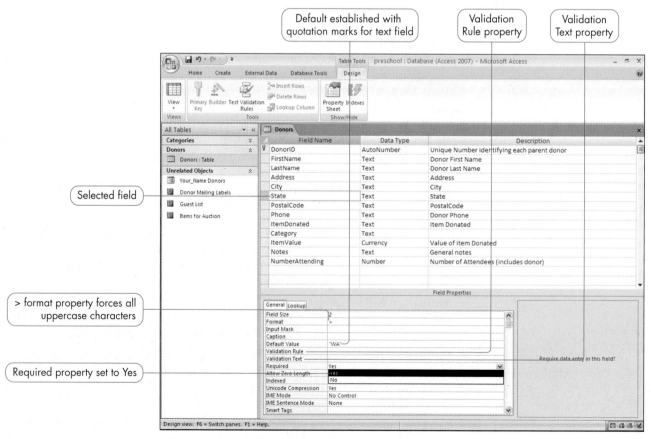

Figure 6.1 Required and Default Properties

When a majority of new records you add contain a common element, such as the same city or state, you can set a default value for that field to reduce data-entry time. You establish a field's default property by selecting the field in the table's Design view in the top part of the grid and then clicking the Default Value property in the Field Properties grid in the lower part of the window. For example, the South Vancouver Pre-school's donors primarily live in Washington. Figure 6.1 displays the default value of the State field set to *WA*. You may enter different two-character state abbreviations when necessary, but the presumption is that the majority of donors live in Washington.

Set a Validation Rule and Generate Validation Text

A *validation rule* is a restriction that specifies which values are allowed in a field.

A *validation rule* is a restriction that specifies that data entered in a field are allowed; data that do not meet the restriction are prevented from being stored in a particular field. For most data types, you can enter one validation rule by specifying an expression in the Validation Rule property. For example, you can type >0 in the Validation Rule property to ensure that only values greater than zero are entered.

When you break a validation rule, you must provide Access with the required information in the desired format before you can move on. You have probably experienced frustration when filling out a data form on a Web site and not being able to move to the next task without knowing why. Good database design not only protects the data by using validation but also tells the user when a rule has been violated and what is needed to fix the situation. Access helps you communicate by entering error message text in the Validation Text property in the Field Properties grid. You use

Validation text informs users about what they have done incorrectly and instructs them about what needs to be done.

validation text to inform users about what they have done incorrectly and instruct them about what they need to do to correct the problem. Examples of good validation text messages might be *Please enter a daytime phone number* or *The birth date needs to be formatted using the MMDDYYYY form of data entry*. Enter the rule and text in the respective properties in the Field Properties grid, as shown in Figure 6.1.

If you add a validation rule to an already populated table, you may violate your own rule because records with inappropriate values may be stored in the table. Access warns you if existing table data violate the newly established rule. You can remove the rule, switch to Datasheet view, find and correct the rule violators, and then return to Design view and reapply the rule.

You may choose to employ different layers of validation. For example, suppose you were developing a table or form for each academic department to use to enter the courses they plan on offering during the summer. You could add a validation rule that forces the course number to fall between 100 and 599 for undergraduate classes: >=100 and <= 599. If a department head attempts to enter 650 for a class that should be 560, he or she receives an error message and a prompt suggesting a method to fix the problem. Simply having a validation rule does not prevent users from skipping the field. Unless you set the Required property to Yes, having a validation rule will not force data entry for the field. Generally, if a field is important enough to require validation, it is also important enough to insist on data entry.

Creating and Modifying a Lookup Field

A **lookup field** provides a predefined list of values from which to select.

Good database planning identifies the database fields containing repetitive data and designs the table and form structure to facilitate the data entry. If all of the donated items are classified as a product, service, gift certificate, or other, then it makes life easier to limit data entry options to a drop-down list. Whoever does the data entry will have their choices limited to the appropriate category. This will help ensure uniformity and consistency during data entry. A **lookup field** provides the user with a predefined list of values to select, which decreases the amount of time for entering data. Frequently, the values that need to be entered in one table have already been stored as a related field in a different table. For example, if all payments are limited to cash, check, credit, or other online payment methods, data entry will be faster and more accurate when clicking and selecting from a list option is available.

Suppose the field might contain only three values, Cash, Credit, or Check. If the data entry operators were typing, they might misspell Credit as Credir or Cerdit. Then, a query set to return all of the purchases made using Credit last month would not include some of the necessary records. The mistyped values would not be selected in the query. Perhaps that query will be used to generate the bills to send to the customer. If the query did not select the record, no request for payment will be sent. Data entry errors add costs to the organization. They add costs because the information they generate is wrong and the decisions made based on the misinformation will also be wrong. Errors add costs because the organization needs to hire someone to find and fix the errors. And finally, incorrect data may lead to poor customer service and result in the loss of a customer. If the database table or form used for data entry contains a lookup field with pre-specified (and correctly typed) values of Cash, Credit, or Check, the chance of data entry error reduces. The lookup will not prevent a data entry misclassification of a Cash sale as a Credit one, but it will prevent misspelling the word Credit. Access provides a Lookup Wizard to help you establish the lookup column and values. The **Lookup Wizard** helps create the lookup field, populates the appropriate values, and if needed, establishes the necessary table relationships.

The **Lookup Wizard** helps create, populate, and relate the lookup field.

Create the Lookup Field

Suppose the South Vancouver Pre-school's auction categorizes donations as Service, Products, Gift Certificates, and Other. Because these values do not exist anywhere in the database, you would create a new table, Categories, and populate the Category field with four records containing the appropriate values. Then you would create Category as a foreign field in the Donors table. Figure 6.2 illustrates the Donor table in Design view with the Data Type column of the Category field set to launch the Lookup Wizard. Although you can simply type the values into a list using the Lookup Wizard, it is not recommended. It can create problems later when you run queries or reports that are query-based. Having a separate table to look up values also means that you can establish referential integrity between the tables. This uses the database power to protect queried results. Using a lookup list violates the rules of good database design.

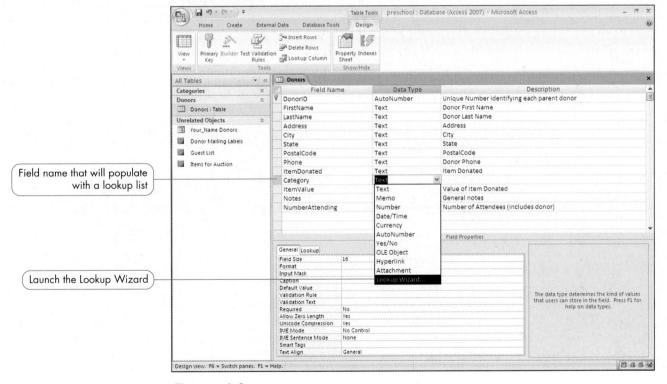

Figure 6.2 Launch the Lookup Wizard

The first screen in the Lookup Wizard asks that you identify the source data. Figure 6.3 shows the Categories table selection. The next screen asks you to select the field or fields for the lookup column (see Figure 6.4). Next, the wizard asks that you specify a sort order for the list box (see Figure 6.5). The next screen asks you to establish the column width for the lookup column. You want to make it wide enough to display the longest value, but not so wide that it obscures the rest of the form or table in which it is used (see Figure 6.6). You make width adjustments by moving your mouse over the right column boundary, and when the pointer changes to the double-headed arrow, click and drag to the appropriate width. Figure 6.7 shows the name of the lookup field and gives you a choice of single (default) or multiple values. Most lookups will not need a multiple value. Figure 6.8 shows a category being selected from the populated lookup field in Datasheet view.

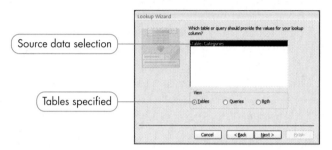

Figure 6.3 Lookup Column Data Source Specification

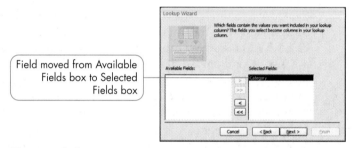

Figure 6.4 Select the Necessary Field(s)

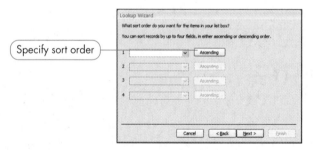

Figure 6.5 Lookup Column Sort Order

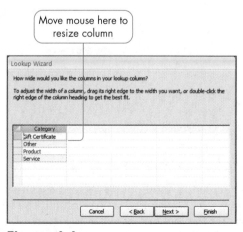

Figure 6.6 Column Width Adjustment

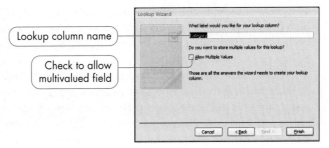

Figure 6.7 Name Specification

Figure 6.8 Lookup Column in Use

Modify a Lookup by Adding and Deleting Values

Data needs change. You can edit, delete, or add values to the lookup field to accommodate changed data needs. For example, the school workers cataloging the auction donations complain that the categories are too restrictive. They want the Other category removed from the lookup column list and the Service category changed to be Personal Service and Sports Services. You agree to make the necessary changes. You begin changing a lookup column by identifying the source of the lookup data. These lookup data are stored in the Category table. You need to open the Category table, delete Other, and add (or edit) Personal Service and Sports Services. Move off the record and close the Category table. As soon as the changes are made, the new lookup values are available for use in the lookup column in the Donors table (see Figure 6.9). Someone would need to go through the table data and reclassify all of the former other categories.

Figure 6.9 Edited Lookup Column in Use

Creating and Modifying a Multivalued Lookup Field

Often, data do not fit easily into narrowly defined classifications. For example, you have Sports Services and Gift Certificate categories. Would you classify the donation of golf lessons as Sports Services or Gift Certificate? Once the Donors table is populated with hundreds of items, it will become difficult for prospective bidders at the auction to find the items on which they wish to bid. The event chair plans on publishing auction lists by category to help bidders find items. However, the existing classification system will list the golf lessons only under the Sports Services category. You want to also display the golf lessons in the Gift Certificate category. Other items should also be listed in two categories. For example, the football tickets should be classified as Sports Services and Product.

These situations describe a need for a database that will support multiple choices. A **multivalued field** is one that accepts multiple choices for a single field without requiring you to create a complex design. You have worked in one-to-many relationships between table data. One customer ID can show up on multiple orders, but many customers cannot place a single order. These situations describe events that should be structurally designed in a many-to-many relationship. Access 2007 provides a way to do this. By checking the Allow Multiple Values check box in the appropriate Lookup Wizard (see Figure 6.7), you produce a field that accepts multiple values. Figure 6.10 shows the results of a field with multiple values in the first record. The values display in the table separated by commas. The second record displays the Category Field List box after Allow Multiple Values was selected. The user specifies one or more categories by checking the appropriate check boxes.

These steps are deceptively simple. Access works hard so that you do not need to. Access creates a succession of hidden system tables and the affiliated relationships for them. It appears as though you are working with a single field. Under the surface, Access creates a series of juncture tables and stores them independently.

> A **multivalued field** is one defined to accept multiple choices for a single field.

> (Access works hard so that you do not need to.)

TIP When Not to Use a Multivalued Lookup Field

Most databases (including earlier versions of Access) could not do multivalued fields—or at least not do them easily. If a possibility exists that your database will start its life in an Access environment and eventually migrate to a larger, SQL-based environment, you should not create any multivalued fields. Using them violates the basic premise of the relational model in database design. A multivalued field will not export to a SQL environment because it cannot function in a relational environment with rigidly enforced referential integrity. The database administrator cannot accurately predict the results of queries or query-based reports when the parameter field is multivalued.

> Commas separate multivalued field choices

> Check boxes select multivalued field choices

Figure 6.10 Multivalued Field Specifications

Working with Input Masks

> An **input mask** specifies the exact formatting of the input data while minimizing data storage.

Designing databases well requires that the designers anticipate how the users will interact with and populate the tables. Good designers facilitate data entry and minimize the required storage space in their databases. An **input mask** specifies the exact formatting of the input data while minimizing data storage requirements. For example, you are used to viewing (and thinking about) Social Security numbers with hyphens (e.g., 123-45-6789) and telephone numbers with parentheses and hyphens, such as (405) 555-1234. In a database with thousands of records, the parentheses and hyphens consume unnecessary storage space, take time for data entry operators to type, and may interfere with sorting the data. The parentheses and hyphens add value and help data users understand the information stored in the data with greater accuracy. People need them, but the computer does not. Because people in the United States are accustomed to seeing the Social Security number with the hyphens in place, you can create an input mask to display the data with the hyphens in position but store and use the data in a "hyphenless" format. In the case of the phone number, the input mask also serves as a prompt to the data entry operator to remember to enter the area code as well as the seven-digit phone number. It also helps ensure consistency in data entry. Different data entry operators might enter a phone number in a variety of ways, such as (810) 555-2222, 801-555-2222, or with the international form, 810.555.2222. Good database design anticipates and eliminates inconsistent data input. You may use the Input Mask Wizard or create a customized input mask.

Use the Input Mask Wizard

The *Input Mask Wizard* helps generate and test masks.

The *Input Mask Wizard* helps generate and test masks so you spend less time creating and correcting data masks. You launch the Input Mask Wizard by opening the table in Design view and activating the field you want to mask in the top portion of the Design grid. Click the Input Mask property in the Field Properties grid. After you click in the Input Mask property, click Builder in the Tools group on the Design tab or click Build on the right side of the Input Mask property (see Figure 6.11) to launch the Input Mask Wizard. Specify settings in the Input Mask dialog box. Figure 6.12 shows the first screen in the Input Mask Wizard dialog box. In this step, you select or edit an existing mask.

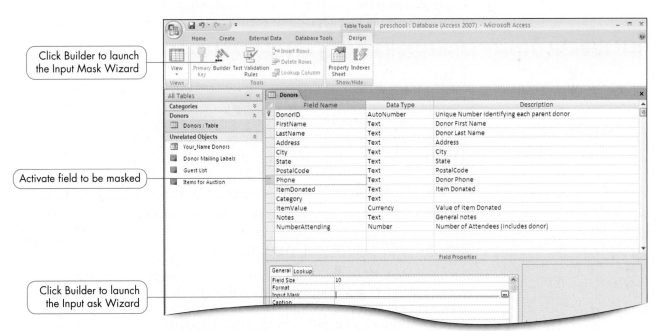

Figure 6.11 Launching the Input Mask Wizard

Figure 6.12 Input Mask Wizard

The second step in the Input Mask Wizard enables you to select a placeholder character, such as an underscore (_) or a pound sign (#), to display in the field in Datasheet view until you type the data. The last step enables you to specify if you want the symbols, such as the parentheses and hyphens, to be stored with the data. After you apply the mask, the correct syntax !(999) 000-0000;;_ appears in the Input Mask property. This mask prompts the data entry operator to enter an area code with each phone number entered in the database table or form (see Figure 6.13). The underscore placeholder appears for each digit as you type the phone number.

Figure 6.13 Datasheet View of a Field with an Input Mask

Create a Customized Input Mask

The Input Mask Wizard provides many of the commonly used masks. Because each organization and each database needs differently described data, you may need to create a custom input mask. Suppose your database was used in a jewelry store. The items in inventory all begin with FJ (Fall's Jewelers), followed by two characters describing the item type (WA–watch, RI–ring, BR–bracelet, etc.), followed by a five-digit inventory number. FA-RI-02345 might identify an emerald ring. The mask would be !"FJ-">AA"-"00000.

The exclamation point forces the data input to move from left to right. The "FJ-" is a character literal. All inventory numbers will begin with what is enclosed in the hyphens, in this case, FJ. The greater than symbol (>) in the mask converts whatever is typed to uppercase characters. Using it will mean that the data entry operators do not need to press Shift on the keyboard to produce uppercase letters. The next part is another character literal to produce the next hyphen. Finally, a five-digit identification number is mandatory. The data entry operator types ri02345, and Access displays FA-RI-02345. Table 6.1 describes the characters and uses of input mask codes.

Table 6.1 Some Common Input Mask Characters and Uses

Character	Description	Requires Entry
0	Digit (0 to 9) Plus + and Minus – not allowed	Yes
9	Digit or space Plus + and Minus – not allowed	No
#	Digit or Space Plus + and Minus – allowed Spaces display as blanks but are not stored	No
L	Letter (A to Z)	Yes
?	Letter (A to Z)	No
A	Letter (A to Z)	Yes
a	Letter (A to Z)	No
<	Converts all characters entered to lowercase letters	No
>	Converts all characters entered to uppercase letters	No
\	Turns the next character into a literal \(displays (\Q displays Q	No
.(period)	Decimal placeholder	No
- or /	Date separators Jun-5-2008 or 6/5/2008	No
!	Forces the value to be input from left to right	Not Applicable

In the first hands-on exercise, you will use Access features that help protect data from data entry errors, facilitate the data entry process, and ensure that the decision makers have all of the data necessary to answer their questions. You will create field properties that require information, notify data entry operators of rule violations, simplify data entry, and prompt data entry operators to enter data in the desired format.

Hands-On Exercises

1 | Data Protection

Skills covered: 1. Establish Required and Default Field Properties **2.** Create and Test Validation Rules and Text **3.** Create a Lookup Field **4.** Modify a Lookup Field Value **5.** Create a Multivalued Lookup Field **6.** Create and Edit Input Masks

---

Step 1
Establish Required and Default Field Properties

Refer to Figure 6.14 as you complete Step 1.

a. Use Windows Explorer to locate the file named *chap6_ho1-3_nationalbank.accdb.* Copy the file to your production folder and rename the copied file as **chap6_ho1-3_nationalbank_solution.accdb.**

b. Open *chap6_ho1-3_nationalbank_solution.accdb* and click **Options** on the Security Warning toolbar, click **Enable this content** in the Microsoft Office Security Options dialog box, and click **OK.**

c. Rename the *Your_Name Loan Payment* query with your name.

d. Open the **Customers table** in Datasheet view and replace *Your_Name* in the First Name and Last Name fields with your name.

e. Right-click the **Customers tab** and select **Design View** from the shortcut menu.

f. In the top portion of the table Design grid, click in the **PhoneNumber** field to select it. In the Field Properties grid, click in the **Required** property. Click the **drop-down arrow** on the right of the Required property, and then select **Yes** from the list.

You changed the data entry process so that a phone number is required for each customer.

g. In the top portion of the table Design grid, click in the **AccountType** field to select it. In the Field Properties grid, click in the **Default Value** property and type **Gold**. Press **Enter.**

As soon as you click outside the Default Value property, Access adds quotation marks around the default property because it is a text string. Because most of the bank's customers are Gold level accounts, you set the default value to display the most frequently occurring field value. You need to test the changes you made to the table design.

h. Click **Save** on the Quick Launch Toolbar. Right-click the **Customers tab** and select **Datasheet View** from the shortcut menu. If you get a warning about testing the data integrity rules, click **Yes.** Because this is a small database, testing the data integrity will not take a long time.

Look at the new record row. The AccountType field has already been entered as Gold.

i. Create a new record. Type **Aaron, Thomasson, 409 Cook Road, Stoneboro, PA, 16137,** in the appropriate fields. When you get to the Phone Number field, skip it and type **Platinum** in the **AccountType** field.

j. Click into a different record. An error message appears, reminding you that you must enter a value in the Customers.PhoneNumber field. Click **OK** and type **7245551212.** Close the Customers table.

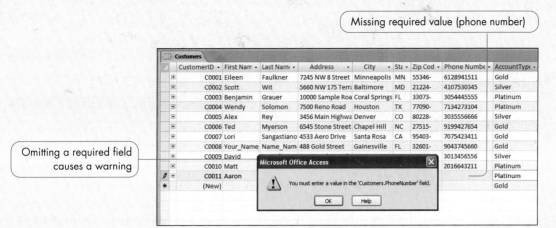

Missing required value (phone number)

Omitting a required field causes a warning

Customers								
CustomerID	First Name	Last Name	Address	City	Sta	Zip Cod	Phone Numbe	AccountTyp
C0001	Eileen	Faulkner	7245 NW 8 Street	Minneapolis	MN	55346-	6128941511	Gold
C0002	Scott	Wit	5660 NW 175 Terr	Baltimore	MD	21224-	4107530345	Silver
C0003	Benjamin	Grauer	10000 Sample Roa	Coral Springs	FL	33073-	3054445555	Platinum
C0004	Wendy	Solomon	7500 Reno Road	Houston	TX	77090-	7134273104	Platinum
C0005	Alex	Rey	3456 Main Highwa	Denver	CO	80228-	3035556666	Silver
C0006	Ted	Myerson	6545 Stone Street	Chapel Hill	NC	27515-	9199427654	Gold
C0007	Lori	Sangastiano	4533 Aero Drive	Santa Rosa	CA	95403-	7075423411	Gold
C0008	Your_Name	Name_Nam	488 Gold Street	Gainesville	FL	32601-	9043745660	Gold
C0009	David						3013456556	Silver
C0010	Matt						2016643211	Platinum
C0011	Aaron							Platinum
(New)								Gold

Microsoft Office Access — You must enter a value in the 'Customers.PhoneNumber' field. OK Help

Figure 6.14 Data Validation

Step 2
Create and Test Validation Rules and Text

Refer to Figure 6.15 as you complete Step 2.

a. Right-click the **Loans table** in the All Tables pane and select **Design View** from the shortcut menu.

b. Click the **InterestRate** field on the top of the Design grid.

c. Click in the **Validation Rule** property in the Field Properties grid.

You will establish a rule that notifies data entry operators if they attempt to enter an interest rate that is greater than an acceptable boundary. Notice that an ellipsis button appears at the right of the property row. If the validation rule is complicated, you can launch the Expression Builder and use it to establish correct syntax. This rule is simple, and you do not need to use the Builder.

d. Type **>0.25** in the Validation Rule property box.

e. Click in the **Validation Text** property and type **The interest rate you entered is too high. Enter this value as a decimal, e.g. type .055 to enter 5.5%.**

When a data entry operator enters an interest rate that is too high, a message will appear, giving guidance about what needs to be done differently.

f. Save the design changes. Read the message about changed data integrity rules. Click **Yes**. Right-click the **Loans tab** and select **Datasheet View** from the shortcut menu.

Access tests the data in the table to make sure that none of the interest rates are too high.

g. Click in the **InterestRate** field of the first record. Edit the value by typing **.26**. Press **Enter**.

You should receive an error message containing the validation text you typed in Step 2e.

h. Read the message. Click **OK** in the error message box. Edit the first record to display **.062** for the interest rate field. Press **Enter**.

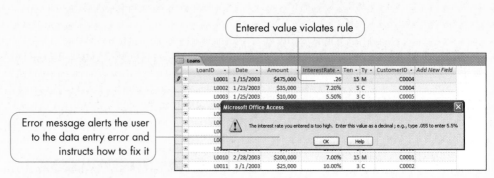

Entered value violates rule

Error message alerts the user to the data entry error and instructs how to fix it

Figure 6.15 Error Message Displays when Validation Rule Is Violated

Refer to Figure 6.16 as you complete Step 3.

a. Click the **Datasheet tab** and click **Lookup Column** in the Fields & Columns group.

The Lookup Wizard launches.

b. Verify that the **I want the lookup column to look up the values in a table or query** option is selected. Click **Next**.

c. Click the **Table: LoanTypes** and click **Next**.

d. Click the **LoanName** field in the Available Fields box to select it. Click the **Move to Selected Fields button** to move the field to the Selected Fields box. Click **Next**.

You decide that the ascending sort order meets your needs.

e. Click **Next**. Make sure that the **Hide key column (recommended) check box** is selected. Adjust the column width by moving your mouse over the LoanName column heading's right boundary. When the mouse pointer shape changes to a two-headed arrow, click and drag right about one-fourth inch. Click **Next**.

f. Name the lookup column **LoanType**. Click **Finish**. Click in the first record of the LoanType field. Click the **arrow** and select **Mortgage**. Press **Enter**. The next record is a car loan. Type **C**. Press **Enter**. Use the Type column as a reference to populate the LoanType field for the rest of the records.

A new column, LoanType, has been added. If you had the InterestRate field active at the end of Step 2, the new column inserts to the left of the interest rate column.

TROUBLESHOOTING: It does not matter where the Loan type column appears in your file. It only matters that it has been created. If necessary, switch to Design view and reorder the fields to match the order in Figure 6.16.

The Type field tells what type of loan

Arrow to facilitate data entry

Typing the first letter of the loan type permits quick data entry

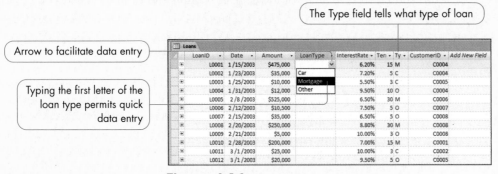

Figure 6.16 A Lookup Column

Step 4
Modify a Lookup Field Value

Refer to Figure 6.17 as you complete Step 4.

a. Open the **LoanTypes** table in Datasheet view.

b. Click in the **LoanName** field in the third record, Other, to select it. Type **Personal** and press **Enter.**

You decide that the Other loan category would be more professional if named Personal.

c. Close the LoanTypes table.

The Loans table should still be open in Datasheet view. If it is not, open it.

d. Examine the data in the LoanType field.

The word Other no longer appears. It has been replaced with Personal. You wonder why the changes in the LoanType table change the Loans table. You decide to do some research.

e. Click the **Database Tools tab** and click **Relationships** in the Show/Hide group.

The Relationships window displays a relationship between the Loans and LoanType table. Access created the relationship for you as you worked through the Lookup Wizard.

f. Close the Relationships window.

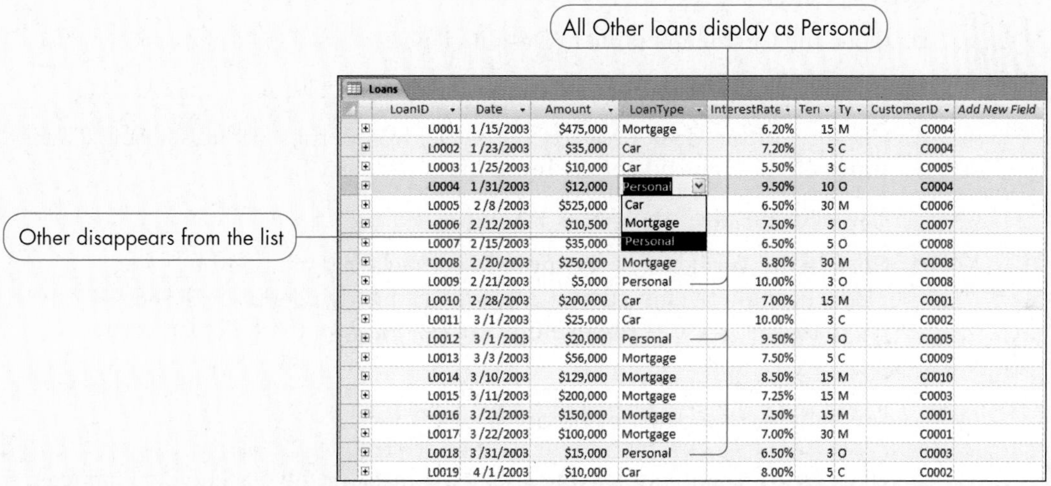

LoanID	Date	Amount	LoanType	InterestRate	Ter	Ty	CustomerID	Add New Field
L0001	1/15/2003	$475,000	Mortgage	6.20%	15	M	C0004	
L0002	1/23/2003	$35,000	Car	7.20%	5	C	C0004	
L0003	1/25/2003	$10,000	Car	5.50%	3	C	C0005	
L0004	1/31/2003	$12,000	Personal	9.50%	10	O	C0004	
L0005	2/8/2003	$525,000		6.50%	30	M	C0006	
L0006	2/12/2003	$10,500		7.50%	5	O	C0007	
L0007	2/15/2003	$35,000		6.50%	5	O	C0008	
L0008	2/20/2003	$250,000	Mortgage	8.80%	30	M	C0008	
L0009	2/21/2003	$5,000	Personal	10.00%	3	O	C0008	
L0010	2/28/2003	$200,000	Car	7.00%	15	M	C0001	
L0011	3/1/2003	$25,000	Car	10.00%	3	C	C0002	
L0012	3/1/2003	$20,000	Personal	9.50%	5	O	C0005	
L0013	3/3/2003	$56,000	Mortgage	7.50%	5	C	C0009	
L0014	3/10/2003	$129,000	Mortgage	8.50%	15	M	C0010	
L0015	3/11/2003	$200,000	Mortgage	7.25%	15	M	C0003	
L0016	3/21/2003	$150,000	Mortgage	7.50%	15	M	C0001	
L0017	3/22/2003	$100,000	Mortgage	7.00%	30	M	C0001	
L0018	3/31/2003	$15,000	Personal	6.50%	3	O	C0003	
L0019	4/1/2003	$10,000	Car	8.00%	5	C	C0002	

Figure 6.17 Edited Lookup Column

Step 5
Create a Multivalued Lookup Field

Refer to Figure 6.18 as you complete Step 5.

a. Right-click the **Loans tab** and select **Design View** from the shortcut menu.

b. Click the **LoanType** field in the Field Name list to select it. Click the **Lookup Tab** in the Field Properties grid.

Now that a Lookup column exists, you can modify its properties to make adjustments to it.

c. Click the **Allow Multiple Values** property to select it. Click the arrow on the right of the property box and select **Yes**. Click **Yes** in the warning box.

Access warns you that you will not be able to undo this change after the table is saved. You are sure about this change.

d. Save the changes to the design of the Loans table. Right-click the **Loans tab** and select **Datasheet View** from the shortcut menu.

e. Click the arrow in the first record of the LoanType field. Add a check to the **Car check box**. Click **OK**.

You have identified that this loan is a mortgage that was also used to purchase a car. The new loan type displays as Car, Mortgage.

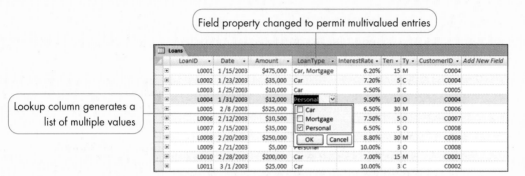

Figure 6.18 Expanded Information

Step 6
Create and Edit Input Masks

Refer to Figure 6.19 as you complete Step 6.

a. Open the **Customers table** in Design view.

b. Click the **PhoneNumber** field in the FieldName column.

c. Click the **Input Mask** property in the Field Properties grid to select it. Click **Build** on the right side of the Input Mask property box.

This activates the Input Mask Wizard.

d. Click in the **Try It** box of the Input Mask Wizard dialog box. (___) ___-____ displays. Position the insertion point at the right edge and type **5556667777** to see if the mask displays the phone numbers as you want them displayed.

TROUBLESHOOTING: You need to reposition the insertion point next to the open parentheses to make the number fit.

e. Click **Next**. You do not need to adjust the mask or the placeholder character, so click **Next** again.

f. Click the **With the symbols in the mask** option. Click **Next** and click **Finish**. Save the table, right-click the **Customers tab**, and select **Datasheet View** from the shortcut menu.

The phone numbers display in an easier-to-read format. Parentheses enclose the area codes, and hyphens separate the prefix and suffix portions of the number. You worry that all of the extra characters will consume too much storage space and decide to edit the mask. The easiest edit method is to launch the Input Mask Wizard again.

g. Right-click the **Customers tab** and select **Design View** from the shortcut menu. Click **Build** on the right side of the Input Mask property box. Click **Next** twice.

h. Make sure that **Without the symbols in the mask** is selected and click **Finish**. Save the table, right-click the **Customers tab**, and select **Datasheet View** from the shortcut menu.

i. Click the **Office Button**, select **Manage**, and select **Compact and Repair Database**.

j. Click the **Office Button**, select **Manage**, and then select **Back Up Database**. Type **chap6_ho1_nationalbank_solution** and click **Save**.

You just created a backup of the database after completing the first hands-on exercise. The original database *chap6_ho1-3_nationalbank_solution* remains onscreen. If you ruin the original database as you complete the second hands-on exercise, you can use the backup file you just created.

k. Close the file and exit Access if you do not want to continue with the next exercise at this time.

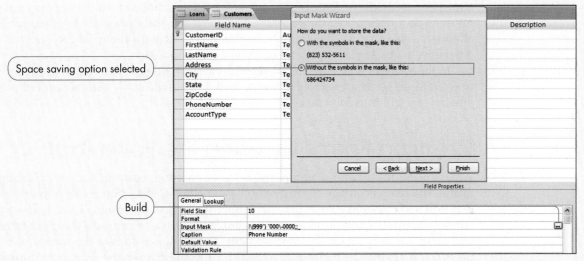

Figure 6.19 Input Mask Wizard Displaying Corrected Options

Forms

Although some data entry operators prefer entering data in the grids provided in Access tables because they find it to be quicker, most database data entry users and designers prefer forms for data entry control. Grid data entry speed may introduce errors. Especially in very long or wide tables, the data entry operators entering the data can accidentally change records in the middle of an edit. They correctly enter the data for the first five fields of the record, then jump to the previous row and overwrite existing data with values that belong in the next record. Now, two records have incorrect or incomplete data.

Typically, a form user sees only a single record at a time, so this eliminates the record-jumping problem. Using forms enables data entry to multiple tables concurrently. If a field in a record is stored as an object, like an Excel chart or a Word memo, viewing the record in a form will display the actual object. Viewing the same record in the Datasheet view of a table will display only an icon or text displaying the object's file name. Finally, forms may be designed to emulate the paper documents already in use in the organization. This facilitates the transition from the paper environment to an electronic data storage environment. Databases do not necessarily eliminate paper forms; they supplement and coexist with them. Therefore, it is a good idea to design the paper and electronic forms to match.

In this section, you learn the basics of good form design. You will discover multiple methods to create and edit Access forms. You will work with action buttons. Finally, you will learn how to create calculated controls.

Creating Forms by Using the Form Tool

Access provides several different methods of creating, editing, and embellishing forms. The reference page summarizes these methods. Once you create a form, you may edit and customize the form using either the Layout or Design views. Forms are almost never born fully functional. The designer creates a form, and the users test it and offer suggestions for its improvement. The designer adjusts the form and the users test it again. The collaborative design process between the database administrative and use staff continues throughout the life of the form. Because data needs in the organization change, forms designed long ago and used for years sometimes need to be redesigned. The form creation process provides the database administration staff a window into how the rest of the organization functions. It empowers the database users with the ability to alter the tools they use daily. Ideally, a form should simplify data entry. Form users may need access to only a few fields in a table that contains many. The form designer needs to strike a delicate balance between providing users access to everything they need to do their jobs without cluttering the form with extraneous fields. The users of the data know what they need and often offer detailed descriptions of what they want. By listening to their suggestions, your forms will function more effectively, the users' work will be easier, and your data will suffer fewer user-generated errors.

> (Ideally, a form should simplify data entry.)

Form Creation Methods | Reference

Method	Location	Use
Form Tool	With a table or query open, Create Tab, Forms group	Creates a simple form displaying all of the fields in the source object.
Split Form Tool	With a table or query open, Create Tab, Forms group	Creates a two-part form that includes all of the source fields. In it, one view is a form displaying a single record and the other is a Datasheet view of the source object. The two views synchronize and edits made in either place update the other.
Multiple Items Tool	With a table or query open, Create Tab, Forms group	Creates a tabular form that includes all of the fields from the source. It closely resembles a datasheet of a table or query. This creation method moves beyond the datasheet view by permitting inclusion of action buttons, graphic elements, and other controls.
Datasheet Tool	With a table or query open, Create Tab, Forms group, More Forms Tool, Datasheet Tool	Creates a form that looks exactly like the data source. This creation method moves beyond the Datasheet view by permitting inclusion of action buttons, graphic elements, and other controls while locking the source data in a split database environment.
Form Wizard	Close source object. Create Tab, Forms Group, More Forms, Form Wizard	Creates a form that may source one or more tables or queries and may include or exclude fields. It is more selective than the three earlier methods. You may define data grouping and sorting. You may select from a number of themes to enhance your form.
Blank Form Tool	Close source object. Create Tab, Forms Group, Blank Form	Very quick form creation tool—especially suitable for forms containing only a few fields.
PivotChart Tool	With a table, form or query open, Create Tab, Forms group, PivotChart	Like the PivotChart view of a table or query, you can create and save forms in pivot views. Often, multiple different pivots of the data need to be stored. Saving a pivot as a form provides additional storage capabilities.
PivotTable Tool	With a table, form or query open, Create Tab, Forms group, More Forms, PivotTable	Like the PivotTable view of a table or query, you can create and save forms in pivot views. Often, multiple different pivots of the data need to be stored. Saving a pivot as a form provides additional storage capabilities.
Modal Dialog Tool	Close source object. Create Tab, Forms Group, More Forms, Modal Dialog	Creates a dialog box that empowers the form user to filter and select only the fields and records necessary.
Form Design	Close source object. Create Tab, Forms Group, Form Design Tool	Creates a blank form in Design view. You may completely customize all aspects of the form.

The **Form Tool** gives you a one-click method of form creation.

The **Form Tool** gives you a one-click method of form creation. Have the source object open, click the Create tab, and then click Form in the Forms group. The newly created form opens in Layout view ready for customizing edits. You may generate many forms, even complicated ones, using this method, and then use the Layout view to edit and customize your work. Figure 6.20 shows an open table with the form tool highlighted ready to generate a form. Figure 6.21 shows the form open in Layout view ready to customize.

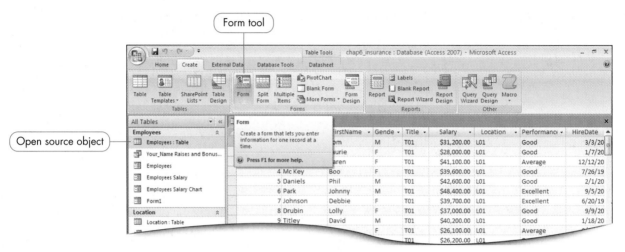

Figure 6.20 Setup for Form Creation

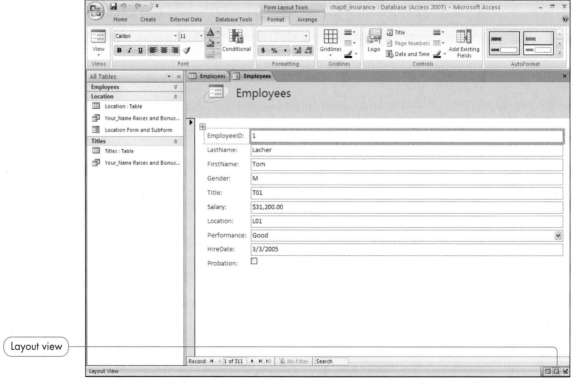

Figure 6.21 Newly Created Form Opened in Layout View

You need to understand the boxes displayed in the Layout view prior to editing the new form. Every item on the form is a control. Form controls operate like report controls. They may be bound, unbound, or calculated.

- **Bound Controls**—contain the data fields from the underlying source document. Each record is tied to the underlying data source. Every field on a form must have a unique bound control.

- **Unbound Controls**—contain labels (text boxes) providing the user with guidance on what to do with the bound control boxes. For example, the unbound control might display a label, FAX Number, and the bound control for that record would store the FAX for that employee. Unbound controls also contain aesthetic elements, lines, or borders. Use unbound controls to perform calculations in a form.

- **Calculated Controls**—contain the instructions (formulas) that generate the calculations displayed in a form.

Good form design generally dictates that you should have at least one unbound control for every bound control to identify or label the form data. As you edit the form, you will discover that each bound control generates an unbound label. If you move the label, the bound control moves along with it. If you move the bound control, the label moves, too. You may ungroup the controls and move them separately, but the default is that they are a matched set.

Use Design Elements

Attractive form design can enhance the form and make it more usable. You will generally use sans serif fonts for the form labels and a different font or color for the user-entered information. This approach helps the form user distinguish between the places where they are expected to interact with the data and the labels. Form designers frequently shade the background of the bound controls a different color from the labels. You may consider right-aligning the labels and following them with a colon while left-aligning the bound controls. You should group like objects together and separate the group visually from the rest of the form by drawing a box around it. Simply altering the white space between the group and the rest of the form will provide a sufficient visual boundary. You often see these techniques used in recurrent groups on a form like addresses. In an address group on a form, the street, suite, city, state, and postal code will be arranged as though on an envelope's address, and knitted together by having a box drawn around them. The users will guide you in effective design. They will request a larger font or a different background color if they believe making those changes will make it easier for them to see the record's data.

Create a Split Form

A ***split form*** provides a data interaction method that combines a form with a datasheet.

The ***form splitter bar*** divides the two portions of the form.

New to Access 2007, ***split forms*** provide a data interaction method that combines a form with a datasheet. Although forms are intended to provide a user-friendly interface for entering and updating data, they are not universally well received. Some users, especially those who do data entry exclusively, complain that form usage slows them down. You can imagine that in an organization that rewards data entry operators for efficiency and accuracy, anything that slows the data entry engenders complaints. Using a split form (see Figure 6.22) helps designers because they can apply data protection afforded by viewing a single record at a time. It helps the users because they can locate records quickly using the datasheet portion of the form. Then they can edit the record using the form. The users see the same data presented in both views. The views are synchronized at all times. If you select a field in one part of the form, the same field selects in the same record in the other part of the form. You may add, edit, or delete records in either view. The *form splitter bar* divides the two portions of the form. Users may reallocate space between the views by clicking and dragging the form splitter bar up or down. The form designer may disable this ability and hide the splitter bar from the users' view by setting the splitter bar property to No. The splitter bar position can be set to default to the designed position each time the form is launched by setting the save splitter position property to Yes. You can create a split form by opening the record source in Datasheet view. Click the Create tab and click the Split Form tool in the Forms group.

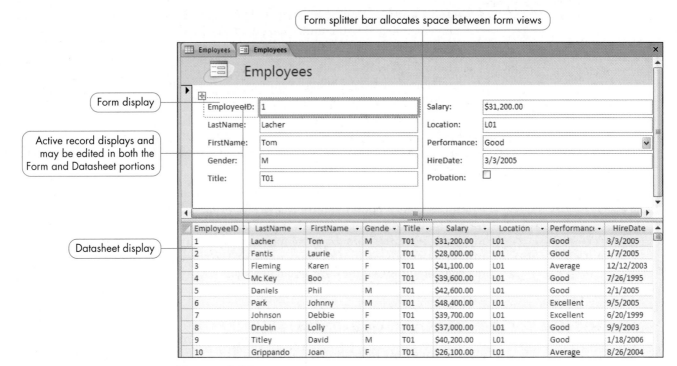

Figure 6.22 Split Form

Create a Multiple Items Form

The ***multiple items form*** creates a form that shows many records in a datasheet with one item in each row.

A form created using the Form Tool displays only a single record at a time. The ***multiple items form*** creates a form that shows many records in a datasheet with one item in each row. This facilitates data entry and updates because scrolling the records in a multiple items form is faster than navigating the form that shows only a single record at a time. Like the split form, the multiple items form is new to Access 2007. It provides developers another tool that will help them deliver the organization's users what they want. You create a multiple items form by first opening the data source and clicking Multiple Items in the Forms group on the Create tab. Figure 6.23 shows a multiple items form.

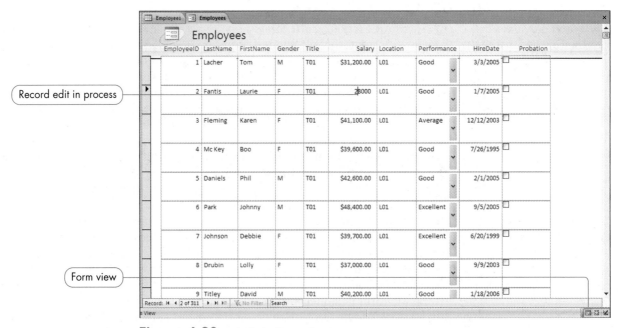

Figure 6.23 Multiple Items Form

Create a Datasheet Form

A ***datasheet form*** creates a form that looks exactly like the underlying data source.

Access provides a ***datasheet form*** that creates a form that looks exactly like the underlying data source, generally a table. This might be especially useful when a split database environment is introduced. The database managers can lock down the tables and protect the data from accidental damage while providing the users a form that looks exactly like the datasheet they were accustomed to using. One hallmark of introducing procedural change in data management is making the change transparent to the user. In other words, change the way the data are protected, but do not change the daily interaction of the users with the data. The datasheet form accomplishes this. Figure 6.24 shows a datasheet form.

Figure 6.24   Datasheet Form

Create PivotTable and PivotChart Forms

The PivotTable and PivotChart features of a form operate almost the same as they do in a query or table view. You use PivotTables and PivotCharts to summarize lengthy data using complex criteria and to represent the summary graphically. You may create a PivotChart by clicking the PivotChart in the Forms group on the Create tab. The PivotTable is found in More Forms in the Forms group on the Create tab. Once you create the Pivot grid, you drag field names from the Field List box and drop them on the appropriate position in the drop zones. Unlike the PivotTable and PivotChart views of a table or query, PivotTables and PivotCharts in forms exist independently of each other. Although you may choose to display the same data in PivotTable and PivotChart, you may also choose to display one set of criteria graphically and another in tabular form. You may change either the PivotTable or PivotChart without affecting the other. Figures 6.25 and 6.26 display Pivot Forms.

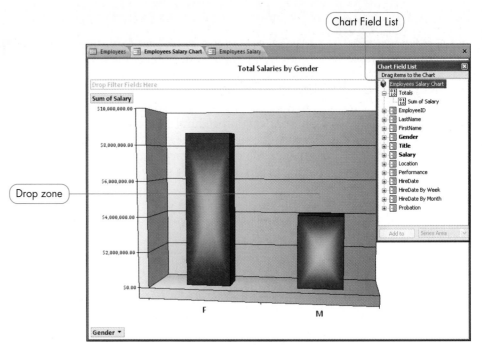

Figure 6.25 PivotChart Form

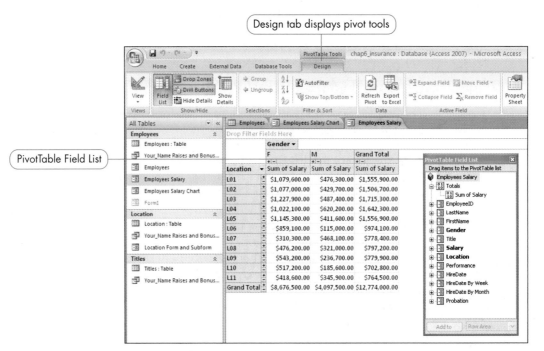

Figure 6.26 PivotTable Form May Display Different Data from PivotChart

 Form Wizard

Access 2007 moved the Form Wizard to a less prominent position than in earlier versions. You may use it by clicking More Forms in the Forms group on the Design tab. The Form Wizard closely resembles the Report Wizard. However, you may find it easier to generate a form using the Form, Split Form, Datasheet Form, or Multiple Items Form tools. Once you create a form, you may edit the form in either the Layout view or Design view.

In the second hands-on exercise, you will create a series of forms using the many form creation tools available in Access 2007.

Hands-On Exercises

2 | Form Creation Tools

Skills covered: 1. Use the Form Tool and Identify Form Controls **2.** Create a Split Form **3.** Create a Multiple Items Form **4.** Create a Datasheet Form **5.** Create PivotTable and PivotChart Forms

<table>
<tr><td>

Step 1

Use the Form Tool and Identify Form Controls

</td><td>

Refer to Figure 6.27 as you complete Step 1.

a. Open the *chap6_ho1-3_nationalbank_solution* file, if necessary, and click **Options** on the Security Warning toolbar. Then click **Enable this content** in the Microsoft Office Security Options dialog box and click **OK**.

> **TROUBLESHOOTING:** If you create unrecoverable errors while completing this hands-on exercise, you can delete the *chap6_ho1-3_nationalbank_solution* file, copy the *chap6_ho1_nationalbank_solution* backup database you created at the end of the first hands-on exercise, and open the copy of the backup database to start the second hands-on exercise again.

b. Open the **Payments table**. Click the **Create tab** and click **Form** in the Forms group.

You created a simple form that may be used to record customers' loan payments. The form opens in Layout view ready to edit.

c. Slowly move your mouse over the top of the **P** in *P0001*.

As you move up, the mouse pointer shape changes to a double-headed arrow. Continue moving the pointer up until the pointer shape changes to a bold down arrow.

d. When the pointer shape changes to the bold down arrow, click.

Gold selection boxes appear around the form's four bound controls. These items are bound to the values stored in the underlying table.

e. With the gold borders displayed, move your mouse over the right margin. When the pointer shape changes to a double-headed arrow, click and drag the right boundary left about five inches.

The Payments table is open.

f. Click the **Payment table tab** to switch to the table. The first record indicates a payment of $4,242.92. Click in the first record in the AmountReceived field. Type **4342.92** and press **Enter**.

g. Click the **Payments form tab** to return to the form. Look at the amount received in the first record. It should show $4,342.92.

This value is a bound control. It is tied to the value stored in the underlying data source.

h. Click the **PaymentID** label to select it. Click it again to turn on Edit mode. Move the insertion point to the left of *I* and insert a space between *Payment* and *ID*.

This is an unbound control. While working in Layout view, you may edit the unbound control. This label is cosmetic. It might say anything without having any effect on any table data. Of course, you want to label the controls in your forms descriptively, so you would not want it to say just anything.

</td></tr>
</table>

i. Type **Ctrl+S** to save the form and name it **Your_Name Payments Form**. Click **OK**. Close the form.

TROUBLESHOOTING: If you cannot easily recover from an error you make altering a form's layout, you can close the form without saving changes. This will return you to the table. Simply click the Form tool and recreate the form to start over again.

The column heading for the first column in the Payments table still says PaymentID (no space). That is because the edit you performed was on the unbound label control. It had no effect on the table data because they are not tied or bound to the table.

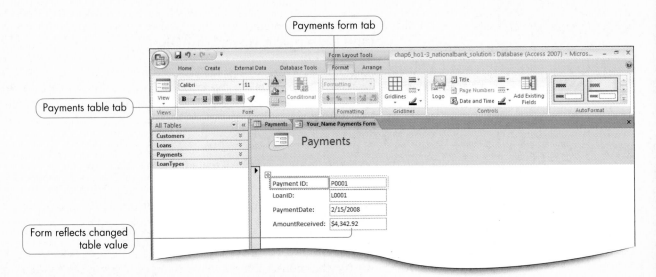

Figure 6.27 Edited Payments Form

Step 2
Create a Split Form

Refer to Figure 6.28 as you complete Step 2.

a. With the Payments table open, click the **Create tab**, and then click **Split Form** in the Forms group.

You created a new form using the split view. The top half of the screen displays the form, and the lower portion displays the table data in a close representation of the Datasheet view.

b. Click the **AmountReceived** field in the sixth record, P0006. Edit it to be **260.40**. Press **Shift+Enter**.

Shift+Enter saves the changes without changing to a different record.

c. Look at the form in the top portion of the window.

It displays $260.40 for the payment in March for record 6.

d. Right-click the **Payments form tab** and switch to **Form View** from the shortcut menu.

You will edit this record further by changing the payment date. Most forms open in the Layout view when they are first created. You cannot modify form data in the Layout view.

e. Click in the **PaymentDate** field in the form and edit it to display **3/10/2008**.

f. Click the **Next Record** navigation. Look at the date for record 6 in the Datasheet view.

The date now displays 3/10/2008. It does not matter whether changes are made to the split form by using the top or the bottom portion of the form. Any change in either place affects the other.

g. Move your mouse over the boundary between the form and datasheet portions of the window. When the pointer shape changes to a double-headed arrow, click and drag the datasheet portion of the window up about two inches.

h. Save your form as **Your_Name Payments Split**. Close the form.

Both the Payments and Split Payments forms are sourced on the same table. Any changes you make in either form will immediately reflect in the Payments table.

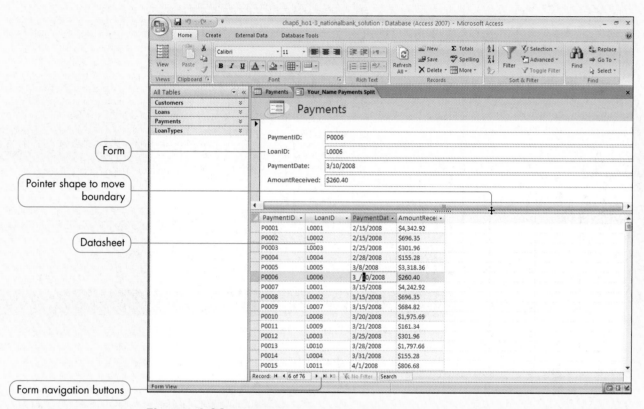

Figure 6.28 Split Form

Refer to Figure 6.29 as you complete Step 3.

Step 3
Create a Multiple Items Form

a. Open the **Payments table** (if necessary), click the **Create tab**, and click **Multiple Items** in the Forms group.

You created a multiple items form. It opens in Layout view for you to edit. You decide that if the row heights were shortened, more records would display on the screen at a time.

b. Click any value in the **PaymentID** field. Move your mouse pointer over the bottom of the cell. When the pointer shape changes to a double-headed arrow, click and drag up about a quarter of an inch.

The rows move closer together.

c. Right-click the value and select **Properties** from the shortcut menu to display the Property Sheet window.

d. Click the **Height property box** on the Format tab and edit it to display **0.2"**.

e. Save the form as **Your_Name Payments Multi**. Close the form.

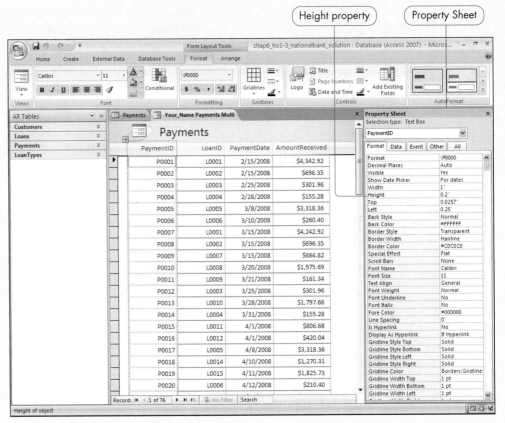

Figure 6.29 Multiple Items Form in Layout View

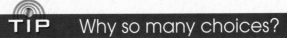

TIP   Why so many choices?

Access provides numerous choices for form creation because most database users interact with the database through forms. Users have strong opinions about how the forms they use should look and behave.

Step 4

Create a Datasheet Form

Refer to Figure 6.30 as you complete Step 4.

a. Open the **Payments table** (if necessary), click the **Create tab**, and click **More Forms** in the Forms group. Then select **Datasheet**.

The form opens in the Datasheet view.

b. Right-click the **Payments form tab**. This form is different from the others with which you have worked. It displays only a Datasheet and Design view. Click **Design View**.

Although the form in Datasheet view looks exactly like the table, you can see the dramatic difference in structure when you switch and look at the form in Design view. This does not look anything like a table Design view. It does not act like the Design view of a table, either. Make no mistake; this is a form.

c. Right-click the **Payments Form tab** and select **Datasheet View**.

d. Click the **Payments table tab**. Return to the **Payments form**.

The only cosmetic difference between the two is the form and table icons on the tabs.

e. Save the form as **Your_Name Payments Datasheet** and keep the form open for the next step.

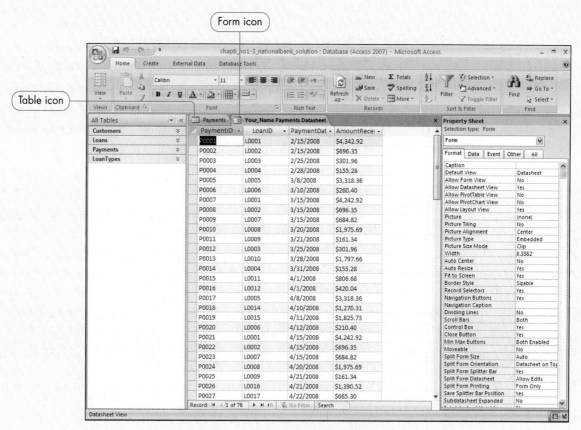

Figure 6.30 Datasheet Form in Datasheet View

Step 5
Create PivotTable and PivotChart Forms

Refer to Figure 6.31 as you complete Step 5.

a. Open the **Your_Name Payments Datasheet form** (if necessary), click the **Create tab**, and click **More Forms** in the Forms group. Then select **PivotTable**.

The form opens in the PivotTable view Design grid.

b. Click in the middle of the Design grid.

The PivotTable Field list box should turn on.

TROUBLESHOOTING: If the PivotTable Field List box fails to open, click the Field List Tool in the Show/Hide group on the Design tab.

c. Click the **AmountReceived** field in the PivotTable Field List box and drag it to the **Drop Totals or Detail Fields Here drop zone**.

d. Click the **LoanID** field in the PivotTable Field List box and drag it to the **Drop Row Fields Here drop zone**.

e. Click the **PaymentDate by Month** field in the PivotTable Field List box and drag it to the **Drop Column Fields Here drop zone**.

f. Click the **AmountReceived** column to make it the active column in the PivotTable, and then click **AutoCalc** in the Tools group and select **Sum**.

g. Click **Hide Details** in the Show/Hide group.

h. Click **Expand Details** next to 2008 (the box containing the plus sign) to display quarterly details.

The yearly data expands to display totals by quarter.

i. Save the PivotTable form as **Your_Name Payments PivotTable**.

j. Click the **Create tab** and click **PivotChart**.

k. Click anywhere in the gray part of the chart to turn on the Chart Field List box.

l. Drag the **LoanID** field from the Chart Field List box to the **Drop Category Fields Here** box.

m. Drag the **AmountReceived** field from the Chart Field List box to the **Plot area**.

n. Save the chart as **Your_Name Payments PivotChart**. Close the PivotChart.

Although you based the PivotChart on the PivotTable, the table does not change when you change the chart.

o. Close the open database objects. Click the **Office Button**, select **Manage**, and then select **Compact and Repair Database**.

p. Click the **Office Button** again, select **Manage**, and then select **Back Up Database**. Type **chap6_ho2_nationalbank_solution** as the file name and click **Save**.

You just created a backup of the database after completing the second hands-on exercise. The original database *chap6_ho1-3_nationalbank_solution* remains onscreen. If you ruin the original database as you complete the third hands-on exercise, you can use the backup file you just created.

q. Close the file and exit Access if you do not want to continue with the next exercise at this time.

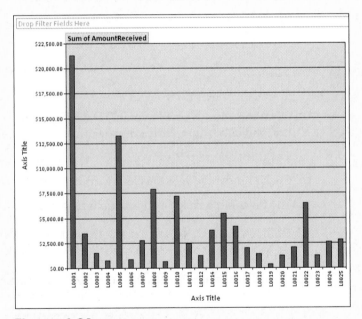

Figure 6.31 PivotChart Form

Form Customization

You can now create a variety of forms, but everything you have accomplished so far has been standard. Because much of the day-to-day work in an organization's database is accomplished using forms, you need to develop skills to make your forms fit the tasks. Your forms need to facilitate the users' work and make their lives easier. Designers spend many hours conversing with the form users, watching them work, and developing innovations that (hopefully) make the users' work lives easier.

In this section, you will learn how to create a form using Design view, add action buttons, perform calculations, create and modify subforms, and apply formatting and conditional formatting to enhance your form's usability.

Creating Custom Forms in Design View

Access provides several ways of creating forms. You have already used many of them. Design view gives you the power to completely customize the form. The Design view of a form is like a blueprint for a building. You do not see the data in a form Design view, you see only the controls, or placeholders, that will store and display your data. The form does not run while you are in Design view, and updates and changes to data do not display. There are some actions which may only be accomplished in Design view. Other actions, like applying or modifying formats or styles, may be done in either Design or Layout views. You will need to experiment to see which method suits your style. Use Design view when you need to do the following:

- Modify Form Properties, i.e., Default View or Allow Form View
- Change the form section sizes
- Add different types of controls, i.e., pictures, lines, rectangles, and calculations
- Edit control source properties directly in the text box

Use the Design Grid

You launch a new form in Design view by clicking the Create tab and then clicking Form Design. A blank workspace and the tools that you will use to create the form display. Figure 6.32 identifies many of the tools. You probably do not need to memorize each icon's purpose because the tip boxes and Microsoft Help will always remind you. Most form designers use only a select few of these tools and generally customize their Ribbons to display only the tools they employ.

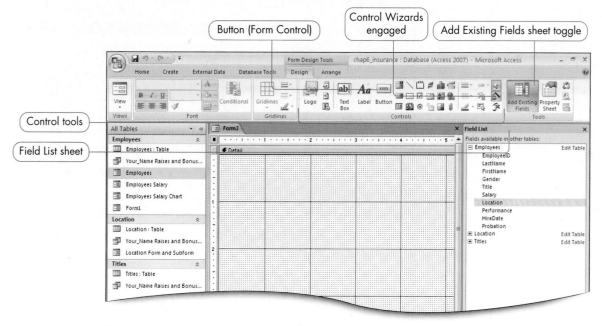

Figure 6.32 Blank Form in Design View

The Add Existing Fields tool is engaged, and the Field List displays in Figure 6.32. To add fields to the form, you need only click them in the Field List sheet and drag them onto the Design grid. Notice that the Design grid contains two grids, a fine and a wide hatch. These provide you with placement guides to help you align the form data. Do not worry about positioning a control incorrectly; after the control is on the Design grid, you can select it and move it easily. The default Design grid displays only the detail section of the form. You will use the tools to add additional sections, for example a header. You click the Title tool to create both the form header area and the label that will eventually contain the form title.

> ### TIP   Text Box or Label
>
> You may wonder when to use a text box and when to use a label on a form. If the control is bound, use a text box because it creates two boxes on the form. The first contains the control's label and the second is a placeholder for the record value to display. The values displayed in the right box will change as the user navigates through the records displayed in the form. Use a label when you need something displayed on the form that does not change as the user navigates through records. Examples of when to use labels might include form titles, indications of form author-ship or the date of last revision, or the company slogan.

Figure 6.33 displays a form in Design view with some controls and design elements added. By clicking the Title tool in the controls group, you may add a form header and the label to contain the form title. The label is selected, and it contains size handles that you may use to change its size. The Property Sheet displays that the caption is Form1. It is a good idea to change to a more descriptive form title. You can change the space allocation between the form header and detail areas by moving your mouse over the boundary bar until its shape changes to the move cross and then clicking and dragging to the desired location. This form also displays an example of a

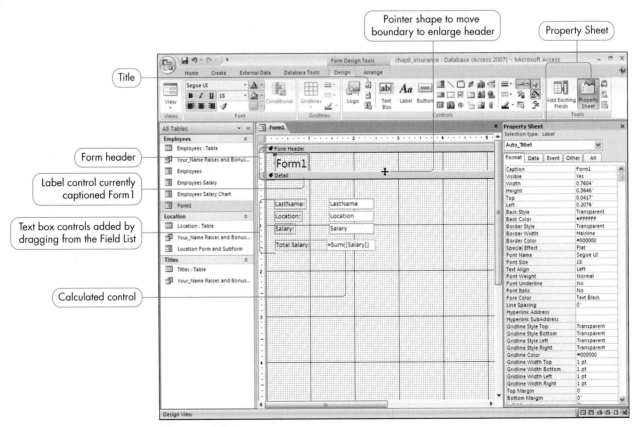

Figure 6.33 Simple Form in Design View

calculated control. The last control uses the sum function (generated with the Expression Builder) to calculate the total of all employees' salaries.

Add Action Buttons

The Button tool in the Controls group provides powerful and user-friendly form additions. When you click it, your mouse pointer shape changes to a rectangle attached to a plus sign. This means that you need to click and drag on the Design grid to position and size the button you want to create. The Command Button Wizard launches as soon as you release the mouse. Access provides many alternatives for form commands. The first wizard screen, shown in Figure 6.34, offers different categories of actions. The second screen of the wizard gives you options about the button content. In this case, the default printer picture communicates the button's action well. You could browse to a different picture or simply use text to describe the button's action (see Figure 6.35). The last wizard screen lets you name the button. Figure 6.36 shows the form as the user will engage it in Form view.

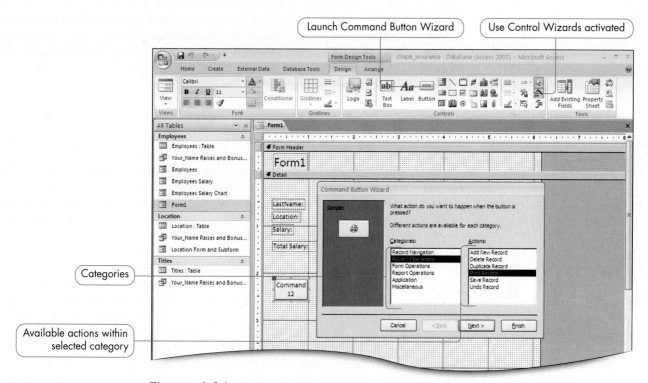

Figure 6.34 First Command Button Wizard Screen

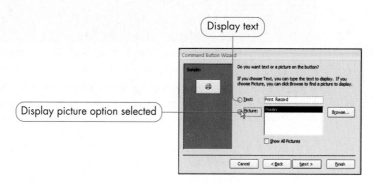

Figure 6.35 Button Information Selected

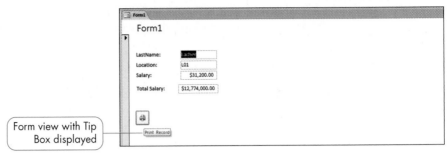

Form view with Tip Box displayed

Figure 6.36 Form Displayed in Form View

TIP   Adjust, View, and Save Often

Working with the Design view can be confusing because data do not display. The secret is to make a small adjustment, switch from Design view to Form view, look at the change, and if you like the results, save your form. If you do not like the results, return to Design view, click Undo on the Quick Access Toolbar, and try again. You do not want to make multiple changes without viewing them in Form view as you make each change. You will probably not be able to undo several changes at once.

Creating Subforms

A **subform** is a form that exists inside another form.

A *subform* is a form that exists inside another form. Sometimes subforms are called parent/child or nested form structures. The primary form (parent) may be edited separately from the subform (child) and the subform is stored and edited separately from the parent. Alternatively, both forms may be viewed and edited at the same time. You use subforms to show information that sources two or more related tables. For example, you might need to see the order history displayed as a subform in the Customers table. That way, a customer service representative can scroll past orders to tell the customer the name of the product that he or she purchased last month. This presupposes that a relationship, generally one-to-many, exists between the Customers and Orders tables. The primary form (customers) is the one portion of the one-to-many relationship, whereas the subform (orders) is the many part. The forms are linked so that when a specific customer's data display in the primary form, only the related items in the Orders table display in the subform. If the forms linkages were broken, all of the records in the Orders table would display in the subform.

TIP   Establish the Relationships Prior to Creating Subforms

Because the subform depends on the one-to-many relationship with the parent form to display only the related records, it is much less work if the relationship exists before you create either the form or subform. When the relationship exists, open the parent table and use the Form tool. The default is a form containing the appropriate subform.

Access provides several methods of subform creation. You can use the Form tool in the Forms group on the Create tab when a table is open that displays its relationships to a related table with the Expand Detail symbols displayed. Figure 6.37 shows a location table with the Kansas City employees (the related table) with the details displayed. Figure 6.38 shows the form created from this table opened to the fourth record, Kansas City. A user in the firm could easily scroll the performance ratings of the Kansas City employees to get an overview of the supervisor's rating style.

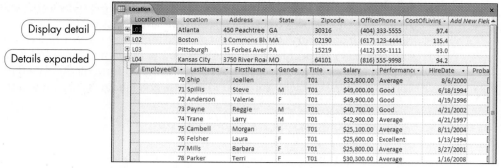

Display detail

Details expanded

Figure 6.37 Table with Relationship Indicated

Only Kansas City employees display

Main form

Subform

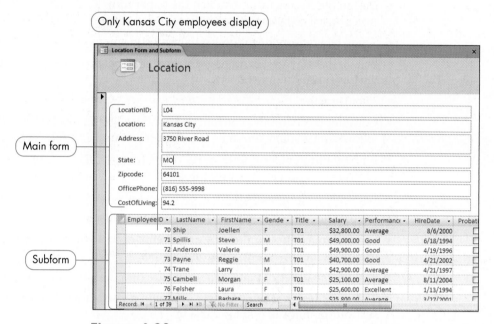

Figure 6.38 Form with Subform Displayed in Form View

The **Link Child Field** property governs which field or fields in the subform link to the main form.

The **Link Master Field** property governs which field or fields in the main form link to the subform.

Another way to generate a form with a subform is to create both forms separately. Open the main form in Design view and make sure the Control Wizard tool in the controls group is engaged. Drag the form that you wish to make the subform from the Navigation Pane and drop it on the main form's design grid. Access will create the subform and establish the linkages between the form and its subform based on the predetermined relationships in the database. If Access cannot determine how to establish the relationship, you will need to do so yourself. You would need to use the Link Child and Link Master properties in the Property Sheet. The *Link Child Field* property governs which field or fields in the subform link to the main form. The *Link Master Field* property governs which field or fields in the main form link to the subform.

You can create a form with a subform by using the Form Wizard. If you specify more than one table as the data source for the form, you will be given an option of specifying how to view the data. Make sure that you select the table that will become the main form to answer the wizard. Finally, you can create a form and its subforms completely in Design view. You may have more than one subform in a form. You may also nest multiple subforms if the appropriate relationships preexist.

Designing Functional Formats

Access provides an extremely wide range of formatting options. You can change foreground and background colors and patterns, add emphasis by shadowing or embossing controls or by changing fonts, and add boxes and lines to visually group form elements. You might add other graphic elements like pictures or designs to add clarity or excitement to the form. You can improve a form's usability by changing the form navigation tab order. Just because you *can* do these things does not necessarily mean that you *should* do them. Especially in large organizations, some employees do nothing but data entry. They might look at a single Access form all day long. The colors and patterns you decide to use might have the unintended effect of making the data entry operators' lives unpleasant. A poorly designed form might even damage the data entry operators' eyesight. You need to exercise good judgment about your form's design.

Adhere to Form Design Guidelines

(When in doubt, leave it out)

When you create a form, you should adhere to the following design guidelines to ensure a professional, readable form.

- Design the Access form to match the paper form as closely as possible if the Access form coexists with or replaces a paper form.
- Abide by your organization's published style manual if such a style manual exists.
- Ensure that navigation among the form controls progresses from the upper left to the lower right in most forms.
- Avoid scrolling.
- Consider the Windows convention of right-aligning text boxes with labels and follow with a colon, and then left-align the bound control.
- Employ different fonts and/or fill colors for controls the form user engages and controls that provide the user information.
- Right-align all numeric fields with the possible exception of an ID field.
- Ensure that control boxes are large enough to display data completely.
- Space form controls uniformly and evenly except when you use empty space as a design element to group controls together.
- Test the tab order of your form to ensure that the navigation sequence is logical.
- Test your design using a variety of monitor resolutions. Even though you might set your monitor to display 2,084 by 786 pixels, your form's users might prefer 800 by 600.
- Select font and background colors and/or patterns with sufficient contrast to make the data easily visible.
- When there is any indication that a special effect (i.e., shadowing or embossing) detracts from the form's utility, omit it. When in doubt, leave it out.
- If the primary users of the form come from outside your organization (customers or business partners), build in contact information on every screen. This might include your logo, organization name, address, your Web site's link, and telephone number.
- Ask yourself if you would like to interact with the form you created—all day, every day. Would the themes and colors you select give you a headache after staring at them for a few hours? If so, the form users will also get headaches and complain.

Add Themes and Design Elements

Access makes forms easily. Customizing the form sometimes takes more work. Figure 6.39 shows a newly created Access form in Layout view with the controls selected. You decide that the controls for the first- and last-name fields should be on the same row. To change the form layout, you must first remove the default layout, using either Layout or Design views. Click the box with the four-headed arrow in the upper left, and the controls select. Employ the Remove tool in the Control Layout group on the Arrange tab. This "ungroups" the controls and enables you to position the controls on the form where you want them. Click the control you wish to reposition and drag it. You may reposition several controls at once by shift-clicking. You may also adjust the order in which the controls respond as the data entry operator presses Tab to navigate the form. This will open a dialog box where you can click and drag the field names to change the tab navigation order.

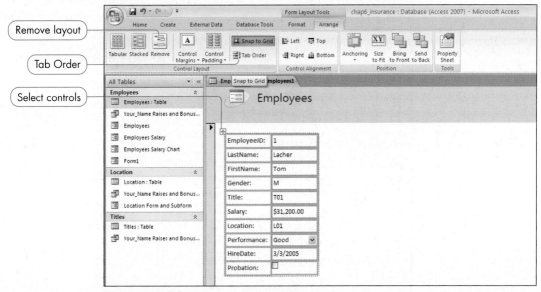

Figure 6.39 Removing the Default Layout Permits Individual Control Placement

Figure 6.40 shows the repositioned controls and adds a theme. Add themes to your forms by using AutoFormat on the Format tab. If you need more extensive design enhancement, you will need to use Design view. Figure 6.41 displays a form in Design view. Additional unbound controls add information and visual appeal. The designer added a label to the left of the FirstName field control and format-painted from the existing controls. Adding a rectangle using the rectangle control visually grouped the part of the form that serves to identify the employee. You may do this by using the rectangle tool in the Controls group on the Design tab. The mouse pointer shape changes to a rectangle attached to a crosshair. Click on the form and drag to create the appropriately sized rectangle (see Figure 6.42). With the newly added rectangle active, the designer added a shadowed special effect. Finally, the designer added

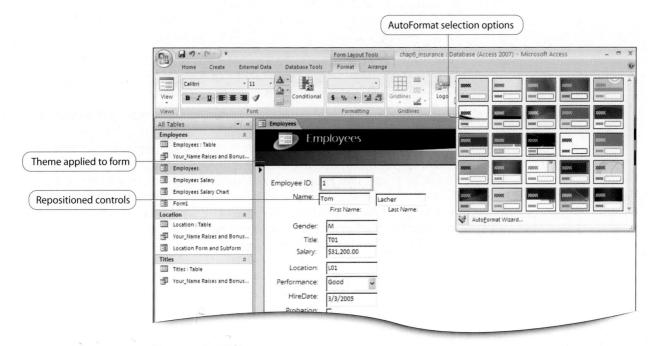

Figure 6.40 Repositioned and Formatted Form

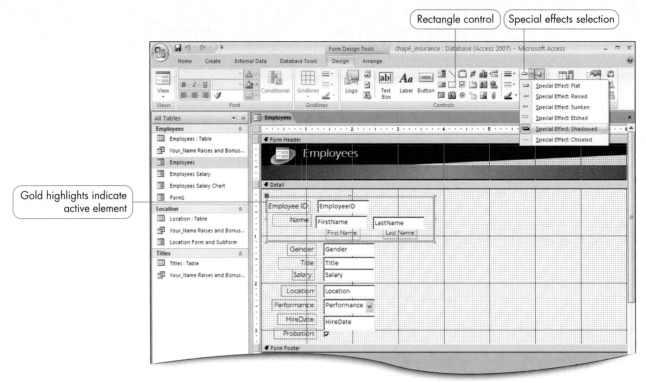

Figure 6.41 Add Controls Using Design View

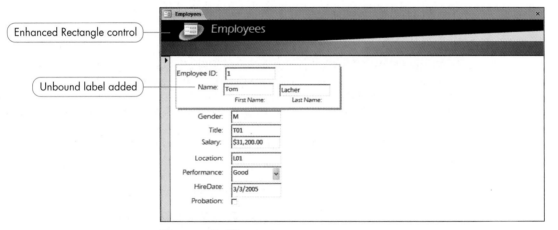

Figure 6.42 Completed Form in Form View

special effects to the controls to indicate where the user should enter data. Figure 6.42 shows the completed form as the user will encounter it in Form view.

In the third hands-on exercise, you will calculate employee pay raises by using a Cost of Living Index. Because this organization employs workers in locations across the country, you will need to make adjustments to worker salaries to compensate them for cost of living differences. For example, it is more expensive to live and work in New York City than it is in Pittsburgh or Phoenix. Your company recognizes this and adjusts employees' salaries to compensate them for the increased living expenses incurred in some places.

Hands-On Exercises

3 | Customizing Forms

Skills covered: 1. Use the Blank Form Tool to Create a Form **2.** Create a Form in Design View **3.** Add Action Buttons and Controls **4.** Create and Edit a Form with a Subform **5.** Customize a Form by Moving Controls and Adding a Theme

Step 1 **Use the Blank Form Tool to Create a Form**	Refer to Figure 6.43 as you complete Step 1. **a.** Open the *chap6_ho1-3_nationalbank_solution* file if necessary, click the **Options** button in the Security Alert toolbar, click the **Enable this content option** in the Security Alerts dialog box, and click **OK**. **TROUBLESHOOTING:** If you create unrecoverable errors while completing this hands-on exercise, you can delete the *chap6_ho1-3_nationalbank_solution* file, copy the *chap6_ho2_nationalbank_solution* database you created at the end of the second hands-on exercise, and open the copy of the backup database to start the third hands-on exercise again. **b.** Close any open objects in the database and click the **Create tab**. Click **Blank Form** in the Forms group. A blank form opens in Layout view with the Field List pane open. You should see collapsed views of the tables in the database. Click the plus boxes to view the lists of the fields in each table. **TROUBLESHOOTING:** If the Field List pane fails to open, click Add Existing Fields in the Controls group on the Format tab. If the Field list displays but no table names are displayed, click the Show all tables link at the top of the Field List pane. **c.** Click the **plus** sign next to the **Loans table** in the Field List pane to expand it. The available fields in the Loans table display under the table name. The LoanType field contains another plus. That is the field you created a Multivalued lookup for earlier in the chapter. **d.** Double-click the **Date** field in the Field List pane to add it to the form. The Date field moves to the default position in the upper left of the form. A tip box with a lightning symbol displays under the control. **e.** Click the **lightning box**, and then click **Show in Tabular Layout**. The form layout changes to tabular, like a spreadsheet with the column heads above the data. You determine that you want the default Stacked layout for this form. **f.** Click the **lightning box**, and then click **Show in Stacked Layout**. **g.** Double-click the **Amount and LoanType** fields in the Field List pane to add them to the form. Because the LoanType field is a lookup field, it adds to the form as a Smart Tag, and the form user may select one or more options from a drop-down list. **h.** Click **Title** in the Controls group on the Format tab. Type **Your_Name Payment Receipt** in the title control at the top of the form. Save the form as **Your_Name Payment Receipt**. Close the form. The Title's control expands to accommodate the form title.

i. Open the form in Form view. Click the **Office Button** and select **Print**. Click **Selected Record(s)** in the Print dialog box and click **OK**. Close the form.

Lookup inherited from source

Figure 6.43 Payment Receipt in Form View

Step 2
Create a Form in Design View

Refer to Figure 6.44 as you complete Step 2.

a. Close all database objects if necessary. Click **Form Design** in the Forms group on the Create tab.

A blank form opens in Design view with the Field List pane open. You should see collapsed views of the tables in the database. Click the plus boxes to view the lists of the fields in each table.

TROUBLESHOOTING: If the Field List pane fails to open, click Add Existing Fields in the Controls group on the Format tab. If the Field List displays but no table names are displayed, click the Show all tables link at the top of the Field List box.

b. Click the **CustomerID** field in the Field List pane and drag it to the *Detail Fields* area of the Pivot grid. Drop it at the intersection of the second vertical line and the first horizontal line.

TROUBLESHOOTING: If you position the control boxes incorrectly, you can click and drag to reposition them or, if the controls remain active, use the cursor (arrow) keys to reposition the controls. Both the text box and label boxes move together.

c. Double-click the **FirstName, LastName, and AccountType** fields to add them to the Design grid. Position them in columns under the CustomerID field.

> **TIP** Shift-Click to Select Multiple Controls
>
> If you click a control in Design view, release the mouse, and press and hold Shift, you can select multiple items and interact with them collectively.

d. Click **Title** in the Controls group on the Format tab. Type **Your_Name Customer** in the box that says **Form1**.

e. Right-click the **Form1 tab** and select **Form View** from the shortcut menu. Check to make sure the controls align. Right-click the **Form1 tab** and select **Design View** from the shortcut menu. If necessary, adjust the control layout.

You look at the form as the user will encounter it in Form view but make adjustments to it in Design view or Layout view.

f. Save your form and name it **Your_Name Customer**.

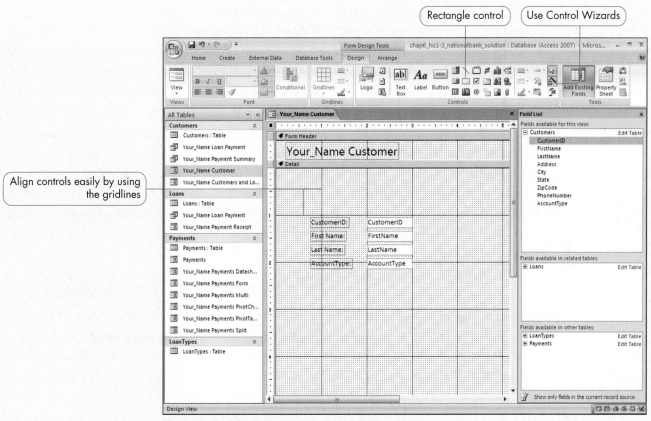

Figure 6.44 Design View of the Customer Form

Step 3
Add Action Buttons and Controls

Refer to Figure 6.45 as you complete Step 3.

a. Check to make sure the Use Control Wizards tool is engaged (see Figure 6.44). Click **Button** in the Controls group on the Design tab.

The Button tool turns gold and waits for instruction from you about where to position the button on the form.

b. Click on the first vertical grid under the AccountType control box.

Access places a button named, for the time being, Command1. (Your button may have a different number. That is OK.) The Command Button Wizard dialog box launches. This button will provide form users a navigation tool to go to the next record.

c. Select, if necessary, **Record Navigation** in the Categories box and **Go To Next Record** in the Actions box. Click **Next**.

You decide that you want a picture on this button.

d. Select the **Picture** option and **Go To Next**. Click **Next**.

e. Name the button **Next** and click **Finish**.

Your Button changes shape and shows a right triangle.

f. Switch to **Form View** by right-clicking the **Your_Name Customer tab** and use the button. Navigate through a few records to make sure it works. If it functions as expected, return to **Design View** (right-click the tab) and save your changes.

You want to add the Bank Name to the form header area. To do this, you need a control.

g. Click **Label** in the Controls group on the Design tab. Click the vertical Gridline on the **four-inch mark** in the Form Header area and drag to the **six-inch mark**.

You created a control. The insertion point is flashing inside the label, ready for you to type the name of the bank.

h. Type **National Bank**. Click the **Your_Name Customer** control. Click the **Format Painter**. Click the **National Bank** control.

You painted the title control's format on the new control.

i. Switch to Form view to examine your changes. Return to Design view. Make any needed adjustments. Compare your work to Figure 6.45. If it is correct, save and close the form.

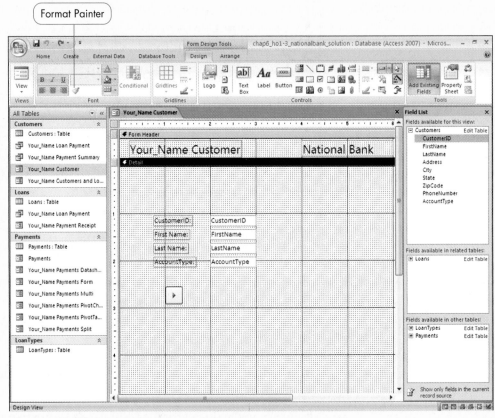

Figure 6.45 National Bank Customer Form in Design View

Step 4
Create and Edit a Form with a Subform

Refer to Figure 6.46 as you complete Step 4.

a. Open the **Customers table** in Datasheet view. Click the **Create tab** and click **Form** in the Forms group.

Access creates the form and associated subform and opens them in Layout view ready for editing. Notice that both the form and subform have separate navigation bars. The first customer has three mortgages with the bank. The subform record indicator displays record 1 of 3 and the form record indicates record 1 of 11.

b. Click the Form Navigation **Next Record** button.

You see data about Scott Wit, who has two car loans.

c. Click the Subform Navigation **Next Record** button.

The active record becomes Mr. Wit's $10,000 car loan.

d. Click the column leading **Term** in the subform. A gold border surrounds the Term column. Click and drag the **right boundary right** to make the column wider.

e. Switch to **Design View** by right-clicking the tab. Click **Yes** in the Save dialog box and save the form as **Your_Name Customers and Loans**.

The subform appears as a link to the table data and looks blank.

f. Right-click the subform and select **Properties** from the shortcut menu. Click the **Data tab** in the Property Sheet, if necessary. Examine the Link Master Fields and Link Child Fields properties.

Access used the existing relationships among the tables to generate the form and subform with all of the properties appropriately selected.

g. Save the form.

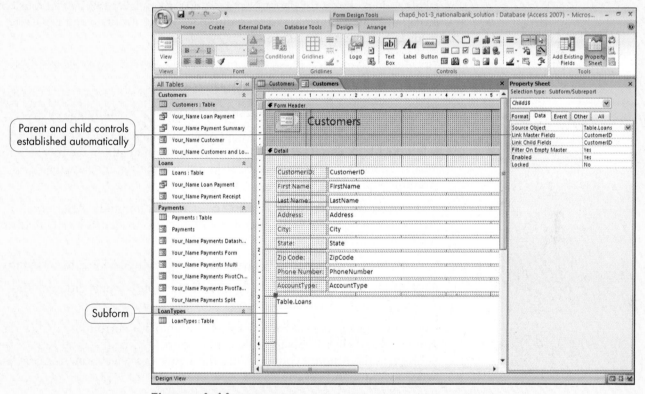

Parent and child controls established automatically

Subform

Figure 6.46 Form with Subform in Design View

Refer to Figure 6.47 as you complete Step 5.

a. Click the **CustomerID field** in the main form. Locate the box in the upper left that contains the plus sign. Click the box.

All of the controls in the main form select. You want to move the city, state, and Zip fields to the same row to conserve space. You must first remove the currently applied layout.

b. Click the **Arrange tab** and click **Remove** in the Control Layout group. Close the Property Sheet.

The controls are still selected, but each control has a size handle permitting you to interact with the fields separately.

c. Click the **City Field Text** box (the right one) to select it. The gold selection boundary should be only around the right city box. Move your mouse over the right edge of the City control and when the pointer shape changes to a two-headed arrow, click and drag the boundary left to the three-inch mark. Repeat with the **State** and **Zip Code** boxes. Make the Zip Code box about one inch wide.

d. Move the mouse pointer over any boundary of the Zip Code box and when the pointer shape changes to the **four-headed move arrow**, click and drag it **up** and position it so the *right boundary* is on the **8" vertical grid** mark and it is on the same row as the City field.

e. Click the **State Field** text box to select it and move the mouse over a boundary. When the pointer shape changes to the **four-headed move arrow**, click and drag it **up** and position it between the City and Zip Code fields on the same row.

f. Click the **Phone Number label** to select it and make it **wider** so the word Number is no longer cut off, if necessary. Press **Shift** as you click to select the labels and text boxes for Phone Number and Account Type. When all four boxes are selected, move them **up** to close the space where the State and Zip Code fields used to be positioned.

TROUBLESHOOTING: If you select too many controls, simply click off onto the Design grid to deselect everything and try again.

g. Edit the labels so that spaces appear in field names and nothing is cut off.

h. Click **Tab Order** in the Control Layout group on the Arrange tab. Click the row selector beside **CustomerID**. With your mouse pointer still in the row selector area, drag the selected CustomerID field **down** and drop it below the AccountType field. Click **OK**.

You altered the order that the form accepts tab commands. After entering the AccountType, the data entry operator will move to the CustomerID field at the top of the main form.

i. Save the form and change to the **Layout view** by right-clicking the form tab.

j. Click **More** to see the list of AutoFormats in the AutoFormats group on the Format tab. Select **Concourse** (second row, first column).

k. Click anywhere in the **subform** to select it. A gold box surrounds it. Click the **Home tab** and click **Totals** in the Records group. Click in the **Total Row** of the subform in the **Amount** column. Click the **arrow** and select **Sum** from the listed functions. Save and close the form.

The Totals tool enables you to use common aggregating functions in a form exactly like you may do in a table or query. You notice that the Column headings in the subform need spaces in them. You may not alter a field property in a subform. You may add a caption to the table that the subform sources.

l. Open the **Loans table** in Design view. Create a caption that includes a space for the LoanID, LoanType, and InterestRate fields. Save the changes and close the Loans table. Reopen the Your_Name Customers and Loans form in Layout view. Look in the subform for any necessary column-width adjustments and make them.

m. Look at your form in Form view and press **Tab** on the keyboard to test the tab order change. Save and close the form.

n. Click the **Office Button**, select **Manage**, and select **Compact and Repair**. Close the file and exit Access.

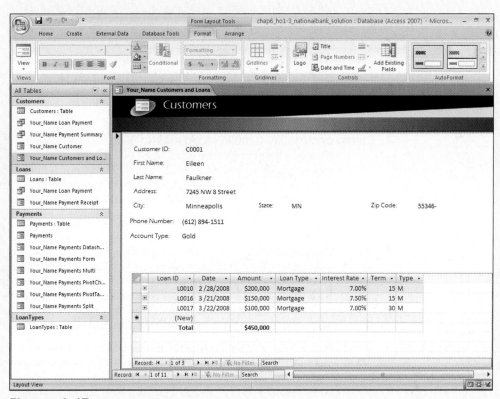

Figure 6.47 Formatted Form

Summary

1. **Establish data validity.** Database administrators establish safeguards on table data to protect them from data-entry and user error. As you learn these skills you shift from being a person in the organization who uses data to becoming the individual in the organization who administers, manages, and protects the organization's data. Data validation is a set of tools that help control the type and accuracy of the data entered into a field. Although Access provides some data validation automatically, you will need to augment the validation to help defend the data against user errors. Simply requiring that a field be filled out can help. Use a default value when the majority of your data will be the same value. Validation text informs users about what they have done incorrectly and instructs them about what needs to be done. When you break a validation rule, you must provide Access with the required information in the desired format before you can move on.

2. **Create and modify a lookup field.** Increase data entry speed and accuracy by providing the user with a predefined list of values. The Lookup Wizard helps create, populate, and relate the lookup field. Users select field values from a drop-down list. Change the values of a lookup table by opening the lookup table and changing the values in the table. The changes are immediately available.

3. **Create and modify a multivalued lookup field.** Sometimes, a database needs to support multiple choices. These choices are often represented by check boxes on a form in which you can choose multiple options. A multivalued field is one defined to accept multiple choices for a single field without requiring you to create a complex design. It is similar to a many-to-many relationship. Select the Allow Multiple Values check box in the appropriate Lookup Wizard to define this. Under the surface, Access creates a series of juncture tables and stores them independently.

4. **Work with input masks.** An input mask specifies the exact formatting of the input data while minimizing data storage requirements. You are used to viewing (and thinking about) Social Security numbers with hyphens in them, for example 123-45-6789, and telephone numbers with parentheses and hyphens. To conserve space in an Access database using an input mask for a Social Security number field, only the digits are stored in the table as 123456789, but the mask displays with the hyphens to make the data more readable for the user.

5. **Create forms by using the Form Tool.** Forms enable data entry in one or more tables with more flexibility in presentation to the user. They often resemble paper forms and facilitate the switch from paper to electronic data storage. For example, the last time you entered your name, e-mail address, and other information and clicked a submit button, you worked in a form. They also enable displaying objects such as graphics, charts, or other Office files. Access provides several different methods of creating, editing, and embellishing forms. After a form is created, you will edit it many times to satisfy the users' data entry needs. The Form tool gives you a one-click method of form creation. Split Forms provide a data interaction method that combines a form with a datasheet. The Multiple Items form creates a form that shows many records in a datasheet with one item in each row. Access provides a Datasheet Form that creates a form that looks exactly like the underlying data source. You use PivotTables and PivotCharts to summarize lengthy data using complex criteria and to represent the summary graphically.

6. **Create custom forms using Design view.** You can create a form using Design view, add action buttons, perform calculations, create and modify subforms, and apply formatting and conditional formatting to enhance your form's usability. Design view gives you the power to completely customize the form. The Design view of a form is like a blueprint for a building. You do not see the data in a Design view form; you see only the controls, or placeholders, that will store and display your data. Some actions may only be accomplished in Design view. Other actions, like applying or modifying formats or styles, may be done in either Design or Layout views. Use the Design grid. You launch a new form in Design view by clicking the Create tab and then clicking the Design View Tool. A blank workspace and the tools that you will use to create the form display. The Design grid contains two grids, a fine and a wide hatch. These provide you with placement guides to help you align the form data. The default Design grid displays only the detail section of the form. You will use the tools to add additional sections and controls, for example a header and a calculated control such as a sum. The Button tool in the Control group provides powerful and user-friendly form additions. The Command

...continued on Next Page

Button Wizard launches as soon as you create a button on a form. Access provides many alternatives for form commands, such as print, next record, and go to.

7. **Create subforms.** A subform is a form that exists inside another form. The primary form (parent) may be edited separately from the subform (child), and the subform is stored and edited separately from the parent. Alternatively, both forms may be viewed and edited at the same time. You use subforms to show information that sources two or more related tables such as customers and orders. Access provides several ways to create nested forms, including through an option in the Form Wizard.

8. **Design functional formats.** The colors and patterns you decide to use might have the unintended effect of making the data entry workers' lives unpleasant. You may need to rearrange the controls on a form. To change the form layout you must first remove the default layout using either Layout or Design views. Click the box with the four-headed arrow in the upper left and the controls select. Employ the Remove tool in the Control Layout group on the Arrange tab. You can apply themes, colors, and special effects to most form elements. If you are not sure that the special effects add to the form's utility, omit them.

Key Terms

Multiple Choice

1. Database administrators establish safeguards on table data to protect it from data-entry and user error to ensure:

   (a) Referential integrity

   (b) Data validity

   (c) Hierarchical structure

   (d) Normalization

2. Which of the following is not an example of a data validation tool?

   (a) You cannot enter text into a date field.

   (b) Primary keys can contain duplicate values.

   (c) Defined default values.

   (d) Input masks, Lookup lists, Multiple Value Fields, Logical rule.

3. To make a field required, you should:

   (a) Set the required value in the Form Wizard.

   (b) Set the required button on the form design toolbox.

   (c) Set the required value in the field properties box in the table's Design view.

   (d) Click the Required/Default command in the table design group.

4. A good validation text message should:

   (a) Be generic, e.g., "You made a mistake."

   (b) Tell the users what they did incorrectly.

   (c) Offer the user guidance.

   (d) Inform the user about the error and offer guidance on correction.

5. This is the field from the source data that contains values to be summarized in a lookup table.

   (a) Lookup field

   (b) Page field

   (c) Item

   (d) Data field

6. To alter available selections in a lookup table, you should:

   (a) Add, change, or delete the records in the underlying table.

   (b) Type the desired value in the drop-down list in the form as you fill it out.

   (c) Modify the lookup property.

   (d) Click the lookup table command on the lookup table group.

7. A multivalued lookup field would most likely be represented on a form by:

   (a) An option where you put a dot in a circle to select

   (b) A drop-down list where you Ctrl + click multiple options

   (c) Check boxes beside items in a list where you put an X in the box to select

   (d) Both b and c

8. Which of the following is true about input masks?

   (a) Input masks store extra characters in records such as hyphens in Social Security numbers and parentheses and hyphens in U.S. phone numbers to speed data entry.

   (b) Input masks display the hyphens in a Social Security number field or parentheses and hyphens in a U.S. phone number field and store them in the record.

   (c) Input masks display the hyphens in a Social Security number field or parentheses and hyphens in a U.S. phone number field, but do not store them in the record.

   (d) Input masks should not be overused because they use slightly more storage space.

9. You have a Customers table open in Datasheet view. It is related to an Orders table, and you can click an expand button and examine the orders placed by the customer. If you click the Form tool, what will result?

   (a) You will create a form based on the Customers table and a subform based on the Orders table. The Customers table will be the child.

   (b) You will create a form based on the Customers table and a subform based on the Orders table. The Customers table will be the parent.

   (c) You will create a form based on the Orders table and a subform based on the Customers table. The Customers table will be the parent.

   (d) You will create a form based on the Orders table and a subform based on the Customers table. The Customers table will be the child.

10. This type of form provides a data interaction method that combines a form with a datasheet:

    (a) Multiple items form

    (b) Tabular form

    (c) Datasheet form

    (d) Split form

11. The following are examples of forms available to create in Access except:

    (a) Multiple items forms

    (b) Datasheet forms

    (c) Spreadsheet forms

    (d) PivotTable and PivotChart forms

12. The Design view for a form gives you the power to:

    (a) Customize the form.

    (b) Make formatting and style changes, but not alter the functionality of the form.

    (c) View the data as it will be presented in the form.

    (d) All of the above.

13. Where do you find the tools to add Action buttons to a form you are designing?

    (a) You can download button code from Microsoft.com to use as an add-in.

    (b) The Button Wizard in the controls toolbox

    (c) The Button tool in the Control group launches the Command Button Wizard and creates buttons per your specifications.

    (d) Buttons have to be programmed in Visual Basic and imported to Access for forms.

14. Which of the following is not true about subforms?

    (a) The primary form (parent) may be edited separately from the subform (child), and the subform is stored and edited separately from the parent.

    (b) Subforms are created automatically when you use the Subform Design Wizard.

    (c) Both forms may be viewed and edited at the same time.

    (d) You use subforms to show information that sources two or more related tables such as customers and orders.

15. Why should you design forms for your databases?

    (a) To present users with a format that is familiar and easy to use

    (b) To make the database run more quickly and efficiently

    (c) To display differing views of PivotTables and PivotCharts

    (d) a and c but not b

Practice Exercises

1 National Conference Data Entry

You are the intern assigned to the Dean of Students' Office and spend most of your time scheduling and planning the National Conference. Others in the office also work on the conference, but you find that sometimes they omit needed information or make errors that you must find and fix. For example, some people in the office enter phone numbers as (910) 555-1101, while others enter them as 910-555-1101. Some people skip the phone number field completely. You decide to add some verification and requirement properties to the database to help protect the data. Refer to Figure 6.48 to verify your work.

a. Copy the partially completed file *chap6_pe1_natconf.accdb* from the Exploring Access folder to your production folder. Rename it **chap6_pe1_natconf_solution**. Double-click the file name to open it. Click **Options** on the Security Warning toolbar, click **Enable this content** in the Microsoft Office Security Options dialog box, and click **OK**.

b. Open the **Speakers table** and replace *Your_Name* with your name in the FirstName and LastName fields.

c. Right-click the table tab and select **Design View** from the shortcut menu. Click the **PhoneNumber** field in the Field Name column to activate it. Change the Required property in the Field Properties pane to **Yes**.

d. Click the Input Mask property for the PhoneNumber field and click **Build** on the right side. Click **Yes** to the alert message on saving the changes to the table. Click **Yes** in the Data Integrity Warning dialog box. In the Input Mask Wizard dialog box, make sure that the **Phone Number** is selected in the Input Mask Column.

e. Click the **Try It box**. Click to the left edge of the phone number placeholders and type **2227775555**. Click **Next**.

f. In the next wizard screen, click the **Placeholder character drop-down arrow** and select #. Click in the **Try it** box and make sure that the mask displays **(###) ###-####**. Click **Next**.

g. Store the data **Without the symbols in the mask**. Click **Next**. Click **Finish**.

h. Make sure that the PhoneNumber field is still active. Capture a screenshot by pressing **Prnt Scrn**. Launch Word. Type your name and section number on the first line, and then press **Enter**. Paste the screenshot in the Word document, print, and save the file as **chap6_pe1_natconf_solution.docx**.

i. Toggle back to the Access database. Save the changes to the table design.

j. Click the **Office Button**, select **Manage**, and select **Compact and Repair** the file. Close the file.

...continued on Next Page

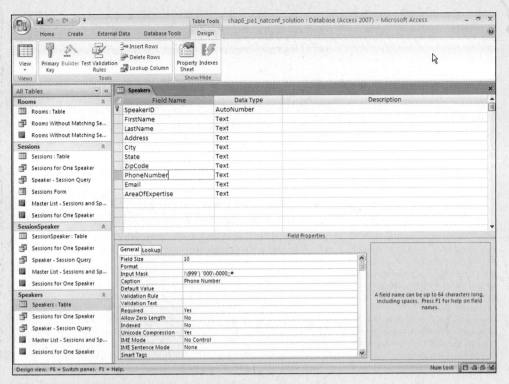

Figure 6.48 Table Property Changes

2 National Conference Form Design

You discover that a coworker entered information in the Speakers table incorrectly. He entered the first half of a new record correctly, but then jumped to a different record and overwrote the information correctly stored with incorrect data. When you discovered the error, it took you a long time to find the correct information and correct both records. You decide that a form would help your coworkers enter data more accurately and help eliminate a stray mouse click damaging data in other records. You need to create a form that will help the office workers add new speakers and sessions to the database as plans are finalized. After creating the form, you will need to customize it to be more attractive and functional. Refer to Figure 6.49 to verify your work.

a. Copy the partially completed file *chap6_pe2_natconf.accdb* from the Exploring Access folder to your production folder. Rename it **chap6_pe2_natconf_solution**. Double-click the file name to open it. Enable the security content by clicking the **Options** button in the Security Warning bar. Select **Enable this content**, and then click **OK**.

b. Open the **Speakers table** and replace *Your_Name* with your name in the FirstName and LastName fields. Close the Speakers table.

c. Open the **Speaker-Session query** in Datasheet view. Click **Form** in the Forms group on the Create tab.

d. Move the mouse to the right boundary of the selected control. When the pointer shape changes to the double-headed arrow, click and drag the right boundary left to make the column about one-half as wide.

e. Locate and click the **box with the plus sign** in it in the *upper-left corner* of the form in Layout view. All the controls select. Click the **Arrange tab**, and then click the **Remove Tool** in the Control Layout group. Click anywhere on the white space to deselect the controls.

f. Click the control for the Session ID, **S01**. Move your mouse over the right boundary. When the pointer shape changes to the double-headed arrow, click and drag the right boundary **right** to make the column about *one-half inch wide*.

g. Click the control for the Session Title, **Understanding Diversity within the University**. With the mouse pointer in the four-headed-arrow, move the control **up** and position it beside the *Session ID, S01*.

...continued on Next Page

TROUBLESHOOTING: You can click on the S01 control box, and then Shift+click on the Session Title control to select both boxes. Then on the Arrange tab, in the Control Alignment group, click Top to align the Session Title box even with the top edge of the S01 control box.

h. Click the **SessionTitle label** and press **Delete**. Edit the SessionID and StartingTime labels to add **spaces**. Edit the form title to be **Speaker – Session Form**.

i. Make the text boxes wider to match the Session Title text box width. (You might find it easier to use the Design view grid to align the boxes.) Save the form as **Your_Name Speaker-Session Form**.

j. Right-click the form tab and select **Form View** from the shortcut menu. Navigate to the third record.

k. Capture a screenshot of the third record by pressing **Prnt Scrn**. Open a Word document. Type your name and section number on the first line, then press **Enter**. Paste the screenshot into the Word document and save the file as **chap6_pe2_natconf_solution.docx**. Print the Word document. Close Word.

l. Save and close the form and any open objects. Click the **Office Button**, select **Manage**, and then select **Compact and Repair**. Close the file.

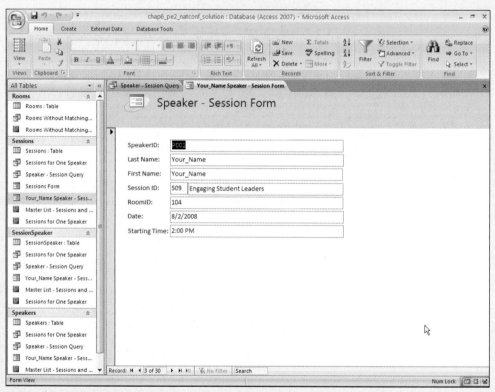

Figure 6.49 Edited Form

3 Lifelong Learning

The Lifelong Learning Physicians Association asks that you help simplify their data entry tasks. They want a form that will enroll new physicians as members. Because the data entry clerks sometimes misspell the members' specializations, you decide to create a lookup table. If all of the specialty areas are spelled uniformly, a query or a filter to examine data subsets by specialty will return predictable and accurate results. After creating the lookup and the form, you will populate the table with each physician's area of specialty. Refer to Figure 6.50 to verify your work.

a. Copy the partially completed file *chap6_pe3_physicians.accdb* from the Exploring Access folder to your production folder. Rename it **chap6_pe3_physicians_solution.accdb**.

...continued on Next Page

Double-click the file name to open it. Click **Options** in the Security Warning bar, select **Enable this content**, and click **OK**.

b. Open the **Physicians table** in Datasheet view. Click in the Add New Field column in the first row. Click the **Datasheet tab**, and then click **Lookup Column** in the Fields & Column group to launch the Lookup Wizard.

c. In the first wizard screen, select **I want the lookup column to look up the values in a table or query**. Click **Next**. In the second screen, select **Table:Specialization**. Click **Next**. In the next screen, double-click the **Specialization** field to move it to the *Selected Fields box*. Click **Next twice**. Adjust the column width to make sure that all of *Exercise Physiology* displays. Ensure that the **Hide Key column check box** is selected. Click **Next**. In the final screen, name the lookup **Specialization**. Click **Finish**. Save the table.

d. Click the **Create tab**, and then click **Form** in the Forms group. Click the **subform boundary** at the bottom of the form to select it. With the large gold rectangle surrounding the subform, press **Delete**.

e. Right-click the **Physicians form tab** and Switch to **Form View** by selecting it from the shortcut menu. Use the form to populate the Specialization Field with the following information. Add yourself as a new record. Your specialization is Gerontology.

First Name	Last Name	Specialization
Bonnie	Clinton	Obstetrics
Warren	Brasington	Hematology
James	Shindell	General Medicine
Edward	Wood	Cardiology
Michelle	Quintana	Internal Medicine
Kristine	Park	Exercise Physiology
William	Williamson	General Medicine
Holly	Davis	Cardiology
Steven	Fisher	Internal Medicine
David	Tannen	Hematology
Jeffrey	Jacobsen	Internal Medicine
Patsy	Clark	Cardiology

f. Save the form as **Your_Name Physicians**. Capture a screenshot of the form with your record displayed by pressing **Prnt Scrn**. Launch Word, and then type **Your_Name and section number** at the top of the page. Press **Enter**. Paste the screenshot into the Word document. Keep the Word document open.

g. Return to Access. Click the **Physicians table tab** to display the table data. Close and open the Physicians table again. Check to make sure that your newly added record displays.

h. Capture a screenshot of the Physicians table by pressing **Prnt Scrn**. Return to Word and press **Enter** after the screenshot of the form. Paste the screenshot into the Word document and save the file as **chap6_pe3_physicians_solution.docx**. Print and close the Word document.

i. Save and close the table and form. Click the **Office Button**, select **Manage**, and select **Compact and Repair**. Close the file.

...continued on Next Page

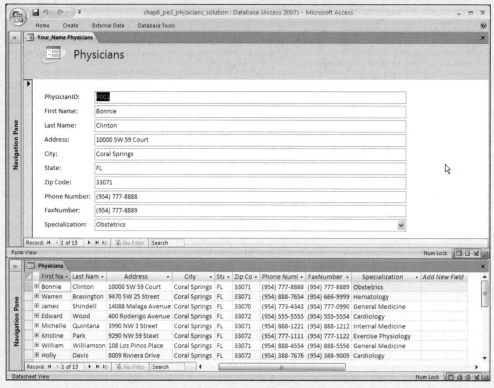

Figure 6.50 Form and Table

4 Custom Coffee

The Custom Coffee Company is a small service organization that provides coffee, tea, and snacks to offices. Custom Coffee also provides and maintains the equipment for brewing the beverages. Although the firm is small, its excellent reputation for providing outstanding customer service has helped it grow. Part of its good customer service record is because the firm owner set up a database to organize and keep track of customer purchases. You need to add a form to help track customer purchases. Because the Customers and Orders tables have a one-to-many relationship, the form created needs to be a form based on the Customers table and a subform showing the Orders each customer has placed. You will also need to add additional fields to the form. Refer to Figure 6.51 to verify your work..

a. Copy the partially completed file *chap6_pe4_coffee.accdb* from the Exploring Access folder to your production folder. Rename it **chap6_pe4_coffee_solution.accdb**. Double-click the file name to open the file. Click **Options** in the Security Warning bar, select **Enable this content**, and click **OK**.

b. Double-click the **Sales Rep table** to open it. Replace *Your_Name* with your name. Close the table by clicking Close in the database window.

c. Double-click the **Customers table** to open it. Click **Form** in the Forms group on the Create tab. The form and subform are too long to fit on a single screen, so you need to rearrange the controls.

d. Move your mouse over the *right boundary* of the first control and when the pointer shape changes to the double-headed arrow, click and drag **left** until all of the control text boxes are about two inches wide.

e. Click the **Box with the plus sign** in it in the upper-left corner of the form. Click the **Arrange tab** and click **Remove** in the Control Layout group. **Click** the *Contact label* and **Shift+click** the *text box* controls to select them both, drag them up, and position them in the same row as the Customer Name.

...continued on Next Page

f. Reposition the remaining main form controls as shown in Figure 6.51. Delete the label controls for Address2, City, State, and Zip.

g. Click the *subform border* to activate it. Find the Move box in the upper-left corner. Click and drag the Move box up. Save your form as **Your_Name Customers**.

h. Right-click the Form tab and select **Design View** from the shortcut menu. Display the **Field List pane** by clicking **Add Existing Fields** in the Tools group on the Design tab.

i. Click the **plus sign** beside the Sales Reps table to display the fields. Find and select the **LastName** field in the Sales Reps table. Drag the **LastName** field to the form and drop it *above the Sales Rep ID field*. Save the form. Close the Field List pane.

j. Right-click the form tab and select **Form View** from the shortcut menu. Click the **Sales Rep ID** label and use Format Painter to copy the formatting to the **LastName** label. Click the **Next Record** button six times to view Record 7. Press **Tab** to test the tab order of the form controls. The LastName field is out of order. Right-click the *form tab* and select **Layout View** from the shortcut menu. Click **Tab Order** in the Control Layout group on the Arrange tab.

k. Click the **LastName field row selector** (the gray box to the left of the field name). Once selected, drag the row selector box and the associated field name **up** and drop it *under the Fax field*.

l. Move the Tab Order box to the upper-right corner of the screen and press **Prnt Scrn**. Click **OK** to close the Tab Order box.

m. Launch Word, change to **Landscape** orientation, and type **Your_name** and **section number**. Press **Enter**. Paste the screenshot into the Word document and save the file as **chap6_pe4_coffee_solution.docx**. Print and close the Word document.

n. Save the form. Click the **Office Button**, select **Manage**, and then select **Compact and Repair**. Close the file.

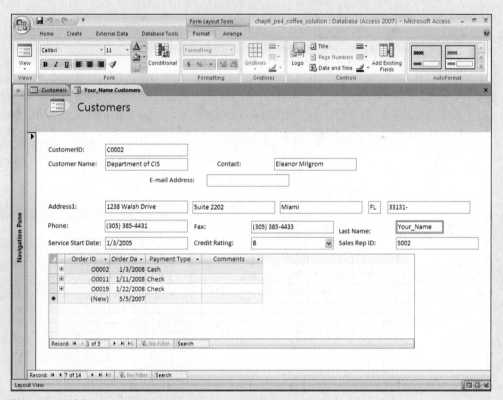

Figure 6.51 Form, Subform, and Rearranged Controls

The Parent Teachers Organization (PTO) at the South Vancouver Pre-school holds a silent auction each spring to help supply the classrooms. Parents and grandparents donate items to the auction and are invited to a dinner at which they can place bids. To help the school keep track of the donations, you prepared an Access form. You gave the form to the chairperson of the Auction Committee, who requested changes to the form design. You need to add a button that will print the form. You also need to create a lookup field to categorize donated items. The form also needs to display the items' value. Refer to Figure 6.52 to verify your work.

a. Locate the file named *chap6_mid1_preschool.accdb*, copy it to your production folder, and rename it **chap6_mid1_preschool_solution.accdb**. Open the file and enable the content.

b. Rename the *Donors* form as **Your_Name Donors**. Open the Donor table and replace Shelly Martin's name in the first and last name fields with your name.

c. Create a multivalued lookup field that uses the Category field in the Categories table as the data source. Name the field **Category**. Look at the ItemDonated field and use your best judgment to populate the new field with data.

d. Open the **Your_Name Donor** form in Layout view. Add the **ItemValue** field to the form under the Item Donated field. Add the **Category** field under the Number Attending field. Match the formatting of the other controls on the form.

e. Switch to **Design view**. Add a button between the Add New Record and Close Form buttons that prints the active record.

f. Change to **Form View** to test the Tab navigation. Fix any Tab order problems in Layout or Design views. Test the action buttons.

g. Capture a screenshot of the form that has the Tab Order dialog box open. Move the **Tab Order box** to the *top-right corner* of the screen before capturing the screenshot.

h. Launch Word, type **Your_Name and section number**, and press **Enter**. Paste the screenshot and save the file as **chap6_mid1_preschool_solution.docx**.

i. Print and close the Word document. Compact and repair the database. Close the database.

Figure 6.52 Edited Donation Form

...continued on Next Page

You are the general manager of a large hotel chain. Your establishment provides a variety of guest services ranging from rooms and conferences to weddings. You and your staff need to quickly determine how often the customer uses your services. You need a form that will show an individual record's detail as well as showing other records. Refer to Figure 6.53 to verify your work.

a. Locate the file named *chap6_mid2_memrewards.accdb*, copy it to your production folder, and rename it **chap6_mid2_memrewards_solution.accdb**. Open the file and enable the content. Rename the *Revenue* query as **Your_Name Revenue**. Open it in Datasheet view.

b. Create a split form. Select a control in the right column in the top of the form and make the second column about two inches wide. Save the form.

c. Change the Text Align property for the PerPerson Charge and Revenue fields to be right-aligned. Add spaces in the Controls in the left column where needed. Save the form.

d. Right-click the City field for the first record and select **Equals "Las Vegas"**. Sort the records by last name.

e. Click **Totals** in the Records group on the Home tab to turn on the Total row. Click into the Total row in the Revenue column, click the **arrow**, and select **Sum**.

f. Capture a screenshot of your form displaying only Las Vegas activities. Paste it into Word under a line giving your name and section number.

g. Return to Access and remove the filters. Apply a new filter that displays only records for Joe Little.

h. Capture a screenshot of your form displaying only Joe's activities. Paste it into Word under the other screenshot. Save and print the Word document.

i. Return to Access. Compact, repair, and close the database.

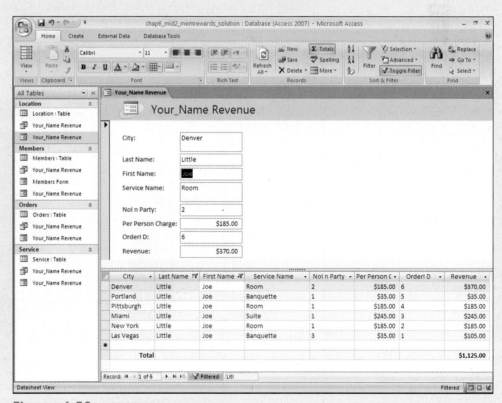

Figure 6.53 Sorted, Filtered Table

...continued on Next Page

You are the marketing manager of an international specialty food wholesaler. You need a form that will help you track sales performance and profitability by product line and employee. You will need to calculate profit by subtracting total costs from revenue. You want to have the ability to examine both aggregates and details. Refer to Figure 6.54 to verify your work.

a. Locate the file named *chap6_mid3_traders.accdb* copy it to your production folder, and rename it **chap6_mid3_traders_solution.accdb**. Open the file and enable the content. Rename the *Revenue query* as **Your_Name Revenue**. Open the **Employees** table and replace *Your_Name* with your first and last names. Close the table and open the query.

b. Create a PivotTable (located in More Forms in the Forms group on the Create tab). Display the PivotTable Field List pane.

c. Add the **CategoryName** field to the Drop Row Fields Here zone. Add the **LastName** field to the Drop Column Fields Here zone. Add the **Revenue** and **TotalCost** fields to the Detail Drop zone.

d. Calculate **Profit** for each order by using the **Create Calculated Detail Field** tool under Formulas in the Tools group on the Design tab. Profit is the difference between Revenue and TotalCost. Name the newly created field **Profit**. Format it as **Currency**.

e. Click the *Profit* column head to select all of the records and calculate a sum by using the **AutoCalc** tool. Calculate the sum of Revenue and Total Cost.

f. Hide the details. Display only your sales figures. Save the form as **Your_Name Revenue Pivot Form**. Print the PivotTable form.

g. Create a PivotChart that uses the PivotTable as its data source. Use Figure 6.54 as a guide to format your chart. Print the chart in landscape orientation. Save it as **Your_Name Revenue Pivot Chart**.

h. Save your query. Compact, repair, and close the database.

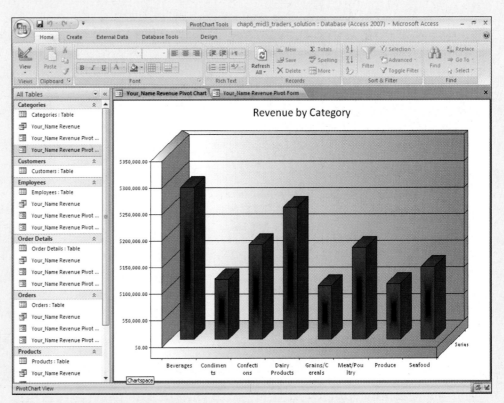

Figure 6.54 Pivot Views of Data

Capstone Exercise

(Replacements, Ltd. exists. The data in the case file are actual data. The customer and employee information has been changed to ensure privacy. However, the inventory and sales records reflect actual transactions.)

You work as an associate information technology trainee at Replacements, Ltd. In preparation for your first day on the job you have browsed the Replacements Web site, www.replacements.com. There you learned that Replacements, Ltd. (located in Greensboro, NC) has the world's largest selection of old and new dinnerware, including china, stoneware, crystal, glassware, silver, stainless, and collectibles. Your task is to create a form that data entry associates may use to add new items to the inventory. You will create a lookup table to classify merchandise as China, Crystal, or Flatware. After you test the newly created form's function, you will compact and repair the database.

Database File Setup

You need to copy an original database file, rename the copied file, and then open the copied database to complete this capstone exercise. After you open the copied database, you will replace an existing employee's name with your name. Finally, you will create a new table that will be the source for a lookup.

a. Locate the file named *chap6_cap_replacements.accdb* and copy it to your production folder.

b. Rename the copied file as **chap6_cap_ replacements_solution.accdb**.

c. Open the *chap6_cap_replacements_solution.accdb* file and enable the content.

d. Open the **Employees table**.

e. Navigate to record 33 and replace *Sherol Cowan's* name with your name. Press **Enter** and close the table.

f. Create a new table.

g. Populate the new table by clicking in the first row in the *Add New Field* column. Type **China** and press **Enter**. Click in the second row in the column (now named *Field1*) and type **Flatware**. In the next row, type **Crystal**. Right-click the column head, Field1, and rename it **Category**. Save the table and name it **Product Lines**. Close the table.

Establish Validation Rules and Text

You need to edit the Inventory table design to validate data. Specifically, you need to require the SKU for each new record and set a validation rule to contain values of 0 or higher.

a. Open the **Inventory table** in Design view.

b. Set the property to require a value for the SKU field.

c. Establish a validation rule for the OnHandQty field that is at least zero. Require this field.

d. Create validation text for the OnHandQty: **Please enter the number of this product in inventory. If there are none on hand enter 0 (zero).**

e. Save the table and test the data with the new rules. Switch to Datasheet view.

Test the Validation Rule

You need to test the newly created rule to see if it works and if the error message is helpful.

a. Click any field in the OnHandQty column and write down the value it contains.

b. Delete the value and press **Enter**. You receive the required field error message. Read it and click **OK**.

c. Type a negative number, such as –3. Read the validation text.

d. Click **Undo** or type the original OnHandValue in the table.

Create and Format a Form

You need to create a form that will be used to check new purchases into inventory.

a. Create a form. Because the table is in relationship with the Orders table, the form generates a subform.

b. Delete the subform.

c. Apply the Opulent (second column, fourth row) AutoFormat.

d. Apply the **Currency Format** to the **Retail** field.

e. Right-align all of the labels. Add a sunken special effect to the text box controls.

f. Delete the form icon image in the title. Change the title to Your_Name Inventory. Add spaces where necessary in the control labels and align them.

g. Make the form controls about three inches wide. Remove the default layout and make the width of the last three controls about 1.5".

Create a Lookup

Now that you are satisfied that the form shows the necessary information, you can begin to make it easy to use.

a. Switch to Design view and deselect the controls.

b. Click the **Combo Box** tool in the Controls group on the Design tab. Click on the Design grid below the ProductCategoryId controls.

c. In the List Box Wizard, select an existing table as the source and select the **Product Lines** table. Select the Category field and instruct Access to remember this value for later use.

d. Save the form as Your_Name Inventory. Print a single record.

e. Compact and repair the database. Close the file.

Mini Cases

Use the rubric following the case as a guide to evaluate your work, but keep in mind that your instructor may impose additional grading criteria or use a different standard to judge your work.

Determining What Fields to Include on a Form

GENERAL CASE

The *chap6_mc1_traders.accdb* file contains data from an international specialty foods distribution firm. Copy the *chap6_mc1_traders.accdb* file to your production folder, name it **chap6_mc1_traders_solution.accdb**, and open the copied file. Use the skills from this chapter to perform several tasks. Open the Orders table and use it to create a form. The form will be used in the warehouse to tell the packers what items to place in each box. It will be printed on custom dye-cut labels and used in three places. One part of the form needs to group the shipping address information together. Another should generate a packing list (i.e., how many of each item have been boxed and shipped). It needs to include the name of the product (not just the identification numbers). The third grouping of information on the form needs to show the order number, the company name, the date of shipment, and the name of the shipping company (use a lookup table). Format the labels to have spaces where needed and apply an attractive format. Save and title the form as **Your_Name Packing Form**. Adjust the tab order as necessary. Compact and repair the database.

Performance Elements	Exceeds Expectations	Meets Expectations	Below Expectations
Group arrangement	Controls are grouped logically and functionally. The groups are visually separated from each other.	Most of the items that should be together are grouped; there is some visual distinction between groups.	Output missing or incorrect.
Lookup	Appropriate and functional lookups created. Unnecessary fields removed.	Lookups created and function. Unnecessary fields exist.	Output missing or inaccurate.
Detail manipulation	Appropriate levels of details displayed and formatted correctly.	Appropriate levels of details displayed with some formatting problems.	Insufficient understanding of detail manipulation.

Identifying Good and Poor Form Design

RESEARCH CASE

This chapter introduced you to the power of using Access forms, but you have much more to explore. Now that you have learned a little about form design and usage, go to the Web and find one form that you consider well designed and easy to use. Capture a screenshot of the good form and paste it into a Word file. Write a paragraph describing why you selected this form as an illustration of a well-designed, easy-to-use form. Identify which fields in your form are required. Describe the features like validation text messages that made the form useful. Identify how the form used lookups and other labor-saving features. Return to the Web and find a form that you believe has design flaws. The flaws may be aesthetic (you might dislike the background color) or they might be functional (the tab order is not logical). Capture a screenshot and paste it in the Word document. Write a paragraph describing what is wrong with this form and how you would fix it. Save the file as **chap6_mc2_goodform_solution.docx**.

Performance Elements	Exceeds Expectations	Meets Expectations	Below Expectations
Found examples of a well-designed and a poorly designed form	Both forms located and presented as directed. There were clear distinctions between the good and poor designs.	Both forms located and presented as directed. There were some distinctions between the good and poor designs.	Forms not found or there was insufficient evidence of design differences.
Form element identification	The screenshots were clearly labeled, identifying most relevant form elements.	Screenshots labeled with many relevant form design items.	Labels missing or incorrect.
Summarize and communicate	Identifications and descriptions clearly written and accurate.	Identifications and descriptions clearly written and mostly accurate, indicating some understanding but also weaknesses.	Identifications and descriptions missing, inaccurate, or incomprehensible.
Diagnosis and treatment	Most of the problems with the poorly designed form diagnosed, and the recommended actions would solve most problems.	Many problems identified, and most of the recommended actions would solve the problems.	Problems only partially identified, and no clear understanding of how to resolve presented.

Design a Form That Functions

DISASTER RECOVERY

A coworker called you into his office, explained that he was having difficulty with Access 2007, and asked you to look at his work. Copy the *chap6_mc3_physicians.accdb* file to your production folder, name it **chap6_mc3_physicians_solution.accdb**, and open the file. Your coworker explains he cannot use the form. He intended that it should provide an easy method of enrolling new volunteers into medical studies. However, he indicates several problems. The phone numbers are accurate but difficult to understand. The form controls need to be grouped more logically, with one grouping for the contact information for the volunteers, a second for their medical information, and a third for the study they are interested in joining. The study needs to be identified by name, not ID number. Rework the form with these guides in mind. Add formatting. Test the tab order. Compact, repair, and back up your database.

Performance Elements	Exceeds Expectations	Meets Expectations	Below Expectations
Error identification	Correct identification and correction of all errors.	Correct identification of all errors and correction of some errors.	Errors neither located nor corrected.
Data interaction	The phone number and study title display appropriately.	One but not both controls have been fixed.	Neither control repaired.
Grouping	Form controls visually grouped logically and attractively.	Most controls grouped logically, but there may be an item or two out of position.	No visual definition of form groupings.

Introduction to PowerPoint

Presentations Made Easy

bjectives

After you read this chapter, you will be able to:

1. Identify PowerPoint user interface elements **(page 1129)**.
2. Use PowerPoint views **(page 1134)**.
3. Open and save a slide show **(page 1139)**.
4. Get Help **(page 1142)**.
5. Create a storyboard **(page 1147)**.
6. Use slide layouts **(page 1150)**.
7. Apply design themes **(page 1150)**.
8. Review the presentation **(page 1152)**.
9. Add a table **(page 1159)**.
10. Insert clip art **(page 1159)**.
11. Use transitions and animations **(page 1161)**.
12. Run and navigate a slide show **(page 1170)**.
13. Print with PowerPoint **(page 1172)**.

Hands-On Exercises

Exercises	Skills Covered
1. INTRODUCTION TO POWERPOINT (page 1143) **Open:** chap1_ho1_intro.pptx **Save as:** chap1_ho1_intro_solution.pptx	• Start PowerPoint • Open an Existing Presentation • Type a Speaker's Note • View the Presentation • Save the Presentation with a New Name • Locate Information Using Help
2. CREATING A PRESENTATION (page 1153) **Open:** none **Save as:** chap1_ho2_content_solution.pptx	• Create a New Presentation • Add Slides • Check Spelling and Use the Thesaurus • Modify Text and Layout • Reorder Slides • Apply a Design Theme
3. STRENGTHENING A PRESENTATION (page 1164) **Open:** chap1_ho2_content _solution.pptx (from Exercise 2) **Save as:** chap1_ho3_content_solution.pptx (additional modifications)	• Add a Table • Insert, Move, and Resize Clip Art • Apply a Transition • Animate Objects
4. NAVIGATING AND PRINTING (page 1175) **Open:** chap1_ho3_content_solution.pptx (from Exercise 3) **Save as:** chap1_ho4_content_solution.pptx (additional modifications)	• Display a Slide Show • Navigate to Specific Slides • Annotate a Slide • Print Audience Handouts

CASE STUDY

Be a Volunteer

While watching television one evening, you see a public service announcement on the volunteer organization Big Brothers Big Sisters. The Big Brothers Big Sisters organization seeks to help children ages 6 through 18 reach their potential by providing mentors through their growing years. The organization matches "Bigs" (adults) with "Littles" (children) in one-on-one relationships with the goal of having the mentor make a positive impact on the child's life. Being intrigued, you attend an informational open house where volunteers and board members give an overview of the program and share personal experiences. At the open house you discover that the organization has been helping at-risk children for more than 100 years and that in 2003 Big Brothers Big Sisters was selected by *Forbes Magazine* as one of its top ten charities that it believes are worthy of donor consideration.

Case Study

You choose to answer Big Brothers Big Sisters' call to "Be a friend. Be a mentor. Just be there." You call the local organization for further information and you are invited to come in and meet representatives, introduce yourself, and complete an application. Because "Bigs" and "Littles" are matched by interests, you decide to create a presentation to introduce you and give information about your interests. Your assignment is to create a PowerPoint slide show about yourself to use in your presentation. You may want to include a slide about a mentor who has positively impacted your life. Forget modesty at this point—toot your own horn!

Your Assignment

- Read the chapter, paying special attention to how to create and enhance a presentation.
- Create a new presentation with a title slide that includes your name. Save the presentation as **chap1_case_introduction_solution**.
- Storyboard a presentation that includes four to six slides that introduce you, your background, and your interests. Include an introduction slide and a summary or conclusion slide as well as your main point slides introducing you.
- Use the storyboard to create a PowerPoint slide show about you.
- Apply a design theme and add a transition to at least one slide.
- Insert at least one clip art image in an appropriate location.
- Display your slide show to at least one class member, or to the entire class if asked by your instructor.
- Print handouts, four slides per page, framed.

Introduction to PowerPoint

This chapter introduces you to PowerPoint 2007, one of the major applications in Microsoft Office 2007. PowerPoint enables you to create a professional presentation without relying on others, and then lets you deliver that presentation in a variety of ways. You can show the presentation from your computer, on the World Wide Web, or create traditional overhead transparencies. You can even use PowerPoint's Package for CD feature to package your presentation with a viewer so those without PowerPoint may still view your presentation.

A PowerPoint presentation consists of a series of slides such as those shown in Figures 1.1–1.6. The various slides contain different elements (such as text, images, and WordArt), yet the presentation has a consistent look with respect to its overall design and color scheme. Creating this type of presentation is relatively easy, and that is the power in PowerPoint. In essence, PowerPoint enables you to concentrate on the content of a presentation without worrying about its appearance. You supply the text and supporting elements and leave the formatting to PowerPoint. If, however, you wish to create your own presentation design, PowerPoint provides you with powerful tools to use in the design process.

Figure 1.1 Title Slide

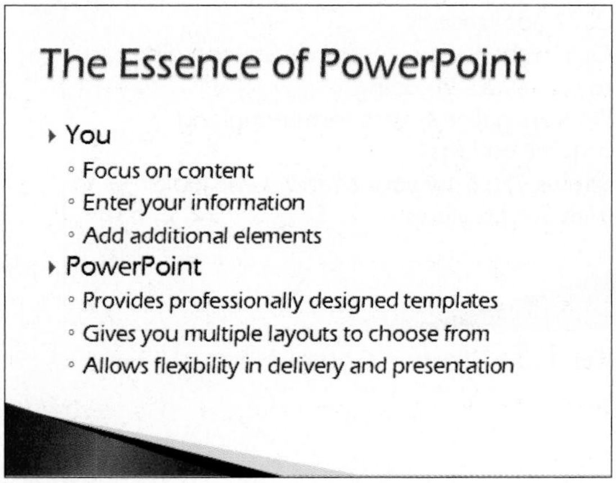

Figure 1.2 Title and Content Slide

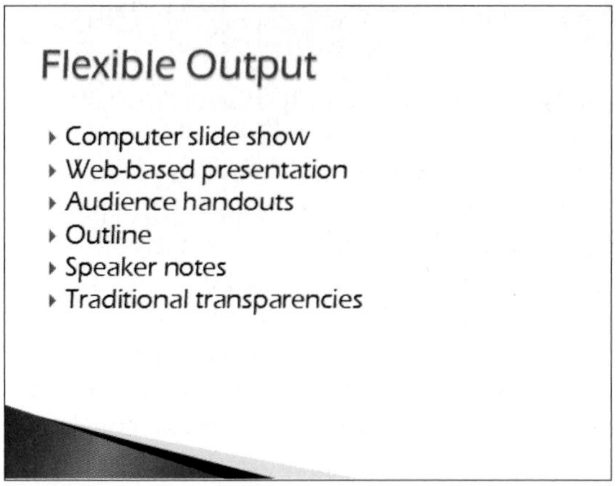
Flexible Output
Computer slide show
Web-based presentation
Audience handouts
Outline
Speaker notes
Traditional transparencies

Figure 1.3 Title and Content Slide

Enhanced Presentations
Include photographs, clip art and other objects
Bob
Cyndi
Add sound and animation

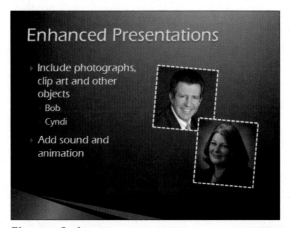

Figure 1.4 Title and Two Content Slides with Images

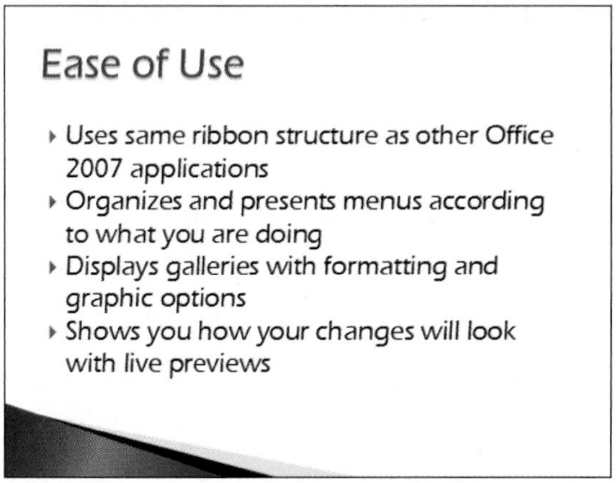
Ease of Use
Uses same ribbon structure as other Office 2007 applications
Organizes and presents menus according to what you are doing
Displays galleries with formatting and graphic options
Shows you how your changes will look with live previews

Figure 1.5 Title and Content Slide

Figure 1.6 Title Slide with WordArt

In addition to helping you create the presentation, PowerPoint provides a variety of ways to deliver it. You can show the presentation on a computer monitor as a slide show or Web presentation, or you can project the slide show onto a screen or a wall for an audience. You can include sound and video in the presentation, provided your system has a sound card and speakers. You can automate the presentation and display it at a convention booth or kiosk. If you cannot show the presentation on a computer with a monitor or projector, you can easily convert it to overhead transparencies or print the presentation in various ways to distribute to your audience.

In this section, you start your exploration of PowerPoint by viewing a previously completed presentation so that you can better appreciate what PowerPoint is all about. You examine the PowerPoint interface and various views to discover the advantages of each view. You modify and save an existing presentation, and then you create your own. Finally, you use Help to obtain assistance within PowerPoint.

Delivery Tips | Reference

Practice the following delivery tips to gain confidence and polish your delivery:

- Look at the audience, not at the screen, as you speak and you will open communication and gain credibility. Use the three-second guide: look into the eyes of a member of the audience for three seconds and then scan the entire audience. Continue doing this throughout your presentation. Use your eye contact to keep members of the audience involved.

- Do not read from a prepared script or your PowerPoint Notes. Know your material thoroughly. Glance at your notes infrequently. Never post a screen full of small text, and then torture your audience by saying "I know you cannot read this so I will..."

- Practice or rehearse your presentation with your PowerPoint at home until you are comfortable with the material and its corresponding slides.

- Speak slowly and clearly and try to vary your delivery. Show emotion or enthusiasm for your topic. If you do not care about your topic, why should the audience?

- Pause to emphasize key points when speaking.

- Speak to the person farthest away from you to be sure the people in the last row can hear you.

- Do not overwhelm your audience with your PowerPoint animations, sounds, and special effects. These features should not overpower you and your message, but should enhance your message.

- Arrive early to set up so you do not keep the audience waiting while you manage equipment. Have a backup in case the equipment does not work: overhead transparencies or handouts work well. Again, know your material well enough that you can present without the slide show if necessary.

- Prepare handouts for your audience so they can relax and participate in your presentation rather than scramble taking notes.

- Thank the audience for their attention and participation. Leave on a positive note.

Identifying PowerPoint User Interface Elements

If you have completed the Exploring Series Office Fundamentals chapter on Office 2007, many of the PowerPoint 2007 interface features will be familiar to you. If this is your first experience with an Office 2007 application, you will quickly feel comfortable in PowerPoint, and because the interface is core to all of the Office 2007 applications, you will quickly be able to apply the knowledge in Word, Excel, Access, and Outlook. In Office 2007, Microsoft organizes features and commands to correspond directly to the common tasks people perform, making it possible for you to find the features you need quickly.

In PowerPoint 2007, you work with two windows: the PowerPoint application window and the document window for the current presentation. The PowerPoint application window contains the Minimize, Maximize (or Restore), and Close buttons. The PowerPoint application window also contains the title bar, which indicates the file name of the document on which you are working and the name of the application (Microsoft PowerPoint). Figure 1.7 shows the default PowerPoint view, the *Normal view*, with three panes that provide maximum flexibility in working with the presentation. The pane on the left side of the screen shows either thumbnails or an outline of the presentation, depending on whether you select the Slides tab or the Outline tab. The Slide pane on the right displays the currently selected slide in your presentation. The final pane, the Notes pane, is located at the bottom of the screen where you enter notes pertaining to the slide or the presentation.

Normal view is the tri-pane default PowerPoint view.

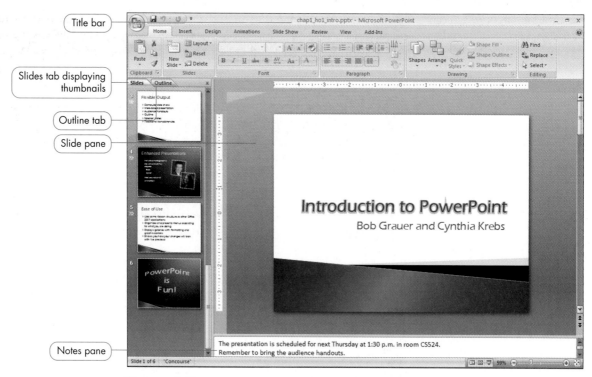

Figure 1.7 The Default PowerPoint View (Normal View)

Refer to Figure 1.8 to see the Microsoft Office Button, hereafter referred to as the Office Button, displayed below the title bar. This button provides you with an easy way to access commands for saving and printing, and includes features for finalizing your work and sharing your work with others. To the right of the Office Button is the Quick Access Toolbar, which gives you quick access to the commands that you may need at any time: Save, Undo, and Redo. You also can add other commands to the Quick Access Toolbar.

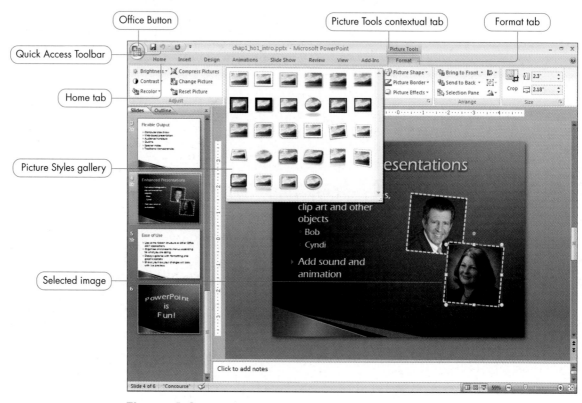

Figure 1.8 PowerPoint's Interface

The **Ribbon** is a command center that organizes commands into groups accessed from tabs.

Beneath the Office Button and the Quick Access Toolbar is the **Ribbon**, a command center that organizes commands into groups. The Ribbon makes it easy for you to find the features you need. Locate the Ribbon in Figure 1.8.

TIP   View Hidden Commands

If, when you look at your PowerPoint screen, it does not show all of the commands, your monitor could be set to display at a low resolution. For example, a resolution of 800 by 600 pixels used with small notebooks and older 13" CRT screens will not show all the commands. To see the hidden commands, click the ▶ on the vertical bar on the far right of the Ribbon. The remaining commands will appear. Changing your resolution to 1026 by 768 pixels or a higher resolution will enable all commands to display.

A **tab** sits above the Ribbon and is used to organize or group like features for quick access.

A **tab** sits above the Ribbon and organizes commands by grouping the most commonly used features related to your task for quick access. Once you select a tab based on the task you wish to perform, the commands that relate to one another when working on that task appear together in groups. For example, when you click the Home tab, the core PowerPoint commands appear in groups such as Clipboard, Slides, Font, Paragraph, Drawing, and Editing. PowerPoint has seven tabs: Home, Insert, Design, Animations, Slide Show, Review, and View. You may see an additional tab, Add-Ins, if you have any supplemental programs that add features to Microsoft Office. The author installed a supplemental image-capturing program, so all figures in this text display the Add-Ins tab. Table 1.1 lists each of the tabs, the groups that appear when the tab is selected, and a general description of the available commands.

TIP   Minimize the Ribbon

To increase the size of the working area on your screen, you can minimize the Ribbon by clicking any active tab, located above the Ribbon. To restore the Ribbon, click any tab. As an alternative, use the keyboard shortcut by pressing **Ctrl+F1**.

An **object** is any type of information that can be inserted in a slide.

A **contextual tab** is a specialty tab that appears only when certain types of objects are being edited.

> Microsoft . . . "pick and click" formatting . . . gives you results that look good without much design effort.

A **gallery** displays a set of predefined options that can be clicked to apply to an object.

When you add text, a graphic, a table, a chart, or any other form of information to a slide, you are adding an **object** to the slide. When you select certain types of objects for editing, **contextual tabs** containing commands specific to that object appear. The contextual tabs appear above the Ribbon and, when clicked, open a tab containing multiple tools you need. For example, in Figure 1.8, because the image of Cyndi is selected for editing, the Picture Tools contextual tab displays. Clicking the Picture Tools tab opened the Format tab. The Format tab is organized into groups related to specific tasks (Picture Tools, Picture Styles, Arrange, and Size).

As you examine Figure 1.8, notice the large box that appears on top of the Ribbon, showing a wide variety of styles that could be applied to a picture. This is the Picture Styles gallery, one of many galleries within PowerPoint. A **gallery** provides you with a set of visual options to choose from when working with your presentation. You click an option, and the styles in that option are applied to your object. Microsoft refers to this feature as "pick and click" formatting. "Picking and clicking" gives you results that look good without much design effort.

Table 1.1 Tab, Group, and Description

Tab and Group	Description
Home Clipboard Slides Font Paragraph Drawing Editing	The core PowerPoint tab. Contains basic editing functions such as cut and paste, and finding and replacing text. Includes adding slides and changing slide layout. Formatting using font, paragraph, and drawing tools is available.
Insert Tables Illustrations Links Text Media Clips	Contains all insert functions in one area. Includes ability to create tables and illustrations. Hyperlinks, text boxes, headers and footers, WordArt, and media clips are inserted here.
Design Page Setup Themes Background	Contains all functions associated with slide design including themes and backgrounds. Change page setup and slide orientation here.
Animations Preview Animations Transition To This Slide	Controls all aspects of animation including transitions, advanced options, and customizing.
Slide Show Start Slide Show Set Up Monitors	Includes slide show setup, monitor set up, and timing. Options for starting the slide show available.
Review Proofing Comments Protect	Contains all reviewing tools in PowerPoint, including such things as spelling and the use of comments.
View Presentation Views Show/Hide Zoom Color/Grayscale Window Macros	Contains Presentation Views. Advanced view options include showing or hiding slides, zooming, and available color choices. Set window arrangement here. Enables macro creation.
Add-Ins Custom Toolbars	Displays programs added to system that extend PowerPoint functionality. Does not display if supplemental programs are not installed.

A **ScreenTip** is a small window that describes a command.

Figure 1.9 shows a **ScreenTip**, or small window that appears when the mouse pointer moves over a command. The ScreenTip states the name or more descriptive explanation of a command. Enhanced ScreenTips also contain an icon that you can click to get more assistance from Help. ScreenTips can be invaluable when you need to identify a selected style. In this case, the ScreenTip gives the name of a WordArt choice, Fill–Accent 2, Warm Matte Bevel, and a preview of how it would look if selected. In some instances, an Enhanced ScreenTip provides brief description of the feature and includes a link to a Help topic relating to the command.

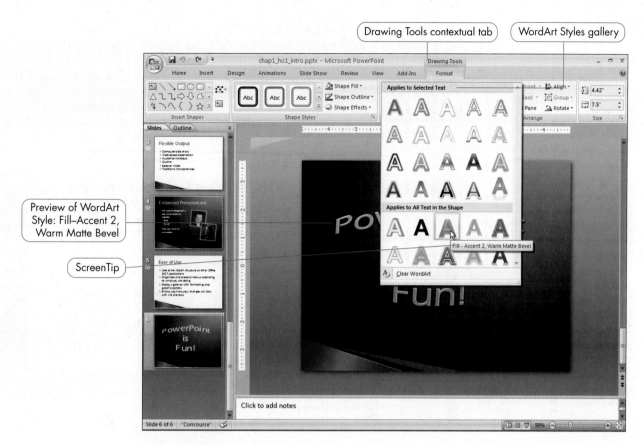

Figure 1.9 WordArt Gallery with ScreenTip

The **Mini toolbar** is a small, semitransparent toolbar that you can use to format text.

The **status bar** is a bar that contains the slide number, the Design Theme name, and view options.

The **Mini toolbar** is a small semitransparent toolbar that appears above selected text (see Figure 1.10) and gives you quick and easy access to the formatting commands commonly applied to text (such as font, font styles, font size, text alignment, text color, indent levels, and bullet features). Because the Mini toolbar appears above the selected text, you do not have to move the mouse pointer up to the Ribbon. When you first select text, the Mini toolbar appears as a semitransparent image, but if you move the mouse pointer over the toolbar, it fades in and becomes active for your use. As the mouse pointer moves away from the toolbar, or if a command is not selected, the Mini toolbar disappears.

Figure 1.10 also shows PowerPoint's unique **status bar**, a bar that contains the slide number, the design theme name, and options that control the view of your presentation: view buttons, the Zoom level button, the Zoom Slider, and the *Fit slide to current window* button. The status bar is located at the bottom of your screen, and can be customized. To customize the status bar, right-click the bar and then click the options you want displayed from the Customize Status Bar list.

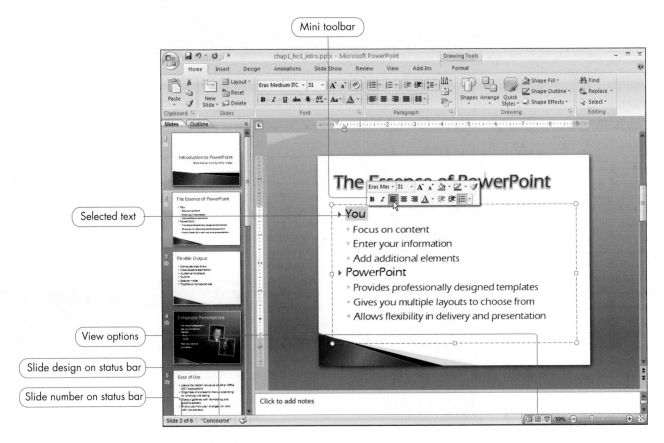

Figure 1.10 Mini Toolbar and Status Bar

Using PowerPoint Views

PowerPoint offers four primary views in which to create, modify, and deliver a presentation: Normal, Slide Sorter, Notes Page, and Slide Show. Each view represents a different way of looking at the presentation and each view has unique capabilities. (You will find some redundancy among the views in that certain tasks can be accomplished from multiple views.) The View tab gives you access to the four primary views, plus three additional views for working with masters. If you prefer, you may use the view buttons on the status bar to switch from one view to another, but only three views are available from the status bar: Normal, Slide Sorter, and Slide Show.

You looked at the default Normal view earlier in the chapter, (refer to Figure 1.7) but you will examine it in more detail now and compare it to other PowerPoint views. Knowing the benefits of each view enables to you work more efficiently. Figure 1.11 shows Normal view with the screen divided into three panes: the Outline tab pane showing the text of the presentation, the Slide pane displaying an enlarged view of one slide, and the Notes pane showing a portion of any associated speaker notes for the selected slide. The Outline tab pane provides the fastest way to type or edit text for the presentation. You type directly into the outline pane and move easily from one slide to the next. You also can use the outline pane to move and copy text from one slide to another or to rearrange the order of the slides within a presentation. The outline pane is limited, however, in that it does not show graphic elements that may be present on individual slides. Thus, you may want to switch to the Normal view that shows the Slides tab containing *thumbnail* images (slide miniatures) rather than the outline. In this view, you can change the order of the slides by clicking and dragging a slide to a new position. The Outline and Slides tabs let you switch between the two variations of the Normal view.

A ***thumbnail*** is a miniature of a slide that appears in the Slides tab.

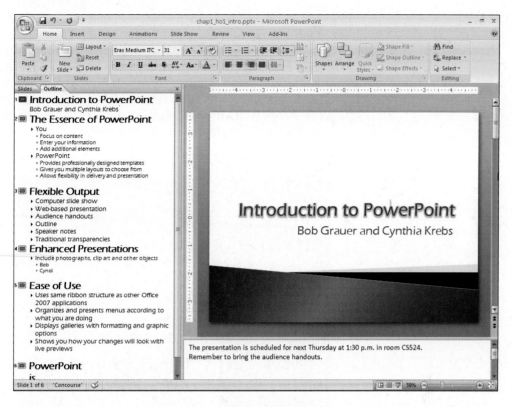

Figure 1.11 Normal View with Outline Tab Selected

The Normal view also provides access to the individual slides and speaker notes, each of which appears in its own pane. The Slide pane is the large pane on the right of the window. The Notes pane displays on the bottom of the window. You can change the size of these panes by dragging the splitter bar (border) that separates one pane from another. Figure 1.12 shows the Slides tab selected, the size of the Slide pane reduced, and the size of the Notes pane enlarged to provide for more space in which to create speaker notes.

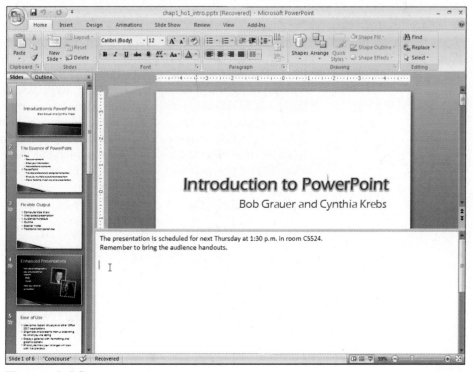

Figure 1.12 Normal View with Resized Panes

The Normal view is probably all that you need, but some designers like to close the left pane completely to see just an individual slide. This variation of the Normal view enlarges the individual slide so you can see more detail. Because the individual slide is where you change or format text, add graphical elements, or apply various animation effects an enlarged view is helpful. Figure 1.13 shows the individual slide in Normal view with the left pane closed. If you close the left pane, you can restore the screen to its usual tri-pane view by clicking the View tab, and then clicking Normal in the Presentation Views group.

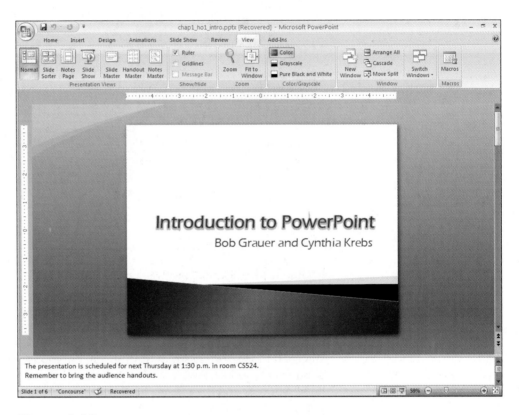

Figure 1.13 Individual Slide View

The **Notes Page view** is used for entering and editing large amounts of text that the speaker can refer to when presenting.

Rather than create speaker notes in the small pane available in the Normal view, you can work in the **Notes Page view**, a view specifically created to enter and edit large amounts of text that the speaker can refer to when presenting. If you have a large amount of technical detail in the speaker notes, you also may want to print audience handouts of this view since each page contains a picture of the slide plus the associated speaker notes. The notes do not appear when the presentation is shown, but are intended to help the speaker remember the key points about each slide. To switch from Normal view to Notes Page view, click the View tab, and then click Notes Page view in the Presentation Views group. Figure 1.14 shows an example of the Notes Page view.

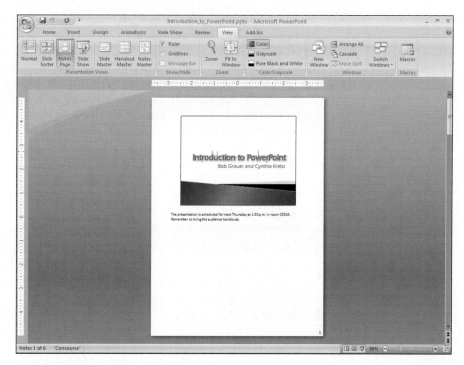

Figure 1.14 Notes Page View

The **Slide Sorter view** displays thumbnails of slides.

The **Slide Sorter view** enables you to see miniatures of your presentation slides to view multiple slides simultaneously (see Figure 1.15). This view is helpful when you wish to reorder the slides in a presentation. It also provides a convenient way to delete one or more slides. It lets you set transition effects for multiple slides. Any edit that you perform in one view is automatically updated in the other views. If, for example, you change the order of the slides in the Slide Sorter view, the changes automatically are reflected in the outline or thumbnail images within the Normal view. To switch to Slide Sorter view, click the View tab, and then click Slide Sorter in the Presentation Views group. If you are in Slide Sorter view and double-click a thumbnail, PowerPoint returns to the Normal view.

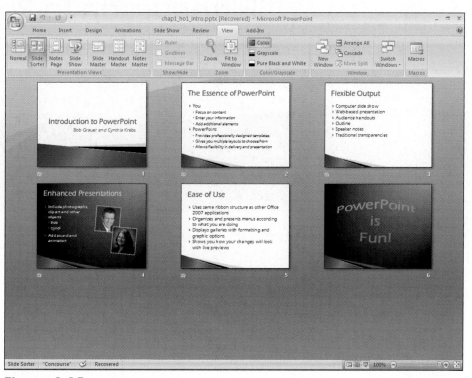

Figure 1.15 Slide Sorter View

The **Slide Show view** displays a full-screen view of a presentation.

The **Slide Show view** is used to deliver the completed presentation full screen to an audience, one slide at a time, as an electronic presentation on the computer (see Figure 1.16). The slide show can be presented manually, where the speaker clicks the mouse to move from one slide to the next, or automatically, where each slide stays on the screen for a predetermined amount of time, after which the next slide appears. A slide show can contain a combination of both methods for advancing. You can insert transition effects to impact the look of how one slide moves to the next. To view the presentation in Slide Show view, click the View tab and then click Slide Show in the Presentation Views group. This step begins the show with Slide 1. To end the slide show, press Escape on the keyboard.

TIP   Start the Slide Show

To choose whether you start a slide show from the beginning, Slide 1, or from the current slide, click the Slide Show tab, and then click either From Beginning or From Current Slide in the Start Slide Show group.

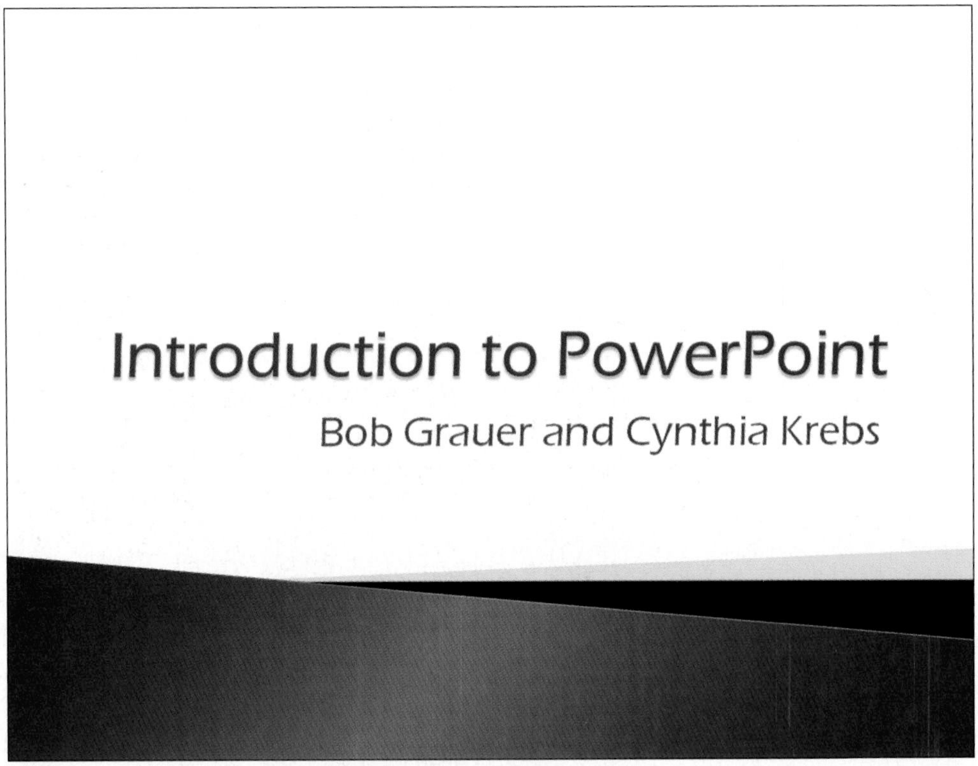

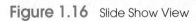

Introduction to PowerPoint
Bob Grauer and Cynthia Krebs

Figure 1.16   Slide Show View

Have you been in an audience watching a presenter use PowerPoint to deliver an electronic presentation? Did the presenter look professional at all times? While this is the desired scenario, consider another real-life scenario—the presenter holds a remote in one hand, printed speaker notes in the other hand, and is wearing a watch. The presenter is conscious of the time allotted for the presentation and attempts to look at the watch to see how much time has elapsed. Using the remote, the presenter attempts to slide a long sleeve up and reveal the watch. The remote catches on the printed speaker notes, the notes start to fall, the presenter grabs to catch them . . . and chaos results. Presenter Fumble lives! You can avoid "Presenter Fumble" by using Presenter view.

(. . . avoid "Presenter Fumble" by using Presenter view!)

Presenter view delivers a presentation on two monitors simultaneously.

Presenter view delivers a presentation on two monitors simultaneously. Typically, one monitor is a projector that delivers the full-screen presentation to the audience and one monitor is a laptop or computer at the presenter's station. Having two monitors enables your audience to see your presentation at the same time you are seeing a special view of the presentation that includes the slide, speaker notes, slide thumbnails so you can jump between slides as needed, navigation arrows that advance your slide or return to the previous slide, options to enable a marking on the slide, and a timer that displays the time elapsed since you began. Figure 1.17 shows the audience view on the left side of the figure and the Presenter view on the right side.

Figure 1.17 Presenter View

In order to use Presenter view, you must use a computer that has multiple monitor capability, and multiple monitor support must be turned on. If you need information about how to enable multiple monitor support, see Microsoft Windows Help. After you enable multiple monitor support, click Show Presenter View in the Monitors group on the Slide Show tab, and then click from Beginning in the Start Slide Show group under the same tab.

Opening and Saving a Slide Show

The Office Button gives you access to an important menu. The available options include the New command so that you can create a new document in this case, a presentation that is blank or that is based upon a template. You use the Open command to retrieve a presentation saved on a storage device and place it in the RAM memory of your computer so you can work on it. The Print command opens a dialog box so that you may choose print settings and then print. The Close command closes the current presentation but leaves PowerPoint open. To exit PowerPoint, click the X located on the top right of the application window.

While you are working on a previously saved presentation, it is being saved in the temporary memory or RAM memory of your computer. The Save As command copies the presentation that you are working on to the hard drive of your computer or to a storage device such as a flash drive. When you activate the Save As command, the Save As dialog box appears (see Figure 1.18). The dialog box requires you to specify the drive or folder in which to store the presentation, the name of the presentation, and the type of file you wish the presentation to be saved as. All subsequent executions of the Save command save the presentation under the assigned name, replacing the previously saved version with the new version. If you wish to change the name of the presentation, use Save As again. Pressing Ctrl+S also displays the Save As dialog box if it is the first time you are saving the slide show.

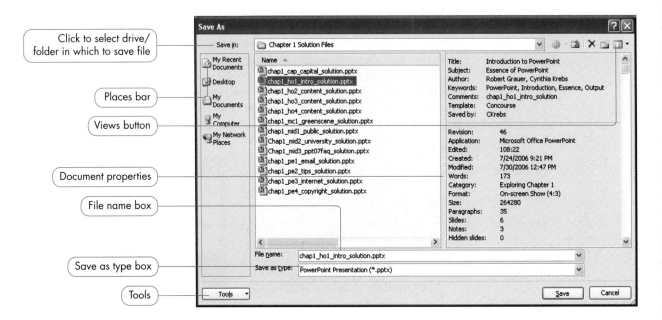

Figure 1.18 Save As Dialog Box

The file name (e.g., chap1_ho1_intro_solution) can contain up to 255 characters including spaces, commas, and/or periods. Periods are discouraged, however, since they are too easily confused with the file extensions explained in the next paragraph. Click the *Save in* drop-down arrow to select the drive and the folder in which the presentation file will be saved.

The file type defaults to a PowerPoint presentation. You can save to other formats including a Web page. When you save a PowerPoint file, it is assigned a .pptx extension. This file type is an XML (eXtensible Markup Language) format. This file format compresses data, which greatly reduces file sizes, thereby saving storage space on your hard drive or storage device. Another benefit of using the XML file format is that it reduces the chance of file corruption and helps you recover corrupted documents. This file format also provides increased security. One caution must be noted, however: Files created in the XML format cannot be opened in earlier versions of Office software unless the Microsoft Compatibility Pack is installed. Your colleagues who share files with you should download the Compatibility Pack on all computers that may be used to open your XML files.

TIP   New Folder Creation

By default, all Office documents are stored in the My Documents folder. It is helpful, however, to create additional folders, especially if you work with a large number of different documents. You can create one folder for school and another for personal work, or you can create different folders for different applications. To create a folder, click the Office Button, select Save As, and then click the Create New Folder button to display the New Folder dialog box. Type the name of the folder, and then click OK to create the folder. The next time you open or save a presentation, use the *Look in* or *Save in* box to navigate to that folder. For this class, you may wish to create a folder with your assignment solutions for each chapter so you can quickly locate them.

The Open command retrieves a copy of an existing presentation into memory, enabling you to work with that presentation. The Open command displays the Open dialog box in which you specify the file name, the drive (and optionally, the folder) that contains the file, and the file type. PowerPoint will then list all files of that type on the designated drive (and folder), enabling you to open the file you want. To aid you in selecting the correct file, click the Views button. The Preview view shows the first slide in a presentation, without having to open the presentation.

TIP   Use the Tools Button for File Management

Both the Open and the Save As dialog boxes contain a Tools button on the bottom left of their dialog boxes. Once you select any existing file and click the Tools button, you can perform basic file management functions. You can delete or rename the file. You also are able to print the file.

Metadata is data that describes other data.

Document properties is the collection of metadata.

The Properties view shows the document *metadata*, or the data that describes the document data. The collection of metadata is referred to as the *document properties*. Author name, keywords, and date created are all examples of metadata displayed in the Properties view. Figure 1.19 shows the Open dialog box in Properties view with the document properties of our sample slideshow displayed.

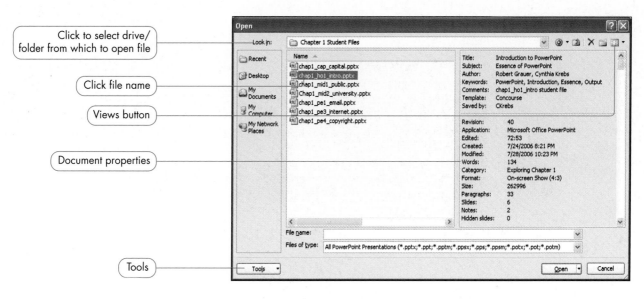

Figure 1.19 Open Dialog Box

TIP Sort by Name, Date, or File Size

The files in the Save As and Open dialog boxes can be displayed in ascending or descending sequence by name, size, file type, or date modified. Change to the Details view, then click the heading of the desired column; for example, click the Modified column to list the files according to the date they were last changed. Click the column heading a second time to reverse the sequence—that is, to switch from ascending to descending, and vice versa.

Getting Help

Microsoft Help is designed to give you all the information you need, whether it is locating information about a specific feature, troubleshooting to solve a problem, searching for software updates, finding a template, or receiving additional training. Help is installed on your computer system at the same time your Office software applications are installed. You can use Help online or offline, depending on whether you are connected to the Internet.

To access Help, you click the Microsoft Office PowerPoint Help button located at the top right of the screen below the Close button. Or, if you prefer, you can use the Help keyboard shortcut by pressing F1. The Help window will appear. This window is designed to make Help easier for you to use. You can navigate and locate information by clicking one of the hyperlinked Help topics, or you can enter a topic in the Search box. The bottom portion of the Help Window gives you access to Office Online where you can obtain clip art, download templates or training, or read articles. Clicking the *Get up to speed with Microsoft Office 2007* hyperlink and then reading the resulting Help screen will help you review the information covered thus far.

Hands-On Exercises

1 | Introduction to PowerPoint

Skills covered: 1. Start PowerPoint **2.** Open an Existing Presentation **3.** Type a Speaker's Note **4.** View the Presentation **5.** Save the Presentation with a New Name **6.** Locate Information Using Help

---

Step 1
Start PowerPoint

a. Click **Start** on your Windows taskbar, and then click **All Programs**.

b. Click **Microsoft Office**, and then click **Microsoft Office PowerPoint 2007**.

You should see a blank PowerPoint presentation in Normal view.

Step 2
Open an Existing Presentation

Refer to Figure 1.20 as you complete Step 2.

a. Click the **Office Button** and select **Open**.

The Open dialog box will appear. Do not be concerned that your file list does not match Figure 1.20.

b. Click the **Look in drop-down arrow**, and then click the appropriate drive depending on the storage location of your data.

c. Double-click the **Exploring PowerPoint folder** to make it active.

This is the folder from which you will retrieve files and into which you will save your assignment solutions.

TROUBLESHOOTING: If you do not see an Exploring PowerPoint folder, it is possible that the student files for this text were saved to a different folder for your class. Check with your instructor to find out where to locate your student files.

d. Click the **Views button** repeatedly to cycle through the different views.

As you cycle through the various views, in the Open dialog box observe the differences in each view. Identify a reason you might use each view. Figure 1.20 is displayed in Preview view.

e. Double-click the *chap1_ho1_intro* presentation.

The slide show opens to the *Introduction to PowerPoint* title slide.

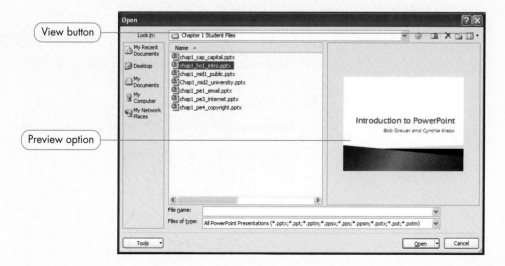

Figure 1.20 Open Dialog Box

Step 3
Type a Speaker's Note

Refer to Figure 1.21 as you complete Step 3.

a. Click the **Slide 4 thumbnail** in the Slides tab.

Slide 4 is selected and the slide appears in the Slide pane.

b. Drag the splitter bar between the Slide pane and the Notes pane upward to create more room in the Notes pane area.

c. Type the following information in the Notes pane: **Among the objects that can be inserted into PowerPoint are tables, clip art, diagrams, charts, hyperlinks, text boxes, headers and footers, movies, sound, and objects from other software packages.**

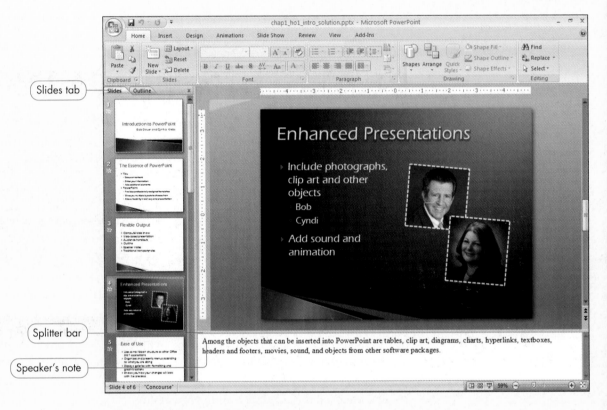

Figure 1.21 Speaker's Note

Step 4
View the Presentation

a. Click **From Beginning** in the Start Slide Show group on the Slide Show tab.

The presentation begins with the title slide, the first slide in all slide shows. The title and subtitle have animations assigned, so they come in automatically.

b. Press **Spacebar** to advance to the second slide.

The text on the second slide wipes down and creates each bullet point.

c. Click the left mouse button to advance to the third slide.

The text on the third slide, and all following slides, has the same animation applied to create consistency in the presentation.

d. Click to advance to the fourth slide, which has sound added to the image animations.

e. Continue to view the show until you come to the end of the presentation.

f. Press **Esc** to return to the PowerPoint Normal view.

Refer to Figure 1.22 as you complete Step 3.

a. Click the **Office Button**, and then select **Save As**.

b. Click the **Save in drop-down arrow**.

c. Click the appropriate drive, depending on where you are storing your data.

d. Double-click the *Exploring PowerPoint* folder to make it the active folder.

   If you have created a different folder to store your solutions, change to that folder.

e. Type **chap1_ho1_intro_solution** as the file name for the presentation.

f. Click **Save**.

TIP   Change the Default Folder

The default folder is where PowerPoint goes initially to open an existing presentation or to save a new presentation. You may find it useful to change the default folder if you are working on your own computer and not in a classroom lab. Click the Office Button, and then select Application Settings, which enables you to modify your document settings and customize how PowerPoint behaves by default. Click Saving from the frame on the left side. Click in the box that contains the default file location, enter the new drive or the new folder where you wish your files to be saved, and click OK. The next time you open or save a file, PowerPoint will go automatically to that location. This feature may not work in a classroom lab, however, if the lab has a "deep freeze" program to ensure students work from default settings.

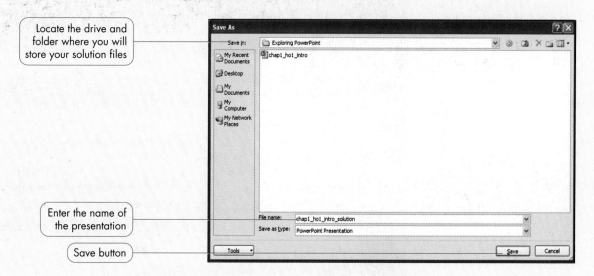

Figure 1.22   Save the Presentation with a New Name

Refer to Figure 1.23 as you complete Step 6.

a. Click **Microsoft Office PowerPoint Help** on the top right side of the screen.

The PowerPoint Help window opens.

TROUBLESHOOTING: If you do not see the same Help viewer as displayed in Figure 1.23, you may not have an active Internet connection. If you do not have an active Internet connection, the Help feature retrieves the Help information that was installed on your computer. Also, because Help Online is a dynamic feature, Microsoft frequently adds content. Each time you open a Help Online topic, you are asked to give Microsoft feedback on the value of the topic. Due to this feature, topics may be added and links changed.

b. Click the *What's New* hyperlink, and then click the *Use the Ribbon* hyperlink.

c. Scroll to the bottom of the Help window until the *See Also* box is visible. Click *Use the keyboard to work with Ribbon programs*, and then read the article on using access keys with the Ribbon.

d. Close Help, and then press **F1** on the keyboard.

F1 is the shortcut for opening Help.

e. Type **print preview** in the Search box, and then click Search.

f. Click *Print a Help topic* and read the article.

g. Close Help, and then close the *chap1_ho1_intro_solution* presentation.

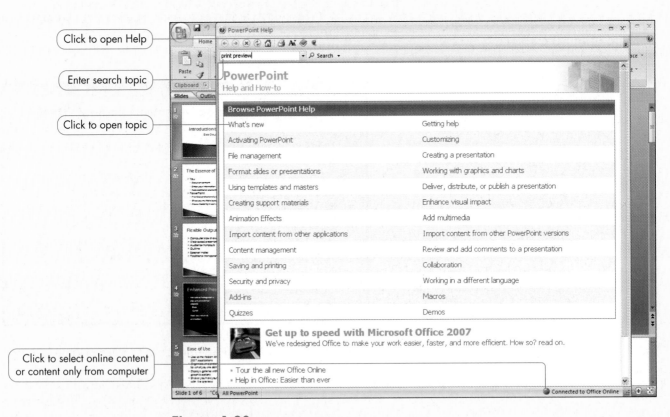

Figure 1.23 The Help Window

Presentation Creation

You are ready to create your own presentation, a process that requires you to develop its content and apply the formatting through the use of a template or design specification. You can do the steps in either order, but by starting with the content, you can concentrate on your message and the structure of your message without getting distracted by the formatting and design of the presentation.

Before you start the presentation in PowerPoint, you can complete several tasks that could make your presentation more effective and save you time.

Before you start the presentation in PowerPoint, you can complete several tasks that could make your presentation more effective and save you time. While you know the topic you are going to present, the way you present it should be tailored to your audience. Research your audience—determine who makes up your audience, what their needs are, and what their expectations are. By tailoring your presentation to the audience, you will have a much more interesting presentation and an involved audience. After researching your audience, begin brainstorming on how to deliver your information and message to the audience. Sketch out your thoughts to help you organize them.

After you have sketched out your thoughts, enter them into the PowerPoint presentation and apply a theme to give your presentation a polished look. Review the presentation for spelling errors and word choice problems so your presentation is professional.

In this section, you create a visual plan known as a storyboard. You learn how to change layouts, apply design themes, and use the Spell Check and the Thesaurus to review your presentation for errors.

Creating a Storyboard

A **storyboard** is a visual plan that displays the content of each slide in the slideshow.

A **storyboard** is a visual plan for your presentation. It can be a very rough draft you sketch out while brainstorming, or it can be an elaborate plan that includes the text and objects drawn as they would appear on a slide. The complexity of your storyboard is your choice, but the key point is that the storyboard helps you plan the direction of your presentation. Remember the old adage, "If you don't know where you are going, you are going to end up somewhere else!"

A simple PowerPoint storyboard is divided into sections representing individual slides. The first block in the storyboard is used for the title slide. The title slide should have a short title that indicates the purpose of the presentation and introduces the speaker. Try to capture the title in two to five words. The speaker introduction information is usually included in a subtitle and can include the speaker's name and title, the speaker's organization, the organization's logo, and the date of the presentation.

While a title slide may serve as the introduction, having a separate introduction sets a professional tone for the presentation. The introduction should get the audience's attention and convince them your presentation will be worth their time. Creating an agenda showing the topics to be covered in the presentation can serve as an introduction because as you review the agenda with the audience you start them thinking about the topics. Often, presenters use a thought-provoking quotation or question as the introduction, and pause for a short time to give the audience time to think. An image can be particularly moving if it relates to the topic and is displayed in silence for a moment. The presenter may then introduce the idea behind the image or question the audience to extract the meaning of the image from them, thereby inducing the audience to introduce the topic.

Following the title slide and the introduction, you have slides containing the main body of information you want your audience to have. Each key thought deserves a slide, and on that slide, text bullets or other objects should develop that key thought. When preparing these slides, ask yourself what you want your audience to know that they did not know before. Ask yourself what it is you want them to remember. Create the slides to answer these questions and support these main points on the slides with facts, examples, charts or graphs, illustrations, images, or video clips.

Finally, end your presentation with a summary or conclusion. This is your last chance to get your message across to your audience. It should review main points, restate the purpose of the presentation, or invoke a call to action. The summary will solidify your purpose with the audience. Remember the old marketing maxim, "Tell 'em what you're going to tell 'em, tell 'em, then tell 'em what you told 'em,"—or in other words, "Introduction, Body, Conclusion."

After you create the storyboard, review what you wrote. Now is a good time to edit your text. Shorten complete sentences to phrases. As you present, you can expand on the information shown on the slide. The phrases on the slide help your audience organize the information in their minds. Edit phrases to use as bullet points. Review and edit the phrases so they begin with an active voice when possible to involve the user. Active voice uses action verbs—action verbs ACT! Passive verbs can be recognized by the presence of linking verbs (is, am, are, was, were).

TIP The "7 x 7" Guideline

Keep the information on your slide concise. The slide is merely a tool to help your audience "chuck into memory" the information you give. Your delivery will cover the detail. To help you remember to stay concise, follow the 7 x 7 guideline that suggests you limit the words on a visual to no more than seven words per line and seven lines per slide. This guideline gives you a total of 49 or fewer words per slide. While you may be forced to exceed this guideline on occasion, follow it as often as possible.

After you complete your planning, you are ready to prepare your PowerPoint presentation. Now instead of wasting computer time trying to decide what to say, you spend your computer time entering information, formatting, and designing. Figure 1.24 shows a working copy of a storyboard for planning presentation content. The storyboard is in rough draft form and shows changes made during the review process. The PowerPoint presentation (Figure 1.25) incorporates the changes.

Presentation Storyboard

Purpose of Presentation: *Educational presentation*

Audience: *IAAP membership*   Location: *Marriott Hotel*   Date: *9/20/08*

Content	Layout	Visual Element(s)
Title Slide *Planning Before Creating a Presentation Content*	*Title Slide*	○ Shapes ○ Chart ○ Table ○ WordArt ○ Picture ○ Movie ○ Clip Art ○ Sound ○ SmartArt ○ _____ *Description:*
Introduction (Key Points, Quote, Image, Other) *"If you don't know where you are going, you might end up someplace else" Casey Stengel*	*Section Header ? ? ?*	○ Shapes ○ Chart ○ Table ○ WordArt ○ Picture ○ Movie ◉ Clip Art ○ Sound ○ SmartArt ○ _____ *Description: Stengel pic* *Confusion image*
Support for Key Point #1 *Identify Purpose* *Selling (E-Commerce) Persuading Informing Advertising Building Good Will Entertaining Educating Motivation*	*Two Content*	○ Shapes ○ Chart ○ Table ○ WordArt ○ Picture ○ Movie ○ Clip Art ○ Sound ○ SmartArt ○ _____ *Description:*
Support for Key Point #2 *Define Audience* *Who is going to be in the audience?* *What are the audience's expectations?* *How much do they audience already know?*	*Title & Content*	○ Shapes ○ Chart ○ Table ○ WordArt ◉ Picture ○ Movie ○ Clip Art ○ Sound ○ SmartArt ○ _____ *Description: Audience pic*
Support for Key Point #3 *Develop the Content* *Brainstorm and write ideas down* *Research the topic and take notes* *Storyboard a rough draft and then refine*	*Title & Content*	○ Shapes ○ Chart ○ Table ○ WordArt ○ Picture ○ Movie ○ Clip Art ○ Sound ○ SmartArt ○ _____ *Description: SmartArt*
Support for Key Point #4 *Edit the Content* *Shorten the text from sentences* *Phrases make it concise* *Make bullets parallel + use active verbs*	*Title & Content*	○ Shapes ○ Chart ○ Table ○ WordArt ○ Picture ○ Movie ○ Clip Art ○ Sound ○ SmartArt ○ _____ *Description:*
Summary (Restatement of Key Points, Quote, Other) *The key to an effective presentation is planning ahead.*	*Title*	○ Shapes ○ Chart ○ Table ○ WordArt ○ Picture ○ Movie ◉ Clip Art ○ Sound ○ SmartArt ○ _____ *Description: Key*

Title slide — Title Slide
Introduction — Introduction (Key Points, Quote, Image, Other)
Key topics with main points — Support for Key Points
Conclusion — Summary

Figure 1.24 Rough Draft Storyboard

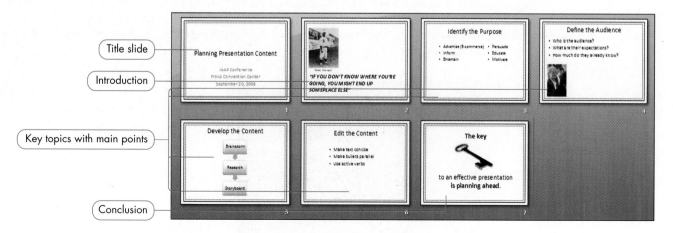

Title slide
Introduction
Key topics with main points
Conclusion

Figure 1.25 Presentation from Storyboard

Presentation Creation | **PowerPoint 2007**   **1149**

Using Slide Layouts

When you first begin a new slide show, PowerPoint presents you with a slide for use as a title slide. New slides from that point on are typically created as content slides, consisting of a slide title and a defined area for content. You can enter content in the defined area or add new elements manually. If the slide arrangement does not meet your needs, you can change it by changing the slide layout.

A slide *layout* determines the position of objects containing content on the slide.

PowerPoint provides a set of predefined slide *layouts* that determine the position of the objects or content on a slide. Slide layouts contain any number and combination of placeholders, and are available each time you click New Slide on the Home tab. When you click New Slide, the gallery of layouts is displayed for you to choose from. All of the layouts except the Blank layout include placeholders. *Placeholders* hold content and determine the position of the objects, or content, on the slide. After you select the layout, you simply click the appropriate placeholder to add the content you desire. Thus, you would click the placeholder for the title and enter the text of the title as indicated. In similar fashion, you click the placeholder for text and enter the associated text. By default, the text appears as bullets. You can change the size and position of the placeholders by moving the placeholders just as you would any object.

A *placeholder* is a container that holds content and is used in the layout to determine the position of objects on the slide.

Applying Design Themes

PowerPoint enables you to concentrate on the content of a presentation without concern for its appearance. You focus on what you are going to say, and then utilize PowerPoint features to format the presentation attractively. The simplest method to format a slide show is to select a design theme. A design *theme* is a collection of formatting choices that includes colors, fonts, and special theme effects such as shadowing or glows. PowerPoint designers have created beautiful design themes for your use, and the themes are available in other Office applications, which lets you unify all of the documents you create.

A *theme* is a set of design elements that gives the slide show a unified, professional appearance.

When you apply a theme, the formatting implements automatically. To select and apply a theme, click the Design tab and click the More button in the Themes group. From the Themes gallery that appears, choose the theme you like. PowerPoint formats the entire presentation according to the theme you choose. Do not be afraid to apply new themes. As you gain experience with PowerPoint and design, you can rely less on PowerPoint and more on your own creativity for your design. Figures 1.26–1.29 show a title slide with four different themes applied. Note the color, font, and text alignment in each theme.

Figure 1.26 Opulent Theme

Figure 1.27 Urban Theme

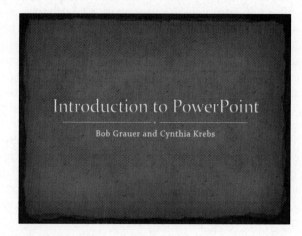

Figure 1.28 Paper Theme

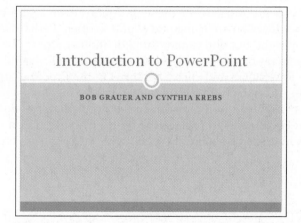

Figure 1.29 Civic Theme

Reviewing the Presentation

After you create the presentation, check for spelling errors and incorrect word usage. This step can be done before or after you apply the design theme, but sometimes applying the theme before checking for spelling errors helps you see errors you did not see before. It gives you a fresh look at the slide, which helps you revisualize what is displaying.

Check Spelling

The first step to checking your spelling is to visually check the slide after you create the text in the placeholders. A red wavy line under a word indicates that a word is misspelled. In the case of a proper name, the word may be spelled correctly but is not in the standard dictionary shared by the software in the Microsoft Office suite. In either event, point to the underlined word and click the right mouse button to display a shortcut menu. Select the appropriate spelling from the list of suggestions. If the word does not appear in the list of suggestions, you can add the word to the *custom dictionary*, a supplemental dictionary Microsoft Office uses to store items such as proper names, acronyms, or specialized words for your business or industry.

A *custom dictionary* is a supplemental dictionary Microsoft Office uses to store items such as proper names, acronyms, or specialized words.

After you complete the presentation and have visually checked each slide, use PowerPoint's Spelling feature to check the entire presentation again. Click the Review tab, and then click Spelling in the Proofing group. If a word does not appear in the dictionary, the Spelling dialog box appears. Use the options on the right side to choose whether you wish to accept the word and resume spell checking, ignore all occurrences of the word, change the word to one of the listed choices, add the word to your custom dictionary, look at other suggested spellings, add the word to AutoCorrect, or close the dialog box.

Finally, display the presentation in Slide Show view and read each word on each slide out loud. Reading the words in the Slide Show view eliminates the distractions in PowerPoint's creation screen and enables you to concentrate fully on the text. Although the Spelling feature is a valuable tool, it does **NOT** catch commonly misused words like to, too, and two, or for, fore, and four. While proofreading three times may seem excessive to you, if you ever flash a misspelled word before an audience in full Slide Show view, you will wish you had taken the time to proofread carefully. Nothing is more embarrassing and can make you seem less professional than a misspelled word enlarged on a big screen for your audience so they cannot miss it.

Use the Thesaurus

As you proofread your presentation, or even while you are creating it, you may notice that you are using one word too often. Perhaps you find a word that does not seem right, but you cannot think of another word. The Thesaurus, which gives you synonyms or words with the same meaning, is ideal to use in these situations. Click the Review tab and click Thesaurus in the Proofing group. The Research task pane appears on the right side of the screen and displays synonyms for the selected word. Point to the desired replacement key, click the drop-down arrow to display a menu, and click Insert to replace the word. Click Undo on the Quick Access Toolbar to return to the original text if you prefer the original word.

 TIP   The Research Task Pane

Microsoft Office 2007 brings the resources of the Web directly into the application. Click Research in the Proofing group on the Review tab. Type the entry you are searching for, click the down arrow to choose a reference book, and then click the green arrow to initiate the search. You have access to reference, research, business, and financial sites. You even have an online bilingual dictionary. Research has never been easier.

Hands-On Exercises

2 | Creating a Presentation

Skills covered: 1. Create a New Presentation **2.** Add Slides **3.** Check Spelling and Use the Thesaurus **4.** Modify Text and Layout **5.** Reorder Slides **6.** Apply a Design Theme

---

<table>
<tr>
<td>

Step 1

Create a New Presentation

</td>
<td>

Refer to Figure 1.30 as you complete Step 1.

a. Click the **Office Button**, select **New**, and then double-click **Blank Presentation**.

PowerPoint opens with a new blank presentation.

b. Click inside the placeholder containing the *Click to add title* prompt, and then type the presentation title **Creating Presentation Content**.

c. Click inside the placeholder containing the *Click to add subtitle* prompt and enter your name.

Type your name as it shows on the class roll. Do not enter a nickname or the words *Your Name*.

d. Click in the Notes pane and type today's date and the name of the course for which you are creating this slide show.

e. Save the presentation as **chap1_ho2_content_solution**.

</td>
</tr>
</table>

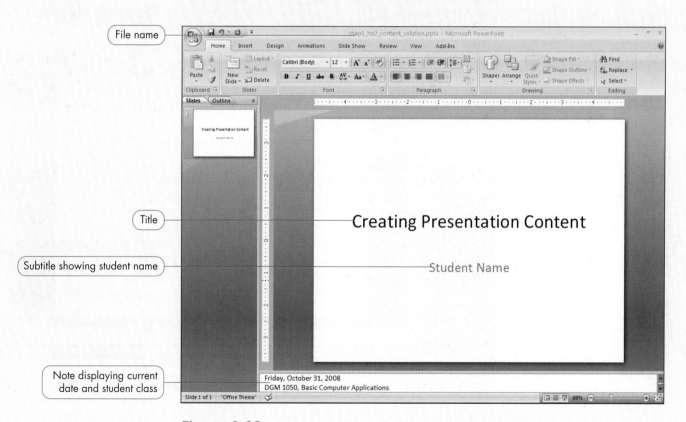

Figure 1.30 Creating Presentation Content Title Slide

Refer to Figure 1.31 as you complete Step 2.

a. Click **New Slide** in the Slides group on the Home tab.

b. Select the **Title and Content** layout from the gallery.

Slide 2 is created with two placeholders: one for the title and one for body content. You can insert an object by clicking on the bar in the center of the content placeholder, or you can enter bullets by typing text in the placeholder.

c. Type **Simplify the Content** in the title placeholder.

d. Click in the content placeholder and type **Use one main concept per slide**, and then press **Enter**.

e. Type **Use the 7 x 7 guideline** and press **Enter** again.

f. Click **Increase List Level** in the Paragraph group on the Home tab.

Clicking Increase List Level creates a new bullet level that you can use for detail related to the main bullet. If you wish to return to the main bullet level, click Decrease List Level.

g. Type **Limit slide to seven or fewer lines** and press **Enter**.

h. Type **Limit lines to seven or fewer words**.

i. Save the *chap1_ho2_content_solution* presentation.

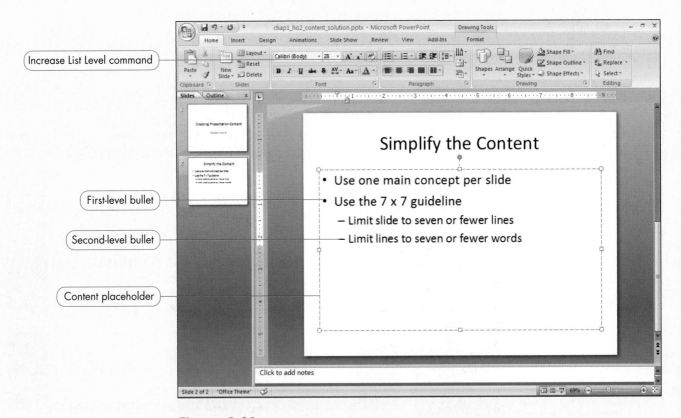

Figure 1.31 New Slide

Refer to Figure 1.32 as you complete Step 3.

a. Use the **New Slide** command to create four more slides with the Title and Content layout.

b. Type the following text in the appropriate slide.

Slide	Slide Title	Level 1 Bullets	Level 2 Bullets
3	Define the Audience	Who is the audience? What are their needs? What are their expectations? How much do they already know? How can you help them understand message?	
4	Develop the Content	Identify purpose Research topic Brainstorm Create storyboard	Title slide Introduction Key points Conclusion
5	Edit the Content	Make text concise Use consistent verb tense Utilize strong active verbs Eliminate excess adverbs and adjectives Use few prepositions	
6		The key to an effective presentation is planning ahead!	

c. Click **Spelling** in the Proofing group on the Review tab.

The result of the spelling check depends on how accurately you entered the text of the presentation. If the spell checker locates a word not in its dictionary, you will be prompted to resume checking, change the word, ignore the word in that occurrence or in all occurrences, or add the word to your dictionary so it is not identified as misspelled in the future. Select one of these options, and then continue checking the presentation for spelling errors, if necessary.

d. Move to **Slide 2** and click anywhere within the word *main*.

e. Click **Thesaurus** in the Proofing group on the Review tab.

The Research task pane opens and displays a list of synonyms from which to choose a replacement word.

f. Point to the word *key*, click the drop-down arrow, and click **Insert**.

The word *main* is replaced with the word *key*.

TROUBLESHOOTING: If you click the replacement word in the Research pane list instead of clicking the drop-down arrow and choosing Insert, the replacement word you clicked will replace the original word in the Search for box, and the Research pane changes to display the synonyms of the replacement word. The word in your presentation will not change.

g. Save the *chap1_ho2_content_solution* presentation.

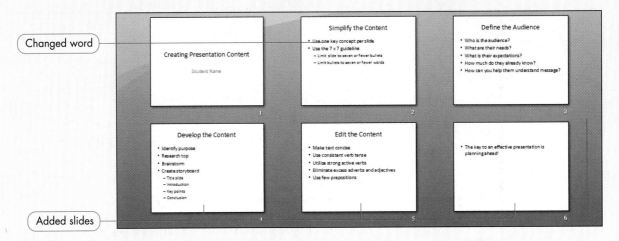

Changed word

Added slides

Figure 1.32 Proofed Slide Show

<table>
<tr><td>

Step 4
Modify Text and Layout

</td><td>

Refer to Figure 1.33 as you complete Step 4.

a. Click the **Slide 6 thumbnail** in the Slide tab pane.

You wish to end the slide show with a statement emphasizing the importance of planning. You created the statement in a content placeholder in a slide using the Title and Content layout. You decide to modify the text and layout of the slide to give the statement more emphasis.

b. Click the **Home tab** and click **Layout** in the Slides group.

c. Click **Title Slide**.

The layout for Slide 6 changes to the Title Slide layout. Layouts can be used on any slide in a slide show if their format meets your needs.

d. Click the border of the Title placeholder, press **Delete** twice on the keyboard, and then drag the Subtitle placeholder containing your text upward until it is slightly above the center of your slide.

The layout in Slide 6 has now been modified.

e. Drag across the text in the subtitle placeholder to select it, and then move your pointer upwards until the Mini toolbar appears.

f. Click **Bold**, and then click **Italic** on the Mini toolbar.

Using the Mini toolbar to modify text is much faster than moving back and forth to the commands in the Font group on the Home tab to make changes.

g. Save the *chap1_ho2_content_solution* presentation.

</td></tr>
</table>

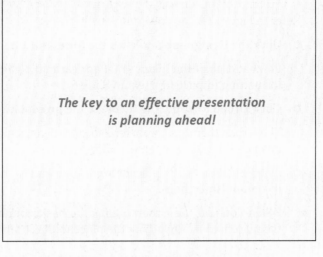

Figure 1.33 Slide with Modified Text and Layout

Refer to Figure 1.34 as you complete Step 5.

a. Click the **View tab** and click **Slide Sorter** in the Presentation Views group.

The view changes to thumbnail views of the slides in the slide show with the current slide surrounded by a heavy border to indicate it is selected. Your view may differ from Figure 1.34 depending on what your zoom level is set at. Notice that the slides do not follow logical order. The Slide Sorter view is ideal for checking the logical sequence of slides and for changing slide position if necessary.

b. Select **Slide 2**, and then drag it so that it becomes Slide 5, the slide before the summary slide.

As you drag Slide 2 to the right, the pointer becomes a move cursor and a vertical bar appears to indicate the position of the slide when you drop it. After you drop the slide, all slides renumber.

c. Double-click **Slide 6**.

Double-clicking a slide in the Slide Sorter view returns you to Normal view.

d. Save the *chap1_ho2_content_solution* presentation.

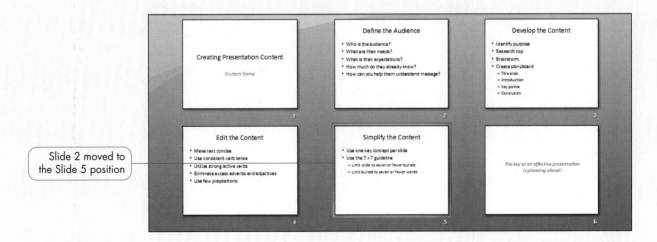

Slide 2 moved to the Slide 5 position

Figure 1.34 Reordered Slide Show

Step 6
Apply a Design Theme

Refer to Figure 1.35 as you complete Step 6.

a. Click the **Design tab** and click the **More button** in the Themes group.

Point at each of the themes that appear in the gallery and note how the theme formatting impacts the text in Slide 6.

b. Click **Urban** to apply the theme to the presentation.

The Urban theme is characterized by a clean, simple background with a business-like color scheme, making it a good choice for this presentation.

c. Drag the Slide 6 Title placeholder down and to the left, and then resize it so that it contains three lines.

When you add the Urban theme, the background of the theme hides the text in the placeholder. You adjust the placeholder location and size to fit the theme.

TROUBLESHOOTING: You may not see the Title placeholder on Slide 6. However, click in the middle of the dark gray area of the slide. The sizing handles appear around the placeholder when you click it. Then you can click and drag the placeholder into its new location specified by Step 6c.

d. Save the *chap1_ho2_content_solution* presentation. Close the file and exit PowerPoint if you do not want to continue to the next exercise at this time.

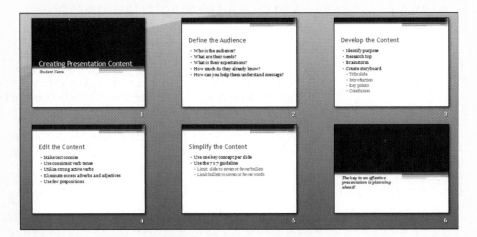

Figure 1.35 Slide Show with Urban Theme Applied

Presentation Development

Thus far, our presentation is strictly text. You can strengthen your slide show by adding objects that relate to the message. PowerPoint enables you to include a variety of visual objects to add impact to your presentation. You can add clip art, images, WordArt, sound, animated clips, or video clips to increase your presentation's impact. You can add tables, charts and graphs, and diagrams to provide more information for the audience. These objects can be created in PowerPoint, or you can insert objects that were created in other applications, such as a chart from Microsoft Excel or a table from Microsoft Word.

> (*... clip art, images, WordArt, sound, animated clips, or video clips ... increase your presentation's impact.*)

In this section, you add a table to organize data in columns and rows. Then you insert clip art objects that relate to your topics. You move and resize the clip art to position it attractively on the slide. Finally, you apply transitions to your slide to control how one slide changes to another, and you apply animations to your text and clip art to help maintain your audience's attention.

Adding a Table

A **table** is an illustration that places information in columns and rows.

A **table** is an illustration that places information in columns and rows. Tables are a great way for you to present related information in an orderly manner. Tables can be simple and include just words or images, or they can be complex and include a great deal of structured numerical data. Because tables organize information for the viewer, they are a great way to augment your presentation.

You can add a table to your presentation by creating it in PowerPoint or by reusing a table created in Word or Excel. In this chapter, you create a basic table in PowerPoint. To create a table, you can select the Title and Content layout and then click the Table icon on the Content bar, or you can select the Title Only layout and click the Insert tab and then click Table in the Tables group. These two options create the table with slightly different sizing, however. Figure 1.36 shows the same data entered into tables created in each of these ways.

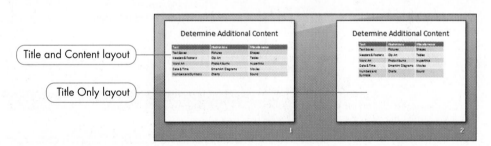

Figure 1.36 Table Layout

Inserting Clip Art

In addition to inserting tables from the Insert tab, you can insert other objects and media in your presentation. From the Illustrations group, click Picture and browse to locate a picture or image that has been saved to a storage device, click Clip Art to insert clip art from the Microsoft Clip Organizer, click Photo Album to create a photo album from images you have saved, click Shape to insert a shape, click SmartArt to insert a diagram, or click Chart to insert a chart.

A **clip** is any media object that you can insert in a document.

In this chapter, you concentrate on adding clip art from the Microsoft Clip Organizer, although inserting other types of clips uses the same procedure. The Microsoft Clip Organizer contains a variety of **clips**, or media objects such as clip art, photographs, movies, or sounds, that may be inserted in a presentation. The Microsoft Clip Organizer brings order by cataloging the clips that are available to you. Clips installed locally are cataloged in the My Collections folder; clips installed in conjunction with Office are cataloged in the Office Collections folder; and clips downloaded from the Web are cataloged in the Web Collections folder. If you are connected to the Internet, clips located in Microsoft Online also display in the Clip Organizer. You can insert a specific clip into your presentation if you know its location, or you can search for a clip that will enhance your presentation.

To search for a clip, you enter a keyword that describes the clip you are looking for, specify the collections that are to be searched, and indicate the type of clip(s) you are looking for. The results are displayed in the Clip Art task pane, as shown in Figure 1.37. This figure shows clips that were located using the keyword *key*. The example searches all collections for all media types to return the greatest number of potential clips. When you point to a clip displaying in the gallery, the clip's keywords, an indication if the clip is scaleable, the clip's file size, and file format appear. When you see the clip that you want to use, point to the clip, click the drop-down arrow, and then click the Insert command from the resulting menu. You also can click the clip to insert it in the center of the slide, or drag the clip onto the slide.

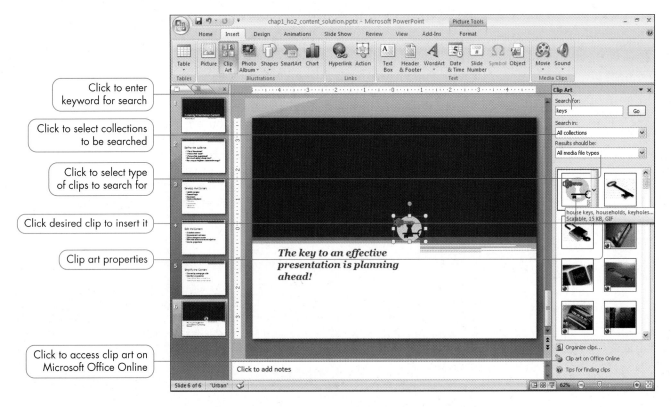

Figure 1.37 Clip Art Task Pane

TIP   Reorganizing Clip Collections

You can access the Microsoft Clip Organizer (to view the various collections) by clicking the Organize clips link at the bottom of the task pane. You also can access the Clip Organizer outside of PowerPoint by clicking the Start button on the task bar, and then clicking All Programs, Microsoft Office, Microsoft Office Tools, and Microsoft Clip Organizer. Once in the Organizer, you can search through the clips in the various collections, reorganize the existing collections, add new collections, and even add new clips (with their associated keywords) to the collections.

Move and Resize Clip Art

Just like any Windows object, clip art can be moved and sized. When you click the clip art, the clip art displays editing handles. Position the mouse pointer inside the boundaries of the handles, and it will change to a four-headed arrow. While the pointer has this shape, you can drag the clip art image to a new location. When you position the mouse pointer on one of the editing handles, a double-headed arrow appears. Use this arrow to resize the image. Dragging one of the corner handles resizes the image and keeps it in proportion. Dragging one of the interior handles distorts the image's width or height. Figure 1.38 shows the clip dragged to a new position.

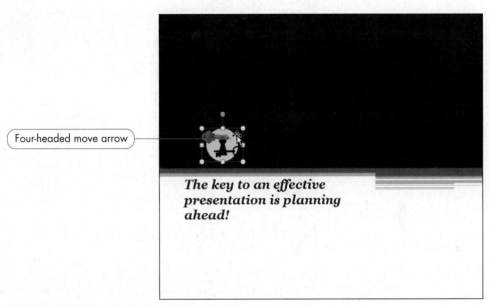

Four-headed move arrow

The key to an effective presentation is planning ahead!

Figure 1.38 Repositioned Clip Art

Using Transitions and Animations

You have successfully created a PowerPoint presentation, but the most important step is yet to come—the delivery of the presentation to an audience. Typically, the slide show is projected on a screen through a projection device. While the slide show is being displayed, the slides change. This process can be enhanced through the use of *transitions*, or movement special effects that take place as you move from slide to slide while in Slide Show view.

A *transition* is a movement special effect that takes place as one slide replaces another in Slide Show view.

An *animation* is movement applied to individual elements on a single slide.

While transitions apply to the slide as a whole and control the way a slide moves onto the screen, *animations* are movements that control the entrance, emphasis, path, and/or exit of individual objects on a single slide. Multiple animations can be applied to a single object. Animating objects can help focus the audience's attention on an important point, can control the flow of information on a slide, and can help you keep the audience's attention.

Apply Transitions and Animations

Transition special effects include fades and dissolves, wipes, push and cover, stripes and bars, and random effects. The gallery in Figure 1.39 displays the available transition effects. The Transition Gallery contains 58 transitions. To display the Transitions Gallery, click the More button in the Transitions To This Slide group on the Animations tab. To see the effect of a transition on the slide, point to a transition in the Transitions Gallery to see the Live Preview, which shows how the change will affect the slide show before you select the transition.

Figure 1.39 The Transitions Gallery

After you choose the effect you desire, you can select a sound to play when the transition takes effect and you can select a speed for the transition. If you wish the transition to impact all slides, click Apply to All in the Transition to This Slide group on the Animations tab. Click Preview Slide Show in the Preview group on the Animations tab to move directly to the show and see what you have accomplished. (Transition effects also can be applied from the Slide Sorter view, where you can apply the same transition to multiple slides by selecting the slides prior to applying the effect.)

Another determination you must make is how you want to start the transition process. Do you want to manually click or press a key to advance to the next slide or do you want the slide to automatically advance after a specified number of seconds? The Advance Slide options in the Transition To This Slide group enable you to determine if you want to mouse click to advance or if you want the slide to advance automatically. You set the number of seconds for the slide to display in the same area.

> ### TIP Effectively Adding Media Objects
>
> When you select your transitions, sounds, and animations, remember that a presentation is not a high-speed music video. Too many transition and animation styles are distracting. The audience wonders what is coming next rather than paying attention to your message. Transitions that are too fast or too slow can lose the interest of the audience. Slow transitions will bore your audience while you stand there saying, "The next slide will load soon." Too many sound clips can be annoying. Consider whether you need to have the sound of applause with the transition of every slide. Is a typewriter sound necessary to keep your audience's attention or will it grate on their nerves if it is used on every set. Ask a classmate to review your presentation and let you know if there are annoying or jarring elements.

Animate Objects

You can animate objects such as text, clip art, diagrams, charts, sound, and hyperlinks. You can apply a preset **animation scheme**, which is a built-in, standard animation created by Microsoft to simplify the animation process, or you can apply a **custom animation** where you determine the animation effect, the speed for the effect, the properties of the effect, and the way the animation begins. The properties available with animations are determined by the animation type. For example, if you choose a wipe animation effect, you can determine the direction property. If you choose a color wave effect, you can determine the color to be added to the object.

To apply an animation scheme, select the object you want to animate, click the Animations tab, and then click the Animate down arrow in the Animations group. A list of animation schemes opens. If you have text selected, options will appear for you to choose how you wish the text to animate.

To apply a custom animation to an object, select the object that you want to animate, and then click Custom Animation in the Animations group on the Animations tab. In the Custom Animation task pane, click Add Effect. Point to Entrance, Emphasis, Exit, or Motion Paths. Select an effect from the resulting list. Once the effect has been selected, you can determine the start, property, and speed of the transition. In this chapter, you will apply an animation scheme and a basic custom animation.

The slide in Figure 1.40 shows an animation effect added to the title and the subtitle. The title will animate first, because it was selected first. A tag with the number one is attached to the placeholder to show it is first. The subtitle animates next, and a tag with the number 2 is attached to the subtitle placeholder. Examine the Custom Animation task pane and note the effect that was added to the subtitle, the way it will start, the direction and the speed of the animation.

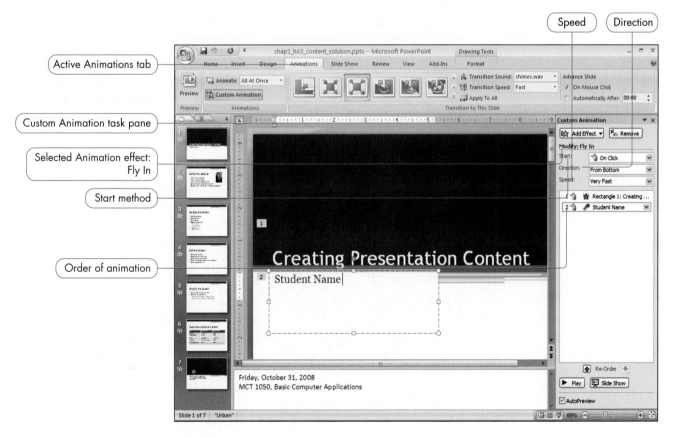

Figure 1.40 The Custom Animation Task Pane

3 | Strengthening a Presentation

Skills covered: **1.** Add a Table **2.** Insert, Move, and Resize Clip Art **3.** Apply a Transition **4.** Animate Objects

Step 1 **Add a Table**	Refer to Figure 1.41 as you complete Step 1.

a. Open the *chap1_ho2_content_solution* presentation if you closed it after the last exercise, and then save it as **chap1_ho3_content_solution**.

b. Move to **Slide 5**, click the **Home tab**, and click **New Slide** in the Slides group.

c. Click the **Title and Content** layout.

A new slide with the Title and Content layout is inserted after Slide 5.

d. Click inside the title placeholder and type **Determine Additional Content**.

e. Click the **Insert Table icon** on the toolbar in the center of the content placeholder.

The Insert Table dialog box appears for you to enter the number of columns and the number of rows you desire.

f. Type **3** for the number of columns and **6** for the number of rows.

PowerPoint creates the table and positions it on the slide. The first row of the table is formatted differently from the other rows so that it can be used for column headings.

g. Click in the top left cell of the table and type **Text**. Press **Tab** to move to the next cell and type **Illustrations**. Press **Tab**, and then type **Miscellaneous** in the last heading cell.

h. Type the following text in the remaining table cells.

Text Boxes	Pictures	Shapes
Headers & Footers	Clip Art	Tables
WordArt	Photo Albums	Hyperlinks
Date & Time	SmartArt Diagrams	Movies
Symbols	Charts	Sound

i. Save the *chap1_ho3_content_solution* presentation.

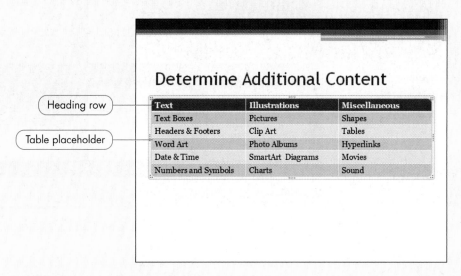

Figure 1.41 PowerPoint Table

Refer to Figure 1.42 as you complete Step 2.

a. Move to **Slide 2**, click the **Insert tab**, and click **Clip Art** in the Illustrations tab group.

b. Type **groups** in the *Search for* box. Make sure the *Search in* box is set to **All collections**.

c. Click the down arrow next to *Results should be*, deselect all options except Photographs, and then click **Go**.

d. Refer to Figure 1.42 to determine the group image to select, and then click the image to insert it in Slide 2.

If you cannot locate the image in Figure 1.42, select another group photograph that looks like an audience.

e. Position your pointer in the center of the image and drag the image to the top right of the slide so that the top of the image touches the bars.

f. Position your pointer over the bottom-left sizing handle of the image and drag inward to reduce the size of the photograph.

The photograph is too large. Not only is it overpowering the text, it is blocking text so that it cannot be read. As you drag the sizing handle inward, all four borders are reduced equally so the photograph no longer touches the bars.

g. If necessary, reposition the clip art image so that it is positioned attractively on the slide.

h. Move to **Slide 7**, change the keyword to **keys**, change the results to show **All media types**, and then click **OK**.

i. Refer to Figure 1.42 to determine the keys clip to select, and then click the image to insert it in Slide 7. Close the Clip Art task pane.

j. Reposition the clip so that it is over the word *key* but do not resize it.

This clip is an animated move clip. If it is enlarged, the image will become pixelated and unattractive.

k. Save the *chap1_ho3_content_solution* presentation.

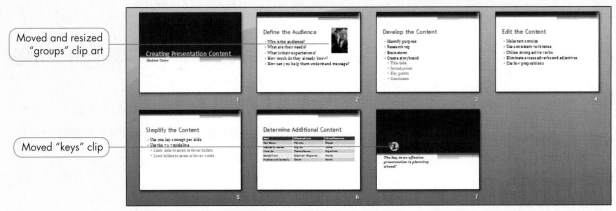

Moved and resized "groups" clip art

Moved "keys" clip

Figure 1.42 Inserted Clip Art

Step 3
Apply a Transition

Refer to Figure 1.43 as you complete Step 3.

a. Click the **Animations tab** and click **More** in the Transitions To This Slide group.

b. Point at several of the transition effects to see how they impact the slide, and then click the **Box Out** wipe transition.

c. Click **Apply To All** in the Transitions To This Slide group on the Animation tab.

The Apply To All will apply the transition set for the current slide to all slides in the slide show.

d. Move to **Slide 1**, click the **Transition Sound down arrow** in the Transitions To This Slide group on the Animations tab, and then click **Chimes**.

The Chimes sound will play as Slide 1 enters. Presenters often use a sound or an audio clip to focus the audience's attention on the screen as the presentation begins.

e. Click **Preview** in the Preview group on the Animations tab.

Because Slide 1 is active, you hear the chimes sound as the Box Out transition occurs.

TROUBLESHOOTING: If you are completing this activity in a classroom lab, you may need to plug in headphones or turn on speakers to hear the sound.

f. Click the **View tab** and click **Slide Sorter** in the Presentation Views group.

Notice the small star beneath each slide. The star indicates a transition has been applied to the slide.

g. Click any of the stars to see a preview of the transition applied to that slide.

h. Save the *chap1_ho3_content_solution* presentation.

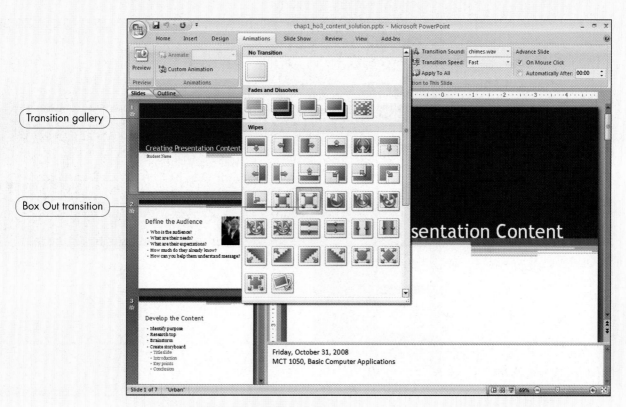

Figure 1.43 The Transition Gallery

Step 4
Animate Objects

Refer to Figure 1.44 as you complete Step 4.

a. Double-click **Slide 1** to open it in Normal view, and then select the Title placeholder.

b. Click the **Animations tab** and click the **Animate down arrow** in the Animations group.

c. Click **Fade**.

The Fade animation scheme is applied to the Title placeholder. The title placeholder dissolves into the background until it is fully visible.

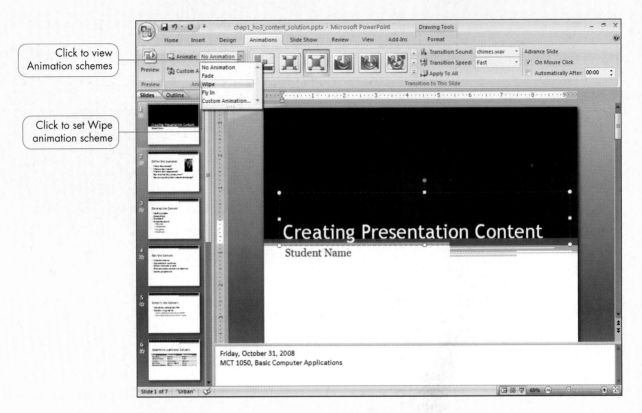

Click to view Animation schemes

Click to set Wipe animation scheme

Creating Presentation Content
Student Name

Friday, October 31, 2008
MCT 1050, Basic Computer Applications

Figure 1.44 Object Animation schemes

d. Select the Subtitle placeholder on Slide 1, and then click the **Animate dropdown arrow** in the Animations group on the Animations tab.

e. Click the **All at once** button located under Fly In.

f. Move to **Slide 2** and select the photograph.

You decide to use a custom animation on the photograph so that you can have more animation choices and can control the speed with which the photograph animates.

g. Click **Custom Animation** in the Animations group on the Animations tab.

The Custom Animation task pane opens, which enables you to add an animation effect to the selected object.

h. Click the **Add Effect button**, point at **Entrance**, and then click **More Effects** from the animation list.

The Add Entrance Effect dialog box appears. The animation effects are separated into categories: Basic, Subtle, Moderate, and Exciting.

i. Scroll down and select **Curve Up** in the Exciting category.

A preview of the Curve Up animation plays, but the dialog box remains open so that you can continue previewing animations until you find the one you like. Experiment with the Entrance Effects so you can see the impact they will have.

j. Select **Boomerang**, and then click **OK**.

k. Click the **Start drop-down arrow**, and then select **After Previous**.

You can choose to start the animation with a mouse click, or by having the animation start automatically. If you wish to begin the animation automatically, you can choose to have it begin at the same time as a previous animation by selecting Start With Previous, or having it begin after a previous animation by selecting Start After Previous.

l. Click the **Speed drop-down arrow**, and then click **Medium**.

m. Save the *chap1_ho3_content_solution* presentation. Close the file and exit PowerPoint if you do not want to continue to the next exercise at this time.

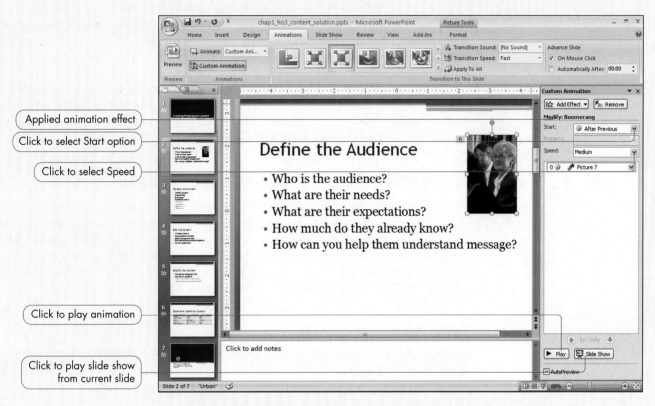

Figure 1.45 Custom Animation Task Pane

Navigation and Printing

In the beginning of this chapter, you opened a slide show and advanced one by one through the slides by clicking the mouse button. This task is possible because PowerPoint is, by default, a linear software tool that advances each slide one after another in a straight line order. Audiences, however, are seldom comfortable with a linear slide show. If they are involved in the presentation, they want to ask questions. As you respond to the questions, you may find yourself needing to jump to a previous slide or needing to move to a future slide. PowerPoint's navigation options enable you to do this maneuver.

To help your audience follow your presentation, you can choose to provide them with a handout. You may give it to them at the beginning of your presentation for them to take notes on, or you tell them you will be providing them with notes and let them relax and enjoy your slide show. A variety of options are available for audience handouts. All you need do is be aware of the options and choose the one that best suits your audience's needs.

> A variety of options are available for audience handouts . . . be aware of the options and choose the one that best suits your audience's needs.

In this section, you run a slide show and navigate within the show. You will practice a variety of methods for advancing to new slides or returning to previously viewed slides. You will annotate slides during a presentation, and change from screen view to black-screen view. Finally, you print the slide show.

Running and Navigating a Slide Show

PowerPoint provides multiple methods you can use to advance through your slide show. You also can go backwards to a previous slide, if desired. Use Table 1.2 to identify the navigation options, and then experiment with each method for advancing and going backwards. Find the method that you are most comfortable using and stay with that method. That way you will not get confused during the slide show and advance to a new slide before you mean to do so.

Table 1.2 Navigation Options

Navigation Option	Navigation Method
To Advance Through the Slide Show	Press the Spacebar
	Press Page Down
	Press the letter **N** or **n** for next
	Press the right arrow or down arrow
	Press Enter
To Return to a Previous Slide or Animation	Right-click and choose Previous from the Popup menu
	Press the Page Up button
	Press the letter **P** or **p** for previous
	Press the left arrow or up arrow
	Press Backspace
To End the Slide Show	Press Esc on the keyboard
	Press the hyphen key
To Go to a Specific Slide	Type Slide number and press Enter
	Right-click, click Go to Slide, then click the slide desired

Annotate the Slide Show

An **_annotation_** is a note that can be written or drawn on a slide for additional commentary or explanation.

You may find it helpful to add **_annotations_**, or notes, to your slides. You can write or draw on your slides during a presentation. To do so, right-click to bring up the shortcut menu, and then click Pointer Options to select your pen type. You can change the color of the pen from the Popup menu, too. To create the annotation, hold down the left mouse button as you write or draw on your slide. To erase what you have drawn, press the letter **E** or **e** on the keyboard. Keep in mind that the mouse was never intended to be an artist's tool. Your drawings or added text will be clumsy efforts at best, unless you use a tablet and pen. The annotations you create are not permanent unless you save the annotations when exiting the slide show and then save the changes upon exiting the file.

Printing with PowerPoint

A printed copy of a PowerPoint slide show is very beneficial. It can be used by the presenter for reference during the presentation. It can be used by the audience for future reference, or as backup during equipment failure. It can even be used by students as a study guide. A printout of a single slide with text on it can be used as a poster or banner.

Print Slides

Use the Print Slides option to print each slide on a full page. One reason to print the slides as full slides is to print the slides for use as a backup. You can print the full slides on overhead transparencies that could be projected with an overhead projector during a presentation. You will be extremely grateful for the backup if your projector bulb blows out or your computer quits working during a presentation. Using the Print Slides option also is valuable if you want to print a single slide that has been formatted as a sign or a card.

If you are printing the slides on transparencies, or on paper smaller than the standard size, be sure to set the slide size and orientation before you print. By default PowerPoint sets the slides for landscape orientation, or printing where the width is greater than the height (11 x 8.5"). If you are going to print on a transparency for an overhead projector, however, you need to set PowerPoint to portrait orientation, or printing where the height is greater than the width (8.5 x 11").

To change your slide orientation, or to set PowerPoint to print for a different size, click the Design tab and click Page Setup in the Page Setup group to open the Page Setup dialog box. Click in the *Slides sized for* list to select the size or type of paper on which you will print. To print overhead transparency, you click Overhead. You also can set the slide orientation in this dialog box. If you wish to create a custom size of paper to print, enter the height and width. Figure 1.46 displays the Page Setup options. Note that the slide show we have been creating has been changed so that it can be printed on overhead transparencies.

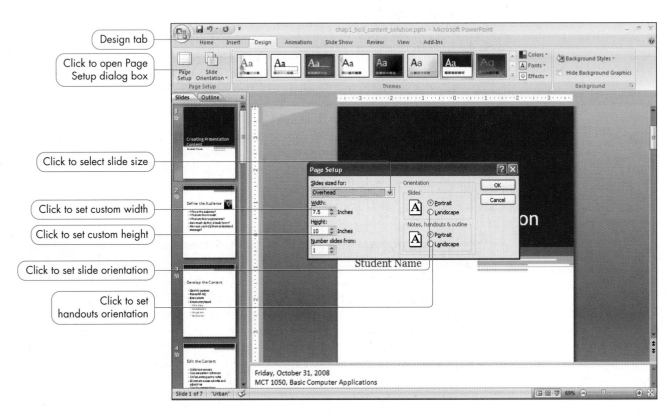

Figure 1.46 Page Setup Options

Once you have determined your page setup, you are ready to print the slides. To print, click the Office Button, select Print, and then select Print in the submenu. The Print dialog box opens so that you can select your printer, your print range, and number of copies—options available to all Office applications. In addition to the standard print options, PowerPoint has many options that tailor the printout to your needs. You can click the *Print what* drop-down arrow and select whether you want to print slides, handouts, notes pages, or outlines.

You can determine the color option with which to print. Selecting Color prints your presentation in color if you have a color printer or grayscale if you are printing on a black-and-white printer. Selecting the Grayscale option prints in shades of gray, but be aware that backgrounds do not print when using the Grayscale option. By not printing the background, you make the text in the printout easier to read and you save a lot of ink or toner. Printing with the Pure Black and White option prints with no gray fills. Try using Microsoft clip art and printing in Pure Black and White to create coloring pages for children.

If you have selected a custom size for your slide show, or if you have set up the slide show so that is it larger than the paper you are printing on, be sure to check the *Scale to fit paper* box. Doing so will ensure that each slide prints on one page. The Frame slides option puts a back border around the slides in the printout, giving the printout a more polished appearance. If you have applied shadows to text or objects, you may want to check the *Print shadows* option so that the shadows print. The final two options, *Print comments and ink markup* and *Print hidden slides*, are only active if you have used these features.

Print Handouts

The principal purpose for printing handouts is to give your audience something they can use to follow during the presentation and give them something on which to take notes. With your handout and their notes, the audience has an excellent resource for the future. Handouts can be printed with one, two, three, four, six, or nine slides per page. Printing three handouts per page is a popular option because it places thumbnails of the slides on the left side of the printout and lines on which the audience can write on the right side of the printout. Figure 1.47 shows the *Print what* option set to Handouts and the Slides per page option set to 3.

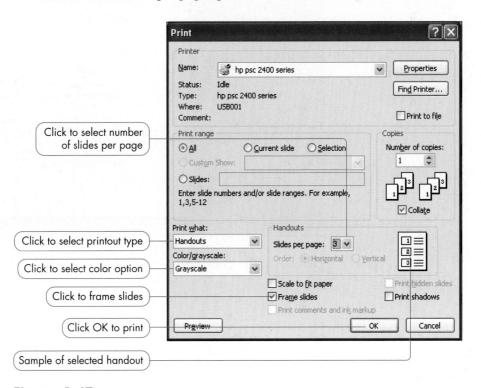

Figure 1.47 Page Setup Options

Print Notes Pages

In the first exercise in this chapter, you created a note in the Notes pane. If you include charts or technical information in your notes, you will want to print the notes for reference. You also may want to print the detailed notes for your audience, especially if your notes contain references. To print your notes, click the Office Button, select Print, select Print from the submenu, and then click Notes Pages in the *Print what* box.

Print Outlines

You may print your presentation as an outline made up of the slide titles and main text from each of your slides. This is a good option if you only want to deal with a few pages instead of a page for each slide as is printed for Notes pages. The outline generally gives you enough detail to keep you on track with your presentation.

You can print the outline following the methods discussed for the other three printout types, but you also can preview it and print from the preview screen. To preview how a printout will look, click the Office Button, and then point to the arrow next to Print. In the list that displays, click Print Preview. Click the arrow next to the *Print what* box, and then click Outline View. If you decide to print, click Print. Figure 1.48 shows the outline for the presentation we have been creating in Print Preview.

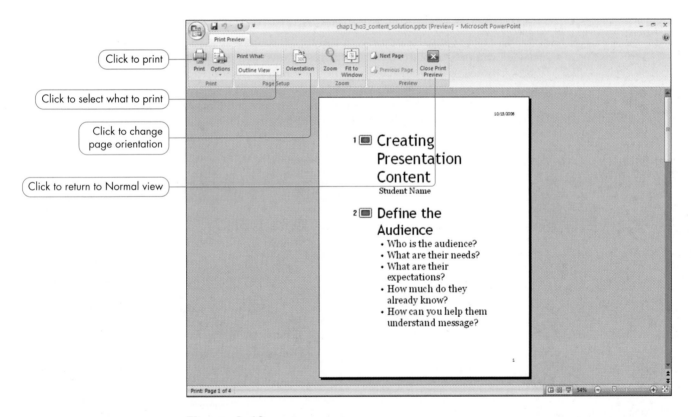

Figure 1.48 Outline View in Print Preview

Hands-On Exercises

4 | Navigating and Printing

Skills covered: 1. Display a Slide Show **2.** Navigate to Specific Slides **3.** Annotate a Slide **4.** Print Audience Handouts

---

Step 1
Display a Slide Show

a. Open the *chap1_ho3_content_solution* presentation if you closed it after the last exercise, and then save it as **chap1_ho4_content_solution**. Type your class under your name in the title placeholder.

b. Click the **Slide Show tab** and click **From Beginning** in the Start Slide Show group.

   Note the transition effect and sound you applied in Hands-On Exercise 3.

c. Press **Spacebar** to animate the title, press **Spacebar** again to animate the subtitle.

   Pressing Spacebar advances to the next animation or the next slide.

d. Click to advance to Slide 2.

   Note that the photograph animation plays automatically.

e. Press **Page Down** to advance to Slide 3.

f. Press **Page Up** to return to Slide 2.

g. Press **Enter** to advance to Slide 3.

h. Press **N** on the keyboard to advance to Slide 4.

i. Press **Backspace** to return to Slide 3.

Step 2
Navigate to Specific Slides

a. Right-click, select **Go to Slide**, and then select **5 Simply the Content**.

   Slide 5 displays.

b. Press the number **3** on the keyboard, and then press **Enter**.

   Slide 3 displays.

c. Press **F1** and read the Slide Show Help menu showing the shortcut tips that are available during the display of a slide show.

d. Close the Help menu.

Step 3
Annotate a Slide

a. Press **Ctrl + P**.

   The mouse pointer becomes a pen.

b. Circle and underline several words on the slide.

c. Press the letter **E**.

   The annotations erase.

d. Press the letter **B**.

   The screen blackens.

e. Press the letter **B** again.

The slide show displays again.

f. Press **Esc** to end the slide show.

Step 4

Print Audience Handouts

a. Click the **Office Button** and select **Print**.

b. Click the **Print what drop-down arrow**, and then click **Handouts**.

c. Specify **4** slides per page, and then click **OK** to print the presentation.

d. Save the *chap1_ho4_content_solution* presentation and close it.

Summary

1. **Identify PowerPoint user interface elements.** PowerPoint features are designed to aid you in creating slide shows in support of presentations you give. Slide shows are electronic presentations that enable you to advance through slides containing content that will help your audience understand your message. PowerPoint 2007 is one of the four main applications in the Office 2007 Suite that uses a new interface designed for easier access to features. PowerPoint has different views, each with unique capabilities. The Normal view is a tri-pane view that displays either thumbnail images or an outline in one pane, the slide in one pane, and a Notes pane. The Slide Sorter view displays thumbnails of multiple slides. The Notes view shows a miniature of the slide and the associated speaker notes. The Slide Show view.

2. **Use PowerPoint views.** PowerPoint contains multiple views to fit the user's needs. The default view is the Normal view—a tri-pane view used predominantly for slideshow creation. The Slide Sorter view enables the user to quickly reorder or delete slides to enhance organization. The Notes Page view displays a thumbnail of the slide and the notes the user has entered for that slide. The Slide Show view displays the slide show in full-screen view for an audience. If a presenter has multiple monitors, the Presenter's view gives the presenter options for greater control of the playback.

3. **Open and save a slide show.** Previously created slide shows can be opened so that they can be modified. After editing, they can be saved with the same file name using the Save feature, or saved with a new file name using the Save As feature. When slide shows are saved, they are assigned an extension of .pptx, indicating they are in XML (eXtensible Markup Language) file format.

4. **Get Help.** PowerPoint's Help can be used to locate information about a specific feature, to troubleshoot, to search for software updates, to find a template, or to locate additional training. Help is available online or offline.

5. **Create a storyboard.** Before creating your slide show you should spend a considerable amount of time analyzing your audience, researching your message, and organizing your ideas. Organize your ideas on a storyboard, and then create your presentation in PowerPoint. After completing the slide show, you should spend a considerable amount of time practicing your presentation so that you are comfortable with your slide content and the technology you will use to present it with.

6. **Use slide layouts.** PowerPoint provides a set of predefined slide layouts that determine the position of the objects or content on a slide. Slide layouts contain any number and combination of placeholders. Placeholders hold content and determine the position of the objects on the slide.

7. **Apply design themes.** PowerPoint themes enable you to focus on the content of a presentation. You create the text and supporting elements, and then you apply a design theme to give the presentation a consistent look. The theme controls the font, background, layout, and colors.

8. **Review the presentation.** To ensure there are no typographical errors or misspelled words in a presentation, use the Check Spelling feature to complete an initial check for errors. You also need to review each slide yourself because the Check Spelling feature does not find all errors. An example of an error that the Check Spelling feature does not find is the misuse of the word "to" or "two" when the correct word is "too." Use the Thesaurus to locate synonyms for overused words in the slide show.

9. **Add a table.** Tables can be created to help organize information needed in the slide show. PowerPoint's table features can be used to specify the number of columns and rows needed in the table. Tables can be inserted from the Content bar in the Content placeholder or through the Insert tab.

10. **Insert clip art.** A variety of clips can be added to slides. Clips are media objects such as clip art, images, movies, and sound. The Microsoft Clip Organizer contains media objects you can insert, or you can locate clips and insert them through the Insert tab. Clips you gather can be added to the Microsoft Clip Organizer to help you locate them more easily.

11. **Use transitions and animations.** Transitions and animations show in Slide Show view. Transitions control the movements of slides as one slide changes to another, while an animation controls the movement of an object on the slide. Both features can aid in keeping the attention of the audience, but animations are especially valuable in directing attention to specific elements you wish to emphasize.

...continued on Next Page

12. **Run and navigate a slide show.** While displaying the slide show, you need flexibility in moving between slides. Various navigation methods advance the slide show, return to previously viewed slides, or go to specific slides. Slides can be annotated during a presentation to add emphasis or comments to slides.

13. **Print with PowerPoint.** PowerPoint has four ways to print the slideshow, each with specific benefits. The Slides method of printing prints each slide on a full page. The Handouts method prints miniatures of the slides in 1, 2, 3, 4, 6, or 9 per page format. The Notes Pages method prints each slide on a separate page and is formatted to display a single thumbnail of a slide with its associated notes. The Outline method prints the titles and main points of the presentation in outline format.

Key Terms

Multiple Choice

1. Which of the following methods does not save changes in a PowerPoint presentation?

   (a) Click the Office Button, and then click the Save As command.
   (b) Click the Save button on the Quick Access toolbar.
   (c) Press Ctrl+S.
   (d) Press F1.

2. The Quick Access Toolbar, containing commands you may need at any time regardless of what tab is active, includes which of the following commands?

   (a) Cut and Paste
   (b) Undo and Redo
   (c) Find and Replace
   (d) Spelling and Grammar

3. You have created a very complex table with great detail on a slide. You want to give the audience a printout of the slide showing all the detail so they can review it with you during your presentation. Which of the following print methods would show the necessary detail?

   (a) Audience handout, 4 per page
   (b) Outline
   (c) Notes page
   (d) Full slide

4. While displaying a slide show, which of the following will display a list of shortcuts for navigating?

   (a) F1
   (b) F11
   (c) Ctrl+Enter
   (d) Esc

5. The predefined slide formats in PowerPoint are:

   (a) Layout views
   (b) Slide layouts
   (c) Slide guides
   (d) Slide displays

6. If you need to add an object such as clip art or a picture to a slide, which tab would you select?

   (a) Add-ins
   (b) Design
   (c) Slide
   (d) Insert

7. The Open command:

   (a) Brings a presentation from a storage device into RAM memory
   (b) Removes the presentation from the storage device and brings it into RAM memory
   (c) Stores the presentation in RAM memory to a storage device
   (d) Stores the presentation in RAM memory to a storage device, and then erases the presentation from RAM memory

8. The Save command:

   (a) Brings a presentation from a storage device into RAM memory
   (b) Removes the presentation from the storage device and brings it into RAM memory
   (c) Stores the presentation in RAM memory to a storage device
   (d) Stores the presentation in RAM memory to a storage device, and then erases the presentation from RAM memory

9. Which of the following provides a ghost image of a toolbar for use in formatting selected text?

   (a) Styles command
   (b) Quick Access Toolbar
   (c) Formatting Text gallery
   (d) Mini toolbar

10. Which of the following is a true statement?

   (a) A design theme must be applied before slides are created.
   (b) The design theme can be changed after all of the slides have been created.
   (c) Design themes control fonts and backgrounds but not placeholder location.
   (d) Placeholders positioned by a design theme cannot be moved.

11. Microsoft Clip Organizer searches:

   (a) May be limited to a specific media type
   (b) Locate clips based on keywords
   (c) May be limited to specific collections
   (d) All of the above

12. Which of the following views is best for reordering the slides in a presentation?

   (a) Presenter view
   (b) Slide Show view
   (c) Reorder view
   (d) Slide Sorter view

Multiple Choice Continued...

13. Normal view contains which of the following components?

(a) The slide sorter pane, the tabs pane, and the slide pane

(b) The tabs pane, the slide pane, and the slide sorter pane

(c) The tabs pane, the slide pane, and the notes pane

(d) The outline pane, the slide pane, and the tabs pane

14. Which of the following cannot be used to focus audience attention on a specific object on a slide during a slide show?

(a) Apply a transition to the object

(b) Apply an animation to the object

(c) Use the pen tool to circle the object

(d) Put nothing on the slide but the object

15. What is the animation effect that controls how one slide changes to another slide?

(a) Custom animation

(b) Animation scheme

(c) Transition

(d) Advance

The presentation in Figure 1.49 reviews the basics of e-mail and simultaneously provides you with practice opening, modifying, and saving an existing PowerPoint presentation. The presentation contains two slides on computer viruses and reminds you that your computer is at risk whenever you receive an e-mail message with an attachment. Notes containing explanations are included for some slides. You create a summary of what you learn and enter it as a note for the last slide.

a. Click the **Office Button** and select **Open**. Click the **Look in drop-down arrow**, and then locate the drive and folder where your student files are saved. Select the *chap1_pe1_email* presentation, and then click **Open**.

b. Click the **Slide Show tab** and click **From Beginning** in the Start Slide Show group. Read each of the slides by pressing **Spacebar** to advance through the slides. Press **Esc** to exit the Slide Show View.

c. Click in the **Slide 1 title placeholder**, and then replace the words *Student Name* with your name as it appears on the instructor's rolls. Replace *Student Class* with the name of the class you are taking.

d. Click in the **Slide 10 Notes pane**, and then type a short note about what you learned regarding e-mail by reviewing this slide show.

e. Click the **Slide 4 thumbnail** in the Tabs pane to move to Slide 4. Select the sample e-mail address, and then type your e-mail address to replace the sample.

f. Move to **Slide 3** and then click inside the content placeholder. Type **Inbox**, and then press **Enter**. Continue typing the following bullet items: **Outbox**, **Sent items**, **Deleted items**, **Custom folders**.

g. Move to **Slide 8**, select the first protocol, *POP Client – Post Office Protocol Client*, and then move your pointer slightly upward until the Mini toolbar appears. Apply **Bold** and **Italics** to the first protocol. Repeat the process for the second protocol, *IMAP – Internet Message Access Protocol*.

h. Click the **Design tab** and click the **More button** in the Themes group.

i. Click **Technic** to apply the Technic theme to all slides in the slide show.

j. Move to **Slide 1** and adjust the size of the Title placeholder so the complete title fits on one line.

k. Click the **Office Button**, point to **Print**, and then click **Print** in the submenu. Click **Current slide** option in the *Print range* section. Click the **Frame slides check box** to activate it, and then click **OK**. Slide 1 will print for your use as a cover page.

l. Open the Print dialog box again, and then click the **Slides** option in the *Print range* section. Type the slide range **2–10**.

m. Click the **Print what drop-down arrow**, and then select **Handouts**. Click the **Slides per page drop-down arrow** in the *Handouts* section, and then select **3**.

n. Click the **Frame slides check box** to activate it, and then click **OK**. Slides 2–10 will print 3 per page with lines for audience note taking. Staple the cover page to the handouts, and then submit it to your instructor if requested to do so.

o. Click the **Office Button** and select **Save As**. Click the **Save in drop-down arrow** and locate the drive and folder where you are saving your file solutions. Type **chap1_pe1_email_solution** as the file name for the presentation. Click **Save**.

...continued on Next Page

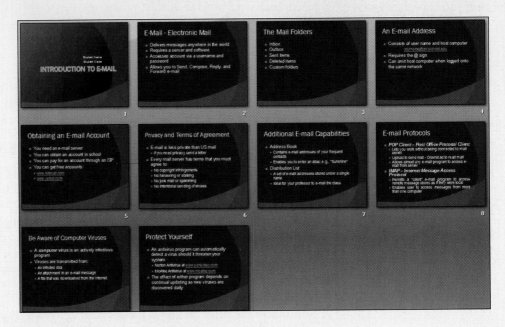

Figure 1.49 Introduction to E-Mail Presentation

2 Successful Presentations

Your employer is a successful author who often presents to various groups. He has been asked by the local International Association of Administrative Professionals (IAAP) to give the group tips for presenting successfully using PowerPoint. He created a storyboard of his presentation and has asked you to create the presentation from the storyboard. Refer to Figure 1.50 as you complete this assignment.

a. Click the **Office Button**, select **New**, click **Blank**, and then click **Create**.

b. Click the **Office Button** and select **Save As**. Click the **Save in drop-down arrow** and locate the drive and folder where you are saving your file solutions. Type **chap1_pe2_tips_solution** as the file name for the presentation. Click **Save**.

c. Click in the **Slide 1 title placeholder**, and then type **Successful Presentations**. Click in the subtitle placeholder and type **Robert Grauer and your name** as it appears on the instructor's rolls.

d. Click the **Home tab**, click the **New Slide down arrow** in the Slides group, and click **Title Only**.

e. Click in the title placeholder and type **Techniques to Consider**.

f. Click **Table** in the Tables group on the Insert tab, and then drag the grid to highlight two columns and five rows.

g. Type the following information in the table cells. Press **Tab** to move from cell to cell.

Feature	Use
Rehearse Timings	Helps you determine the length of your presentation
Header/Footer	Puts information on the top and bottom of slides, notes, and handouts
Hidden Slides	Hides slides until needed
Annotate a Slide	Write on the slide

h. Click the **Home tab**, click the **New Slide down arrow** in the Slides group, and then click **Title and Content**. Type **The Delivery is Up to You**.

i. Click in the content placeholder and type the following bullet text: **Practice makes perfect, Arrive early on the big day, Maintain eye contact, Speak slowly, clearly, and with sufficient volume, Allow time for questions**.

j. Click the **Home tab**, click the **New Slide down arrow** in the Slides group, and then click **Title and Content**. Type **Keep Something in Reserve**.

...continued on Next Page

k. Click in the content placeholder and type the following bullet text: **Create hidden slides to answer difficult questions that might occur, Press Ctrl+S to display hidden slides**.

l. Click the **Home tab**, click **New Slide** in the Slides group, and then click **Title and Content**. Type **Provide Handouts.**

m. Click in the content placeholder and type the following bullet text: **Allows the audience to follow the presentation, Lets the audience take the presentation home**.

n. Click the **Review tab** and click **Spelling** in the Proofing group.

o. Correct any misspelled words Check Spelling locates. Proofread the presentation and correct any misspelled words Check Spelling missed.

p. Click the **Design tab** and click the **More button** in the Themes group.

q. Click **Oriel**.

r. Click the **Slide Show tab** and click **From Beginning** in the Start Slide Show group. Press **Page Down** to advance through the slides.

s. When you reach the end of the slide show, press the number **2**, and then press **Enter** to return to Slide 2. Press **Esc.**

t. Press **Ctrl+S** to save the *chap1_pe2_tips_solution* presentation and close.

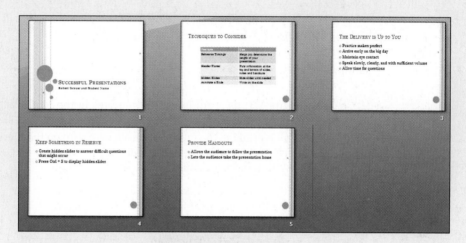

Figure 1.50 Successful Presentations Slide Show

3 Introduction to the Internet

You have been asked to give a presentation covering the basics of the Internet. You created a storyboard and entered the content in a slide show. After viewing the slide show, you realize the slides are text intensive and that transitions and animations would make the show more interesting. You modify the slide show and remove some of the detail from the slides. You put the detail in the Notes pane. You add a transition and apply it to all slides, and you apply custom animations to two images. You print the Notes for you to refer to as you present.

a. Click the **Office Button** and select **Open**. Click the **Look in drop-down arrow**, and then locate the drive and folder where your student files are saved. Click the *chap1_pe3_internet* presentation, and then click **Open**.

b. Click in the **Slide 1** title placeholder and replace the words *Your Name* with your name as it appears on the instructor's rolls. Replace *Your Class* with the name of the class you are taking.

c. Click in the **Slide 2 content placeholder** and modify the text so that it is shortened to brief, easy-to-remember chunks, as displayed in Figure 1.51.

...continued on Next Page

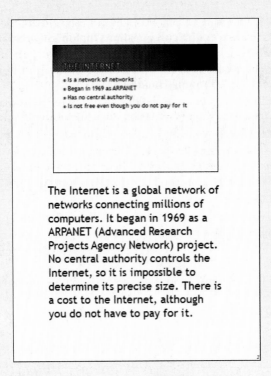

Figure 1.51 Internet Slide 2 Modifications

d. Click the **View tab**. Click **Notes Page** in the Presentation Views group, and then using Figure 1.51 as a guide, enter the notes in the Notes placeholder, which provides the appropriate place for the text omitted in the previous step.

e. Click **Normal** in the Presentation Views group on the View tab, and then move to **Slide 3**. Click in the content placeholder and modify the text so that it is shortened to brief, easy-to-remember chunks, as displayed in Figure 1.52.

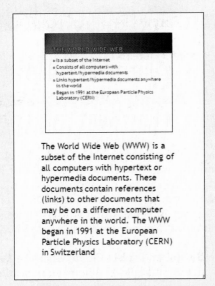

Figure 1.52 Internet Slide 3 Modifications

...continued on Next Page

f. Click the **View tab**, click **Notes Page** in the Presentation Views group, and then using Figure 1.52 as a guide, enter the notes in the Notes placeholder.

g. Click **Normal** in the Presentation Views group, and then click the **Animations tab**. Click the **More button** in the Transition To This Slide group.

h. Click the **Cover Right-Down** option and click **Apply To All**.

i. Move to **Slide 5**, and then click the image of the computer network to select it.

j. Click the down arrow next to **Animate** in the Animations group on the Animations tab and then click **Fly In**. Repeat this process for the image of the modem and telephone.

k. Click the **View tab**, click **Slide Show** in the Presentation Views group, and then advance through the slide show. Press **Esc** to end the slide show after you have viewed the last slide.

l. Click the **Office Button**, select **Print**, and then select **Print Preview**.

m. Select **Notes Pages** from the Print what list, and then press **Page Down** on the keyboard to advance through the slides. If your instructor asks you to print the Notes Pages, click **Print** in the Print group on the Print Preview tab. Click **Close Print Preview** in the Preview group on the Print Preview tab.

n. Click the **Office Button**, and then select **Save As**. Click the **Save in drop-down arrow** and locate the drive and folder where you are saving your file solutions. Type **chap1_pe3_internet_solution** as the file name for the presentation. Click **Save**.

4 Copyright and the Law

The ethics and values class you are taking this semester requires a final presentation to the class. Although a PowerPoint slide show is not required, you feel it will strengthen your presentation. You create a presentation to review basic copyright law and software licensing and add clip art, a transition, and an animation.

a. Click the **Office Button** and select **Open**. Click the **Look in drop-down arrow**, and then locate the drive and folder where your student files are saved. Select the *chap1_pe4_copyright* presentation, and then click **Open**.

b. Click the **Slide Show tab**, and then click **From Beginning** in the Start Slide Show group. Read each of the slides and note the length of some bullets. Press **Esc** to return to Normal view.

c. Click the **Design tab**, click the **More button** in the Themes group, and select the **Flow theme**.

d. Click in the **Slide 1 title placeholder**, if necessary, and then replace the words *Your Name* with your name as it appears on the instructor's rolls. Replace *Your Class* with the name of the class you are taking.

e. Click the **Insert tab** and click **Clip Art** in the Illustrations group. Type **copyright** in the **Search for** box. Select the animated copyright symbol and drag it to the title slide next to your name. Refer to Figure 1.53 to help you identify the copyright logo.

TROUBLESHOOTING: If the animated copyright clip does not appear when you search for the copyright keyword, change the keyword to **law**, and then select an image that relates to the presentation content and uses the same colors.

f. Click the **Animations tab** and click the **More button** in the Transition To This Slide group.

g. Click the **Fade Through Black** option, and then click **Apply To All**.

h. Move to **Slide 6**, and then select the blue object containing text located at the bottom of the slide.

i. Click **Custom Animation** in the Animations group on the Animations tab.

j. Click **Add Effect** in the Custom Animations task pane, click **More Effects** at the bottom of the Entrance group, and then choose **Faded Zoom** from the Subtle category.

k. Click the **Start** drop-down arrow, and then click **After Previous**.

...continued on Next Page

l. Click **Play** at the bottom of the Custom Animation task pane to see the result of your custom animation.

m. Move to the last slide in the slide show, **Slide 9**, click the **Home tab**, and then click **New Slide** in the Slides group.

n. Click **Section Header** from the list of layouts.

o. Click in the title placeholder and type **Individuals who violate copyright law and/or software licensing agreements may be subject to criminal or civil action by the copyright or license owners**. Press **Ctrl + A** to select the text and change the font size to 40 pts.

p. Click the border of the subtitle placeholder and press **Delete**.

q. Drag the title placeholder downward until all of the text is visible and is centered vertically on the slide.

r. Select the text, move your pointer upward until the Mini toolbar appears, and then click the **Center Align** button.

s. Click the **Office Button** and select **Save As**. Click the **Save in drop-down arrow** and locate the drive and folder where you are saving your file solutions. Type **chap1_pe4_copyright_solution** as the file name for the presentation. Click **Save**.

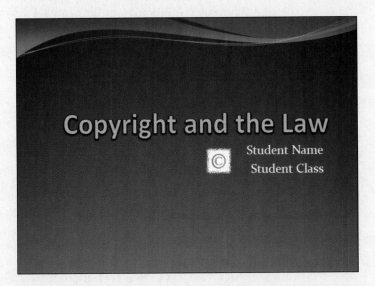

Figure 1.53 Copyright and the Law Presentation

PowerPoint will help you to create an attractive presentation, but the delivery is still up to you. It is easier than you think, and you should not be intimidated at the prospect of facing an audience. You can gain confidence and become an effective speaker by following the basic tenets of good public speaking. Refer to Figure 1.54 as you complete this exercise.

a. Open the *chap1_mid1_public* presentation and save it as **chap1_mid1_public_solution**.

b. Add your name and e-mail address to the title slide. Add your e-mail address to the summary slide as well.

c. Print the notes for the presentation, and then view the slide show while looking at the appropriate notes for each slide. Which slides have notes attached? Are the notes redundant, or do they add something extra? Do you see how the notes help a speaker to deliver an effective presentation?

d. Which slide contains the phrase, "Common sense is not common practice"? In what context is the phrase used within the presentation?

e. Which personality said, "You can observe a lot by watching?" In what context is the phrase used during the presentation?

f. Join a group of three or four students, and then have each person in the group deliver the presentation to his or her group. Were they able to follow the tenets of good public speaking? Share constructive criticism with each of the presenters. Constructive criticism means you identify both positive aspects of their presentations and aspects that could be improved with practice. The goal of constructive criticism is to help one another improve.

g. Summarize your thoughts about this exercise in an e-mail message to your instructor.

h. Save the *chap1_mid1_public_solution* presentation and close.

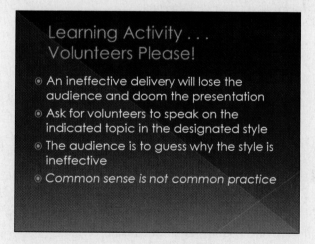

Figure 1.54 Public Speaking 101

...continued on Next Page

The Provost's Office at your university manages policies and practices that affect the academic life of the university as a whole. The new provost, Dr. Richard Shaw, has asked the housing office administrator to meet with him and update him about the purpose and goals of the housing office. As a work-study student employed by the housing office, you have been asked to take the administrator's notes and prepare a presentation for the provost. Refer to Figure 1.55 as you complete this exercise.

a. Open the *chap1_mid2_university* presentation and save it as **chap1_mid2_university_solution**.

b. Add your name and the name of the class you are taking to the title slide.

c. Insert a new slide using the Title and Content layout as the second slide in the presentation. Type **Mission** as the title.

d. Type the mission in the content placeholder: **The mission of the University Housing Office is to provide a total environment that will enrich the educational experience of its residents. It seeks to promote increased interaction between faculty and students through resident masters, special programs, and intramural activities.**

e. Move to the end of the presentation and insert a new slide with the Blank layout. Insert two photograph clips related to college life from the Microsoft Clip Organizer or Office Online.

f. Move to **Slide 4** and create a table using the following information:

Dorm Name	Room Revenue	Meal Revenue	Total Revenue
Ashe Hall	$2,206,010	$1,616,640	$3,822,650
Memorial	$1,282,365	$934,620	$2,216,985
Ungar Hall	$2,235,040	$1,643,584	$3,878,624
Merrick Hall	$1,941,822	$1,494,456	$3,346,278
Fort Towers	$1,360,183	$981,772	$2,341,955
Totals	$9,025,420	$6,581,072	$15,606,492

g. Select the cells containing numbers, and then use the Mini toolbar to right-align the numbers Select the cells containing the column titles, and then use the Mini toolbar to center-align the text..

h. Apply the Cut transition theme to all slides in the slide show.

i. Add the Curve Up custom animation to each of the images on Slide 6. Curve Up is located in the Exciting category of Entrance Effects. Set the animations so that they start automatically after the previous event.

j. Print the handouts, 3 per page, framed.

k. Save the *chap1_mid2_university_solution* presentation and close.

...continued on Next Page

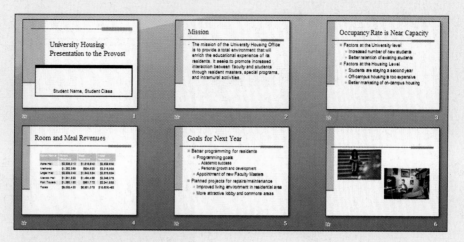

Figure 1.55 University Housing

3 PowerPoint FAQ

As a volunteer in the computer room at the local library, you get a barrage of questions about PowerPoint 2007. To help library personnel and library patrons and to reduce having to repeatedly answer the same questions, you decide to create a PowerPoint FAQ (Frequently Asked Questions) slide show that people can watch when needed. You use Help to help you prepare the FAQ slide show, and as you navigate through Help and read the associated articles, you summarize what you learn in the FAQ slide show. Refer to Figure 1.56 as you complete this exercise.

a. Create a new slide show and save it as **chap1_mid3_ppt07faq_solution**.

b. Type **PowerPoint 2007 Frequently Asked Questions** as the presentation title, and then add your name and the name of the class you are taking to the title slide.

c. Create a new slide for each of the following PowerPoint interfaces using these titles:

- What is the Microsoft Office Button?

- What is the Quick Access Toolbar?

- What is the Ribbon?

- What is a Gallery?

d. Move to **Slide 2** and open Help. Type **Office Button** as the keyword for the search and then conduct the search. When the results page displays, click the link for *What and where is the Microsoft Office Button?*

e. Read the resulting article and close the Help dialog box. In the content placeholder, enter a summary of what you learned. For example, *The Office Button provides access to the basic commands such as open, save, and print, and replaces the File menu.*

f. Use Help to find information about the remaining features, and then enter a summary about each feature in the content placeholder of each slide.

g. Apply the **Origin** design theme to your slide show.

h. Apply the **Fade Smoothly** transition theme to all slides in the slide show.

i. Check the spelling in your presentation, and then proofread carefully to catch any errors that Spelling may have missed.

j. Print the handouts as directed by your instructor.

k. Save the *chap1_mid3_ppt07faq_solution* presentation and close.

...continued on Next Page

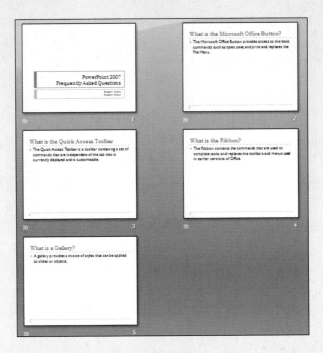

Figure 1.56 FAQ Presentation

Capstone Exercise

Definitely Needlepoint is a successful retail store owned by four close friends. One of them is your mother. The store has been in operation for three years and has increased its revenue and profit each year. The partners are looking to expand their operation by requesting venture capital. They have an important meeting scheduled next week. Help your mother prepare a PowerPoint slide show to help them present their case.

Presentation Setup

You need to open the presentation that you already started, rename the file, and save it. You add your name to the title slide and then you apply a design theme.

a. Locate the file named *chap1_cap_capital*, and then save it as **chap1_cap_capital_solution**.

b. Replace *Your Name* with your name as it appears on your instructor's roll book in the title placeholder of Slide 1.

c. Apply the **Metro** design theme.

Create a Mission Statement Slide

You need to create a slide for the Definitely Needlepoint mission statement. The mission statement created by the four owners clearly reflects their personality and their attitude about their customers. This attitude is a clear factor in the success of the business, so you decide it should be preeminent in the presentation and use it as the introduction slide.

a. Insert a new slide after Slide 1 with the Title Only layout.

b. Type the following mission statement in the title placeholder: **Definitely Needlepoint provides a friendly and intimate setting in which to stitch. Our customers are not just customers, but friends who participate in a variety of social and educational activities that encourage and develop the art of needlepoint.**

c. Select the text, use the Mini toolbar to change the Font size to **28 pts**, and then apply **Italics**.

d. Reposition the placeholder so that the entire statement fits on the slide.

e. Save the *chap1_cap_capital_solution* presentation.

Create Tables

You create tables to show the increase in sales from last year to this year, the sales increase by category, and the sales increase by quarters.

a. Move to **Slide 4**, click the **Insert tab**, and then click **Table** in the Tables group.

b. Create a table with four columns and seven rows. Type the following data in your table:

Category	Last Year	This Year	Increase
Canvases	$75,915	$115,856	$39,941
Fibers	$47,404	$77,038	$29,634
Accessories	$31,590	$38,540	$6,950
Classes	$19,200	$28,200	$9,000
Finishing	$25,755	$46,065	$20,310
Totals	$199,864	$305,699	$105,835

c. Use the Mini toolbar to right-align the numbers and to bold the bottom row of totals.

d. Reposition the table on the slide so that it does not block the title.

e. Move to **Slide 5** and insert a table of six columns and three rows.

f. Type the following data in your table:

Year	Canvases	Fibers	Accessories	Classes	Finishing
Last Year	$75,915	$47,404	$31,590	$19,200	$25,755
This Year	$115,856	$77,038	$38,540	$28,200	$46,065

g. Use the Mini toolbar to change the text font to 16 points and then right-align the numbers.

h. Reposition the table on the slide so that it does not block the title.

i. Move to **Slide 6** and insert a table of five columns and three rows.

j. Type the following data in your table:

...continued on Next Page

Year	Qtr 1	Qtr 2	Qtr 3	Qtr 4
Last Year	$37,761	$51,710	$52,292	$58,101
This Year	$61,594	$64,497	$67,057	$112,551

k. Spell-check the presentation, check the presentation for errors not caught by spell checking, and then carefully compare the numbers in the tables to your text to check for accuracy.

l. Save the *chap1_cap_capital_solution* presentation.

Insert Clip

Definitely Needlepoint uses a needle and thread as its logo. You decide to use a needle and thread clip on the title slide to continue this identifying image.

a. Move to **Slide 1** and open the Clip Organizer.

b. Type **stitching** in the Search for box and press **Go**.

c. Refer to Figure 1.57 to aid you in locating the needle and thread image.

d. Insert the needle and thread image and position it so that the needle is above the word *Needlepoint* and the tread appears to wrap in and out of the word.

e. Save the *chap1_cap_capital_solution* presentation.

Add Custom Animation

To emphasize the profits that Definitely Needlepoint has made over the last two years, you created two text boxes on Slide 4. You decide to animate these text boxes so that they fly in as you discuss each year. You create custom animations for each box.

a. Move to **Slide 4** and click to select the *Our first year was profitable* text box.

b. Open the Custom Animation task pane and apply a Fly In animation from the Entrance category.

c. Keep the text box selected and click the Add Effect button again. Apply a Fly Out animation from the Exit category. Note the non-printing tags now appear on the text box placeholder indicating the order of the animations.

d. Select the *Our second year was significantly better* text box and then apply a Fly In animation from the Entrance category.

e. Change the Start option to **With Previous**, which will cause this text box to fly in as the other text box flies out.

f. Save the *chap1_cap_capital_solution* presentation.

View and Print the Presentation

You view the presentation to proofread it without the distraction of the PowerPoint creation tools and to check to see if the transitions and animations are applied correctly. When you have proofed the presentation, you print a handout with 4 slides per page to give to the owners so they can see how the presentation is progressing.

a. Click the **Slide Show tab**, and then advance through the presentation. When you get to the table slides, compare the figures with the figures in your text to ensure there are no typographical errors.

b. Exit the slide show and correct any errors.

c. Print handouts in Grayscale, 4 slides per page, and framed.

d. Save the *chap1_cap_capital_solution* presentation and close.

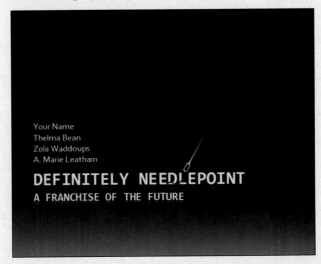

Figure 1.57 Definitely Needlepoint Title Slide

Mini Cases

Use the rubric following the case as a guide to evaluate your work, but keep in mind that your instructor may impose additional grading criteria or use a different standard to judge your work.

Green Scene Lawn Service

GENERAL CASE

You create a yard care service to help supplement your income while going to school. You name the yard service "Green Scene." You decide that one way to get your message out to potential customers is to create a presentation about your services and burn it to a CD. You'll deliver the CD to homes around your neighborhood, knowing that by delivering your message in this format, you are most likely to catch the interest of people with technological savvy—those who are busy spending their time in front of a computer instead of doing yard work.

You provide multiple services that customers can choose from. You mow once a week and cut the lawn one-third of its length at a time, you trim and edge along the foundation of the home and any fence lines, and you use a blower to remove the debris left from the trimming. You aerate the lawn in the spring to relieve soil compaction and increase water infiltration. You fertilize using natural-based, granular fertilizers and include lawn, tree, and shrub fertilization. You apply broadleaf weed control and include a surface insect control when this service is ordered. In the spring, you remove winter debris, dethatch the lawn, and restock mulch beds. In the fall you remove fall leaves and you seed and mulch bare soil patches. Your tree and shrub service includes trimming and removing of trees and shrubs as well as stump removal. You treat the shrubs and trees to protect them from disease.

Create a title slide for your presentation that includes the name of your company and your name. Save your file as **chap1_mc1_greenscene_solution**. Do not worry about burning the presentation to a CD.

Slide 2 should be an introduction slide listing your services:

- Lawn Mowing, Trimming, and Edging
- Aeration, Fertilization,Weed Control
- Spring and Fall Clean-up
- Tree and Shrub Service

Create a slide for each of these topics using the Title and Content layout. The titles for the slides should match the above bullets. Use the case study introductory material to create the content for each slide. Create a summary slide using the Title Slide layout and type **Call today for a free estimate!** in the title placeholder. Include your name and telephone number in the subtitle placeholder. Insert several appropriate clips throughout the presentation, and then resize and position the clips as desired. Apply the design theme of your choice. Reposition placeholders and modify text as desired. Apply a transition of your choice to all slides.

Performance Elements	Exceeds Expectations	Meets Expectations	Below Expectations
Organization	Presentation is easy to follow because information is presented in a logical interesting sequence.	Presentation is generally easy to follow.	Presentation cannot be understood because there is no sequence of information.
Visual aspects	Presentation background, themes, clip art, and animation are appealing and enhance the understanding of presentation purpose and content. There is a consistent visual theme.	Clip art is related to the topic. Animation enhances the presentation.	The background or theme is distracting to the topic. Clip art does not enhance understanding of the content or is unrelated.
Layout	The layout is visually pleasing and contributes to the overall message with appropriate use of headings, subheadings, bullet points, clip art, and white space.	The layout shows some structure, but placement of some headings, subheadings, bullet points, clip art, and/or white space can be improved.	The layout is cluttered and confusing. Placement of headings, subheadings, bullet points, clip art, and/or white space detracts from readability.
Mechanics	Presentation has no errors in spelling, grammar, word usage, or punctuation. No typographical errors present. Bullet points are parallel.	Presentation has no more than one error in spelling, grammar, word usage, or punctuation. Bullet points are inconsistent in no more than one slide.	Presentation readability is impaired due to repeated errors in spelling, grammar, word usage, or punctuation. Most bullet points are not parallel.

The National Debt

RESEARCH CASE

The national debt is staggering—more than $8 trillion, or approximately $28,000 for every man, woman, and child in the United States. The annual budget is approximately $2 trillion. Use the Internet to obtain exact figures for the current year, then use this information to create a presentation about the national debt. A good place to start your research is the Web site for the United States Department of the Treasury (http://www.treas.gov) where entering National Debt in the FAQ (Frequently Asked Questions) search box brings up several interesting hyperlinks to information that you can use to develop your presentation.

Do some additional research and obtain the national debt for the years 1945 and 1967. The numbers may surprise you. For example, how does the debt for the current year compare to the debt in 1967 (at the height of the Vietnam War)? To the debt in 1945 (at the end of World War II)? Include your references on a Reference slide at the end of your presentation. Save the presentation as **chap1_mc2_debt_solution**.

Performance Elements	Exceeds Expectations	Meets Expectations	Below Expectations
Organization	Presentation indicates accurate research and significant facts. Evidence exists that information has been evaluated and synthesized showing an understanding of the topic.	Presentation indicates some research has taken place and that information was included in the content.	Presentation demonstrates a lack of research or understanding of the topic. Content misinterpreted or incorrect.
Visual aspects	Presentation background, themes, clip art, and animation are appealing and enhance the understanding of presentation purpose and content. There is a consistent visual theme.	Clip art is related to the topic. Animation is not distracting.	The background or theme is distracting to the topic. Clip art does not enhance understanding of the content or is unrelated.
Layout	The layout is visually pleasing and contributes to the overall message with appropriate use of headings, subheadings, bullet points, clip art, and white space.	The layout shows some structure, but placement of some headings, subheadings, bullet points, clip art, and/or white space can be improved.	The layout is cluttered and confusing. Placement of headings, subheadings, bullet points, clip art, and/or white space detracts from readability.
Mechanics	Presentation has no errors in spelling, grammar, word usage, or punctuation. Bullet points are parallel.	Presentation has no more than one error in spelling, grammar, word usage, or punctuation. Bullet points are inconsistent in one slide.	Presentation readability is impaired due to repeated errors in spelling, grammar, word usage, or punctuation. Most bullet points are not parallel.

Planning for Disaster

DISASTER RECOVERY

This case is perhaps the most important case of this chapter as it deals with the question of backup. Do you have a backup strategy? Do you even know what a backup strategy is? This is a good time to learn, because sooner or later you will need to recover a file. The problem always seems to occur the night before an assignment is due. You accidentally erased a file, are unable to read from a storage device like a flash drive, or worse yet, suffer a hardware failure in which you are unable to access the hard drive. The ultimate disaster is the disappearance of your computer, by theft or natural disaster.

Use the Internet to research ideas for backup strategies. Create a title slide and three or four slides related to a backup strategy or ways to protect files. Include a summary on what you plan to implement in conjunction with your work in this class. Choose the design theme, transition, and animations. Save the new presentation as **chap1_mc3_disaster_solution**.

Performance Elements	Exceeds Expectations	Meets Expectations	Below Expectations
Organization	Presentation indicates accurate research and significant facts. Evidence exists that information has been evaluated and synthesized showing an understanding of the topic.	Presentation indicates some research has taken place and the information was included in the content.	Presentation demonstrates a lack of research or understanding of the topic. Content misinterpreted or incorrect.
Visual aspects	Presentation background, themes, clip art, and animation are appealing and enhance the understanding of presentation purpose and content. There is a consistent visual theme.	Clip art is related to the topic. Animation is not distracting.	The background or theme is distracting to the topic. Clip art does not enhance understanding of the content or is unrelated.
Layout	The layout is visually pleasing and contributes to the overall message with appropriate use of headings, subheadings, bullet points, clip art, and white space.	The layout shows some structure, but placement of some headings, subheadings, bullet points, clip art, and/or white space can be improved.	The layout is cluttered and confusing. Placement of headings, subheadings, bullet points, clip art, and/or white space detracts from readability.
Mechanics	Presentation has no errors in spelling, grammar, word usage, or punctuation. Bullet points are parallel.	Presentation has no more than one error in spelling, grammar, word usage, or punctuation. Bullet points are inconsistent in no more than one slide.	Presentation readability is impaired due to repeated errors in spelling, grammar, word usage, or punctuation. Most bullet points are not parallel.

Presentation Development

Planning and Preparing a Presentation

bjectives

After you read this chapter, you will be able to:

1. Create a presentation using a template **(page 1199)**.

2. Modify a template **(page 1201)**.

3. Create a presentation in Outline view **(page 1209)**.

4. Modify an outline structure **(page 1211)**.

5. Print an outline **(page 1212)**.

6. Import an outline **(page 1217)**.

7. Add existing content to a presentation **(page 1218)**.

8. Examine slide show design principles **(page 1222)**.

9. Apply and modify a Design Theme **(page 1222)**.

10. Insert a header or footer **(page 1226)**.

Hands-On Exercises

Exercises	Skills Covered
1. USING A TEMPLATE (page 1204) **Open:** New presentation **Insert:** chap2_ho1_photo1.tif **Save as:** chap2_ho1_nature_solution.pptx	• Create a New Presentation Based on an Installed Template • Modify Text in a Placeholder • Add a Slide and Select a Layout • Add a Picture and a Caption • Change a Layout
2. CREATING AND MODIFYING AN OUTLINE (page 1213) **Open:** New presentation **Save as:** chap2_ho2_presentations_solution.pptx	• Create a Presentation in Outline View • Enter an Outline • Edit a Presentation • Modify the Outline Structure and Print
3. IMPORTING AN OUTLINE AND REUSING SLIDES (page 1220) **Import:** chap2_ho3_success.docx, chap2_ho3_development.pptx **Save as:** chapt2_ho3_guide_solution.pptx	• Import a Microsoft Word Outline • Reuse Slides from Another Presentation
4. APPLYING AND MODIFYING A DESIGN THEME (page 1229) **Open:** chap2_ho3_guide_solution.pptx (from Exercise 3) **Save as:** chap2_ho4_guide_solution.pptx (additional modifications)	• Apply a Theme to a Presentation • Apply a Color Scheme • Add a Font Scheme • Apply a Background Style • Hide Background Graphics on a Slide • Save Current Theme • Create a Slide Footer • Create a Handout Header and Footer

CASE STUDY

Go Back in Time

Dr. Thien Ngo, your professor in world history, has created a very interesting assignment this semester. Each student is to choose a particular voyage, trip, expedition, or journey of interest and create a 10-minute presentation from the perspective of the individual(s) who traveled. You were instructed to create the presentation as an outline in PowerPoint, and to keep it to 6–10 slides. However, Professor Ngo added a twist to the presentation—the audience you are presenting to represents the financial sponsors of your travels (i.e., those who are providing you with whatever provisions you will need to successfully complete your trip). It is up to you to convince them that your idea is worthy of their sponsorship. In addition, you need to request what you will want in return for completing a successful expedition!

Professor Ngo cited several explorers; among them were Lewis and Clark, Amerigo Vespucci, Marco Polo, Queen Hatshepsut, Ferdinand Magellan, Neil Armstrong, Jacques Cousteau, and Christopher Columbus. You can choose from other explorers—it is up to you to determine who you would want to be and what you might like to have discovered!

Your Assignment

- Read the chapter, paying special attention to how to locate and download a template, how to create and modify an outline, and how to apply and modify theme effects in a presentation.
- Locate and download a template from Microsoft Office Online to use for your presentation. Choose a template that enhances the "exploration" theme, such as the Spinning globe template located in the Design slides group, Business category, or the Papyrus extract template, or the Writing on the wall template in the Design slides group Whimsy category. Or, try the Globe on water design in the Presentations group, Design category. Create a title slide with the title **Honoring Our Explorers,** and then enter your choice of explorer as the subtitle. Save the presentation as **chap2_case_explorer_solution**.
- Create an introduction slide indicating to whom the presentation will be given, slides covering main points, and a summary slide reiterating the need for the voyage. Possible slides for main points could cover the current situation, potential reasons or benefits for the voyage, a brief outline of the plan, a list of provisions, the personal qualifications needed for the leaders for this voyage or why you (as that leader) think you have what it takes to make the journey, and what you want in return for your services.
- Modify the theme color scheme or the font scheme, and then save the modified theme.
- Add at least one related clip art image and add animation to at least one slide. Apply a transition to all slides.
- Create a handout with your name in the header, and your instructor's name and your class in the footer.
- Print the Outline View.

Templates

One of the hardest things about creating a presentation is getting started. You may have a general idea of what you want to say, but the words do not come easily to you. You may know what you want to say, but you do not want to spend time designing the look for the slides. Microsoft gives you a potential solution to both of these circumstances by providing templates for your use. Microsoft's templates enable you to create very professional-looking presentations and may include content to help you decide what to say. While previous versions of PowerPoint included an AutoContent Wizard to help you with content development, PowerPoint 2007 incorporates content within some templates to give you more freedom when developing your presentation.

In this section, you learn how to create a presentation using a template. Second, you learn how to modify the template to create a unique appearance.

Creating a Presentation Using a Template

A ***template*** is a file that incorporates a theme, a layout, and content that can be modified.

A ***template*** provides for the formatting of design elements like the background, theme, and color scheme, and also font selections for titles and text boxes. Some templates include suggestions for how to modify the template. These suggestions can help you learn to use many of the features in PowerPoint. Content templates include ideas about what you could say to inform your audience about your topic.

> By visiting Microsoft Office Online, you can quickly and easily download. . . professional templates in a variety of categories.

PowerPoint 2007 offers professional built-in templates for you to use, but by visiting Microsoft Office Online you can quickly and easily download additional templates in a variety of categories. These templates are suitable for virtually every presentation. For example, from the Business and Legal template category at Microsoft Office Online, you can download a template for a bank loan request for a small business, a pre-incorporation agreement for a new business, or a project plan for a new business.

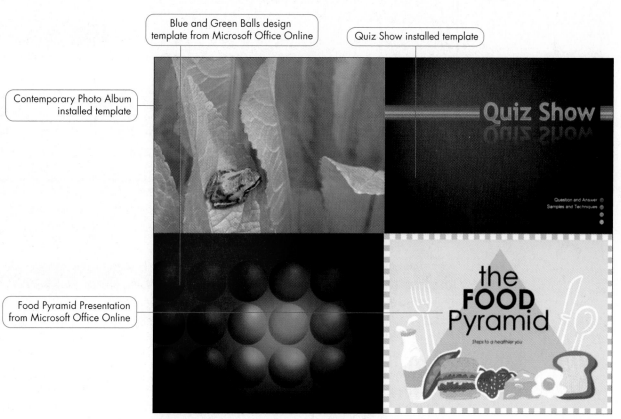

Figure 2.1 Microsoft PowerPoint Templates

Figure 2.1 shows the title slides for featured templates featured on Microsoft Office Online.

Templates are available when you create a new presentation. Click the Office Button and select New. The New Presentation dialog box displays. Template categories display on the left showing the installed templates and links for categories of templates available from Microsoft Office Online. The top center of the dialog box displays the options needed to create a new blank PowerPoint presentation. The left side of the dialog box displays an option to create a new presentation from a blank presentation, from installed templates and from installed themes. Another option enables you to create a presentation from templates you have previously created and saved. Finally, you can create a presentation from an existing presentation. A preview of a selected template is displayed on the far right. Select the Featured category under the Microsoft Office Online section and hyperlinks to check for updates, training, and additional templates appear. Check with your instructor to find out if you are able to download and save Microsoft Office Online Templates in your lab. Figure 2.2 displays the New Presentation dialog box resized to show the entire box. Your dialog box may be different from Figure 2.2 because Microsoft may change its online content.

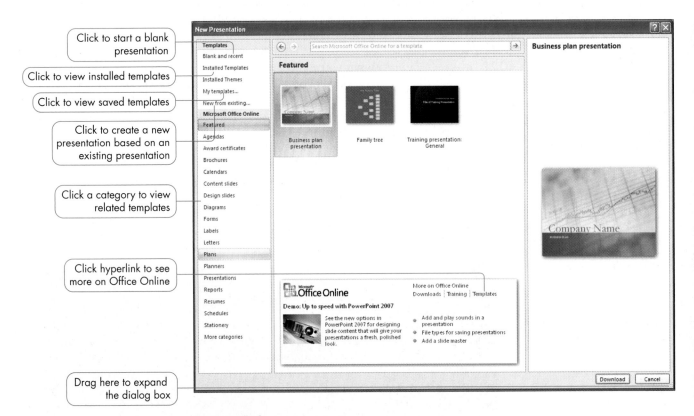

Figure 2.2 New Presentation Dialog Box

TIP   Expanding a Dialog Box

To resize a dialog box to see all available options without having to use the scroll bars, position the pointer on the dots in the bottom-right corner of the dialog box. When the pointer changes to a diagonal two-headed arrow, drag until the full dialog box is visible.

When you select the Installed Templates option in the New Presentation dialog box, the templates installed with PowerPoint 2007 display. Currently, Microsoft includes six templates, but future releases of PowerPoint 2007 may install more. Figure 2.3 shows the Classic Photo Album selected and the preview of the title page for the template.

Modifying a Template

After you download an installed template, you can modify it, perhaps by adding a unifying corporate logo, changing a font style or size, or moving an object on the slide. After you modify the template, you can save it and use it over and over. This feature can save you a tremendous amount of time, as you will not have to redo your modifications the next time you use the template.

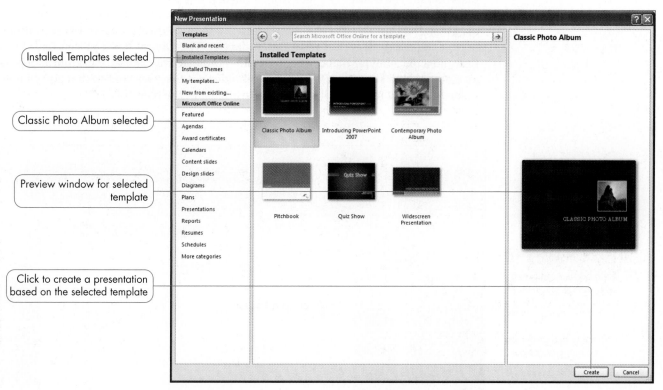

Figure 2.3 PowerPoint Installed Templates

A slide **layout** controls the position of objects containing content on the slide.

A **placeholder** is a container that holds content and is used in the layout to determine the position of objects on the slide.

When you change an object's location on a slide, you are modifying the template *layout* that defines, or controls, the objects on the slide. PowerPoint, as do all Microsoft Office applications, includes standard layouts for your use. The templates you download may have custom layouts unique to that particular template. To modify the location of an object, you must select the *placeholder* containing the object.

Placeholders contain content and are positioned in the layout of a slide. The layout can include any number or combination of placeholders, and every layout can have additional placeholders added to it. You can easily identify placeholders because they are boxes with dotted or hatch-marked borders. In addition to holding text, placeholders can contain elements such as a table, chart, clip art, diagrams, pictures, or media clips. The behavior of the content in a placeholder varies depending on the type of placeholder used. For example, a text placeholder uses internal margins to set the distance between the placeholder borders and the text, while a picture placeholder centers and crops an image that is inserted in it.

A layout may even have no placeholders. PowerPoint also includes a Blank Slide layout with no placeholders so that you can design and create your own layout. If you apply a layout that contains placeholders you do not need, you can delete the placeholder by clicking its border and then pressing Delete. If the placeholder has text, you must delete the text first, and then delete the placeholder.

You can resize a placeholder by clicking on the placeholder to select it, and then pointing at one of the *sizing handles* of the placeholder. When you point at one of the sizing handles, the pointer becomes a two-headed arrow. After your pointer changes into the two-headed arrow, drag the handle until your object is the size you desire. To move a placeholder, select the placeholder and point to any of the placeholder borders. When the pointer becomes a four-headed arrow, drag the placeholder to the location you desire.

You can use text placeholders to quickly change all text contained in the placeholder. First, click to select the placeholder, and then click the border of the placeholder. The border changes from a dashed line to a solid line indicating that all the text is selected. After you select the text, you can change the font, size, case, color, or spacing within the placeholder. Figure 2.4 shows PowerPoint's most commonly used slide layout, the Title and Content layout. This layout has a placeholder for a title and a placeholder that can contain either bulleted text points or graphical objects available from a small icon set. The placeholder has been selected so that any change made to the text format will be applied to all text in the placeholder.

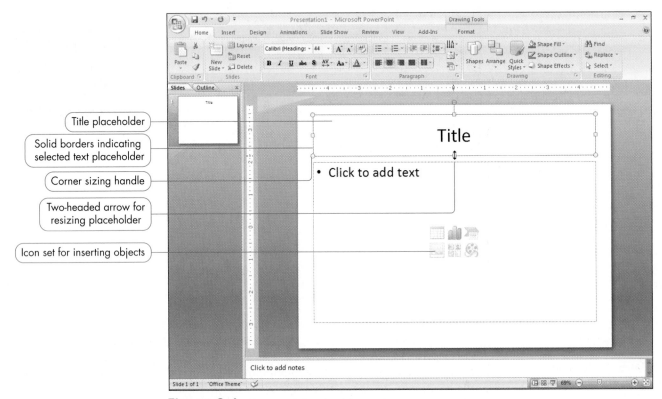

Figure 2.4 Title and Content Layout

Figure 2.5 shows the standard layouts when you open PowerPoint. By default, when you launch PowerPoint, the Home tab is active and displays the Layout command in the Slides group. Clicking Layout brings up the standard layouts for the Office Theme, the default theme. If you cannot determine which layout you need, position the mouse pointer over a layout to show the descriptive name of the layout. The descriptive name indicates the types of placeholders the layout includes.

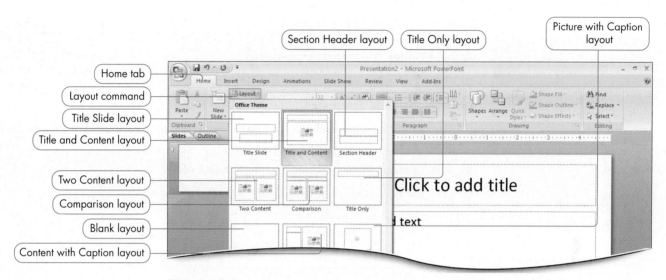

Figure 2.5 Standard Layouts

Hands-On Exercises

1 | Using a Template

Skills covered: 1. Create a New Presentation Based on an Installed Template **2.** Modify Text in a Placeholder **3.** Add a Slide and Select a Layout **4.** Add a Picture and a Caption **5.** Change a Layout

Refer to Figure 2.6 as you complete Step 1.

a. Open PowerPoint, click the **Office Button**, and then select **New**.

b. Click **Installed Templates** in the Templates Category.

The New Presentation dialog box changes to display thumbnails of the Installed Templates.

c. Select **Classic Photo Album**, and then click **Create**.

d. Save the presentation as **chap2_ho1_nature_solution**.

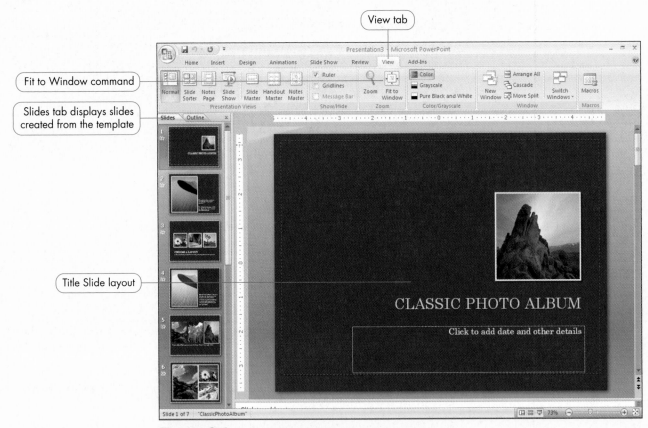

Figure 2.6 The Classic Photo Album Template

Step 2
Modify Text in a Placeholder

Refer to Figure 2.7 as you complete Step 2.

a. Select the text *CLASSIC PHOTO* in the title placeholder, and then type **NATURE**.

The newly entered text replaces the selected text.

b. Replace the subtitle text, *Click to add date and other details*, with **Favorite Pictures 2008!**

c. Click the subtitle placeholder light blue border.

The placeholder's dashed border is replaced with a solid border indicating that all of the content in the placeholder is selected.

d. Click the **Home tab** and click **Italic** and **Shadow** in the Font group.

Italic and shadowing are applied to all text in the placeholder. The shadowing is subtle, but the black shadow helps the white text stand out.

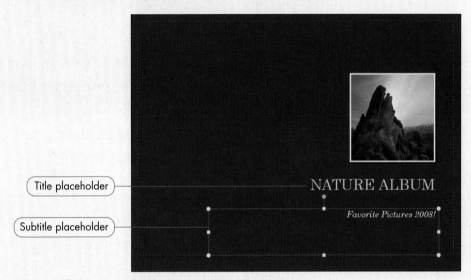

Figure 2.7 Modified Text on the Title Page

Step 3
Add a Slide and Select a Layout

Refer to Figure 2.8 as you complete Step 3.

a. Click the **Slide 2 thumbnail** displayed in the Slides tab, and then click anywhere in the text to display the placeholder.

b. Click the border of the caption placeholder, and then press **Delete**.

Pressing Delete deletes the text but not the placeholder. Because the placeholder does not print or view, you do not need to worry about it displaying. If, however, you wish to remove the placeholder, you simply click the placeholder border again and press Delete.

c. Click the **Home tab** and click the **New Slide arrow** to display the Classic Photo Album template gallery.

d. Select the **Portrait with Caption** template.

A new slide is created from the template and is inserted after Slide 2.

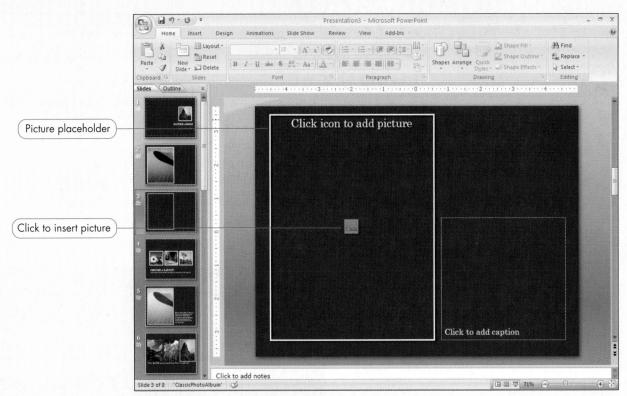

Picture placeholder

Click to insert picture

Figure 2.8 The Portrait with Caption Template

Step 4
Add a Picture and a Caption

Refer to Figure 2.9 as you complete Step 4.

a. Click the **Insert Picture button** located in the picture placeholder.

The Insert Picture dialog box displays for your use as you navigate to the location of the files for your textbook.

b. Locate *chap2_ho1_photo1* and click the **Insert button**.

c. Click inside the caption placeholder and type **Each moment of the year has its own beauty.** Press **Enter** twice, and then type **Ralph Waldo Emerson**.

d. Click the border of the caption placeholder to select the text within.

e. Click the **Home tab** and click **Center** in the Paragraph group.

f. Drag the caption placeholder to the left side of the slide, and then drag the picture placeholder to the right side of the slide.

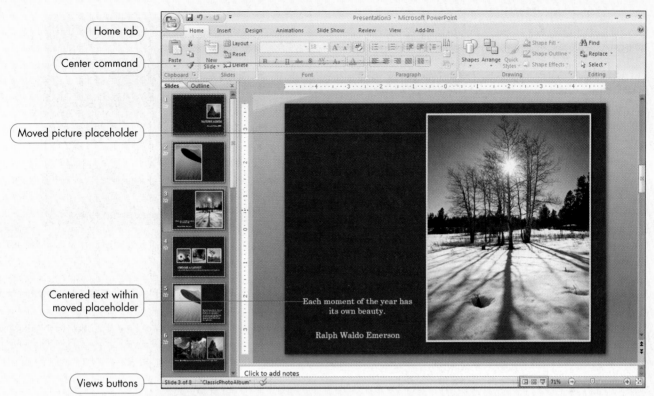

Figure 2.9 The Modified Layout

Labels for Figure 2.9:
- Home tab
- Center command
- Moved picture placeholder
- Centered text within moved placeholder
- Views buttons

Text within the figure:
Each moment of the year has its own beauty.

Ralph Waldo Emerson

Step 5
Change a Layout

Refer to Figure 2.10 as you complete Step 5.

a. Select **Slide 4**, and then click the **Home tab**, if necessary.

b. Click **Layout** in the Slides group on the Home tab.

c. Click the **2-Up Landscape with Captions** layout to apply it to the slide.

The Classic Photo Album includes a large number of layouts to provide you with a variety of pages in your album.

d. Select the extra photograph and press **Delete**. Select a border surrounding one of the caption placeholders and press **Delete**. Repeat selecting and deleting until the remaining caption placeholders have all been deleted.

When you select a new layout, placeholders may not fit the new layout perfectly. You can move or delete placeholders as necessary.

e. Select the thumbnails for **Slides 5** and **6** in the Slides tab and press **Delete**.

f. Click the **Slide Show tab**, and then click **From Beginning** in the Start Slide Show to view your presentation. Press **Esc** when you are done viewing the presentation.

g. Click **Slide Sorter** in the Views buttons area on the status bar to view all the slides showing the wide variety of layouts.

h. Save the *chap2_ho1_nature_solution* presentation and close the file.

Figure 2.10   The Completed Album

Outlines

Creating an **outline** is a method of organizing text using a **hierarchy** with main points and subpoints to denote the levels of importance of the text. An outline is the fastest way to enter or edit text for the presentation. Think of an outline as the road map you use to create your presentation. You created a basic outline when you created a storyboard for your presentation, and now you are ready to input the storyboard information into your presentation. Rather than having to enter the text in each placeholder on each slide separately, a time-consuming process, you type the text directly into an outline.

In this section, you create a presentation in Outline view. After creating the presentation, you modify the outline structure. Finally, you print the outline.

Creating a Presentation in Outline View

To create an outline for your presentation, you must be in Normal view and you need to have the Outline tab selected in the pane that contains the Outline and Slides tabs. This view is considered the **Outline view**. In this view, PowerPoint shows your presentation as an outline made up of the titles and text in each slide. Each slide will display a slide icon and a slide number. The slide title appears next to the slide icon and slide number. Main text on the slide is shown indented under the slide title.

One benefit of working in the Outline view is that you can get a good overview of your presentation. While in this view, you can move easily from one slide to the next. You can copy text from one slide to another and you can rearrange the order of the slides within a presentation. You can change the sequence of the individual bullets (subpoints) in a slide, or move points to another slide. The global overview makes it easy to see relationships between points and determine where information belongs. Figure 2.11 shows a portion of a presentation in Outline view.

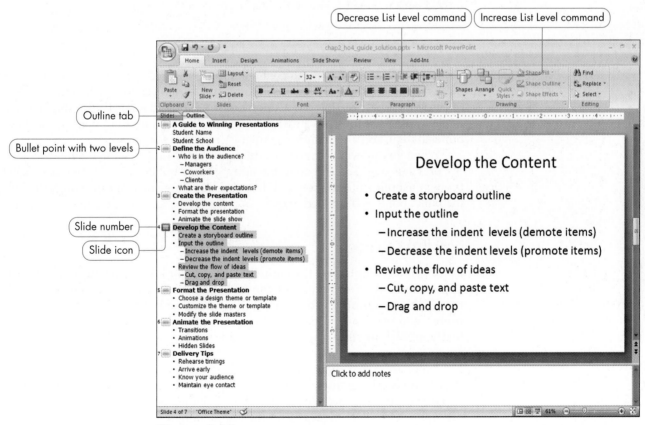

Figure 2.11   The Outline View

> Remember the lower the level of an item in an outline, the greater the importance of the item.

While Figure 2.11 shows only two levels of information in the bullet points, PowerPoint 2007 accommodates nine levels of indentation. Previous versions of PowerPoint accommodated only five. Levels make it possible to show hierarchy, or importance, of the data you enter. The main points appear on Level 1. Subsidiary items are indented below the main point to which they apply. Any item can be promoted to a higher level or demoted to a lower level, either before or after the text is entered. This is accomplished clicking Increase List Level or Decrease List Level in the Paragraph group on the Home tab. Consider carefully the number of subsidiary items you add to a main point. Too many levels of hierarchy within a single slide can make the slide difficult to read or understand as the text size automatically re-sizes to a smaller size with each additional level. Remember the lower the level of an item in an outline, the greater the importance of the item. Level 1 items are your main points. Level 9 items would be insignificant in comparison.

TIP | Changing List Levels in an Outline

As a quick keyboard alternative to using Increase and Decrease List Level commands on the Home tab, you can use a keyboard shortcut. Pressing Tab will demote an item or move it to the next level. The result is the same as increasing the indention by clicking Increase List Level. Pressing Shift+Tab promotes an item or moves it back in the list. This action decreases the indention the same as clicking Decrease List Level.

Consider, for example, Slide 4 in Figure 2.11. The title of the slide, *Develop the Content*, appears immediately after the slide number and icon. The first bullet, *Create a storyboard outline*, is indented under the title. The second bullet, *Input the outline*, has two subsidiary bullets at the next level. The next bullet, *Review the flow of ideas*, is moved back to Level 1, and it, too, has two subsidiary bullets.

Enter the Outline

The outline is an ideal way to create and edit the presentation. The insertion point marks the place where new text is entered and is established by clicking anywhere in the outline. (The insertion point automatically is placed at the title of the first slide in a new presentation.) Press Enter after typing the title or after entering the text of a bulleted item, and a new slide or bullet is created, respectively.

When you press Enter, the insertion point stays at the same indentation level as the previous one. You can continue adding more bullet points at the same level by typing the bullet information and then pressing Enter, or you can change the level of the bullet point as described above.

Edit the Outline

Editing is accomplished through the same techniques used in other Windows applications. For example, you can use the Cut, Copy, and Paste commands in the Clipboard group on the Home tab to move and copy selected text. Or, if you prefer, you can simply drag and drop text from one place to another. To locate text you wish to edit, you can click Find or Replace in the Editing group on the Home tab.

Note, too, that you can format text in the outline by using the *select-then-do* approach common to all Office applications; that is, you select the text, then you execute the appropriate command or click the appropriate command. For example, you could select the text, and then apply a new font. The selected text remains highlighted and is affected by all subsequent commands until you click elsewhere in the outline.

Modifying an Outline Structure

Because the Outline view gives you the global picture of your presentation, you can use the view to change the structure of your outline. You can shift bullets or slides around until your outline's structure is refined. To make this process simple, you can collapse or expand your view of the outline contents. A *collapsed outline* view displays only the title of the slides, while the *expanded outline* view displays the title and the content of the slides. You can collapse or expand the content in individual slides or all slides.

A *collapsed outline* displays the title of slides only in the Outline view.

An *expanded outline* displays the title and content of slides in the Outline view.

Figure 2.12 displays a collapsed view of the outline, which displays only the title of each slide. When a slide is collapsed, a wavy line appears below the slide title letting you know additional levels are collapsed. Positioning the pointer over a slide icon causes it to become a four-headed arrow. To select the slide, click the icon. To move the slide, drag the icon to the desired position.

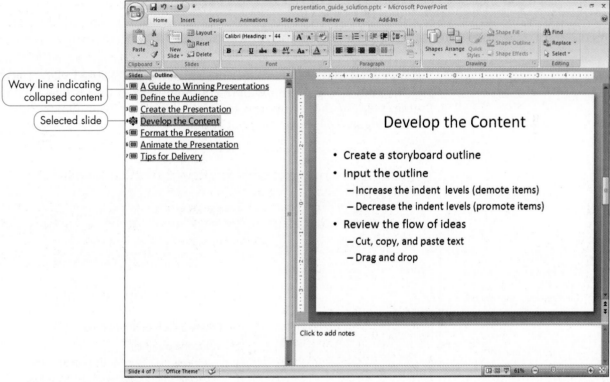

Figure 2.12 The Collapsed Outline View

To collapse a slide, select the text of the slide and right-click. The shortcut menu that appears contains the Collapse command. When you click the Collapse arrow, two new commands appear: Select Collapse or Collapse All. To expand a collapsed slide, select the slide icon and right-click Select Expand or Expand All. See Figure 2.13 for the process involved for collapsing a slide.

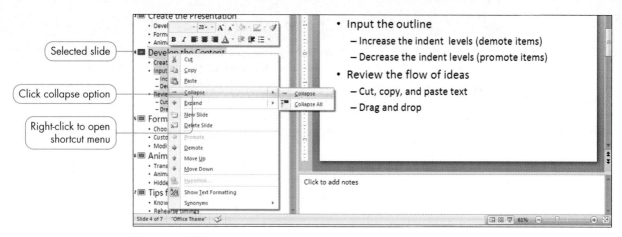

Figure 2.13 Collapse Process

Printing an Outline

You may print the outline in either the expanded or collapsed view. The slide icon and slide number will print with the outline. To print the outline, click the Office Button, point at the arrow next to Print, and select Print, Quick Print, or Print Preview. Figure 2.14 shows the print options.

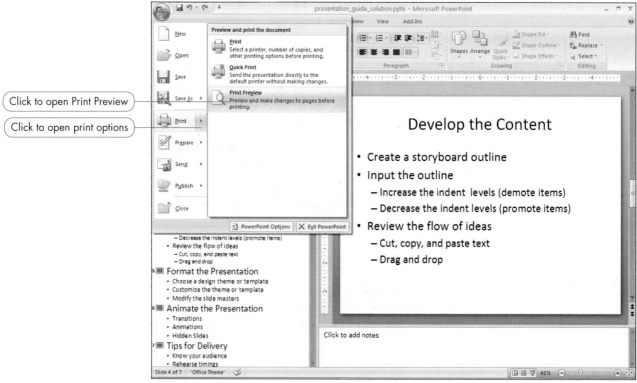

Figure 2.14 Print Options

Hands-On Exercises

2 | Creating and Modifying an Outline

Skills covered: 1. Create a Presentation in Outline View **2.** Enter an Outline **3.** Edit a Presentation **4.** Modify the Outline Structure and Print

---

Step 1

Create a Presentation in Outline View

Refer to Figure 2.15 as you complete Step 1.

a. Start a new presentation, click the **View tab** and click the **Outline tab** below the Presentation Views group.

b. Click the **Slide 1 icon** on the Outline tab.

c. Type the title of your presentation, **A Guide to Successful Presentations** in the Outline tab panes, and then press **Enter**.

   When you pressed Enter, a new slide was created. To change the level from a new slide to a subtitle, you must increase the indent level.

d. Click the **Home tab** and click **Increase List Level** in the Paragraph group.

e. Enter the first line of the subtitle, the words **Presented by**, and then press **Shift+Enter**.

   Pressing Shift+Enter moves the insertion point to the next line and keeps the same level.

f. Enter your name in the subtitle.

g. Save the file as **chap2_ho2_presentations_solution**.

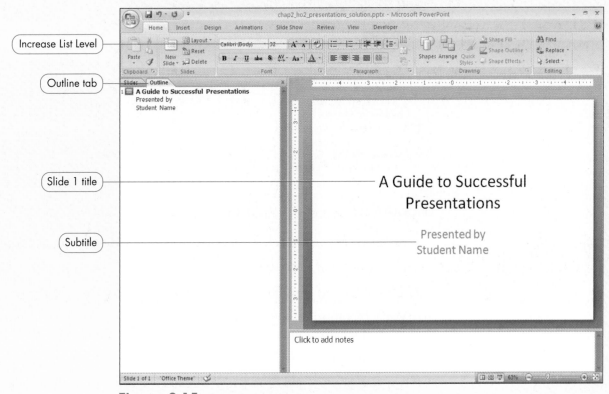

Figure 2.15   Slide 1, Title Slide

Refer to Figure 2.16 as you complete Step 2.

a. Press **Enter**, and then click **Decrease List Level** in the Paragraph group on the Home tab.

A new slide, Slide 2, is created.

b. Type the title for Slide 2, **Define the Audience**, and then press **Enter**.

c. Press **Tab** to move to the next level.

Pressing Tab is a keyboard shortcut that accomplishes the same task as clicking the Increase List Level button.

d. Type **Who is in the audience?**, and then press **Enter**.

e. Press **Tab** to move to the next level and enter the text **Managers**.

Managers becomes Level 2 text.

f. Press **Enter** and type **Coworkers**.

g. Press **Enter**, and then press **Shift+Tab** twice to return to Level 1 and create Slide 3.

h. Continue entering the text of the outline, and then save the *chap2_ho2_presentations_solution* file. Figure 2.16 contains the text to be typed.

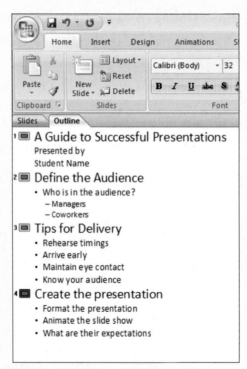

Figure 2.16 Successful Presentations Outline

Refer to Figure 2.17 as you complete Step 3.

a. Click at the end of the text *Coworkers* in Slide 2.

While proofreading your outline, you discover that you did not identify one of your audiences. You need to enter your customers as an audience.

b. Press **Enter** and type **Customers**.

TROUBLESHOOTING: If your text does not appear in the correct position, check to see if the insertion point was in the wrong location. To enter a blank line for a new bullet, the insertion point must be at the end of an existing bullet point and not at the beginning.

c. Select the text *slide show* in the second bullet point in Slide 4 and replace it with **presentation**.

After replacing the text, you notice that you left off the first step of creating a presentation—developing the content.

d. Click at the end of the title in Slide 4, and then press **Enter**.

e. Press **Tab**, type **Develop the content**, and then press **Enter**.

f. Save the *chap2_ho2_presentations_solution* file.

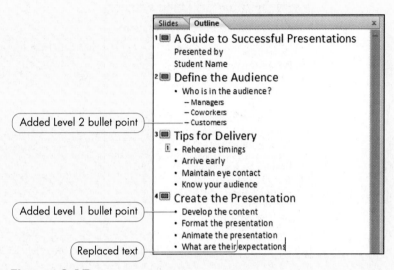

Figure 2.17 The Edited Outline

Step 4	Refer to Figure 2.18 as you complete Step 4.

Step 4
Modify the Outline Structure and Print

Refer to Figure 2.18 as you complete Step 4.

a. Position the pointer over the last bullet in **Slide 4**. When the mouse pointer looks like a four-headed arrow, click to select the text in the bullet point, What are their expectations.

The last bullet in Slide 4 is out of position. It belongs at the end of Slide 2.

b. Right-click and select **Cut**.

c. Click at the end of the last bullet point in **Slide 2** and press **Enter**. Click **Decrease List Level** in the Paragraph group on the Home tab.

d. Right-click and select **Paste**. Then type a question mark at the end of the question you just moved.

In the final review of the presentation, you realize that the slides are out of order. The *Tips for Delivery* slide should be the last slide in the presentation. Collapsing the bullets will make it easy to move the slide.

e. Right-click any bullet point, point at Collapse, and then select **Collapse All**.

f. Click the **Slide 3 icon** to select the collapsed slide.

g. Drag the **Slide 3 icon** below the Slide 4 icon and release.

h. Click the **Office Button**, point at the triangle to the right of the **Print button**, and then select **Print Preview**.

i. Click the **Print What down arrow** in the Page Setup group on the Print Preview tab, and then select **Outline View**.

j. Click **Orientation down arrow** in the Page Setup group on the Print Preview tab, and then select **Landscape**.

k. Click **Close Print Preview** in the preview group and return to editing the presentation.

l. Select all of the slides in the outline.

m. Right-click, point at the Expand button, and then click **Expand All**.

n. Repeat Steps 4h–j to view the presentation in Print Preview and change the orientation to **Portrait**.

o. Close Print Preview and save the *chap2_ho2_presentations_solution* file. Close the file.

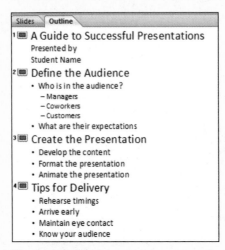

Figure 2.18 The Expanded Outline with Structural Changes

Data Imports

At some time, you may receive an outline created by a colleague using Microsoft Word or another word processing program and you need to create a presentation from that outline. Or perhaps you prefer creating your outlines in a word processing program rather than within PowerPoint. This preference poses no problems as PowerPoint can create slides based on Microsoft Word outlines or outlines saved in a format that PowerPoint recognizes.

Rich Text Format (.rtf) is a file type that retains structure and most text formatting when used to transfer documents between applications or platforms.

Plain Text Format (.txt) is a file type that retains only text when used to transfer documents between applications or platforms.

PowerPoint recognizes outlines created and saved in a *Rich Text Format (.rtf)*, a file type you can use to transfer text documents with formatting between applications such as any word processing program and PowerPoint, or even between platforms such as Macintosh and IBM. You must save the document in the RTF format with the .rtf extension if you wish to use it in PowerPoint. When you save the document in this format, the extension .rtf is assigned to it. The outline structure and most of the text formatting is retained when you import the outline into PowerPoint.

PowerPoint also recognizes outlines created and saved in a *Plain Text format (.txt)*, a file format that retains text only. When .txt outlines are imported, the hierarchical structure is lost and each line of the outline becomes a slide. No text formatting is saved. Another alternative is to import a Web document (.htm), but in this case, all the text from the file appears in one placeholder on one slide.

In this section, you learn how to import an outline into a PowerPoint presentation. You also learn how to add existing content from another presentation into the current presentation.

Importing an Outline

To create a new presentation from an outline created in another format, click the Office Button, and then select Open. When the Open dialog box displays, click All Outlines in the *Files of type* box. Any files in a format PowerPoint recognizes will be listed. Double-click the document you wish to use as the basis for your presentation. Figure 2.19 displays the same outline in three different formats. All three formats appear in the list as they are all formats PowerPoint recognizes.

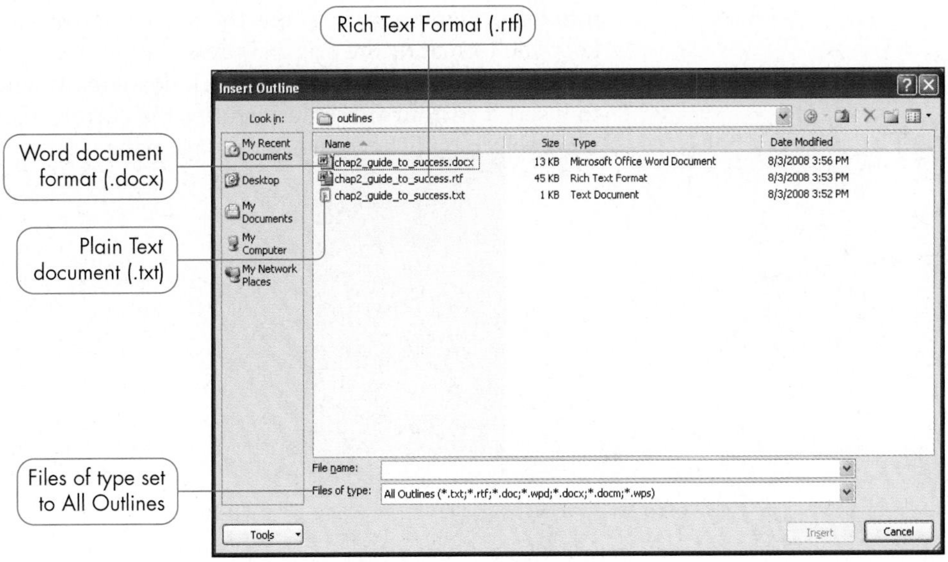

Figure 2.19 Document Formats for Importing

Adding Existing Content to a Presentation

> With each presentation you create, you create resources for the future.

After you prepare a presentation, you can reuse the content in other presentations. With each presentation you create, you create resources for the future. To obtain the content from other presentations, click New Slide in the Slides group on the Home tab. The bottom of the New Slide gallery contains options for duplicating selected slides, for inserting all the slides from an existing outline, and for reusing slides you select.

When you select the Slides from Outline command, the Insert Outline dialog box displays. By default, only outlines are displayed. You can, however, change the *Files of type* to display other files. Double-click the file you wish to use, and the outline is inserted after the current slide.

For greater flexibility, however, use the Reuse Slides to select the slides you want to use rather than insert all slides. When you select Reuse Slides, a task pane opens on the right side of your window. The Reuse Slides task pane includes a Browse button for locating the file containing the slides you wish to include in your current presentation. When you locate the file and open it, thumbnail images of your slides are displayed in the task pane. Running the pointer over a thumbnail enlarges the image so that text may be read.

At the bottom of the task pane is a check box. By default, when you insert a slide into the presentation, it retains the format of the current presentation. If you wish to keep the format or the original presentation from which you are obtaining the slide, click the *Keep source formatting* check box. Finally, click the thumbnail of your choice to insert it in your presentation after the current slide. The task pane stays open for more selections. The Reuse Slides task pane is shown in Figure 2.20.

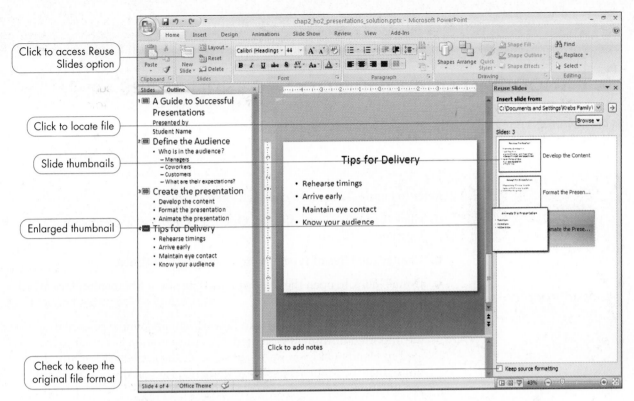

Figure 2.20 Reuse Slides Task Pane

Hands-On Exercises

3 | Importing an Outline and Reusing Slides

Skills covered: 1. Import a Microsoft Word Outline **2.** Reuse Slides from Another Presentation

---

Step 1
Import a Microsoft Word Outline

Refer to Figure 2.21 as you complete Step 1.

a. Click the **Office Button**, select **Open**, and then navigate to your classroom file location.

b. Change the **Files of type** option to show **All Outlines**.

c. Double-click to open the file *chap2_ho3_success*, a Microsoft Office Word document.

The Word outline is opened into PowerPoint and a new presentation based upon the imported document is created. This presentation is similar to the one you created in Hands-On Exercise 1, but some of the content is slightly different. Also, notice that the font is Times New Roman, based on the outline imported into the presentation.

d. Click the **Outline tab**, and select **Slide 3**, *Create the Presentation*.

e. Save the file as **chap2_ho3_guide_solution**.

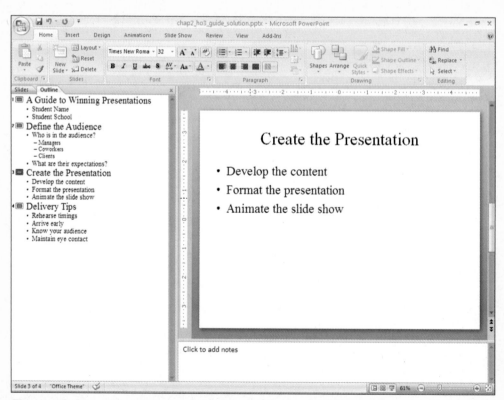

Figure 2.21   New Presentation Based on a Word Outline

Refer to Figure 2.22 as you complete Step 2.

a. Click the **Home tab** and click **New Slide** in the Slides group.

The New Slide gallery appears.

b. Click **Reuse Slides** at the bottom of the gallery.

The Reuse Slides pane appears on the right side of your screen.

c. Click the **Browse button**, click **Browse File**, and locate your student files.

d. Click to select the file *chap2_ho3_development*, and then click **Open**.

TROUBLESHOOTING: If you do not see the *chap2_ho3_development* presentation, change the *Files of type* option to All PowerPoint Presentations.

e. Click each of the slides in the Reuse Slides task pane to insert the slides into the slide show.

f. Close the Reuse Slides task pane.

g. Refer to Figure 2.22. Move slides as needed to obtain the correct structure, if necessary.

Ignore font changes, as we will handle design issues in the next section of this chapter.

h. Save the *chap2_ho3_guide_solution* file and keep it onscreen if you plan to continue to the next hands-on exercise. Close the file and exit PowerPoint if you do not want to continue with the next exercise at this time.

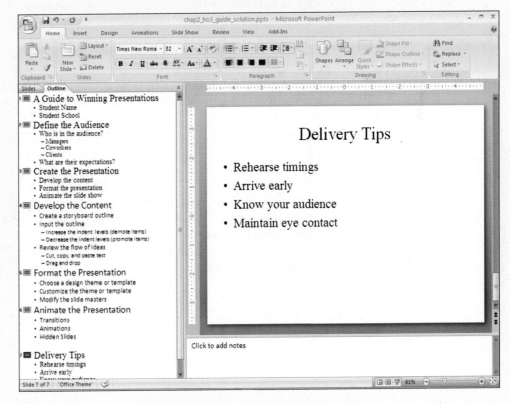

Figure 2.22   Reused Slides Added to Presentation

Design

> You should evaluate many aspects when considering the visual design of your presentation.

When you work with the content of a presentation, it can be helpful to work with the blank template, as you did when we worked with the outlines. Working in the blank template lets you concentrate on what you want to say. After you are satisfied with the content, however, you need to consider the visual aspects of the presentation. You should evaluate many aspects when considering the visual design of your presentation. Those aspects include layout, background, typography, color, and animation.

Because the majority of people using PowerPoint are not graphic artists and do not have a strong design background, Microsoft designers created a variety of methods to help users deal with design issues. By now, you should have explored themes and templates that are used to help people create an attractively designed slide show without a background in design.

In this section, you explore additional Microsoft features to aid with design. After you are comfortable using these features, you can modify the design to reflect your own taste. Before doing so, however, you need to examine some basic visual design principles for PowerPoint.

Examining Slide Show Design Principles

Basic design principles are universal. When applied to a project, they can increase its appeal and professionalism. While basic principles are universal, some aspects may be applied in specific ways to the various types of modern communication: communicating through print mediums such as flyers or brochures, through audio mediums such as narrations or music, or through a visual medium such as a slide show. You will focus on a few of the principles that apply to slide shows and examine examples of slides that illustrate the principles.

Remember that these principles are guidelines. You may chose to avoid applying one of these principles, but you should be aware of the principle and why you are not following it. If you are in doubt about your design, ask a classmate or colleague to review the design and make suggestions. Fresh eyes can see things you may not.

Applying and Modifying a Design Theme

You should already have experience applying a theme. You can tweak the theme once it is applied. You can change the colors used in the theme, the fonts used, and effects used. You can even change the background styles. Each of these options is on the Design tab, and each has its own gallery. Figure 2.30 shows the locations for accessing the galleries.

Examples of Designs for Various Audiences | Reference

Figure 2.23 Examples of Choosing a Template for Audience

- All design elements should be appropriate for the audience. Carefully consider your audience and their background, and then use a design that fits the background of the audience. For example, for a presentation to elementary students, you may use bright primary colors in your color scheme and cartoon-like clip art to keep their attention. Fonts should be large and easy to read. For a presentation to landscape designers, however, you may choose muted earth tones and more photographs than text to convey your message. Photographs give the slide show a more professional appearance. In a formal presentation to a group of stockholders, however, you may choose a traditional blue color scheme with tables, charts, and graphs to convey your message. Figure 2.23 shows design examples suitable for grade-schoolers and business people respectively.

Figure 2.24 Examples of a Cluttered Design (left) and a Clean Design (right)

- Keep the design neat and clean. This principle is often referred to as KISS: Keep it simple, sweetie! • Avoid using multiple fonts and colors on a slide. • Too many fonts and colors make the slide look cluttered and busy. • Avoid using more than five colors on a slide and three fonts. • Avoid using multiple clip art images. • Use white space, or empty space, to open your design.

Figure 2.25 Examples of an Ineffective Focal Point (left) and an Effective Focal Point (right)

- Create a focal point, or main area of interest, on your slide and have everything else lead the viewer's eyes to that location. Images should always lead the viewer's eyes to the focal point, not away from it. Images should not be so large they detract from the focal point, unless your goal is to make the image the focal point.

Sans Serif   Serif

Figure 2.26   Sans Serif and Serif Fonts

- Carefully consider the output of your presentation. If your presentation is to be delivered through a projection device, consider using sans serif fonts with short text blocks. If your presentation will be delivered as a printout, consider using a serif font, as the serifs help guide the reader's eyes across the page. You may use longer text blocks in printed presentations. Figure 2.26 displays an example of a sans serif font—a font that does not have serifs, or small lines, at the ends of letters. It also shows an example of a serif font with the serifs on the letter "S" circled. Decorative fonts are also available. When choosing a font, remember that readability is critical in a presentation.

Figure 2.27   Unified Design Elements

- Use a unified design for a professional look. Visual unity creates a harmony between the elements of the slide and the slides in the slide show. Unity gives the viewer a sense of order and peace. Create unity by repeating colors and shapes. Use clip art in one style so the design is unified.

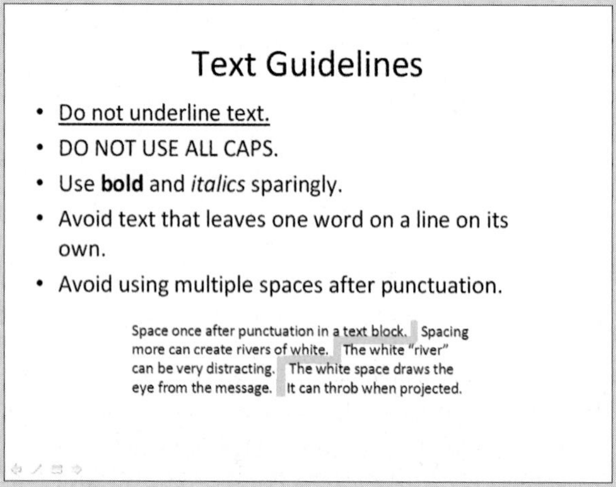

Text Guidelines

- <u>Do not underline text.</u>
- DO NOT USE ALL CAPS.
- Use **bold** and *italics* sparingly.
- Avoid text that leaves one word on a line on its own.
- Avoid using multiple spaces after punctuation.

Space once after punctuation in a text block.   Spacing more can create rivers of white.   The white "river" can be very distracting.   The white space draws the eye from the message.   It can throb when projected.

Figure 2.28   Appropriate and Inappropriate Text Examples

- Text is also a visual element. Text guidelines are:
  - Do not underline text. Underlined text is harder to read, and it is generally assumed that the text is a hyperlink.
  - Avoid using all capital letters in titles, bulleted lists, or long text blocks. In addition to being difficult to read, it is considered to be yelling at the audience.
  - Use italic and bold sparingly. They can create visual clutter. Also, too much emphasis confuses the audience about what is important and creates the impression of no emphasis.
  - Avoid creating lines of text that leave a single word hanging on a line of its own.
  - Use just one space after punctuation in text blocks. This practice avoids distracting "rivers of white space" in the text block.

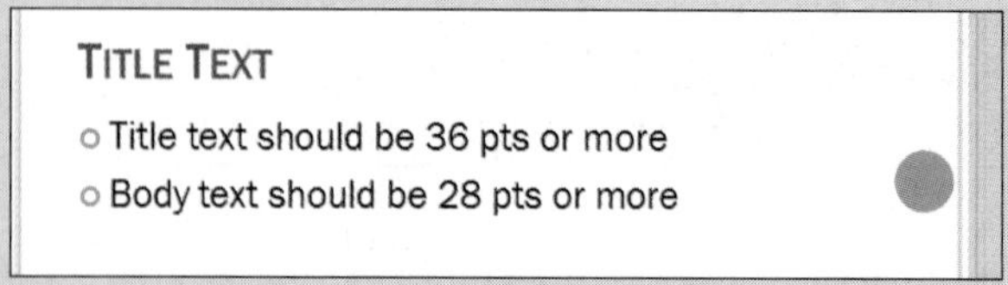

TITLE TEXT

○ Title text should be 36 pts or more
○ Body text should be 28 pts or more

Figure 2.29   Readable Text Guidelines

- Make text readable. Title text should use title case and be 36 pts or higher. Bullet text should be in sentence case and be 28 pts or higher. Remember the 7 × 7 guideline. When you create more than seven lines on a slide, PowerPoint automatically resizes the font to a smaller size that is difficult to read when projected.

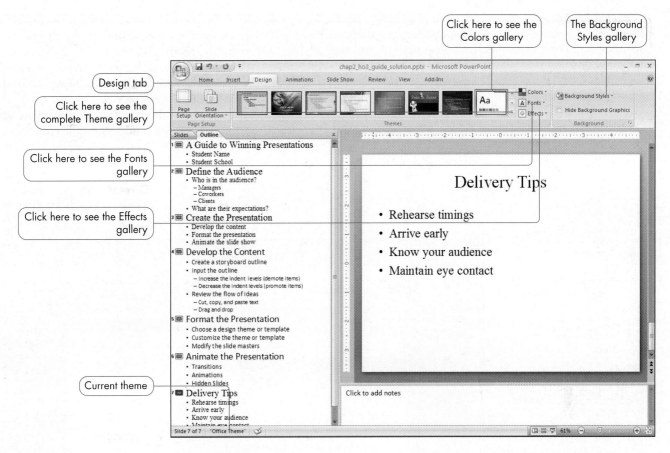

Figure 2.30 Design Galleries

The **Colors gallery** is a gallery with a set of colors for every available theme.

Each PowerPoint theme includes a **Colors gallery**, a gallery that provides a set of colors. Each color in the gallery is assigned to a different element in the theme design. Once the theme is selected, you can click the Colors down arrow to display the Built-In gallery. Clicking one of the color themes applies it to the theme, thereby applying it to the presentation. You can even create your own color theme set by selecting Create New Theme Colors at the bottom of the gallery.

The **Fonts gallery** contains font sets for title text and body text.

Selecting a font for the title and one for the bullets or body text of your presentation can be difficult. Without a background in typography, it is hard to determine which fonts go together well. The **Fonts gallery** is a gallery that pairs a title font and a body font for your use. Click any of the samples in the Fonts gallery, and the font pair is applied to your theme. You do not need to select the slides because the change applies to all slides.

The **Effects gallery** includes a range of effects for shapes used in the presentation.

The **Effects gallery** is a gallery that displays a full range of special effects that can be applied to all shapes in the presentation. This aids you in maintaining the consistency of the look of your presentation. Effects in the gallery include a soft glow, soft edges to the shape, shadows, or a three-dimensional (3-D) look.

You can change the background style of the theme by accessing the **Background Styles gallery**, a gallery containing backgrounds consistent with the color theme. The backgrounds fall into one of three areas: subtle, moderate, or intense. Subtle backgrounds are a solid color, while intense backgrounds are designed with patterns such as checks, stripes, blocks, or dots. Simply changing your background style can liven up a presentation and give it your individual style.

Some of the themes, like Equity, include shapes on their background to create the design. If the background shapes are interfering with other objects on the slide, however, you can click the Hide Background Graphics check box and the background shapes will not display for that slide.

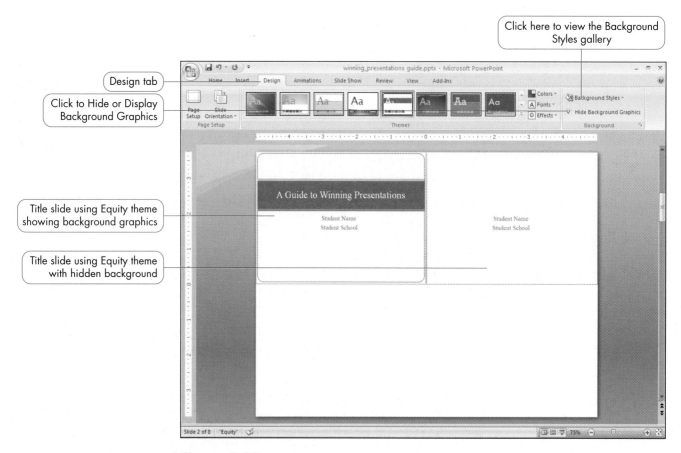

Figure 2.31 Equity Theme

Inserting a Header or Footer

You will find that many times there is information that you want to appear on every slide, handout, or notes page. As a student, your instructor may want your name on every handout you turn in or the date you completed the assignment. Use the Header and Footer feature to do this. A **header** contains information that appears at the top of pages in a handout or on a notes page. A **footer** contains information that appears at the bottom of slides in a presentation or at the bottom of pages in a handout or a notes page.

Common uses of headers and footers are to insert slide numbers, the time and date, a company logo, the presenter's name, or even the presentation's file name. Headers and footers can contain text or graphics. To insert text in a header or footer, you use the Header and footers command. To insert graphics, you modify the header or footer fields in the Slide Master. For now, you will use the Header and footer command. You can use Help to learn how to customize a Slide Master to include a logo graphic in a footer. Figure 2.32 shows an example of a title slide with a footer.

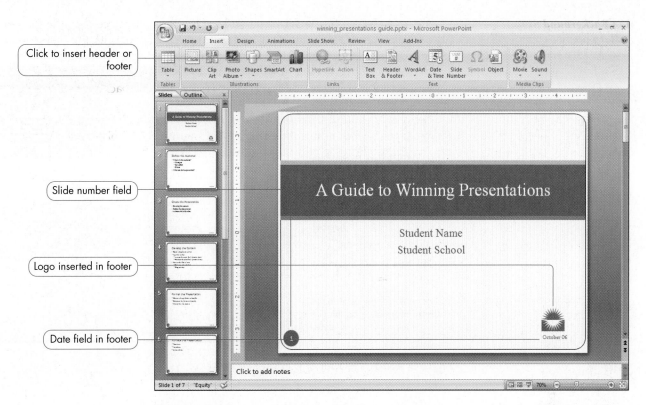

Figure 2.32 Title Slide with Footer

To create a footer for a slide, click the Insert tab, and then click Header & Footer in the Text group. Click the Slide tab when the Header and Footer dialog box displays. Click the Date and time check box in the *Include on slide* section to insert the current date and time. Click *Update automatically* if you wish the date to always be current. Once you select *Update automatically*, you can select the date format you prefer. Alternatively, you can choose the option to enter a fixed date that will not change. You use a fixed date to preserve the original date you created the presentation, which could help you keep track of versions.

A check box also activates the Slide number field. Click the Footer check box to activate the footer field. When you click the check box, the insertion point is placed inside the Footer box, and you can enter any information you desire. The Preview window lets you see the position of these fields. If you do not want the footer to appear on the title slide, click the *Don't show on title slide* check box. The last step is to click Apply to apply the footer to the selected slide or to click Apply All to apply the footer to every slide in the presentation. Figure 2.33 shows the Header and Footer dialog box with the Slide tab selected.

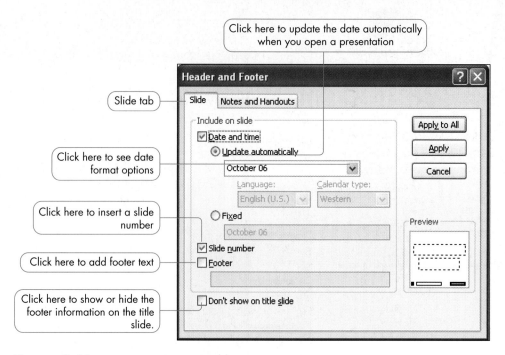

Figure 2.33 Header and Footer Dialog box

The Notes and Handouts tab gives you many of the same options available in the Slides tab. You can add more information in this tab, however, because it gives you an extra field box for information—the Header field. Since this feature is used for printouts, the slides are not numbered, but the pages in the handout are. As you activate the fields, the preview window shows the location of the fields. The Date and Time field is located on the top right of the printout. The Header field is located on the top left. The page number is located on the bottom right, and the Footer field is on the bottom left.

Hands-On Exercises

4 | Applying and Modifying a Design Theme

Skills covered: 1. Apply a Theme to a Presentation **2.** Apply a Color Scheme **3.** Add a Font Scheme **4.** Apply a Background Style **5.** Hide Background Graphics on a Slide **6.** Save Current Theme **7.** Create a Slide Footer **8.** Create a Handout Header and Footer

Step 1	Refer to Figure 2.34 as you complete Step 1.
Apply a Theme to a Presentation	**a.** Open the *chap2_ho3_guide_solution* file if you closed it after the last hands-on exercise. Save the file as **chap2_ho4_guide_solution**.

b. Click the **Design tab** and click the **More button** in the Themes group.

The Themes gallery opens for you to select from Themes in This Presentation, from the Built-In themes, from Office Online, or enables you to Browse for Themes you have previously created and saved.

c. Click the **Solstice theme**.

The theme is applied to all slides in the presentation.

d. Save the *chap2_ho4_guide_solution* presentation.

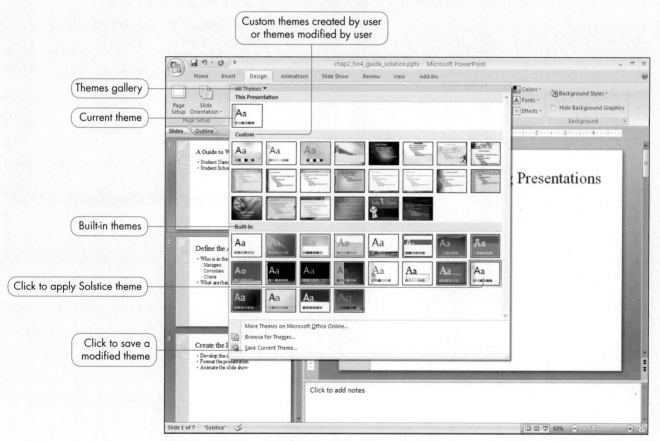

Figure 2.34 Solstice Theme

Step 2
Apply a Color Scheme

Refer to Figure 2.35 as you complete Step 2.

a. With *chap2_ho4_guide_solution* open, point at the Colors button in the Themes group.

Note the ScreenTip that appears showing the currently applied color scheme applied—Solstice.

b. Click **Colors** in the Themes group on the Design tab to see the Built-In gallery.

c. Point to several of the color schemes to see the effects they have on the title slide.

The color scheme is not applied until you click.

d. Click the **Origin color scheme**.

The color scheme is applied to your presentation.

e. Save the *chap2_ho4_guide_solution* presentation.

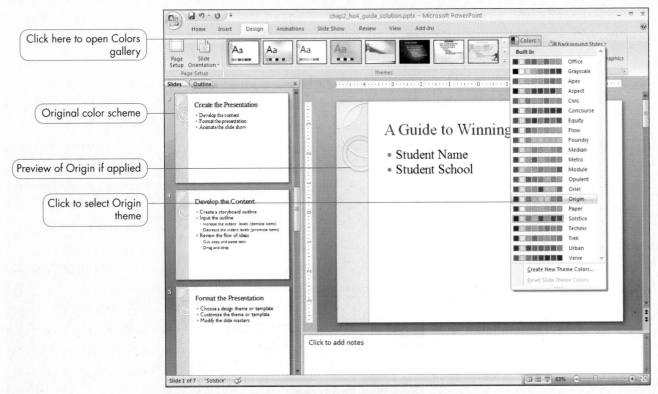

Figure 2.35 Solstice Theme with Origin Color Theme

Refer to Figure 2.36 as you complete Step 3.

a. With *chap2_ho4_guide_solution* open, click the **Outline tab**.

b. Note that Slides 1, 2, 3, and 7 use different fonts than Slides 4, 5, and 6.

Slides 4, 5, and 6 were created by reusing slides from another presentation, causing the font shift. Slides 1, 2, 3, and 7 use a serif font—Times New Roman. Slides 4, 5, and 6 use a sans serif font—Gill Sans.

c. Click the **Design tab** and click **Fonts** in the Themes group.

The Built-In fonts appear in the gallery.

d. Click the **Flow font scheme** to apply it to your presentation.

The Flow font scheme applies the Calibri font to titles and the Constantia font to body text.

TROUBLESHOOTING: If the font scheme does not apply to all slides, select the slide that did not have the scheme applied and then change the title and bullets manually.

e. Save the *chap2_ho4_guide_solution* presentation.

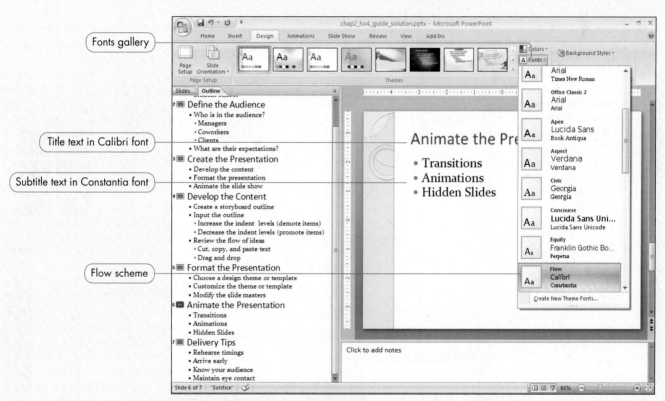

Figure 2.36 The Flow Font Scheme

Refer to Figure 2.37 as you complete Step 4.

a. With *chap2_ho4_guide_solution* open, click the **Slides tab**.

Changing to the Slides tab enables you to see the background style you apply on several slides.

b. Click **Background Styles** in the Background group on the Design tab.

c. Point at each of the styles and note the changes to the background graphic on the side of the slide.

TIP Choosing Backgrounds Based on Lighting

A dark background choice is appropriate if you will be giving your presentation in a very light room. If you use a light background in a light room, your audience may not see your text because there would not be enough contrast. If you give your presentation in a dark room, select a light background. A dark background in a dark room gives your audience an invitation to sleep!

---

d. Click **Style 6**.

e. Save the *chap2_ho4_guide_solution* presentation.

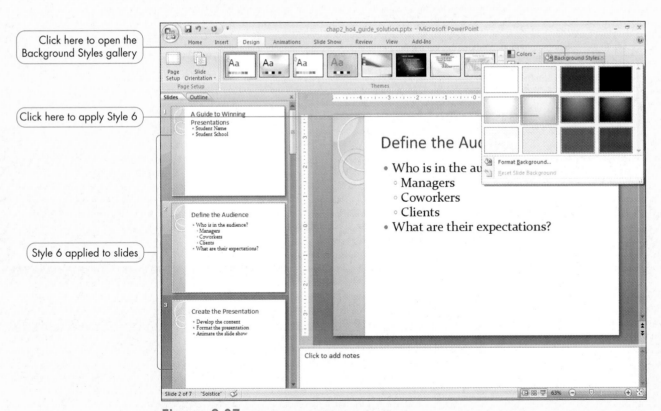

Figure 2.37 Background Style 6 Applied

Step 5
Hide Background Graphics on a Slide

Refer to Figure 2.38 as you complete Step 5.

a. With *chap2_ho4_guide_solution* open, click to select **Slide 1**, if necessary.

You decide to put a photograph related to presenting on the bottom of the title slide to add color. To keep the slide from being cluttered, you decide to remove the background graphics.

b. Click the **Hide Background Graphics check box** in the Background group on the Design tab.

c. Click the **Insert tab** and click **Clip Art** in the Illustrations group.

d. In the Clip Art task pane, type **presenter** in the **Search for** box.

e. Click the **Results should be arrow**, remove the check marks from all media types except Photographs, and then click **GO**.

f. Click the image of the presenter in the red jacket, drag it to the lower right of your slide, and then close the Clip Art task pane.

The red jacket adds more color to the title slide. Your clip art gallery may have more images if you are connected to Microsoft Online, but you can drag the scroll bar to locate this image. Figure 2.38 indicates the image to click. Because the image is positioned on the lower left, the audience's eyes would flow down to the image after reading the title. The image is looking away, which leads their eyes off the slide—a visual clue that the slide is finished. If the image was placed higher on the slide, you would flip it so that it looks inward to the focal point, the title text. Figure 2.39 displays the completed slide.

g. Click the **Home tab**, click **Layout** in the Slides group, and click **Title Slide**.

The first slide was formatted by the Title and Text layout when you import the Word outline in Hand-On Excercise 2. You applied Title Slide layout to convert the bullet-list items to a subtitle.

h. Save the *chap2_ho4_guide_solution* presentation.

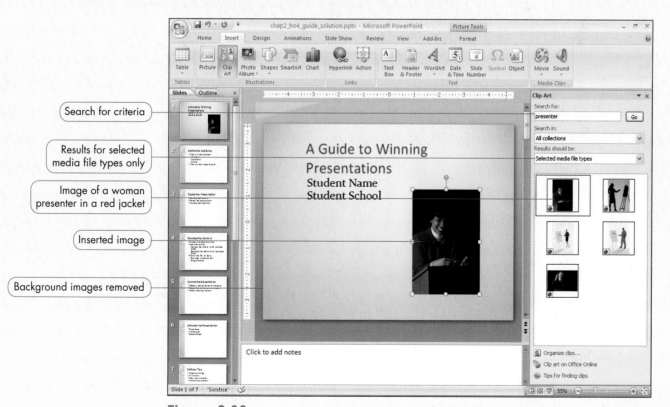

Figure 2.38 Background Image Removed and Clip Art Added

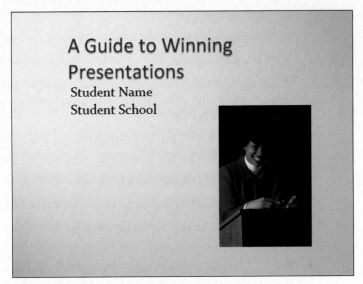

A Guide to Winning
Presentations
Student Name
Student School

Figure 2.39 Modified Title Slide

Refer to Figure 2.40 as you complete Step 6.

a. With *chap2_ho4_guide_solution* open, click **More** in the Themes group on the Design tab.

To save time in the future, you save the theme you created when you customized the Solstice theme.

b. Click **Save Current Theme**.

c. Type **presenter_theme** in the **File name** box and click **Save**.

d. Click **More** in the Themes group on the Design tab.

A new theme category has been added to the All Themes gallery—the Custom category.

e. Point at the theme displaying in the Custom category. Note the ScreenTip showing the theme name. This is the presenter_theme you just created.

f. Save the *chap2_ho4_guide_solution* presentation.

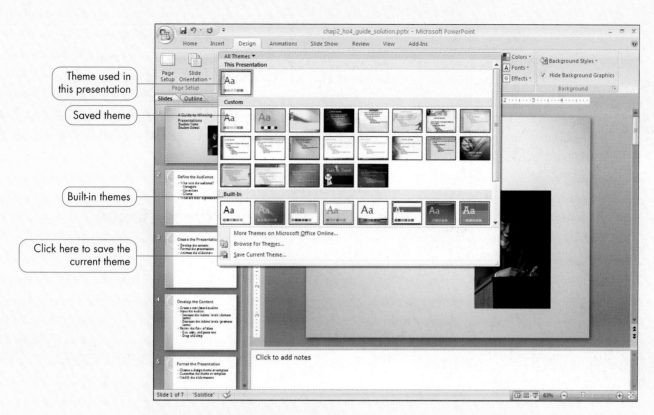

Theme used in this presentation

Saved theme

Built-in themes

Click here to save the current theme

Figure 2.40 All Themes Gallery

Refer to Figure 2.41 as you complete Step 7.

a. With *chap2_ho4_guide_solution* open, click the **Insert tab**, and then click **Header & Footer** in the Text group.

b. In the Header and Footer dialog box, click the **Date and time check box** in the *Include on slide* section.

c. Click **Update automatically**, if it is not already selected.

d. Click the **drop-down arrow** and select the sixth date format in the list.

The sixth date format spells out the month and then includes the year, such as June 08.

e. Click the **Slide number check box**.

f. Click the **Don't show on title slide option check box**.

Clicking this check box adds a check mark hiding the footer on the title slide.

g. Click **Apply to All**.

h. Click the **Slide 1 thumbnail** to display the slide in the Slides pane.

Notice that the footer does not appear on this slide because you selected the option to hide the footer on the title slide.

i. Save the *chap2_ho4_guide_solution* presentation.

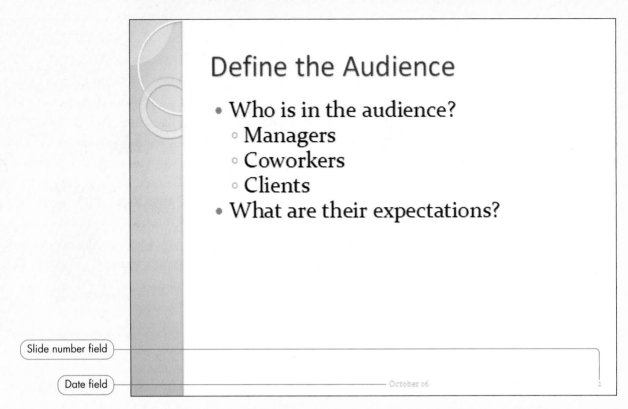

Figure 2.41 The Slide Footer

Refer to Figure 2.42 as you complete Step 8.

a. With *chap2_ho4_guide_solution* open, click the **Insert tab**, if necessary, and then click **Header & Footer** in the Text group.

b. Click the **Notes and Handouts tab**.

In the previous exercise, you created a footer that displays when the slide show plays. In this exercise, you create a header and footer that only displays on printouts.

c. Click the **Date and time check box**.

d. Click **Update automatically**, if needed.

By selecting the Update automatically option, you ensure that any printouts will display the current date and not the date the presentation originally was created.

e. Click the **drop-down arrow** and select the sixth date format in the list.

f. Click the **Header check box** and enter your name in the text box.

g. Click the **Footer check box** and enter your instructor's name and your class.

Footers often are used for identifying information.

h. Click the **Apply to All button**.

i. Click the **Office Button**, point at the **Print arrow**, and then select **Print Preview**.

j. Change the *Print What* option to **Handouts (4 Slides Per Page)**.

k. Note the placement of the header, date, footer, and slide number. Click **Close Print Preview**.

l. Save the *chap2_ho4_guide_solution* presentation. Close the presentation.

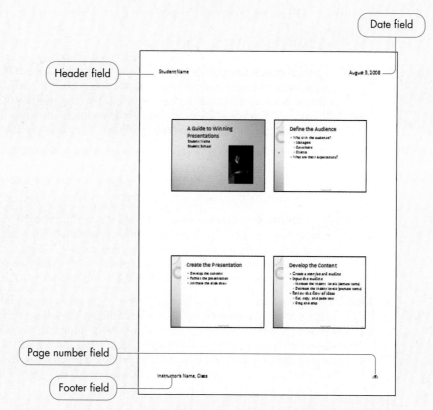

Figure 2.42 Handout Header and Footer

Summary

1. **Create a presentation using a template.** Using a template saves you a great deal of time and enables you to create a more professional presentation. Templates incorporate a theme, a layout, and content that can be modified. You can use templates that are installed when Microsoft Office is installed, or you can download templates from Microsoft Office Online. Microsoft is constantly adding templates to the online site for your use.

2. **Modify a template.** In addition to changing the content of a template, you can modify the structure and design. The structure is modified by changing the layout of a slide. To change the layout, drag placeholders to new locations or resize placeholders. You can even add placeholders so that elements such as logos can be included.

3. **Create a presentation in Outline view.** When you use a storyboard to determine your content, you create a basic outline. Then you can enter your presentation in Outline view, which enables you to concentrate on the content of the presentation. Using Outline view keeps you from getting buried in design issues at the cost of your content. It also saves you time because you can enter the information without having to move from placeholder to placeholder.

4. **Modify an outline structure.** Because the Outline view gives you a global view of the presentation, it helps you see the underlying structure of the presentation. You are able to see where content needs to be strengthened, or where the flow of information needs to be revised. If you find a slide with content that would be presented better in another location in the slide show, you can use the Collapse and Expand features to easily move it. By collapsing the slide content, you can drag it to a new location and then expand it. To move individual bullet points, cut and paste the bullet point or drag-and-drop it.

5. **Print an outline.** When you present, using the outline version of your slide show as a reference is a boon. No matter how well you know your information, it is easy to forget to present some information when facing an audience. While you would print speaker's notes if you have many details, you can print the outline as a quick reference. The outline can be printed in either the collapsed or the expanded form, giving you far fewer pages to shuffle in front of an audience than printing speaker's notes would.

6. **Import an outline.** You do not need to re-enter information from an outline created in Microsoft Word or another word processor. You can use the Open feature to import any outline that has been saved in a format that PowerPoint can read. In addition to a Word outline, you can use the common generic formats Rich Text Format and Plain Text Format.

7. **Add existing content to a presentation.** After you spend time creating the slides in a slide show, you may find that slides in the slide show would be appropriate in another show at a later date. Any slide you create can be reused in another presentation, thereby saving you considerable time and effort. You simply open the Reuse Slides pane, locate the slide show with the slide you need, and then click the thumbnail of the slide to insert a copy of it in the new slide show.

8. **Examine slide show design principles.** With a basic understanding of slide show design principles, you can create presentations that reflect your personality in a professional way. The goal of applying these principles is to create a slide show that focuses the audience on the message of the slide without being distracted by clutter or unreadable text.

9. **Apply and modify a design theme.** PowerPoint provides you with themes to help you create a clean, professional look for your presentation. Once a theme is applied, you can modify the theme by changing the color scheme, the font scheme, the effects scheme, or the background style.

10. **Insert a header or footer.** Identifying information can be included in a header or footer. You may, for example, wish to include the group to whom you are presenting, the location of the presentation, or a copyright notation for original work. You can apply footers to slides, handouts, and Notes pages. Headers may be applied to handouts and Notes pages.

Key Terms

Multiple Choice

1. A file that incorporates a theme, a layout, and content that can be modified is known as a:

   (a) Hierarchy
   (b) Footer
   (c) Speaker note
   (d) Template

2. To create a presentation based on an installed template, click the:

   (a) File tab and then Open
   (b) Office Button and then New
   (c) Insert tab and then Add Template
   (d) Design tab and then New

3. What advantage, if any, is there to collapsing the outline so only the slide titles are visible?

   (a) More slides are displayed at one time, making it easier to rearrange the slides in the presentation.
   (b) Transition and animations can be added.
   (c) Graphical objects become visible.
   (d) All of the above.

4. Which of the following is true?

   (a) Slides cannot be added to a presentation after a template has been chosen.
   (b) The slide layout can be changed before the template has been chosen.
   (c) Placeholders downloaded with a template cannot be modified.
   (d) The slide layout can be changed after the template has been chosen.

5. How do you insert identifying information on every slide in a presentation?

   (a) Click the Design tab and click Events.
   (b) Click the Insert tab and click Headers and Footers.
   (c) Click the View tab and click Headers and Footers.
   (d) Click the Home tab and click Events.

6. Which of the following is true?

   (a) PowerPoint supplies many different templates, but each template has only one color scheme.
   (b) You cannot change the color scheme of a presentation.
   (c) PowerPoint supplies many different templates, and each template in turn has multiple color schemes.
   (d) You cannot change a template once it has been selected.

7. Which of the following is the fastest and most efficient method for reusing a slide layout you have customized in another presentation?

   (a) Open the slide with the customized layout, delete the content, and enter the new information.
   (b) Open the slide with the customized layout and cut and paste the placeholders to a new slide.
   (c) Save the custom slide layout and reuse it in the new presentation.
   (d) Drag the placeholders from one slide to the next.

8. You own a small business and decide to institute an Employee of the Month award program. Which of the following would be the fastest way to create the award certificate with a professional look?

   (a) Access Microsoft Office Online and download an Award certificate template.
   (b) Select a Design Theme, modify the placeholders, and then enter the award text information.
   (c) Open Microsoft Word, insert a table, enter the award text in the table, and then add clip art.
   (d) Enter the text in the title placeholder of a slide, change the font for each line, and drag several clip art images of awards onto the slide.

9. Which of the following moves a bullet point from the first level to the second level in an outline?

   (a) Shift+Tab
   (b) Tab
   (c) Decrease List Level
   (d) Ctrl+Tab

10. The Increase List Level and Decrease List Level commands are available from which tab?

    (a) Home
    (b) Insert
    (c) Design
    (d) Slide Show

11. Which of the following formats cannot be imported to use as an outline for a presentation?

    (a) .docx
    (b) .rtf
    (c) .txt
    (d) .tiff

12. You create a presentation for a local volunteer organization. When you arrive to present at its office, you find the room you are presenting in has many windows. Which of the following procedures should you follow?

    (a) Change the theme of the presentation to a theme with a dark background.

    (b) Change the background style to a dark background.

    (c) Close the blinds to darken the room.

    (d) Any of the above.

13. Which of the following statements is a true text design guideline?

    (a) Title text should be 36 pts or larger.

    (b) Use underlining to emphasize key points.

    (c) Create all titles in ALL CAPS.

    (d) Bold all bullet points.

14. Which of the following is not a field in the Header and Footer dialog box?

    (a) Date and time

    (b) Slide number

    (c) File name

    (d) Footer

15. To add existing content to a presentation, use which of the following features?

    (a) Duplicate Selected Slides

    (b) Slides from Outline

    (c) Reuse Slides

    (d) All of the above

Practice Exercises

1 Download and Modify a Template

Figure 2.43 displays an Employee of the Year Award for Olsen Cabinets. It was created from a template downloaded from Microsoft Office Online. A small business owner who runs a cabinet shop might use an award program to motivate employees and could create this award quickly by downloading the template and modifying it. Assume you are the owner of Olsen Cabinets and you want to present your employee, Michael Mulhern, with the Employee of the Year Award.

a. Click the **Office Button**, and then select **New**.
b. Click **Award certificates** in the Microsoft Office Online category.
c. Click the **Employee of the year award**, and then click **Download**.
d. Save the file as **chap2_pe1_award_solution**.
e. Drag to select the text *Company Name* and type **OLSEN CABINETS**.
f. Drag to select the text *EMPLOYEE NAME* and type **Michael Mulhern**.
g. Select *Michael Mulhern* and move your pointer slightly upward to activate the Mini toolbar with text options.
h. Click **Bold**, and then click **Italic**.
i. Drag to select the text *Presenter's Name and Title*, and then enter your name and your class.
j. Save the *chap2_pe1_award_solution* file and close it.

Figure 2.43   Download and Modify a Template

2 Create an Outline

The Wellness Education Center at your school promotes the overall wellness among students and employees. The center provides many services and needs to make the campus community aware of these services. You volunteer to create a presentation that can be shown to campus groups to inform them about the center and its mission. Figure 2.44 shows the outline of the presentation.

a. In a new presentation, click the **View tab**, and then click **Normal** in the Presentation Views group (if necessary).
b. Click the **Outline tab**.
c. Type the title of your presentation, **Wellness Education Center**, and then press **Enter**.
d. Save the file as **chap2_pe2_center_solution**.
e. Click the **Home tab** and click **Increase List Level** in the Paragraph group.
f. Enter the first line of the subtitle, **Dedicated to**.

...continued on Next Page

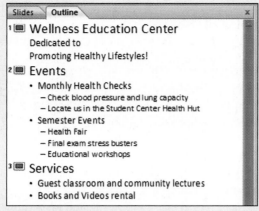

Figure 2.44 Create an Outline

g. Press **Shift+Enter** to move the point of insertion to the next line of the subtitle placeholder.

h. Type the second line of the subtitle, **Promoting Healthy Lifestyles!**

i. Press **Enter**, and then click **Decrease List Level** in the Paragraph group on the Home tab.

j. Type the title **Events**, and then press **Enter**.

k. Press **Tab**, and then type **Monthly Health Checks**.

l. Press **Enter**, and then press **Tab**.

m. Type **Check blood pressure and lung capacity**, and then press **Enter**.

n. Type **Locate us in the Student Center Health Hut**, and then press **Enter**.

o. Press **Shift+Tab**.

p. Continue entering the text of the outline, as shown in Figure 2.44.

q. Save the *chap2_pe2_center_solution* file and keep it onscreen if you plan to continue to the next exercise. Close the file and exit PowerPoint if you do not want to continue to the next exercise at this time.

3 Modify an Outline

The director at the Wellness Education Center reviews your outline. While she is pleased with its development thus far, she would like you to include more information about the Center Services, and she would like the services slide to be the second slide in the presentation. Figure 2.45 shows additional information in the outline.

a. Open the *chap2_pe2_center_solution* presentation if you closed it after the last exercise and save it as **chap2_pe3_center_solution**.

b. Click the **Outline tab**, click at the end of the word *lectures* in Slide 3, and add **including:**

c. Proofread the bullet point you created and note that the word *including* is on a line by itself. To avoid this hanging line, remove the word *Guest* from the bullet and capitalize the word *Classroom*.

d. Position the point of insertion at the end of the line, press **Enter**, and then press **Tab**.

e. Type the following bullet points:

- **Health and Fitness**

- **Alcohol Use and Misuse**

- **Substance/Drug Abuse**

f. Position the pointer over the bullet next to the text *Books and Videos rental* so that the pointer becomes a four-headed arrow, and then click to select the bullet.

g. Replace the existing text by typing **Lending library**.

h. Press **Enter**, and then press **Tab**.

...continued on Next Page

i. Type the two bullet points for the *Lending library*, as shown in Figure 2.45.

j. Drag to select all of the text in the outline.

k. Right-click in the selected area, select **Collapse**, and then select **Collapse All**.

l. Position the pointer over the slide icon for Slide 3, *Services*, and then drag *Services* above Slide 2.

m. Click the **Office Button**, point at the arrow to the right of the Print button, and then select **Print Preview**.

n. Click the **Print What arrow** in the Page Setup group, and select **Outline View**. Print the collapsed outline if directed to do so by your instructor.

o. Close Print Preview and return to the presentation.

p. Drag to select all of the slides in the outline, and then right-click the selected area.

q. Click **Expand**, and then click **Expand All**.

r. Save the *chap2_pe3_center_solution* file and keep it onscreen if you plan to continue to the next exercise. Close the file and exit PowerPoint if you do not want to continue to the next exercise at this time.

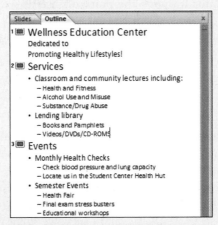

Figure 2.45 Modify an Outline

4 Add Existing Content

While reviewing the Wellness Center presentation, you realize that you do not have an introduction slide or a summary slide. You remember another slide show that has slides that would fit well in this presentation. To save time and maintain consistency, you reuse these slides. Figure 2.46 shows the outline after inserting slides into the presentation.

a. Open the *chap2_pe3_center_solution* presentation if you closed it after the last exercise, then save it as **chap2_pe4_center_solution**.

b. Click the **Outline tab**, if necessary, and then click at the end of the word *Lifestyles* in Slide 1.

c. Click the **Home tab** and click **New Slide** in the Slides group.

d. Click **Reuse Slides** at the bottom of the gallery.

e. Click the **Browse button** that appears in the Reuse Slides task pane, click **Browse File**, and then navigate to the location of your student files.

f. Click to select the file *chap2_pe4_mission*, and then click **Open**.

g. Click the Mission Statement thumbnail to enter it in your presentation as Slide 2.

h. Position your point of insertion at the end of your outline, and then click the thumbnail for the remaining slide in the presentation, the slide beginning *We strive. . . .*

i. Close the Reuse Slides Task Pane.

j. Save the *chap2_pe4_center_solution* file and keep it onscreen if you plan to continue to the next exercise. Close the file and exit PowerPoint if you do not want to continue to the next exercise at this time.

...continued on Next Page

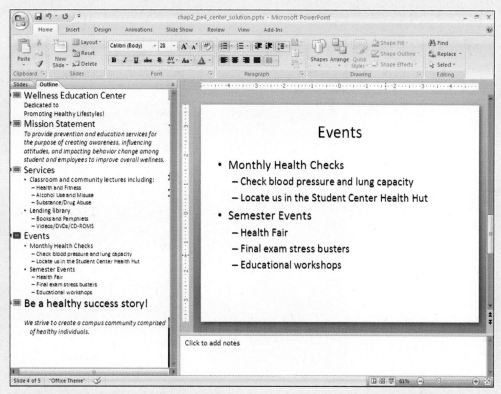

Figure 2.46 Add Existing Content

5 Apply and Modify a Theme

Both you and the director of the Wellness Education Center are satisfied with the content of the presentation, so now you concentrate on the design of the presentation. The director of the center specifies that she would like a calming blue background and a clean look. After you are satisfied with the design, you save it for future presentations you create for the center. Figure 2.47 shows the slide show after changing the theme and background color.

a. Start PowerPoint and open the *chap2_pe4_center_solution* presentation if you closed it after the last exercise, then save it as **chap2_pe5_center_solution**.

b. Click the **Design tab** and click the **More button** in the Themes group on the Design tab.

c. Click the **Trek theme**.

d. Click **Colors** in the Themes group on the Design tab.

e. Click the **Flow color scheme**.

f. Click **Font** in the Themes group on the Design tab.

g. Click the **Opulent font scheme**, which applies the Trebuchet MS font to the title and content placeholders.

h. Click **Background Styles** in the Background group on the Design tab.

i. Click **Style 11**.

j. Click the **More button** in the Themes group on the Design tab.

k. Click **Save Current Theme**.

l. Enter **wellness_theme** in the *File name* box, and then click **Save**.

m. Save the *chap2_pe5_center_solution* file and keep it onscreen if you plan to continue to the next exercise. Close the file and exit PowerPoint if you do not want to continue to the next exercise at this time.

...continued on Next Page

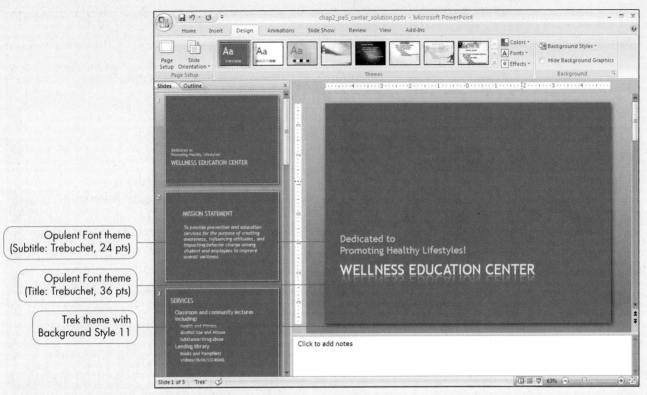

Figure 2.47 Apply and Modify a Theme

6 Create a Header and a Footer

The director of the Wellness Education Center wants to show the presentation to a colleague at a conference she is attending. Because the director does not want to bring a laptop computer on the plane, you prepare a printout using a handout format. You add a header and footer to the presentation with identifying information before printing. Figure 2.48 shows one slide with the header, and Figure 2.49 shows the notes and handouts printout.

    a. Open the *chap2_pe5_center_solution* presentation if you closed it after the last exercise, then save it as **chap2_pe6_center_solution**.

    b. Click the **Insert tab**, and then click **Header & Footer** in the Text group on the Insert tab.

    c. Click the **Slide number check box** to insert a slide number on each slide in the presentation.

    d. Click the **Footer check box** and type **Wellness Education Center**.

    e. Click the **Don't show on title slide check box**, if necessary. The footer is not necessary on the title slide.

    f. Click **Apply to All**. Note that this Microsoft theme moves the footer text to the top of the slide.

    g. Click the **Insert tab** and click **Header & Footer** in the Text group.

    h. Click the **Notes and Handouts tab**.

    i. Click the **Date and time check box**.

    j. Click **Update automatically**, and then click the **drop-down arrow**.

    k. Click the sixth date format in the list.

    l. Click the **Header check box** and then enter your name (your name represents the director's name) in the text box.

    m. Click the **Footer check box** and type **Wellness Education Center**.

    n. Click **Apply to All**. Note that with this theme Microsoft has positioned the slide Footer at the top of the slide and not at the bottom as is common. Note also that the theme has

...continued on Next Page

a very slight change in color between the background and the Footer text causing the Footer to be almost hidden.

o. Click the **Office Button**, point at the triangle next to Print, and then select **Print Preview**.

p. Change the **Print What** option to **Handouts** (6 slides per page).

q. Click **Print** if directed to do so by your instructor or click **Close Print Preview**.

r. Save the *chap2_pe6_center_solution* file and close the file.

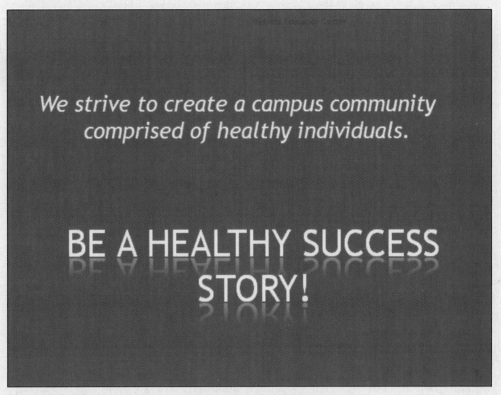

Figure 2.48 Wellness Center Slide with Header & Footer

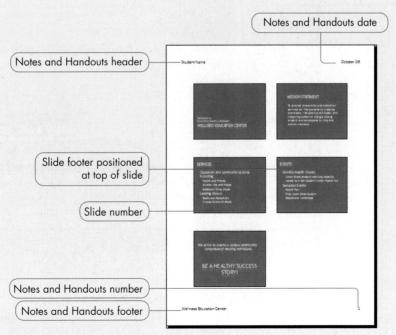

Figure 2.49 Wellness Center Handout

You have been asked to help in a local elementary school. The teacher would like you to teach the children about nutrition and healthy eating. You decide to create a presentation about the U.S. Department of Agriculture (USDA)–recommended food pyramid. (Visit http://www.mypyramid .gov.) You locate a Microsoft Office Online template based on the food pyramid that will help you organize the presentation. Figure 2.50 displays the downloaded template, and Figure 2.51 displays the conclusion slide of your presentation.

a. Download the **Food pyramid presentation**, which is available from Microsoft Office Online. It can be found in the Presentations category, Healthcare subcategory. Immediately save it as **chap2_mid1_pyramid_solution**.

b. Move to **Slide 2** and copy the information on the slide, and then paste it into the notes area. After reading the content tips on the template slides, you think they would make excellent speaker notes for you to refer to when presenting. As you create each new slide in the rest of the exercise, copy the information on the slide and paste it to the notes as you did in this step.

c. Type the following bullet points. The completed slide is displayed in Figure 2.50.

- **Choosing the right foods helps you feel better**

- **Eating a good diet keeps you healthier**

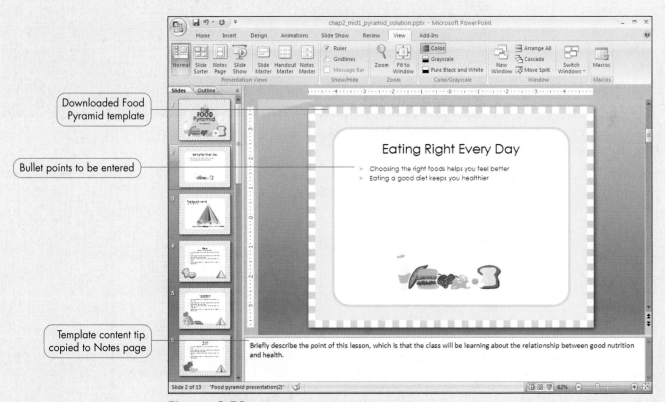

Figure 2.50 Food Pyramid Content Slide

...continued on Next Page

d. Move to **Slide 4** and type the following bullet points.

- **Great grains!**
- **Whole-wheat flour**
- **Cracked wheat**
- **Oatmeal**
- **Whole cornmeal**
- **Brown rice**

e. Make changes to the slides as shown below.

Slide	Level 1 Bullet	Level 2 Bullets
5	Very Cool Veggies!	Broccoli
		Spinach
		Carrots
		Cauliflower
		Mushrooms
		Green beans
6	Fresh Fruit!	Apples
		Bananas
		Grapes
		Peaches
		Oranges
7	Only a Little Oil!	Sunflower oil
		Margarine
		Butter
		Mayonnaise
8	Magnificent Milk!	Milk
		Cheese
		Yogurt
		Pudding
9	Mighty Meats and Beans!	Chicken
		Turkey
		Beef
		Pork
		Fish
		Beans and nuts

10	• Provide bonus calories to give you energy
	• Use for:
	  • Eating more of the food on the list
	  • Eating higher calorie food
	• Eat more than advised and you will gain weight.	

12	Use the MyPyramid Worksheet provided by the USDA.	
13	Follow the Food Pyramid Steps for a healthier you!	

...continued on Next Page

f. Delete **Slide 11**.

g. Change the layout for **Slide 12**, the conclusion, to a Title Slide format.

h. Delete the graphic box with the white background that was left over when you changed the layout.

i. Check the spelling of your presentation and ignore any references to MyPyramid, the USDA worksheet name.

j. Create a handout header with your name and a handout footer with your instructor's name and your class time. Print as required by your instructor.

k. Save the *chap2_mid1_pyramid_solution* file and close the file.

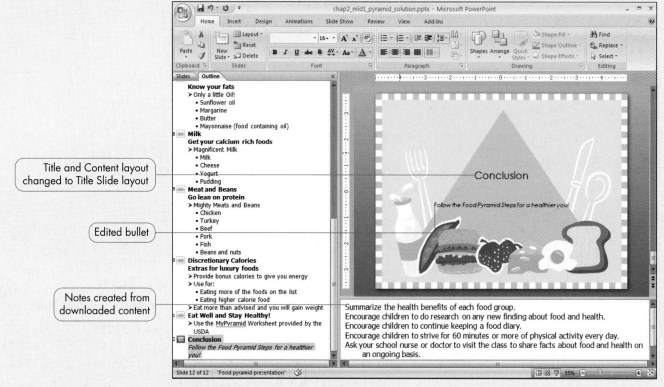

Figure 2.51 Food Pyramid Conclusion

2 Go-Digital

The local senior citizen's center has asked you to speak on photography. The center has many interested seniors—but the center has indicated to you that the seniors are unsure about whether they want information on traditional photography or digital photography. You feel that digital photography would be a good option for amateur photographers, so you decide to slant the presentation in favor of digital photography. Figure 2.52 shows the completed presentation.

a. Save a blank presentation as **chap2_mid2_digital_solution**.

b. Type the title **Go Digital, Get Creative!** so that it is on two lines in the title placeholder. Enter your name in the subtitle placeholder.

...continued on Next Page

c. Use the Outline view to create these slides.

- **Why Go Digital?**
  - **Inexpensive**
  - **Improved pictures**
  - **Instant feedback**
  - **Image sharing**
- **Inexpensive**
  - **No film cost**
  - **Free experimentation**
  - **Cameras in all price ranges**
- **Improved Pictures**
  - **Image editing with software**
    - **Remove red eye**
    - **Improve exposure**
    - **Crop the pictures**
  - **Free experimentation**
    - **Take extra pictures for practice**
    - **Try new camera settings**
- **Instant Feedback**
  - **Viewing screen**
- **Image Sharing**
  - **Traditional**
  - **Web pages/Online photo albums**
  - **E-mail**

d. Review the presentation in Outline view and note that *Free experimentation* appears in two locations, that the Instant feedback slide does not have enough information to be a slide on its own, and that the presentation does not contain a conclusion slide.

e. Move the two bullets under *Free experimentation* on **Slide 4** to the correct location on **Slide 3**, and then delete the *Free experimentation* bullet in **Slide 4**.

f. Move the information in **Slide 5** so that it becomes the first bullet point in Slide 4.

g. Collapse the outline, move the Improved Pictures slide to the **Slide 4** position, and then Expand the outline.

h. Spell-check your presentation.

i. Save the *chap2_mid2_digital_solution* presentation and close the file.

j. Download the **Seasons in sage** design template, which is located on Microsoft Office Online in the Design slides category, Nature Subcategory.

k. Display the Add Slide gallery and click **Slides from Outline**.

l. Browse to where you save your files, change *Files of type* to **All Files**, and then insert your *chap2_mid2_digital_solution* presentation.

m. Drag **Slide 1** so that it becomes the last slide of the presentation, and then type **Go Digital:** in the title placeholder, and **Unleash Your Creativity!** in the subtitle placeholder.

n. Create a handout header with your name, and a handout footer with your instructor's name and your class. Print as required by your instructor.

o. Save the **chap2_mid2_digital_solution** presentation and click **Yes** when asked if you wish to replace the original file. Close the file.

...continued on Next Page

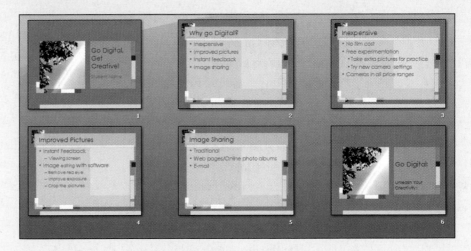

Figure 2.52 Go Digital Presentation with Seasons in Sage Template

3 The Impressionists

The paintings of the Impressionists are some of the most loved paintings in the world. Their paintings may be viewed by going to the Web page of the WebMuseum, Paris (www.ibiblio.org/wm), navigating to the Famous Artworks collections page, and then navigating to the Impressionism page. The museum is maintained by Nicolas Pioch and is not part of any official or supported project. He maintains the site for your pleasure and his. In a continuing project throughout this text, you create an album celebrating the Impressionists and their works. Figure 2.53 shows the completed slide show in the Slide Sorter view.

a. Save a blank presentation as **chap2_mid 3_impressionists_solution**.

b. Type the title **Impressionism**, and then enter your name in the subtitle place holder. Also include the following text in the subtitle placeholder: **All images may be viewed at the WebMuseum**. (You will insert the hyperlink for the WebMuseum in a later project.)

c. Use the Outline view to create these slides.

- **Impressionist Paintings**
  - **Characterized by small brush strokes**
  - **Reproduced the artist's visual impression**
  - **Studied**
    - **Light**
    - **Atmosphere**
    - **Reflections**
    - **Color**
- **Impressionist Artists**
  - **Claude Monet**
  - **Pierre-Auguste Renoir**
  - **Berthe Morisot**
  - **Edgar Degas**

d. Apply the **Flow theme**.

e. Apply the **Metro color theme**.

...continued on Next Page

f. Insert the **Oriel font theme**.

g. Insert the *chap2_mid3_artists* Word outline after the last slide in your presentation.

h. Rearrange the bullets in **Slide 3** so the artists are listed alphabetically by last name.

i. Collapse the outline and move **Slides 4–7** so they are listed alphabetically by last name, and then expand the outline.

j. Create a conclusion slide using the Content with Caption layout.

k. Modify the conclusion slide layout by deleting the text placeholder and moving the title placeholder so that its bottom border is even with the bottom border of the large content placeholder.

l. Leave the audience with one last thought about Impressionism by entering the following text in the title placeholder on the conclusion slide: **Work at the same time on sky, water, branches, ground, keeping everything going on an equal basis . . . Don't be afraid of putting on colour . . . Paint generously and unhesitatingly, for it is best not to lose the first impression. Camille Pissarro.**

m. Italicize the Pissarro name.

n. Spell-check your presentation.

o. Create a handout header with your name and a handout footer with your instructor's name and your class. Print as required by your instructor.

p. Save the *chap2_mid 3_impressionists_solution* presentation and close the file.

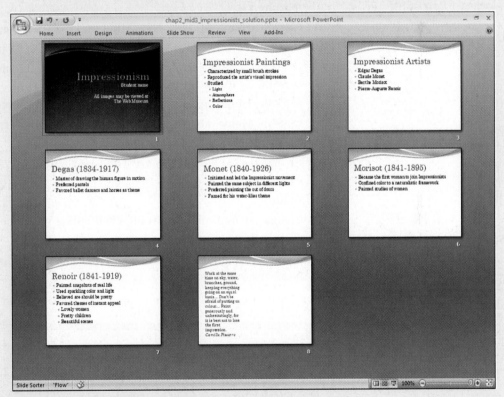

Figure 2.53 Impressionist Presentation in Slide Sorter View

4 Audience Analysis

Your community is experiencing a strong economic growth pattern, and part of this growth is because new business is encouraged and supported. Part of the support structure includes a city-sponsored Small Business Development Center (SBDC). One way the SBDC helps encourage small business owners and future business owners is to provide training on a wide variety of

...continued on Next Page

topics such as developing business plans, refining strategies, and overcoming challenges. A small business owner has requested the next training session cover giving presentations.

The SBDC maintains a list of local speakers, and as a humorous, popular speaker you are invited to address this group. You question the person issuing the invitation about the audience and find out you will be presenting to a small casual group of 8 to 10 men and women over lunch in a very informal room with no windows. You may bring your notebook computer and connect it to the center's projector. When you ask what the audience wants to get from your presentation, the SBDC representative tells you that the attendees want to know how to relax as they present. He adds that since it is a break in the middle of a busy day for them, they will probably be laughing and joking a lot. You decide to begin your presentation by addressing what you believe is the key to being a successful speaker—understanding the audience, but to do it in a humorous way. You want to show them that if a speaker knows his or her material well and analyzes the audience well, the speaker can relax while presenting and still be able to inject personality into the presentation. You also decide to create speaker notes to distribute to the group so that they can see how jotting down ideas of what to say in speaker notes can help them plan what to say to fill in around the bullet points. Figure 2.54 shows the completed slide show in Slide Sorter view.

a. Open *chap2_mid4_audience* and save it as **chap2_mid4_audience_solution**.

b. Read the Note at the bottom of Slide 1 and notice that this is a good location to keep track of when and where a presentation will be given. Move to **Slide 2** and switch to **Outline View**.

c. Click the **Home tab**, click **New Slide**, and then click **Reuse Slides**.

d. Use **Browse** in the Reuse Slides pane and open *chap2_mid4_analysis*.

e. Insert the second slide of the *chap2_mid4_analysis* into the current slideshow, and then close the Reuse Slides task pane.

f. Click the **Home tab**, click **Layout**, and then click **Comparison**.

g. Click the **Home tab, New Slide**, and then click **Slides from Outline**.

h. Insert the *chap2_mid4_outline* file.

i. Change the **Layout** of Slide 4 to **Title and Content**.

j. Change the title font on the slides you imported to **Comic Sans Serif** and the bullets to **Calibri**.

k. Change the font color for the titles and bullets you imported to black.

l. Change **Background Styles** to **Style 5**.

m. Create a handout header with your name and a handout footer with your instructor's name and your class. Print as required by your instructor.

n. Save the *chap2_mid 4_audience_solution* presentation and close the file.

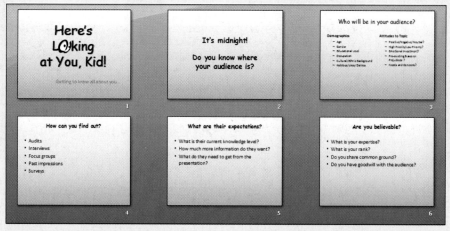

Figure 2.54 Audience Analysis Presentation in Slide Sorter View

Capstone Exercise

Your neighbors in your small southwestern subdivision are concerned about drought, fire danger, and water conservation. You volunteer to gather information about possible solutions and share the information with them at the next neighborhood association meeting. You decide a PowerPoint presentation would be an excellent way to inform them of their options. In this capstone exercise, you concentrate on developing the content. In a later chapter capstone exercise, you will enhance the project with illustrations, images, charts, and hyperlinks.

Design Template

You download a Microsoft Office Online template to create the basic design and structure for your presentation, name the presentation, and create the title slide.

a. Download the **Sun spots** design template from Microsoft Office Online, Design slides category, Abstract subcategory.

b. Save the presentation with the file name **chap2_cap_waterwise_solution**.

c. Type **Conserve** as the title on the title slide. Reduce the font size of the title until it fits on one line.

d. Type the subtitle **Waterwise Landscaping**.

Outline and Modifications

Based on the storyboard you created after researching water conservation on the Internet, you create the outline for your presentation. As you create the outline, you also modify the outline structure.

a. Click the **Outline tab**.

b. Type **Waterwise Options** as the title for Slide 2.

c. Enter each of the following as Level 1 bullets for Slide 2: **Zeroscaping, Xeriscaping**

d. Type **Purpose of Landscaping** as the title for Slide 3.

e. Type each of the following as Level 1 bullets for Slide 3: **Beauty, Utility, Conservation**.

f. Modify the outline structure by reversing Slides 2 and 3.

Imported Outline

You originally started your task intending to hold two information sessions for your neighbors. You began by creating an outline on zeroscaping in Microsoft Word. You determined that using a PowerPoint slide show would let you show images, so you create a slide show on xeriscaping. After going to this work, however, you decide that it is better to make the comparison in one presentation so that

homeowners are more easily able to see the overall picture. You do not want to lose the work you have already done, so you import the zeroscaping outline and reuse the xeriscaping slides.

a. Position the point of insertion at the end of the outline and add a new slide.

b. Use the **Slides from Outline option** to insert the *chap2_cap_zeroscaping* outline.

c. Change the layout of Slide 4 from Title slide to Picture with Caption so that you may insert a picture illustrating zeroscaping later.

d. Position the point of insertion at the end of the outline.

e. Use the appropriate option to reuse slides from *chap2_cap_xeriscaping*.

f. Insert all the slides from *chap2_cap_xeriscaping*.

Design

When you preview the slide show, you note that a lack of contrast makes the text difficult to read. You decide to change the color theme and font scheme to increase the visibility of the text. You realize that you may want to use this changed theme in later presentations, so you save the theme.

a. Change the color theme to **Solstice**.

b. Change the font theme to **Trek**.

TROUBLESHOOTING: If the Picture and Caption layouts in Slides 4 and 8 do not accept the new font change because they were imported, change the caption font to Franklin Gothic Medium, 36 pts.

c. Click the **More button** in the Themes group on the Design tab.

d. Save the current theme as *heat_theme*.

e. Spell-check the presentation.

f. Apply the **Fade Through Black animation scheme** to all slides.

g. Create a handout header with your name and a handout footer with your instructor's name and your class. Print as required by your instructor.

h. Save the *chap2_cap_waterwise_solution* presentation and close the file. Exit PowerPoint if you do not want to continue to the mini cases at this time.

Mini Cases

Use the rubric following the case as a guide to evaluate your work, but keep in mind that your instructor may impose additional grading criteria or use a different standard to judge your work.

Identity Theft

GENERAL CASE

The partially completed *chap2_mc1_identity* presentation is intended to aid you in recognizing the global value of the outline view and how it can be used to modify the structure of a presentation. A combination of slides containing only titles and slides containing content are randomly entered as if they were created from brainstorming. Organize the presentation so there is content under each topic and that the content matches the topic in the slide title. Create an appropriate conclusion. You may add additional slides, if desired. Good resources for your presentation include the Federal Trade Commission Web site (www.consumer.gov/idtheft) and the Social Security Online Electronic Fact Sheet (www.ssa.gov/pubs/idtheft).

Be sure to spell-check and carefully proofread the content of the presentation. Save the presentation as **chap2_mc1_identity_solution**. Locate a template to use for the design and reuse the *chap2_mc1_identity_solution* presentation slides to create a new presentation. Apply a font scheme, color scheme, and background style as desired. You also may modify layouts. Add appropriate clip art to at least two slides. Remember the design guidelines as you insert the clip art. Match the colors of the clips to your background and try to locate clips that are similar—do not apply a cartoon-like clip on one slide and a professional clip on another. Apply a transition to all slides and add a custom animation to the clip art you added. Create a handout header with your name and a handout footer with the file name, your instructor's name, and your class. Print as directed by your instructor. Save the file as **chap2_mc1_identity_solution** and click Yes when asked if you want to save over the original file.

Performance Elements	Exceeds Expectations	Meets Expectations	Below Expectations
Organization	Presentation is easy to follow because information is presented in a logical, interesting sequence.	Presentation is generally easy to follow.	Presentation cannot be understood because there is no sequence of information.
Visual aspects	Presentation background, themes, clip art, and animation are appealing and enhance the understanding of presentation purpose and content.	Clip art is related to topic.	The background, theme, or animation is distracting to the topic.
	There is a consistent visual theme.	Animation is not distracting.	Clip art does not enhance understanding of the content or is unrelated.
Layout	The layout is visually pleasing and contributes to the overall message with appropriate use of headings, subheadings, bullet points, clip art, and white space.	The layout shows some structure, but placement of some headings, subheadings, bullet points, clip art, and/or white space can be improved.	The layout is cluttered and confusing. Placement of headings, subheadings, bullet points, clip art, and/or white spaces detracts from readability.
Mechanics	Presentation has no errors in spelling, grammar, word usage, or punctuation.	Presentation has no more than one error in spelling, grammar, word usage, or punctuation.	Presentation readability is impaired due to repeated errors in spelling, grammar, word usage, or punctuation.
	Bullet points are parallel.	Bullet points are inconsistent in one slide.	Most bullet points are not parallel.

You have a bright, creative, and energetic personality and you are using these talents in college as a senior majoring in Digital Film within the Multimedia Communication Technology Department. You hope to become a producer for a major film company, following the footsteps of your grandfather. This term, you are taking MCT 4000: Administration of Studio Operations. The final project requires every student to create his or her own feature film company and present an overview of the company to the class. The presentation is to be in the form of an employee orientation: It should include the company purpose, the company's history, past and present projects, and a final slide giving the resources you used to create your presentation. Your instructor asks you to write notes for each slide.

The assignment was given at the beginning of the semester with the understanding that it would be developed as the topics were presented. It is now the end of the semester, and you, a creative procrastinator by nature, are in a real bind. You have 24 hours to complete the entire presentation before presenting it to the class. You remember Microsoft Office Online Templates and wonder if it has a template you can use. Using **film** as your keyword, search Microsoft Office Online for templates and then download a template to use in creating your presentation. You will, however, have to research what a feature film company does and add your own content to comply with the case requirements. Add clip art, transitions, and animations as desired. Create a handout header with your name and a handout footer with your instructor's name and your class time. Print as directed by your instructor. Save the presentation as **chap2_mc2_film_solution**.

Performance Elements	Exceeds Expectations	Meets Expectations	Below Expectations
Organization	Presentation indicates accurate research and significant facts. Evidence exists that information has been evaluated and synthesized showing an understanding of the topic.	Presentation indicates some research has taken place and that information was included in the content.	Presentation demonstrates a lack of research or understanding of the topic. Content is misinterpreted or incorrect.
Visual aspects	Presentation background, themes, clip art, and animation are appealing and enhance the understanding of presentation purpose and content.	Clip art is related to the topic.	The background or theme is distracting to the topic.
	There is a consistent visual theme.	Animation is not distracting.	Clip art does not enhance understanding of the content or is unrelated.
Layout	The layout is visually pleasing and contributes to the overall message with appropriate use of headings, subheadings, bullet points, clip art, and white space.	The layout shows some structure, but placement of some headings, subheadings, bullet points, clip art, and/or white space can be improved.	The layout is cluttered and confusing. Placement of headings, subheadings, bullet points, clip art, and/or white spaces detracts from readability.
Mechanics	Presentation has no errors in spelling, grammar, word usage, or punctuation.	Presentation has no more than one error in spelling, grammar, word usage, or punctuation.	Presentation readability is impaired due to repeated errors in spelling, grammar, word usage, or punctuation.
	Bullet points are parallel.	Bullet points are inconsistent in one slide.	Most bullet points are not parallel.

My State

DISASTER RECOVERY

Your little sister prepared a report on your state for a youth organization merit badge on research, and she is going to present the information to her leader and team members. She spent a lot of time researching the state and created a presentation with the information she wants included. Unfortunately, she is frustrated because the presentation she worked so hard on looks "ugly" to her. She asks you to help her create a presentation that "won't embarrass" her. You sit down with her and show her how to download the presentation for Report on State template from the Microsoft Office Online site, Presentations Category, Academic Subcategory. Save the new presentation as **chap2_mc3_florida_solution**. You reuse her slides saved as *chap2_mc3_florida* to bring them into the new template. From there, you cut and paste the images she gathered into the correct placeholders and move bullet points to the correct slide. Resize placeholders as needed. As you edit the presentation with her, you tell your sister that mixing clip art and pictures is contributing to the cluttered look and ask her what she prefers. She cannot decide, so you use your preference, but be consistent. The template does not have slides for all her information, so you create new slides with appropriate layouts when needed. You remind her that although federal government organizations allow use of their images in an educational setting, your sister should give proper credit if she is going to use their data. Also give credit to the State of Florida's Web site for the information obtained from MyFlorida.com (**http://dhr.dos.state.fl.us/facts/symbols**). Give credit to the U.S. Census Bureau (**www.census.gov**) for the Quick Facts.

You delete any slide for which your sister does not have information. Be sure to spell-check and carefully proofread the content of the presentation as your sister freely admits she "wasn't worried about that stuff." You pick an animation to apply to all slides with her help and resist her pleas to do "something different" on every slide. You explain to her that this is not an MTV music video; rather, it is an informational presentation, and multiple animations are distracting. Create a handout header with your name and a handout footer with your instructor's name and your class time. Print as directed by your instructor.

Performance Elements	Exceeds Expectations	Meets Expectations	Below Expectations.
Organization	Presentation is easy to follow because information is presented in a logical, interesting sequence.	Presentation is generally easy to follow.	Presentation cannot be understood because there is no sequence of information.
Visual aspects	Presentation background, themes, clip art, and animation are appealing and enhance the understanding of presentation purpose and content.	Clip art is related to the topic.	The background or theme is distracting to the topic.
	There is a consistent visual theme.	Animation is not distracting.	Clip art does not enhance understanding of the content or is unrelated.
Layout	The layout is visually pleasing and contributes to the overall message with appropriate use of headings, subheadings, bullet points, clip art, and white space.	The layout shows some structure, but placement of some headings, subheadings, bullet points, clip art, and/or white space can be improved.	The layout is cluttered and confusing. Placement of headings, subheadings, bullet points, clip art, and/or white spaces detracts from readability.
Mechanics	Presentation has no errors in spelling, grammar, word usage, or punctuation.	Presentation has no more than one error in spelling, grammar, word usage, or punctuation.	Presentation readability is impaired due to repeated errors in spelling, grammar, word usage, or punctuation.
	Bullet points are parallel.	Bullet points are inconsistent in one slide.	Most bullet points are not parallel.

Getting Started with Windows XP

bjectives

After you read this chapter, you will be able to:

1. Identify components on the Windows desktop **(page 1261)**.

2. Work with windows and menus **(page 1264)**.

3. Identify dialog box components **(page 1268)**.

4. Use the Help and Support Center **(page 1269)**.

5. Work with folders **(page 1274)**.

6. Manage folders and files in Windows Explorer **(page 1276)**.

7. Delete items and manage the Recycle Bin **(page 1278)**.

8. Change the display settings **(page 1286)**.

9. Change computer settings using the Control Panel **(page 1287)**.

10. Create shortcuts on the desktop and Quick Launch toolbar **(page 1291)**.

11. Use Windows Desktop Search **(page 1293)**.

Hands-On Exercises

Exercises	Skills Covered
1. INTRODUCTION TO WINDOWS XP (page 1271)	• Turn On the Computer and Select a Username • Modify the Start Menu • Move, Size, and Close a Window • Get Help
2. FILE AND FOLDER MANAGEMENT (page 1281)	• Change a Window View • Create and Rename a Folder • Move and Delete a Folder • Create and Save a File
3. CUSTOMIZING YOUR SYSTEM (page 1295)	• Customize the Desktop • Create a Desktop Shortcut • Use Windows Desktop Search to Locate Files • Use Control Panel to Customize System Settings • Add a User Account • Add a Shortcut to the Quick Launch Toolbar

CASE STUDY
Virginia Beach Properties

Jessica and Brian Street own Virginia Beach Properties, a property management company specializing in managing vacation and long-term rental homes. It is a small and very successful business, due to the business acumen of its owners. Jessica recently graduated with an MBA; Brian has an MIS degree. Both love living and working out of their home on the beach. Brian is in charge of maintaining their database, which contains information about the rental homes and their owners, existing tenants, and pending rental requests. It is an elaborate, user-friendly system that is backed up daily. The backup files are stored onsite for easy access.

Case Study

The idea for the business stemmed from Jessica's initial experience renting her family's beach home. Her parents were unable to enjoy the home as often as they would like but they were reluctant to sell. They wanted to keep the property in the family and wanted the additional income it could provide. Jessica and Brian started with one property and built the business from there. That was five years ago, and the business has prospered. No major problems existed until the day that Hurricane Isabel came to town.

Brian backed up his files regularly. He assured Jessica that they were protected against computer crashes, viruses, lost files, and so on. He never anticipated a hurricane. Their home was completely destroyed, and the backup media were lost in the ensuing flood damage. Brian was stunned. All he could say to Jessica as they sifted through the wreckage was, "It should not have happened."

Your Assignment

- Read the chapter, paying special attention to the topic of file management.
- Think about how the owners of this business could have avoided the disaster had an appropriate backup strategy been in place.
- Summarize your thoughts in a one-page report, describing the elements of a basic backup strategy. Refer to the Windows XP Help and Support Center for specific information on backing up files and include that research in your report.
- In your report, give several other examples of unforeseen circumstances that can cause data to be lost.
- Save your report as **chap1_case_report_solution.docx**.

Basics of Windows XP

Windows XP is the primary operating system for personal computers.

(You have seen the Windows interface many times, but do you really understand it?)

Windows Vista is the newest version of the Windows operating system.

Windows XP Home Edition focuses on entertainment and home use.

Windows XP Professional Edition is designed to support business systems.

Windows XP Media Center Edition coordinates multimedia elements.

Fast user switching is a Windows feature that enables you to quickly move from one user account to another.

Windows XP is a popular version of the very successful series of Windows operating systems. Although *Windows Vista* is newer and more powerful, you will continue to see Windows XP utilized on many home and business computers for quite some time. Windows XP looks slightly different from earlier versions, but it maintains the conventions of its various predecessors. You have seen the Windows interface many times, but do you really understand it? Can you move and copy files with confidence? Do you know how to back up the Excel spreadsheets, Access databases, and other documents that you work so hard to create? If not, now is the time to learn.

Windows XP is available in several versions. *Windows XP Home Edition* is intended for entertainment and home use. It includes a media player, support for digital photography, and an instant messenger. *Windows XP Professional Edition* has all of the features of the Home Edition plus additional security to encrypt files and protect data. It includes support for high-performance multiprocessor systems. It also lets you connect to your computer from a remote station. *Windows XP Media Center Edition* enables you to enjoy video, audio, pictures, and television on your computer monitor. Along with a remote control, the simple layout and intuitive menus enhance the multimedia experience.

A login screen is displayed when the computer is powered on initially or when you switch from one user account to another. Windows XP makes it possible to create several user accounts, each with unique privileges. As the primary user of your computer, your account possesses administrative privileges, enabling you to create other user accounts and maintain your system. Individual *user accounts* retain individual desktop settings, a lists of favorite and recently visited Web sites, and other customized Windows settings (such as desktop background). Multiple users can be logged on simultaneously through a feature known as *fast user switching*.

In this section, you begin by identifying components on the Windows desktop and taskbar. Then you learn how to work with windows. In particular, you learn how to move and size windows, use menus within windows, and identify components of a dialog box.

Identifying Components on the Windows Desktop

The **desktop** contains icons and a taskbar. It is displayed when a computer first boots up.

An **icon** is a pictorial element representing a program, file, Web site, or shortcut.

Windows XP creates a working environment for your computer that parallels the working environment at home or in an office. You work at a desk. Windows operations take place on the *desktop*. You can place physical objects, such as folders, a dictionary, a calculator, or a phone, on a desk. The computer equivalents of those objects appear as *icons* (pictorial symbols) on the desktop. Each object on a real desk has attributes (properties) such as size, weight, and color. In similar fashion, Windows assigns properties to every object on its desktop. And just as you can move objects on a real desk, you can rearrange the objects on the Windows desktop. The Windows XP desktop (see Figure 1.1) contains standard elements that enable you to access files and other system resources.

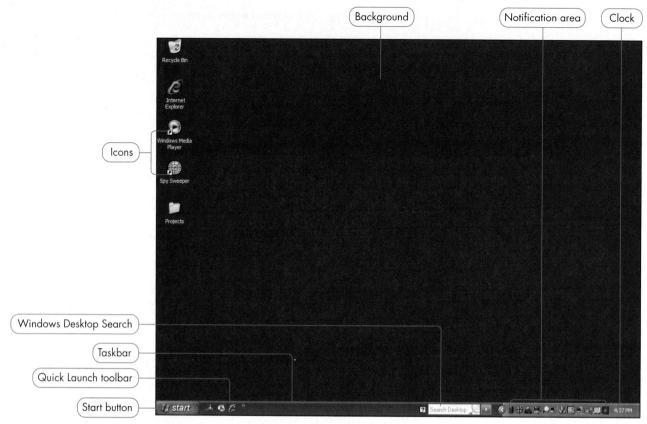

Figure 1.1 The Windows XP Desktop

Your desktop may contain different icons or may be arranged differently than desktops on other computers. That is because each computer has different programs, and each desktop can be customized to suit a user's preferences. Moreover, you are likely to work on different systems—at school, at work, or at home—so desktops are likely to be different. What is important is that you recognize the common functionality that is present on all desktops.

Use the Taskbar

The **taskbar** is the horizontal bar that enables you to move among open windows and provides access to system resources.

The **Start button** provides access to programs and other system resources.

The **Start menu** is displayed when you click the Start button.

At the bottom of the desktop is the **taskbar**, a horizontal strip that contains the Start button, the Quick Launch toolbar, button area, Windows Desktop Search, and the Notification area. These taskbar sections are discussed in the following paragraphs.

The **Start button**, as its name suggests, is where you begin. Click Start to see a menu of programs and other functions. The **Start menu** is divided into two columns (see Figure 1.2). The left column displays the pinned items list, typically an Internet browser program and an e-mail program that are "pinned" to the top of the column, and a list of the most recently used programs. As you work with programs, the recently used program list changes based on the frequency of usage. The bottom of the left column also contains the All Programs option. Position the mouse over All Programs to see a list of all programs installed on your computer. The right column of the Start menu provides access to Windows folders such as My Music, My Documents, and My Pictures. The right column also contains entries for the Control Panel, Help and Support, and Search.

Although the Windows XP Start menu is typically a two-column display, you can modify the menu so that it appears as only one column. Right-click an empty area of the taskbar and select Properties. Click the Start menu tab in the Taskbar and Start Menu Properties dialog box. Click the Classic Start menu option and click OK.

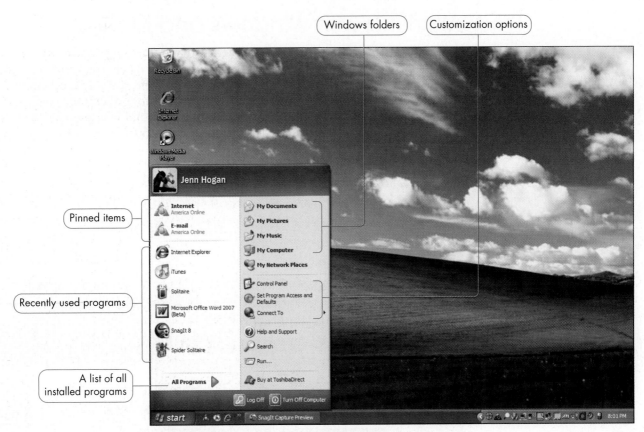

Figure 1.2 The Windows XP Start Menu

The *Quick Launch toolbar* contains program icons, making it possible to open programs with a single click.

The *Quick Launch toolbar* is located just to the right of the Start button. Each button on the Quick Launch toolbar represents a program that you can quickly launch with a single click. For example, the Quick launch toolbar in Figure 1.2 contains icons that you can click to quickly launch America Online and Internet Explorer. If the Quick Launch toolbar is not visible on your taskbar, you can right-click a blank area of the taskbar, select Toolbars from the shortcut menu, and then select Quick Launch.

The third section of the taskbar displays buttons for all open programs. In Figure 1.1, the button area is empty because no programs are open. The clock at the far right side of the taskbar displays the time. If your mouse pointer hovers over the time, you also will see the day of the week and the current date. To the left of the clock is the *Notification area* that displays buttons for such items as volume control, wireless network connections, Windows updates, and background programs (programs that are active when your computer is on, like anti-virus software). It also provides a button that enables you to safely remove hardware, such as a flash (USB) drive (described later in this chapter). If you have installed *Windows Desktop Search*, the search bar will appear to the left of the Notification area. Using Desktop Search, you can quickly find files, folders, programs, e-mail, and calendar appointments.

The *Notification area*, found at the right side of the taskbar, displays icons for background programs and system processes.

Windows Desktop Search helps you find anything on your computer.

Working with Windows and Menus

A **window** is an enclosed rectangular area representing a program or data.

Multitasking is the ability to run more than one program at a time.

Each *window* displays a program or a folder that is currently in use. Figure 1.3 displays a desktop with four open program windows. The ability to run several programs at the same time is known as *multitasking*, and it is a major benefit of the Windows environment. For example, you can create a document using a word processor in one window, create a spreadsheet in a second window, surf the Internet in a third window, play a game in a fourth window, and so on. You can work in a program as long as you want and then change to a different program by clicking its window or clicking its button on the taskbar.

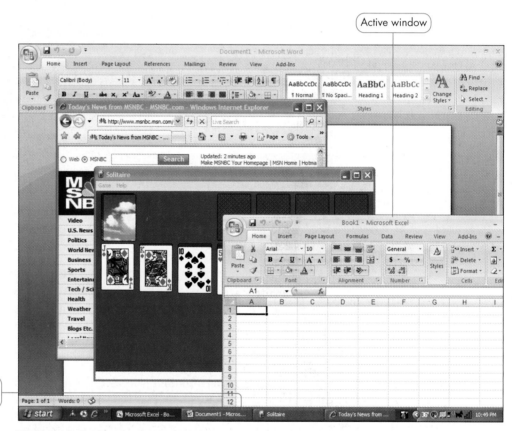

Figure 1.3 Multiple Windows

Move and Size a Window

At times, you will need to resize or move a window. Perhaps you need to resize a window so that you can see icons on the desktop. Or maybe you just want to move a window because part of it appears off screen and you cannot see a critical component. To resize a window, point to any border (the pointer changes to a double arrow) and drag the border in the direction you want to go—inward to shrink the window or outward to enlarge it. You also can drag a corner, instead of a border, to change both dimensions at the same time. To move a window, click and drag the title bar (the shaded bar at the top of the window) to a new position on the desktop. When you release the mouse button, the window moves to its new location.

Identify the Anatomy of a Window

All Windows applications share a common user interface and exhibit a consistent command structure. That means that every Windows application works essentially the same way, providing a sense of familiarity from one application to another. In other words, once you learn the basic concepts and techniques in one application, you can apply that knowledge to every other application.

The *task pane* is a bar that provides support for a currently selected item or window.

The My Computer window in Figure 1.4 displays the storage drives on a particular computer system. The computer has one hard drive and a DVD/CD-RW drive. The *task pane*, displayed at the left of the window, provides easy access to various commands such as viewing system information and adding or removing programs.

Figure 1.4 My Computer

The *title bar* is the shaded bar at the top of every window.

The *Minimize button* removes a window from view but not from memory.

The *Maximize button* causes a window to fill the screen.

The *Restore Down button* returns a window to the size it was before it was maximized.

The *title bar* appears at the top of every window, displaying the name of the folder or application. The icon at the extreme left of the title bar identifies the window and also provides access to a control menu with operations relevant to the window, such as moving it or sizing it. Three buttons appear at the right of the title bar. The *Minimize button* shrinks the window to a button on the taskbar but leaves the window open in memory. The *Maximize button* enlarges the window so that it fills the entire desktop. The *Restore Down button* (not shown in Figure 1.4) appears instead of the Maximize button after a window has been maximized, displaying the window in its previous size. The *Close button* closes the window and removes it from memory and the desktop.

The **Close button** removes a window from memory.

A **drop-down menu** displays more selections pertaining to the menu item.

A **menu bar** is a horizontal bar at the top of a window containing options to enable you to work with an application.

A **toolbar**, usually found at the top or side of a window, contains buttons that are accessed more quickly than menu selections.

A **status bar** displays summary information about the selected window or object.

A **scroll bar** enables you to control which part of a window is in view at any time.

The **menu bar** appears immediately below the title bar. When you click an item on the menu bar, you will see a **drop-down menu** with more selections pertaining to the menu item. One or more **toolbars** appear below the menu bar and let you execute a command by clicking a button, as opposed to selecting from a menu. Figure 1.4 includes a Standard Buttons toolbar.

The **status bar** at the bottom of a window, as shown in Figure 1.5, displays information about the entire window or about a selected object within a window. A vertical (or horizontal) **scroll bar** appears at the right (or bottom) border of a window when the window's contents are not completely visible. The scroll bar provides access to unseen areas. The vertical scroll bar along the right border of the contents pane in Figure 1.5 implies that additional items are available that are not currently visible. A horizontal scroll bar does not appear because the display of objects in the currently selected folder extends out of view vertically, but not horizontally, on the screen.

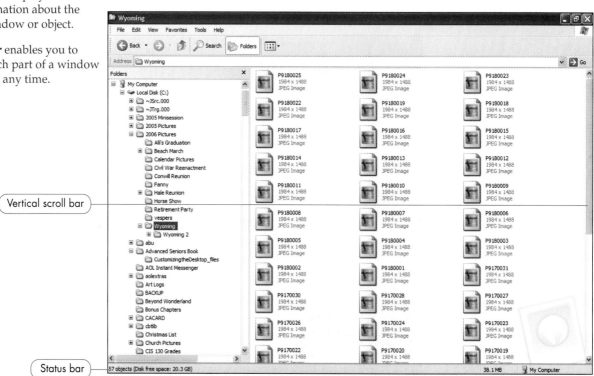

Figure 1.5 Common Window Elements (Status Bar and Scroll Bar)

Display Menus

The menu bar provides access to commands within an application (program). When you click a menu bar item, a drop-down menu appears, listing commands that relate to the menu name. You also can activate a menu bar item by pressing the Alt key plus the underlined letter in the menu name; for example, press Alt+V to select from the View menu.

From a drop-down menu, you can make a selection by clicking a command or by typing the underlined letter. Figure 1.6 shows the menu that results from clicking Edit on the menu bar. From the menu, you can click a selection or you can bypass the menu entirely if you know the equivalent shortcuts shown to the right of the command in the menu. For example, the shortcut key combinations Ctrl+X, Ctrl+C, and Ctrl+V respectively cut, copy, and paste. A dimmed (ghosted) command, such as the Paste command, means that the command is not currently available and that some additional action has to be taken for the command to become available. In the case of the Paste command, you would first have to copy an item or text before it could be pasted.

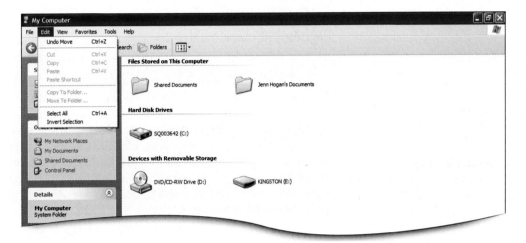

Figure 1.6 Edit Menu

An ellipsis (. . .) following a menu selection indicates that additional information is required to execute the command. For example, if you select Format from the File menu (after having selected a disk drive), as shown in Figure 1.7, you will have to provide or confirm additional information about the formatting process, such as which disk to format. A dialog box, which is a special window that enables you to change settings or make selections, appears after such a menu item is selected.

Figure 1.7 File Menu

A check next to a menu command is a toggle switch indicating whether the command is on or off. Figure 1.8 shows a check next to Status Bar in the View menu, which means that the status bar is displayed. Click Status Bar and the check disappears suppressing the display of the status bar. Click the command a second time and the check reappears, as does the status bar in the associated window.

Figure 1.8 View Menu

A *thumbnail* is a miniature display of a folder or page.

A bullet next to an item, such as Tiles in the View menu, indicates a selection from a set of mutually exclusive choices. Click a different option within the group, such as *thumbnails*, and the bullet will move from the previous selection (Tiles) to the new selection (Thumbnails), providing a different view.

An arrow after a command, like the one beside Arrange Icons by in the View menu, indicates that a submenu (also known as a cascaded menu) will display additional menu options. To access such a submenu, you do not actually have to click the main selection (Arrange Icons by, in this case). Simply pointing to it with the mouse pointer should cause the submenu to appear.

Identify Dialog Box Components

A *dialog box* is a special window that requests input or presents information.

A *dialog box* appears when additional information is necessary to execute a command. Figure 1.9 shows a typical dialog box, displayed when you are printing a document. The dialog box requests information about precisely what to print and how to print it. The information is entered into the dialog box in different ways, depending on the type of information that is required.

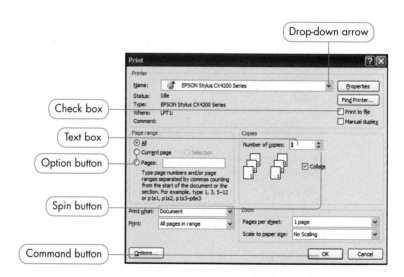

Figure 1.9 Print Dialog Box

An *option button*, or *radio button*, is a mutually exclusive selection in a dialog box.

Option buttons, sometimes called *radio buttons*, indicate mutually exclusive choices, one of which *must* be chosen, such as the page range. In this example you can print all pages, the selection (if it is available), the current page, or a specific set of pages (such as pages 1–4), but you can choose *one and only one* option. Any time you select (click) an option, the previous option is automatically deselected.

A *text box* enables you to give an instruction by typing in a box.

A *text box*, such as the one shown beside the *Pages* option in Figure 1.9, enables you to enter specific information. In this case, you could type *1–5* in the text box if

A **spin button** is a dialog box feature with an up or down arrow to increase or decrease a value.

A **check box** enables you to select one or more items that are not mutually exclusive.

A **list box** presents several items, any of which can be selected.

A **command button** is a dialog box item that you click to accept or cancel selections.

you wanted only the first five pages to print. A **spin button** is a common component of a dialog box, providing a quick method of increasing or decreasing a setting. For example, clicking the spin button (or spinner) beside *Number of copies* enables you to increase or decrease the number of copies of the document to print. You also can enter the information explicitly by typing it into the text box beside the spin button.

Check boxes are used instead of option buttons if the choices are not mutually exclusive. The Collate check box in Figure 1.9 is checked; Print to file is not. You can select or clear options by clicking the appropriate check box, which toggles the operation on and off. A *list box* (not shown in Figure 1.9) displays some or all of the available choices, any of which can be selected by clicking the list item.

The Help button (a question mark at the right end of the title bar) provides help for any item in the dialog box. Click the button, and then click the item in the dialog box for which you want additional information. The Close button (the X at the extreme right of the title bar) closes the dialog box without accepting any changes that you might have made.

All dialog boxes also contain one or more *command buttons* that provide options to either accept or cancel your selections. The OK button in Figure 1.9, for example, initiates the printing process. The Cancel button does just the opposite. It ignores (cancels) any changes made to the settings and closes the dialog box.

Using the Help and Support Center

The **Help and Support Center** provides assistance on Windows topics.

The *Help and Support Center* combines such traditional features as a search function and an index of help topics. It also lets you request remote help from other Windows XP users, or you can access the Microsoft Knowledge Base on the Microsoft Web site. Access Help and Support by clicking Start and Help and Support. As shown in Figure 1.10, Help and Support combines a toolbar, a Search bar, and basic information, some of which is updated daily.

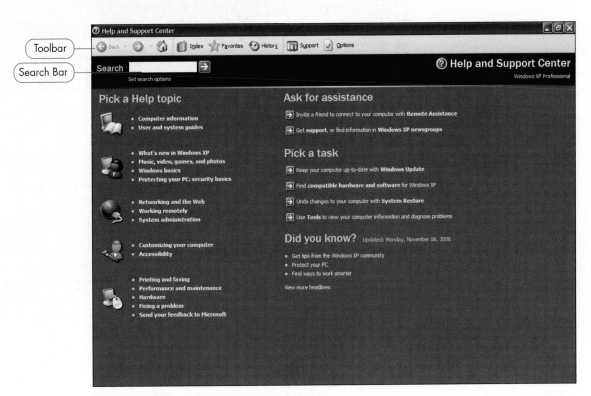

Figure 1.10 Help and Support Center

Windows provides several ways to obtain help on a particular topic. To get quick assistance with a Windows topic, you can use the index feature. Click Index on the toolbar and type a topic in the "Type in the keyword to find" text box. As you type, the Help center narrows the results to match your text. By the time you finish typing, you should see a list of subtopics, if any are available. If you see none, you might try rephrasing the search topic in the index box. You might think, for example, that there is not much to know about the mouse, except how to click and double-click. However, take a look at Figure 1.11, which shows resulting subtopics from an index search on *mouse*. Just about everything you would ever want to know about the mouse is there!

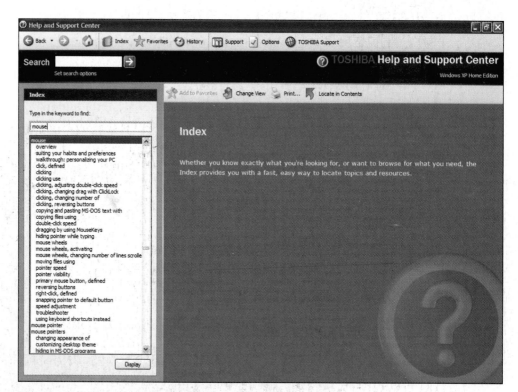

Figure 1.11 Mouse Subtopics

Help and Support also provides a broader search tool that includes information from the Microsoft Knowledge Base, a collection of support on Microsoft tools. Type a topic in the *Search* box and click the green arrow to the right. Results are presented in order of relevance, with the most relevant shown first.

The toolbar at the top of the window contains several buttons that make it easy to navigate through Help and Support. The Back and Forward buttons enable you to move through the various pages that were viewed in the current session. The Favorites button displays a list of previously saved Help topics from previous sessions. The History button shows all pages that were visited in this session. The Support button enables you to get help from a friend or a support professional. You can customize your view of the Help and Support Center through the Options button.

Hands-On Exercise

1 | Introduction to Windows XP

Skills covered: 1. Turn On the Computer and Select a Username **2.** Modify the Start Menu **3.** Move, Size, and Close a Window **4.** Get Help

---

Step 1
Turn on the Computer and Select a Username

Refer to Figure 1.12 as you complete Step 1.

a. Power on the computer by pressing the power switch.

b. If presented with a choice of one or more user accounts, click the appropriate account. Respond to a password request if prompted.

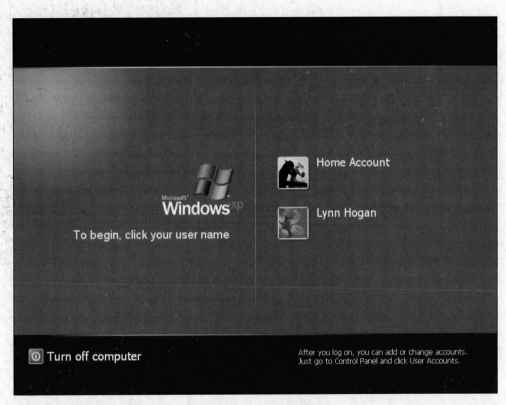

Figure 1.12 User Accounts

Step 2
Modify the Start Menu

Refer to Figure 1.13 as you complete Step 2.

a. Right-click a blank area of the taskbar and select **Properties**.

The Taskbar and Start Menu Properties dialog box appears.

b. Click the **Start Menu tab**, click the **Classic Start menu option**, and then click **OK**.

The Start menu will display in the standard one-column Classic view instead of the Windows XP view.

TROUBLESHOOTING: If you do not see a menu containing the Properties option, you right-clicked an occupied area of the taskbar instead of an empty part. Try the procedure again, this time being careful to click an unoccupied area.

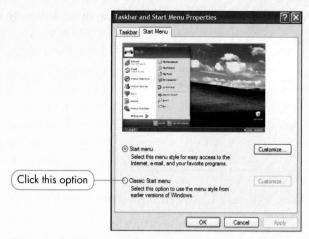

Figure 1.13 Taskbar and Start Menu Properties

Click this option (callout pointing to "Classic Start menu" option)

   c. Change the Start menu back to the Windows XP view by repeating the directions given in Steps 1a and b, but click the **Start menu option**.

   The Start menu now displays in the two-column Windows XP view.

Step 3
Move, Size, and Close a Window

Refer to Figure 1.14 as you complete Step 3.

   a. Click the **Start button**, and then click **My Computer**. Move and size the window to match that shown in Figure 1.14.

   TROUBLESHOOTING: The My Computer window may open as a maximized window. In that case, you cannot move or resize it. You must first Restore Down by clicking the middle control button before you can move or resize it.

Figure 1.14 Moving and Resizing a Window

To move a window, click and drag the title bar. To resize a window, click and drag a border or corner of the window.

b. Click the **Minimize button** to minimize the window.

My Computer is still open, although you no longer see the window. You should see a button on the taskbar letting you know the window is still open.

c. Click **My Computer** on the taskbar to display the window on the desktop again.

d. Click the **Maximize button** to expand the My Computer window.

e. Click the **Restore Down button** to return the window to its previous size.

f. Click the **Close button** to close My Computer.

Step 4
Get Help

Refer to Figure 1.15 as you complete Step 4.

a. Click **Start** and click **Help and Support**.

b. Click **Index**. The insertion point appears in a text box where you can enter a search topic. Type **mouse** to see an immediate list of topics that relate to *mouse*.

Suppose that you are left-handed and are seeking help for adjusting the mouse so that the buttons are reversed. You can use Help and Support to get assistance.

c. Find and click the *reversing buttons* topic. Click the **Display** button at the bottom of the task pane. Your results should be similar to Figure 1.15.

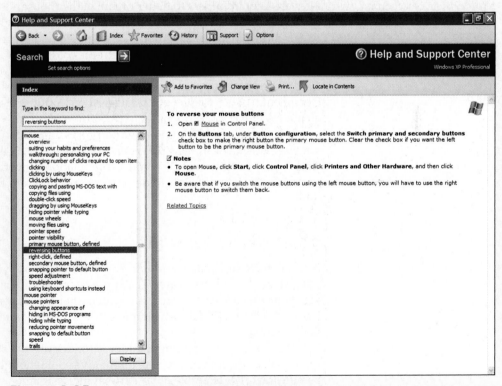

Figure 1.15 Help with Reversing Mouse Buttons

d. Click **Print** to print the Help topic.

e. Click the **Close button** to close Help and Support.

Files and Folders

A *file* is a collection of data or information that has a name.

A *program file* is part of a software program, such as Microsoft Word.

A *data file* is an item that you create and to which you give a name, such as a document.

A *file name* is an identifier that you give a file when you save it.

A *file* is a set of instructions or data that has been given a name and stored. Two basic types of files exist: *program files* and *data files*. Microsoft Word and Microsoft Excel are examples of program files. The documents and workbooks that you create using these programs are called data files. A program file is executable; it contains instructions that tell the computer what to do. A data file is not executable; it can be used only in conjunction with a specific program. In other words, by using a program file, such as Microsoft Word, you can create data files, like documents that are important to you.

Every file has a *file name* that identifies it to the operating system. The file name can contain up to 255 characters and may include spaces and other punctuation. File names cannot contain the following characters: \, /, :, *, ?, ", <, >, and |. Rather than remember the characters to avoid, you might find it easier to limit the characters in a file name to letters, numbers, and spaces. In the Exploring series, underlines are used rather than spaces.

$\Big($ It is important that you learn to work with folders so that you can better organize your storage devices. $\Big)$

In this section, you work with folders. Specifically, you learn how to create, rename, and delete folders. Then you learn how to change the view of folder contents. It is important that you learn to work with folders so that you can better organize your storage devices. Just as you can design your own method of organizing folders in a filing cabinet, you also can design folder structure on your hard drive or another storage medium.

Working with Folders

A *folder* is an object or container that can hold multiple files and subfolders.

Files are kept in *folders* to better organize the thousands of files on a typical system. A computer folder is similar to a file folder that you might keep in your office to hold one or more documents. Although your office folder probably is kept in a filing cabinet, Windows stores its files in electronic folders that are located on a hard drive, CD, flash drive, or other storage device.

Windows XP creates many folders automatically, such as My Computer or My Documents. Other folders are created when you install new software. You can even create folders to hold documents and other files that you develop. You might, for example, create a folder for your word processing documents and a second folder for your spreadsheets. You could create a folder to hold all of your work for a specific class, which in turn might contain a combination of word processing documents and spreadsheets. Remember, a folder can contain program files, data files, or even other folders.

Create, Rename, and Delete Folders

As you create files, such as letters or worksheets, you will want to save them so that you can easily find them later. The key is to create and name folders appropriately, so that your files are categorized in a system that makes sense to you. Creating, renaming, and deleting folders is a simple process and one with which you should become very familiar.

The first step in creating a folder is to identify the storage device on which you plan to place the folder. You also might give some thought to any subfolders that will be necessary. For example, if you are saving assignments for all classes in which you are enrolled this semester, you might create a folder named Spring Semester on your flash drive. Within the Spring Semester folder, you could include a separate folder for each class, such as English Composition and Biology. To create a folder, open My Computer by clicking Start and then My Computer. Click the Folders button on the Standard buttons toolbar to display a folder hierarchy in the left (folders) pane. Click My Computer (in the left pane) to expand the folder view. You should see all of the storage devices on your system. Because you want to place the Spring Semester folder on your flash drive, click the drive letter that corresponds with your flash drive, such as Removable Disk (E:). Click File in the menu bar and point to New. When a cascaded menu appears, select Folder. You will see a New Folder icon. Type a folder name, such as Spring Semester, and press Enter. You now have a folder named Spring Semester. Although the folder does not yet contain any files, the folder is available. As you create subsequent folders and subfolders, remember to first click the drive or folder under which you want the new folder to appear before creating the folder.

At times, a folder may be named inappropriately. Perhaps you misspelled a word, or the folder's purpose has changed so that a new name is necessary. Renaming a folder is a simple process. First, open My Computer and change the view to Folders by clicking Folders on the Standard buttons toolbar. Expand My Computer by clicking it (in the left pane) and navigate to the folder that you want to rename. When you locate the folder, right-click it and select Rename on the shortcut menu. Type the folder's new name and press Enter.

TIP   Using F2 to Rename Folders

You can rename a folder by clicking it, and then pressing F2 on the keyboard. Type the new folder name, and press Enter.

When you delete a folder, the folder and all of its subfolders and files are removed. It is important, therefore, to be certain that you no longer need a folder or its contents before you delete it. To delete a folder, right-click the folder and select Delete from the shortcut menu. You also will have to respond to a dialog box asking if you are certain that you want to remove the folder. If you later decide that you need the folder, you can recover it from the Recycle Bin if you deleted it from the hard drive. However, if it was deleted from a CD or other storage medium, you cannot retrieve it. The Recycle Bin is discussed in a later section of this chapter.

Change Folder Views

Figure 1.16 displays the contents of a folder containing two documents. The folder contents are displayed in Tiles view. Figure 1.17 displays the same folder in Details view, which shows the date the files were created or last modified, along with other file information. Both views display a file icon next to each file to indicate the file type or application that was used to create the file. *Introduction to E-mail*, for example, is a PowerPoint presentation. *Basic Financial Documents* is an Excel workbook. Other views include Icons, which is much like Tiles except only the file name is displayed, and List, which presents folder contents in a columnar format with the file name and a small icon for each file. If the files are digital photos or other graphics, you might like to view them in either Filmstrip, or Thumbnails view. Filmstrip which is only an option if the selected folder contains picture files, shows a miniature image of each file along with a large display of the currently selected (or first in line) image. Similarly, Thumbnails shows a miniature image of each graphic, but does not enlarge a selected file.

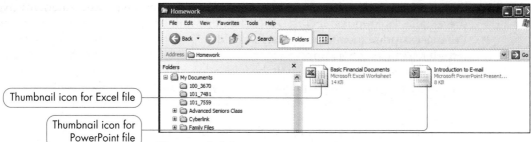

Figure 1.16 Tiles View

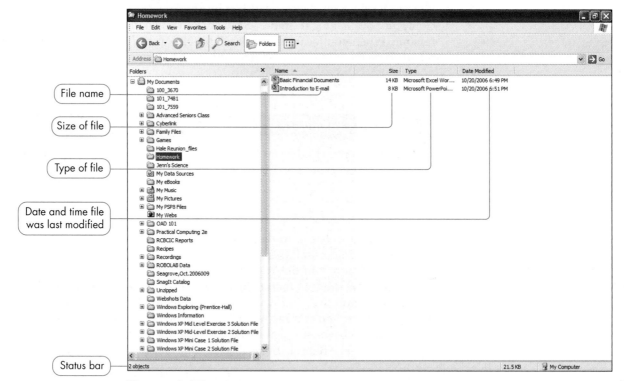

Figure 1.17 Details View

Figures 1.16 and 1.17 have more similarities than differences, such as the name of the folder (*Homework*), which appears in the title bar of the open folder. The Minimize, Restore Down, and Close buttons are found at the right of the title bar. A menu bar appears below the title bar. The Standard buttons toolbar is shown below the menu, with the Address bar (indicating the drive and folder) appearing below the toolbar. A status bar is shown at the bottom of the folder window, giving summary information about the *Homework* folder. For a review of the parts of a window, see Figure 1.4 earlier in this chapter.

Managing Folders and Files in Windows Explorer

Windows Explorer displays a tree structure of the devices and folders on your computer.

Windows Explorer is a program that displays a hierarchical (tree) structure of the devices and folders on your computer. Figure 1.18 displays the contents of the Reports folder (on drive F, which is a removable USB drive). The folder structure is displayed in the left pane, while the contents of the selected object (the Reports folder) are shown in the right pane. To open Windows Explorer, click Start, All Programs, Accessories, Windows Explorer.

Although by default, Windows Explorer displays folders in the left pane, you occasionally might see the left pane used as a task pane, which does not display folder hierarchy. To display the folder structure, click Folders in the toolbar. Alternatively, if the folder structure displays, but you want to work with the task pane (which contains tasks appropriate to a selected item), click Folders. The Folders button is a toggle button that switches back and forth between task pane and folders views.

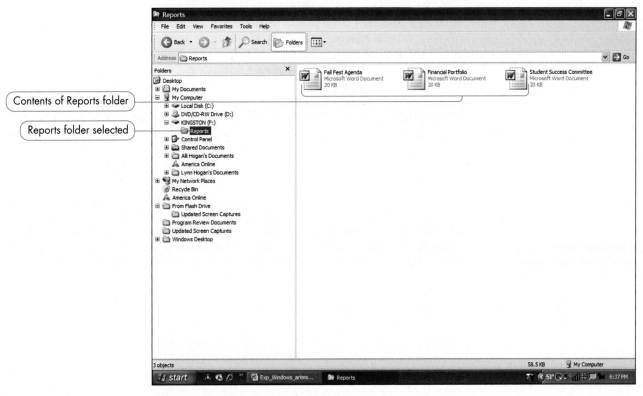

Contents of Reports folder

Reports folder selected

Figure 1.18 A Folder and Its Contents

Take a look at the folders pane (left pane). A plus sign appears beside the icon for My Documents to indicate that the folder has not been expanded to show its subfolders. Clicking the plus sign will expand My Documents to show more detail. The contents of drive C (the hard drive) also are not visible. Look closely and you see that both drive F and drive C are indented under My Computer, which in turn is indented under the desktop. In other words, the desktop is at the top of the hierarchy, containing the My Computer folder, which in turn contains drive F and drive C. The desktop also contains the My Documents folder, but the plus sign next to My Documents indicates the folder is collapsed. My Computer, on the other hand, has a minus sign indicating the folder is expanded. You can see its contents, which consist of the drives on your system as well as other special folders (Control Panel and Shared Documents).

Look at the icon next to the Reports folder in the left pane of Figure 1.18. The icon is an open folder, indicating that the Reports folder is the active folder. The folder's name also is shaded, and it appears in the title bar and address bar. Only one folder can be active at a time, with its contents displayed in the right pane. If you want to work with a document in the Reports folder, you could double-click the document to open it, or click to select it so that you could rename, move, copy, or delete the document. To see the contents of a different folder, such as My Documents, you would select the icon for that folder in the left pane (which automatically closes the Reports folder). The contents of My Documents would then appear in the right pane.

Move and Copy a File or Folder

Basic file management involves moving and copying a file or folder from one location to another. This can be done in various ways. The method of copying and moving files is the same as that for folders. The easiest way to copy or move is to click and drag the file icon from the source drive or folder to the destination drive or folder within Windows Explorer. Whether a file is moved or copied, however, depends on whether the source and destination are on the same or different drives. Dragging a file from one folder to another folder on the same drive moves the file. When you drag a file to a folder on a different drive, you create a copy of the file.

This process is not as arbitrary as it seems. Windows assumes that if you drag an item to a different drive, such as from drive C to drive E, you want the object to appear in both places. Therefore, the default action when you click and drag an object to a different drive is to *copy* the object. You can, however, override the default and move the object by pressing and holding the Shift key as you drag. When you make a copy of an item, the copy is usually on another disk drive, for backup purposes. You might copy a file from the hard drive to a CD or USB drive.

Windows also assumes that you do not want two copies of an object on the same drive, as that would result in wasted disk space. Thus, the default action when you click and drag an item to a different folder on the same drive is to *move* the object. You can override the default and copy the object by pressing and holding Ctrl on the keyboard as you drag the file from one location to another.

Fortunately, you have an alternative to learning the rules related to clicking and dragging (whether a file is moved or copied). Simply right-click and drag a file to another location, regardless of whether the new location is on the same drive as the original file. When you release the mouse button, you will respond to a ***shortcut menu*** choosing to either *copy* or *move* the file. Using this method, you do not have to remember when, or if, to hold down Shift or Ctrl.

If the disk to which you are copying or moving is a removable media, such as a USB drive, you should follow a few safety tips before removing the drive. When you are ready to disconnect the drive, click the Safely Remove Hardware icon in the Notification area. To identify the Safely Remove Hardware icon, place the pointer over each icon and wait for a ScreenTip to appear, informing you of each icon's purpose. When you find the Safely Remove Hardware icon, click it and select the device from the list of hardware devices. Click the Stop button and the OK button. When the Safe to Remove Hardware screen tip displays, remove the drive. Close the Safely Remove Hardware dialog box.

A ***shortcut menu*** displays a list of commands when you right-click an item or screen element.

Backup Files

It is not a question of *if* it will happen, but *when* it will happen. Hard drives die, files are lost, or viruses infect a system. You certainly do not want to lose any files, but you should be especially attentive to your data files, creating backup copies on different drive media so that you can always recover your work. The essence of a good ***backup*** strategy is to decide which files to back up, how often to copy them, and where to keep the backup.

A ***backup*** is a copy of a file.

Your strategy should be very simple—copy what you cannot afford to lose, do so on a regular basis, and store the backup away from your computer. You need not copy every file, every day. Instead, copy just the files that changed during the current session. Realize, too, that it is much more important to copy your data files than your program files. You can always reinstall program files from the original CD, or if necessary, locate another copy of an application. You, however, are the only one who has a copy of the term paper that is due tomorrow. Once you decide on a strategy, follow it, and follow it on a regular basis.

Deleting Items and Managing the Recycle Bin

Deleting a file or folder is a very easy task. In Windows Explorer, you can simply click to select the item and then press Delete on the keyboard. Alternatively, you can right-click the file or folder and select Delete. If you are deleting an item from the hard drive, you can recover it later because it is actually only moved to the Recycle Bin. However, files and folders deleted from a removable disk, such as a CD/RW or USB drive, are not placed in the Recycle Bin and cannot be recovered.

The **Recycle Bin** holds files and folders deleted from the hard drive.

The *Recycle Bin* is a special folder on the hard drive that contains files and folders that have been deleted from a hard drive. Think of the Recycle Bin as similar to the wastebasket in your room. You throw out (delete) a report by tossing it into a wastebasket. You can still get it back by taking it out of the wastebasket as long as the basket has not been emptied. The Recycle Bin works the same way. Files are not actually removed from the hard drive, but they are instead moved to the Recycle Bin. You can retrieve discarded files and restore them to their original locations as long as it has not been emptied. To view the contents of the Recycle Bin, double-click the Recycle Bin on the desktop. Figure 1.19 shows an open Recycle Bin.

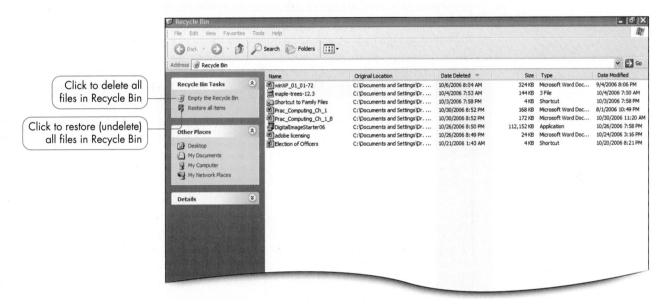

Figure 1.19 Recycle Bin

Windows provides several ways to place a file or folder in the Recycle Bin. In Windows Explorer, you can simply click a file or folder and press Delete. Or you can right-click the item and select Delete. In either case, you will be asked to confirm the deletion. You also can click and drag a file or folder to the Recycle Bin. If you can see the Recycle Bin in the left folders pane of Windows Explorer, simply click and drag the file or folder to the Recycle Bin. If you do not see the Recycle Bin in the left pane, you must click Folders in the Standard buttons toolbar to change the left pane view to folders. You also can drag items to the Recycle Bin on the desktop.

Remember that only items removed from the hard drive are placed in the Recycle Bin, not files deleted from removable media. The Recycle Bin is a type of safety net—if you later decide that you want to recover a deleted item, you can recover it from the Recycle Bin, as long as the Recycle Bin is not full. Because the Recycle Bin reserves 10% of your hard drive space for deleted files, it is very likely that a file will still be there if you retrieve it within a few weeks of removing it. To retrieve a deleted file or folder, open the Recycle Bin by double-clicking the icon on the desktop. If you want to recover all files and folders, click *Restore all items*. If, however, you are retrieving only one item, click it and click *Restore this item*.

The Recycle Bin is an area of hard drive space reserved for deleted items. Therefore, when you delete an item, you are not actually freeing hard drive space, but are instead simply moving an item from one location to another. If your goal is to remove unnecessary items from the hard drive, and you are certain that you will not need them later, you can empty the Recycle Bin. To do so, open the Recycle Bin and click Empty the Recycle Bin. You also can simply right-click the Recycle Bin and click Empty Recycle Bin. If you want to delete some items permanently, but retain others in the Recycle Bin, open the Recycle Bin, right-click any item to be deleted, and select Delete. Remember, when the file or folder is deleted, it is permanently removed and cannot be recovered.

Given the ever-increasing sizes of hard drives, you might determine that the Recycle Bin is requiring too much of that space. At 10% of your hard drive space, the reserved area for deleted files could be excessive. You can adjust the Recycle Bin properties to decrease the amount of space reserved. Right-click the Recycle Bin and click Properties. Click and drag the slider to adjust the percentage of space reserved, as shown in Figure 1.20. Click OK to accept the new settings.

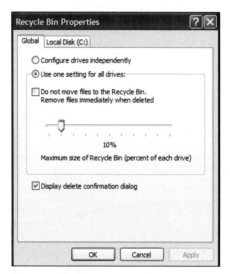

Figure 1.20 Recycle Bin Properties

Hands-On Exercises

2 | File and Folder Management

Skills covered: 1. Change a Window View **2.** Create and Rename a Folder **3.** Move and Delete a Folder **4.** Create and Save a File.

Step 1 Change a Window View	Refer to Figure 1.21 as you complete Step 1.

a. Click **Start**, point to **All Programs**, point to **Accessories**, and then click **Windows Explorer**.

Windows Explorer enables you to view files and folders saved on your computer. You can modify the view to display large, tiled, or detailed icons. If you are viewing picture files, the *Thumbnails* or *Filmstrip* view provides a preview of each picture.

b. Click **View**. On the menu, Status Bar should be checked. Select **Status Bar** to clear the check mark.

The status bar is no longer displayed at the bottom of the window. The status bar, which can be displayed or hidden, is shown along the lower edge of the Windows Explorer window, giving additional information about the selected item.

c. Click **View** and check to see which option has a small black circle to the left. That option is the selected icon display. Select **Tiles** (even if it already has a black dot to the left).

The icons display in a tiled format.

d. Click **View** and point to **Toolbars**. From the submenu that appears, make sure a check mark appears beside both **Standard Buttons** and **Address Bar**. If either is not selected, click to select that option.

e. Click **Folders** on the Standard Buttons toolbar to toggle (change) the contents of the left pane. Click **Folders** again to display the folder structure. End with Windows Explorer displayed, as shown in Figure 1.21.

f. Close Windows Explorer.

Figure 1.21 Windows Explorer

Step 2	Refer to Figure 1.22 as you complete Step 2.

Step 2

Create and Rename a Folder

Refer to Figure 1.22 as you complete Step 2.

a. Connect your USB (flash) drive to a USB port. Wait a few seconds. Close any dialog box that appears.

When a flash drive, DVD, or CD is identified, Windows XP displays a dialog box providing suggestions for opening or otherwise accessing the new unit. You can either select an option, or close the dialog box.

b. Click **Start**, point to **All Programs**, point to **Accessories**, and then click **Windows Explorer**. Scroll the left pane up or down, if necessary, to locate My Computer. Click the **My Computer +** to expand the view. Click the removable drive (probably drive E or F). Check the contents displayed in the right pane. Depending on what the drive has been used for, you may or may not see folders and files.

c. Select **File**, select **New**, and then select **Folder**. Type **Computer Class** and press **Enter**.

You should see a new folder named Computer Class in the right pane to store assignments for your computer class. Giving the folder an appropriate name and saving it to a removable drive make it easy to take class work to and from class.

TROUBLESHOOTING: Instead of the name that you intend to give it, your renamed folder might be called **New Folder** because you clicked or pressed a key before typing the new name. To correct this problem, you can rename the folder by right-clicking it, clicking **Rename**, and typing the correct name. Or select it and press F2.

d. Right-click **Computer Class** (in either the right or left pane). Select **Rename** from the shortcut menu. Type **CIS 100** and press **Enter**.

Because you are taking a couple of computer classes this term, you want to differentiate between them by using course numbers, instead of generic identification.

e. Click the removable drive. Select **File**, select **New**, and then select **Folder**. Type **CIS 150** and press **Enter**.

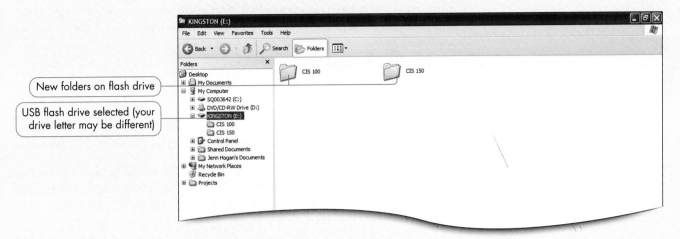

New folders on flash drive

USB flash drive selected (your drive letter may be different)

Figure 1.22 Creating New Folders

<table>
<tr><td>**Step 3**
Move and Delete
a Folder</td><td>Refer to Figure 1.23 as you complete Step 3.

a. Click the removable drive in the left pane. Select **File**, select **New**, and then select **Folder**. Type **Computer Classes** and press **Enter**.

Since you have two computer classes, you plan to create a folder called Computer Classes, in which to place the two folders from Step 1.

b. Right-click and drag **CIS 100** to **Computer Classes** (in either the left or right pane). Click **Move Here**.

c. Move the **CIS 150** folder to the **Computer Classes** folder by repeating Step b. Click "+" beside **Computer Classes**, if necessary, to expand the folder view. Your folder structure should appear, as shown in Figure 1.23.</td></tr>
</table>

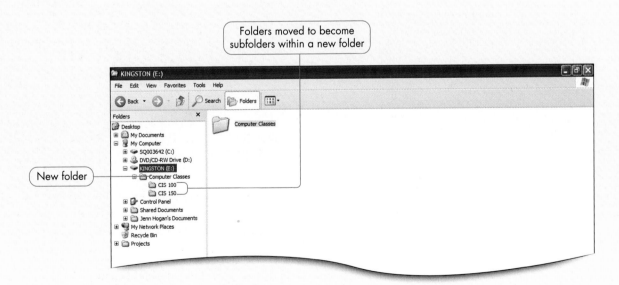

Folders moved to become subfolders within a new folder

New folder

Figure 1.23 Computer Class Folders

d. Right-click the **CIS 150 folder** (in either the right or left pane) and then select **Delete**. Confirm the deletion by clicking **Yes**.

Unfortunately, you have overloaded your schedule this semester and find it necessary to drop the CIS 150 class. Therefore, you no longer need the folder and want to delete it.

e. Close Windows Explorer.

Step 4
Create and Save a File

Refer to Figure 1.24 as you complete Step 4.

a. Click **Start**, point to **All Programs**, point to **Accessories**, and then click **WordPad**.

Your first assignment for the CIS 100 class is to use WordPad to type a paragraph about your favorite vacation place. WordPad is a word processing accessory program included in Windows installations. You will create the document using WordPad and save it in the CIS 100 folder.

b. Type a paragraph about your favorite vacation destination. Do not press Enter, but enable WordPad to automatically wrap lines for you. Include a description of the destination and explain why it is special to you. So that the file can be used in a later hands-on exercise, include the word *vacation* somewhere in the document.

c. Click **File** and select **Save**. Click **My Computer** in the left frame of the Save As dialog box. Double-click the removable drive.

d. Double-click **Computer Classes**. Double-click **CIS 100**. Click in the File name box and type **chap1_ho2_assignment2_solution**. Click **Save**.

e. Close WordPad.

f. Click **Start**, click **All Programs**, click **Accessories**, and click **Windows Explorer**. Click **My Computer**. (You might have to scroll down slightly to find **My Computer**.) Click the removable drive. Click **Computer Classes**. Click **CIS 100**.

Look to the right. You should see *chap1_ho2_assignment2_solution*.

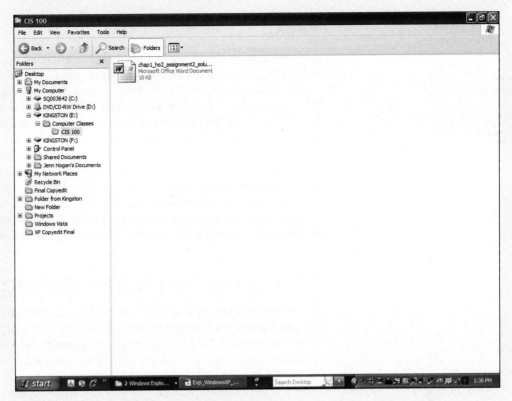

Figure 1.24 File Saved in CIS 100 Folder

g. Right-click **chap1_ho2_assignment2_solution**, select **Open With**, and select **WordPad**. After checking the assignment, click the **Close button** to close WordPad.

h. Close Windows Explorer.

i. Double-click the **Safely Remove Hardware** icon in the Notification area of the taskbar. Select the device, click the Stop button and OK. When the Safe to Remove Hardware ScreenTip appears, remove the USB drive, and close the Safely Remove Hardware dialog box. Disconnect the USB drive.

Windows Customization

You are likely to spend a great deal of time enjoying a computer and using it in the workplace. Windows XP not only enables you to access programs, but it also enables you to customize your Windows experience. What that means is that you can change the appearance of the desktop, create and manage user accounts, select a screen saver, change printer and mouse settings, and use the Control Panel to uninstall programs. As you begin to customize your system, you will identify even more ways to fine-tune Windows settings so that you get the most from your computer.

In this section, you change display settings. Specifically, you learn how to change the background and activate a screen saver. Then you learn how to use the Control Panel to customize Windows settings. You learn how to install and uninstall programs, change the mouse settings, and manage user accounts. Then you learn how to create shortcuts on the desktop and Quick Launch toolbar.

Changing the Display Settings

One of the first things that you will want to do is to modify your display settings. You can change such things as desktop theme, background, screen saver, and screen resolution through the Display Properties dialog box. A simple way to access display settings is to right-click an empty area of the desktop. From the shortcut menu, select Properties. Figure 1.25 shows the Display Properties dialog box. As you can see, tabs at the top of the dialog box enable you to change various display settings.

Figure 1.25 Changing the Desktop Background

Change the Background

The **background** is the area of a display screen behind the desktop icons.

The desktop **background** is the graphic or color that appears behind the icons on the desktop. The background is not displayed in windows or dialog boxes—only on the desktop. Although you can select a favorite photograph as your background, Windows XP has many pre-designed backgrounds from which you can choose. Click Start and click Control Panel. Next, click Appearance and Themes. Click Change the desktop background. Scroll among the background choices, clicking any that look interesting. A sample screen above the background area displays your choice. If your selection does not fill the screen, or if it appears in a checkerboard pattern, click the drop-down arrow beside Position and click Stretch. If you like the background, click OK. Otherwise, make another selection.

To include a favorite photograph saved to your hard drive, click Browse. Navigate through the folder structure to locate the photograph. Double-click the file. Click OK.

Select a Screen Saver

A *screen saver* is a moving graphic or image that takes over the display screen when the user is idle.

A *screen saver* is a moving pattern or image that occupies your desktop when you are idle for a specified period of time. Originally, screen savers were designed to keep static images from "burning" into the monitor, which they were prone to do with earlier monitors. However, now screen savers are popular because they are entertaining and because they provide a level of security. If you set a password on your screen saver, no one can stop the screen saver by moving the mouse or by pressing a key unless he or she knows the password. You can step away from your computer without the risk of leaving it open for anyone to work with.

Windows XP includes several screen savers from which you can choose. You also can buy screen savers or build them yourself from digital photographs. To select a screen saver, right-click an empty part of the desktop. Click Properties. Click the Screen Saver tab. Click the Screen saver drop-down arrow and make a selection, as shown in Figure 1.26. The screen saver will appear in miniature on the sample screen. To adjust the "wait" time, which is the amount of time that you must be idle before the screen saver displays, click the spinner beside Wait and modify the selected time. To view the screen saver in full-screen size, click Preview. Move the mouse or press any key to stop the screen saver. If you like your selection, click OK.

If you have included favorite photographs in the My Pictures folder and want to use them as your screen saver, visit the screen saver settings dialog box, as described in the previous paragraph. Click the Screen saver drop-down arrow and select My Pictures Slideshow. Click OK to accept the new screen saver.

Figure 1.26 Selecting a Screen Saver

Changing Computer Settings Using the Control Panel

The *Control Panel* enables you to change system settings.

The *Control Panel* enables you to change system settings, such as your background, screen saver, screen fonts, and accessibility options. It also provides information about system configuration and hardware performance. You can, for example, change the way your mouse behaves by switching the function of the left and right mouse buttons and/or by replacing the standard mouse pointers with animated icons that move across the screen. Working with the Control Panel, you can customize your computer system and Desktop to reflect your preferences.

The Control Panel can be organized as categories or as folders; the Category View is shown in Figure 1.27. Point to any category to display a ScreenTip that describes the specific tasks within that category. Appearance and Themes, for example, lets you select a screen saver or customize the Start menu and taskbar. You can switch to the Classic view by clicking the appropriate link in the Task pane. The Classic view displays all tools in a single screen.

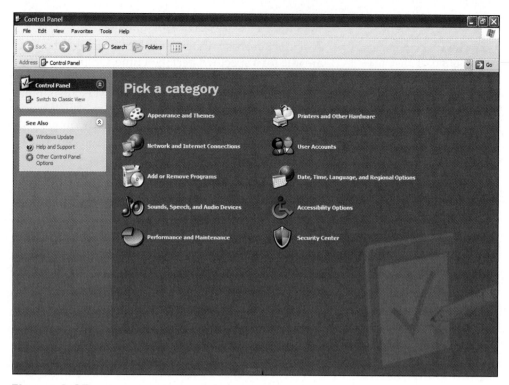

Figure 1.27   Control Pane in Category View

Check System Settings

The Control Panel is also a tool for checking your system settings—displaying your operating system version, amount of RAM, processor speed, power settings, and other performance and maintenance readings. To view those settings, click Start and Control Panel. Click Performance and Maintenance. Click System to view general computer settings, or click Power Options to adjust power settings such as stand-by and hibernation. After clicking System, the General tab should be selected, displaying a dialog box similar to Figure 1.28. From there, you can view information related to your operating system and any service packs, RAM, and processor speed. Figure 1.29 displays the Power Options dialog box.

Figure 1.28   System Settings

Figure 1.29 Power Options

Install and Uninstall Programs

When you visit the software aisle of an office supply store, you will likely find many titles in which you have an interest. Software, or programs, must be installed on your computer before you can enjoy them. Luckily, installation is usually very simple. As you open the software package, you will find a CD. Place the CD in your CD drive and wait for onscreen instructions. Most software opens in an installation *wizard*, which is a step-by-step guided set of instructions. Most often, simply clicking Next and being affirmative to requests for input result in successful installation. Once installed, evidence of the software appears in several locations. It always will be listed as a program on your program list, accessible by clicking Start, All Programs. Sometimes, it also is installed as an icon on your desktop so that you can simply double-click the icon to run the program. Less often, it also is placed as an icon on the Quick Launch toolbar.

> A **wizard** is a set of guided instructions.

Uninstalling software is a relatively simple task, but one with which you should become familiar so that you can maintain your computer. Undoubtedly, you will find that a program you once enjoyed immensely has become unnecessary. Hard drive space is limited, so you may elect to remove software that you no longer need. To uninstall software, click Start, and Control Panel. Click Add or Remove Programs. In a few seconds, you will see a list of all software installed on your computer (Figure 1.30). Find the program that you want to uninstall and click it. Click Remove. Respond affirmatively to any prompts. The software will be completely removed from your system. If you have the original software CD, you can always reinstall it later.

Figure 1.30 Uninstalling Software in Control Panel

Manage the Mouse and Printers

There are times when you will need to make adjustments to your mouse and printer. If you are left-handed, you might want to reverse the mouse buttons so that you can use the mouse effectively with your left hand. If the speed at which you have to double-click is a little fast you can slow it down slightly to make using the mouse more comfortable. As you send documents to the printer, they are buffered (placed in a holding area until they can all be printed) and printed. Sometimes, you might unknowingly send multiple documents to the printer and then find it necessary to cancel printing because too many are lined up in the buffer and the printer is producing page after page. In all those instances, you can use the Control Panel to manage the mouse and printer.

To adjust the mouse, click Start, and then click Control Panel. Click Printers and Other Hardware. Click Mouse. Click Buttons, if necessary. The dialog box shown in Figure 1.31 enables you to adjust the double-click speed and reverse the mouse buttons. Depending on the mouse type, the dialog box may not be exactly as shown in Figure 1.31. Click OK when done.

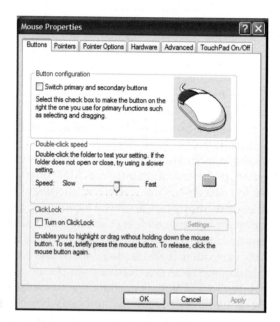

Figure 1.31 Adjusting Mouse

If you are working with more than one printer, you will need to direct the print to the correct printer. One printer will be identified as the default printer, which means that print jobs will be automatically sent to that printer unless you specify otherwise. You might want to change the default printer. Finally, you might need to cancel one or more print jobs if the printer is printing too many pages. All of these tasks can be accomplished through the Control Panel. Click Start, and then click Control Panel. Click Printers and Other Hardware. Click Printers and Faxes. One of the printers listed (if more than one is listed) will have a check mark beside its icon, identifying it as the default printer, as shown in Figure 1.32. To select another printer as the default, right-click another and click Set as Default Printer. If a printer is printing continually and you want to cancel print jobs and stop printing, double-click the printer. A printer dialog box opens, listing all current print jobs. To cancel all print jobs and pause printing, click Printer. From the subsequent menu, click Pause Printing to stop the printer and/or click Cancel All Documents to remove them from the buffer. Be aware, however, that when you pause printing, two things will happen. First, the printer will not immediately stop, since it has some printing left in the buffer. Second, when the printer stops after you have paused printing, it will not begin again until you click to remove the check beside Pause Printing. It is a toggle switch.

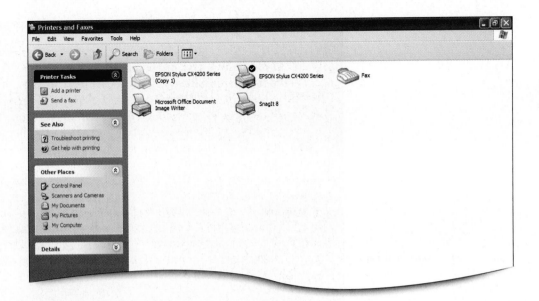

Figure 1.32 Setting a Default Printer

Create and Manage User Accounts

A **user account** specifies a user's settings, permissions, and customizations.

Windows XP includes a **user accounts** feature. Several people can use the same computer but with different accounts and varying privileges. What that means is that each person can have a customized desktop, personal folders, and even password protection in his account. Setting up user accounts is done easily through the Control Panel.

To create a new user account, click Start and Control Panel. Click User accounts. Click Create a new account. Type an account name and click Next. Select either Administrator or Limited. A limited account can only view and work with files created by this user, customize this user's desktop, and change this user's own password, while an administrator can create accounts, make system-wide changes, and install programs. Click Create Account to finalize the user account. As the administrator, you can also change user accounts, deleting them or changing the status.

Creating Shortcuts on the Desktop and Quick Launch Toolbar

A **shortcut** is a special type of file that points to another file or device.

A **shortcut** is a link to any object on your computer, such as a program, file, folder, disk drive, or Web page. Shortcuts can appear anywhere, but most often they are placed on the desktop or on the Start menu. The desktop in Figure 1.33 contains several shortcuts; shortcut icons are identified by a small arrow in the corner. If you double-click the shortcut to *Election of Officers*, for example, the document will open in Word (because it was created in Word). In similar fashion, you might double-click the shortcut for a Web page, folder, or disk drive to open the object and display its contents.

Shortcut to file

Figure 1.33 Desktop with Shortcuts

Creating a shortcut is a two-step process. First, locate the object, such as a file, folder, or disk drive to which you want to create a shortcut. The object might be in a Windows Explorer view, on the Start menu, or in a Windows Desktop Search result (as described later in this chapter). Then select the object, right-click and drag it to the desktop, and click Create Shortcuts Here. You also can right-click and select Send To, Desktop (create shortcut).

In order to see both the desktop and the window in which the object appears (such as Windows Explorer) at the same time, you probably will need to either Restore Down or otherwise resize the window so that a portion of the desktop appears behind it. After dragging the object to the desktop, a shortcut icon will appear on the desktop with the phrase *Shortcut to* as part of the name. You can create as many shortcuts as you like, and you can place them anywhere on the desktop or in individual folders. You also can right-click a shortcut to change its name. Since a shortcut is simply a pointer to the software or object, deleting the shortcut does not remove the software or item to which it directs. Many people make the mistake of thinking that if they remove a program shortcut from the desktop, the software is removed. The best way to remove software is to uninstall in Control Panel. Removing the shortcut does not uninstall software.

Several shortcuts are found in the Quick Launch toolbar that appears to the right of the Start button. Your Quick Launch toolbar might or might not appear, depending on the settings on your computer. To display the Quick Launch toolbar, right-click an empty area of the taskbar, click Toolbars, and Quick Launch. Click any icon on the Quick Launch toolbar, and the associated program will open.

Another location for shortcuts is the Start menu. Windows XP intuitively adds to the Start menu shortcuts to programs that you frequently access. You can manually add a program shortcut to the Start menu or Quick Launch toolbar by right-clicking and dragging the program to the Start button or to the Quick Launch toolbar.

Using Windows Desktop Search

Sooner or later you will create a file and then forget where (in which folder) you saved it. Or you may create a document and forget its name, but remember a key word or phrase in the document. You might want to locate all files of a certain type—for example, all of the sound files on your system. You can use either Windows Desktop Search or the *Search Companion* to locate such items.

Search Companion is a search tool option in Windows XP.

If you have installed Microsoft Office 2007, you might have chosen to install Windows Desktop Search (WDS). You also can download Windows Desktop Search from the Microsoft Web site. If you have not installed WDS, you will work with the Search Companion instead. Because WDS is a more current and complete search tool, however, you will probably want to select it as your primary search tool. WDS appears on the taskbar (see Figure 1.34). To search for an item, click in the WDS text box and type as much as you can remember of the file name or any text that might appear in the file. As you type, WDS begins searching for matches. Figure 1.34 illustrates a search for any documents containing the word *Picture* either in the file name or within file contents. Once a file is found, you can open it by clicking the file name.

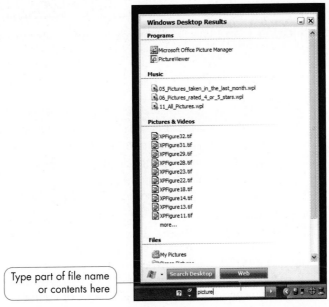

Figure 1.34 Windows Desktop Search

Windows Desktop Search creates a complete index of the files and folders on your system, along with any calendar appointments, contacts, tasks, and e-mails stored in Outlook. That means that you can find items almost instantly, much like a Web search. In fact, as you type an item in the search bar, WDS immediately begins to narrow the results, displaying those that match the text typed so far. Windows Desktop Search can be customized to better reflect your search needs. To explore customization options, click the Deskbar search box. Click the Windows icon (in the bottom-left corner of the Windows Desktop Results box). Click Deskbar Options. In the left pane, click Indexing (see Figure 1.35). In the right pane, you can choose what you want to index and whether you want to automatically run Windows Desktop Search when you log on to Windows.

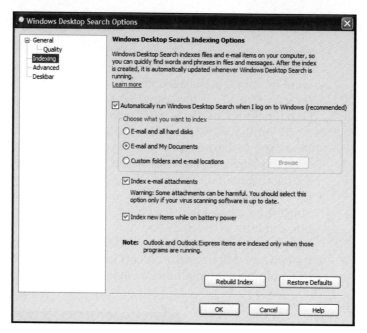

Figure 1.35 Windows Desktop Search Options

TIP   Using Search Companion

If you are accustomed to using the Search Companion instead of Windows Desktop Search, you can still use it. To use Search Companion as a default search tool, click the Desktop Search text box on the taskbar. Click the window icon. Click Deskbar Options. Click General. Click Use Search Companion instead of Desktop Search.

You can initiate a search in one of two ways. Either click the WDS box and type what you can remember of the file name or contents, or click Start Search. If you click Start Search, you will be able to respond to categories that narrow the search. If you scroll to the bottom of the left pane, you can select Click here to use Search Companion instead of WDS if you prefer it.

Hands-On Exercises

3 | Customizing Your System

Skills covered: 1. Customize the Desktop **2.** Create a Desktop Shortcut **3.** Use Windows Desktop Search to Locate Files **4.** Use Control Panel to Customize System Settings **5.** Add a User Account **6.** Add a Shortcut to the Quick Launch Toolbar

---

Step 1

Customize the Desktop

Refer to Figure 1.36 as you complete Step 1.

a. Point to an empty area of the desktop and right-click to display a shortcut menu. Select **Properties**. Click the **Themes tab**, if necessary. Click the drop-down arrow beside **Theme** and click **Windows XP**. Click **OK**.

This step modifies the Theme and Background of your desktop. Before attempting this step, check with your instructor to see if you are allowed to modify the desktop. If you are not able to change settings, move to Step 2.

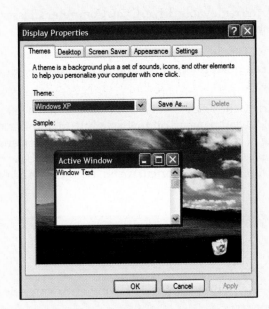

Figure 1.36 Display Properties

b. Right-click an empty part of the desktop, then select **Properties**. Click the **Desktop tab**, select **None** in the Background list box, and click **OK**. The background disappears.

TROUBLESHOOTING: If you do not see None as a choice of background, you might have to scroll up slightly to find the selection.

Refer to Figure 1.37 as you complete Step 2.

a. Click **Start**, click **All Programs**, and click **Accessories**.

Because you often use Windows Explorer, you find it cumbersome to go through the Programs menu structure each time you access the program. Therefore, you want to create a Windows Explorer shortcut on the desktop so that you simply double-click the shortcut to open the program.

b. Right-click and drag **Windows Explorer** to the desktop (visible behind the Programs menu). Click **Copy Here**. A *Shortcut to Windows Explorer* icon displays on the desktop.

c. Connect your USB drive to the USB port on your computer. Wait a few seconds and close any dialog box that appears.

d. Double-click the **Windows Explorer icon** on your desktop. Click "+" beside **My Computer** in the left pane (you might have to scroll the left pane up or down slightly to find My Computer).

TROUBLESHOOTING: If, instead of the folders pane, you see the task pane on the left, click **Folders** in the Standard toolbar. Then repeat Step b.

e. Click the removable drive. Click **Computer Classes**. Click **CIS 100**. To the right, you should see *chap1_ho2_assignment2*.

You will create a shortcut to *chap1_ho2_assignment2* on the desktop. That way, you can quickly open the file at any time by double-clicking the file on the desktop.

f. Return to the Folders pane. Find *Desktop* in the left pane (you might have to scroll the left pane up or down slightly to find Desktop). Do not click it; just locate it. You may have to scroll up to see it. You should still see *chap1_ho2_assignment2* in the right pane. Right-click and drag *chap1_ho2_assignment2* to Desktop. From the shortcut menu, click **Create Shortcuts Here**.

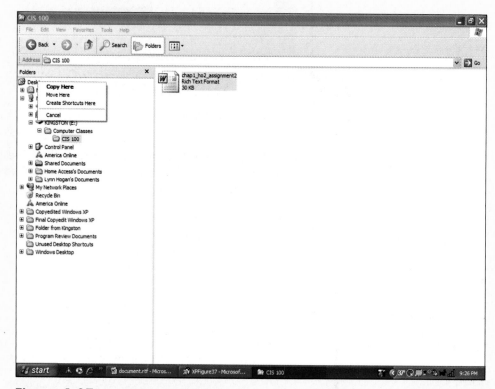

Figure 1.37 Creating a Shortcut

g. Close **Windows Explorer**. Close any open windows. On the desktop, locate the *chap1_ho2_assignment2* shortcut. Right-click the file, select **Open With**, and select **WordPad**. After viewing the file, close WordPad.

h. Right-click Windows Explorer and click **Delete** to remove the Windows Explorer shortcut from the desktop. Confirm the deletion by clicking **Yes**. In similar fashion, remove the *chap1_ho2_assignment2* shortcut from the desktop.

Step 3
Use Windows Desktop Search to Locate Files

Refer to Figure 1.38 as you complete Step 3.

a. Click in the Windows Desktop Search bar on the taskbar. Type **document**.

You will search the hard drive for all files and folders containing the word **document**.

b. Click **My Documents**, a folder that should have displayed as a result of your search.

c. Close the resulting **My Documents** window as well as any remaining open windows.

You will use the Search Companion to search for the document on your USB drive containing the word **vacation** (from Step 4 of Hands-On Exercise 2: File and Folder Management).

d. Click **Start** and click **Search**. Maximize the **Desktop Search** window. Scroll to the bottom of the left pane and click **Click here to use Search Companion**.

e. Click **Documents (word processing, spreadsheet, etc.)**. Maximize the Search Results window.

f. Click **Use advanced search options**. Click the box beneath **A word or phrase in the document**. Type **vacation** (because you remember that your document contained the word "vacation").

g. Scroll down slightly to view the *Look in* area. Click the drop-down arrow beside the disk drive selection and click to select your removable drive.

h. Click **Search**.

Because *chap1_ho2_assignment2* contains the text, *vacation*, the file should be displayed in the right pane, as shown in Figure 1.38. To open the file, you could double-click it.

i. Close all open windows.

j. Double-click the **Safely Remove Hardware** icon in the Notification area of the taskbar. Select the device, click the Stop button and OK. When the Safe to Remove Hardware ScreenTip appears, remove the USB drive and close the Safely Remove Hardware dialog box.

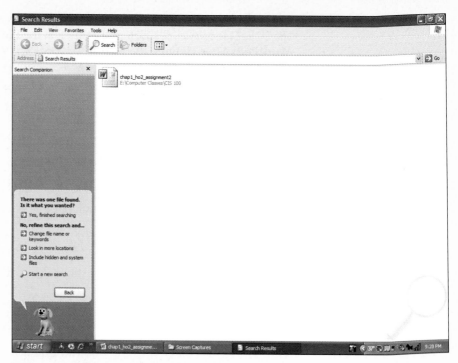

Figure 1.38 Finding a File

Refer to Figure 1.39 as you complete Step 4.

a. Click **Start** and click **Control Panel**.

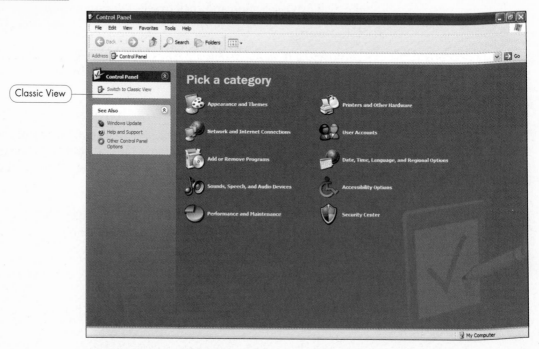

Classic View

Figure 1.39 Control Panel

b. Click **Date, Time, Language,** and **Regional Options**.

c. Click **Change the date and time**.

d. Double-click the **minutes** portion of the time displayed below the clock. When minutes are selected (shaded), type a new minutes setting. Click **OK**.

e. In the Control Panel, click **Back**.

f. Click **Performance and Maintenance**.

g. Click **See basic information about your computer**. Click the **General tab**, if necessary. You should see information including the version of Windows and amount of RAM.

h. Click **Cancel**. Click **Back**.

i. Click **Appearance and Themes**. Click **Choose a screen saver**.

j. Click the drop-down arrow beside the screen saver area. Click 3D Flower Box. Click Preview. If necessary, click to end the preview. If you want to keep the screen saver, click OK. However, if you are in a classroom or lab setting, click Cancel.

k. Close the Control Panel.

Step 5
Add a User Account

Refer to Figure 1.40 as you complete Step 5.

a. Click **Start**, click **Control Panel**, and then click **User Accounts**.

If you are in a computer lab, you might not be allowed to work with user accounts. Please check with your instructor before completing this exercise.

b. Click **Create a New Account**.

c. Type **Home Access** in the "type a name for the new account" text box and click **Next**.

d. Click the **Limited option** to grant only basic privileges to the new account.

e. Click **Create Account**. Figure 1.40 displays the new account. From the User Accounts window, you can change an existing account or create another.

f. Click **Home Access**. You can easily remove an account, but be aware that the user might also lose some data and personal information.

g. Click **Delete the Account**. Click **Delete Files**. Click **Delete Account**. Close all open windows.

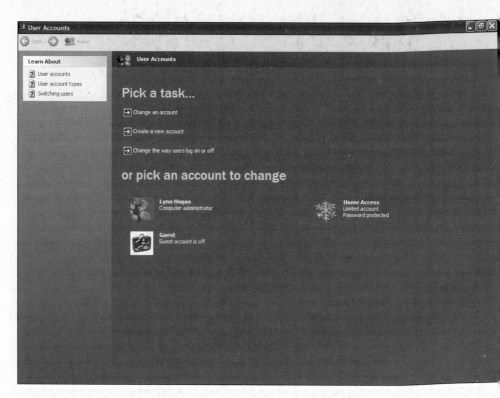

Figure 1.40 User Accounts

Step 6	**a.** Right-click an empty area of the taskbar. Point to **Toolbars**. If there is no check mark beside Quick Launch, click **Quick Launch**. If a check mark already appears, click outside the menu to close it.

Step 6
Add a Shortcut to the
Quick Launch Toolbar

a. Right-click an empty area of the taskbar. Point to **Toolbars**. If there is no check mark beside Quick Launch, click **Quick Launch**. If a check mark already appears, click outside the menu to close it.

b. Click and drag the Recycle Bin icon to the Quick Launch toolbar. When a small black vertical line appears on the toolbar, release the mouse button.

c. Click **Recycle Bin** on the taskbar. Does the Recycle Bin open? Close the Recycle Bin.

d. Right-click the **Recycle Bin icon** on the Quick Launch toolbar. Click **Delete**. When asked to confirm the deletion, click **Yes**.

Remember that removing a shortcut icon only deletes the pointer, not the actua program. Therefore, the Recycle Bin is only removed from the **Quick Launch** toolbar, not the desktop.

Summary

1. **Identify components on the Windows desktop.** The desktop is displayed when the computer is first powered on. Just like a normal desktop that you might use at home, the computer desktop is an area to hold projects, software, and files (in bordered areas called windows). Icons on the desktop represent software, files, Web sites, and shortcuts. You can maintain your computer desktop, keeping clutter to a minimum and customizing the background and other settings.

2. **Work with windows and menus.** A window can be minimized, maximized, resized, moved, and closed. Menus organize commands within an application and enable you to make selections relevant to the current task.

3. **Identify dialog box components.** A dialog box is a window that presents options for the user to select to process instructions. An option button enables you to select only one option in a group. A text box enables you to type information. A spin button enables you to increase or decrease a value. A check box enables you to select one or more items in a group. A list box displays a list of items from which to select. Clicking a command button processes a command to accept or cancel changes or displays another dialog box.

4. **Use the Help Support Center.** Although no printed reference manuals are packaged with Windows XP, there is a wealth of information in the Help and Support Center. Available as a Start menu selection, Help and Support is an indexed tool whereby you can search for information on just about any Windows-related topic.

5. **Work with folders.** A folder is a storage area on a disk in which you can place files and subfolders. You can use My Computer or Windows Explorer to create folders. You can organize folders in any way that you like.

6. **Manage folders and files in Windows Explorer.** Windows XP provides tools that assist you in managing files and folders. Windows Explorer is a program that enables you to view the contents of disks as well as to create folders and move or copy items into them. When you copy an item, a duplicate is saved in another folder or on another drive. When you move an item, the file or folder is removed from its original location and placed in another. The easiest way to move or copy items is to right-click and drag them from one area to another in Windows Explorer.

7. **Delete items and manage the Recycle Bin.** The Recycle Bin is a holding area for items that have been deleted from the hard drive. It does not, however, retain items removed from other media, such as CDs or USB drives. If you decide that you want to retrieve a deleted item, you can open the Recycle Bin, click the item, and click **Restore this item**.

8. **Change the display settings.** As you work with a computer, you probably will want to change the display to a more colorful or personal background. You also might select a screen saver and adjust the screen resolution. All of those activities are possible by working with the Display Properties dialog box.

9. **Change computer settings using the Control Panel.** The Control Panel is a Windows feature that enables you to change certain computer settings, such as the desktop background, screen saver, mouse buttons and pointers, and clock. Through the Control Panel, you also can view system settings, create user accounts, uninstall software, and manage printers and other peripheral devices.

10. **Create shortcuts on the desktop and Quick Launch toolbar.** A shortcut is a file that points to another file or device. You might want to create a shortcut on the desktop so that you can simply double-click it when you want to open the program to which the shortcut points. Shortcuts are most often placed on the desktop by right-clicking and dragging the file to the desktop. Similarly, you can create shortcuts on the Quick Launch toolbar by clicking and dragging items to the toolbar.

11. **Use Windows Desktop Search.** In a perfect world, you would never lose files or misplace them. Realistically, though, you are very likely to create a file and misplace it or download an item from the Internet and not pay attention to where it is saved on your system. Windows Desktop Search makes it easy to find a lost item if you know anything about it, such as part of the file name or file content. Windows Desktop Search indexes files, folders, and e-mail so that items can be found quickly.

Key Terms

Multiple Choice

1. Which of the following is true regarding a dialog box?
   - (a) Option buttons indicate mutually exclusive choices
   - (b) Check boxes imply that multiple options may be selected
   - (c) Both A and B
   - (d) Neither A nor B

2. Which of the following is the first step in sizing a window?
   - (a) Point to the title bar.
   - (b) Pull down the View menu to display the toolbar.
   - (c) Point to any corner or border.
   - (d) Pull down the View menu and change to large icons.

3. Which of the following is the first step in moving a window?
   - (a) Point to the title bar.
   - (b) Pull down the View menu to display the toolbar.
   - (c) Point to any corner or border.
   - (d) Pull down the View menu and change to large icons.

4. Which button appears immediately after a window has been maximized?
   - (a) Close
   - (b) Minimize
   - (c) Maximize
   - (d) Restore Down

5. What happens to a window that has been minimized?
   - (a) The window is still visible but it no longer has a Minimize button.
   - (b) The window shrinks to a button on the taskbar.
   - (c) The window is closed and the application is removed from memory.
   - (d) The window is still open but the application has been removed from memory.

6. What is the significance of a faded (dimmed) command in a drop-down menu?
   - (a) The command is not currently accessible.
   - (b) A dialog box appears if the command is selected.
   - (c) A Help window appears if the command is selected.
   - (d) There are no equivalent keystrokes for the particular command.

7. The Recycle Bin enables you to restore a file that was deleted from:
   - (a) The CD drive
   - (b) Drive C
   - (c) Both A and B
   - (d) Neither A nor B

8. Which of the following is suggested as essential to a backup strategy?
   - (a) Back up all program files at the end of every session
   - (b) Store backup files at another location
   - (c) Both A and B
   - (d) Neither A nor B

9. A shortcut may be created for:
   - (a) An application or a document
   - (b) A folder or a drive
   - (c) Both A and B
   - (d) Neither A nor B

10. What happens if you click the Folders button (on the Standard Buttons toolbar in the My Computer folder) twice in a row?
    - (a) The left pane displays a task pane with commands for the selected object.
    - (b) The left pane displays a hierarchical view of the devices on your system.
    - (c) The left pane displays either a task pane or the hierarchical view depending on what was displayed prior to clicking the button initially.
    - (d) The left pane displays both the task pane and a hierarchical view.

11. Windows Desktop Search can:
    - (a) Locate all files containing a specified phrase
    - (b) Locate all files of a certain type
    - (c) Both A and B
    - (d) Neither A nor B

12. Which views display miniature images of photographs within a folder?
    - (a) Tiles view and Icons view
    - (b) Thumbnails view and Filmstrip view
    - (c) Details view and List view
    - (d) All views display a miniature image

13. Which of the following statements is true?

(a) A plus sign next to a folder indicates that its contents are hidden.

(b) A minus sign next to a folder indicates that its contents are hidden.

(c) A plus sign appears next to any folder that has been expanded.

(d) A minus sign appears next to any folder that has been collapsed.

14. To create a screen saver using your own pictures, the pictures must be saved in what folder?

(a) My Documents

(b) Favorites

(c) My Photos

(d) My Pictures

15. When is a file permanently deleted?

(a) When you delete the file from Windows Explorer

(b) When you empty the Recycle Bin

(c) When you turn the computer off

(d) All of the above

Practice Exercises

1 Lakeview Heritage Day

Lakeview High School is sponsoring Lakeview Heritage Day, a day of activities and entertainment honoring the heritage of the 50-year-old high school. Your class is coordinating activities for alumni who are 60 years old or older. An alumni survey of students in that age group indicated an interest in basic computer training. Your computer instructor asked you to test some training materials for a class introducing Windows XP to the older alumni, and gave you a suggested outline. Pretend to be a "senior student" and go through the activities given below.

a. Turn on the computer and select an account (entering a password, if necessary).

b. To make sure icons are set to auto-arrange, right-click an empty area of the desktop. Point to **Arrange Icons by**. If a check mark does not appear beside **Auto Arrange**, click **Auto Arrange**.

c. Click **Start** and **Control Panel**. Click **Appearance and Themes**. Click **Change the desktop background**. Select the Windows XP background and click **OK**. Close the Control Panel.

d. Click **Start**, select **All Programs**, select **Accessories**, and then **Calculator**. Practice a calculation: **2025/15**, which is 2025 divided by 15 (the slash is the division operator). You can either type the calculation or use the mouse to enter the calculation. Then press **Enter** or click **=**. What is the result? Close the calculator.

e. Double-click the **Recycle Bin** icon on the desktop. If the window opens as a maximized window (filling the screen), click the **Restore Down button** (the middle button). Your window should be less than full size. Make the window smaller by clicking and dragging a border or corner. Move the window by clicking and dragging the title bar. Click the **Close button** to close the Recycle Bin.

f. Get help. You have heard about hibernation and wonder what that has to do with a computer! Click **Start**, select **Help and Support**, and select **Index**. Click in the Type in the keyword to find text box and type *hibernation*. In the index, click **overview**. Click **Display**. Compare to Figure 1.41. Close Help and Support.

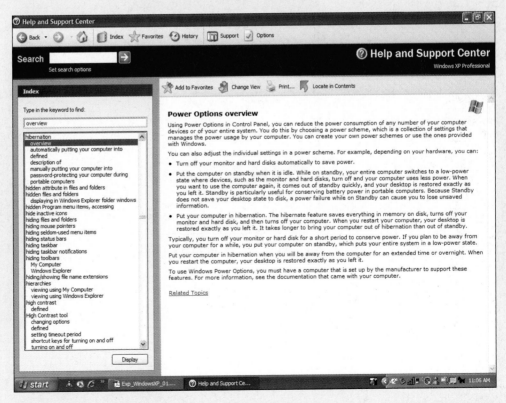

Figure 1.41 Index Keyword

...continued on Next Page

g. Find all pictures on your system. You think there may be some appropriate photographs that you could use for publicizing the computer class. To find all pictures, click the **Windows Desktop Search bar on the taskbar**. Type ***.jpg**. (The * is a wildcard character that represents any file name, while .jpg narrows results to picture files.) All pictures will be displayed. To preview a picture, click it. The picture will appear in the preview pane to the right. Close all open windows.

2 Friends of the Library

As a community service, you have volunteered to work with *Friends of the Library*, a group of people dedicated to raising money for the local public library. A benefactor donated a computer, but it needs to be cleaned up—unnecessary icons should be removed and an appropriate background selected. You also need to take a look at the computer and identify the operating system in use and the configuration of disk drives and programs.

a. To assure a relatively "clean" desktop, you will isolate those desktop icons that are not used often. Right-click an empty area of the desktop. Click **Properties**. Click the **Desktop tab**. Click **Customize Desktop**. Click **Clean Desktop Now**. Click **Next**. Take a look at the icons that are to be placed in an *Unused Desktop Shortcuts* folder. If you are in a classroom or lab setting, check with your instructor, or click **Cancel** to end the activity. If you are at home, or if your instructor approves, click **Next**, and click **Finish**. Close all open windows.

b. Right-click an empty area of the desktop and select **Properties**. Click **Desktop**. Select Tulips. Click **OK**.

c. Click **Start** and click **Control Panel**. Click **Performance and Maintenance**. Click **System**. What operating system is installed on the computer? How much memory (RAM) is available? Close all open windows. Compare to Figure 1.42.

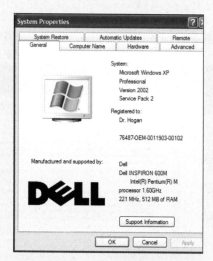

Figure 1.42 System Properties

...continued on Next Page

d. Click **Start** and click **My Computer**. What type of disk drives do you see? How much free space is available on the hard drive? Place your mouse pointer over the local drive to check the availability.

e. Because the computer will be in a public space, you want to set a screen saver so that when the computer is idle, a moving image obscures the screen. Click **Start** and click **Control Panel**. Click **Appearance and Themes**. Click **Choose a screen saver**. Click the **Screen saver drop-down arrow** and select **Starfield**. Change the wait time to 8 minutes. Click **OK**. Close all open windows.

f. You are not sure what programs are already installed on the system so you want to display a complete list. Click **Start** and **Control Panel**. Click **Add or Remove Programs**. Wait a few seconds for the list to appear. Scroll through the list, familiarizing yourself with the programs. You will not remove any programs, but if you were actually working with a donated computer, you could click any program to uninstall and click **Remove**. Close all open windows.

3 College Bound

This is your first semester in college, and you are determined to be as organized as possible. Since most of your instructors require electronic submission of assignments in the form of Word documents and PowerPoint presentations, you will create a folder for each class and its assignments.

a. Click **Start**, click **All Programs**, click **Accessories**, and click **Windows Explorer**. If you do not see the folder hierarchy in the left pane, but instead see the task pane, click **Folders** in the Standard toolbar. Click "+" beside **My Computer** to expand the folders structure. Click **Local Disk (C:)**.

b. Because you plan to be in college for a few years, you will identify your assignments not only by class, but by semester. With the local hard drive selected (shaded) in the left pane, click **File**, **New**, and **Folder**. Type **Fall 2008** and press **Enter**. You should see the new folder in the right pane as well as underneath the local drive in the left pane. If you do not see it in the left pane, click "+" beside **Local Disk (C:)** to display it.

c. You are registered for two classes this term—*Speech 101* and *Biology 100*. Click **Fall 2008** in the left pane. Select **File**, select **New**, and select **Folder**. Type **Speech 101** and press **Enter**. Click **Fall 2008** in the left pane. Select **File**, select **New**, and select **Folder**. Type **Biology 101** and press **Enter**. In the left pane, you should see the two new folders underneath **Fall 2008**, as shown in Figure 1.43. If you do not see the folders, click "+" beside **Fall 2008** to expand the view. If you make a mistake with naming or placing a folder, right-click the folder, click **Rename**, type the correct name, and press **Enter**. To remove a folder that is in the wrong place, right-click the folder and click Delete. Confirm the deletion. Close Windows Explorer.

...continued on Next Page

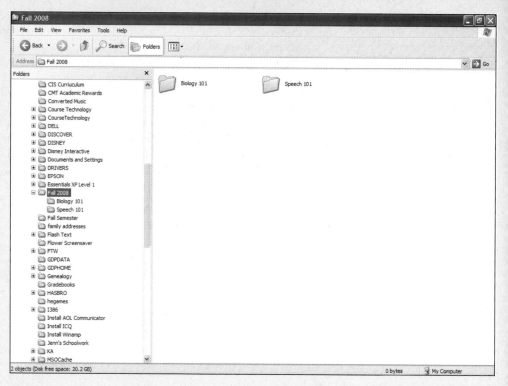

Figure 1.43 Folder Hierarchy

d. Your first Speech assignment is to write a short paragraph about your career goals and save it in WordPad. Click **Start**, select **All Programs**, select **Accessories**, and then select **WordPad**. Type a paragraph, describing your career goals. Click **File** and **Save**. Click **My Computer** in the left frame of the dialog box. Double-click **Local Disk (C:)**. Double-click **Fall 2008**. Double-click **Speech 101**. Click in the **File name** box and type **chap1_pe3_career_solution**. Click **Save**. Close WordPad.

e. To make sure your career paragraph was saved correctly, open Windows Explorer. If necessary, click **Folders** to display the folder structure in the left pane. If **My Computer** is not expanded (showing folders below), click "+" beside **My Computer**. If a "+" appears beside **Local Disk (C:)**, click it. Click **Fall 2008**. Click **Speech 101**. You should see your career goals assignment in the right pane. Right-click the file. Click **Open With**. Click **WordPad**. Close WordPad.

f. Since you probably are working on a school computer, you need to delete the folders that you just created. If you delete a major folder, such as **Fall 2008**, all subfolders and all files also will be removed. Therefore, you will remove **Fall 2008**. In the left pane of Windows Explorer, right-click **Fall 2008**. Click **Delete**. When asked if you want to place the folder in the Recycle Bin, click **Yes**. Confirm that the folder no longer shows in Windows Explorer. Close Windows Explorer.

g. Double-click **Recycle Bin**. Do you see **Fall 2008**? If you ever want to restore the folder and its contents, click the folder and click **Restore this item**. Close the Recycle Bin.

h. For one-click access to the Recycle Bin, you will drag it to the Quick Launch toolbar. First, make sure the Quick Launch toolbar is open on the taskbar. If not, right-click an empty area of the taskbar and point to **Toolbars**. Click **Quick Launch** (if a check mark is not already beside it). Right-click and drag the Recycle Bin to the Quick Launch toolbar. Click **Create shortcuts here**.

i. Right-click the **Recycle Bin icon** on the Quick Launch toolbar, select **Delete**, and confirm the deletion.

The Read-It-Again Bookstore is a new business venture in your community. It stocks new and used books in a unique coffee shop setting so that patrons can enjoy coffee and coffee blends while perusing the book collection. Obviously, maintaining accurate records of inventory is important. Your aunt has just purchased the bookstore and has asked for your help in setting up and maintaining a computer for her store records. You will first become familiar with the computer and change a few basic settings.

a. Customize the computer by selecting the Bliss background and the 3D FlowerBox screen saver.

b. Make sure the clock on the taskbar is correct. If not, adjust it.

c. Display the Quick Launch toolbar if it is not already displayed.

d. Open **My Computer**. Maximize the window if it does not fill the screen. Make sure the left pane displays the folder structure of your system. Click **My Documents**. Click **My Pictures**. (You might have to work your way through the folder structure of **My Documents** to find the **My Pictures** folder.) Change the view to **Thumbnails**.

e. Select **My Documents**. Create a folder for an inventory of used books. At the same level (underneath **My Documents**), create a folder for an inventory of new books.

f. Create a shortcut on the Quick Launch toolbar for the Recycle Bin.

g. Get help on copying files and folders to a CD-RW. Because you plan to use a CD-RW for backing up the inventory files, you need to know the proper procedure of copying. In the Help and Support window, you might begin with the keyword **CD-RW** and narrow the search from there. If a printer is installed, print the help screen that explains how to copy files and folders to a CD-RW.

h. Close all open windows.

2 Fitness Challenge

Several people in your neighborhood are interested in forming a fitness group. Having done a good bit of Internet research, you are aware of several weight maintenance and fitness programs that can be customized for the group. You have summarized the programs in Word documents. You plan to print and distribute them for the group to consider. You also have a PowerPoint presentation in mind to further motivate members during the group's first meeting. In preparing the material, you will create and modify some files and folders on your computer.

a. You want to know what Windows can tell you about searching the Internet. In the Help and Support window, click in the **Search** bar and type **Web Search**. Do you find any results on searching the Internet? Close Help and Support.

b. Using Windows Explorer, create a folder as a subfolder of **My Documents** to contain the Word documents that you have created. Name the folder Fitness Resources. Close Windows Explorer.

...continued on Next Page

c. Using WordPad, create a document outlining suggestions for warming up before exercise. Save the file in your new folder as **chap1_mid2_warmups_solution**. Close WordPad.

d. Using Windows Explorer, right-click and drag the folder that you created in Step b to the Desktop to create a shortcut there. Close Windows Explorer.

e. Suppose that you cannot find the *chap1_mid2_warmups_solution* file. Using Windows Desktop Search, search for and locate the file. Close any open windows.

f. You have found some software containing fitness exercises and tips. The software requires a minimum of 10 MB space to install and 256 MB RAM. Check your system to assure that you have enough space for the software.

g. Click **My Documents** and navigate to the folder that you created in Step b. Delete the folder.

h. Close all open windows.

3 Job Search

Nearing graduation from college, you are preparing for a job search. Your first interview includes not only an oral presentation, but a computer skills test to evaluate your preparedness in that area. Although you have completed the required computer literacy component of your degree, you want to refresh your memory and get a little practice before you go for that all-important evaluation. The following skills review should help.

a. Choose the 3D Pipes screen saver. Set the wait time to 5 minutes.

b. Auto Arrange the icons on your desktop.

c. If a Quick Launch toolbar appears on the taskbar, remove it. If it is not there, open it. Be sure to leave the taskbar as you found it by reversing your previous action.

d. Search for help on pausing printing.

e. Create a shortcut to WordPad on the desktop.

f. Change the desktop background to Wind.

g. Open Windows Explorer. Select the **My Pictures** folder (a subfolder of **My Documents**). Change the view to Thumbprints or **Filmstrip**.

h. Connect your USB drive to a USB port. Wait a few seconds for a dialog box to appear. Close the dialog box. Create a folder on the USB drive called **Sample Folder**.

i. Create a subfolder of **Sample Folder** called **Subfolder A**. Create another subfolder of **Sample Folder** called **Subfolder B**.

j. Suppose you place a music selection in the **My Music** folder on the hard drive, but cannot find the **My Music** folder. Using Windows Desktop Search, find the **My Music** folder.

k. Close all open windows.

Mini Cases

Use the rubric following the case as a guide to evaluate your work, but keep in mind that your instructor may impose additional grading criteria or use a different standard to judge your work.

Paint and WordPad

GENERAL CASE

Paint and WordPad are programs included as Accessories in Windows XP. Paint is a graphics program that enables you to create graphics and work with clip art and photographs at an elementary level. WordPad is a basic word processor that is capable of producing text-based documents, but it does not incorporate graphics. Use WordPad to create an invitation to a cookout at your home. Using Paint, you will create a map of your neighborhood. Finally, you will create a folder on your USB (flash) drive to store files related to the cookout. Find and open Paint. Explore the toolbar and determine how to draw a map. *Hint: As you learn to work with Paint, you probably will want to erase your effort and begin anew. Click **File**, **New** and indicate that you do not want to save changes to open a new Paint screen.* Save the map to the newly created folder on the USB drive. Save the file as **chap1_mc1_cookout_solution**. Similarly, open WordPad and create an invitation to your home. Explore WordPad text and alignment features in creating the document. Save it to the same folder as your map, calling the file **chap1_mc1_invitation_solution**.

Performance Elements	Exceeds Expectations	Meets Expectations	Below Expectations
Organization	Files are saved in an appropriately named folder. They are complete and would serve the purpose of a mailed invitation.	Files are adequate, but do not appear neat or finished. The end result is not a polished product that could be sent to friends; however, it is recognizable as a map and invitation to a cookout.	Files are poorly designed with incomplete elements. The folder is either inappropriately named or is missing.
Visual aspects	The theme of the map and invitation is consistent, resulting in a pleasing presentation. The invitation contains no errors, and the map is bright, informative, and appealing.	Either the invitation or the map contains elements that are difficult to read or are not related to the topic. There seems to be very little connection between the two files.	The cookout map is not visually appealing and does not take full advantage of Paint's tools. The WordPad invitation includes obvious typos and lack of attention to formatting detail.
Mechanics	The folder is appropriately named and placed. The files are in the folder and are named correctly. The Paint file utilizes at least three different tools and is very readable. The WordPad file contains no mistakes or misspellings.	The folder is not named in a way that suggests its purpose. The Paint file utilizes at least one, but fewer than three tools. The WordPad file contains a mistake.	The folder is missing. The Paint file is a very simple drawing, utilizing little or no color and very few tools. The WordPad document is very short and not informative. The invitation contains multiple errors.

Windows XP enables you to access Web information by entering a URL in the address bar of either **My Computer** or **Windows Explorer**. Open **My Computer**. Click in the address bar and type www.microsoft.com/windowsxp. Press Enter or click Go. In the left frame, click your edition of Windows (**Home Edition**, **Media Center Edition**, or **Professional**). Following relevant links, find as much information as you can about your product, including system requirements, package options (student or academic versions, etc.), and general features. Create a folder called **Windows XP Cases** on a USB drive. Use WordPad or Word to create a one-page report, summarizing your findings. Save the report as **chap1_mc2_report_solution** in the Windows XP Cases folder.

Performance Elements	Exceeds Expectations	Meets Expectations	Below Expectations
Organization	The report is well researched, with findings outlined in a very readable manner. Complete coverage includes a product overview, system requirements, and purchasing options.	Although the basic required elements of the report are included, they are not presented in a coherent fashion. The report may be shorter than one full page.	The report is very short, with an obvious lack of preparation. There is little or no coverage of product details, system requirements, and/or purchasing options.
Visual aspects	The report is well developed, with appropriate paragraph divisions and no typos.	The report contains a few mistakes, but the basic elements are presented in a readable manner.	There is little or no paragraph structure, and it is difficult to identify the major points of the report. Obvious mistakes detract from the subject matter.
Mechanics	The report is saved in the folder on the required storage drive. Both the file and folder are named as directed in the mini case. All required elements are present in the report.	The report is saved in the folder on the required storage drive. However, the file contains several spelling and formatting mistakes and/or the folder and file are not named as required.	The folder is missing or named incorrectly. The report contains multiple mistakes and is very poorly prepared with regard to sentence and paragraph structure.

Glossary

All key terms appearing in this book (in bold italic) are listed alphabetically in this Glossary for easy reference. If you want to learn more about a feature or concept, use the Index to find the term's other significant occurrences.

Absolute cell reference A cell reference that stays the same no matter where you copy a formula.

Access function Predefined formula that performs an operation using input supplied as arguments and returns a value.

Access speed Measures the time it takes for the storage device to make the file content available for use.

Active cell The cell you are working in; the cell where information or data will be input.

Aggregate A collection of many parts that come together from different sources and are considered a whole.

Amortization The payment schedule for a loan that is based on a fixed interest rate over a specified period of time.

AND function Accepts two or more conditions and returns true if all conditions are true and false if any of the conditions are false.

And operator Returns only records that meet all criteria.

Animation Movement applied to individual elements on a single slide.

Animation scheme A built-in, standard animation effect.

Annotation A note that can be written or drawn on a slide for additional commentary or explanation.

Append Process of adding new records to the end of the table.

Argument A necessary input component required to produce the output for a function.

Ascending order Arranges data in alphabetical or sequential order from lowest to highest.

AutoFill An Excel operation that enables users to copy the content of a cell or a range of cells by dragging the fill handle over an adjacent cell or range of cells.

AutoFit The command used when formatting a spreadsheet to automatically adjust the height and width of cells.

AutoFormat A feature that evaluates an entire document, determines how each paragraph is used, then it applies an appropriate style to each paragraph.

Automatic replacement Makes a substitution automatically.

AutoNumber field A field that assigns a unique identifying number to each record.

AutoText A feature that substitutes a predefined item for specific text but only when the user initiates it.

AVERAGE function The function that determines the arithmetic mean, or average, for the values in a range of cells.

AVERAGEIF function Returns the average of all the cells in a range that meet a given criterion.

AVERAGEIFS function Returns the average of all the cells that meet multiple criteria.

Axes The vertical and horizontal scales displaying plotted data in a line, column, bar, or scatter chart.

Back end Protects and stores data so that users cannot inadvertently destroy or corrupt the organization's vital data.

Background The area of a display screen found behind the desktop icons.

Background Styles gallery Provides both solid color and background styles for application to a theme.

Backup A copy of a file.

Bar chart A chart that displays quantitative data horizontally to compare values across categories; useful when categorical labels are long.

Bar tab Does not position text or decimals, but inserts a vertical bar at the tab setting; useful as a separator for text printed on the same line.

Bibliography A list of works cited or consulted by an author and should be included with the document when published.

Bookmark An electronic marker for a specific location in a document, enabling the user to go to that location quickly.

Border A line that surrounds a paragraph, a page, a table, or an image, similar to how a picture frame surrounds a photograph or piece of art.

Bound control A control that enables you to pull information from the underlying table or query data.

Breakpoint The lowest numeric value for a specific category or in a series of a lookup table to produce a corresponding result to return for a lookup function.

Brightness The ratio between lightness and darkness of an image.

Building Blocks Document components used frequently, such as disclaimers, company addresses, or a cover page.

Bulleted list Itemizes and separates paragraph text to increase readability.

Calculated control Uses an expression as opposed to a record value as its data source.

Calculated detail field The portion of a PivotTable or PivotChart that generates a new field and performs the stipulated calculation on all of the detail records.

Calculated field A field that derives its value from a formula that references one or more existing fields.

Calculated total field A field used to customize aggregated data.

CamelCase notation Field-naming style that uses no spaces in multi-word field names, but uses uppercase letters to distinguish the first letter of each new word.

Caption A descriptive title for an image, a figure, or a table.

Caption property Specifies a label other than the field name that appears at the top of a column in Datasheet view, forms, and reports.

Cascade delete Searches the database and deletes all of the related records.

Cascade update Connects any primary key changes to the tables in which it is a foreign key.

Cascades Permit data changes to travel from one table to another.

Case-insensitive search Finds a word regardless of any capitalization used.

Case-sensitive search Matches not only the text but also the use of upper- and lowercase letters.

Category label Textual information, such as column and row headings (cities, months, years, product names, etc.), used for descriptive entries.

Cell The intersection of a column and row in a table or in an Excel spreadsheet.

Cell margin The amount of space between data and the cell border in a table.

Cell reference The intersection of a column and row designated by a column letter and a row number.

Center tab Sets the middle point of the text you type; whatever you type will be centered on that tab setting.

Change Case Feature that enables you to change capitalization of text to all capital letters, all lowercase letters, sentence case, or toggle case.

Character spacing The horizontal space between characters.

Character style Stores character formatting (font, size, and style) and affects only the selected text.

Chart A graphic or visual representation of data.

Chart area The entire chart and all of its elements.

Chart title The area of a chart that displays a name describing the data depicted in a chart.

Check box Enables you to select one or more items that are not mutually exclusive in a dialog box.

Circular reference Occurs when a formula is created that relies on its own value. For example, if cell C10 contains =C5+C10, a circular reference occurs because cell C10 contains a reference to itself.

Citation A note recognizing a source of information or a quoted passage.

Clip Any media object that you can insert in a document.

Clip art A graphical image, illustration, drawing, or sketch.

Clipboard A memory location that holds up to 24 items for you to paste into the current document, another file, or another application.

Close button Removes a window from memory.

Clustered column chart A chart that groups similar data together in columns making visual comparison of the data easier to determine.

Collapsed outline View that displays the title of slides only in the Outline view.

Color scales A conditional formatting technique that formats cells with colors based on the relative value of a cells compared to other cells.

Colors gallery A gallery with a set of colors for every available theme.

Column Formats a section of a document into side-by-side vertical blocks in which the text flows down the first column and then continues at the top of the next column.

Column chart A chart that displays quantitative data vertically in columns to compare values across different categories.

Column field The data field that you assign to group data vertically into columns.

Column index number A number, indicated by col_index_num in the function, that refers to the number of the column in the lookup table that contains the return values.

Column width The horizontal space or width of a column in a table or in a spreadsheet.

Combine Feature that incorporates all changes from multiple documents into a new document.

Command An icon on the Quick Access Toolbar or in a group on the Ribbon that you click to perform a task. A command can also appear as text on a menu or within a dialog box.

Command button A dialog box item that you click to accept or cancel selections.

Comment A private note, annotation, or additional information to the author, another reader, or to yourself.

Compare Feature that evaluates the contents of two or more documents and displays markup balloons that show the differences between the documents.

Compatibility checker Looks for features that are not supported by previous versions of Word, Excel, PowerPoint, or Access.

Compress The process of reducing the file size of an object.

CONCATENATE function Joins two or more text strings into one text string and permits you to include the comma or space separators in the text string.

Conditional formatting Apply specific formats automatically to cells that contain particular values or content.

Constant An unchanging value, like a birthdate.

Contextual tab A specialty tab that appears on the Ribbon only when certain types of objects are being edited.

Continuous data Classification of data in which values fall on a continuum, such as continuum of ounces in a container.

Contrast The difference between the darkest and lightest areas of a image.

Control Panel Windows control center that enables you to change system settings, such as your background, screen saver, screen fonts, and accessibility options.

Controls Position, display, format, and calculate the report data.

Copy The process of making a duplicate copy of the text or object leaving the original intact.

Copyright The legal protection afforded to a written or artistic work.

COUNT function The function that counts the number of cells in a range that contain numerical data.

COUNTA function The function that counts the number of cells in a range that are not blank.

COUNTIF function Calculates the number of cells in a range that match the specified criteria rather than the number of all cells in a range that would be calculated using the COUNT function.

COUNTIFS function Counts the number of cells within a range that meet multiple criteria.

Criteria range An area within the worksheet that specifies the conditions to filter the table. The first row of the criteria range displays column headings, and the second and succeeding rows specify the conditions.

Criteria row Position in a query design grid where criteria may be entered.

Criterion (criteria, pl) A rule or norm that is the basis for making judgments.

Cropping Process of reducing an image size by eliminating unwanted portions of an image.

Cross-reference A note that refers the reader to another location for more information about a topic.

Crossfooting The sum of a total row compared to the sum of a column total to verify that the two totals match.

Currency The medium of exchange, in the United States, currency formatted values display with a dollar sign.

Current List Includes all citation sources you use in the current document.

Custom animation An animation where the user determines the animation settings.

Custom dictionary A supplemental dictionary Microsoft Office uses to store items such as proper names, acronyms, or specialized words.

Cut Process of removing the original text or an object from its current location.

Data Facts about a specific record or sets of records.

Data aggregate A collection of many parts that come together from different sources to form a whole, such as a sum or average derived from many values.

Data bars The conditional formatting technique that applies gradient-colored bars to help you visualize the value of a cell relative to other cells.

Data file An item that you create and to which you give a name, such as a document.

Data label The value or name of a data point in a chart.

Data mining The process of analyzing large volumes of data to identify patterns and relationships.

Data point A numeric value that describes a single item on a chart.

Data redundancy Occurs when unnecessary duplicate information exists in a database.

Data series A group of related data points that appear in row(s) or column(s) in the worksheet.

Data type Determines the type of data that can be entered and the operations that can be performed on that data.

Data validation A set of constraints or rules that help control the type and accuracy of the data entered into a field or cell.

Database A file that consists of one or more tables and the supporting objects used to get data into and out of the tables.

Database functions Predefined formulas that analyze data only for selected records in a table.

Dataset A container for records that satisfy the criteria specified in the query, provides the answers to the user's questions.

Datasheet form A form that has the same appearance as the Datasheet view of a table.

Datasheet view A grid containing columns (fields) and rows (records) where you add, edit, and delete records in an Access database table.

Date arithmetic A mathematical expression that calculates lapsed time.

Date formatting Affects the date's display without changing the serial value.

Date/time field A field that facilitates calculations for dates and times.

DatePart function Enables users to identify a specific part of a date, such as only the year.

DAVERAGE function Determines the arithmetic mean, or average, of numeric entries in a field of records in a list or database that match conditions you specify.

DAY function Returns the day of a date represented by a serial number.

DCOUNT function Counts the cells that contain numbers in a field of records in a list or database that match conditions you specify.

Decimal tab Marks where numbers align on a decimal point as you type.

Delete operation The operation that removes all content from a cell or from a selected cell range.

Delimiter Character used to separate one column from another in a text file.

Demographics Data describing population segments by age, race, education, and other variables.

Dependent cells Contain formulas that refer to other cells such as the formula for gross pay depending on the hourly wage and regular hours.

Descending order Arranges data in alphabetical or sequential order from highest to lowest.

Design view Displays the infrastructure of a table, form, or report without displaying the data.

Desktop Contains icons and a taskbar. It is displayed when a computer first boots up.

Detail field The data field that contains individual values to be summarized.

Detail section Repeats once for each record in the underlying record source.

Dialog box A window that provides an interface for a user to select commands.

Dialog Box Launcher A small icon that, when clicked, opens a related dialog box.

Discrete data Classification of data that is measured and quantified in discrete, unique increments, such as the number of males and females in a class.

DMAX function Returns the highest value of numeric entries in a field of records in a list or database that match conditions you specify.

DMIN function Returns the lowest value of numeric entries in a field of records in a list or database that match conditions you specify.

Document Information panel Provides descriptive information about a document, such as a title, subject, author, keywords, and comments.

Document Inspector Checks for and removes different kinds of hidden and personal information from a document.

Document Map A pane that lists the structure of headings in your document.

Document properties The collection of metadata associated with a file.

Documentation worksheet A worksheet that describes the contents of each worksheet within the workbook.

Doughnut chart A chart that displays values as percentages of the whole for multiple data series.

Draft view Shows a simplified work area, removing white space and other elements from view.

Drill button The plus (+) or minus (–) sign that enables you to show or collapse details, respectively, in a PivotTable.

Drop zone An area in the PivotTable or PivotChart design grid where you drop fields to organize the data. Primary drop zones include row field, column field, data field, and filter field.

Drop-down menu Lists commands that relate to the menu name.

DSUM function Adds up or sums the numeric entries in a field of records in a list or database that match conditions you specify.

Duplex printer A printing device that prints on both sides of the page.

Effects gallery Includes a range of effects for shapes used in a presentation.

Endnote A citation that appears at the end of a document.

Enhanced ScreenTip Displays when you rest the pointer on a command on the Quick Access Toolbar or Ribbon.

Expanded outline Displays the title and content of slides in the Outline view.

Exploded pie chart A chart that separates one or more slices of the pie for emphasis.

Expression A formula used to calculate new fields from the values in existing fields.

Expression Builder A tool to help you create a formula that performs calculations easily.

Fast user switching A Windows feature that enables you to quickly move from one user account to another.

Field A basic entity, data element, or category, such as a book title or telephone number.

Field List pane Displays a list of all of the tables and fields in the database.

Field row The area in the query design grid that specifies fields to be used in a query.

Field size property Defines how much space to reserve for each field.

File A collection of data or information that has a name.

File name An identifier that you give a file when you save it.

Fill handle A small black solid square in the bottom-right corner of a selected cell. It is used to duplicate formulas.

Filter Condition that helps you find a subset of data meeting your specifications.

Filter by Form Permits selecting the criteria from a drop-down list, or applying multiple criterion.

Filter by Selection Selects only the records that match the pre-selected criteria.

Filter field The data field that you use to create criteria to filter data in a PivotTable.

Final Showing Markup A view that displays inserted text in the body of the document and shows deleted text in a balloon.

Find Locates a word or group of words in a file.

First line indent Marks the location to indent only the first line in a paragraph.

Flat or non-relational Data contained in a single page or sheet (not multiple).

Folder An object that can hold multiple files and subfolders.

Font A complete set of characters—upper- and lowercase letters, numbers, punctuation marks, and special symbols with the same design.

Fonts gallery Contains font sets for title text and body text.

Footer Information printed at the bottom of document pages.

Footnote A citation that appears at the bottom of a page.

Foreign key A field in one table that also is stored in a different table as a primary key.

Form An interface that enables you to enter or modify record data.

Form splitter bar Divider between the form and datasheet areas of a split form; enables you to click and drag it up or down to change the height of the two areas.

Form Tool A tool that creates an automatic form for the open table; uses all fields from the table in the form.

Format Cells Operations that control the formatting for numbers, alignment, fonts, borders, colors, and patterns in a particular cell.

Format Painter Feature that enables you to copy existing text formats to other text to ensure consistency.

Formatting text Changes an individual letter, a word, or a body of selected text.

Formula The combination of constants, cell references, arithmetic operations, and/or functions displayed in a calculation.

Formula auditing A process of displaying or tracing relationships between cells and formulas. Helps identify errors contained in formulas.

Formula bar The area used to enter or edit cell contents.

Freezing The process that enables you to keep headings on the screen as you work with large worksheets, rows and column.

Full Screen Reading view Eliminates tabs and makes it easier to read your document.

Function A preconstructed formula that makes difficult computations less complicated.

FV function The function that returns the future value of an investment if you know the interest rate, the term, and the periodic payment.

Gallery Displays a set of predefined options that can be clicked to apply to an object or to text.

Go To Moves the insertion point to a specific location in the file.

Gridlines The lines that extend across the plot area of a chart; help guide the reader's eyes from the axis values to the data points.

Group Categories that organize similar commands together within each tab on the Ribbon.

Group footer section(s) Appear at the end of each grouping level.

Group header section(s) Appear once at the start of each new grouping level in the report.

Hanging indent Aligns the first line of a paragraph at the left margin and indents the remaining lines.

Hard page break Forces the next part of a document to begin on a new page.

Hard return Created when you press Enter to move the insertion point to a new line.

Header Information printed at the top of document pages.

Help and Support Center Provides assistance on Windows topics.

Hidden In Excel, the process of making rows, columns, and sheets invisible.

Hidden text Document text that does not appear onscreen.

Hierarchy Denotes levels of importance in a structure.

Highlight tool Background color used to mark text that you want to stand out or locate easily.

Horizontal alignment The placement of text between the left and right margins.

Icon A pictorial element representing a program, file, Web site, or shortcut.

Icon sets A conditional formatting technique that applies little graphics or symbols that display in cells to classify data into three to five categories, based on the contents of the cells.

IF function, Excel The function that returns one value when a condition is met and returns another value when the condition is not met.

IFERROR function Returns a value you specify if a formula evaluates to an error.

IIF function, Access The function that evaluates a condition and executes one action when the condition is true and an alternate action when the condition is false.

Importing The process of inserting data from another application, such as bringing in data from a text delimited file into an Excel worksheet.

Index An alphabetical listing of topics covered in a document, along with the page numbers where the topic is discussed.

INDEX function Returns a value or the reference to a value within a table or range.

Indexed property A list that relates the field values to the records that contain the field value.

Inequity Examines a mathematical relationship such as equals, not equals, greater than, less than, greater than or equal to, or less than or equal to.

Information Data that have been arranged or processed to view in some usable form.

Input mask Specifies the exact formatting of the input data while minimizing data storage; useful to ensure consistent data entry of phone numbers, zip codes, etc. Displays placeholder for required characters until data entry is complete for the field for a particular record.

Input Mask Wizard The tool that helps you generate and test an input mask for a field.

Input message Part of the data validation process that provides descriptive text or instructions for data entry.

Insert The process of adding text in a document, spreadsheet cell, database object, or presentation slide.

Insertion point The blinking vertical line in the document, cell, slide show, or database table designating the current location where text you type displays.

Iteration The repeated recalculation of a worksheet until a specific numeric condition is met.

Kerning Automatically adjusts spacing between characters to achieve a more evenly spaced appearance.

Key Tip The letter or number that displays over each feature on the Ribbon and Quick Access Toolbar and is the keyboard equivalent that you press. Press Alt by itself to display Key Tips.

Keys The fields that records are sorted on. Keys dictate the sequence of the records in a worksheet table.

Label Wizard Asks you questions and then, depending on how you answer, generates the report formatted to print on mailing labels.

Landscape orientation Page orientation is wider than it is long, resembling a landscape scene.

Layout Determines the position of objects containing content on a slide, form, report, document, or spreadsheet.

Layout view Alter the report design while viewing the data.

Leader character Typically dots or hyphens that connect two items, to draw the reader's eye across the page.

Left tab Sets the start position on the left so as you type, text moves to the right of the tab setting.

Legend The area of a chart that identifies which color represents the data for each data series.

Line chart A chart that plots data points to compare trends over time. Lines connect the data points for a particular data series.

Line spacing The vertical space between the lines in a paragraph and between paragraphs.

Link Child Field Property that specifies which field or fields in the subform link to the main form.

Link Master Field Property that specifies which field or fields in the main form link to the subform.

Linking The process of using formulas that reference cells in other workbooks or applications in which changes made in the original location are reflected in the target workbook.

List box Presents several items, any of which can be selected.

Live Preview A feature that provides a preview of how a gallery option will affect the current text or object when the mouse pointer hovers over the gallery option.

Logic error An error that is the result of a syntactically correct formula but logically incorrect construction, which produces inaccurate results. For example, multiplying when dividing is the correct mathematical operation is a logic error.

Lookup field A filed that provides a predefined list of values from which to select.

Lookup table The table that Excel searches using a lookup function

Lookup value The location in a table that represents the cell containing the value to look up the result in a table.

Lookup Wizard A tool that helps create, populate, and relate the lookup field.

LOWER function Converts all uppercase letters in a text string to lowercase.

Macro Small program that automates tasks in a file.

Mailing labels Self-stick, die-cut labels that you print with names, addresses, and postal barcodes.

Manual duplex Operation that enables you to print on both sides of the paper by printing first on one side and then on the other.

Margin The amount of white space around the top, bottom, left, and right edges the page.

Markup balloon Colored circles that contain comments, insertions, and deletions in the margin with a line drawn to where the insertion point was in the document prior to inserting the comment or editing the document.

Master document A document that acts like a binder for managing smaller documents.

Master List A database of all citation sources created in Word on a particular computer.

MATCH function Returns the relative position of an item in an array that matches a specified value in a specified order.

MAX function The function that determines the highest value of all cells in a list of arguments.

Maximize button Causes a window to fill the screen.

MEDIAN function The function that finds the midpoint value in a set of values.

Menu bar A horizontal bar at the top of a window containing options that enable you to work with an application.

Merge and center cells The action that merges the content of several cells into one cell and centers the content of the merged cell.

Metadata Data that describes other data.

Microsoft Clip Organizer Catalogs pictures, sounds, and movies stored on your hard drive.

Microsoft WordArt An application within Microsoft Office that creates decorative text that can be used to add interest to a document.

MIN function The function that determines the smallest value of all cells in a list of arguments.

Mini toolbar A semitransparent toolbar of often-used font, indent, and bullet commands that displays when you position the mouse over selected text and disappears when you move the mouse away from the selected text.

Minimize button Removes a window from view, but not from memory.

Mixed cell reference References that occur when you create a formula that combines an absolute reference with a relative reference ($C13 or C$13). As a result, either the row number or column letter does not change when the cell is copied.

Monospaced typeface Uses the same amount of horizontal space for every character.

MONTH function Returns the month represented by a serial number.

Move operation The operation that transfers the content of a cell or cell range from one location in the worksheet to another with the cells where the move originated becoming empty.

Multilevel list Extends a numbered list to several levels, and is updated automatically when topics are added or deleted.

Multiple data series Series that compare two or more sets of data in one chart.

Multiple items form A continuous form that shows many records in a datasheet with one item in each row.

Multitasking The ability to run more than one program at a time.

Multivalued field A field defined to accept multiple choices for a single field.

Name box Displays the cell reference of the active cell in Excel.

Nested function A function within another function. For example, =UPPER(CONCATENATE(B4,", ",A4) nests the CONCATENATE function within the UPPER function.

Nested groups Provide a power-layering tool to organize information.

Nonbreaking hyphen Keeps text on both sides of the hyphen together, thus preventing the hyphenated word from becoming separated at the hyphen.

Nonbreaking space A special character that keeps two or more words together.

Normal view The tri-pane default PowerPoint view.

NOT function Reverses the value of its argument.

Not operator Returns the opposite of the specified criteria.

Notes Page view Used for entering and editing large amounts of text that the speaker can refer to when presenting.

Notification area Found at the right side of the taskbar; displays icons for background programs and system processes.

NOW function The function that uses the computer's clock to display the current date and time side by side in a cell.

Numbered list Sequences and prioritizes the items and is automatically updated to accommodate additions or deletions.

Object, Access An entity that contains the basic elements of the database. Access uses six types of objects—tables, queries, forms, reports, macros, and modules.

Object, PowerPoint Any type of information that can be inserted in slide.

Office Button Icon that, when clicked, displays the Office menu.

Office menu List of commands (such as New, Open, Save, Save As, Print, and Options) that work with an entire file or with the specific Microsoft Office program.

One-to-many relationship Exists when each record in the first table may match one, more than one, or no records in the second table. Each record in the second table matches one and only one record in the first table.

Operand Field or value being operated or manipulated in an expression.

Operators Are plus, minus, equals, greater than, less than, multiply (*), divide (/) and not equals (<>).

Option button A mutually exclusive selection in a dialog box.

OR function Accepts two or more conditions and returns true if any of the conditions are met.

Or operator Returns records meeting any of the specified criteria.

Order of precedence Rules that establish the sequence by which values are calculated.

Original Showing Markup A view that shows deleted text within the body of the document (with a line through the deleted text) and displays inserted text in a balloon to the right of the actual document.

Orphan The first line of a paragraph appearing by itself at the bottom of a page.

Outline A method of organizing text in a hierarchy to depict relationships.

Outline view Displays varying amounts of detail; a structural view of a document that can be collapsed or expanded as necessary.

Overtype mode Replaces the existing text with text you type character by character.

Page Break Preview The command that shows you where page breaks currently occur and gives you the opportunity to change where the page breaks occur when a worksheet is printed.

Page footers Appear once for each page in the report at the bottom of the pages.

Page headers Appear once for each page in the report at the top of the pages.

Paragraph spacing The amount of space before or after a paragraph.

Paragraph style Stores paragraph formatting such as alignment, line spacing, indents, as well as the font, size, and style of the text in the paragraph.

Paste Places the cut or copied text or object in the new location.

Picture style A gallery that contains preformatted options that can be applied to a graphical object.

Pie chart A chart that shows proportion of each category to the whole for a single data series.

PivotChart An interactive graphical representation of the data in a PivotTable.

PivotChart view Displays a chart of the associated PivotTable view.

PivotTable A powerful, interactive data mining feature that enables you to quickly summarize and analyze large amounts of data in tables.

PivotTable view Provides a convenient way to summarize and organize data about groups of records.

Placeholder A container that holds content and is used in the layout to determine the position of objects on the slide.

Plagiarism The act of using and documenting the ideas or writings of another as one's own.

Plain Text Format (.txt) A file type that retains only text when used to transfer documents between applications or platforms.

Plot area The area containing the graphical representation of the values in a data series.

PMT function Calculates a periodic loan payment given a constant interest rate, term, and original value.

PNPI Federal laws governing the safeguarding of personal, non-public information such as Social Security numbers (SSNs), credit card or bank account numbers, medical or educational records, or other sensitive data.

Pointing The use of the mouse or arrow keys to select a cell directly when creating a formula.

Portrait orientation Page orientation is longer than it is wide—like the portrait of a person.

Position Raises or lowers text from the baseline without creating superscript or subscript size.

Precedent cells Cells that are referred to by a formula in another cell, such as hourly wage and regular hours being referred to by a formula to calculate gross pay.

Precision A measure of the degree of accuracy for a calculation.

Presentation graphics software A computer application, such as Microsoft PowerPoint, that is used primarily to create electronic slide shows.

Presenter view Delivers a presentation on two monitors simultaneously.

Primary key The field that makes each record in a table unique.

Print Layout view The default view that closely resembles the printed document.

Print Preview view Displays the report as it will be printed.

Program file Part of a software program, such as Microsoft Word.

PROPER function Capitalizes the first letter of each word in a text string, such as converting *exploring EXCEL* to *Exploring Excel.*

Property A characteristic or attribute of an object that determines how the object looks and behaves.

Proportional typeface Allocates horizontal space to the character.

Query A database object that enables you to ask questions about the data stored in a database and returns the answers in the order from the records that match your instructions.

Query design grid Displays when you select a query's Design view; it divides the window into two parts.

Query sort order Determines the order of items in the query datasheet view.

Query Wizard An Access tool that facilitates new query development.

Quick Access Toolbar A customizable row of buttons for frequently used commands, such as Save and Undo.

Quick Launch toolbar Contains program icons, making it possible to open programs with a single click.

Radio button A mutually exclusive selection in a dialog box.

Range A rectangular group of cells. A range may be as small as a single cell or as large as the entire worksheet.

Range name Word or string of characters, to represent a cell, range of cells, or constant value. May be used within a formula instead of a cell reference.

Record A complete set of all of the data (fields) about one person, place, event, or idea.

Recycle Bin Holds files and folders deleted from the hard drive.

Redo Command that reinstates or reserves an action performed by the Undo command.

Referential integrity The set of rules that ensure that data stored in related tables remain consistent as the data are updated.

Relational Database Management System Data are grouped into similar collections, called tables, and the relationships between tables are formed by using a ' common field.

Relational database software A computer application, such as Microsoft Access, that is used to store data and convert it into information.

Relational operator A symbol used to compare cell contents to another cell or specific value. Used to specify conditions in a criteria range to filter a list or to make comparisons within the logical test of an IF statement.

Relative cell reference A cell reference that changes relative to the direction in which the formula is being copied.

Repeat Provides limited use because it repeats only the last action you performed. The Repeat icon is replaced with the Redo icon after you use the Undo command.

Replace The process of finding and replacing a word or group of words with other text.

Report A printed document that displays information professionally from a database.

Report footer section Prints once at the conclusion of each report.

Report header section Prints once at the beginning of each report.

Report view Provides you the ability to see what the printed report will look like and to make temporary changes to how the data are viewed.

Report Wizard Asks you questions and then, depending on how you answer, generates the report.

Restore Down button Returns a window to the size it was before it was maximized.

Reviewing Pane A window that displays all comments and editorial changes made to the main document.

Revision mark Indicates where text is added, deleted, or formatted while the Track Changes feature is active.

Ribbon The Microsoft Office 2007 GUI command center that organizes commands into related tabs and groups.

Rich Text Format (.rtf) A file type that retains structure and most text formatting when used to transfer documents between applications or platforms.

Right tab Sets the start position on the right so as you type, text moves to the left of that tab setting and aligns on the right.

ROUND function Rounds a value to a specified number of digits.

Row field The source field that you assign to group data horizontally into rows.

Row height The vertical space from the top to the bottom of a row in a table or in a spreadsheet.

Run a query Access processes the query instructions and displays records that meet the conditions.

Sans serif typeface A typeface that does not contain thin lines on characters.

Sarbanes Oxley Act (SOX) Protects the general public and companies' shareholders against fraudulent practices and accounting errors.

Scale or scaling Increases or decreases text or a graphic as a percentage of its size.

Scatter plot (XY) chart A chart that shows a relationship between two variables.

Screen saver A moving graphic or image that takes over the display screen when the user is idle.

ScreenTip A small window that describes a command.

Scroll bar Enables you to control which part of a window is in view at any time.

Search Companion Helps you locate files.

Section break A marker that divides a document into sections thereby allowing different formatting in each section.

Select All button The square at the intersection of the rows and column headings used to select all elements of the worksheet.

Select query Searches the underlying tables to retrieve the data that satisfy the query parameters.

Selective replacement Lets you decide whether to replace text.

Serif typeface A typeface that contains a thin line or extension at the top and bottom of the primary strokes on characters.

Shading A background color that appears behind text in a paragraph, a page, a table, or a spreadsheet cell.

Sheet tabs The tabs located at the bottom left of the Excel window that tell the user what sheets of a workbook are available.

Shortcut A special type of file that points to another file or device.

Shortcut menu A list of commands that appears when you right-click an item or screen element.

Show Markup Enables you to view document revisions by reviewer; it also allows you to choose which type of revisions you want to view such as comments, insertions and deletions, or formatting changes.

Show row Area in a query design grid that controls whether the field will display in the query results.

Show/Hide feature Reveals where formatting marks such as spaces, tabs, and returns are used in the document.

Sizing handle The small circles and squares that appear around a selected object and enable you to adjust the height and width of a selected object.

Slide Show view Used to deliver the completed presentation full screen to an audience, one slide at a time, as an electronic presentation on the computer.

Slide Sorter view Displays thumbnails of slides.

Soft page break Inserted when text fills an entire page then continues on the next page.

Soft return Created by the word processor as it wraps text to a new line.

Sort Lists those records in a specific sequence, such as alphabetically by last name or rearranges data based on a certain criteria.

Sort Ascending Provides an alphabetical list of text data or a small-to-large list of numeric data.

Sort command The command that puts lists in ascending or descending order according to specified keys.

Sort Descending Arranges the records with the highest value listed first.

Sort row The area in the query design grid in which to indicate if you want the query results sorted in ascending or descending order for a specific field.

Sorting The action that arranges records in a table by the value of one or more fields within a table.

Spelling and Grammar Feature that attempts to catch mistakes in spelling, punctuation, writing style, and word usage by comparing strings of text within a document to a series of predefined rules.

Spin button A dialog box feature whereby you can click an up or down arrow to increase or decrease a selection.

Split form A data interaction method that combines a form with a datasheet so that you can see data for a single record in the form area and view a list of table records in the datasheet at the same time.

Splitter control The two-headed arrow at the top of the vertical scroll bar and at the right of the horizontal scroll bar, and it is used to divide a window into panes.

Splitting a window The process of dividing a worksheet window into two or four resizable panes so you can view widely separated parts of a worksheet at the same time.

Spreadsheet The computerized equivalent of a ledger that is a grid of rows and columns enabling users to organize data, recalculate formulas when any changes in data are made, and make decisions based on quantitative data.

Spreadsheet program A computer application, such as Microsoft Excel, that is used to build and manipulate electronic spreadsheets.

Stacked column chart A chart that places (stacks) data in one column with each data series a different color for each category.

Start button Provides access to programs and other system resources.

Start menu Displayed when you click the Start button.

Status bar The horizontal bar at the bottom of a Microsoft Office application that displays summary information about the selected window or object and contains View buttons and the Zoom slider. The Word status bar displays the page number and total words, while the Excel status bar displays the average, count, and sum of values in a selected range. The PowerPoint status bar displays the slide number and the Design Theme name.

Stock chart A chart that shows the high, low, and close prices for individual stocks over a period of time.

Storyboard A visual plan that displays the content of each slide in the slideshow.

Style A set of formatting options you apply to characters or paragraphs.

Subdocument A smaller document that is a part of a master document.

Subform A form that exists within another form; used to show the one-to-many relationship between two tables. When a record is selected in the main form, the subform shows the related records from the related table.

SUBSTITUTE function Substitutes new text for old text in a text string.

Subtotal command Inserts a subtotal row, such as the sum or average of values by category, where the value of the designated field changes.

SUM function The function that adds or sums numeric entries within a range of cells and then displays the result in the cell containing the function.

SUMIF function Similar to the SUM function except that it enables you to calculate a sum of values in a range that satisfies a specific condition you specify instead of calculating the sum of an entire range.

SUMIFS function Adds the cells in a range that meet multiple criteria.

Synchronous scrolling Enables you to scroll through documents at the same time in Side by Side view.

Syntax The set of rules by which the words and symbols of an expression are correctly combined.

Syntax error An error that occurs because a formula or function violates correct construction, such as a misspelled function name or illegal use of an operator.

Tab Looks like a folder tab and divides the Ribbon into task-oriented categories.

Tab, Word Markers that specify the position for aligning text and add organization to a document.

Table A series of rows and columns that organize data effectively.

Table alignment The position of a table between the left and right document margins.

Table of authorities Used in legal documents to reference cases, and other documents referred to in a legal brief.

Table of contents Lists headings in the order they appear in a document and the page numbers where the entries begin.

Table of figures A list of the captions in a document.

Table row The second row of the query design grid that specifies the tables from which the fields are selected to create a query.

Table style Contain borders, shading, font sizes, and other attributes that enhance readability of a table.

Table, Access A collection of records. Every record in a table contains the same fields in the same order.

Table, Excel An area in a worksheet that contains rows and columns of similar or related information. A table can be used as part of a database or organized collection of related information, where the worksheet rows represent the records and the worksheet columns represent the fields in a record. The first row of a table contains the column labels or field names.

Task pane A bar that provides support for a currently selected item or window.

Taskbar The horizontal bar that allows you to move among open windows and provides access to system resources.

Template A file that incorporates a theme, a layout, and content that can be modified.

Text Any combination of entries from the keyboard and includes letters, numbers, symbols, and spaces.

Text box An object that enables you to place text anywhere on a slide or in a document or within a dialog box.

Text direction The degree of rotation in which text displays.

Text wrapping style The way text wraps around an image.

Theme A set of design elements that gives the slide show a unified, professional appearance.

Three-dimensional (3-D) formula A formula that refers to the same cell or range on multiple worksheets.

Three-dimensional pie chart A type of pie chart that contains a three-dimensional view.

Thumbnail A miniature display of an image, page, or slide.

Title bar The shaded bar at the top of every window; often displays the program name and filename.

TODAY function The function that is a date-related function that places the current date in a cell.

Toggle switch Causes the computer to alternate between two states. For example, you can toggle between the Insert mode and the Overtype mode.

Toolbar Usually found at the top or side of a window, contains buttons that are accessed more quickly than menu selections.

Total row Displays as the last row in the Datasheet view of a table or query and provides a variety of summary statistics.

Totals query Organizes query results into groups by including a grouping field and a numeric field for aggregate calculations.

Track Changes Monitors all additions, deletions, and formatting changes you make in a document.

Transition A movement special effect that takes place as one slide replaces another in Slide Show view.

Typeface A complete set of characters—upper- and lower-case letters, numbers, punctuation marks, and special symbols.

Typography The arrangement and appearance of printed matter.

Unbound controls Do not have any record source for their contents.

Undo Command cancels your last one or more operations.

UPPER function Converts text strings to uppercase letters.

User account A relationship between a user and a computer (requiring a username and password) defining individual desktop settings and file storage.

User interface The meeting point between computer software and the person using it.

Validation rule A restriction that specifies which values are allowed in a field.

Validation text Message that informs users about what they have done incorrectly and instructs them about what needs to be done.

Value Number entered in a cell that represent a quantity, an amount, a date, or time.

View Side by Side Enables you to display two documents on the same screen.

Virus checker Software that scans files for a hidden program that can damage your computer.

VLOOKUP function The function that evaluates a value and looks up this value in a vertical table to return a value, text, or formula.

Web Layout view View to display how a document will look when posted on the Web.

Widow The last line of a paragraph appearing by itself at the top of a page.

Window An enclosed rectangular area representing a program or data.

Windows Desktop Search Helps you find anything on your computer by simply typing one or more keywords.

Windows Explorer Displays a tree structure of the devices and folders on your computer.

Windows Vista The newest version of the Windows operating system.

Windows XP The primary operating system (OS) for personal computers.

Windows XP Home Edition Focuses on entertainment and home use.

Windows XP Media Center Edition Coordinates multimedia elements.

Windows XP Professional Edition Designed to support business systems.

Wizard A set of guided instructions.

Word processing software A computer application, such as Microsoft Word, that is used primarily with text to create, edit, and format documents.

Word wrap The feature that automatically moves words to the next line if they do not fit on the current line.

Work-around Acknowledges that a problem exists, and develops a sufficing solution.

Workbook A collection of related worksheets contained within a single file.

Worksheet A single spreadsheet consisting of columns and rows that may contain formulas, functions, values, text, and graphics.

Worksheet reference Reference to a cell on a worksheet not currently active.

X or horizontal axis The axis that depicts categorical labels.

Y or vertical axis The axis that depicts numerical values.

YEAR function Returns the year corresponding to a date.

Zoom slider Enables you to increase or decrease the magnification of the file onscreen.

Multiple Choice Answer Keys

Office Fundamentals, Chapter 1

1. b
2. c
3. d
4. a
5. d
6. c
7. b
8. c
9. d
10. a
11. c
12. d
13. c
14. a
15. d

Word 2007, Chapter 1

1. c
2. b
3. a
4. c
5. b
6. a
7. c
8. d
9. b
10. c
11. d
12. d
13. b
14. a
15. c
16. d

Word 2007, Chapter 2

1. d
2. c
3. b
4. a
5. d
6. d
7. d
8. d
9. d
10. d
11. b
12. d
13. c
14. d
15. c
16. a
17. b
18. a
19. a

Word 2007, Chapter 3

1. d
2. a
3. a
4. d
5. c
6. b
7. a
8. d
9. a
10. d
11. b
12. b
13. d
14. b
15. a
16. c
17. d

Word 2007, Chapter 4

1. c
2. d
3. b
4. a
5. c
6. b
7. c
8. c
9. a
10. d
11. b
12. a
13. d
14. a
15. b

Excel 2007, Chapter 1

1. b
2. a
3. a
4. c
5. c
6. c
7. c
8. a
9. b
10. b
11. b
12. b
13. a
14. a
15. b
16. c
17. a
18. c
19. b

Excel 2007, Chapter 2

1. d
2. b
3. b
4. c
5. d
6. b
7. a
8. a
9. b
10. b
11. c
12. d
13. b
14. b
15. b

Excel 2007, Chapter 3

1. a
2. a
3. a
4. d
5. c
6. d
7. a
8. d
9. a
10. d
11. a
12. c
13. a
14. a
15. c
16. d
17. c

Excel 2007, Chapter 4

1. a
2. a
3. d
4. c
5. b
6. c
7. b
8. d
9. c
10. a
11. b
12. d
13. b
14. d
15. b
16. d

Excel 2007, Chapter 5

1. b
2. c
3. a
4. b
5. c
6. c
7. d
8. d
9. b
10. b
11. b
12. b
13. d
14. d
15. c
16. d
17. b
18. a

Excel 2007, Chapter 6

1. b
2. d
3. a
4. c
5. a
6. d
7. c
8. b
9. b
10. c
11. c
12. a
13. c
14. a
15. c
16. b

Excel 2007, Chapter 7

1. d
2. b
3. b
4. c
5. a
6. b
7. c
8. a
9. d
10. b
11. a
12. b
13. c
14. b
15. c
16. c
17. c
18. b
19 . d

Access 2007, Chapter 1

1. b
2. b
3. d
4. d
5. b
6. b
7. b
8. c
9. c
10. c
11. c
12. a
13. c
14. d
15. a

Access 2007, Chapter 2

1. b
2. c
3. b
4. a
5. d
6. b
7. d
8. c
9. b
10. b
11. d
12. d
13. b
14. c
15. c
16. b
17. c
18. b
19. d
20. b

Access 2007, Chapter 3

1. a
2. c
3. e
4. d
5. b
6. c
7. a
8. a
9. a
10. c
11. a
12. b
13. b
14. c
15. d

Access 2007, Chapter 4

1. b
2. d
3. d
4. c
5. c
6. b
7. d
8. c
9. b
10. d
11. a
12. c
13. a
14. c
15. d
16. a
17. b
18. b

Access 2007, Chapter 5

1. a
2. b
3. d
4. d
5. a
6. a
7. c
8. b
9. d
10. a
11. d
12. c
13. b
14. a
15. c

PowerPoint 2007, Chapter 1

1. d
2. b
3. d
4. a
5. b
6. d
7. a
8. c
9. d
10. b
11. d
12. d
13. c
14. a
15. c

Windows XP, Chapter 1

1. c
2. c
3. a
4. d
5. b
6. a
7. b
8. b
9. c
10. c
11. c
12. b
13. a
14. d
15. b

Access 2007, Chapter 6

1. b
2. a
3. c
4. d
5. a
6. a
7. d
8. c
9. b
10. d
11. c
12. a
13. c
14. b
15. d

PowerPoint 2007, Chapter 2

1. d
2. b
3. a
4. d
5. b
6. c
7. c
8. a
9. b
10. a
11. d
12. d
13. a
14. c
15. d

Index

A

Absolute cell references, 382–383, 412
  F4 key and, 383
Accept/reject changes, in documents, 255, 261–262
Access 2007, Microsoft, 3
  data management with, 772–773, 789
  data sharing between Excel and, 828–832, 837–839, 861, 868–871
  Excel v., 767, 772–773, 789
  file formats for, 23
  help feature in, 14–15, 57
  introduction to, 747–805
  Office menu in, 5
  Print Preview in, 57
  relational database software and, 3
  saving feature in, 24
Access databases. *See* Databases, Access
Access functions, 892, 914. *See also* Function(s)
  Expression Builder with, 893
Access objects. *See* Objects, Access
Access reports. *See* Report(s)
Access Ribbon, 752. *See also* Ribbons
  groups on, 752
  tabs on, 752
Access speed, 757, 758
Accounting number format, 345
Accuracy counts worksheet exercise, 377
Action buttons
  custom forms with, 1093–1094
  forms with, 1101–1102
Active cells, 317, 318
ActiveX settings, 109
Add-ins
  tab, 1132
  Word, 109
Addition function, 328, 329
Addition symbol, 881
Advanced Filter dialog box, 565, 566
Advanced filters. *See also* Filter(s)
  application of, 565–566
  criteria range and, 577–578
Advanced formatting, 554. *See also* Conditional formatting; Formatting
Aggregate(s), 854. *See also* Data aggregates
  functions, 1003
  statistics, 1002–1004, 1039
Ajax College band exercise, 636–640
Ajax Medical Society donors exercise, 667–670
Alaska document exercise, 247
Alice Bar Realty exercise, 541
Alignment, 148–149, 179
  cells and text, 199
  centered, 148, 149
  horizontal, 148–149
  image, 224
  justified, 148, 149, 154
  keyboard shortcuts for, 149
  left, 148, 149
  right, 148, 149
  tables and, 206, 208, 216–217
Alignment group, 200, 346
Alignment tab, 346
All About Training exercise, 124–125
Allow Zero Length property, 819
Alphabetic sort sequence, 514

American Psychological Association style. *See* APA style
Amortization, 651
Amortization schedule
  exercise, 655–661
  completion of, 659–661
  formulas for first payment in, 656, 657
  formulas for second payment in, 658–659
  IF function in, 657, 658
  loan parameters in, 655
  naming of cell in, 657
Amortization tables, 651–661, 663
  car loan, 651
  defining of, 651–652
  dump truck, 679–680
  exercise with, 655–661
  functions in, 652–654, 663
  Golf Shoppe, 679–680
  house, 652
  multiple choice test for, 665, 666
Ampersand (&) operator, 623
And criteria, 849, 850
AND function, 644, 662
  nested, in IF function, 648–649
And operator, 850
Animal concerns exercise, 128
Animation(s), 1161, 1177
  custom, 1163
  objects with, 1163, 1168–1169
  presentations with, 1161–1162
  tab, 1132
Animation schemes, 1163, 1168
Annotations
  definition of, 1171
  shortcuts for, 1171
  slide shows with, 1171, 1175–1176, 1178
AnytimeTalk exercise, 473
APA (American Psychological Association) style, 280, 284
Append, 829
Application window, 1129
Appreciation letter exercise, 128
Arboretum exercise, 876
Arguments, 387, 892, 914
  IF function with, 399, 412
  PMT function with, 408, 412, 893
Arithmetic operators, 328, 329
  order of precedence for, 330, 360
Arithmetic symbols, 329, 360
Art collection exercise, 423–424
Ascending order
  for sorting, 209
  sorting in, 513
Asset allocation exercise, 617
Asterisk wild cards, 847
Astronomy lab worksheet exercise, 368–369
Athletic department eligibility grade book exercise, 403–406
Auction exercise, 530–531
Audience analysis exercise, 1253–1254
Auditing
  commands for, 722
  of formulas, 319, 718–721, 740–741
  multiple choice test and, 730, 731
  quarterly sales and, 724
  of workbooks, 715–717

AutoCalc, 1003, 1004
  changing of, 1025
AutoComplete feature, 323
  Function, 392
AutoCorrect feature
  AutoText feature v., 76, 77
  symbol insertion and, 227
AutoFill, 334, 360
  Best Restaurant Corporate Sales and, 709
AutoFilters, 514–515
  Custom, 576–577
  multiple, 515, 524
  Top Ten, 363–365, 565
AutoFit Column Width, 342
AutoFit command, 342
AutoFit Row Height, 342
AutoFormat, 163
  forms and, 1097
  report formatting with, 946–948
  Report Wizard and, 974
AutoMark command, 176
Automatic replacement, 94
Automatic Spell and Grammar Check, 40
AutoNumber data type, 815
AutoNumber field, 815
  definition of, 816
AutoRecover feature, 105, 116. *See also* Backup options, for files
AutoSum, 389, 412
AutoText feature, 76–78, 115
  AutoCorrect feature v., 76, 77
  creation of, 84
  insertion of, 83
AVERAGE function, 390, 393, 412, 1003
  exercise with, 394, 395
AVERAGEIF function, 642, 662
  exercise with, 646
AVERAGEIFS function, 642–643, 662
  exercise with, 647, 648
Axes, 1016, 1039

B

Back end, of databases, 855, 861
Background Styles gallery, 1226, 1232
Backgrounds, 1286
  changing of, 1286
  slides and, 1232–1233
Backspace key, 76
Backup options, for files, 104, 105–106, 116, 122
  AutoRecover and, 105, 116
  document exercise for, 122–123
Backups, 1278
  of Access databases, 758, 766, 789
  slide show exercise, 1194
  strategies, 1194
Bank loans exercise, 1046–1048
  PivotTable in, 1047
Banquet inventory exercise, 421
Bar charts, 434, 468, 1015, 1022, 1039
  clustered, 434
  purpose of, 440
Bar code, 997
Bar tabs, 143
Basic tasks, 31–47
  exercise with, 48–52
Bayside Restaurant exercise, 63

Function Library, 319, 387, 388
Function Wizard, 387
Fundraiser exercise, 125
Future Value (FV) function, 393, 409, 412, 416
  exercise with, 416–417
FV function. *See* Future Value function

G

Galleries. *See also specific galleries*
  Background Styles, 1226, 1232
  Colors, 1225
  definition of, 7, 1131
  Design, 1225
  Effects, 1225
  Fonts, 1225
  Picture Styles, 1130
  Themes, 1235
  Transition, 1161, 1162, 1167
  WordArt, 1133, 1161
Garbage In, Garbage Out (GIGO), 509, 883, 1061
Gee Airlines human resources department exercise, 556–560, 574–581
Get External Data
  group, 548, 549
  process, 829
Get External Data - Excel Spreadsheet wizard, 828–832
  available worksheets/preview data in, 830
  data description for Access in, 830
  field properties stipulation in, 831
  naming of Access table in, 832
  primary key designation in, 831
  saving of import specifications in, 832
  source/destination of data in, 829
Get up to speed with Microsoft Office 2007 hyperlink, 1142
GIGO. *See* Garbage In, Garbage Out
GLBA. *See* Gramm-Leach-Bliley Act
Go Digital exercise, 1250–1252
Go To command, 36, 38–39, 53, 95, 101, 102, 116
  large worksheets and, 487
Golf Shoppe exercise, 613–614
  amortization table for, 679–680
  auditing formulas in, 740–741
Grade book exercise, 316
  COUNTIF function and, 678
  freshman seminar, 374–375
  linking worksheets and, 738–739
  nested IF function and, 677–678
Grammar
  automatic checking for, 40
  checking of, 40–41, 50, 53
Grammar and Spelling feature, 103, 116
  exercise for, 110
  memo exercise with, 120–121
Gramm-Leach-Bliley Act (GLBA), 812
Graphic elements. *See also* Images
  reports with, 944, 945
Graphic shapes
  charts with, 442, 453, 468
  software sales worksheet with, 458
Graphic tools, 219–231
  brightness feature in, 222–223
  clip art/images in documents and, 219–220, 227, 228, 232
  Clip Organizer in, 219, 220
  compress feature in, 223
  contrast feature in, 222–223
  cropping in, 222
  editing features in, 224
  formatting with, 221–224
  multiple choice test for, 233–234
  recolor feature in, 224

scaling in, 222
  sizing handles in, 221
  text wrapping styles in, 221, 224
Greater Latrobe art exercise, 423–424
Green Scene exercise, 1193
Gridlines, 1016
Group & Sort tool, 953
Group footer section, 949, 951, 977
Group header section, 951, 977
Grouped reports, 952
  creation of, 953–957, 960, 977
  Report Wizard and, 952, 968–969, 977
Grouped worksheets, 693–694
  Best Restaurant Corporate sales and edited, 700, 701
  Best Restaurant Corporate Sales and formatted, 701, 702
  Plumber Corporation and, 739–740
Grouping feature, 630, 631, 639, 663
Grouping levels, in reports, 952–957, 977
  additional, 956–957, 961
  Group & Sort tool and, 953
  hide/display details in, 954–955
  nested groups and, 953, 977
  removal of, 963–964
  reordering of, 964–965
  selection of primary, 953–954
  summary statistics in, 955–956, 962
Groups, definition of, 6
Grow Font command, 46

H

Handouts
  footers on, 1236, 1237, 1238
  headers on, 1236, 1237, 1238
Handouts method, of printing, 1173, 1176, 1178
Hanging indents, 149
Hard page breaks, 89, 90
  insertion of, 97, 98
  keyboard shortcut for, 90
Hard returns, 75
Header(s), 91–92, 354–355, 1226, 1238
  exercise with, 358
  formatting buttons for, 355
  handout with, 1236, 1237, 1238
  insertion of, 98–99
  insertion of footers and, 91–92, 115
  slides with, 1226–1228, 1238
Header and Footer dialog box, 1228
Header/Footer tab, 354–355
Heading 3 style, modification of, 166
Health First Insurance exercise, 64
Health Insurance Portability and Accountability Act (HIPAA), 812
Healthy living tips exercise, 189–190
Heart disease prevention exercise, 125–126
Help and Support Center, 1269–1270, 1273, 1301
Help feature, Office 2007, 10, 53
  Access and, 14–15, 57
  dialog boxes and, 11, 53
  Excel and, 10
  Microsoft Office Online and, 53
  PowerPoint and, 12, 1142, 1146, 1177
  Word and, 16–17
Help Online, 1146
Help Window, 1142, 1146
Hidden commands, 1131
Hidden text, 135
Hide Detail, 632
Hide/Show feature, 76, 115
Hiding feature, 489–490, 498–499
  columns and, 489–490, 498–499, 527
  rows and, 489–490, 498–499, 527
  worksheets and, 460, 489–490, 498–499, 527

Hierarchies, 1209
  outlines with, 1209
Highlight cell rules, conditional formatting and, 552
Highlighter tool, 136–137, 142, 179
HLOOKUP function, 402. *See also* VLOOKUP function
Holiday greeting card exercise, 246
Home Arts exercise, 479
Home Health Consultants document, 242
Home tab, 72, 73, 319, 1130
  description of, 1132
Horizontal alignment, 148–149
Horizontal axis, 432
Hotel chain
  nesting pivoted data in, 1053–1054
  PivotChart for, 1054
  PivotTable for, 1054
  stacked column chart for, 1052
House amortization table, 652
Housing office worksheet exercise, 377
Hyperlink data type, 815
Hyperlink field, 815
Hyphens
  nonbreaking, 137–138, 139, 140–141, 179
  regular, 139

I

Icon sets conditional formatting, 553
  exercise with, 559, 560
Icons, 1261
  Safely Remove Hardware, 1285
Identifiers, 882
Identity theft, 812
  exercise, 310, 1256
IF functions, 387, 393, 399–400, 412
  amortization schedule with, 657, 658
  arguments of, 399, 412
  comparison operators in, 400
  evaluation and result in, 400
  exercise with, 403, 405
  formulas for, 643
  nested, 643–644, 650, 663, 677–678
  nested AND function in, 648–649
  nested OR function in, 649
  tip for, 644
IFERROR function, 644, 645, 662
Ignore Error, 724
IIf function, 893–894
Images. *See also* Clip art
  alignment of, 224
  border feature for, 224
  copyrights for, 219
  formatting of, 220–224, 232
  height/width adjustment of, 221, 224
  insertion of, 219–220, 227, 228, 232
  recolor feature for, 224
  rotating of, 224
  shadow applied to, 224
  text wrapping styles and, 221, 224
IME Mode property, 819
IME Sentence Mode property, 819
Import Wizard, 861
Importing process, 548. *See also* Data sharing, Access/Excel
  Access database and, 550–551, 558–559, 600
  data from other sources and, 551
  outlines and, 1217–1218, 1220, 1238
  SQL Server Analysis Services cube and, 551
  SQL Server Table and, 551
  text files and, 548–550, 600